Alternate Third Edition

FINANCIAL ACCOUNTING
The Impact on Decision Makers

Harcourt College Publishers

Where Learning Comes to Life

TECHNOLOGY

Technology is changing the learning experience, by increasing the power of your textbook and other learning materials; by allowing you to access more information, more quickly; and by bringing a wider array of choices in your course and content information sources.

Harcourt College Publishers has developed the most comprehensive Web sites, e-books, and electronic learning materials on the market to help you use technology to achieve your goals.

PARTNERS IN LEARNING

Harcourt partners with other companies to make technology work for you and to supply the learning resources you want and need. More importantly, Harcourt and its partners provide avenues to help you reduce your research time of numerous information sources.

Harcourt College Publishers and its partners offer increased opportunities to enhance your learning resources and address your learning style. With quick access to chapter-specific Web sites and e-books . . . from interactive study materials to quizzing, testing, and career advice . . . Harcourt and its partners bring learning to life.

Harcourt's partnership with Digital:Convergence™ brings :CRQ™ technology and the :CueCat™ reader to you and allows Harcourt to provide you with a complete and dynamic list of resources designed to help you achieve your learning goals. Just swipe the cue to view a list of Harcourt's partners and Harcourt's print and electronic learning solutions.

http://www.harcourtcollege.com/partners/

Alternate Third Edition

FINANCIAL ACCOUNTING
The Impact on Decision Makers

GARY A. PORTER
The University of Montana

CURTIS L. NORTON
Northern Illinois University

Harcourt College Publishers

Fort Worth   Philadelphia   San Diego   New York   Orlando   Austin
San Antonio   Toronto   Montreal   London   Sydney   Tokyo

Publisher	Mike Roche
Acquisitions Editor	Craig Avery
Market Strategist	Charlie Stutesman
Developmental Editor	Emma Guttler
Project Editor	Jim Patterson
Art Director	April Eubanks
Production Manager	Lois West

Cover Design: Bill Brammer

ISBN: 0-03-033563-9
Library of Congress Catalog Card Number: 2001086105

Copyright © 2002 by Harcourt, Inc.

Requests for permission to make copies of any part of the work should be mailed to the following address: Permissions Department, Harcourt, Inc., 6277 Sea Harbor Drive, Orlando, FL 32887-6777.

Portions of this work were published in previous editions.

Copyrights and Acknowledgments appear on page H-1, which constitutes a continuation of the copyright page.

Address for Domestic Orders
Harcourt, Inc., 6277 Sea Harbor Drive, Orlando, FL 32887-6777
800-782-4479

Address for International Orders
International Customer Service
Harcourt, Inc., 6277 Sea Harbor Drive, Orlando, FL 32887-6777
407-345-3800
(fax) 407-345-4060
(e-mail) hbintl@harcourt.com

Address for Editorial Correspondence
Harcourt College Publishers, 301 Commerce Street, Suite 3700, Fort Worth, TX 76102

Web Site Address
http://www.harcourtcollege.com

Printed in the United States of America

1 2 3 4 5 6 7 8 9 0   048   9 8 7 6 5 4 3 2 1

Harcourt College Publishers

To those who really "count":
Melissa
Kathy, Amy, Andrew

The Harcourt Series in Accounting

PRINCIPLES OF ACCOUNTING
INTEGRATED FINANCIAL/MANAGERIAL
Cunningham, Nikolai, and Bazley
ACCOUNTING: Information for Business Decisions

TECHNOLOGY COMPONENTS
Guided Exploration, LLC
Interactive Decision Cases for Financial Accounting

Bell, Kirby, and Gantt
Guide to Understanding and Using Annual Reports
Second Edition

Davis
OMAR (Online Multimedia Accounting Review):
The Accounting Cycle

COMMUNICATION
McKay and Rosa
The Accountant's Guide to Professional Communication:
Writing and Speaking the Language of Business

FINANCIAL
Hanson and Hamre
Financial Accounting
Eighth Edition

Porter and Norton
Financial Accounting: The Impact on Decision Makers
Third Edition

Porter and Norton
Financial Accounting: The Impact on Decision Makers
Alternate Third Edition

Stickney and Weil
Financial Accounting: An Introduction to Concepts,
Methods, and Uses
Ninth Edition

Knechel
The Monopoly Game Practice Set

MANAGERIAL
Jackson and Sawyers
Managerial Accounting: A Focus on Decision Making

Maher, Stickney, and Weil
Managerial Accounting: An Introduction to Concepts, Methods,
and Uses
Seventh Edition

INTERMEDIATE
Williams, Stanga, and Holder
Intermediate Accounting
Fifth Edition
1998 Update

ADVANCED
Pahler and Mori
Advanced Accounting: Concepts and Practice
Seventh Edition

FINANCIAL STATEMENT ANALYSIS
Stickney and Brown
Financial Reporting and Statement Analysis:
A Strategic Perspective
Fourth Edition

AUDITING
Guy, Alderman, and Winters
Auditing
Fifth Edition

Rittenberg and Schwieger
Auditing: Concepts for a Changing Environment
Third Edition

THEORY
Bloom and Elgers
Foundations of Accounting Theory and Policy: A Reader

Bloom and Elgers
Issues in Accounting Policy: A Reader

GOVERNMENTAL AND NOT-FOR-PROFIT
Douglas
Governmental and Nonprofit Accounting: Theory and Practice
Second Edition

REFERENCE
Bailey
Miller GAAS Guide
College Edition

Williams
Miller GAAP Guide
College Edition

To the Instructor

THE ALTERNATIVE TO DEBITS AND CREDITS

Financial Accounting: The Impact on Decision Makers, first published in 1995 and revised in 1998 and again in 2001, has achieved an unparalleled level of success. Many factors contributed to this success; certainly one was the number of instructors who were making a change in how they teach financial accounting and were prepared to de-emphasize procedures, focus on introductory accounting concepts, and teach financial accounting to their predominantly non-majors from an increased financial statement user-perspective. A large portion of financial accounting instructors are at this point now, balancing the use of financial information with its preparation, and for them the regular Third Edition of *Financial Accounting* will continue to be of great help.

But since the publication of the first edition of *Financial Accounting,* a number of instructors have told us that they are taking further steps away from the preparation of financial information as part of their move to a more fully user-oriented course. An increasing number of instructors remove debits and credits substantially or entirely from the classroom. They do so in part to broaden the scope of the course for their majors to include larger business issues, and in part to help prepare nonmajors to appreciate the financial information that will dominate their professional lives. Still other instructors are offloading debits and credits to the accounting lab or to online materials while devoting more time in the classroom to foster the skills and judgment required in how to read, interpret, and analyze financial information and how to make informed business decisions.

These instructors have issued a challenge: Provide a more user-oriented book without eliminating the features, pedagogy, and package that have been so successful. From this challenge came the idea for an Alternate Edition of *Financial Accounting,* one that focuses even more on external users over preparers, emphasizing the concepts and minimizing the procedures. The emphasis is on learning how to read and analyze financial information and make decisions. So just as we have in past years, for these instructors we offer a version of our Third Edition that we call **"An Alternative to Debits and Credits."** This edition simply extends the conceptual, user emphasis by eliminating references to debits and credits, removing journal entries, and further reducing procedural detail. Rather, we replace journal entries with a <u>transaction effects equation</u> that shows graphically how each business and accounting transaction affects the accounting equation and the financial statements.

In this way, students think about how a business transaction affects the income statement, for example, rather than whether to debit or credit the accounts. The result is a book with an enhanced conceptual, user-oriented focus having the features, pedagogy, and student-friendly style that leads to effective, motivated learning for majors and non-majors alike.

A HEAD START FOR THE STUDENTS

Because there *are* so many new features and ideas embodied in the Third Edition—and because of our intensified commitment to students and their learning needs—we have organized this introductory material a little differently, as you'll soon see. By directing students to their own introduction, we believe they can get started in the course just that much more efficiently. Naturally you'll want to turn to the Student section on page xxiii when you've finished exploring here.

STUDENT-FRIENDLY FINANCIAL STATEMENT OPTIONS

This edition contains financial information of public companies that is organized and highlighted in a colorful way to focus efficiently on both what is important about those companies and what is vital for beginning students. For the Third Edition, we've increased our financial statement flexibility in the book and the support materials:

- For the Third Edition we've replaced ice cream with pizza in our flagship company financial statements. Rather than Ben & Jerry's, as in past editions, students are introduced to **Uno Restaurant Corporation,** a national chain of full-service restaurants known for its signature deep-dish pizza. We believe Uno is a company that students will find not only fun to get to know, but similar to Ben & Jerry's and relatively easy to understand.

- To further expand students' awareness of annual reports we have added a second flagship company. We chose to add **Gateway, Inc.** because it is a high-technology company that students can identify with and, like Uno, has financial statements that can be read and understood by beginning accounting students. The complete 1999 annual reports for both companies are reprinted in the back of the textbook for easy reference.

- Our marginal Concept to Practice boxes, three per chapter, provide instructors with the flexibility of focusing on applying selected text concepts to the relevant financial statements of both these two flagship companies as well as the company highlighted in each chapter, such as JCPenney or IBM. As the instructor, you choose the company with which your students practice the text's concepts. (You'll see an example of this feature later.)

- User-oriented support materials such as an annual report project (*Understanding and Using Annual Reports,* discussed later), coupled with an online web search tool for all our real companies' financial and news web pages, allow instructors to assign the annual reports of any public company covered in the book as well as any other public company you choose.

- Many instructors ask for the latest financial information as a means to keeping students as current as possible and to keep motivation high throughout the course. To meet this need, we provide updates of the book's features that refer to Uno and Gateway, along with access to the latest-year annual reports, online via our Web site. Also on our web site is a Resources page containing company news, features, and links to late-breaking information about these two key companies, as well as updates for the companies highlighted in other chapters.

With this guiding element—student-friendly financial information choices updated online—we've added a new emphasis on evolving student needs that, we believe, will keep the Third Edition on target with the needs of your students in their introductory accounting course.

NEW "GETTING STARTED" MODULE: A ROAD MAP FOR STUDENTS

Students and instructors alike have said that getting started in financial accounting can be difficult. So for the Third Alternate Edition we've made the start of the course a priority. One key to getting started is our "To the Student" introduction, starting on page xxiii. Another key is the module that opens the book before Chapter 1.

For the Third Alternate Edition, we provide you and your students with a road map to the financial accounting course in the form of an introductory module, **"Getting Started in Business."** It is designed to help students orient themselves to the business world—from how one enterprising individual started a business, to the importance of decision-making, to the forms businesses take and the activities of a business entity.

A major focus of this revision is making the book even more student-friendly—and getting students off on the right foot in the course is the most friendly thing we can do for them. After checking out "To the Student," and "Getting Started in Business," students are better prepared to focus on the core introductory topics which we've streamlined in Chapters 1 and 2.

ORGANIZATION, PEDAGOGY, AND PACKAGE DESIGNED FOR *ENHANCED LEARNING*

For the Third Alternate Edition, we remain committed to four principles that have been instrumental to the success of the first two editions:

- An emphasis on *pedagogy and student appeal that accommodates most learning styles.*
- A focus on *financial statements.*
- A focus on *actual public companies.*
- A *decision-making* emphasis.

Students learn and understand in a variety of ways, so we have provided a variety of features, including a number of **NEW** features, to help them along the way. The first of these student-oriented features is our book's revised organization and topical changes, which are designed to improve students' ability to focus on what's important.

ORGANIZATION AND TOPICAL CHANGES TO ENHANCE LEARNING

Combined with "Getting Started in Business," Chapters 1 and 2 provide a true "first gear" for the course.

Chapter 1, "Accounting as a Form of Communication," has been revised and streamlined to <u>highlight the key introductory issues</u>:

- We moved the first section on the startup of a company, Uno in this edition, to the "Getting Started in Business" module.
- We provide a **NEW** Exhibit 1-1 on typical questions of users of financial information.
- We revised the text's introduction of the balance sheet to better focus on the relationship of the balance sheet to the accounting equation.
- We annotate and highlight the balance sheet of Uno to focus on this accounting equation relationship.
- We include a **NEW** Exhibit 1-3 on the accounting equation and the balance sheet.
- We add **NEW** brief examples of typical balance sheet items.
- We annotate the income statement to provide students with simple summaries of the two line items introduced in Chapter 1—sales and cost of sales.
- We removed the statement of stockholders' equity and refer students to the annual report for this statement.
- We moved the introduction to the statement of cash flows, and the statement itself, to Chapter 2.
- We revised the conceptual framework for greater understanding.
- We simplified the introduction of the standard-setting organizations and included this material in Learning Objective 3.

Chapter 2, "Financial Statements and the Annual Report," has been shortened and streamlined to make it <u>more accessible to beginning accounting students</u>.

- Rather than show financial statements for both a hypothetical and a real-world company in each section as in the past, the chapter progresses from enhanced, more graphic coverage of the hypothetical (i.e. "textbook") company statements to example real-world statements using Gateway, Inc.

- We have simplified the language of the objectives of financial reporting.
- We have simplified the explanations of the qualitative characteristics.
- We have focused on introducing the objectives and qualitative characteristics so as to better place them in the context of the use of financial statements.
- We have simplified Exhibit 2-1, "The Application of Financial Reporting Objectives," for better use as a study aid.
- We no longer introduce the details of different depreciation methods in this chapter.
- We have revised Exhibit 2-3 on the operating cycle to be more graphic and to introduce the length of the operating cycle into the exhibit to reinforce the importance of that concept.
- We have annotated the Dixon balance sheet to summarize long-term vs. current assets and liabilities and to aid its use as a study reference.
- We have eliminated several ratios from this introductory chapter, as their coverage in Chapter 2 duplicated coverage elsewhere in the book.
- We have annotated and highlighted Exhibits 2-5 and 2-6 on the income statement for the hypothetical company to better focus on the differences between the single-step and the multi-step formats and as a study reference for the multiple-step concept.
- We have annotated and highlighted Exhibit 2-8 on the hypothetical company's statement of cash flows, to aid study of the three types of activities shown on the statement.
- For simplicity, we have changed the method illustrated on this cash flows statement to the direct method.
- We have minimally annotated Gateway's income statement and balance sheet to show the line items that would be used for simple ratio analysis.
- To avoid adding a level of complication, we have replaced the use of an actual public company in the review problem with a generic company, Grizzly, Inc.

Changes to other chapters are equally exciting for instructors and students. Here are just some of those revisions:

Chapter 5, "Merchandise Accounting and Internal Control," continues to serve as an introduction to inventory accounting in Chapter 6. A new Exhibit 5-4 more graphically illustrates the cost of goods sold model, and a sample of the privacy and security policy for The Gap from its website has been added in the internal control section of the chapter.

Chapter 6, "Inventories and Cost of Goods Sold," has been revised to focus attention on the fundamental differences in inventory costing methods. Inventory errors have been moved to later in the chapter, and a consignments example has been removed from the errors section as a move toward streamlining.

Chapter 8, "Operating Assets: Property, Plant, and Equipment, Natural Resources, and Intangibles," has been updated with new financial statements for all companies and has also been updated for new FASB developments concerning goodwill and the amortization of intangible assets. The AOL/Time Warner merger is introduced.

Chapter 9, "Current Liabilities, Contingent Liabilities, and the Time Value of Money," has been updated with new financial statements for all companies. It continues to cover current liabilities, contingent liabilities and the time value of money concepts for those instructors who wish to provide that background material. The appendix concerning payroll accounting has been retained because students find it applicable to their daily work lives.

Chapter 10, "Long-Term Liabilities," now utilizes the real-world statements of both Coca-Cola and PepsiCo to allow instructors to compare two companies within the same industry. The section on analysis of long-term liabilities has been moved toward the end of the chapter. Finally, the chapter has been simplified by moving the more advanced topics of deferred tax and pensions to an appendix.

Chapter 11, "Stockholders' Equity," now utilizes the financial statements from Delta Air Lines and other companies from the airline industry. A section has been added to stress the role of retained earnings as a link between the income statement and balance sheet, and a new exhibit illustrates this important concept graphically.

Chapter 12, "The Statement of Cash Flows," and **Chapter 13,** "Financial Statement Analysis," allow the instructor the maximum flexibility. In Chapter 12, instructors can emphasize either the concepts of cash flows or the preparation of the cash flows statement, or both, or they can defer the chapter to a later course. Chapter 13 consolidates the coverage of ratios that was integrated into the chapters, allowing instructors to teach financial statement analysis throughout the course, only in this chapter, or in another course. Thus we have made only minimal changes to these well-received chapters.

PEDAGOGY DESIGNED TO *ENHANCE LEARNING*

We place greater emphasis in the Third Edition on making learning financial accounting enjoyable, relevant, and interesting. New features combine with successful approaches used in previous editions to accommodate the variety of learning and instructional styles emerging across the country.

■ *Study Links* at the beginning of each chapter give the student an integrated perspective on the material. They review the previous chapter, introduce the current chapter, and look forward to applications for the following chapter.

NEW: Key topics in the *current chapter* are highlighted with underlining as a time saver and study aid.

■ *Learning Objectives* are stated at the beginning of each chapter and keyed in the margin and used throughout the book and package as a study aid.

Study Links

A Look at This Chapter
We begin the study of accounting by considering what accounting is and who uses the information it provides. We will see that accounting is an important form of communication and that financial statements are the medium that accountants use to communicate with those who in some way have an interest in the financial affairs of a company.

This is the part of the Study Link that focuses on the current chapter. Look at the Chapter 2 opener on page 44 to see how the previous, current, and next chapters are linked.

LEARNING OBJECTIVES	AT START OF CHAPTER
After studying this chapter, you should be able to:	
LO 1 Identify the primary users of accounting information and their needs. (p. 6)	**LO 3** Identify and explain the primary assumptions made in preparing financial statements. (p. 14)
LO 2 Explain the purpose of each of the financial statements and the relationships among them and prepare a set of simple statements. (p. 8)	**LO 4** Describe the various roles of accountants in organizations. (p. 16)

NEW: Page references have been added to the initial listing for easier use.

LO 1 Identify the primary users of accounting information and their needs.

BESIDE CHAPTER SECTION

Multi-Concept Exercises　　　IN HOMEWORK ASSIGNMENTS

LO 1, 2 **Exercise 1-12** Users of Accounting Information and the Financial Statements
Listed below are a number of users of accounting information and examples of questions they need answered before making decisions. Fill in each blank to indicate whether the user is most likely to find the answer by looking at the income statement (IS), the balance sheet (BS), or the statement of retained earnings (RE).

■ **NEW!** *Study Tips* in the margin focus students on key concepts in a section.
■ **NEW!** *Two-Minute Review* boxes at the ends of selected sections invite students to pause, think, and review concepts just learned before continuing on:

Study Tip

The operating cycle of a business is the basis for deciding which assets are current and which ones are noncurrent.

Two-Minute Review

1. *Give at least three examples of current assets.*
2. *Give the three common categories of noncurrent assets.*

Answers:

1. *Cash, accounts receivable, inventory, short-term investments, and prepaid expenses.*
2. *Investments, property, plant and equipment, and intangibles.*

From *Concept*

TO PRACTICE 1.2

READING UNO'S AUDITORS' REPORT Note the date at the bottom of the report. Why do you think it takes one month after the end of the year to issue this report?

■ *From Concept to Practice* boxes in the margins invite students to apply what they have learned in the text and class to financial statements of the chapter-opening companies, Uno and Gateway.

■ **NEW!** *Warmup Exercises with Suggested Solutions* give students a preview of assignments to come. These simple exercises, like the Two-Minute Reviews and Key Terms Quizzes, help students move from reading the text to doing the end-of-chapter assignments. Warmup Exercises precede the Review Problem and Solution in each chapter.

WARMUP EXERCISES

LO 2 **Warmup Exercise 1-3** Uno and the Accounting Equation

Place Uno's total assets, total liabilities, and total owners' equity in the form of the accounting equation.

Key to the Solution

Recall Exhibit 1-2. You will have to separate the liabilities and the stockholders' equity because they are not subtotaled for you.

SOLUTIONS TO WARMUP EXERCISES

Warmup Exercise 1-3 Uno and the Accounting Equation

$$\text{Assets} = \text{Liabilities} + \text{Owners' Equity}$$
$$\$149{,}612 \qquad \$68{,}633 + \qquad \$80{,}979$$

■ *Review Problem with Suggested Solutions.* At the end of every chapter is a review problem and a suggested solution to test students' understanding of some of the major ideas presented in the chapter. (For example, see page 23)

■ **NEW** We've *doubled the number of problems* from the Second Edition, adding a set of **Alternate Problems** to complement our end-of-chapter material. These Alternate Problems include Alternate Multi-concept Problems for added challenge. Instructors can use this additional assignment material as extra homework, test preparation, or quiz material.

FINANCIAL STATEMENT FOCUS USING PUBLIC COMPANIES

Through the first two editions, our hallmark has been the use of actual financial statements as examples throughout the book. For the Third Alternate Edition we are remaining true to this principle with significant improvements.

■ Our chapter-opening vignettes, called "Focus on Financial Results," have been updated and rewritten using many **NEW** companies. They focus on a key aspect of the company and the financial information it presents that relates to the chapter.

   • To view a sample and see how students may use these vignettes effectively, turn to "To the Student," page xxiii.

   • To review the focus of each vignette, see the Table of Contents. In the margin we have included the key issue discussed by the vignette and illustrated in a related financial statement.

■ **NEW** **Business Strategy** boxes, one per chapter, generally focus on a competitor to the chapter-opening company and a key business strategy that is reflected in its financial statements. This is part of one Business Strategy box:

BUSINESS STRATEGY

California Pizza Kitchen (CPK). is a casual dining restaurant chain that, like the east coast's Pizzeria Uno chain, specializes in premium pizza for the mainstream market. Like Uno, it both owns and franchises its restaurants, which feature such best sellers as BBQ Chicken Pizza and Thai Chicken Pizza, along with the Philly Cheesesteak Pizza and Grilled Garlic Shrimp Pizza. Pastas, salads, soups, and desserts round out the menu.

■ **All real-world financial statements have been updated in the text to the latest possible 1999 or 2000 annual report year**. Many have been further highlighted or annotated to focus attention on the specific line item or section being discussed.

■ Because many instructors prefer to use the latest financial statements available, we are putting renewed emphasis on **accessing the latest annual report information online. NEW:** The **URLs** of real companies cited are now listed in the margins, and in the chapter openers.

www.pizzeriauno.com
www.gateway.com
www.hoovers.com

■ An updated **Internet Research Case** is again included at the back of each chapter.

INTERNET RESEARCH CASE

Case 2-8 Gateway

You can probably do this from your everyday knowledge, but this is good practice in researching a company using the internet. Find a WWW site or a source of information that will list the competitors to Gateway. Choose the top two competitors and answer the following questions:

1. Looking at their balance sheets, what are their total current assets and their total current liabilities? From these numbers, calculate each company's working capital and current ratio. How do they compare to the ratios for Gateway, shown on page 65?

2. From their income statements, calculate their profit margin for the latest year available. How do they compare to those of Gateway, which you were asked to calculate in the From Concept to Practice box on page 67?

Optional Research: From the financial information available on their WWW sites, what other comparisons can you make about these companies? Based on your research, are the companies themselves comparable in such areas as size, products, assets, liabilities, and net income? If not, explain five ways in which they differ. Is the financial information itself comparable for the three companies? Explain.

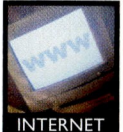
INTERNET

Fill in your source for industry information:
www._____.com

Gateway and its main competitors:
www.gateway.com
www._____.com
www._____.com

■ Actual WWW graphics of financial information for selected companies are used throughout. The text's WWW site is enhanced for better research capabilities.

■ **Financial information from more public companies** has been included in the end-of-chapter material.

FEATURES THAT SUPPORT OUR DECISION-MAKING EMPHASIS

Practice in decision making using financial information has been an important principle in past editions. For the Third Edition, we have strengthened the use of financial information to make business and personal financial decisions.

■ **Accounting for Your Decisions** boxes in each chapter place the student in a role-playing situation as a user of financial statements, as a decision-maker, and as a future businessperson.

■ **Focus on Users** boxes are **NEW** interviews with young businesspersons who use financial information in their everyday decision making. **NEW:** Now included in *every* chapter.

About our Use of Icons Icons are like signposts helping students identify their way along the route. For the Third Edition, we include icons for selected functions.

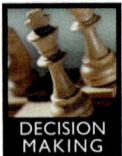

Decision Making opportunities in the text and end-of-chapter material are identified with this icon.

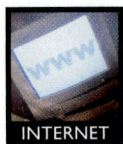

Internet resources are identified by a general Internet icon. Specific Web addresses are provided in the margins with this notation: www.harcourtcollege.com.

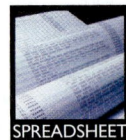

Problems that are supported by the **spreadsheet** problem support tool accompanying the text are identified with this icon.

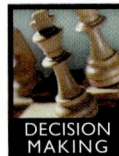

- **Making Financial Decisions cases** and **Accounting and Ethics cases** at the end of the chapter provide additional end-of-chapter support for decision-making using financial information.
- **Internet Research Cases** give the perspective of an actual user or company, provide engaging questions, place the students in a role-playing situation, and give them directions to specific Internet resources for decision-oriented projects.
- **NEW** Video Cases at the end of each of the four parts of the textbook are based on **NEW** videos that focus on financial accounting and business decision-making in four public companies: Tweeter Home Entertainment Inc.; Stride-Rite Inc.; Uno Restaurant Corp., and Lycos.

SUPPLEMENTS FOR THE INSTRUCTOR

A number of ancillary items are available for the instructor's use:

- **NEW! Instructor's Resource CD**: Includes the Solutions Manual, Instructor's Manual, Test Bank in Word, Lectures in PowerPoint, Spreadsheet Problem Support (instructor version).
- **Solutions Manual** by the text authors, with Donna Hetzel (Western Michigan University) and Barbara Reider (University of Montana). Solutions are included for every Question, Exercise, Problem, and Case in the text with the exception of the Internet Research Cases. (Solutions and suggested answers to the internet research cases are on the book's website.)
- **Test Bank** by Diane Tanner (University of Northern Florida). We have made a special effort to assure that test items are well correlated with the end-of-chapter assignments. This test bank is also available in a **Computerized Test Bank** from ExaMaster.
- **Instructor's Manual** by Walter Austin (Mercer University) contains chapter outlines, projects and activities, and a bibliography of readings. Numerous activities throughout are keyed to public companies; their URLs are included to facilitate further research.
- **Teaching and Solutions Transparencies** consist of 100 exhibits from the text and other lecture aids, along with acetates of exercises, problems, and solutions in the text.
- **Web site.** Company research, downloads of instructor and student supplements, and a whole range of activities for students can be found at www.harcourtcollege.com/ accounting/porteralt3e. Included is Getting Started, an online supplement for Financial Accounting organized by topic that contains resources, review questions, including company profiles with financial information. (For a preview, see the front endpapers.)
- **NEW** WebCT course administration tools for two student WebCT courses to accompany the textbook:
  - **WebCourse** The WebCourse to accompany the Third Alternate Edition, by Sarah Brown (University of North Alabama), allows instructors to develop and manage their course using tools and resources provided by the publisher as well as their own teaching

www.harcourtcollege.com/
accounting/porteralt3e

materials. Examples include a conferencing system, online chat, student progress tracking, group project organization, grade maintenance and distribution, access control, navigation tools, auto-graded quizzes, e-mail, course calendar, and syllabus generator.

- **OMAR: Online Multimedia Accounting Review** OMAR, by Charles Davis (Baylor University), is Harcourt's new highly graphical and interactive computer-based tutorial short course on the concepts and mechanics of the accounting cycle. It may be used in conjunction with Chapters 3 and 4 if the instructor believes that additional review and drill-and-practice in accounting cycle procedures is needed for his or her students. Built on a WebCT platform, OMAR is available as an e-commerce product. Access is also available via a personal information number (PIN) found within a custom student guide to OMAR and WebCT sold to students through the bookstore. (Students can also purchase this guide online.)

  Basic administration of OMAR is simple and uncomplicated—instructors can track student progress through the frequent lesson exercises and module-ending mastery exams, viewing percent completed, time to complete, and which test items were completed.

A little about WebCT. WebCT is a software tool that facilitates the creation of sophisticated World Wide Web-based educational environments by non-technical users. Using web browsers as the interface, WebCT can be used to create entire on-line courses, or to simply publish materials that supplement existing courses. For more information about WebCT, and to see current Harcourt courses using WebCT, go to Harcourt College Online Learning Center at www.webct.harcourtcollege.com, or to www.webct.com

A little about OMAR. OMAR has four modules covering the concepts and procedures of the accounting cycle:

- The Double Entry System
- The Accounting Cycle—Part 1
- Accrual Accounting
- The Accounting Cycle—Part 2

Lessons in each module contain interactive activities, quizzes, graphics, and animations. Each module ends with a grade-reported one-time mastery exam.

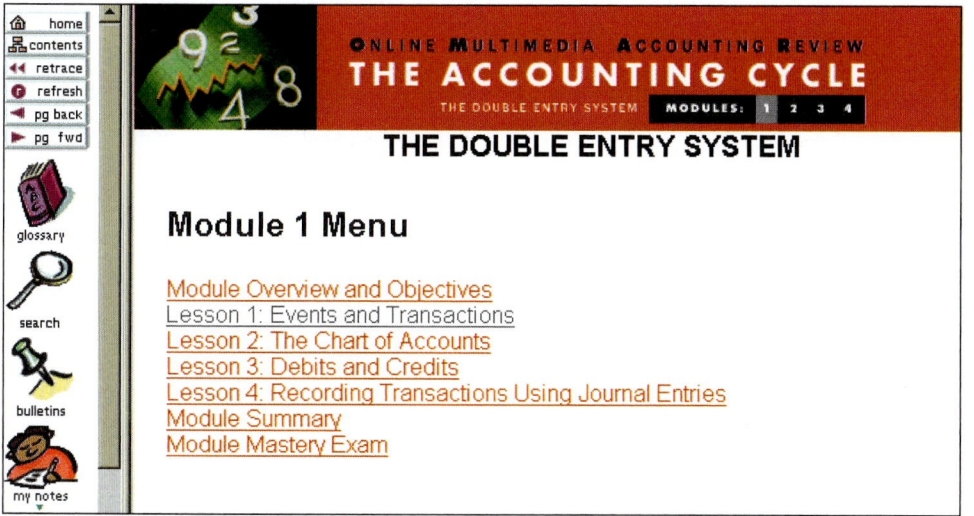

- ■ **NEW Video segments,** tied to a new Video Case at the end of each of the four parts of the textbook, focus on financial information and management issues for four public companies, Tweeter Home Entertainment, Stride-Rite, Uno's Restaurant Corp., and Lycos.

Availability of all instructor ancillaries, including the Solutions Manual, is restricted to instructors only under their pre-designated ISBNs. Instructors desiring to make any instructor ancillaries available to their students must contact their local Harcourt representative or the Harcourt College Publishers Marketing Department for special arrangement exceptions.

For Student Supplements
see "To the Student" on page xxiii following Meet the Authors

A NEW MANAGERIAL TITLE TO PAIR WITH *FINANCIAL ACCOUNTING*

Harcourt's NEW *Managerial Accounting: A Focus on Decision Making* by Steve Jackson, The University of Tennessee—Martin, and Roby Sawyers, North Carolina State University, uses a 4-step **decision-making model** throughout the text and end-of-chapter material to

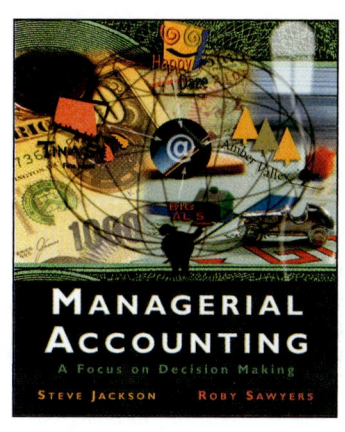

facilitate learning the decision-making process. It contains extensive coverage of contemporary topics such as ABC, ABM, the value chain, just-in-time inventories, and the balanced scorecard. It also contains a unique chapter (13) on the development of **knowledge management** and the integration of accounting information throughout the whole organization's information systems.

Just as Porter/Norton focuses on the use of accounting information for outside decision-maker, Jackson/Sawyers focuses on the use of accounting and other relevant information for managers within the company.

Ask your sales representative about combining these two books for a one-book principles course.

ACKNOWLEDGMENTS

To develop, write, and publish a book to meet the changing needs of students and instructors truly requires a team effort. We appreciate the sincere and devoted work of all those who have contributed to our books in the first three editions.

REVIEWERS AND FOCUS GROUP PARTICIPANTS FOR THE FIRST EDITION (1995):

Diane Tanner
University of North Florida
Saul Ahiaria
SUNY at Buffalo
Mike Akers
Marquette University
Marcia Anderson
University of Cincinnati
David Angelovich
San Francisco State University
Alana Baier
Marquette University
Amelia A. Baldwin-Morgan
Eastern Michigan University
Bobbe M. Barnes
University of Colorado at Denver
Maj. Curt Barry
U.S. Military Academy
Peter Battell
University of Vermont
Paul Bayes
East Tennessee State University
Mark Bettner
Bucknell University
Frank Biegbeder
Rancho Santiago Community College
Francis Bird
University of Richmond
Karen Bird
University of Michigan
Eddy Birrer
Gonzaga University
Michelle Bissonnette
California State University–Fresno
John Blahnik
Lorain County Community College
Ed Bresnahan
American River College
Sarah Brown
University of North Alabama
Philip Buchanan
George Washington University

Rosie Bukics
Lafayette College
Carolyn Callahan
University of Notre Dame
Linda Campbell
University of Toledo
Jim Cashell
Miami University
Charles Caufield
Loyola University Chicago
Gyan Chandra
Miami University
Mayer Chapman
California State University at Long Beach
Alan Cherry
Loyola Marymount University
Mike Claire
College of San Mateo
David C. Coffee
Western Carolina University
David Collins
Eastern Kentucky University
Judith Cook
Grossmont College
John C. Corless
California State University–Sacramento
Dean Crawford
University of Toledo
Shirley J. Daniel
University of Hawaii at Manoa
Alan Davis
Community College of Philadelphia
Henry H. Davis
Eastern Illinois University
Lyle E. Dehning
Metropolitan State College–Denver
Patricia Doherty
Boston University
Margaret Douglas
University of Arkansas
Kathy Dunne
Rider College

Kenneth Elvik
Iowa State University
Anette Estrada
Grand Valley State University
Ed Etter
Syracuse University
Alan Falcon
Loyola Marymount University
Charles Fazzi
Robert Morris College
Anita Feller
University of Illinois
Howard Felt
Temple University
David Fetyko
Kent State University
Richard File
University of Nebraska–Omaha
Ed Finkhauser
University of Utah
Jeannie M. Folk
College of DuPage
J. Patrick Forrest
Western Michigan University
Patrick Fort
University of Alaska–Fairbanks
Diana Franz
University of Toledo
Tom Frecka
University of Notre Dame
Gary Freeman
University of Tulsa
Veronique Frucot
Rutgers University–Camden
Joe Gallo
Cuyahoga Community College
Michelle Gannon
Western Connecticut State University
Will Garland
Coastal Carolina University
John Gartska
Loyola Marymount University

Roger Gee
San Diego Mesa College
Cynthia Van Gelderen
Aquinas College
Linda Genduso
Nova University
Don E. Giacomino
Marquette University
Claudia Gilbertston
Anoka Ramsey Community College
Lorraine Glascock
University of Alabama
Larry Godwin
University of Montana
Lynn Grace
Edison Community College
Marilyn Greenstein
Lehigh University
Paul Griffin
University of California–Davis
Leon Hanouille
Syracuse University
Joseph Hargadon
Widener University
Robert Hartwig
Worcester State College
Jean Hatcher
University of South Carolina at Sumner
Donna Sue Hetzel
Western Michigan University
Thomas F. Hilgeman
St. Louis Community College–Meramec
Robert E. Holtfreter
Ft. Hays State University
Kathy Horton
University of Illinois, Chicago
Bruce Ikawa
Loyola Marymount University
Danny Ivancevich
University of Nevada–Las Vegas
Janet Jackson
Wichita State University
Sharon Jackson
Auburn University at Montgomery
Randy Johnston
Pennsylvania State University
William Jones
Seton Hall University
Naida Kaen
University of New Hampshire
Manu Kai'ama
University of Hawaii at Manoa
Jane Kapral
Clark University
Marcia Kertz
San Jose State University
Jean Killey
Midlands Technical College
Ronald King
Washington University
William Kinsella
Loyola Marymount University
Jay LaGregs
Tyler Junior College
Michael Lagrone
Clemson University
Lucille E. Lammers
Illinois State University

Ellen Landgraf
Loyola University Chicago
Horace Landry
Syracuse University
Kristine Lawyer
North Carolina State University
Terry Lease
Loyola Marymount University
Susan Lightle
Wright State University
Tom Linsmeier
University of Iowa
Chao-Shin Liu
University of Notre Dame
Bruce Lubich
Syracuse University
Catherine Lumbattis
Southern Illinois University
Patsy Lund
Lakewood Community College
Raymond D. MacFee, Jr.
University of Colorado
David Malone
University of Idaho
Janice Mardon
Green River Community College
Mary D. Maury
St. John's University
Al Maypers
University of North Texas
John C. McCabe
Ball State University
Nancy McClure
Lock Haven University
Margaret McCrory
Marist College
Christine McKeag
University of Evansville
Thomas D. McLaughlin
Monmouth College
Laura McNally
Black Hills State College
Mallory McWilliams
San Jose State University
E. James Meddaugh
Ohio University
Cynthia Miller
GM Institute
William Mister
Colorado State University
Tami Mittelstaedt
University of Notre Dame
Perry Moore
David Lipscomb University
Barbara Morris
Angelo State University
Mike Morris
University of Notre Dame
Theodore D. Morrison
Valparaiso University
Howard E. Mount
Seattle Pacific University
Rafael Munoz
University of Notre Dame
Mary J. Nisbet
University of California–Santa Barbara
Curtis L. Norton
Northern Illinois University

Priscilla O'Clock
Xavier University
Phil Olds
Virginia Commonwealth University
Michael O'Neill
Gannon University
Janet O'tousa
University of Notre Dame
Rimona Palas
William Paterson College of New Jersey
Beau Parent
Tulane University
Paul Parkison
Ball State University
Sue Pattillo
University of Notre Dame
Ron Pawliczek
Boston College
Donna Philbrick
Portland State University
Gary A. Porter
Loyola University Chicago
Harry V. Poynter
Central Missouri State University
Joseph Ragan
St. Joseph's University
Mitchell Raiborn
Bradley University
Ann Riley
American University
Mary Rolfes
Mankato State University
Leo A. Ruggle
Mankato State University
Victoria Rymer
University of Maryland
George Sanderson
Moorhead State University
Karen Saurlander
University of Toledo
Warren Schlesinger
Ithaca College
Edward S. Schwan
Susquehanna University
Don Schwartz
National University
Richard Scott
University of Virginia
Richard Sherman
St. Joseph's University
Ray Slager
Calvin College
Amy Spielbauer
St. Norbert College
Charles Stanley
Baylor University
Catherine Staples
Virginia Commonwealth University
Anita Stellenwerf
Ramapo College
Stephen Strange
Indiana University at Kokomo
Linda Sugarman
University of Akron
Kathy Sullivan
George Washington University
Jeanie Sumner
Pacific Lutheran University

Judy Swingen
Rochester Institute of Technology
Tim Tancy
University of Notre Dame
Bente Villadsen
Washington University
Alan K. Vogel
Cuyahoga Community College–Western
Vicki Vorell
Cuyahoga Community College–Western
Phil Walter
Bellevue Community College
Ann Watkins
Louisiana State University

Judy Wenzel
Gustavus Adolphus College
Charles Werner
Loyola University Chicago
Michael Werner
University of Miami
Paul Wertheim
Pepperdine University
Shari Wescott
Houston Baptist University
T. Sterling Wetzel
Oklahoma State University
Steven D. White
Western Kentucky University

Samuel Wild
Loyola Marymount University
Jack Wilkerson
Wake Forest University
Lyle Wimmergren
Worcester Polytechnic Institute
Carol Wolk
University of Tennessee
Steve Wong
San Jose City College
Robert Zahary
California State University at Los Angeles
Thomas L. Zeller
Loyola University Chicago

SURVEY RESPONDENTS FOR THE SECOND EDITION (1998):

Ray Bainbridge
Lehigh University
Dorcas Berg
Wingate University
Bruce Bolick
University of Mary Hardin Baylor
Frank Bouchlers
North Carolina State University
Thomas Brady
University of Dayton
Bob Brill
St. Bonaventure University
Sarah Brown
University of North Alabama
David Brunn
Carthage College
Gary Bulmash
American University
Brian Burks
Harding University
Judith Cadle
Tarleton State University
John E. Coleman
University of Massachusetts at Boston
Carrie Cristea
Augustana College, South Dakota
Fred Current
Furman University
Jim Davis
Clemson University
Les Dlabay
Lake Forest College
Patricia Douglas
Loyola Marymount University
Joan Friedman
Illinois Wesleyan University
Sharon Garvin
Wayne State College
Art Goldman
University of Kentucky
Bud Granger
Mankato State University
Jack Grinnell
University of Vermont
Al Hannan
College of Notre Dame
Suzanne Hartley
Franklin University

Donna Hetzel
Western Michigan University
Nathan Hindi
Shippensburgh University of Pennsylvania
Betty Horn
Southern Connecticut State University
Fred Ihrke
Winona State University
Patricia Johnson
Canisius College
Becky Jones
Baylor University
Don Kellogg
Rock Valley College
Rita Kiugery
University of Delaware
Paul Kleichman
University of Richmond
George Klersey
Birmingham Southern College
Lynn Koshiyama
University of Alaska
Bobby Kuhlmann
Chaffey College
James Kurtenbach
Iowa State University
Jay LaGregs
Tyler Junior College
Laurie Larson
Valencia Community College
Chao Liu
Tarleton State University
Gina Lord
Santa Rosa Junior College
George Macklin
Susquehanna University
Jim Martin
University of Montevallo
Laurie McWhorter
University of Kentucky
Paul Mihalek
University of Hartford
Charles Milliner
Glendale Community College
Marcia Niles
University of Idaho
Mary Ellen O'Grady
Ramapo College

Bruce Oliver
Rochester Institute of Technology
Paul Parkison
Ball State University
Victor Pastena
SUNY Buffalo
Charles A. Pauley
Gannon University
Chris Pew
Galivan College
Al Rainford
Greenfield Community College
Keith Richardson
Indiana State University
Joseph Rue
Syracuse University
Rick Samuelson
San Diego State University
Gail Sanderson
Lebanon Valley College
Richard Sathe
University of St. Thomas
Ron Singer
University of Wisconsin–Parkside
David Smith
Metropolitan State University
David Smith
University of Dayton
Kim Sorenson
Eastern Oregon State University
Jens Stephan
University of Cincinnati
David Strupeck
Indiana University NW
Larry Tartaligno
Cabrillo College
Dewey Ward
Michigan State University
Jennifer Wells
University of San Francisco
Paul Wertheim
Pepperdine University
Jill Whitley
Sioux Falls College
Jane Wiese
Valencia Community College
David Willis
Illinois Wesleyan University

REVIEWERS AND FOCUS GROUP PARTICIPANTS FOR THE SECOND EDITION (1998):

Angela Bell
Jacksonville University
Bryan Burks
Harding University
Judith Cook
Grossmont Community College
Rosalind Cranor
Virginia Polytechnic Institute
Les Dlabay
Lake Forest College
Jaime Doran
Muhlenberg College
Alan Doyle
Pima Community College East
Alan Drebin
Northwestern University
Dean Edmiston
Emporia State University
Leo Gabriel
Bethel College
Lorraine Glasscock
University of North Alabama
Bonnie Hairrell
Birmingham Southern
Sharon Jackson
Auburn University, Montgomery
Stanley Jenne
University of Montana

Mary Keim
California State University–Bakersfield
Anne Marie Keinath
Indiana University Northwest
Robert Kelly
Corning Community College
Charles Konkol
University of Wisconsin–Milwaukee
Frank Korman
Mountain View College
James Kurtenbach
Iowa State University
Tom Lee
Winona State University
Alan Lord
Bowling Green State University
Bruce Lubich
American University
Jim Martin
University of Montevallo
Daniel O'Mara
Quinnipiac College
John Osborn
California State University–Fresno
Prakash Pai
Kent State University
John Rhode
University of San Francisco

Marilyn Sagrillo
University of Wisconsin–Green Bay
Karen Sedatole
Stephen F. Austin
John Sherman
University of Texas, Dallas
Richard Silkoff
Quinnipiac College
Jill Smith
Idaho State University
Donna Street
James Madison University
Martha Turner
Bowling Green State University
Karen Walton
John Carroll University
Dewey Ward
Michigan State University
Michael Welker
Drexel University
Jane Wells
University of Kentucky
Betty Wolterman
St. John's University, MN
Steven Wong
San Jose City College
Gail Wright
Bryant College

We wish to thank Donna Street (James Madison University) for her suggestions leading to the inclusion of international accounting issues. Jeannie Folk (College of DuPage) and Donna Hetzel (Western Michigan University) provided invaluable help in revising end-of-chapter problem material and the Solutions Manual. We also wish to thank Sylvia Ong (Paradise Valley Community College), Les Dlabay (Lake Forest College), Stuart Weiss, and Karen Hill for their help in revising the features.

REVIEWERS, FOCUS GROUP PARTICIPANTS, AND SURVEY RESPONDENTS FOR THE THIRD EDITION (2001):

Sheila Ammons
Austin Community College
Sarah Brown
University of Northern Alabama
Ronnie Burrows
University of Dayton
David N. Champagne
Antelope Valley College
Gail Cook
University of Wisconsin, Parkside
Susan Coomer Galbreath
Tennessee Tech University
Betty Driver
Murray State University
Paquita Y. Friday
University of Notre Dame
Hubert Gill
University of North Florida

Jeanne Hamilton
Cypress College
Christopher Jones
George Washington University
Greg Krippel
Coastal Carolina University
James Kurtenbach
Iowa State University
Tom Lee
Winona State University
Gina Lord
Santa Rosa Junior College
Don Loster
University of California, Santa Barbara
Spencer Martin
University of Rhode Island

Muroki Mwaura
William Paterson University
Jane Park
California State University, Los Angeles
Kathy Petroni
Michigan State University
Robert Rouse
College of Charleston
Donna Rudderow
Franklin University
Judith Sage
University of Southern Colorado
David P. Weiner
University of San Francisco
Michael Williams
Century College

For the Alternate Edition:

The following reviewers gave invaluable advice on the central issues confronting the development of the alternate edition, and for that we are especially grateful: Robert Bal-lenger, Babson College; Teddy L. Coe, University of North Texas; Patricia Doherty,

Boston University; David Fetyko, Kent State University; Diana Franz, University of Toledo; Claudia Gilbertson, Anoka-Ramsey Community College; Shirley Glass, Macomb Community College; Lee Hendrick, University of Tennessee; Kathy Horton, University of Illinois, Chicago; Don Loster, University of California–Santa Barbara; Barbara Merino, University of North Texas; William Morris, Jr., University of North Texas; Mary Nisbet, University of California–Santa Barbara; Nanne Olds, Doane College; Marc Rubin, Miami University; Jane Park, California State University–Los Angeles; Ray Slager, Calvin College; H. Lee Tatum, University of Nebraska–Omaha.

We are grateful to the following reviewers and survey respondents of the **alternate second edition** for their insightful comments: Mel Auerbach, California State University Dominguez Hills; Eddy G. Birrer, Gonzaga University; Doris Brown, Central Methodist University; Charles G. Carpenter, Miami University; Araya Debessay, University of Delaware; Anita Feller, University of Illinois; David Fetyko, Kent State University; Richard G. File, University of Nebraska–Omaha; Don Foster, Tacoma Community College; Jay LeGregs, Tyler Junior College; Cynthia Miglietti, Bowling Green State University at Firelands; Les Price, Pierce College, University of Puget Sound; Marilyn Sagrillo, University of Wisconsin–Green Bay; Bradley Schwieger, St. Cloud State University; William E. Smith, Xavier University; Diane Tanner, University of North Florida; Larry Tartaligno, Cabrillo College; George Violette, University of Southern Maine; and Philip M. Walter, Bellevue Community College.

We wish to thank the following survey respondents and contributors for their assistance to the **alternate third edition:** Robert Ballenger, University of Alabama, Huntsville; Bob Bauman, Allan Hancock College; Charles G. Carpenter, Berry College; Alice Cash, University of Southern Maine; Araya Debassay, University of Delaware; Teddy L. Coe, University of North Texas; Patricia Doherty, Boston University; Richard File, University of Nebraska–Omaha; Don Foster, Tacoma Community College; Diana Franz, University of Toledo; Lee Hendrick, University of Tennessee; Jay LeGregs, Tyler Junior College; Don Loster, University of California–Santa Barbara; Jim Meir, Cleveland State Community College; Barbara Merino, University of North Texas; Cynthia Miglietti, Bowling Green State University at Firelands; William Morris, Jr., University of North Texas; Marilyn Sagrillo, University of Wisconsin–Green Bay; William E. Smith, Xavier University; George Violette, University of Southern Maine; Katherine Xenophon-Rybowiak; and Linda Zucca, Kent State University.

We also wish to thank the following for their efforts in creating the ancillaries to the alternate third edition: Barbara Reider, University of Alaska, Anchorage; Donna Hetzel, Western Michigan University; Diane Tanner, University of Northern Florida; Coby Harmon, University of California, Santa Barbara; Walter Austin, Mercer University; Sandra Devona, Northern Illinois University; Leo Gabriel, Bethel College; and Sarah Brown, University of North Alabama.

We are grateful to the editorial, marketing, and production team at Harcourt College Publishers for its invaluable efforts: Craig Avery, Emma Guttler, Laura Hayes, Charlie Stutesman, Heather Hogan, Jim Patterson, Lois West, April Eubanks, and Linda Blundell.

Finally, we are grateful to Uno Restaurant Corporation and Gateway, Inc., for their cooperation in our partnership between education and the real world of business.

Gary A. Porter
Curtis L. Norton

Meet the Authors

Gary A. Porter, CPA, is Professor and Chair of the Department of Accounting and Finance at the University of Montana. He earned Ph.D. and M.B.A. degrees from the University of Colorado and his B.S.B.A. from Drake University. He has published in the *Journal of Accounting Education*, *Journal of Accounting, Auditing & Finance*, and *Journal of Accountancy*, among others and has conducted numerous workshops on the subject of introductory accounting education.

Dr. Porter's professional activities include experience as a staff accountant with Deloitte & Touche in Denver, a participant in KPMG Peat Marwick Foundation's Faculty Development program and as a leader in numerous bank training programs. He has won an Excellence in Teaching award from the University of Colorado and an Outstanding Professor Award from San Diego State University.

He served on the Illinois CPA Society's Innovations in Accounting Education Grants Committee, the steering committee of the midwest region of the American Accounting Association, and the board of directors of the Chicago chapter of the Financial Executives Institute. Dr. Porter is also a member of the Montana Society of Certified Public Accountants. At the University of Montana, Dr. Porter was recently selected as Beta Alpha Psi's Outstanding Undergraduate Accounting Professor and also received university-wide recognition from Mortar Board for his teaching excellence.

Curtis L. Norton, is Deloitte & Touche Professor of Accountancy at Northern Illinois University. He earned his Ph.D. from Arizona State University, his M.B.A. from the University of South Dakota, and his B.S. from Jamestown College, North Dakota. His extensive list of publications includes articles in *Accounting Horizons*, *The Journal of Accounting Education*, *Journal of Accountancy*, *Journal of Corporate Accounting*, *Journal of the American Taxation Association*, *Real Estate Review*, *The Accounting Review*, *CPA Journal*, and many others. In 1988-89, Dr. Norton received the University Excellence in Teaching Award, the highest university-wide teaching recognition at NIU. He is also a consultant and has conducted training programs for governmental authorities, banks, utilities, and other entities.

Dr. Norton is a member of the American Accounting Association and a member and officer of the Financial Executives Institute.

To the Student

Now that you've enrolled in Financial Accounting, and have bought your books and assigned supplements, you probably have more questions than answers:

- How can I get the most out of the book and its features?
- How can study aids help me be more successful in the course?

For many, Financial Accounting will be your first course in business. "So what is business, anyway?" you may ask. The strategies in this section, and the *Getting Started in Business* module that follows next before Chapter 1, will start you out on the right foot in the course.

FEATURES TO HELP YOU LEARN

We're dedicated to getting you out of the gate fast in Financial Accounting. In "To the Instructor," we've described and shown images of these features. Here we give you an overview of how you might use them.

Apart from reading the chapter, you can use the study aids in every part of the book:

1. *Get a feel for the chapter—turn to the chapter-opening spread.* Financial accounting is about companies, how they operate and how their managers think. So we've provided you with an actual company in each chapter as a study example—complete with a profile, a sample financial statement, some questions that will help put the company in context, and their Web address.

FOCUS ON FINANCIAL RESULTS

- Chapter-opening introduction illustrates a key financial issue related to the chapter.

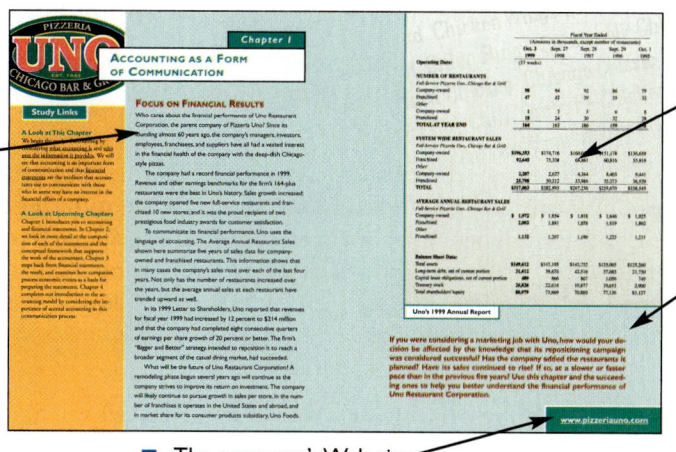

- A financial statement or excerpt from the company's annual report.

- Thought-provoking questions relates the company back to the chapter.

- The company's Web site.

These companies will be referred to in the chapter, so use the opener as a model of your growing understanding of how this company—and all companies—perform.

A Business Strategy box later in the chapter can help you better understand the company, its strategies for success, and its competitors. It's background that may help you if your instructor assigns homework to research the company.

2. *Organize your study using the Learning Objectives.* They are keyed to sections in the text, to the homework assignments, and to the Study Guide. Look them over first, then use them to organize your study.

3. *Make sure to check out the Study Tips in the margins.* These brief aids are designed to help by focusing on making connections between what you've read before and the current topic, or stating a point in a different way.

> **Study Tip**
>
> Use the Study Links at the left of the opening spread to see, chapter-by-chapter, where you are in the course.

> **Study Tip**
>
> To see some sample Learning Objectives and how they will appear, turn back to page xi.

Study Tip

To see a sample Two-Minute Review, turn back to page xi.

Study Tip

To see a sample Warmup Exercise, turn back to page xii.

4. *Use the Two-Minute Reviews in the middle of each chapter to help keep you on track.* These quick reviews have the answers underneath, but going through the process will help you understand the concepts you've just read about in the section.

5. *Prepare for the homework assignments using Warmup Exercises.* These exercises at the end of the chapter, with answers following, focus on helping you learn to format and prepare homework assignments.

6. *Look for key terms in boldface.* This helps you recognize key concepts when they're first used. These terms and their definitions are later tested in the Key Terms Quiz at the end of the chapter.

THE GETTING STARTED IN BUSINESS MODULE: HOW CAN IT HELP?

"Getting Started in Business," following next after the table of contents, will help you answer these questions before you start Chapter 1:

■ What is business?

■ Could I start a successful business?

■ What are the forms that businesses take?

■ What are some of the activities that businesses engage in?

Use this module to get a head start on understanding how accounting fits into the business scheme.

STUDENT SUPPLEMENTS ARE THERE TO HELP

Your instructor may not require all of these ancillaries, but it's still good to know that Harcourt publishes them if you need a little help. You can obtain these ancillaries online from Harcourt College Store at *www.harcourtcollege.com/store/*.

www.harcourtcollege.com/store/

NEW Student CD You'll be up and running with your homework assignments the **Student CD** containing **NEW** spreadsheet homework problem support, PowerPoint slides, and other resources.

www.harcourtcollege.com/ accounting/porteralt3e

Web Site An extensive book web-site is provided for performing **research on each public company** mentioned in the text. **Online quizzing and testing** is available for each chapter. There are also many non-text-specific **activities and resources** that are useful for accounting students, such as the Getting Started tour with resources, review questions, company profiles by topic. Play a stock market game, learn to select stocks, and conduct company research all at *www.harcourtcollege.com/accounting/porteralt3e*. (For a preview, see the front endpapers.)

A sample page from OMAR

Easy navigation, plenty of activities, links to key terms, and audio commentary are some of the features that make **OMAR** a great way to study the basic concepts and skills of accounting— the accounting cycle.

OMAR (Online Multimedia Accounting Review) is a graphical, interactive web-based minicourse that helps you to master the concepts and skills of basic accounting procedures. This four-module course gets you started by identifying events in a company's operations. And, using activities and animation, you'll be preparing financial statements by the end of Module 4. You can take the course and the quizzes again and again to master the material. Your instructor may assign you to take the one-time Mastery Exam for a grade. OMAR's student manual may be purchased online at www.harcourtcollege.com/store/ and is also available through the bookstore. Ask your instructor for details about setting up the course for your class.

WebCourse Your instructor has the option of using the course management web tools available with this book. If so, here is a preview of what's in store for you.

■ **Course Notes** will help guide you through the textbook.

■ **Online Quizzing and Testing** supports the text and extends the chapter homework.

■ **Glossary**—You'll be able to review terminology online along with other online resources found here.

- ■ **Syllabus**—Your instructor's syllabus is online, on one site with the other course materials.
- ■ **Web activities**—Porter/Norton already includes a number of opportunities to use the web, especially for the Internet Research Case at the end of the chapter. These are separate activities to keep you up-to-date with the financials of public companies.
- ■ **Discussion Questions**—Your instructor may use this feature to keep classes interesting and lively.
- ■ **Group projects**—Again, your instructor can choose to assign several of these projects to deepen your learning.

Guide to Understanding and Using Annual Reports, by Angela Sandberg, Floyd W. Kirby, and Elise M. Gantt (all of Jacksonville State University). This popular annual report project, revised and enhanced for the Third Edition, is a step-by step guide to understanding and using any annual report your instructor may assign. This guide allows you to apply the concepts in the text to any public company. From the book's website, you have the ability to download both the horizontal and vertical analysis as well.

Study Guide, by Coby Harmon (University of California, Santa Barbara). Use the Study Guide to review the chapter's main focus, key concepts, key terms, and brush up your homework and test-taking skills (including solutions).

Procedural Review, by Douglas Schneider and Mark McCarthy (both of East Carolina University). This supplement provides you with more opportunity to practice the accounting procedures covered in the book. Arranged by Learning Objective for each chapter, the Procedural Review can be an invaluable tool if you need more help in building your skills.

Working Papers by Diana Tanner (University of North Florida). Why use notebook paper for your homework when you can save time by simply entering the answers in the format preferred by your instructor? This handy book provides all the forms you'll need when your instructor asks you to manually prepare the homework assignments at the back of each chapter.

Tamije Garden Supply, Inc., a Corporate Practice Set by Leon Hanouille (Syracuse University) and Jerry Funk (Brazosport College, Business Branch Office, Inc.) This booklet, with general ledger program CD, allows you to sharpen your accounting cycle skills. Can be started any time after Chapter 3 of the textbook and completed any time after Chapter 9.

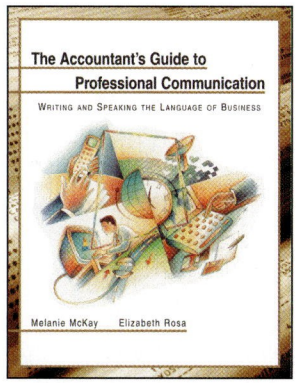

Also available to enhance your business education

The Accountant's Guide to Professional Communication: Writing and Speaking the Language of Business by Melanie McKay (Loyola University of New Orleans) and Elizabeth Rosa (Allentown College of St. Francis de Sales). This supplement can help you write and speak more effectively in this course, and throughout your business education. From written communication to oral presentations and visual aids, this guide includes actual examples from the careers of accounting professionals. One chapter even helps you get a job in the accounting field.

Interactive Decision Cases for Financial Accounting by Guided Exploration LLC With this CD, you gain hands-on practice in making accounting and business decisions while you learn and practice key financial accounting skills applied to today's business. Each of the 8 cases uses data from public companies like Whirlpool, Kmart, Dell, Seagrams, and Apple.

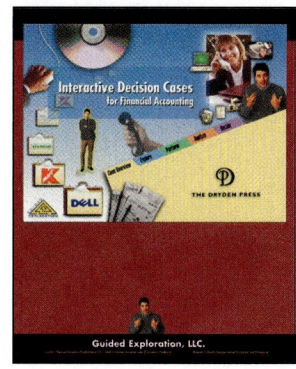

Now turn to the opening module, *Getting Started in Business!*

Brief Contents

Contents

Pizzeria Uno
Boosting sales while continuing to
expand.

Each chapter contains the following material: Warmup Exercises, Solutions to
Warmup Exercises, Review Problem, Solution to Review Problem, Chapter Highlights,
Key Terms Quiz, Alternate Terms, Questions, Exercises, Problems, Cases, Solutions to
Key Terms Quiz

Gateway Inc.
A doubling of cash and equivalents,
and an increase in property, plant,
and equipment.

K2

Increasing net sales with a diversity
of products.

McDonald's
Maintaining growth in revenue will require global strategies.

The Gap
Managing for success in retail: doubling of net sales in two years, and a decrease in cost of goods sold.

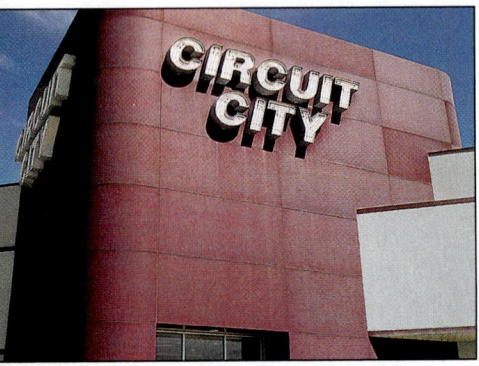

Circuit City
Managing inventory using in-store Build-to-Order stations. Inventory is half of total assets.

PepsiCo
Effect of business and brand changes on accounts and notes receivable, as well as cash and equivalents and short-term investments.

Time Warner / AOL
Merger with AOL. Tangible and intangible operating assets, and "originating brands as engines of growth."

PART III ACCOUNTING FOR LIABILITIES AND OWNERS' EQUITY   394

JCPenney
Improving profitability means managing accounts payable and other current liabilities.

e-business

IBM
With record revenues, and with healthy investments in three key areas, substantial cash is left over for shareholders and stock buybacks.

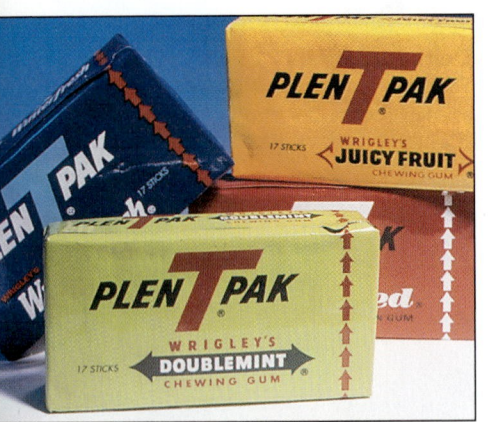

Wrigley
With record net earnings, paying dividends is a tradeoff against greater investments in key markets.

Getting Started in Business

Pick your favorite company. Maybe it is The Gap, because you buy all your clothes there. Or maybe it is The Tribune Company, because they own your favorite team, the Chicago Cubs. Or is it Gateway, because you like their commercials? At any rate, have you ever wondered how the company got started? Here is the abbreviated story of the birth of Uno Restaurant Corporation:

LO 1 Explain why financial information is important in making decisions.

www.pizzeriauno.com

> In 1943, the first Pizzeria Uno opened at the corner of Wabash and Ohio in downtown Chicago. Word began to spread that something new and truly original was happening. If you wanted the world's best deep-dish pizza served in a warm, fun atmosphere, Ike Sewell's upstart restaurant was the only place to go.[1]

PIZZERIA UNO: THE NEED TO MAKE FINANCIAL DECISIONS

From these humble beginnings, Pizzeria Uno made tremendous strides in the second half of the past century. Revenues in 1999 exceeded $214 million. Numerous factors account for the company's phenomenal success. From its beginning, the company has relied on its signature product, the deep-dish pizza, not only to keep customers coming back but also to grow. However, any company owes a major part of its success to its ability to make *financial decisions*. Initially, Ike Sewell made the decision to invest his own money and open a pizzeria. Would *you* have been willing to risk your savings to start a new business? This was a financial decision Ike had to make.

As is often the case with successful businesses, Uno faced a major decision in 1955: whether to expand by opening a larger restaurant. The company took a financial risk and opened a second pizzeria—called Pizzeria Due—in a former mansion one block away. An even tougher decision faced Ike Sewell when he agreed in 1978 to work with Aaron Spencer to expand beyond Chicago and take the deep-dish pizza concept to the nation. This decision obviously involved a much larger commitment of money and risk, and it required Ike to think carefully about the potential for his company. If you had been in his shoes, would you have been willing to risk your personal finances as well as the future of your existing restaurants for the chance to grow even larger?

---

[1]This information, and that in the following section, is provided in more detail in Uno's 1999 annual report.

Beginning with its famous Chicago-style deep dish pizza, Uno has expanded its menu over the years as well as its markets. Uno now operates company-owned and franchised restaurants as well as a consumer products division.

Many restaurants grow through franchising. Uno seized this opportunity in 1980 when it opened the first franchised unit in Washington, D.C. This financial decision proved a fruitful one for the business: Twenty years later, the number of franchised units had grown to over 60.

One of the most important chapters in Uno's history began to unfold in the mid-1980s. Many successful companies reach a point in their existence when it becomes necessary to consider "going public." A public offering of Uno's stock in 1987 provided the company with the financial resources to grow and expand into new markets. For Uno, this monumental decision appears to have been a wise one: Five years later it opened its 100th restaurant, and five years after that the 150th restaurant opened. Not bad for the company that had its roots as a neighborhood pizzeria barely 50 years earlier!

All the major events in the history of Uno involved a need to take risks and make decisions. And in each of these situations, the decision makers needed to rely on financial information. All of us use financial information in making decisions. For example, when you were deciding whether to enroll at your present school, you needed information on the tuition and room-and-board costs at the different schools you were considering. When a stockbroker decides whether to recommend to a client the purchase of stock in a company, the broker needs information on the company's profits and whether it pays dividends. When trying to decide whether to lend money to a company, a banker must consider the company's current debts.

In this book, we explore how accounting can help all of us in making informed financial decisions. Before we turn to the role played by accounting in decision making, we need to explore business in more detail. What *is* business? What forms of organization carry on business activity? In what types of business activity do those organizations engage?

WHAT IS BUSINESS?

LO 2 Understand what business is about.

Just as Pizzeria Uno got its start in downtown Chicago, your study of accounting has to start somewhere. All disciplines have a foundation on which they rest. For accounting, that foundation is business.

Broadly defined, **business** consists of all the activities necessary to provide the members of an economic system with goods and services. Certain business activities focus on the providing of goods or products, such as pizza, automobiles, and computers. Some of these companies produce or manufacture the products. Others are involved in the distribution of the goods, either as wholesalers (who sell to retail outlets) or retailers (who sell to consumers). Other business activities by their nature are service oriented. Corporate giants, such as Citicorp, Walt Disney, Time Warner and United Airlines, remind us of the prominence of service activities in the world today. The relatively recent phenomenon of various "service providers," such as health-care organizations and Internet companies, are a testimony to the growing importance of the service sector in the U.S. economy.

To appreciate the kinds of business enterprises in our economy, consider the various types of companies that have a stake in the delivery of a pint of ice cream to the grocery store. We will use as an example the case of Ben & Jerry's, a Vermont-based producer of super premium ice cream. First, Ben & Jerry's must contract with a *supplier* of milk. The company buys much of its milk from a local company, St. Albans Cooperative Creamery. As a *manufacturer* or *producer*, Ben & Jerry's takes the milk and other various raw materials, such as sugar and chocolate, and transforms them into a finished product. At this stage, a *distributor* or *wholesaler* gets involved. For example, Ben & Jerry's sells a considerable amount of its ice cream to Dreyer's Grand Ice Cream. Dreyer's, in turn, sells the products to many different *retailers,* such as Albertsons and Safeway. Although maybe less obvious, any number of *service* companies are involved in the process. For example, various trucking companies transport the milk to Ben & Jerry's for production, and others move the ice cream along to Dreyer's. Still others get it to supermarkets and other retail outlets. Exhibit GS-1 summarizes the process.

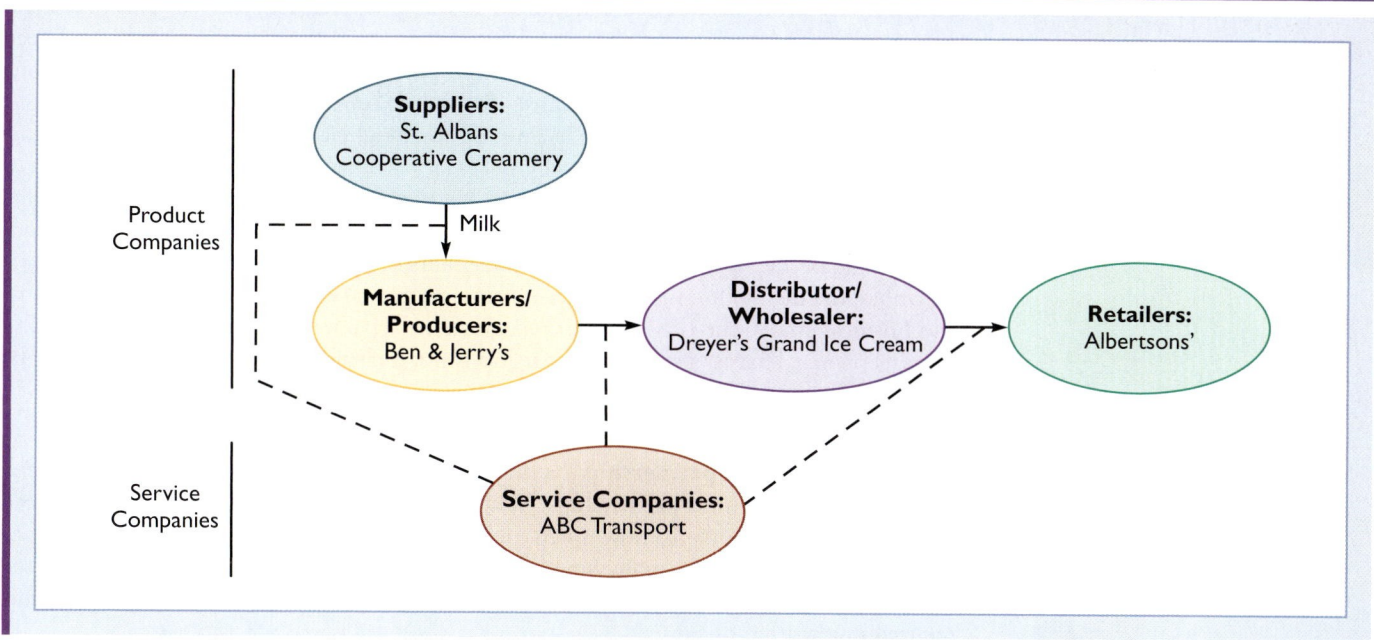

FORMS OF ORGANIZATION

There are many different types of organizations in our society. One convenient way to categorize the myriad types is to distinguish between those that are organized to earn money and those that exist for some other purpose. Although the lines can become blurred, *business entities* generally are organized to earn a profit, whereas *nonbusiness entities* generally exist to serve various segments of society. Both types are summarized in Exhibit GS-2.

LO 3 Distinguish among the forms of organization.

BUSINESS ENTITIES

Business entities are organized to earn a profit. Legally, a profit-oriented company is one of three types: sole proprietorships, partnerships, and corporations.

EXHIBIT GS-2 Forms of Organization

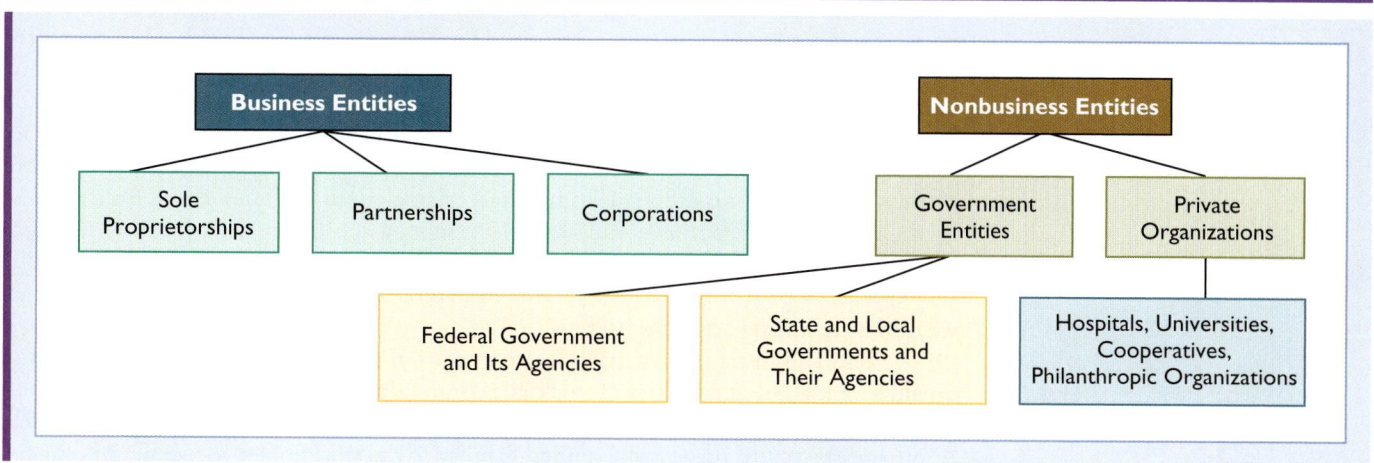

Sole Proprietorships This form of organization is characterized by a single owner. Many small businesses are organized as **sole proprietorships.** Very often the business is owned and operated by the same person. Because of the close relationship between the owner and the business, the affairs of the two must be kept separate. This is one example in accounting of the **economic entity concept,** which requires that a single, identifiable unit of organization be accounted for in all situations. For example, assume that Bernie Berg owns a neighborhood grocery store. In paying the monthly bills, such as utilities and supplies, Bernie must separate his personal costs from the costs associated with the grocery business. In turn, financial statements prepared for the business must not intermingle Bernie's personal affairs with the affairs of the company.

Unlike the distinction made for accounting purposes between an individual's personal and business affairs, the IRS does not recognize the separate existence of a proprietorship from its owner. That is, a sole proprietorship is not a taxable entity; any profits earned by the business are taxed on the return of the individual.

Partnerships A **partnership** is a business owned by two or more individuals. Many small businesses begin as partnerships. When two or more partners start out, they need some sort of agreement as to how much each will contribute to the business and how they will divide any profits. In many small partnerships, the agreement is often just an oral understanding between the partners. In large businesses, the partnership agreement is formalized in a written document.

Although a partnership may involve just two owners, some have thousands of partners. Public accounting firms, law firms, and other types of service companies are often organized as partnerships. Like a sole proprietorship, a partnership is not a taxable entity. The individual partners pay taxes on their proportionate shares of the profits of the business.

Corporations Although sole proprietorships and partnerships dominate in sheer number, corporations control an overwhelming majority of the private resources in this country. A **corporation** is an entity organized under the laws of a particular state. Each of the 50 states is empowered to regulate the creation and operation of businesses organized as corporations in it.

To start a corporation, one must file articles of incorporation with the state. If the articles are approved by the state, a corporate charter is issued, and the corporation can begin to issue stock. A **share of stock** is a certificate that acts as evidence of ownership in a corporation. Although not always the case, stocks of many corporations are traded on organized stock exchanges, such as the New York and American Stock Exchanges.

What are the advantages of running a business as a corporation? This was the question the owners of Uno had to ask themselves. The company enjoyed early success in the market, and to capitalize on that success, it needed to grow. To grow meant that it would need to add more restaurants, which obviously costs money. Where would the money come from?

One of the primary advantages of the corporate form of organization is the ability to raise large amounts of money in a relatively brief period of time. This is what prompted Uno to "go public" in 1987. To raise money, the company sold a specific type of security: stocks. As stated earlier, a share of stock is simply a certificate that evidences ownership in a corporation. Sometimes corporations issue another type of security, called a bond. A **bond** is similar to a share of stock in that it is a certificate or piece of paper issued to someone. However, it is different from a share of stock in that a bond represents a promise by the company to repay a certain amount of money at a future date. In other words, if you were to buy a bond from a company, you would be lending it money. Interest on the bond is usually paid semiannually. We will have more to say about stocks and bonds when we discuss financing activities later.

The ease of transfer of ownership in a corporation is another advantage of this form of organization. If you hold shares of stock in a corporation whose stock is actively traded and you decide that you want out, you simply call your broker and put in an order to sell. Another distinct advantage is the limited liability of the stockholder. Generally speaking, a stockholder is liable only for the amount contributed to the business. That is, if a company goes out of business, the most the stockholder stands to lose is the amount invested. On the other hand, both proprietors and general partners usually can be held personally liable for the debts of the business.

NONBUSINESS ENTITIES

Most **nonbusiness entities** are organized for a purpose other than to earn a profit. They exist to serve the needs of various segments of society. For example, a hospital is organized to provide health care to its patients. A municipal government is operated for the benefit of its citizens. A local school district exists to meet the educational needs of the youth in the community.

All these entities are distinguished by the lack of an identifiable owner. The lack of an identifiable owner and of the profit motive changes to some extent the type of accounting used by nonbusiness entities. This type, called *fund accounting,* is discussed in advanced accounting courses. Regardless of the lack of a profit motive in nonbusiness entities, there is still a demand for the information provided by an accounting system. For example, a local government needs detailed cost breakdowns in order to levy taxes. A hospital may want to borrow money and will need financial statements to present to the prospective lender.

ORGANIZATIONS AND SOCIAL RESPONSIBILITY

Although nonbusiness entities are organized specifically to serve members of society, U.S. business entities also have become more sensitive to their broader social responsibilities. Because they touch the lives of so many members of society, most large corporations recognize the societal aspects of their overall mission and have established programs to meet their social responsibilities. Some companies focus their efforts on local charities while others donate to national or international causes. Certainly all the companies showcased in the chapter openers of this book have programs in place to meet their objectives in the area of corporate giving.

THE NATURE OF BUSINESS ACTIVITY

Because corporations dominate business activity in the United States, in this book we will focus on this form of organization. Corporations engage in a multitude of different types of activities. It is possible to categorize all of them into one of three types, however: financing, investing, and operating.

LO 4 Describe the various types of business activity.

FINANCING ACTIVITIES

All businesses must start with financing. Simply put, money is needed to start a business. Ike Sewell needed money in 1943 to open his first pizzeria. As described earlier, the company found itself in need of additional financing in 1987 to expand, and it made the decision to sell stock to the public. At other times during its history, Uno has raised money by borrowing.

As you will see throughout this book, accounting has its own unique terminology. In fact, accounting is often referred to as *the language of business.* The discussion of financing activities brings up two important accounting terms: liabilities and capital stock. A **liability** is an obligation of a business; it can take many different forms. When a company borrows money at a bank, the liability is called a *note payable.* When a company sells bonds, the obligation is termed *bonds payable.* Amounts owed to the government for taxes are called *taxes payable.* Assume Uno buys cheese to use in making pizzas from the ABC Dairy. Assume ABC gives Uno 30 days to pay for puchases. During this 30-day period, Uno has an obligation called *accounts payable.*

Capital stock is the term used by accountants to indicate the dollar amount of stock sold to the public. Capital stock differs from liabilities in one very important respect.

Those who buy stock in a corporation are not lending money to the business, as are those who buy bonds in the company or make a loan in some other form to the company. Someone who buys stock in a company is called a **stockholder,** and that person is providing a *permanent* form of financing to the business. In other words, there is not a due date at which time the stockholder will be repaid. Normally, the only way for a stockholder to get back his or her original investment from buying stock is to sell it to someone else. Occasionally, a corporation buys back the stock of one of its stockholders. Someone who buys bonds in a company or in some other way makes a loan to it is called a **creditor.** A creditor does *not* provide a permanent form of financing to the business. That is, the creditor expects repayment of the amount loaned and, in many instances, payment of interest for the use of the money as well.

INVESTING ACTIVITIES

There is a natural progression in a business from financing activities to investing activities. That is, once funds are generated from creditors and stockholders, money is available to invest. Uno used the money it received from selling stock to open more restaurants.

An **asset** is a future economic benefit to a business. For example, cash is an asset to a company. Uno's land, buildings, and equipment are assets to it. At any point in time, Uno has ingredients, beverages, and supplies on hand. These items are called *inventory* and are another valuable asset of a company.

An asset represents the right to receive some sort of benefit in the future. The point is that not all assets are tangible in nature, as are inventories and plant and equipment. For example, a majority of Uno's sales are made directly to customers who pay immediately. However, Uno also makes pizzas for sale to hotels, movie theaters, and airlines, such as American Airlines. Assume Uno gives the airline 30 days to pay for a bulk purchase of pizzas. At the time of sale, Uno doesn't have cash yet, but it has another valuable asset. The right to collect the amount due from the customer in 30 days is an asset called an *account receivable.* As a second example, assume that a company acquires from an inventor a patent that will allow the company the exclusive right to manufacture a certain product. The right to the future economic benefits from the patent is an asset. In summary, an asset is a valuable resource to the company that controls it.

At this point, you should notice the inherent tie between assets and liabilities. How does a company satisfy its liabilities, that is, its obligations? Although there are some exceptions, most liabilities are settled by transferring assets. The asset most often used to settle a liability is cash.

OPERATING ACTIVITIES

Once funds are obtained from financing and investments are made in productive assets, a business is ready to begin operations. Every business is organized with a purpose in mind. The purpose of some businesses is to sell a *product.* Ike Sewell organized his company to sell pizza. Other companies provide *services.* Service-oriented businesses are becoming an increasingly important sector of the U.S. economy. Some of the largest corporations in this country, such as banks and airlines, sell services rather than products. Some companies sell both products and services.

Accountants have a name for the sale of products and services. **Revenue** is the inflow of assets resulting from the sale of products and services. When a company makes a cash sale, the asset it receives is cash. When a sale is made on credit, the asset received is an account receivable. For now, you should understand that revenue represents the dollar amount of sales of products and services for a specific period of time.

We have thus far identified one important operating activity: the sale of products and services. However, costs must be incurred to operate a business. Employees must be paid salaries and wages. Suppliers must be paid for purchases of inventory, and the utility company has to be paid for heat and electricity. The government must be paid the taxes owed it. All these are examples of important operating activities of a business. As you might expect by now, accountants use a specific name for the costs incurred in

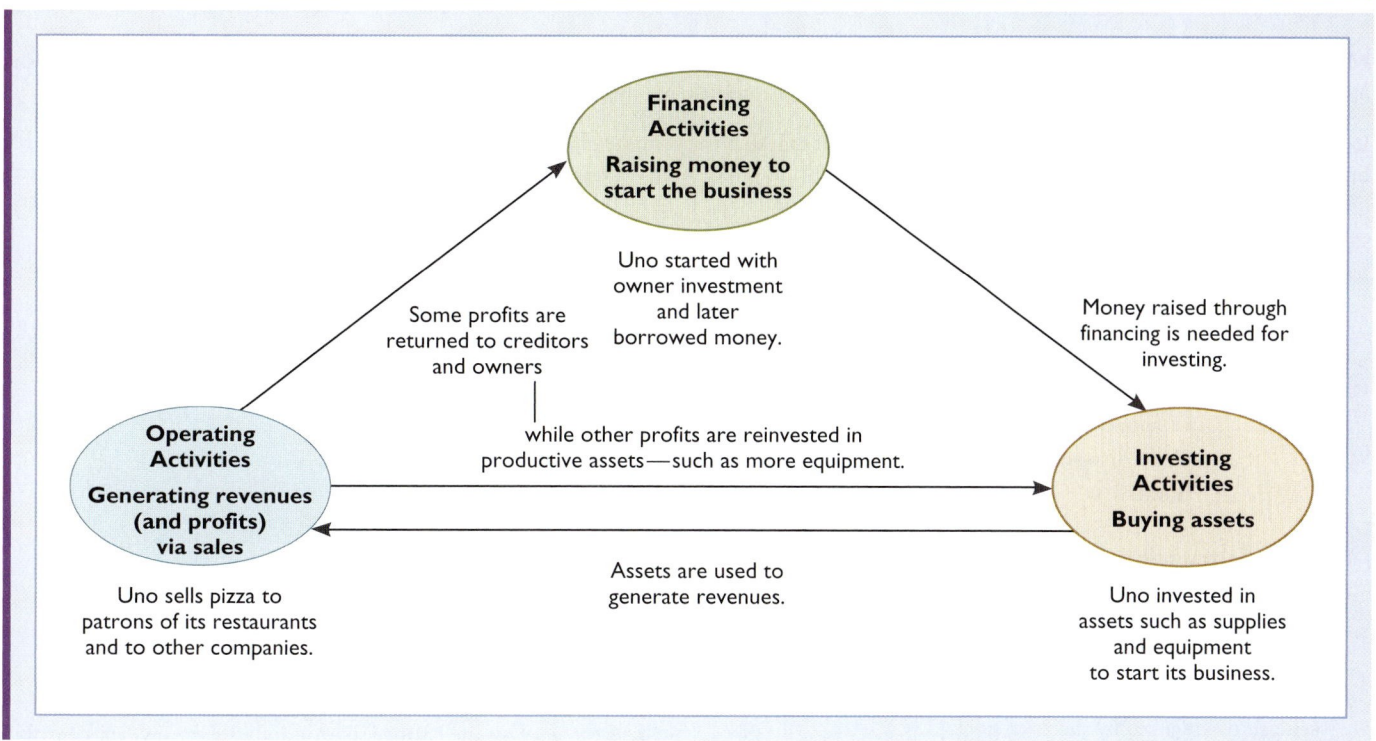

operating a business. An **expense** is the outflow of assets resulting from the sale of goods and services.

Exhibit GS-3 summarizes the three types of activities conducted by a business. Our discussion and the exhibit present a simplification of business activity, but actual businesses are in a constant state of motion with many different financing, investing, and operating activities going on at any one time. The model as portrayed in Exhibit GS-3 should be helpful as you begin the study of accounting, however. To summarize, a company obtains money from various types of financing activities, uses the money raised to invest in productive assets, and then provides goods and services to its customers.

STARTING THE STUDY OF ACCOUNTING

The purpose of this module was to introduce you to business and help you to understand why it is the foundation on which accounting is based. Now that you have a basic understanding of what business is, the types of organizations that engage in business, and the various activities they conduct, you are ready to begin the study of accounting itself.

This module introduced you to business and decision making by telling a brief story of how Uno got started. You will learn more about the company and its financial statements in Chapter 1. Beginning in Chapter 2, another new feature company will start off each chapter as a way of introducing the material in that chapter.

If you do not own stock in one of these companies, how can you get access to its financial statements and other information about it? One way is by calling or writing to the company's investor relations department. A much more efficient and timely approach to gathering this information, however, is to use the Internet. Nearly all major corporations, as well as many smaller ones, now post financial statements and other information on their Web sites. To help in your search, each chapter contains the URLs of the companies discussed there.

KEY TERMS QUIZ

Note to the student: We conclude each chapter with a quiz on the key terms, which are in bold where they appear in the chapter. We have included a quiz for the numerous important terms introduced in this Getting Started module.

Read each definition below and then write the number of that definition in the blank beside the appropriate term it defines. The first one has been done for you. The solution appears at the end of this module. When reviewing terminology, come back to your completed key terms quiz. Study tip: Also check the glossary at the end of the book.

___	Business	___	Nonbusiness entity
___	Business entity	___	Liability
___	Sole proprietorship	___	Capital stock
___	Economic entity concept	___	Stockholder
___	Partnership	___	Creditor
___	Corporation	_1_	Asset
___	Share of stock	___	Revenue
___	Bond	___	Expense

1. **A future economic benefit.**

2. A business owned by two or more individuals; organization form often used by accounting firms and law firms.

3. An inflow of assets resulting from the sale of goods and services.

4. A form of entity organized under the laws of a particular state; ownership evidenced by shares of stock.

5. Organization operated for some purpose other than to earn a profit.

6. An outflow of assets resulting from the sale of goods and services.

7. An obligation of a business.

8. A certificate that acts as ownership in a corporation.

9. A certificate that represents a corporation's promise to repay a certain amount of money and interest in the future.

10. One of the owners of a corporation.

11. Someone to whom a company or person has a debt.

12. The assumption that a single, identifiable unit must be accounted for in all situations.

13. Form of organization with a single owner.

14. A category on the balance sheet to indicate the owners' contributions to a corporation.

15. All the activities necessary to provide the members of an economic system with goods and services.

16. Organization operated to earn a profit.

QUESTIONS

1. What is business about? What do all businesses have in common?

2. What is an asset? Give three examples.

3. What is a liability? How does the definition of *liability* relate to the definition of *asset*?

4. Business entities are organized as one of three distinct forms. What are these three forms?

5. What are the three distinct types of business activities in which companies engage? Assume you start your own company to rent bicycles in the summer and skis in the winter. Give an example of at least one of each of the three types of business activities in which you would engage.

SOLUTIONS TO KEY TERMS QUIZ

_15_	Business (p. GS2)	_5_	Nonbusiness entity (p. GS5)
_16_	Business entity (p. GS3)	_7_	Liability (p. GS5)
_13_	Sole proprietorship (p. GS4)	_14_	Capital stock (p. GS5)
_12_	Economic entity concept (p. GS4)	_10_	Stockholder (p. GS6)
_2_	Partnership (p. GS4)	_11_	Creditor (p. GS6)
_4_	Corporation (p. GS4)	_1_	Asset (p. GS6)
_8_	Share of stock (p. GS4)	_3_	Revenue (p. GS6)
_9_	Bond (p. GS4)	_6_	Expense (p. GS7)

FINANCIAL ACCOUNTING
The Impact on Decision Makers

THE ACCOUNTING MODEL

A WORD TO STUDENTS ABOUT THIS COURSE

Knowing accounting is just smart for everyone in today's job market. Thus this book is not just for accounting majors—it's for anyone who wants to learn how to read and understand financial information. You'll manipulate numbers in this course. But at every turn, this book and its study aids—not to mention your instructor—will walk you through the details. You'll write some memorandums backing up your calculations, pitting your analytical skills against real financial statements and problems. And you'll have the chance to put yourself in different business roles. **In fact, this book will help you think, talk, and write skillfully about accounting information.**

Chapter 1

ACCOUNTING AS A FORM OF COMMUNICATION

Study Links

A Look at This Chapter

We begin the study of accounting by considering <u>what accounting is</u> and <u>who uses the information it provides</u>. We will see that accounting is an important form of communication and that <u>financial statements</u> are the medium that accountants use to communicate with those who in some way have an interest in the financial affairs of a company.

A Look at Upcoming Chapters

Chapter 1 introduces you to accounting and financial statements. In Chapter 2, we look in more detail at the composition of each of the statements and the conceptual framework that supports the work of the accountant. Chapter 3 steps back from financial statements, the result, and examines how companies process economic events as a basis for preparing the statements. Chapter 4 completes our introduction to the accounting model by considering the importance of accrual accounting in this communication process.

FOCUS ON FINANCIAL RESULTS

Who cares about the financial performance of Uno Restaurant Corporation, the parent company of Pizzeria Uno? Since its founding almost 60 years ago, the company's managers, investors, employees, franchisees, and suppliers have all had a vested interest in the financial health of the company with the deep-dish Chicago-style pizzas.

The company had a record financial performance in 1999. Revenue and other earnings benchmarks for the firm's 164-plus restaurants were the best in Uno's history. Sales growth increased; the company opened five new full-service restaurants and franchised 10 new stores; and it was the proud recipient of two prestigious food industry awards for customer satisfaction.

To communicate its financial performance, Uno uses the language of accounting. The Average Annual Restaurant Sales shown here summarize five years of sales data for company-owned and franchised restaurants. This information shows that in many cases the company's sales rose over each of the last four years. Not only has the number of restaurants increased over the years, but the average annual sales at each restaurant have trended upward as well.

In its 1999 Letter to Shareholders, Uno reported that revenues for fiscal year 1999 had increased by 12 percent to $214 million and that the company had completed eight consecutive quarters of earnings per share growth of 20 percent or better. The firm's "Bigger and Better" strategy, intended to reposition it to reach a broader segment of the casual dining market, had succeeded.

What will be the future of Uno Restaurant Corporation? A remodeling phase begun several years ago will continue as the company strives to improve its return on investment. The company will likely continue to pursue growth in sales per store, in the number of franchises it operates in the United States and abroad, and in market share for its consumer products subsidiary, Uno Foods.

	Fiscal Year Ended				
	(Amounts in thousands, except number of restaurants)				
	Oct. 3 1999	Sept. 27 1998	Sept. 28 1997	Sept. 29 1996	Oct. 1 1995
Operating Data:	(53 weeks)				
NUMBER OF RESTAURANTS					
Full-Service Pizzeria Uno...Chicago Bar & Grill					
Company-owned	98	94	92	86	79
Franchised	47	42	39	35	33
Other					
Company-owned	1	3	5	6	8
Franchised	18	24	30	32	28
TOTAL AT YEAR END	164	163	166	159	148
SYSTEM WIDE RESTAURANT SALES					
Full-Service Pizzeria Uno...Chicago Bar & Grill					
Company-owned	$196,353	$174,716	$160,045	$151,178	$136,659
Franchised	92,645	75,338	68,861	60,816	55,916
Other					
Company-owned	2,207	2,627	4,344	8,403	9,441
Franchised	25,798	30,212	33,986	35,273	36,529
TOTAL	$317,003	$282,893	$267,236	$255,670	$238,545
AVERAGE ANNUAL RESTAURANT SALES					
Full-Service Pizzeria Uno...Chicago Bar & Grill					
Company-owned	$ 1,972	$ 1,854	$ 1,818	$ 1,846	$ 1,925
Franchised	2,002	1,881	1,858	1,819	1,862
Other					
Franchised	1,132	1,207	1,199	1,223	1,231
Balance Sheet Data:					
Total assets	$149,612	$143,195	$143,732	$135,065	$125,260
Long-term debt, net of current portion	31,612	38,676	42,516	37,085	21,750
Capital lease obligations, net of current portion	489	666	867	1,056	749
Treasury stock	26,826	22,616	19,877	10,653	2,900
Total shareholders' equity	80,979	73,669	70,880	77,136	83,127

Uno's 1999 Annual Report

If you were considering a marketing job with Uno, how would your decision be affected by the knowledge that its repositioning campaign was considered successful? Has the company added the restaurants it planned? Have its sales continued to rise? If so, at a slower or faster pace than in the previous five years? Use this chapter and the succeeding ones to help you better understand the financial performance of Uno Restaurant Corporation.

www.pizzeriauno.com

After studying this chapter, you should be able to:

LO 1 Identify the primary users of accounting information and their needs. (p. 6)

LO 2 Explain the purpose of each of the financial statements and the relationships among them and prepare a set of simple statements. (p. 8)

LO 3 Identify and explain the primary assumptions made in preparing financial statements. (p. 14)

LO 4 Describe the various roles of accountants in organizations. (p. 16)

WHAT IS ACCOUNTING?

Many people have preconceived notions about what accounting is. They think of it as a highly procedural activity practiced by people who are "good in math." This notion of accounting is very narrow and focuses only on the record-keeping or bookkeeping aspects of the discipline. Accounting is in fact much broader than this in its scope. Specifically, **accounting** is "the process of identifying, measuring, and communicating economic information to permit informed judgments and decisions by users of the information."[1]

Each of the three activities in this definition—*identifying, measuring,* and *communicating*—requires the judgment of a trained professional. We will return later in this chapter to accounting as a profession and the various roles of accountants in our society. Note that the definition refers to the users of economic information and the decisions they make. Who *are* the users of accounting information? We turn now to this important question.

USERS OF ACCOUNTING INFORMATION AND THEIR NEEDS

LO 1 Identify the primary users of accounting information and their needs.

It is helpful to categorize users of accounting information on the basis of their relationship to the organization. Internal users, primarily the managers of a company, are involved in the daily affairs of the business. All other groups are external users.

INTERNAL USERS

The management of a company is in a position to obtain financial information in a way that best suits its needs. For example, if an Uno's restaurant manager needs to know how much it costs to make a large pizza with all the toppings, this information exists in the accounting system and can be reported. If the same manager wants to find out if the monthly payroll is more or less than the budgeted amount, a report can be generated to provide the answer. **Management accounting** is the branch of accounting concerned with providing internal users (management) with information to facilitate planning and control. The ability to produce management accounting reports is limited only by the extent of the data available and the cost involved in generating the relevant information.

EXTERNAL USERS

External users, those not involved directly in the operations of a business, need information that differs from that needed by internal users. In addition, the ability of external users to obtain the information is more limited. Without the day-to-day contact with the affairs of the business, outsiders must rely on the information presented to them by the management of the company.

---

[1]American Accounting Association, *A Statement of Basic Accounting Theory* (Evanston, Ill.: American Accounting Association, 1966), p. 1.

Certain external users, such as the Internal Revenue Service, require that information be presented in a very specific manner, and they have the authority of the law to ensure that they get the required information. Stockholders, bondholders, and other creditors must rely on *financial statements* for their information.[2] **Financial accounting** is the branch of accounting concerned with communication with outsiders through financial statements.

Stockholders and Potential Stockholders   Both existing and potential stockholders need financial information about a business. If you currently own stock in a company, you need information that will aid in your decision either to continue to hold the stock or to sell it. If you are considering buying stock in a company, you need financial information that will help in choosing among competing alternative investments. What has been the recent performance of the company in the stock market? What were its profits for the most recent year? How do these profits compare with those of the prior year? How much did the company pay in dividends? One source for much of this information is the company's financial statements.

BUSINESS STRATEGY

California Pizza Kitchen (CPK). is a casual dining restaurant chain that, like the east coast's Pizzeria Uno chain, specializes in premium pizza for the mainstream market. Like Uno, it both owns and franchises its restaurants, which feature such best sellers as BBQ Chicken Pizza and Thai Chicken Pizza, along with the Philly Cheesesteak Pizza and Grilled Garlic Shrimp Pizza. Pastas, salads, soups, and desserts round out the menu.

California Pizza Kitchen cooking areas are centered around an open-flame oven that forms the centerpiece of the restaurant. The atmosphere is designed to be family-friendly with broad consumer appeal. Through a strategic alliance with Kraft Pizza Company, CPK is also distributing a line of premium frozen pizzas through supermarkets and retail outlets. The frozen product line includes some of the restaurant's most popular items. Says CPK President and CEO Fred Hipp, "We are committed to serving unique and delicious pizzas in our restaurants, and Kraft combined our creativity with their proprietary self-rising crust technology, manufacturing, and marketing expertise to deliver premium quality pizzas that are among the best in the grocer's freezer."

The strategies that have worked so well for Uno—distinctive pizza dining in a friendly upscale atmosphere, plus expansion to the consumer retail market—have worked impressively so far for CPK, too. While the two firms have more or less split the country between them, with Uno in Chicago and the East Coast and CPK mostly in the Western States and District of Columbia, they may soon be closer rivals. CPK is expanding abroad, as Uno has already done, and both plan further expansion at home in the future. There seems little doubt that their geographic market areas will converge, and their market segments are already the same. Is there room for both of them? American diners will be deciding for themselves.

SOURCES: "Profile—California Pizza Kitchen," *Yahoo! Finance*, accessed at http://biz.yahoo.com/p/c/cpki.html, Jan. 12, 2001; "California Pizza Kitchen," *Market Guide*, accessed at http://yahoo.marketgide.com/mgi/frameset.asp?nss=yahoo&rt=news&m=A260D, Jan. 12, 2001; "California Pizza Kitchen Is Stocking More Shelves in the Frozen Food Aisle in Denver, Washington D.C., and Baltimore," *Business Wire*, Dec. 18, 2000.

Bondholders, Bankers, and Other Creditors   Before buying a bond in a company (remember you are lending money to the company), you need to feel comfortable that the company will be able to pay you the amount owed at maturity and the periodic

---

[2]Technically, stockholders are insiders because they own stock in the business. In most large corporations, however, it is not practical for stockholders to be involved in the daily affairs of the business. Thus, they are better categorized here as external users because they normally rely on general-purpose financial statements, as do creditors.

EXHIBIT 1-1   Users of Accounting Information

Categories of Users	Examples of Users	Common Decision	Relevant Question
Internal	Management	Should we open a new restaurant?	What will be the cost to open a new restaurant, and how profitable will it be?
External	Stockholder	Should I buy shares of Uno's stock?	How much did the company earn last year?
	Banker	Should I lend money to Uno's?	What existing debts or liabilities does the company have?
	Employee	Should I ask for a raise?	How much is the company generating in sales, and how much is it paying out in salaries and wages? Is it paying out too much in compensation compared to its sales?
	Supplier	Should I allow Uno's to buy pepperoni from me and pay me later?	What is the current amount of the company's accounts payable?

interest payments. Financial statements can help you to decide whether to purchase a bond. Similarly, before lending money, a bank needs information that will help it to determine the company's ability to repay both the amount of the loan and interest. Therefore, a set of financial statements is a key ingredient in a loan proposal.

Government Agencies   Numerous government agencies have information needs specified by law. For example, the Internal Revenue Service (IRS) is empowered to collect a tax on income from both individuals and corporations. Every year a company prepares a tax return to report to the IRS the amount of income it earned. Another government agency, the Securities and Exchange Commission (SEC), was created in the aftermath of the Great Depression. This regulatory agency sets the rules under which financial statements must be prepared for corporations that sell their stock to the public on organized stock exchanges. Similar to the IRS, the SEC prescribes the manner in which financial information is presented to it. Companies operating in specialized industries submit financial reports to other regulatory agencies, such as the Interstate Commerce Commission and the Federal Trade Commission.

www.irs.gov

www.sec.gov

Other External Users   Many other individuals and groups rely on financial information given to them by businesses. A supplier of raw material needs to know the credit-worthiness of a company before selling it a product on credit. To promote its industry, a trade association must gather financial information on the various companies in the industry. Other important users are stockbrokers and financial analysts. They use financial reports in advising their clients on investment decisions. In reaching their decisions, all of these users rely to a large extent on accounting information provided by management. Exhibit 1-1 summarizes the various users of financial information and the types of decisions they must make.

FINANCIAL STATEMENTS: HOW ACCOUNTANTS COMMUNICATE

LO 2 Explain the purpose of each of the financial statements and the relationships among them and prepare a set of simple statements.

The primary focus of this book is financial accounting. This branch of accounting is concerned with informing management and outsiders about a company through financial statements. We turn our attention now to the composition of three of the major statements: the balance sheet, the income statement, and the statement of retained earnings.[3]

---

[3]The fourth major financial statement is the statement of cash flows. This important statement will be introduced in Chapter 2.

THE ACCOUNTING EQUATION AND THE BALANCE SHEET

Study Tip

The accounting equation and the financial statements are at the heart of this course. Memorize the accounting equation, and make sure you study this introduction to how the financial statements should look, how to read them, and what they say about a company.

The *accounting equation* is the foundation for the entire accounting system:

Assets = Liabilities + Owners' Equity

The left side of the accounting equation refers to the *assets* of the company. Those items that are valuable economic resources and will provide future benefit to it should appear on the left side of the equation. The right side of the equation indicates who provided, or has a claim to, those assets. Some of the assets were provided by creditors, and they have a claim to them. For example, if a company has a delivery truck, the dealer that provided the truck to the company has a claim to the assets until the dealer is paid. The delivery truck would appear on the left side of the equation as an asset to the company; the company's *liability* to the dealer would appear on the right side of the equation. Other assets are provided by the owners of the business. Their claim to these assets is represented by the portion of the right side of the equation called **owners' equity.**

The term *stockholders' equity* is used to refer to the owners' equity of a corporation. **Stockholders' equity** is the mathematical difference between a corporation's assets and its obligations or liabilities. That is, after the amounts owed to bondholders, banks, suppliers, and other creditors are subtracted from the assets, the amount remaining is the stockholders' equity, the amount of interest or claim that the owners have on the assets of the business.

Stockholders' equity arises in two distinct ways. First, it is created when a company issues stock to an investor. As we noted earlier, capital stock reflects ownership in a corporation in the form of a certificate. It represents the amounts contributed by the owners to the company. Second, as owners of shares in a corporation, stockholders have a claim on the assets of a business when it is profitable. **Retained earnings** represents the owners' claims to the company's assets that result from its earnings that have not been paid out in dividends. It is the earnings accumulated or retained by the company.

The **balance sheet** (sometimes called the *statement of financial position*) is the financial statement that summarizes the assets, liabilities, and owners' equity of a company. It is a "snapshot" of the business at a certain date. A balance sheet can be prepared on any day of the year, although it is most commonly prepared on the last day of a month, quarter, or year. At any point in time, the balance sheet must be "in balance." That is, assets must equal liabilities and owners' equity.

Balance sheets for Uno Corporation at the end of two recent years are shown in Exhibit 1-2. Note that Uno's most recent year ended on October 3, 1999, and that the prior year ended on September 27, 1998. The variance in year ends is explained by the company's policy to end each year on the close of business on the Sunday closest to September 30. As the exhibit makes clear, there are the three main sections of the balance sheet corresponding to the three elements of the accounting equation: Assets, Liabilities, and Stockholders' Equity (Uno calls this Shareholders' Equity).

www.pizzeriauno.com

In the following table, note some of the main types of items that appear on the balance sheet:

1 Cash: Includes cash on hand as well as cash in various checking and savings accounts

2 Accounts Receivable: Arises from selling products to customers and allowing them to pay later

3 Inventory: Refers to food, beverages, and supplies currently on hand

4 Property, Equipment, and Leasehold Improvements: Includes the restaurants and the equipment in them that is used to make pizza

5 Accounts Payable: Arises from buying supplies and other items and being allowed to pay later

6 Retained Earnings: Amount of income earned over the life of the company (Uno does not pay any dividends)

Exhibit 1-3 summarizes the relationship between the accounting equation and the items that appear on a balance sheet.

EXHIBIT 1-2 Uno's Balance Sheets

Consolidated Balance Sheets

Year ended	October 3 1999	September 27 1998
(Amounts in thousands, except per share data) $A = L + SE$		
Assets $\boxed{A}$		
Current assets:		
[1] Cash	$752	$2,030
[2] Accounts receivable, net	2,398	1,784
[3] Inventory	2,436	2,296
Prepaid expenses	1,757	815
Total current assets	7,343	6,925
[4] **Property, equipment and leasehold improvements, net**	128,746	125,323
Deferred income taxes	10,020	7,450
Liquor licenses and other assets	3,503	3,497
	$149,612	$143,195

Liabilities and shareholders' equity =		
Current liabilities: $\boxed{L}$		
[5] Accounts payable	$7,798	$6,589
Accrued expenses	8,668	7,949
Accrued compensation and taxes	3,369	2,666
Income taxes payable	2,914	995
Current portions of long-term debt and capital lease obligation	4,075	4,081
Total current liabilities	26,824	22,280
Long-term debt, net of current portion	31,612	38,676
Capital lease obligations, net of current portion	489	666
Other liabilities	9,708	7,904

+

Commitments and contingencies $\boxed{SE}$		
Shareholders' equity:		
Preferred Stock, $1.00 par value; 1,000 shares authorized; no shares issued or outstanding		
Common Stock, $.01 par value, 25,000 shares authorized;		
15,375 shares in 1999 and 15,153 shares in 1998 issued	154	152
Additional paid-in capital	55,648	53,930
[6] Retained earnings	52,003	42,203
	107,805	96,285
Treasury Stock (4,100 shares in 1999 and 3,492 shares in 1998) at cost	(26,826)	(22,616)
Total shareholders' equity	80,979	73,669
	$149,612	$143,195

See accompanying notes.

Assets	=	Liabilities	+	Owners' Equity

Economic resources Examples: • Cash • Accounts receivable • Inventory	**Creditors' claims to the assets** Examples: • Accounts payable • Notes payable	**Owners' claims to the assets** Examples: • Capital stock • Retained earnings

Exhibit 1-3 refers to Owners' Equity while Exhibit 1-2 refers to Shareholders' Equity. Remember, both are correct! "Owners' equity" is the general term by which we refer to ownership. "Shareholders' (or Stockholders') equity" refers only to ownership of a corporation by shareholders.

THE INCOME STATEMENT

An **income statement,** or statement of income, as it is sometimes called, summarizes the revenues and expenses of a company for a period of time. Comparative income statements for Uno for three recent years are shown in Exhibit 1-4. Unlike the balance sheet, an income statement is a *flow* statement. That is, it summarizes the flow of revenues and expenses for the year. As was the case for the balance sheet, you are not expected at this point to understand fully all the complexities involved in preparing an income statement. However, note the two largest items on the income statement: Restaurant Sales, and Labor and Benefits. For now, it is sufficient to understand that Restaurant Sales is Uno's primary source of revenue and Labor and Benefits is its most significant expense.

THE STATEMENT OF RETAINED EARNINGS

As discussed earlier, Retained Earnings represents the accumulated earnings of a corporation less the amount paid in dividends to stockholders. **Dividends** are distributions of the net income or profits of a business to its stockholders. Not all businesses pay cash dividends. Uno's rationale for not paying dividends to stockholders is stated in its annual report:

> The Company has not paid any cash dividends on its Common Stock and for the foreseeable future intends to continue its policy of retaining earnings to finance the development and growth of the Company.

A **statement of retained earnings** explains the change in retained earnings during the period. The basic format for the statement is as follows:

Beginning balance	$xxx,xxx
Add: Net income for the period	xxx,xxx
Deduct: Dividends for the period	xxx,xxx
Ending balance	$xxx,xxx

Revenues minus expenses, or net income, is an increase in retained earnings, and dividends are a decrease in the balance. Why are dividends shown on a statement of retained earnings instead of on an income statement? Dividends are not an expense and thus are

From Concept
TO PRACTICE 1.1

READING GATEWAY'S INCOME STATEMENT Now that you've seen Uno's income statement, turn to the end of the book to Gateway's income statement. Note the large amount of Cost of Sales—$6,745,744,000— on Gateway's 1999 income statement (consolidated income statement). What types of costs would fall into the Cost of Sales category for Gateway?

EXHIBIT 1-4   Uno's Income Statements

Consolidated Statements of Income

Year ended	October 3 1999	September 27 1998	September 28 1997
(Amounts in thousands, except per share data)	(53 weeks)		
Revenues:			
Restaurant sales	$198,560	$177,343	$164,389
Consumer product sales	10,568	9,384	9,115
Franchise income	5,105	4,549	4,516
	214,233	191,276	178,020
Costs and expenses:			
Cost of food and beverages	54,683	48,567	43,994
Labor and benefits	64,700	58,139	54,183
Occupancy costs	29,199	27,988	27,045
Other operating costs	18,333	18,086	16,067
General and administrative	16,629	13,661	13,384
Depreciation and amortization	12,702	12,183	12,469
Special charges			4,000
	196,246	178,624	171,142
Operating income	17,987	12,652	6,878
Other expense (income):			
Interest expense	3,160	3,527	2,695
Other expense (income)	(21)	134	132
	3,139	3,661	2,827
Income before income taxes	14,848	8,991	4,051
Provision for income taxes	5,048	2,968	1,378
Income before cumulative effect **of change in accounting principle**	9,800	6,023	2,673
Cumulative effect of change in accounting principle for pre-opening costs, net of income tax benefit of $313		636	
Net income	$9,800	$ 5,387	$2,673

See accompanying notes.

Uno's primary source of revenue

Uno's most significant expense

not a component of net income, as are expenses. Instead, they are a *distribution of* the income of the business to its stockholders.

Recall that stockholders' equity consists of two parts: capital stock and retained earnings. In lieu of a separate statement of retained earnings, many corporations prepare a comprehensive statement to explain the changes both in the various capital stock accounts and in retained earnings during the period. Uno, for example, presents the more comprehensive statement of stockholders' equity. (It is not shown here, but you will find it in the printed annual report or online with Uno's other financial statements.) Because Uno does not pay dividends, the only activity reported in the Retained Earnings column of its statement of stockholders' equity is net income.

RELATIONSHIPS AMONG UNO'S FINANCIAL STATEMENTS

Because the statements of a company such as Uno are complex, it may not be easy at this point to see the important links among them. The relationships among the statements are summarized for you in Exhibit 1-5. Recall that in its annual report, Uno does not present a separate statement of retained earnings. The information for the statement of retained earnings in Exhibit 1-5 appears as one of the columns in Uno's statement of stockholders' equity. Two important relationships are seen by examining the exhibit (NOTE: Here and throughout the book, the numbers that follow correspond to the highlighted numbers in the exhibit; numbers in this exhibit are stated in thousands of dollars):

1 The 1999 income statement reports net income of $9,800. Net income increases retained earnings, as reported on the statement of retained earnings.

2 The ending balance of $52,003 in retained earnings, as reported on the statement of retained earnings for 1999, is transferred to the balance sheet at the end of 1999.

Two-Minute Review

1. State the accounting equation, and indicate what each term means.

2. What are the three financial statements presented in this chapter?

3. How do amounts in the three statements interrelate?

Answers:

1. Assets = Liabilities + Owners' Equity
Assets are economic resources. Liabilities are creditors' claims against assets. Owners' Equity is owners' claims against assets. See Exhibit 1-3.

2. The three financial statements are the balance sheet, the income statement, and the statement of retained earnings.

3. Net income on the income statement increases retained earnings on the statement of retained earnings. The ending balance in retained earnings is transferred to the balance sheet. See Exhibit 1-5.

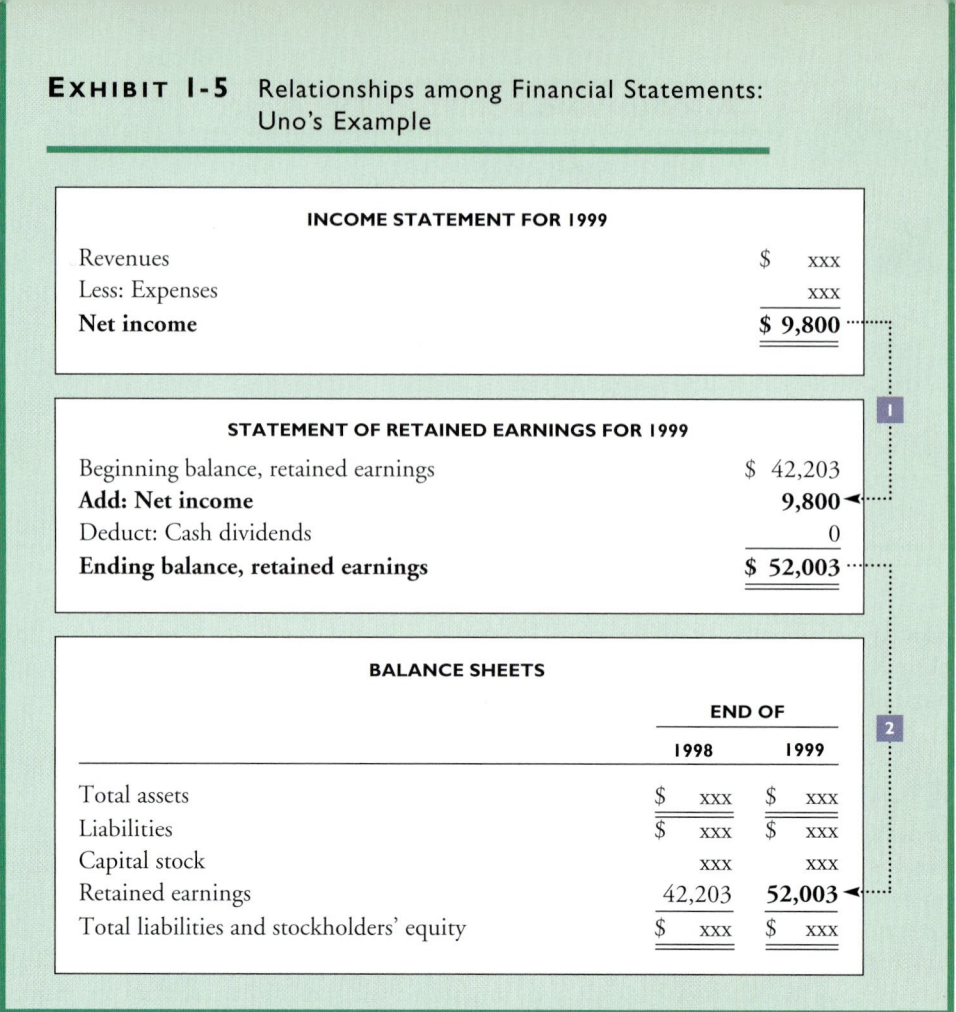

EXHIBIT 1-5 Relationships among Financial Statements: Uno's Example

---

INCOME STATEMENT FOR 1999

Revenues	$ xxx
Less: Expenses	xxx
Net income	**$ 9,800**

STATEMENT OF RETAINED EARNINGS FOR 1999

Beginning balance, retained earnings	$ 42,203
Add: Net income	**9,800**
Deduct: Cash dividends	0
Ending balance, retained earnings	**$ 52,003**

BALANCE SHEETS

	END OF	
	1998	**1999**
Total assets	$ xxx	$ xxx
Liabilities	$ xxx	$ xxx
Capital stock	xxx	xxx
Retained earnings	42,203	**52,003**
Total liabilities and stockholders' equity	$ xxx	$ xxx

THE CONCEPTUAL FRAMEWORK: FOUNDATION FOR FINANCIAL STATEMENTS

LO 3 Identify and explain the primary assumptions made in preparing financial statements.

Study Tip

The concepts in this section underlie everything you will learn throughout the course. You'll encounter them later in the context of specific topics.

Many people perceive the work of an accountant as being routine. In reality, accounting is anything but routine and requires a great deal of judgment on the part of the accountant. The record-keeping aspect of accounting—what we normally think of as bookkeeping—is the routine part of the accountant's work and only a small part of it. Most of the job deals with communicating relevant information to financial statement users.

The accounting profession has developed a *conceptual framework for accounting* that aids accountants in their role as interpreters and communicators of relevant information. The purpose of the framework is to act as a foundation for the specific principles and standards needed by the profession. An important part of the conceptual framework is a set of assumptions accountants make in preparing financial statements. We will briefly consider these assumptions, returning to a more detailed discussion of them in later chapters.

The *economic entity concept* was introduced in "Getting Started" when we first discussed different types of business entities. This assumption requires that an identifiable, specific entity be the subject of a set of financial statements. For example, assume that you own 100 shares of Uno's stock. Even though you own part of Uno, your personal affairs must be kept separate from the business affairs of the company. When we look at a balance sheet for the pizza business, we need assurance that it shows the financial position of that entity only and does not intermingle the personal assets and liabilities of you or any of the other stockholders.

The **cost principle** requires that accountants record assets at the cost paid to acquire them and continue to show this amount on all balance sheets until the company disposes of them. With a few exceptions, companies do not carry assets at their market value (how much they could sell the asset for today) but at original cost. Accountants use the term *historical cost* to refer to the original cost of an asset. Why not show an asset, such as land, at market value? The *subjectivity* inherent in determining market values supports the practice of carrying assets at their historical cost. The cost of an asset is verifiable by an independent observer and is much more *objective* than market value.

Accountants assume that the entity being accounted for is a **going concern.** That is, they assume that Uno is not in the process of liquidation and that it will continue indefinitely into the future. Another important reason for using historical cost rather than market value to report assets is the going concern assumption. If we assume that a business is *not* a going concern, then we assume that it is in the process of liquidation. If this is the case, market value might be more relevant than cost as a basis for recognizing the assets. But if we are able to assume that a business will continue indefinitely, cost can be more easily justified as a basis for valuation. The **monetary unit** used in preparing the statements of Uno was the dollar. The dollar is used as the monetary unit because it is the recognized medium of exchange in the United States. It provides a convenient yardstick to measure the position and earnings of the business. As a yardstick, however, the dollar, like the currencies of all other countries, is subject to instability. We are all well aware that a dollar will not buy as much today as it did 10 years ago.

Inflation is evidenced by a general rise in the level of prices in an economy. Its effect on the measuring unit used in preparing financial statements is an important concern to the accounting profession. Although accountants have experimented with financial statements adjusted for the changing value of the measuring unit, the financial statements now prepared by corporations are prepared under the assumption that the monetary unit is relatively stable. At various times in the past, this has been a reasonable assumption and at other times not so reasonable.

Under the **time period** assumption, accountants assume that it is possible to prepare an income statement that accurately reflects net income or earnings for a specific time period. In the case of Uno, this time period was one year. It is somewhat artificial to measure the earnings of a business for a period of time indicated on a calendar, whether it be a month, a quarter, or a year. Of course, the most accurate point in time to measure the earnings of a business would be at the end of its life. Accountants prepare periodic statements, however, because the users of the statements demand information about the entity on a regular basis.

Financial statements prepared by accountants must conform to **generally accepted accounting principles (GAAP).** This term refers to the various methods, rules, practices, and other procedures that have evolved over time in response to the need for some form of regulation over the preparation of financial statements. As changes have taken place in the business environment over time, GAAP have developed in response to these changes.

ACCOUNTING AS A SOCIAL SCIENCE

Accounting is a service activity. As we have seen, its purpose is to provide financial information to decision makers. Thus, accounting is a *social* science. Accounting principles are much different from the rules that govern the *physical* sciences. For example, it is a rule of nature that an object dropped from your hand will eventually hit the ground rather than be suspended in air. There are no rules comparable to this in accounting. The principles that govern financial reporting are not governed by nature but instead develop in response to changing business conditions. For example, consider the lease of an office building. Leasing has developed in response to the need to have access to valuable assets, such as office space, without spending the large sum necessary to buy the asset. As leasing has increased in popularity, it has been left to the accounting profession to develop guidelines, some of which are quite complex, to be followed in accounting for leases. Those guidelines are now part of GAAP.

Is this company a going concern?
One firm goes out of business; another thrives in the same location. The difference may lie in making the best decisions possible based on high-quality financial information.

Two-Minute Review

1. Name the four concepts (other than the economic entity concept) in the conceptual framework presented in this section.

2. Give a brief example of each concept.

3. What is "GAAP"?

Answers:

1. Cost principle, going concern, monetary unit, and time period assumption.

2. Under the cost principle, we record assets at their cost rather than at market value. Example: Uno would record a new pizza oven at its purchase price. Under going concern, we assume that the company will continue existing indefinitely. Example: Uno will continue to operate rather than begin liquidating its assets. The monetary unit, such as the dollar, is the company's recognized medium of exchange. Example: Uno uses the dollar as the monetary unit. The time period assumption imposes, for reporting purposes, an arbitrary time period (such as a year) that is shorter than the company's life span. Example: Uno's income statement is for the fiscal year ended October 3, 1999.

3. GAAP are the methods, rules, practices, and other procedures that have evolved to govern the preparation of financial statements.

WHO DETERMINES THE RULES OF THE GAME?

Who determines the rules to be followed in preparing an income statement or a balance sheet? No one group is totally responsible for setting the standards or principles to be followed in preparing financial statements. The process is a joint effort among the following groups.

www.sec.gov

The federal government, through the **Securities and Exchange Commission (SEC),** has the ultimate authority to determine the rules for preparing financial statements by companies whose securities are sold to the general public. However, for the most part, the SEC has allowed the accounting profession to establish its own rules.

www.fasb.org

The **Financial Accounting Standards Board (FASB)** sets these accounting standards in the United States. A small independent group with a large staff, the board has issued more than 130 financial accounting standards, and six statements of financial accounting concepts, since its creation in the early 1970s. These standards deal with a variety of financial reporting issues, such as the proper accounting for lease arrangements and pension plans, and the concepts are used to guide the board in setting accounting standards.

www.aicpa.org

The **American Institute of Certified Public Accountants (AICPA)** is the professional organization of certified public accountants. It advises the FASB, but actually sets the auditing standards to be followed by public accounting firms.

Finally, if you are considering buying stock in Porsche, the German-based car manufacturer, you'll want to be sure that the rules Porsche followed in preparing its statements are similar to those the FASB requires for U.S. companies. Unfortunately, accounting standards can differ considerably from one country to another. The **International**

www.iasc.org.uk

Accounting Standards Committee (IASC) was formed in 1973 to develop worldwide accounting standards. More than 100 organizations from 80 different countries, including the FASB in this country, participate in the IASC's efforts to develop international reporting standards. Although the group has made considerable progress, compliance with the standards of the IASC is strictly voluntary, and much work remains to be done in developing international accounting standards.

THE ACCOUNTING PROFESSION

LO 4 Describe the various roles of accountants in organizations.

Accountants play many different roles in society. Understanding the various roles will help you to appreciate more fully the importance of accounting in organizations.

EXHIBIT 1-6 Partial Organization Chart

This partial organization chart does not show details of the other departments in the company—such as marketing, sales, production, and so on. That does not mean they are unimportant to the flow of accounting information. In fact, accounting information for internal decision making forms a complex system of reporting, responsibility, and control collectively known as management accounting.

EMPLOYMENT BY PRIVATE BUSINESS

Many accountants work for business entities. Regardless of the types of activities companies engage in, accountants perform a number of important functions for them. A partial organization chart for a corporation is shown in Exhibit 1-6. The chart indicates that three individuals report directly to the chief financial officer: the controller, the treasurer, and the director of internal auditing.

The **controller** is the chief accounting officer for a company and typically has responsibility for the overall operation of the accounting system. Accountants working for the controller record the company's activities and prepare periodic financial statements. In this organization, the payroll function is assigned to the controller's office, as is responsibility for the preparation of budgets.

The **treasurer** of an organization is typically responsible for the safeguarding, as well as the efficient use, of the company's liquid resources, such as cash. Note that the director of the tax department in this corporation reports to the treasurer. Accountants in the tax department are responsible for both preparing the company's tax returns and planning transactions in such a way that the company pays the least amount of taxes possible within the laws of the Internal Revenue Code.

Internal auditing is the department responsible in a company for the review and appraisal of accounting and administrative controls. The department must determine whether the company's assets are properly accounted for and protected from losses. Recommendations are made periodically to management for improvements in the various controls.

EMPLOYMENT BY NONBUSINESS ENTITIES

Nonbusiness organizations, such as hospitals, universities, and various branches of the government, have as much need for accountants as do companies organized to earn a profit. Although the profit motive is not paramount to nonbusiness entities, all organizations must have financial information to operate efficiently. A county government needs detailed cost information in determining the taxes to levy on its constituents. A university must pay close attention to its various operating costs in setting the annual tuition rates. Accountants working for nonbusiness entities perform most of the same tasks as their counterparts in the business sector. In fact, many of the job titles in business entities, such as controller and treasurer, are also used by nonbusiness entities.

EMPLOYMENT IN PUBLIC ACCOUNTING

Public accounting firms provide valuable services in much the same way as do law firms or architectural firms. They provide a professional service for their clients in return for a fee. The usual services provided by public accounting firms include auditing and tax and management consulting services.

Auditing Services   The auditing services rendered by public accountants are similar in certain respects to the work performed by internal auditors. However, there are key differences between the two types of auditing. Internal auditors are more concerned with the efficient operation of the various segments of the business, and, therefore, the work they do is often called *operational auditing.* On the other hand, the primary objective of the external auditor, or public accountant, is to assure stockholders and other users that the statements are fairly presented. In this respect, **auditing** is the process of examining the financial statements and the underlying records of a company in order to render an opinion as to whether the statements are fairly presented.

As we discussed earlier, the financial statements are prepared by the company's accountants. The external auditor performs various tests and procedures to be able to render his or her opinion. The public accountant has a responsibility to the company's stockholders and any other users of the statements. Because most stockholders are not actively involved in the daily affairs of the business, they must rely on the auditors to ensure that management is fairly presenting the financial statements of the business.

Note that the **auditors' report** is an *opinion,* not a statement of fact. For example, one important procedure performed by the auditor to obtain assurance as to the validity of a company's inventory is to observe the year-end physical count of inventory by the company's employees. However, this is done on a sample basis. It would be too costly for the auditors to make an independent count of every single item of inventory.

The auditors' report on the financial statements for Uno is shown in Exhibit 1-7. Note first that the report is directed to the company's board of directors. The company is audited by Ernst & Young, a large international accounting firm. Public accounting firms range in size from those with a single owner to others, such as Ernst & Young, that have thousands of partners. The opinion given by Ernst & Young on the company's financial statements is the *standard auditors' report.* The first paragraph indicates that the firm has examined the company's balance sheet and the related statements of income, stockholders' equity, and cash flows. Note that the second paragraph of the report indicates that evidence supporting the amounts and disclosures in the statements was examined on a *test* basis. The third paragraph states the firm's *opinion* that the financial statements are fairly presented in conformity with GAAP. (We have highlighted these paragraphs for clarity.)

Tax Services   In addition to auditing, public accounting firms provide a variety of tax services. Firms often prepare the tax returns for the companies they audit. They also usually work throughout the year with management to plan acquisitions and other transactions to take full advantage of the tax laws. For example, if tax rates are scheduled to decline next year, a public accounting firm would advise its client to accelerate certain expenditures this year as much as possible to receive a higher tax deduction than would be possible by waiting until next year.

Management Consulting Services   By working closely with management to provide auditing and tax services, a public accounting firm becomes very familiar with various aspects of a company's business. This vantage point allows the firm to provide expert

From *Concept*

TO PRACTICE 1.2

READING UNO'S AUDITORS' REPORT   Note the date at the bottom of the report. Why do you think it takes one month after the end of the year to issue this report?

www.ey.com

EXHIBIT 1-7 Uno's Auditors' Report

Report of Ernst & Young LLP, Independent Auditors

The Board of Directors
Uno Restaurant Corporation

We have audited the accompanying consolidated balance sheets of Uno Restaurant Corporation and subsidiaries (the Company) as of October 3, 1999 and September 27, 1998, and the related consolidated statements of income, shareholders' equity, and cash flows for each of the three years in the period ended October 3, 1999. These financial statements are the responsibility of the Company's management. Our responsibility is to express an opinion on these financial statements based on our audits.

We conducted our audits in accordance with generally accepted auditing standards. Those standards require that we plan and perform the audit to obtain reasonable assurance about whether the financial statements are free of material misstatement. An audit includes examining, on a test basis, evidence supporting the amounts and disclosures in the financial statements. An audit also includes assessing the accounting principles used and significant estimates made by management, as well as evaluating the overall financial statement presentation. We believe that our audits provide a reasonable basis for our opinion.

In our opinion, the financial statements referred to above present fairly, in all material respects, the consolidated financial position of Uno Restaurant Corporation and subsidiaries at October 3, 1999 and September 27, 1998, and the consolidated results of their operations and their cash flows for each of the three years in the period ended October 3, 1999, in conformity with generally accepted accounting principles.

As discussed in Note 1 to the consolidated financial statements, during fiscal year 1998, the Company adopted the provisions of the American Institute of Certified Public Accountants' Statement of Position 98-5, "Reporting the Costs of Start-up Activities."

Ernst & Young LLP

Boston, Massachusetts
October 29, 1999, except for Note 14,
  as to which the date is November 30, 1999

Standard Auditor's Report

First Paragraph	Second Paragraph	Third Paragraph
says that the auditor has examined the statements.	indicates that evidence was gathered on a test basis.	states the auditor's opinion.

EXHIBIT 1-8 Salaries in the Accounting Profession

Position	Salary Range	
Public Accounting		
➤ Staff Auditors (1–3 years' experience)	$31,250–$44,250	$
Managers	$57,500–$97,000	$$
Partners	$150,000+	$$$
Industry		
➤ Staff Accountants (1–3 years' experience)	$32,250–$45,000	$
Corporate Controllers	$52,000–$150,250	$$–$$$
Chief Financial Officers	$73,500–$335,000	$$–$$$$
➤ **Government (entry-level)**		
Federal	$28,863 average	$
State/Local	$28,571 average	$

Accounting graduates start here.

advice to the company to improve its operations. The management consulting services rendered by public accounting firms to their clients take a variety of forms. For example, the firm might advise the company on the design and installation of a computer system to fill its needs. The services provided in this area have grown dramatically to include such diverse activities as advice on selection of a new plant site or an investment opportunity.

ACCOUNTANTS IN EDUCATION

Some accountants choose a career in education. As the demand for accountants in business entities, nonbusiness organizations, and public accounting has increased, so has the need for qualified professors to teach this discipline. Accounting programs range from two years of study at community colleges to doctoral programs at some universities. All these programs require the services of knowledgeable instructors. In addition to their teaching duties, many accounting educators are actively involved in research. The **American Accounting Association** is a professional organization of accounting educators and others interested in the future of the profession. The group advances its ideas through its many committees and the publication of a number of journals.

www.aaa-edu.org

ACCOUNTING AS A CAREER

As you can see, a number of different career paths in accounting are possible. The stereotypical view of the accountant as a "numbers person and not a people person" is seriously

ACCOUNTING FOR YOUR DECISIONS

You Are a Student

As a student, you decide to go into the accounting profession. However, you are not sure which area to focus on: private, nonbusiness, public, or education. What information would you seek to help you make this decision?

ANS: You may want to consider the following (not necessarily in this order): (1) both starting and potential increases in salaries; (2) education requirements; (3) advancement opportunities; (4) fringe benefits; and (5) challenging work.

FOCUS ON USERS

Using Financial Data to Make Career Decisions

Most people are faced with tough financial decisions at one point or another during their lives. Understanding the principles of accounting and putting them to work, both in professional and personal situations, can make these decisions easier to manage. Lynn Homburg, a general sales manager for a promotional marketing company in New York, has relied on accounting principles since the day she entered the work force. But, she has made use of these same principles since college, when her quality of life depended on her ability to budget.

In college, Lynn wanted to take advantage of her school's program to study abroad. Because of the expense involved, she decided that she needed to start bringing in more money. She took two part-time jobs during the year leading up to the summer trip, both of which helped her to finance the program. After college, Lynn took the idea of financial management a step further. She initiated a monthly budgeting system based on her income, accounting for everything from rent to magazine subscriptions. She immediately started to notice the positive effects of this regimen. As she says, "I was aware of my tendency to overextend myself financially, so I knew that the only way for me to reach my financial goals was to know where my money was going each month. By implementing this system, I've been able to live the Manhattan lifestyle I want and to invest in my future." Lynn's budget has also helped her to make periodic spending decisions. As she explains, "I knew I wanted to take a long vacation to Spain. Figuring out the costs of this and then plugging them into my overall budget made me realize that getting a ski house with my friends that winter wouldn't make sense."

Personal decisions such as these mirror the decisions Lynn faces in her professional life today. She says, "As a sales manager, it is my responsibility to ensure that my team is meeting our sales and profit goals. By closely following these numbers, I am able to figure out what the team needs to be doing to reach those goals: Do we need to do a sales blitz to generate more sales, increase our profit margin by 5 percent on each sale, or scale back on entertainment expenses? It's very similar to the questions I ask with regard to my own finances: Do I need to increase my income, put more into investments, or cut my expenses?"

Name: Lynn Homburg
Education: B.S., Miami University (Oxford, Ohio)
College Major: Marketing
Occupation: General Sales Manager, Boise Marketing Services, Inc., New York
Age: 30

---

outdated. Various specialties are now emerging, including tax accounting, environmental accounting, forensic accounting, software development, and accounting in the entertainment and telecommunications industries. Some of these opportunities exist in both the business and the nonbusiness sectors. For example, forensic accounting has become an exciting career field as both corporations and various agencies of the federal government, such as the FBI, concern themselves with fraud and white-collar crime.

As in any profession, salaries in accounting vary considerably depending on numerous factors, including educational background and other credentials, number of years of experience, and size of the employer. For example, most employers pay a premium for candidates with a master's degree and professional certification, such as the CPA. Exhibit 1-8 indicates salaries for various positions within the accounting field.[4]

---

[4]The information in this section regarding career opportunities and salaries was drawn primarily from the AICPA's Web site (http://www.aicpa.org). The AICPA's Web site is based on the 2000 Robert Half and Accounttemps Salary Guide.

ACCOUNTANTS AND ETHICAL JUDGMENTS

Remember the primary goal of accounting: to provide useful information to aid in the decision-making process. As we discussed, the work of the accountant in providing useful information is anything but routine and requires the accountant to make subjective judgments about what information to present and how to present it. The latitude given accountants in this respect is one of the major reasons accounting is a profession and its members are considered professionals. Along with this designation as a professional, however, comes a serious responsibility. As we noted, financial statements are prepared for external parties who must rely on these statements to provide information on which to base important decisions.

At the end of each chapter are cases titled "Accounting and Ethics: What Would You Do?" The cases require you to evaluate difficult issues and make a decision. Judgment is needed in deciding which accounting method to select or how to report a certain item in the statements. As you are faced with these decisions, keep in mind the trust placed in the accountant by various financial statement users. This is central to reaching an ethical decision.

A FINAL NOTE ABOUT UNO AND GATEWAY

As you have seen in this chapter, accounting is a practical discipline. Financial statements of real companies, including Uno and Gateway, are used throughout the remainder of the book to help you learn more about this practical discipline. For example, some of the From Concept to Practice sidebars in future chapters will require you to return to the financial statements of these two companies, as will some of the cases at the end of the chapters. Because no two sets of financial statements look the same, however, you will be introduced to the financial statements of many other real companies as well. Use this opportunity to learn more not only about accounting but also about each of these companies.

WARMUP EXERCISES

> **Study Tip**
>
> Use these exercises to get accustomed to the assignments that follow.

LO 2 **Warmup Exercise 1-1** Your Assets and Liabilities
Consider your own situation in terms of assets and liabilities.

Required

1. Name three of your financial assets.
2. Name three of your financial liabilities.

Key to the Solution
Recall Exhibit 1-3 for definitions of assets and liabilities.

LO 2 **Warmup Exercise 1-2** Uno's Assets and Liabilities

www.pizzeriauno.com   Think about Uno's business in balance sheet terms.

Required

1. Name three of Uno's assets.
2. Name three of Uno's liabilities.

Key to the Solution
Recall Exhibit 1-2 if you need to see Uno's balance sheet. Also consult the list on page 9.

LO 2 **Warmup Exercise 1-3** Uno and the Accounting Equation

www.pizzeriauno.com   Place Uno's total assets, total liabilities, and total owners' equity in the form of the accounting equation.

Key to the Solution

Recall Exhibit 1-2. You will have to separate the liabilities and the stockholders' equity because they are not subtotaled for you.

SOLUTIONS TO WARMUP EXERCISES

Warmup Exercise 1-1   Your Assets and Liabilities

1. Possible personal financial assets might include: checking accounts, savings accounts, certificates of deposit, money market accounts, stocks, bonds, and mutual funds.

2. Possible personal financial liabilities might include: student loans, car loans, home mortgage, and amounts borrowed from relatives.

Warmup Exercise 1-2   Uno's Assets and Liabilities

1. Uno's assets are: Cash; Accounts receivable; Inventory; Prepaid expenses; Property, equipment, and leasehold improvements; Deferred income taxes; and Liquor licenses and other assets.

2. Uno's liabilities are: Accounts payable; Accrued expenses; Accrued compensation and taxes; Income taxes payable; Current portion of long-term debt and capital lease obligation, Long-term debt, net of current portion; Capital lease obligation, net of current portion; and Other liabilities.

Warmup Exercise 1-3   Uno and the Accounting Equation

$$\text{Assets} = \text{Liabilities} + \text{Owners' Equity}$$
$$\$149,612 \quad \$68,633 \ + \quad \$80,979$$

REVIEW PROBLEM

Greenway Corporation is organized on June 1, 2001. The company will provide lawn-care and tree-trimming services on a contract basis. Following is an alphabetical list of the items that should appear on its income statement for the first month and on its balance sheet at the end of the first month (you will need to determine on *which* statement each should appear).

Accounts payable	$ 800
Accounts receivable	500
Building	2,000
Capital stock	5,000
Cash	3,300
Gas, utilities, and other expenses	300
Land	4,000
Lawn-care revenue	1,500
Notes payable	6,000
Retained earnings (beginning balance)	–0–
Salaries and wages expense	900
Tools	800
Tree-trimming revenue	500
Truck	2,000

Required

1. Prepare an income statement for the month of June.

2. Prepare a balance sheet at June 30, 2001. *Note:* You will need to determine the balance in Retained Earnings at the end of the month.

3. The financial statements you have just prepared are helpful, but in many ways they are a starting point. Assuming this is your business, what additional questions do they raise that you need to consider?

> **Study Tip**
>
> **Note to the student:** At the end of each chapter is a problem to test your understanding of some of the major ideas presented in the chapter. Try to solve the problem before turning to the solution that follows it.

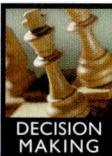

DECISION MAKING

y

Review Problem | **23**

Solution to Review Problem

1.

GREENWAY CORPORATION
INCOME STATEMENT
FOR THE MONTH ENDED JUNE 30, 2001

Revenues:		
Lawn care	$1,500	
Tree trimming	500	$2,000
Expenses:		
Salaries and wages	$ 900	
Gas, utilities, and other expenses	300	1,200
Net income		$ 800

2.

GREENWAY CORPORATION
BALANCE SHEET
AT JUNE 30, 2001

Assets		Liabilities and Owners' Equity	
Cash	$ 3,300	Accounts payable	$ 800
Accounts receivable	500	Notes payable	6,000
Truck	2,000	Capital stock	5,000
Tools	800	Retained earnings	800
Building	2,000		
Land	4,000		
		Total Liabilities and	
Total Assets	$12,600	Owners' Equity	$12,600

3. Following are examples of questions that the financial statements raise:

- During June, 75% of the revenue was from lawn care and the other 25% from trimming trees. Will this relationship hold in future months?

- Are the expenses representative of those that will be incurred in the future? Will any other expenses arise, such as advertising and income taxes?

- When can we expect to collect the accounts receivable? Is there a chance that not all will be collected?

- How soon will the accounts payable need to be paid?

- What is the interest rate on the note payable? When is interest paid? When is the note itself due?

CHAPTER HIGHLIGHTS

1. **LO 1** Both individuals external to a business and those involved in the internal management of the company use accounting information. External users include present and potential stockholders, bankers and other creditors, government agencies, suppliers, trade associations, labor unions, and other interested groups.

2. **LO 2** The accounting equation is the basis for the entire accounting system: **Assets = Liabilities + Owners' Equity.** Assets are valuable economic resources. Liabilities are the claims of outsiders to the assets of a business. Owners' equity is the residual interest that remains after deducting liabilities from assets.

3. **LO 2** A balance sheet summarizes the financial position of a company at a *specific point in time.* An income statement reports on its revenues and expenses for a *period of time.* A statement of

retained earnings explains the changes in retained earnings *during a particular period.*

4. **LO 3** A number of assumptions are made in preparing financial statements. Accounting is not an exact science, and judgment must be used in deciding what to report on financial statements and how to report the information. Generally accepted accounting principles (GAAP) have evolved over time and are based on a conceptual framework. The *Securities and Exchange Commission* in the public sector and the *Financial Accounting Standards Board* in the private sector have the most responsibility for developing GAAP at the present time.

5. **LO 4** Accountants are employed by business entities, nonbusiness entities, public accounting firms, and educational institutions. Public accounting firms provide audit services for their clients, as well as tax and management consulting services.

KEY TERMS QUIZ

Read each definition below and then write the number of that definition in the blank beside the appropriate term it defines. The solution appears at the end of the chapter.

_____ Accounting
_____ Management accounting
_____ Financial accounting
_____ Owners' equity
_____ Stockholders' equity
_____ Retained earnings
_____ Balance sheet
_____ Income statement
_____ Dividends
_____ Statement of retained earnings
_____ Cost principle
_____ Going concern
_____ Monetary unit

_____ Time period
_____ Generally accepted accounting principles (GAAP)
_____ Securities and Exchange Commission (SEC)
_____ Financial Accounting Standards Board (FASB)
_____ American Institute of Certified Public Accountants (AICPA)
_____ International Accounting Standards Committee (IASC)
_____ Controller
_____ Treasurer
_____ Internal auditing
_____ Auditing
_____ Auditors' report
_____ American Accounting Association

1. A statement that summarizes revenues and expenses for a period of time.

2. The statement that summarizes the income earned and dividends paid over the life of a business.

3. The owners' equity of a corporation.

4. The process of identifying, measuring, and communicating economic information to various users.

5. The branch of accounting concerned with communication with outsiders through financial statements.

6. The owners' claim to the assets of an entity.

7. The financial statement that summarizes the assets, liabilities, and owners' equity at a specific point in time.

8. The part of owners' equity that represents the income earned less dividends paid over the life of an entity.

9. The branch of accounting concerned with providing management with information to facilitate the planning and control functions.

10. A distribution of the net income of a business to its stockholders.

11. The various methods, rules, practices, and other procedures that have evolved over time in response to the need to regulate the preparation of financial statements.

12. Assets recorded and reported at the cost paid to acquire them.

13. The federal agency with ultimate authority to determine the rules in preparing statements for companies whose stock is sold to the public.

14. The professional organization for accounting educators.

15. The officer of an organization who is responsible for the safeguarding and efficient use of the company's liquid assets.

16. The assumption that an entity is not in the process of liquidation and that it will continue indefinitely.

17. The group in the private sector with authority to set accounting standards.

18. The yardstick used to measure amounts in financial statements; the dollar in the United States.

19. The professional organization for certified public accountants.

20. The department in a company responsible for the review and appraisal of a company's accounting and administrative controls.

21. A length of time on the calendar used as the basis for preparing financial statements.

22. The chief accounting officer for a company.

23. The process of examining the financial statements and the underlying records of a company in order to render an opinion as to whether the statements are fairly presented.

24. The organization formed to develop worldwide accounting standards.

25. The opinion rendered by a public accounting firm concerning the fairness of the presentation of the financial statements.

ALTERNATE TERMS

Auditors' report   Report of independent accountants
Balance sheet   Statement of financial position
Cost principle   Original cost; historical cost
Creditor   Lender

Income statement   Statement of income
Net income   Profits or earnings
Stockholder   Shareholder

1. What is accounting? Define it in terms understandable to someone without a business background.

2. How do financial accounting and management accounting differ?

3. What are five different groups of users of accounting information? Briefly describe the types of decisions each group must make.

4. How does owners' equity fit in to the accounting equation?

5. What are the two distinct elements of owners' equity in a corporation? Define each element.

6. What is the purpose of a balance sheet?

7. How should a balance sheet be dated: as of a particular day or for a particular period of time? Explain your answer.

8. What does the term *cost principle* mean?

9. What is the purpose of an income statement?

10. How should an income statement be dated: as of a particular day or for a particular period of time? Explain your answer.

11. Rogers Corporation starts the year with a Retained Earnings balance of $55,000. Net income for the year is $27,000. The ending balance in Retained Earnings is $70,000. What was the amount of dividends for the year?

12. How do the duties of the controller of a corporation typically differ from those of the treasurer?

13. What are the three basic types of services performed by public accounting firms?

14. How would you evaluate the following statement: "The auditors are in the best position to evaluate a company because they have prepared the financial statements"?

15. What is the relationship between the cost principle and the going concern assumption?

16. Why does inflation present a challenge to the accountant? Relate your answer to the monetary unit assumption.

17. What is meant by the phrase *generally accepted accounting principles?*

18. What role has the Securities and Exchange Commission played in setting accounting standards? Contrast its role with that played by the Financial Accounting Standards Board.

EXERCISES

LO 1 Exercise 1-1 Users of Accounting Information and Their Needs

Listed below are a number of the important users of accounting information. Below the list are descriptions of a major need of each of these various users. Fill in the blank with the one user group that is most likely to have the need described to the right of the blank.

Company management	Banker
Stockholder	Supplier
Securities and Exchange Commission	Labor union
Internal Revenue Service	

User Group

_____

_____

_____

_____

_____

_____

_____

Needs Information About

1. The profitability of each division in the company

2. The prospects for future dividend payments

3. The profitability of the company since the last contract with the workforce was signed

4. The financial status of a company issuing securities to the public for the first time

5. The prospects that a company will be able to meet its interest payments on time

6. The prospects that a company will be able to pay for its purchases on time

7. The profitability of the company based on the tax code

LO 2 Exercise 1-2 The Accounting Equation

For each of the following independent cases, fill in the blank with the appropriate dollar amount.

	Assets	=	Liabilities	+	Owners' Equity
Case 1	$125,000		$ 75,000		$ _____
Case 2	400,000		_____		100,000
Case 3	_____		320,000		95,000

LO 2 Exercise 1-3 The Accounting Equation

Ginger Enterprises began the year with total assets of $500,000 and total liabilities of $250,000. Using this information and the accounting equation, answer each of the following independent questions.

Required

1. What was the amount of Ginger's owners' equity at the beginning of the year?
2. If Ginger's total assets increased by $100,000 and its total liabilities increased by $77,000 during the year, what was the amount of Ginger's owners' equity at the end of the year?
3. If Ginger's total liabilities increased by $33,000 and its owners' equity decreased by $58,000 during the year, what was the amount of its total assets at the end of the year?
4. If Ginger's total assets doubled to $1,000,000 and its owners' equity remained the same during the year, what was the amount of its total liabilities at the end of the year?

LO 2   Exercise 1-4   The Accounting Equation
Using the accounting equation, answer each of the following independent questions.

1. Burlin Company starts the year with $100,000 in assets and $80,000 in liabilities. Net income for the year is $25,000, and no dividends are paid. How much is owners' equity at the end of the year?
2. Chapman Inc. doubles the amount of its assets from the beginning to the end of the year. Liabilities at the end of the year amount to $40,000, and owners' equity is $20,000. What is the amount of Chapman's assets at the beginning of the year?
3. During the year, the liabilities of Dixon Enterprises triple in amount. Assets at the beginning of the year amount to $30,000, and owners' equity is $10,000. What is the amount of liabilities at the end of the year?

LO 2   Exercise 1-5   Changes in Owners' Equity
The following amounts are available from the records of Coaches and Carriages Inc. at the end of the years indicated:

December 31	Total Assets	Total Liabilities
1999	$ 25,000	$ 12,000
2000	79,000	67,000
2001	184,000	137,000

Required

1. Compute the changes in Coaches and Carriages' owners' equity during 2000 and 2001.
2. Compute the amount of Coaches and Carriages' net income (or loss) for 2000 assuming that no dividends were paid during the year.
3. Compute the amount of Coaches and Carriages' net income (or loss) for 2001 assuming that dividends paid during the year amounted to $10,000.

LO 2   Exercise 1-6   The Accounting Equation
For each of the following independent cases, fill in the blank with the appropriate dollar amount.

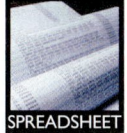
SPREADSHEET

	Case 1	Case 2	Case 3	Case 4
Total assets, end of period	$40,000	$ 34,000	$75,000	$50,000
Total liabilities, end of period	9,000	15,000	25,000	10,000
Capital stock, end of period	10,000	5,000	20,000	15,000
Retained earnings, beginning of period	15,000	8,000	10,000	20,000
Net income for the period	8,000	7,000	23,000	9,000
Dividends for the period	2,000	1,000	3,000	4,000

LO 2   Exercise 1-7   Classification of Financial Statement Items
Classify each of the following items according to (1) whether it belongs on the income statement (IS) or balance sheet (BS) and (2) whether it is a revenue (R), expense (E), asset (A), liability (L), or owners' equity (OE) item.

Item	Appears on the	Classified As
Example: Cash	BS	A
1. Salaries expense	_____	_____
2. Equipment	_____	_____
3. Accounts payable	_____	_____
4. Membership fees earned	_____	_____
5. Capital stock	_____	_____
6. Accounts receivable	_____	_____
7. Buildings	_____	_____
8. Advertising expense	_____	_____
9. Retained earnings	_____	_____

LO 2 Exercise 1-8 Net Income (or Loss) and Retained Earnings

The following information is available from the records of Prestige Landscape Design Inc. at the end of the 2001 calendar year:

Accounts payable	$ 5,000	Office equipment	$ 7,500
Accounts receivable	4,000	Rent expense	6,500
Capital stock	8,000	Retained earnings,	
Cash	13,000	beginning of year	8,500
Dividends paid		Salary and wage expense	12,000
during the year	3,000	Supplies	500
Landscaping revenues	25,000		

Required

Use the information above to answer the following questions:

1. What was Prestige's net income for the year ended December 31, 2001?
2. What is Prestige's retained earnings balance at the end of the year?
3. What is the total amount of Prestige's assets at the end of the year?
4. What is the total amount of Prestige's liabilities at the end of the year?
5. How much owners' equity does Prestige have at the end of the year?
6. What is Prestige's accounting equation at December 31, 2001?

LO 2 Exercise 1-9 Statement of Retained Earnings

Ace Corporation has been in business for many years. Retained earnings on January 1, 2001, is $235,800. The following information is available for the first two months of 2001:

	January	February
Revenues	$83,000	$96,000
Expenses	89,000	82,000
Dividends paid	–0–	5,000

Required

Prepare a statement of retained earnings for the month ended February 28, 2001.

LO 3 Exercise 1-10 Accounting Principles and Assumptions

The following basic accounting principles and assumptions were discussed in the chapter:

Economic entity   **Going concern**

Monetary unit   **Time period**

Cost principle

Fill in each of the blanks with the accounting principle or assumption that is relevant to the situation described.

Going Concern

Cost Principle

Economic Entity

Monetary Unit

Time Period

1. Genesis Corporation is now in its 30th year of business. The founder of the company is planning to retire at the end of the year and turn the business over to his daughter.
2. Nordic Company purchased a 20-acre parcel of property on which to build a new factory. The company recorded the property on the records at the amount of cash given to acquire it.
3. Jim Bailey enters into an agreement to operate a new law firm in partnership with a friend. Each partner will make an initial cash investment of $10,000. Jim opens a checking account in the name of the partnership and transfers $10,000 from his personal account into the new account.
4. Multinational Corp. has a division in Japan. Prior to preparing the financial statements for the company and all its foreign divisions, Multinational translates the financial statements of its Japanese division from yen to U.S. dollars.
5. Camden Company has always prepared financial statements annually, with a year-end of June 30. Because the company is going to sell its stock to the public for the first time, quarterly financial reports will also be required by the Securities and Exchange Commission.

LO 3   Exercise 1-11   Organizations and Accounting
Match each of the organizations listed below with the statement that most adequately describes the role of the group.

      Securities and Exchange Commission

      International Accounting Standards Committee

      Financial Accounting Standards Board

      American Institute of Certified Public Accountants

      American Accounting Association

1. Federal agency with ultimate authority to determine rules used in preparing financial statements for companies whose stock is sold to the public
2. Professional organization for accounting educators
3. Group in the private sector with authority to set accounting standards
4. Professional organization for certified public accountants
5. Organization formed to develop worldwide accounting standards

Multi-Concept Exercises

LO 1, 2   Exercise 1-12   Users of Accounting Information and the Financial Statements
Listed below are a number of users of accounting information and examples of questions they need answered before making decisions. Fill in each blank to indicate whether the user is most likely to find the answer by looking at the income statement (IS), the balance sheet (BS), or the statement of retained earnings (RE).

User	Question	Financial Statement
Stockholder	How did this year's sales compare to last year's?	
Banker	How much debt does the company already have on its books?	
Supplier	How much does the company currently owe to its suppliers?	
Stockholder	How much did the company pay in dividends this past year?	
Advertising account manager	How much did the company spend this past year to generate sales?	
Banker	What collateral or security can the company provide to ensure that any loan I make will be repaid?	

LO 2, 3 **Exercise 1-13** Uno's Inventory

Refer to Uno's balance sheet reproduced in the chapter.

Required

What was the amount of Inventory at October 3, 1999? What monetary unit is this amount based on? Give some examples of the types of inventory you would expect Uno to carry. Given the types of inventory Uno would carry, do you think the stability of the monetary unit is a concern? Explain your answer.

LO 1, 4 **Exercise 1-14** Roles of Accountants

One day on campus, you overhear two nonbusiness majors discussing the reasons each did not major in accounting. "Accountants are bean counters. They just sit in a room and play with the books all day. They do not have people skills, but I suppose it really doesn't matter because no one ever looks at the statements they prepare," said the first student. The second student replied, "Oh, they are very intelligent, though, because they must know all about the tax laws, and that's too complicated for me."

Required

Comment on the students' perceptions of the roles of accountants in society. Do you agree that no one ever looks at the statements they prepare? If not, identify who the primary users are.

PROBLEMS

LO 1 **Problem 1-1** You Won the Lottery

You have won a lottery! You will receive $200,000, after taxes, each year for the next five years.

Required

Describe the process you will go through in determining how to invest your winnings. Consider at least two options and make a choice. You may consider the stock of a certain company, bonds, real estate investments, bank deposits, and so on. Be specific. What information did you need to make a final decision? How was your decision affected by the fact that you will receive the winnings over a five-year period rather than in one lump sum? Would you prefer one payment? Explain.

LO 1 **Problem 1-2** Users of Accounting Information and Their Needs

Havre Company would like to buy a building and equipment to produce a new product line. Some information about Havre is more useful to some people involved in the project than to others.

Required

Complete the following chart by identifying the information listed on the right with the user's need to know the information. Identify the information as

a. *need* to know;

b. *helpful* to know; or

c. *not necessary* to know.

User of the Information			
Management	Stockholders	Banker	Information
_____	_____	_____	1. Amount of current debt, repayment schedule, and interest rate
_____	_____	_____	2. Fair market value of the building
_____	_____	_____	3. Condition of the roof and heating and cooling, electrical, and plumbing systems
_____	_____	_____	4. Total cost of the building, improvements, and equipment to set up production
_____	_____	_____	5. Expected sales from the new product, variable production costs, related selling costs

LO 2 **Problem 1-3** Balance Sheet

The following items are available from records of Freescia Corporation at the end of the 2001 calendar year:

Accounts payable	$12,550
Accounts receivable	23,920
Advertising expense	2,100
Buildings	85,000
Capital stock	25,000
Cash	4,220
Notes payable	50,000
Office equipment	12,000
Retained earnings, end of year	37,590
Salary and wage expense	8,230
Sales revenue	14,220

Required

Prepare a balance sheet. *Hint:* Not all the items listed should appear on a balance sheet. For each of these items, indicate where it should appear.

LO 2 **Problem 1-4** Corrected Balance Sheet

Dave is the president of Avon Consulting Inc. Avon began business on January 1, 2001. The company's controller is out of the country on business. Dave needs a copy of the company's balance sheet for a meeting tomorrow and asks his secretary to obtain the required information from the company's records. She presents Dave with the following balance sheet. He asks you to review it for accuracy.

AVON CONSULTING INC.
BALANCE SHEET
FOR THE YEAR ENDED DECEMBER 31, 2001

Assets		Liabilities and Owners' Equity	
Accounts payable	$13,000	Accounts receivable	$16,000
Cash	21,000	Capital stock	20,000
Cash dividends paid	16,000	Net income for 2001	72,000
Furniture and equipment	43,000	Supplies	9,000

Required

1. Prepare a corrected balance sheet.
2. Draft a memo explaining the major differences between the balance sheet Dave's secretary prepared and the one you prepared.

LO 2 **Problem 1-5** Income Statement, Statement of Retained Earnings, and Balance Sheet

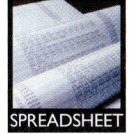
SPREADSHEET

Shown below, in alphabetical order, is a list of the various items that regularly appear on the financial statements of Maple Park Theatres Corp. The amounts shown for balance sheet items are balances as of September 30, 2001 (with the exception of Retained Earnings, which is the balance on September 1, 2001), and the amounts shown for income statement items are balances for the month ended September 30, 2001:

✓ Accounts payable	$17,600
✓ Accounts receivable	6,410
✓ Advertising expense	14,500
✓ Buildings	60,000
✓ Capital stock	50,000
✓ Cash	15,230
✓ Concessions revenue	60,300
✓ Cost of concessions sold	23,450
✓ Dividends paid during the month	8,400
✓ Furniture and fixtures	34,000
✓ Land	26,000
✓ Notes payable	20,000
✓ Projection equipment	25,000

✓ Rent expense—movies	50,600
✓ Retained earnings	73,780
✓ Salaries and wages expense	46,490
✓ Ticket sales	95,100
✓ Water, gas, and electricity	6,700

Required

1. Prepare an income statement for the month ended September 30, 2001.

2. Prepare a statement of retained earnings for the month ended September 30, 2001.

3. Prepare a balance sheet at September 30, 2001.

4. You have $1,000 to invest. On the basis of the statements you prepared, would you use it to buy stock in Maple Park? What other information would you want before making a final decision?

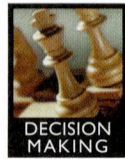

DECISION MAKING

LO 2   Problem 1-6   Income Statement and Balance Sheet

Green Bay Corporation began business in July 2001 as a commercial fishing operation and passenger service between islands. Shares of stock were issued to the owners in exchange for cash. Boats were purchased by making a down payment in cash and signing a note payable for the balance. Fish are sold to local restaurants on open account, and customers are given 15 days to pay their account. Cash fares are collected for all passenger traffic. Rent for the dock facilities is paid at the beginning of each month. Salaries and wages are paid at the end of the month. The following amounts are from the records of Green Bay Corporation at the end of its first month of operations:

Accounts receivable	$18,500
Boats	80,000
Capital stock	40,000
Cash	7,730
Dividends	5,400
Fishing revenue	21,300
Notes payable	60,000
Passenger service revenue	12,560
Rent expense	4,000
Retained earnings	???
Salary and wage expense	18,230

Required

1. Prepare an income statement for the month ended July 31, 2001.

2. Prepare a balance sheet at July 31, 2001.

3. What information would you need about Notes Payable to assess fully Green Bay's long-term viability? Explain your answer.

LO 2   Problem 1-7   Corrected Financial Statements

Hometown Cleaners Inc. operates a small dry-cleaning business. The company has always maintained a complete and accurate set of records. Unfortunately, the company's accountant left in a dispute with the president and took the 2001 financial statements with him. The balance sheet and the income statement shown below were prepared by the company's president.

HOMETOWN CLEANERS INC.
INCOME STATEMENT
FOR THE YEAR ENDED DECEMBER 31, 2001

Revenues:		
Accounts receivable	$15,200	
Cleaning revenue—cash sales	32,500	$47,700
Expenses:		
Dividends	$ 4,000	
Accounts payable	4,500	
Utilities	12,200	
Salaries and wages	17,100	37,800
Net income		$ 9,900

HOMETOWN CLEANERS INC.
BALANCE SHEET
DECEMBER 31, 2001

Assets		Liabilities and Owners' Equity	
Cash	$ 7,400	Cleaning revenue—	
Building and equipment	80,000	credit sales	$26,200
Less: Notes payable	(50,000)	Capital stock	20,000
Land	40,000	Net income	9,900
		Retained earnings	21,300
		Total liabilities and	
Total assets	$77,400	owners' equity	$77,400

The president is very disappointed with the net income for the year because it has averaged $25,000 over the last 10 years. She has asked for your help in determining whether the reported net income accurately reflects the profitability of the company and whether the balance sheet is prepared correctly.

Required

1. Prepare a corrected income statement for the year ended December 31, 2001.

2. Prepare a statement of retained earnings for the year ended December 31, 2001. (The actual balance of retained earnings on January 1, 2001, was $42,700. Note that the December 31, 2001, balance shown above is incorrect. The president simply "plugged" this amount in to make the balance sheet balance.)

3. Prepare a corrected balance sheet at December 31, 2001.

4. Draft a memo to the president explaining the major differences between the income statement she prepared and the one you prepared.

LO 2 Problem 1-8 Statement of Retained Earnings for Wendy's

Wendy's International reported the following amounts in various statements included in its 1999 annual report (all amounts are stated in thousands of dollars):   **www.wendy.com**

Net income for 1999*	$ 166,585
Dividends declared and paid in 1999	29,305
Retained earnings, January 3, 1999	931,603
Retained earnings, January 2, 2000	1,068,883

*The 1999 fiscal year ended on January 2, 2000.

Required

1. Prepare a statement of retained earnings for Wendy's for the year ended January 2, 2000.

2. Wendy's does not actually present a statement of retained earnings in its annual report. Instead, it presents a broader statement of stockholders' equity. Describe the information that would be included on this statement and that is not included on a statement of retained earnings.

LO 4 Problem 1-9 Role of the Accountant in Various Organizations

The following positions in various entities require a knowledge of accounting practices:

1. Chief financial officer for the subsidiary of a large company

2. Tax adviser to a consolidated group of entities

3. Independent computer consultant

4. Financial planner in a bank

5. Real estate broker in an independent office

6. Production planner in a manufacturing facility

7. Quality control adviser

8. Superintendent of a school district

9. Manager of one store in a retail clothing chain

10. Salesperson for a company that offers subcontract services to hospitals, such as food service and maintenance

Required

For each position listed above, identify the entity in which it occurs as business or nonbusiness and describe the kind of accounting knowledge (such as financial, managerial, taxes, not-for-profit) required by each position.

www.timewarner.com **LO 1   Problem 1-10**   Information Needs and Setting Accounting Standards

The Financial Accounting Standards Board requires companies to supplement their consolidated financial statements with disclosures about segments of their businesses. To comply with this standard, Time Warner's 1998 annual report provides various disclosures for the five segments in which it operates: Cable Systems, Cable Networks, Publishing, Filmed Entertainment, and Music.

Required

Which users of accounting information do you think the Financial Accounting Standards Board had in mind when it set this standard? What types of disclosures do you think these users would find helpful?

Multi-Concept Problem

LO 2, 3   Problem 1-11   Primary Assumptions Made in Preparing Financial Statements

Joe Hale opened a machine repair business in leased retail space, paying the first month's rent of $300 and a $1,000 security deposit with a check on his personal account. He took the tools and equipment, worth about $7,500, from his garage to the shop. He also bought some more equipment to get started. The new equipment had a list price of $5,000, but Joe was able to purchase it on sale at Sears for only $4,200. He charged the new equipment on his personal Sears charge card. Joe's first customer paid $400 for services rendered, so Joe opened a checking account for the company. He completed a second job, but the customer has not paid Joe the $2,500 for his work. At the end of the first month, Joe prepared the following balance sheet and income statement.

JOE'S MACHINE REPAIR SHOP
BALANCE SHEET
JULY 31, 2001

Cash	$ 400		
Tools	5,000	Equity	$5,400
Total	$5,400	Total	$5,400

JOE'S MACHINE REPAIR SHOP
INCOME STATEMENT
FOR MONTH ENDED JULY 31, 2001

Sales		$2,900
Rent	$ 300	
Tools	4,200	4,500
Loss		($1,600)

Joe believes that he should show a greater profit next month because he won't have large expenses for such items as tools.

Required

Identify the assumptions that Joe has violated and explain how each event should have been handled. Prepare a corrected balance sheet and income statement.

ALTERNATE PROBLEMS

LO 1   Problem 1-1A   What to Do with a Million Dollars

You have inherited $1 million!

Required

Describe the process you will go through in determining how to invest your inheritance. Consider at least two options and choose one. You may consider the stock of a certain company, bonds, real estate investments, bank deposits, and so on. Be specific. What information did you need to make a final decision? Where did you find the information you needed? What additional information will you need to consider if you want to make a change in your investment?

LO 1 Problem I-2A Users of Accounting Information and Their Needs

Billings Inc. would like to buy a franchise to provide a specialized service. Some information about Billings is more useful to some people involved in the project than to others.

Required

Complete the following chart by identifying the information listed on the left with the user's need to know the information. Identify the information as

a. *need* to know;

b. *helpful* to know; or

c. *not necessary* to know.

Information	User of the Information		
	Manager	Stockholders	Franchisor
1. Expected revenue from the new service.	___	___	___
2. Cost of the franchise fee and recurring fees to be paid to the franchisor.	___	___	___
3. Cash available to Billings, the franchisee, to operate the business after the franchise is purchased.	___	___	___
4. Expected overhead costs of the service outlet.	___	___	___
5. Billings's required return on its investment.	___	___	___

LO 2 Problem I-3A Balance Sheet

The following items are available from the records of Victor Corporation at the end of its fiscal year ended July 31, 2001:

Accounts payable	$16,900
Accounts receivable	5,700
Buildings	35,000
Butter and cheese inventory	12,100
Capital stock	25,000
Cash	21,800
Computerized mixers	25,800
Delivery expense	4,600
Notes payable	50,000
Office equipment	12,000
Retained earnings, end of year	26,300
Salary and wage expense	8,230
Sales revenue	14,220
Tools	5,800

Required

Prepare a balance sheet. *Hint:* Not all the items listed should appear on a balance sheet. For each of these items, indicate where it should appear.

LO 2 Problem I-4A Corrected Balance Sheet

Pete is the president of Island Enterprises. Island Enterprises began business on January 1, 2001. The company's controller is out of the country on business. Pete needs a copy of the company's balance sheet for a meeting tomorrow and asks his secretary to obtain the required information from the company's records. She presents Pete with the following balance sheet. He asks you to review it for accuracy.

ISLAND ENTERPRISES
BALANCE SHEET
FOR THE YEAR ENDED DECEMBER 31, 2001

Assets		Liabilities and Owners' Equity	
Accounts payable	$ 29,600	Accounts receivable	$ 23,200
Cash	14,750	Capital stock	100,000
Cash dividends paid	16,000	Net income for 2001	113,850
Building and equipment	177,300	Supplies	12,200

Required

1. Prepare a corrected balance sheet.

2. Draft a memo explaining the major differences between the balance sheet Pete's secretary prepared and the one you prepared.

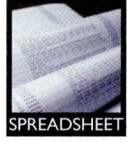

LO 2   Problem 1-5A   Income Statement, Statement of Retained Earnings, and Balance Sheet
Shown below, in alphabetical order, is a list of the various items that regularly appear on the financial statements of Sterns Audio Book Rental Corp. The amounts shown for balance sheet items are balances as of December 31, 2001 (with the exception of retained earnings, which is the balance on January 1, 2001), and the amounts shown for income statement items are balances for the year ended December 31, 2001:

Accounts payable	$ 4,500
Accounts receivable	300
Advertising expense	14,500
Audio tape inventory	70,000
Capital stock	50,000
Cash	2,490
Display fixtures	45,000
Dividends paid during the year	12,000
Notes payable	10,000
Rental revenue	125,900
Rent paid on building	60,000
Retained earnings	35,390
Salaries and wages expense	17,900
Water, gas, and electricity	3,600

Required

1. Prepare an income statement for the year ended December 31, 2001.

2. Prepare a statement of retained earnings for the year ended December 31, 2001.

3. Prepare a balance sheet at December 31, 2001.

4. You have $1,000 to invest. On the basis of the statements you prepared, would you use it to buy stock in this company? What other information would you want before making a final decision?

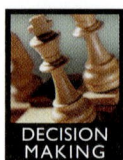

LO 2   Problem 1-6A   Income Statement and Balance Sheet
Fort Worth Corporation began business in January 2001 as a commercial carpet cleaning and drying service. Shares of stock were issued to the owners in exchange for cash. Equipment was purchased by making a down payment in cash and signing a note payable for the balance. Services are performed for local restaurants and office buildings on open account, and customers are given 15 days to pay their account. Rent for office and storage facilities is paid at the beginning of each month. Salaries and wages are paid at the end of the month. The following amounts are from the records of Fort Worth Corporation at the end of its first month of operations:

Accounts receivable	$24,750
Capital stock	80,000
Cash	51,650
Cleaning revenue	45,900
Dividends	5,500

Equipment	62,000	
Notes payable	30,000	
Rent expense	3,600	
Retained earnings	???	
Salary and wage expense	8,400	

Required

1. Prepare an income statement for the month ended January 31, 2001.

2. Prepare a balance sheet at January 31, 2001.

3. What information would you need about Notes Payable to fully assess Fort Worth's long-term viability? Explain your answer.

LO 2 Problem 1-7A Corrected Financial Statements

Heidi's Bakery Inc. operates a small pastry business. The company has always maintained a complete and accurate set of records. Unfortunately, the company's accountant left in a dispute with the president and took the 2001 financial statements with her. The balance sheet and the income statement shown below were prepared by the company's president.

HEIDI'S BAKERY INC.
INCOME STATEMENT
FOR THE YEAR ENDED DECEMBER 31, 2001

Revenues:		
Accounts receivable	$15,500	
Pastry revenue—cash sales	23,700	$39,200
Expenses:		
Dividends	$ 5,600	
Accounts payable	6,800	
Utilities	9,500	
Salaries and wages	18,200	40,100
Net loss		$ (900)

HEIDI'S BAKERY INC.
BALANCE SHEET
DECEMBER 31, 2001

Assets		Liabilities and Owners' Equity	
Cash	$ 3,700	Pastry revenue—	
Building and equipment	60,000	credit sales	$22,100
Less: Notes payable	(40,000)	Capital stock	30,000
Land	50,000	Net loss	(900)
		Retained earnings	22,500
		Total liabilities and	
Total assets	$73,700	owners' equity	$73,700

The president is very disappointed with the net loss for the year because net income has averaged $21,000 over the last 10 years. He has asked for your help in determining whether the reported net loss accurately reflects the profitability of the company and whether the balance sheet is prepared correctly.

Required

1. Prepare a corrected income statement for the year ended December 31, 2001.

2. Prepare a statement of retained earnings for the year ended December 31, 2001. (The actual amount of Retained Earnings on January 1, 2001, was $39,900. The December 31, 2001, balance shown above is incorrect. The president simply "plugged" this amount in to make the balance sheet balance.)

3. Prepare a corrected balance sheet at December 31, 2001.

4. Draft a memo to the president explaining the major differences between the income statement he prepared and the one you prepared.

LO 2 **Problem 1-8A** Statement of Retained Earnings for Brunswick Corporation

Brunswick Corporation reported the following amounts in various statements included in its 1999 annual report (all amounts are stated in millions of dollars):

Net earnings for 1999	$ 37.9
Cash dividends declared and paid in 1999	45.9
Retained earnings, December 31, 1998	1,189.5
Retained earnings, December 31, 1999	1,181.5

Required

1. Prepare a statement of retained earnings for Brunswick for the year ended December 31, 1999.

2. Brunswick does not actually present a statement of retained earnings in its annual report. Instead, it presents a broader statement of shareholders' (stockholders') equity. Describe the information that would be included on this statement and that is not included on a statement of retained earnings.

LO 4 **Problem 1-9A** Role of the Accountant in Various Organizations

The following positions in various entities require a knowledge of accounting practices:

_____ 1. Chief financial officer for the subsidiary of a large company

_____ 2. Tax adviser to a consolidated group of entities

_____ 3. Accounts receivable computer analyst

_____ 4. Financial planner in a bank

_____ 5. Budget analyst in a real estate office

_____ 6. Production planner in a manufacturing facility

_____ 7. Quality control adviser

_____ 8. Manager of the team conducting an audit on a state lottery

_____ 9. Assistant superintendent of a school district

_____ 10. Manager of one store in a retail clothing chain

_____ 11. Controller in a company that offers subcontract services to hospitals, such as food service and maintenance

_____ 12. Staff accountant in a large audit firm

Required

For each position listed above, fill in the blank to classify the position as one of the general categories of accountants listed below.

Financial accountant

Managerial accountant

Tax accountant

Accountant for not-for-profit organization

Auditor

Not an accounting position

LO 1 **Problem 1-10A** Information Needs and Setting Accounting Standards

The Financial Accounting Standards Board requires companies to supplement their consolidated financial statements with disclosures about segments of their businesses. To comply with this standard, Marriott International's 1999 annual report provides various disclosures for the three segments in which it operates: Lodging, Senior Living Services, and Distribution Services (a wholesale food-distribution business).

Required

Which users of accounting information do you think the Financial Accounting Standards Board had in mind when it set this standard? What types of disclosures do you think these users would find helpful?

Alternate Multi-Concept Problem

LO 2, 3 **Problem 1-11A** Primary Assumptions Made in Preparing Financial Statements

Millie Abrams opened a ceramic studio in leased retail space, paying the first month's rent of $300 and a $1,000 security deposit with a check on her personal account. She took molds and paint, worth about $7,500, from her home to the studio. She also bought a new firing kiln to start the business. The new kiln had a list price of $5,000, but Millie was able to trade in her old kiln, worth $500 at the time of trade, on the new kiln, and, therefore, she paid only $4,500 cash. She wrote a check on her personal checking account. Millie's first customers paid a total of $1,400 to attend classes for the next two months. She opened a checking account in the company's name with the $1,400. She has conducted classes for one month and has sold for $3,000 unfinished ceramic pieces called *greenware*. Greenware sales are all cash. Millie incurred $1,000 of personal cost in making the greenware. At the end of the first month, Millie prepared the following balance sheet and income statement.

MILLIE'S CERAMIC STUDIO
BALANCE SHEET
JULY 31, 2001

Cash	$1,400		
Kiln	5,000	Equity	$6,400
Total	$6,400	Total	$6,400

MILLIE'S CERAMIC STUDIO
INCOME STATEMENT
FOR THE MONTH ENDED JULY 31, 2001

Sales		$4,400
Rent	$300	
Supplies	600	900
Income		$3,500

Millie needs to earn at least $3,000 each month for the business to be worth her time. She is pleased with the results.

Required

Identify the assumptions that Millie has violated and explain how each event should have been handled. Prepare a corrected balance sheet and income statement.

CASES

Reading and Interpreting Financial Statements

LO 1, 2 **Case 1-1** An Annual Report as Ready Reference

Refer to the Gateway annual report, and identify where each of the following users of accounting information would first look to answer their respective questions about Gateway: **www.gateway.com**

1. Investors: How much did the company earn for each share of stock I own? How much of those earnings did I receive, and how much was reinvested in the company?

2. Potential investors: What amount of earnings can I expect to see from Gateway in the near future?

3. Bankers and creditors: Should I extend the short-term borrowing limit to Gateway? Do they have sufficient cash or cash-like assets to repay short-term loans?

4. IRS: How much does Gateway owe for taxes?

5. Employees: How much money did the president and vice presidents earn? Should I ask for a raise?

LO 2 **Case 1-2** Reading and Interpreting Uno Financial Statements

Refer to the financial statements for Uno reproduced in the chapter and answer the following   **www.pizzeriauno.com**
questions:

1. What was the company's net income for 1999?

2. State Uno's financial position on October 3, 1999, in terms of the accounting equation.

3. Explain the reason for the change in retained earnings from a balance of $42,203 on September 27, 1998, to a balance of $52,003 on October 3, 1999. Also, what amount of dividends did the company pay in 1999?

Making Financial Decisions

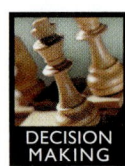

LO 1   Case I-3   An Investment Opportunity

You have saved enough money to pay for your college tuition for the next three years when a high school friend comes to you with a deal. He is an artist who has spent most of the past two years drawing on the walls of old buildings. The buildings are about to be demolished and your friend thinks you should buy the walls before the buildings are demolished and open a gallery featuring his work. Of course, you are levelheaded and would normally say "No!" Recently, however, your friend has been featured on several local radio and television shows and is talking to some national networks about doing a feature on a well-known news show. To set up the gallery would take all your savings, but your friend feels that you will be able to sell his artwork for 10 times the cost of your investment. What kinds of information about the business do you need before deciding to invest all your savings? What kind of profit split would you suggest to your friend if you decide to open the gallery?

LO 2   Case I-4   Preparation of Projected Statements for a New Business

Upon graduation from MegaState University, you and your roommate decide to start your respective careers in accounting and salmon fishing in Remote, Alaska. Your career as a CPA in Remote is going well, as is your roommate's job as a commercial fisher. After one year in Remote, he approaches you with a business opportunity.

As we are well aware, the video rental business has yet to reach Remote, and the nearest rental facility is 250 miles away. We each put up our first year's savings of $5,000 and file for articles of incorporation with the state of Alaska to do business as Remote Video World. In return for our investment of $5,000, we will each receive equal shares of capital stock in the corporation. Then we go to the Corner National Bank and apply for a $10,000 loan. We take the total cash of $20,000 we have now raised and buy 2,000 videos at $10 each from a mail-order supplier. We rent the movies for $3 per title and sell monthly memberships for $25, allowing a member to check out an unlimited number of movies during the month. Individual rentals would be a cash-and-carry business, but we would give customers until the 10th of the following month to pay for a monthly membership. My most conservative estimate is that during the first month alone, we will rent 800 movies and sell 200 memberships. As I see it, we will have only two expenses. First, we will hire two high school students to run the store for 30 hours each per week and pay them $5 per hour. Second, the landlord of a vacant store in town will rent us space in the building for $1,000 per month.

Required

1. Prepare a projected income statement for the first month of operations.

2. Prepare a balance sheet as it would appear at the end of the first month of operations.

3. Assume that the bank is willing to make the $10,000 loan. Would you be willing to join your roommate in this business? Explain your response. Also, indicate any information other than what he has provided that you would like to have before making a final decision.

Accounting and Ethics: What Would You Do?

LO 1, 2   Case I-5   Identification of Errors in Financial Statements and Preparation of Revised Statements

Lakeside Slammers Inc. is a minor-league baseball organization that has just completed its first season. You and three other investors organized the corporation; each put up $10,000 in cash for shares of capital stock. Because you live out of state, you have not been actively involved in the daily affairs of the club. However, you are thrilled to receive a dividend check for $10,000 at the end of the season—an amount equal to your original investment! Included with the check are the following financial statements, along with supporting explanations.

LAKESIDE SLAMMERS INC.
INCOME STATEMENT
FOR THE YEAR ENDED DECEMBER 31, 2001

Revenues:		
Single-game ticket revenue	$420,000	
Season-ticket revenue	140,000	
Concessions revenue	280,000	
Advertising revenue	100,000	$940,000
Expenses:		
Cost of concessions sold	$110,000	
Salary expense—players	225,000	
Salary and wage expense—staff	150,000	
Rent expense	210,000	695,000
Net Income		$245,000

LAKESIDE SLAMMERS INC.
STATEMENT OF RETAINED EARNINGS
FOR THE YEAR ENDED DECEMBER 31, 2001

Beginning balance, January 1, 2001	$ –0–
Add: Net income for 2001	245,000
Deduct: Cash dividends paid in 2001	(40,000)
Ending balance, December 31, 2001	$205,000

LAKESIDE SLAMMERS INC.
BALANCE SHEET
AT DECEMBER 31, 2001

Assets		Liabilities and Owners' Equity	
Cash	$ 5,000	Notes payable	$ 50,000
Accounts receivable		Capital stock	40,000
Season tickets	140,000	Additional owners' capital	80,000
Advertisers	100,000	Parent club's equity	125,000
Auxiliary assets	80,000	Retained earnings	205,000
Equipment	50,000		
Player contracts	125,000	Total liabilities and	
Total assets	$500,000	owners' equity	$500,000

Additional information:

a. Single-game tickets sold for $4 per game. The team averaged 1,500 fans per game. With 70 home games × $4 per game × 1,500 fans, single-game ticket revenue amounted to $420,000.

b. No season tickets were sold during the first season. During the last three months of 2001, however, an aggressive sales campaign resulted in the sale of 500 season tickets for the 2002 season. Therefore, the controller (who is also one of the owners) chose to record an Account Receivable—Season Tickets and corresponding revenue for 500 tickets × $4 per game × 70 games, or $140,000.

c. Advertising revenue of $100,000 resulted from the sale of the 40 signs on the outfield wall at $2,500 each for the season. However, none of the advertisers has paid its bills yet (thus, an account receivable of $100,000 on the balance sheet) because the contract with Lakeside required them to pay only if the team averaged 2,000 fans per game during the 2001 season. The controller believes that the advertisers will be sympathetic to the difficulties of starting a new franchise and be willing to overlook the slight deficiency in the attendance requirement.

d. Lakeside has a working agreement with one of the major-league franchises. The minor-league team is required to pay $5,000 *every* year to the major-league team for each of the 25 players on its roster. The controller believes that each of the players is certainly an asset to the organization and has therefore recorded $5,000 × 25, or $125,000, as an asset called Player Contracts. The item on the right side of the balance sheet entitled Parent Club's Equity is the amount owed to the major league team by February 1, 2002, as payment for the players for the 2001 season.

e. In addition to the cost described in **d,** Lakeside directly pays each of its 25 players a $9,000 salary for the season. This amount—$225,000—has already been paid for the 2001 season and is reported on the income statement.

f. The items on the balance sheet entitled Auxiliary Assets on the left side and Additional Owners' Capital on the right side represent the value of the controller's personal residence. She has a mortgage with the bank for the full value of the house.

g. The $50,000 note payable resulted from a loan that was taken out at the beginning of the year to finance the purchase of bats, balls, uniforms, lawn mowers, and other miscellaneous supplies needed to operate the team (equipment is reported as an asset for the same amount). The loan, with interest, is due on April 15, 2002. Even though the team had a very successful first year, Lakeside is a little short of cash at the end of 2001 and has, therefore, asked the bank for a three-month extension of the loan. The controller reasons, "By the due date of April 15, 2002, the cash due from the new season ticket holders will be available, things will be cleared up with the advertisers, and the loan can be easily repaid."

Required

1. Identify any errors that you think the controller has made in preparing the financial statements.

2. On the basis of your answer in **1,** prepare a revised income statement, statement of retained earnings, and balance sheet.

3. On the basis of your revised financial statements, identify any ethical dilemma you now face. Do you have a responsibility to share these revisions with the other three owners? What is your responsibility to the bank?

INTERNET RESEARCH CASE

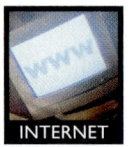

www.pizzeriauno.com

www.sec.com

Case 1-6 Pizzeria Uno

Imagine pepperoni, lots of mozzarella cheese, and zesty tomato sauce on a deep-dish crust. These are just some of the ingredients that make up Pizzeria Uno's famous Chicago-style pizza and attract so many customers from all over the country. Every purchase of a Pizzeria Uno's product influences the company's sales, cost of sales, net income, and other financial aspects and is a major contributor to its aggressive growth.

Pizzeria Uno's parent company, Uno Restaurant Corporation, has been around for almost 60 years and during that time it has established a name for itself not only in the "pizza business" but as corporation that has continued to grow to 170-plus restaurants. And as a corporation and publicly traded company its earnings, sales, net income, etc. are reported to the Securities and Exchange Commission (SEC) through the annual report. You can access Uno Restaurant Corporation's annual reports either by using the company's Web site or EDGAR Online, a database of SEC filings at its Web site, and compare its growth from the 1999 annual reports to the current online report.

To track the growth of the company, access Uno Restaurant Corporation's Web site, EDGAR Online at the SEC's WEB site, and business news pages. Then answer the following questions.

1. Locate Uno's net sales and cost of sales in its current statement of income. How do these numbers compare with the amounts for these items in the Selected Financial Data for 1999 in the opening vignette shown at the start of the chapter?

2. From Uno's current income statement, what is its gross profit? How has this amount changed from 1999? What may have caused this change?

3. Access business news sites to find out what announcements have been made by the corporation.

4. How well is Uno Restaurant Corporation performing? Where did you find this information?

SOLUTIONS TO KEY TERMS QUIZ

 4 Accounting (p. 6)

 9 Management accounting (p. 6)

 5 Financial accounting (p. 7)

 6 Owners' equity (p. 9)

 3 Stockholders' equity (p. 9)

 8 Retained earnings (p. 9)

 7 Balance sheet (p. 9)

 1 Income statement (p. 11)

 10 Dividends (p. 11)

 2 Statement of retained earnings (p. 11)

 12 Cost principle (p. 15)

 16 Going concern (p. 15)

 18 Monetary unit (p. 15)

 21 Time period (p. 15)

 11 Generally accepted accounting principles (GAAP) (p. 15)

 13 Securities and Exchange Commission (SEC) (p. 16)

 17 Financial Accounting Standards Board (FASB) (p. 16)

 19 American Institute of Certified Public Accountants (AICPA) (p. 16)

 24 International Accounting Standards Committee (IASC) (p. 16)

 22 Controller (p. 17)

 15 Treasurer (p. 17)

 20 Internal auditing (p. 17)

 23 Auditing (p. 18)

 25 Auditors' report (p. 18)

 14 American Accounting Association (p. 20)

Chapter 2

FINANCIAL STATEMENTS AND THE ANNUAL REPORT

Study Links

A Look at the Previous Chapter

Chapter 1 introduced the role of accounting in our society. We explored how investors, creditors, and others use accounting and the outputs of an accounting system—financial statements—in making informed decisions.

A Look at This Chapter

In this chapter, we take a closer look at the financial statements, as well as the other elements that make up an annual report. In the first part of the chapter, we explore the underlying conceptual framework of accounting. Every discipline has a set of interrelated concepts, principles, and conventions that guide daily practice. In the second part of the chapter, we will see how the concepts introduced in the first part of the chapter are used in the development of financial statements.

A Look at Upcoming Chapters

Chapter 2 focuses on the end result by examining the outputs of an accounting system, the financial statements. We will take a step back in Chapters 3 and 4, to consider how economic events are processed in an accounting system and are then summarized in the financial statements.

FOCUS ON FINANCIAL RESULTS

Gateway, the computer manufacturer and retailer, had a banner year in 1999, increasing revenues by 16 percent, enjoying 42 percent unit growth in its U.S. consumer business and 65 percent growth in Asia, and ending the year with its stock 170 percent higher than it began. Some important strategies for building the business spurred these impressive gains.

In 1999 Gateway became the first PC maker to bundle Internet access with the sale of a computer and also struck a deal with America Online that gives Gateway access to AOL's content and portal capabilities. Gateway also launched an innovative online software and peripheral store, working with an e-commerce firm called NECX to create SpotShop.com. The company grew its online and CD-based training programs in more than 400 classrooms in its Gateway Country retail locations around the country and continued to introduce new products to its bread-and-butter business, PC systems. And to kick off its growth in 2000, Gateway sealed a new partnership to bring a Gateway store-within-a-store to nearly one thousand Office Max locations across the United States. Quick response to competitors and continued change are critical in this fast-paced industry.

All these strategies cost money, but Gateway sees it as money well spent. Investments in the future make sense to this successful and growing firm. In fact, the firm also plans to expand its unique, direct retail model overseas in the near future.

Gateway's executives believe that a company has three kinds of resources: human, technological, and financial. Gateway's 1999 balance sheet highlights the big changes in the firm's financial resources. As can be seen, total assets rose dramatically during 1999. Are these the financial results you would expect from a firm committed to improving all three kinds of resources?

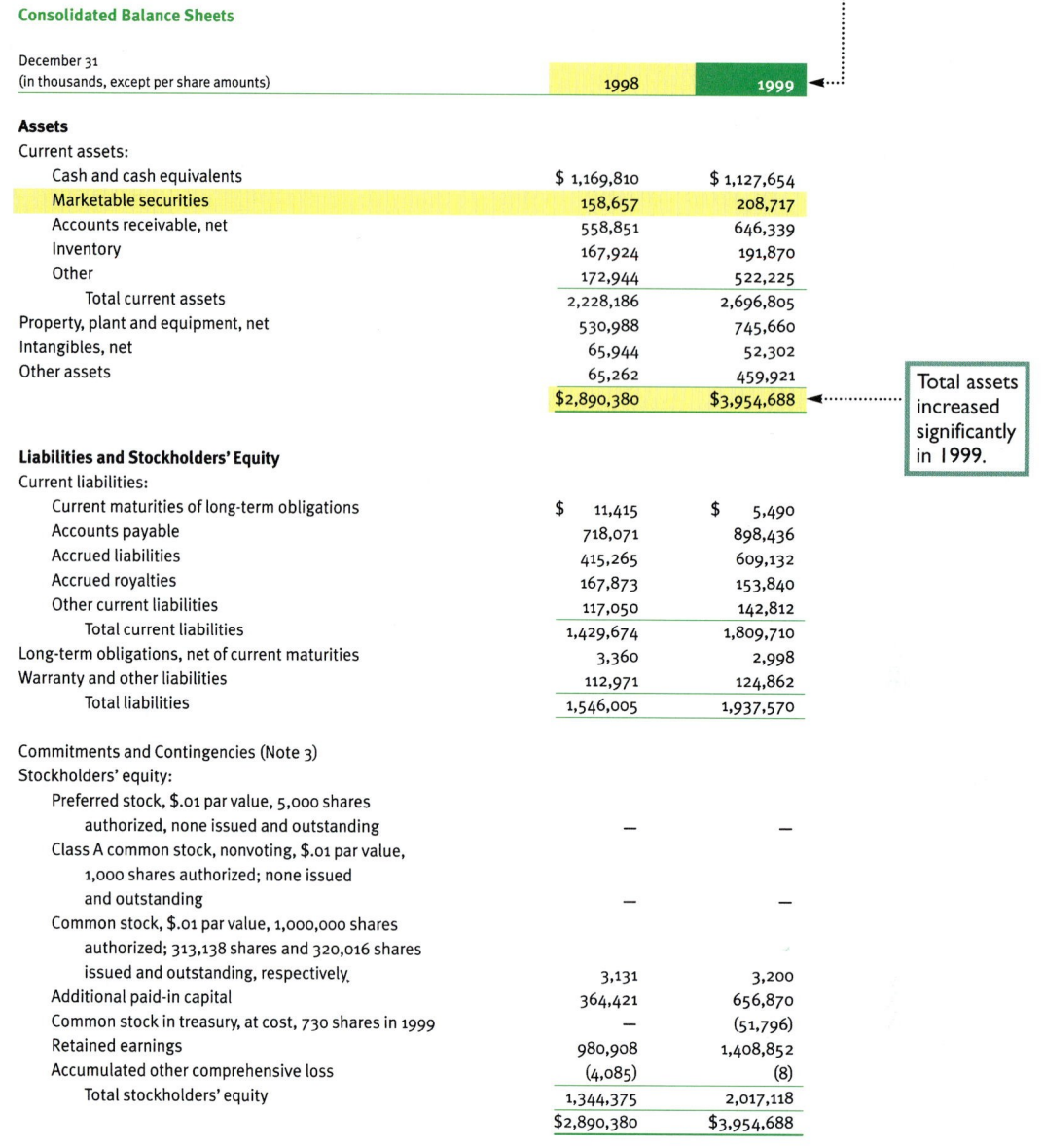

Consolidated Balance Sheets

December 31
(in thousands, except per share amounts)

	1998	1999
Assets		
Current assets:		
Cash and cash equivalents	$ 1,169,810	$ 1,127,654
Marketable securities	158,657	208,717
Accounts receivable, net	558,851	646,339
Inventory	167,924	191,870
Other	172,944	522,225
Total current assets	2,228,186	2,696,805
Property, plant and equipment, net	530,988	745,660
Intangibles, net	65,944	52,302
Other assets	65,262	459,921
	$2,890,380	$3,954,688
Liabilities and Stockholders' Equity		
Current liabilities:		
Current maturities of long-term obligations	$ 11,415	$ 5,490
Accounts payable	718,071	898,436
Accrued liabilities	415,265	609,132
Accrued royalties	167,873	153,840
Other current liabilities	117,050	142,812
Total current liabilities	1,429,674	1,809,710
Long-term obligations, net of current maturities	3,360	2,998
Warranty and other liabilities	112,971	124,862
Total liabilities	1,546,005	1,937,570
Commitments and Contingencies (Note 3)		
Stockholders' equity:		
Preferred stock, $.01 par value, 5,000 shares authorized, none issued and outstanding	—	—
Class A common stock, nonvoting, $.01 par value, 1,000 shares authorized; none issued and outstanding	—	—
Common stock, $.01 par value, 1,000,000 shares authorized; 313,138 shares and 320,016 shares issued and outstanding, respectively	3,131	3,200
Additional paid-in capital	364,421	656,870
Common stock in treasury, at cost, 730 shares in 1999	—	(51,796)
Retained earnings	980,908	1,408,852
Accumulated other comprehensive loss	(4,085)	(8)
Total stockholders' equity	1,344,375	2,017,118
	$2,890,380	$3,954,688

Total assets increased significantly in 1999.

The accompanying notes are an integral part of the consolidated financial statements.

Gateway 1999 Annual Report

If you were thinking of buying shares of Gateway stock, what questions about Gateway's future plans would you want answered? Use this chapter, Gateway's annual report, and its Web site to help you identify and evaluate information about the company's financial performance and management's plans for use of the firm's resources.

www.gateway.com

After studying this chapter, you should be able to:

LO 1 Describe the objectives of financial reporting. (p. 46)

LO 2 Describe the qualitative characteristics of accounting information. (p. 47)

LO 3 Explain the concept and purpose of a classified balance sheet and prepare the statement. (p. 53)

LO 4 Use a classified balance sheet to analyze a company's financial position. (p. 58)

LO 5 Explain the difference between a single-step and a multiple-step income statement and prepare each type of income statement. (p. 60)

LO 6 Use a multiple-step income statement to analyze a company's operations. (p. 62)

LO 7 Identify the components of the statement of retained earnings and prepare the statement. (p. 62)

LO 8 Identify the components of the statement of cash flows and prepare the statement. (p. 63)

LO 9 Read and use the financial statements and other elements in the annual report of a publicly held company. (p. 64)

WHY DOES ACCOUNTING INFORMATION NEED TO BE USEFUL? OBJECTIVES OF FINANCIAL REPORTING

LO 1 Describe the objectives of financial reporting.

The users of financial information are the main reason financial statements are prepared. After all, it is the investors, creditors, and other groups and individuals outside and inside the company who must make economic decisions based on these statements. Therefore, as we learned in Chapter 1, financial statements must be based on agreed-upon assumptions like time-period, going concern, and other generally accepted accounting principles.

Moreover, when the accountants for companies like Uno and Gateway prepare their financial statements, they must keep in mind financial reporting objectives, which are focused on providing the most understandable and useful information possible. Financial reporting has one overall objective and a set of related objectives, all of them concerned with how the information may be most useful to the readers.

THE PRIMARY OBJECTIVE: PROVIDE INFORMATION FOR DECISION MAKING

The primary objective of financial reporting is *to provide economic information to permit users of the information to make informed decisions.* Users include both the management of a company (internal users) and others not involved in the daily operations of the business (external users). Without access to the detailed records of the business and without the benefit of daily involvement in the affairs of the company, external users make their decisions based on *financial statements* prepared by management. According to the Financial Accounting Standards Board (FASB), "Financial reporting should provide information that is useful to present and potential investors and creditors and other users in making rational investment, credit, and similar decisions."[1]

We see from this statement how closely the objective of financial reporting is tied to decision making. *The purpose of financial reporting is to help the users reach their decisions in an informed manner.*

---

[1]*Statement of Financial Accounting Concepts [SFAC] No. 1,* "Objectives of Financial Reporting by Business Enterprises" (Stamford, Conn.: Financial Accounting Standards Board, November 1978), par. 34.

SECONDARY OBJECTIVE: REFLECT PROSPECTIVE CASH RECEIPTS TO INVESTORS AND CREDITORS

Present stockholders must decide whether to hold their stock in a company or sell it. For potential stockholders, the decision is whether to buy the stock in the first place. Bankers, suppliers, and other types of creditors must decide whether to lend money to a company. In making their decisions, all these groups rely partially on the information provided in financial statements. (Other sources of information are sometimes as important, or more important, in reaching a decision. For example, the most recent income statement may report the highest profits in the history of a company. However, a potential investor may choose not to buy stock in a company if *The Wall Street Journal* or *Business Week* reports that a strike is likely to shut down operations for an indeterminable period of time.)

www.wsj.com
www.businessweek.com

If you buy stock in a company, your primary concern is the *future cash to be received from the investment*. First, how much, if anything, will you periodically receive in *cash dividends?* Second, how much cash will you receive from the *sale of the stock?* The interests of a creditor, such as a banker, are similar. The banker is concerned with receiving the original amount of money lent and the interest on the loan. In summary, another objective of financial reporting is to "provide information to help present and potential investors and creditors and other users in assessing the amounts, timing, and uncertainty of prospective cash receipts from dividends or interest and the proceeds from the sale, redemption, or maturity of securities or loans."[2]

SECONDARY OBJECTIVE: REFLECT PROSPECTIVE CASH FLOWS TO THE ENTERPRISE

As an investor, your ultimate concern is not the company's cash flows—how much comes in and goes out in the course of doing business—but the cash you receive from your investment. But since your investment depends to some extent on the company's business skills in managing its cash flows, another objective of accounting is to provide information that will allow users to make decisions about the cash flows of a company. (We will discuss cash flows briefly later in the chapter and will return to them in Chapter 12.)

SECONDARY OBJECTIVE: REFLECT THE ENTERPRISE'S RESOURCES AND CLAIMS TO ITS RESOURCES

The FASB emphasizes the roles of the balance sheet and the income statement in providing useful information. These financial statements should reflect what *resources* (or assets) the company or enterprise has, what *claims to these resources* (liabilities and stockholders' equity) there are, and the effects of transactions and events that change these resources and claims.[3] Thus, another objective of financial reporting is to show the effect of transactions on the entity's "accounting equation."

Exhibit 2-1 summarizes the objectives of financial reporting as they pertain to someone considering whether to buy stock in Gateway. The exhibit should help you to understand how something as abstract as a set of financial reporting objectives can be applied to a decision-making situation.

WHAT MAKES ACCOUNTING INFORMATION USEFUL? QUALITATIVE CHARACTERISTICS

Since accounting information must be useful for decision making, what makes this information useful? This section focuses on the qualities that accountants strive for in

LO 2 Describe the qualitative characteristics of accounting information.

---

[2]*SFAC No. 1,* par. 37.
[3]*SFAC No. 1,* par. 40.

EXHIBIT 2-1 The Application of Financial Reporting Objectives

Financial Reporting Objective	Potential Investor's Questions
1. The primary objective: Provide information for decision making.	"Based on the financial information, should I buy shares of stock in Gateway?"
2. Secondary objective: Reflect prospective cash receipts to investors and creditors.	"How much cash will I receive in dividends each year and from the sale of the stock of Gateway in the future?"
3. Secondary objective: Reflect prospective cash flows to the enterprise.	"After paying its suppliers and employees, and meeting all its obligations, how much cash will Gateway take in during the time I own the stock?"
4. Secondary objective: Reflect the enterprise's resources and claims to its resources.	"How much has Gateway invested in new plant and equipment?"

their financial reporting and on some of the challenges they face in making reporting judgments. It also reveals what users of financial information expect from financial statements.

Quantitative considerations, such as tuition costs, certainly were a concern when you chose your current school. In addition, your decision required you to make subjective judgments about the *qualitative* characteristics you were looking for in a college. Similarly, there are certain qualities that make accounting information useful.

UNDERSTANDABILITY

For anything to be useful, it must be understandable. Usefulness and understandability go hand in hand. However, **understandability** of financial information varies considerably, depending on the background of the user. For example, should financial statements be prepared so that they are understandable by anyone with a college education? Or should it be assumed that all readers of financial statements have completed at least one accounting course? Is a background in business necessary for a good understanding of financial reports, regardless of one's formal training? As you might expect, there are no simple answers to these questions. However, the FASB believes that financial information should be comprehensible to *those who are willing to spend the time to understand it:* "Financial information is a tool and, like most tools, cannot be of much direct help to those who are unable or unwilling to use it or who misuse it. Its use can be learned, however, and financial reporting should provide information that can be used by all—nonprofessionals as well as professionals—who are willing to learn to use it properly."[4]

RELEVANCE

Understandability alone is certainly not enough to render information useful. To be useful, information must be relevant. **Relevance** is the capacity of information to make a difference in a decision.[5] For example, assume that you are a banker evaluating the financial statements of a company that has come to you for a loan. All the financial statements point to a strong and profitable company. However, today's newspaper revealed that the company has been named in a multimillion-dollar lawsuit. Undoubtedly, this information would be relevant to your talks with the company, and disclosure of the lawsuit in the financial statements would make them even more relevant to your lending decision.

[4]*SFAC No. 1,* par. 36.
[5]*Statement of Financial Accounting Concepts [SFAC] No. 2,* "Qualitative Characteristics of Accounting Information" (Stamford, Conn.: Financial Accounting Standards Board, May 1980), par. 47.

ACCOUNTING FOR YOUR DECISIONS

You Are the Stockholder

ABC Technology produces a highly technical product used in the computer industry. You are a stockholder and are currently in the process of reading this year's annual report. You find that you can't understand the report because it contains so much accounting jargon. But the annual report contains an 800 number for shareholder inquiries. You call the number and complain about the annual report, but the corporate spokesman politely tells you that "that's the way people talk in accounting." Is your complaint valid?

ANS: One of the purposes of an annual report is to interest potential stockholders in the company. A small percentage of those potential investors are professional money managers who are familiar with the accounting terminology. However, most readers are individual investors who probably don't have a sophisticated accounting background. It is true that the report must assume a minimum level of formal education; accountants expect those who read the report to take the time to understand it. Technicalities aside, however, it is important to write an annual report for as broad an audience as possible.

RELIABILITY

What makes accounting information reliable? According to the FASB, "Accounting information is reliable to the extent that users can depend on it to represent the economic conditions or events that it purports to represent."[6]

Reliability has three basic characteristics:

■ *Verifiability* Information is verifiable when we can make sure that it is free from error—for example, by looking up the cost paid for an asset in a contract or an invoice.

■ *Representational faithfulness* Information is representationally faithful when it corresponds to an actual event—such as when the purchase of land corresponds to a transaction in the company's records.

■ *Neutrality* Information is neutral when it is not slanted to portray a company's position in a better or worse light than the actual circumstances would dictate—such as when the probable losses from a major lawsuit are disclosed accurately in the notes to the financial statements, with all its potential effects on the company, rather than minimized as a very remote possible loss.

COMPARABILITY AND CONSISTENCY

Comparability allows comparisons to be made *between or among companies.* Generally accepted accounting principles (GAAP) allow a certain amount of freedom in choosing among competing alternative treatments for certain transactions.

For example, under GAAP, companies may choose from a number of methods of accounting for the depreciation of certain long-term assets. **Depreciation** is the *process of allocating* the cost of a long-term tangible asset, such as a building or equipment, over its useful life. Each method may affect the value of the assets differently. (We discuss depreciation in Chapter 8.) How does this freedom of choice affect the ability of investors to make comparisons between companies?

Assume you were considering buying stock in one of three companies. As their annual reports indicate, two of the companies use what is called the "accelerated" depreciation method, and the other company uses what is called the "straight-line" depreciation method. (We'll learn about these methods in a later chapter.) Does this lack of a common depreciation method make it impossible for you to compare the performance of the three companies?

---

[6]*SFAC No. 2,* par. 62.

Dell Computers, like Gateway, is in the business of selling computers directly to consumers and to business and government organizations. It makes each machine to order and, like Gateway, carries a very small inventory at any one time. Dell also shares with Gateway a strategy of growth, seeking to enlarge its market share against such established giants as Compaq and IBM. However, focusing only on growth can be risky, as Dell found in the mid-1990s when it expanded its product line with notebook computers that fell short of quality standards and had to be withdrawn from the market.

More recently, Dell experienced fulfillment problems during the 2000 holiday selling season. Some shoppers, despite ordering their new Dell computers in November, experienced lengthy delays in shipment of their new Dimension 8100 desktops and Inspiron 8000 notebook computers, both high-profile, high-margin consumer systems. Two separate problems created the delays—an ordering glitch allowed customers to inadvertently order incompatible parts in shipments of the Dimension 8100, and supply problems with CD-RW drives and graphics cards slowed Inspiron 8000 orders.

Analysts called the problems particularly serious since consumer PC sales were down between 18 and 30 percent from the previous holiday season, although Dell placed part of the blame for the Inspiron 8000 problem on higher-than-expected demand. "The (demand for) 32MB graphics cards beat all forecasts," said Tom Kehoe, a Dell spokesperson, "so we did have a supply issue." The week before Christmas, the problem had been solved with the supplier, and Dell began quoting normal shipping lead times again. The firm also solved the incompatible-parts problem by simply shipping the right mouse with the Dimension 8100, instead of the incompatible one customers ordered, and used its support Web site to reach out to frustrated customers, even offering sweetening extras to some. But a "black eye" was something Dell could ill afford.

SOURCES: Lawrence M. Fisher, "Inside Dell Computer Corporation: Managing Working Capital," *Strategy and Business* 10 (first quarter 1998): 68–75; Joe Wilcox, "Dell Struggles with PC Shipment Delays," CNET news, Dec. 18, 2000, accessed at http://news/cnet.com/news/0-1006-200-4197427.html?tag=st.ne.1430735, Jan. 15, 2001.

Obviously, comparisons among the companies would be easier and more meaningful if all three used the same depreciation method. However, comparisons are not impossible just because companies use different methods. Certainly, the more alike—that is, uniform—statements are in terms of the principles used to prepare them, the more comparable they will be. However, the profession allows a certain freedom of choice in selecting from among alternative generally accepted accounting principles.

To render statements of companies using different methods more meaningful, *disclosure* assumes a very important role. For example, as we will see later in this chapter, the first footnote in the annual report of a publicly traded company is the disclosure of its accounting policies. The reader of this footnote for each of the three companies is made aware that the companies do not use the same depreciation method. Disclosure of accounting policies allows the reader to make some sort of subjective adjustment to the statements of one or more of the companies and thus to compensate for the different depreciation method being used.

Consistency is closely related to the concept of comparability. Both involve the relationship between two numbers. *However, whereas financial statements are comparable when they can be compared between one company and another, statements are consistent when they can be compared within a single company from one accounting period to the next.*

Occasionally, companies decide to change from one accounting method to another. Will it be possible to compare a company's earnings in a period in which it switches methods with its earnings in prior years if the methods differ? Like the different methods used by different companies, changes in accounting methods from one period to the next do not

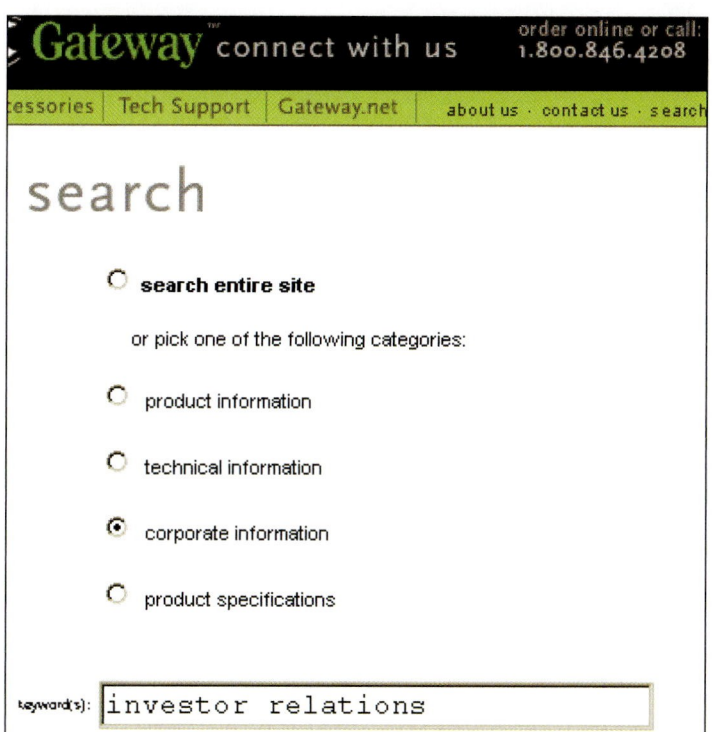

Companies still produce printed annual reports as a way to summarize the past year's business activities, discuss the firm's performance, preview upcoming products and business trends, and give investors and other users of financial information a format for analyzing the financial information. But most companies also provide annual report information—along with news reports and current information—at the *Investor Relations* page on their Web sites. You can search for Gateway's at www.gateway.com.

make comparisons impossible, only more difficult. When a company makes an accounting change, accounting standards require various disclosures to help the reader evaluate the impact of the change.

MATERIALITY

For accounting information to be useful, it must be relevant to a decision. The concept of **materiality** is closely related to relevance and deals with the size of an error in accounting information. The issue is whether the error is large enough to affect the judgment of someone relying on the information. Consider the following example. A company pays cash for two separate purchases: one for a $5 pencil sharpener and the other for a $50,000 computer. Theoretically, each expenditure results in the acquisition of an asset that should be depreciated over its useful life. However, what if the company decides to account for the $5 as an expense of the period rather than treat it in the theoretically correct manner by depreciating it over the life of the pencil sharpener? *Will this error in any way affect the judgment of someone relying on the financial statements?* Because such a slight error will *not* affect any decisions, minor expenditures of this nature are considered *immaterial* and are accounted for as an expense of the period.

The *threshold* for determining materiality will vary from one company to the next, depending to a large extent on the size of the company. Many companies establish policies that *any* expenditure under a certain dollar amount should be accounted for as an expense of the period. The threshold might be $50 for the corner grocery store but $1,000 for a large corporation. Finally, in some instances, the amount of a transaction may be immaterial by company standards but may still be considered significant by financial statement users. For example, a transaction involving either illegal or unethical behavior by a company officer would be of concern, regardless of the dollar amounts involved.

CONSERVATISM

The concept of **conservatism** is a holdover from earlier days when the primary financial statement was the balance sheet and the primary user of this statement was the banker. It was customary to deliberately understate assets in the balance sheet because this resulted

EXHIBIT 2-2   Qualitative Characteristics of Accounting Information

SITUATION A bank is trying to decide whether to extend a $1 million loan to Russell Corporation. Russell presents the bank with its most recent balance sheet, showing its financial position on a historical cost basis. Each quality of the information is summarized in the form of a question.

Quality	Question
Understandability	Can the information be used by those willing to learn to use it properly?
Relevance	Would the information be useful in deciding whether to loan money to Russell?
Reliability Verifiability	Can the information be verified? Is the information free from error?
Representational faithfulness	Is there agreement between the information and the events represented?
Neutrality	Is the information slanted in any way to present the company more favorably than is warranted?
Comparability	Are the methods used in assigning amounts to assets the same as those used by other companies?
Consistency	Are the methods used in assigning amounts to assets the same as those used in prior years?
Materiality	Will a specific error in any way affect the judgment of someone relying on the financial statements?
Conservatism	If there is any uncertainty about any of the amounts assigned to items in the balance sheet, are they recognized using the least optimistic estimate?

in an even larger margin of safety that the assets being provided as collateral for a loan were sufficient.

Today, the balance sheet is not the only financial statement, and deliberate understatement of assets is no longer considered desirable. The practice of conservatism is reserved for those situations in which there is *uncertainty* about how to account for a particular item or transaction: "Thus, if two estimates of amounts to be received or paid in the future are about equally likely, conservatism dictates using the less optimistic estimate; however, if two amounts are not equally likely, conservatism does not necessarily dictate using the more pessimistic amount rather than the more likely one."[7]

Various accounting rules are based on the concept of conservatism. For example, inventory held for resale is reported on the balance sheet at the *lower-of-cost-or-market value.* This rule requires a company to compare the cost of its inventory with the market price, or current cost to replace that inventory, and report the lower of the two amounts on the balance sheet at the end of the year. In Chapter 6, we will more fully explore the lower-of-cost-or-market rule as it pertains to inventory.

Exhibit 2-2 summarizes the qualities that make accounting information useful as these characteristics pertain to a banker's decision regarding whether to lend money to a company.

FINANCIAL REPORTING: AN INTERNATIONAL PERSPECTIVE

In Chapter 1, we introduced the International Accounting Standards Committee (IASC) and its efforts to improve the development of accounting standards around the world. Interestingly, four of the most influential members of this group, representing the standard-setting bodies in the United States, the United Kingdom, Canada, and Australia, agree on

---

[7] *SFAC No. 2,* par. 95.

the primary objective of financial reporting. All recognize that the primary objective is to provide information useful in making economic decisions.

The standard-setting body in the United Kingdom distinguishes between qualitative characteristics that relate to *content* of the information presented and those that relate to *presentation.* Similar to the FASB, this group recognizes relevance and reliability as the primary characteristics related to content. Comparability and understandability are the primary qualities related to the presentation of the information.

The concept of conservatism is also recognized in other countries. For example, both the IASC and the standard-setting body in the United Kingdom list "prudence" among their qualitative characteristics. Prudence requires the use of caution in making the various estimates required in accounting. Like the U.S. standard-setting body, these groups recognize that prudence does not justify the deliberate understatement of assets or revenues or the deliberate overstatement of liabilities or expenses.

THE CLASSIFIED BALANCE SHEET

Now that we have learned about the conceptual framework of accounting, we turn to the outputs of the system: the financial statements. First, we will consider the significance of a *classified balance sheet.* We will then examine the *income statement,* the *statement of retained earnings,* and the *statement of cash flows.* The chapter concludes with a brief look at the financial statements of a real company, Gateway, and at the other elements in an annual report.

LO 3 Explain the concept and purpose of a classified balance sheet and prepare the statement.

WHAT ARE THE PARTS OF THE BALANCE SHEET? UNDERSTANDING THE OPERATING CYCLE

In the first part of this chapter, we stressed the importance of *cash flow.* For a company that sells a product, the **operating cycle** begins when cash is invested in inventory and ends when cash is collected by the enterprise from its customers.

Assume that on August 1 a retailer, Laptop Computer Sales, buys a computer for $5,000 from the manufacturer, BIM Corp. At this point, Laptop has merely substituted one asset, cash, for another, inventory. On August 20, 20 days after buying the computer, Laptop sells it to an accounting firm, Arthur & Company, for $6,000. Under the purchase agreement, Arthur will pay for the computer within the next 30 days. At this point, both the form of the asset and the amount have changed. The form of the asset held by Laptop has changed from inventory to accounts receivable. Also, because the inventory has been sold for $1,000 more than its cost of $5,000, the size of the asset held, the account receivable, is now $6,000. Finally, on September 20, Arthur pays $6,000 to Laptop, and the operating cycle is complete. As we will explore more fully in later chapters, Laptop has earned $1,000, the difference between what it sold the computer for and what it initially paid for the computer. The cycle starts again when Laptop buys another computer for resale.

Laptop's operating cycle is summarized in Exhibit 2-3. The length of the company's operating cycle was 50 days. The operating cycle consisted of two distinct parts. From the time Laptop purchased the inventory, 20 days elapsed before it sold the computer. Another 30 days passed before the account receivable was collected. The length of the operating cycle depends to a large extent on the nature of a company's business. For example, in our illustration, the manufacturer of the computer, BIM Corp., received cash immediately from Laptop and did not have to wait to collect a receivable. However, additional time is added to the operating cycle of BIM Corp. to *manufacture* the computer.

The operating cycle of the accounting firm in our example, Arthur & Company, differs from that of either the manufacturer or the retailer. Arthur sells a service rather

> **Study Tip**
>
> The operating cycle of a business is the basis for deciding which assets are current and which are noncurrent. When you look at a company's balance sheet, be sure you understand the length of its operating cycle so you are clear about how it classifies its assets.

EXHIBIT 2-3   The Operating Cycle for a Retailer

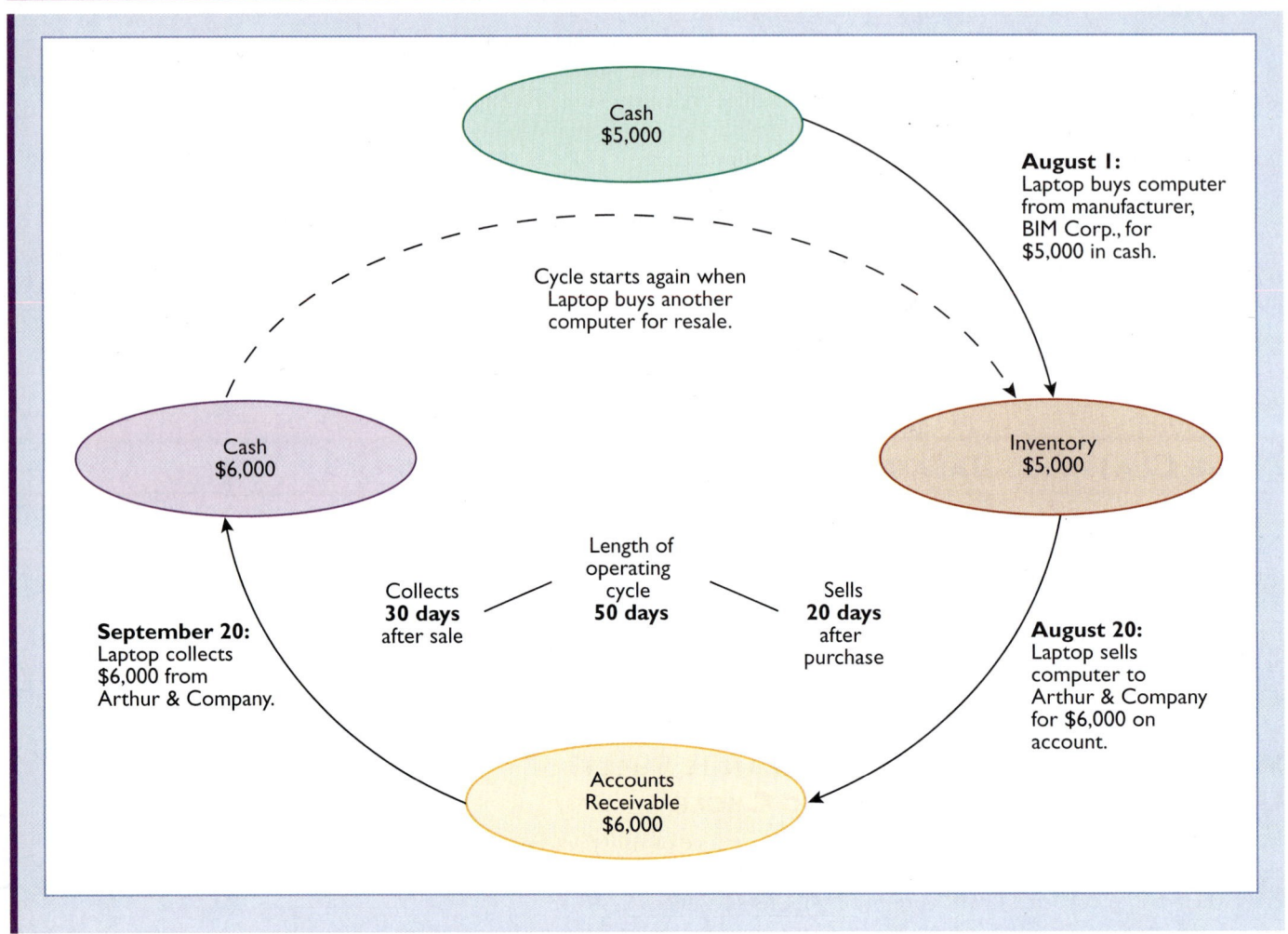

than a product. Its operating cycle is determined by two factors: the length of time involved in providing a service to the client and the amount of time required to collect any account receivable.

A classified balance sheet for a hypothetical company, Dixon Sporting Goods Inc., is shown in Exhibit 2-4. You will want to refer to it as you learn about the different categories on a classified balance sheet. (The bulleted numbers below refer to Exhibit 2-4.)

CURRENT ASSETS ■

The basic distinction on a classified balance sheet is between current and noncurrent items. **Current assets** are "cash and other assets that are reasonably expected to be realized in cash or sold or consumed during the normal operating cycle of a business or within one year if the operating cycle is shorter than one year."[8]

Most businesses have an operating cycle shorter than one year. The operating cycle for Laptop Computer Sales in our illustration was 50 days. Therefore, cash, accounts receivable, and inventory are classified as current assets because they *are* cash, will be *realized* in (converted to) cash (accounts receivable), or will be *sold* (inventory) within one year.

---

[8]Accounting Principles Board, *Statement of the Accounting Principles Board, No. 4,* "Basic Concepts and Accounting Principles Underlying Financial Statements of Business Enterprises" (New York: American Institute of Certified Public Accountants, 1970), par. 198.

EXHIBIT 2-4   Balance Sheet for Dixon Sporting Goods

DIXON SPORTING GOODS INC.
BALANCE SHEET
AT DECEMBER 31, 2001

ASSETS

These assets are realizable, sold, or consumed in one year or operating cycle.

Current assets

Cash	$ 5,000	
Marketable securities	11,000	
Accounts receivable	23,000	
Merchandise inventory	73,500	
Prepaid insurance	4,800	
Store supplies	700	
Total current assets		$118,000

These assets will not be realizable, sold, or consumed within one year or operating cycle.

Investments

Land held for future office site			150,000

Property, plant, and equipment

Land		100,000	
Buildings	$150,000		
Less: Accumulated depreciation	60,000	90,000	
Store furniture and fixtures	$ 42,000		
Less: Accumulated depreciation	12,600	29,400	
Total property, plant, and equipment			219,400

Intangible assets

Franchise agreement		55,000
Total assets		$542,400

LIABILITIES

These are liabilities that will be satisfied within one year or operating cycle.

Current liabilities

Accounts payable	$ 15,700	
Salaries and wages payable	9,500	
Income taxes payable	7,200	
Interest payable	2,500	
Bank loan payable	25,000	
Total current liabilities		$ 59,900

These are liabilities that will not be satisfied within one year or operating cycle.

Long-term debt

Notes payable, due December 31, 2011		120,000
Total liabilities		$179,900

STOCKHOLDERS' EQUITY

These are owners' claims on assets.

Contributed capital

Capital stock, $10 par, 5,000 shares issued and outstanding	$ 50,000	
Paid-in capital in excess of par value	25,000	
Total contributed capital	$ 75,000	
Retained earnings	287,500	
Total stockholders' equity		362,500
Total liabilities and stockholders' equity		$542,400

Can you think of a situation in which a company's operating cycle is longer than one year? A construction company is a good example. A construction company essentially builds an item of inventory, such as an office building, to a customer's specifications. The entire process, including constructing the building and collecting the sales amount from the customer, may take three years to complete. According to our earlier definition, because the inventory will be sold and the account receivable will be collected within the operating cycle, they will still qualify as current assets.

In addition to cash, accounts receivable, and inventory, the two other most common types of current assets are marketable securities and prepaid expenses. Excess cash is often

Compare the length of the operating cycle of a builder of an office building (or of communications equipment for the Internet) to that of a computer retailer. The time from the "launch" of a construction project to cash collection may be years, not weeks or months.

www.ibm.com

www.uswest.com

www.microsoft.com

invested in the stocks and bonds of other companies, as well as in various government instruments. If the investments are made for the short term, they are classified as current and are typically called either *short-term investments* or *marketable securities*. (Alternatively, some investments are made for the purpose of exercising influence over another company and thus are made for the long term. These investments are classified as noncurrent assets.) Various prepayments, such as office supplies, rent, and insurance, are classified as *prepaid expenses* and thus are current assets. These assets qualify as current because they will usually be *consumed* within one year.

NONCURRENT ASSETS 2

Any assets that do not meet the definition of a current asset are classified as *long-term* or *noncurrent assets*. Three common categories of long-term assets are: investments; property, plant, and equipment; and intangibles.

Investments Recall, from the discussion of current assets, that stocks and bonds expected to be sold within the next year are classified as current assets. Securities that are *not* expected to be sold within the next year are classified as *investments*. In many cases, the investment is in the common stock of another company. Sometimes companies invest in another company either to exercise some influence or actually to control the operation of the other company. Other types of assets classified as investments are land held for future use and buildings and equipment not currently used in operations. Finally, a special fund held for the retirement of debt or for the construction of new facilities is also classified as an investment.

Property, Plant, and Equipment This category consists of the various *tangible, productive assets* used in the operation of a business. Land, buildings, equipment, machinery, furniture and fixtures, trucks, and tools are all examples of assets held for use in the *operation* of a business rather than for *resale*. The distinction between inventory and equipment, for example, depends on the company's *intent* in acquiring the asset. For example, IBM classifies a computer system as inventory because its intent in manufacturing the asset is to offer it for resale. However, this same computer in the hands of a law firm would be classified as equipment because its intent in buying the asset from IBM is to use it in the long-term operation of the business.

The relative size of property, plant, and equipment depends largely on a company's business. Consider US West, a telecommunications company with over $23 billion in total assets at the end of 1999. Over 70% of the total assets was invested in property, plant, and equipment. On the other hand, property and equipment represented less than 5% of the total assets of Microsoft, the highly successful software company. Regardless of the relative size of property, plant, and equipment, all assets in this category are subject to depreciation, with the exception of land. A separate accumulated depreciation account is used to account for the depreciation recorded on each of these assets over its life.

Intangibles Intangible assets are similar to property, plant, and equipment in that they provide benefits to the firm over the long term. The distinction, however, is in the *form* of the asset. *Intangible assets lack physical substance.* Trademarks, copyrights, franchise rights, patents, and goodwill are examples of intangible assets. The cost principle governs the accounting for intangibles, just as it does for tangible assets. For example, the amount paid to an inventor for the patent rights to a new project is recorded as an intangible asset. Similarly, the amount paid to purchase a franchise for a fast-food restaurant for the exclusive right to operate in a certain geographic area is recorded as an intangible asset. Like tangible assets, intangibles are written off to expense over their useful lives. *Depreciation* is the name given to the process of writing off tangible assets; the same process for intangible assets is called *amortization*. Depreciation and amortization are both explained more fully in Chapter 8.

ACCOUNTING FOR YOUR DECISIONS

You Are a Student

Identify any assets you currently have, and then categorize them as either current or noncurrent.

ANS: Among your current assets would be cash (both on hand and in savings and checking accounts) and any investments you expect to sell in the near future. Your car would be a noncurrent asset.

CURRENT LIABILITIES 3

The definition of a current liability is closely tied to that of a current asset. A **current liability** is an obligation that will be satisfied within the next operating cycle or within one year, if the cycle is shorter than one year. For example, the classification of a note payable on the balance sheet depends on its maturity date. If the note will be paid within the next year, it is classified as current; otherwise, it is classified as a long-term liability. On the other hand, accounts payable, wages payable, and income taxes payable are all short-term or current liabilities.

Most liabilities, such as those for purchases of merchandise on credit, are satisfied by the payment of cash. However, certain liabilities are eliminated from the balance sheet when the company performs services. For example, the liability Subscriptions Received in Advance, which would appear on the balance sheet of a magazine publisher, is satisfied not by the payment of any cash but by the delivery of the magazine to the customers. Finally, it is possible to satisfy one liability by substituting another in its place. For example, a supplier might ask a customer to sign a written promissory note to replace an existing account payable if the customer is unable to pay at the present time.

LONG-TERM LIABILITIES 4

Any obligation that will not be paid or otherwise satisfied within the next year or the operating cycle, whichever is longer, is classified as a long-term liability, or long-term debt. Notes payable and bonds payable, both promises to pay money in the future, are two common forms of long-term debt. Some bonds have a life as long as 25 or 30 years.

STOCKHOLDERS' EQUITY 5

Recall that stockholders' equity represents the owners' claims on the assets of the business. These claims arise from two sources: *contributed capital* and *earned capital*. Contributed capital appears on the balance sheet in the form of capital stock, and earned capital takes the form of retained earnings. *Capital stock* indicates the owners' investment in the business. *Retained earnings* represents the accumulated earnings, or net income, of the business since its inception less all dividends paid during that time.

Most companies have a single class of capital stock called *common stock*. This is the most basic form of ownership in a business. All other claims against the company, such as those of *creditors* and *preferred stockholders,* take priority. *Preferred stock* is a form of capital stock that, as the name implies, carries with it certain preferences. For example, the company must pay dividends on preferred stock before it makes any distribution of dividends on common stock. In the event of liquidation, preferred stockholders have priority over common stockholders in the distribution of the entity's assets.

Capital stock may appear as two separate items on the balance sheet: *Par Value* and *Paid-in Capital in Excess of Par Value.* The total of these two items tells us the amount that has been paid by the owners for the stock. We will take a closer look at these items in Chapter 11.

USING A CLASSIFIED BALANCE SHEET

LO 4 Use a classified balance sheet to analyze a company's financial position.

As we have now seen, a classified balance sheet separates both assets and liabilities into those that are current and those that are noncurrent. This distinction is very useful in any analysis of a company's financial position.

WORKING CAPITAL

Investors, bankers, and other interested readers use the balance sheet to evaluate the liquidity of a business. **Liquidity** is a relative term and deals with the ability of a company to pay its debts as they come due. As you might expect, bankers and other creditors are particularly interested in the liquidity of businesses to which they have lent money. A comparison of current assets and current liabilities is a starting point in evaluating the ability of a company to meet its obligations. **Working capital** is the difference between current assets and current liabilities at a point in time. Referring back to Exhibit 2-4, we see that the working capital for Dixon Sporting Goods on December 31, 2001, is as follows:

WORKING CAPITAL

FORMULA	FOR DIXON SPORTING GOODS
Current Assets − Current Liabilities	$118,000 − $59,900 = $58,100

The management of working capital is an important task for any business. A company must continually strive for a *balance* in managing its working capital. For example, too little working capital—or, in the extreme, negative working capital—may signal the inability to pay creditors on a timely basis. However, an overabundance of working capital could indicate that the company is not investing enough of its available funds in productive resources, such as new machinery and equipment.

CURRENT RATIO

Because it is an absolute dollar amount, working capital is limited in its informational value. For example, $1 million may be an inadequate amount of working capital for a large corporation but far too much for a smaller company. In addition, a certain dollar amount of working capital may have been adequate for a company earlier in its life but is inadequate now. However, a related measure of liquidity, the **current ratio,** allows us to *compare* the liquidity of companies of different sizes and of a single company over time. The ratio is computed by dividing current assets by current liabilities. Dixon Sporting Goods has a current ratio of just under 2 to 1:

CURRENT RATIO

FORMULA	FOR DIXON SPORTING GOODS
$\dfrac{\text{Current Assets}}{\text{Current Liabilities}}$	$\dfrac{\$118,000}{\$59,900} = 1.97 \text{ to } 1$

Some analysts use a rule of thumb of 2 to 1 for the current ratio as a sign of short-term financial health. However, as is always the case, rules of thumb can be dangerous. Historically, companies in certain industries have operated quite efficiently with a current ratio of less than 2 to 1, whereas a ratio much higher than this is necessary to survive in other industries. Consider Tommy Hilfiger Corp., the popular clothing company. At the end of the fiscal year 1999, it had a current ratio of 2.72 to 1. On the other hand, companies in the telephone communication business routinely have current ratios well under 1 to 1. Sprint's current ratio at the end of 1999 was only .82 to 1.

www.tommy.com

www.sprint.com

Unfortunately, neither the amount of working capital nor the current ratio tells us anything about the *composition* of current assets and current liabilities. For example, assume two companies both have total current assets equal to $100,000. Company A has cash of $10,000, accounts receivable of $50,000, and inventory of $40,000. Company B also has cash of $10,000 but accounts receivable of $20,000 and inventory of $70,000. All other things being equal, Company A is more liquid than Company B because more of its total current assets are in receivables than inventory. Receivables are only one step away from being cash, whereas inventory must be sold and then the receivable collected. Note that Dixon's inventory of $73,500 makes up a large portion of its total current assets of $118,000. An examination of the *relative* size of the various current assets for a company may reveal certain strengths and weaknesses not evident in the current ratio.

In addition to the composition of the current assets, the *frequency* with which they are "turned over" is important. For instance, how long does it take to sell an item of inventory? How long is required to collect an account receivable? Many companies could not exist with the current ratio of .48 reported by the McDonald's Corporation at the end of 1999. However, think about the nature of the fast-food business. The frequency of its sales and thus the numerous operating cycles within a single year mean that it can operate with a much lower current ratio than a manufacturing company, for example.

www.mcdonalds.com

THE INCOME STATEMENT

The income statement is used to summarize the results of operations of an entity for a *period of time.* At a minimum, all companies prepare income statements at least once a year. Companies that must report to the Securities and Exchange Commission prepare financial statements, including an income statement, every three months. Monthly income statements are usually prepared for internal use by management.

www.sec.gov

WHAT APPEARS ON THE INCOME STATEMENT?

From an accounting perspective, it is important to understand what transactions of an entity should appear on the income statement. In general, the income statement reports the excess of *revenue over expense,* that is, the *net income,* or in the event of an excess of *expense over revenue,* the *net loss* of the period. As a reference to the "bottom line" on an income statement, it is common to use the terms *profits* or *earnings* as synonyms for *net income.*

As discussed in Chapter 1, *revenue* is the inflow of assets resulting from the sale of products and services. It represents the dollar amount of sales of products and services for a period of time. An *expense* is the outflow of assets resulting from the sale of goods and services for a period of time. The cost of products sold, wages and salaries, and taxes are all examples of expenses.

Certain special types of revenues, called *gains,* are sometimes reported on the income statement, as are certain special types of expenses, called *losses.* For example, assume that Sanders Company holds a parcel of land for a future building site. The company paid $50,000 for the land 10 years ago. The state pays Sanders $60,000 for the property to use in a new highway project. Sanders has a special type of revenue from the condemnation of its property. It will recognize a *gain* of $10,000: the excess of the cash received from the state, $60,000, over the cost of the land, $50,000.

FORMAT OF THE INCOME STATEMENT

LO 5 Explain the difference between a single-step and a multiple-step income statement and prepare each type of income statement.

Different formats are used by corporations to present their results. The major choice a company makes is whether to prepare the income statement in a single-step or a multiple-step form. Both forms are generally accepted. According to the AICPA's annual survey of 600 companies, more than twice as many use the multiple-step form than the single-step form. Next, we'll explain the differences between the two forms and their variations.

Single-Step Format for the Income Statement In a **single-step income statement,** all expenses and losses are added together and then are deducted *in a single step* from all revenues and gains to arrive at net income. A single-step format for the income statement of Dixon Sporting Goods is presented in Exhibit 2-5. The primary advantage of the single-step form is its simplicity. No attempt is made to classify either revenues or expenses or to associate any of the expenses with any of the revenues.

Multiple-Step Format for the Income Statement The purpose of the **multiple-step income statement** is to subdivide the income statement into specific sections and provide the reader with important subtotals. This format is illustrated for Dixon Sporting Goods in Exhibit 2-6.

The multiple-step income statement for Dixon indicates three important subtotals. First, ∎ cost of goods sold is deducted from sales to arrive at **gross profit:**

$$\text{Gross profit} = \text{Sales} - \text{Cost of goods sold}$$

Sales	$357,500
Cost of goods sold	218,300
Gross profit	$139,200

Cost of goods sold, as the name implies, is the cost of the units of inventory sold during the year. It is logical to associate cost of goods sold with the sales revenue for the year because the latter represents the *selling price* of the inventory sold during the period.

EXHIBIT 2-5 Income Statement (Single-Step Format) for Dixon Sporting Goods Inc.

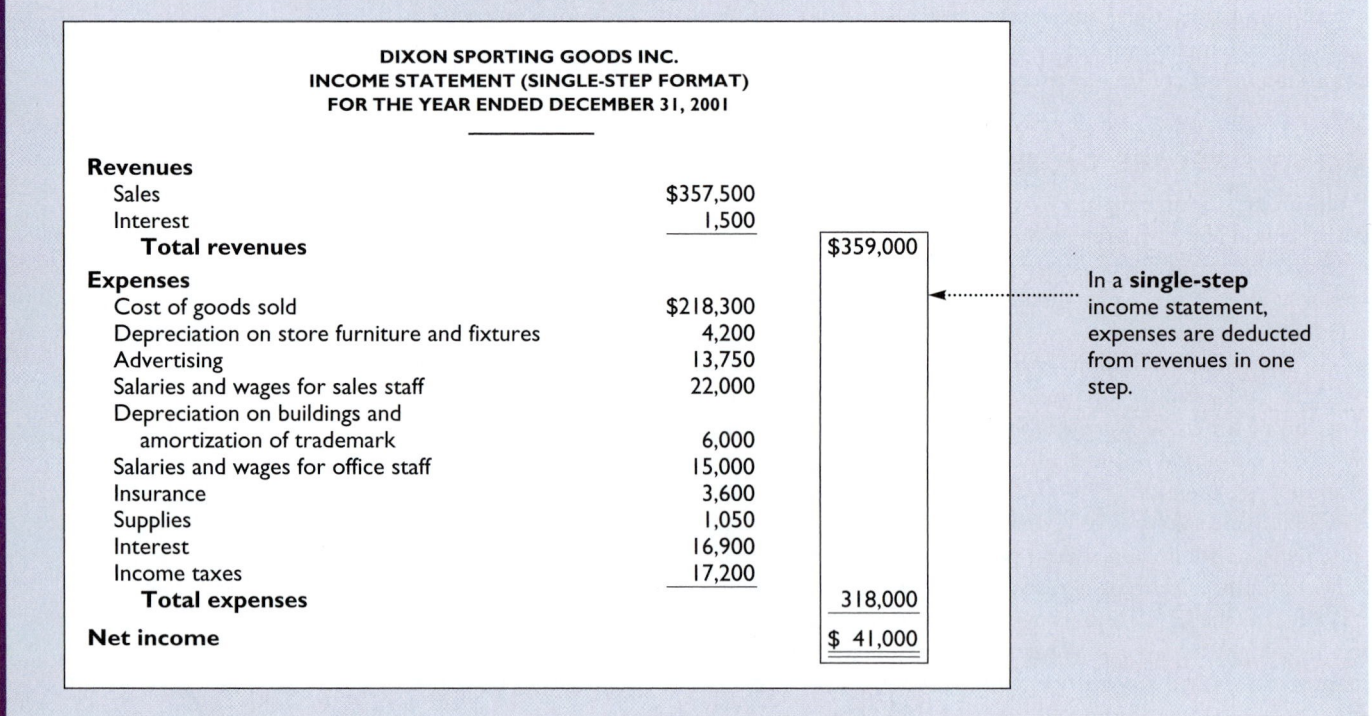

DIXON SPORTING GOODS INC.
INCOME STATEMENT (SINGLE-STEP FORMAT)
FOR THE YEAR ENDED DECEMBER 31, 2001

Revenues		
Sales	$357,500	
Interest	1,500	
Total revenues		$359,000
Expenses		
Cost of goods sold	$218,300	
Depreciation on store furniture and fixtures	4,200	
Advertising	13,750	
Salaries and wages for sales staff	22,000	
Depreciation on buildings and amortization of trademark	6,000	
Salaries and wages for office staff	15,000	
Insurance	3,600	
Supplies	1,050	
Interest	16,900	
Income taxes	17,200	
Total expenses		318,000
Net income		$ 41,000

In a **single-step** income statement, expenses are deducted from revenues in one step.

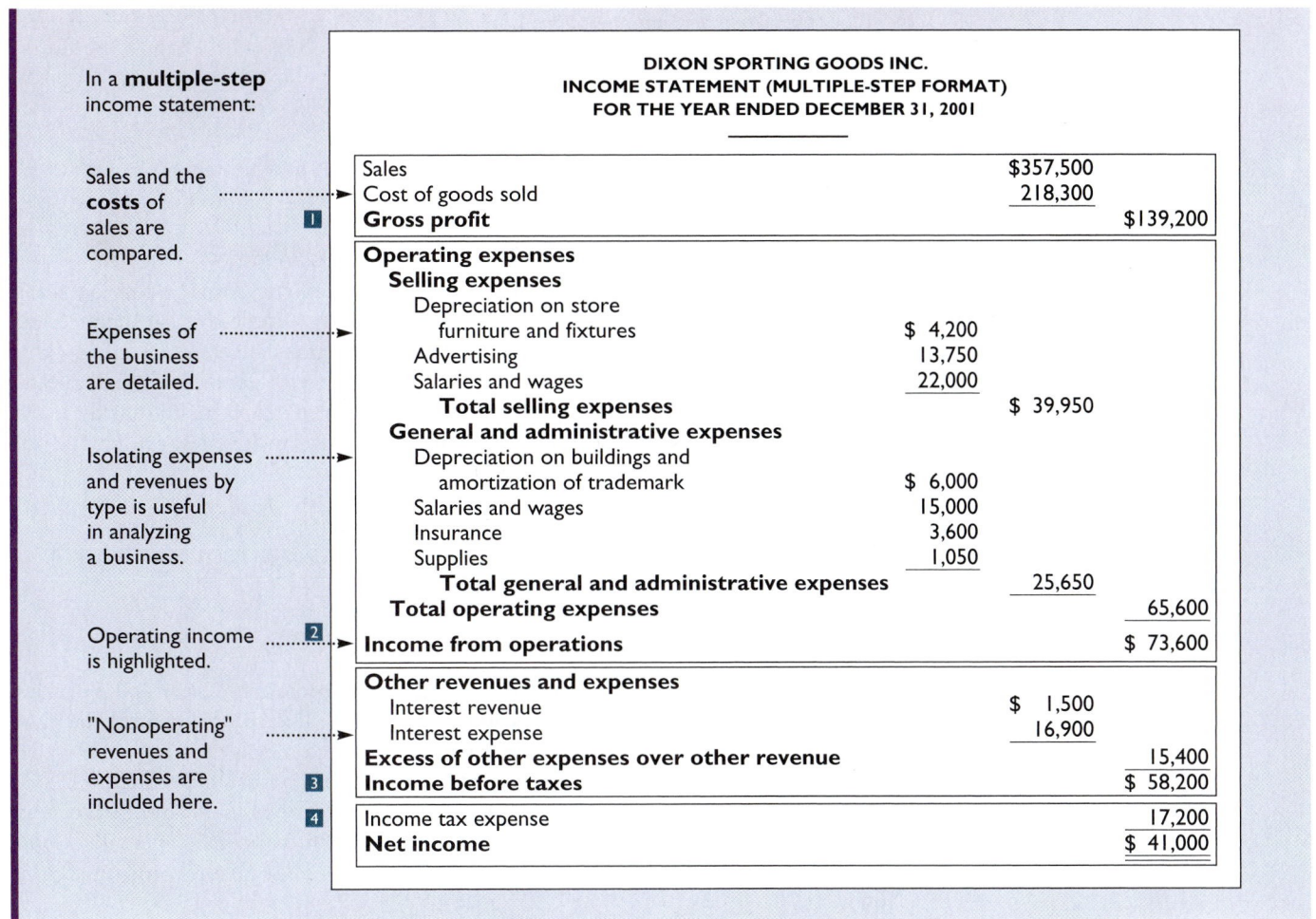

In a **multiple-step** income statement:

Sales and the **costs** of sales are compared. **1**

Expenses of the business are detailed.

Isolating expenses and revenues by type is useful in analyzing a business.

Operating income is highlighted. **2**

"Nonoperating" revenues and expenses are included here. **3**

4

DIXON SPORTING GOODS INC.
INCOME STATEMENT (MULTIPLE-STEP FORMAT)
FOR THE YEAR ENDED DECEMBER 31, 2001

Sales		$357,500	
Cost of goods sold		218,300	
Gross profit			$139,200
Operating expenses			
Selling expenses			
Depreciation on store			
furniture and fixtures	$ 4,200		
Advertising	13,750		
Salaries and wages	22,000		
Total selling expenses		$ 39,950	
General and administrative expenses			
Depreciation on buildings and			
amortization of trademark	$ 6,000		
Salaries and wages	15,000		
Insurance	3,600		
Supplies	1,050		
Total general and administrative expenses		25,650	
Total operating expenses			65,600
Income from operations			$ 73,600
Other revenues and expenses			
Interest revenue		$ 1,500	
Interest expense		16,900	
Excess of other expenses over other revenue			15,400
Income before taxes			$ 58,200
Income tax expense			17,200
Net income			$ 41,000

The second important subtotal on Dixon's income statement is **2** *income from operations* of $73,600. This is found by subtracting *total operating expenses* of $65,600 from the gross profit of $139,200. Operating expenses are further subdivided between *selling expenses* and *general and administrative expenses*. For example, note that two depreciation amounts are included in operating expenses. Depreciation on store furniture and fixtures is classified as a selling expense because the store is where sales take place. On the other hand, we will assume that the buildings are offices for the administrative staff and thus depreciation on the buildings is classified as a general and administrative expense.

The third important subtotal on the income statement is **3** *income before taxes* of $58,200. Interest revenue and interest expense, neither of which is an operating item, are included in *other revenues and expenses*. The excess of interest expense of $16,900 over interest revenue of $1,500, which equals $15,400, is subtracted from income from operations to arrive at income before taxes. Finally, **4** *income tax expense* of $17,200 is deducted to arrive at *net income* of $41,000.

Two-Minute Review

1. Give at least two examples of items that would appear on a multiple-step income statement but not a single-step statement.

2. Classify each of the following expenses as either selling or general and administrative: advertising, depreciation on office building, salespersons' commissions, and office salaries.

Answers on next page.

USING A MULTIPLE-STEP INCOME STATEMENT

LO 6 Use a multiple-step income statement to analyze a company's operations.

An important advantage of the multiple-step income statement is that it provides additional information to the reader. Although all the amounts needed to calculate certain ratios are available on a single-step statement, such calculations are easier to figure with a multiple-step statement. For example, the deduction of cost of goods sold from sales to arrive at gross profit, or *gross margin* as it is sometimes called, allows us to quickly calculate the **gross profit ratio.** The ratio of Dixon's gross profit to its sales, rounded to the nearest percent, is as follows:

GROSS PROFIT RATIO

FORMULA	FOR DIXON SPORTING GOODS
$\dfrac{\text{Gross Profit}}{\text{Sales}}$	$\dfrac{\$139,200}{\$357,500} = 39\%$

The gross profit ratio tells us that after paying for the product, for every dollar of sales, 39¢ is available to cover other expenses and earn a profit. The complement of the gross profit ratio is the ratio of cost of goods sold to sales. For Dixon, this ratio is $1 - .39 = .61$, or 61%. For every dollar of sales, Dixon spends $.61 on the cost of the product.

An important use of the income statement is to evaluate the *profitability* of a business. For example, a company's **profit margin** is the ratio of its net income to its sales. Some analysts refer to a company's profit margin as its *return on sales.* Dixon's profit margin is as follows:

PROFIT MARGIN

FORMULA	FOR DIXON SPORTING GOODS
$\dfrac{\text{Net Income}}{\text{Sales}}$	$\dfrac{\$41,000}{\$357,500} = 11\%$

For every dollar of sales, Dixon has $.11 in net income.

Two important factors should be kept in mind in evaluating any financial statement ratio. First, how does this year's ratio differ from ratios of prior years? For example, a decrease in the profit margin may indicate that the company is having trouble this year controlling certain costs. Second, how does the ratio compare with industry norms? For example, in some industries the profit margin is considerably lower than in many others, such as in mass merchandising (Wal-Mart's profit margin was only 3.3% for the year ended January 31, 2000). It is always helpful to compare key ratios, such as the profit margin, with an industry average or with the same ratio for a close competitor of the company.

From Concept

TO PRACTICE 2.1

READING UNO'S INCOME STATEMENT Which income statement format does Uno use: single-step or multiple-step? Calculate Uno's 1999 and 1998 gross profit ratio. Explain what happened from 1998 to 1999.

www.walmart.com

THE STATEMENT OF RETAINED EARNINGS

LO 7 Identify the components of the statement of retained earnings and prepare the statement.

The purpose of a statement of stockholders' equity is to explain the changes in the components of owners' equity during the period. Retained earnings and capital stock are the two primary components of stockholders' equity. If there are no changes during the period in a company's capital stock, it may choose to present a statement of retained earnings instead

DIXON SPORTING GOODS INC.
STATEMENT OF RETAINED EARNINGS
FOR THE YEAR ENDED DECEMBER 31, 2001

Retained earnings, January 1, 2001	$271,500
Add: Net income for 2001	41,000
	$312,500
Less: Dividends declared and paid in 2001	(25,000)
Retained earnings, December 31, 2001	$287,500

of a statement of stockholders' equity.[9] A statement of retained earnings for Dixon Sporting Goods is shown in Exhibit 2-7.

The statement of retained earnings provides an important link between the income statement and the balance sheet. Dixon's net income of $41,000, as detailed on the income statement, is an *addition* to retained earnings. Note that the dividends declared and paid of $25,000 do not appear on the income statement because they are a payout, or *distribution,* of net income to stockholders rather than one of the expenses deducted to arrive at net income. Accordingly, they appear as a direct deduction on the statement of retained earnings. The beginning balance in retained earnings is carried forward from last year's statement of retained earnings.

THE STATEMENT OF CASH FLOWS

All publicly held corporations are required to present a statement of cash flows in their annual reports. The purpose of the statement is to summarize the cash flow effects of a company's operating, investing, and financing activities for the period.

LO 8 Identify the components of the statement of cash flows and prepare the statement.

THE CASH FLOW STATEMENT FOR DIXON SPORTING GOODS

The statement for Dixon Sporting Goods is shown in Exhibit 2-8. The statement consists of three categories: operating activities, investing activities, and financing activities. Each of these three categories can result in a net inflow of cash or a net outflow of cash.

Dixon's *operating activities* generated $56,100 of cash during the period. Operating activities **1** concern the purchase and sale of a product, in this case the acquisition of sporting goods from distributors and the subsequent sale of those goods. As we can readily see, Dixon had one major source of cash, the collection from its customers of $362,500. Similarly, Dixon's largest use of cash was the $217,200 it paid for inventory. In Chapter 12, we will discuss the statement of cash flows in detail and the preparation of this section of the statement.

Financing and investing activities were described in "Getting Started." *Investing activities* **2** involve the acquisition and sale of long-term assets, such as long-term investments, property, plant, and equipment, and intangible assets. *Financing activities* **3** result from the issuance and repayment, or retirement, of long-term liabilities and capital stock. The one investing activity on Dixon's statement of cash flows, the purchase of land for a future office site, required the use of cash and thus is shown as a net outflow of $150,000. Dixon

[9]According to the AICPA's annual survey, most corporations (almost 85%) present a statement of stockholders' equity. A separate statement of retained earnings, or a combined statement of income and retained earnings, is used by a small minority of companies.

EXHIBIT 2-8   Statement of Cash Flows for Dixon Sporting Goods Inc.

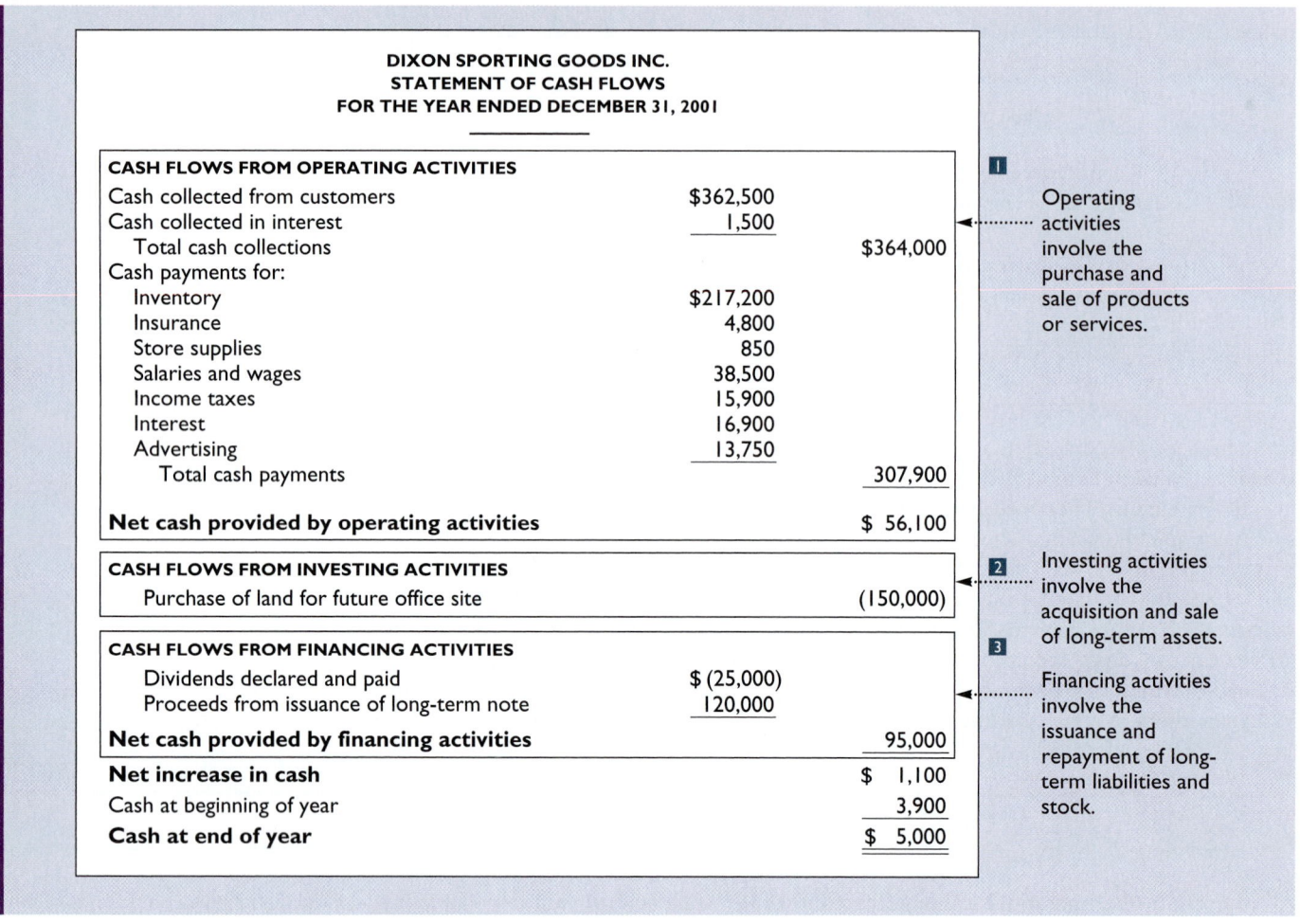

DIXON SPORTING GOODS INC.
STATEMENT OF CASH FLOWS
FOR THE YEAR ENDED DECEMBER 31, 2001

CASH FLOWS FROM OPERATING ACTIVITIES		
Cash collected from customers	$362,500	
Cash collected in interest	1,500	
Total cash collections		$364,000
Cash payments for:		
Inventory	$217,200	
Insurance	4,800	
Store supplies	850	
Salaries and wages	38,500	
Income taxes	15,900	
Interest	16,900	
Advertising	13,750	
Total cash payments		307,900
Net cash provided by operating activities		$ 56,100
CASH FLOWS FROM INVESTING ACTIVITIES		
Purchase of land for future office site		(150,000)
CASH FLOWS FROM FINANCING ACTIVITIES		
Dividends declared and paid	$ (25,000)	
Proceeds from issuance of long-term note	120,000	
Net cash provided by financing activities		95,000
Net increase in cash		$ 1,100
Cash at beginning of year		3,900
Cash at end of year		$ 5,000

1 Operating activities involve the purchase and sale of products or services.

2 Investing activities involve the acquisition and sale of long-term assets.

3 Financing activities involve the issuance and repayment of long-term liabilities and stock.

had two financing activities: dividends of $25,000 required the use of cash, and the issuance of a long-term note generated cash of $120,000. The balance in cash on the bottom of the statement of $5,000 must agree with the balance for this item as shown on the balance sheet in Exhibit 2-4.

THE FINANCIAL STATEMENTS FOR GATEWAY

LO 9 Read and use the financial statements and other elements in the annual report of a publicly held company.

The financial statements for our hypothetical company, Dixon Sporting Goods Inc., introduced the major categories on each of the statements. We now turn to the financial statements of an actual company, Gateway. These statements are more complex and require additional analysis and a better understanding of accounting to fully appreciate them. However, we will concentrate on certain elements of the statements. At this stage in your study, look for the similarities rather than the differences between these statements and those of Dixon.

www.gateway.com

Gateway was founded by Ted Waitt in 1985 in an empty farmhouse near Sioux City, Iowa. What began as a mail-order business has grown to the point that sales in 1999 exceeded $8.6 billion. Early on, Gateway adopted a cow as its mascot and began to ship all its products in boxes that looked like the markings on a Holstein cow.[10]

---

[10]*International Directory of Company Histories,* vol. 10 (St. James Press, 1995), p. 308.

As we will see later, the notes to a set of financial statements give the reader a variety of information about a company. Like the statements of many other companies, Gateway's financials include a note that describes its business:

> Gateway, Inc. (the "Company") is a direct marketer of personal computers ("PCs") and PC-related products and services. The Company develops, manufactures, markets and supports a broad line of desktop and portable PCs, servers, workstations, and PC-related products used by individuals, families, businesses, government agencies and educational institutions. The Company also offers and supports PC-related services, including training, financing, and Internet service.[11]

GATEWAY'S BALANCE SHEET

The balance sheets for Gateway at the end of each of two years are shown in Exhibit 2-9. Like most other companies, Gateway chose an accounting or fiscal year that corresponds to the calendar—that is, beginning on January 1 and ending on December 31. However, some companies choose a fiscal year that ends at a point when sales are at their lowest in the annual cycle. For example, Wal-Mart ends its fiscal year on January 31, after the busy holiday season.

www.walmart.com

Gateway releases what are called *consolidated financial statements,* which reflect the position and results of all operations that are controlled by a single entity. Like most other large corporations, Gateway owns other companies. Often these companies are legally separate and are called *subsidiaries.* How a company accounts for its investment in a subsidiary is covered in advanced accounting courses.

Gateway presents comparative balance sheets to indicate its financial position at the end of each of the last two years. As a minimum standard, the Securities and Exchange Commission requires that the annual report include balance sheets as of the two most recent years and income statements for each of the three most recent years. Note that all amounts on the balance sheet are stated in thousands of dollars. This type of rounding is a common practice in the financial statements of large corporations and is justified under the materiality concept. Knowing the exact dollar amount of each asset would not change a decision made by an investor.

The presentation of comparative balance sheets allows the reader to make comparisons between years. For example, Gateway's *working capital* increased during 1999:

WORKING CAPITAL

	December 31, 1998	December 31, 1999
Current Assets − Current Liabilities	$2,228,186 − $1,429,674 = $798,512	$2,696,805 − $1,809,710 = $887,095

Gateway's *current ratio* at each of the two dates follows:

CURRENT RATIO

	December 31, 1998	December 31, 1999
$\dfrac{\text{Current Assets}}{\text{Current Liabilities}}$	$\dfrac{\$2,228,186}{\$1,429,674} = 1.56 \text{ to } 1$	$\dfrac{\$2,696,805}{\$1,809,710} = 1.49 \text{ to } 1$

Although the amount of working capital increased between 1998 and 1999, the current ratio actually decreased. This occurred because current liabilities increased by a higher percentage than did current assets.

On the liability side of its balance sheet, Gateway lists two noncurrent liabilities: long-term obligations, net of current maturities, and warranty and other liabilities. Given the nature of the products it sells (PCs), Gateway provides its customers with warranties. (As we will see in Chapter 9, warranties often create a liability for companies. Long-term obligations will be discussed more fully in Chapter 10.)

---

[11] *Gateway 1999 Annual Report*, p. 29.

EXHIBIT 2-9 Comparative Balance Sheets for Gateway

Consolidated Balance Sheets

December 31
(in thousands, except per share amounts)

	1998	1999
Assets		
Current assets:		
Cash and cash equivalents	$ 1,169,810	$ 1,127,654
Marketable securities	158,657	208,717
Accounts receivable, net	558,851	646,339
Inventory	167,924	191,870
Other	172,944	522,225
Total current assets	2,228,186	2,696,805
Property, plant and equipment, net	530,988	745,660
Intangibles, net	65,944	52,302
Other assets	65,262	459,921
	$2,890,380	$3,954,688
Liabilities and Stockholders' Equity		
Current liabilities:		
Current maturities of long-term obligations	$ 11,415	$ 5,490
Accounts payable	718,071	898,436
Accrued liabilities	415,265	609,132
Accrued royalties	167,873	153,840
Other current liabilities	117,050	142,812
Total current liabilities	1,429,674	1,809,710
Long-term obligations, net of current maturities	3,360	2,998
Warranty and other liabilities	112,971	124,862
Total liabilities	1,546,005	1,937,570
Commitments and Contingencies (Note 3)		
Stockholders' equity:		
Preferred stock, $.01 par value, 5,000 shares		
authorized, none issued and outstanding	—	—
Class A common stock, nonvoting, $.01 par value,		
1,000 shares authorized; none issued		
and outstanding	—	—
Common stock, $.01 par value, 1,000,000 shares		
authorized; 313,138 shares and 320,016 shares		
issued and outstanding, respectively	3,131	3,200
Additional paid-in capital	364,421	656,870
Common stock in treasury, at cost, 730 shares in 1999	—	(51,796)
Retained earnings	980,908	1,408,852
Accumulated other comprehensive loss	(4,085)	(8)
Total stockholders' equity	1,344,375	2,017,118
	$2,890,380	$3,954,688

Use these to find:
• Working capital
• Current ratio

The accompanying notes are an integral part of the consolidated financial statements.

GATEWAY'S INCOME STATEMENT

We have examined two basic formats for the income statement: the single-step format and the multiple-step format. In practice, numerous variations on these two basic formats exist, depending to a large extent on the nature of a company's business. For example, the multiple-step form, with its presentation of gross profit, is not used by service businesses because they do not sell a product. (Remember that gross profit is sales less cost of goods sold.) As we will see for Gateway, the form of the income statement is a reflection of a company's operations.

EXHIBIT 2-10   Comparative Income Statements for Gateway

Consolidated Income Statements

For the years ended December 31
(in thousands, except per share amounts)

	1997	1998	1999
Net sales	$6,293,680	$7,467,925	$8,645,561
Cost of goods sold	5,217,239	5,921,651	6,745,744
Gross profit	1,076,441	1,546,274	1,899,817
Selling, general and administrative expense	786,168	1,052,047	1,304,147
Nonrecurring expenses	113,842	—	—
Operating income	176,431	494,227	595,670
Other income, net	27,189	47,021	67,809
Income before income taxes	203,620	541,248	663,479
Provision for income taxes	93,823	194,849	235,535
Net income	$ 109,797	$ 346,399	$ 427,944
Net income per share:			
Basic	$ 0.36	$ 1.11	$ 1.36
Diluted	$ 0.35	$ 1.09	$ 1.32
Weighted-average shares outstanding:			
Basic	307,680	311,084	313,974
Diluted	312,402	317,857	324,421

The accompanying notes are an integral part of the consolidated financial statements.

Use these to find:
• Gross profit ratio

Multiple-step income statements for Gateway for a three-year period are presented in Exhibit 2-10. Note the increase in Gateway's *gross profit ratio* from 1998 to 1999:

GROSS PROFIT RATIO

	1998	1999
$\dfrac{\text{Gross Profit}}{\text{Net Sales}}$	$\dfrac{\$1,546,274}{\$7,467,925} = 21\%$	$\dfrac{\$1,899,817}{\$8,645,561} = 22\%$

Both Gateway's management and its stockholders should be pleased with this improvement in the gross profit ratio. It is a clear sign that the company has successfully increased its sales while controlling the costs to make its products. Also, note the inclusion of net income per share information at the bottom of the statement. The per share information helps users of the statement in various ways and is discussed in more detail in Chapter 13.

OTHER ELEMENTS OF AN ANNUAL REPORT

No two annual reports look the same. The appearance of an annual report depends not only on the size of a company but also on the budget devoted to the preparation of the report. Some companies publish "bare-bones" annual reports, whereas others issue a glossy report complete with pictures of company products and employees. In recent years, many companies, as a cost-cutting measure, have scaled back the amount spent on the annual report. The creativity in annual reports varies as well. Starbuck's 1998 annual report included a coupon good for a 12-ounce beverage at any of its stores. The 1998 Wal-Mart annual report was designed to give the appearance of a magazine, complete with feature articles and an ad for Sam's Club.

Privately held companies tend to distribute only financial statements, without the additional information normally included in the annual reports of public companies. For the annual reports of public companies, however, certain basic elements are considered standard.

From Concept

TO PRACTICE 2.2

READING GATEWAY'S INCOME STATEMENT   Compute Gateway's profit margin for the past two years. Did it go up or down from the prior year to the current year?

www.starbucks.com
www.walmart.com

EXHIBIT 2-11 Report of Independent Accountants for Gateway

Report of Independent Accountants

To the Stockholders and Board of Directors of Gateway, Inc.

In our opinion, the accompanying consolidated balance sheets and the related consolidated statements of income, cash flows and changes in stockholders' equity and comprehensive income present fairly, in all material respects, the consolidated financial position of Gateway, Inc. at December 31, 1998 and 1999, and the consolidated results of its operations and its cash flows for each of the three years in the period ended December 31,1999, in conformity with accounting principles generally accepted in the United States. These financial statements are the responsibility of the Company's management; our responsibility is to express an opinion on these financial statements based on our audits. We conducted our audits of these statements in accordance with auditing standards generally accepted in the United States which require that we plan and perform the audit to obtain reasonable assurance about whether the financial statements are free of material misstatement. An audit includes examining, on a test basis, evidence supporting amounts and disclosures in the financial statements, assessing the accounting principles used and significant estimates made by management, and evaluating the overall financial statement presentation. We believe that our audits provide a reasonable basis for the opinion expressed above.

PricewaterhouseCoopers LLP

PricewaterhouseCoopers LLP
San Diego, California

January 20, 2000

A letter to the stockholders from either the president or the chairman of the board of directors appears in the first few pages of most annual reports. A section describing the company's products and markets is usually included. At the heart of any annual report is the financial report or review, which consists of the financial statements accompanied by footnotes to explain various items on the statements. We will now consider these other elements as presented in the 1999 annual report of Gateway.

Report of Independent Accountants   As you see in Exhibit 2-11, Gateway is audited by PricewaterhouseCoopers LLP, one of the largest international accounting firms. Two key phrases should be noted in the first sentence of the independent accountants' report: *in our opinion* and *present fairly.* The report indicates that responsibility for the statements rests with Gateway and that the auditors' job is to *express an opinion* on the statements, based on certain tests. It would be impossible for an auditing firm to spend the time or money to retrace and verify every single transaction entered into during the year by Gateway. Instead, the auditing firm performs various tests of the accounting records to be able to assure itself that the statements are free of *material misstatement.* Auditors do not "certify" the total accuracy of a set of financial statements but render an opinion as to the reasonableness of those statements. Finally, note that this format for the auditors' report differs from the one for Uno presented in Chapter 1. However, both formats contain the same basic information.

The Ethical Responsibility of Management and the Auditors   The management of a company and its auditors share a common purpose: to protect the interests of stockholders. In large corporations, the stockholders are normally removed from the daily affairs of the business. The need for a professional management team to run the business is a practical necessity, as is the need for a periodic audit of the company's records. Because stockholders cannot run the business themselves, they need assurances that the business is being oper-

> "I was familiar with the basic elements of the [annual] report, but the line-by-line specifics were foreign to me."
> —Matthew Butler

Using Financial Statements Becomes Second Nature

Annual reports reveal a company's financial health. For this reason, all kinds of professionals use reports and their financial statements as a guide in making business decisions or in helping others make investment decisions.

Matthew Butler, a financial advisor for a large brokerage firm in Washington, D.C., has learned along the way how important the financial statements are in the business world. "I knew what an annual report was to the extent that I knew that every year a company sends a formal accounting of its financial status to shareholders. I was familiar with the basic elements of the report, but the line-by-line specifics were foreign to me," Matthew says. "Then, when I went to get licensed as a financial advisor, I was required to pass a group of financial exams, including the Series 7. Studying for and acing this exam taught me everything I would ever want to know about financial statements and how to interpret them. Now, I use them every day without even thinking about it."

As a financial advisor, Matthew's job is to provide potential investors with opinions about stocks and the companies behind them. "The first thing I do when a client asks me about a particular stock is look at the numbers. On the income statement, I look at the net income and revenues to find out how much the company is making and at the costs to see how much it is spending. From there, I go to the 'earnings per share'—net income divided by the total number of shares outstanding—and to the 'price/earnings ratio'—which is the current price of the stock divided by earnings per share. These calculations are huge in my business. They're the most important numbers I can provide my clients."

By looking at corporate financial statements day to day and doing what is called "fundamental analysis" for his clients, Matthew now has the experience to render, in an instant, an opinion on the financial health of a company. As he says, "It's what I do for a living."

ated effectively and efficiently and that the financial statements presented by management are a fair representation of the company's operations and financial position. The management and the auditors have a very important ethical responsibility to their constituents, the stockholders of the company.

Management Discussion and Analysis   Preceding the financial statements is a section of Gateway's annual report titled "Management's Discussion and Analysis of Financial Condition and Results of Operations." This report gives management the opportunity to discuss the financial statements and provide the stockholders with explanations for certain amounts reported in the statements. For example, management explains the increase in sales as follows:

> Gateway set new sales records in 1999, shipping more than 4.6 million systems and generating more than $8.6 billion in sales during the year. The Company's 1999 performance eclipsed the prior year's record results, besting 1998 unit shipments and sales by 32% and 16%, respectively, compared to an increase in unit shipments and sales of 37% and 19% in 1998. Domestic and international sales grew 15% and 19%, respectively.[12]

---

[12]*Gateway 1999 Annual Report,* p. 20.

Notes to Consolidated Financial Statements The sentence "The accompanying notes are an integral part of the consolidated financial statements" appears at the bottom of each of Gateway's four financial statements. These comments, or *footnotes*, as they are commonly called, are necessary to satisfy the need for *full disclosure* of all the facts relevant to a company's results and financial position. The first footnote in all annual reports is a summary of *significant accounting policies*. A company's policies for valuing inventories, depreciating assets, and recognizing revenue are among the important items contained in this footnote. For example, Gateway describes its policy for depreciating assets as follows: "Depreciation is provided using straight-line methods over the assets' estimated useful lives, ranging from four to forty years."[13] In addition to the summary of significant accounting policies, other footnotes discuss such topics as income taxes and retirement savings plans.

This completes our discussion of the makeup of the annual report. By now you should appreciate the flexibility that companies have in assembling the report, aside from the need to follow generally accepted accounting principles in preparing the statements. The accounting standards followed in preparing the statements, as well as the appearance of the annual report itself, differ in other countries. As has been noted elsewhere, although many corporations operate internationally, accounting principles are far from being standardized.

WARMUP EXERCISES

LO 4, 6 Warmup Exercise 2-1   Identifying Ratios

State the equation for each of the following ratios:

1. Current ratio
2. Gross profit ratio
3. Profit margin

Key to the Solution

Review the various ratios as discussed in the chapter.

LO 4, 6   Warmup Exercise 2-2   Calculating Ratios

Bridger reported net income of $150,000, sales of $1,000,000, and cost of goods sold of $800,000.

Required

Compute each of the following ratios for Bridger:

1. Gross profit ratio
2. Profit margin

Key to the Solution

Recall the equation for each of these ratios as presented in the chapter.

LO 4   Warmup Exercise 2-3   Determining Liquidity

Big has current assets of $500,000 and current liabilities of $400,000. Small reports current assets of $80,000 and current liabilities of $20,000.

Required

Which company is more liquid? Why?

Key to the Solution

Calculate the current ratio for each company and compare them.

---

[13]*Gateway 1999 Annual Report,* p. 30.

Warmup Exercise 2-1

1. $\text{Current ratio} = \dfrac{\text{Current Assets}}{\text{Current Liabilities}}$

2. $\text{Gross profit ratio} = \dfrac{\text{Gross Profit}}{\text{Sales}}$

3. $\text{Profit margin} = \dfrac{\text{Net income}}{\text{Sales}}$

Warmup Exercise 2-2

1. $\dfrac{\$1,000,000 - \$800,000}{\$1,000,000} = \dfrac{\$200,000}{\$1,000,000} = \underline{\underline{20\%}}$

2. $\dfrac{\$150,000}{\$1,000,000} = \underline{\underline{15\%}}$

Warmup Exercise 2-3

Small Company appears on the surface to be more liquid. Its current ratio of $80,000/$20,000 or 4 to 1 is significantly higher than Big's current ratio of $500,000/$400,000 or 1.25 to 1.

The following review problem will give you the opportunity to apply what you have learned by preparing both an income statement and a balance sheet.

REVIEW PROBLEM

The following items, in alphabetical order, are taken from the records of Grizzly Inc., a chain of outdoor recreational stores in the Northwest. Use the items to prepare two statements. First, prepare an income statement for the year ended December 31, 2001. The income statement should be in multiple-step form. Second, prepare a classified balance sheet at December 31, 2001. All amounts are in thousands of dollars.

Accounts payable	$ 6,500
Accounts receivable	8,200
Accumulated depreciation—buildings	25,000
Accumulated depreciation—furniture and fixtures	15,000
Advertising expense	3,100
Buildings	80,000
Capital stock, $1 par, 10,000 shares issued and outstanding	10,000
Cash	2,400
Commissions expense	8,600
Cost of goods sold	110,000
Depreciation on buildings	2,500
Depreciation on furniture and fixtures	1,200
Furniture and fixtures	68,000
Income taxes payable	2,200
Income tax expense	13,000
Insurance expense	2,000
Interest expense	12,000
Interest payable	1,000
Interest revenue	2,000
Land	100,000
Long-term notes payable, due December 31, 2009	120,000
Merchandise inventories	6,000

Office supplies	900
Paid-in capital in excess of par value	40,000
Prepaid rent	3,000
Rent expense for salespersons' autos	9,000
Retained earnings	48,800
Salaries and wages for office staff	11,000
Sales revenue	190,000

Solution to Review Problem

1. Multiple-step income statement:

GRIZZLY INC.
INCOME STATEMENT
FOR THE YEAR ENDED DECEMBER 31, 2001
(IN THOUSANDS OF DOLLARS)

Sales revenue		$190,000	
Cost of goods sold		110,000	
Gross profit			$ 80,000
Operating expenses:			
Selling expenses:			
Advertising	$ 3,100		
Depreciation on furniture and fixtures	1,200		
Rent for salespersons' autos	9,000		
Commissions	8,600		
Total selling expenses		$ 21,900	
General and administrative expenses:			
Depreciation on buildings	$ 2,500		
Insurance	2,000		
Salaries and wages for office staff	11,000		
Total general and administrative expenses		15,500	
Total operating expenses			37,400
Income from operations			$ 42,600
Other revenues and expenses:			
Interest revenue		$ 2,000	
Interest expense		12,000	
Excess of other expenses over other revenue			10,000
Income before taxes			$ 32,600
Income tax expense			13,000
Net income			$ 19,600

2. Classified Balance Sheet:

GRIZZLY INC.
BALANCE SHEET
AT DECEMBER 31, 2001
(IN THOUSANDS OF DOLLARS)

Assets

Current assets:		
Cash	$ 2,400	
Accounts receivable	8,200	
Merchandise inventories	6,000	
Office supplies	900	
Prepaid rent	3,000	
Total current assets		$ 20,500

Property, plant, and equipment:

Land			$100,000	
Buildings		$ 80,000		
Less: Accumulated depreciation		25,000	55,000	
Furniture and fixtures		$ 68,000		
Less: Accumulated depreciation		15,000	53,000	
Total property, plant, and equipment				208,000
Total assets				$228,500

Liabilities

Current liabilities:				
Accounts payable			$ 6,500	
Income taxes payable			2,200	
Interest payable			1,000	
Total current liabilities				$ 9,700
Long-term notes payable, due December 31, 2009				120,000
Total liabilities				$129,700

Stockholders' Equity

Contributed capital:				
Capital stock, $1 par, 10,000 shares				
issued and outstanding			$ 10,000	
Paid-in capital in excess of par value			40,000	
Total contributed capital			$ 50,000	
Retained earnings			48,800	
Total stockholders' equity				98,800
Total liabilities and stockholders' equity				$228,500

CHAPTER HIGHLIGHTS

1. **LO 1** The primary objective of financial reporting is to provide information that is useful in making investment, credit, and similar decisions.

2. **LO 1** Investors and creditors are ultimately interested in their own prospective cash receipts from dividends or interest and the proceeds from the sale, redemption, or maturity of securities or loans. Because these expected cash flows are related to the expected cash flows to the company, its cash flows are of interest to investors and creditors. The entity's economic resources, claims to them, and the effects of transactions that change resources and claims to those resources are also of interest.

3. **LO 2** Financial information should be understandable to those who are willing to spend the time to understand it. To be useful, the information should be relevant and reliable. Relevant information has the capacity to make a difference in a decision. Reliable information can be depended on to represent the economic events that it purports to represent.

4. **LO 2** *Comparability* is the quality that allows for comparisons to be made between two or more companies, whereas *consistency* is the quality that allows for comparisons to be made within a single company from one period to the next. These two qualities of useful accounting information are aided by full disclosure—in the footnotes to the financial statements—of all relevant information.

5. **LO 3** The operating cycle depends to a large extent on the nature of a company's business. For a retailer, it encompasses the period

of time from the investment of cash in inventory to the collection of any account receivable from sale of the product. The operating cycle for a manufacturer is expanded to include the period of time required to convert raw materials into finished products.

6. **LO 3** Current assets will be realized in cash or sold or consumed during the operating cycle or within one year if the cycle is shorter than one year. Because most businesses have numerous operating cycles within a year, the cutoff for classification as a current asset is usually one year. Cash, accounts receivable, inventory, and prepaid expenses are all examples of current assets.

7. **LO 3** The definition of *current liability* is related to that of *current asset*. A current liability is an obligation that will be satisfied within the operating cycle or within one year if the cycle is shorter than one year. Many liabilities are satisfied by making a cash payment. However, some obligations are settled by rendering a service.

8. **LO 4** A classified balance sheet is helpful in evaluating the liquidity of a business. Working capital, the difference between current assets and current liabilities, indicates the buffer of protection for creditors. The current ratio, current assets divided by current liabilities, provides the reader with a relative measure of liquidity.

9. **LO 5, 6** All expenses are added together and subtracted from all revenues in a single-step income statement. The multiple-step income statement provides the reader with classifications of revenues and expenses as well as with important subtotals. Cost of goods sold is subtracted from sales revenue on a multiple-step

statement, with the result reported as gross profit. Profitability analysis includes such measures as the gross profit ratio (the ratio of gross profit to sales) and the profit margin (the ratio of net income to sales).

10. **LO 7, 8** If there are no changes in the capital stock accounts, some companies present a statement of retained earnings or a combined statement of income and retained earnings in lieu of a statement of stockholders' equity. The statement of cash flows summarizes the operating, investing, and financing activities of an entity for the period.

11. **LO 9** No two annual reports are the same. However, certain basic elements are included in most of them. In addition to the financial statements, annual reports include, among other items, the independent accountants' report, management's discussion of the amounts appearing in the statements, and footnotes to the statements.

KEY TERMS QUIZ

Read each definition below and then write the number of that definition in the blank beside the appropriate term it defines. The solution appears at the end of the chapter.

____ Understandability
____ Relevance
____ Reliability
____ Comparability
____ Depreciation
____ Consistency
____ Materiality
____ Conservatism
____ Operating cycle
____ Current asset

____ Current liability
____ Liquidity
____ Working capital
____ Current ratio
____ Single-step income statement
____ Multiple-step income statement
____ Gross profit
____ Gross profit ratio
____ Profit margin

1. An income statement in which all expenses are added together and subtracted from all revenues.

2. The magnitude of an omission or a misstatement in accounting information that will affect the judgment of someone relying on the information.

3. The capacity of information to make a difference in a decision.

4. An income statement that provides the reader with classifications of revenues and expenses as well as with important subtotals.

5. The practice of using the least optimistic estimate when two estimates of amounts are about equally likely.

6. The quality of accounting information that makes it comprehensible to those willing to spend the necessary time.

7. Gross profit divided by sales.

8. Current assets divided by current liabilities.

9. The quality of accounting information that makes it dependable in representing the events that it purports to represent.

10. An obligation that will be satisfied within the next operating cycle or within one year if the cycle is shorter than one year.

11. The period of time between the purchase of inventory and the collection of any receivable from the sale of the inventory.

12. Current assets minus current liabilities.

13. Net income divided by sales.

14. The quality of accounting information that allows a user to analyze two or more companies and look for similarities and differences.

15. An asset that is expected to be realized in cash or sold or consumed during the operating cycle or within one year if the cycle is shorter than one year.

16. The ability of a company to pay its debts as they come due.

17. The quality of accounting information that allows a user to compare two or more accounting periods for a single company.

18. Sales less cost of goods sold.

19. The allocation of the cost of a tangible, long-term asset over its useful life.

ALTERNATE TERMS

Balance sheet   Statement of financial position or condition

Capital stock   Contributed capital

Cost of goods sold   Cost of sales

Gross profit   Gross margin

Income statement   Statement of income

Income tax expense   Provision for income taxes

Long-term assets   Noncurrent assets

Long-term liability   Long-term debt

Net income   Profits or earnings

Report of independent accountants   Auditors' report

Retained earnings   Earned capital

Stockholders' equity   Shareholders' equity

QUESTIONS

1. How would you evaluate the following statement: "The cash flows to a company are irrelevant to an investor; all the investor cares about is the potential for receiving dividends on the investment"?

2. A key characteristic of useful financial information is understandability. How does this qualitative characteristic relate to the background of the user of the information?

3. What does *relevance* mean with regard to the use of accounting information?

4. What is the qualitative characteristic of comparability, and why is it important in preparing financial statements?

5. What is the difference between comparability and consistency as they relate to the use of accounting information?

6. How does the concept of materiality relate to the size of a company?

7. How does the operating cycle of a retailer differ from that of a service company?

8. How does the concept of the operating cycle relate to the definition of a current asset?

9. What are two examples of the way a company's intent in using an asset affects classification of the asset on the balance sheet?

10. How would you evaluate the following statement: "A note payable with an original maturity of five years will be classified on the balance sheet as a long-term liability until it matures"?

11. How do the two basic forms of owners' equity items for a corporation—capital stock and retained earnings—differ?

12. What are the limitations of working capital as a measure of the liquidity of a business as opposed to the current ratio?

13. What is meant by a company's capital structure?

14. What is the major weakness of the single-step form for the income statement?

15. Why might a company's gross profit ratio increase from one year to the next but its profit margin ratio decrease?

16. How does a statement of retained earnings act as a link between an income statement and a balance sheet?

17. In auditing the financial statements of a company, does a certified public accountant *certify* that the statements are totally accurate and without errors of any size or variety?

18. What is the first footnote in the annual report of all publicly held companies, and what is its purpose?

EXERCISES

LO 2 **Exercise 2-1** Characteristics of Useful Accounting Information

Fill in the blank with the qualitative characteristic for each of the following descriptions:

_____ 1. Information that users can depend on to represent the events that it purports to represent

_____ 2. Information that has the capacity to make a difference in a decision

_____ 3. Information that is valid, that indicates an agreement between the underlying data and the events represented

_____ 4. Information that allows for comparisons to be made from one accounting period to the next

_____ 5. Information that is free from error

_____ 6. Information that is meaningful to those who are willing to learn to use it properly

_____ 7. Information that is not slanted to portray a company's position any better or worse than the circumstances warrant

_____ 8. Information that allows for comparisons to be made between or among companies

LO 3 **Exercise 2-2** Classification of Assets and Liabilities

Indicate the appropriate classification of each of the following as a current asset (CA), noncurrent asset (NCA), current liability (CL), or long-term liability (LTL):

_____ 1. Inventory

_____ 2. Accounts payable

_____ 3. Cash

_____ 4. Patents

_____ 5. Notes payable, due in six months

_____ 6. Taxes payable

_____ 7. Prepaid rent (for the next nine months)

_____ 8. Bonds payable, due in 10 years

_____ 9. Machinery

LO 5 Exercise 2-3 Selling Expenses and General and Administrative Expenses

Operating expenses are subdivided between selling expenses and general and administrative expenses when a multiple-step income statement is prepared. From the following list, identify each item as a selling expense (S) or general and administrative expense (G&A):

_____ 1. Advertising expense

_____ 2. Depreciation expense—store furniture and fixtures

_____ 3. Office rent expense

_____ 4. Office salaries expense

_____ 5. Store rent expense

_____ 6. Store salaries expense

_____ 7. Insurance expense

_____ 8. Supplies expense

_____ 9. Utilities expense

LO 5 Exercise 2-4 Missing Income Statement Amounts

For each of the following independent cases, fill in the blank with the appropriate dollar amount:

	Sara's Coffee Shop	Amy's Deli	Jane's Bagels
Net sales	$35,000	$ _____	$78,000
Cost of goods sold	_____	45,000	_____
Gross profit	7,000	18,000	_____
Selling expenses	3,000	_____	9,000
General and administrative expenses	1,500	2,800	_____
Total operating expenses	_____	8,800	13,600
Net income	$ 2,500	$ 9,200	$25,400

LO 6 Exercise 2-5 Income Statement Ratios

The 2001 income statement of Holly Enterprises shows net income of $45,000, comprising net sales of $134,800, cost of goods sold of $53,920, selling expenses of $18,310, general and administrative expenses of $16,990, and interest expense of $580. Holly's stockholders' equity was $280,000 at the beginning of the year and $320,000 at the end of the year. The company has 20,000 shares of stock outstanding at December 31, 2001.

Required

Compute Holly's (1) gross profit ratio and (2) profit margin. What other information would you need to be able to comment on whether these ratios are favorable?

LO 7 Exercise 2-6 Statement of Retained Earnings

Landon Corporation was organized on January 2, 1999, with the investment of $100,000 by each of its two stockholders. Net income for its first year of business was $85,200. Net income increased during 2000 to $125,320 and to $145,480 during 2001. Landon paid $20,000 in dividends to each of the two stockholders in each of the three years.

Required

Prepare a statement of retained earnings for the year ended December 31, 2001.

LO 8 Exercise 2-7 Components of the Statement of Cash Flows

From the following list, identify each item as operating (O), investing (I), financing (F), or not on the statement of cash flows (N):

_____ 1. Paid for supplies

_____ 2. Collected cash from customers

_____ 3. Purchased land (held for resale)

_____ 4. Purchased land (for construction of new building)

_____ 5. Paid dividend

_____ 6. Issued stock

_____ 7. Purchased computers (for use in the business)

_____ 8. Sold old equipment

LO 9   **Exercise 2-8**   Basic Elements of Financial Statements

Most financial reports contain the following list of basic elements. For each element, identify the person(s) who prepared the element and describe the information a user would expect to find in each element. Some information is verifiable; other information is subjectively chosen by management. Comment on the verifiability of information in each element.

1. Letter from the president
2. Product/markets of company
3. Financial statements
4. Notes to financial statements
5. Independent accountants' report

Multi-Concept Exercises

LO 3, 5, 7   **Exercise 2-9**   Financial Statement Classification

Potential stockholders and lenders are interested in a company's financial statements. For the following list, identify the statement—balance sheet (BS), income statement (IS), retained earnings statement (RE)—on which each item would appear.

_____ 1. Accounts payable	_____ 11. Dividends
_____ 2. Accounts receivable	_____ 12. Land held for future expansion
_____ 3. Advertising expense	_____ 13. Loss on the sale of equipment
_____ 4. Bad debt expense	_____ 14. Office supplies
_____ 5. Bonds payable	_____ 15. Organizational costs
_____ 6. Buildings	_____ 16. Patent amortization expense
_____ 7. Cash	_____ 17. Retained earnings
_____ 8. Common stock	_____ 18. Sales
_____ 9. Deferred income taxes	_____ 19. Unearned revenue
_____ 10. Depreciation expense	_____ 20. Utilities expense

LO 5, 6   **Exercise 2-10**   Single- and Multiple-Step Income Statement

Some headings and/or items are used on either the single-step or the multiple-step income statement. Some are used on both. For the list below, indicate the following: single-step (S), multiple-step (M), both formats (B), or not used on either income statement (N).

_____ 1. Sales
_____ 2. Cost of goods sold
_____ 3. Selling expenses
_____ 4. Total revenues
_____ 5. Utilities expense
_____ 6. Administrative expense
_____ 7. Net loss
_____ 8. Supplies on hand
_____ 9. Accumulated depreciation
_____ 10. Gross profit

LO 5, 6   **Exercise 2-11**   Multiple-Step Income Statement

Gaynor Corporation's partial income statement follows:

Sales	$1,200,000
Cost of sales	450,000
Selling expenses	60,800
General and administrative expenses	75,000

Required

Determine the gross profit ratio and profit margin. Would you consider investing in Gaynor Corporation? Explain your answer.

LO 2 **Problem 2-1** Materiality

Joseph Knapp, a newly hired accountant, wanted to impress his boss, so he stayed late one night to analyze the office supplies expense. He determined the cost by month, for the past 12 months, of each of the following: computer paper, copy paper, fax paper, pencils and pens, note pads, postage, stationery, and miscellaneous items.

1. What did Joseph think his boss would learn from this information? What action might be taken as a result of knowing it?

2. Would this information be more relevant if Joseph worked for a hardware store or for a real estate company? Discuss.

LO 2 **Problem 2-2** Costs and Expenses

The following costs are incurred by a retailer:

Depreciation
1. Display fixtures in a retail store
2. Advertising
3. Merchandise for sale
4. Incorporation (i.e., legal costs, stock issue costs)
5. Cost of a franchise
6. Office supplies
7. Wages in a restaurant
8. Computer software
Depreciation 9. Computer hardware *current asset*

Required

For each of these costs, explain whether all of the cost or only a portion of the cost would appear as an expense on the income statement for the period in which the cost was incurred. If not all of the cost would appear on the income statement for that period, explain why not.

LO 3 **Problem 2-3** Classified Balance Sheet

The following balance sheet items, listed in alphabetical order, are available from the records of Ruth Corporation at December 31, 2001:

Accounts payable	$ 18,255
Accounts receivable	23,450
Accumulated depreciation—automobiles	22,500
Accumulated depreciation—buildings	40,000
Automobiles	112,500
Bonds payable, due December 31, 2005	160,000
Buildings	200,000
Capital stock, $10 par value	150,000
Cash	13,230
Income taxes payable	6,200
Interest payable	1,500
Inventory	45,730
Land	250,000
Long-term investments	85,000
Notes payable, due June 30, 2002	10,000
Office supplies	2,340
Paid-in capital in excess of par value	50,000
Patents	40,000
Prepaid rent	1,500
Retained earnings	311,095
Salaries and wages payable	4,200

Required

1. Prepare in good form a classified balance sheet as of December 31, 2001.

2. Compute Ruth's current ratio.

3. On the basis of your answer to requirement **2**, does Ruth appear to be *liquid?* What other information do you need to fully answer this question?

LO 4   Problem 2-4   Financial Statement Ratios

The following items, in alphabetical order, are available from the records of Walker Corporation as of December 31, 2001 and 2000:

	December 31, 2001	December 31, 2000
Accounts payable	$ 8,400	$ 5,200
Accounts receivable	13,230	19,570
Cash	10,200	9,450
Cleaning supplies	450	700
Interest payable	–0–	1,200
Inventory	24,600	26,200
Marketable securities	6,250	5,020
Note payable, due in six months	–0–	12,000
Prepaid rent	3,600	4,800
Taxes payable	1,450	1,230
Wages payable	1,200	1,600

Required

1. Calculate the following, as of December 31, 2001, and December 31, 2000:

   a. Working capital

   b. Current ratio

2. On the basis of your answers to **1**, comment on the relative liquidity of the company at the beginning and the end of the year. As part of your answer, explain the change in the company's liquidity from the beginning to the end of 2001.

LO 4   Problem 2-5   Working Capital and Current Ratio

The balance sheet of Stevenson Inc. includes the following items:

Cash	$ 23,000
Accounts receivable	13,000
Inventory	45,000
Prepaid insurance	800
Land	80,000
Accounts payable	54,900
Salaries payable	1,200
Capital stock	100,000
Retained earnings	5,700

Required

1. Determine the current ratio and working capital.

2. Beyond the information provided in your answers to **1**, what does the composition of the current assets tell you about Stevenson's liquidity?

3. What other information do you need to fully assess Stevenson's liquidity?

LO 5   Problem 2-6   Single-Step Income Statement

The following income statement items, arranged in alphabetical order, are taken from the records of Shaw Corporation for the year ended December 31, 2001:

Advertising expense	$ 1,500
Commissions expense	2,415
Cost of goods sold	29,200
Depreciation expense—office building	2,900
Income tax expense	1,540
Insurance expense—salesperson's auto	2,250
Interest expense	1,400
Interest revenue	1,340
Rent revenue	6,700
Salaries and wages expense—office	12,560
Sales revenue	48,300
Supplies expense—office	890

Required

1. Prepare a single-step income statement for the year ended December 31, 2001.

2. What weaknesses do you see in this form for the income statement?

LO 5   Problem 2-7   Multiple-Step Income Statement

Refer to the list of income statement items in Problem 2-6. Assume that Shaw Corporation classifies all operating expenses into two categories: (1) selling and (2) general and administrative.

1. Prepare a multiple-step income statement for the year ended December 31, 2001.

2. Compute Shaw's gross profit percentage.

3. What does this percentage tell you about Shaw's markup on its products?

LO 6   Problem 2-8   Albertsons' Gross Profit Ratio

www.albertsons.com   Albertsons Inc. is a large, retail food and drug chain, with nearly 2,500 stores in 37 states across the country. The following items appeared in the company's 1999 annual report (all amounts are in millions of dollars):

	53 Weeks February 3, 2000	52 Weeks January 28, 1999	52 Weeks January 29, 1998
Sales	$37,478	$35,872	$33,828
Cost of sales	27,164	26,156	24,821

Required

1. Note that Albertsons' fiscal year ends toward the end of January (actually, on the Thursday nearest to January 31 each year). Why do you think this particular company would choose this time, rather than December 31, to end its accounting year?

2. Compute Albertsons' gross profit and its gross profit ratio for each of the three years.

3. Comment on the *change* in the gross profit ratio over the three-year period. What possible explanations are there for the change?

LO 8   Problem 2-9   Statement of Cash Flows

Colorado Corporation was organized on January 1, 2001, with the investment of $250,000 in cash by its stockholders. The company immediately purchased an office building for $300,000, paying $210,000 in cash and signing a three-year promissory note for the balance. Colorado signed a five-year, $60,000 promissory note at a local bank during 2001 and received cash in the same amount. During its first year, Colorado collected $93,970 from its customers. It paid $65,600 for inventory, $20,400 in salaries and wages, and another $3,100 in taxes. Colorado paid $5,600 in cash dividends.

1. Prepare a statement of cash flows for the year ended December 31, 2001.

2. What does this statement tell you that an income statement does not?

LO 9   Problem 2-10   Basic Elements of Financial Reports

Comparative income statements for Grammar Inc. follow.

	2001	2000
Sales	$1,000,000	$500,000
Cost of sales	500,000	300,000
Gross margin	$ 500,000	$200,000
Operating expenses	120,000	100,000
Operating income	$ 380,000	$100,000
Loss on sale of subsidiary	(400,000)	—
Net income	$ (20,000)	$100,000

Required

The president and management believe that the company performed better in 2001 than it did in 2000. Write the president's letter to be included in the 2001 annual report. Explain why the company is financially sound and why shareholders should not be alarmed by the $20,000 loss in a year when sales have doubled.

Multi-Concept Problems

LO 2, 4 **Problem 2-11** Comparing Coca-Cola and PepsiCo

The following current items, listed in alphabetical order, are taken from the consolidated balance sheets of Coca-Cola and PepsiCo as of December 31, 1999, and December 25, 1999, respectively (all amounts are in millions of dollars):

www.cocacola.com
www.pepsico.com

SPREADSHEET

Coca-Cola

Accounts payable and accrued expenses	$3,714
Accrued income taxes	769
Cash and cash equivalents	1,611
Current maturities of long-term debt	261
Inventories	1,076
Loans and notes payable	5,112
Marketable securities	201
Prepaid expenses and other assets	1,794
Trade accounts receivable, less allowance of $26	1,798

PepsiCo

Accounts and notes receivable, net	$1,704
Accounts payable and other current liabilities	3,399
Cash and cash equivalents	964
Income taxes payable	156
Inventories	899
Prepaid expenses and other current assets	514
Short-term borrowings	233
Short-term investments, at cost	92

Required

1. Compute working capital and the current ratio for both companies.
2. On the basis of your answers to **1,** which company appears to be more liquid?
3. As you know, other factors affect a company's liquidity in addition to its working capital and current ratio. Comment on the *composition* of each company's current assets and how this composition affects its liquidity.

LO 2, 5 **Problem 2-12** Comparability and Consistency in Income Statements

The following income statements were provided by Gleeson Company, a retailer:

2001 Income Statement		2000 Income Statement	
Sales	$1,700,000	Sales	$1,500,000
Cost of sales	520,000	Cost of sales	450,000
Gross profit	$1,180,000	Sales salaries	398,000
Selling expense	702,000	Advertising	175,000
Administrative expense	95,000	Office supplies	54,000
Total selling and		Depreciation—building	40,000
administrative expense	$ 797,000	Delivery expense	20,000
		Total expenses	$1,137,000
Net income	$ 383,000	Net income	$ 363,000

Required

1. Identify each income statement as either single-step or multiple-step format.

2. Convert the 2000 income statement to the same format as the 2001 income statement.

LO 3, 5, 7 Problem 2-13 Classified Balance Sheet, Multiple-Step Income Statement, and Statement of Retained Earnings for Kellogg's

www.kelloggs.com

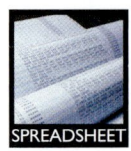

SPREADSHEET

The following items, in alphabetical order, are taken from Kellogg's 1999 consolidated financial statements:

	(in millions)
Accounts payable	$ 305.3
Accounts receivable, net	678.5
Accumulated other comprehensive income (reduction of owners' equity listed after treasury stock)	(331.4)
Capital in excess of par value	104.5
Cash and cash equivalents	150.6
Cash dividends	388.7
Common stock	103.8
Cost of goods sold	3,325.1
Current maturities of long-term debt	2.9
Disposition-related charges (listed after interest expense)	168.5
Income taxes (expense)	198.4
Interest expense	118.8
Inventories	503.8
Long-term debt	1,612.8
Net sales	6,984.2
Notes payable (current liability)	518.6
Other assets (long-term assets)	598.6
Other current assets	236.3
Other current liabilities	761.0
Other income (expense), net	(4.8)
Other liabilities (long-term liabilities)	794.9
Property, net	2,640.9
Restructuring charges (operating expense)	244.6
Retained earnings, beginning of year	1,367.7
Selling, general and administrative expense	2,585.7
Stock options exercised and other (reduction of retained earnings)	(.1)
Treasury stock (reduction of owners' equity listed after retained earnings)	(380.9)

(NOTE: The descriptions in parentheses are not part of the items but have been added to provide you with hints as you complete this problem.)

Required

1. Prepare a multiple-step income statement for Kellogg's for the year ended December 31, 1999.

2. Prepare a statement of retained earnings for Kellogg's for the year ended December 31, 1999.

3. Prepare a classified balance sheet for Kellogg's at December 31, 1999.

LO 4, 6   Problem 2-14   Using Kellogg's Classified Balance Sheet and Multiple-Step Income Statement

(**Note:** Consider completing this problem after Problem 2-13 to ensure that you have the various items on the financial statements properly classified.)

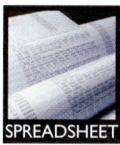
www.kelloggs.com

SPREADSHEET

Refer to the information set forth in Problem 2-13.

Required

1. Compute Kellogg's working capital and its current ratio at December 31, 1999.

2. Does Kellogg's appear to be liquid? What other factors need to be considered in answering this question?

3. Compute Kellogg's gross profit ratio and its profit margin for 1999.

4. As a Kellogg's stockholder, would you be satisfied with the company's gross profit ratio and its profit margin? What other factors need to be considered in answering this question?

LO 1, 4, 8   Problem 2-15   Cash Flow

Franklin Co., a specialty retailer, has a history of paying quarterly dividends of $.50 per share. Management is trying to determine whether the company will have adequate cash on December 31, 2001, to pay a dividend if one is declared by the board of directors. The following additional information is available:

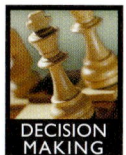
DECISION MAKING

■ All sales are on account, and accounts receivable are collected one month after the sale. Sales volume has been increasing 5% each month.

■ All purchases of merchandise are on account, and accounts payable are paid one month after the purchase. Cost of sales is 40% of the sales price. Inventory levels are maintained at $75,000.

■ Operating expenses in addition to the mortgage are paid in cash. They amount to $3,000 per month and are paid as they are incurred.

FRANKLIN CO.
BALANCE SHEET
SEPTEMBER 30, 2001

Cash	$ 5,000	Accounts payable	$ 5,000
Accounts receivable	12,500	Mortgage note†	150,000
Inventory	75,000	Common stock—$1 par	50,000
Note receivable*	10,000	Retained earnings	66,500
Building/Land	169,000	Total liabilities	
Total assets	$271,500	and stockholders' equity	$271,500

*Note receivable represents a one-year, 5% interest-bearing note, due November 1, 2001.

†Mortgage note is a 30-year, 7% note due in monthly installments of $1,200.

Required

Determine the cash that Franklin will have available to pay a dividend on December 31, 2001. Round all amounts to the nearest dollar. What can Franklin's management do to increase the cash available? Should management recommend that the board of directors declare a dividend?

ALTERNATE PROBLEMS

LO 2   Problem 2-1A   Materiality

Jane Erving, a newly hired accountant, wanted to impress her boss, so she stayed late one night to analyze the long-distance calls by area code and time of day placed. She determined the monthly cost, for the past 12 months, by hour and area code called.

Required

1. What did Jane think her boss would learn from this information? What action might be taken as a result of knowing it?

2. Would this information be more relevant if Jane worked for a hardware store or for a real estate company? Discuss.

LO 2 Problem 2-2A Costs and Expenses

The following costs are incurred by a retailer:

1. Point-of-sale systems in a retail store
2. An ad in the yellow pages
3. An inventory-control computer software system
4. Shipping merchandise for resale to chain outlets

For each of these costs, explain whether all of the cost or only a portion of the cost would appear as an expense on the income statement for the period in which the cost is incurred. If not all of the cost would appear on the income statement for that period, explain why not.

LO 3 Problem 2-3A Classified Balance Sheet

The following balance sheet items, listed in alphabetical order, are available from the records of Singer Company at December 31, 2001:

Accounts payable	$ 34,280
Accounts receivable	26,700
Accumulated depreciation—buildings	40,000
Accumulated depreciation—equipment	12,500
Bonds payable, due December 31, 2007	250,000
Buildings	150,000
Capital stock, $1 par value	200,000
Cash	60,790
Equipment	84,500
Income taxes payable	7,500
Interest payable	2,200
Land	250,000
Marketable securities	15,000
Merchandise inventory	112,900
Notes payable, due April 15, 2002	6,500
Office supplies	400
Paid-in capital in excess of par value	75,000
Patents	45,000
Prepaid rent	3,600
Retained earnings	113,510
Salaries payable	7,400

Required

1. Prepare a classified balance sheet as of December 31, 2001.
2. Compute Singer's current ratio.
3. On the basis of your answer to **2,** does Singer appear to be *liquid?* What other information do you need to fully answer this question?

LO 4 Problem 2-4A Financial Statement Ratios

The following items, in alphabetical order, are available from the records of Quinn Corporation as of December 31, 2001 and 2000:

	December 31, 2001	December 31, 2000
Accounts payable	$10,500	$ 6,500
Accounts receivable	16,500	26,000
Cash	12,750	11,800
Interest receivable	200	–0–
Note receivable, due 12/31/2003	12,000	12,000
Office supplies	900	1,100
Prepaid insurance	400	250
Salaries payable	1,800	800
Taxes payable	10,000	5,800

Required

1. Calculate the following, as of December 31, 2001, and December 31, 2000:

   a. Working capital

   b. Current ratio

2. On the basis of your answers to **1,** comment on the relative liquidity of the company at the beginning and the end of the year. As part of your answer, explain the change in the company's liquidity from the beginning to the end of 2001.

LO 4 **Problem 2-5A** Working Capital and Current Ratio

The balance sheet of Kapinski Inc. includes the following items:

Cash	$ 23,000
Accounts receivable	43,000
Inventory	75,000
Prepaid insurance	2,800
Land	80,000
Accounts payable	84,900
Salaries payable	3,200
Capital stock	100,000
Retained earnings	35,700

Required

1. Determine the current ratio and working capital.

2. Kapinski appears to have a positive current ratio and a large net working capital. Why would it have trouble paying bills as they come due?

3. Suggest three things that Kapinski can do to help pay its bills on time.

LO 5 **Problem 2-6A** Single-Step Income Statement

The following income statement items, arranged in alphabetical order, are taken from the records of Corbin Enterprises, a software sales firm, for the year ended December 31, 2001:

Advertising expense	$ 9,000
Cost of goods sold	150,000
Depreciation expense—computer	4,500
Dividend revenue	2,700
Income tax expense	30,700
Interest expense	1,900
Rent expense—office	26,400
Rent expense—salesperson's car	18,000
Sales revenue	350,000
Supplies expense—office	1,300
Utilities expense	6,750
Wages expense—office	45,600

Required

1. Prepare a single-step income statement for the year ended December 31, 2001.

2. What weaknesses do you see in this form for the income statement?

LO 5 **Problem 2-7A** Multiple-Step Income Statement

Refer to the list of income statement items in Problem 2-6A. Assume that Corbin Enterprises classifies all operating expenses into two categories: (1) selling and (2) general and administrative.

Required

1. Prepare a multiple-step income statement for the year ended December 31, 2001.

2. Compute Corbin's gross profit percentage.

3. What does this percentage tell you about Corbin's markup on its products?

LO 6   **Problem 2-8A**   Saks Gross Profit Ratio

Saks Incorporated is a national retailer operating department stores under various names, with the most recognizable being Saks Fifth Avenue. The following items appeared in the company's 1999 annual report (all amounts are in thousands of dollars):

	Year Ended		
	January 29, 2000	**January 30, 1999**	**January 31, 1998**
Net sales	$6,423,819	$5,955,242	$5,508,728
Cost of sales	4,022,522	3,788,794	3,477,770

Required

1. Note that Saks' fiscal year ends toward the end of January (actually, on the Saturday closest to January 31 each year). Why do you think this particular company would choose this time to end its accounting year rather than December 31?

2. Compute Saks' gross profit and its gross profit ratio for each of the three years.

3. Comment on any *change* in the gross profit ratio over the three-year period. What possible explanations are there for the change?

LO 8   **Problem 2-9A**   Statement of Cash Flows

Wisconsin Corporation was organized on January 1, 2001, with the investment of $400,000 in cash by its stockholders. The company immediately purchased a manufacturing facility for $300,000, paying $150,000 in cash and signing a five-year promissory note for the balance. Wisconsin signed another five-year note at the bank for $50,000 during 2001 and received cash for the same amount. During its first year, Wisconsin collected $310,000 from its customers. It paid $185,000 for inventory, $30,100 in salaries and wages, and another $40,000 in taxes. Wisconsin paid $4,000 in cash dividends.

Required

1. Prepare a statement of cash flows for the year ended December 31, 2001.

2. What does this statement tell you that an income statement does not?

LO 9   **Problem 2-10A**   Basic Elements of Financial Reports

Comparative income statements for Thesaurus Inc. are presented below:

	2001	**2000**
Sales	$1,000,000	$500,000
Cost of sales	500,000	300,000
Gross margin	$ 500,000	$200,000
Operating expenses	120,000	100,000
Operating income	$ 380,000	$100,000
Gain on the sale of subsidiary	—	400,000
Net income	$ 380,000	$500,000

Required

The president and management believe that the company performed better in 2001 than it did in 2000. Write the president's letter to be included in the 2001 annual report. Explain why the company is financially sound and why shareholders should not be alarmed by the reduction in income in a year when sales have doubled.

Alternate Multi-Concept Problems

LO 2, 4   **Problem 2-11A**   Comparing Compaq and Dell

The following current items, listed in alphabetical order, are taken from the consolidated balance sheets of Compaq Computer Corporation and Dell Computer Corporation as of December 31, 1999, and January 28, 2000, respectively (all amounts are in millions of dollars):

Compaq

Accounts payable	$4,380
Accounts receivable, net	6,685
Accrued restructuring costs	1,002

Cash and cash equivalents	2,666
Deferred income (liability)	972
Deferred income taxes (asset)	1,460
Inventories	2,008
Other current assets	394
Other current liabilities	5,031
Short-term borrowings	453
Short-term investments	636

Dell

Accounts payable	$3,538
Accounts receivable, net	2,608
Accrued and other (liabilities)	1,654
Cash and cash equivalents	3,809
Inventories	391
Other (assets)	550
Short-term investments	323

(NOTE: The descriptions in parentheses are not part of the items but have been added to provide you with assistance as you complete this problem.)

Required

1. Compute working capital and the current ratio for both companies.
2. On the basis of your answers to **1,** which company appears to be more liquid?
3. As you know, other factors affect a company's liquidity in addition to its working capital and current ratio. Comment on the *composition* of each company's current assets and how this composition affects its liquidity.

LO 2, 5 Problem 2-12A Comparability and Consistency in Income Statements
The following income statements were provided by Chisholm Company, a wholesale food distributor:

	2001	2000
Sales	$1,700,000	$1,500,000
Cost of sales	612,000	450,000
Sales salaries	427,000	398,000
Delivery expense	180,000	175,000
Office supplies	55,000	54,000
Depreciation—truck	40,000	40,000
Computer line expense	23,000	20,000
Total expenses	$1,337,000	$1,137,000
Net income	$ 363,000	$ 363,000

Required

1. Identify each income statement as either single-step or multiple-step format.
2. Restate each item in the income statements as a percentage of sales. Why did net income remain unchanged when sales increased in 2001?

LO 3, 5, 7 Problem 2-13A Classified Balance Sheet, Multiple-Step Income Statement, and Statement of Retained Earnings for Walgreen's
Shown below, in alphabetical order, are items taken from Walgreen's 2000 consolidated financial statements. Walgreen Co. has a fiscal year ending August 31. **www.walgreens.com**

	(in millions)
Accounts receivable, net	$ 614.5
Accrued expenses and other liabilities (current liability)	847.7
Cash and cash equivalents	12.8

Cash dividends declared	$ 136.1
Common stock	79.0
Cost of sales	15,465.9
Deferred income taxes (long-term liabilities)	101.6
Income taxes (current liability)	92.0
Income tax provision (expense)	486.4
Interest expense	0.4
Interest income	6.1
Inventories	2,830.8
Net sales	21,206.9
Other current assets	92.0
Other income	33.5
Other non-current assets	125.4
Other non-current liabilities	464.4
Paid-in capital	367.2
Property and equipment (net)	3,428.2
Retained earnings, beginning of year	3,147.0
Selling, occupancy, and administration (expense)	4,516.9
Trade accounts payable	1,364.0

(NOTE: The descriptions in parentheses are not part of the items but have been added to provide you with hints as you complete this problem.)

Required

1. Prepare a multiple-step income statement for Walgreen's for the year ended August 31, 2000.
2. Prepare a statement of retained earnings for Walgreen's for the year ended August 31, 2000.
3. Prepare a classified balance sheet for Walgreen's at August 31, 2000.

LO 4, 6   Problem 2-14A   Using Walgreen's Classified Balance Sheet and Multiple-Step Income Statement

www.walgreens.com   (**Note:** Consider completing this problem after Problem 2-13A to ensure that you have the various items on the financial statements properly classified.)

Refer to the information set forth in Problem 2-13A.

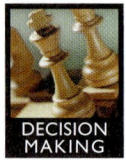

DECISION MAKING

Required

1. Compute Walgreen's working capital and its current ratio at August 31, 2000.
2. Does Walgreen's appear to be liquid? What other factors need to be considered in answering this question?
3. Compute Walgreen's gross profit ratio and its profit margin for the year ended August 31, 2000.
4. As a Walgreen's stockholder, would you be satisfied with the company's gross profit ratio and its profit margin? What other factors need to be considered in answering this question?

LO 1, 4, 8   Problem 2-15A   Cash Flow

Roosevelt Inc., a consulting service, has a history of paying annual dividends of $1 per share. Management is trying to determine whether the company will have adequate cash on December 31, 2001, to pay a dividend if one is declared by the board of directors. The following additional information is available:

■ All sales are on account, and accounts receivable are collected one month after the sale. Sales volume has been decreasing 5% each month.

■ Operating expenses are paid in cash in the month incurred. Average monthly expenses are $10,000 (excluding the biweekly payroll).

■ Biweekly payroll is $4,500, and it will be paid December 15 and December 31.

■ Unearned revenue is expected to be earned in December. This amount was taken into consideration in the expected sales volume.

ROOSEVELT INC.
BALANCE SHEET
DECEMBER 1, 2001

Cash	$ 15,000	Unearned Revenue	$ 2,000
Accounts receivable	40,000	Note payable*	30,000
Computer equipment	120,000	Common stock—$2 par	50,000
		Retained earnings	93,000
		Total liabilities and	
Total assets	$175,000	stockholder's equity	$175,000

*The note payable plus 3% interest for six months is due January 15, 2002.

Required

Determine the cash that Roosevelt will have available to pay a dividend on December 31, 2001. Round all amounts to the nearest dollar. Should management recommend that the board of directors declare a dividend?

CASES

Reading and Interpreting Financial Statements

LO 3   Case 2-1   Boeing's Operating Cycle

In Boeing's annual report, footnote 1, "Summary of Significant Accounting Policies," includes the following explanation of Boeing's Inventories:

www.boeing.com

Inventories

Inventoried costs on commercial aircraft programs and long-term contracts include direct engineering, production and tooling costs, and applicable overhead, not in excess of estimated realizable value. In accordance with industry practice, inventoried costs include amounts relating to programs and contracts with long production cycles, a portion of which is not expected to be realized within one year. Commercial spare parts and general stock materials are stated at average cost not in excess of realizable value.[14]

Required

1. Based on the preceding note, describe Boeing's inventory. That is, what types of items would you expect to find in the inventory of this type of company?

2. Why would Boeing expect that a portion of its inventoried costs would *not* be realized within one year?

3. Based on your answer to **2,** should Boeing classify its inventories as current or as noncurrent assets? Explain your answer.

LO 4   Case 2-2   Uno's Current Assets and Current Liabilities

Refer to Uno's balance sheets as of October 3, 1999 and September 27, 1998.

www.pizzeriauno.com

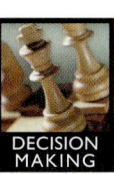

DECISION MAKING

Required

1. Compute Uno's working capital as of each of the two balance sheet dates. Also, compute the change in working capital from the end of 1998 to the end of 1999.

2. Compute Uno's current ratio as of each of the two balance sheet dates. Compute the percentage change in the ratio from the end of 1998 to the end of 1999.

3. Assume that you are a dairy farmer and are considering whether to sell cheese to Uno in return for its promise to pay any amounts owed within sixty days. On the basis of your answers to **1** and **2,** what would your decision be? Justify your decision.

LO 3, 4   Case 2-3   Interpreting Gateway's Liabilities

Refer to Gateway's balance sheet as of December 31, 1999.

www.gateway.com

---

[14]*Boeing Company 1999 Annual Report,* p. 56.

Required

1. The first current liability Gateway reports is titled "Current maturities of long-term obligations." Explain *why* a long-term obligation would be classified as a current liability.

2. Directly below the current liabilities is an account titled "Long-term obligations, net of current maturities." Explain the meaning of this account—specifically, what Gateway means by the term *net*.

3. The last liability reported on the balance sheet is titled "Warranty and other liabilities." Explain why warranties result in the recognition of a liability to Gateway.

Making Financial Decisions

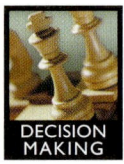

DECISION MAKING

LO 8 **Case 2-4** Analysis of Cash Flow for a Small Business

Charles, a financial consultant, has been self-employed for two years. His list of clients has grown, and he is earning a reputation as a shrewd investor. Charles rents a small office, uses the pool secretarial services, and has purchased a car that he is depreciating over three years. The following income statements cover Charles's first two years of business:

	Year 1	Year 2
Commissions revenue	$ 25,000	$65,000
Rent	12,000	12,000
Secretarial services	3,000	9,000
Car expenses, gas, insurance	6,000	6,500
Depreciation	15,000	15,000
Net income	$(11,000)	$22,500

Charles believes that he should earn more than $11,500 for working very hard for two years. He is thinking about going to work for an investment firm where he can earn $40,000 per year. What would you advise Charles to do?

LO 9 **Case 2-5** Factors Involved in an Investment Decision

As an investor, you are considering purchasing stock in a fast-food restaurant chain. The annual reports of several companies are available for comparison.

Required

Prepare an outline of the steps you would follow to make your comparison. Start by listing the first section that you would read in the financial reports. What would you expect to find there, and why did you choose that section to read first? Continue with the other sections of the financial report.

Many fast-food chains are owned by large conglomerates. What limitation does this create in your comparison? How would you solve it?

Accounting and Ethics: What Would You Do?

LO 2 **Case 2-6** The Expenditure Approval Process

Roberto is the plant superintendent of a small manufacturing company that is owned by a large corporation. The corporation has a policy that any expenditure over $1,000 must be approved by the chief financial officer in the corporate headquarters. The approval process takes a minimum of three weeks. Roberto would like to order a new labeling machine that is expected to reduce costs and pay for itself in six months. The machine costs $2,200, but Roberto can buy the sales rep's demo for $1,800. Roberto has asked the sales rep to send two separate bills for $900 each.

What would you do if you were the sales rep? Do you agree or disagree with Roberto's actions? What do you think about the corporate policy?

LO 4, 6 **Case 2-7** Barbara Applies for a Loan

Barbara Bites, owner of Bites of Bagels, a drive-through bagel shop, would like to expand her business from its current one location to a chain of bagel shops. Sales in the bagel shop have been increasing an average of 8% each quarter. Profits have been increasing accordingly. Barbara is conservative in spending and a very hard worker. She has an appointment with a banker to apply for a loan to expand the business. To prepare for the appointment, she instructs you, as the chief financial officer and payroll clerk, to copy the quarterly income statements for the past two years but not to include a balance sheet. Barbara already has a substantial loan from another bank. In fact, she has very little of her own money invested in the business.

What should you do? Do you think the banker will lend Barbara more money?

INTERNET RESEARCH CASE

Case 2-8 Gateway

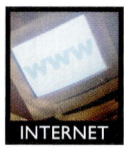

You can probably do this from your everyday knowledge, but this is good practice in researching a company using the internet. Find a WWW site or a source of information that will list the competitors to Gateway. Choose the top two competitors and answer the following questions:

1. Looking at their balance sheets, what are their total current assets and their total current liabilities? From these numbers, calculate each company's working capital and current ratio. How do they compare to the ratios for Gateway, shown on page 65?

2. From their income statements, calculate their profit margin for the latest year available. How do they compare to those of Gateway, which you were asked to calculate in the From Concept to Practice box on page 67?

Optional Research: From the financial information available on their WWW sites, what other comparisons can you make about these companies? Based on your research, are the companies themselves comparable in such areas as size, products, assets, liabilities, and net income? If not, explain five ways in which they differ. Is the financial information itself comparable for the three companies? Explain.

Fill in your source for industry information:

www._____.com

Gateway and its main competitors:

www.gateway.com

www._____.com

www._____.com

SOLUTION TO KEY TERMS QUIZ

6 Understandability (p. 48)

3 Relevance (p. 48)

9 Reliability (p. 49)

14 Comparability (p. 49)

19 Depreciation (p. 49)

17 Consistency (p. 50)

2 Materiality (p. 51)

5 Conservatism (p. 51)

11 Operating cycle (p. 53)

15 Current asset (p. 54)

10 Current liability (p. 57)

16 Liquidity (p. 58)

12 Working capital (p. 58)

8 Current ratio (p. 58)

1 Single-step income statement (p. 60)

4 Multiple-step income statement (p. 60)

18 Gross profit (p. 60)

7 Gross profit ratio (p. 62)

13 Profit margin (p. 62)

Chapter 3

PROCESSING ACCOUNTING INFORMATION

Study Links

A Look at Previous Chapters

Up to this point, we have focused our attention on the role of accounting in decision making and the way accountants use financial statements to communicate useful information to the various users of the statements.

A Look at This Chapter

In this chapter, we consider how accounting information is processed. We begin by considering the *inputs* to an accounting system, that is, the transactions entered into by a business. We look at how transactions are analyzed, and then we turn to a number of accounting tools and procedures designed to facilitate the preparation of the *outputs* of the system, the financial statements. Ledger accounts, journal entries, and trial balances are tools that allow a company to process vast amounts of data efficiently.

A Look at Upcoming Chapters

Chapter 4 concludes our overview of the accounting model. We will examine the accrual basis of accounting and its effect on the measurement of income. Adjustments, which are the focus of the accrual basis, will be discussed in detail in Chapter 4, along with the other steps in the accounting cycle.

FOCUS ON FINANCIAL RESULTS

When snowboarding became a full-medal sport at the 1998 Winter Olympics, two companies took note. One was Ride Inc., a successful new manufacturer of snowboards and related equipment. The other was K2, a leading designer, manufacturer, and marketer of brand-name sporting goods. K2 purchased Ride in 1999.

K2 is a company that wants to grow, and it measures growth in terms of sales. It markets a broad range of sports products, including K2 and Olin Alpine skis; K2 snowboards, boots, and bindings; K2 in-line skates and bikes; Stearns sports equipment; Shakespeare fishing tackle; and Dana Design backpacks. In 1999, a newly created division for small-wheeled products successfully introduced the Kickboard, a three-wheeled scooter sold primarily in Europe. Diversity helps K2 survive the ups and downs of its market.

Sales are affected by weather, changing consumer tastes and interests, retailers' shifting inventory strategies, and K2's own ability to deliver products on time—or not. Sales can be buoyed by the birth of new products like the Kickboard, by crossovers into related product categories, and by increases in K2's market share, which its purchase of Ride helped accomplish. K2 hopes to use all these strategies—product innovation, line expansion, and growth of market share—to fulfill its goal of enhancing shareholder value through sales.

In addition, part of the company's strategy is to grow earnings by reducing costs. K2 has various cost initiatives in place, which include the relocation of certain operations to lower-cost areas and improvements in sourcing.

Year ended December 31	1999	1998	1997
	[In thousands, except per share figures]		
Net sales	$635,105	$574,510	$559,030
Cost of products sold	462,033	418,950	391,860
Gross profit	173,072	155,560	167,170
Selling expenses	95,774	87,389	79,832
General and administrative expenses	40,341	39,030	38,303
Research and development expenses	12,113	12,391	11,979
Operating income	24,844	16,750	37,056
Interest expense	12,741	12,163	10,560
Other income, net	(413)	(236)	(619)
Income from continuing operations before provision for income taxes	12,516	4,823	27,115
Provision for income taxes	4,005	955	7,815
Income from continuing operations	8,511	3,868	19,300
Discontinued operations, net of taxes	1,332	975	2,600
Net Income	$ 9,843	$ 4,843	$ 21,900
Basic earnings per share:			
Continuing operations	$ 0.50	$ 0.23	$ 1.17
Discontinued operations	0.08	0.06	0.15
Net income	$ 0.58	$ 0.29	$ 1.32
Diluted earnings per share:			
Continuing operations	$ 0.50	$ 0.23	$ 1.15
Discontinued operations	0.08	0.06	0.16
Net income	$ 0.58	$ 0.29	$ 1.31
Basic shares outstanding	16,880	16,554	16,541
Diluted shares outstanding	16,883	16,637	16,713

K2 concentrates on growing sales (annotation beside Net sales)

fairly unusual → means closing down an operation (handwritten note beside Discontinued operations)

See notes to consolidated financial statements

K2's 1999 Annual Report

K2's income statement, pictured here, tells a story of the need for growth and a decrease in costs. As you study the accounting process introduced in this chapter, consider how the accounting system would help you process information for K2. How would you record sales figures or the effects of your cost-cutting campaign?

www.K2sports.com

LEARNING OBJECTIVES

After studying this chapter, you should be able to:

LO 1 Explain the difference between an external and an internal event. (p. 94)

LO 2 Explain the role of source documents in an accounting system. (p. 94)

LO 3 Analyze the effects of transactions on the accounting equation. (p. 95)

LO 4 Define the concept of a general ledger and understand the use of the T account as a method for analyzing transactions. (p. 103)

LO 5 Explain the rules of debits and credits. (p. 103)

LO 6 Explain the purposes of a journal and the posting process. (p. 108)

LO 7 Explain the purpose of a trial balance. (p. 111)

ECONOMIC EVENTS: THE BASIS FOR RECORDING TRANSACTIONS

LO 1 Explain the difference between an external and an internal event.

Many different types of economic events affect an entity during the year. A sale is made to a customer. Inventory is purchased from a supplier. A loan is taken out at the bank. A fire destroys a warehouse. A new contract is signed with the union. In short, "An **event** is a happening of consequence to an entity."[1]

EXTERNAL AND INTERNAL EVENTS

Two types of events affect an entity: internal and external. An **external event** "involves interaction between the entity and its environment."[2] For example, the *purchase* of raw material from a supplier is an external event, as is the *sale* of inventory to a customer. An **internal event** occurs entirely within the entity. The *transfer* of raw material into production is an internal event, as is the use of a piece of equipment. We will use the term **transaction** to refer to any event, external or internal, that is recognized in a set of financial statements.[3]

What is necessary to recognize an event in the records? Are all economic events recognized as transactions by the accountant? The answers to these questions involve the concept of *measurement*. An event must be measured to be recognized. Certain events are relatively easy to measure: the payroll for the week, the amount of inventory destroyed by an earthquake, or the sales for the day. Not all events that affect an entity can be measured *reliably*, however. For example, how does a manufacturer of breakfast cereal measure the effect of a drought on the price of wheat? A company hires a new chief executive. How can it reliably measure the value of the new officer to the company? There is no definitive answer to the measurement problem in accounting. It is a continuing challenge to the accounting profession and something we will return to throughout the text.

From Concept

TO PRACTICE 3.1

READING K2'S FINANCIAL STATEMENTS K2 Inc. purchases materials to use in making snowboards. Is this an internal or an external event? The company subsequently uses the materials in the production process. Is this an internal or an external event?

THE ROLE OF SOURCE DOCUMENTS IN RECORDING TRANSACTIONS

LO 2 Explain the role of source documents in an accounting system.

The first step in the recording process is *identification*. A business needs a systematic method for recognizing events as transactions. A **source document** provides the evidence needed in an accounting system to record a transaction. Source documents take many different forms. An invoice received from a supplier is the source document for a purchase of inventory on credit. A cash register tape is the source document used by a retailer to recognize a cash sale.

---

[1]*Statement of Financial Accounting Concepts (SFAC) No. 3,* "Elements of Financial Statements of Business Enterprises" (Stamford, Conn.: Financial Accounting Standards Board, 1982), par. 65.

[2]*SFAC No. 3.*

[3]Technically, a *transaction* is defined by the Financial Accounting Standards Board as a special kind of external event in which the entity exchanges something of value with an outsider. Because the term *transaction* is used in practice to refer to any event that is recognized in the statements, we will use this broader definition.

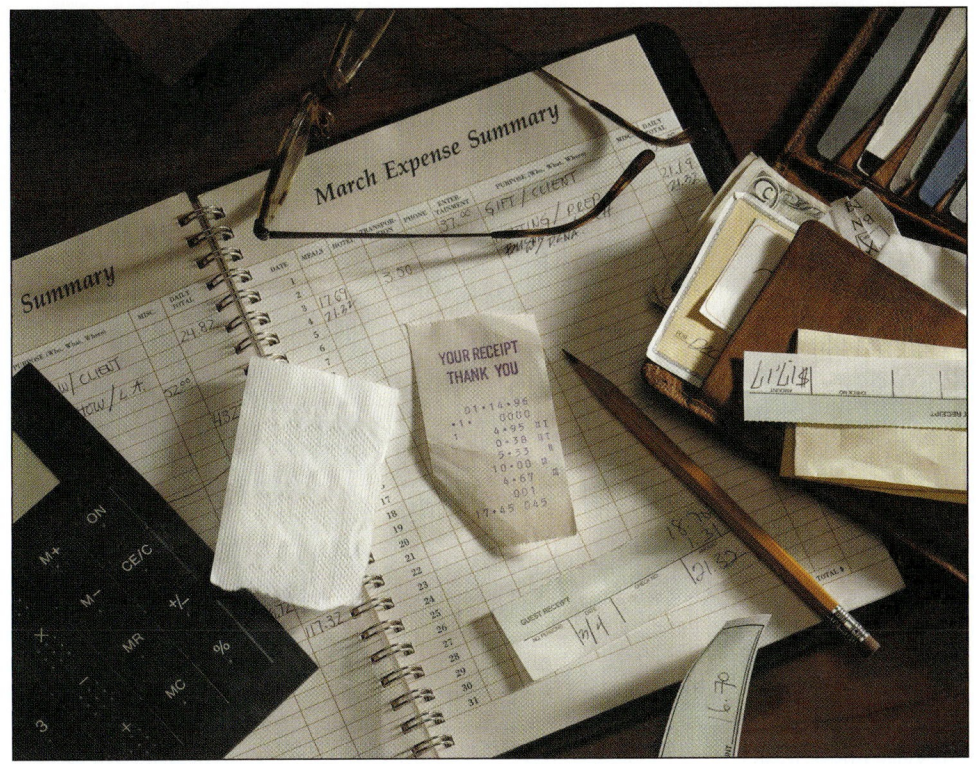

The payroll department sends the accountant the time cards for the week as the necessary documentation to record wages.

Not all recognizable events are supported by a standard source document. For certain events, some form of documentation must be generated. For example, no standard source document exists to recognize the financial consequences from a fire or the settlement of a lawsuit. Documentation is just as important for these types of events as it is for standard, recurring transactions.

ANALYZING THE EFFECTS OF TRANSACTIONS ON THE ACCOUNTING EQUATION

Economic events are the basis for recording transactions in an accounting system. For every transaction, it is essential to analyze its effect on the accounting equation:

LO 3 Analyze the effects of transactions on the accounting equation.

Assets = Liabilities + Owners' Equity

We will now consider a series of events and their recognition as transactions for a hypothetical corporation, Glengarry Health Club. The transactions are for the month of January 2001, the first month of operations for the new business.

(1) *Issuance of capital stock.* The company is started when Mary-Jo Kovach and Irene McGuinness file articles of incorporation with the state to obtain a charter. Each invests $50,000 in the business. In return, each receives 5,000 shares of capital stock. Thus, at this point, each of them owns 50 percent of the outstanding stock of the company and has a claim to 50 percent of its assets. The effect of this transaction on the accounting equation is to increase both assets and owners' equity:

	Assets					=	Liabilities		+	Owners' Equity	
TRANSACTION NUMBER	CASH	ACCOUNTS RECEIVABLE	EQUIPMENT	BUILDING	LAND		ACCOUNTS PAYABLE	NOTES PAYABLE		CAPITAL STOCK	RETAINED EARNINGS
1	$100,000									$100,000	
Totals			$100,000							$100,000	

As you see, each side of the accounting equation increases by $100,000. Cash is increased, and because the owners contributed this amount, their claim to the assets is increased in the form of Capital Stock.

(2) *Acquisition of property in exchange for a note.* The company buys a piece of property for $200,000. The seller agrees to accept a five-year promissory note. The note is given by the health club to the seller and is a written promise to repay the principal amount of the loan at the end of five years. To the company, the promissory note is a liability. The property consists of land valued at $50,000 and a newly constructed building valued at $150,000. The effect of this transaction on the accounting equation is to increase both assets and liabilities by $200,000:

TRANSACTION NUMBER	CASH	ACCOUNTS RECEIVABLE	Assets EQUIPMENT	BUILDING	LAND	=	ACCOUNTS PAYABLE	Liabilities NOTES PAYABLE	+	CAPITAL STOCK	Owners' Equity RETAINED EARNINGS
Bal.	$100,000									$100,000	
2				$150,000	$50,000			$200,000			
Bal.	$100,000			$150,000	$50,000			$200,000		$100,000	
Totals			$300,000						$300,000		

(3) *Acquisition of equipment on an open account.* Mary-Jo and Irene contact an equipment supplier and buy $20,000 of exercise equipment: treadmills, barbells, and stationary bicycles. The supplier agrees to accept payment in full in 30 days. The health club has acquired an asset and at the same time incurred a liability:

TRANSACTION NUMBER	CASH	ACCOUNTS RECEIVABLE	Assets EQUIPMENT	BUILDING	LAND	=	ACCOUNTS PAYABLE	Liabilities NOTES PAYABLE	+	CAPITAL STOCK	Owners' Equity RETAINED EARNINGS
Bal.	$100,000			$150,000	$50,000			$200,000		$100,000	
3			$20,000				$20,000				
Bal.	$100,000		$20,000	$150,000	$50,000		$20,000	$200,000		$100,000	
Totals			$320,000						$320,000		

(4) *Sale of monthly memberships on account.* The owners open their doors for business. During January, they sell 300 monthly club memberships for $50 each, or a total of $15,000. The members have until the 10th of the following month to pay. Glengarry does not have cash from the new members but instead has a promise from each member to pay cash in the future. The promise from a customer to pay an amount owed is an asset called an *account receivable*. The other side of this transaction is an increase in the owners' equity (specifically, Retained Earnings) in the business. In other words, the assets have increased by $15,000 without any increase in a liability or decrease in another asset. The increase in owners' equity indicates that the owners' residual interest in the assets of the business has increased by this amount. More specifically, an inflow of assets resulting from the sale of goods and services by a business is called *revenue*. The change in the accounting equation follows:

TRANSACTION NUMBER	CASH	ACCOUNTS RECEIVABLE	Assets EQUIPMENT	BUILDING	LAND	=	ACCOUNTS PAYABLE	Liabilities NOTES PAYABLE	+	CAPITAL STOCK	Owners' Equity RETAINED EARNINGS
Bal.	$100,000		$20,000	$150,000	$50,000		$20,000	$200,000		$100,000	
4		$15,000									$15,000
Bal.	$100,000	$15,000	$20,000	$150,000	$50,000		$20,000	$200,000		$100,000	$15,000
Totals			$335,000						$335,000		

(5) *Sale of court time for cash.* In addition to memberships, Glengarry sells court time. Court fees are paid at the time of use and amount to $5,000 for the first month:

TRANSACTION NUMBER	Assets					=	Liabilities		+	Owners' Equity	
	CASH	ACCOUNTS RECEIVABLE	EQUIPMENT	BUILDING	LAND		ACCOUNTS PAYABLE	NOTES PAYABLE		CAPITAL STOCK	RETAINED EARNINGS
Bal.	$100,000	$15,000	$20,000	$150,000	$50,000		$20,000	$200,000		$100,000	$15,000
5	5,000										5,000
Bal.	$105,000	$15,000	$20,000	$150,000	$50,000		$20,000	$200,000		$100,000	$20,000
Totals			$340,000						$340,000		

The only difference between this transaction and **(4)** is that cash is received rather than a promise to pay at a later date. Both transactions result in an increase in an asset and an increase in the owners' claim to the assets. In both cases, there is an inflow of assets, in the form of either Accounts Receivable or Cash. Thus, in both cases, the company has earned revenue.

(6) *Payment of wages and salaries.* The wages and salaries for the first month amount to $10,000. The payment of this amount results in a decrease in Cash and a decrease in the owners' claim on the assets—that is, a decrease in Retained Earnings. More specifically, an outflow of assets resulting from the sale of goods or services is called an *expense*. The effect of this transaction is to decrease both sides of the accounting equation:

TRANSACTION NUMBER	Assets					=	Liabilities		+	Owners' Equity	
	CASH	ACCOUNTS RECEIVABLE	EQUIPMENT	BUILDING	LAND		ACCOUNTS PAYABLE	NOTES PAYABLE		CAPITAL STOCK	RETAINED EARNINGS
Bal.	$105,000	$15,000	$20,000	$150,000	$50,000		$20,000	$200,000		$100,000	$20,000
6	− 10,000										−10,000
Bal.	$ 95,000	$15,000	$20,000	$150,000	$50,000		$20,000	$200,000		$100,000	$10,000
Totals			$330,000						$330,000		

(7) *Payment of utilities.* The cost of utilities for the first month is $3,000. Glengarry pays this amount in cash. Both the utilities and the salaries and wages are expenses, and they have the same effect on the accounting equation. Cash is decreased, accompanied by a corresponding decrease in the owners' claim on the assets of the business:

TRANSACTION NUMBER	Assets					=	Liabilities		+	Owners' Equity	
	CASH	ACCOUNTS RECEIVABLE	EQUIPMENT	BUILDING	LAND		ACCOUNTS PAYABLE	NOTES PAYABLE		CAPITAL STOCK	RETAINED EARNINGS
Bal.	$95,000	$15,000	$20,000	$150,000	$50,000		$20,000	$200,000		$100,000	$10,000
7	− 3,000										− 3,000
Bal.	$92,000	$15,000	$20,000	$150,000	$50,000		$20,000	$200,000		$100,000	$ 7,000
Totals			$327,000						$327,000		

(8) *Collection of accounts receivable.* Even though the January monthly memberships are not due until the 10th of the following month, some of the members pay their bills by the end of January. The amount received from members in payment of their accounts is $4,000. The effect of the collection of an open account is to increase Cash and decrease Accounts Receivable:

TRANSACTION NUMBER	Assets					=	Liabilities		+	Owners' Equity	
	CASH	ACCOUNTS RECEIVABLE	EQUIPMENT	BUILDING	LAND		ACCOUNTS PAYABLE	NOTES PAYABLE		CAPITAL STOCK	RETAINED EARNINGS
Bal.	$92,000	$15,000	$20,000	$150,000	$50,000		$20,000	$200,000		$100,000	$7,000
8	4,000	− 4,000									
Bal.	$96,000	$11,000	$20,000	$150,000	$50,000		$20,000	$200,000		$100,000	$7,000
Totals			$327,000						$327,000		

This is the first transaction we have seen that affects only one side of the accounting equation. In fact, the company simply traded assets: Accounts Receivable for Cash. Thus, note that the totals for the accounting equation remain at $327,000. Also note that Retained Earnings is not affected by this transaction because revenue was recognized earlier, in **(4),** when Accounts Receivable was increased.

(9) *Payment of dividends.* At the end of the month, Mary-Jo and Irene, acting on behalf of Glengarry Health Club, decide to pay a dividend of $1,000 on the shares of stock owned by each of them, or $2,000 in total. The effect of this dividend is to decrease both Cash and Retained Earnings. That is, the company is returning cash to the owners, based on the profitable operations of the business for the first month. The transaction not only reduces Cash but also decreases the owners' claims on the assets of the company. Dividends are not an expense but rather a direct reduction of Retained Earnings. The effect on the accounting equation follows:

| TRANSACTION NUMBER | Assets | | | | | = | Liabilities | | + | Owners' Equity | |
	CASH	ACCOUNTS RECEIVABLE	EQUIPMENT	BUILDING	LAND		ACCOUNTS PAYABLE	NOTES PAYABLE		CAPITAL STOCK	RETAINED EARNINGS
Bal.	$96,000	$11,000	$20,000	$150,000	$50,000		$20,000	$200,000		$100,000	$7,000
9	− 2,000										−2,000
Bal.	$94,000	$11,000	$20,000	$150,000	$50,000		$20,000	$200,000		$100,000	$5,000
Totals			$325,000					$325,000			

The Cost Principle   An important principle governs the accounting for both the exercise equipment in **(3)** and the building and land in **(2).** The *cost principle* requires that we record an asset at the cost to acquire it and continue to show this amount on all balance sheets until we dispose of the asset. With a few exceptions, an asset is not carried at its market value but at its original cost. Why not show the land on future balance sheets at its market value? Although this might seem more appropriate in certain instances, the *subjectivity* inherent in determining market values is a major reason behind the practice of carrying assets at their historical cost. The cost of an asset can be verified by an independent observer and is much more *objective* than market value.

Companies engage in transactions in many ways. The shoe company from whom this woman is ordering supports sales transactions over the phone using a credit card number. A sales representative may be inputting the card number and the order information into an order database. The company links its order-processing system and other business systems to this customer input.

> **Two-Minute Review**
> Assume that on February 1 Glengarry buys additional exercise equipment for $10,000 in cash.
>
> 1. Indicate which two accounts are affected and the increase or decrease in each.
>
> 2. What will be the total dollar amount of each of the two sides of the accounting equation after this transaction is recorded?
>
> **Answers:**
>
> 1. Equipment will increase by $10,000, and Cash will decrease by $10,000.
>
> 2. $325,000 (the effect of the transaction is to increase and decrease assets by the same amount).

BALANCE SHEET AND INCOME STATEMENT FOR THE HEALTH CLUB

To summarize, Exhibit 3-1 indicates the effect of each transaction on the accounting equation, specifically the individual items increased or decreased by each transaction. Note the *dual* effect of each transaction. At least two items were involved in each transaction. For example, the initial investment by the owners resulted in an increase in an asset and an increase in Capital Stock. The payment of the utility bill caused a decrease in an asset and a decrease in Retained Earnings.

You can now see the central idea behind the accounting equation: Even though individual transactions may change the amount and composition of the assets and liabilities, the

		ASSETS				=	LIABILITIES		+	OWNERS' EQUITY	
TRANS. NO.	CASH	ACCOUNTS RECEIVABLE	EQUIPMENT	BUILDING	LAND		ACCOUNTS PAYABLE	NOTES PAYABLE		CAPITAL STOCK	RETAINED EARNINGS
1	$100,000									$100,000	
2				$150,000	$50,000			$200,000			
Bal.	$100,000			$150,000	$50,000			$200,000		$100,000	
3			$20,000				$20,000				
Bal.	$100,000		$20,000	$150,000	$50,000		$20,000	$200,000		$100,000	
4		$15,000									$15,000
Bal.	$100,000	$15,000	$20,000	$150,000	$50,000		$20,000	$200,000		$100,000	$15,000
5	5,000										5,000
Bal.	$105,000	$15,000	$20,000	$150,000	$50,000		$20,000	$200,000		$100,000	$20,000
6	− 10,000										−10,000
Bal.	$ 95,000	$15,000	$20,000	$150,000	$50,000		$20,000	$200,000		$100,000	$10,000
7	− 3,000										− 3,000
Bal.	$ 92,000	$15,000	$20,000	$150,000	$50,000		$20,000	$200,000		$100,000	$ 7,000
8	4,000	− 4,000									
Bal.	$ 96,000	$11,000	$20,000	$150,000	$50,000		$20,000	$200,000		$100,000	$ 7,000
9	− 2,000										− 2,000
Bal.	$ 94,000	$11,000	$20,000	$150,000	$50,000		$20,000	$200,000		$100,000	$ 5,000

Total assets: $325,000   Total liabilities and owners' equity: $325,000

equation must always balance *for* each transaction, and the *balance sheet* must balance *after* each transaction.

A balance sheet for Glengarry Health Club appears in Exhibit 3-2. All the information needed to prepare this statement is available in Exhibit 3-1. The balances at the bottom of this exhibit are entered on the balance sheet, with assets on the left side and liabilities and owners' equity on the right side.

An income statement for Glengarry is shown in Exhibit 3-3. An income statement summarizes the revenues and expenses of a company for a period of time. In our example, the statement is for the month of January, as indicated on the third line of the heading of the statement. Glengarry earned revenues from two sources: (1) memberships and (2) court fees. Two types of expenses were incurred: (1) salaries and wages and (2) utilities.

EXHIBIT 3-2   Balance Sheet for Glengarry Health Club

GLENGARRY HEALTH CLUB
BALANCE SHEET
JANUARY 31, 2001

Assets		**Liabilities and Owners' Equity**	
Cash	$ 94,000	Accounts payable	$ 20,000
Accounts receivable	11,000	Notes payable	200,000
Equipment	20,000	Capital stock	100,000
Building	150,000	Retained earnings	5,000
Land	50,000		
		Total liabilities	
Total assets	$325,000	and owners' equity	$325,000

EXHIBIT 3-3 Income Statement for Glengarry Health Club

GLENGARRY HEALTH CLUB
INCOME STATEMENT
FOR THE MONTH ENDED JANUARY 31, 2001

Revenues:		
Memberships	$15,000	
Court fees	5,000	$20,000
Expenses:		
Salaries and wages	10,000	
Utilities	3,000	13,000
Net income		$ 7,000

BUSINESS STRATEGY

While snowboard companies like K2 and Ride, which K2 recently purchased, rely on diversification and acquisitions as means of growth, Burton Snowboards, the leading snowboard manufacturer in the world, relies on something a little harder to analyze: the passion of its founder, Jake Burton.

A native of New York, Burton always loved sports. He studied economics in college and started his first snowboard manufacturing company with a small inheritance. Unfortunately, after going through 100 unsuccessful prototypes, Burton had sold a few hundred boards, but used up his funds. He spent the next few years teaching tennis, tending bar, and working to get snowboarding allowed in ski resorts to build a market for the product he still hoped to make. Stratton Mountain Resort finally agreed to allow snowboards on its slopes, and interest in snowboarding began to spread.

Still, Burton's first big success was in Europe, where interest was stronger, and where he lived and worked for three years in the mid 1980s, finding a subcontractor for Burton's designs and establishing distribution channels. Today, Burton Snowboards is headquartered in Burlington, Vermont, and makes a line of 120 different snowboards, as well as boots, bindings, packs, apparel, and outwear. It does business in more than 30 countries, has operations in Austria and Japan, and employs almost 400 people in the United States.

The inclusion of snowboarding in the 1998 Olympics at Nagano, Japan, and the boost that gave the snowboard market meant a lot to Burton, who feels he can now concentrate on what he loves most: snowboarding.

In spite of his success, Burton has resisted the lure to take his company public. "I'll take a pretty good businessperson for whom snowboarding is a passion over somebody who's a brilliant businessperson but doesn't really care about the sport," Burton says. "I'm first and foremost a snowboarder, and I use the fact that I don't have to be [in the office] every day like I used to, as an opportunity to get more immersed in the sport." His only quantifiable goal? To ride 100 days every year.

SOURCES: "Burton Snowboards," accessed at www.fortune.com/fortune/, November 21, 2000; Portland Helmich, "Chairman of the Board," *Business People Vermont*, accessed at www.vermontguides.com/2000/8-aug/aig1.htm, January 17, 2001.

The difference between the total revenues of $20,000 and the total expenses of $13,000 is the net income for the month of $7,000. Finally, remember that dividends appear on a statement of retained earnings rather than on the income statement. They are a *distribution* of net income of the period, not a *determinant* of net income as are expenses.

We have seen how transactions are analyzed and how they affect the accounting equation and ultimately the financial statements. Although the approach we took in analyzing the nine transactions of the Glengarry Health Club was manageable, can you imagine using this type of analysis for a company with *thousands* of transactions in any one month? We now turn our attention to various *tools* used by the accountant to process a large volume of transactions effectively and efficiently.

THE ACCOUNT: THE BASIC UNIT FOR RECORDING TRANSACTIONS

An **account** is the record used to accumulate monetary amounts for each asset, liability, and component of owners' equity, such as Capital Stock, Retained Earnings, and Dividends. It is the basic recording unit for each element in the financial statements. Each revenue and expense has its own account. In the Glengarry Health Club example, nine accounts were used: Cash, Accounts Receivable, Equipment, Building, Land, Accounts Payable, Notes Payable, Capital Stock, and Retained Earnings. (Recall that revenues, expenses, and dividends were recorded directly in the Retained Earnings account. Later in the chapter we will see that normally each revenue and expense is recorded in a separate account.) In the real world, a company might have hundreds, or even thousands, of individual accounts.

No two entities have exactly the same set of accounts. To a certain extent, the accounts used by a company depend on its business. For example, a manufacturer normally has three inventory accounts: Raw Materials, Work in Process, and Finished Goods. A retailer uses just one account for inventory, a Merchandise Inventory account. A service business has no need for an inventory account.

From **Concept**

TO PRACTICE 3.2

READING UNO'S BALANCE SHEET AND FOOTNOTES How many liability accounts does the company report on its balance sheet? What is Uno's largest liability at the end of the most recent year?

CHART OF ACCOUNTS

Companies need a way to organize the large number of accounts they use to record transactions. A **chart of accounts** is a numerical list of all the accounts an entity uses. The numbering system is a convenient way to identify accounts. For example, all asset accounts might be numbered from 100 to 199, liability accounts from 200 to 299, equity accounts from 300 to 399, revenues from 400 to 499, and expenses from 500 to 599. A chart of accounts for a hypothetical company, Widescreen Theaters Corporation, is shown in Exhibit 3-4. Note the division of account numbers within each of the financial statement categories. For example, within the asset category, the various cash accounts are numbered from 100 to 109, receivables from 110 to 119, and so forth. Not all the numbers are currently assigned. For example, only three of the available nine numbers are currently utilized for cash accounts. This allows the company to add accounts as the need arises.

EXHIBIT 3-4 Chart of Accounts for a Theater

100–199:	ASSETS
100–109:	Cash
101:	Cash, Checking, Second National Bank
102:	Cash, Savings, Third State Bank
103:	Cash, Change, or Petty Cash Fund (coin and currency)
	(continued)

EXHIBIT 3-4 Chart of Accounts for a Theater *(continued)*

110–119:	Receivables	
111:		Accounts Receivable
112:		Due from Employees
113:		Notes Receivable
120–129:	Prepaid Assets	
121:		Cleaning Supplies
122:		Prepaid Insurance
130–139:	Property, Plant, and Equipment	
131:		Land
132:		Theater Buildings
133:		Projection Equipment
134:		Furniture and Fixtures
200–299:	LIABILITIES	
200–209:	Short-Term Liabilities	
201:		Accounts Payable
202:		Wages and Salaries Payable
203:		Taxes Payable
203.1:		Income Taxes Payable
203.2:		Sales Taxes Payable
203.3:		Unemployment Taxes Payable
204:		Short-Term Notes Payable
204.1:		Six-Month Note Payable to First State Bank
210–219:	Long-Term Liabilities	
211:		Bonds Payable, due in 2013
300–399:	STOCKHOLDERS' EQUITY	
301:		Preferred Stock
302:		Common Stock
303:		Retained Earnings
400–499:	REVENUES	
401:		Tickets
402:		Video Rentals
403:		Concessions
404:		Interest
500–599:	EXPENSES	
500–509:	Rentals	
501:		Films
502:		Videos
510–519:	Concessions	
511:		Candy
512:		Soda
513:		Popcorn
520–529:	Wages and Salaries	
521:		Hourly Employees
522:		Salaries
530–539:	Utilities	
531:		Heat
532:		Electric
533:		Water
540–549:	Advertising	
541:		Newspaper
542:		Radio
550–559:	Taxes	
551:		Income Taxes
552:		Unemployment Taxes

THE GENERAL LEDGER

Companies store their accounts in different ways, depending on their accounting system. In a manual system, a separate card or sheet is used to record the activity in each account. A **general ledger** is simply the file or book that contains the accounts.[4] For example, the general ledger for Widescreen Theaters Corporation might consist of a file of cards in a cabinet, with a card for each of the accounts listed in the chart of accounts.

In today's business world, most companies have an automated accounting system. The computer is ideally suited for the job of processing vast amounts of data rapidly. *All the tools discussed in this chapter are as applicable to computerized systems as they are to manual systems. It is merely the appearance of the tools that differs between manual and computerized systems.* For example, the ledger in an automated system might be contained on a computer file server rather than stored in a file cabinet. Throughout the book, we will use a manual system to explain the various tools, such as ledger accounts, because it is easier to illustrate and visualize the tools in a manual system. However, all the ideas apply just as well to a computerized system of accounting.

THE DOUBLE-ENTRY SYSTEM

The origin of the double-entry system of accounting can be traced to Venice, Italy, in 1494. In that year, Fra Luca Pacioli, a Franciscan monk, wrote a mathematical treatise. Included in his book was the concept of debits and credits that is still used almost universally today.

THE T ACCOUNT

The form for a general ledger account will be illustrated later in the chapter. However, the form of account often used to analyze transactions is called the *T account,* so named because it resembles the capital letter T. The name of the account appears across the horizontal line. One side is used to record increases and the other side decreases, but as you will see, the same side is not used for increases for every account. As a matter of convention, the *left* side of an *asset* account is used to record *increases* and the *right* side to record *decreases.* To illustrate a T account, we will look at the Cash account for Glengarry Health Club. The transactions recorded in the account can be traced to Exhibit 3-1.

Debit		CASH	Credit	
INCREASES			**DECREASES**	
Investment by owners	100,000		Wages and salaries	10,000
Court fees collected	5,000		Utilities	3,000
Accounts collected	4,000		Dividends	2,000
	109,000			15,000 ← footings
Bal.	94,000			

The amounts $109,000 and $15,000 are called *footings.* They represent the totals of the amounts on each side of the account. Neither these amounts nor the balance of $94,000 represents transactions. They are simply shown to indicate the totals and the balance in the account.

DEBITS AND CREDITS

Rather than refer to the left or right side of an account, accountants use specific labels for each side. The *left* side of any account is the **debit** side, and the *right* side of any account is the **credit** side. We will also use the terms *debit* and *credit* as verbs. If we *debit* the Cash

---

[4]In addition to a general ledger, many companies maintain subsidiary ledgers. For example, an accounts receivable subsidiary ledger contains a separate account for each customer. The use of a subsidiary ledger for Accounts Receivable is discussed further in Chapter 7.

account, we enter an amount on the left side. Similarly, if we want to enter an amount on the right side of an account, we *credit* the account. To *charge* an account has the same meaning as to *debit* it. No such synonym exists for the act of crediting an account.

Note that *debit* and *credit* are *locational* terms. They simply refer to the left or right side of a T account. They do *not* represent increases or decreases. As we will see, when one type of account is increased (for example, the Cash account), the increase is on the left or *debit* side. When certain other types of accounts are increased, however, the entry will be on the right or *credit* side.

As you would expect from your understanding of the accounting equation, the conventions for using T accounts for assets and liabilities are opposite. Assets are future economic benefits, and liabilities are obligations to transfer economic benefits in the future. If an asset is *increased* with a *debit,* how do you think a liability would be increased? *Because assets and liabilities are opposites, if an asset is increased with a debit, a liability is increased with a credit.* Thus, the right side, or credit side, of a liability account is used to record an increase. Like liabilities, owners' equity accounts are on the opposite side of the accounting equation as are assets. *Thus, like a liability, an owners' equity account is increased with a credit.* We can summarize the logic of debits and credits, increases and decreases, and the accounting equation in the following way:

ASSETS		=	LIABILITIES		+	OWNERS' EQUITY	
Debits	Credits		Debits	Credits		Debits	Credits
Increases	Decreases		Decreases	Increases		Decreases	Increases
+	−		−	+		−	+

Note again that debits and credits are location-oriented. Debits are always on the left side of an account and credits on the right side.

ACCOUNTING FOR YOUR DECISIONS

You Are a Student

A classmate comes to you with a question about the bank statement she has received. Why does the bank credit her account when she makes a deposit to her account, but accounting rules state that cash is increased with a debit?

ANS: The bank is looking at customer deposits from its perspective and not the customers'. Checking account deposits represent liabilities to the bank, such as "Deposits Payable." Thus, when customers make deposits, the bank has increased its liability to those customers, with a credit to its "Deposits Payable."

DEBITS AND CREDITS FOR REVENUES, EXPENSES, AND DIVIDENDS

In our Glengarry Health Club example, revenues were an increase in Retained Earnings. The sale of memberships was not only an increase in the asset Accounts Receivable but also an increase in the owners' equity account Retained Earnings. The transaction resulted in an increase in the owners' claim on the assets of the business. Rather than being recorded directly in Retained Earnings, however, each revenue item is maintained in a separate account. The following logic is used to arrive at the rules for increasing and decreasing revenues:[5]

1. Retained Earnings is increased with a credit.

2. Revenue is an increase in Retained Earnings.

---

[5]We normally think of both revenues and expenses as being only increased, not decreased. Because we will need to decrease them as part of the closing procedure, it is important to know how to reduce these accounts as well as increase them.

3. Revenue is increased with a credit.

4. Because revenue is increased with a credit, it is decreased with a debit.

The same logic is applied to the rules for increasing and decreasing expense accounts:

1. Retained Earnings is decreased with a debit.

2. Expense is a decrease in Retained Earnings.

3. Expense is increased with a debit.

4. Because expense is increased with a debit, it is decreased with a credit.

Recall that dividends reduce cash. But they also reduce the owners' claim on the assets of the business. Earlier we recognized this decrease in the owners' claim as a reduction of Retained Earnings. As we do for revenue and expense accounts, we will use a separate Dividends account:

1. Retained Earnings is decreased with a debit.

2. Dividends are a decrease in Retained Earnings.

3. Dividends are increased with a debit.

4. Because dividends are increased with a debit, they are decreased with a credit.

SUMMARY OF THE RULES FOR INCREASING AND DECREASING ACCOUNTS

The rules for increasing and decreasing the various types of accounts are summarized as follows:

Type of Account	Debit	Credit
Asset	Increase	Decrease
Liability	Decrease	Increase
Owners' Equity	Decrease	Increase
Revenue	Decrease	Increase
Expense	Increase	Decrease
Dividends	Increase	Decrease

NORMAL ACCOUNT BALANCES

Each account has a "normal" balance. For example, assets normally have debit balances. Would it be possible for an asset such as Cash to have a credit balance? Assume that a company has a checking account with a bank. A credit balance in the account would indicate that the decreases in the account, from checks written and other bank charges, were more than the deposits into the account. If this were the case, however, the company would no longer have an asset, Cash, but instead would have a liability to the bank. The normal balances for the accounts we have looked at are as follows:

Type of Account	Normal Balance
Asset	Debit
Liability	Credit
Owners' Equity	Credit
Revenue	Credit
Expense	Debit
Dividends	Debit

DEBITS AREN'T BAD, AND CREDITS AREN'T GOOD

Students often approach their first encounter with debits and credits with preconceived notions. The use of the terms *debit* and *credit* in everyday language leads to many of these notions. "Joe is a real credit to his team." "Nancy should be credited with saving Mary's career." These both appear to be very positive statements. You must resist the temptation to associate the term *credit* with something good or positive and the term *debit* with something bad or negative. *In accounting, debit means one thing: an entry made on the left side of an account. A credit means an entry made on the right side of an account.*

DEBITS AND CREDITS APPLIED TO TRANSACTIONS

Recall the first transaction recorded by Glengarry Health Club earlier in the chapter: the owners invested $100,000 cash in the business. The transaction resulted in an increase in the Cash account and an increase in the Capital Stock account. Applying the rules of debits and credits, we would *debit* the Cash account for $100,000 and *credit* the Capital Stock account for the same amount:[6]

CASH	CAPITAL STOCK
(1) 100,000	100,000 (1)

You now can see why we refer to the **double-entry system** of accounting. Every transaction is recorded so that the equality of debits and credits is maintained, and in the process, the accounting equation is kept in balance. *Every transaction is entered in at least two accounts on opposite sides of T accounts. Our first transaction resulted in an increase in an asset account and an increase in an owners' equity account. For every transaction, the debit side must equal the credit side. The debit of $100,000 to the Cash account equals the credit of $100,000 to the Capital Stock account.* It naturally follows that if the debit side must equal the credit side for every transaction, at any point in time the total of all debits recorded must equal the total of all credits recorded. Thus, the fundamental accounting equation remains in balance.

TRANSACTIONS FOR GLENGARRY HEALTH CLUB

Three distinct steps are involved in recording a transaction in the accounts.

1. First, we *analyze* the transaction. That is, we decide what accounts are increased or decreased and by how much.

2. Second, we *recall* the rules of debits and credits as they apply to the transaction we are analyzing.

3. Finally, we *record* the transaction using the rules of debits and credits.

We return to the transactions of the health club. We have already explained the logic for the debit to the Cash account and the credit to the Capital Stock account for the initial investment by the owners. We will now analyze the remaining eight transactions for the month. Refer to Exhibit 3-1 for a summary of the transactions.

(2) A building and land are exchanged for a promissory note.
  (a) *Analyze:* Two asset accounts are increased: Building and Land. The liability account Notes Payable is also increased.
  (b) *Recall the rules of debits and credits:* An asset is increased with a debit, and a liability is increased with a credit.
  (c) *Record the transaction:*

BUILDING	NOTES PAYABLE
(2) 150,000	200,000 (2)

LAND	
(2) 50,000	

---

[6]We will use the numbers of each transaction, as they were labeled earlier in the chapter, to identify the transactions. In practice, a formal ledger account is used, and transactions are entered according to their date.

(3) Exercise equipment is purchased from a supplier on open account. The purchase price is $20,000.

    (a) *Analyze:* An asset account, Equipment, is increased. A liability account, Accounts Payable, is also increased. Thus, the transaction is identical to the last transaction in that an asset or assets are increased and a liability is increased.

    (b) *Recall the rules of debits and credits:* An asset is increased with a debit, and a liability is increased with a credit.

    (c) *Record the transaction:*

EQUIPMENT		ACCOUNTS PAYABLE	
(3) 20,000			**20,000 (3)**

(4) Three hundred club memberships are sold for $50 each. The members have until the 10th of the following month to pay.

    (a) *Analyze:* The asset account Accounts Receivable is increased by $15,000. This amount is an asset because the company has the right to collect it in the future. The owners' claim to the assets is increased by the same amount. Recall, however, that we do not record these claims—revenues—directly in an owners' equity account but instead use a separate revenue account. We will call the account Membership Revenue.

    (b) *Recall the rules of debits and credits:* An asset is increased with a debit. Owners' equity is increased with a credit. Because revenue is an increase in owners' equity, it is increased with a credit.

    (c) *Record the transaction:*

ACCOUNTS RECEIVABLE		MEMBERSHIP REVENUE	
(4) 15,000			**15,000 (4)**

(5) Court fees are paid at the time of use and amount to $5,000 for the first month.

    (a) *Analyze:* The asset account Cash is increased by $5,000. The owners' claim to the assets is increased by the same amount. The account used to record the increase in the owners' claim is Court Fee Revenue.

    (b) *Recall the rules of debits and credits:* An asset is increased with a debit. Owners' equity is increased with a credit. Because revenue is an increase in owners' equity, it is increased with a credit.

    (c) *Record the transaction:*

CASH		COURT FEE REVENUE	
(1) 100,000			**5,000 (5)**
(5) 5,000			

(6) Wages and salaries amount to $10,000, and they are paid in cash.

    (a) *Analyze:* The asset account Cash is decreased by $10,000. At the same time, the owners' claim to the assets is decreased by this amount. However, rather than record a decrease directly to Retained Earnings, we set up an expense account, Wage and Salary Expense.

    (b) *Recall the rules of debits and credits:* An asset is decreased with a credit. Owners' equity is decreased with a debit. Because expense is a decrease in owners' equity, it is increased with a debit.

    (c) *Record the transaction:*

CASH		WAGE AND SALARY EXPENSE	
(1) 100,000	**10,000 (6)**	**(6) 10,000**	
(5) 5,000			

(7) The utility bill of $3,000 for the first month is paid in cash.

    (a) *Analyze:* The asset account Cash is decreased by $3,000. At the same time, the owners' claim to the assets is decreased by this amount. However, rather than record a decrease directly to Retained Earnings, we set up an expense account, Utility Expense.

(b) *Recall the rules of debits and credits:* An asset is decreased with a credit. Owners' equity is decreased with a debit. Because expense is a decrease in owners' equity, it is increased with a debit.

(c) *Record the transaction:*

CASH				UTILITY EXPENSE		
(1) 100,000	10,000 (6)			(7)	**3,000**	
(5) 5,000	**3,000** (7)					

(8) Cash of $4,000 is collected from members for their January dues.

(a) *Analyze:* Cash is increased by the amount collected from the members. Another asset, Accounts Receivable, is decreased by the same amount. Glengarry has simply traded one asset for another.

(b) *Recall the rules of debits and credits:* An asset is increased with a debit and decreased with a credit. Thus, one asset is debited, and another is credited.

(c) *Record the transaction:*

CASH				ACCOUNTS RECEIVABLE		
(1) 100,000	10,000 (6)			(4) 15,000	**4,000** (8)	
(5) 5,000	3,000 (7)					
(8) **4,000**						

(9) Dividends of $2,000 are distributed to the owners.

(a) *Analyze:* The asset account Cash is decreased by $2,000. At the same time, the owners' claim to the assets is decreased by this amount. Earlier in the chapter, we decreased Retained Earnings for dividends paid to the owners. Now we will use a separate account, Dividends, to record these distributions.

(b) *Recall the rules of debits and credits:* An asset is decreased with a credit. Retained earnings is decreased with a debit. Because dividends are a decrease in retained earnings, they are increased with a debit.

(c) *Record the transaction:*

CASH				*Retained Earnings*		
				DIVIDENDS		
(1) 100,000	10,000 (6)			(9) **2,000**		
(5) 5,000	3,000 (7)					
(8) 4,000	**2,000** (9)					

Two-Minute Review

1. Assume Glengarry pays the supplier the amount owed on open account. Record this transaction in the appropriate T accounts.

2. Assume Glengarry collects the remaining amount owed by members for dues. Record this transaction in the appropriate T accounts.

Answers:

1.

CASH		ACCOUNTS PAYABLE	
	20,000	20,000	

2.

CASH		ACCOUNTS RECEIVABLE	
11,000			11,000

THE JOURNAL: THE FIRM'S CHRONOLOGICAL RECORD OF TRANSACTIONS

LO 6 Explain the purposes of a journal and the posting process.

Each of the nine transactions was entered directly in the ledger accounts. By looking at the Cash account, we see that it increased by $5,000 in transaction **(5)**. But what was the other side of this transaction? That is, what account was credited? To have a record of *each* *entry,* transactions are recorded first in a journal. A **journal** is a chronological record of transactions entered into by a business. Because a journal lists transactions in the order in which they took place, it is called the *book of original entry.* Transactions are recorded first in a journal and then are posted to the ledger accounts. **Posting** is the process of transferring a journal entry to the ledger accounts:

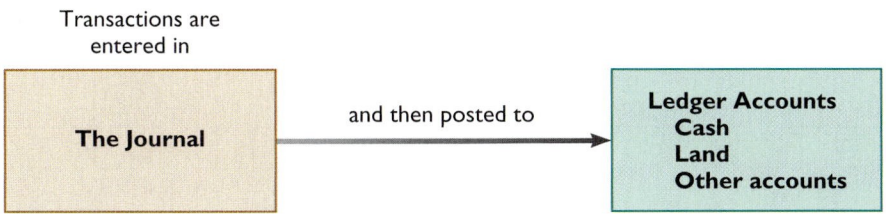

Note that posting does not result in any change in the amounts recorded. It is simply a process of re-sorting the transactions from a chronological order to a topical arrangement.

A journal entry is recorded for each transaction. **Journalizing** is the process of recording entries in a journal. A standard format is normally used for recording journal entries. Consider the original investment by the owners of Glengarry Health Club. The format of the journal entry is as follows:

			DEBIT	CREDIT
Jan.	xx	Cash	100,000	
		Capital Stock *credited*		100,000
		To record the issuance of 10,000 shares of stock for cash.		

Each journal entry contains a date with columns for the amounts debited and credited. Accounts credited are indented to distinguish them from accounts debited. A brief explanation normally appears on the line below the entry.

Transactions are normally recorded in a **general journal.** Specialized journals may be used to record repetitive transactions. For example, a cash receipts journal may be used to record all transactions in which cash is received. Special journals accomplish the same purpose as a general journal, but they save time in recording similar transactions. In this chapter, we will use a general journal to record all transactions.

An excerpt from Glengarry Health Club's general journal appears in the top portion of Exhibit 3-5. One column needs further explanation. *Post. Ref.* is an abbreviation for *Posting Reference.* As part of the posting process explained below, the debit and credit amounts are posted to the appropriate accounts, and this column is filled in with the number assigned to the account.

Journal entries and ledger accounts are both *tools* used by the accountant. The result, a set of financial statements, is the most important part of the process. Journalizing provides us with a chronological record of each transaction. So why not just prepare financial statements directly from the journal entries? Isn't it just extra work to *post* the entries to the ledger accounts? In our simple example of Glengarry Health Club, it would be possible to prepare the statements directly from the journal entries. In real-world situations, however, the number of transactions in any given period is so large that it would be virtually impossible, if not terribly inefficient, to bypass the accounts. Accounts provide us with a convenient summary of the activity, as well as the balance, for a specific financial statement item.

The posting process for Glengarry Health Club is illustrated in Exhibit 3-5 for the health club's fifth transaction, in which cash is collected for court fees. Rather than a T-account format for the general ledger accounts, the *running balance form* is illustrated. A separate column indicates the balance in the ledger account after each transaction. The use of the explanation column in a ledger account is optional. Because an explanation of the entry in the account can be found by referring to the journal, this column is often left blank.

Note the cross-referencing between the journal and the ledger. As amounts are entered in the ledger accounts, the Posting Reference column is filled in with the page number of the journal. At the same time, the Posting Reference column of the journal is filled in with the appropriate account number (for example, GJ1 to indicate page 1 from general journal).

From **Concept**

TO PRACTICE 3.3

READING GATEWAY'S FINANCIAL STATEMENTS Refer to Gateway's income statement and its balance sheet. Using the appropriate accounts from these statements, prepare the journal entry Gateway would record if it sold a computer for $2,000 and gave the customer 30 days to pay.

EXHIBIT 3-5   Posting from the Journal to the Ledger

General Journal   Page No. 1

Date		Account Titles and Explanation		Post. Ref.	Debit	Credit
2001 Jan.	XX	Accounts Receivable		5	1 5 0 0 0	
		Membership Revenue		40		1 5 0 0 0
		Sold 300 memberships at $50 each.				
	XX	Cash		1	5 0 0 0	
		Court Fee Revenue		44		5 0 0 0
		Collected court fees.				

General Ledger
Cash   Account No. 1

Date		Explanation		Post. Ref.	Debit	Credit	Balance
2001 Jan.	XX			GJ1	1 0 0 0 0 0		1 0 0 0 0 0
	XX			GJ1	5 0 0 0		1 0 5 0 0 0

Court Fee Revenue   Account No. 44

Date		Explanation		Post. Ref.	Debit	Credit	Balance
2001 Jan.	XX			GJ1		5 0 0 0	5 0 0 0

ACCOUNTING FOR YOUR DECISIONS

You Are the Manager

You are the community relations manager for a company. You need to determine whether the company is spending its money wisely in promoting its image in the local community.

1. What types of accounts would you examine? Give examples of the possible names for some of these accounts.

2. Would a general journal or a general ledger be more useful to you in making your determination? Explain your answer.

ANS: 1. Among the possible accounts that you want to examine are Entertainment, Travel, Promotions, Advertising, and Miscellaneous, in addition to any accounts that might contain expenditures related to community relations.

2. You may want to examine the general ledger for each of the accounts listed in part 1. The ledger contains a record for each of the accounts and the activity in them during the period.

FOCUS ON USERS

Name: Mark Gleason Jr.
Education: B.A., Georgetown University; M.S., Medill School of Journalism
College Major: American Studies
Occupation: President and Publisher, West Egg Communications LLC
Age: 34

This New Company Relies Heavily on Its Account-Processing System

As the owner of a start-up company in its second year of business, Mark Gleason knows how important it is to keep good accounting records from the time the first transaction takes place. Without an accountant for the first few weeks of operation, it was up to Mark to initiate a processing system for his new business. "It's amazing how fast even a small business's accounting can get complicated. In the very early days, it was just a matter of keeping a checkbook ledger, but after a couple of months, we wanted to know how we were doing in terms of our budget. I remember in the beginning, before we computerized, I sorted expenses into about a dozen file folders. A year later, we've got well over a hundred expense accounts that are recorded electronically on a regular and systematic basis."

There are many reasons to keep tight controls on the way accounting information is processed in a working business, whether it be new or old, big or small. For Mark, whose company launched a national magazine, the benefits of meticulous recordkeeping are obvious. As he says, "It ensures that we pay bills on time, which is critical to maintaining good relationships. It forces us to keep track of expenses, rein them in if necessary, and plan future cash flow." But probably the most valuable result of a good processing system is having a quantifiable basis for analysis. Mark explains, "When a strategic decision needs to be made, it helps to be able to look at the financial history—at what happened in a similar situation—and see how much money came in, what kind of pressure was put on cash flow, and what the tax impact was." If the accounts are always kept up to date, the data we need for analysis will always be there when those critical decisions come up.

The frequency of posting differs among companies, partly based on the degree to which their accounting system is automated. For example, in some computerized systems, amounts are posted to the ledger accounts at the time an entry is recorded in the journal. In a manual system, posting is normally done periodically, for example, daily, weekly, or monthly. Regardless of when performed, the posting process changes nothing. It simply reorganizes the transactions by account.

THE TRIAL BALANCE

Accountants use one other tool to facilitate the preparation of a set of financial statements. A **trial balance** is a list of each account and its balance at a specific point in time. The trial balance is *not* a financial statement but merely a convenient device to prove the equality of the debit and credit balances in the accounts. It can be as informal as an adding-machine tape with the account titles penciled in next to the debit and credit amounts. A trial balance for Glengarry Health Club as of January 31, 2001, is shown in Exhibit 3-6. The balance in each account was determined by adding the increases and subtracting the decreases for the account for the transactions detailed earlier.

Certain types of errors are detectable from a trial balance. For example, if the balance of an account is incorrectly computed, the total of the debits and credits in the trial balance will not equal. If a debit is posted to an account as a credit, or vice versa, the trial

LO 7 Explain the purpose of a trial balance.

Study Tip

Remember from p. 105 that every account has a normal balance, either debit or credit. Note the normal balances for each account on this trial balance.

EXHIBIT 3-6   Trial Balance for Glengarry Health Club

GLENGARRY HEALTH CLUB
TRIAL BALANCE
AT JANUARY 31, 2001

Account Title	Debits	Credits
Cash	$ 94,000	
Accounts Receivable *owed to you at end of the year*	11,000	
Building	150,000	
Land	50,000	
Equipment	20,000	
Accounts Payable		$ 20,000
Notes Payable		200,000
Capital Stock		100,000
Membership Revenue		15,000
Court Fee Revenue		5,000
Wage and Salary Expense	10,000	
Utility Expense	3,000	
Dividends	2,000	
Totals	$340,000	$340,000

ACCOUNTING FOR YOUR DECISIONS

You Are the Stockholder

You own 100 shares of stock in General Motors. Every year you receive GM's annual report, which includes a chairman's letter, a description of new models, a financial section, and footnotes to financial statements. Nowhere in the report do you see a general ledger or a trial balance. Is General Motors hiding something?

ANS: GM's balance sheet, income statement, and statement of cash flows are derived from the company's journal entries, general ledgers, trial balances, and so on. These documents are the building blocks of the final statements. There could literally be millions of transactions during the year—which even the most diehard accounting fan would tire of reading.

balance will be out of balance. The omission of part of a journal entry in the posting process will also be detected by the preparation of a trial balance.

Do not attribute more significance to a trial balance, however, than is warranted. It does provide a convenient summary of account balances for preparing financial statements. It also assures us that the balances of all the debit accounts equal the balances of all the credit accounts. But an equality of debits and credits does not necessarily mean that the *correct* accounts were debited and credited in an entry. For example, the entry to record the purchase of land by signing a promissory note *should* result in a debit to Land and a credit to Notes Payable. If the accountant incorrectly debited Cash instead of Land, the trial balance would still show an equality of debits and credits. A trial balance can be prepared at any time; it is usually prepared before the release of a set of financial statements.

In the first part of this chapter, we analyzed the effects of the transactions of Glengarry Health Club on the accounting equation. *Because the accounting equation is the basis for financial statements, the ability to analyze transactions in terms of their effect on the equation is an essential skill to master.* In the second part of the chapter, we briefly examined tools used by the accountant to effectively and efficiently process large volumes of transactions during the period. We saw that debits and credits are simply words that accountants use to indicate increases and decreases in various accounts.

The emphasis throughout this book is on the *use* of financial statements to make decisions, as opposed to the tools used by accountants to process information. Therefore, in future chapters, our emphasis will not be on the accountant's various tools, such as debits and credits, but on the effects of transactions on the accounting equation and financial statements. Recall transaction 4 for the Glengarry Health Club, as it was originally summarized in Exhibit 3-1:

		Assets				=	Liabilities		+	Owners' Equity	
NUMBER	CASH	ACCOUNTS RECEIVABLE	EQUIPMENT	BUILDING	LAND		ACCOUNTS PAYABLE	NOTES PAYABLE		CAPITAL STOCK	RETAINED EARNINGS
4		$15,000									$15,000

Recall also that the increase in retained earnings is the result of an increase in revenue from the sale of memberships. In future chapters, we will use a variation of the format in Exhibit 3-1 to demonstrate the effects of various transactions on the accounting equation. For example, the sale of memberships would appear as follows in this version of the equation:

BALANCE SHEET						INCOME STATEMENT
ASSETS	=	LIABILITIES	+	OWNERS' EQUITY	+	REVENUES – EXPENSES
Accounts Receivable 15,000						Membership Revenue 15,000

Note two important changes in this version of the equation. First, rather than having a separate column for each individual financial statement item, the items are simply listed under the appropriate categories. For example, this transaction results in an increase in Accounts Receivable, which is shown in the assets category. Second, in this expanded version of the accounting equation, the income statement is viewed as an extension of the balance sheet. Thus, rather than show Membership Revenue as an increase in retained earnings as in Exhibit 3-1, it is shown as an increase in revenue on the income statement. As you are aware, revenues do result in an increase in retained earnings and thus owners' equity, but they must first be recorded on the income statement.

To illustrate one additional transaction with this new format, recall transaction 6 for Glengarry in which $10,000 was paid in wages and salaries. The effect of this transaction on the accounting equation is:

BALANCE SHEET						INCOME STATEMENT
ASSETS	=	LIABILITIES	+	OWNERS' EQUITY	+	REVENUES – EXPENSES
Cash (10,000)						Wage and Salary Expense (10,000)

Exhibit 3-7 summarizes how the new transaction effects equation will be used in Chapters 4–13.

EXHIBIT 3-7 Using the Transaction Effects Equation

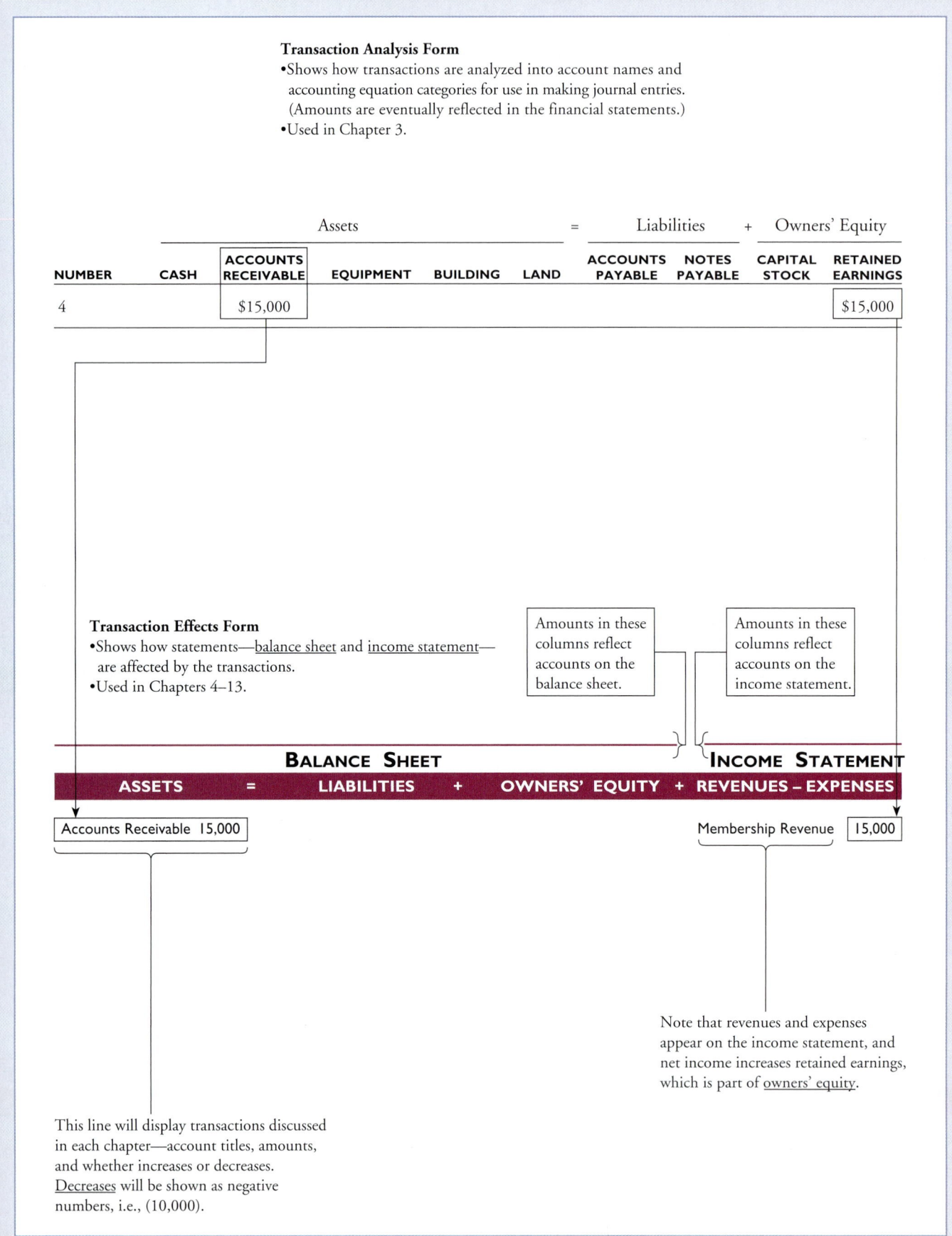

Transaction Analysis Form
•Shows how transactions are analyzed into account names and
accounting equation categories for use in making journal entries.
(Amounts are eventually reflected in the financial statements.)
•Used in Chapter 3.

| | | Assets | | | | = | Liabilities | + | Owners' Equity | |
NUMBER	CASH	ACCOUNTS RECEIVABLE	EQUIPMENT	BUILDING	LAND		ACCOUNTS PAYABLE	NOTES PAYABLE	CAPITAL STOCK	RETAINED EARNINGS
4		$15,000								$15,000

Transaction Effects Form
•Shows how statements—balance sheet and income statement—
are affected by the transactions.
•Used in Chapters 4–13.

Amounts in these
columns reflect
accounts on the
balance sheet.

Amounts in these
columns reflect
accounts on the
income statement.

BALANCE SHEET

INCOME STATEMENT

ASSETS = LIABILITIES + OWNERS' EQUITY + REVENUES – EXPENSES

Accounts Receivable 15,000

Membership Revenue   15,000

Note that revenues and expenses
appear on the income statement, and
net income increases retained earnings,
which is part of owners' equity.

This line will display transactions discussed
in each chapter—account titles, amounts,
and whether increases or decreases.
Decreases will be shown as negative
numbers, i.e., (10,000).

WARMUP EXERCISES

LO 3, 5 **Warmup Exercise 3-1**   Your Debits and Credits

Assume that you borrow $1,000 from your roommate by signing an agreement to repay the amount borrowed in six months.

Required

1. What is the effect of this transaction on your own accounting equation?
2. Prepare the journal entry to record this transaction in your own records.

Key to the Solution

Recall Exhibit 3-1 for the effects of transactions on the accounting equation, and refer to the summary of the rules for increasing and decreasing accounts on p. 105.

LO 3, 5 **Warmup Exercise 3-2**   A Bank's Debits and Credits

The Third State Bank loans a customer $5,000 in exchange for a promissory note.

Required

1. What is the effect of this transaction on the bank's accounting equation?
2. Prepare the journal entry to record this transaction in the bank's records.

Key to the Solution

Recall Exhibit 3-1 for the effects of the transaction on the accounting equation, and refer to the summary of the rules for increasing and decreasing accounts on p. 105.

LO 3, 5 **Warmup Exercise 3-3**   Debits and Credits for Uno

Assume Uno goes to its bank and borrows $10,000 by signing a promissory note. The next day the company uses the money to buy a pizza oven.

Required

1. What is the effect of each of these two transactions on Uno's accounting equation?
2. Prepare the journal entries to record both transactions in Uno's records.

Key to the Solution

Recall Exhibit 3-1 for the effects of transactions on the accounting equation, and refer to the summary of the rules for increasing and decreasing accounts on p. 105.

SOLUTIONS TO WARMUP EXERCISES

Warmup Exercise 3-1
1. If you borrow $1,000 from your roommate, assets, in the form of cash, increase $1,000, and liabilities, in the form of a note payable, increase $1,000.
2. Cash   1,000
       Notes Payable   1,000

Warmup Exercise 3-2
1. If a bank loans a customer $5,000, the bank's assets, in the form of a note receivable, increase $5,000, and its assets, in the form of cash, decrease $5,000.
2. Notes Receivable   5,000
       Cash   5,000

Warmup Exercise 3-3
1. If Uno borrows $10,000 from its bank, assets, in the form of cash, increase $10,000, and liabilities, in the form of a note payable, increase $10,000. If the company uses the money to buy an oven, assets, in the form of equipment, increase $10,000, and assets, in the form of cash, decrease $10,000.

				2.	Cash	10,000	

2. | Cash | 10,000 | |
Notes Payable		10,000
Equipment	10,000	
Cash		10,000

REVIEW PROBLEM

The following transactions are entered into by Sparkle Car Wash during its first month of operations:

a. Articles of incorporation are filed with the state, and 20,000 shares of capital stock are issued. Cash of $40,000 is received from the new owners for the shares.

b. A five-year promissory note is signed at the local bank. The cash received from the loan is $120,000.

c. An existing car wash is purchased for $150,000 in cash. The values assigned to the land, building, and equipment are $25,000, $75,000, and $50,000, respectively.

d. Cleaning supplies are purchased on account for $2,500 from a distributor. All the supplies are used in the first month.

e. During the first month, $1,500 is paid to the distributor for the cleaning supplies. The remaining $1,000 will be paid next month.

f. Gross receipts from car washes during the first month of operations amount to $7,000.

g. Wages and salaries paid in the first month amount to $2,000.

h. The utility bill of $800 for the month is paid.

i. A total of $1,000 in dividends is paid to the owners.

Required

1. Prepare a table to summarize the preceding transactions as they affect the accounting equation. Use the format in Exhibit 3-1. Identify each transaction by letter.

2. Prepare an income statement for the month.

3. Prepare a balance sheet at the end of the month.

Solution to Review Problem

1.
SPARKLE CAR WASH
TRANSACTIONS FOR THE MONTH

	Assets				=	Liabilities + Owners' Equity			
TRANS.	CASH	LAND	BUILDING	EQUIPMENT		ACCOUNTS PAYABLE	NOTES PAYABLE	CAPITAL STOCK	RETAINED EARNINGS
a.	$ 40,000							$40,000	
b.	120,000						$120,000		
Bal.	$160,000						$120,000	$40,000	
c.	−150,000	$25,000	$75,000	$50,000					
Bal.	$ 10,000	$25,000	$75,000	$50,000			$120,000	$40,000	
d.						$2,500			$–2,500
Bal.	$ 10,000	$25,000	$75,000	$50,000		$2,500	$120,000	$40,000	$–2,500
e.	−1,500					−1,500			
Bal.	$ 8,500	$25,000	$75,000	$50,000		$1,000	$120,000	$40,000	$–2,500
f.	7,000								7,000
Bal.	$ 15,500	$25,000	$75,000	$50,000		$1,000	$120,000	$40,000	$ 4,500
g.	−2,000								−2,000
Bal.	$ 13,500	$25,000	$75,000	$50,000		$1,000	$120,000	$40,000	$ 2,500
h.	−800								−800
Bal.	$ 12,700	$25,000	$75,000	$50,000		$1,000	$120,000	$40,000	$ 1,700
i.	−1,000								−1,000
Bal.	$ 11,700	$25,000	$75,000	$50,000		$1,000	$120,000	$40,000	$ 700

Total Assets: $161,700   Total Liabilities and Owners' Equity: $161,700

2.

SPARKLE CAR WASH
INCOME STATEMENT
FOR THE MONTH ENDED XX/XX/XX

Car wash revenue		$7,000
Expenses:		
Supplies	$2,500	
Wages and salaries	2,000	
Utilities	800	5,300
Net income		$1,700

3.

SPARKLE CAR WASH
BALANCE SHEET
XX/XX/XX

Assets		Liabilities and Owners' Equity	
Cash	$ 11,700	Accounts payable	$ 1,000
Land	25,000	Notes payable	120,000
Building	75,000	Capital stock	40,000
Equipment	50,000	Retained earnings	700
		Total Liabilities	
Total Assets	$161,700	and Owners' Equity	$161,700

CHAPTER HIGHLIGHTS

1. **LO 1** Both internal and external events affect an entity. External events, such as the purchase of materials, involve the entity and its environment. Internal events, such as the placement of the materials into production, do not involve an outside entity. For any event to be recorded, it must be measurable.

2. **LO 2** Source documents are used as the basis for recording events as transactions. For certain repetitive transactions, a standard source document is used, such as a time card to document the payroll for the week. For other nonrepetitive transactions, a source document has to be generated for the specific event.

3. **LO 3** Economic events are the basis for recording transactions. These transactions result in changes in the company's financial position. Transactions change the amount of individual items on the balance sheet, but the statement must balance after each transaction is recorded.

4. **LO 4** A separate account is used for each identifiable asset, liability, revenue, expense, and component of owners' equity. No standard set of accounts exists, and the types of accounts used depend to a certain extent on the nature of a company's business. A chart of accounts is a numerical list of all the accounts used by an entity. The general ledger in a manual system might consist of a set of cards, one for each account, in a file cabinet. In a computerized system, a magnetic tape or diskette might be used to store the accounts.

5. **LO 4** Accountants use T accounts as the basic form of analysis of transactions. The left side of an account is used for debits, and the right side is for credits. Transactions are recorded in the ledger in more formal accounts than the typical T account.

6. **LO 5** By convention, the left side of an asset account is used to record increases. Thus, an asset account is increased with a debit. Because liabilities are on the opposite side of the accounting equation, they are increased with a credit. Similarly, owners' equity accounts are increased with a credit. Because revenue is an increase in owners' equity, it is increased with a credit. Thus, an expense, as well as a dividend, is increased with a debit. According to the double-entry system, there are two sides to every transaction. For each transaction, the debit or debits must equal the credit or credits.

7. **LO 6** Transactions are not recorded directly in the accounts but are recorded initially in a journal. A separate entry is recorded in the journal for each transaction. The account(s) debited appears first in the entry, with the account(s) credited listed next and indented. Separate columns for debits and credits are used to indicate the amounts for each. A general journal is used in lieu of any specialized journals.

8. **LO 6** Amounts appearing in journal entries are posted to the ledger accounts. Posting can be done either at the time the entry is recorded or periodically. The Post. Ref. column in a journal indicates the account number to which the amount is posted, and a similar column in the account acts as a convenient reference back to the particular page number in the journal.

9. **LO 7** A trial balance proves the equality of the debits and credits in the accounts. If only one side of a transaction is posted to the accounts, the trial balance will not balance. Other types of errors are detectable from the process of preparing a trial balance. It cannot, however, detect all errors. A trial balance could be in balance even though the wrong asset account is debited in an entry.

KEY TERMS QUIZ

Read each definition below, and then write the number of the definition in the blank beside the appropriate term it defines. The solution appears at the end of the chapter.

_____ Event
_____ External event
_____ Internal event
_____ Transaction
_____ Source document
_____ Account
_____ Chart of accounts
_____ General ledger

_____ Debit
_____ Credit
_____ Double-entry system
_____ Journal
_____ Posting
_____ Journalizing
_____ General journal
_____ Trial balance

1. A numerical list of all the accounts used by a company.
2. A list of each account and its balance at a specific point in time; used to prove the equality of debits and credits.
3. A happening of consequence to an entity.
4. An entry on the right side of an account.
5. An event occurring entirely within an entity.
6. A piece of paper, such as a sales invoice, that is used as the evidence to record a transaction.
7. The act of recording journal entries.
8. An entry on the left side of an account.
9. The process of transferring amounts from a journal to the appropriate ledger accounts.
10. An event involving interaction between an entity and its environment.

11. The record used to accumulate monetary amounts for each individual asset, liability, revenue, expense, and component of owners' equity.
12. A book, file, hard drive, or other device containing all of a company's accounts.
13. A chronological record of transactions, also known as the _book of original entry._
14. Any event, external or internal, that is recognized in a set of financial statements.
15. The journal used in place of a specialized journal.
16. A system of accounting in which every transaction is recorded with equal debits and credits and the accounting equation is kept in balance.

ALTERNATE TERMS

Credit side of an account   Right side of an account
Debit an account   Charge an account
Debit side of an account   Left side of an account
General ledger   Set of accounts

Journal   Book of original entry
Journalize an entry   Record an entry
Posting an account   Transferring an amount from the journal to the ledger

QUESTIONS

1. What are the two types of events that affect an entity? Describe each.
2. What is the significance of source documents to the recording process? Give two examples of source documents.
3. What are four different forms of cash?
4. How does an account receivable differ from a note receivable?
5. What is meant by the statement "One company's account receivable is another company's account payable"?
6. What do accountants mean when they refer to the "double-entry system" of accounting?
7. Owners' equity represents the claim of the owners on the assets of the business. What is the distinction relative to the owners'

claim between the Capital Stock account and the Retained Earnings account?
8. If an asset account is increased with a debit, what is the logic for increasing a liability account with a credit?
9. A friend comes to you with the following plight: "I'm confused. An asset is something positive, and it is increased with a debit. However, an expense is something negative, and it is also increased with a debit. I don't get it." How can you straighten your friend out?
10. The payment of dividends reduces cash. If the Cash account is reduced with a credit, why is the Dividends account debited when dividends are paid?
11. If Cash is increased with a debit, why does the bank credit your account when you make a deposit?

12. Your friend presents the following criticism of the accounting system: "Accounting involves so much duplication of effort. First, entries are recorded in a journal, and then the same information is recorded in a ledger. No wonder accountants work such long hours!" Do you agree with this criticism?

13. How does the T account differ from the running balance form for an account? How are they similar?

14. What is the benefit of using a cross-referencing system between a ledger and a journal?

15. How often should a company post entries from the journal to the ledger?

16. What is the purpose of a trial balance?

EXERCISES

LO 1 Exercise 3-1 Types of Events
For each of the following events, identify whether it is an external event that would be recorded as a transaction (E), an internal event that would be recorded as a transaction (I), or not recorded (NR):

_____ **1.** A supplier of a company's raw material is paid an amount owed on account.

_____ **2.** A customer pays its open account.

_____ **3.** A new chief executive officer is hired.

_____ **4.** The biweekly payroll is paid.

_____ **5.** Raw materials are entered into production.

_____ **6.** A new advertising agency is hired to develop a series of newspaper ads for the company.

_____ **7.** The advertising bill for the first month is paid.

_____ **8.** The accountant determines the federal income taxes owed based on the income earned during the period.

LO 2 Exercise 3-2 Source Documents Matched with Transactions
Following are a list of source documents and a list of transactions. Indicate by letter next to each transaction the source document that would serve as evidence for the recording of the transaction.

Source Documents

a. Purchase invoice

b. Sales invoice

c. Cash register tape

d. Time cards

e. Promissory note

f. Stock certificates

g. Monthly statement from utility company

h. No standard source document would normally be available

Transactions

_____ **1.** Utilities expense for the month is recorded.

_____ **2.** A cash settlement is received from a pending lawsuit.

_____ **3.** Owners contribute cash to start a new corporation.

_____ **4.** The biweekly payroll is paid.

_____ **5.** Cash sales for the day are recorded.

_____ **6.** Equipment is acquired on a 30-day open account.

_____ **7.** A sale is made on open account.

_____ **8.** A building is acquired by signing an agreement to repay a stated amount plus interest in six months.

LO 3 Exercise 3-3 The Effect of Transactions on the Accounting Equation
For each of the following transactions, indicate whether it increases (I), decreases (D), or has no effect (NE) on the total dollar amount of each of the elements of the accounting equation.

Transactions	Assets	= Liabilities	+ Owners' Equity
Example: Common stock is issued in exchange for cash.	I	NE	I

1. Equipment is purchased for cash.
2. Sales are made on account.
3. Cash sales are made.
4. An account payable is paid off.
5. Cash is collected on an account receivable.
6. Buildings are purchased in exchange for a three-year note payable.
7. Advertising bill for the month is paid.
8. Dividends are paid to stockholders.
9. Land is acquired by issuing shares of stock to the owner of the land.

LO 3 Exercise 3-4   Types of Transactions

As you found out in reading the chapter, there are three elements to the accounting equation: assets, liabilities, and owners' equity. You also learned that every transaction affects at least two of these elements. Although other possibilities exist, five types of transactions are described below. For *each* of these five types, write out descriptions of at least *two* transactions that illustrate these types of transactions.

Type of Transaction	Assets	= Liabilities	+ Owners' Equity
1.	Increase	Increase	
2.	Increase		Increase
3.	Decrease	Decrease	
4.	Decrease		Decrease
5.	Increase Decrease		

LO 3 Exercise 3-5   Analyzing Transactions

Prepare a table to summarize the following transactions as they affect the accounting equation. Use the format in Exhibit 3-1.

1. Sales on account of $1,530.
2. Purchases of supplies on account for $1,365.
3. Cash sales of $750.
4. Purchase of equipment for cash of $4,240.
5. Issuance of a promissory note for $2,500.
6. Collections on account for $890.
7. Sale of capital stock in exchange for a parcel of land. The land is appraised at $50,000.
8. Payment of $4,000 in salaries and wages.
9. Payment of open account in the amount of $500.

LO 4 Exercise 3-6   Balance Sheet Accounts and Their Use

Choose from the following list of account titles the one that most accurately fits the description of that account or is an example of that account. An account title may be used more than once or not at all.

Cash	Accounts Receivable	Notes Receivable
Prepaid Asset	Land	Buildings
Investments	Accounts Payable	Notes Payable
Taxes Payable	Retained Earnings	Common Stock
Preferred Stock		

_____ 1. A written obligation to repay a fixed amount, with interest, at some time in the future

_____ 2. Twenty acres of land held for speculation

_____ 3. An amount owed by a customer

_____ 4. Corporate income taxes owed to the federal government

_____ 5. Ownership in a company that allows the owner to receive dividends before common share-holders receive any distributions

_____ 6. Five acres of land used as the site for a factory

_____ 7. Amounts owed on an open account to a supplier of raw materials, due in 90 days

_____ 8. A checking account at the bank

_____ 9. A warehouse used to store merchandise

_____ 10. Claims by the owners on the undistributed net income of a business

_____ 11. Rent paid on an office building in advance of use of the facility

LO 5 **Exercise 3-7** Normal Account Balances

Each account has a normal balance. For the following list of accounts, indicate whether the normal balance of each is a debit or a credit.

Account	Normal Balance
1. Cash	_____
2. Prepaid Insurance	_____
3. Retained Earnings	_____
4. Bonds Payable	_____
5. Investments	_____
6. Capital Stock	_____
7. Advertising Fees Earned	_____
8. Wages and Salaries Expense	_____
9. Wages and Salaries Payable	_____
10. Office Supplies	_____
11. Dividends	_____

LO 5 **Exercise 3-8** Debits and Credits

The new bookkeeper for Darby Corporation is getting ready to mail the daily cash receipts to the bank for deposit. Because his previous job was at a bank, he is aware that the bank "credits" your account for all deposits and "debits" your account for all checks written. Therefore, he makes the following entry before sending the daily receipts to the bank:

June 5	Accounts Receivable	10,000	
	Sales Revenue	2,450	
	Cash		12,450
	To record cash received on June 5: $10,000 collections on account and $2,450 in cash sales.		

Required

Explain why this entry is wrong, and prepare the correct journal entry. Why does the bank refer to cash received from a customer as a _credit_ to that customer's account?

LO 7 **Exercise 3-9** Trial Balance

The following list of accounts was taken from the general ledger of Spencer Corporation on December 31, 2001. The bookkeeper thought it would be helpful if the accounts were arranged in alphabetical order. Each account contains the balance normal for that type of account (for example, Cash normally has a debit balance). Prepare a trial balance as of this date, with the accounts arranged in the following order: (1) assets, (2) liabilities, (3) owners' equity, (4) revenues, (5) expenses, and (6) dividends.

Account	Balance
Accounts Payable	$ 7,650
Accounts Receivable	5,325

Automobiles	9,200
Buildings	150,000
Capital Stock	100,000
Cash	10,500
Commissions Expense	2,600
Commissions Revenue	12,750
Dividends	2,000
Equipment	85,000
Heat, Light, and Water Expense	1,400
Income Tax Expense	1,700
Income Taxes Payable	2,500
Interest Revenue	1,300
Land	50,000
Notes Payable	90,000
Office Salaries Expense	6,000
Office Supplies	500
Retained Earnings	110,025

Multi-Concept Exercises

LO 3, 4, 5 **Exercise 3-10** Journal Entries Recorded Directly in T Accounts

Record each transaction shown below directly in T accounts, using the numbers preceding the transactions to identify them in the accounts. Each account involved needs a separate T account.

1. Received contribution of $6,500 from each of the three principal owners of the We-Go Delivery Service in exchange for shares of stock.
2. Purchased office supplies for cash of $130.
3. Purchased a van for $15,000 on an open account. The company has 25 days to pay for the van.
4. Provided delivery services to residential customers for cash of $125.
5. Billed a local business $200 for delivery services. The customer is to pay the bill within 15 days.
6. Paid the amount due on the van.
7. Received the amount due from the local business billed in transaction **5.**

LO 3, 4, 5 **Exercise 3-11** Determining an Ending Account Balance

Jessie's Bead Shop was organized on June 1, 2001. The company received a contribution of $1,000 from each of the two principal owners. During the month, Jessie's Bead Shop had cash sales of $1,400, had sales on account of $450, received $250 from customers in payment of their accounts, purchased supplies on account for $600 and equipment on account for $1,350, received a utility bill for $250 that will not be paid until July, and paid the full amount due on the equipment. Use a T account to determine the company's Cash balance on June 30, 2001.

LO 3, 4, 5 **Exercise 3-12** Reconstructing a Beginning Account Balance

During the month, services performed for customers on account amounted to $7,500, and collections from customers in payment of their accounts totaled $6,000. At the end of the month, the Accounts Receivable account had a balance of $2,500. What was the Accounts Receivable balance at the beginning of the month?

LO 3, 5, 6 **Exercise 3-13** Journal Entries

Following is a list of transactions entered into during the first month of operations of Gardener Corporation, a new landscape service. Prepare in journal form the entry to record each transaction.

April 1: Articles of incorporation are filed with the state, and 100,000 shares of common stock are issued for $100,000 in cash.

April 4: A six-month promissory note is signed at the bank. Interest at 9% per annum will be repaid in six months along with the principal amount of the loan of $50,000.

April 8: Land and a storage shed are acquired for a lump sum of $80,000. On the basis of an appraisal, 25% of the value is assigned to the land and the remainder to the building.

April 10: Mowing equipment is purchased from a supplier at a total cost of $25,000. A down payment of $10,000 is made, with the remainder due by the end of the month.

April 18: Customers are billed for services provided during the first half of the month. The total amount billed of $5,500 is due within 10 days.

April 27: The remaining balance due on the mowing equipment is paid to the supplier.

April 28: The total amount of $5,500 due from customers is received.

April 30: Customers are billed for services provided during the second half of the month. The total amount billed is $9,850.

April 30: Salaries and wages of $4,650 for the month of April are paid.

PROBLEMS

LO 1 Problem 3-1 Events to Be Recorded in Accounts

The following events take place at Dillon's Drive-In:

1. Food is ordered from vendors, who will deliver the food within the week.
2. Vendors deliver food on account, payment due in 30 days.
3. Employees take frozen food from the freezers and prepare it for customers.
4. Food is served to customers, and sales are rung up on the cash register; sales will be totaled at the end of the day.
5. Trash is taken to dumpsters, and the floors are cleaned.
6. Cash registers are cleared at the end of the day.
7. Cash is deposited in the bank night depository.
8. Employees are paid weekly paychecks.
9. Vendors noted in item 2 are paid for the food delivered.

Required

Identify each event as internal (I) or external (E), and indicate whether each event would be recorded in the *accounts* of the company. For each event that is to be recorded, identify the names of at least two accounts that would be affected.

LO 3 Problem 3-2 Transaction Analysis and Financial Statements

Just Rolling Along Inc. was organized on May 1, 2001, by two college students who recognized an opportunity to make money while spending their days at a beach along Lake Michigan. The two entrepreneurs plan to rent bicycles and in-line skates to weekend visitors to the lakefront. The following transactions occurred during the first month of operations:

May 1: Received contribution of $9,000 from each of the two principal owners of the new business in exchange for shares of stock.

May 1: Purchased 10 bicycles for $300 each on an open account. The company has 30 days to pay for the bicycles.

May 5: Registered as a vendor with the city and paid the $15 monthly fee.

May 9: Purchased 20 pairs of in-line skates at $125 per pair, 20 helmets at $50 each, and 20 sets of protective gear (knee and elbow pads and wrist guards) at $45 per set for cash.

May 10: Purchased $100 in miscellaneous supplies on account. The company has 30 days to pay for the supplies.

May 15: Paid $125 bill from local radio station for advertising for the last two weeks of May.

May 17: Customers rented in-line skates and bicycles for cash of $1,800.

May 24: Billed the local park district $1,200 for in-line skating lessons provided to neighborhood kids. The park district is to pay one-half of the bill within 5 working days and the rest within 30 days.

May 29: Received 50% of the amount billed to the park district.

May 30: Customers rented in-line skates and bicycles for cash of $3,000.

May 30: Paid wages of $160 to a friend who helped out over the weekend.

May 31: Paid the balance due on the bicycles.

Required

1. Prepare a table to summarize the preceding transactions as they affect the accounting equation. Use the format in Exhibit 3-1. Identify each transaction with the date.

2. Prepare an income statement for the month ended May 31, 2001.

3. Prepare a classified balance sheet at May 31, 2001.

4. Why do you think the two college students decided to incorporate their business rather than operate it as a partnership?

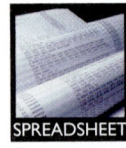
SPREADSHEET

LO 3   Problem 3-3 Transaction Analysis and Financial Statements

Expert Consulting Services Inc. was organized on March 1, 2001, by two former college roommates. The corporation will provide computer consulting services to small businesses. The following transactions occurred during the first month of operations:

March 2: Received contributions of $20,000 from each of the two principal owners of the new business in exchange for shares of stock.

March 7: Signed a two-year promissory note at the bank and received cash of $15,000. Interest, along with the $15,000, will be repaid at the end of the two years.

March 12: Purchased $700 in miscellaneous supplies on account. The company has 30 days to pay for the supplies.

March 19: Billed a client $4,000 for services rendered by Expert in helping to install a new computer system. The client is to pay 25% of the bill upon its receipt and the remaining balance within 30 days.

March 20: Paid $1,300 bill from the local newspaper for advertising for the month of March.

March 22: Received 25% of the amount billed the client on March 19.

March 26: Received cash of $2,800 for services provided in assisting a client in selecting software for its computer.

March 29: Purchased a computer system for $8,000 in cash.

March 30: Paid $3,300 of salaries and wages for March.

March 31: Received and paid $1,400 in gas, electric, and water bills.

Required

1. Prepare a table to summarize the preceding transactions as they affect the accounting equation. Use the format in Exhibit 3-1. Identify each transaction with the date.

2. Prepare an income statement for the month ended March 31, 2001.

3. Prepare a classified balance sheet at March 31, 2001.

4. From reading the balance sheet you prepared in part **3,** what events would you expect to take place in April? Explain your answer.

LO 3   Problem 3-4 Transactions Reconstructed from Financial Statements

The following financial statements are available for Elm Corporation for its first month of operations:

ELM CORPORATION
INCOME STATEMENT
FOR THE MONTH ENDED JUNE 30, 2001

Service revenue		$93,600
Expenses:		
Rent	$ 9,000	
Salaries and wages	27,900	
Utilities	13,800	50,700
Net income		$42,900

ELM CORPORATION
BALANCE SHEET
JUNE 30, 2001

Assets		Liabilities and Owners' Equity	
Cash	$ 22,800	Accounts payable	$ 18,000
Accounts receivable	21,600	Notes payable	90,000
Equipment	18,000		
Building	90,000	Capital stock	30,000
Land	24,000	Retained earnings	38,400
Total	$176,400	Total	$176,400

Required

Using the format illustrated in Exhibit 3-1, prepare a table to summarize the transactions entered into by Elm Corporation during its first month of business. State any assumptions you believe are necessary in reconstructing the transactions.

Multi-Concept Problems

LO 1, 2 Problem 3-5   Identification of Events with Source Documents

Many events are linked to a source document. The following is a list of events that occurred in an entity:

a. Paid a one-year insurance policy.

b. Paid employee payroll.

c. Sold merchandise to a customer on account.

d. Identified supplies in the storeroom destroyed by fire.

e. Received payment of bills from customers.

f. Purchased land for future expansion.

g. Calculated taxes due.

h. Entered into a car lease agreement and paid the tax, title, and license.

Required

For each item **a** through **h,** indicate whether the event should or should not be recorded in the entity's accounts. For each item that should be recorded in the entity's books:

1. Identify one or more source documents that are generated from the event.

2. Identify which source document would be used to record an event when it produces more than one source document.

3. For each document, identify the information that is most useful in recording the event in the accounts.

LO 3, 5 Problem 3-6   Accounts Used to Record Transactions

A list of accounts, with an identifying number for each, is shown below. Following the list of accounts is a series of transactions entered into by a company during its first year of operations.

Required

For each transaction, indicate the account or accounts that should be debited and credited.

1. Cash	**9.** Notes Payable
2. Accounts Receivable	**10.** Capital Stock
3. Office Supplies	**11.** Retained Earnings
4. Buildings	**12.** Service Revenue
5. Automobiles	**13.** Wage and Salary Expense
6. Land	**14.** Selling Expense
7. Accounts Payable	**15.** Utilities Expense
8. Income Tax Payable	**16.** Income Tax Expense

Transactions	Accounts Debited	Credited
Example: Purchased land and building in exchange for a three-year promissory note.	4, 6	9
a. Issued capital stock for cash.	_____	_____
b. Purchased 10 automobiles; paid part in cash and signed a 60-day note for the balance.	_____	_____
c. Purchased land in exchange for a note due in six months.	_____	_____
d. Purchased office supplies; agreed to pay total bill by the 10th of the following month.	_____	_____
e. Billed clients for services performed during the month, and gave them until the 15th of the following month to pay.	_____	_____
f. Received cash on account from clients for services rendered to them in past months.	_____	_____
g. Paid employees salaries and wages earned during the month.	_____	_____
h. Paid newspaper for company ads appearing during the month.	_____	_____
i. Received monthly gas and electric bill from the utility company; payment is due anytime within the first 10 days of the following month.	_____	_____
j. Computed amount of taxes due based on the income of the period; amount will be paid in the following month.	_____	_____

LO 3, 4, 5 **Problem 3-7** Analysis and Journal Entries Recorded Directly in T Accounts

Four brothers organized Beverly Entertainment Enterprises on October 1, 2001. The following transactions occurred during the first month of operations:

October 1: Received contribution of $10,000 from each of the four principal owners of the new business in exchange for shares of stock.

October 2: Purchased the Arcada Theater for $125,000. The seller agreed to accept a down payment of $12,500 and a seven-year promissory note for the balance. The Arcada property consists of land valued at $35,000 and a building valued at $90,000.

October 3: Purchased new seats for the theater at a cost of $5,000, paying $2,500 down and agreeing to pay the remainder in 60 days.

October 12: Purchased candy, popcorn, cups, and napkins for $3,700 on an open account. The company has 30 days to pay for the concession supplies.

October 13: Sold tickets for the opening-night movie for cash of $1,800, and took in $2,400 at the concession stand.

October 17: Rented out the theater to a local community group for $1,500. The community group is to pay one-half of the bill within 5 working days and has 30 days to pay the remainder.

October 23: Received 50% of the amount billed to the community group.

October 24: Sold movie tickets for cash of $2,000, and took in $2,800 at the concession stand.

October 26: The four brothers, acting on behalf of Beverly Entertainment, paid a dividend of $750 on the shares of stock owned by each of them, or $3,000 in total.

October 27: Paid $500 for utilities.

October 30: Paid wages and salaries of $2,400 total to the ushers, the projectionist, concession stand workers, and the maintenance crew.

October 31: Sold movie tickets for cash of $1,800, and took in $2,500 at the concession stand.

Required

1. Prepare a table to summarize the preceding transactions as they affect the accounting equation. Use the format in Exhibit 3-1. Identify each transaction with a date.

2. Record each transaction directly in T accounts, using the dates preceding the transactions to identify them in the accounts. Each account involved in the problem needs a separate T account.

Required

Identify each e
recorded in the
of at least two a

LO 3 Probl
Beachway Ente
an opportunity
preneurs plan to
of operations:

June   1: Rece
              busi

June   1: Purc
              pay f

June   5: Regis

June 10: Purcl
              to pa

June 15: Paid

June 17: Cust

June 24: Billed
              being
              withi

June 29: Recei

June 30: Cust

June 30: Paid

June 30: Paid t

Required

1. Prepare a tab
     Use the form

2. Prepare an in

3. Prepare a clas

LO 3 Probler
Dynamic Service
corporation will
curred during the

March   2: Rec
               char

March   7: Sign
               alon

March 12: Purc

March 19: Bille
               twee
               rema

March 20: Paid

March 22: Rece

March 26: Rece
               tax r

March 29: Purc

March 30: Paid

March 31: Rece

LO 4, 7   Problem 3-8   Trial Balance and Financial Statements
Refer to the table for Beverly Entertainment Enterprises in part **1** of Problem 3-7.

Required

1. Prepare a trial balance at October 31, 2001.

2. Prepare an income statement for the month ended October 31, 2001.

3. Prepare a statement of retained earnings for the month ended October 31, 2001.

4. Prepare a classified balance sheet at October 31, 2001.

LO 3, 5, 6   Problem 3-9   Journal Entries
Atkins Advertising Agency began business on January 2, 2001. Listed below are the transactions
entered into by Atkins during its first month of operations.

a. Acquired its articles of incorporation from the state, and issued 100,000 shares of capital stock
     in exchange for $200,000 in cash.

b. Purchased an office building for $150,000 in cash. The building is valued at $110,000, and the
     remainder of the value is assigned to the land.

c. Signed a three-year promissory note at the bank for $125,000.

d. Purchased office equipment at a cost of $50,000, paying $10,000 down and agreeing to pay
     the remainder in 10 days.

e. Paid wages and salaries of $13,000 for the first half of the month. Office employees are paid
     twice a month.

f. Paid the balance due on the office equipment.

g. Sold $24,000 of advertising during the first month. Customers have until the 15th of the
     following month to pay their bills.

h. Paid wages and salaries of $15,000 for the second half of the month.

i. Recorded $3,500 in commissions earned by the salespeople during the month. They will be
     paid on the fifth of the following month.

Required

Prepare in journal form the entry to record each transaction.

LO 3, 4, 5   Problem 3-10   Journal Entries Recorded Directly in T Accounts
Refer to the transactions for Atkins Advertising Agency in Problem 3-9.

Required

Record each transaction directly in T accounts, using the letters preceding the transactions to identify
them in the accounts. Each account involved in the problem needs a separate T account.

LO 1, 3   Problem 3-11   Transaction Analysis and Financial Statements
Blue Jay Delivery Service is incorporated on January 2, 2001, and enters into the following transactions during its first month of operations:

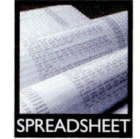
SPREADSHEET

January   2: Filed articles of incorporation with the state, and issued 100,000 shares of capital
                 stock. Cash of $100,000 is received from the new owners for the shares.

January   3   Purchased a warehouse and land for $80,000 in cash. An appraiser values the land at
                 $20,000 and the warehouse at $60,000.

January   4: Signed a three-year promissory note at the Third State Bank in the amount of $50,000.

January   6: Purchased five new delivery trucks for a total of $45,000 in cash.

January 31: Performed services on account that amounted to $15,900 during the month. Cash
                 amounting to $7,490 was received from customers on account during the month.

January 31: Established an open account at a local service station at the beginning of the month.
                 Purchases of gas and oil during January amounted to $3,230. Blue Jay has until the
                 10th of the following month to pay its bill.

Required

1. Prepare a table to summarize the preceding transactions as they affect the accounting equation.
     Ignore depreciation expense and interest expense. Use the format in Exhibit 3-1.

Required

1. Prepare a table to summarize the preceding transactions as they affect the accounting equation. Use the format in Exhibit 3-1. Identify each transaction with the date.

2. Prepare an income statement for the month ended March 31, 2001.

3. Prepare a classified balance sheet at March 31, 2001.

4. From reading the balance sheet you prepared in part **3,** what events would you expect to take place in April? Explain your answer.

LO 3 Problem 3-4A Transactions Reconstructed from Financial Statements

The following financial statements are available for Oak Corporation for its first month of operations:

OAK CORPORATION
INCOME STATEMENT
FOR THE MONTH ENDED JULY 31, 2001

Service revenue		$75,400
Expenses:		
Rent	$ 6,000	
Salaries and wages	24,600	
Utilities	12,700	43,300
Net income		$32,100

OAK CORPORATION
BALANCE SHEET
JULY 31, 2001

Assets		Liabilities and Owners' Equity	
Cash	$ 13,700	Wages payable	$ 6,000
Accounts receivable	25,700	Notes payable	50,000
Equipment	32,000	Unearned service revenue	4,500
Furniture	14,700	Capital stock	30,000
Land	24,000	Retained earnings	19,600
Total	$110,100	Total	$110,100

Required

Describe as many transactions as you can that were entered into by Oak Corporation during the first month of business.

Alternate Multi-Concept Problems

LO 1, 2 Problem 3-5A Identification of Events with Source Documents

Many events are linked to a source document. The following is a list of events that occurred in an entity:

a. Paid a security deposit and six months' rent on a building.

b. Hired three employees and agreed to pay them $400 per week.

c. Sold merchandise to a customer for cash.

d. Reported a fire that destroyed a billboard that is on the entity's property and is owned and maintained by another entity.

e. Received payment of bills from customers.

f. Purchased stock in another entity to gain some control over it.

g. Signed a note at the bank and received cash.

h. Contracted with a cleaning service to maintain the interior of the building in good repair. No money is paid at this time.

Required

For each item **a** through **h,** indicate whether the event should or should not be recorded in the entity's accounts. For each item that should be recorded in the entity's books:

1. Identify one or more source documents that are generated from the event.

2. Identify which source document would be used to record an event when it produces more than one source document.

3. For each document, identify the information that is most useful in recording the event in the accounts.

LO 3, 5 **Problem 3-6A** Accounts Used to Record Transactions

A list of accounts, with an identifying number for each, is shown below. Following the list of accounts is a series of transactions entered into by a company during its first year of operations.

Required

For each transaction, indicate the account or accounts that should be debited and credited.

1. Cash	9. Notes Payable
2. Accounts Receivable	10. Capital Stock
3. Prepaid Insurance	11. Retained Earnings
4. Office Supplies	12. Service Revenue
5. Automobiles	13. Wage and Salary Expense
6. Land	14. Utilities Expense
7. Accounts Payable	15. Income Tax Expense
8. Income Tax Payable	

		Accounts	
Transactions		**Debited**	**Credited**
Example: Purchased office supplies for cash.		4	1
a.	Issued capital stock for cash.	_____	_____
b.	Purchased an automobile and signed a 60-day note for the total amount.	_____	_____
c.	Acquired land in exchange for capital stock.	_____	_____
d.	Received cash from clients for services performed during the month.	_____	_____
e.	Paid employees salaries and wages earned during the month.	_____	_____
f.	Purchased flyers and signs from a printer, payment due in 10 days.	_____	_____
g.	Paid for the flyers and signs purchased in part **f.**	_____	_____
h.	Received monthly telephone bill; payment is due within 10 days of receipt.	_____	_____
i.	Paid for a six-month liability insurance policy.	_____	_____
j.	Paid monthly telephone bill.	_____	_____
k.	Computed amount of taxes due based on the income of the period and paid the amount.	_____	_____

LO 3, 4, 5 **Problem 3-7A** Transaction Analysis and Journal Entries Recorded Directly in T Accounts

Three friends organized Rapid City Roller Rink on October 1, 2001. The following transactions occurred during the first month of operations:

October 1: Received contribution of $22,000 from each of the three principal owners of the new business in exchange for shares of stock.

October 2: Purchased land valued at $15,000 and a building valued at $75,000. The seller agreed to accept a down payment of $9,000 and a five-year promissory note for the balance.

October 3: Purchased new tables and chairs for the lounge at the roller rink at a cost of $25,000, paying $5,000 down and agreeing to pay for the remainder in 60 days.

October 9: Purchased 100 pairs of roller skates for cash at $35 per pair.

October 12: Purchased food and drinks for $2,500 on an open account. The company has 30 days to pay for the concession supplies.

October 13: Sold tickets for cash of $400 and took in $750 at the concession stand.

October 17: Rented out the roller rink to a local community group for $750. The community group is to pay one-half of the bill within 5 working days and has 30 days to pay the remainder.

October 23: Received 50% of the amount billed to the community group.

October 24: Sold tickets for cash of $500, and took in $1,200 at the concession stand.

October 26: The three friends, acting on behalf of Rapid City Roller Rink, paid a dividend of $250 on the shares of stock owned by each of them, or $750 in total.

October 27: Paid $1,275 for utilities.

October 30: Paid wages and salaries of $2,250.

October 31: Sold tickets for cash of $700, and took in $1,300 at the concession stand.

Required

1. Prepare a table to summarize the preceding transactions as they affect the accounting equation. Use the format in Exhibit 3-1. Identify each transaction with a date.

2. Record each transaction directly in T accounts, using the dates preceding the transactions to identify them in the accounts. Each account involved in the problem needs a separate T account.

LO 4, 7 Problem 3-8A Trial Balance and Financial Statements
Refer to the table for Rapid City Roller Rink in part **1** of Problem 3-7A.

Required

1. Prepare a trial balance at October 31, 2001.
2. Prepare an income statement for the month ended October 31, 2001.
3. Prepare a statement of retained earnings for the month ended October 31, 2001.
4. Prepare a classified balance sheet at October 31, 2001.

LO 3, 5, 6 Problem 3-9A Journal Entries
Castle Consulting Agency began business in February 2001. Listed below are the transactions entered into by Castle during its first month of operations.

a. Acquired articles of incorporation from the state, and issued 10,000 shares of capital stock in exchange for $150,000 in cash.

b. Paid monthly rent of $400.

c. Signed a five-year promissory note for $100,000 at the bank.

d. Received $5,000 cash from a customer for services to be performed over the next two months.

e. Purchased software to be used on future jobs. The software costs $950 and is expected to be used on five to eight jobs over the next two years.

f. Billed customers $12,500 for work performed during the month.

g. Paid office personnel $3,000 for the month of February.

h. Received a utility bill of $100. The total amount is due in 30 days.

Required

Prepare in journal form the entry to record each transaction.

LO 3, 4, 5 Problem 3-10A Journal Entries Recorded Directly in T Accounts
Refer to the transactions for Castle Consulting Agency in Problem 3-9A.

Required

Record each transaction directly in T accounts, using the letters preceding the transactions to identify them in the accounts. Each account involved in the problem needs a separate T account.

LO 1, 3 Problem 3-11A Transaction Analysis
Overnight Delivery Inc. is incorporated on January 2, 2001, and enters into the following transactions during its second month of operations:

February 2: Paid $400 for wages earned by employees for the week ending January 31.

February 3: Paid $3,230 for gas and oil billed on an open account in January.

February 4: Declared and paid $2,000 cash dividends to stockholders.

February 15: Received $8,000 cash from customer accounts.

February 26: Provided $16,800 of services on account during the month.

February 27: Received a $3,400 bill from the local service station for gas and oil used during February.

Required

1. Prepare a table to summarize the preceding transactions as they affect the accounting equation. Use the format in Exhibit 3-1.

2. For the transactions on February 2, 3, 4, and 27, indicate whether the amount is an expense of operating in the month of January or February or is not an expense in either month.

LO 1, 3 Problem 3-12A Transaction Analysis and a Balance Sheet

Krittersbegone Inc. was organized on July 1, 2001, by a group of technicians to provide termite inspections and treatment to homeowners and small businesses. The following transactions occurred during the first month of business:

July 2: Received contributions of $3,000 from each of the six owners in exchange for shares of stock.

July 3: Paid $1,000 rent for the month of July.

July 5: Purchased flashlights, tools, spray equipment, and ladders for $18,000, with a down payment of $5,000 and the balance due in 30 days.

July 17: Paid a $200 bill for the distribution of door-to-door advertising.

July 28: Paid August rent and July utilities to the landlord in the amounts of $1,000 and $450, respectively.

July 30: Received $8,000 in cash from homeowners for services performed during the month. In addition, billed $7,500 to other customers for services performed during the month. Billings are due in 30 days.

July 30: Paid commissions of $9,500 to the technicians for July.

July 31: Received $600 from a business client to perform services over the next two months.

Required

1. Prepare a table to summarize the preceding transactions as they affect the accounting equation. Use the format in Exhibit 3-1.

2. Prepare a classified balance sheet dated July 31, 2001. From the balance sheet, what cash inflow and what cash outflow can you predict in the month of August? Who would be interested in the cash flow information and why?

CASES

Reading and Interpreting Financial Statements

LO 3 Case 3-1 Reading and Interpreting Uno's Statement of Cash Flows

Refer to Uno's statement of cash flows for the year ended October 3, 1999.

Required

1. What amount did the company spend on additions to property, plant, equipment, and leasehold improvements during 1999? Determine the effect on the accounting equation from these additions, assuming cash was paid.

2. What amount did the company receive from borrowing on its line of credit during 1999? Determine the effect on the accounting equation from this borrowing.

LO 4 Case 3-2 Reading and Interpreting Gateway's Balance Sheet and Footnotes

Refer to Gateway's balance sheet as of December 31, 1999 and Footnote 9 titled "Selected Balance Sheet Information."

Required

1. Using Exhibit 3-4 from the chapter as an example, prepare the asset section of a chart of accounts for Gateway. Do not go beyond the major categories of assets on your chart.

2. For the Property, plant, and equipment section of your chart of accounts, extend it to the next level to include the various types of these assets.

3. Which type of asset is the most significant among Gateway's property, plant, and equipment? What is the dollar amount of this asset at December 31, 1999? What does this dollar amount represent—that is, what attribute is being measured?

www.delta-air.com

LO 1, 3 Case 3-3 Reading and Interpreting Delta's Balance Sheet

The following item appears in the current liabilities section of Delta Airlines' balance sheet at June 30, 2000.

    Air traffic liability $1,920 million

In addition, one of Delta's footnotes states: "We record sales of passenger tickets and cargo services as air traffic liability on our Consolidated Balance Sheets. Passenger and cargo revenues are recognized and the related air traffic liability is reduced when we provide the transportation. We periodically evaluate the estimated air traffic liability. Any resulting adjustments, which can be significant, are included in the Consolidated Statements of Income in the period that the evaluations are completed."

Required

1. What economic event caused Delta to incur this liability? Was it an external or an internal event?

2. Assume that one customer purchases a $500 ticket in advance. Determine the effect on the accounting equation from this transaction.

3. What economic event will cause Delta to reduce its air traffic liability? Is this an external or an internal event?

Making Financial Decisions

LO 2, 3 Case 3-4 Cash Flow versus Net Income

Shelia Young started a real estate business in December of last year. After approval by the state for a charter to incorporate, she issued 1,000 shares of stock to herself and deposited $20,000 in a bank account under the name Young Properties. Because business was "booming," she spent all her time during the first month selling properties rather than keeping financial records.

At the end of January, Shelia comes to you with the following plight:

I put $20,000 in to start this business last month. My January 31 bank statement shows a balance of $17,000. After all my efforts, it appears as if I'm "in the hole" already! On the other hand, that seems impossible—we sold five properties for clients during the month. The total sales value of these properties was $600,000, and I receive a commission of 5% on each sale. Granted, one of the five sellers still owes me an $8,000 commission on the sale, but the other four have been collected in full. Three of the sales, totaling $400,000, were actually made by my assistants. I pay them 4% of the sales value of a property. Sure, I have a few office expenses for my car, utilities, and a secretary, but that's about it. How can I have possibly lost $3,000 this month?

You agree to help Shelia figure out how she really did this month. The bank statement is helpful. The total deposits during the month amount to $22,000. Shelia explains that this amount represents the commissions on the four sales collected so far. The canceled checks reveal the following expenditures:

Check No.	Payee—Memo at Bottom of Check	Amount
101	Stevens Office Supply	$ 2,000
102	Why Walk, Let's Talk Motor Co.—new car	3,000
103	City of Westbrook—heat and lights	500

Check No.	Payee—Memo at Bottom of Check	Amount
104	Alice Hill—secretary	2,200
105	Ace Property Management—office rent for month	1,200
106	Jerry Hayes (sales assistant)	10,000
107	Joan Harper (sales assistant)	6,000
108	Don's Fillitup—gas and oil for car	100

According to Shelia, the $2,000 check to Stevens Office Supply represents the down payment on a word processor and a copier for the office. The remaining balance is $3,000, and it must be paid to Stevens by February 15. Similarly, the $3,000 check is the down payment on a car for the business. A $12,000 note was given to the car dealer and is due along with interest in one year.

1. Prepare an income statement for the month of January for Young Properties.

2. Prepare a statement of cash flows for the month of January for Young Properties.

3. Draft a memorandum to Shelia Young explaining as simply and as clearly as possible why she *did* in fact have a profitable first month in business but experienced a decrease in her cash account. Support your explanation with any necessary figures.

4. The down payments on the car and the office equipment are reflected on the statement of cash flows. They are assets that will benefit the business for a number of years. Do you think that *any* of the cost associated with the acquisition of these assets should be recognized in some way on the income statement? Explain your answer.

LO 3, 7 Case 3-5 Loan Request

Simon Fraser started a landscaping and lawn-care business in April 2001 by investing $20,000 cash in the business in exchange for capital stock. Because his business is in the Midwest, the season begins in April and concludes in September. He prepared the following trial balance (with accounts in alphabetical order) at the end of the first season in business.

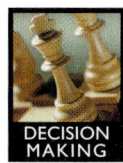
DECISION MAKING

FRASER LANDSCAPING
TRIAL BALANCE
SEPTEMBER 30, 2001

	Debits	Credits
Accounts Payable		$13,000
Accounts Receivable	$23,000	
Capital Stock		20,000
Cash	1,200	
Gas and Oil Expense	15,700	
Insurance Expense	2,500	
Landscaping Revenue		33,400
Lawn Care Revenue		24,000
Mowing Equipment	5,000	
Rent Expense	6,000	
Salaries Expense	22,000	
Truck	15,000	
Totals	$90,400	$90,400

Simon is pleased with his first year in business. "I paid myself a salary of $22,000 during the year and still have $1,200 in the bank. Sure, I have a few bills outstanding, but my accounts receivable will more than cover those." In fact, Simon is so happy with the first year that he has come to you in your role as a lending officer at the local bank to ask for a $20,000 loan to allow him to add another truck and mowing equipment for the second season.

Required

1. From your reading of the trial balance, what does it appear to you that Simon did with the $20,000 in cash he originally contributed to the business? Determine the effect on the accounting equation from the transaction you think took place.

2. Prepare an income statement for the six months ended September 30, 2001.

3. The mowing equipment and truck are assets that will benefit the business for a number of years. Do you think that any of the costs associated with the purchase of these assets should have been recognized as expenses in the first year? How would this have affected the income statement?

4. Prepare a classified balance sheet as of September 30, 2001. As a banker, what two items on the balance sheet concern you the most? Explain your answer.

5. As a banker, would you loan Simon $20,000 to expand his business during the second year? Draft a memo to respond to Simon's request for the loan, indicating whether you will make the loan.

Accounting and Ethics: What Would You Do?

LO 3, 5, 6 **Case 3-6** Delay in the Posting of a Journal Entry

As assistant controller for a small consulting firm, you are responsible for recording and posting the daily cash receipts and disbursements to the ledger accounts. After you have posted the entries, your boss, the controller, prepares a trial balance and the financial statements. You make the following entries on June 30, 2001:

2001			
June 30	Cash	1,430	
	Accounts Receivable	1,950	
	Service Revenue		3,380
	To record daily cash receipts.		
June 30	Advertising Expense	12,500	
	Utilities Expense	22,600	
	Rent Expense	24,000	
	Salary and Wage Expense	17,400	
	Cash		76,500
	To record daily cash disbursements.		

The daily cash disbursements are much larger on June 30 than any other day because many of the company's major bills are paid on the last day of the month. After you have recorded these two transactions and *before* you have posted them to the ledger accounts, your boss comes to you with the following request:

> As you are aware, the first half of the year has been a tough one for the consulting industry and for our business in particular. With first-half bonuses based on net income, I am concerned whether you or I will get any bonus this time around. However, I have a suggestion that should allow us to receive something for our hard work and at the same time will not hurt anyone. Go ahead and post the June 30 cash receipts to the ledger but don't bother to post that day's cash disbursements. Even though the treasurer writes the checks on the last day of the month and you normally journalize the transaction on the same day, it is pretty silly to bother posting the entry to the ledger, since it takes at least a week for the checks to clear the bank.

Required

1. Explain *why* the controller's request will result in an increase in net income.

2. Do you agree with the controller that the omission of the entry on June 30 "will not hurt anyone"? If not, be explicit as to why you don't agree. Whom could it hurt?

3. What would you do? Whom should you talk to about this issue?

LO 5, 6 **Case 3-7** Revenue Recognition

You are controller for an architectural firm whose accounting year ends on December 31. As part of the management team, you receive a year-end bonus directly related to the firm's earnings for the year. One of your duties is to review the journal entries recorded by the bookkeepers. A new bookkeeper prepared the following journal entry:

Dec. 3	Cash	10,000	
	Service revenue		10,000
	To record deposit from client.		

You notice that the explanation for the journal entry refers to the amount as a deposit, and the bookkeeper explains to you that the firm plans to provide the services to the client in March of the following year.

1. Did the bookkeeper prepare the correct journal entry to account for the client's deposit? Explain your answer.

2. What would you do as controller for the firm? Do you have a responsibility to do anything to correct the books?

INTERNET RESEARCH CASE

Case 3-8 K2 Inc.

Although K2 Inc. does not currently post its financial statements or annual report on its Web site, you can research the company in a number of ways to answer the following questions. Use the URLs in the margin to learn more about the company, and go to K2's home page to get product, company history, and related information.

finance.yahoo.com
www.hoovers.com
www.k2sports.com

1. Investigate K2 Inc. as though you were interested in the company as a whole—its lines of products, its divisions, its means of distribution.

   a. How are K2 products distributed?
   b. How many lines of products does K2 have?
   c. See K2's history page. What aspects of its recent history are emphasized there? What does that tell you about the financial focus of the company?

2. Investigate K2 Inc. from its available financial information.

   a. What is K2's stock symbol and where is it traded?
   b. How has K2's acquisition of Ride, Inc. impacted its profit?
   c. Consider the diversity of its products as well as its measures to cut costs. Have these been successful in increasing profit?

SOLUTION TO KEY TERMS QUIZ

3	Event (p. 94)		8	Debit (p. 103)
10	External event (p. 94)		4	Credit (p. 103)
5	Internal event (p. 94)		16	Double-entry system (p. 106)
14	Transaction (p. 94)		13	Journal (p. 109)
6	Source document (p. 94)		9	Posting (p. 109)
11	Account (p. 101)		7	Journalizing (p. 109)
1	Chart of accounts (p. 101)		15	General journal (p. 109)
12	General ledger (p. 103)		2	Trial Balance (p. 111)

INCOME MEASUREMENT AND ACCRUAL ACCOUNTING

Study Links

A Look at Previous Chapters

We focused our attention in Chapter 3 on how accounting information is processed. Debits and credits, journal entries, accounts, and trial balances were introduced as convenient tools to aid in the preparation of periodic financial statements.

A Look at This Chapter

We begin this chapter by considering the roles of recognition and measurement in the process of preparing financial statements. We explore in detail the accrual basis of accounting and its effect on the measurement of income. The recognition of revenues and expenses in an accrual system is examined, and we look at the role of adjustments in this process.

A Look at Upcoming Chapters

Chapter 4 completes our overview of the accounting model. In the next section, we will examine accounting for the various types of assets. We begin by looking at accounting by merchandise companies in Chapter 5.

FOCUS ON FINANCIAL RESULTS

McDonald's operates nearly 28,000 quick-service restaurants in 119 countries and has more than two-thirds of globally branded quick-service restaurant sales. Its remarkable performance continues a pattern of growth that Chairman and CEO Jack M. Greenberg refers to as McDonald's "unique heritage—a history of success and innovation."

The consolidated statement of income excerpted here shows that tradition of growth continuing. Total revenues increased in each of the three years shown. Two kinds of revenue are reported—sales by company-operated restaurants and revenues from franchised and affiliated restaurants, whose operators pay McDonald's a fee plus a share of their income for the right to operate as part of the chain. Thus, only a portion of the franchisees' revenue appears in the second line of the income statement, while all the revenue of the company-operated restaurants appears in the first line.

How will revenue growth be sustained? McDonald's 1999 annual report provides some clues. In that year, McDonald's acquired Aroma Café, a small chain of British coffeehouses, and Donatos Pizza, a U.S. chain. The firm also gained a majority ownership in Chipotle Mexican Grill, a chain of shops specializing in gourmet burritos and tacos, and concluded an agreement to purchase the family-style restaurants of Boston Market. In 2001, McDonald's also announced a New Tastes Menu that added a number of pork dishes to its other offerings. These events are all part of the company's worldwide strategy of achieving "enduring profitable growth by expanding the brand and leveraging the strengths of the McDonald's System through innovation and technology."

Consolidated statement of income

(In millions, except per share data)	Years ended December 31,	1999	1998	1997
Revenues	Sales by Company-operated restaurants	$ 9,512.5	$ 8,894.9	$ 8,136.5
	Revenues from franchised and affiliated restaurants	3,746.8	3,526.5	3,272.3
	Total revenues	13,259.3	12,421.4	11,408.8
Operating costs and expenses	Food and packaging	3,204.6	2,997.4	2,772.6
	Payroll and employee benefits	2,418.3	2,220.3	2,025.1
	Occupancy and other operating expenses	2,206.7	2,043.9	1,851.9
	Total Company-operated restaurant expenses	7,829.6	7,261.6	6,649.6
	Franchised restaurants–occupancy expenses	737.7	678.0	613.9
	Selling, general and administrative expenses	1,477.6	1,458.5	1,450.5
	Other operating (income) expense	(124.1)	(60.2)	(113.5)
	Made For You costs	18.9	161.6	
	Special charge		160.0	
	Total operating costs and expenses	9,939.7	9,659.5	8,600.5
	Operating income	3,319.6	2,761.9	2,808.3
	Interest expense–net of capitalized interest of $14.3, $17.9 and $22.7	396.3	413.8	364.4
	Nonoperating (income) expense	39.2	40.7	36.6
	Income before provision for income taxes	2,884.1	2,307.4	2,407.3
	Provision for income taxes	936.2	757.3	764.8
	Net income	$ 1,947.9	$ 1,550.1	$ 1,642.5
	Net income per common share	$ 1.44	$ 1.14	$ 1.17
	Net income per common share–diluted	1.39	1.10	1.15
	Dividends per common share	$ .20	$ .18	$ .16
	Weighted-average shares	1,355.3	1,365.3	1,378.7
	Weighted-average shares–diluted	1,404.2	1,405.7	1,410.2

> Maintaining growth in revenues will require global strategies.

McDonald's 1999 Annual Report

How long can McDonald's continue to surpass its past performance, and how will its two types of revenue affect profits? Will it matter that 85 percent of its restaurants are franchises? As you study this chapter, you'll understand the effect of the timing of revenues and expenses and their impact on reported profits.

www.mcdonalds.com

After studying this chapter, you should be able to:

LO 1 Explain the significance of recognition and measurement in the preparation and use of financial statements. (p. 140)

LO 2 Explain the differences between the cash and accrual bases of accounting. (p. 142)

LO 3 Describe the revenue recognition principle and explain its application in various situations. (p. 146)

LO 4 Describe the matching principle and the various methods for recognizing expenses. (p. 146)

LO 5 Identify the four major types of adjustments and determine their effect on the accounting equation. (p. 148)

LO 6 Explain the steps in the accounting cycle and the significance of each step. (p. 160)

RECOGNITION AND MEASUREMENT IN FINANCIAL STATEMENTS

LO 1 Explain the significance of recognition and measurement in the preparation and use of financial statements.

Accounting is a communication process. To successfully communicate information to the users of financial statements, accountants and managers must answer two questions:

1. What economic events should be communicated, or *recognized,* in the statements?

2. How should the effects of these events be *measured* in the statements?

The dual concepts of recognition and measurement are crucial to the success of accounting as a form of communication.

RECOGNITION

"**Recognition** is the process of formally recording or incorporating an item into the financial statements of an entity as an asset, liability, revenue, expense, or the like. Recognition includes depiction of an item in both words and numbers, with the amount included in the totals of the financial statements."[1] We see in this definition the central idea behind general-purpose financial statements. They are a form of communication between the entity and external users. Stockholders, bankers, and other creditors have limited access to relevant information about a company. They depend on the periodic financial statements issued by management to provide the necessary information to make their decisions. Acting on behalf of management, accountants have a moral and ethical responsibility to provide users with financial information that will be useful in making their decisions. The process by which the accountant depicts, or describes, the effects of economic events on the entity is called *recognition*.

The items, such as assets, liabilities, revenues, and expenses, depicted in financial statements are *representations.* Simply stated, the accountant cannot show a stockholder or other user the company's assets, such as cash and buildings. What the user sees in a set of financial statements is a depiction of the real thing. That is, the accountant describes, with words and numbers, the various items in a set of financial statements. The system is imperfect at best and, for that reason, is always in the process of change. As society and the business environment have become more complex, the accounting profession has striven for ways to improve financial statements as a means of communicating with statement users.

MEASUREMENT

Accountants depict a financial statement item in both words and *numbers.* The accountant must *quantify* the effects of economic events on the entity. It is not enough to decide

---

[1]*Statement of Financial Accounting Concepts No. 5,* "Recognition and Measurement in Financial Statements of Business Enterprises" (Stamford, Conn.: Financial Accounting Standards Board, December 1984), par. 6.

that an event is important and, thus, warrants recognition in the financial statements. To be able to recognize it, the statement preparer must measure the financial effects of the event on the company.

Measurement of an item in financial statements requires that two choices be made. First, the accountant must decide on the *attribute* to be measured. Second, a scale of measurement, or *unit of measure,* must be chosen.

The Attribute to Be Measured

Assume that a company holds a parcel of real estate as an investment. What attribute—that is, *characteristic*—of the property should be used to measure and, thus, recognize it as an asset on the balance sheet? The cost of the asset at the time it is acquired is the most logical choice. *Cost* is the amount of cash, or its equivalent, paid to acquire the asset. But how do we report the property on a balance sheet a year from now?

- The simplest approach is to show the property on the balance sheet at its original cost, thus the designation **historical cost.** The use of historical cost is not only simple but also *verifiable.* Assume that two accountants are asked to independently measure the cost of the asset. After examining the sales contract for the land, they should arrive at the same amount.

- An alternative to historical cost as the attribute to be measured is **current value.** Current value is the amount of cash, or its equivalent, that could be received currently from the sale of the asset. For the company's piece of property, current value is the *estimated* selling price of the land, reduced by any commissions or other fees involved in making the sale. But the amount is only an estimate, not an actual amount. If the company has not yet sold the property, how can we know for certain its selling price? We have to compare it to similar properties that *have* sold recently.

The choice between current value and historical cost as the attribute to be measured is a good example of the trade-off between *relevance* and *reliability.* As indicated earlier, historical cost is verifiable and is, thus, to a large extent a reliable measure. But is it as relevant to the needs of the decision makers as current value? Put yourself in the position of a banker trying to decide whether to lend money to the company. In evaluating the company's assets as collateral for the loan, is it more relevant to your decision to know what the firm paid for a piece of land 20 years ago or what it could be sold for today? But what *could* the property be sold for today? Two accountants might not necessarily arrive at the same current value for the land. Whereas value or selling price may be more relevant to your decision on the loan, the reliability of this amount is often questionable.

Because of its objective nature, historical cost is the attribute used to measure many of the assets recognized on the balance sheet. However, certain other attributes, such as current value, have increased in popularity in recent years. In other chapters of the book, we will discuss some of the alternatives to historical cost.

The Unit of Measure

Regardless of the attribute of an item to be measured, it is still necessary to choose a yardstick or unit of measure. The yardstick we currently use is units of money. *Money* is something accepted as a medium of exchange or as a means of payment. The unit of money in the United States is the dollar. In Japan, the medium of exchange is the yen, and in Great Britain, it is the pound.

The use of the dollar as a unit of measure for financial transactions is widely accepted. The *stability* of the dollar as a yardstick is subject to considerable debate, however. Consider an example. You are thinking about buying a certain parcel of land. As part of your decision process, you measure the dimensions of the property and determine that the lot is 80 feet wide and 120 feet deep. Thus, the unit of measure used to determine the lot's size is the square foot. The company that owns the land offers to sell it for $10,000. Although the offer sounds attractive, you decide against the purchase today.

You return in one year to take a second look at the lot. You measure the lot again and, not surprisingly, find the width to still be 80 feet and the depth 120 feet. The owner is still willing to sell the lot for $10,000. This may appear to be the same price as last year. But the *purchasing power* of the unit of measure, the dollar, may very possibly have changed since last year. Even though the foot is a stable measuring unit, the dollar often is not. A *decline*

EXHIBIT 4-1 Recognition and Measurement in Financial Statements

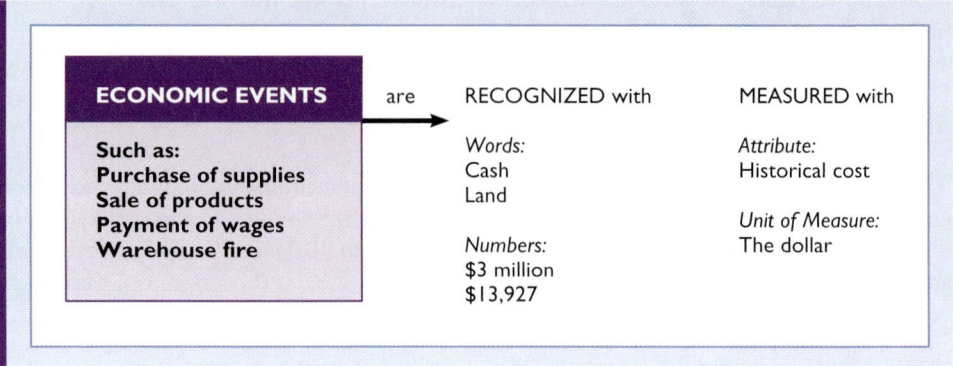

What events have economic consequences to a business? The destructive effects of a warehouse fire, for example, will result in losses to buildings and other business assets. These losses will surely be reflected in the next year's financial statements of the affected companies—possibly in the income statement, as a downturn in revenues due to lost sales. What other financial statements would be affected by a big fire?

in the purchasing power of the dollar is evidenced by a continuing *rise* in the general level of prices in an economy. For example, rather than paying $10,000 last year to buy the lot, you could have spent the $10,000 on other goods or services. However, a year later, the same $10,000 may very well not buy the same amount of goods and services.

Inflation, or a rise in the general level of prices in the economy, results in a decrease in purchasing power. In the past, the accounting profession has experimented with financial statements adjusted for the changing value of the dollar. As inflation has declined in recent years in the United States, the debate over the use of the dollar as a stable measuring unit has somewhat subsided.[2] It is still important to recognize the inherent weakness in the use of a measuring unit that is subject to change, however.

SUMMARY OF RECOGNITION AND MEASUREMENT IN FINANCIAL STATEMENTS

The purpose of financial statements is to communicate various types of economic information about a company. The job of the accountant is to decide which information should be recognized in the financial statements and how the effects of that information on the entity should be measured. Exhibit 4-1 summarizes the role of recognition and measurement in the preparation of financial statements.

Ansammlung

THE ACCRUAL BASIS OF ACCOUNTING

LO 2 Explain the differences between the cash and accrual bases of accounting.

The accrual basis of accounting is the foundation for the measurement of income in our modern system of accounting. The best way to understand the accrual basis is to compare it with the simpler cash approach.

COMPARING THE CASH AND ACCRUAL BASES OF ACCOUNTING

The cash and accrual bases of accounting differ with respect to the *timing* of the recognition of revenues and expenses. For example, assume that on July 24, Barbara White, a salesperson for Spiffy House Painters, contracts with a homeowner to repaint a house for $1,000. A large crew comes in and paints the house the next day, July 25. The customer

---

[2]The rate of inflation in some countries, most noticeably those in South America, has far exceeded the rate in the United States. Companies operating in some of these countries with hyperinflationary economies are required to make adjustments to their statements.

has 30 days from the day of completion of the job to pay and does, in fact, pay Spiffy on August 25. *When* should Spiffy recognize the $1,000 as revenue? As soon as the contract is signed on July 24? Or on July 25, when the work is done? Or on August 25, when the customer pays the bill?

In an income statement prepared on the **cash basis,** revenues are recognized when cash is *received.* Thus, on a cash basis, the $1,000 would not be recognized as revenue until the cash is collected, on August 25. On an **accrual basis,** revenue is recognized when it is *earned.* On this basis, the $1,000 would be recognized as revenue on July 25, when the house is painted. This is the point at which the revenue is earned.

Although cash has not yet been received on July 25, another asset, Accounts Receivable, is recognized. This asset represents the right to receive cash in the future. The effect on Spiffy's accounting equation when revenue is recognized before cash is received is as follows:

		BALANCE SHEET				INCOME STATEMENT	
ASSETS	**=**	**LIABILITIES**	**+**	**OWNERS' EQUITY**	**+**	**REVENUES – EXPENSES**	
Accounts Receivable 1,000						Service Revenue	1,000

At the time cash is collected, accounts receivable is reduced and cash is increased. The effect on the accounting equation from this event is this:

		BALANCE SHEET				INCOME STATEMENT	
ASSETS	**=**	**LIABILITIES**	**+**	**OWNERS' EQUITY**	**+**	**REVENUES – EXPENSES**	
Cash 1,000							
Accounts Receivable (1,000)							

Assume that Barbara White is paid a 10% commission for all contracts and is paid on the 15th of the month following the month a house is painted. Thus, for this job, she will receive a $100 commission check on August 15. When should Spiffy recognize her commission of $100 as an expense? On July 24, when White gets the homeowner to sign a contract? When the work is completed, on July 25? Or on August 15, when she receives the commission check? Again, on a cash basis, commission expense would be recognized on August 15, when cash is *paid* to the salesperson. But on an accrual basis, expenses are recognized when they are *incurred.* In our example, the commission expense is incurred when the house is painted, on July 25.

Exhibit 4-2 summarizes the essential differences between recognition of revenues and expenses on a cash basis and recognition on an accrual basis.

EXHIBIT 4-2 Comparing the Cash and Accrual Bases of Accounting

	Cash Basis	Accrual Basis
Revenue is recognized	**When Received**	**When Earned**
Expense is recognized	**When Paid**	**When Incurred**

BUSINESS STRATEGY

McDonald's has experienced a long run of rapid and continuous growth, both at home and abroad. In 1999 the company added 1,790 McDonald's restaurants to its chain, of which more than 90 percent were outside the United States. At most of the locations in the 118 foreign countries in which McDonald's operates, a combination of locally tailored menus and the attraction of U.S. culture has made the restaurants an immediate hit, and it is not unusual for thousands of eager customers to line up outside new stores in Belarus and Kuwait.

But the novelty that keeps customers excited about eating at McDonald's is a little harder to come by at home, where hamburgers and fries are overly familiar and easy to find at competitors' restaurants—or even in the family backyard. How does McDonald's plan to keep its U.S. customers loyal?

One strategy that has served the company very well is its ability to partner with other firms like Disney and Ty (maker of Beanie Babies) to bring popular children's toys into the mix through promotional giveaways included in the chain's trademark Happy Meals. But what brings people to a restaurant day after day is, above all, the food. So, McDonald's installed a new "Made for You" food preparation system in more than 13,000 of its kitchens in the United States and Canada to help support its new product roster, known as the New Tastes Menu, which rolled out in the United States in 2001.

New Tastes expands McDonald's menu and introduces the idea of rotating items. Local managers can select up to four items from 40 products that aren't part of the regular menu nationwide. The selections, which can include Sausage Breakfast Burrito, BBQ Bacon Crispy Chicken sandwich, Crispy Chicken McClub, and Bacon Egg and Cheese Bagel, can be changed every few weeks and are based on regional preferences. Todd Duvick, a Bank of America food industry analyst, said the main strategy behind the New Tastes Menu was a hedge against expected shifts in consumer habits in the event the U.S. economy continued to slow.

SOURCES: Bob Burgdorfer, "McDonald's New Menu Seen Eyeing Economy," Reuters Limited, January 18, 2001, accessed at http://news.excite.com/news/r/010118/17/business-food-mcdonalds-dc; "McDonald's to Launch Rotating Menu," AP, January 17, 2001, accessed at http://news.excite.com/news/ap/010117/18/mcdonalds-menu; Kate MacArthur, "McDonald's Announces New Menu Launch," *Advertising Age*, January 17. 2001, accessed at http://adage.com/news_and_features/features/20010117/article1.html.

WHAT THE INCOME STATEMENT AND THE STATEMENT OF CASH FLOWS REVEAL

Most business entities, other than the very smallest, use the accrual basis of accounting. Thus, the income statement reflects the accrual basis. Revenues are recognized when they are earned and expenses when they are incurred. At the same time, however, stockholders and creditors are also interested in information concerning the cash flows of an entity. The purpose of a statement of cash flows is to provide this information. Keep in mind that even though we present a statement of cash flows in a complete set of financial statements, the accrual basis is used for recording transactions and for preparing a balance sheet and an income statement.

Recall the example of Glengarry Health Club in Chapter 3. The club earned revenue from two sources, memberships and court fees. Both of these forms of revenue were recognized on the income statement presented in that chapter and are reproduced in the top portion of Exhibit 4-3. Recall, however, that members have 30 days to pay and that, at the end of the first month of operation, only $4,000 of the membership fees of $15,000 had been collected.

Now consider the statement of cash flows for the first month of operation, partially reproduced in the bottom portion of Exhibit 4-3. Because we want to compare the income statement to the statement of cash flows, only the Operating Activities section of the state-

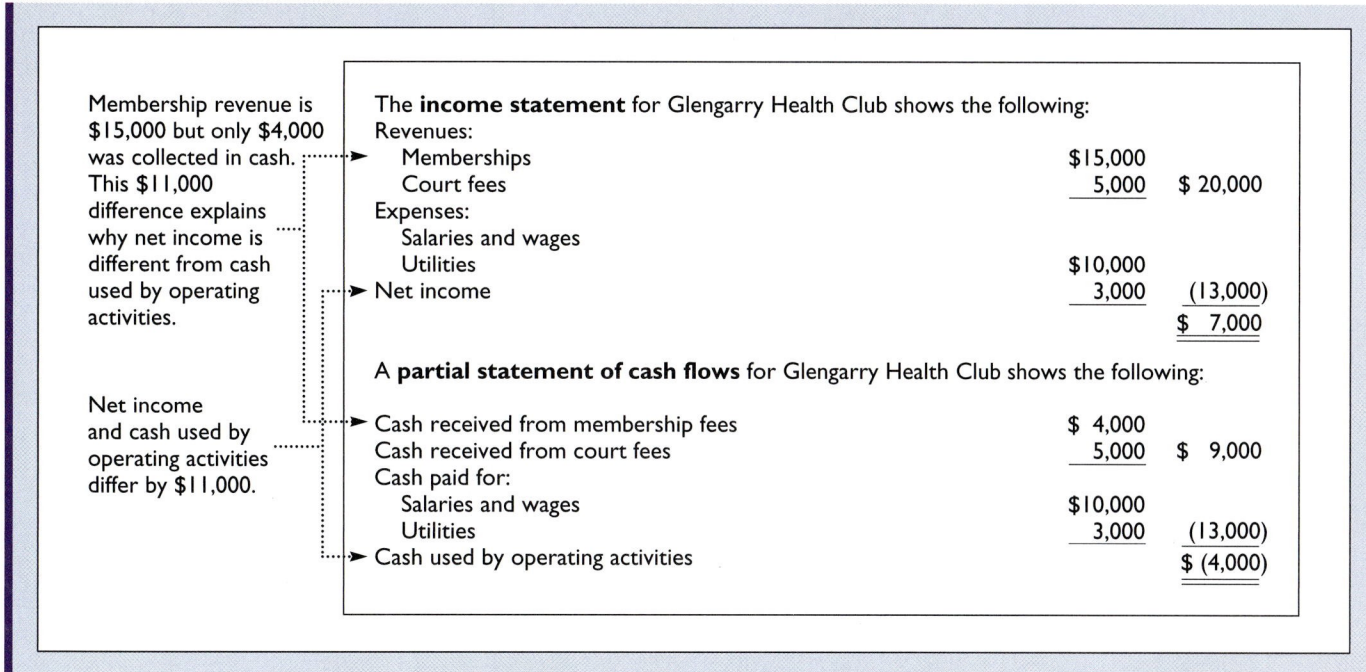

Membership revenue is $15,000 but only $4,000 was collected in cash. This $11,000 difference explains why net income is different from cash used by operating activities.	**The income statement** for Glengarry Health Club shows the following:	
	Revenues:	
	Memberships	$15,000
	Court fees	5,000 $ 20,000
	Expenses:	
	Salaries and wages	
	Utilities	$10,000
	Net income	3,000 (13,000)
		$ 7,000
Net income and cash used by operating activities differ by $11,000.	A **partial statement of cash flows** for Glengarry Health Club shows the following:	
	Cash received from membership fees	$ 4,000
	Cash received from court fees	5,000 $ 9,000
	Cash paid for:	
	Salaries and wages	$10,000
	Utilities	3,000 (13,000)
	Cash used by operating activities	$ (4,000)

ment is shown. (The Investing and Financing Activities sections have been omitted from the statement.) Why is net income for the month a *positive* $7,000 but cash from operating activities a *negative* $4,000? Of the membership revenue of $15,000 reflected on the income statement, only $4,000 was collected in cash. Glengarry has accounts receivable for the other $11,000. Thus, cash from operating activities, as reflected on a statement of cash flows, is $11,000 *less* than net income of $7,000, or a negative $4,000.

Each of these two financial statements serves a useful purpose. The income statement reflects the revenues actually earned by the business, regardless of whether cash has been collected. The statement of cash flows tells the reader about the actual cash inflows during a period of time. The need for the information provided by both statements is summarized by the Financial Accounting Standards Board as follows:

> Statements of cash flows commonly show a great deal about an entity's current cash receipts and payments, but a cash flow statement provides an incomplete basis for assessing prospects for future cash flows because it cannot show interperiod relationships. Many current cash receipts, especially from operations, stem from activities of earlier periods, and many current cash payments are intended or expected to result in future, not current, cash receipts. Statements of earnings and comprehensive income, especially if used in conjunction with statements of financial position, usually provide a better basis for assessing future cash flow prospects of an entity than do cash flow statements alone.[3]

ACCRUAL ACCOUNTING AND TIME PERIODS

The *time period* assumption was introduced in Chapter 1. We assume that it is possible to prepare an income statement that fairly reflects the earnings of a business for a specific period of time, such as a month or a year. It is somewhat artificial to divide the operations of a business into periods of time as indicated on a calendar. The conflict arises because earning income is a *process* that takes place *over a period of time* rather than *at any one point in time*.

Consider an alternative to our present system of reporting on the operations of a business on a periodic basis. A new business begins operations with an investment of $50,000. The business operates for 10 years, during which time no records are kept other than a

---

[3]*SFAC No. 5,* par. 24c.

checkbook for the cash on deposit at the bank. At the end of the 10 years, the owners decide to go their separate ways and convert all their assets to cash. They split among them the balance of $80,000 in the bank account. What is the profit of the business for the 10-year period? The answer is $30,000, the difference between the original cash of $50,000 contributed and the cash of $80,000 available at liquidation.

The point of this simple example is that we could be very precise and accurate in our measurement of the income of a business if it were not necessary to artificially divide operations according to a calendar. Stockholders, bankers, and other interested parties cannot wait until a business liquidates to make decisions, however. They need information on a periodic basis. Thus, the justification for the accrual basis of accounting lies in the needs of financial statement users for periodic information on the financial position as well as the profitability of the entity.

THE REVENUE RECOGNITION PRINCIPLE

LO 3 Describe the revenue recognition principle and explain its application in various situations.

"**Revenues** are inflows or other enhancements of assets of an entity or settlements of its liabilities (or a combination of both) from delivering or producing goods, rendering services, or other activities that constitute the entity's ongoing major or central operations."[4] Two points should be noted about this formal definition of revenues. First, an asset is not always involved when revenue is recognized. The recognition of revenue may result from the settlement of a liability rather than from the acquisition of an asset. Second, entities generate revenue in different ways: some companies produce goods, others distribute or deliver the goods to users, and still others provide some type of service.

On the accrual basis, revenues are recognized when earned. However, the **revenue recognition principle** involves two factors. Revenues are recognized in the income statement when they are both *realized* and *earned*. Revenues are *realized* when goods or services are exchanged for cash or claims to cash. As a practical rule, revenue is usually recognized at the time of sale. This is normally interpreted to mean at the time of delivery of the product or service to the customer. However, the nature of some businesses requires considerable judgment by the accountant to determine when revenue should be recognized. For example, when should McDonald's recognize revenue from the various fees it charges its franchisees? Some of the fees are recognized as McDonald's assists a new franchisee in selecting a site and hiring employees; other fees are recognized as the franchisee makes its sales and remits a percentage of these sales to the company.

From Concept

TO PRACTICE 4.1

READING MCDONALD'S INCOME STATEMENT Refer to McDonald's comparative income statements for 1999, 1998, and 1997 in the chapter opener. What percentage of total revenues was derived from franchised restaurants? Has this percentage changed over the three-year period?

EXPENSE RECOGNITION AND THE MATCHING PRINCIPLE

LO 4 Describe the matching principle and the various methods for recognizing expenses.

Companies incur a variety of costs. A new office building is constructed. Inventory is purchased. Employees perform services. The electric meter is read. In each of these situations, the company incurs a cost, regardless of when it pays cash. Conceptually, *any time a cost is incurred, an asset is acquired.* However, according to the definition in Chapter 1, an asset represents a future economic benefit. An asset ceases being an asset and becomes an expense when the economic benefits from having incurred the cost have expired. Assets are unexpired costs, and expenses are expired costs.

At what point do costs expire and become expenses? The expense recognition principle requires that we recognize expenses in different ways, depending on the nature of the cost. The ideal approach to recognizing expenses is to match them with revenues. Under the **matching principle,** the accountant attempts to associate revenues of a period with the costs necessary to generate those revenues. For certain types of expenses, a direct form of matching is possible; for others, it is necessary to associate costs with a particular period. The classic example of direct matching is cost of goods sold expense with sales revenue. Cost of goods sold is the cost of the inventory associated with a particular sale. A cost is incurred and an asset is recorded when the inventory is purchased. The asset, inventory, becomes an expense when it is sold. Another example of a cost that can be matched directly with revenue is commissions. The commission paid to a salesperson can be matched directly with the sale.

---

[4]*Statement of Financial Accounting Concepts No. 6,* "Elements of Financial Statements" (Stamford, Conn.: Financial Accounting Standards Board, December 1985), par. 78.

An indirect form of matching is used to recognize the benefits associated with certain types of costs, most noticeably long-term assets, such as buildings and equipment. These costs benefit many periods, but usually it is not possible to match them directly with a specific sale of a product. Instead, they are matched with the periods during which they will provide benefits. For example, an office building may be useful to a company for 30 years. *Depreciation* is the process of allocating the cost of a tangible long-term asset to its useful life. Depreciation Expense is the account used to recognize this type of expense.

The benefits associated with the incurrence of certain other costs are treated in accounting as expiring simultaneously with their acquisition. The justification for this treatment is that no future benefits from the incurrence of the cost are discernible. This is true of most selling and administrative costs. For example, the costs of heat and light in a building benefit only the current period and therefore are recognized as expenses as soon as the costs are incurred. Likewise, income taxes incurred during the period do not benefit any period other than the current period and are thus written off as an expense in the period incurred.

The relationships among costs, assets, and expenses are depicted in Exhibit 4-4 using three examples. First, costs incurred for purchases of merchandise result in an asset, Merchandise Inventory, and are eventually matched with revenue at the time the product is sold. Second, costs incurred for office space result in an asset, Office Building, which is recognized as Depreciation Expense over the useful life of the building. Third, the cost of heating and lighting benefits only the current period and is thus recognized immediately as Utilities Expense.

According to the FASB, **expenses** are "outflows or other using up of assets or incurrences of liabilities (or a combination of both) from delivering or producing goods, rendering services, or carrying out other activities that constitute the entity's ongoing major or central operations."[5] The key point to note about expenses is that they come about in two different ways: from the use of an asset or from the recognition of a liability. For example, when a retailer sells a product, the asset sacrificed is Inventory. Cost of Goods Sold is the expense account that is increased, and the Inventory account is decreased. As we will see in the next section, the incurrence of an expense may also result in a liability.

---

[5]*SFAC No. 6*, par. 80.

EXHIBIT 4-4   Relationships among Costs, Assets, and Expenses

Various types of **costs** are incurred:
Purchases of merchandise
Office space
Heating and lighting

Unexpired costs are called **assets:**
(reported on the balance sheet)
Merchandise Inventory
Office Building

Expired costs are called **expenses:**
(reported on the income statement)
Cost of Goods Sold Expense
Depreciation Expense
Utilities Expense

Two-Minute Review

1. Explain the difference between the attribute to be measured and the unit of measure.

2. Explain when revenues are normally recognized.

3. Explain the different ways in which expenses are matched with revenues.

Answers:

1. Accountants must decide whether to use historical cost or another attribute or characteristic of an asset, such as its current value, to measure it. Regardless of the attribute measured, it is necessary to choose a yardstick, or unit of measure. In this country, accountants use the dollar to measure assets and other financial statement items.

2. Revenues are normally recognized in the income statement when they are both realized and earned. Revenues are realized when goods or services are exchanged for cash or claims to cash.

3. For certain costs, such as cost of goods sold, it is possible to directly match the expense with revenue generated. For other costs, such as depreciation, an indirect form of matching is necessary in which expenses are allocated to the periods benefited, rather than matched with specific revenues. Finally, the benefits associated with the incurrence of certain costs, such as utilities, expire immediately and therefore expense is recognized as soon as the cost is incurred.

ACCRUAL ACCOUNTING AND ADJUSTMENTS

LO 5 Identify the four major types of adjustments and determine their effect on the accounting equation.

The accrual basis of accounting necessitates a number of adjustments at the end of a period. **Adjusting entries** are the journal entries the accountant makes at the end of a period for a company on the accrual basis of accounting. *Adjusting entries are not needed if a cash basis is used. It is the very nature of the accrual basis that results in the need for adjusting entries.* The frequency of the adjustment process depends on how often financial statements are prepared. Most businesses make adjustments at the end of each month. Recall from Chapter 3 that the emphasis throughout this book is on the *use* of financial statements rather than their preparation. Thus, rather than focus on the adjusting *entries* that the accountant makes, we will concern ourselves with the effect of these adjustments on the accounting equation.

TYPES OF ADJUSTMENTS

Why are there four basic types, or categories, of adjusting entries? The answer lies in the distinction between the cash and the accrual bases of accounting. On an accrual basis, revenue can be earned either *before* or *after* cash is received. *Expenses* can be incurred either *before* or *after* cash is paid. Each of these four distinct situations requires a different type of adjustment at the end of the period. We will consider each of the four categories and look at some examples of each.

(1) Cash Paid before Expense Is Incurred (Deferred Expense)

Assets are often acquired before their actual use in the business. Insurance policies typically are prepaid, as often is rent. Office supplies are purchased in advance of their use, as are all types of property and equipment. Recall from our earlier discussion that unexpired costs are assets. As the costs expire and the benefits are used up, the asset must be written off and replaced with an expense.

Assume that on September 1, a company prepays $2,400 in rent on its office space for the next 12 months. The effect of the prepayment on the accounting equation follows:

BALANCE SHEET						INCOME STATEMENT
ASSETS	=	LIABILITIES	+	OWNERS' EQUITY	+	REVENUES – EXPENSES
Prepaid Rent 2,400						
Cash (2,400)						

The asset Prepaid Rent represents the benefits that the company will receive over the next 12 months. Because the rent is for a 12-month period, $200 of benefits from the asset expire at the end of each month. The adjustment at the end of September to record this expiration accomplishes two purposes: (1) it recognizes the reduction in the asset Prepaid Rent, and (2) it recognizes the expense associated with using up the benefits for one month. On September 30, the accountant makes an adjustment to recognize the expense and reduce the asset:

BALANCE SHEET						INCOME STATEMENT	
ASSETS	=	LIABILITIES	+	OWNERS' EQUITY	+	REVENUES – EXPENSES	
Prepaid Rent	(200)					Rent Expense	(200)

The balance in Prepaid Rent represents the unexpired benefits from the prepayment of rent for the remaining 11 months: $200 × 11 = $2,200. Rent Expense reflects the expiration of benefits during the month of September.

As discussed earlier in the chapter, depreciation is the process of allocating the cost of a long-term tangible asset over its estimated useful life. The accountant does not attempt to measure the decline in *value* of the asset but simply tries to allocate its cost over its useful life. Thus, the adjustment for depreciation is similar to the one we made for rent expense. Assume that on January 1, a company buys a delivery truck, for which it pays $21,000. At this point, one asset is simply traded for another. The effect of the purchase of the truck on the accounting equation is as follows:

From **Concept**

TO PRACTICE 4.2

READING UNO'S BALANCE SHEET
Refer to the balance sheet in Uno's annual report. How does Uno classify prepaid expenses? What types of prepaid expenses would you expect the company to have?

BALANCE SHEET						INCOME STATEMENT
ASSETS	=	LIABILITIES	+	OWNERS' EQUITY	+	REVENUES – EXPENSES
Delivery Truck 21,000						
Cash (21,000)						

Two estimates must be made in depreciating the delivery truck: (1) the useful life of the asset and (2) the salvage value of the truck at the end of its useful life. Estimated salvage value is the amount a company expects to be able to receive when it sells an asset at the end of its estimated useful life. Assume a five-year estimated life for the truck and an estimated salvage value of $3,000 at the end of that time. Thus, the *depreciable cost* of the truck is $21,000 − $3,000, or $18,000. In a later chapter, we will consider alternative methods for allocating the depreciable cost over the useful life of an asset. For now, we will use the simplest approach, called the **straight-line method,** which assigns an equal amount of depreciation to each period. The monthly depreciation is found by dividing the depreciable cost of $18,000 over the estimated useful life of 60 months, which equals $300 per month.

ACCOUNTING FOR YOUR DECISIONS

You Are the Store Manager

You are responsible for managing a new running-shoe store. The landlord requires a security deposit as well as prepayment of the first year's rent. The security deposit is refundable at the end of the first year. After the first year, rent is payable on a monthly basis. After three months in business, the owner asks you for an income statement. How should the security deposit and the prepayment of the first year's rent be recognized on this income statement?

ANS: The security deposit will not affect the income statement. It is an asset that will be converted to cash at the end of the first year, assuming that you are entitled to a full refund. One-fourth of the prepayment of the first year's rent should be recognized as an expense on the income statement for the first three months.

The adjustment to recognize depreciation is conceptually the same as the adjustment to write off Prepaid Rent. That is, the asset account is reduced, and an expense is recognized. However, accountants normally use a contra account to reduce the total amount of long-term tangible assets by the amount of depreciation. A **contra account** is any account that is used to offset another account. For example, Accumulated Depreciation is used to record the decrease in a long-term asset, such as the delivery truck:

BALANCE SHEET					INCOME STATEMENT
ASSETS	**=**	**LIABILITIES**	**+**	**OWNERS' EQUITY**	**+ REVENUES – EXPENSES**
Accumulated Depreciation (300)					Depreciation Expense (300)

Study Tip

Think of the Accumulated Depreciation account as simply an extension of the related asset account—in this case, the truck. Therefore, although the truck account is not directly reduced for depreciation, an increase in its companion account, Accumulated Depreciation, has the effect of reducing the asset.

Why do companies use a contra account for depreciation rather than simply reducing the long-term asset directly? If the asset account were reduced each time depreciation is recorded, its original cost would not be readily determinable from the accounting records. Businesses need to know the original cost of each asset, for various reasons. One of the most important of these reasons is the need to know historical cost for computation of depreciation for tax purposes.

On a balance sheet prepared on January 31, the contra account is shown as a reduction in the carrying value of the truck:

Delivery Truck	$21,000	
Less: Accumulated Depreciation	300	$20,700

(2) Cash Received before Revenue Is Earned (Deferred Revenue)

You can benefit greatly in your study of accounting by recognizing its *symmetry.* By this we mean that one company's asset is another company's liability. In the earlier example involving the rental of office space, a second company, the landlord, received the cash paid by the first company, the tenant. At the time cash is received, the landlord has a liability because it has taken cash from the tenant but has not yet performed the service to earn the revenue. The revenue will be earned with the passage of time. The effect on the accounting equation from the collection of cash on September 1 is as follows:

BALANCE SHEET						INCOME STATEMENT
ASSETS	**=**	**LIABILITIES**	**+**	**OWNERS' EQUITY**	**+**	**REVENUES – EXPENSES**
Cash 2,400		Rent Collected in Advance 2,400				

The account Rent Collected in Advance is a liability. The landlord is obligated to provide the tenant uninterrupted use of the office facilities for the next 12 months. With the passage of time, the liability is satisfied as the tenant is provided the use of the space. The adjustment at the end of each month accomplishes two purposes: It recognizes (1) the reduction in the liability and (2) the revenue earned each month as the tenant occupies the space:

BALANCE SHEET						INCOME STATEMENT
ASSETS	**=**	**LIABILITIES**	**+**	**OWNERS' EQUITY**	**+**	**REVENUES – EXPENSES**
		Rent Collected in Advance (200)				Rent Revenue 200

After the adjustment is made, the landlord's remaining liability is $2,400 − $200, or $2,200, which represents 11 months of unearned rent at $200 per month.

In another example, many magazine subscriptions require the customer to pay in advance. For example, you pay $12 for a one-year subscription to your favorite magazine, and the publisher in turn sends you 12 monthly issues. At the time you send money to the publisher, it incurs a liability. It has taken your money but has not yet done anything to earn it. The publisher has an obligation either to provide you with the magazine over the next 12 months or to refund your $12.

At what point should the publisher recognize revenue from magazine sales? The publisher receives cash at the time the subscription is sold. The revenue has not been *earned* until the company publishes the magazine and mails it to you, however. Thus, a publisher usually recognizes revenue at the time of delivery. An excerpt from the 1999 annual report of Time Warner Inc. (the publisher of such popular magazines as *Time, People,* and *Sports Illustrated*) reflects this policy:

> The unearned portion of paid subscriptions is deferred until magazines are delivered to subscribers. Upon each delivery, a proportionate share of the gross subscription price is included in revenues.

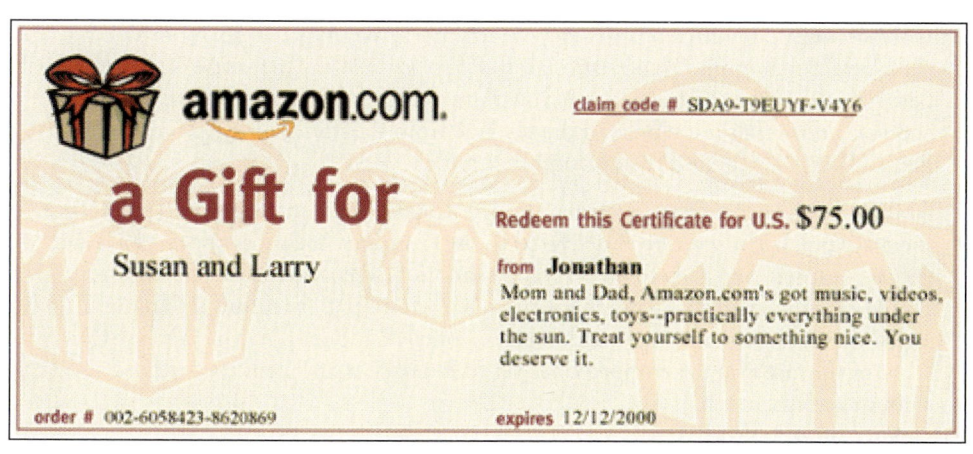

A gift certificate like this is a good example of a deferred revenue. Amazon.com has received the $75 in payment for the certificate, but because it must wait for the recipient of the gift to pick out a book, it considers the obligation to deliver the book in the future a liability.

Assume that on March 1, Time Warner sells 500 one-year subscriptions to a monthly magazine at a price of $12 each. At this point, Time Warner has an obligation to deliver magazines over the next 12 months:

BALANCE SHEET					INCOME STATEMENT
ASSETS	=	LIABILITIES	+	OWNERS' EQUITY	+ REVENUES – EXPENSES
Cash 6,000		Subscriptions Collected in Advance 6,000			

Assuming that each of the subscriptions starts with the March issue of the magazine, at the end of March, Time Warner accountants would adjust the records to reflect the revenue earned for the first month:

BALANCE SHEET					INCOME STATEMENT
ASSETS	=	LIABILITIES	+	OWNERS' EQUITY	+ REVENUES – EXPENSES
		Subscriptions Collected in Advance (500)			Subscription Revenue 500

After the adjustment is made, Time Warner's remaining liability is $6,000 − $500, or $5,500, which represents 11 months of unearned revenue at $500 per month.

As you know by now, accounting terminology differs among companies. The account title Subscriptions Collected in Advance is only one of any number of possible titles for the liability related to subscriptions. For example, some companies call this account Unearned Portion of Paid Subscriptions.

(3) Expense Incurred before Cash Is Paid (Accrued Liability)

This situation is just the opposite of (1). That is, cash is paid *after* an expense is actually incurred rather than *before* its incurrence, as was the case in (1). Many normal operating costs, such as payroll and utilities, fit this situation. The utility bill is received at the end of the month, but the company has 10 days to pay it. Or consider the biweekly payroll for Jones Corporation. The company pays a total of $28,000 in wages on every other Friday. Assume that the last payday was Friday, May 31. The next two paydays will be Friday, June 14, and Friday, June 28. The effect on the accounting equation on each of the two paydays is the same:

ACCOUNTING FOR YOUR DECISIONS

You Are the Banker

A new midwestern publisher comes to you for a loan. Through an aggressive ad campaign, the company sold a phenomenal number of subscriptions to a new sports magazine in its first six months and needs additional money to go national. The first issue of the magazine is due out next month. The publisher presents you an income statement for its first six months, and you notice that it includes all the revenue from the initial subscriptions sold in the Midwest. What concerns do you have?

ANS: First, the accounting treatment for the magazine revenue is improper. Because the magazine has not yet been delivered to the customer, the subscriptions have not yet been earned, and therefore no revenue should be recognized. As a banker, you should be concerned that a potential customer would present improper financial statements and deny the loan on that basis alone. That does not even take into account the fact that the company has yet to establish a sufficient track record to warrant the credit risk.

BALANCE SHEET						**INCOME STATEMENT**	
ASSETS	**=**	**LIABILITIES**	**+**	**OWNERS' EQUITY**	**+**	**REVENUES – EXPENSES**	
Cash	(28,000)					Wage Expense	(28,000)

On a balance sheet prepared as of June 30, a liability must be recognized. Even though the next payment is not until July 12, Jones *owes* employees wages for the last two days of June and must recognize an expense for the wages earned by employees for these two days. We will assume that the company operates seven days a week and that the daily cost is 1/14th of the biweekly amount of $28,000, or $2,000. In addition to recognizing a liability on June 30, Jones must adjust the records to reflect an expense associated with the cost of wages for the last two days of the month:

BALANCE SHEET						**INCOME STATEMENT**	
ASSETS	**=**	**LIABILITIES**	**+**	**OWNERS' EQUITY**	**+**	**REVENUES – EXPENSES**	
		Wages Payable	4,000			Wages Expense	(4,000)

What adjustment will be made on the next payday, July 12? Jones will need to eliminate the liability of $4,000 for the last two days of wages recorded on June 30 because the amount has now been paid. An additional $24,000 of expense has been incurred for the $2,000 cost per day associated with the first 12 days in July. Finally, cash is reduced by $28,000, which represents the biweekly payroll:

BALANCE SHEET						**INCOME STATEMENT**	
ASSETS	**=**	**LIABILITIES**	**+**	**OWNERS' EQUITY**	**+**	**REVENUES – EXPENSES**	
Cash	(28,000)	Wages Payable	(4,000)			Wages Expense	(24,000)

The following time line illustrates the amount of expense incurred in each of the two months, June and July, for the biweekly payroll:

```
2 days' expense              12 days' expense
in June: $4,000              in July: $24,000

|_____|_____|

Friday, June 28:    Friday, June 30:        Friday, July 12:
Last payday         End of accounting        Next payday
                    period
```

Another typical expense incurred before the payment of cash is interest. In many cases, the interest on a short-term loan is repaid with the amount of the loan, called the *principal*, on the maturity date. For example, Granger Company takes out a 9%, 90-day, $20,000 loan with its bank on March 1. The principal and interest will be repaid on May 30. On March 1, both an asset, Cash, and a liability, Notes Payable, are increased:

BALANCE SHEET						**INCOME STATEMENT**	
ASSETS	**=**	**LIABILITIES**	**+**	**OWNERS' EQUITY**	**+**	**REVENUES – EXPENSES**	
Cash	20,000	Notes Payable	20,000				

The basic formula for computing interest follows:

$$I = P \times R \times T,$$

where I = The dollar amount of interest

P = The principal amount of the loan

R = The annual rate of interest as a percentage

T = Time in years (often stated as a fraction of a year).

The total interest on Granger's loan is as follows:

90 days

$$\$20{,}000 \times .09 \times 3/12 = \$450$$

Therefore, the amount of interest that must be recognized as expense at the end of March is one-third of $450 because one month of a total of three has passed. Alternatively, the formula for finding the total interest on the loan can be modified to compute the interest for one month:[6]

$$\$20{,}000 \times .09 \times 1/12 = \$150$$

On March 31 and April 30, the accountant records adjustments to recognize interest both as an expense and as an obligation. The effect on the accounting equation from the adjustments for the two months combined is as follows:

BALANCE SHEET					INCOME STATEMENT	
ASSETS	**=**	**LIABILITIES**	**+**	**OWNERS' EQUITY**	**+**	**REVENUES – EXPENSES**
		Interest Payable 300				Interest Expense (300)

The effect on Granger's accounting equation on May 30 when it repays the principal and interest is

BALANCE SHEET					INCOME STATEMENT	
ASSETS	**=**	**LIABILITIES**	**+**	**OWNERS' EQUITY**	**+**	**REVENUES – EXPENSES**
Cash (20,450)		Interest Payable (300)				Interest Expense (150)
		Notes Payable (20,000)				

Recognition of this transaction accomplishes three purposes. First, the $20,000 of principal and the total interest of $450 for three months is recognized as a decrease in Cash. Second, Interest Expense of $150 for the month of May is recognized. Finally, the two liabilities remaining on the books, Interest Payable and Notes Payable, are removed.[7]

From Concept

TO PRACTICE 4.3

READING GATEWAY'S BALANCE SHEET Refer to the balance sheet in Gateway's annual report. How does Gateway classify accrued liabilities? By how much did they go up or down from 1998 to 1999? What types of accrued liabilities would you expect the company to have?

(4) Revenue Earned before Cash Is Received (Accrued Asset)

Revenue is sometimes earned before the receipt of cash. Rent and interest are both earned with the passage of time and require an adjustment if cash has not yet been received. For example, assume that Grand Management Company rents warehouse space to a number of tenants. Most of its contracts call for prepayment of rent for six months at a time. Its agreement with one tenant, however, allows the tenant to pay Grand $2,500 in monthly rent anytime within the first 10 days of the following month. The adjustment on April 30, the end of the first month of the agreement, is as follows:

BALANCE SHEET					INCOME STATEMENT	
ASSETS	**=**	**LIABILITIES**	**+**	**OWNERS' EQUITY**	**+**	**REVENUES – EXPENSES**
Rent Receivable 2,500						Rent Revenue 2,500

---

[6]In practice, interest is calculated on the basis of days rather than months. For example, the interest for March would be $20,000 × .09 × 30/365, or $147.95, to reflect 30 days in the month out of a total of 365 days in the year. The number of days in March is 30 rather than 31 because in computing interest, businesses normally count the day a note matures but not the day it is signed. To simplify the calculations, we will use months, even though the result is slightly inaccurate.

[7]This assumes that Granger did not make an adjustment prior to this to recognize interest expense for the month of May. If a separate adjustment had been made, Interest Payable would be reduced by $450.

When the tenant pays its rent on May 7, the effect on Grand's accounting equation is as follows:

BALANCE SHEET						INCOME STATEMENT
ASSETS	=	LIABILITIES	+	OWNERS' EQUITY	+	REVENUES – EXPENSES
Cash 2,500						
Rent Receivable (2,500)						

Although we used the example of rent to illustrate this category, the membership revenue of Glengarry Health Club in Chapter 3 also could be used as an example. Whenever a company records revenue before cash is received, some type of receivable is increased and revenue is also increased. In that chapter, the health club earned membership revenue even though members had until the following month to pay their dues.

ACCRUALS AND DEFERRALS

One of the challenges in learning accounting concepts is to gain an understanding of the terminology. Part of the difficulty stems from the alternative terms used by different accountants to mean the same thing. For example, the asset created when insurance is paid for in advance is termed a *prepaid asset* by some and a *prepaid expense* by others. Someone else might refer to it as a *deferred expense.*

We will use the term **deferral** to refer to a situation in which cash has been either paid or received but the expense or revenue has been deferred to a later time. A **deferred expense** indicates that cash has been paid but the recognition of expense has been deferred. Because a deferred expense represents a *future benefit* to a company, it is an *asset.* An alternative name for deferred expense is *prepaid expense.* Prepaid insurance and office supplies are deferred expenses. An adjustment is made periodically to record the portion of the deferred expense that has expired. A **deferred revenue** means that cash has been received but the recognition of any revenue has been deferred until a later time. Because a deferred revenue represents an *obligation* to a company, it is a *liability.* An alternative name for deferred revenue is *unearned revenue.* Rent collected in advance is deferred revenue. The periodic adjustment recognizes the portion of the deferred revenue that is earned in that period.

In this chapter, we have discussed in detail the accrual basis of accounting, which involves recognizing changes in resources and obligations as they occur, not simply when cash changes hands. More specifically, we will use the term **accrual** to refer to a situation in which no cash has been paid or received yet but it is necessary to recognize, or accrue, an expense or a revenue. An **accrued liability** is recognized at the end of the period in cases in which an expense has been incurred but cash has not yet been paid. Wages payable and interest payable are examples of accrued liabilities. An **accrued asset** is recorded when revenue has been earned but cash has not yet been collected. Rent receivable is an accrued asset.

SUMMARY OF ADJUSTMENTS

The four types of adjustments are summarized in Exhibit 4-5. Common examples of each are shown, along with the accounts affected by each. Finally, the following generalizations should help you in gaining a better understanding of adjustments and how they are used:

1. An adjustment is an internal transaction. It does not involve another entity.

2. Because it is an internal transaction, an adjustment *never* involves an increase or decrease in Cash.

3. At least one balance sheet account and one income statement account are involved in an adjustment. It is the nature of the adjustment process that an asset or liability account is adjusted with a corresponding change in either a revenue or an expense account.

> *Study Tip*
>
> Now that we have seen examples of all four types of adjustments, think about a key difference between deferrals (the first two categories) and accruals (the last two categories). When we make adjustments involving deferrals, we must consider any existing balance in a deferred account. Conversely, there is no existing account when making an accrual.

EXHIBIT 4-5 Accruals and Deferrals

Type	Situation	Examples	Accounts Affected During Period	Accounts Affected At End of Period
Deferred expense	Cash paid before expense incurred	Insurance policy Supplies Rent Buildings, equipment	Increase in Prepaid Asset Decrease in Cash	Increase in Expense Decrease in Prepaid Asset
Deferred revenue	Cash received before revenue earned	Deposits, rent Subscriptions Gift certificates	Increase in Cash Increase in Liability	Decrease in Liability Increase in Revenue
Accrued liability	Expense incurred before cash paid	Salaries, wages Interest Taxes Rent	No Adjustment	Increase in Expense Increase in Liability
Accrued asset	Revenue earned before cash received	Interest Rent	No Adjustment	Increase in Asset Increase in Revenue

Two-Minute Review

Assume a company wants to prepare financial statements at the end of its first month of operations. Each of the following transactions was recorded on the company's books on the first day of the month.

1. Purchased a 24-month insurance policy for $3,600.

2. Collected $4,800 from a tenant for office space that the tenant has rented for the next 12 months.

3. Took out a 6%, 180-day, $10,000 loan at the bank.

For each of these transactions, determine the effect on the accounting equation of the adjustment required at the end of the month.

Answers:

BALANCE SHEET ASSETS	=	LIABILITIES	+	OWNERS' EQUITY	+	INCOME STATEMENT REVENUES – EXPENSES	
1. Prepaid Insurance (150)						Insurance Expense	(150)
2.		Rent Collected in Advance	(400)			Rent Revenue	400
3.		Interest Payable	50			Interest Expense	(50)

COMPREHENSIVE EXAMPLE OF ADJUSTMENTS

We will now consider a comprehensive example involving the transactions for the first month of operations and the end-of-period adjustments for a hypothetical business, Duffy Transit Company. A list of accounts and their balances is shown for Duffy Transit at January 31, the end of the first month of operations (prior to making any adjustments):

Assets:
Cash $ 50,000
Prepaid Insurance   48,000
Land   20,000

Buildings—Garage	160,000
Equipment—Buses	300,000
Liabilities:	
Discount Tickets Sold in Advance	25,000
Notes Payable	150,000
Owners' Equity	
Capital Stock	400,000
Revenues:	
Daily Ticket Revenue	30,000
Expenses:	
Gas, Oil, and Maintenance Expense	12,000
Wage and Salary Expense	10,000
Dividends	5,000

Duffy wants to prepare a balance sheet at the end of January and an income statement for its first month of operations. Use of the accrual basis necessitates a number of adjustments to update certain asset and liability accounts and to recognize the correct amounts for the various revenues and expenses.

ADJUSTMENTS AT THE END OF JANUARY

(1) At the beginning of January, Duffy issued an 18-month, 12%, $150,000 promissory note for cash. Although interest will not be repaid until the loan's maturity date, Duffy must accrue interest for the first month. The calculation of interest for one month is $150,000 \times .12 \times 1/12$. The adjustment is

BALANCE SHEET						INCOME STATEMENT	
ASSETS	=	LIABILITIES	+	OWNERS' EQUITY	+	REVENUES – EXPENSES	
		Interest Payable	1,500			Interest Expense	(1,500)

(2) Wages and salary expense of $10,000 reflects the amount paid to employees during January. Duffy owes employees an additional $2,800 in salaries and wages at January 31. The effect of the adjustment is as follows:

BALANCE SHEET						INCOME STATEMENT	
ASSETS	=	LIABILITIES	+	OWNERS' EQUITY	+	REVENUES – EXPENSES	
		Wages and Salaries Payable	2,800			Wage and Salary Expense	(2,800)

(3) At the beginning of January, Duffy acquired a garage to house the buses at a cost of $160,000. Land is not subject to depreciation. The cost of the land acquired in connection with the purchase of the building will remain on the books until the property is sold. The garage has an estimated useful life of 20 years and an estimated salvage value of $16,000 at the end of its life. The monthly depreciation is found by dividing the depreciable cost of $144,000 by the useful life of 240 months:

$$\frac{\$160,000 - \$16,000}{20 \text{ years} \times 12 \text{ months}} = \frac{\$144,000}{240 \text{ months}} = \underline{\$600} \text{ per month.}$$

The adjustment to recognize the depreciation on the garage for January for a full month is

BALANCE SHEET						INCOME STATEMENT	
ASSETS	=	LIABILITIES	+	OWNERS' EQUITY	+	REVENUES – EXPENSES	
Accumulated Depreciation—Garage	(600)					Depreciation Expense— Garage	(600)

(4) Duffy purchased 10 buses for $30,000 each at the beginning of January. The buses have an estimated useful life of five years at which time the company plans to sell them for $6,000 each. The monthly depreciation on the 10 buses is

$$10 \times \frac{\$30,000 - \$6,000}{5 \text{ years} \times 12 \text{ months}} = 10 \times \frac{\$24,000}{60 \text{ months}} = \underline{\underline{\$4,000}} \text{ per month.}$$

The adjustment to recognize the depreciation on the buses for the first month is

BALANCE SHEET						INCOME STATEMENT	
ASSETS	**=**	**LIABILITIES**	**+**	**OWNERS' EQUITY**	**+**	**REVENUES – EXPENSES**	
Accumulated Depreciation—Buses (4,000)						Depreciation Expense Buses	(4,000)

(5) An insurance policy was purchased for $48,000 on January 1. It provides property and liability protection for a 24-month period. The adjustment to allocate the cost to expense for the first month is

BALANCE SHEET						INCOME STATEMENT	
ASSETS	**=**	**LIABILITIES**	**+**	**OWNERS' EQUITY**	**+**	**REVENUES – EXPENSES**	
Prepaid Insurance (2,000)						Insurance Expense	(2,000)

(6) In addition to selling tickets on the bus, Duffy sells discount tickets at the terminal. The tickets are good for a ride anytime within 12 months of purchase. Thus, as these tickets are sold, Duffy increases Cash, as well as a liability account, Discount Tickets Sold in Advance. The sale of $25,000 worth of these tickets was recorded during January. At the end of the first month, Duffy counts the number of tickets that have been redeemed. Because $20,400 worth of tickets has been turned in, this is the amount by which the company reduces its liability and recognizes revenue for the month:

BALANCE SHEET						INCOME STATEMENT	
ASSETS	**=**	**LIABILITIES**	**+**	**OWNERS' EQUITY**	**+**	**REVENUES – EXPENSES**	
		Discount Tickets Sold in Advance (20,400)				Discount Ticket Revenue	20,400

(7) Duffy does not need all the space in its garage and rents a section of it to another company for $2,500 per month. The tenant has until the 10th day of the following month to pay its rent. The adjustment on Duffy's books on the last day of the month is

BALANCE SHEET						INCOME STATEMENT	
ASSETS	**=**	**LIABILITIES**	**+**	**OWNERS' EQUITY**	**+**	**REVENUES – EXPENSES**	
Rent Receivable 2,500						Rent Revenue	2,500

(8) Corporations pay estimated taxes on a quarterly basis. Because Duffy is preparing an income statement for the month of January, it must estimate its taxes incurred for the month, which will be paid at the end of the quarter. We will assume a corporate tax rate of 34% on income before tax. The computation of Income Tax Expense is as follows (the amounts shown for the revenues and expenses reflect the effect of the adjustments):

Revenues:		
Daily Ticket Revenue	$30,000	
Discount Ticket Revenue	20,400	
Rent Revenue	2,500	$52,900
Expenses:		
Gas, Oil, and Maintenance Expense	$12,000	
Wage and Salary Expense	12,800	
Depreciation Expense	4,600	
Insurance Expense	2,000	
Interest Expense	1,500	32,900
Net Income before Tax		$20,000
Times the Corporate Tax Rate		× .34
Income Tax Expense		$ 6,800

Based on this estimate of taxes, the final adjustment Duffy makes is

BALANCE SHEET						INCOME STATEMENT	
ASSETS	=	LIABILITIES		+	OWNERS' EQUITY	+	REVENUES – EXPENSES
		Income Tax Payable	6,800			Income Tax Expense	(6,800)

INCOME STATEMENT AND BALANCE SHEET FOR DUFFY TRANSIT

Now that the adjustments have been made, financial statements can be prepared. An income statement for January and a balance sheet as of January 31 are shown in Exhibit 4-6. Each of the account balances on the statements was determined by taking the balances in the list of accounts on pages 156 and 157 and adding or subtracting as appropriate the necessary adjustments. Note the balance in Retained Earnings of $8,200. This amount was found by taking the net income of $13,200 and deducting the dividends of $5,000.

ETHICAL CONSIDERATIONS FOR A COMPANY ON THE ACCRUAL BASIS

As you have seen, the accrual basis requires the recognition of revenues when earned and expenses when incurred, regardless of when cash is received or paid. It was also noted earlier that adjusting entries are *internal* transactions in that they do not involve an exchange with an outside entity. Because adjustments do not involve another company, accountants may at times feel pressure from others within the organization to either speed or delay the recognition of certain adjustments.

Consider the following two examples for a construction company that is concerned about its "bottom line," that is, its net income. A number of jobs are in progress, but because of inclement weather, none of them is very far along. Management asks the accountant to recognize 50% of the revenue from a job in progress even though by the most liberal estimates it is only 25% complete. Further, the accountant has been asked to delay the recognition of various short-term accrued liabilities (and, of course, the accompanying expenses) until the beginning of the new year.

The "correct" response of the accountant to each of these requests may seem obvious: only 25% of the revenue on the one job should be recognized, and all accrued liabilities should be expensed at year-end. The pressures of the daily work environment make these decisions difficult for the accountant, however. The accountant must always remember that his or her primary responsibility in preparing financial statements is to accurately portray the affairs of the company to the various outside users. Bankers, stockholders, and others rely on the accountant to serve their best interests.

EXHIBIT 4-6   Financial Statements for Duffy Transit Company

DUFFY TRANSIT COMPANY
INCOME STATEMENT
FOR THE MONTH OF JANUARY

Revenues:

Daily ticket revenue	$30,000	
Discount ticket revenue	20,400	
Rent revenue	2,500	$52,900

Expenses:

Gas, oil, and maintenance	$12,000	
Wages and salaries	12,800	
Depreciation—garage	600	
Depreciation—buses	4,000	
Insurance	2,000	
Interest	1,500	
Income taxes	6,800	$39,700
Net income		$13,200

DUFFY TRANSIT COMPANY
BALANCE SHEET
JANUARY 31

Assets			Liabilities and Owners' Equity	
Cash		$ 50,000	Discount tickets	
Rent receivable		2,500	sold in advance	$ 4,600
Prepaid insurance		46,000	Notes payable	150,000
Land		20,000	Interest payable	1,500
Buildings—garage	$160,000		Wages and salaries	
Accumulated			payable	2,800
depreciation	600	159,400	Income tax payable	6,800
Equipment—buses	$300,000		Capital stock	400,000
Accumulated			Retained earnings	8,200
depreciation	4,000	296,000	Total liabilities and	
Total assets		$573,900	owners' equity	$573,900

THE ACCOUNTING CYCLE

LO 6 Explain the steps in the accounting cycle and the significance of each step.

We have focused our attention in this chapter on accrual accounting and the adjusting entries it necessitates. The adjustments the accountant makes are one key component in the **accounting cycle.** The accountant for a business follows a series of steps each period. The objective is always the same: *Collect the necessary information to prepare a set of financial statements.* Together, these steps make up the accounting cycle. The name comes from the fact that the steps are repeated each period. It is possible that a company performs all the steps in the accounting cycle once a *month,* although in practice, certain steps in the cycle may be carried out only once a *year.*

The steps in the accounting cycle are shown in Exhibit 4-7. Note that step 1 involves not only *collecting* information but also *analyzing* it. Transaction analysis is probably the most challenging of all the steps in the accounting cycle. It requires the ability to think

EXHIBIT 4-7   Steps in the Accounting Cycle

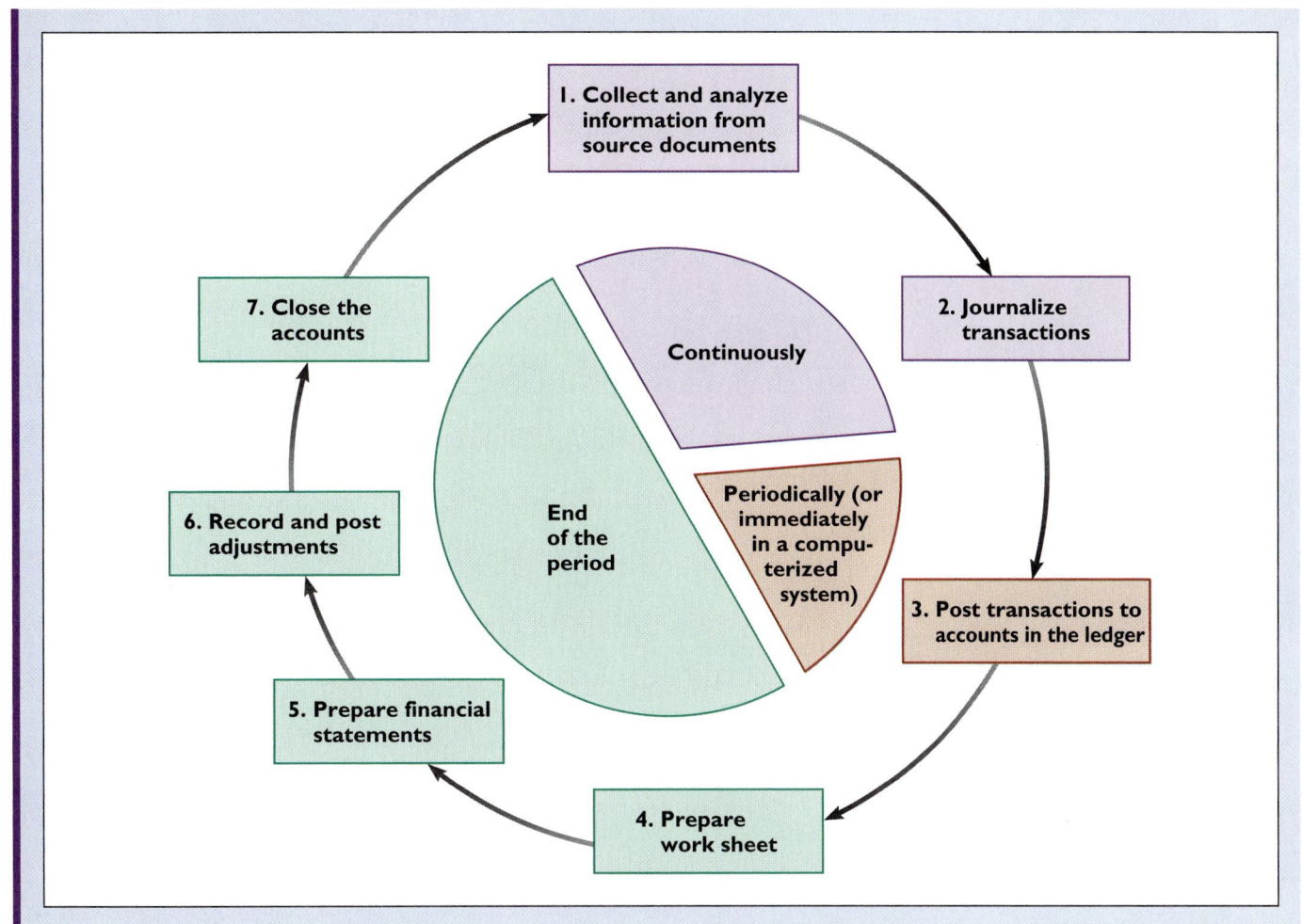

logically about an event and its effect on the financial position of the entity. Once the transaction is analyzed, it is recorded in the journal, as indicated by the second step in the exhibit. The first two steps in the cycle take place continuously.

Transactions are posted to the accounts on a periodic basis. The frequency of posting to the accounts depends on two factors: the type of accounting system employed by a company and the volume of transactions. In a manual system, entries might be posted daily, weekly, or even monthly, depending on the amount of activity. The larger the number of transactions a company records, the more often it posts. In an automated accounting system, posting is likely done automatically by the computer each time a transaction is recorded.

THE USE OF A WORK SHEET

Step 4 in Exhibit 4-7 calls for the preparation of a work sheet. The end of an accounting period is a busy time. In addition to recording daily recurring transactions, adjustments must be recorded as the basis for preparing financial statements. The time available to prepare the statements is usually very limited. The use of a **work sheet** allows the accountant to gather and organize the information required to adjust the accounts without actually recording and posting the adjustments to the accounts. Actually recording adjustments and posting them to the accounts can be done after the financial statements are prepared. *A work sheet itself is not a financial statement.* Instead, it is a useful device to *organize* the information needed to prepare the financial statements at the end of the period.

It is not essential that a work sheet be used before preparing financial statements. If it is not used, step 6, recording and posting adjustments, comes before step 5, preparing the financial statements.

The Closing Process   Step 7 in Exhibit 4-7 is the closing process. For purposes of closing the books, accountants categorize accounts into two types. Balance sheet accounts are called **real accounts** because they are permanent in nature. For this reason, they are never closed. The balance in each of these accounts is carried over from one period to the next. In contrast, revenue, expense, and dividend accounts are temporary or **nominal accounts.** The balances in the income statement accounts and the Dividends account are *not* carried forward from one accounting period to the next. For this reason, these accounts are closed at the end of the period.

Closing entries serve two important purposes: (1) to return the balances in all temporary or nominal accounts to zero to start the next accounting period and (2) to transfer the net income (or net loss) and the dividends of the period to the Retained Earnings account.

INTERIM FINANCIAL STATEMENTS

We mentioned earlier in this chapter that certain steps in the accounting cycle are sometimes carried out only once a year rather than each month, as in our example. For ease of illustration, we assumed a monthly accounting cycle. Many companies adjust and close the accounts only once a year, however. They use a work sheet more frequently than this as the basis for preparing interim statements. Statements prepared monthly, quarterly, or at other intervals less than a year in duration are called **interim statements.** Many companies prepare monthly financial statements for their own internal use. Similarly, corporations whose shares are publicly traded on one of the stock exchanges are required to file quarterly financial statements with the Securities and Exchange Commission.

Suppose that a company prepares monthly financial statements for internal use and completes the accounting cycle in its entirety only once a year. In this case, a work sheet is prepared each month as the basis for interim financial statements. Formally adjusting and closing the books is done only at the end of each year. The adjustments that appear on the monthly work sheet are not posted to the accounts. They are entered on the work sheet simply as a basis for preparing the monthly financial statements.

WARMUP EXERCISES

LO 5 Warmup Exercise 4-1 Prepaid Insurance
ABC Corp. purchases a 24-month fire insurance policy on January 1, 2001, for $5,400.

Required

Determine the effect on the accounting equation on January 31, 2001.

Key to the Solution

Determine what proportion and therefore what dollar amount of the policy has expired after one month.

LO 5 Warmup Exercise 4-2 Depreciation
ABC Corp. purchased a new car for one of its salespeople on January 1, 2001, for $25,000. The estimated useful life of the car is four years with an estimated salvage value of $1,000.

Required

Determine the effect on the accounting equation on January 31, 2001.

Key to the Solution

Determine what dollar amount of the cost of the car should be depreciated and then how much should be depreciated each month.

LO 5 Warmup Exercise 4-3 Interest on a Note
On January 1, 2001, ABC Corp. took out a 12%, 120-day, $10,000 loan at its bank.

Required

Determine the effect on the accounting equation on January 31, 2001.

Key to the Solution

Determine the monthly interest cost on a loan that accrues interest at the rate of 12% per year.

SOLUTIONS TO WARMUP EXERCISES

		BALANCE SHEET				INCOME STATEMENT	
ASSETS	**=**	**LIABILITIES**	**+**	**OWNERS' EQUITY**	**+**	**REVENUES – EXPENSES**	
1. Prepaid Insurance	(225)					Insurance Expense	(225)
2. Accumulated Depreciation	(500)					Depreciation Expense	(500)
3.		Interest Payable	100			Interest Expense	(100)

REVIEW PROBLEM

A list of accounts for Northern Airlines at January 31 is shown here. It reflects the recurring transactions for the month of January, but it does not reflect any month-end adjustments.

Cash	$ 75,000
Parts Inventory	45,000
Land	80,000
Buildings—Hangars	250,000
Accumulated Depreciation—Hangars	24,000
Aircraft	650,000
Accumulated Depreciation—Aircraft	120,000
Tickets Sold in Advance	85,000
Capital Stock	500,000
Retained Earnings	368,000
Ticket Revenue	52,000
Maintenance Expense	19,000
Wage and Salary Expense	30,000

The following additional information is available:

a. Airplane parts needed for repairs and maintenance are purchased regularly, and the amounts paid are added to the asset account Parts Inventory. At the end of each month, the inventory is counted. At the end of January, the amount of parts on hand is $36,100. *Hint:* What adjustment is needed to reduce the asset account to its proper carrying value? Any expense involved should be included in Maintenance Expense.

b. The estimated useful life of the hangar is 20 years with an estimated salvage value of $10,000 at the end of its life. The original cost of the hangar was $250,000.

c. The estimated useful life of the aircraft is 10 years with an estimated salvage value of $50,000. The original cost of the aircraft was $650,000.

d. As tickets are sold in advance, the amounts are added to Cash and to the liability account Tickets Sold in Advance. A count of the redeemed tickets reveals that $47,000 worth of tickets were used during January.

e. Wages and salaries owed to employees, but unpaid, at the end of January total $7,600.

f. Northern rents excess hangar space to other companies. The amount owed to Northern but unpaid at the end of January is $2,500.

g. Assume a corporate income tax rate of 34%.

Required

1. For each of the preceding items of additional information, determine the effect on the accounting equation.

2. Prepare an income statement for January and a balance sheet as of January 31.

SOLUTION TO REVIEW PROBLEM

1.

a.

BALANCE SHEET						INCOME STATEMENT	
ASSETS	=	LIABILITIES	+	OWNERS' EQUITY	+	REVENUES − EXPENSES	
Parts Inventory (8,900)						Maintenance Expense	(8,900)

b.

BALANCE SHEET						INCOME STATEMENT
ASSETS	=	LIABILITIES	+	OWNERS' EQUITY	+	REVENUES – EXPENSES
Accumulated Depreciation—Hangars (1,000)						Depreciation Expense—Hangars (1,000)

c.

BALANCE SHEET						INCOME STATEMENT
ASSETS	=	LIABILITIES	+	OWNERS' EQUITY	+	REVENUES – EXPENSES
Accumulated Depreciation—Aircraft (5,000)						Depreciation Expense—Aircraft (5,000)

d.

BALANCE SHEET						INCOME STATEMENT
ASSETS	=	LIABILITIES	+	OWNERS' EQUITY	+	REVENUES – EXPENSES
		Tickets Sold in Advance (47,000)				Ticket Revenue 47,000

e.

BALANCE SHEET						INCOME STATEMENT
ASSETS	=	LIABILITIES	+	OWNERS' EQUITY	+	REVENUES – EXPENSES
		Salaries and Wages Payable 7,600				Wage and Salary Expense (7,600)

f.

BALANCE SHEET						INCOME STATEMENT
ASSETS	=	LIABILITIES	+	OWNERS' EQUITY	+	REVENUES – EXPENSES
Rent Receivable 2,500						Rent Revenue 2,500

g.

BALANCE SHEET						INCOME STATEMENT
ASSETS	=	LIABILITIES	+	OWNERS' EQUITY	+	REVENUES – EXPENSES
		Income Tax Payable 10,200				Income Tax Expense (10,200)

2. Financial statements:

NORTHERN AIRLINES
INCOME STATEMENT
FOR THE MONTH OF JANUARY

Revenues:		
Ticket revenue	$99,000	
Rent revenue	2,500	$101,500
Expenses:		
Maintenance	$27,900	
Wages and salaries	37,600	
Depreciation—hangars	1,000	
Depreciation—aircraft	5,000	
Income taxes	10,200	81,700
Net income		$ 19,800

NORTHERN AIRLINES
BALANCE SHEET
JANUARY 31

Assets			Liabilities and Owners' Equity	
Cash		$ 75,000	Tickets sold in advance	$ 38,000
Rent receivable		2,500	Salaries and wages	
Parts inventory		36,100	payable	7,600
Land		80,000	Income tax payable	10,200
Buildings—Hangars	$250,000		Capital stock	500,000
Accumulated			Retained earnings	387,800
depreciation	25,000	225,000		
Aircraft	$650,000			
Accumulated				
depreciation	125,000	525,000	Total liabilities and	
Total assets		$943,600	owners' equity	$943,600

CHAPTER HIGHLIGHTS

1. **LO 1** The success of accounting as a form of communication depends on two concepts: recognition and measurement. The items depicted in financial statements are representations. The accountant cannot show the reader an asset but instead depicts it with words and numbers.

2. **LO 1** Measurement in accounting requires choosing an attribute and a unit of measure. Historical cost is the attribute used for many of the assets included in financial statements. One alternative to historical cost is current value. The dollar as a unit of measure is subject to instability, depending on the level of inflation.

3. **LO 2** Under the accrual basis of accounting, revenues are recognized when earned and expenses when incurred. The income statement is prepared on an accrual basis, and the statement of cash flows complements it by providing valuable information about the operating, financing, and investing cash flows of a business.

4. **LO 3** According to the revenue recognition principle, revenues are recognized when they are realized and earned. On a practical basis, revenue is normally recognized at the time a product or service is delivered to the customer. Certain types of sales arrangements, such as franchises, present special problems in applying the principle.

5. **LO 4** The matching principle attempts to associate with the revenue of the period all costs necessary to generate that revenue. A direct form of matching is possible for certain types of costs, such as cost of goods sold and commissions. Costs, such as depreciation, are recognized as expenses on an indirect basis. Depreciation is the allocation of the cost of a tangible, long-term asset over its useful life. The benefits from most selling and administrative expenses expire immediately and are recognized as expenses in the period the costs are incurred.

6. **LO 5** The accrual basis necessitates adjustments at the end of a period. The four types of adjustments result from differences between the recognition of revenues and expenses on an accrual basis and the receipt or payment of cash.

7. **LO 5** Cash paid before expense is incurred results in a deferred expense, which is recognized as an asset on the balance sheet. The adjustment reduces the asset and recognizes a corresponding amount of expense. Cash received before revenue is earned requires the recognition of a liability, a deferred revenue. The adjustment reduces the liability and recognizes a corresponding amount of revenue.

8. **LO 5** If cash is paid after an expense is incurred, an adjustment is needed to recognize the accrued liability and the related expense. Similarly, if cash is received after the revenue is earned, the adjustment recognizes the accrued asset and the corresponding revenue. The liability or asset is eliminated in a later period when cash is either paid or received.

9. **LO 6** Steps in the accounting cycle are carried out each period as a basis for the preparation of financial statements. Some of the steps, such as journalizing transactions, are performed continuously, while others, such as recording adjustments, are performed only at the end of the period.

10. **LO 7** After adjustments are recorded and posted to the accounts, certain accounts are closed. Closing serves two important purposes: (1) to return the balances in all revenue, expense, and dividend accounts to zero to start the following accounting period and (2) to transfer the net income (or net loss) and the dividends of the period to the Retained Earnings account.

KEY TERMS QUIZ

Read each definition below and then write the number of the definition in the blank beside the appropriate term it defines. The solution appears at the end of the chapter.

____ Recognition
____ Historical cost
____ Current value
____ Cash basis
____ Accrual basis
____ Revenues
____ Revenue recognition principle
____ Matching principle
____ Expenses
____ Adjusting entries
____ Straight-line method
____ Contra account

____ Deferral
____ Deferred expense
____ Deferred revenue
____ Accrual
____ Accrued liability
____ Accrued asset
____ Accounting cycle
____ Work sheet
____ Real accounts
____ Nominal accounts
____ Closing entries
____ Interim statements

1. A device used at the end of the period to gather the information needed to prepare financial statements without actually recording and posting adjusting entries.

2. Inflows or other enhancements of assets or settlements of liabilities from delivering or producing goods, rendering services, or other activities.

3. Journal entries made at the end of a period by a company using the accrual basis of accounting.

4. Journal entries made at the end of the period to return the balance in all nominal accounts to zero and transfer the net income or loss and the dividends of the period to Retained Earnings.

5. A liability resulting from the receipt of cash before the recognition of revenue.

6. The name given to balance sheet accounts because they are permanent and are not closed at the end of the period.

7. An asset resulting from the recognition of a revenue before the receipt of cash.

8. The amount of cash, or its equivalent, that could be received by selling an asset currently.

9. The assignment of an equal amount of depreciation to each period.

10. Cash has either been paid or received, but expense or revenue has not yet been recognized.

11. A system of accounting in which revenues are recognized when earned and expenses when incurred.

12. Cash has not yet been paid or received, but expense has been incurred or revenue earned.

13. Financial statements prepared monthly, quarterly, or at other intervals less than a year in duration.

14. Revenues are recognized in the income statement when they are realized and earned.

15. The process of recording an item in the financial statements as an asset, a liability, a revenue, an expense, or the like.

16. An asset resulting from the payment of cash before the incurrence of expense.

17. The name given to revenue, expense, and dividend accounts because they are temporary and are closed at the end of the period.

18. A system of accounting in which revenues are recognized when cash is received and expenses when cash is paid.

19. A liability resulting from the recognition of an expense before the payment of cash.

20. The association of revenue of a period with all the costs necessary to generate that revenue.

21. An account with a balance that is opposite that of a related account.

22. The amount that is paid for an asset and that is used as a basis for recognizing it on the balance sheet and carrying it on later balance sheets.

23. Outflows or other using up of assets or incurrences of liabilities resulting from delivering goods, rendering services, or carrying out other activities.

24. A series of steps performed each period and culminating with the preparation of a set of financial statements.

ALTERNATE TERMS

Historical cost   Original cost

Asset   Unexpired cost

Deferred expense   Prepaid expense, prepaid asset

Deferred revenue   Unearned revenue

Expense   Expired cost

Nominal account   Temporary account

Real account   Permanent account

1. What is meant by the following statement? "The items depicted in financial statements are merely *representations* of the real thing."

2. What is the meaning of the following statement? "The choice between historical cost and current value is a good example of the trade-off in accounting between relevance and reliability."

3. A realtor earns a 10% commission on the sale of a $150,000 home. The realtor lists the home on June 5, the sale occurs on June 12, and the seller pays the realtor the $15,000 commission on July 8. When should the realtor recognize revenue from the sale, assuming (a) the cash basis of accounting and (b) the accrual basis of accounting?

4. What does the following statement mean? "If I want to assess the cash flow prospects for a company down the road, I look at the company's most recent statement of cash flows. An income statement prepared under the accrual basis of accounting is useless for this purpose."

5. What is the relationship between the time period assumption and accrual accounting?

6. Is it necessary for an asset to be acquired when revenue is recognized? Explain your answer.

7. When should a publisher of magazines recognize revenue?

8. A friend says to you: "I just don't get it. Assets cost money. Expenses reduce income. There must be some relationship among *assets, costs,* and *expenses*—I'm just not sure what it is!" What is the relationship? Can you give an example of it?

9. What is the meaning of *depreciation* to the accountant?

10. What are the four basic types of adjustments? Give an example of each.

11. What is the difference between a real account and a nominal account?

12. What two purposes are served in making closing entries?

EXERCISES

LO 3   Exercise 4-1   Revenue Recognition

The highway department contracted with a private company to collect tolls and maintain facilities on a turnpike. Users of the turnpike can pay cash as they approach the toll booth, or they can purchase a pass. The pass is equipped with an electronic sensor that subtracts the toll fee from the pass balance as the motorist slowly approaches a special toll booth. The passes are issued in $10 increments. Refunds are available to motorists who do not use the pass balance, but these are issued very infrequently. Last year $3,000,000 was collected at the traditional toll booths, $2,000,000 of passes were issued, and $1,700,000 of passes were used at the special toll booth. How much should the company recognize as revenue for the year? Explain how the revenue recognition rule should be applied in this case.

LO 4   Exercise 4-2   The Matching Principle

Three methods of matching costs with revenue were described in the chapter: (a) directly match a specific form of revenue with a cost incurred in generating that revenue, (b) indirectly match a cost with the periods during which it will provide benefits or revenue, and (c) immediately recognize a cost incurred as an expense because no future benefits are expected. For each of the following costs, indicate how it is normally recognized as expense by indicating either *a, b,* or *c.* If you think there is more than one possible answer for any of the situations, explain why.

 C = no future benefits

    b **1.** New office copier

    c **2.** Monthly bill from the utility company for electricity

    b or c **3.** Office supplies

    c **4.** Biweekly payroll for office employees

    a **5.** Commissions earned by salespeople *matches specific form of rev. with a cost incurred in generating that revenue*

    c **6.** Interest incurred on a six-month loan from the bank *immediately recognise 1/6 per month*

    a **7.** Cost of inventory sold during the current period

    c **8.** Taxes owed on income earned during current period

    b **9.** Cost of three-year insurance policy *1/36 each month*

LO 5   Exercise 4-3   Accruals and Deferrals

For the following situations, indicate whether each involves a deferred expense (DE), a deferred revenue (DR), an accrued liability (AL), or an accrued asset (AA).

Example: ___DE___   Office supplies purchased in advance of their use

___AL___ **1.** Wages earned by employees but not yet paid

OR ___IA___ **2.** Cash collected from subscriptions in advance of publishing a magazine

AA ___II___ **3.** Interest earned on a customer loan for which principal and interest have not yet been collected

___DE___ **4.** One year's premium on life insurance policy paid in advance

___OE___ **5.** Office building purchased for cash

___OR___ **6.** Rent collected in advance from a tenant

___AL___ **7.** State income taxes owed at the end of the year

___AA___ **8.** Rent owed by a tenant but not yet collected

LO 5   Exercise 4-4   Office Supplies

Somerville Corp. purchases office supplies once a month and prepares monthly financial statements. The asset account Office Supplies on Hand has a balance of $1,450 on May 1. Purchases of supplies during May amount to $1,100. Supplies on hand at May 31 amount to $920. Determine the effect on the accounting equation of the adjustment necessary on May 31. What would be the effect on net income for May if this entry is *not* recorded?

LO 5   Exercise 4-5   Prepaid Rent—Quarterly Adjustments

On September 1, Northhampton Industries signed a six-month lease, effective September 1, for office space. Northhampton agreed to prepay the rent and mailed a check for $12,000 to the landlord on September 1. Assume that Northhampton prepares adjustments only four times a year, on March 31, June 30, September 30, and December 31.

Required

1. Compute the rental cost for each full month.
2. Determine the effect on the accounting equation of the entry necessary on September 1.
3. Determine the effect on the accounting equation of the adjustment necessary on September 30.
4. Assume that the accountant prepares the adjustment on September 30 but forgets to record an adjustment on December 31. Will net income for the year be understated or overstated? By what amount?

LO 5   Exercise 4-6   Depreciation

On July 1, 2001, Red Gate Farm buys a combine for $100,000 in cash. Assume that the combine is expected to have a seven-year life and an estimated salvage value of $16,000 at the end of that time.

Required

1. Determine the effect on the accounting equation of the purchase of the combine on July 1, 2001.
2. Compute the depreciable cost of the combine.
3. Using the straight-line method, compute the monthly depreciation.
4. Determine the effect on the accounting equation of the adjustment necessary to record depreciation at the end of July 2001.
5. Compute the combine's carrying value that will be shown on Red Gate's balance sheet prepared on December 31, 2001.

LO 5   Exercise 4-7   Prepaid Insurance—Annual Adjustments

On April 1, 2001, Briggs Corp. purchases a 24-month property insurance policy for $72,000. The policy is effective immediately. Assume that Briggs prepares adjusting entries only once a year, on December 31.

Required

1. Compute the monthly cost of the insurance policy.   3,000
2. Determine the effect on the accounting equation of the purchase of the policy on April 1, 2001.

3. Determine the effect on the accounting equation of the adjustment necessary on December 31, 2001.

4. Assume that the accountant forgets to record an adjustment on December 31, 2001. Will net income for the year ended December 31, 2001, be understated or overstated? Explain your answer.

LO 5 **Exercise 4-8** Subscriptions

Country Living publishes a monthly magazine for which a 12-month subscription costs $30. All subscriptions require payment of the full $30 in advance. On August 1, 2001, the balance in the Subscriptions Received in Advance account was $40,500. During the month of August, the company sold 900 yearly subscriptions. After the adjustment at the end of August, the balance in the Subscriptions Received in Advance account is $60,000.

Required

1. Determine the effect on the accounting equation of the sale of the 900 yearly subscriptions during the month of August.

2. Determine the effect on the accounting equation of the adjustment necessary on August 31.

3. Assume that the accountant made the correct entry during August to record the sale of the 900 subscriptions but forgot to make the adjustment on August 31. Would net income for August be overstated or understated? Explain your answer.

LO 5 **Exercise 4-9** Customer Deposits

Wolfe & Wolfe collected $9,000 from a customer on April 1 and agreed to provide legal services during the next three months. Wolfe & Wolfe expects to provide an equal amount of services each month.

Required

1. Determine the effect on the accounting equation of the receipt of the customer deposit on April 1.

2. Determine the effect on the accounting equation of the adjustment necessary on April 30.

3. What would be the effect on net income for April if the adjustment in **(2)** is not recorded?

LO 5 **Exercise 4-10** Wages Payable

Denton Corporation employs 50 workers in its plant. Each employee is paid $10 per hour and works seven hours per day, Monday through Friday. Employees are paid every Friday. The last payday was Friday, October 20.

Required

1. Compute the dollar amount of the weekly payroll.

2. Determine the effect on the accounting equation of the payment of the weekly payroll on Friday, October 27.

3. Denton prepares monthly financial statements. Determine the effect on the accounting equation of the adjustment necessary on Tuesday, October 31, the last day of the month.

4. Determine the effect on the accounting equation of the payment of the weekly payroll on Friday, November 3.

5. Would net income for the month of October be understated or overstated if Denton doesn't bother with an adjustment on October 31? Explain your answer.

LO 5 **Exercise 4-11** Interest Payable

Billings Company takes out a 12%, 90-day, $100,000 loan with First National Bank on March 1, 2001.

Required

1. Determine the effect on the accounting equation of the borrowing on March 1, 2001.

2. Determine the effect on the accounting equation of the adjustments necessary for the months of March and April 2001.

3. Determine the effect on the accounting equation on May 30, 2001, when Billings repays the principal and interest to First National.

LO 5 Exercise 4-12 Property Taxes Payable—Annual Adjustments

Lexington Builders owns property in Kaneland County. Lexington's 2000 property taxes amounted to $50,000. Kaneland County will send out the 2001 property tax bills to property owners during April 2002. Taxes must be paid by June 1, 2002. Assume that Lexington prepares adjusting entries only once a year, on December 31, and that property taxes for 2001 are expected to increase by 5% over those for 2000.

Required

1. Determine the effect on the accounting equation of the adjustment necessary to record the property taxes payable on December 31, 2001.

2. Determine the effect on the accounting equation of the payment of the 2001 property taxes on June 1, 2002.

LO 5 Exercise 4-13 Interest Receivable

On June 1, 2001, MicroTel Enterprises lends $60,000 to MaxiDriver Inc. The loan will be repaid in 60 days with interest at 10%.

Required

1. Determine the effect on the accounting equation of the loan on MicroTel's books on June 1, 2001.

2. Determine the effect on the accounting equation of the adjustment necessary on MicroTel's books on June 30, 2001.

3. Determine the effect on the accounting equation for MicroTel's books on July 31, 2001, when MaxiDriver repays the principal and interest.

LO 5 Exercise 4-14 Unbilled Accounts Receivable

Mike and Cary repair computers for small local businesses. Heavy thunderstorms during the last week of June resulted in a record number of service calls. Eager to review the results of operations for the month of June, Mike prepared an income statement and was puzzled by the lower-than-expected amount of revenues. Cary explained that he had not yet billed the company's customers for $40,000 of work performed during the last week of the month.

Required

1. Should revenue be recorded when services are performed or when customers are billed? Explain your answer.

2. Determine the effect on the accounting equation of the adjustment necessary on June 30.

LO 5 Exercise 4-15 The Effect of Ignoring Adjusting Entries on Net Income

For each of the following independent situations, determine whether the effect of ignoring the required adjustment will result in an understatement (U), an overstatement (O), or no effect (NE) on net income for the period.

Situation	Effect on Net Income
Example: Taxes owed but not yet paid are ignored.	O
1. A company fails to record depreciation on equipment.	O
2. Sales made during the last week of the period are not recorded.	U
3. A company neglects to record the expired portion of a prepaid insurance policy (its cost was originally recorded in an asset account).	O
4. Interest due but not yet paid on a long-term note payable is ignored.	O
5. Commissions earned by salespeople but not payable until the 10th of the following month are ignored.	NE
6. A landlord receives cash on the date a lease is signed for the rent for the first six months and records Unearned Rent Revenue. The landlord fails to make any adjustment at the end of the first month.	

LO 5 Exercise 4-16 The Effect of Adjusting Entries on the Accounting Equation

Determine whether recording each of the following adjustments will increase (I), decrease (D), or have no effect (NE) on each of the three elements of the accounting equation.

	Assets =	Liabilities +	Owners' Equity
Example: Wages earned during the period but not yet paid are accrued.	NE	I	D

1. Prepaid insurance is reduced for the portion of the policy that has expired during the period. _____ _____ _____

2. Interest incurred during the period but not yet paid is accrued. _____ _____ _____

3. Depreciation for the period is recorded. _____ _____ _____

4. Revenue is recorded for the earned portion of a liability for amounts collected in advance from customers. _____ _____ _____

5. Rent revenue is recorded for amounts owed by a tenant but not yet paid. _____ _____ _____

6. Income taxes owed but not yet paid are accrued. _____ _____ _____

LO 6   **Exercise 4-17**   The Accounting Cycle

The steps in the accounting cycle are listed below in random order. Fill in the blank next to each step to indicate its *order* in the cycle. The first step in the cycle is filled in as an example.

Order	Procedure
_____	Prepare a work sheet.
_____	Close the accounts.
1	Collect and analyze information from source documents.
_____	Prepare financial statements.
_____	Post transactions to accounts in the ledger.
_____	Record and post adjusting entries.
_____	Journalize daily transactions.

Multi-Concept Exercises

LO 1, 2, 3   **Exercise 4-18**   Revenue Recognition, Cash and Accrual Basis

Hathaway Health Club sold three-year memberships at a reduced rate during its opening promotion. It sold 1,000 three-year, nonrefundable memberships for $366 each. The club expects to sell 100 additional three-year memberships for $900 each over each of the next two years. Membership fees are paid when clients sign up. The club's bookkeeper has prepared the following income statement for the first year of business and projected income statements for Years 2 and 3.

Cash-basis income statements:

	Year 1	Year 2	Year 3
Sales	$366,000	$90,000	$90,000
Equipment*	100,000	–0–	–0–
Salaries and Wages	50,000	50,000	50,000
Advertising	5,000	5,000	5,000
Rent and Utilities	36,000	36,000	36,000
Income (Loss)	$175,000	$ (1,000)	$ (1,000)

*Equipment was purchased at the beginning of Year 1 for $100,000 and is expected to last for three years and then to be worth $1,000.

Required

1. Convert the income statements for each of the three years to the accrual basis.

2. Describe how the revenue recognition principle applies. Do you believe that the cash-basis or the accrual-basis income statements are more useful to management? To investors? Why?

LO 4, 5 Exercise 4-19 Depreciation Expense

During 2001, Carter Company acquired three assets with the following costs, estimated useful lives, and estimated salvage values:

Date	Asset	Cost	Estimated Useful Life	Estimated Salvage Value
March 28	Truck	$ 18,000	5 years	$ 3,000
June 22	Computer	55,000	10 years	5,000
October 3	Building	250,000	30 years	10,000

The company uses the straight-line method to depreciate all assets and computes depreciation to the nearest month. For example, the computer system will be depreciated for six months in 2001.

Required

1. Compute the depreciation expense that Carter will record on each of the three assets for 2001.

2. Comment on the following statement: "Accountants could save time and money by simply expensing the cost of long-term assets when they are purchased. In addition, this would be more accurate because depreciation requires estimates of useful life and salvage value."

LO 4, 5 Exercise 4-20 Accrual of Interest on a Loan

On July 1, 2001, Paxson Corporation takes out a 12%, two-month, $50,000 loan at Friendly National Bank. Principal and interest are to be repaid on August 31.

Required

1. Determine the effects on the accounting equation of each of the following: (a) the borrowing on July 1 (b) the necessary adjustment for the accrual of interest on July 31 (c) repayment of the principal and interest.

2. Evaluate the following statement: "It would be much easier not to bother with an adjustment on July 31 and simply record interest expense on August 31 when the loan is repaid."

PROBLEMS

LO 5 Problem 4-1 Adjustments

Water Corporation prepares monthly financial statements and therefore adjusts its accounts at the end of every month. The following information is available for March 2001:

a. Water Corporation takes out a 90-day, 8%, $15,000 note on March 1, 2001, with interest and principal to be paid at maturity.

b. The asset account Office Supplies on Hand has a balance of $1,280 on March 1, 2001. During March, Water adds $750 to the account for the purchases of the period. A count of the supplies on hand at the end of March indicates a balance of $1,370.

c. The company purchased office equipment last year for $62,600. The equipment has an estimated useful life of six years and an estimated salvage value of $5,000.

d. The company's plant operates seven days per week with a daily payroll of $950. Wage earners are paid every Sunday. The last day of the month is Saturday, March 31.

e. The company rented an idle warehouse to a neighboring business on February 1, 2001, at a rate of $2,500 per month. On this date, Water Corporation recorded Rent Collected in Advance for six months' rent received in advance.

f. On March 1, 2001, Water Corporation created a liability account, Customer Deposits, for $4,800. This sum represents an amount that a customer paid in advance and that will be earned evenly by Water over a four-month period.

g. Based on its income for the month, Water Corporation estimates that federal income taxes for March amount to $3,900.

Required

1. For each of the preceding situations, determine the effect on the accounting equation of the adjustment necessary on March 31, 2001.

2. Assume that Water reports income of $23,000 before any of the adjustments. What net income will Water report for March?

LO 5 Problem 4-2 Annual Adjustments

Palmer Industries prepares annual financial statements and adjusts its accounts only at the end of the year. The following information is available for the year ended December 31, 2001:

a. Palmer purchased computer equipment two years ago for $15,000. The equipment has an estimated useful life of five years and an estimated salvage value of $250.

b. The Office Supplies account had a balance of $3,600 on January 1, 2001. During 2001, Palmer added $17,600 to the account for purchases of office supplies during the year. A count of the supplies on hand at the end of December 2001 indicates a balance of $1,850.

c. On August 1, 2001, Palmer created a liability account, Customer Deposits, for $24,000. This sum represents an amount that a customer paid in advance and that will be earned evenly by Palmer over a six-month period.

d. Palmer rented some office space on November 1, 2001, at a rate of $2,700 per month. On that date, Palmer recorded Prepaid Rent for three months' rent paid in advance.

e. Palmer took out a 120-day, 9%, $200,000 note on November 1, 2001, with interest and principal to be paid at maturity.

f. Palmer operates five days per week with an average daily payroll of $500. Palmer pays its employees every Friday. December 31, 2001, is a Monday.

Required

1. For each of the preceding situations, determine the effect on the accounting equation of the adjustment necessary on December 31, 2001.

2. Assume that Palmer's accountant forgets to record the adjustments on December 31, 2001. Will net income for the year be understated or overstated? By what amount? (Ignore the effect of income taxes.)

LO 5 Problem 4-3 Recurring Transactions and Adjustments

The following are Butler Realty Corporation's accounts, identified by number. The company has been in the real estate business for 10 years and prepares financial statements monthly. Following the list of accounts is a series of transactions entered into by Butler. For each transaction, enter the number of the account(s) affected.

Accounts

1. Cash	11. Notes Payable
2. Accounts Receivable	12. Capital Stock, $10 par
3. Prepaid Rent	13. Paid-in Capital in Excess of Par
4. Office Supplies	14. Commissions Revenue
5. Automobiles	15. Office Supply Expense
6. Accumulated Depreciation	16. Rent Expense
7. Land	17. Salaries and Wages Expense
8. Accounts Payable	18. Depreciation Expense
9. Salaries and Wages Payable	19. Interest Expense
10. Income Tax Payable	20. Income Tax Expense

Transaction

a. **Example:** Issued additional shares of stock to owners at amount in excess of par.   1, 12, 13

b. Purchased automobiles for cash.   _____

c. Purchased land; made cash down payment and signed a promissory note for the balance.   _____

Transaction

d. Paid cash to landlord for rent for next 12 months. _____

e. Purchased office supplies on account. _____

f. Collected cash for commissions from clients for the properties sold during the month. _____

g. Collected cash for commissions from clients for the properties sold in the prior month. _____

h. During the month, sold properties for which cash for commissions will be collected from clients next month. _____

i. Paid for office supplies purchased on account in an earlier month. _____

j. Recorded an adjustment to recognize wages and salaries incurred but not yet paid. _____

k. Recorded an adjustment for office supplies used during the month. _____

l. Recorded an adjustment for the portion of prepaid rent that expired during the month. _____

m. Made required month-end payment on note taken out in **(c)**; payment is part principal and part interest. _____

n. Recorded adjustment for monthly depreciation on the autos. _____

o. Recorded adjustment for income taxes. _____

LO 5 Problem 4-4 Use of Account Balances as a Basis for Annual Adjustments

The following account balances are taken from the records of Chauncey Company at December 31, 2001. The Prepaid Insurance account represents the cost of a three-year policy purchased on August 1, 2001. The Rent Collected in Advance account represents the cash received from a tenant on June 1, 2001, for 12 months' rent, beginning on that date. The Note Receivable represents a nine-month promissory note received from a customer on September 1, 2001. Principal and interest at an annual rate of 9% will be received on June 1, 2002.

Prepaid Insurance	$ 7,200
Rent Collected in Advance	6,000
Note Receivable	50,000

Required

1. For each of the three situations described above, determine the effect on the accounting equation of the adjustments necessary on December 31, 2001. Assume that Chauncey records adjustments only once a year, on December 31.

2. Assume that adjustments are made at the end of each month rather than only at the end of the year. What would be the balance in Prepaid Insurance *before* the December adjustment is recorded? Explain your answer.

LO 5 Problem 4-5 Use of Account Balances as a Basis for Adjustments

Bob Reynolds operates a real estate business. A list of accounts on April 30, 2001, *before* recording any adjustments, appears as follows:

Cash	$15,700
Prepaid Insurance	450
Office Supplies	250
Office Equipment	50,000
Accumulated Depreciation—Office Equipment	5,000
Automobile	12,000
Accumulated Depreciation—Automobile	1,400
Accounts Payable	6,500
Unearned Commissions	9,500
Notes Payable	2,000
Capital Stock	10,000
Retained Earnings	40,000
Dividends	2,500

Commissions Earned		17,650
Utility Expense		2,300
Salaries Expense		7,400
Advertising Expense		1,450

Other Data

a. The monthly insurance cost is $50.

b. Office supplies on hand on April 30, 2001, amount to $180.

c. The office equipment was purchased on April 1, 2000. On that date, it had an estimated useful life of 10 years.

d. On September 1, 2000, the automobile was purchased; it had an estimated useful life of five years.

e. A deposit is received in advance of providing any services for first-time customers. Amounts received in advance are recorded initially in the account Unearned Commissions. Based on services provided to these first-time customers, the balance in this account at the end of April should be $5,000.

f. Repeat customers are allowed to pay for services one month after the date of the sale of their property. Services rendered during the month but not yet collected or billed to these customers amount to $1,500.

g. Interest owed on the note payable but not yet paid amounts to $20.

h. Salaries owed to employees but unpaid at the end of the month amount to $2,500.

Required

1. For each of the items of other data, **a** through **h,** determine the effect on the accounting equation.

2. Compute the net increase or decrease in net income for the month from the recognition of the adjustments in part **1.** (Ignore income taxes.)

3. Note the balance in Accumulated Depreciation—Office Equipment is $5,000. Explain *why* the account contains a balance of $5,000 on April 30, 2001.

LO 5 Problem 4-6 Reconstruction of Adjustments from Account Balances

Taggart Corp. records adjustments each month before preparing monthly financial statements. The following selected account balances on May 31, 2001 and June 30, 2001 reflect month-end adjustments.

Account Title	May 31, 2001	June 30, 2001
Prepaid Insurance	$3,600	$3,450
Equipment	9,600	9,600
Accumulated Depreciation	1,280	1,360
Notes Payable	9,600	9,600
Interest Payable	2,304	2,448

Required

1. The company purchased a 36-month insurance policy on June 1, 2000. Determine the effect on the accounting equation of the adjustment that was made for insurance on June 30, 2001.

2. What was the original cost of the insurance policy? Explain your answer.

3. The equipment was purchased on February 1, 2000, for $9,600. Taggart uses straight-line depreciation and estimates that the equipment will have no salvage value. Determine the effect on the accounting equation of the adjustment that was made for depreciation on June 30, 2001.

4. What is the equipment's estimated useful life in months? Explain your answer.

5. Taggart signed a two-year note payable on February 1, 2000, for the purchase of the equipment. Interest on the note accrues on a monthly basis and will be paid at maturity along with the principal amount of $9,600. Determine the effect on the accounting equation of the adjustment that was made for interest on June 30, 2001.

6. What is the *monthly* interest rate on the loan? Explain your answer.

Problem 4-7 Use of Account Balances as a Basis for Adjustments

The following is a list of accounts for Four Star Video at May 31, 2001. It reflects the recurring transactions for the month of May but does not reflect any month-end adjustments.

Cash	$ 4,000
Prepaid Rent	6,600
Video Inventory	25,600
Display Stands	8,900
Accumulated Depreciation	5,180
Accounts Payable	3,260
Customer Subscriptions	4,450
Capital Stock	5,000
Retained Earnings	22,170
Rental Revenue	9,200
Wage and Salary Expense	2,320
Utility Expense	1,240
Advertising Expense	600

The following additional information is available:

a. Four Star rents a store in a shopping mall and prepays the annual rent of $7,200 on April 1 of each year.

b. The asset account Video Inventory represents the cost of videos purchased from suppliers. When a new title is purchased from a supplier, its cost is added to this account. When a title has served its useful life and can no longer be rented (even at a reduced price), it is removed from the inventory in the store. Based on the monthly count, the cost of titles on hand at the end of May is $23,140.

c. The display stands have an estimated useful life of five years and an estimated salvage value of $500.

d. Wages and salaries owed to employees but unpaid at the end of May amount to $1,450.

e. In addition to individual rentals, Four Star operates a popular discount subscription program. Customers pay an annual fee of $120 for an unlimited number of rentals. Based on the $10 per month earned on each of these subscriptions, the amount earned for the month of May is $2,440.

f. Four Star accrues income taxes using an estimated tax rate equal to 30% of the income for the month.

Required

1. For each of the items of additional information **a** through **f**, determine the effect on the accounting equation.

2. On the basis of the information you have, does Four Star appear to be a profitable business? Explain your answer.

Multi-Concept Problems

Problem 4-8 Cash and Accrual Income Statements for a Manufacturer

Drysdale Company was established to manufacture components for the auto industry. The components are shipped the same day they are produced. The following events took place during the first year of operations.

a. Issued common stock for a $50,000 cash investment.

b. Purchased delivery truck at the beginning of the year at a cost of $10,000 cash. The truck is expected to last five years and will be worthless at the end of that time.

c. Manufactured and sold 500,000 components the first year. The costs incurred to manufacture the components are (1) $1,000 monthly rent on a facility that included utilities and insurance, (2) $400,000 of raw materials purchased on account ($100,000 is still unpaid as of year-end, but all materials were used in manufacturing), and (3) $190,000 paid in salaries and wages to employees and supervisors.

d. Paid $100,000 to sales and office staff for salaries and wages.

e. Sold all components on account for $2 each. As of year-end, $150,000 is due from customers.

Required

1. How much revenue will Drysdale recognize under the cash basis and under the accrual basis?

2. Describe how Drysdale should apply the matching principle to recognize expenses.

3. Prepare an income statement under the accrual basis. Ignore income taxes.

LO 3, 4 Problem 4-9 Revenue and Expense Recognition

Two years ago, Darlene Darby opened a delivery service. Darby reports the following accounts on her income statement:

Sales	$69,000
Advertising expense	3,500
Salaries expense	39,000
Rent expense	10,000

These amounts represent two years of revenue and expenses. Darby has asked you how she can tell how much of the income is from the first year of business and how much is from the second year. She provides the following additional data:

a. Sales in the second year were double those of the first year.

b. Advertising expense is for a $500 opening promotion and weekly ads in the newspaper.

c. Salaries represent one employee for the first nine months and then two employees for the remainder of the time. Each is paid the same salary. No raises have been granted.

d. Rent has not changed since the business opened.

Required

Prepare income statements for Years 1 and 2.

LO 5, 6 Problem 4-10 Monthly Transactions, Adjustments, and Financial Statements

Moonlight Bay Inn is incorporated on January 2, 2001, by its three owners, each of whom contributes $20,000 in cash in exchange for shares of stock in the business. In addition to the sale of stock, the following transactions are entered into during the month of January:

January   2:   A Victorian inn is purchased for $50,000 in cash. An appraisal performed on this date indicates that the land is worth $15,000 and the remaining balance of the purchase price is attributable to the house. The owners estimate that the house will have an estimated useful life of 25 years and an estimated salvage value of $5,000.

January   3:   A two-year, 12%, $30,000 promissory note was signed at the Second State Bank. Interest and principal will be repaid on the maturity date of January 3, 2003.

January   4:   New furniture for the inn is purchased at a cost of $15,000 in cash. The furniture has an estimated useful life of 10 years and no salvage value.

January   5:   A 24-month property insurance policy is purchased for $6,000 in cash.

January   6:   An advertisement for the inn is placed in the local newspaper. Moonlight Bay pays $450 cash for the ad, which will run in the paper throughout January.

January   7:   Cleaning supplies are purchased on account for $950. The bill is payable within 30 days.

January 15:   Wages of $4,230 for the first half of the month are paid in cash.

January 16:   A guest mails the business $980 in cash as a deposit for a room to be rented for two weeks. The guest plans to stay at the inn during the last week of January and the first week of February.

January 31:   Cash receipts from rentals of rooms for the month amount to $8,300.

January 31:   Cash receipts from operation of the restaurant for the month amount to $6,600.

January 31:   Each stockholder is paid $200 in cash dividends.

Required

1. Determine the effect on the accounting equation of each of the preceding transactions.

2. Prepare a list of accounts for Moonlight Bay Inn at January 31, 2001. Reflect the recurring transactions for the month of January but not the necessary month-end adjustments.

3. Determine the effect on the accounting equation of the necessary adjustments at January 31, 2001, for each of the following:

   a. Depreciation of the house

   b. Depreciation of the furniture

   c. Interest on the promissory note

   d. Recognition of the expired portion of the insurance

   e. Recognition of the earned portion of the guest's deposit

   f. Wages earned during the second half of January amount to $5,120 and will be paid on February 3.

   g. Cleaning supplies on hand on January 31 amount to $230.

   h. A gas and electric bill that is received from the city amounts to $740 and is payable by February 5.

   i. Income taxes are to be accrued at a rate of 30% of income before taxes.

4. Prepare in good form the following financial statements:

   a. Income statement for the month ended January 31, 2001

   b. Statement of retained earnings for the month ended January 31, 2001

   c. Balance sheet at January 31, 2001

5. Assume that you are the loan officer at Second State Bank (refer to the transaction on January 3). What are your reactions to Moonlight's first month of operations? Are you comfortable with the loan you made?

ALTERNATE PROBLEMS

LO 5 **Problem 4-1A** Adjustments

Flood Relief Inc. prepares monthly financial statements and therefore adjusts its accounts at the end of every month. The following information is available for June 2001:

a. Flood received a $10,000, 4%, two-year note receivable from a customer for services rendered. The principal and interest are due on June 1, 2003. Flood expects to be able to collect the note and interest in full at that time.

b. Office supplies totaling $5,600 were purchased during the month. The asset account Supplies is increased whenever a purchase is made. A count in the storeroom on June 30, 2001, indicated that supplies on hand amount to $507. The supplies on hand at the beginning of the month total $475.

c. The company purchased machines last year for $170,000. The machines are expected to be used for four years and have an estimated salvage value of $2,000.

d. On June 1, the company paid $4,650 for rent for June, July, and August, and increased the asset Prepaid Rent. It did not have a balance on June 1.

e. The company operates seven days per week with a weekly payroll of $7,000. Wage earners are paid every Sunday. The last day of the month is Saturday, June 30.

f. Based on its income for the month, Flood estimates that federal income taxes for June amount to $2,900.

Required

For each of the preceding situations, determine the effect on the accounting equation of the adjustment necessary on June 30, 2001.

LO 5 **Problem 4-2A** Annual Adjustments

Ogonquit Enterprises prepares annual financial statements and adjusts its accounts only at the end of the year. The following information is available for the year ended December 31, 2001:

a. Ogonquit purchased office furniture last year for $25,000. The furniture has an estimated useful life of seven years and an estimated salvage value of $4,000.

b. The Supplies account had a balance of $1,200 on January 1, 2001. During 2001, Ogonquit added $12,900 to the account for purchases of supplies during the year. A count of the supplies on hand at the end of December 2001 indicates a balance of $900.

c. On July 1, 2001, Ogonquit created a liability account, Customer Deposits, for $8,800. This sum represents an amount that a customer paid in advance and that will be earned evenly by Ogonquit over an eight-month period.

d. Ogonquit rented some warehouse space on September 1, 2001, at a rate of $4,000 per month. On that date, Ogonquit recorded Prepaid Rent for six months' rent paid in advance.

e. Ogonquit took out a 90-day, 6%, $30,000 note on November 1, 2001, with interest and principal to be paid at maturity.

f. Ogonquit operates five days per week with an average weekly payroll of $4,150. Ogonquit pays its employees every Friday. December 31, 2001, is a Monday.

Required

1. For each of the preceding situations, determine the effect on the accounting equation of the adjustment necessary on December 31, 2001.

2. Assume that Ogonquit's accountant forgets to record the adjustments on December 31, 2001. Will net income for the year be understated or overstated? By what amount? (Ignore the effect of income taxes.)

LO 5 **Problem 4-3A** Recurring Transactions and Adjustments

The following are the accounts of Dominique Inc., an interior decorator. The company has been in the decorating business for 10 years and prepares quarterly financial statements. Following the list of accounts is a series of transactions entered into by Dominique. For each transaction, enter the number of the account(s) affected.

Accounts

1. Cash	**11.** Capital Stock, $1 par
2. Accounts Receivable	**12.** Paid-in Capital in Excess of Par
3. Prepaid Rent	**13.** Consulting Revenue
4. Office Supplies	**14.** Office Supply Expense
5. Office Equipment	**15.** Rent Expense
6. Accumulated Depreciation	**16.** Salaries and Wages Expense
7. Accounts Payable	**17.** Depreciation Expense
8. Salaries and Wages Payable	**18.** Interest Expense
9. Income Tax Payable	**19.** Income Tax Expense
10. Interim Financing Notes Payable	

Transaction

a.	**Example:** Issued additional shares of stock to owners; shares issued at greater than par.	1, 11, 12
b.	Purchased office equipment for cash.	_____
c.	Collected open accounts receivable from customer.	_____
d.	Purchased office supplies on account.	_____
e.	Paid office rent for the next six months.	_____
f.	Paid interest on an interim financing note.	_____
g.	Paid salaries and wages.	_____
h.	Purchased office equipment; made a down payment in cash and signed an interim financing note.	_____
i.	Provided services on account.	_____
j.	Recorded depreciation on equipment.	_____
k.	Recorded income taxes due next month.	_____
l.	Recorded the used office supplies.	_____
m.	Recorded the used portion of prepaid rent.	_____

LO 5 **Problem 4-4A** Use of Account Balances as a Basis for Annual Adjustments

The following account balances are taken from the records of Laugherty Inc. at December 31, 2001. The Supplies account represents the cost of supplies on hand at the beginning of the year plus all purchases. A physical count on December 31, 2001, shows only $1,520 of supplies on hand. The Unearned Revenue account represents the cash received from a customer on May 1, 2001, for 12 months of service, beginning on that date. The Note Payable represents a six-month promissory note signed with a supplier on September 1, 2001. Principal and interest at an annual rate of 10% will be paid on March 1, 2002.

Supplies	$ 5,790
Unearned Revenue	1,800
Note Payable	60,000

Required

1. For each of the three situations described above, determine the effect on the accounting equation of the adjustments necessary on December 31, 2001. Assume that Laugherty records adjustments only once a year, on December 31.

2. Assume that adjustments are made at the end of each month rather than only at the end of the year. What would be the balance in Unearned Revenue *before* the December adjustment is made? Explain your answer.

LO 5 **Problem 4-5A** Use of Account Balances as a Basis for Adjustments

Lori Matlock operates a graphic arts business. A list of accounts on June 30, 2001, *before* recording any adjustments, appears as follows:

Cash	$ 7,000
Prepaid Rent	18,000
Supplies	15,210
Office Equipment	46,120
Accumulated Depreciation—Equipment	4,000
Accounts Payable	1,800
Notes Payable	2,000
Capital Stock	50,000
Retained Earnings	24,350
Dividends	8,400
Revenue	46,850
Utility Expense	2,850
Salaries Expense	19,420
Advertising Expense	12,000

Other Data

a. The monthly rent cost is $600.

b. Supplies on hand on June 30, 2001, amount to $1,290.

c. The office equipment was purchased on June 1, 2000. On that date, it had an estimated useful life of 10 years and a salvage value of $6,120.

d. Interest owed on the note payable but not yet paid amounts to $50.

e. Salaries of $620 are owed to employees but unpaid at the end of the month.

Required

1. For each of the items of other data, **a** through **e,** determine the effect on the accounting equation.

2. Note the balance in Accumulated Depreciation—Equipment is $4,000. Explain *why* the account contains a balance of $4,000 on June 30, 2001.

LO 5 **Problem 4-6A** Reconstruction of Adjustments from Account Balances

Zola Corporation records adjustments each month before preparing monthly financial statements. The following selected account balances on May 31, 2001 and June 30, 2001 reflect month-end adjustments.

Account Title	May 31, 2001	June 30, 2001
Prepaid Rent	$4,000	$3,000
Equipment	9,600	9,600
Accumulated Depreciation	800	900
Notes Payable	9,600	9,600
Interest Payable	768	864

Required

1. The company paid for a six-month lease on April 1, 2001. Determine the effect on the accounting equation of the adjustment that was made for the lease on June 30, 2001.

2. What amount was prepaid on April 1, 2001? Explain your answer.

3. The equipment was purchased on September 30, 2000, for $9,600. Zola uses straight-line depreciation and estimates that the equipment will have no salvage value. Determine the effect on the accounting equation of the adjustment that was made for depreciation on June 30, 2001.

4. What is the equipment's estimated useful life in months? Explain your answer.

5. Zola signed a two-year note on September 30, 2000, for the purchase of the equipment. Interest on the note accrues on a monthly basis and will be paid at maturity along with the principal amount of $9,600. Determine the effect on the accounting equation of the adjustment that was made for interest expense on June 30, 2001.

6. What is the *monthly* interest rate on the loan? Explain your answer.

LO 5 Problem 4-7A Use of Account Balances as a Basis for Adjustments

Lewis and Associates has been in the termite inspection and treatment business for five years. The following is a list of accounts for Lewis at June 30, 2001. It reflects the recurring transactions for the month of June, but does not reflect any month-end adjustments.

Cash	$ 6,200
Accounts Receivable	10,400
Prepaid Rent	4,400
Chemical Inventory	9,400
Equipment	18,200
Accumulated Depreciation	1,050
Accounts Payable	1,180
Capital Stock	5,000
Retained Earnings	25,370
Treatment Revenue	40,600
Wages and Salary Expense	22,500
Utility Expense	1,240
Advertising Expense	860

The following additional information is available:

a. Lewis rents a warehouse with office space and prepays the annual rent of $4,800 on May 1 of each year.

b. The asset account Equipment represents the cost of treatment equipment, which has an estimated useful life of 10 years and an estimated salvage value of $200.

c. Chemical inventory on hand equals $1,300.

d. Wages and salaries owed to employees but unpaid at the end of the month amount to $1,080.

e. Lewis accrues income taxes using an estimated tax rate equal to 30% of the income for the month.

Required

1. For each of the items of additional information, a through e, determine the effect on the accounting equation.

2. On the basis of the information you have, does Lewis appear to be a profitable business? Explain your answer.

Alternate Multi-Concept Problems

LO 2, 3, 4 **Problem 4-8A** Cash and Accrual Income Statements for a Manufacturer

Marie's Catering makes sandwiches for vending machines. The sandwiches are delivered to the vendor on the same day that they are made. The following events took place during the first year of operations.

a. On the first day of the year, issued common stock for a $20,000 cash investment and a $10,000 investment of equipment. The equipment is expected to last 10 years and will be worthless at the end of that time.

b. Purchased a delivery truck at the beginning of the year at a cost of $14,000 cash. The truck is expected to last five years and will be worthless at the end of that time.

c. Made and sold 50,000 sandwiches during the first year of operations. The costs incurred to make the sandwiches are (1) $800 monthly rent on a facility that included utilities and insurance, (2) $25,000 of meat, cheese, bread, and condiments (all food was purchased on account, and $4,000 is still unpaid at year-end even though all of the food has been used), and (3) $35,000 paid in salaries and wages to employees and supervisors.

d. Paid $12,000 for part-time office staff salaries.

e. Sold all sandwiches on account for $2 each. As of year-end, $25,000 is still due from the vendors.

Required

1. How much revenue will Marie's Catering recognize under the cash basis and under the accrual basis?

2. Explain how accountants apply the revenue recognition principle to Marie's small business. What conditions would allow Marie's to use the cash method to recognize revenue?

3. Prepare an income statement according to the accrual method. Ignore income taxes.

LO 3, 4 **Problem 4-9A** Revenue and Expense Recognition

Two years ago, Sue Stern opened an audio book rental shop. Sue reports the following accounts on her income statement:

Sales	$84,000
Advertising expense	10,500
Salaries expense	12,000
Depreciation on tapes	5,000
Rent expense	18,000

These amounts represent two years of revenue and expenses. Sue has asked you how she can tell how much of the income is from the first year and how much is from the second year of business. She provides the following additional data:

a. Sales in the second year are triple those of the first year.

b. Advertising expense is for a $1,500 opening promotion and weekly ads in the newspaper.

c. Salaries represent one employee who was hired eight months ago. No raises have been granted.

d. Rent has not changed since the shop opened.

Required

Prepare income statements for Years 1 and 2.

LO 5, 6, 8 **Problem 4-10A** Adjustments and Financial Statements

The following account balances are available for Tenfour Trucking Company on January 31, 2001 (before any adjustments are made):

Cash	$ 27,340
Accounts Receivable	41,500
Prepaid Insurance	18,000
Warehouse	40,000
Accumulated Depreciation—Warehouse	21,600
Truck Fleet	240,000
Accumulated Depreciation—Truck Fleet	112,500

Land	20,000
Accounts Payable	32,880
Notes Payable	50,000
Interest Payable	4,500
Customer Deposits	6,000
Capital Stock	100,000
Retained Earnings	40,470
Freight Revenue	165,670
Gas and Oil Expense	57,330
Maintenance Expense	26,400
Wage and Salary Expense	43,050
Dividends	20,000

Required

1. Determine the effect on the accounting equation of the necessary adjustments at January 31, 2001, for each of the following:

   a. Prepaid insurance represents the cost of a 24-month policy purchased on January 1, 2001.

   b. The warehouse has an estimated useful life of 20 years and an estimated salvage value of $4,000.

   c. The truck fleet has an estimated useful life of six years and an estimated salvage value of $15,000.

   d. The promissory note was signed on January 1, 2000. Interest at an annual rate of 9% and the principal of $50,000 are due on December 31, 2001.

   e. The customer deposits represent amounts paid in advance by new customers. A total of $4,500 of the balance in Customer Deposits was earned during January 2001.

   f. Wages and salaries earned by employees at the end of January but not yet paid amount to $8,200.

   g. Income taxes are accrued at a rate of 30% at the end of each month.

2. Prepare in good form the following financial statements:

   a. Income statement for the month ended January 31, 2001

   b. Statement of retained earnings for the month ended January 31, 2001

   c. Balance sheet at January 31, 2001

3. Compute Tenfour's current ratio. What does this ratio tell you about the company's liquidity?

4. Explain why it is not possible to compute a gross profit ratio for Tenfour. Describe a ratio that you believe would be a meaningful measure of profitability for a trucking company. Feel free to "invent" a ratio if you think it would be a meaningful measure of profitability.

CASES

Reading and Interpreting Financial Statements

LO 3 Case 4-1   Reading and Interpreting Uno's Footnotes—Revenue Recognition

www.pizzeriauno.com Refer to page 21 of its annual report where Uno explains how it recognizes franchise fees as revenue.

Required

1. Is the way in which Uno recognizes franchise fees for individual restaurants as revenue in accordance with the revenue recognition principle? Explain your answer.

2. Refer to Uno's financial statements. How important are franchise fees as a form of revenue for the company? Support your answer with any necessary computations.

LO 3 Case 4-2   Reading and Interpreting Gateway's Footnotes—Revenue Recognition

www.gateway.com Refer to Gateway's first footnote, "Summary of Significant Accounting Policies," and specifically the section that discusses revenue recognition.

Required

1. At what point in time does Gateway recognize revenue?

2. Explain what Gateway means by "extended service plans."

3. Why would Gateway recognize the revenue from these programs over "the extended service period" rather than in the period a product is sold?

LO 3   Case 4-3   Reading and Interpreting Sears, Roebuck's Footnotes—Revenue Recognition

The following excerpt is taken from Sears' 1999 annual report: "The Company sells extended service contracts with terms of coverage generally between 12 and 36 months. Revenues and incremental direct acquisition costs from the sale of these contracts are deferred and amortized over the lives of the contracts. Costs related to performing the services under the contracts are expensed as incurred."   www.searsroebuck.com

Required

1. Why do retailers recognize the revenue over the life of the service contract even though cash is received at the time of the sale?

2. If a product is sold in Year 1 for $2,500, including a $180 service contract that will cover three years, how much revenue is recognized in Years 1, 2, and 3? (Assume a straight-line approach.) What corresponding account can you look for in the financial statements to determine the amount of service contract revenue that will be recognized in the future?

Making Financial Decisions

LO 2, 3, 4   Case 4-4   The Use of Net Income and Cash Flow to Evaluate a Company

After you have gained five years of experience with a large CPA firm, one of your clients, Duke Inc., asks you to take over as chief financial officer for the business. Duke advises its clients on the purchase of software products and assists them in installing the programs on their computer systems. Because the business is relatively new (it began servicing clients in January 2001), its accounting records are somewhat limited. In fact, the only statement available is an income statement for the first year:

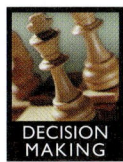

DECISION
MAKING

DUKE INC.
STATEMENT OF INCOME
FOR THE YEAR ENDED DECEMBER 31, 2001

Revenues		$1,250,000
Expenses:		
Salaries and wages	$480,000	
Supplies	65,000	
Utilities	30,000	
Rent	120,000	
Depreciation	345,000	
Interest	138,000	
Total expenses		$1,178,000
Net income		$ 72,000

Based on its relatively modest profit margin of 5.76% (net income of $72,000 divided by revenues of $1,250,000), you are concerned about joining the new business. To alleviate your concerns, the president of the company is able to give you the following additional information:

a. Clients are given 90 days to pay their bills for consulting services provided by Duke. On December 31, 2001, $230,000 of the revenues is yet to be collected in cash.

b. Employees are paid on a monthly basis. Salaries and wages of $480,000 include the December payroll of $40,000, which will be paid on January 5, 2002.

c. The company purchased $100,000 of operating supplies when it began operations in January. The balance of supplies on hand at December 31 amounts to $35,000.

d. Office space is rented in a downtown high-rise building at a monthly rental of $10,000. When the company moved into the office in January, it prepaid its rent for the next 18 months, beginning January 1, 2001.

e. On January 1, 2001, Duke purchased its own computer system and related accessories at a cost of $1,725,000. The estimated useful life of the system is five years.

f. The computer system was purchased by signing a three-year, 8% note payable for $1,725,000 on the date of purchase. The principal amount of the note and interest for the three years are due on January 1, 2004.

Required

1. Based on the income statement and the additional information given, prepare a statement of cash flows for Duke for 2001. (*Hint:* Simply list all the cash inflows and outflows that relate to operations.)

2. On the basis of the income statement given and the statement of cash flows prepared in part **1,** do you think it would be a wise decision on your part to join the company as its chief financial officer? Include in your response any additional questions that you believe are appropriate to ask before joining the company.

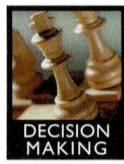

DECISION MAKING

LO 4   Case 4-5   Depreciation

Jenner Inc., a graphic arts studio, is considering the purchase of computer equipment and software for a total cost of $18,000. Jenner can pay for the equipment and software over three years at the rate of $6,000 per year. The equipment is expected to last 10 to 20 years, but because of changing technology, Jenner believes it may need to replace the system as soon as three to five years. A three-year lease of similar equipment and software is available for $6,000 per year. Jenner's accountant has asked you to recommend whether the company should purchase or lease the equipment and software and to suggest the length of the period over which to depreciate the software and equipment if the company makes the purchase.

Required

Ignoring the effect of taxes, would you recommend the purchase or the lease? Why? Referring to the definition of *depreciation,* what is the appropriate useful life to use for the equipment and software?

Accounting and Ethics: What Would You Do?

LO 2, 3, 4, 5   Case 4-6   Revenue Recognition and the Matching Principle

Listum & Sellum Inc. is a medium-size midwestern real estate company. It was founded five years ago by its two principal stockholders, Willie Listum and Dewey Sellum. Willie is president of the company, and Dewey is vice-president of sales. Listum & Sellum has enjoyed tremendous growth since its inception by aggressively seeking out listings for residential real estate and paying a very generous commission to the selling agent.

The company receives a 6% commission for selling a client's property and gives two-thirds of this, or 4% of the selling price, to the selling agent. For example, if a house sells for $100,000, Listum & Sellum receives $6,000 and pays $4,000 of this to the selling agent. At the time of the sale, the company records $6,000 of Accounts Receivable and $6,000 of Sales Revenue. The accounts receivable is normally collected within 30 days. Also at the time of sale, the company records $4,000 of Commissions Expense and $4,000 of Commissions Payable. Sales agents are paid by the 15th of the month following the month of the sale. In addition to the commissions expense, Listum & Sellum's other two major expenses are advertising of listings in local newspapers and depreciation of the company fleet of Cadillacs (Dewey has always believed that all the sales agents should drive Cadillacs). The newspaper ads are taken for one month, and the company has until the 10th of the following month to pay that month's bill. The automobiles are depreciated over four years (Dewey doesn't believe that any salesperson should drive a car that is more than four years old).

Due to a downturn in the economy in the Midwest, sales have been sluggish for the first 11 months of the current year, which ends on June 30. Willie is very disturbed by the slow sales this particular year because a large note payable to the local bank is due in July and the company plans to ask the bank to renew the note for another three years. Dewey seems less concerned by the unfortunate timing of the recession and has some suggestions as to how they can "paint the rosiest possible picture for the banker" when they go for the loan extension in July. In fact, he has some very specific recommendations for you as to how to account for transactions during June, the last month in the fiscal year.

You are the controller for Listum & Sellum and have been treated very well by Willie and Dewey since joining the company two years ago. In fact, Dewey insists that you personally drive the top-of-the-line Cadillac. Following are his suggestions:

> First, for any sales made in June, we can record the 6% commission revenue immediately but delay recording the 4% commission expense until July, when the sales agent is paid.

We record the sales at the same time we always have, the sales agents get paid when they always have, the bank sees how profitable we have been, we get our loan, and everybody is happy!

Second, since we won't be paying our advertising bills for the month of June until July 10, we can just wait until then to record the expense. The timing seems perfect, given that we are to meet with the bank for the loan extension on July 8.

Third, since we will be depreciating the fleet of Caddys for the year ending June 30, how about just changing the estimated useful life on them to eight years instead of four years? We won't say anything to the sales agents; no need to rile them up about having to drive their cars for eight years. Anyhow, the change to eight years would just be for accounting purposes. In fact, we could even switch back to four years for accounting purposes next year. Likewise, the changes in recognizing commission expense and advertising expense don't need to be permanent either; these are just slight bookkeeping changes to help us get over the hump!

Required

1. Explain why each of the three proposed changes in accounting will result in an increase in net income for the year ending June 30.

2. Identify any concerns you have with each of the three proposed changes in accounting from the perspective of generally accepted accounting principles.

3. Identify any concerns you have with each of the three proposed changes in accounting from an ethical perspective.

4. What would you do? Draft your response to Willie and Dewey in the form of a business memo.

LO 4 Case 4-7 Advice to a Potential Investor

Century Company was organized 15 months ago as a management consulting firm. At that time, the owners invested a total of $50,000 cash in exchange for stock. Century purchased equipment for $35,000 cash and supplies to be used in the business. The equipment is expected to last seven years with no salvage value. Supplies are purchased on account and paid for in the month after the purchase. Century normally has about $1,000 of supplies on hand. Its client base has increased so dramatically that the president and chief financial officer have approached an investor to provide additional cash for expansion. The balance sheet and income statement for the first year of business are presented here:

CENTURY COMPANY
BALANCE SHEET
DECEMBER 31, 2001

Assets		Liabilities and Owners' Equity	
Cash	$10,100	Accounts payable	$ 2,300
Accounts receivable	1,200	Common stock	50,000
Supplies	16,500	Retained earnings	10,500
Equipment	35,000		
Total	$62,800	Total	$62,800

CENTURY COMPANY
INCOME STATEMENT
FOR THE YEAR ENDED DECEMBER 31, 2001

Revenues		$82,500
Wages and salaries	$60,000	
Utilities	12,000	72,000
Net income		$10,500

Required

The investor has asked you to look at these financial statements and give an opinion about Century's future profitability. Are the statements prepared in accordance with generally accepted accounting principles? If not, explain why. Based on only these two statements, what would you advise? What additional information would you need in order to give an educated opinion?

INTERNET RESEARCH CASE

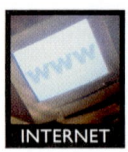

INTERNET

www.mcdonalds.com

Case 4-8 McDonald's

McDonald's is the largest and best known fast-food supplier in the world, with worldwide (system-wide) sales of nearly $38 billion in 1999. Yet it claims to serve only 1% of the world's population. One of its strategic goals is to increase market share, and to this end it has acquired several different restaurant chains, further diversifying its interests.

Review the chapter opening introduction to McDonald's and the Business Strategy box. Then go to McDonald's Web site, examine its most recent annual report, and research how the company can fulfill management's goals of greater market share, higher customer satisfaction, and increased profitability.

1. McDonald's total revenues includes all the revenues from company-operated restaurants and a portion of the revenues of franchisees' restaurants.

   a. Looking at the latest year's income statement, what are McDonald's total revenues for the current year?

   b. McDonald's also refers to a total "systemwide" sales in the management section of its annual report. By looking at the current year's annual report, find its systemwide sales for the current year and indicate what the term refers to.

   c. Why is total revenue reported in the income statement and systemwide revenue not reported there? That is, why can't McDonald's place systemwide sales on its income statement?

2. Look at McDonald's Web site and its latest annual report carefully. How is the company working to achieve its strategic goals mentioned above? In what financial statements and line items might you see these goals reflected? Do you see evidence of their goals paying off?

SOLUTION TO KEY TERMS QUIZ

15	Recognition (p. 140)		**10**	Deferral (p. 155)
22	Historical cost (p. 141)		**16**	Deferred expense (p. 155)
8	Current value (p. 141)		**5**	Deferred revenue (p. 155)
18	Cash basis (p. 143)		**12**	Accrual (p. 155)
11	Accrual basis (p. 143)		**19**	Accrued liability (p. 155)
2	Revenues (p. 146)		**7**	Accrued asset (p. 155)
14	Revenue recognition principle (p. 146)		**24**	Accounting cycle (p. 160)
20	Matching principle (p. 146)		**1**	Work sheet (p. 161)
23	Expenses (p. 147)		**6**	Real accounts (p. 162)
3	Adjusting entries (p. 148)		**17**	Nominal accounts (p. 162)
9	Straight-line method (p. 150)		**4**	Closing entries (p. 162)
21	Contra account (p. 150)		**13**	Interim statements (p. 163)

Part I

INTEGRATIVE PROBLEM

Completing Financial Statements, Computing Ratios, Comparing Accrual vs. Cash Income, and Evaluating the Company's Cash Needs

Mountain Home Health Inc. was formed in 1993 to provide home nursing services in the Great Smoky Mountains of Tennessee. When contacted by a client or referred by a physician, nurses visit with the patient and discuss needed services with the physician.

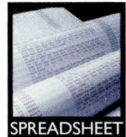

SPREADSHEET

Mountain Home Health earns revenue from patient services. Most of the revenue comes from billing either insurance companies, the state of Tennessee, or the Medicare program. Amounts billed are recorded in the Billings Receivable account. Insurance companies, states, and the federal government do not fully fund all procedures. For example, the state of Tennessee pays an average 78% of billed amounts. Mountain Home Health has already removed the uncollectible amounts from the Billings Receivable account and reports it and Medical Services Revenue at the net amount. Services extended on Saturday, December 30, and Sunday, December 31, 2000, totaled $16,000, net of allowances for uncollectible amounts. The firm earns a minor portion of its total revenue directly from patients in the form of cash.

Employee salaries, medical supplies, depreciation, and gasoline are the major expenses. Employees are paid every Friday for work performed during the Saturday-to-Friday pay period. Salaries amount to $800 per day. In 2000, December 31 falls on a Sunday. Medical supplies (average use of $1,500 per week) are purchased periodically to support health care coverage. The inventory of supplies on hand on December 31 amounted to $8,653.

The firm owns five automobiles (all purchased at the same time) that average 50,000 miles per year and are replaced every 3 years. They typically have no residual value. The building has an expected life of 20 years with no residual value. Straight-line depreciation is used on all firm assets. Gasoline costs, which are a cash expenditure, average $375 per day. The firm purchases a 3-year, extended warranty contract to cover maintenance costs. The contract costs $9,000 (assume equal use each year).

On December 29, 2000, Mountain Home Health declared a dividend of $10,000, payable on January 15, 2001. The firm makes annual payments of principal and interest each June 30 on the mortgage. The interest rate on the mortgage is 6%.

The following account balances are available for Mountain Home Health on December 31, 2000 (before any adjustments have been made).

Cash	$ 75,000
Billings Receivable (net)	151,000
Medical Supplies	73,000
Extended Warranty	3,000
Automobiles	90,000
Accumulated Depreciation—Automobiles	60,000
Building	200,000
Accumulated Depreciation—Building	50,000
Accounts Payable	22,000
Dividend Payable	10,000
Mortgage Payable	100,000
Capital Stock	100,000
Additional Paid-in-Capital	50,000
Retained Earnings	99,900
Medical Services Revenue	550,000
Salary and Wages Expense	290,400
Gasoline Expense	137,500
Utilities Expense	12,000
Dividends	10,000

Required

1. Determine the effect on the accounting equation of the necessary adjustments on December 31, 2000.

2. Prepare a statement of income and a statement of retained earnings for Mountain Home Health for the year ended December 31, 2000.

3. Prepare a balance sheet for Mountain Home Health as of December 31, 2000.

4. Compute the following as of December 31, 2000: **a.** Working capital **b.** Current ratio

5. Which of the adjustments might cause a difference between cash and accrual based income?

6. Mary Francis, controller of Mountain Home, became concerned about the company's cash flow after talking to a local bank loan officer. The firm tries to maintain a 7-week supply of cash to meet the demands of payroll, medical supply purchases, and gasoline. Determine the amount of cash Mountain Home needs to meet the 7-week supply.

VIDEO CASE I   TWEETER HOME ENTERTAINMENT GROUP

Tweeter Home Entertainment Group (www.tweeter.com) is a leading retailer of mid- to high-end audio and video electronics products. Its stores feature an extensive selection of home and car audio systems and components, portable audio equipment, cellular phones, and home video products. Installation and repair services are offered, and Tweeter also has a corporate sales division.

Tweeter opened its first store in Boston in 1972 and grew to 18 stores in New England over the next 20 years. By growing in new regional markets, today Tweeter maintains 95 stores in 14 mid-Atlantic states, the Southeast, Texas, and California. It operates these stores under the Tweeter name as well as Bryn Mawr Stereo & Video, HiFi Buys, United Audio Centers, and Douglas TV. The firm's future plans include adding stores in its current markets and relocating some stores to more favorable sites. It employs 2,200 people and went public in 1998.

Tweeter has a growth strategy for the Internet, too. In October 1999, the firm entered a joint venture with Cyberian Outpost to jointly market and sell consumer electronics over the Internet. Making an equity investment of $1 million in Cyberian's common stock, Tweeter chose to enter the world of e-commerce with a proven partner. Sandy Bloomberg, chairman and founder of Tweeter, and Jeffrey Stone, president and CEO, both thought this strategy would minimize the firm's risk, limit Tweeter's investment in Web infrastructure by allowing it to use Outpost.com's existing facilities, and provide a proven structure for customer fulfillment instead of building a system from scratch. Both partners in the venture, known as Tweeter.Outpost.com, jointly market the

site, which produced $6.3 million in sales for the fiscal quarter ending December 31, 2000.

Selling strategies have evolved to help manage the product mix, which generally includes higher-end items from over 50 vendors. Video products have yielded lower growth margins than audio products, although total sales of video have increased at faster rates than audio. To enhance the overall gross margin, Tweeter adopted a "Sell Audio with Video" strategy. Purchasing strategies are important, too. Tweeter is a member of a national volume-buying group that often saves costs by getting additional vendor rebates and product discounts.

With the huge amount of information needed to manage the chain, Tweeter has developed a sophisticated management information system. It is automatically updated after every transaction, and information is accessible in real time to managers, sales associates, and buyers alike. Store managers and retail associates have access to real-time data on sales volume by category, and upper management and store managers can view sales volume, gross margin, and product mix on a per-store or per-sales-associate basis. Store managers are evaluated and compensated based on this information.

Like most retailers, Tweeter experiences seasonal variations in its business. A significant portion of total revenue and net income are realized during the first and fourth fiscal quarters, with most of the net income being realized in the first fiscal quarter. The biggest single influence on the firm's financial condition is the holiday shopping season, although the timing of new store openings, acquisitions, and unexpected changes in supplier prices or the competitive environment are also important.

Required

1. How do you think the joint venture with Cyberian Outpost has affected Tweeter's financial position? Where in its financial statements will the results be shown?

2. Describe the decision-making process at Tweeter as well as you can. What roles does financial information seem to play? What role do you think information about the external or competitive environment plays?

3. Select one of Tweeter's long-term goals as identified in the video. Explain how you think the firm's managers can use financial information to determine how well Tweeter is reaching that goal.

Accounting for Assets

A Word to Students about Part II

In Part I you learned how companies communicate their activities and financial results to users of financial information. You also discovered new ways of thinking about events as transactions, and how these business transactions culminate in a company's financial statements. You learned specialized terminology, used the accounting equation, and began to understand the basis for making financial decisions.

Part II tells what happens when assets flow into the business. Chapter 5 introduces the effects of buying and selling merchandise on the financial statements, and the internal control necessary for keeping a business running smoothly. Chapter 6 expands on inventory issues and shows how inventory transactions affect the statement of cash flows. Chapter 7 covers the inflow of cash and receivables into the business and investments that a company makes. Chapter 8 recognizes that the business must invest its cash and receivables in operating assets.

Finally, you'll focus on how investors and other financial statement users evaluate companies with ratios and make decisions based on that information.

MERCHANDISE ACCOUNTING AND INTERNAL CONTROL

FOCUS ON FINANCIAL RESULTS

With over 3,650 stores in the United States, Canada, France, Germany, Japan, and the United Kingdom, The Gap has become a global success story. This youth-oriented retailer of casual fashions, accessories, and personal care products encompasses three distinct brands—Gap, Banana Republic, and Old Navy. AOL showcases all three on its popular Internet shopping site, and each also has a Web site of its own. Gap Inc.'s sales exceed $11.6 billion a year, and 1999 was the best overall year in the company's 30-plus years.

Like its competitors, Gap Inc. has sometimes suffered from the uncertainties of the retail fashion industry, but it has a record of making solid comebacks by constantly reinventing itself as a fashion leader and using smart merchandising to regain market share. Although 2000 was somewhat disappointing for the firm, with earnings below expectations, sales were strong, and most observers expect the firm to rebound once again.

As a retailer, Gap Inc. measures its success in terms of what it earns from buying and selling merchandise. Sales are a fundamental measure of that goal, and as you can see from its 1999 statement of earnings, pictured here, net sales almost doubled from two years ago. At the same time, cost of goods sold as a percentage of net sales steadily decreased. This measure indicated that Gap Inc. was successfully managing the difference between what it cost the firm to acquire goods and what it earned by selling them. By 1999, according to the company's annual report, only about 58 cents of every sales dollar went to cover costs of goods sold.

Consolidated Statements of Earnings

($000 except per share amounts)	Fifty-two Weeks Ended January 29, 2000	Percentage to Sales	Fifty-two Weeks Ended January 30, 1999	Percentage to Sales	Fifty-two Weeks Ended January 31, 1998	Percentage to Sales
Net sales	$11,635,398	100.0%	$9,054,462	100.0%	$6,507,825	100.0%
Costs and expenses						
Cost of goods sold and occupancy expenses	6,775,262	58.2	5,318,218	58.7	4,021,541	61.8
Operating expenses	3,043,432	26.2	2,403,365	26.5	1,635,017	25.1
Net interest expense (income)	31,755	0.3	13,617	0.2	(2,975)	0.0
Earnings before income taxes	1,784,949	15.3	1,319,262	14.6	854,242	13.1
Income taxes	657,884	5.6	494,723	5.5	320,341	4.9
Net earnings	$ 1,127,065	9.7%	$ 824,539	9.1%	$ 533,901	8.2%
Weighted-average number of shares–basic	853,804,924		864,062,060		891,404,945	
Weighted-average number of shares–diluted	895,029,176		904,374,383		922,951,706	
Earnings per share–basic	$1.32		$0.95		$0.60	
Earnings per share–diluted	1.26		0.91		0.58	

See Notes to Consolidated Financial Statements.

Cost of goods sold has decreased as a percentage of sales from 1997 to 1999 fiscal years.

Net sales of over $11.6 billion are almost double 1997's $6.5 billion

Gap Inc.'s 1999 Annual Report

If you were a Gap Inc. manager, you would want the cost of goods sold percentage to keep decreasing and sales to continue increasing. How would the use of AOL and the company's own Web sites to market its products be likely to affect GAP Inc.'s sales and cost of goods sold, and the relationship between them?

www.gapinc.com

After studying this chapter, you should be able to:

LO 1 Understand how wholesalers and retailers account for sales of merchandise. (p. 197)

LO 2 Explain the differences between periodic and perpetual inventory systems. (p. 202)

LO 3 Understand how wholesalers and retailers account for cost of goods sold. (p. 204)

LO 4 Explain the importance of internal control to a business. (p. 208)

LO 5 Describe the basic internal control procedures. (p. 211)

LO 6 Describe the various documents used in recording purchases of merchandise and their role in controlling cash disbursements (Appendix 5A). (p. 219)

THE INCOME STATEMENT FOR A MERCHANDISER

From **Concept**

TO PRACTICE 5.1

READING UNO'S ANNUAL REPORT

According to one of the footnotes, what form does Uno's inventory take? Would you consider Uno to be a merchandiser? Explain your answer.

www.gapinc.com
www.circuitcity.com

To this point, we have concentrated on the accounting for businesses that sell *services*. Banks, hotels, airlines, health clubs, real estate offices, law firms, and accounting firms are all examples of service companies. In this chapter, we turn to accounting by merchandisers. Both retailers and wholesalers are merchandisers. They purchase inventory in finished form and hold it for resale. This is in contrast to manufacturers' inventory, which takes three different forms: raw materials, work in process, and finished goods. (Accounting for the three different forms of inventory for a manufacturer is more complex and is covered in a follow-up course to this one.) We focus in this chapter on accounting for merchandise— that is, inventory held by either a wholesaler or a retailer.

A *condensed* multiple-step income statement for Grizzly Hardware Stores is presented in Exhibit 5-1. First, note the period covered by the statement: for the year ended December 31, 2001. Grizzly ends its fiscal year on December 31; however, many merchandisers end their *fiscal year* on a date other than December 31. Retailers often choose a date toward the end of January because the busy holiday shopping season is over and time can be devoted to closing the records and preparing financial statements. For example, The Gap Inc. ends its fiscal year on the Saturday closest to January 31, and Circuit City closes its books on the last day of February each year.

We will concentrate on the first two items on Grizzly's statement: net sales and cost of goods sold. The major difference between this income statement and that for a service

EXHIBIT 5-1   Condensed Income Statement for a Merchandiser

GRIZZLY HARDWARE STORES INCOME STATEMENT FOR THE YEAR ENDED DECEMBER 31, 2001	
Net sales	$100,000
Cost of goods sold	60,000
Gross margin	$ 40,000
Selling and administrative expenses	29,300
Net income before tax	$ 10,700
Income tax expense	4,280
Net income	$ 6,420

company is the inclusion of cost of goods sold. Because a service company does not sell a product, it does not report cost of goods sold. On the income statement of a merchandising company, cost of goods sold is deducted from net sales to arrive at gross margin or gross profit.

Gross margin as a percentage of net sales is a common analytical tool for merchandise companies. Analysts compare the gross margin percentages for various periods or for several companies and express concern if a company's gross margin is dropping. Every industry in the retail sector tracks its average gross margin ratio, average overhead cost per square foot, and average sales per square foot of retail space. Analysts can use these facts to see how one company is performing in comparison with others in the same industry. If analysts looked at The Gap's 10-year summary in its annual report, they would find that sales per square foot have increased from $438 in 1990 to $548 in 1999.

www.gap.com

NET SALES OF MERCHANDISE

The first section of Grizzly's income statement is presented in Exhibit 5-2. Two deductions—for sales returns and allowances and sales discounts—are made from sales revenue to arrive at **net sales.** Sales revenue, or simply sales, as it is often called, is a *representation of the inflow of assets,* either cash or accounts receivable, from the sale of merchandise during the period:

LO 1 Understand how wholesalers and retailers account for sales of merchandise.

■ In a merchandising business, *cash sales* are recorded daily in the journal and are based on the total amount shown on the cash register tape. For example, suppose that the cash register tape in the paint department of Grizzly Hardware Stores shows sales on March 31, 2001, of $350. The sale of merchandise for cash increases both sides of the accounting equation:

BALANCE SHEET						INCOME STATEMENT	
ASSETS	=	LIABILITIES	+	OWNERS' EQUITY	+	REVENUES – EXPENSES	
Cash	350					Sales Revenue	350

■ Further assume that on May 4, Grizzly makes a sale for $125 on an open account. Sales on credit do not result in the immediate inflow of cash but in an accounts receivable, a promise by the customer to pay cash at a later date:

BALANCE SHEET						INCOME STATEMENT	
ASSETS	=	LIABILITIES	+	OWNERS' EQUITY	+	REVENUES – EXPENSES	
Accounts Receivable	125					Sales Revenue	125

EXHIBIT 5-2 Net Sales Section of the Income Statement

GRIZZLY HARDWARE STORES
PARTIAL INCOME STATEMENT
FOR THE YEAR ENDED DECEMBER 31, 2001

Sales revenue	$103,500	
Less: Sales returns and allowances	2,000	
Sales discounts	1,500	
Net sales		$100,000

SALES RETURNS AND ALLOWANCES

www.nordstrom.com

Study Tip

Recall Accumulated Depreciation, a contra account introduced in Chapter 4. It reduces a long-term asset. In other cases, such as this one involving sales, a contra account reduces an income statement account.

The cornerstone of marketing is to satisfy the customer. Most companies have standard policies that allow the customer to *return* merchandise within a stipulated period of time. Nordstrom, the Seattle-based retailer, has a very liberal policy regarding returns. That policy has, in large measure, fueled its growth. A company's policy might be that a customer who is not completely satisfied can return the merchandise anytime within 30 days of purchase for a full refund. Alternatively, the customer may be given an *allowance* for spoiled or damaged merchandise—that is, the customer keeps the merchandise but receives a credit for a certain amount in the account balance. Typically, a single account, **Sales Returns and Allowances,** is used to account both for returns and for allowances. If the customer has already paid for the merchandise, either a cash refund is given or the credit amount is applied to future purchases.

The accounting for a return or an allowance depends on whether the customer is given a cash refund or credit on an account. Assume that Grizzly's paint department gives a $25 cash refund on spoiled paint returned by a customer. The effect of this transaction follows:

BALANCE SHEET					INCOME STATEMENT	
ASSETS	**=**	**LIABILITIES**	**+**	**OWNERS' EQUITY**	**+**	**REVENUES – EXPENSES**
Cash (25)					Sales Returns and Allowances	(25)

Sales Returns and Allowances is a *contra-revenue* account. A contra account is used to offset a related account and is deducted from that account on the statement.

The purpose of this transaction is to reduce the amount of previously recorded sales. So why didn't the accountant simply reduce Sales Revenue by $25? The reason is that management needs to be able to *monitor* the amount of returns and allowances. If Sales Revenue is reduced for returns and at some point the company needs to determine the total dollars of returns for the period, it would need to add up all the individual reductions to the Sales Revenue account. A much more efficient method is to split the sales revenue into two accounts, one that includes only sales and another that includes only returns. In this way, the total amount of returns is readily available, and the decision-making process is more efficient and thus more effective.

The previous entry illustrates the accounting for a return of merchandise. The same account is normally used when a credit is given and the customer keeps the merchandise. Assume that on May 7 the customer who made the $125 purchase from Grizzly on May 4 notifies it that one of the purchased tools is defective. Grizzly agrees to reduce the customer's unpaid account by $10 because of the defect. The effect of this transaction is as follows:

BALANCE SHEET					INCOME STATEMENT	
ASSETS	**=**	**LIABILITIES**	**+**	**OWNERS' EQUITY**	**+**	**REVENUES – EXPENSES**
Accounts Receivable (10)					Sales Returns and Allowances	(10)

The Sales Returns and Allowances account gives management and stockholders an important piece of data: that merchandise is being returned or is not completely acceptable. It does not answer the following questions, however. Why is the merchandise being returned? Why are customers getting partial refunds? Is the merchandise shoddy? Are salespeople too aggressive? Should the store's liberal policy regarding returns be changed? Answers to these questions require management to look beyond the accounting data.

TRADE DISCOUNTS AND QUANTITY DISCOUNTS

Various types of discounts to the list price are given to customers. A **trade discount** is a selling price reduction offered to a special class of customers. For example, Grizzly's plumbing department might offer a special price to building contractors. The difference between normal selling price and this special price is called a *trade discount*. A **quantity discount** is sometimes offered to customers who are willing to buy in large quantities.

Trade discounts and quantity discounts are *not* recorded in the accounts. Although a company might track the amount of these discounts for control purposes, the reason for ignoring the quantity and trade discounts in the accounting records is that the list price is not the actual selling price. The *net* amount is a more accurate reflection of the amount of a sale. For example, assume that Grizzly gives a 20% discount from the normal selling price to any single customer who buys between 10 and 25 kitchen sinks, and a 30% discount on purchases of more than 25 sinks. The list price for each unit is $200. The selling price and the amount recorded for a customer's purchase of 40 sinks on July 2 are as follows:

List price	$ 200
Less: 30% quantity discount	60
Selling price	140
× Number of sinks sold	× 40
Sales revenue	$5,600

Merchandisers stock and sell products that other companies manufacture. Whether they are retail shops like this one or wholesalers selling their merchandise to retail stores, merchandisers keep inventories of the different products they stock. Merchandisers must track these items and their cost as they are delivered to the store, as they leave the store as sold—and sometimes as they come back as returned merchandise.

CREDIT TERMS AND SALES DISCOUNTS

Most companies have a standard credit policy. Special notation is normally used to indicate a particular firm's policy for granting credit. For example, credit terms of *n/30* mean that the *net* amount of the selling price—that is, the amount determined after deducting any returns or allowances—is due within 30 days of the date of the invoice. *Net, 10 EOM* means that the net amount is due anytime within 10 days after the end of the month in which the sale took place.

Another common element of the credit terms offered to customers is sales discounts, a reduction from the selling price given for early payment. For example, assume that Grizzly offers a building contractor credit terms of *1/10, n/30*. This means that the customer may deduct 1% from the selling price if the bill is paid within 10 days of the date of the invoice. Normally, the discount period begins with the day *after* the invoice date. If the customer does not pay within the first 10 days, the full invoice amount is due within 30 days. Finally, note that the use of *n* for *net* in this notation is really a misnomer. Although the amount due is net of any returns and allowances, it is the *gross* amount that is due within 30 days. That is, no discount is given if the customer does not pay early.

How valuable to the customer is a 1% discount for payment within the first 10 days? Assume that a $1,000 sale is made. If the customer pays at the end of 10 days, the cash paid will be $990, rather than $1,000, a net savings of $10. The customer has saved $10 by paying 20 days earlier than required by the 30-day term. If we assume 360 days in a year, there are 360/20 or 18 periods of 20 days each in a year. Thus, a savings of $10 for 20 days is equivalent to a savings of $10 times 18, or $180 for the year. An annual return of $180/$990, or 18.2%, would be difficult to match with any other type of investment. In fact, a customer might want to consider borrowing the money to pay off the account early.

Some companies record sales *net* of any discounts for early payment; others record the *gross* amount of sales and then track sales discounts separately. Because the effect on the accounting equation does not differ between the two methods, we will concern ourselves only with the *gross method,* which assumes that customers will not necessarily take advantage of the discount offered for early payment. Sales discounts are rarely material, and companies do not normally disclose the method used on their financial statements.

Assume a sale of $1,000 with credit terms of 2/10, net 30. The effect on the accounting equation from the sale is as follows:

BALANCE SHEET						INCOME STATEMENT	
ASSETS	**=**	**LIABILITIES**	**+**	**OWNERS' EQUITY**	**+**	**REVENUES – EXPENSES**	
Accounts Receivable 1,000						Sales Revenue	1,000

Net Sales of Merchandise	**199**

If the customer pays within the discount period, a *contra revenue* account called **Sales Discounts,** reflecting a reduction in revenue, is used to record the discount of $20. Note in Exhibit 5-2 that sales discounts are deducted from sales on the income statement. The effect of the payment within the discount period on the accounting equation is as follows:

BALANCE SHEET						INCOME STATEMENT	
ASSETS	=	LIABILITIES	+	OWNERS' EQUITY	+	REVENUES – EXPENSES	
Accounts Receivable	(1,000)					Sales Discounts	(20)
Cash	980						

THE COST OF GOODS SOLD

The cost of goods sold section of the income statement for Grizzly is shown in Exhibit 5-3. We will soon turn to each line item in this section. First, let us take a look at the basic model for cost of goods sold.

THE COST OF GOODS SOLD MODEL

The recognition of cost of goods sold as an expense is an excellent example of the *matching principle.* Sales revenue represents the *inflow* of assets, in the form of cash and accounts receivable, from the sale of products during the period. Likewise, cost of goods sold represents the *outflow* of an asset, inventory, from the sale of those same products. The company

EXHIBIT 5-3   Cost of Goods Sold Section of the Income Statement

GRIZZLY HARDWARE STORES
PARTIAL INCOME STATEMENT
FOR THE YEAR ENDED DECEMBER 31, 2001

Cost of goods sold:		
Inventory, January 1, 2001		$15,000
Purchases	$65,000	
Less: Purchase returns and allowances	1,800	
Purchase discounts	3,700	
Net purchases	$59,500	
Add: Transportation-in	3,500	
Cost of goods purchased		63,000
Costs of goods available for sale		$78,000
Less: Inventory, December 31, 2001		18,000
Cost of goods sold		$60,000

needs to match the revenue of the period with one of the most important costs necessary to generate the revenue, the *cost* of the merchandise sold.

It may be helpful in understanding cost of goods sold to realize what it is *not. Cost of goods sold is not necessarily equal to the cost of purchases of merchandise during the period.* Except in the case of a new business, a merchandiser starts the year with a certain stock of inventory on hand, called *beginning inventory.* For Grizzly, beginning inventory is the dollar cost of merchandise on hand on January 1, 2001. During the year, Grizzly purchases merchandise. When the cost of goods purchased is added to beginning inventory, the result is **cost of goods available for sale.** Just as the merchandiser starts the period with an inventory of merchandise on hand, a certain amount of *ending inventory* is usually on hand at the end of the year. For Grizzly, this is its inventory on December 31, 2001.

As shown in Exhibit 5-4, think of cost of goods available for sale as a "pool" of costs to be distributed between what we sold and what we did not sell. If we subtract from the pool the cost of what we did *not* sell, the *ending inventory,* we will have the amount we *did*

EXHIBIT 5-4   The Cost of Goods Sold Model

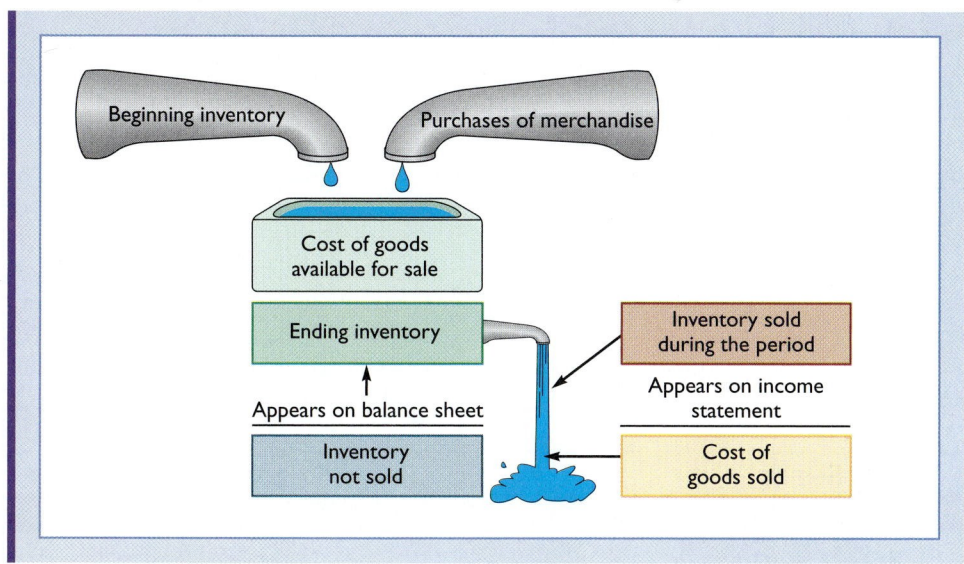

EXHIBIT 5-5   The Cost of Goods Sold Model: Example for a Merchandiser

Description	Item	Amount
Merchandise on hand to start the period	Beginning inventory	$15,000
Acquisitions of merchandise during the period	+ Cost of goods purchased	63,000
The pool of merchandise available for sale during the period	= Cost of goods available for sale	$78,000
Merchandise on hand at end of period	− Ending inventory	(18,000)
The expense recognized on the income statement	= Cost of goods sold	$60,000

A $3,000 excess of ending inventory over beginning inventory means the company bought $3,000 more than it sold ($63,000 bought versus $60,000 sold).

sell, the **cost of goods sold.** Cost of goods sold is simply the difference between the cost of goods available for sale and the ending inventory:

Beginning inventory	What is on hand to start the period
+ Purchases	What was acquired for resale during the period
= Cost of goods available for sale	The "pool" of costs to be distributed
− Ending inventory	What was not sold during the period and therefore is on hand to start the next period
= Cost of goods sold	What was sold during the period

The cost of goods sold model for a merchandiser is illustrated in Exhibit 5-5. The amounts used for the illustration are taken from the cost of goods sold section of Grizzly's income statement as shown in Exhibit 5-3. Notice that ending inventory exceeds beginning inventory by $3,000. That means that the cost of goods purchased exceeds cost of goods sold by that same amount. Indeed, a key point for stockholders, bankers, and other users is whether inventory is building up—that is, whether a company is not selling as much inventory during the period as it is buying. A buildup may indicate that the company's products are becoming less desirable or that prices are becoming uncompetitive.

INVENTORY SYSTEMS: PERPETUAL AND PERIODIC

LO 2 Explain the differences between periodic and perpetual inventory systems.

Before we look more closely at the accounting for cost of goods sold, it is necessary to understand the difference between the periodic and the perpetual inventory systems. All businesses use one of these two distinct approaches to account for inventory. With the **perpetual system,** the Inventory account is updated *perpetually,* or after each sale or purchase of merchandise. Conversely, with the **periodic system,** the Inventory account is updated only at the end of the *period.*

In a perpetual system, every time goods are purchased, the Inventory account is increased, with a corresponding increase in Accounts Payable for a credit purchase or a decrease in the Cash account for a cash purchase. In addition to recognizing the increases in Accounts Receivable or Cash and in Sales Revenue when goods are sold, the accountant also records an entry that has the following effect on the accounting equation:

BALANCE SHEET					INCOME STATEMENT	
ASSETS	**=**	**LIABILITIES**	**+**	**OWNERS' EQUITY**	**+**	**REVENUES − EXPENSES**
Inventory	(xxx)				Cost of Goods Sold	(xxx)

Thus, at any point during the period, the inventory account is up-to-date. It has been increased for the cost of purchases during the period and reduced for the cost of the sales.

Why don't all companies use the procedure we just described, the perpetual system? Depending on the volume of inventory transactions—that is, purchases and sales of merchandise—a perpetual system can be extremely costly to maintain. Historically, businesses that have a relatively small volume of sales at a high unit price have used perpetual systems. For example, dealers in automobiles, furniture, appliances, and jewelry normally use a perpetual system. Each purchase of a unit of merchandise, such as an automobile, can be easily identified and an increase recorded in the Inventory account. When the auto is sold, the dealer can easily determine the cost of the particular car sold by looking at a perpetual inventory record.

Can you imagine, however, a similar system for a supermarket or a hardware store? Consider a checkout stand in a grocery store. Through the use of a cash register tape, the sales revenue for that particular stand is recorded at the end of the day. Because of the tremendous volume of sales of various items of inventory, from cans of vegetables to boxes of soap, it may not be feasible to record the cost of goods sold every time a sale takes place. This illustrates a key point in financial information: the cost of the information should never exceed its benefit. If a store manager had to stop and update the records each time a can of Campbell's soup was sold, the retailer's business would obviously be disrupted.

To a certain extent, the ability of mass merchandisers to maintain perpetual inventory records has improved with the advent of point-of-sale terminals. When a cashier runs a can of corn over the sensing glass at the checkout stand and the bar code is read, the company's computer receives a message that a can of corn has been sold. In some companies, however, updating the inventory record is in units only and is used as a means to determine when a product needs to be reordered. The company still relies on a periodic system to maintain the *dollar* amount of inventory. In the remainder of this chapter, we limit our discussion to the periodic system. We discuss the perpetual system in detail in Chapter 6.

BEGINNING AND ENDING INVENTORIES IN A PERIODIC SYSTEM

In a periodic system, the Inventory account is *not* updated each time a sale or purchase is made. Throughout the year, the Inventory account contains the amount of merchandise on hand at the beginning of the year. The account is adjusted only at the end of the year. A company using the periodic system must physically *count* the units of inventory on hand at the end of the period. The number of units of each product is then multiplied by the cost per unit, to determine the dollar amount of ending inventory. Refer to Exhibit 5-3 for Grizzly Hardware Stores. The procedure just described was used to determine its ending

From Concept

TO PRACTICE 5.2

UNDERSTANDING GATEWAY'S INVENTORY SYSTEM   Given the nature of its products, would you expect that Gateway uses a perpetual or a periodic inventory system? Explain your answer.

inventory of $18,000. Because one period's ending inventory is the next period's beginning inventory, the beginning inventory of $15,000 was based on the count at the end of the prior year.

In summary, the ending inventory in a periodic system is determined by counting the merchandise, not by looking at the Inventory account at the end of the period. The periodic system results in a trade-off. Use of the periodic system reduces record keeping but at the expense of a certain degree of control. Losses of merchandise due to theft, breakage, spoilage, or other reasons may go undetected in a periodic system because management may assume that all merchandise not on hand at the end of the year was sold. In a retail store, some of the merchandise may have been shoplifted rather than sold. In contrast, with a perpetual inventory system, a count of inventory at the end of the period serves as a *control device.* For example, if the Inventory account shows a balance of $45,000 at the end of the year but only $42,000 of merchandise is counted, management is able to investigate the discrepancy. No such control feature exists in a periodic system.

In addition to the loss of control, the use of a periodic system presents a dilemma when a company wants to prepare *interim* financial statements. Because most companies that use a periodic system find it cost-prohibitive to count the entire inventory more than once a year, they use estimation techniques to determine inventory for monthly or quarterly statements. (These techniques are discussed in Chapter 6.)

THE COST OF GOODS PURCHASED

LO 3 Understand how wholesalers and retailers account for cost of goods sold.

The cost of goods purchased section of Grizzly's income statement is shown in Exhibit 5-6. The company purchased $65,000 of merchandise during the period. Two amounts are deducted from purchases to arrive at net purchases: purchase returns and allowances of $1,800 and purchase discounts of $3,700. The cost of $3,500 incurred by Grizzly to ship the goods to its place of business is called **transportation-in** and is added to net purchases of $59,500 to arrive at the cost of goods purchased of $63,000. Another name for transportation-in is *freight-in.*

Purchases Assume that Grizzly buys merchandise on account from one of its wholesalers at a cost of $4,000. **Purchases** is the temporary account used in a periodic inventory system to record acquisitions of merchandise. The effect of this transaction is to increase liabilities and increase cost of goods sold, which is an expense:

	BALANCE SHEET				INCOME STATEMENT
ASSETS	=	LIABILITIES	+	OWNERS' EQUITY	+	REVENUES – EXPENSES
		Accounts Payable 4,000			Purchases *cost of goods sold* (4,000)

EXHIBIT 5-6 Cost of Goods Purchased

GRIZZLY HARDWARE STORES
PARTIAL INCOME STATEMENT
FOR THE YEAR ENDED DECEMBER 31, 2001

Purchases	$65,000	
Less: Purchase returns and allowances	1,800	
Purchase discounts	3,700	
Net purchases	$59,500	
Add: Transportation-in	3,500	
Cost of goods purchased		$63,000

It is important to understand that Purchases is *not* an asset account. It is included in the income statement as an integral part of the calculation of cost of goods sold and is therefore shown as a reduction on the income statement in the accounting equation.

Purchase Returns and Allowances   We discussed returns and allowances earlier in the chapter from the seller's point of view. From the standpoint of the buyer, purchase returns and allowances are reductions in the cost to purchase merchandise. Rather than record these reductions directly in the Purchases account, the accountant uses a separate account. The account, **Purchase Returns and Allowances,** is a *contra account* to Purchases. The use of a contra account allows management to monitor the amount of returns and allowances. For example, a large number of returns during the period relative to the amount purchased may signal that the purchasing department is not buying from reputable sources.

Suppose that Grizzly returns $850 of merchandise to a wholesaler for credit on its account. The return decreases both liabilities and purchases. Note that because a return reduces purchases, it actually *increases* net income:

BALANCE SHEET						INCOME STATEMENT
ASSETS	**=**	**LIABILITIES**	**+**	**OWNERS' EQUITY**	**+**	**REVENUES – EXPENSES**
		Accounts Payable (850)				Purchase Returns and Allowances 850

The effect of an allowance for merchandise retained rather than returned is the same as that for a return.

ACCOUNTING FOR YOUR DECISIONS

You Are the President

You are the president of a mail-order computer business. Your company buys computers and related parts directly from manufacturers and sells them to consumers via direct mail. Recently, you have noticed an increase in the amount of purchase returns and allowances relative to the amount of purchases. What are some possible explanations for this increase?

ANS: Any number of explanations are possible. It is possible that the products are being damaged while in transit. Or it may be that the company has changed suppliers and the merchandise is not of the quality expected. Or it may be that the customers are becoming more demanding in what they accept than they used to be.

Purchase Discounts   Discounts were discussed earlier in the chapter, from the seller's viewpoint. Merchandising companies often purchase inventory on terms that allow for a cash discount for early payment, such as 2/10, net 30. To the buyer, a cash discount is called a *purchase discount* and results in a reduction of the cost to purchase merchandise. For example, assume a purchase of merchandise for $500, with credit terms of 1/10, net 30. If all purchases are recorded at the gross amount, the effect of the purchase is:

BALANCE SHEET						INCOME STATEMENT
ASSETS	**=**	**LIABILITIES**	**+**	**OWNERS' EQUITY**	**+**	**REVENUES – EXPENSES**
		Accounts Payable 500				Purchases (500)

Any discount taken by a customer is recorded in the **Purchase Discounts** account and deducted from purchases on the income statement. Assuming that the customer pays on time, the effect of the collection of the open account is as follows:

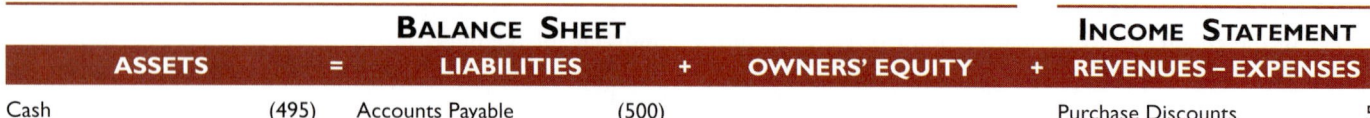

BALANCE SHEET						INCOME STATEMENT
ASSETS	**=**	**LIABILITIES**	**+**	**OWNERS' EQUITY**	**+**	**REVENUES – EXPENSES**
Cash (495)		Accounts Payable (500)				Purchase Discounts 5

The Purchase Discounts account is contra to the Purchases account and thus increases net income, as shown in the accounting equation above. Also note in Exhibit 5-6 that purchase discounts are deducted from Purchases on the income statement.

Shipping Terms and Transportation Costs

The *cost principle* governs the recording of all assets. All costs necessary to prepare an asset for its intended use should be included in its cost. The cost of an item to a merchandising company is not necessarily limited to its invoice price. For example, any sales tax paid should be included in computing total cost. Any transportation costs incurred by the buyer should likewise be included in the cost of the merchandise.

The buyer does not always pay to ship the merchandise. This depends on the terms of shipment. Goods are normally shipped either **FOB destination point** or **FOB shipping point**; *FOB* stands for *free on board*. When merchandise is shipped FOB destination point, it is the responsibility of the seller to deliver the products to the buyer. Thus, the seller either delivers the product to the customer or pays a trucking firm, railroad, or other carrier to transport it. Alternatively, the agreement between the buyer and the seller may provide for the goods to be shipped FOB shipping point. In this case, the merchandise is the responsibility of the buyer as soon as it leaves the seller's premises. When the terms of shipment are FOB shipping point, the buyer incurs transportation costs.

Refer to Exhibit 5-6. Transportation-in represents the freight costs Grizzly paid for in-bound merchandise. These costs are added to net purchases, as shown in the exhibit, and increase the cost of goods purchased. Assume that on delivery of a shipment of goods, Grizzly pays an invoice for $300 from the Rocky Mountain Railroad. The terms of shipment are FOB shipping point. The effect on the accounting equation is as follows:

BALANCE SHEET						INCOME STATEMENT
ASSETS	**=**	**LIABILITIES**	**+**	**OWNERS' EQUITY**	**+**	**REVENUES – EXPENSES**
Cash (300)						Transportation-in (300)

The Transportation-in account is an *adjunct* account because it is *added* to the net purchase of the period. The total of net purchases and transportation-in is called the *cost of goods purchased*. In summary, cost of goods purchased consists of the following:

> Purchases
> Less: Purchase returns and allowances
>   Purchase discounts
> Equals: Net purchases
> Add: Transportation-in
> Equals: Cost of goods purchased

How should the *seller* account for the freight costs it pays when the goods are shipped FOB destination point? This cost, sometimes called *transportation-out,* is not an addition to the cost of purchases of the seller but is instead one of the costs necessary to *sell* the merchandise. Transportation-out is classified as a *selling expense* on the income statement.

EXHIBIT 5-7 Shipping Terms and Transfer of Title to Inventory

FACTS   On December 28, 2001, Horton Wholesale ships merchandise to Grizzly Hardware Stores. The trucking company delivers the merchandise to Grizzly on January 2, 2002. Grizzly's fiscal year-end is December 31.

		If Merchandise Is Shipped FOB	
Company		Destination Point	Shipping Point
		seller pays transport	*buyer pays*
Horton	Pay freight costs?	Yes	No
(seller)	Record sale in 2001?	No	Yes
	Include inventory on balance sheet at December 31, 2001?	Yes	No
Grizzly	Pay freight costs?	No	Yes
(buyer)	Record purchase in 2001?	No	Yes
	Include inventory on balance sheet at December 31, 2001?	No	Yes

Shipping Terms and Transfer of Title to Inventory   Terms of shipment take on additional significance at the end of an accounting period. It is essential that a company establish a proper cutoff at year-end. For example, what if Grizzly purchases merchandise that is in transit at the end of the year? To whom does the inventory belong, Grizzly or the seller? The answer depends on the terms of shipment. If goods are shipped FOB destination point, they remain the legal property of the seller until they reach their destination. Alternatively, legal title to goods shipped FOB shipping point passes to the buyer as soon as the seller turns the goods over to the carrier.

The example in Exhibit 5-7 is intended to summarize our discussion about shipping terms and ownership of merchandise. The example involves a shipment of merchandise in transit at the end of the year. Horton, the seller of the goods, pays the transportation charges only if the terms are FOB destination point. Horton records a sale for goods in transit at year-end, however, only if the terms of shipment are FOB shipping point. If Horton does not record a sale, because the goods are shipped FOB destination point, the inventory appears on its December 31 balance sheet. Grizzly, the buyer, pays freight costs only if the goods are shipped FOB shipping point. Only in this situation does Grizzly record a purchase of the merchandise and include it as an asset on its December 31 balance sheet.

ACCOUNTING FOR YOUR DECISIONS

You Are the Manager

You manage the student bookstore. To get ready for the spring term, in December you order a large shipment of books from a publisher, with terms of FOB shipping point. On December 31, the books have not yet arrived. Should this shipment be included in the year-end inventory count even though it is not on hand to count? Assume a periodic inventory system.

ANS: Because the books were shipped FOB shipping point, they should be included in the year-end count even though they are not on hand to count. You should review the purchase invoice to determine the number of books ordered and the unit costs.

Two-Minute Review

On April 13, 2001, Bitterroot Distributing sells merchandise to Darby Corp. for $1,000 with credit terms of 2/10, net 30. On April 19, Darby returns $150 of defective merchandise and receives a credit on account from Bitterroot. On April 23, Darby pays the amount due.

1. Determine the effects on Bitterroot's accounting equation from April 13 through April 23. Assume Bitterroot uses a periodic inventory system.

2. Determine the effects on Darby's accounting equation from April 13 through April 23. Assume Darby uses a periodic inventory system.

Answers:

			BALANCE SHEET					INCOME STATEMENT	
ASSETS		=	LIABILITIES		+	OWNERS' EQUITY	+	REVENUES – EXPENSES	
1. April 13:									
Accounts Receivable	1,000							Sales Revenue	1,000
April 19:									
Accounts Receivable	(150)							Sales Returns and Allowances	(150)
April 23:									
Cash	833							Sales Discounts	(17)
Accounts Receivable	(850)								
2. April 13:			Accounts Payable	1,000				Purchases	(1,000)
April 19:			Accounts Payable	(150)				Purchases Returns and Allowances	150
April 23:									
Cash	(833)		Accounts Payable	(850)				Purchases Discounts	17

AN INTRODUCTION TO INTERNAL CONTROL

LO 4 Explain the importance of internal control to a business.

An employee of a large auto parts warehouse routinely takes spare parts home for personal use. A payroll clerk writes and signs two checks for an employee and then splits the amount of the second check with the worker. Through human error, an invoice is paid for merchandise never received from the supplier. These cases sound quite different from one another, but they share one important characteristic. They all point to a deficiency in a company's internal control system. An **internal control system** consists of the policies and procedures necessary to ensure the safeguarding of an entity's assets, the reliability of its accounting records, and the accomplishment of its overall objectives.

Three assets are especially critical to the operation of a merchandising company: cash, accounts receivable, and inventory. Activities related to these three assets compose the operating cycle of a business. Cash is used to buy inventory, the inventory is eventually sold, and, assuming a sale on credit, the account receivable from the customer is collected. We turn now to the ways in which a company attempts to *control* the assets at its disposal. This section introduces the important topic of internal control, which is explored further at appropriate points in the book. For example, controls to safeguard cash are discussed in Chapter 7.

THE REPORT OF MANAGEMENT: SHOWING RESPONSIBILITY FOR CONTROL

Modern business is characterized by absentee ownership. In most large corporations, it is impossible for the owners—the stockholders—to be actively involved in the daily affairs of the business. Professional managers have the primary responsibility for the business's smooth operation. They are also responsible for the content of the financial statements.

EXHIBIT 5-8 Report of Management—The Gap Inc.

Management's Report on Financial Information

Management is responsible for the integrity and consistency of all financial information presented in the Annual Report. The financial statements have been prepared in accordance with generally accepted accounting principles and necessarily include certain amounts based on Management's best estimates and judgments.

In fulfilling its responsibility for the reliability of financial information, Management has established and maintains accounting systems and procedures appropriately supported by internal accounting controls. Such controls include the selection and training of qualified personnel, an organizational structure providing for division of responsibility, communication of requirement for compliance with approved accounting control and business practices and a program of internal audit. The extent of the Company's system of internal accounting control recognizes that the cost should not exceed the benefits derived and that the evaluation of those factors requires estimates and judgments by Management. Although no system can ensure that all errors or irregularities have been eliminated, Management believes that the internal accounting controls in use provide reasonable assurance, at reasonable cost, that assets are safeguarded against loss from unauthorized use or disposition, that transactions are executed in accordance with Management's authorization and that the financial records are reliable for preparing financial statements and maintaining accountability for assets. The financial statements of the Company have been audited by Deloitte & Touche LLP, independent auditors whose report appears below.

The Audit and Finance Committee (the "Committee") of the Board of Directors is comprised solely of directors who are not officers or employees of the Company. The Committee is responsible for recommending to the Board of Directors the selection of independent auditors. It meets periodically with Management, the independent auditors and the internal auditors to assure that they are carrying out their responsibilities. The Committee also reviews and monitors the financial, accounting and auditing procedures of the Company in addition to reviewing the Company's financial reports. Deloitte & Touche LLP and the internal auditors have full and free access to the Committee, with and without Management's presence.

First Paragraph
Management's responsibility for the financial information

Second Paragraph
System of internal controls

Third Paragraph
Role of the Audit and Finance Committee

Most annual reports now include a **report of management** to the stockholders. A typical management report, in this case for The Gap Inc., is shown in Exhibit 5-8. The first paragraph of the report clearly spells out management's responsibility for the financial information presented in the annual report. The second paragraph refers to the system of internal controls within the company. One of the features of The Gap's internal control system is the use of an **internal audit staff.** Most large corporations today have a full-time staff of internal auditors who have the responsibility for evaluating the entity's internal control system.

The primary concern of the independent public accountants, or external auditors, is whether the financial statements have been presented fairly. Internal auditors focus more on the efficiency with which the organization is run. They are responsible for periodically reviewing both accounting and administrative controls, which we discuss later in this chapter. The internal audit staff also helps to ensure that the company's policies and procedures are followed.

The second paragraph of the report states that the company's independent public accountants have audited the company's financial statements. The management of most corporations would consider it cost-prohibitive for the auditors to verify the millions of transactions recorded in a single year. Instead, the auditors rely to a certain degree on the system of internal control as assurance that transactions are properly recorded and reported. The degree of reliance that they are able to place on the company's internal controls is a significant factor in determining the extent of their testing. The stronger the system of internal control, the less testing is necessary. A weak system of internal control requires that the auditors extend their tests of the records.

The **board of directors** of a corporation usually consists of key officers of the corporation as well as a number of directors whom it does not directly employ. For example, The Gap's board of 12 directors consists of 4 insiders and 8 outsiders. The outsiders often include presidents and key executive officers of other corporations and sometimes business school faculty. The board of directors is elected by the stockholders.

As referred to in the third paragraph of Exhibit 5-8, the **audit committee** (or the Audit and Finance Committee for The Gap) of the board of directors provides direct contact between the stockholders and the independent accounting firm. Audit committees have assumed a much more active role since the passage of the **Foreign Corrupt Practices Act** in 1977. This legislation was passed in response to a growing concern over various types of improprieties by top management, such as kickbacks to politicians and bribes of foreign officials. The act includes a number of provisions intended to increase the accountability of management and the board of directors to stockholders. According to the act, management is responsible for keeping accurate records, and various provisions deal with the system of internal controls necessary to ensure the safeguarding of assets and the reliability of the financial statements. Audit committees have become much more involved in the oversight of the financial reporting system since the enactment of the act.

From Concept

TO PRACTICE 5.3

READING THE GAP'S MANAGE-MENT REPORT Refer to the management report for The Gap in Exhibit 5-8. What is the composition of its Audit and Finance Committee? Why do you think it is composed the way it is?

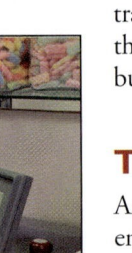

This woman is using the paper source document in her hand as a reference for entering data into the accounting system. From the standpoint of internal control, should she be the one who is ordering inventory, receiving it, and entering the information into the system? Is she authorized to make journal entries? If so, does her laptop have safeguards that prevent access by unauthorized personnel? These and other internal control procedures are part of the control environment within every company.

THE CONTROL ENVIRONMENT

The success of an internal control system begins with the competence of the people in charge of it. Management's operating style will have a determinable impact on the effectiveness of various policies. An autocratic style in which a few key officers tightly control operations will result in an environment different from that of a decentralized organization in which departments have more freedom to make decisions. Personnel policies and practices form another factor in the internal control of a business. An appropriate system for hiring competent employees and firing incompetent ones is crucial to an efficient operation. After all, no internal control system will work very well if employees who are dishonest or poorly trained are on the payroll. On the other hand, too few people doing too many tasks defeats the purpose of an internal control system. Finally, the effectiveness of internal control in a business is influenced by the board of directors, particularly its audit committee.

THE ACCOUNTING SYSTEM

An **accounting system** consists of all the methods and records used to accurately report an entity's transactions and to maintain accountability for its assets and liabilities. Regardless of the degree of computer automation, the use of a journal to record transactions is an integral part of all accounting systems. Refinements are sometimes made to the basic components of the system, depending on the company's needs. For example, most companies use specialized journals to record recurring transactions, such as sales of merchandise on credit.

An accounting system can be completely manual, fully computerized, or as is often the case, a mixture of the two. Internal controls are important to all businesses, regardless of the degree of automation of the accounting system. The system must be capable of handling both the volume and the complexity of transactions entered into by a business. Most businesses use computers because of the sheer volume of transactions. The computer is ideally suited to the task of processing large numbers of repetitive transactions efficiently and quickly.

The cost of computing has dropped so substantially that virtually every business can now afford a system. Today some computer software programs that are designed for home-based businesses cost under $100 and are meant to run on machines that cost less than $1,000. Inexpensive software programs that categorize expenses and print checks, produce financial statements, and analyze financial ratios are available.

INTERNAL CONTROL PROCEDURES

Management establishes policies and procedures on a number of different levels to ensure that corporate objectives will be met. Some procedures are formalized in writing. Others may not be written but are just as important. Certain **administrative controls** within a company are more concerned with the efficient operation of the business and adherence to managerial policies than with the accurate reporting of financial information. For example, a company policy that requires all prospective employees to be interviewed by the personnel department is an administrative control. Other **accounting controls** primarily concern safeguarding assets and ensuring the reliability of the financial statements. We now turn to a discussion of some of the most important internal control procedures:

LO 5 Describe the basic internal control procedures.

> Proper authorizations
>
> Segregation of duties
>
> Independent verification
>
> Safeguarding assets and records
>
> Independent review and appraisal
>
> The design and use of business documents

Proper Authorizations Management grants specific departments the authority to perform various activities. Along with the *authority* goes *responsibility*. Most large organizations give the authority to hire new employees to the personnel department. Management authorizes the purchasing department to order goods and services for the company and the credit department to establish specific policies for granting credit to customers. By specifically authorizing certain individuals to carry out specific tasks for the business, management is able to hold these same people responsible for the outcome of their actions.

The authorizations for some transactions are general in nature; others are specific. For example, a cashier authorizes the sale of a book in a bookstore by ringing up the transaction (a general authorization). It is likely, however, that the bookstore manager's approval is required before a book can be returned (a specific authorization).

Segregation of Duties What might happen if one employee is given the authority both to prepare checks and to sign them? What could happen if a single employee is allowed to order inventory and receive it from the shipper? Or what if the cashier at a checkout stand also records the daily receipts in the journal? If the employee in each of these situations is honest and never makes mistakes, nothing bad will happen. However, if the employee is dishonest or makes human errors, the company can experience losses. These situations all point to the need for the segregation of duties, which is one of the most fundamental of all internal control procedures. Without segregation of duties, an employee is able not only to perpetrate a fraud but also to conceal it. A good system of internal control requires that the *physical custody* of assets be separated from the *accounting* for those same assets.

Like most internal control principles, the concept of segregation of duties is an ideal that is not always completely attainable. For example, many smaller businesses simply do not have adequate personnel to achieve complete segregation of key functions. In certain instances, these businesses need to rely on the direct involvement of the owners in the business and on independent verification.

Independent Verification Related to the principle of segregation of duties is the idea of independent verification. The work of one department should act as a check on the work of another. For example, the physical count of the inventory in a perpetual inventory system provides such a check. The accounting department maintains the general ledger card for inventory and updates it as sales and purchases are made. The physical count of the inventory by an independent department acts as a check on the work of the accounting department. As another example, consider a bank reconciliation as a control device. The reconciliation of a company's bank account with the bank statement by

someone not responsible for either the physical custody of cash or the cash records acts as an independent check on the work of these parties. (We will take a closer look at the use of a bank reconciliation as a control device in Chapter 7.)

Safeguarding Assets and Records Adequate safeguards must be in place to protect assets and the accounting records from losses of various kinds. Cash registers, safes, and lockboxes are important safeguards for cash. Secured storage areas with limited access are essential for the safekeeping of inventory. Protection of the accounting records against misuse is equally important. For example, access to a computerized accounting record should be limited to those employees authorized to prepare journal entries. This can be done with the use of a personal identification number and a password to access the system.

Independent Review and Appraisal A well-designed system of internal control provides for periodic review and appraisal of the accounting system as well as the people operating it. The group primarily responsible for review and appraisal of the system is the internal audit staff. Internal auditors provide management with periodic reports on the effectiveness of the control system and the efficiency of operations.

The Design and Use of Business Documents *Business documents* are the crucial link between economic transactions entered into by an entity and the accounting record of these events. They are often called *source documents*. Some source documents are manual; others are computer-generated. The source document for the recognition of the expense of an employee's wages is the time card. The source documents for a sale include the sales order, the sales invoice, and the related shipping document. Business documents must be designed so that they capture all relevant information about an economic event. They are also designed to ensure that related transactions are properly classified.

Business documents themselves must be properly controlled. For example, a key feature for documents is a *sequential numbering system* just like you have for your personal checks. This system results in a complete accounting for all documents in the series and negates the opportunity for an employee to misdirect one. Another key feature of well-designed business documents is the use of *multiple copies*. The various departments involved in a particular activity, such as sales or purchasing, are kept informed of the status of outstanding orders through the use of copies of documents. Appendix 5A provides an example of the use of business documents for a merchandiser.

Inventory Control Helps Avoid Upset Customers

At J. W. Homes & Neighborhoods, a large residential builder in the Southeast, Julie Weston has been responsible for inventory control in the company's lighting division. The corporate income statement has been critical in Julie's management of inventory because it accounts for the cost of goods sold relative to sales, allowing her to make judgments about how to purchase and manage inventory going forward and to affect future profitability. She says: "To find our profits, we take our net sales minus cost of goods sold minus operating costs, which gives us our profit. If we were to look only at our net sales, we might outspend what our budget allows. We have to keep buying more finished goods to sell to homeowners to generate more profit." In addition to staying on top of the relationship between cost of goods sold and sales, being responsible for inventory control means constantly monitoring the level of inventories that are on hand for sale. As Julie explains: "We run reports to check inventory weekly and monthly. If we don't have an accurate count, we may promise our customers items we can't deliver. In the lighting division, our homeowners [customers] come in to select their lighting fixtures months before their homes go up. You can imagine how upset a customer would be if the closing of a house is delayed because of an inventory problem." This is just one example of how line items on the financial statements can affect corporate decision making and profitability.

Name: Julie Weston
Education: B.A., Purdue University
College Major: Communications/Public Relations
Occupation: Design Operations Manager, John Wieland Homes & Neighborhoods, Atlanta
Age: 26

LIMITATIONS ON INTERNAL CONTROL

Internal control is a relative term. No system of internal control is totally foolproof. An entity's size affects the degree of control that it can obtain. In general, large organizations are able to devote a substantial amount of resources to safeguarding assets and records because these companies have the assets to justify the cost. Because the installation and maintenance of controls can be costly, an internal audit staff is a luxury that many small businesses cannot afford. The mere segregation of duties can result in added costs if two employees must be involved in a task previously performed by only one.

Segregation of duties can be effective in preventing collusion, but no system of internal control can ensure that it will not happen. It does no good to have one employee count

privacy and security

privacy policy

Gap collects customer information through its web site and retail stores. We use this information to process orders, enhance our customers' shopping experience, and communicate with our customers about products, services, and promotions. We do not share the information you provide us online with any outside company or third party.

When you place an order at Gap Online, we collect your name, mailing address, phone number, and credit card information. We also collect your email address when you order from

Internal control has taken on a whole new meaning now that transactions are occurring on the Web. Nearly every online retailer—The Gap Inc. included—has developed privacy and security policies that are designed to ensure that the customer's information—including personal information as well as credit card information—is secure from unauthorized use or reuse.

the cash at the end of the day and another to record it if the two act in concert to steal from the company. Rotation of duties can help to lessen the likelihood for problems of this sort. An employee is less likely to collude with someone to steal if the assignment is a temporary one. Another control feature, a system of authorizations, is meaningless if management continually overrides it. Management must believe in a system of internal control enough to support it.

Intentional acts to misappropriate company assets are not the only problem. All sorts of human errors can weaken a system of internal control. Misunderstood instructions, carelessness, fatigue, and distraction can all lead to errors. A well-designed system of internal control should result in the best-possible people being hired to perform the various tasks, but no one is perfect.

Two-Minute Review

1. Explain why an internal control system is important to the operation of a merchandising company.

2. Explain the difference between administrative controls and accounting controls.

3. Explain how the concept of segregation of duties involves an evaluation of costs versus benefits.

Answers:

1. An effective system of internal controls is critical to protecting a merchandiser's investment in three of its major assets: cash, accounts receivable, and inventory. Without an effective system, these assets are subject to misuse.

2. Administrative controls are concerned with the efficient operation of a business and adherence to managerial policies. Alternatively, accounting controls deal with safeguarding assets and ensuring the reliability of the financial statements.

3. Involving more than one employee in a specific function reduces the likelihood of theft or other misuse of company assets. However, all businesses must decide whether the benefit of segregation of duties outweighs the additional cost of involving more than one employee in a specific function, such as the preparation and distribution of the payroll.

WARMUP EXERCISES

LO 1 Warmup Exercise 5-1 Net Sales
Victor Merchandising reported sales revenue, sales returns and allowances, and sales discounts of $57,000, $1,500, and $900, respectively, in 2001.

Required

Prepare the net sales section of Victor's 2001 income statement.

Key to the Solution
Refer to Exhibit 5-2.

LO 3 Warmup Exercise 5-2 Cost of Goods Sold
The following amounts are taken from Redfield Inc.'s records (all amounts are for 2001):

Inventory, January 1	$14,200
Inventory, December 31	10,300
Purchases	87,500
Purchase Discounts	4,200
Purchase Returns and Allowances	1,800
Transportation-in	4,500

Required

Prepare the cost of goods sold section of Redfield's 2001 income statement.

Key to the Solution
Refer to Exhibit 5-3.

LO 5   Warmup Exercise 5-3   Internal Control
List the internal control procedures discussed in the text.

Key to the Solution
Refer to the section in the chapter that discusses internal control procedures.

SOLUTIONS TO WARMUP EXERCISES

Warmup Exercise 5-1

VICTOR MERCHANDISING
PARTIAL INCOME STATEMENT
FOR THE YEAR ENDED DECEMBER 31, 2001

Sales revenue	$57,000	
Less: Sales returns and allowances	1,500	
Sales discounts	900	
Net sales		$54,600

Warmup Exercise 5-2

REDFIELD INC.
PARTIAL INCOME STATEMENT
FOR THE YEAR ENDED DECEMBER 31, 2001

Inventory, January 1, 2001		$ 14,200	
Purchases	$87,500		
Less: Purchase returns and allowances	1,800		
Purchase discounts	4,200		
Net purchases	$81,500		
Add: Transportation-in	4,500		
Cost of goods purchased		86,000	
Cost of goods available for sale		$100,200	
Less: Inventory, December 31, 2001		10,300	
Cost of goods sold			$ 89,900

Warmup Exercise 5-3
1. Proper authorizations
2. Segregation of duties
3. Independent verification
4. Safeguarding assets and records
5. Independent review and appraisal
6. Design and use of business documents

REVIEW PROBLEM

Mickey's Marts, which operates a chain of department stores, uses the periodic inventory system. The cost of inventory on hand at January 1 amounts to $12,000, and on January 31, it is $9,500. The following transactions are entered into by Mickey's during January:

a. Purchased merchandise on account from various vendors for $25,000. All merchandise is bought with terms of 1/10, net 30. All purchases are recorded initially at the gross amount.

b. Reduced the total amount owed to vendors by $20,000. This is *not* the amount paid but the amount before taking the 1% discount. All accounts are paid within 10 days of the date of the invoice.

c. Recognized purchase returns and allowances of $1,900 during the month.

d. Recognized total sales of $42,000 for the month, of which $28,000 is cash sales and the remainder is on account.

e. Made collections on account of $17,000 for the month.

f. Applied $3,200 of sales returns and allowances for the month to customers' account balances.

g. Paid the freight cost of $2,700 on *incoming* purchases of merchandise.

Required

1. For each of the transactions **a** through **g,** determine the effect on the accounting equation.

2. Prepare a *partial* income statement for the month of January. The last line on the partial statement should be gross margin.

SOLUTION TO REVIEW PROBLEM

1. a.

	BALANCE SHEET				INCOME STATEMENT	
ASSETS	**=**	**LIABILITIES**	**+**	**OWNERS' EQUITY**	**+**	**REVENUES – EXPENSES**
		Accounts Payable	25,000		Purchases	(25,000)

b.

	BALANCE SHEET				INCOME STATEMENT	
ASSETS	**=**	**LIABILITIES**	**+**	**OWNERS' EQUITY**	**+**	**REVENUES – EXPENSES**
Cash (19,800)		Accounts Payable	(20,000)		Purchase Discounts	200

c.

	BALANCE SHEET				INCOME STATEMENT	
ASSETS	**=**	**LIABILITIES**	**+**	**OWNERS' EQUITY**	**+**	**REVENUES – EXPENSES**
		Accounts Payable	(1,900)		Purchase Returns and Allowances	1,900

d.

	BALANCE SHEET				INCOME STATEMENT	
ASSETS	**=**	**LIABILITIES**	**+**	**OWNERS' EQUITY**	**+**	**REVENUES – EXPENSES**
Cash 28,000					Sales Revenue	42,000
Accounts Receivable 14,000						

e.

	BALANCE SHEET				INCOME STATEMENT	
ASSETS	**=**	**LIABILITIES**	**+**	**OWNERS' EQUITY**	**+**	**REVENUES – EXPENSES**
Cash 17,000						
Accounts Receivable (17,000)						

f.

BALANCE SHEET						INCOME STATEMENT
ASSETS	=	LIABILITIES	+	OWNERS' EQUITY	+	REVENUES – EXPENSES
Accounts Receivable (3,200)						Sales Returns and Allowances (3,200)

g.

BALANCE SHEET						INCOME STATEMENT
ASSETS	=	LIABILITIES	+	OWNERS' EQUITY	+	REVENUES – EXPENSES
Cash (2,700)						Transportation-in (2,700)

2. Partial income statement:

MICKEY'S MARTS
PARTIAL INCOME STATEMENT
FOR THE MONTH OF JANUARY

Sales revenue			$42,000
Less: Sales returns and allowances			3,200
Net sales			$38,800
Cost of goods sold:			
Inventory, January 1		$12,000	
Purchases	$25,000		
Less: Purchase discounts	200		
Purchase returns and allowances	1,900		
Net purchases	$22,900		
Add: Transportation-in	2,700		
Cost of goods purchased		25,600	
Cost of goods available for sale		$37,600	
Less: Inventory, January 31		9,500	
Cost of goods sold			28,100
Gross margin			$10,700

APPENDIX 5A

ACCOUNTING TOOLS: INTERNAL CONTROL FOR A MERCHANDISING COMPANY

Specific internal controls are necessary to control cash receipts and cash disbursements in a merchandising company. In addition to the separation of the custodianship of cash from the recording of it in the accounts, two other fundamental principles apply to its control. First, all cash receipts should be deposited *intact* in the bank on a *daily* basis. *Intact* means that no disbursements should be made from the cash received from customers. The second basic principle is related to the first: all cash disbursements should be made by check. The use of sequentially numbered checks results in a clear record of all disbursements. The only exception to this rule is the use of a petty cash fund to make cash disbursements for minor expenditures such as postage stamps and repairs.

CONTROL OVER CASH RECEIPTS

Most merchandisers receive checks and currency from customers in two distinct ways: (1) cash received over the counter—that is, from cash sales—and (2) cash received in the mail—that is, cash collections from credit sales. Each of these types of cash receipts poses its own particular control problems.

Cash Received over the Counter Several control mechanisms are used to handle these receipts. First, cash registers allow the customer to see the display, which deters the salesclerk from ringing up a sale for less than the amount received from the customer and pocketing the difference. A locked-in cash register tape is another control feature. At various times during the day, an employee other than the clerk unlocks the register, removes the tape, and forwards it to the accounting department. At the end of the shift, the salesclerk remits the coin and currency from the register to a central cashier. Any difference between the amount of cash remitted to the cashier and the amount on the tape submitted to the accounting department is investigated.

Finally, prenumbered customer receipts, prepared in duplicate, are a useful control mechanism. The customer is given a copy, and the salesclerk retains another. The salesclerk is accountable for all numbers in a specific series of receipts and must be able to explain any differences between the amount of cash remitted to the cashier and the amount collected per the receipts.

Cash Received in the Mail Most customers send checks rather than currency through the mail. Any form of cash received in the mail from customers should be applied to their account balances. The customer wants assurance that the account is appropriately reduced for the amount of the payment. The company must be assured that all cash received is deposited in the bank and that the account receivable is reduced accordingly.

To achieve a reasonable degree of control, two employees should be present when the mail is opened.[1] The first employee opens the mail in the presence of the second employee, counts the money received, and prepares a control list of the amount received on that particular day. The list is often called a *prelist* and is prepared in triplicate. The second employee takes the original to the cashier along with the total cash received on that day. The cashier is the person who makes the bank deposit. One copy of the prelist is forwarded to the accounting department to be used as the basis for recording the increase in Cash and the decrease in Accounts Receivable. The other copy is retained by one of the two persons opening the mail. A comparison of the prelist to the bank deposit slip is a timely way to detect receipts that do not make it to the bank. Because the two employees acting in concert could circumvent the control process, rotation of duties is important.

Monthly customer statements act as an additional control device for customer payments received in the mail. Assume that the two employees responsible for opening the mail and remitting checks to the cashier decide to pocket a check received from a customer. Checks made payable to a company *can* be stolen and cashed. The customer provides the control element. Because the check is not remitted to the cashier, the accounting department will not be notified to reduce the customer's account for the payment. The monthly statement, however, should alert the customer to the problem. The amount the customer thought was owed will be smaller than the balance due on the statement. At this point, the customer should ask the company to investigate the discrepancy. As evidence of its payment on account, the customer will be able to point to a canceled check—which was cashed by the unscrupulous employees.

Finally, keep in mind that the use of customer statements as a control device will be effective only if the employees responsible for the custody of cash received through the mail, for record keeping, and for authorization of adjustments to customers' accounts are not allowed to prepare and mail statements to customers. Employees allowed to do so are in a position to alter customers' statements.

Cash Discrepancies Discrepancies occur occasionally due to theft by dishonest employees and to human error. For example, if a salesclerk either intentionally or unin-

---

[1]In some companies, this control procedure may be omitted because of the cost of having two employees present when the mail is opened.

tentionally gives the wrong amount of change, the amount remitted to the cashier will not agree with the cash register tape. Any material differences should be investigated. Of particular significance are *recurring* differences between the amount remitted by any one cashier and the amount on the cash register tape.

THE ROLE OF COMPUTERIZED BUSINESS DOCUMENTS IN CONTROLLING CASH DISBURSEMENTS

A company makes cash payments for a variety of purposes: to purchase merchandise, supplies, plant, and equipment; to pay operating expenditures; and to cover payroll expenses, to name a few. We will concentrate on the disbursement of cash to purchase goods for resale, focusing particularly on the role of business documents in the process. Merchandising companies rely on a smooth and orderly inflow of quality goods for resale to customers. It is imperative that suppliers be paid on time so that they will continue to make goods available.

Business documents play a vital role in the purchasing function. The example that follows begins with a requisition for merchandise by the tool department of Grizzly Hardware Stores. The example continues through the receipt of the goods and the eventual payment to the supplier. The entire process is summarized in Exhibit 5-9. You will want to refer to this exhibit throughout the remainder of this appendix.

Purchase Requisition The tool department at Grizzly Hardware Stores weekly reviews its stock to determine whether any items need replenishing. On the basis of its needs, the supervisor of the tool department fills out the **purchase requisition form** shown in Exhibit 5-10. The form indicates the preferred supplier or vendor, A-1 Tool.

The purchasing department has the responsibility for making the final decision on a vendor. Giving the purchasing department this responsibility means that it is held accountable for acquiring the goods at the lowest price, given certain standards for merchandise quality. Grizzly assigns a separate item number to each of the thousands of individual items of merchandise it stocks. Note that the requisition also indicates the vendor's number for each item. The unit of measure for each item is indicated in the quantity column. For example, "24 ST" means 24 sets, and "12 CD" means 12 cards. The original and a copy of the purchase requisition are sent to the purchasing department. The tool department keeps one copy for its records.

Purchase Order Like many other businesses, Grizzly uses a computerized purchasing system. Most companies either have purchased software or have developed software internally to perform such functions as purchasing, sales, and payroll. The software is capable not only of increasing the speed and accuracy of the process but also of generating the necessary documents.

A computer-generated **purchase order** is shown in Exhibit 5-11. Purchase orders are usually prenumbered; a company should periodically investigate any missing numbers. The purchasing department uses its copy of the purchase requisition as a basis for preparing the purchase order. An employee in the purchasing department keys in the relevant information from the purchase requisition and adds the unit cost for each item gathered from the vendor's price guide. The software program generates the purchase order as shown in Exhibit 5-11. You should trace all the information for at least one of the three items ordered from the purchase requisition to the purchase order. The purchase order indicates the instructions for shipping, FOB destination point, and the terms for payment, 2/10, net 30.

The system generates the original purchase order and three copies. As indicated in Exhibit 5-9, the original is sent to the supplier after a supervisor in the purchasing department approves it. One copy is sent to the accounting department, where it will be matched with the original requisition. A second copy is sent to the tool department as confirmation that its request for the items has been attended to by the purchasing department. The purchasing department keeps the third copy for its records.

LO 6 Describe the various documents used in recording purchases of merchandise and their role in controlling cash disbursements.

EXHIBIT 5-9 Document Flow for the Purchasing Function

Requesting Department
prepares
Purchase Requisition
sends original and a copy to

Purchasing Department
uses
Purchase Requisition
sends copy to

as basis for preparing
Purchase Order
sends copy to
Purchase Order
which is sent to

Supplier uses the
Purchase Order
to bill customer
Invoice
mail to
and ship
Merchandise
copies of
Check and Remittance Advice

Accounting Department
compares
Purchase Requisition
and
Purchase Order
and
Invoice
and
Receiving Report
as a basis for preparing
Invoice Approval Form
which is sent with the invoice to

Receiving Department
inspects and counts
Merchandise
and prepares
Receiving Report
sends original to*
to

Finance Department
uses
Invoice Approval Form and Invoice
to prepare
Check and Remittance Advice
which is mailed to the supplier

* Copies to Requesting and Purchasing Departments

EXHIBIT 5-10 Purchase Requisition

Grizzly Hardware Stores
676 Sentinel St.
Missoula, MT

PURCHASE REQUISITION

Date 5/28/01   **PR 75638**

Preferred vendor A-1 Tool Co.

Date needed by 6/5/01

The following items are requested for   weekly dept. order

Item No.	Quantity	Description/Vendor No.
314627	24 ST	Hobby tool set/5265
323515	12 CD	Hobby blades 5 pk/7512
323682	6 ST	Screwdriver set 5/PC/1589

Requested by *Joe Smith*   **Department** Tool department

A purchase order is not the basis for recording a purchase and a liability. Legally, the order is merely an offer by the company to purchase goods from the supplier. Technically, the receipt of goods from the supplier is the basis for the purchaser's recognition of a liability. As a matter of practice, however, most companies record the payable upon receipt of the invoice.

EXHIBIT 5-11 Computer-Generated Purchase Order

Grizzly Hardware Stores
676 Sentinel St.
Missoula, MT

PURCHASE ORDER

TO: PO 54296
A-1 Tool Co.
590 West St.
Milwaukee, WI
Date 5/30/01   Ship by   Best Express   Instructions   FOB destination point
Terms 2/10, net 30   Date required 6/5/01

Item No.	Quantity	Description/Vendor No.	Unit price	Amount
314627	24 ST	Hobby tool set/5265	$28.59	$686.16
323515	12 CD	Hobby blades 5 pk/7512	.69	8.28
323682	6 ST	Screwdriver set 5/PC/1589	4.49	26.94
				$721.38

Approved by *Mary Jones*

EXHIBIT 5-12 Invoice

NO. 427953

A-1 Tool Co.
590 West St.
Milwaukee, WI

INVOICE

Sold to Grizzly Hardware Stores   **Date** 6/2/01
676 Sentinel St.   **Order No.** 54296
Missoula, MT   **Shipped via** Best Express
Ship to Same   **Date shipped** 6/2/01
Terms 2/10, net 30   **Ship terms** FOB destination

Quantity	Description/No.	Price	Amount
24 ST	Hobby tool set/5265	$28.59	$686.16
12 CD	Hobby blades 5 pk/7512	.69	8.28
6 ST	Screwdriver set 5 PC/1589	4.49	26.94
			$721.38

Invoice When A-1 Tool ships the merchandise, it also mails an invoice to Grizzly, requesting payment according to the agreed-upon terms, in this case 2/10, net 30. The **invoice** may be mailed separately or included with the shipment of merchandise. A-1 Tool, the seller, calls this document a *sales invoice;* it is the basis for recording a sale and an account receivable. Grizzly, the buyer, calls the same document a *purchase invoice,* which is the basis for recording a purchase and an account payable. The invoice that A-1 sent to Grizzly's accounting department is shown in Exhibit 5-12.

Receiving Report The accounting department receives the invoice for the three items ordered. Within a few days before or after the receipt of the invoice, the merchandise arrives at Grizzly's warehouse. As soon as the items are unpacked, the receiving department inspects and counts them. The same software program that generated the purchase order also generates a receiving report, as shown in Exhibit 5-13.

Grizzly uses a **blind receiving report.** The column for the quantity received is left blank and is filled in by the receiving department. Rather than being able simply to indicate that the number ordered was received, an employee must count the items to determine that the number ordered is actually received. You should trace all the relevant information for one of the three items ordered from the purchase order to the receiving report. The accounting system generates an original receiving report and three copies. The receiving department keeps one copy for its records and sends the original to the accounting department. One copy is sent to the purchasing department to be matched with the purchase order, and the other copy is sent to the tool department as verification that the items it originally requested have been received.

Invoice Approval Form At this point, Grizzly's accounting department has copies of the purchase requisition from the tool department, the purchase order from the purchasing department, the invoice from the supplier, and the receiving report from the warehouse. The accounting department uses an **invoice approval form** to document the accuracy of

EXHIBIT 5-13   Computer-Generated Receiving Report

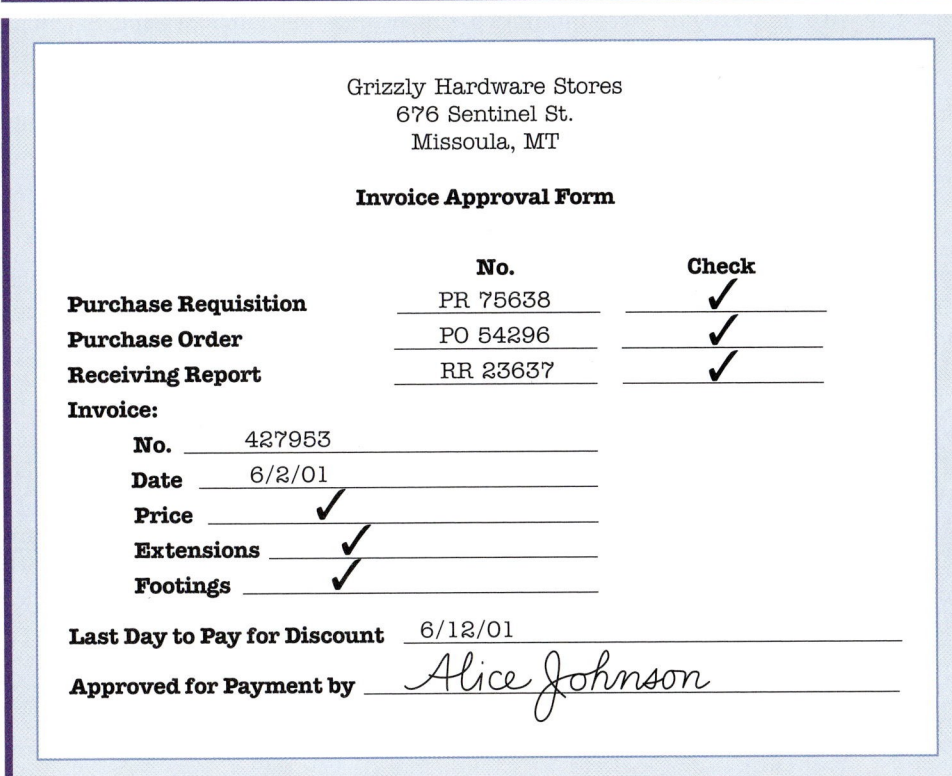

```
                        Grizzly Hardware Stores
                             676 Sentinel St.
                             Missoula, MT

                           Receiving Report

                                                        RR 23637

  Purchase Order No.  54296          Date ordered  5/30/01
  Vendor  A-1 Tool Co.               Date required  6/5/01
  Ship via  Best Express             Instructions  FOB Destination
  Terms  2/10, net 30

  Quantity received    Our Item No.    Description/Item No.       Remarks
                                                              Box damaged but
      24 ST            314627     Hobby tool set/5265          merchandise ok
      12 CD            323515     Hobby blades 5 pk/7512
       6 ST            323682     Screwdriver set 5/PC/1589

  Received by   Bob Reed                       Date      6/4/01
```

the information on each of these other forms. The invoice approval form for Grizzly Hardware is shown in Exhibit 5-14.

The invoice is compared to the purchase requisition to ensure that the company is billed for goods that it requested. A comparison of the invoice with the purchase order ensures that the goods were in fact ordered. Finally, the receiving report is compared with the invoice to verify that all goods the company is being billed for were received. An

EXHIBIT 5-14   Invoice Approval Form

```
                        Grizzly Hardware Stores
                             676 Sentinel St.
                             Missoula, MT

                        Invoice Approval Form

                                    No.             Check

  Purchase Requisition         PR 75638               ✓
  Purchase Order               PO 54296               ✓
  Receiving Report             RR 23637               ✓
  Invoice:
      No.    427953
      Date   6/2/01
      Price            ✓
      Extensions       ✓
      Footings         ✓

  Last Day to Pay for Discount   6/12/01

  Approved for Payment by   Alice Johnson
```

EXHIBIT 5-15   Check with Remittance Advice

3690

Grizzly Hardware Stores
676 Sentinel St.
Missoula, MT

<u>June 12</u> 20 <u>01</u>

PAY TO THE
ORDER OF ____<u>A-1 Tool Co.</u>_____   <u>$706.95</u>

<u>Seven hundred six and 95/100</u>_____   DOLLARS

Second National Bank
Missoula, MT
3690 035932 9321

John B. Martin

Purchase Order No.	Invoice No.	Invoice Date	Description	Amount
PO 54296	427953	6/2/01	24 ST Hobby tool set	$686.16
			12 CD Hobby blades 5pk	8.28
			6 ST Screwdriver set 5PC	26.94
			Total	721.38
			Less: 2% discount	14.43
			Net remitted	706.95

accounting department employee must also verify the mathematical accuracy of the amounts that appear on the invoice. The date the invoice must be paid to take advantage of the discount is noted so that the finance department will be sure to send the check by this date. At this point, the accounting department increases Purchases and Accounts Payable. The invoice approval form and the invoice are then sent to the finance department. Some businesses call the invoice approval form a *voucher;* it is used for all expenditures, not just for purchases of merchandise. Finally, it is worth noting that some businesses do not use a separate invoice approval form but simply note approval directly on the invoice itself.

Check with Remittance Advice   Grizzly's finance department is responsible for issuing checks. This results from the need to segregate custody of cash (the signed check) from record-keeping (the updating of the ledger). On receipt of the invoice approval form from the accounting department, a clerk in the finance department types a check with a remittance advice attached, as shown in Exhibit 5-15.[2]

Before the check is signed, the documents referred to on the invoice approval form are reviewed and canceled to prevent reuse. The clerk then forwards the check to one of the company officers authorized to sign checks. According to one of Grizzly's internal control policies, only the treasurer and the assistant treasurer are authorized to sign checks. Both officers must sign check amounts above a specified dollar limit. To maintain separation of duties, the finance department should mail the check. The remittance advice informs the supplier as to the nature of the payment and is torn off by the supplier before cashing the check.

---

[2]In some companies, an employee in the accounting department prepares checks and sends them to the finance department for review and signature. Also, many companies use computer-generated checks, rather than manually typed ones.

1. **LO 1** Merchandise is inventory purchased in finished form and held for resale. Both wholesalers and retailers sell merchandise. Sales revenue is a representation of the inflow of assets from the sale of merchandise during the period. Two deductions are made from sales revenue on the income statement. Sales returns and allowances and sales discounts are both subtracted from sales revenue to arrive at net sales.

2. **LO 2** A perpetual inventory system requires the updating of the Inventory account at the time of each purchase and each sale of merchandise. With the periodic system, the Inventory account is updated only at the end of the year. Separate accounts are used during the period to record purchases, purchase returns and allowances, purchase discounts, and transportation-in. The periodic system relies on a count of the inventory on the last day of the period to determine ending inventory.

3. **LO 3** Cost of goods sold is recognized as an expense under the matching principle. It represents the cost associated with the merchandise sold during the period and is matched with the revenue of the period.

4. **LO 3** The purchases of the period are reduced by purchase returns and allowances and by purchase discounts. Any freight costs paid to acquire the merchandise, called *transportation-in,* are added. The result, cost of goods purchased, is added to the beginning inventory to determine cost of goods available for sale. Cost of goods sold is found by deducting ending inventory from cost of goods available for sale.

5. **LO 3** *FOB destination point* means that the seller is responsible for the cost of delivering the merchandise to the buyer. Title to the goods does not transfer to the buyer until the buyer receives the merchandise from the carrier. *FOB shipping point* means that the buyer pays shipping costs. Title to the goods transfers to the buyer as soon as the seller turns them over to the carrier.

6. **LO 4** The purpose of an internal control system is to provide assurance that overall company objectives are met. Specifically, accounting controls are designed to safeguard the entity's assets and provide the company with reliable accounting records. Management has the primary responsibility for the reliability of the financial statements. Many companies employ a full-time internal audit staff to monitor and evaluate the internal control system.

7. **LO 5** Segregation of duties is the most fundamental of all internal control procedures. Possession of assets must be kept separate from the record-keeping function. Other important control procedures include a system of independent verifications, proper authorizations, adequate safeguards for assets and their records, independent review and appraisal of the accounting system, and the design and use of business documents.

8. **LO 5** Control over cash requires that all receipts be deposited intact on a daily basis and that all disbursements be made by check. Control procedures are important for cash received over the counter as well as for cash received in the mail. Any material discrepancies between the cash actually on hand and the amount that should be on hand need to be investigated.

9. **LO 6** Business documents play a vital role in various business activities, such as the purchase of merchandise. The requesting department fills out a purchase requisition form and sends it to the purchasing department. The purchasing department uses the requisition to complete a purchase order, which it sends to the supplier. The supplier mails an invoice to the buyer's accounting department. The accounting department also gets a receiving report from the warehouse to indicate the quantity and condition of the goods delivered. The accounting department fills out an invoice approval form, which it sends with the invoice to the finance department, which uses them as the basis for preparing and sending a check to the supplier. (Appendix 5A)

KEY TERMS QUIZ

Because of the large number of terms introduced in this chapter, there are two key terms quizzes. Read each definition below and then write the number of the definition in the blank beside the appropriate term it defines. The solution appears at the end of the chapter.

Quiz 1: Merchandise Accounting

____ Net sales

____ Sales Returns and Allowances

____ Trade discount

____ Quantity discount

____ Sales Discounts

____ Cost of goods available for sale

____ Cost of goods sold

____ Perpetual system

____ Periodic system

____ Transportation-in

____ Purchases

____ Purchase Returns and Allowances

____ Purchase Discounts

____ FOB destination point

____ FOB shipping point

1. A reduction in selling price for buying a large number of units of a product.

2. The contra-revenue account used to record both refunds to customers and reductions of their accounts.

3. The adjunct account used to record freight costs paid by the buyer.

4. A selling price reduction offered to a special class of customers.

5. The system in which the Inventory account is increased at the time of each purchase of merchandise and decreased at the time of each sale.

6. The contra-purchases account used in a periodic inventory system when a refund is received from a supplier or a reduction given in the balance owed to the supplier.

7. The contra-revenue account used to record discounts given customers for early payment of their accounts.

8. Terms that require the seller to pay for the cost of shipping the merchandise to the buyer.

9. Terms that require the buyer to pay the shipping costs.

10. The system in which the Inventory account is updated only at the end of the period.

11. Beginning inventory plus cost of goods purchased.

12. The contra-purchases account used to record reductions in purchase price for early payment to the supplier.

13. The account used in a periodic inventory system to record acquisitions of merchandise.

14. Sales revenue less sales returns and allowances and sales discounts.

15. Cost of goods available for sale minus ending inventory.

Quiz 2: Internal Control

____ Internal control system
____ Report of management
____ Internal audit staff
____ Board of directors
____ Audit committee
____ Foreign Corrupt Practices Act
____ Accounting system

____ Administrative controls
____ Accounting controls
____ Purchase requisition form (Appendix 5A)
____ Purchase order (Appendix 5A)
____ Invoice (Appendix 5A)
____ Blind receiving report (Appendix 5A)
____ Invoice approval form (Appendix 5A)

1. The form sent by the seller to the buyer as evidence of a sale.

2. The group composed of key officers of a corporation and outside members responsible for the general oversight of the affairs of the entity.

3. The methods and records used to accurately report an entity's transactions and to maintain accountability for its assets and liabilities.

4. The board of directors subset that acts as a direct contact between the stockholders and the independent accounting firm.

5. Procedures concerned with safeguarding the assets or the reliability of the financial statements.

6. The form a department uses to initiate a request to order merchandise.

7. A form the accounting department uses before making payment to document the accuracy of all the information about a purchase.

8. A written statement in the annual report indicating the responsibility of management for the financial statements.

9. A form used by the receiving department to account for the quantity and condition of merchandise received from a supplier.

10. Legislation intended to increase the accountability of management for accurate records and reliable financial statements.

11. Procedures concerned with efficient operation of the business and adherence to managerial policies.

12. The form sent by the purchasing department to the supplier.

13. The department responsible for monitoring and evaluating the internal control system.

14. Policies and procedures necessary to ensure the safeguarding of an entity's assets, the reliability of its accounting records, and the accomplishment of overall company objectives.

ALTERNATE TERMS

Gross margin Gross profit
Invoice Purchase invoice, sales invoice
Invoice approval form Voucher
Merchandiser Wholesaler, retailer

Report of management Management's report
Sales revenue Sales
Transportation-in Freight-in

QUESTIONS

1. When a company gives a cash refund on returned merchandise, why doesn't it just reduce Sales Revenue instead of using a contra-revenue account?

2. Why are trade discounts and quantity discounts not accorded accounting recognition? (The sale is simply recorded net of either of these types of discounts.)

3. What do credit terms of *3/20, n/60* mean? How valuable to the customer is the discount offered in these terms?

4. What is the difference between a periodic inventory system and a perpetual inventory system?

5. How have point-of-sale terminals improved the ability of mass merchandisers to use a perpetual inventory system?

6. In a periodic inventory system, what kind of account is Purchases? Is it an asset or an expense or neither?

7. Why are shipping terms, such as FOB shipping point or FOB destination point, important in deciding ownership of inventory at the end of the year?

8. How and why are transportation-in and transportation-out recorded differently?

9. How do the duties of an internal audit staff differ from those of the external auditors?

10. What is the typical composition of a board of directors of a publicly held corporation?

11. An order clerk fills out a purchase requisition for an expensive item of inventory and the receiving report when the merchandise arrives. The clerk takes the inventory home and then sends the invoice to the accounting department so that the supplier will be paid. What basic internal control procedure could have prevented this misuse of company assets?

12. What are some of the limitations on a company's effective system of internal control?

13. What two basic procedures are essential to an effective system of internal control over cash? (Appendix 5A)

14. How would you evaluate the following statement? "The only reason a company positions its cash register so that the customers can see the display is so that they feel comfortable they are being charged the correct amount for a purchase." (Appendix 5A)

15. Which document, a purchase order or an invoice, is the basis for recording a purchase and a corresponding liability? Explain your answer. (Appendix 5A)

16. What is a blind receiving report, and how does it act as a control device? (Appendix 5A)

17. What is the purpose in comparing a purchase invoice with a purchase order? in comparing a receiving report with a purchase invoice? (Appendix 5A)

EXERCISES

LO 1   Exercise 5-1   Sales Transactions and Returns

For each of the following transactions of Ace Corporation on March 3, 2001, determine the effect on the accounting equation:

a.   Sold merchandise on credit for $500 with terms of 2/10, net 30. Ace records all sales at the gross amount.

b.   Recorded cash sales for the day of $1,250 from the cash register tape.

c.   Granted a cash refund of $135 to a customer for spoiled merchandise returned.

d.   Granted a customer a credit of $190 on its outstanding bill and allowed the customer to keep a defective product.

e.   Applied cash of $2,300, received through the mail, to customers' accounts. All amounts received qualify for the discount for early payment.

LO 1   Exercise 5-2   Credit Terms

Ling Company sold merchandise on credit for $800 on September 10, 2001, to Letson Inc. For each of the following terms, indicate the last day Letson could take the discount, the amount Letson would pay if it took the discount, and the date full payment is due.

a.   2/10, n/30

b.   3/15, n/45

c.   1/7, n/21

d.   5/15, n/30

LO 1   Exercise 5-3   Sales Discounts

For each of the following transactions of Rambler Corporation, determine the effect on the accounting equation, assuming it uses the gross method to record sales discounts (all sales on credit are made with terms of 2/10, net 30).

June   2:   Sold merchandise on credit to Huskie Corp. for $1,200.

June   4:   Sold merchandise on credit to Hawkeye Company for $2,000.

June 13:   Collected cash from Hawkeye Company.

June 30:   Collected cash from Huskie Corp.

LO 2 Exercise 5-4 Perpetual and Periodic Inventory Systems

Following is a partial list of account balances for two different merchandising companies. The amounts in the accounts represent the balances at the end of the year *before* any adjustments are made or the books are closed.

Company A		Company B	
Sales revenue	$50,000	Sales revenue	$85,000
Sales discounts	3,000	Sales discounts	2,000
Merchandise inventory	12,000	Merchandise inventory	9,000
Cost of goods sold	38,000	Purchases	41,000
		Purchase discounts	4,000
		Purchase returns and allowances	1,000

Required

1. Identify which inventory system, perpetual or periodic, each of the two companies uses. Explain how you know which system each uses by looking at the types of accounts on their books.

2. How much inventory does Company A have on hand at the end of the year? What is its cost of goods sold for the year?

3. Explain why you cannot determine Company B's cost of goods sold for the year from the information available.

LO 2 Exercise 5-5 Perpetual and Periodic Inventory Systems

From the following list, identify whether the merchandisers described would most likely use a perpetual or periodic inventory system.

_____ Appliance store

_____ Car dealership

_____ Drugstore

_____ Furniture store

_____ Grocery store

_____ Hardware store

_____ Jewelry store

How might changes in technology affect the ability of merchandisers to use perpetual inventory systems?

LO 3 Exercise 5-6 Missing Amounts in Cost of Goods Sold Model

For each of the following independent cases, fill in the missing amounts:

	Case 1	Case 2	Case 3
Beginning inventory	$ (a)	$2,350	$1,890
Purchases (gross)	6,230	5,720	(e)
Purchase returns and allowances	470	800	550
Purchase discounts	200	(c)	310
Transportation-in	150	500	420
Cost of goods available for sale	7,110	(d)	8,790
Ending inventory	(b)	1,750	1,200
Cost of goods sold	5,220	5,570	(f)

LO 3 Exercise 5-7 Purchase Discounts

For each of the following transactions of Buckeye Corporation, determine the effect on the accounting equation, assuming it uses the gross method to record purchase discounts (all purchases on credit are made with terms of 1/10, net 30, and Buckeye uses the periodic system of inventory):

July 3: Purchased merchandise on credit from Wildcat Corp. for $3,500.

July 6: Purchased merchandise on credit from Cyclone Company for $7,000.

July 12: Paid amount owed to Wildcat Corp.

August 5: Paid amount owed to Cyclone Company.

LO 3 Exercise 5-8 Purchases—Periodic System

For each of the following transactions of Wolverine Corporation, determine the effect on the accounting equation. The company uses the periodic system and the gross method to record purchase discounts.

March   3: Purchased merchandise from Spartan Corp. for $2,500 with terms of 2/10, net/30. Shipping costs of $250 were paid to Neverlate Transit Company.

March   7: Purchased merchandise from Boilermaker Company for $1,400 with terms of net/30.

March 12: Paid amount owed to Spartan Corp.

March 15: Received a credit of $500 on defective merchandise purchased from Boilermaker Company. The merchandise was kept.

March 18: Purchased merchandise from Gopher Corp. for $1,600 with terms of 2/10, net 30.

March 22: Received a credit of $400 from Gopher Corp. for spoiled merchandise returned to them. This is the amount of credit exclusive of any discount.

April   6: Paid amount owed to Boilermaker Company.

April   18: Paid amount owed to Gopher Corp.

LO 3 Exercise 5-9 Shipping Terms and Transfer of Title

On December 23, 2001, Miller Wholesalers ships merchandise to Michael Retailers with terms of FOB destination point. The merchandise arrives at Michael's warehouse on January 3, 2002.

Required

1. Identify who pays to ship the merchandise.

2. Determine whether the inventory should be included as an asset on Michael's December 31, 2001, balance sheet. Should the sale be included on Miller's 2001 income statement?

3. Explain how your answers to part **2** would have been different if the terms of shipment had been FOB shipping point.

LO 3 Exercise 5-10 Transfer of Title to Inventory

From the following list, identify whether the transactions described should be recorded by Cameron Companies during December 2001 or January 2002.

Purchases of merchandise that are in transit from vendors to Cameron Companies on December 31, 2001:

_____ Shipped FOB shipping point

_____ Shipped FOB destination point

Sales of merchandise that are in transit to customers of Cameron Companies on December 31, 2001:

_____ Shipped FOB shipping point

_____ Shipped FOB destination point

LO 5 Exercise 5-11 Internal Control

The university drama club is planning a raffle. The president overheard you talking about internal control to another accounting student, so she has asked you to set up some guidelines to "be sure" that all money collected for the raffle is accounted for by the club.

Required

1. Describe guidelines that the club should follow to achieve an acceptable level of internal control.

2. Comment on the president's request that she "be sure" all money is collected and recorded.

LO 5 Exercise 5-12 Segregation of Duties

The following tasks are performed by three employees, each of whom is capable of performing all of them. Do not concern yourself with the time required to perform the tasks but with the need to provide for segregation of duties. Assign the duties by using a check mark to indicate which employee should perform each task. Remember that you may assign any one of the tasks to any of the employees.

Task	Employee		
	Mary	**Sue**	**John**
Prepare invoices			
Mail invoices			
Pick up mail from post office			
Open mail, separate checks			
List checks on deposit slip in triplicate			
Post payment to customer's account			
Deposit checks			
Prepare monthly schedule of accounts receivable			
Reconcile bank statements			

Multi-Concept Exercises

LO 1, 3   Exercise 5-13   Income Statement for a Merchandiser

Fill in the missing amounts in the following income statement for Carpenters Department Store Inc.:

Sales revenue		$125,600	
Less: Sales returns and allowances		(a) ?	
Net sales			$122,040
Cost of goods sold:			
Beginning inventory		23,400	
Purchases	(b) ?		
Less: Purchase discounts	1,300		
Net purchases	(c) ?		
Add: Transportation-in	6,550		
Cost of goods purchased		81,150	
Cost of goods available for sale		104,550	
Less: Ending inventory		(e) ?	
Cost of goods sold			(d) ?
Gross margin			38,600
Operating expenses			$ (f) ?
Income before tax			26,300
Income tax expense			10,300
Net income			$ (g) ?

LO 1, 3   Exercise 5-14   Partial Income Statement—Periodic System

LaPine Company has the following account balances as of December 31, 2001:

Purchase returns and allowances	$ 400
Inventory, January 1	4,000
Sales	80,000
Transportation-in	1,000
Sales returns and allowances	500
Purchase discounts	800
Inventory, December 31	3,800
Purchases	30,000
Sales discounts	1,200

Required

Prepare a partial income statement for LaPine Company for 2001 through gross margin. Calculate LaPine's gross margin (gross profit) ratio for 2001.

PROBLEMS

LO 1 Problem 5-1 Trade Discounts

Essex Inc. offers the following discounts to customers who purchase large quantities:

> 10% discount: 10–25 units
>
> 20% discount: >25 units

Mr. Essex, the president, would like to record all sales at the list price and record the discount as an expense.

Required

1. Explain to Mr. Essex why trade discounts do not enter into the accounting records.

2. Even though trade discounts do not enter into the accounting records, is it still important to have some record of these? Explain your answer.

LO 1 Problem 5-2 Calculation of Gross Margins for Wal-Mart and Kmart

The following information was summarized from the consolidated statements of income of Wal-Mart Stores Inc. and Subsidiaries for the years ended January 31, 2000 and 1999, and the consolidated statements of operations of Kmart Corporation for the years ended January 26, 2000, and January 27, 1999 (for each company, years are labeled as 1999 and 1998, respectively):

www.walmart.com
www.bluelight.com

(in Millions)	1999		1998	
	Sales	**Cost of Sales***	**Sales**	**Cost of Sales***
Wal-Mart	$165,013	$129,664	$137,634	$108,725
Kmart	$ 35,925	$ 28,102	$ 33,674	$ 26,319

*Described as "cost of sales, buying and occupancy" by Kmart Corporation.

Required

1. Calculate the gross margin (gross profit) ratios for Wal-Mart and Kmart for 1999 and 1998.

2. Which company appears to be performing better? What factors might cause the difference in the gross margin ratios of the two companies? What other information should you consider to determine how these companies are performing in this regard?

LO 5 Problem 5-3 Internal Control Procedures

You are opening a summer business, a chain of three drive-thru snow-cone stands. You have hired other college students to work and have purchased a cash register with locked-in tapes. You retain one key, and the other is available to the lead person on each shift.

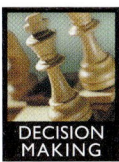

DECISION MAKING

Required

1. Write a list of the procedures for all employees to follow when ringing up sales and giving change.

2. Write a list of the procedures for the lead person to follow in closing out at the end of the day. Be as specific as you can so that employees will have few if any questions.

3. What is your main concern in the design of internal control for the snow-cone stands? How did you address that concern? Be specific.

LO 6 Problem 5-4 The Design of Internal Control Documents (Appendix 5A)

Motel $49.99 has purchased a large warehouse to store all supplies used by housekeeping departments in the company's expanding chain of motels. In the past, each motel bought supplies from local distributors and paid for the supplies from cash receipts.

Required

1. Name some potential problems with the old system.

2. Design a purchase requisition form and a receiving report to be used by the housekeeping departments and the warehouse. Indicate how many copies of each form should be used and who should receive each copy.

Multi-Concept Problems

LO 1, 2, 3 **Problem 5-5** Transactions of a Merchandiser

The following transactions were entered into by North Coast Tires Inc. during the month of June:

June   2: Purchased 1,000 tires at a cost of $60 per tire. Terms of payment are 1/10, net 45.

June   4: Paid trucking firm $1,200 to ship the tires purchased on June 2.

June   5: Purchased 600 tires at a cost of $60 per tire. Terms of payment are 2/10, net 30.

June   6: Paid trucking firm $800 to ship the tires purchased on June 5.

June   7: Returned 150 of the tires purchased on June 2 because they were defective. Received a credit on open account from the seller.

June 11: Paid for tires purchased on June 2.

June 13: Sold 700 tires from those purchased on June 2. The selling price was $90 per tire. Terms are 1/10, net 30.

June 22: Received cash from sale of tires on June 13.

June 30: Paid for tires purchased on June 5.

Required

1. For each of the preceding transactions of North Coast Tires Inc., determine the effect on the accounting equation. The company uses the gross method of recording purchase and sales discounts. North Coast uses a periodic inventory system.

2. Given the nature of its product, do you think it would be feasible for North Coast to use a perpetual inventory system? Why? If so, what advantages would accrue to the company by using a perpetual system?

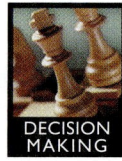

DECISION MAKING

LO 1, 2, 3 **Problem 5-6** Transactions of a Merchandiser

Leisure Time Furniture Store entered into the following transactions in the month of April:

April   3: Purchased 50 lounge chairs at $150 each with terms 2/10, net 45. The chairs were shipped FOB destination.

April   7: Sold 6 chairs for $320 each, terms 2/10, net 30.

April   8: Purchased 20 patio umbrella tables for $120 each, FOB shipping point, terms 1/10, net 30.

April   9: Due to defects, returned 5 lounge chairs purchased on April 3. Received a credit memorandum, indicating that amount due has been reduced.

April 10: Paid the trucking firm $360 for delivery of the tables purchased on April 8.

April 13: Paid for the chairs purchased on April 3.

April 17: Received payment for the chairs sold on April 7.

April 20: Paid for the tables purchased on April 8.

Required

1. For each of the preceding transactions of Leisure Time, determine the effect on the accounting equation. Leisure Time uses the gross method of recording purchase and sales discounts. The company uses a periodic inventory system.

2. Do you think Leisure Time should change to a perpetual inventory system, given the nature of its business? Why? What advantages would a company have using the perpetual system instead of the periodic system?

LO 1, 3 **Problem 5-7** Trade and Cash Discounts

Billings Inc. publishes books and offers trade discounts to customers who purchase in large quantities: 30% for purchases of more than 50 units. It also offers credit terms of 2/10, net 30 to induce early payment. The list price of one book is $60. Columbus Company purchased 100 of these books on September 12. Payment was made on September 21.

Required

1. Determine the effects on Billings's accounting equation from the transactions to record the sale and the receipt of cash.

2. Determine the effects on Columbus's accounting equation from the transactions to record the purchase and the payment.

LO 1, 3 **Problem 5-8** Transactions of a Merchandiser and Partial Income Statement

Weekend Wonders Inc. operates a chain of discount hardware stores. The company uses a periodic inventory system. Inventory on hand on June 1, 2001, amounts to $25,670; on June 30, 2001, it is $30,200. The company uses the gross method to record purchase and sales discounts. The following transactions take place during the month of June:

a. Purchased merchandise from suppliers at a cost of $80,000 with credit terms of 2/10, net 30.

b. Paid freight costs of $4,250 to the common carrier for merchandise purchased.

c. Returned defective merchandise to suppliers and received credits of $2,300, the amount of credit before taking into account any purchase discounts.

d. Realized $92,000 in sales for the month, of which $68,000 is on credit; the remainder was received in cash. The credit sales are made with terms of 2/10, net 45.

e. Gave sales returns and allowances on credit sales of $4,000 during the month.

f. Made cash payments of $62,000 to suppliers for earlier purchases on account. All amounts paid during the month are made within the discount period.

g. Received $56,000 in cash collections on account from customers. All amounts received during the month are within the discount period.

Required

1. For each of the preceding transactions of Weekend Wonders Inc., determine the effect on the accounting equation.

2. Prepare a partial income statement for the month of June. The last line on the statement should be gross margin.

3. Assume that Weekend Wonders decides as a matter of policy to forgo the discount for early payment on purchases (credit terms are 2/10, net 30). What return would Weekend Wonders need to earn on the money it invests by not paying early to justify this decision? Provide any necessary calculations to support your answer.

LO 1, 2, 3 **Problem 5-9** Purchases and Sales of Merchandise, Cash Flows

Two Wheeler, a bike shop, opened for business on April 1. It uses a periodic inventory system and records purchases at gross. The following transactions occurred during the first month of business:

April 1: Purchased five units from Duhan Co. for $500 total, with terms 3/10, net 30, FOB destination.

April 10: Paid for the April 1 purchase.

April 15: Sold one unit for $200 cash.

April 18: Purchased 10 units from Clinton Inc. for $900 total, with terms 3/10, net/30, FOB destination.

April 25: Sold three units for $200 each, cash.

April 28: Paid for the April 18 purchase.

Required

1. For each of the preceding transactions of Two Wheeler, determine the effect on the accounting equation.

2. Determine net income for the month of April. Two Wheeler incurred and paid $100 for rent and $50 for miscellaneous expenses during April. Ending inventory is $967 (ignore income taxes).

3. Assuming that the only transactions during April are given (including rent and miscellaneous expenses), compute net cash flow from operating activities.

4. Explain why cash outflow is so much larger than expenses on the income statement.

LO 1, 3 **Problem 5-10** The Gap's Sales, Cost of Goods Sold, and Gross Margin

The consolidated balance sheets of The Gap Inc. included merchandise inventory in the amount **www.gap.com** of $1,462,045,000 as of January 29, 2000 (the end of fiscal year 1999) and $1,056,444,000 as of January 30, 1999 (the end of fiscal year 1998). Refer also to The Gap's consolidated statements of earnings for fiscal 1999 and 1998, which are set forth in the opening vignette of this chapter.

Required

1. Unlike most other merchandisers, The Gap doesn't include accounts receivable on its balance sheet. Why doesn't The Gap's balance sheet include this account?

2. The Gap sets forth net sales but not gross sales on its income statement. What type(s) of deduction(s) would be made from gross sales to arrive at the amount of net sales reported? Why might the company decide not to report the amount(s) of the deduction(s) separately?

3. Reconstruct the cost of goods sold section of The Gap's 1999 income statement.

4. Calculate the gross margin (gross profit) ratios for The Gap for 1999, 1998, and 1997, and comment on the changes noted, if any. Is the company's performance improving? What factors might have caused the change in the gross margin ratio?

LO 4, 5 Problem 5-11   Internal Control

At Morris Mart Inc. all sales are on account. Mary Morris-Manning is responsible for mailing invoices to customers, recording the amount billed, opening mail, and recording the payment. Mary is very devoted to the family business and never takes off more than one or two days for a long weekend. The customers know Mary and sometimes send personal notes with their payments. Another clerk handles all aspects of accounts payable. Mary's brother, who is president of Morris Mart, has hired an accountant to help with expansion.

Required

1. List some problems with the current accounts receivable system.

2. What suggestions would you make to improve internal control?

3. How would you explain to Mary that she personally is not the problem?

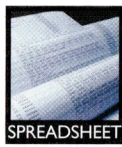

SPREADSHEET

LO 1, 3 Problem 5-12   Financial Statements

A list of accounts for Maple Inc. at 12/31/01 follows:

Accounts Receivable	$ 2,359
Advertising Expense	4,510
Buildings and Equipment, Net	55,550
Capital Stock	50,000
Cash	590
Depreciation Expense	2,300
Dividends	6,000
Income Tax Expense	3,200
Income Tax Payable	3,200
Interest Receivable	100
Inventory:	
January 1, 2001	6,400
December 31, 2001	7,500
Land	20,000
Purchase Discounts	800
Purchases	40,200
Retained Earnings, January 1, 2001	32,550
Salaries Expense	25,600
Salaries Payable	650
Sales	84,364
Sales Returns	780
Transportation-in	375
Utilities Expense	3,600

Required

1. Determine cost of goods sold for 2001.

2. Determine net income for 2001.

3. Prepare a balance sheet dated December 31, 2001.

LO 1 **Problem 5-1A** Discounts

Whitefish Inc., a recording distributor, would like to offer discounts to customers who purchase large quantities. Whitefish is unsure about the terms to use and how to account for discounts extended to customers. The company also wants to consider a cash discount for early payment by customers. Whitefish expects sales of about $3 million this year. All sales are on account to about 100 different outlets located within 500 miles of the warehouse. Deliveries are made by Whitefish's own trucks and cost about $25 per 100 miles driven. A full truck will hold 1,000 units.

Required

1. Explain the difference between a quantity discount and a discount for early payment. How is each accounted for in the accounting records? What are the reasons to extend the different discounts to customers?

2. Set up a quantity discount plan and a sales discount plan for Whitefish to extend to customers. Be able to explain why you chose your bases for the discounts and the amount of discounts.

LO 1 **Problem 5-2A** Calculation of Gross Margins for Sears and JCPenney

The following information was summarized from the 1999 and 1998 consolidated statements of income of Sears, Roebuck and Co. (for the years ended January 1, 2000, and January 2, 1999), and JCPenney Company, Inc. and Subsidiaries (for the years ended January 29, 2000, and January 30, 1999). For each company, years are labeled as 1999 and 1998).

www.sears.com
www.jcpenney.com

	1999		1998	
(in Millions)	Sales*	Cost of Sales**	Sales*	Cost of Sales**
Sears	$36,728	$27,212	$36,957	$27,444
JCPenney	$31,391	$23,374	$29,439	$21,642

*Described as "merchandise sales and services" by Sears and "retail sales, net" by JCPenney.
**Described as "cost of sales, buying and occupancy" by Sears and "cost of goods sold" by JCPenney.

Required

1. Calculate the gross margin (gross profit) ratios for Sears and JCPenney for 1999 and 1998.

2. Which company appears to be performing better? What factors might cause the difference in the gross margin ratios of the two companies? What other information should you consider to determine how these companies are performing in this regard?

LO 5 **Problem 5-3A** Internal Control Procedures

The loan department in a bank is subject to regulation. Internal auditors work for the bank to ensure that the loan department complies with requirements. The internal auditors must verify that each car loan file has a note signed by the maker, verification of insurance, and a title issued by the state that names the bank as co-owner.

Required

1. Explain why the bank and the regulatory agency are concerned with these documents.

2. Describe the internal control procedures that should be in place to ensure that these documents are obtained and safeguarded.

LO 6 **Problem 5-4A** The Design of Internal Control Documents (Appendix 5A)

Tiger's Group is a newly formed company that produces and sells children's movies about an imaginary character. The movies are in such great demand that they are shipped to retail outlets as soon as they are produced. The company must pay a royalty to several actors for each movie that it sold to retail outlets.

Required

1. Describe some internal control features that should be in place to ensure that all royalties are paid to the actors.

2. Design the shipping form that Tiger's Group should use for the movies. Be sure to include authorizations and indicate the number of copies and the routing of the copies.

Alternate Multi-Concept Problems

LO 1, 3 **Problem 5-5A** Transactions of a Merchandiser

The following transactions were entered into by Maxwell Inc. during the month of July:

July 2: Purchased 1,000 pounds of steak at a cost of $3 per pound. Terms of payment are 2/10, net 30.

July 4: Paid trucking firm $500 to ship the steak purchased on July 2.

July 5: Purchased 600 pounds of steak at a cost of $3 per pound. Terms of payment are 2/10, net 45.

July 6: Paid trucking firm $300 to ship the steak purchased on July 5.

July 7: Due to expired dates on some packages, returned 100 pounds of the steak purchased on July 2. Received a credit on open account from the seller.

July 11: Paid for steak purchased on July 2.

July 13: Sold 1,200 pounds of steak from those purchased on July 2 and July 5. The selling price was $7 per pound, cash.

July 30: Paid for steak purchased on July 5.

Required

1. For each of the preceding transactions of Maxwell Inc., determine the effect on the accounting equation. The company uses the gross method of recording purchase discounts. Maxwell uses a periodic inventory system.

2. Maxwell assumes a $3 per pound cost of inventory when planning profit and setting prices. Is this accurate? Explain.

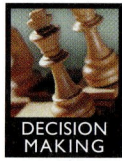
DECISION MAKING

LO 1, 2, 3 **Problem 5-6A** Transactions of a Merchandiser

Deckside Furniture Store entered into the following transactions in the month of April:

April 3: Purchased 50 lounge chairs at $120 each with terms 2/10, net 45. The chairs were shipped FOB destination.

April 7: Sold 6 chairs for $256 each, terms 2/10, net 30.

April 8: Purchased 20 patio umbrella tables for $96 each, FOB shipping point, terms 1/10, net 30.

April 9: Due to defects, returned 5 lounge chairs purchased on April 3. Received a credit memorandum.

April 10: Paid the trucking firm $288 for delivery of the tables purchased on April 8.

April 13: Paid for the chairs purchased on April 3.

April 17: Received payment for the chairs sold on April 7.

April 20: Paid for the tables purchased on April 8.

Required

1. For each of the preceding transactions of the furniture company, determine the effect on the accounting equation. Deckside uses the gross method of recording purchase and sales discounts. The company uses a periodic inventory system.

2. Do you think Deckside should change to a perpetual inventory system, given the nature of their business? Why? What advantages would a company have using the perpetual system instead of the periodic system?

LO 1, 3 **Problem 5-7A** Trade and Cash Discounts

Kalispell Inc. publishes books and offers trade discounts to customers who purchase in large quantities: 20% for purchases of more than 50 units. It also offers credit terms of 2/10, net 30 to induce early payment. The list price of one book is $50. Glacier Company purchased 100 of these books on September 12. Payment was made on September 21.

Required

1. Determine the effect on Kalispell's accounting equation from the transactions to record the sale and the receipt of cash.

2. Determine the effect on Glacier's accounting equation from the transactions to record the purchase and the payment.

LO 1, 3 Problem 5-8A Transactions of a Merchandiser

Toppsie Turn Inc. operates a chain of T-shirt stores. The company uses a periodic inventory system. Inventories on hand on June 1 and June 30, 2001, amount to $12,840. The company uses the gross method to record purchase discounts. The following transactions take place during the month of June:

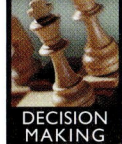

DECISION MAKING

a. Purchased merchandise from suppliers at a cost of $62,000 with credit terms of 2/10, net 30.

b. Paid freight cost of $3,400 to the common carrier for merchandise purchased.

c. Realized $124,000 of sales for the month, all of which are cash sales.

d. Paid for merchandise purchased during the month within the discount period.

e. Accepted $500 in returned merchandise during the month.

Required

1. For each of the preceding transactions of Toppsie Turn Inc., determine the effect on the accounting equation.

2. Determine the gross margin that Toppsie Turn would report on the income statement for the month of June.

3. Toppsie is thinking about extending credit to some of its major customers to encourage credit customers to pay quickly. Toppsie expects existing sales will increase by 10% and that, at the new sales level, 60% of sales will be credit sales. Should Toppsie extend credit terms of 2/10, net 30? Explain your answer.

LO 1, 2, 3 Problem 5-9A Purchases and Sales of Merchandise, Cash Flows

Chestnut Corp., a ski shop, opened for business on October 1. It uses a periodic inventory system and the gross method to record purchase discounts. The following transactions occurred during the first month of business:

October   1: Purchased three units from Oshkosh Inc. for $249 total, terms 2/10, net 30, FOB destination.

October 10: Paid for the October 1 purchase.

October 15: Sold one unit for $200 cash.

October 18: Purchased 10 units from Wausau Company for $800 total, with terms 2/10, net/30, FOB destination.

October 25: Sold three units for $200 each, cash.

October 30: Paid for the October 18 purchase.

Required

1. For each of the preceding transactions of Chestnut, determine the effect on the accounting equation.

2. Determine the number of units on hand on October 31.

3. If Chestnut started the month with $2,000, determine its balance in cash at the end of the month, assuming that these are the only transactions that occurred during October. Why has the cash balance decreased when the company reported net income?

LO 1, 3 Problem 5-10A Walgreen's Sales, Cost of Goods Sold, and Gross Margin

The following information was summarized from the consolidated balance sheets of Walgreen Co. and Subsidiaries as of August 31, 2000, and August 31, 1999, and the consolidated statements of income for the years ended August 31, 2000, and August 31, 1999.

www.walgreens.com

(in millions)	2000	1999
Accounts receivable, net	$ 614.5	$ 486.5
Cost of sales	15,465.9	12,978.6
Inventories	2,830.8	2,462.6
Net sales	21,206.9	17,838.8

Required

1. Walgreen Co. sets forth net sales but not gross sales on its income statement. What type(s) of deduction(s) would be made from gross sales to arrive at the amount of net sales reported? Why might the company decide not to report the amount(s) of the deduction(s) separately?

2. Reconstruct the cost of goods sold section of Walgreen's 2000 income statement.

3. Calculate the gross margin (gross profit) ratios for Walgreen Co. for 2000 and 1999 and comment on the change noted, if any. Is the company's performance improving? What factors might have caused the change in the gross margin ratio?

LO 4, 5   Problem 5-11A   Internal Control

Abbott Inc. is expanding and needs to hire more personnel in the accounting office. Barbara Barker, the chief accounting clerk, knew that her cousin Cheryl was looking for a job. Barbara and Cheryl are also roommates. Barbara offered Cheryl a job as her assistant. Barbara will be responsible for Cheryl's performance reviews and training.

Required

1. List some problems with the proposed personnel situations in the accounting department.

2. Explain why accountants are concerned with the hiring of personnel. What suggestions would you make to improve internal control at Abbott?

3. How would you explain to Barbara and Cheryl that they personally are not the problem?

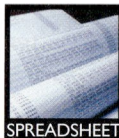
SPREADSHEET

LO 1, 3   Problem 5-12A   Financial Statements

A list of accounts for Lloyd Inc. at December 31, 2001, follows:

Accounts Receivable	$56,359
Advertising Expense	12,900
Capital Stock	50,000
Cash	22,340
Dividends	6,000
Income Tax Expense	1,450
Income Tax Payable	1,450
Inventory	
January 1, 2001	6,400
December 31, 2001	5,900
Purchase Discounts	1,237
Purchases	62,845
Retained Earnings, January 1, 2001	28,252
Salaries Payable	650
Sales	112,768
Sales Returns	1,008
Transportation-in	375
Utilities Expense	1,800
Wages and Salaries Expense	23,000
Wages Payable	120

Required

1. Determine cost of goods sold for 2001.

2. Determine net income for 2001.

3. Prepare a balance sheet dated December 31, 2001.

CASES

Reading and Interpreting Financial Statements

LO 1, 3   Case 5-1   Reading and Interpreting Uno's Financial Statements

www.pizzeriauno.com   Refer to the 1999 financial statements and footnotes included in Uno's annual report.

Required

1. Is Uno a merchandiser, manufacturer, or service provider? Explain your answer.

2. Is it possible to calculate gross margin for Uno? If so, what accounts on the income statement would you use? Explain your answers.

3. Refer to footnote 1 in the annual report. What components make up Uno's inventory?

LO 1, 3 **Case 5-2** Reading and Interpreting Gateway's Financial Statements

Refer to the 1999 financial statements and footnotes included in Gateway's annual report.   **www.gateway.com**

Required

1. Determine the amount of net sales and cost of goods sold for 1999.

2. Is Gateway a merchandiser, manufacturer, or service provider?

3. Compare and contrast the inventory for merchandisers and manufacturers (refer to footnote 9 in Gateway's annual report to assist you).

LO 4 **Case 5-3** Reading and Interpreting Sears' Management Report

Sears, Roebuck and Co.'s 1999 annual report includes a management's report. Included in the re-   **www.sears.com**
port is the following:

> Management maintains a system of internal controls that it believes provides reasonable as-
> surance that, in all material respects, assets are maintained and accounted for in accordance
> with management's authorizations and transactions are recorded accurately in the books
> and records. The concept of reasonable assurance is based on the premise that the cost of
> internal controls should not exceed the benefits derived. To assure the effectiveness of the
> internal control system, the organizational structure provides for defined lines of responsi-
> bility and delegation of authority.

Required

1. Why did management include this report in the annual report?

2. What types of costs does Sears have in mind when it states that "the cost of internal controls should not exceed the benefits derived"?

3. Based on what you know about retail stores, and Sears stores in particular, list the kinds of accounting and system controls the company may have in place to safeguard assets.

Making Financial Decisions

LO 1, 3 **Case 5-4** Gross Margin for a Merchandiser

Emblems For You sells specialty sweatshirts. The purchase price is $10 per unit, plus 10% tax and a shipping cost of 50¢ per unit. When the units arrive, they must be labeled, at an additional cost of 75¢ per unit. Emblems purchased, received, and labeled 1,500 units, of which 750 units were sold during the month for $20 each. The controller has prepared the following income statement:

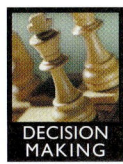

DECISION MAKING

Sales	$15,000
Cost of sales ($11 × 750)	8,250
Gross margin	$ 6,750
Shipping expense	750
Labeling expense	1,125
Net income	$ 4,875

Emblems is aware that a gross margin of 40% is standard for the industry. The marketing manager believes that Emblems should lower the price because the gross margin is higher than the industry average.

Required

1. Calculate Emblems' gross margin ratio.

2. Explain why you believe that Emblems should or should not lower its selling price.

LO 1, 3 **Case 5-5** Pricing Decision

Caroline's Candy Corner sells gourmet chocolates. The company buys chocolates, in bulk, for $5.00 per pound plus 5% sales tax. Credit terms are 2/10, net 25, and the company always pays promptly in order to take advantage of the discount. The chocolates are shipped to Caroline FOB shipping point. Shipping costs are $.05 per pound. When the chocolates arrive at the shop, Caroline's Candy repack-
ages them into one-pound boxes labeled with the store name. Boxes cost $.70 each. The company pays its employees an hourly wage of $5.25 plus a commission of $.10 per pound.

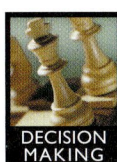

DECISION MAKING

Required

1. What is the cost per one-pound box of chocolates?

2. What price must Caroline's Candy charge in order to have a 40% gross margin?

3. Do you believe this is a sufficient margin for this kind of business? What other costs might the company still incur?

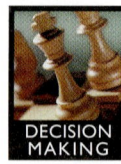
DECISION MAKING

LO 2 Case 5-6 Use of a Perpetual Inventory System
Darrell Keith is starting a new business. He would like to keep a tight control over it. Therefore, he wants to know *exactly* how much gross profit he earns on each unit he sells. Darrell has set up an elaborate numbering system to identify each item as it is purchased and then to match the item with a sales price. Each unit is assigned a number as follows:

0000-000-00-000

a. The first four numbers represent the month and day an item was received.

b. The second set of numbers is the last three numbers of the purchase order that authorized the purchase of the item.

c. The third set of numbers is the two-number department code assigned to different types of products.

d. The last three numbers are a chronological code assigned to units as they are received during a given day.

Required

1. Write a short memo to Darrell explaining the benefits and costs involved in a perpetual inventory system in conjunction with his quest to know exactly how much he will earn on each unit.

2. Comment on Darrell's inventory system, assuming that he is selling (a) automobiles or (b) trees, shrubs, and plants.

Accounting and Ethics: What Would You Do?

LO 1 Case 5-7 Sales Returns and Allowances
You are the controller for a large chain of discount merchandise stores. You receive a memorandum from the sales manager for the midwestern region. He raises an issue regarding the proper treatment of sales returns. The manager urges you to discontinue the "silly practice" of recording Sales Returns and Allowances each time a customer returns a product. In the manager's mind, this is a waste of time and unduly complicates the financial statements. The manager recommends, "Things could be kept a lot simpler by just reducing Sales Revenue when a product is returned."

Required

1. What do you think the sales manager's *motivation* might be for writing you the memo? Is it that he believes the present practice is a waste of time and unduly complicates the financial statements?

2. Do you agree with the sales manager's recommendation? Explain why you agree or disagree.

3. Write a brief memo to the sales manager outlining your position on this matter.

LO 4, 5 Case 5-8 Cash Receipts in a Bookstore
You were recently hired by a large retail bookstore chain. Your training involved spending a week at the largest and most profitable store in the district. The store manager assigned the head cashier to train you on the cash register and closing procedures required by the company's home office. In the process, the head cashier instructed you to keep an envelope for cash over and short that would include cash or IOUs equal to the net amount of overages or shortages in the cash drawer. "It is impossible to balance exactly, so just put extra cash in this envelope and use the cash when you are short." You studied accounting for one semester in college and remembered your professor saying that "all deposits should be made intact, daily."

Required

Draft a memorandum to the store manager detailing any problems you see with the current system.

INTERNET RESEARCH CASE

Case 5-9 The Gap
The Gap, Inc. has over 3,650 stores selling casual clothes worldwide, including GapKids and baby-Gap stores and its Old Navy and Banana Republic stores. While its 1999 revenues were the best in

its 30-year history, it will continue to face competition from other retail clothing, shoe, and accessory companies in the continually changing retail marketplace.

Go to The Gap's Web site, explore the site for company-related information, and view its most recent annual report.

INTERNET

www.gap.com

1. For the most recent year available, what is The Gap's net sales? How does this compare to the previous year? What is shown for cost of goods sold and occupancy expenses? How does this compare to the previous year?

2. Based on the latest accounting year available, what percentage of net sales goes for cost of goods sold and occupancy expenses? How does this compare to the percentage calculated from the Focus on Financial Results chapter opening vignette? What does this tell you about how well The Gap is controlling its costs?

3. As a manager, how might changes in the gross profit percentage influence future actions? What actions might be taken by management to maximize the difference between net sales and cost of goods sold?

4. Find out from a source such as Hoovers.com or finance.yahoo.com what companies are in The Gap's industry segment. Conduct an online search for news articles that compare how well these companies are performing. Then compare the sales revenues and cost of goods sold for The Gap plus two of its competitors.

   a. What are each company's sales revenues?

   b. Over three years, how fast is each company growing in terms of revenues?

   c. Compare each company's cost of goods sold as a percentage of sales.

SOLUTIONS TO KEY TERMS QUIZ

Quiz 1: Merchandise Accounting

14 Net sales (p. 197)

2 Sales Returns and Allowances (p. 198)

4 Trade discount (p. 198)

1 Quantity discount (p. 199)

7 Sales Discounts (p. 200)

11 Cost of goods available for sale (p. 201)

15 Cost of goods sold (p. 202)

5 Perpetual system (p. 202)

10 Periodic system (p. 202)

3 Transportation-in (p. 204)

13 Purchases (p. 204)

6 Purchase Returns and Allowances (p. 205)

12 Purchase Discounts (p. 206)

8 FOB destination point (p. 206)

9 FOB shipping point (p. 206)

Quiz 2: Internal Control

14 Internal control system (p. 208)

8 Report of management (p. 209)

13 Internal audit staff (p. 209)

2 Board of directors (p. 210)

4 Audit committee (p. 210)

10 Foreign Corrupt Practices Act (p. 210)

3 Accounting system (p. 210)

11 Administrative controls (p. 211)

5 Accounting controls (p. 211)

6 Purchase requisition form (Appendix 5A) (p. 219)

12 Purchase order (Appendix 5A) (p. 219)

1 Invoice (Appendix 5A) (p. 222)

9 Blind receiving report (Appendix 5A) (p. 222)

7 Invoice approval form (Appendix 5A) (p. 222)

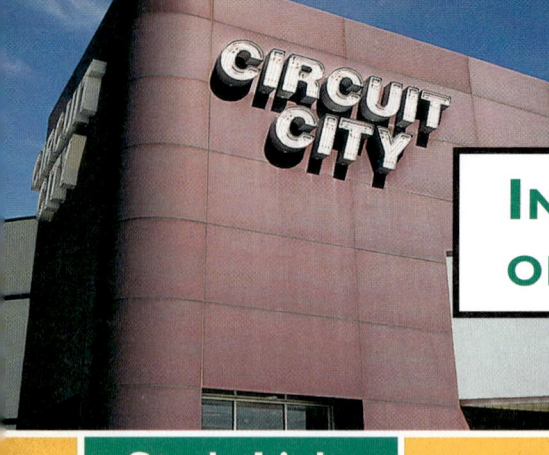

INVENTORIES AND COST OF GOODS SOLD

FOCUS ON FINANCIAL RESULTS

For the last few years the consumer electronics industry has sustained tremendous growth in a fiercely competitive environment. Circuit City remains a top retailer in the U.S. market. High-quality customer service and state-of-the-art merchandise have rewarded Circuit City with steady increases in net sales, which exceeded $12.6 billion in 2000. (Circuit City also maintains a revolutionary used-car business known as CarMax.)

Sales volume is important for any merchandiser, but so is managing <u>inventory</u> effectively. Inventory is a major issue for Circuit City as it continues to grow; you can see from the accompanying partial balance sheets that merchandise represents almost half the firm's total assets.

In July 2000, Circuit City made a strategic decision that dramatically changed the nature of its inventory: The firm discontinued selling major appliances in all its stores to reposition itself exclusively as a retailer of consumer electronics and home office products.

Another change that is having an impact on Circuit City's inventory is its on-line ordering system. Computer Build-to-Order Stations, added to all Circuit City stores in 1999, allow consumers to use a touch screen to select from a broad range of computer features to meet their specific needs. The system searches the configure-to-order capabilities of IBM, NEC, Hewlett-Packard, and Compaq in real time so customers can compare available choices. Best of all, from an inventory standpoint, the products bypass the warehouse and are delivered directly to the customer's home or sent to the store for customer pickup.

CONSOLIDATED BALANCE SHEETS

(Amounts in thousands except share data)

	At February 29 or 28	
	2000	**1999**
ASSETS		
CURRENT ASSETS:		
Cash and cash equivalents	$ 643,933	$ 265,880
Net accounts receivable [NOTE 12]	593,276	574,316
Inventory	**1,689,209**	**1,517,675**
Prepaid expenses and other current assets	16,197	36,644
TOTAL CURRENT ASSETS	2,942,615	2,394,515
Property and equipment, net [NOTES 4 AND 5]	965,181	1,005,773
Other assets	47,552	44,978
TOTAL ASSETS	**$3,955,348**	**$3,445,266**

> Inventory is almost half of Circuit City's total assets

CONSOLIDATED STATEMENTS OF EARNINGS

(Amounts in thousands except per share data)

	Years Ended February 29 or 28					
	2000	%	1999	%	1998	%
NET SALES AND OPERATING REVENUES	$12,614,390	100.0	$10,810,468	100.0	$8,870,797	100.0
Cost of sales, buying and warehousing	9,751,833	77.3	8,354,230	77.3	6,827,133	77.0
GROSS PROFIT	2,862,557	22.7	2,456,238	22.7	2,043,664	23.0
Selling, general and administrative expenses [NOTE 11]	2,309,593	18.3	2,086,838	19.3	1,815,275	20.5
Interest expense [NOTE 5]	24,206	0.2	28,319	0.2	26,861	0.2
TOTAL EXPENSES	2,333,799	18.5	2,115,157	19.5	1,842,136	20.7
Earnings from continuing operations before income taxes	528,758	4.2	341,081	3.2	201,528	2.3
Provision for income taxes [NOTE 6]	200,928	1.6	129,611	1.2	76,581	0.9
EARNINGS FROM CONTINUING OPERATIONS	327,830	2.6	211,470	2.0	124,947	1.4
Discontinued operations [NOTE 15]:						
Loss from discontinued operations of Divx, less income tax benefit	(16,215)	(0.1)	(68,546)	(0.7)	(20,636)	(0.2)
Loss on disposal of Divx, including provision for losses during phase-out period, less income tax benefit	(114,025)	(0.9)	–	–	–	–
Loss from discontinued operations	(130,240)	(1.0)	(68,546)	(0.7)	(20,636)	(0.2)
NET EARNINGS	$ 197,590	1.6	$ 142,924	1.3	$ 104,311	1.2

Circuit City's 2000 annual report

How will the new system help Circuit City better manage its "inventory turns"—the number of times it turns over its merchandise each year? What will lower or higher inventory turns say about the company's effectiveness in choosing, pricing, and promoting its products? While studying this chapter, consider these questions and select the annual report items you need to estimate Circuit City's inventory turns each year.

www.circuitcity.com

After studying this chapter, you should be able to:

LO 1 Identify the forms of inventory held by different types of businesses and the types of costs incurred. (p. 244)

LO 2 Explain the relationship between the valuation of inventory and the measurement of income. (p. 245)

LO 3 Apply the inventory costing methods of specific identification, weighted average, FIFO, and LIFO using a periodic system. (p. 246)

LO 4 Analyze the effects of the different costing methods on inventory, net income, income taxes, and cash flow. (p. 252)

LO 5 Analyze the effects of an inventory error on various financial statement items. (p. 257)

LO 6 Apply the lower-of-cost-or-market rule to the valuation of inventory. (p. 260)

LO 7 Explain why and how the cost of inventory is estimated in certain situations. (p. 263)

LO 8 Analyze the management of inventory turnover. (p. 265)

LO 9 Explain the effects that inventory transactions have on the statement of cash flows. (p. 266)

LO 10 Apply the inventory costing methods using a perpetual system (Appendix 6A). (p. 271)

THE NATURE OF INVENTORY

LO 1 Identify the forms of inventory held by different types of businesses and the types of costs incurred.

Inventory is an asset that is held for *resale* in the normal course of business. The distinction between inventory and an operating asset is the *intent* of the owner. For example, some of the computers that Circuit City owns are operating assets because they are used in various activities of the business, such as the payroll and accounting functions. Many more of the computers Circuit City owns are inventory, however, because the company intends to sell them. This chapter is concerned with the proper valuation of inventory and the related effect on cost of goods sold.

It is important to distinguish between the *types* of inventory costs incurred and the *form* the inventory takes. Wholesalers and retailers incur a single type of cost, the *purchase price,* of the inventory they sell. On the balance sheet they use a single account for inventory, titled **Merchandise Inventory.** Wholesalers and retailers buy merchandise in finished form and offer it for resale without transforming the product in any way. Because they do not use factory buildings, assembly lines, or production equipment, merchandise companies have a relatively small dollar amount in operating assets and a large amount in inventory. For example, on its February 29, 2000, balance sheet, Circuit City reported inventory of approximately $1.7 billion and total assets of $4.0 billion. It is not unusual for inventories to account for half the total assets of a merchandise company.

The cost of inventory to a *merchandiser* is limited to the product's purchase price, which may include other costs we will mention soon. Conversely, three distinct *types* of costs are incurred by a *manufacturer:* direct materials, direct labor, and manufacturing overhead. Direct materials, also called **raw materials,** are the ingredients used in making a product. The costs of direct materials used in manufacturing an automobile include the costs of steel, glass, and rubber. Direct labor consists of the amounts paid to workers to manufacture the product. The $20 per hour paid to an assembly line worker is a primary ingredient in the cost to manufacture the automobile. Manufacturing overhead includes all other costs that are related to the manufacturing process but cannot be directly matched to specific units of output. Depreciation of a factory building and the salary of a supervisor are two examples of overhead costs. Accountants have developed various techniques to assign, or allocate, these manufacturing overhead costs to specific products.

In addition to the three types of costs incurred in a production process, the inventory of a manufacturer takes three distinct *forms.* The three forms or stages in the development

EXHIBIT 6-1 Relationships between Types of Businesses and Inventory Costs

Type of Business	Inventory	Costs Included in Inventory
Retailer/Wholesaler ····▸	Merchandise inventory	Cost to purchase
	Raw materials	Cost of materials before entered into production
Manufacturer ····▸	Work in process	Costs of direct materials used, direct labor, and overhead in unfinished items
	Finished goods	Cost of completed, but unsold, items

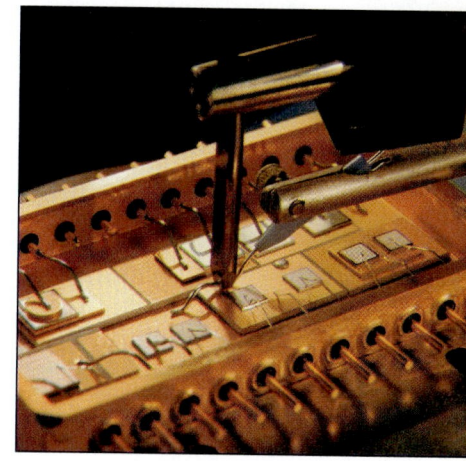

The inventory of a manufacturer consists of raw material, work in process, and finished goods. The electronic device being built here is part of a firm's work in process inventory. The direct materials probably consist of such items as the individual control knobs purchased from another manufacturer. When the manufacturing process is complete, the inventory of finished goods is ready for sale.

of inventory are raw materials, work in process, and finished goods. Direct materials or raw materials enter a production process in which they are transformed into a finished product by the addition of direct labor and manufacturing overhead. At any point in time, including the end of an accounting period, some of the materials have entered the process and some labor costs have been incurred but the product is not finished. The cost of unfinished products is appropriately called **work in process** or *work in progress.* Inventory that has completed the production process and is available for sale is called **finished goods.** Finished goods are the equivalent of merchandise inventory for a retailer or wholesaler in that both represent the inventory of goods held for sale. Many manufacturers disclose the dollar amounts of each of the three forms of inventory in their annual report. For example, Nike disclosed in its 1999 annual report the following amounts, stated in millions of dollars:

www.nike.com

From **Concept**

TO PRACTICE 6.1

READING GATEWAY'S FOOTNOTES
Footnote 9 in Gateway's 1999 annual report includes information about the composition of its inventory. How does Gateway categorize these elements of its inventory? What percentage of its total inventory at the end of 1999 is made up of finished goods?

	Millions
Inventories:	
Finished goods	$1,132.7
Work in progress	44.8
Raw materials	21.8
	$1,199.3

Exhibit 6-1 summarizes the relationships between the types of costs incurred and the forms of inventory for different types of businesses.

INVENTORY VALUATION AND THE MEASUREMENT OF INCOME

Valuation is the major problem in accounting for inventories. Because of the additional complexities involved in valuing the inventory of a manufacturer, we will concentrate in this chapter on the valuation of *merchandise inventory.* (Accounting for the inventory costs incurred by a manufacturing firm is covered in detail in management accounting textbooks.)

One of the most fundamental concepts in accounting is the relationship between *asset valuation* and the *measurement of income.* Recall a point made in Chapter 4: assets are unexpired costs, and expenses are expired costs. Thus, the value assigned to an asset on the balance sheet determines the amount eventually recognized as an expense on the income statement. For example, the amount recorded as the cost of an item of plant and equipment will dictate the amount of depreciation expense recognized on the income statement

LO 2 Explain the relationship between the valuation of inventory and the measurement of income.

over the life of the asset. Similarly, the amount recorded as the cost of inventory determines the amount recognized as cost of goods sold on the income statement when the asset is sold. An error in assigning the proper amount to inventory on the balance sheet will affect the amount recognized as cost of goods sold on the income statement. The relationship between inventory as an asset and cost of goods sold can be understood by recalling the cost of goods sold section of the income statement. Assume the following example:

Beginning inventory	$ 500
Add: Purchases	1,200
Cost of goods available for sale	$1,700
Less: Ending inventory	(600)
Cost of goods sold	$1,100

The amount assigned to ending inventory is deducted from cost of goods available for sale to determine cost of goods sold. If the ending inventory amount is incorrect, cost of goods sold will be wrong, and thus the net income of the period will be in error as well. (We will look at inventory errors later in the chapter.)

INVENTORY COSTS: WHAT SHOULD BE INCLUDED?

All assets, including inventory, are recorded initially at cost. Cost is defined as "the price paid or consideration given to acquire an asset. As applied to inventories, cost means in principle the sum of the applicable expenditures and charges directly or indirectly incurred in bringing an article to its existing condition and location."[1]

Note the reference to the existing *condition* and *location*. This means that certain costs may also be included in the "price paid." Here are examples:

- Any freight costs incurred by the buyer in shipping inventory to its place of business should be included in the cost of the inventory.

- The cost of insurance taken out during the time that inventory is in transit should be added to the cost of the inventory.

- The cost of storing inventory before the time it is ready to be sold should be included in cost.

- Various types of taxes paid, such as excise and sales taxes, are other examples of costs necessary to put the inventory into a position to be able to sell it.

It is often very difficult, however, to allocate many of these incidental costs among the various items of inventory purchased. For example, consider a $500 freight bill that a supermarket paid on a merchandise shipment that includes 100 different items of inventory. To address the practical difficulty in assigning this type of cost to the different products, many companies have a policy by which transportation costs are charged to expense of the period if they are immaterial in amount. Thus, shipments of merchandise are simply recorded at the net invoice price—that is, after taking any cash discounts for early payment. It is a practical solution to a difficult allocation problem. Once again, the company must apply the cost/benefit test to accounting information.

INVENTORY COSTING METHODS WITH A PERIODIC SYSTEM

LO 3 Apply the inventory costing methods of specific identification, weighted average, FIFO, and LIFO using a periodic system.

To this point, we have assumed that the cost to purchase an item of inventory is constant. For most merchandisers, however, the unit cost of inventory changes frequently. Consider a simple example. Everett Company purchases merchandise twice during the first year of business. The dates, the number of units purchased, and the costs are as follows:

---

[1] *Accounting Research Bulletin No. 43,* "Inventory Pricing" (New York: American Institute of Certified Public Accountants, June 1953), ch. 4, statement 3.

| February 4 | 200 units purchased at $1.00 per unit | = $200 |
| October 13 | 200 units purchased at $1.50 per unit | = $300 |

Everett sells 200 units during the first year. Individual sales of the units take place relatively evenly throughout the year. The question is: *which* 200 units did the company sell, the $1.00 units or the $1.50 units or some combination of each? Recall the earlier discussion of the relationship between asset valuation and income measurement. The question is important because the answer determines not only the value assigned to the 200 units of ending inventory *but also* the amount allocated to cost of goods sold for the 200 units sold.

One possible method of assigning amounts to ending inventory and cost of goods sold is to *specifically identify* which 200 units were sold and which 200 units are on hand. This method is feasible for a few types of businesses in which units can be identified by serial numbers, but it is totally impractical in most situations. As an alternative to specific identification, we could make an *assumption* as to which units were sold and which are on hand. Three different answers are possible:

1. 200 units sold at $1.00 each   = $200 cost of goods sold
and 200 units on hand at $1.50 each = $300 ending inventory

or

2. 200 units sold at $1.50 each   = $300 cost of goods sold
and 200 units on hand at $1.00 each = $200 ending inventory

or

3. 200 units sold at $1.25 each   = $250 cost of goods sold
and 200 units on hand at $1.25 each = $250 ending inventory

The third alternative assumes an *average cost* for the 200 units on hand and the 200 units sold. The average cost is the cost of the two purchases of $200 and $300, or $500, divided by the 400 units available to sell, or $1.25 per unit.

If we are concerned with the actual *physical flow* of the units of inventory, all of the three methods illustrated may be incorrect. The only approach that will yield a "correct" answer in terms of the actual flow of *units* of inventory is the specific identification method. In the absence of a specific identification approach, it is impossible to say which particular units were *actually* sold. In fact, there may have been sales from each of the two purchases—that is, some of the $1.00 units may have been sold and some of the $1.50 units may have been sold. To solve the problem of assigning costs to identical units, accountants have developed inventory costing assumptions or methods. Each of these methods makes a specific *assumption* about the *flow of costs* rather than the physical flow of units. The only approach that uses the actual flow of the units in assigning costs is the specific identification method.

To take a closer look at specific identification as well as three alternative approaches to valuing inventory, we will use the following example:

	Units	Unit Cost	Total Cost
Beginning inventory			
January 1	500	$10	$ 5,000*
Purchases			
January 20	300	11	3,300
April 8	400	12	4,800
September 5	200	13	2,600
December 12	100	14	1,400
Total purchases	1,000 units		$12,100
Available for sale	1,500 units		$17,100
Units sold	900 units		?
Units in ending inventory	600 units		?

*Beginning inventory of $5,000 is carried over as the ending inventory from the prior period. It is highly unlikely that each of the four methods we will illustrate would result in the same dollar amount of inventory at any point in time. It is helpful when first learning the methods, however, to assume the same amount of beginning inventory.

The question marks indicate the dilemma. What portion of the cost of goods available for sale of $17,100 should be assigned to the 900 units sold? What portion should be assigned to the 600 units remaining in ending inventory? The purpose of an inventory costing method is to provide a reasonable answer to these two questions.

SPECIFIC IDENTIFICATION METHOD

It is not always necessary to make an assumption about the flow of costs. In certain situations, it may be possible to specifically identify which units are sold and which units are on hand. A serial number on an automobile allows a dealer to identify a car on hand and thus its unit cost. (Circuit City, in fact, uses specific identification for the vehicles it sells in its Car Max Group.) An appliance dealer with 15 refrigerators on hand at the end of the year can identify the unit cost of each by matching a tag number with the purchase records. To illustrate the use of the **specific identification method** for our example, assume that the merchandiser is able to identify the specific units in the inventory at the end of the year and their costs as follows:

serial or tag #

Units on Hand

Date Purchased	Units	Cost	Total Cost
January 20	100	$11	$1,100
April 8	300	12	3,600
September 5	200	13	2,600
Ending inventory	600		$7,300

One of two techniques can be used to find cost of goods sold. We can deduct ending inventory from the cost of goods available for sale:

Cost of goods available for sale		$17,100
Less:	Ending inventory	7,300
Equals:	Cost of goods sold	$ 9,800

Or, we can calculate cost of goods sold independently by matching the units sold with their respective unit costs. By eliminating the units in ending inventory from the original acquisition schedule, the units sold and their costs are as follows:

Units Sold

Date Sold	Units	Cost	Total Cost
January 1	500	$10	$5,000
January 20	200	11	2,200
April 8	100	12	1,200
December 12	100	14	1,400
Cost of goods sold	900		$9,800

The practical difficulty in keeping track of individual items of inventory sold is not the only problem with the use of this method. The method also allows management to *manipulate income.* For example, assume that a company is not having a particularly good year. Management may be tempted to do whatever it can to boost net income. One way it can do this is by *selectively selling units with the lowest-possible unit cost.* By doing so, the company can keep cost of goods sold down and net income up. Because of the potential for manipulation with the specific identification method, coupled with the practical difficulty of applying it in most situations, it is not widely used.

WEIGHTED AVERAGE COST METHOD

The **weighted average cost method** is a relatively easy approach to costing inventory. It assigns the same unit cost to all units available for sale during the period. The weighted average cost is calculated as follows for our example:

$$\frac{\text{Cost of Goods Available for Sale}}{\text{Units Available for Sale}} = \text{Weighted Average Cost}$$

$$\frac{\$17,100}{1,500} = \$11.40$$

Ending inventory is found by multiplying the weighted average unit cost by the number of units on hand:

$$\frac{\text{Weighted Average}}{\text{Cost}} \times \frac{\text{Number of Units in}}{\text{Ending Inventory}} = \text{Ending Inventory}$$

$$\$11.40 \times 600 = \$6,840$$

Cost of goods sold can be calculated in one of two ways:

Cost of goods available for sale		$17,100
Less:	Ending inventory	6,840
Equals:	Cost of goods sold	$10,260

or

$$\frac{\text{Weighted Average}}{\text{Cost}} \times \frac{\text{Number of Units}}{\text{Sold}} = \text{Cost of Goods Sold}$$

$11.40	×	900	=	$10,260

Note that the computation of the weighted average cost is based on the cost of *all* units available for sale during the period, not just the beginning inventory or purchases. Also note that the method is called the *weighted* average cost method. As the name indicates, each of the individual unit costs is multiplied by the number of units acquired at each price. The simple arithmetic average of the unit costs for the beginning inventory and the four purchases is ($10 + $11 + $12 + $13 + $14)/5 = $12. The weighted average cost is slightly less than $12 ($11.40), however, because more units were acquired at the lower prices than at the higher prices.

FIRST-IN, FIRST-OUT METHOD (FIFO)

The **FIFO method** assumes that the first units in, or purchased, are the first units out, or sold. The first units sold during the period are assumed to come from the beginning inventory. After the beginning inventory is sold, the next units sold are assumed to come from the first purchase during the period and so forth. Thus, ending inventory consists of the most recent purchases of the period. In many businesses, this cost-flow assumption is a fairly accurate reflection of the *physical* flow of products. For example, to maintain a fresh stock of products, the physical flow in a grocery store is first-in, first-out.

To calculate *ending inventory*, we start with the *most recent* inventory acquired and work *backward*:

Units on Hand

Date Purchased	Units	Cost	Total Cost
December 12	100	$14	$1,400
September 5	200	13	2,600
April 8	300	12	3,600
Ending inventory	600		$7,600

Cost of goods sold can then be found:

Cost of goods available for sale		$17,100
Less:	Ending inventory	7,600
Equals:	Cost of goods sold	$ 9,500

Or, because the FIFO method assumes that the first units in are the first ones sold, cost of goods sold can be calculated by starting with the *beginning inventory* and working *forward*:

Units Sold

Date Purchased	Units	Cost	Total Cost
January 1	500	$10	$5,000
January 20	300	11	3,300
April 8	100	12	1,200
Units sold	900	Cost of goods sold	$9,500

LAST-IN, FIRST-OUT METHOD (LIFO)

The **LIFO method** assumes that the last units in, or purchased, are the first units out, or sold. The first units sold during the period are assumed to come from the latest purchase made during the period and so forth. Can you think of any businesses where the *physical* flow of products is last-in, first-out? Although this situation is not nearly so common as a first-in, first-out physical flow, a stockpiling operation, such as in a rock quarry, operates on this basis.

To calculate *ending inventory* using LIFO, we start with the *beginning inventory* and work *forward*:

Units on Hand

Date Purchased	Units	Cost	Total Cost
Beginning inventory	500	$10	$5,000
January 20	100	11	1,100
Ending inventory	600		$6,100

Cost of goods sold can then be found:

Cost of goods available for sale		$17,100
Less:	Ending inventory	6,100
Equals:	Cost of goods sold	$11,000

Or, because the LIFO method assumes that the last units in are the first ones sold, *cost of goods sold* can be calculated by starting with the *most recent* inventory acquired and working *backward*:

Units Sold

Date Purchased	Units	Cost	Total Cost
December 12	100	$14	$ 1,400
September 5	200	13	2,600
April 8	400	12	4,800
January 20	200	11	2,200
Units sold	900	Cost of goods sold	$11,000

> **Study Tip**
>
> There may be cases, such as this illustration of LIFO, in which it is easier to determine ending inventory and then deduct it from cost of goods available for sale to find cost of goods sold. This approach is easier in this example because there are fewer layers in ending inventory than in cost of goods sold. In other cases, it may be quicker to determine cost of goods sold first and then deduct it from cost of goods available for sale, to find ending inventory.

LO 4 Analyze the effects of the different costing methods on inventory, net income, income taxes, and cash flow.

The mechanics of each of the inventory costing methods are straightforward. But how does a company decide on the best method to use to value its inventory? According to the accounting profession, *the primary determinant in selecting an inventory costing method should be the ability of the method to accurately reflect the net income of the period.* But how and why does a particular costing method accurately reflect the net income of the period? Because there is no easy answer to this question, a number of arguments have been raised by accountants to justify the use of one method over the others. We turn now to some of these arguments.

COSTING METHODS AND CASH FLOW

Comparative income statements for our example are presented in Exhibit 6-2. Note that with the use of the weighted average method, net income is between the amounts for FIFO and LIFO. Because the weighted average method normally yields results between the other two methods, we concentrate on the two extremes, LIFO and FIFO. The major advantage of using the weighted average method is its simplicity.

The original data for our example involved a situation in which prices were *rising* throughout the period: beginning inventory cost $10 per unit, and the last purchase during the year was at $14. With LIFO, the most recent costs are assigned to cost of goods sold; with FIFO, the older costs are assigned to expense. Thus, in a period of rising prices, the assignment of the *higher* prices to cost of goods sold under LIFO results in a *lower gross margin* under LIFO than under FIFO ($7,000 for LIFO and $8,500 for FIFO). Because operating expenses are not affected by the choice of inventory method, the lower gross margin under LIFO results in lower income before tax, which in turn leads to lower taxes. If we assume a 40% tax rate, income tax expense under LIFO is only $2,000, compared with $2,600 under FIFO, a savings of $600 in taxes. Another way to look at the taxes saved by using LIFO is to focus on the difference in the expense under each method:

LIFO cost of goods sold	$11,000
− FIFO cost of goods sold	9,500
Additional expense from use of LIFO	$ 1,500
× Tax rate	.40
Tax savings from the use of LIFO	$ 600

EXHIBIT 6-2   Income Statements for the Inventory Costing Methods

	Weighted Average	FIFO	LIFO
Sales revenue—$20 each	$18,000	$18,000	$18,000
Beginning inventory	5,000	5,000	5,000
Purchases	12,100	12,100	12,100
Cost of goods available for sale	$17,100	$17,100	$17,100
Ending inventory	**6,840**	**7,600**	**6,100**
Cost of goods sold	**$10,260**	**$ 9,500**	**$11,000**
Gross margin	**$ 7,740**	**$ 8,500**	**$ 7,000**
Operating expenses	2,000	2,000	2,000
Net income before tax	**$ 5,740**	**$ 6,500**	**$ 5,000**
Income tax expense (40%)	**2,296**	**2,600**	**2,000**
Net income	**$ 3,444**	**$ 3,900**	**$ 3,000**

NOTE: Figures that differ among the three methods are in bold.

To summarize, *during a period of rising prices,* the two methods result in the following:

Item	LIFO	Relative To	FIFO
Cost of goods sold	Higher		Lower
Gross margin	Lower		Higher
Income before taxes	Lower		Higher
Taxes	Lower		Higher

Study Tip

During a period of falling prices, all the effects shown here would be just the opposite. For example, cost of goods sold would be lower under LIFO than under FIFO.

In conclusion, lower taxes with the use of LIFO result in cash savings.

The tax savings available from the use of LIFO during a period of rising prices are largely responsible for its popularity. Keep in mind, however, that the cash saved from a lower tax bill with LIFO is only a temporary savings, or what is normally called a *tax deferral.* At some point in the life of the business, the inventory that is carried at the older, lower-priced amounts will be sold. This will result in a tax bill higher than that under FIFO. Yet even a tax deferral is beneficial; given the opportunity, it is better to pay less tax today and more in the future because today's tax savings can be invested.

Two-Minute Review

1. Which of the inventory methods will result in the least amount of income before taxes, assuming a period of rising prices?

2. What is the easiest way to calculate the tax savings from using one method versus another?

Answers:

1. LIFO

2. The easiest approach to calculating the tax savings is to multiply the tax rate times the difference in cost of goods sold between the two methods.

LIFO LIQUIDATION

Recall the assumption made about which costs remain in inventory when LIFO is used. The costs of the oldest units remain in inventory, and if prices are rising, the costs of these units will be lower than the costs of more recent purchases. Now assume that the company *sells more units than it buys during the period.* When a company using LIFO experiences a liquidation, some of the units assumed to be sold will come from the older layers, with a relatively low unit cost. This situation, called a **LIFO liquidation,** presents a dilemma for the company.

A partial or complete liquidation of the older, lower-priced units will result in a low cost of goods sold figure and a correspondingly high gross margin for the period. In turn, the company faces a large tax bill because of the relatively high gross margin. In fact, a liquidation causes the tax advantages of using LIFO to reverse on the company, which is faced with paying off some of the taxes that were deferred in earlier periods. Should a company facing this situation buy inventory at the end of the year to avoid the consequences of a liquidation? This is a difficult question to answer and depends on many factors, including the company's cash position. At the least, the accountant must be aware of the potential for a large tax bill if a liquidation occurs.

Of course, a LIFO liquidation also benefits—and may even distort—reported earnings if the liquidation is large enough. For this reason and the tax problem, many companies are reluctant to liquidate their LIFO inventory. The problem often festers, and companies find themselves with inventory costed at decade-old price levels.

THE LIFO CONFORMITY RULE

Would it be possible for a company to have the best of both worlds? That is, could it use FIFO to report its income to stockholders, thus maximizing the amount of net income reported to this group, and use LIFO to report to the IRS, minimizing its taxable income and the amount paid to the government? Unfortunately, the IRS says that if a company chooses LIFO for reporting cost of goods sold on its tax return, then it must also use LIFO on its books—that is, in preparing its income statement. This is called the **LIFO conformity rule.** Note that the rule applies only to the use of LIFO on the tax return. A company is free to use different methods in preparing its tax return and its income statement as long as the method used for the tax return is *not* LIFO.

THE LIFO RESERVE: ESTIMATING LIFO'S EFFECT ON INCOME AND ON TAXES PAID FOR WHIRLPOOL

If a company decides to use LIFO, an investor can still determine how much more income the company would have reported had it used FIFO. In addition, he or she can approximate the tax savings or the additional taxes to the company from the use of LIFO. Consider the following footnote from the 1999 annual report for Whirlpool Corporation:

www.whirlpool.com

Note 5 Inventories

December 31 (millions of dollars)	1999	1998
Finished products	$ 932	$ 960
Work in process	48	54
Raw materials	253	279
	$1,233	$1,293
Less excess of FIFO cost over LIFO cost	168	193
Total inventories	$1,065	$1,100

LIFO inventories represent approximately 28% and 23% of total inventories at December 31, 1999 and 1998.

Note that Whirlpool uses more than one inventory method and that at the end of 1999, LIFO inventories accounted for only 28% of the total inventory. It is not unusual for companies to use more than one method to value inventories. For now it is important to understand that Whirlpool reported $1,065,000,000 as its total inventory on the December 31, 1999, balance sheet.

The following steps explain the logic for using the information in the inventory footnote to estimate LIFO's effect on income and on taxes:

1. The excess of the value of a company's inventory stated at FIFO over the value stated at LIFO is called the **LIFO reserve.** The *cumulative* excess of the value of Whirlpool's inventory on a FIFO basis over the value on a LIFO basis is $168 million at the end of 1999.

2. Because Whirlpool reports inventory at a lower value on its balance sheet using LIFO, it will report a higher cost of goods sold amount on the income statement. Thus, the LIFO reserve not only represents the excess of the inventory balance on a FIFO basis over that on a LIFO basis but also *represents the cumulative amount by which cost of goods sold on a LIFO basis exceeds cost of goods sold on a FIFO basis.*

3. The decrease in Whirlpool's LIFO reserve in 1999 was $25 million ($193 million − $168 million). This means that the decrease in cost of goods sold for 1999 from using LIFO instead of FIFO was also this amount. Thus, income before tax for 1999 was $25 million higher because the company used LIFO.

4. If we assume a corporate tax rate of 35%, the additional taxes from using LIFO amounted to $25 million × .35, or $8.75 million.

COSTING METHODS AND INVENTORY PROFITS

FIFO, LIFO, and weighted average are all cost-based methods to value inventory. They vary in terms of which costs are assigned to inventory and which to cost of goods sold, but all three assign *historical costs* to inventory. In our previous example, the unit cost for inventory purchases gradually increased during the year from $10 for the beginning inventory to a high of $14 on the date of the last purchase.

An alternative to assigning any of the historical costs incurred during the year to ending inventory and cost of goods sold would be to use **replacement cost** to value each of these. Assume that the cost to replace a unit of inventory at the end of the year is $15. Use of a replacement cost system results in the following:

Ending inventory	=	600 units	×	$15 per unit	=	$ 9,000
Cost of goods sold	=	900 units	×	$15 per unit	=	$13,500

A replacement cost approach is not acceptable under the profession's current standards, but many believe that it provides more relevant information to users. Inventory must be replaced if a company is to remain in business. Many accountants argue that the use of historical cost in valuing inventory leads to what is called **inventory profit,** particularly if FIFO is used in a period of rising prices. For example, cost of goods sold in our illustration was only $9,500 on a FIFO basis, compared with $13,500 if the replacement cost of $15 per unit is used. The $4,000 difference between the two cost of goods sold figures is a profit from holding the inventory during a period of rising prices and is called *inventory profit.* To look at this another way, assume that the units are sold for $20 each. The following analysis reconciles the difference between gross margin on a FIFO basis and on a replacement cost basis:

Sales revenue—900 units × $20 =		$18,000
Cost of goods sold—FIFO basis		9,500
Gross margin—FIFO basis		$ 8,500
Cost of goods sold—replacement cost basis	$13,500	
Cost of goods sold—FIFO basis	9,500	
Profit from holding inventory during a period of inflation		4,000
Gross margin on a replacement cost basis		$ 4,500

Those who argue in favor of a replacement cost approach would report only $4,500 of gross margin. They believe that the additional $4,000 of profit reported on a FIFO basis is simply due to holding the inventory during a period of rising prices. According to this viewpoint, if the 900 units sold during the period are to be replaced, a necessity if the company is to continue operating, the use of replacement cost in calculating cost of goods sold results in a better measure of gross margin than if it is calculated using FIFO.

Given that our current standards require the use of historical costs rather than replacement costs, does any one of the costing methods result in a better approximation of replacement cost of goods sold than the others? Because LIFO assigns the cost of the most

ACCOUNTING FOR YOUR DECISIONS

You Are a Student

The owner/manager of a dairy farm knows that you are an accounting student and has asked your advice about which inventory method to use to measure the cost of both the inventory and the cost of goods sold. Since the inventory of milk and milk byproducts spoils easily, does he have to use the FIFO inventory valuation method? Why or why not?

ANS: No, he does not have to use the FIFO method, just because his products are subject to spoilage. There is a difference between the actual physical flow of the product and the cost flow of that product. From a practical perspective, he would want to sell the milk and milk byproducts on a FIFO basis to minimize spoilage. However, he can keep track of the cost flows for inventory valuation and cost of goods sold purposes using the LIFO method or weighted average cost method.

recent purchases to cost of goods sold, it most nearly approximates the results with a replacement cost system. The other side of the argument, however, is that whereas LIFO results in the best approximation of *replacement cost of goods sold* on the *income statement,* FIFO most nearly approximates replacement cost of the *inventory* on the *balance sheet.* A comparison of the amounts from our example verifies this:

	Ending Inventory	Cost of Goods Sold
Weighted average	$6,840	$10,260
FIFO	7,600	9,500
LIFO	6,100	11,000
Replacement cost	9,000	13,500

CHANGING INVENTORY METHODS

The purpose of each of the inventory costing methods is to *match costs with revenues.* If a company believes that a different method will result in a better matching than that being provided by the method currently being used, it should change methods. A company must be able to justify a change in methods, however. Taking advantage of the tax breaks offered by LIFO is *not* a valid justification for a change in methods.

It is very important for a company to *disclose* any change in accounting principle, including a change in the method of costing inventory. For example, some companies justify a change from LIFO to FIFO on the basis of reduced prices, as illustrated by this excerpt from Fruit of the Loom's 1997 annual report:

www.fruit.com

> During the fourth quarter of 1997, the Company changed its method of determining the cost of inventories from the LIFO method to the FIFO method as it experienced reduced costs from offshore assembly operations and expects continuing cost reductions. The cost of inventories on a LIFO basis at December 31, 1997 was approximately equal to their replacement cost. Accordingly, the Company believes that the FIFO method will result in a better measurement of operating results. All previously reported results have been restated to reflect the retroactive application of this accounting change as required by generally accepted accounting principles. The accounting change increased the net loss for 1997 by $27,800,000, $.37 per share. Due principally to the effect of LIFO reserve liquidations, net earnings previously reported for 1996 were reduced by $4,600,000 or $.06 per share, and the net loss previously reported for 1995 increased by $500,000 or $.01 per share.

POPULARITY OF THE COSTING METHODS

From **Concept**

TO PRACTICE 6.2

READING UNO'S ANNUAL REPORT
Which inventory method does Uno use? Where did you find this information? Do you think the company is justified in using the method it does?

An annual survey conducted by the AICPA indicates the relative popularity of the inventory costing methods. The inventory methods used by the 600 corporations in the survey are reported in Exhibit 6-3. Note that the number of companies each year totals more than 600. This happens because, as we saw for Whirlpool, many companies use more than one method to determine the total cost of inventory. The survey indicates the relatively equal popularity of LIFO and FIFO in practice. Rather than increasing in popularity, as it had during more inflationary times, the use of LIFO appears to have stabilized, as indicated in Exhibit 6-3.

INVENTORY VALUATION IN OTHER COUNTRIES

The acceptable methods of valuing inventory differ considerably around the world. Many countries prohibit the use of LIFO for either tax or financial reporting purposes. Countries in which LIFO is either prohibited or rarely used include the United Kingdom, Canada, New Zealand, Sweden, Denmark, and Brazil. On the other hand, Germany, France, Australia, and Japan allow LIFO for inventory valuation of foreign investments but not for domestic reports.

In Chapter 1, we mentioned the attempts by the International Accounting Standards Committee (IASC) to develop worldwide accounting standards. This group favors the use of either FIFO or weighted average when specific identification is not feasible. The IASC recognizes LIFO as an acceptable alternative if a company discloses information enabling users to reconcile LIFO inventory with either FIFO or weighted average (similar to the idea of a LIFO reserve discussed earlier in this chapter).

EXHIBIT 6-3   Inventory Cost Determination—AICPA Survey

| | Number of Companies | | | |
	1998	1997	1996	1995
Methods				
First-in, first-out (FIFO)	409	415	417	411
Last-in, first-out (LIFO)	319	326	332	347
Average cost	176	188	181	185
Other	40	32	37	40
Use of LIFO				
All inventories	30	17	15	14
50% or more of inventories	152	170	178	191
Less than 50% of inventories	95	99	92	88
Not determinable	42	40	47	54
Companies using LIFO	319	326	332	347

SOURCE: *Accounting Trends & Techniques,* 53rd ed. (New York: American Institute of Certified Public Accountants, 1999).

TWO INVENTORY SYSTEMS: PERIODIC AND PERPETUAL

In the examples presented so far in this chapter, we have assumed a periodic inventory system to concentrate our attention on the various cost-flow assumptions. Recall from Chapter 5 that with this system, a count of the inventory is necessary at the end of the period to determine the number of units sold and the number on hand. The reason is that the Inventory account is not updated each time a purchase is made and each time a sale is made.

For many years, the simplicity of the periodic system resulted in its widespread use. Because of the need in a perpetual system to record the cost of every individual sale when it occurs, use of the perpetual system was limited to businesses that sold products with a relatively high unit cost and low turnover, such as those of an automobile dealer. The ability to computerize the inventory system has resulted, however, in an increase in the use of the perpetual system in all types of businesses. A company can use any one of the costing methods with either a periodic or a perpetual inventory system. The application of the methods when a company maintains a perpetual inventory system is illustrated in Appendix 6A.

INVENTORY ERRORS

Earlier in the chapter, we considered the inherent tie between the valuation of assets, such as inventory, and the measurement of income, such as cost of goods sold. The importance of inventory valuation to the measurement of income can be illustrated by considering inventory errors. Many different types of inventory errors exist. Some errors are mathematical; for example, a bookkeeper may incorrectly add a column total. Other errors relate specifically to the physical count of inventory at year-end. For example, the count might inadvertently omit one section of a warehouse. Other errors arise from cutoff problems at year-end.

For example, assume that merchandise in transit at the end of the year is shipped FOB (free on board) shipping point. Under these shipment terms, the inventory belongs to the buyer at the time it is shipped. Because the shipment has not arrived at the end of the year, however, it cannot be included in the physical count. Unless some type of control is in place, the amount in transit may be erroneously omitted from the valuation of inventory at year-end.

To demonstrate the effect of an inventory error on the income statement, consider the following example. Through a scheduling error, two different inventory teams were assigned to count the inventory in the same warehouse on December 31, 2001. The correct amount of ending inventory is $250,000, but because two different teams counted

LO 5 Analyze the effects of an inventory error on various financial statement items.

EXHIBIT 6-4   Effects of Inventory Error on the Income Statement

	2001			2002		
	Reported	**Corrected**	**Effects of Error**	**Reported**	**Corrected**	**Effects of Error**
Sales	$1,000*	$1,000		$1,500	$1,500	
Costs of goods sold:						
Beginning inventory	200	200		**300**	**250**	$50 OS
Add: Purchases	700	700		1,100	1,100	
Cost of goods available for sale	$ 900	$ 900		**$1,400**	**$1,350**	50 OS
Less: Ending inventory	300	250	$50 OS†	350	350	
Cost of goods sold	$ 600	$ 650	50 US‡	**$1,050**	**$1,000**	50 OS
Gross margin	$ 400	$ 350	50 OS	$ 450	$ 500	50 US
Operating expenses	100	100		120	120	
Net income	$ 300	$ 250	50 OS	$ 330	$ 380	50 US

NOTE: Figures that differ as a result of the error are in bold.   †OS = Overstatement
*All amounts are in thousands of dollars.   ‡US = Understatement

the same inventory in one warehouse, the amount recorded is $300,000. The effect of this error on net income is analyzed in the left half of Exhibit 6-4.

The *overstatement* of *ending inventory* in 2001 leads to an *understatement* of the 2001 cost of goods sold *expense*. Because cost of goods sold is understated, *gross margin* for the year is *overstated*. Operating expenses are unaffected by an inventory error. Thus, *net income* is overstated by the same amount of overstatement of gross margin.[2] The most important conclusion from the exhibit is that an overstatement of ending inventory leads to a corresponding overstatement of net income.

Unfortunately, the effect of a misstatement of the year-end inventory is not limited to the net income for that year. As indicated in the right-hand portion of Exhibit 6-4, the error also affects the income statement for the following year. This happens simply because *the ending inventory of one period is the beginning inventory of the following period*. The *overstatement* of the 2002 *beginning inventory* leads to an *overstatement* of cost of goods available for sale. Because cost of goods available for sale is overstated, *cost of goods sold* is also *overstated*. The *overstatement* of cost of goods sold *expense* results in an *understatement* of *gross margin* and thus an *understatement* of *net income*.

Exhibit 6-4 illustrates the nature of a *counterbalancing error*. The effect of the overstatement of net income in the first year, 2001, is offset or counterbalanced by the understatement of net income by the same dollar amount in the following year. If the net incomes of two successive years are misstated in the opposite direction by the same amount, what is the effect on retained earnings? Assume that retained earnings at the beginning of 2001 is correctly stated at $300,000. The counterbalancing nature of the error is seen by analyzing retained earnings. For 2001, the analysis would indicate the following (OS = overstated and US = understated):

	2001 Reported	2001 Corrected	Effect of Error
Beginning retained earnings	$300,000	$300,000	Correct
Add: Net income	300,000	250,000	$50,000 OS
Ending retained earnings	$600,000	$550,000	$50,000 OS

---

[2]An overstatement of gross margin also results in an overstatement of income tax expense. Thus, because tax expense is overstated, the overstatement of net income is not so large as the overstatement of gross margin. For now, we will ignore the effect of taxes, however.

EXHIBIT 6-5 Effects of Inventory Error on the Balance Sheet

	2001		2002	
	Reported	**Corrected**	**Reported**	**Corrected**
Inventory	$ 300*	$ 250	$ 350	$ 350
All other assets	1,700	1,700	2,080	2,080
Total assets	$2,000	$1,950	$2,430	$2,430
Total liabilities	$ 400	$ 400	$ 500	$ 500
Capital stock	1,000	1,000	1,000	1,000
Retained earnings	600	550	930	930
Total liabilities and stockholders' equity	$2,000	$1,950	$2,430	$2,430

NOTE: Figures that differ as a result of the error are in bold.
*All amounts are in thousands of dollars.

An analysis for 2002 would show the following:

	2002 Reported	2002 Corrected	Effect of Error
Beginning retained earnings	$600,000	$550,000	$50,000 OS
Add: Net income	330,000	380,000	$50,000 US
Ending retained earnings	$930,000	$930,000	Correct

Thus, even though retained earnings is overstated at the end of the first year, it is correctly stated at the end of the second year. This is the nature of a counterbalancing error.

The effect of the error on the balance sheet is shown in Exhibit 6-5. The only accounts affected by the error are Inventory and Retained Earnings. The overstatement of the 2001 ending inventory results in an overstatement of total assets at the end of the first year. Similarly, as our earlier analysis indicates, the overstatement of 2001 net income leads to an overstatement of retained earnings by the same amount. Because the error is counterbalancing, the 2002 year-end balance sheet is correct; that is, ending inventory is not affected by the error, and thus the amount for total assets at the end of 2002 is also correct. The effect of the error on retained earnings is limited to the first year because of the counterbalancing nature of the error.

The effects of inventory errors on various financial statement items are summarized in Exhibit 6-6. Our analysis focused on the effects of an overstatement of inventory. The effects of an understatement are just the opposite and are summarized in the bottom portion of the exhibit.

Not all errors are counterbalancing. For example, if a section of a warehouse *continues* to be omitted from the physical count every year, both the beginning and the ending inventory will be incorrect each year and the error will not counterbalance.

Part of the auditor's job is to perform the necessary tests to obtain reasonable assurance that inventory has not been overstated or understated. If there is an error and inventory is wrong, however, the balance sheet and the income statement will both be distorted. For example, if ending inventory is overstated, inflating total assets, then cost of goods sold will be understated, boosting profits. Thus, such an error overstates the financial health of the organization in two ways. A lender or an investor must make a decision based on the current year's statement and cannot wait until the next accounting cycle, when this error is reversed. This is one reason that investors and creditors insist on audited financial statements.

EXHIBIT 6-6   Summary of the Effects of Inventory Errors

	Effect of Overstatement of Ending Inventory on	
	Current Year	**Following Year**
Cost of goods sold	Understated	Overstated
Gross margin	Overstated	Understated
Net income	Overstated	Understated
Retained earnings, end of year	Overstated	Correctly stated
Total assets, end of year	Overstated	Correctly stated

	Effect of Understatement of Ending Inventory on	
	Current Year	**Following Year**
Cost of goods sold	Overstated	Understated
Gross margin	Understated	Overstated
Net income	Understated	Overstated
Retained earnings, end of year	Understated	Correctly stated
Total assets, end of year	Understated	Correctly stated

Two-Minute Review

Skipper Corp. omits one section of its warehouse in the year-end inventory count.

1. Will the omission understate or overstate cost of goods sold on the income statement in the year the error is made?

2. Will the omission understate or overstate retained earnings on the balance sheet at the end of the year the error is made?

3. Will the omission affect retained earnings on the balance sheet at the end of the following year after the error is made? Explain your answer.

Answers:

1. Cost of goods sold will be overstated because the ending inventory is understated.

2. Retained earnings at the end of the year in which the error is made will be understated because cost of goods sold is overstated, and thus net income, which goes into retained earnings, is understated.

3. Retained earnings at the end of the following year will not be affected because of the counterbalancing nature of this error. Net income in the year of the error is understated, as described above. However, net income of the following year is overstated because cost of goods sold is understated as the result of an understatement of that year's beginning inventory.

VALUING INVENTORY AT LOWER OF COST OR MARKET

LO 6 Apply the lower-of-cost-or-market rule to the valuation of inventory.

One of the components sold by an electronics firm has become economically obsolete. A particular style of suit sold by a retailer is outdated and can no longer be sold at regular price. In each of these instances, it is likely that the retailer will have to sell the merchandise for less than the normal selling price. In these situations, a departure from the cost basis of accounting may be necessary because the *market value* of the inventory may be less than its *cost* to the company. The departure is called the **lower-of-cost-or-market (LCM) rule.**

At the end of each accounting period, the original cost, as determined using one of the costing methods such as FIFO, is compared with the market price of the inventory. If market is less than cost, the inventory is written down to the lower amount.

For example, if cost is $100,000 and market value is $85,000, the accountant makes an adjustment, which has the following effect:

BALANCE SHEET						INCOME STATEMENT
ASSETS	**=**	**LIABILITIES**	**+**	**OWNERS' EQUITY**	**+**	**REVENUES – EXPENSES**
Inventory (15,000)						Loss on Decline in Value of Inventory (15,000)

Note that the adjustment reduces both assets, in the form of inventory, and net income. The reduction in net income is the result of reporting the Loss on Decline in Value of Inventory on the income statement as an item of Other Expense.

WHY REPLACEMENT COST IS USED AS A MEASURE OF MARKET

A better name for the lower-of-cost-or-market rule would be the lower-of-cost-or-replacement-cost rule because accountants define *market* as *replacement cost*.[3] To understand why replacement cost is used as a basis to compare with original cost, consider the following example. A clothier pays $150 for a man's double-breasted suit and normally sells it for $200. Thus, the normal markup on selling price is $50/$200, or 25%, as indicated in the column Before Price Change in Exhibit 6-7. Now assume that double-breasted suits fall out of favor with the fashion world. The retailer checks with the distributor and finds that because of the style change, the cost to the retailer to replace a double-breasted suit is now only $120. The retailer realizes that if double-breasted suits are to be sold at all, they will have to be offered at a reduced price. The selling price is dropped from $200 to $160. If the retailer now buys a suit for $120 and sells it for $160, the gross margin will be $40 and the gross margin percentage will be maintained at 25%, as indicated in the right-hand column of Exhibit 6-7.

To compare the results with and without the use of the LCM rule, assume that the facts are the same as before and that the retailer has 10 double-breasted suits in inventory on December 31, 2001. In addition, assume that all 10 suits are sold at a clearance sale in January 2002 at the reduced price of $160 each. If the lower-of-cost-or-market rule is not used, the results for the two years will be as follows:

LCM Rule Not Used	2001	2002	Total
Sales revenue ($160 per unit)	$–0–	$1,600	$1,600
Cost of goods sold			
(original cost of $150 per unit)	–0–	(1,500)	(1,500)
Gross margin	$–0–	$ 100	$ 100

EXHIBIT 6-7 Gross Margin Percentage before and after Price Change

	Before Price Change	After Price Change
Selling price	$200	$160
Cost	150	120
Gross margin	$ 50	$ 40
Gross margin percentage	25%	25%

---

[3]Technically, the use of replacement cost as a measure of market value is subject to two constraints. First, market cannot be more than the net realizable value of the inventory. Second, inventory should not be recorded at less than net realizable value less a normal profit margin. The rationale for these two constraints is covered in intermediate accounting texts. For our purposes, we assume that replacement cost falls between the two constraints.

If the LCM rule is not applied, the gross margin is distorted. Instead of the normal 25%, a gross margin percentage of $100/$1,600 or 6.25% is reported in 2002 when the 10 suits are sold. If the LCM rule is applied, however, the results for the two years are as follows:

LCM Rule Used	2001	2002	Total
Sales revenue ($160 per unit)	$–0–	$1,600	$1,600
Cost of goods sold (replacement cost of $120 per unit)	–0–	(1,200)	(1,200)
Loss on decline in value of inventory: 10 units × ($150 – $120)	(300)	–0–	(300)
Gross margin	$(300)	$ 400	$ 100

The use of the LCM rule serves two important functions: (1) to report the loss in value of the inventory, $30 per suit or $300 in total, in the year the loss occurs and (2) to report in the year the suits are actually sold the normal gross margin of $400/$1,600, or 25%, which is not affected by a change in the selling price.

CONSERVATISM IS THE BASIS FOR THE LOWER-OF-COST-OR-MARKET RULE

The departure from the cost basis is normally justified on the basis of *conservatism.* According to the accounting profession, conservatism is "a prudent reaction to uncertainties to try to insure that uncertainties and risks inherent in business situations are adequately considered."[4] In our example, the future selling price of a suit is uncertain because of the style changes. The use of the LCM rule serves two purposes. First, the inventory of suits is written down from $150 to $120 each. Second, the decline in value of the inventory is recognized at the time it is first observed rather than waiting until the suits are sold. An investor in a company with deteriorating inventory has good reason to be alarmed. Merchandisers who do not make the proper adjustments to their product lines go out of business as they compete with the lower prices of warehouse clubs and the lower overhead of e-business and home shopping networks.

You should realize that the write-down of the suits violates the historical cost principle, which says that assets should be carried on the balance sheet at their original cost. But the LCM rule is considered a valid exception to the principle because it is a prudent reaction to the uncertainty involved and, thus, an application of conservatism in accounting.

APPLICATION OF THE LCM RULE

We have yet to consider how the LCM rule is applied to the entire inventory of a company. Three different interpretations of the rule are possible:

1. The lower of total cost or total market value for the entire inventory could be reported.

2. The lower of cost or market value for each individual product or item could be reported.

3. The lower of cost or market value for groups of items could be reported.

A company is free to choose any one of these approaches in applying the lower-of-cost-or-market rule. Three different answers are possible, depending on the approach selected.

The item-by-item approach (no. 2 above) is the most popular of the three approaches, for two reasons. First, it produces the most conservative result. The reason is that with either a group-by-group or a total approach, increases in the values of some items of inventory will offset declines in the values of other items. The item-by-item approach, however, ignores

---

[4]*Statement of Financial Accounting Concepts No. 2,* "Qualitative Characteristics of Accounting Information" (Stamford, Conn.: Financial Accounting Standards Board, May 1980), par. 95.

From Concept

TO PRACTICE 6.3

READING CIRCUIT CITY'S FOOTNOTES A footnote to Circuit City's financial statements states "Inventory is stated at the lower of cost or market." Why do you think the application of the lower-of-cost-or-market rule would be important to a business like Circuit City?

increases in value and recognizes all declines in value. Second, the item-by-item approach is the method required for tax purposes, although unlike LIFO, it is not required for book purposes merely because it is used for tax computations.

Consistency is important in deciding which of these approaches to use in applying the LCM rule. As is the case with the selection of one of the inventory costing methods discussed earlier in the chapter, the approach chosen to apply the rule should be used consistently from one period to the next.

METHODS FOR ESTIMATING INVENTORY VALUE

Situations arise in which it may not be practicable or even possible to measure inventory at cost. At times it may be necessary to *estimate* the amount of inventory. Two similar methods are used for very different purposes to estimate the amount of inventory. They are the gross profit method and the retail inventory method.

LO 7 Explain why and how the cost of inventory is estimated in certain situations.

GROSS PROFIT METHOD

A company that uses a periodic inventory system may experience a problem if inventory is stolen or destroyed by fire, flooding, or some other type of damage. Without a perpetual inventory record, what is the cost of the inventory stolen or destroyed? The **gross profit method** is a useful technique to estimate the cost of inventory lost in these situations. The method relies *entirely* on the ability to reliably estimate the *ratio of gross profit to sales.*[5]

Exhibit 6-8 illustrates how the normal income statement model that we use to find cost of goods sold can be rearranged to estimate inventory. The model on the left shows the components of cost of goods sold as they appear on the income statement. Assuming a periodic system, the inventory on hand at the end of the period is counted and is subtracted from cost of goods available for sale to determine cost of goods sold. The model is rearranged on the right as a basis for estimating inventory under the gross profit method. The only difference in the two models is in the reversal of the last two components: ending inventory and cost of goods sold. Rather than attempting to estimate *ending* inventory, we are trying to estimate the amount of inventory that should be on hand at a specific date, such as the date of a fire or flood. The estimate of cost of goods sold is found by estimating gross profit and deducting this estimate from sales revenue.

To understand this method, assume that on March 12, 2001, a portion of Hardluck Company's inventory is destroyed in a fire. The company determines, by a physical count, that the cost of the merchandise not destroyed is $200. Hardluck needs to estimate the cost of the inventory lost for purposes of insurance reimbursement. If the insurance company pays Hardluck an amount equivalent to the cost of the inventory destroyed, no loss

EXHIBIT 6-8 The Gross Profit Method for Estimating Inventory

Income Statement Model	Gross Profit Method Model
Beginning Inventory	Beginning Inventory
+ Purchases	+ Purchases
= Cost of Goods Available for Sale	= Cost of Goods Available for Sale
− Ending Inventory (per count)	− Estimated Cost of Goods Sold
= Cost of Goods Sold	= Estimated Inventory

---

[5]The terms *gross profit* and *gross margin* are synonymous in this context. Although we have used *gross margin* in referring to the excess of sales over cost of goods sold, the method is typically called the *gross profit method.*

will be recognized. If the cost of the inventory destroyed exceeds the amount reimbursed by the insurance company, a loss will be recorded for the excess amount.

Assume that the insurance company agrees to pay Hardluck $250 as full settlement for the inventory lost in the fire. From its records, Hardluck is able to determine the following amounts for the period from January 1 to the date of the fire, March 12:

Net sales from January 1 to March 12	$6,000
Beginning inventory—January 1	1,200
Purchases from January 1 to March 12	3,500

Assume that based on recent years' experience, Hardluck estimates its gross profit ratio as 30% of net sales. The steps it will take to estimate the lost inventory follow:

1. Determine gross profit:

Net Sales $\times$ Gross Profit Ratio = Gross Profit

$6,000 $\times$ 30% = $1,800

2. Determine cost of goods sold:

Net Sales $-$ Gross Profit = Cost of Goods Sold

$6,000 $-$ $1,800 = $4,200

3. Determine cost of goods available for sale at time of fire:

Beginning Inventory $+$ Purchases = Cost of Goods Available for Sale

$1,200 $+$ $3,500 = $4,700

4. Determine inventory at time of the fire:

Cost of Goods Available for Sale $-$ Cost of Goods Sold = Inventory

$4,700 $-$ $4,200 = $500

5. Determine amount of inventory destroyed:

Inventory at Time of Fire $-$ Inventory Not Destroyed = Inventory Destroyed

$500 $-$ $200 = $300

Hardluck would make an adjustment to recognize a loss for the excess of the cost of the lost inventory over the amount of reimbursement from the insurance company. The effect of the adjustment is as follows:

BALANCE SHEET						INCOME STATEMENT	
ASSETS	**=**	**LIABILITIES**	**+**	**OWNERS' EQUITY**	**+**	**REVENUES – EXPENSES**	
Cash	250					Loss on Insurance	(50)
Inventory	(300)					Settlement	

Another situation in which the gross profit method is used is for *interim financial statements.* Most companies prepare financial statements at least once every three months. In fact, the Securities and Exchange Commission requires a quarterly report from corporations whose stock is publicly traded. Companies using the periodic inventory system, however, find it cost-prohibitive to count the inventory every three months. The gross profit method is used to estimate the cost of the inventory at these interim dates. A company is allowed to use the method only in interim reports. Inventory reported in the annual report must be based on actual, not estimated, cost.

www.sec.gov

RETAIL INVENTORY METHOD

The counting of inventory in most retail businesses is an enormous undertaking. Imagine the time involved to count all the various items stocked in a hardware store. Because of the time and cost involved in counting inventory, most retail businesses take a physical inventory only once a year. The **retail inventory method** is used to estimate inventory for interim statements, typically prepared monthly.

The retail inventory method has another important use. Consider the year-end inventory count in a large supermarket. One employee counts the number of tubes of toothpaste on the shelf and relays the relevant information either to another employee or to a tape-recording device: "16 tubes of 8-ounce ABC brand toothpaste at $1.69." The key is that the price recorded is the *selling price* or *retail price* of the product, not its cost. It is much quicker to count the inventory at retail than it would be to trace the cost of each item to purchase invoices. The retail method can then be used to convert the inventory from retail to cost. The methodology used with the retail inventory method, whether for interim statements or at year-end, is similar to the approach used with the gross profit method and is covered in detail in intermediate accounting textbooks.

ANALYZING THE MANAGEMENT OF INVENTORY TURNOVER

Managers must strike a balance between maintaining enough inventory to meet customers' needs and incurring the high cost of carrying inventory. The cost of storage and the lost income from the money tied up to own inventory make it very expensive to keep on hand. Investors are also concerned with a company's inventory management. They pay particular attention to a company's **inventory turnover ratio:**

LO 8 Analyze the management of inventory turnover.

$$\frac{\text{Inventory Turnover}}{\text{Ratio}} = \frac{\text{Cost of Goods Sold}}{\text{Average Inventory}}$$

Refer to Circuit City's financial statements as displayed in the chapter opener. From the information presented, we can compute the company's inventory turnover ratio for fiscal year 2000 (amounts are in thousands of dollars):

www.circuitcity.com

$$\frac{\text{Inventory Turnover}}{\text{Ratio}} = \frac{\text{Cost of Goods Sold}^*}{\text{Average Inventory}} = \frac{\$9,751,833}{(\$1,517,675 + \$1,689,209)/2}$$

$$\underbrace{\qquad\qquad}_{\text{(2/28/99 balance sheet)}} \underbrace{\qquad\qquad}_{\text{(2/29/00 balance sheet)}}$$

$$= \frac{\$9,751,833}{\$1,603,442}$$

$$= 6.1 \text{ times}$$

*Circuit City's income statement displays the line item "Cost of sales, buying and warehousing."

This ratio tells us that in fiscal year 2000, Circuit City turned over its inventory 6.1 times. An alternative way to look at a company's efficiency in managing inventory is to calculate the number of days, on average, that inventory is on hand before it is sold. This measure is called the **number of days' sales in inventory** and is calculated as follows (we will assume 360 days in a year):

$$\text{Number of Days' Sales in Inventory} = \frac{\text{Number of Days in the Period}}{\text{Inventory Turnover Ratio}}$$

$$= \frac{360}{6.1}$$

$$= 59 \text{ days}$$

How efficient was Circuit City in managing its inventory if it took an average of 59 days, or about two months, to sell an item of inventory in fiscal year 2000? There are no easy answers to this question, but a starting point would be to compare this statistic with the same measure for prior years. Another basis for evaluation is to compare the measure with that for other companies in the same industry or business, in this case consumer

EXHIBIT 6-9   Inventory Turnover for Different Types of Companies

Company	Types of Products Sold	Inventory Turnover	Number of Days' Sales in Inventory
Circuit City	Televisions, VCRs, personal computers	6.1 times	59 days
Safeway	Grocery items	9.5 times	38 days

electronics. As you can imagine, inventory turnover varies considerably from one industry to the next because of the differences in products. For example, consider Safeway, one of the country's largest food and drug chains. Safeway's average inventory turnover ratio in 1999 was approximately 9.5 times. This means that on average it takes Safeway only about 360/9.5, or 38 days, to sell its inventory. Given the perishable nature of its products, we would expect Safeway to turn over its inventory more rapidly than a consumer electronics company, such as Circuit City. Exhibit 6-9 summarizes the differences in inventory turnover between the two companies.

HOW INVENTORIES AFFECT THE CASH FLOWS STATEMENT

LO 9 Explain the effects that inventory transactions have on the statement of cash flows.

The effects on the income statement and the statement of cash flows from inventory-related transactions differ significantly. We have focused our attention in the last two chapters on how the purchase and the sale of inventory are reported on the income statement. We found that the cost of the inventory sold during the period is deducted on the income statement as cost of goods sold.

The appropriate reporting on a statement of cash flows for inventory transactions depends on whether the direct or indirect method is used. If the direct method is used to prepare the Operating Activities category of the statement, the amount of cash paid to suppliers of inventory is shown as a deduction in this section of the statement.

If the more popular indirect method is used, it is necessary to make adjustments to net income for the changes in two accounts: Inventories and Accounts Payable. These adjustments are summarized in Exhibit 6-10. An increase in inventory is deducted

EXHIBIT 6-10   Inventories and the Statement of Cash Flows

Item	Cash Flow Statement
	Operating Activities
	Net income xxx
Increase in inventory	–
Decrease in inventory	+
Increase in accounts payable	+
Decrease in accounts payable	–
	Investing Activities
	Financing Activities

> "...[T]he company is able to meet consumer demand while also containing costs, which are captured as cost of goods sold."
>
> —Kim Anne Starke

Timing Inventory Buildup to Anticipate Demand

Name: Kim Anne Starke
Education: B.A., DePauw University; M.B.A., University of South Carolina
College Major: Sociology/Anthropology
Occupation: Senior Manager, Kraft Foods, Inc., Toronto
Age: 31

www.kraftfood.com

In the consumer packaged-goods industry, the rate at which inventory is produced and the valuation of that inventory in the financial statements are two fundamentals that can have a major impact on a company's financial position. As a senior manager in sales finance at Kraft Foods, Kim Anne Starke explains why, for a company like Kraft, which deals with high inventory volumes, the rate of production is so important to her business: "Demand for our products peaks at certain times during the year—for example, holidays. However, it would not be efficient to produce all of the product just prior to these peak periods. Instead, production is planned more evenly to maximize labor and capacity resources, and inventory is built gradually to meet the peak demand. Under such a paced inventory build, the company is able to meet consumer demand while also containing costs, which are captured as cost of goods sold."

Once goods are produced, their costs have to be measured, and those measurements will affect the company's bottom-line earnings. This is why it is important to choose the method for valuing inventory by evaluating company-specific financial patterns. Kim Anne explains: "The key is the timing of when incremental costs or savings are passed on to the income statement as part of cost of goods sold. Under LIFO, these differences are passed immediately through inventory and into the cost of goods sold. Since the differences are not held as part of inventory, the inventory valuation on the balance sheet is more stable, and this, in turn, facilitates a more predictable future inventory position." It is basic accounting principles like this that can make all the difference to financial managers like Kim Anne and to the ultimate bottom line.

because it indicates that the company is building up its stock of inventory and thus expending cash. A decrease in inventory is added to net income. An increase in accounts payable is added because it indicates that during the period, the company has increased the amount it owes suppliers and has therefore conserved its cash. A decrease in accounts payable is deducted because the company actually reduced the amount owed suppliers during the period.

The Operating Activities category of the statement of cash flows for Circuit City is presented in Exhibit 6-11. Note that the company groups accounts payable, accrued expenses, and other current liabilities for purposes of presentation on the statement of cash flows.

The increase in inventory in 2000 is deducted because the additional investments in inventory required an expenditure of cash by the company. On the other hand, a buildup of accounts payable, accrued expenses, and other current liabilities actually conserves Circuit City's cash. Thus, the increase in these items in 2000 is added to net earnings.

CONSOLIDATED STATEMENTS OF CASH FLOWS

| | Years Ended February 29 or 28 | | |
(Amounts in thousands)	2000	1999	1998
OPERATING ACTIVITIES:			
Net earnings..	$ 197,590	$ 142,924	$ 104,311
Adjustments to reconcile net earnings to net cash provided			
by operating activities of continuing operations:			
Loss from discontinued operations [NOTE 15]...	16,215	68,546	20,636
Loss on disposal of discontinued operations [NOTE 15]	114,025	–	–
Depreciation and amortization...	148,164	129,727	114,860
Loss on disposition of property and equipment...	17	3,087	14,093
Provision for deferred income taxes...	43,053	17,235	15,052
Changes in operating assets and liabilities, net of effects			
from business acquisitions:			
Decrease in deferred revenue and other liabilities.....................	(15,565)	(33,022)	(23,024)
(Increase) decrease in net accounts receivable	(18,922)	23,640	(66,061)
Increase in inventory..	(184,507)	(97,597)	(18,182)
Decrease (increase) in prepaid expenses and other current assets............................	81,316	31,257	(6,113)
Decrease (increase) in other assets...	240	(607)	10,359
Increase in accounts payable, accrued expenses and			
other current liabilities...	211,850	24,315	62,276
NET CASH PROVIDED BY OPERATING ACTIVITIES OF CONTINUING OPERATIONS...................................	593,476	309,505	228,207

> Increase here is an expenditure of cash to pay for these assets.

> Increase here conserves cash and thus adds to net earnings.

WARMUP EXERCISES

LO 3   Warmup Exercise 6-1   Inventory Valuation

Busby Corp. began the year with 75 units of inventory that it paid $2 each to acquire. During the year it purchased an additional 100 units for $3 each. Busby sold 150 units during the year.

Required

1. Compute cost of goods sold and ending inventory assuming Busby uses FIFO.
2. Compute cost of goods sold and ending inventory assuming Busby uses LIFO.

Key to the Solution
Review the mechanics of the methods, beginning on page 250.

LO 6   Warmup Exercise 6-2   Lower of Cost or Market

Glendive reports its inventory on a FIFO basis and has inventory with a cost of $78,000 on December 31. The cost to replace the inventory on this date would be only $71,000.

Required

Determine the effect on the accounting equation from any adjustment necessary on December 31.

Key to the Solution
Recall the need to write down inventory when market is less than cost.

LO 8 **Warmup Exercise 6-3** Inventory Turnover

Sidney began the year with $130,000 in merchandise inventory and ended the year with $190,000. Sales and cost of goods sold for the year were $900,000 and $640,000, respectively.

Required

1. Compute Sidney's inventory turnover ratio.
2. Compute the number of days' sales in inventory.

Key to the Solution

Review how these two statistics are computed on page 265.

SOLUTIONS TO WARMUP EXERCISES

Warmup Exercise 6-1

1. Cost of goods sold: $(75 \times \$2) + (75 \times \$3) = \$375$

   Ending Inventory: $25 \times \$3 = $ ___ $\$\ 75$

2. Cost of goods sold: $(100 \times \$3) + (50 \times \$2) = \$400$

   Ending inventory: $25 \times \$2 = $ ___ $\$\ 50$

Warmup Exercise 6-2

	BALANCE SHEET					INCOME STATEMENT
ASSETS	**=**	**LIABILITIES**	**+**	**OWNERS' EQUITY**	**+**	**REVENUES – EXPENSES**
Inventory	(7,000)					Loss on Decline in Value of Inventory (7,000)

Warmup Exercise 6-3

1. Inventory Turnover Ratio $= \dfrac{\text{Cost of Goods Sold}}{\text{Average Inventory}}$

   $= \dfrac{\$640,000}{(\$130,000 + \$190,000)/2}$

   $= \dfrac{\$640,000}{\$160,000} = 4 \text{ times}$

2. $\dfrac{\text{Number of Days'}}{\text{Sales in Inventory}} = \dfrac{\text{Number of Days in the Period}}{\text{Inventory Turnover Ratio}}$

   $= \dfrac{360}{4} = 90 \text{ days}$

REVIEW PROBLEM

Stewart Distributing Company sells a single product for $2 per unit and uses a periodic inventory system. The following data are available for the year:

Date	Transaction	Number of Units	Unit Cost	Total
1/1	Beginning inventory	500	$1.00	$500.00
2/5	Purchase	350	1.10	385.00
4/12	Sale	(550)		
7/17	Sale	(200)		
9/23	Purchase	400	1.30	520.00
11/5	Sale	(300)		

Required

1. Compute cost of goods sold, assuming the use of the weighted average costing method.
2. Compute the dollar amount of ending inventory, assuming the FIFO costing method.
3. Compute gross margin, assuming the LIFO costing method.
4. Assume a 40% tax rate. Compute the amount of taxes saved if Stewart uses the LIFO method rather than the FIFO method.

SOLUTION TO REVIEW PROBLEM

1. Cost of goods sold, weighted average cost method:
   Cost of goods available for sale
$500 + $385 + $520 =	$1,405

   Divided by:
   Units available for sale:
500 + 350 + 400 =	1,250	units
Weighted average cost	$1.124	per unit

   × Number of units sold:
550 + 200 + 300 =	1,050	units
Cost of goods sold	$1,180.20	

2. Ending inventory, FIFO cost method:
Units available for sale	1,250
− Units sold	1,050
= Units in ending inventory	200
× Most recent purchase price of	$ 1.30
= Ending inventory	$ 260

3. Gross margin, LIFO cost method:
Sales revenue: 1,050 units × $2 each	$2,100
Cost of goods sold	
400 units × $1.30 = $520	
350 units × $1.10 = 385	
300 units × $1.00 = 300	1,205
Gross margin	$ 895

4. Taxes saved from using LIFO instead of FIFO:
LIFO Cost of goods sold		$1,205
− FIFO Cost of goods sold:		
Cost of goods available for sale	$1,405	
Ending inventory from part **2**	260	
Cost of goods sold		1,145
Additional expense from use of LIFO		$ 60
× Tax rate		.40
Tax savings from the use of LIFO		$ 24

APPENDIX 6A

ACCOUNTING TOOLS: INVENTORY COSTING METHODS WITH THE USE OF A PERPETUAL INVENTORY SYSTEM

The illustrations of the inventory costing methods in the chapter assumed the use of a periodic inventory system. In this appendix, we will see how the methods are applied when a company maintains a perpetual inventory system. It is important to understand the difference between inventory *costing systems* and inventory *methods*. The two inventory systems differ in terms of how often the inventory account is updated: periodically or perpetually. However, when a company sells identical units of product and the cost to purchase each unit is subject to change, it also must choose an inventory costing method, such as FIFO, LIFO, or weighted average.

Earlier in the chapter, we illustrated the various costing methods with a periodic system. We now use the same data to illustrate how the methods differ when a perpetual system is used. Keep in mind that if a company uses specific identification, the results will be the same regardless of whether it uses the periodic or the perpetual system. To compare the periodic and perpetual systems for the other methods, we must add one important piece of information: the date of each of the sales. The original data as well as number of units sold on the various dates are summarized here:

LO 10 Apply the inventory costing methods using a perpetual system.

Date	Purchases	Sales	Balance
Beginning inventory			500 units @ $10
January 20	300 units @ $11		800 units
February 18		450 units	350 units
April 8	400 units @ $12		750 units
June 19		300 units	450 units
September 5	200 units @ $13		650 units
October 20		150 units	500 units
December 12	100 units @ $14		600 units

FIFO COSTING WITH A PERPETUAL SYSTEM

Exhibit 6-12 illustrates the FIFO method on a perpetual basis. The basic premise of FIFO applies whether a periodic or a perpetual system is used: the first units purchased are assumed to be the first units sold. With a perpetual system, however, this concept is applied *at the time of each sale*. For example, note in the exhibit which 450 units are assumed to be sold on February 18. The 450 units sold are taken from the beginning inventory of 500 units with a unit cost of $10. Thus, the inventory or balance after this sale as shown in the last three columns is 50 units at $10 and 300 units at $11, for a total of $3,800. The purchase on April 8 of 400 units at $12 is added to the running balance. On a FIFO basis, the sale of 300 units on June 19 comes from the remainder of the beginning inventory of 50 units and another 250 units from the first purchase at $11 on January 20. The balance after this sale is 50 units at $11 and 400 units at $12. You should follow through the last three transactions in the exhibit to make sure that you understand the application of FIFO on a perpetual basis. An important point to note about the ending inventory of $7,600 is that it is the same amount that we calculated for FIFO periodic earlier in the chapter:

FIFO periodic (Exhibit 6-2) $7,600
FIFO perpetual (Exhibit 6-12) $7,600

Whether the method is applied each time a sale is made or only at the end of the period, the earliest units in are the first units out, and the two systems will yield the same ending inventory under FIFO.

EXHIBIT 6-12 Perpetual System: FIFO Cost-Flow Assumption

	Purchases				Sales				Balance		
Date	Units	Unit Cost	Total Cost		Units	Unit Cost	Total Cost		Units	Unit Cost	Balance
1/1									500	$10	$5,000
1/20	300	$11	$3,300						500	10	
									300	11	8,300
2/18					450	$10	$4,500		50	10	
									300	11	3,800
4/8	400	12	4,800						50	10	
									300	11	
									400	12	8,600
6/19					50	10	500		50	11	
					250	11	2,750		400	12	5,350
9/5	200	13	2,600						50	11	
									400	12	
									200	13	7,950
10/20					50	11	550		300	12	
					100	12	1,200		200	13	6,200
12/12	100	14	1,400						300	12	
									200	13	
									100	14	7,600

LIFO COSTING WITH A PERPETUAL SYSTEM

A LIFO cost flow with the use of a perpetual system is illustrated in Exhibit 6-13. First, note which 450 units are assumed to be sold on February 18. The sale consists of the most recent units acquired, 300 units at $11, and then 150 units from the beginning inventory at $10. Thus, the balance after this sale is simply the remaining 350 units from the beginning inventory priced at $10. The purchase on April 8 results in a balance of 350 units at $10 and 400 units at $12.

Note what happens with LIFO when it is applied on a perpetual basis. In essence, a gap is created. Units acquired at the earliest price of $10 and units acquired at the most recent price of $12 are on hand, but none of those at the middle price of $11 remains. This situation arises because LIFO is applied every time a sale is made rather than only at the end of the year. Because of this difference, the amount of ending inventory differs, depending on which system is used:

LIFO periodic (Exhibit 6-2) $6,100
LIFO perpetual (Exhibit 6-13) $6,750

MOVING AVERAGE WITH A PERPETUAL SYSTEM

When a weighted average cost assumption is applied with a perpetual system, it is sometimes called a **moving average.** As indicated in Exhibit 6-14, each time a purchase is made, a new weighted average cost must be computed, thus the name *moving average*. For

EXHIBIT 6-13 Perpetual System: LIFO Cost-Flow Assumption

	Purchases				Sales				Balance		
Date	Units	Unit Cost	Total Cost		Units	Unit Cost	Total Cost		Units	Unit Cost	Balance
1/1									500	$10	$5,000
1/20	300	$11	$3,300						500	10	
									300	11	8,300
2/18					300	$11	$3,300				
					150	10	1,500		350	10	3,500
4/8	400	12	4,800						350	10	
									400	12	8,300
6/19					300	12	3,600		350	10	
									100	12	4,700
9/5	200	13	2,600						350	10	
									100	12	
									200	13	7,300
10/20					150	13	1,950		350	10	
									100	12	
									50	13	5,350
12/12	100	14	1,400						350	10	
									100	12	
									50	13	
									100	14	6,750

EXHIBIT 6-14 Perpetual System: Moving Average Cost-Flow Assumption

	Purchases				Sales				Balance		
Date	Units	Unit Cost	Total Cost		Units	Unit Cost	Total Cost		Units	Unit Cost	Balance
1/1									500	$10	$5,000
1/20	300	$11	$3,300						800	10.38*	8,304
2/18					450	$10.38	$4,671		350	10.38	3,633
4/8	400	12	4,800						750	11.24†	8,430
6/19					300	11.24	3,372		450	11.24	5,058
9/5	200	13	2,600						650	11.78‡	7,657
10/20					150	11.78	1,767		500	11.78	5,890
12/12	100	14	1,400						600	12.15§	7,290

The moving average prices per unit are calculated as follows:

*($5,000 + $3,300) / 800 units = $10.38 (rounded to nearest cent) ‡($5,058 + $2,600) / 650 units = $11.78

†($3,633 + $4,800) / 750 units = $11.24 §($5,890 + $1,400) / 600 units = $12.15

example, the goods available for sale after the January 20 purchase consist of 500 units at $10 and 300 units at $11, which results in an average cost of $10.38. This is the unit cost applied to the 450 units sold on February 18. The 400 units purchased on April 8 require the computation of a new unit cost, as indicated in the second footnote to the exhibit. As you might have suspected, the ending inventory with an average cost flow differs, depending on whether a periodic or a perpetual system is used:

Weighted average periodic (Exhibit 6-2)	$6,840
Moving average perpetual (Exhibit 6-14)	$7,290

CHAPTER HIGHLIGHTS

1. **LO 1** A manufacturer's inventory consists of raw materials, work in process, and finished goods. The inventory of a retailer or wholesaler is in a single form called *merchandise inventory*.

2. **LO 2** The amount of cost of goods sold reported on the income statement is inherently tied to the value assigned to ending inventory on the balance sheet. All costs necessary to put inventory into a condition and location for sale should be included in its cost. Freight costs, storage costs, excise and sales taxes, and insurance during the time the merchandise is in transit are all candidates for inclusion in the cost of the asset. As a practical matter, however, some of these costs are very difficult to allocate to individual products and are, therefore, accounted for as expenses of the period.

3. **LO 3** The purchase of identical units of a product at varying prices necessitates the use of a costing method to assign a dollar amount to ending inventory and cost of goods sold. As alternatives to the use of a specific identification method, which is impractical in many instances as well as subject to manipulation, accountants have devised cost-flow assumptions.

4. **LO 3** The weighted average method assigns the same average unit cost to all units available for sale during the period. It is widely used because of its simplicity.

5. **LO 3** The FIFO method assigns the most recent costs to ending inventory. The older costs are assigned to cost of goods sold. A first-in, first-out approach does tend to parallel the physical flow of products in many businesses, although the actual flow is not our primary concern in choosing a costing method.

6. **LO 3** LIFO assigns the most recent costs to cost of goods sold, and the older costs remain in inventory. In a period of rising prices, this method results in a relatively higher amount assigned to cost of goods sold and, thus, a lower amount of reported net income. Lower net income results in a lower amount of taxes due, and the tax advantages have resulted in the widespread use of the LIFO method.

    A company that chooses to take advantage of the tax break from using LIFO on its tax return must also use the method in preparing the income statement. A concern with the use of LIFO is the possibility of a liquidation. If more units are sold than are bought in any one period, some of the units sold will come from the older, lower-priced units, resulting in a low cost of goods sold and a high gross margin. The high gross margin will necessitate a larger tax amount due.

7. **LO 4** Many accountants favor LIFO because it results in the nearest approximation to the current cost of goods sold. On the other hand, under LIFO, the inventory amount on the balance sheet is, in many cases, very outdated. FIFO gives a much closer approximation to current cost on the balance sheet. It leads, how-

ever, to what accountants describe as inventory profit: the portion of the gross margin that is due simply to holding the inventory during an inflationary period.

8. **LO 5** Errors in valuing inventory affect cost of goods sold and, thus, affect the amount of income reported for the period. An understatement of ending inventory will result in an understatement of net income; an overstatement of ending inventory will result in an overstatement of net income.

9. **LO 6** As used in the lower-of-cost-or-market rule, *market* means *replacement cost*. The purpose of valuing inventory at original cost or replacement cost, whichever is lower, is to anticipate declines in the selling price of goods subject to obsolescence, spoilage, and other types of loss. By being conservative and reducing the carrying value of the inventory at the end of the year, a company is more likely to report its normal gross margin when the units are sold at a reduced price in the next period. The rule can be applied to each item, to a group of items, or to the entire inventory.

10. **LO 7** The gross profit method is used to estimate the cost of inventory lost by theft, fire, flooding, and other types of damage. The method is also useful to estimate the amount of inventory on hand for interim reports, such as quarterly financial statements. It relies on a trustworthy estimate of the gross profit ratio.

11. **LO 7** Retailers use the retail inventory method to estimate the cost of inventory for interim financial statements and to convert the year-end inventory, per a physical count, from retail to cost.

12. **LO 8** Different measures are available to analyze how well a company is managing its inventory levels. The inventory turnover ratio indicates how many times during a period a company sells or turns over its inventory, and the number of days' sales in inventory indicates how long it takes, on average, to sell inventory.

13. **LO 9** The payment of cash to suppliers of inventory represents a cash outflow from operating activities on the statement of cash flows. If a company uses the indirect method, however, adjustments are made to net income for the increase or decrease in the Inventory and Accounts Payable accounts.

14. **LO 10** In a perpetual system, the Inventory account is updated at the time of each sale and purchase of merchandise. The computer has made the perpetual system much more feasible for many businesses. Ending inventory costed at FIFO will be the same whether the periodic system or the perpetual system is used. This is not the case when the LIFO method is used: the results under the periodic and the perpetual systems differ. Likewise, ending inventory differs in the periodic system and the perpetual system when a weighted average approach is applied. The average method with a perpetual system is really a moving average approach. (Appendix 6A)

KEY TERMS QUIZ

Read each definition below and then write the number of the definition in the blank beside the appropriate term it defines. The solution appears at the end of the chapter.

___ Merchandise Inventory
___ Raw materials
___ Work in process
___ Finished goods
___ Specific identification method
___ Weighted average cost method
___ FIFO method
___ LIFO method
___ LIFO liquidation
___ LIFO conformity rule

___ LIFO reserve
___ Replacement cost
___ Inventory profit
___ Lower-of-cost-or-market (LCM) rule
___ Gross profit method
___ Retail inventory method
___ Inventory turnover ratio
___ Number of days' sales in inventory
___ Moving average (Appendix 6A)

1. The name given to an average cost method when it is used with a perpetual inventory system.

2. The cost of unfinished products in a manufacturing company.

3. An inventory costing method that assigns the same unit cost to all units available for sale during the period.

4. The account that wholesalers and retailers use to report inventory held for sale.

5. A conservative inventory valuation approach that is an attempt to anticipate declines in the value of inventory before its actual sale.

6. An inventory costing method that assigns the most recent costs to ending inventory.

7. The inventory of a manufacturer before the addition of any direct labor or manufacturing overhead.

8. The current cost of a unit of inventory.

9. An inventory costing method that assigns the most recent costs to cost of goods sold.

10. A measure of how long it takes to sell inventory.

11. A technique used to establish an estimate of the cost of inventory stolen, destroyed, or otherwise damaged or of the amount of inventory on hand at an interim date.

12. A manufacturer's inventory that is complete and ready for sale.

13. A technique used by retailers to convert the retail value of inventory to a cost basis.

14. The IRS requirement that if LIFO is used on the tax return, it must also be used in reporting income to stockholders.

15. An inventory costing method that relies on matching unit costs with the actual units sold.

16. The portion of the gross profit that results from holding inventory during a period of rising prices.

17. The result of selling more units than are purchased during the period, which can have negative tax consequences if a company is using LIFO.

18. The excess of the value of a company's inventory stated at FIFO over the value stated at LIFO.

19. A measure of the number of times inventory is sold during a period.

ALTERNATE TERMS

Gross margin   Gross profit

Interim statements   Quarterly or monthly statements

Market (value for inventory)   Replacement cost

Raw materials   Direct materials

Retail price   Selling price

Work in process   Work in progress

QUESTIONS

1. What are three distinct types of costs that manufacturers incur? Describe each of them.

2. What is the relationship between the valuation of inventory as an asset on the balance sheet and the measurement of income?

3. What is the justification for including freight costs incurred in acquiring incoming goods in the cost of the inventory rather than simply treating the cost as an expense of the period? What is the significance of this decision for accounting purposes?

4. What are the inventory characteristics that would allow a company to use the specific identification method? Give at least two examples of inventory for which the method is appropriate.

5. How can the specific identification method allow management to manipulate income?

6. What is the significance of the adjective *weighted* in the weighted average cost method? Use an example to illustrate your answer.

7. Which inventory method, FIFO or LIFO, more nearly approximates the physical flow of products in most businesses? Explain your answer.

8. York Inc. manufactures notebook computers and has experienced noticeable declines in the purchase price of many of the components it uses, including computer chips. Which inventory costing method should York use if it wants to maximize net income? Explain your answer.

9. Which inventory costing method should a company use if it wants to minimize taxes? Does your response depend on whether prices are rising or falling? Explain your answers.

10. The president of Ace Retail is commenting on the company's new controller: "The woman is brilliant! She has shown us how we can maximize our income and at the same time minimize the amount of taxes we have to pay the government. Because the cost to purchase our inventory constantly goes up, we will use FIFO to calculate cost of goods sold on the income statement to minimize the amount charged to cost of goods sold and thus maximize net income. For tax purposes, however, we will use LIFO because this will minimize taxable income and thus minimize the amount we have to pay in taxes." Should the president be enthralled with the new controller? Explain your answer.

11. What does the term *LIFO liquidation* mean? How can it lead to poor buying habits?

12. Historical-based costing methods are sometimes criticized for leading to inventory profits. In a period of rising prices, which inventory costing method will lead to the most "inventory profit"? Explain your answer.

13. Is it acceptable for a company to disclose, in its annual report, that it is switching from some other inventory costing method to LIFO *to save on taxes?*

14. Delevan Corp. uses a periodic inventory system and is counting its year-end inventory. Due to a lack of communication, two different teams count the same section of the warehouse. What effect will this error have on net income?

15. What is the rationale for valuing inventory at the lower of cost or market?

16. Why is it likely that the result from applying the lower-of-cost-or-market rule using a total approach—that is, by comparing total cost to total market value—and the result from applying the rule on an item-by-item basis will differ?

17. Patterson's controller makes the following suggestion: "I have a brilliant way to save us money. Because we are already using the gross profit method for our quarterly statements, we start using it to estimate the year-end inventory for the annual report and save the money normally spent to have the inventory counted on December 31." What do you think of his suggestion?

18. Why does a company save time and money by using the retail inventory method at the end of the year?

19. Ralston Corp.'s cost of sales has remained steady over the last two years. During this same period, however, its inventory has increased considerably. What does this information tell you about the company's inventory turnover? Explain your answer.

20. In simple terms, how do the inventory costing methods, such as FIFO and LIFO, and the inventory systems, such as periodic and perpetual, differ? (Appendix 6A)

21. Why is the weighted average cost method called a *moving* average when a company uses a perpetual inventory system? (Appendix 6A)

EXERCISES

LO 1   Exercise 6-1   Classification of Inventory Costs

Put an X in the appropriate column next to the inventory item to indicate its most likely classification on the books of a company that manufactures furniture and then sells it in retail company stores.

	Classification			
Inventory Item	Raw Material	Work in Process	Finished Goods	Merchandise Inventory
Fabric				
Lumber				
Unvarnished tables				
Chairs on the showroom floor				
Cushions				
Decorative knobs				
Drawers				
Sofa frames				
Chairs in the plant warehouse				
Chairs in the retail storeroom				

LO 1   Exercise 6-2   Inventoriable Costs

During the first month of operations, ABC Company incurred the following costs in ordering and receiving merchandise for resale. No inventory has been sold.

List price, $100, 200 units purchased

Volume discount, 10% off list price

Paid freight costs, $56

Insurance cost while goods were in transit, $32

Long-distance phone charge to place orders, $4.35

Purchasing department salary, $1,000

Supplies used to label goods at retail price, $9.75

Interest paid to supplier, $46

Required

What amount do you recommend the company record as merchandise inventory on its balance sheet? Explain your answer. For any items not to be included in inventory, indicate their appropriate treatment in the financial statements.

LO 2 **Exercise 6-3** Inventory and Income Manipulation

The president of SOS Inc. is concerned that the net income at year-end will not reach the expected figure. When the sales manager receives a large order on the last day of the fiscal year, the president tells the accountant to record the sale but to ignore any inventory adjustment because the physical inventory has already been taken. How will this affect the current year's net income? Next year's income? What would you do if you were the accountant? Assume that SOS uses a periodic inventory system.

LO 3 **Exercise 6-4** Inventory Costing Methods

VanderMeer Inc. reported the following information for the month of February:

Inventory, February 1	65 units @ $20
Purchases:	
February 7	50 units @ $22
February 18	60 units @ $23
February 27	45 units @ $24

During February, VanderMeer sold 140 units. The company uses a periodic inventory system.

Required

What is the value of ending inventory and cost of goods sold for February under the following assumptions:

1. Of the 140 units sold, 55 cost $20, 35 cost $22, 45 cost $23, and 5 cost $24.
2. FIFO
3. LIFO
4. Weighted average

LO 4 **Exercise 6-5** Evaluation of Inventory Costing Methods

Write the letter of the method that is most applicable to each statement.

a. Specific identification
b. Average cost
c. First-in, first-out (FIFO)
d. Last-in, first-out (LIFO)

_____ a 1. Is the most realistic ending inventory.
_____ b 2. Results in cost of goods sold being closest to current product costs.
_____ d 3. Results in highest income during periods of inflation.
_____ c 4. Results in highest ending inventory during periods of inflation.
_____ b 5. Smooths out costs during periods of inflation.
_____ a 6. Is not practical for most businesses.
_____ b 7. Puts more weight on the cost of the larger number of units purchased.
_____ a 8. Is an assumption that most closely reflects the physical flow of goods for most businesses.

LO 4 **Exercise 6-6** LIFO Liquidation—Sears

The 1999 annual report of Sears, Roebuck & Co. includes the following in the footnote that describes its accounting policies relating to merchandise inventories:

> Partial liquidation of merchandise inventories valued under the LIFO method resulted in a credit of $2 million in 1997. No layer liquidation occurred in 1999 and 1998.

Required

1. What does Sears mean that the partial liquidation resulted in a "credit" in 1997? What was the effect of this credit on cost of sales and on gross margin?

2. Was the LIFO liquidation advantageous to Sears for tax purposes? Explain your answer.

LO 5 **Exercise 6-7** Inventory Errors

For each of the following independent situations, fill in the blanks to indicate the effect of the error on each of the various financial statement items. Indicate an understatement (U), an overstatement (O), or no effect (NE). Assume that each of the companies uses a periodic inventory system.

| | Balance Sheet | | Income Statement | |
Error	Inventory	Retained Earnings	Cost of Goods Sold	Net Income
1. Goods in transit at year end are not included in the physical count: they were shipped FOB shipping point.	U	U	O	U
2. One section of a warehouse is counted twice during the year-end count of inventory.	O	O	U	O
3. During the count at year-end, the inventory sheets for one of the stores of a discount retailer are lost.	U	U	O	U

LO 5 **Exercise 6-8** Transfer of Title to Inventory

For each of the following transactions, indicate which company should include the inventory on its December 31, 2001 balance sheet:

1. Michelson Supplies Inc. shipped merchandise to PJ Sales on December 28, 2001, terms FOB destination. The merchandise arrives at PJ's on January 4, 2002.

2. Quarton Inc. shipped merchandise to Filbrandt on December 25, 2001, FOB destination. Fibrandt received the merchandise on December 31, 2001.

3. James Bros. Inc. shipped merchandise to Randall Company on December 27, 2001, FOB shipping point. Randall Company received the merchandise on January 3, 2002.

4. Hinz Company shipped merchandise to Barner Inc. on December 24, 2001, FOB shipping point. The merchandise arrived at Barner's on December 29, 2001.

LO 7 **Exercise 6-9** Gross Profit Method

On February 12, a hurricane destroys the entire inventory of Suncoast Corporation. An estimate of the amount of inventory lost is needed for insurance purposes. The following information is available:

Inventory on January 1	$ 15,400
Net sales from January 1 to February 12	105,300
Purchases from January 1 to February 12	84,230

Suncoast estimates its gross profit ratio as 25% of net sales. The insurance company has agreed to pay Suncoast $10,000 as a settlement for the inventory destroyed.

Required

Determine the effect on the accounting equation of the adjustment to recognize the inventory loss and the insurance reimbursement.

LO 8 **Exercise 6-10** Inventory Turnover for Sears

The following amounts are available from the 1999 annual report of Sears, Roebuck & Co. (all amounts are in millions of dollars): www.sears.com

Cost of sales, buying, and occupancy	$27,212
Merchandise inventories, January 2, 1999 (the end of fiscal 1998)	4,816
Merchandise inventories, January 1, 2000 (the end of fiscal 1999)	5,069

Required

1. Compute Sears' inventory turnover ratio for 1999.

2. What is the average length of time it takes to sell an item of inventory? Explain your answer.

3. Do you think the average length of time it took Sears to sell inventory in 1999 is reasonable? What other information do you need to fully answer this question?

LO 9 **Exercise 6-11** Impact of Transactions Involving Inventories on Statement of Cash Flows

From the following list, identify whether the change in the account balance during the year would be added to (A) or deducted from (D) net income when the indirect method is used to determine cash flows from operating activities.

_____ Increase in accounts payable

_____ Decrease in accounts payable

_____ Increase in inventories

_____ Decrease in inventories

LO 9 **Exercise 6-12** Effects of Transactions Involving Inventories on the Statement of Cash Flows—Direct Method

Masthead Company's comparative balance sheets included inventory of $180,400 at December 31, 2000, and $241,200 at December 31, 2001. Masthead's comparative balance sheets also included accounts payable of $85,400 at December 31, 2000, and $78,400 at December 31, 2001. Masthead's accounts payable balances are composed solely of amounts due to suppliers for purchases of inventory on account. Cost of goods sold, as reported by Masthead on its 2001 income statement, amounted to $1,200,000.

Required

What is the amount of cash payments for inventory that Masthead will report in the Operating Activities category of its 2001 statement of cash flows assuming that the direct method is used?

LO 9 **Exercise 6-13** Effects of Transactions Involving Inventories on the Statement of Cash Flows—Indirect Method

Refer to all the facts in Exercise 6-12.

Required

Assume instead that Masthead uses the indirect method to prepare its statement of cash flows. Indicate how each item will be reflected as an adjustment to net income in the Operating Activities category of the statement of cash flows.

Multi-Concept Exercises

LO 3, 4 **Exercise 6-14** Inventory Costing Methods—Periodic System

The following information is available concerning the inventory of Carter Inc.:

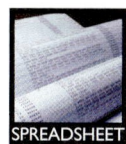
SPREADSHEET

	Units	Unit Cost
Beginning inventory	200	$10
Purchases:		
March 5	300	11
June 12	400	12
August 23	250	13
October 2	150	15

During the year, Carter sold 1,000 units. It uses a periodic inventory system.

Required

1. Calculate ending inventory and cost of goods sold for each of the following three methods:
   a. Weighted average
   b. FIFO
   c. LIFO

2. Assume an estimated tax rate of 30%. How much more or less (indicate which) will Carter pay in taxes by using FIFO instead of LIFO? Explain your answer.

LO 2, 6 Exercise 6-15 Lower-of-Cost-or-Market Rule

Awards Etc. carries an inventory of trophies and ribbons for local sports teams and school clubs. The cost of trophies has dropped in the past year, which pleases the company except for the fact that it has on hand considerable inventory that was purchased at the higher prices. The president is not pleased with the lower profit margin the company is earning. "The lower profit margin will continue until we sell all of this old inventory," he grumbled to the new staff accountant. "Not really," replied the accountant. "Let's write down the inventory to the replacement cost this year, and then next year our profit margin will be in line with the competition."

Required

Explain why the inventory can be carried at an amount less than its cost. Which accounts will be affected by the write-down? What will be the effect on income in the current year and future years?

LO 4, 10 Exercise 6-16 Inventory Costing Methods—Perpetual System (Appendix 6A)

The following information is available concerning Oshkosh Inc.:

	Units	Unit Cost
Beginning inventory	200	$10
Purchases:		
March 5	300	11
June 12	400	12
August 23	250	13
October 2	150	15

Oshkosh, which uses a perpetual system, sold 1,000 units for $22 each during the year. Sales occurred on the following dates:

	Units
February 12	150
April 30	200
July 7	200
September 6	300
December 3	150

Required

1. Calculate ending inventory and cost of goods sold for each of the following three methods:
   a. Moving average
   b. FIFO
   c. LIFO

2. For each of the three methods, compare the results with those for Carter in Exercise 6-14. Which of the methods gives a different answer depending on whether a company uses a periodic or a perpetual inventory system?

3. Assume the use of the perpetual system and an estimated tax rate of 30%. How much more or less (indicate which) will Oshkosh pay in taxes by using LIFO instead of FIFO? Explain your answer.

LO 1   Problem 6-1   Inventory Costs in Various Businesses

Businesses incur various costs in selling goods and services. Each business must decide which costs are expenses of the period and which should be included in the cost of the inventory. Various types of businesses are listed here, along with certain types of costs they incur:

| | | Accounting Treatment | | |
| | | Expense of the Period | Inventory Cost | Other Treatment |
Business	**Types of Costs**			
Retail shoe store	Shoes for sale			
	Shoe boxes			
	Advertising signs			
Grocery store	Canned goods on the shelves			
	Produce			
	Cleaning supplies			
	Cash registers			
Frame shop	Wooden frame supplies			
	Nails			
	Glass			
Walk-in print shop	Paper			
	Copy machines			
	Toner cartridges			
Restaurant	Frozen food			
	China and silverware			
	Prepared food			
	Spices			

Required

Fill in the table to indicate the correct accounting for each of these types of costs by placing an X in the appropriate column. For any costs that receive other treatment, explain what the appropriate treatment is for accounting purposes.

LO 4   Problem 6-2   Evaluation of Inventory Costing Methods

Users of financial statements rely on the information available to them to decide whether to invest in a company or lend it money. As an investor, you are comparing three companies in the same industry. The cost to purchase inventory is rising in the industry. Assume that all expenses incurred by the three companies are the same except for cost of goods sold. The companies use the following methods to value ending inventory:

> Company A—weighted average cost
>
> Company B—first-in, first-out (FIFO)
>
> Company C—last-in, first-out (LIFO)

Required

1. Which of the three companies will report the highest net income? Explain your answer.
2. Which of the three companies will pay the least in income taxes? Explain your answer.
3. Which method of inventory costing do you believe is superior to the others in providing information to potential investors? Explain.
4. Explain how your answers to **1, 2,** and **3** would change if the costs to purchase inventory had been falling instead of rising.

LO 5   Problem 6-3   Inventory Error

The following highly condensed income statements and balance sheets are available for Budget Stores for a two-year period (all amounts are stated in thousands of dollars):

Income Statements	2001	2000
Revenues	$20,000	$15,000
Cost of goods sold	13,000	10,000
Gross profit	$ 7,000	$ 5,000
Operating expenses	3,000	2,000
Net income	$ 4,000	$ 3,000

Balance Sheets	December 31, 2001	December 31, 2000
Cash	$ 1,700	$ 1,500
Inventory	4,200	3,500
Other current assets	2,500	2,000
Long-term assets	15,000	14,000
Total assets	$23,400	$21,000
Liabilities	$ 8,500	$ 7,000
Capital stock	5,000	5,000
Retained earnings	9,900	9,000
Total liabilities and owners' equity	$23,400	$21,000

Before releasing the 2001 annual report, Budget's controller learns that the inventory of one of the stores (amounting to $600,000) was inadvertently omitted from the count on December 31, 2000. The inventory of the store was correctly included in the December 31, 2001, count.

Required

1. Prepare revised income statements and balance sheets for Budget Stores for each of the two years. Ignore the effect of income taxes.

2. If Budget did not prepare revised statements before releasing the 2001 annual report, what would be the amount of overstatement or understatement of net income for the two-year period? What would be the overstatement or understatement of retained earnings at December 31, 2001, if revised statements were not prepared?

3. Given your answers in part **2,** does it matter if Budget bothers to restate the financial statements of the two years to rectify the error? Explain your answer.

LO 7 Problem 6-4 Gross Profit Method of Estimating Inventory Losses

On August 1, an office supply store was destroyed by an explosion in its basement. A small amount of inventory valued at $4,500 was saved. An estimate of the amount of inventory lost is needed for insurance purposes. The following information is available:

Inventory, January 1	$ 3,200
Purchases, January–July	164,000
Sales, January–July	113,500

The normal gross profit ratio is 40%. The insurance company will pay the store $65,000.

Required

1. Using the gross profit method, estimate the amount of inventory lost in the explosion.

2. An adjustment will be made to recognize the inventory loss and the insurance reimbursement. Determine the effect on the accounting equation.

LO 8 Problem 6-5 Inventory Turnover for Compaq Computer and Gateway

www.compaq.com The following information was summarized from the 1999 annual report of Compaq Computer Corporation:

	(in millions)
Product cost of sales for the year ended December 31:	
1999	$25,263
1998	21,383

	(in millions)
Inventories, December 31:	
1999	$ 2,008
1998	2,005
Product revenue for the year ended December 31:	
1999	31,902
1998	27,372

The following information was summarized from the 1999 annual report of Gateway: **www.gateway.com**

	(in thousands)
Cost of goods sold for the year ended December 31:	
1999	$6,745,744
1998	5,921,651
Inventory, December 31:	
1999	191,870
1998	167,924
Net sales for the year ended December 31:	
1999	8,645,561
1998	7,467,925

Required

1. Calculate the gross margin (gross profit) ratios for Compaq Computer and Gateway for 1999 and 1998.

2. Calculate the inventory turnover ratios for both companies for 1999.

3. Which company appears to be performing better? What other information should you consider to determine how these companies are performing in this regard?

LO 9   Problem 6-6 Effects of Changes in Inventory and Accounts Payable Balances on Statement of Cash Flows

Copeland Antiques reported a net loss of $33,200 for the year ended December 31, 2001. The following items were included on Copeland's balance sheets at December 31, 2001 and 2000:

	12/31/01	12/31/00
Cash	$ 65,300	$ 46,100
Trade accounts payable	123,900	93,700
Inventories	192,600	214,800

Copeland uses the indirect method to prepare its statement of cash flows. Copeland does not have any other current assets or current liabilities and did not enter into any investing or financing activities during 2001.

Required

1. Prepare Copeland's 2001 statement of cash flows.

2. Draft a brief memo to the president to explain why cash increased during such an unprofitable year.

Multi-Concept Problems

LO 2, 3, 4   Problem 6-7 Comparison of Inventory Costing Methods—Periodic System

Bitten Company's inventory records show 600 units on hand on October 1 with a unit cost of $5 each. The following transactions occurred during the month of October:

Date	Unit Purchases	Unit Sales
October 4	600 @ 5.00	500 @ $10.00
8	800 @ $5.40	
9		700 @ $10.00
18	700 @ $5.76	
20		800 @ $11.00
29	800 @ $5.90	
	13072	20,800

All expenses other than cost of goods sold amount to $3,000 for the month. The company uses an estimated tax rate of 30% to accrue monthly income taxes.

Required

1. Prepare a chart comparing cost of goods sold and ending inventory using the periodic system and the following costing methods:

	Cost of Goods Sold	Ending Inventory	Total
Weighted average			
FIFO			
LIFO			

2. What does the Total column represent?

3. Prepare income statements for each of the three methods.

4. Will the company pay more or less tax if it uses FIFO rather than LIFO? How much more or less?

LO 2, 4, 10 **Problem 6-8** Comparison of Inventory Costing Methods—Perpetual System (Appendix 6A)

Repeat Problem 6-7 using the perpetual system.

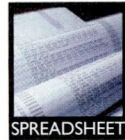
SPREADSHEET

LO 2, 3, 4 **Problem 6-9** Inventory Costing Methods—Periodic System

Oxendine Company's inventory records for the month of November reveal the following:

Inventory, November 1	200 units @ $18.00
November 4, purchase	250 units @ $18.50
November 7, sale	300 units @ $42.00
November 13, purchase	220 units @ $18.90
November 18, purchase	150 units @ $19.00
November 22, sale	380 units @ $42.50
November 24, purchase	200 units @ $19.20
November 28, sale	110 units @ $43.00

Selling and administrative expenses for the month were $10,800. Depreciation expense was $4,000. Oxendine's tax rate is 35%.

Required

1. Calculate the cost of goods sold and ending inventory under each of the following three methods (assume a periodic inventory system): (a) FIFO, (b) LIFO, and (c) weighted average.

2. Calculate the gross margin and net income under each costing assumption.

3. Under which costing method will Oxendine pay the least taxes? Explain your answer.

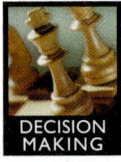
DECISION MAKING

LO 2, 3, 4 **Problem 6-10** Inventory Costing Methods—Periodic System

Following is an inventory acquisition schedule for Weaver Corp. for 2001:

	Units	Unit Cost
Beginning inventory	5,000	$10
Purchases:		
February 4	3,000	9
April 12	4,000	8
September 10	2,000	7
December 5	1,000	6

During the year, Weaver sold 12,500 units at $12 each. All expenses except cost of goods sold and taxes amounted to $20,000. The tax rate is 30%.

Required

1. Compute cost of goods sold and ending inventory under each of the following three methods (assume a periodic inventory system): (a) weighted average, (b) FIFO, and (c) LIFO.

2. Prepare income statements under each of the three methods.

3. Which method do you recommend so that Weaver pays the least amount of taxes during 2001? Explain your answer.

4. Weaver anticipates that unit costs for inventory will increase throughout 2002. Will it be able to switch from the method you recommended it use in 2001 to another method to take advantage, for tax purposes, of the increase in prices? Explain your answer.

LO 1, 4 Problem 6-11   Interpreting Tribune Company's Inventory Accounting Policy
The 1999 annual report of Tribune Company and Subsidiaries includes the following in the foot-note that summarizes its accounting policies:

www.tribune.com

> **Inventories** Inventories are stated at the lower of cost or market. Cost is determined on the last-in, first-out ("LIFO") basis for newsprint and on the first-in, first-out ("FIFO") or aver-age basis for all other inventories.

Required

1. What *types* of inventory cost does Tribune Company carry? What about newspapers? Are news-papers considered inventory?

2. Why would the company choose three different methods to value its inventory?

LO 3, 7 Problem 6-12   Interpreting Sears' Inventory Accounting Policy
The 1999 annual report of Sears, Roebuck and Co. includes the following information in the foot-note that describes its accounting policies relating to merchandise inventories:

www.sears.com

> Approximately 87% of merchandise inventories are valued at the lower of cost (using the last-in, first-out or "LIFO" method) or market using the retail method. To estimate the effects of inflation on inventories, the Company utilizes internally developed price indices.

The footnote also includes the following information about the company's international operations:

> Merchandise inventories of International operations, operations in Puerto Rico, and certain Sears Automotive Store formats, which in total represent approximately 13% of merchandise inventories, are recorded at the lower of cost or market based on the FIFO method.

Your grandfather knows you are studying accounting and asks you what this information means.

Required

1. Sears uses the last-in, first-out method for its domestic merchandise inventories and the first-in, first-out method for its international merchandise inventories. Does this mean it sells its newest mer-chandise first in the United States and its oldest merchandise first overseas? Explain your answer.

2. Does Sears report merchandise inventories on its balance sheet at their retail value? Explain your answer.

ALTERNATE PROBLEMS

LO 1 Problem 6-1A   Inventory Costs in Various Businesses
Sound Traxs Inc. sells and rents videos to retail customers. The accountant is aware that at the end of the year she must account for inventory but is unsure what videos are considered inventory and how to value them. Videos purchased by the company are placed on the shelf for rental. Every three weeks the company performs a detailed analysis of the rental income from each video and decides whether to keep it as a rental or to offer it for sale in the resale section of the store. Resale videos sell for $10 each regardless of the price Sound Traxs paid for the tape.

DECISION MAKING

Required

1. How should Sound Traxs account for each of the two types of tapes—rentals and resales—on its balance sheet?

2. How would you suggest Sound Traxs account for the videos as they are transferred from one department to another?

LO 4 Problem 6-2A   Evaluation of Inventory Costing Methods
Three large mass merchandisers use the following methods to value ending inventory:

      Company X—weighted average cost

      Company Y—first-in, first-out (FIFO)

      Company Z—last-in, first-out (LIFO)

The cost of inventory has steadily increased over the past 10 years of the product life. Recently, however, prices have started to decline slightly due to foreign competition.

Required

1. Will the effect on net income of the decline in cost of goods sold be the same for all three companies? Explain your answer?

2. Company Z would like to change its inventory costing method from LIFO to FIFO. Write an acceptable footnote for its annual report to justify the change.

LO 5 Problem 6-3A Inventory Error

The following condensed income statements and balance sheets are available for Planter Stores for a two-year period (all amounts are stated in thousands of dollars):

Income Statements	2001	2000
Revenues	$35,982	$26,890
Cost of goods sold	12,594	9,912
Gross profit	$23,388	$16,978
Operating expenses	13,488	10,578
Net income	$ 9,900	$ 6,400

Balance Sheets	December 31, 2001	December 31, 2000
Cash	$ 9,400	$ 4,100
Inventory	4,500	5,400
Other current assets	1,600	1,250
Long-term assets, net	24,500	24,600
Total assets	$40,000	$35,350
Current liabilities	$ 9,380	$10,600
Capital stock	18,000	18,000
Retained earnings	12,620	6,750
Total liabilities and owners' equity	$40,000	$35,350

Before releasing the 2001 annual report, Planter's controller learns that the inventory of one of the stores (amounting to $500,000) was counted twice in the December 31, 2000, inventory. The inventory was correctly counted in the December 31, 2001, inventory count.

Required

1. Prepare revised income statements and balance sheets for Planter Stores for each of the two years. Ignore the effect of income taxes.

2. Compute the current ratio at December 31, 2000, before the statements are revised, and then compute the current ratio at the same date after the statements are revised. If Planter applied for a loan in early 2001 and the lender required a current ratio of at least 1-to-1, would the error have affected the loan? Explain your answer.

3. If Planter did not prepare revised statements before releasing the 2001 annual report, what would be the amount of overstatement or understatement of net income for the two-year period? What would be the overstatement or understatement of retained earnings at December 31, 2001, if revised statements were not prepared?

4. Given your answers in parts **2** and **3**, does it matter if Planter bothers to restate the financial statements of the two years to correct the error? Explain your answer.

LO 7 Problem 6-4A Gross Profit Method of Estimating Inventory Losses

On July 1, an explosion destroyed a fireworks supply company. A small amount of inventory valued at $4,500 was saved. An estimate of the amount of inventory lost is needed for insurance purposes. The following information is available:

Inventory, January 1	$14,200
Purchases, January-June	77,000
Sales, January-June	93,500

The normal gross profit ratio is 70%. The insurance company will pay the supply company $50,000.

Required

1. Using the gross profit method, estimate the amount of inventory lost in the explosion.

2. An adjustment will be made to recognize the inventory loss and the insurance reimbursement. Determine the effect on the accounting equation.

LO 8 Problem 6-5A Inventory Turnover for Wal-Mart and Kmart

The following information was summarized from the fiscal year 2000 annual report of Wal-Mart **www.walmart.com** Stores, Inc.:

	(in millions)
Cost of sales for the year ended January 31:	
2000	$129,664
1999	108,725
Inventories, January 31:	
2000	19,793
1999	17,076

The following information was summarized from the fiscal year 1999 annual report of Kmart **www.kmart.com** Corporation:

	(in millions)
Cost of sales, buying, and occupancy for the year ended:	
January 26, 2000	$28,102
January 27, 1999	26,319
Merchandise inventories:	
January 26, 2000	7,101
January 27, 1999	6,536

Required

1. Calculate the inventory turnover ratios for Wal-Mart for the year ending January 31, 2000 and Kmart for the year ending January 26, 2000.

2. Which company appears to be performing better? What other information should you consider to determine how these companies are performing in this regard?

LO 9 Problem 6-6A Effects of Changes in Inventory and Accounts Payable Balances on Statement of Cash Flows

Carpetland City reported net income of $78,500 for the year ended December 31, 2001. The following items were included on Carpetland's balance sheet at December 31, 2001 and 2000:

	12/31/01	12/31/00
Cash	$ 14,400	$26,300
Trade accounts payable	23,900	93,700
Inventories	105,500	84,900

Carpetland uses the indirect method to prepare its statement of cash flows. Carpetland does not have any other current assets or current liabilities and did not enter into any investing or financing activities during 2001.

Required

1. Prepare Carpetland's 2001 statement of cash flows.

2. Draft a brief memo to the president to explain why cash decreased during a profitable year.

Alternate Multi-Concept Problems

LO 2, 3, 4 Problem 6-7A Comparison of Inventory Costing Methods—Periodic System

Stellar Inc.'s inventory records show 300 units on hand on November 1 with a unit cost of $4 each. The following transactions occurred during the month of November:

Date		Unit Purchases	Unit Sales
November	4		200 @ $9.00
	8	500 @ $4.50	
	9		500 @ $9.00
	18	700 @ $4.75	
	20		400 @ $9.50
	29	600 @ $5.00	

All expenses other than cost of goods sold amount to $2,000 for the month. The company uses an estimated tax rate of 25% to accrue monthly income taxes.

Required

1. Prepare a chart comparing cost of goods sold and ending inventory using the periodic system and the following costing methods:

	Cost of Goods Sold	Ending Inventory	Total
Weighted average			
FIFO			
LIFO			

2. What does the Total column represent?

3. Prepare income statements for each of the three methods.

4. Will the company pay more or less tax if it uses FIFO rather than LIFO? How much more or less?

LO 2, 4, 10 Problem 6-8A Comparison of Inventory Costing Methods—Perpetual System
Repeat Problem 6-7A, using the perpetual system.

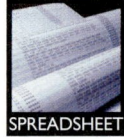

LO 2, 3, 4 Problem 6-9A Inventory Costing Methods—Periodic System
Story Company's inventory records for the month of November reveal the following:

Inventory, November 1	300 units @ $27.00
November 4, purchase	375 units @ $26.50
November 7, sale	450 units @ $63.00
November 13, purchase	330 units @ $26.00
November 18, purchase	225 units @ $25.40
November 22, sale	570 units @ $63.75
November 24, purchase	300 units @ $25.00
November 28, sale	165 units @ $64.50

Selling and administrative expenses for the month were $16,200. Depreciation expense was $6,000. Story's tax rate is 35%.

Required

1. Calculate the cost of goods sold and ending inventory under each of the following three methods (assume a periodic inventory system): (a) FIFO, (b) LIFO, and (c) weighted average.

2. Calculate the gross margin and net income under each costing assumption.

3. Under which costing method will Story pay the least taxes? Explain your answer.

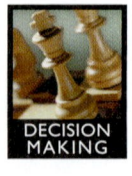

LO 2, 3, 4 Problem 6-10A Inventory Costing Methods—Periodic System
Following is an inventory acquisition schedule for Fees Corp. for 2001:

	Units	Unit Cost
Beginning inventory	4,000	$20
Purchases:		
February 4	2,000	18
April 12	3,000	16
September 10	1,000	14
December 5	2,500	12

During the year, Fees sold 11,000 units at $30 each. All expenses except cost of goods sold and taxes amounted to $60,000. The tax rate is 30%.

Required

1. Compute cost of goods sold and ending inventory under each of the following three methods (assume a periodic inventory system): (a) weighted average, (b) FIFO, and (c) LIFO.

2. Prepare income statements under each of the three methods.

3. Which method do you recommend so that Fees pays the least amount of taxes during 2001? Explain your answer.

4. Fees anticipates that unit costs for inventory will increase throughout 2002. Will it be able to switch from the method you recommended it use in 2001 to another method to take advantage for tax purposes of the increase in prices? Explain your answer.

LO 1, 4 Problem 6-11A Interpreting the New York Times Company's Financial Statements
The 1999 annual report of the New York Times Company includes the following note: www.nytco.com

> Inventories. Inventories are stated at the lower of cost or current market value. Inventory cost is generally based on the last-in, first-out ("LIFO") method for newsprint and magazine paper and the first-in, first-out ("FIFO") method for other inventories.

Required

1. What *types* of inventory costs does the New York Times Company have? What about newspapers? Aren't these considered inventory?

2. Why did the company choose two different methods to value its inventory?

LO 3, 7 Problem 6-12A Interpreting JCPenney's Financial Statements
The 1999 annual report for JCPenney includes the following in the footnote that summarizes its   www.jcpenney.com
accounting policies:

> Merchandise inventory. Substantially all merchandise inventory is valued at the lower of cost (last-in, first-out) or market, determined by the retail method.

A friend knows that you are studying accounting and asks you what this note means.

Required

1. JCPenney uses the last-in, first-out method. Does this mean that it sells its newest merchandise first?

2. Does JCPenney report inventories on its balance sheet at their retail value?

CASES

Reading and Interpreting Financial Statements

LO 1, 3 Case 6-1 Reading and Interpreting Uno's Annual Report
Refer to Uno's financial statements included in its annual report.   www.pizzeriauno.com

Required

1. Before you look at Uno's annual report, what types of inventory accounts do you expect? What types of inventory accounts does Uno actually report? (Refer to the footnote that summarizes its significant accounting policies.)

2. What inventory costing method does Uno use? Look in the footnotes to the financial statements.

3. What portion of total assets is represented by inventory at the end of 1998? At the end of 1999? Do these portions seem reasonable for a company in this business? Explain your answer.

LO 9 Case 6-2 Reading Gateway's Statement of Cash Flows
Refer to the statement of cash flows in Gateway's 1999 annual report and answer the following questions: www.gateway.com

1. Did inventories increase or decrease during 1999? Why was the change in the Inventory account deducted from net income in the Operating Activities category of the statement?

2. Comment on the size of change in inventories over the last three years. Does the level of inventory at the end of 1999 seem appropriate?

3. Did accounts payable increase or decrease during 1999? Why was the change in the account added to net income in the Operating Activities category of the statement?

LO 4 **Case 6-3** Reading and Interpreting JCPenney's Financial Statements

JCPenney reports merchandise inventory in the Current Asset section of the balance sheet in its fiscal 1999 annual report as follows (amounts in millions of dollars):

	1999	1998
Merchandise inventory (including LIFO reserves of $270 and $227)	$5,947	$6,060

Required

1. What method does JCPenney use to report the value of its inventory?
2. What is the amount of the LIFO reserve at the end of each of the two years?
3. Explain the meaning of the increase or decrease in the LIFO reserve during 1999. What does this tell you about inventory costs for the company? Are they rising or falling? Explain your answer.

Making Financial Decisions

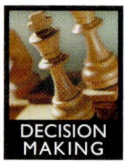

LO 3, 4 **Case 6-4** Inventory Costing Methods

You are the controller for Georgetown Company. At the end of its first year of operations, the company is experiencing cash flow problems. The following information has been accumulated during the year:

Purchases	
January	1,000 units @ $8
March	1,200 units @ 8
October	1,500 units @ 9

During the year, Georgetown sold 3,000 units at $15 each. The expected tax rate is 35%. The president doesn't understand how to report inventory in the financial statements because no record of the cost of the units sold was kept as each sale was made.

Required

1. What inventory *system* must Georgetown use?
2. Determine the number of units on hand at the end of the year.
3. Explain cost-flow assumptions to the president and the method you recommend. Prepare income statements to justify your position, comparing your recommended method with at least one other method.

LO 5 **Case 6-5** Inventory Errors

You are the controller of a rapidly growing mass merchandiser. The company uses a periodic inventory system. As the company has grown and accounting systems have developed, errors have occurred in both the physical count of inventory and the valuation of inventory on the balance sheet. You have been able to identify the following errors as of December 2000:

■ In 1998, one section of the warehouse was counted twice. The error resulted in inventory overstated on December 31, 1998, by approximately $45,600.

■ In 1999, the replacement cost of some inventory was less than the FIFO value used on the balance sheet. The inventory would have been $6,000 less on the balance sheet dated December 31, 1999.

■ In 2000, the company used the gross profit method to estimate inventory for its quarterly financial statements. At the end of the second quarter, the controller made a math error and understated the inventory by $20,000 on the quarterly report. The error was not discovered until the end of the year.

Required

What, if anything, should you do to correct each of these errors? Explain your answers.

Accounting and Ethics: What Would You Do?

LO 6 **Case 6-6** Write-Down of Obsolete Inventory

As a newly hired staff accountant, you are assigned the responsibility of physically counting inventory at the end of the year. The inventory count proceeds in a timely fashion. The inventory is outdated, however. You suggest that the inventory could not be sold for the cost at which it is carried and that the inventory should be written down to a much lower level. The controller replies that experience has taught her how the market changes and she knows that the units in the warehouse will be more marketable again. The company plans to keep the goods until they are back in style.

Required

1. What effect will writing off the inventory have on the current year's income?

2. What effect does not writing off the inventory have on the year-end balance sheet?

3. What factors should you consider in deciding whether to persist in your argument that the inventory should be written down?

LO 4 Case 6-7 Selection of an Inventory Method

As controller of a widely held public company, you are concerned with making the best decisions for the stockholders. At the end of its first year of operations, you are faced with the choice of method to value inventory. Specific identification is out of the question because the company sells a large quantity of diversified products. You are trying to decide between FIFO and LIFO. Inventory costs have increased 33% over the year. The chief executive officer has instructed you to do whatever it takes in all areas to report the highest income possible.

Required

1. Which method will satisfy the CEO?

2. Which method do you believe is in the best interest of the stockholders? Explain your answer.

3. Write a brief memo to the CEO to convince him that reporting the highest income is not always the best approach for the shareholders.

INTERNET RESEARCH CASE

Case 6-8 Circuit City

Circuit City Stores Inc., is a top retailer in the consumer electronics industry (its Circuit City Group), and it is also a significant retailer of autos and trucks (its Carmax Group). The chapter focuses on Circuit City in the opener, in the Business Strategy box, and in the chapter to show how critical inventory is to a business of this type.

www.circuitcity.com

Read the chapter opening text and the Business Strategy box, research the company and its financial information available on its web site, and answer the following questions.

1. What is the inventory amount shown for the most current year?

2. What is the inventory turnover for the Carmax Group? For the entire company as a whole? Is this information significant for evaluating each of the two groups in the company against competition? Is it significant for evaluating the company as a whole? Why or why not?

3. How would Circuit City's rebate program for new CompuServe customers affect inventories at Circuit City?

4. What inventory system would you expect Circuit City to use, perpetual or periodic? What makes you think so?

5. How could Circuit City reduce its costs for carrying inventory?

SOLUTION TO KEY TERMS QUIZ

_4_	Merchandise Inventory (p. 244)	_8_	Replacement cost (p. 255)
_7_	Raw materials (p. 244)	_16_	Inventory profit (p. 255)
_2_	Work in process (p. 245)	_5_	Lower-of-cost-or-market (LCM) rule (p. 260)
_12_	Finished goods (p. 245)		
_15_	Specific identification method (p. 249)	_11_	Gross profit method (p. 263)
_3_	Weighted average cost method (p. 249)	_13_	Retail inventory method (p. 265)
_6_	FIFO method (p. 250)	_19_	Inventory turnover ratio (p. 265)
_9_	LIFO method (p. 251)	_10_	Number of days' sales in inventory (p. 265)
_17_	LIFO liquidation (p. 253)		
_14_	LIFO conformity rule (p. 254)	_1_	Moving average (p. 272)
_18_	LIFO reserve (p. 254)		

Chapter 7

CASH, INVESTMENTS, AND RECEIVABLES

Study Links

A Look at Previous Chapters

In the two preceding chapters, we discussed the accounting for inventories, a major asset for many companies. The emphasis in Chapter 5 was on merchandise inventory and the accounting for purchases and sales of inventory. In Chapter 6, we considered how inventory is valued in the accounts, using a costing method such as weighted average, FIFO, or LIFO.

A Look at This Chapter

We now turn to those assets, namely <u>cash</u> and <u>receivables</u>, that are increased when a company sells its inventory. We also consider the accounting when a company <u>invests some of its cash in the stocks and bonds of other companies</u>. The last part of the chapter covers various valuation issues relative both to accounts receivable and to notes receivable.

A Look at Upcoming Chapters

Chapter 8 focuses on the long-term operational assets, such as property, plant, and equipment and intangibles, necessary to run a business. In Chapters 9 and 10, we explore the use of liabilities to finance the purchase of assets.

FOCUS ON FINANCIAL RESULTS

For the last few years PepsiCo, one of the world's fastest growing consumer products companies, has been in the business of revamping itself. The firm sold off some unrelated businesses around the world (including KFC, Pizza Hut, and Taco Bell) and invested billions of dollars back into the "three great businesses full of opportunity"—Frito-Lay snacks, Pepsi-Cola beverages, and Tropicana juices. After a major investment in new products, new distribution methods (such as 190,000 vending machines and coolers), and extensive advertising and marketing, the company's 1999 results showed healthy growth in revenue, volume, and operating profit in all five of its operating divisions.

Although sales were actually down in 1999, when compared with the four preceding years, earnings were higher, return on invested capital rose from about 15 percent to 20 percent, and operating profit margin rose from 10 percent to 15 percent. Capital spending is down, a result of the company's shifting away from capital-intensive businesses like fast-food outlets, and debt had been reduced from $8 billion all the way down to $2 billion. Operating cash flow was also higher.

Comparing the 1998 and 1999 figures at the right, you can see that the company's <u>cash and cash equivalent</u> figure has more than tripled. The change primarily reflects the fact that the company made fewer acquisitions and investments in affiliate companies than in 1998 and repurchased fewer of its outstanding shares. <u>Accounts and notes receivable</u> are lower, however, and total assets are somewhat lower.

CONSOLIDATED BALANCE SHEET

(in millions except per share amounts)
PepsiCo, Inc. and Subsidiaries
December 25, 1999 and December 26, 1998

	1999	1998
ASSETS		
Current Assets		
Cash and cash equivalents	$ 964	$ 311
Short-term investments, at cost	92	83
	1,056	394
Accounts and notes receivable, net	1,704	2,453
Inventories	899	1,016
Prepaid expenses and other current assets	514	499
Total Current Assets	4,173	4,362
Property, Plant and Equipment, net	5,266	7,318
Intangible Assets, net	4,735	8,996
Investments in Unconsolidated Affiliates	2,846	1,396
Other Assets	531	588
Total Assets	$17,551	$ 22,660

Higher cash and cash equivalents

Higher short-term investments

Lower accounts and notes receivable

PepsiCo's 1999 Annual Report

PepsiCo prides itself on its ability to earn profits for its shareholders. If you owned shares in the company, what questions would you ask about the increase in cash and cash equivalents? Would you be concerned about the decreases in inventories and receivables? Study the chapter to find out how these variables are related.

www.pepsico.com

After studying this chapter, you should be able to:

LO 1 Identify and describe the various forms of cash reported on a balance sheet. (p. 294)

LO 2 Understand various techniques that companies use to control cash. (p. 295)

LO 3 Understand the accounting for various types of investments companies make. (p. 302)

LO 4 Understand how to account for accounts receivable, including bad debts. (p. 312)

LO 5 Understand how to account for interest-bearing notes receivable. (p. 319)

LO 6 Understand how to account for non-interest-bearing notes receivable. (p. 321)

LO 7 Explain various techniques that companies use to accelerate the inflow of cash from sales. (p. 322)

LO 8 Explain the effects of transactions involving liquid assets on the statement of cash flows. (p. 324)

PepsiCo Inc., like all other businesses, relies on *liquid assets* to function smoothly. *Liquidity* is a relative term. It deals with a company's ability to pay its debts as they fall due. Most obligations must be paid in cash, and therefore cash is considered the most liquid of all assets. Accounts and notes receivable are not as liquid as cash. Their collection does result in an inflow of cash, however. Because cash in its purest form does not earn a return, most businesses invest in various types of securities as a way to use idle cash over the short term. The Current Assets section of PepsiCo's balance sheet, as shown in the chapter opener, indicates three highly liquid assets: cash and cash equivalents, short-term investments, and accounts and notes receivable. Inventories are not considered as liquid as these three assets because they depend on a sale to be realized.

We begin the chapter by considering the various forms cash can take and the importance of cash control to a business. Some companies invest cash in various types of financial instruments, as well as in the stocks and bonds of other companies. The chapter illustrates the accounting for these investments. In many instances, the cash available to make these investments comes from the collection of receivables. The chapter concludes with a discussion of the accounting both for accounts receivable and for notes receivable.

WHAT CONSTITUTES CASH?

LO 1 Identify and describe the various forms of cash reported on a balance sheet.

Cash takes many different forms. Coin and currency on hand and cash on deposit in the form of checking, savings, and money market accounts are the most obvious forms of cash. Also included in cash are various forms of checks, including undeposited checks from customers, cashier's checks, and certified checks. The proliferation of different types of financial instruments on the market today makes it very difficult to decide on the appropriate classification of these various items. The key to the classification of an amount as cash is that it be *readily available to pay debts.* Technically, a bank has the legal right to demand that a customer notify it before making withdrawals from savings accounts, or time deposits, as they are often called. Because this right is rarely exercised, however, savings accounts are normally classified as cash. In contrast, a certificate of deposit has a specific maturity date and carries a penalty for early withdrawal and is therefore not included in cash.

CASH EQUIVALENTS AND THE STATEMENT OF CASH FLOWS

Note that the first item on PepsiCo's balance sheet is titled Cash and Cash Equivalents. Examples of items normally classified as cash equivalents are commercial paper issued by corporations, Treasury bills issued by the federal government, and money market funds offered by financial institutions. According to current accounting standards, classification as a **cash equivalent** is limited to those investments that are readily convertible to known amounts of cash and that have an original maturity to the investor of three months or less. Note that according to this definition, a six-month bank certificate of deposit would *not* be classified as a cash equivalent.

The statement of cash flows that accompanies PepsiCo's balance sheet is shown in Exhibit 7-1. Note the direct tie between this statement and the balance sheet (refer to the Current Assets section of PepsiCo's balance sheet as shown in the chapter opener). The cash and cash equivalents of $964 million at the end of 1999, as shown at the bottom of the statement of cash flows, is the same amount that appears as the first line on the balance sheet. The reason for this is that the statement of cash flows traces the flow of cash from the beginning balance of cash for the year—$311 million—to the year's ending balance, $964 million. Cash inflow from operating activities, $3,027 million, minus cash outflow from investing activities, $1,072 million, minus cash outflow from financing activities, $1,304 million, plus the effects of exchange rate changes, $2 million, equals a net increase in cash of $653 million. Add $653 million to the beginning cash balance to arrive at $964 million.

Note the fifth category listed under Investing Activities on the statement of cash flows. The changes in short-term investments represent the net purchases or sales of short-term investments during the year. Later in the chapter we will consider the accounting for both short-term and long-term investments. For now, note that any purchases or sales of items classified as short-term investments are considered significant and worthy of reporting on the statement of cash flows. Any purchases or sales of items classified as cash equivalents, however, are not considered significant activities. Instead, they are included with cash on the balance sheet and are considered to be its "equivalent."

CONTROL OVER CASH

In Chapter 5, we discussed the concept of internal control and the critical role it plays for an asset such as cash. Because cash is universally accepted as a medium of exchange, control over it is critical to the smooth functioning of any business, no matter how large or small.

LO 2 Understand various techniques that companies use to control cash.

CASH MANAGEMENT

In addition to the need to guard against theft and other abuses related to the physical custody of cash, management of this asset is also important. Cash management is necessary to ensure that at any point in time, a company has neither too little nor too much cash on hand. The need to have enough cash on hand is obvious: suppliers, employees, taxing agencies, banks, and all other creditors must be paid on time if an entity is to remain in business. It is equally important that a company not maintain cash on hand and on deposit in checking accounts beyond a minimal amount that is necessary to support ongoing operations, since cash is essentially a nonearning asset. Granted, some checking accounts pay a very meager rate of interest. However, the superior return that could be earned by investing idle cash in various forms of marketable securities dictates that companies carefully monitor the amount of cash on hand at all times.

An important tool in the management of cash, the cash flows statement, is discussed in detail in Chapter 12. Cash budgets, which are also critical to the management of cash, are discussed in management accounting and business finance texts. Cash management is just one important aspect of control over cash. Beyond cash management, companies often use two other cash control features: bank reconciliations and petty cash funds. Before we turn to these control devices, we need to review the basic features of a bank statement.

READING A BANK STATEMENT

Two fundamental principles of internal control discussed in Chapter 5 are worth repeating: all cash receipts should be deposited daily intact, and all cash payments should be made by check. Checking accounts at banks are critical in this regard. These accounts allow a company to carefully monitor and control cash receipts and cash payments. Control is aided

EXHIBIT 7-1 PepsiCo's Statement of Cash Flows

CONSOLIDATED STATEMENT OF CASH FLOWS

(in millions)
PepsiCo, Inc. and Subsidiaries
Fiscal years ended December 25, 1999, December 26, 1998 and December 27, 1997

	1999	1998	1997
Operating Activities			
Income from continuing operations	$ 2,050	$ 1,993	$ 1,491
Adjustments to reconcile income from continuing operations			
to net cash provided by operating activities			
Gain on bottling transactions	(1,000)	–	–
Bottling equity income, net	(83)	–	–
Depreciation and amortization	1,032	1,234	1,106
Noncash portion of 1998 income tax benefit	–	(259)	–
Noncash portion of impairment and restructuring charges	37	254	233
Deferred income taxes	529	150	51
Other noncash charges and credits, net	364	237	342
Changes in operating working capital, excluding effects of acquisitions and dispositions			
Accounts and notes receivable	(149)	(104)	(53)
Inventories	(186)	29	79
Prepaid expenses and other current assets	(203)	(12)	(56)
Accounts payable and other current liabilities	310	(195)	84
Income taxes payable	326	(116)	142
Net change in operating working capital	98	(398)	196
Net Cash Provided by Operating Activities	3,027	3,211	3,419
Investing Activities			
Capital spending	(1,118)	(1,405)	(1,506)
Acquisitions and investments in unconsolidated affiliates	(430)	(4,537)	(119)
Sales of businesses	499	17	221
Sales of property, plant and equipment	126	134	80
Short-term investments, by original maturity			
More than three months-purchases	(2,025)	(525)	(92)
More than three months-maturities	2,008	584	177
Three months or less, net	12	839	(735)
Other, net	(144)	(126)	(96)
Net Cash Used for Investing Activities	(1,072)	(5,019)	(2,070)
Financing Activities			
Proceeds from issuances of long-term debt	3,480	990	
Payments of long-term debt	(1,123)	(2,277)	(1,875)
Short-term borrowings, by original maturity			
More than three months-proceeds	3,691	2,713	146
More than three months-payments	(2,741)	(417)	(177)
Three months or less, net	(2,856)	1,753	(1,269)
Cash dividends paid	(778)	(757)	(736)
Share repurchases	(1,285)	(2,230)	(2,459)
Proceeds from exercises of stock options	308	415	403
Other, net	–	–	5
Net Cash (Used for) Provided by Financing Activities	(1,304)	190	(5,962)
Net Cash Provided by Discontinued Operations	–	–	6,236
Effect of Exchange Rate Changes on Cash and Cash Equivalents	2	1	(2)
Net Increase (Decrease) in Cash and Cash Equivalents	653	(1,617)	1,621
Cash and Cash Equivalents – Beginning of Year	311	1,928	307
Cash and Cash Equivalents – End of Year	$ 964	$ 311	$ 1,928
Supplemental Cash Flow Information			
Interest paid	$ 321	$ 367	$ 462
Income taxes paid	$ 525	$ 521	$ 696
Schedule of Noncash Investing and Financing Activities			
Fair value of assets acquired	$ 717	$ 5,359	$ 160
Cash paid and stock issued	(438)	(4,537)	(134)
Liabilities assumed	$ 279	$ 822	$ 26

This amount appears as first line on the balance sheet

See accompanying Notes to Consolidated Financial Statements.

further by the monthly **bank statement.** Most banks mail their customers a monthly bank statement for each account. The statement provides a detailed list of all activity for a particular account during the month. An example of a typical bank statement is shown in Exhibit 7-2. Note that the bank statement indicates the activity in one of the cash accounts maintained by Weber Products Inc. at the Mt. Etna State Bank.

Before we look at the various items that appear on a bank statement, it is important to understand the route a check takes after it is written. Assume that Weber writes a check on its account at the Mt. Etna State Bank. Weber mails the check to one of its suppliers, Keese Corp., which deposits the check in its account at the Second City Bank. At this point, Second City presents the check to Mt. Etna for payment, and Mt. Etna reduces the balance in Weber's account accordingly. The canceled check has now "cleared" the banking system. Either the canceled check itself or a copy of it is returned with Weber's next bank statement.

The following types of items appear on Weber's bank statement:

> *Canceled checks*—Weber's checks that cleared the bank during the month of June are listed with the corresponding check number and the date paid. Keep in mind that some of these checks may have been written by Weber in a previous month but were not presented for payment to the bank until June. You also should realize

EXHIBIT 7-2 Bank Statement

MT. ETNA STATE BANK
CHICAGO, ILLINOIS
STATEMENT OF ACCOUNT

Weber Products Inc.
502 Dodge St.
Chicago, IL 66606

FOR THE MONTH ENDING   June 30, 2001
ACCOUNT   0371-22-514

DATE	DESCRIPTION	SUBTRACTIONS	ADDITIONS	BALANCE
6-01	Previous balance			3,236.41
6-01	Check 497	723.40		2,513.01
6-02	Check 495	125.60		2,387.41
6-06	Check 491	500.00		1,887.41
6-07	Deposit		1,423.16	3,310.57
6-10	Check 494	185.16		3,125.41
6-13	NSF check	245.72		2,879.69
6-15	Deposit		755.50	3,635.19
6-18	Check 499	623.17		3,012.02
6-20	Check 492	125.00		2,887.02
6-22	Deposit		1,875.62	4,762.64
6-23	Service charge	20.00		4,742.64
6-24	Check 493	875.75		3,866.89
6-24	Check 503	402.10		3,464.79
6-26	Customer note, interest		550.00	4,014.79
6-26	Service fee on note	16.50		3,998.29
6-27	Check 500	1,235.40		2,762.89
6-28	Deposit		947.50	3,710.39
6-30	Check 498	417.25		3,293.14
6-30	Interest earned		15.45	3,308.59
6-30	Statement Totals	5,495.05	5,567.23	

that during June, Weber may have written some checks that do not yet appear on the bank statement because they have not been presented for payment. A check written by a company but not yet presented to the bank for payment is called an **outstanding check.**

Deposits—In keeping with the internal control principle calling for the deposit of all cash receipts intact, most companies deposit all checks, coin, and currency on a daily basis. For the sake of brevity, we have limited to four the number of deposits that Weber made during the month. Keep in mind that Weber also may have made a deposit on the last day or two of the month and that this deposit may not yet be reflected on the bank statement. This type of deposit is called a **deposit in transit.**

NSF check—NSF is an abbreviation for *not sufficient funds*. The NSF check listed on the bank statement on June 13 is a customer's check that Weber recorded on its books, deposited, and thus included in its cash account. When Mt. Etna State Bank learned that the check was not good because the customer did not have sufficient funds on hand in its bank account to cover the check, the bank deducted the amount from Weber's account. Weber needs to contact its customer to collect the amount due; ideally, the customer will issue a new check once it has sufficient funds in its account.

Service charge—Banks charge for various services they provide to customers. Among the most common bank service charges are monthly activity fees and fees charged for new checks, for the rental of a lockbox at the bank in which to store valuable company documents, and for the collection of customer notes by the bank.

Customer note and interest—It is often convenient to have customers pay amounts owed to a company directly to that company's bank. The bank simply acts as a collection agency for the company.

Interest earned—Most checking accounts pay interest on the average daily balance in the account. Rates paid on checking accounts are usually significantly less than could be earned on most other forms of investment.

THE BANK RECONCILIATION

A **bank reconciliation** should be prepared for each individual bank account as soon as the bank statement is received. Ideally, the reconciliation should be performed or, at a minimum, thoroughly reviewed by someone independent of custody, record-keeping, and authorization responsibilities relating to cash. As the name implies, the purpose of a bank reconciliation is to *reconcile* the balance that the bank shows for an account with the balance that appears on the company's books. Differences between the two amounts are investigated, and if necessary, adjustments are made. The following are the steps in preparing a bank reconciliation:

1. Trace deposits listed on the bank statement to the books. Any deposits recorded on the books but not yet shown on the bank statement are deposits in transit. Prepare a list of the deposits in transit.

2. Arrange the canceled checks in numerical order, and trace each of them to the books. Any checks recorded on the books but not yet listed on the bank statement are outstanding. List the outstanding checks.

3. List all items, other than deposits, shown as additions on the bank statement, such as interest paid by the bank for the month and amounts collected by the bank from one of the company's customers. When the bank pays interest or collects an amount owed to a company by one of the company's customers, the bank increases or *credits* its liability to the company on its own books. For this reason, these items are called **credit memoranda.**

4. List all amounts, other than canceled checks, shown as subtractions on the bank statement, such as any NSF checks and the various service charges mentioned earlier. When a company deposits money in a bank, a liability is created on the books of the bank. Therefore, when the bank reduces the amount of its liability for these various

items, it *debits* the liability on its own books. For this reason, these items are called **debit memoranda.**

5. Identify any errors made by the bank or by the company in recording the various cash transactions.

6. Use the information collected in steps 1 through 5 to prepare a bank reconciliation.

Companies use a number of different *formats* in preparing bank reconciliations. For example, some companies take the balance shown on the bank statement and reconcile this amount to the balance shown on the books. Another approach, which we will illustrate for Weber Products, involves reconciling the bank balance and the book balance to an adjusted balance, rather than one to the other. As we will see, the advantage of this approach is that it yields the correct balance and makes it easy for the company to make any necessary adjustments to its books. A bank reconciliation for Weber Products is shown in Exhibit 7-3. The following are explanations for the various items on the reconciliation:

1. The balance per bank statement of $3,308.59 is taken from the June statement as shown in Exhibit 7-2.

2. Weber's records showed a deposit for $642.30 made on June 30 that is not reflected on the bank statement. The deposit in transit is listed as an addition to the bank statement balance.

3. The accounting records indicate three checks written but not yet reflected on the bank statement. The three outstanding checks are as follows:

   496   $ 79.89
   501   $213.20
   502   $424.75

   Outstanding checks are the opposite of deposits in transit and therefore are deducted from the bank statement balance.

Study Tip

Review your own bank statement to see the similarities and differences between it and the one illustrated here. Also, look on the reverse of your statement for the form of a reconciliation the bank provides. It may or may not be the same format as illustrated in Exhibit 7-3.

EXHIBIT 7-3   Bank Reconciliation

WEBER PRODUCTS
BANK RECONCILIATION
JUNE 30, 2001

Balance per bank statement, June 30			$3,308.59
Add:	Deposit in transit		642.30
Deduct:	Outstanding checks:		
	No. 496	$ 79.89	
	No. 501	213.20	
	No. 502	424.75	(717.84)
Adjusted balance, June 30			$3,233.05
Balance per books, June 30			$2,895.82
Add:	Customer note collected	$500.00	
	Interest on customer note	50.00	
	Interest earned during June	15.45	
	Error in recording check 498	54.00	619.45
Deduct:	NSF check	$245.72	
	Collection fee on note	16.50	
	Service charge for lockbox	20.00	(282.22)
Adjusted balance, June 30			$3,233.05

4. The adjusted balance of $3,233.05 is found by adding the deposit in transit and deducting the outstanding checks from the bank statement balance.

5. The $2,895.82 book balance on June 30 is taken from the company's records as of that date.

6. According to the bank statement, $550 was added to the account on June 26 for the collection of a note with interest. We assume that the repayment of the note itself accounted for $500 of this amount and that the other $50 was for interest. The bank statement notifies Weber that the note with interest has been collected. Therefore, Weber must add $550 to the book balance.

7. An entry on June 30 on the bank statement shows an increase of $15.45 for interest earned on the bank account during June. This amount is added to the book balance.

8. A review of the canceled checks returned with the bank statement detected an error made by Weber. The company records indicated that check 498 was recorded incorrectly as $471.25; the check was actually written for $417.25 and reflected as such on the bank statement. This error, referred to as a *transposition error,* resulted from transposing the 7 and the 1 in recording the check in the books. The error is the difference between the amount of $471.25 recorded and the amount of $417.25 that should have been recorded, or $54.00. Because Weber recorded the cash payment at too large an amount, $54.00 must be added back to the book balance.

9. In addition to canceled checks, three other deductions appear on the bank statement. Each of these must be deducted from the book balance:

   a. A customer's NSF check for $245.72 (see June 13 entry on bank statement)

   b. A $16.50 fee charged by the bank to collect the customer's note discussed in item 6 (see June 26 entry on bank statement)

   c. A service fee of $20.00 charged by the bank for rental of a lockbox (see June 23 entry on bank statement)

10. The additions of $619.45 and deductions of $282.22 resulted in an adjusted cash balance of $3,233.05. Note that this adjusted balance agrees with the adjusted bank statement balance on the bank reconciliation (see item 4). Thus, all differences between the two balances have been explained.

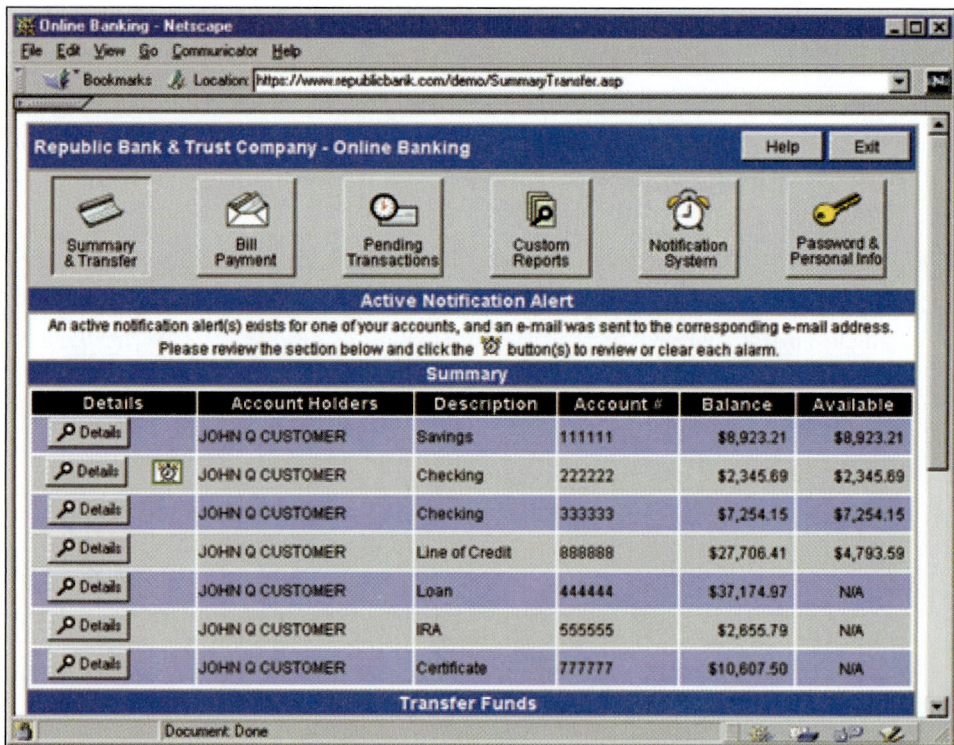

With the popularity of online banking, customers can now access all the account information they need to pay bills and keep their accounts in balance. Some banks offer software that allows the user to pay bills electronically and reconcile their accounts as often as they wish—not once a month as with mailed statements.

THE BANK RECONCILIATION AND THE NEED FOR ADJUSTMENTS TO THE RECORDS

After it completes the bank reconciliation, Weber must prepare a number of adjustments to its records. In fact, all the information for these adjustments will be from one section of the bank reconciliation. Do you think that the additions and deductions made to the bank balance or the ones made to the book balance are the basis for the adjustments? It is logical that the additions and deductions to the Cash account *on the books* should be the basis for the adjustments because these are items that Weber was unaware of before receiving the bank statement. Conversely, the additions and deductions to the bank's balance—that is, the deposits in transit and the outstanding checks, are items that Weber has already recorded on its books.

ESTABLISHING A PETTY CASH FUND

Recall one of the fundamental rules in controlling cash: all disbursements should be made by check. Most businesses make an exception to this rule in the case of minor expenditures, for which they use a **petty cash fund.** This fund consists of coin and currency kept on hand to make minor disbursements. The necessary steps in setting up and maintaining a petty cash fund follow:

1. A check is written for a lump-sum amount, such as $100 or $500. The check is cashed, and the coin and currency are entrusted to a petty cash custodian.
2. A journal entry is made to record the establishment of the fund.
3. Upon presentation of the necessary documentation, employees receive minor disbursements from the fund. In essence, cash is traded from the fund in exchange for a receipt.
4. Periodically, the fund is replenished by writing and cashing a check in the amount necessary to bring the fund back to its original balance.
5. At the time the fund is replenished, an adjustment is made both to record its replenishment and to recognize the various expenses incurred.

The use of this fund is normally warranted on the basis of cost versus benefits. That is, the benefits in time saved in making minor disbursements from cash are thought to outweigh the cost associated with the risk of loss from decreased control over cash disbursements. The fund also serves a practical purpose for certain expenditures, such as taxi fares and messengers, that often must be paid in cash.

ACCOUNTING FOR YOUR DECISIONS

You Are the Sorority Treasurer

You are in charge of the sorority's checking account and bank reconciliation. Each month, you are responsible for purchasing supplies, paying for parties, and paying rent and utilities on the sorority house. You also have a card for an automatic teller machine, which you use to draw out cash to pay for miscellaneous activities. Recently, the president of the sorority asked to see you because the sorority's expenses were exceeding revenues by a significant margin. After examining the checkbook and bank reconciliation, she wanted to know why you were spending roughly $200 per month in cash from an ATM. You told her that since there was no cancelled check for these expenditures, you had no record and couldn't answer her question. How could you have avoided this situation?

ANS: First, an important principle of internal control is that the person writing checks on an account should not be the same person who performs the bank reconciliation. Second, an ATM card confers special responsibilities on the user. Because there is no cancelled check, the person receiving cash from an ATM must document all expenses, obtaining receipts whenever possible or documenting the expenditures in a diary.

ACCOUNTING FOR INVESTMENTS

LO 3 Understand the accounting for various types of investments companies make.

The investments that companies make take a variety of forms and are made for various reasons. Some corporations find themselves with excess cash during certain times of the year and invest this idle cash in various highly liquid financial instruments, such as certificates of deposit and money market funds. Earlier in the chapter it was pointed out that these investments are included with cash and are called cash equivalents if they have an original maturity to the investor of three months or less. Otherwise they are accounted for as short-term investments.

In addition to investments in highly liquid financial instruments, some companies invest in the stocks and bonds of other corporations, as well as bonds issued by various government agencies. Securities issued by corporations as a form of ownership in the business, such as common stock and preferred stock, are called **equity securities.** Because these securities are a form of ownership, they do not have a maturity date. As we will see later, investments in equity securities can be classified as either current or long term, depending on the company's intent. Alternatively, bonds issued by corporations and governmental bodies as a form of borrowing are called **debt securities.** The term of a bond can be relatively short, such as 5 years, or much longer, such as 20 or 30 years. Regardless of the term, classification as a current or noncurrent asset by the investor depends on whether it plans to sell the debt securities within the next year.

INVESTMENTS IN HIGHLY LIQUID FINANCIAL INSTRUMENTS

We now turn our attention to the appropriate accounting for these various types of investments. We begin by considering the accounting for highly liquid financial instruments, such as certificates of deposit, and then turn to the accounting for investments in the stocks and bonds of other companies.

INVESTING IDLE CASH

The seasonal nature of most businesses leads to the potential for a shortage of cash during certain times of the year and an excess of cash during other times. Companies typically deal with _cash shortages_ by borrowing on a short-term basis, either from a bank in the form of notes or from other entities in the form of commercial paper. The maturities of the bank notes or the commercial paper generally range anywhere from 30 days to six months. These same companies use various financial instruments as a way to invest excess cash during other times of the year. We will present the accounting for the most common type of highly liquid financial instrument, a certificate of deposit.

ACCOUNTING FOR AN INVESTMENT IN A CERTIFICATE OF DEPOSIT (CD)

Assume that on October 2, 2001, Creston Corp. invests $100,000 of excess cash in a 120-day certificate of deposit. The CD matures on January 30, 2002, at which time Creston receives the $100,000 invested and interest at an annual rate of 6%. On October 2, 2001, the company has simply traded one asset for another:

BALANCE SHEET					INCOME STATEMENT
ASSETS	=	LIABILITIES	+	OWNERS' EQUITY	+	REVENUES – EXPENSES
Short-Term					
Investments—CD 100,000					
Cash (100,000)					

Assuming December 31 is the end of Creston's fiscal year, an adjustment is needed on this date to record interest earned during 2001, even though no cash will be received until the CD matures in 2002. The adjustment recognizes a new asset as well as an addition on the income statement:

BALANCE SHEET					INCOME STATEMENT
ASSETS	=	LIABILITIES	+	OWNERS' EQUITY	+	REVENUES – EXPENSES
Interest Receivable 1,500					Interest Income 1,500

The basic formula to compute interest is as follows:

$$\text{Interest } (I) = \text{Principal } (P) \times \text{Interest Rate } (R) \times \text{Time } (T)$$

Because interest rates are normally stated on an annual basis, time is interpreted to mean the fraction of a year that the investment is outstanding. The amount of interest is based on the principal or amount invested ($100,000), times the rate of interest (6%), times the fraction of a year the CD was outstanding in 2001 (29 days in October + 30 days in November + 31 days in December = 90 days). To simplify calculations, it is easiest to assume 360 days in a year in computing interest. With the availability of computers to do the work, however, most businesses now use 365 days in a year to calculate interest. Throughout this book, we assume 360 days in a year to allow us to focus on concepts rather than detailed calculations. Thus, in our example, the fraction of a year that the CD is outstanding during 2001 is 90/360 and the amount of interest earned in 2001 is: $100,000 × .06 × 90/360 or $1,500.

The effect of the receipt of the principal amount of the CD of $100,000 and interest for 120 days on January 30 is

BALANCE SHEET						INCOME STATEMENT
ASSETS	=	LIABILITIES	+	OWNERS' EQUITY	+	REVENUES – EXPENSES
Cash	102,000					Interest Income	500
Short-Term						
Investments—CD	(100,000)					
Interest Receivable	(1,500)					

This transaction results in the removal of both the CD and interest receivable from the records and the recognition of $500 in interest earned during the first 30 days of 2002: $100,000 \times .06 \times 30/360 = \$500$.

We now turn our attention to situations in which companies invest in the stocks and bonds of other companies.

INVESTMENTS IN STOCKS AND BONDS

Corporations frequently invest in the securities of other businesses. These investments take two forms: debt securities and equity securities.

Corporations have varying motivations for investing in the stocks and bonds of other companies. We will refer to the company that invests as the *investor* and the company whose stocks or bonds are purchased as the *investee*. In addition to buying certificates of deposit and other financial instruments, companies invest excess funds in stocks and bonds over the short run. The seasonality of certain businesses may result in otherwise idle cash being available during certain times of the year. In other cases, stocks and bonds are purchased as a way to invest cash over the long run. Often, these types of investments are made in anticipation of a need for cash at some distant point in the future. For example, a company may invest today in a combination of stocks and bonds because it will need cash 10 years from today to build a new plant. The investor may be primarily interested in periodic income in the form of interest and dividends, in appreciation in the value of the securities, or in some combination of the two.

Sometimes, shares of stock in another company are bought with a different purpose in mind. If a company buys a relatively large percentage of the common stock of the investee, it may be able to secure significant influence over the policies of this company. For example, a company may buy 30% of the common stock of a supplier of its raw materials to ensure a steady source of inventory. When an investor is able to secure influence over the investee, the *equity method* of accounting is used. According to current accounting standards, this method is appropriate when an investor owns at least 20% of the common stock of the investee.

Finally, a corporation may buy stock in another company with the purpose of obtaining control over that other entity. Normally, this requires an investment in excess of 50% of the common stock of the investee. When an investor owns more than half the stock of another company, accountants normally prepare a set of *consolidated financial statements*. This involves combining the financial statements of the individual entities into a single set of statements. An investor with an interest of more than 50% in another company is called the *parent,* and the investee in these situations is called the *subsidiary.*

We will limit our discussion to how companies account for investments that do *not* give them any significant influence over the other company. (Accounting for investments in which there is either significant influence or control is covered in advanced accounting textbooks.) The following chart summarizes the accounting by an investor for investments in the common stock of another company:

Investor's Percentage Ownership in the Common Stock of Another Company

Fair Value Method | Equity Method | Consolidated Financial Statements

0% — 20% — 50% — 100%

| No Significant Influence | Significant Influence | Control |

We focus on this level of investment

INVESTMENTS WITHOUT SIGNIFICANT INFLUENCE

Companies face a number of major issues in deciding how to account for and report on investments in the stocks and bonds of other companies:

1. What should be the basis for the recognition of periodic income from an investment? That is, what event causes income to be recognized?

2. How should an investment be valued and thus reported at the end of an accounting period? At original cost? At fair value?

3. How should an investment be classified on a balance sheet? As a current asset? As a noncurrent asset?

The answer to each of these questions depends on the type of investment. Accountants classify investments in the securities of other companies into one of three categories.[1]

> **Held-to-maturity securities** are investments in the bonds of other companies when the investor has the positive intent and the ability to hold the securities to maturity. *Note that only bonds can qualify as held-to-maturity securities because shares of stock do not have a maturity date.*

securities = bonds & stocks

> **Trading securities** are stocks and bonds that are bought and held for the purpose of selling them in the near term. These securities are usually held for only a short period of time with the objective of generating profits on short-term appreciation in the market price of the stocks and bonds.

> **Available-for-sale securities** are stocks and bonds that are not classified as either held-to-maturity or trading securities.

INVESTMENTS IN HELD-TO-MATURITY SECURITIES

By their nature, only bonds, not stock, can qualify as held-to-maturity securities. A bond is categorized as a held-to-maturity security if the investor plans to hold it until it matures. An investor may buy the bonds either on the original issuance date or later. If the investor buys them on the date they are originally issued, the purchase is from the issuer. It is also possible, however, for an investor to buy bonds on the *open market* after they have been outstanding for a period of time.

---

[1]*Statement of Financial Accounting Standards No. 115,* "Accounting for Certain Investments in Debt and Equity Securities" (Stamford, Conn.: Financial Accounting Standards Board, May 1993), par. 7–12.

Consider the following example. On January 1, 2001, Simpson issues $10,000,000 of bonds that will mature in ten years. Homer buys $100,000 in face value of these bonds at face value, which is the amount that will be repaid to the investor when the bonds mature. In many instances, bonds are purchased at an amount more or less than face value. We will limit our discussion, however, to the simpler case in which bonds are purchased for face value. The bonds pay 10% interest semiannually on June 30 and December 31. This means Homer will receive 5% of $100,000 or $5,000 on each of these dates. The effect of the purchase on the accounting equation is as follows:

		BALANCE SHEET				INCOME STATEMENT	
ASSETS	**=**	**LIABILITIES**	**+**	**OWNERS' EQUITY**	**+**	**REVENUES – EXPENSES**	
Investment in Bonds	100,000						
Cash	(100,000)						

On June 30, Homer must record the receipt of semiannual interest. The effect of the receipt of interest on this date would be:

		BALANCE SHEET				INCOME STATEMENT	
ASSETS	**=**	**LIABILITIES**	**+**	**OWNERS' EQUITY**	**+**	**REVENUES – EXPENSES**	
Cash	5,000					Interest Income	5,000

Note that income was recognized when interest was received. If interest is not received at the end of an accounting period, a company should accrue interest earned but not yet received. Also note that an investment in held-to-maturity bonds is normally classified as a *noncurrent asset.* Any held-to-maturity bonds that are one year or less from maturity, however, are classified in the current assets section of a balance sheet.

Assume that before the maturity date, Homer needs cash and decides to sell the bonds. Keep in mind that this is a definite change in Homer's plans, since the bonds were initially categorized as held-to-maturity securities. Any difference between the proceeds received from the sale of the bonds and the amount paid for the bonds is recognized as either a gain or a loss.

Assume that on January 1, 2002, Homer sells all its Simpson bonds at 99. This means that the amount of cash received is .99 × $100,000, or $99,000. The effect on the accounting equation from the sale of the bonds is

		BALANCE SHEET				INCOME STATEMENT	
ASSETS	**=**	**LIABILITIES**	**+**	**OWNERS' EQUITY**	**+**	**REVENUES – EXPENSES**	
Cash	99,000					Loss on Sale of Bonds	(1,000)
Investment in Bonds	(100,000)						

The $1,000 loss on the sale of the bonds is the excess of the amount paid for the purchase of the bonds of $100,000 over the cash proceeds from the sale of $99,000. The loss is reported in the other income and expenses section on the 2002 income statement.

INVESTMENTS IN TRADING SECURITIES

A company invests in trading securities as a way to profit from increases in the market prices of these securities over the short term. Because the intent is to hold them for the short term, trading securities are classified as current assets. All trading securities are recorded initially at cost, including any brokerage fees, commissions, or other fees paid to acquire the securities. Trading securities could be either stock or bonds. We will illustrate the concepts using stock. Assume that Dexter Corp. invests in the following securities on November 30, 2001:

Security	Cost
Stuart common stock	$50,000
Menlo preferred stock	25,000
Total cost	$75,000

When Dexter buys the stocks, investments are increased and cash is reduced:

BALANCE SHEET						INCOME STATEMENT	
ASSETS	**=**	**LIABILITIES**	**+**	**OWNERS' EQUITY**	**+**	**REVENUES – EXPENSES**	
Investment in Stuart							
Common Stock	50,000						
Investment in Menlo							
Preferred Stock	25,000						
Cash	(75,000)						

Many companies attempt to pay dividends every year as a signal of overall financial strength and profitability.[2] Assume that on December 10, 2001, Dexter received dividends of $1,000 from Stuart and $600 from Menlo. The dividends received from trading securities are recognized as income, as shown in the accounting equation:

BALANCE SHEET						INCOME STATEMENT	
ASSETS	**=**	**LIABILITIES**	**+**	**OWNERS' EQUITY**	**+**	**REVENUES – EXPENSES**	
Cash	1,600					Dividend Income	1,600

Unlike interest on a bond or a note, dividends do not accrue over time. In fact, a company does not have a legal obligation to pay dividends until its board of directors declares them. Up to that point, the investor has no guarantee that dividends will ever be paid.

As noted earlier, trading securities are purchased with the intention of holding them for a short period of time. Assume that Dexter sells the Stuart stock on December 15, 2001, for $53,000. In this case, Dexter recognizes a gain for the excess of the cash proceeds, $53,000, over the amount recorded on the books, $50,000:

BALANCE SHEET						INCOME STATEMENT	
ASSETS	**=**	**LIABILITIES**	**+**	**OWNERS' EQUITY**	**+**	**REVENUES – EXPENSES**	
Cash	53,000					Gain on Sale of Stock	3,000
Investment in Stuart							
Common Stock	(50,000)						

For accounting purposes, the gain is considered realized and is classified on the income statement as other income.

Assume that on December 22, 2001, Dexter replaces the Stuart stock in its portfolio by purchasing Canby common stock for $40,000:

BALANCE SHEET						INCOME STATEMENT	
ASSETS	**=**	**LIABILITIES**	**+**	**OWNERS' EQUITY**	**+**	**REVENUES – EXPENSES**	
Investment in Canby							
Common Stock	40,000						
Cash	(40,000)						

---

[2]IBM's March 2000 dividend was the computer company's 340th consecutive quarterly dividend, an uninterrupted string of 85 years in which it paid dividends.

Now, assume that Dexter ends its accounting period on December 31. Should it adjust the carrying value of its investments to reflect their fair values on this date? According to the accounting profession, fair values should be used to report investments in trading securities on a balance sheet. The fair values are thought to be relevant information to the various users of financial statements. Assume the following information for Dexter on December 31, 2001:

Security	Total Cost	Total Fair Value on December 31, 2001	Gain (Loss)
Menlo preferred stock	$25,000	$27,500	$2,500
Canby common stock	40,000	39,000	(1,000)
Totals	$65,000	$66,500	$1,500

On December 31, Dexter will make an adjustment in its records that has the following effect on the accounting equation:

BALANCE SHEET						INCOME STATEMENT
ASSETS	=	LIABILITIES	+	OWNERS' EQUITY	+	REVENUES – EXPENSES
Investment in Menlo Preferred Stock 2,500						Unrealized Gain—Trading Securites 1,500
Investment in Canby Common Stock (1,000)						

Note that this adjustment results in each security being written up or down so that it will appear on the December 31 balance sheet at its market or fair value. This type of fair value accounting for trading securities is often referred to as a *mark to market* approach because at the end of each period, the value of each security is adjusted to its current market value. Also, it is important to realize that for trading securities, the changes in value are recognized on the income statement. The difference of $1,500 between the original cost of the two securities, $65,000, and their fair value, $66,500, is recorded in the account Unrealized Gain—Trading Securities to call attention to the fact that the securities have not been sold. Even though the gain or loss is *unrealized,* it is recognized on the income statement as a form of other income or loss.

Assume one final transaction in our Dexter example. On January 20, 2002, Dexter sells the Menlo stock for $27,000. The effect on the accounting equation of the sale is as follows:

BALANCE SHEET						INCOME STATEMENT
ASSETS	=	LIABILITIES	+	OWNERS' EQUITY	+	REVENUES – EXPENSES
Cash 27,000						Loss on Sale of Stock (500)
Investment in Menlo Preferred Stock (27,500)						

The important point to note about this entry is that the $500 loss represents the difference between the cash proceeds of $27,000 and the *fair value of the stock at the most recent reporting date,* $27,500. Because the Menlo stock was adjusted to a fair value of $27,500 on December 31, the excess of this amount over the cash proceeds of $27,000 results in a loss of $500. Keep in mind that a gain of $2,500 was recognized last year when the stock was adjusted to its fair value at the end of the year. Thus, the *net* gain from the Menlo stock is the excess of the sales price of $27,000 over the cost of $25,000, or $2,000. The result is that this net amount is recognized in two periods: as a $2,500 holding gain in 2001 and a $500 loss on sale in 2002.

INVESTMENTS IN AVAILABLE-FOR-SALE SECURITIES

Stocks and bonds that do not qualify as trading securities and bonds that are not intended to be held to maturity are categorized as available-for-sale securities. If an available-for-sale security is to be sold within the next year, it should be classified as a current asset. Otherwise, these securities are classified as long-term assets. The accounting for these securities is similar to the accounting for trading securities, with one major exception: *even though fair value accounting is used to report available-for-sale securities at the end of an accounting period, any gains or losses resulting from marking to market are not reported on the income statement but instead are accumulated in a stockholders' equity account.* This inconsistency is justified by the accounting profession on the grounds that the inclusion in income of fluctuations in the value of securities that are available for sale but that are not necessarily being actively traded could lead to volatility in reported earnings. Regardless, reporting gains and losses on the income statement for one class of securities but not for others is a subject of considerable debate.

To understand the use of fair value accounting for available-for-sale securities, assume that Lenox Corp. purchases two different stocks late in 2001. The costs and fair values at the end of 2001 are as follows:

Security	Total Cost	Fair Value on December 31, 2001	Gain (Loss)
Adair preferred stock	$15,000	$16,000	$ 1,000
Casey common stock	35,000	32,500	(2,500)
Totals	$50,000	$48,500	$(1,500)

On December 31, Lenox adjusts it records to reflect the changes in value of the two securities:

		BALANCE SHEET					INCOME STATEMENT
ASSETS	**=**	**LIABILITIES**	**+**	**OWNERS' EQUITY**	**+**	**REVENUES – EXPENSES**	
Investment in Adair				Unrealized Gain/Loss—			
Preferred stock 1,000				Available-for-Sale			
Investment in Casey				Securities (1,500)			
Common Stock (2,500)							

Note the similarity between this adjustment and the one we made at the end of the period in the example for trading securities. In both instances, the individual investments are adjusted to their fair values for purposes of presenting them on the year-end balance sheet. The unrealized loss of $1,500 does not, however, affect income in this case. Instead, the loss is shown as a reduction of stockholders' equity on the balance sheet.

Now assume that Lenox sells its Casey stock for $34,500 on June 30, 2002. The effect of the sale on the accounting equation is as follows:

		BALANCE SHEET				INCOME STATEMENT	
ASSETS	**=**	**LIABILITIES**	**+**	**OWNERS' EQUITY**	**+**	**REVENUES – EXPENSES**	
Cash 34,500				Unrealized Gain/Loss—		Loss on Sale of Stock	(500)
Investment in Casey				Available-for-Sale			
Common Stock (32,500)				Securities 2,500			

Lenox recognizes a *realized* loss of $500, which represents the excess of the cost of the stock of $35,000 over the cash proceeds of $34,500. Note, however, that the Investment in Casey Common Stock is removed from the books at $32,500, the fair value at the end of the prior period. Thus, it is also necessary to adjust the Unrealized Gain/Loss account for the difference between the original cost of $35,000 and the fair value at the end of 2001 of $32,500.

Finally, assume that Lenox does not buy any additional securities during the remainder of 2002 and that the fair value of the one investment it holds, the Adair preferred stock, is $19,000 on December 31, 2002. The adjustment on this date is as follows:

BALANCE SHEET						INCOME STATEMENT
ASSETS	=	LIABILITIES	+	OWNERS' EQUITY	+	REVENUES − EXPENSES
Investment in Adair Preferred Stock 3,000				Unrealized Gain/Loss— Available-for-Sale Securities 3,000		

From Concept

TO PRACTICE 7.1

READING GATEWAY'S FOOTNOTES

According to Footnote 1D in Gateway's 1999 annual report, how are its investments classified? In what types of securities does the company invest?

The increase in the Investment in Adair Preferred Stock account results in a balance of $19,000 in this account, the fair value of the stock. The stockholders' equity account now has a *positive* balance of $4,000 as follows:

Adjustment on December 31, 2001	$(1,500)
Adjustment on June 30, 2002	2,500
Adjustment on December 31, 2002	3,000
Balance on December 31, 2002	4,000

The balance of $4,000 in this account represents the excess of the $19,000 fair value of the one security now held over its original cost of $15,000.

SUMMARY OF ACCOUNTING AND REPORTING REQUIREMENTS

A summary of the accounting and reporting requirements for each of the three categories of investments is shown in Exhibit 7-4. Periodic income from each of these types of investments is recognized in the form of interest and dividends. Held-to-maturity bonds are reported on the balance sheet at *amortized cost* (see second footnote in Exhibit 7-4). Both trading securities and available-for-sale securities are reported on the balance sheet at fair value. Unrealized gains and losses from holding trading securities are recognized on the income statement, whereas these same gains and losses for available-for-sale securities are accumulated in a stockholders' equity account.

THE CONTROVERSY OVER FAIR VALUE ACCOUNTING

Only recently have accounting standards changed to require that certain investments be reported at fair value. Before the change, the lower-of-cost-or-market rule was followed when accounting for these investments. The use of market or fair values is clearly an exception to the cost principle as first introduced in Chapter 1. Whether the exception is justified has been, and will continue to be, a matter of debate.

EXHIBIT 7-4 Accounting for Investments without Significant Influence

Categories	Types	Asset Classified on Balance Sheet as	Recognize as Income	Report on Balance Sheet at	Report Changes in Fair Value on
Held-to-maturity	Bonds	Noncurrent*	Interest	Cost†	Not applicable
Trading	Bonds, stock	Current	Interest, dividends	Fair value	Income statement
Available-for-sale	Bonds, stock	Current or noncurrent	Interest, dividends	Fair value	Balance sheet (in stockholders' equity)

*Reclassified as current if they mature within one year of the balance sheet date.

†As mentioned earlier, bonds are often purchased at an amount more or less than face value. When this is the case, the bond account must be adjusted periodically and the asset is reported on the balance sheet at amortized cost.

A big change took place in Pepsi-Cola's market in 1998: its biggest customers, grocery store chains, began to merge at an increasing rate. The result was fewer, bigger chains of retail grocers spread out over much larger geographic regions than a few years earlier. Parent company PepsiCo believed the change would fundamentally alter Pepsi-Cola's bottling business, making size the most important factor in achieving both economies of scale (decreases in cost that result from high volumes of production) and the high level of service that the new chains demanded.

So, the company set out to restructure its bottling business, consolidating volume among a few large "anchor bottlers" that are closely aligned with PepsiCo and that focus solely on manufacturing, selling, and distributing. For its company-owned bottling operations, it also created a separate new Pepsi Bottling Group (PBG), which quickly grew into the world's largest seller, manufacturer, and distributor of Pepsi-Cola beverages, with operations in the United States, Canada, Greece, Spain, and Russia. PBG now accounts for about one-third of the company's beverages sold worldwide.

If PepsiCo's best customers, the retail grocery chains, believe that bigger is better, the company wants them to know it thinks so too.

SOURCES: PepsiCo's 1998 annual report; "Pepsi Bottling Creates Pres/COO Post, Names CFO," Reuters Company News Aug. 9, 2000, accessed at http://www.hoovershbn.hoovers.com/bin/story?StoryId= Cozdxqb9DtJa5mJC4ndCX&Print=1&FQ=c%25PBG=&Title=Headlines=for:=PBG=Nav=&StartDate=now.

One concern of financial statement users is the hybrid system now used to report assets on a balance sheet. Consider the following types of assets and how we report them on the balance sheet:

Asset	Reported on the Balance Sheet at
Inventories	Lower of cost or market
Investments	Either cost or fair value
Property, plant, and equipment	Original cost, less accumulated depreciation

It is difficult to justify so many different valuation methods to report the assets of a single company. Recall that the lower-of-cost-or-market approach to valuing inventory is based on conservatism. Why should it be used for inventories while fair value is used for investments? Proponents of fair values believe that the information provided to the reader of the statements is more relevant, and they argue that the subjectivity inherent in valuing other types of assets is not an issue when dealing with securities that have a ready market. The controversy surrounding the valuation of assets on a balance sheet is likely to continue.

Two-Minute Review

1. What are the three categories of investments?

2. Two of the three categories of investments can contain either stocks or bonds. Which one of the three can only contain bonds? Explain your answer.

3. What is the one major distinction between the reporting requirements for trading securities and those for available-for-sale securities?

Answers:

1. Held-to-maturity, trading, and available-for-sale.

2. Bonds are the only securities that can be held to maturity. Stocks do not have a maturity date.

3. Any changes in fair value of trading securities are reported on the income statement. Changes in fair value of available-for-sale securities are reported in stockholders' equity on the balance sheet.

LO 4 Understand how to account for accounts receivable, including bad debts.

www.sears.com

To appreciate the significance of credit sales for many businesses, consider the case of Sears, Roebuck & Co. Sears operates retail outlets throughout the United States and around the world. The balance sheet of Sears reported total assets of approximately $37 billion at the end of 1999. Of this total amount, credit card receivables accounted for over $18 billion, or almost one-half of total assets. Sears or any other company would rather not sell on credit but would prefer to make all sales for cash. Selling on credit causes two problems: it slows down the inflow of cash to the company, and it raises the possibility that the customer may not pay its bill on time or possibly ever. To remain competitive, however, Sears and most other businesses must sell their products and services on credit. Large retailers such as Sears often extend credit through the use of their own credit cards.

www.pepsico.com

The types of receivables reported on a corporate balance sheet depend to some extent on a company's business. The "credit card receivables" on the balance sheet of Sears represent the interest-bearing accounts it carries with its retail customers. Alternatively, consider the case of PepsiCo. The beverage and snack-food businesses usually sell their products to distributors. The asset resulting from a sale by Pepsi on credit, with an oral promise that the customer will pay within a specified period of time, is called an account receivable. This type of account does not bear interest and often gives the customer a discount for early payment. For example, the terms of sale might be 2/10, net 30, which means the customer can deduct 2% from the amount due if the bill is paid within 10 days of the date of sale; otherwise, payment in full is required within 30 days. In some instances, PepsiCo requires from a customer at the time of sale a written promise in the form of a promissory note. The asset resulting from a sale on credit, with a written promise that the customer will pay within a specified period of time, is called a note receivable. This type of account usually bears interest.

THE USE OF A SUBSIDIARY LEDGER

As mentioned earlier, PepsiCo sells its beverages and snack foods through distributors. Assume that it sells $25,000 of Fritos to ABC Distributors on an open account. The sale results in the recognition of an asset and additional revenue:

BALANCE SHEET				INCOME STATEMENT
ASSETS	=	LIABILITIES	+ OWNERS' EQUITY	+ REVENUES – EXPENSES
Accounts Receivable 25,000				Sales Revenue 25,000

Delivering such products as Pepsi's Frappuccino drink to retail stores on account creates large receivables for PepsiCo. Indeed, receivables are a large and important part of the asset side of balance sheets of many companies.

It is important for control purposes that PepsiCo keeps a record of *whom* the sale was to and includes this amount on a periodic statement or *bill* sent to the customer. What if a company has a hundred or a thousand different customers? Some mechanism is needed to track the balance owed by each of these customers. The mechanism companies use is called a **subsidiary ledger.**

A subsidiary ledger contains the necessary detail on each of a number of items that collectively make up a single general ledger account, called the **control account.** In theory, any one of the accounts in the general ledger could be supported by a subsidiary ledger. In addition to Accounts Receivable, two other common accounts supported by subsidiary ledgers are Plant and Equipment and Accounts Payable. An accounts payable subsidiary ledger contains a separate account for each of the suppliers or vendors from which a company purchases inventory. A plant and equipment subsidiary ledger consists of individual accounts, along with their balances, for each of the various long-term tangible assets the company owns.

It is important to understand that a subsidiary ledger does *not* take the place of the control account in the general ledger. Instead, at any point in time, the balances of the accounts that make up the subsidiary ledger should total to the single balance in the related control account. In the remainder of this chapter we will illustrate the use of only the control account. Whenever a specific customer's account is increased or decreased we will, however, note the name of the customer next to the control account in the accounting equation.

THE VALUATION OF ACCOUNTS RECEIVABLE

The following presentation of accounts receivable is taken from footnote 9 in Gateway's 1999 annual report:

December 31 (in thousands)	1998	1999	
Accounts receivable, net:			
Accounts receivable	$573,799	$662,811	← *gross amount*
Allowance for uncollectible accounts	(14,948)	(16,472)	← *write off losses*
	$558,851	$646,339	← *net recoverable amount*

Gateway does not sell its products to customers under the assumption that any particular company will *not* pay its bill. In fact, the credit department of a business is responsible for performing a credit check on all potential customers before they are granted credit. Management of Gateway is not naive enough, however, to believe that all customers will be able to pay their accounts when due. This would be the case only if (1) all customers are completely trustworthy and (2) customers never experience unforeseen financial difficulties that make it impossible to pay on time.

The reduction in Gateway's accounts receivable for an allowance is the way in which most companies deal with bad debts in their accounting records. Bad debts are unpaid customer accounts that a company gives up trying to collect. Some companies describe the allowance more fully as the allowance for doubtful accounts, and others, such as Gateway, call it the allowance for uncollectible accounts. Using the end of 1999 as an example, Gateway believes that the *net recoverable amount* of its receivables is $646,339 thousand, even though the *gross* amount of receivables is $662,811 thousand. The company has reduced the gross receivables for an amount that it believes is necessary to reflect the asset on the books at the *net recoverable amount* or *net realizable value* (you may want to verify that $646,339 is in fact the amount that appears on Gateway's balance sheet at December 31, 1999). We now take a closer look at how a company accounts for bad debts.

allowance - potential uncollectibles

TWO METHODS TO ACCOUNT FOR BAD DEBTS

Assume that Roberts Corp. makes a $500 sale to Dexter Inc. on November 10, 2001, with credit terms of 2/10, net 60. The effect on the accounting equation of the sale is as follows:

BALANCE SHEET						INCOME STATEMENT	
ASSETS	=	LIABILITIES	+	OWNERS' EQUITY	+	REVENUES – EXPENSES	
Accounts Receivable—Dexter 500						Sales Revenue	500

Assume further that Dexter not only misses taking advantage of the discount for early payment but also is unable to pay within 60 days. After pursuing the account for four months into 2002, the credit department of Roberts informs the accounting department that it has given up on collecting the $500 from Dexter and advises that the account should be written off. To do so, the accounting department makes an adjustment:

BALANCE SHEET						INCOME STATEMENT	
ASSETS	=	LIABILITIES	+	OWNERS' EQUITY	+	REVENUES – EXPENSES	
Accounts Receivable—Dexter (500)						Bad Debts Expense	(500)

This approach to accounting for bad debts is called the **direct write-off method.** Do you see any problems with its use? What about Roberts's balance sheet at the end of 2001? By ignoring the possibility that not all its outstanding accounts receivable will be collected,

Roberts is overstating the value of this asset at December 31, 2001. Also, what about the income statement for 2001? By ignoring the possibility of bad debts on sales made during 2001, Roberts has violated the *matching principle.* This principle requires that all costs associated with making sales in a period should be matched with the sales of that period. Roberts has overstated net income for 2001 by ignoring bad debts as an expense. The problem is one of *timing:* Even though any one particular account may not prove to be uncollectible until a later period (e.g., the Dexter account), the cost associated with making sales on credit (bad debts) should be recognized in the period of sale.

Accountants use the **allowance method** to overcome the deficiencies of the direct write-off method. They *estimate* the amount of bad debts before these debts actually occur. For example, assume that Roberts's total sales during 2001 amount to $600,000 and that at the end of the year, the outstanding accounts receivable total $250,000. Also assume that Roberts estimates that on the basis of past experience, 1% of the sales of the period, or $6,000, eventually will prove to be uncollectible. Under the allowance method, Roberts makes the following adjustment at the end of 2001:

BALANCE SHEET						INCOME STATEMENT
ASSETS	**=**	**LIABILITIES**	**+**	**OWNERS' EQUITY**	**+**	**REVENUES – EXPENSES**
Allowance for Doubtful Accounts (6,000)						Bad Debts Expense (6,000)

Bad Debts Expense represents the cost associated with the reduction in value of the asset, Accounts Receivable. A contra asset account is used to reduce the asset to its net realizable value. This is accomplished by using a valuation allowance account, Allowance for Doubtful Accounts. Roberts presents accounts receivable as follows on its December 31, 2001, balance sheet:

Accounts receivable	$250,000
Less: Allowance for doubtful accounts	(6,000)
Net accounts receivable	$244,000

WRITE-OFFS OF UNCOLLECTIBLE ACCOUNTS WITH THE ALLOWANCE METHOD

Like the direct write-off method, the allowance method reduces Accounts Receivable to write off a specific customer's account. If the account receivable no longer exists, there is no need for the related allowance account and thus this account is reduced as well. For example, assume, as we did earlier, that Dexter's $500 account is written off on May 1, 2002. Under the allowance method, the effect of the write-off is as follows:

		BALANCE SHEET				INCOME STATEMENT
ASSETS	=	LIABILITIES	+	OWNERS' EQUITY	+	REVENUES – EXPENSES
Allowance for Doubtful Accounts	500					
Accounts Receivable— Dexter	(500)					

To summarize, whether the direct write-off method or the allowance method is used, the write-off of a specific customer's account reduces the *gross* amount of accounts receivable. However, under the direct write-off method, an *expense* is recognized and under the allowance method, the *allowance* account is reduced.

TWO APPROACHES TO THE ALLOWANCE METHOD OF ACCOUNTING FOR BAD DEBTS

Because the allowance method results in a better *matching,* accounting standards require the use of this method rather than the direct write-off method unless bad debts are immaterial in amount. Accountants use one of two different variations of the allowance method to estimate bad debts. One approach emphasizes matching bad debts expense with revenue on the income statement and bases bad debts on a percentage of the sales of the period. This was the method we illustrated earlier for Roberts Corp. The other approach emphasizes the net realizable amount (value) of accounts receivable on the balance sheet and bases bad debts on a percentage of the accounts receivable balance at the end of the period.

Percentage of Net Credit Sales Approach   If a company has been in business for enough years, it may be able to use the past relationship between bad debts and *net* credit sales to predict bad debt amounts. *Net* means that credit sales have been adjusted for sales discounts and returns and allowances. Assume that the accounting records for Bosco Corp. reveal the following:

Year	Net Credit Sales	Bad Debts
1996	$1,250,000	$ 26,400
1997	1,340,000	29,350
1998	1,200,000	23,100
1999	1,650,000	32,150
2000	2,120,000	42,700
	$7,560,000	$153,700

Although the exact percentage varied slightly over the five-year period, the average percentage of bad debts to net credit sales is very close to 2% ($153,700/$7,560,000 = .02033). Bosco needs to determine whether this estimate is realistic for the current period. For example, are current economic conditions considerably different from those in the prior years? Has the company made sales to any new customers with significantly different credit terms? If the answers to these types of questions are yes, Bosco should consider adjusting the 2% experience rate to estimate future bad debts. Otherwise, it should proceed with this estimate. Assuming that it uses the 2% rate and that its net credit sales during 2001 are $2,340,000, Bosco makes the following adjustment:

BALANCE SHEET					INCOME STATEMENT
ASSETS	=	LIABILITIES	+	OWNERS' EQUITY	+	REVENUES – EXPENSES
Allowance for Doubtful Accounts (46,800)					Bad Debts Expense (46,800)

Thus, Bosco matches bad debt expense of $46,800 with sales revenue of $2,340,000.

Percentage of Accounts Receivable Approach   Some companies believe they can more accurately estimate bad debts by relating them to the balance in the Accounts Receivable account at the end of the period rather than to the sales of the period. The objective with both approaches is the same, however: to use past experience with bad debts to predict future amounts. Assume that the records for Cougar Corp. reveal the following:

Year	Balance in Accounts Receivable December 31	Bad Debts
1996	$ 650,000	$ 5,250
1997	785,000	6,230
1998	854,000	6,950
1999	824,000	6,450
2000	925,000	7,450
	$4,038,000	$32,330

The ratio of bad debts to the ending balance in Accounts Receivable over the past five years is $32,330/$4,038,000, or approximately .008 (.8%). Assuming balances in Accounts Receivable and the Allowance for Doubtful Accounts on December 31, 2001, of $865,000 and $2,100, respectively, Cougar adjusts its records as follows:

BALANCE SHEET					INCOME STATEMENT
ASSETS	=	LIABILITIES	+	OWNERS' EQUITY	+	REVENUES – EXPENSES
Allowance for Doubtful Accounts (4,820)					Bad Debts Expense (4,820)

The logic for the amount recognized as bad debts is as follows:

Balance required in allowance account after adjustment	$6,920 0.8%
Less: Balance in allowance account before adjustment	2,100
Amount of adjustment	$4,820

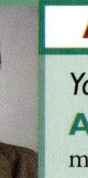

ACCOUNTING FOR YOUR DECISIONS

You Are the Owner

Assume you own a retail business that offers credit sales. To estimate bad debts, your business uses the percentage of net credit sales approach. For the new fiscal year, how would you decide what percentage to use to estimate your bad debts?

ANS: To determine the bad debt percentage for the new fiscal year, you can (1) review historical records to see what the actual percentages of bad debts were, (2) check to see if credit policies have substantially changed, (3) consider current and future economic conditions, and (4) consult with your managers and salespeople to see if they are aware of any changes in customers' paying habits.

Note the one major difference between this approach and the percentage of sales approach: *under the percentage of net credit sales approach, the balance in the allowance account is ignored, and the bad debts expense is simply a percentage of the sales of the period; under the percentage of accounts receivable approach, however, the balance in the allowance account must be considered.* The net realizable value of Accounts Receivable is determined as follows:

Accounts receivable	$865,000
Less: Allowance for doubtful accounts	(6,920)
Net realizable value	$858,080

Aging of Accounts Receivable   Some companies use a variation of the percentage of accounts receivable approach to estimate bad debts. This variation is actually a refinement of the approach because it considers the length of time that the receivables have been outstanding. It stands to reason that the older an account receivable is, the less likely it is to be collected. An **aging schedule** categorizes the various accounts by length of time outstanding. An example of an aging schedule is shown in Exhibit 7-5. We assume that the company's policy is to allow 30 days for payment of an outstanding account. After that time, the account is past due. An alphabetical list of customers appears in the first column, with the balance in each account shown in the appropriate column to the right. The dotted lines after A. Matt's account indicate that many more accounts appear in the records; we have included just a few to show the format of the schedule. The totals on the aging schedule are used as the basis for estimating bad debts, as shown in Exhibit 7-6.

Note that the estimated percentage of uncollectibles increases as the period of time the accounts have been outstanding lengthens. If we assume that the Allowance for Doubtful Accounts has a balance of $1,230 before adjustment, the accountant makes the following adjustments:

BALANCE SHEET						INCOME STATEMENT	
ASSETS	=	LIABILITIES	+	OWNERS' EQUITY	+	REVENUES – EXPENSES	
Allowance for Doubtful Accounts (13,324)						Bad Debts Expense	(13,324)

EXHIBIT 7-5   Aging Schedule

	Number of Days Past Due				
Customer	Current	1–30	31–60	61–90	Over 90
L. Ash	$ 4,400				
B. Budd	3,200				
C. Cox		$ 6,500			
E. Fudd					$6,300
G. Hoff			$ 900		
A. Matt	5,500				
......					
......					
......					
T. West				$ 3,100	
M. Young				4,200	
Totals*	$85,600	$31,200	$24,500	$18,000	$9,200

*Only a few of the customer accounts are illustrated; thus, the column totals are higher than the amounts for the accounts illustrated.

Exhibit 7-6 Use of an Aging Schedule to Estimate Bad Debts

Category	Amount	Estimated Percent Uncollectible	Estimated Amount Uncollectible
Current	$ 85,600	1%	$ 856
Past due:			
1–30 days	31,200	4%	1,248
31–60 days	24,500	10%	2,450
61–90 days	18,000	30%	5,400
Over 90 days	9,200	50%	4,600
Totals	$168,500		$14,554

From Concept

TO PRACTICE 7.2

READING UNO'S FINANCIAL STATEMENTS Does Uno disclose in its annual report which method it uses to estimate bad debts? In what line item on the income statement would you expect bad debts expense to be included?

The logic for the amount recognized as bad debts is as follows:

Balance required in allowance account after adjustment	$14,554
Less: Balance in allowance account before adjustment	1,230
Amount of adjustment	$13,324

The net realizable value of accounts receivable would be determined as follows:

Accounts receivable	$168,500
Less: Allowance for doubtful accounts	14,554
Net realizable value	$153,946

Two-Minute Review

1. What is the theoretical justification for recognizing bad debts under the allowance method?

2. What accounts are adjusted at the end of the period to recognize bad debts?

3. Two approaches are available to recognize bad debts. What are they? Which one of the two takes into account any existing balance in the Allowance for Doubtful Accounts account when the adjustment is made to recognize bad debts for the period?

Answers:

1. Use of the allowance method is an attempt by accountants to match bad debts as an expense with the revenue of the period in which a sale on credit took place.

2. Bad Debts Expense, and Allowance for Doubtful Accounts are both increased.

3. The two approaches are the percentage of net credit sales approach and the percentage of accounts receivable approach. Only the latter takes into account the balance in the Allowance for Doubtful Accounts account.

From Concept

TO PRACTICE 7.3

READING PEPSICO'S FINANCIAL STATEMENTS PepsiCo's 1999 income statement reports net sales of $20,367 (in millions). Using this information and that included in the chapter opener, compute the company's receivable turnover for 1999 (note that PepsiCo combines accounts and notes receivable on its balance sheet). What is the average length of time it takes to collect a receivable? Does this seem reasonable for the company's type of business?

ANALYZING THE ACCOUNTS RECEIVABLE RATE OF COLLECTION

Managers, investors, and creditors are keenly interested in how well a company manages its accounts receivable. One simple measure is to compare a company's sales to its accounts receivable. The result is the accounts receivable turnover ratio:

$$\text{Accounts Receivable Turnover} = \frac{\text{Net Credit Sales}}{\text{Average Accounts Receivable}}$$

Typically, the faster the turnover is, the better. For example, if a company has sales of $10 million and an average accounts receivable of $1 million, it turns over its accounts receivable 10 times per year. If we assume 360 days in a year, that is once every 36 days. An observer would compare that figure with historical figures to see if the company is experiencing slower or faster collections. A comparison could also be made to other companies in the same industry. If receivables are turning over too slowly, that could mean that the company's credit department is not operating effectively and the company therefore is missing opportunities with the cash that isn't available. On the other hand, a turnover rate that is too fast might mean that the company's credit policies are too stringent and that sales are being lost as a result.

NOTES RECEIVABLE

A **promissory note** is a written promise to repay a definite sum of money on demand or at a fixed or determinable date in the future. Promissory notes normally require the payment of interest for the use of someone else's money. The party that agrees to repay money is the **maker** of the note, and the party that receives money in the future is the **payee**. A company that holds a promissory note received from another company has an asset, called a **note receivable;** the company that makes or gives a promissory note to another company has a liability, a **note payable.** Over the life of the note, the maker incurs interest expense on its note payable, and the payee earns interest revenue on its note receivable. The following summarizes this relationship:

Party	Recognizes on Balance Sheet	Recognizes on Income Statement
Maker	Note payable	Interest expense
Payee	Note receivable	Interest revenue

Promissory notes are used for a variety of purposes. Banks normally require a company to sign a promissory note to borrow money. Promissory notes are often used in the sale of consumer durables with relatively high purchase prices, such as appliances and automobiles. At times, a promissory note is issued to replace an existing overdue account receivable.

IMPORTANT TERMS CONNECTED WITH PROMISSORY NOTES

It is important to understand the following terms when dealing with promissory notes:

Principal—the amount of cash received, or the fair value of the products or services received, by the maker when a promissory note is issued.

Maturity date—the date that the promissory note is due.

Term—the length of time a note is outstanding; that is, the period of time between the date it is issued and the date it matures.

Maturity value—the amount of cash the maker is to pay the payee on the maturity date of the note.

Interest—the difference between the principal amount of the note and its maturity value.

In some cases, the interest rate on a promissory note is stated explicitly on the face of the note. Even though the note's term may be less than a year, the interest rate is stated on an annual basis. In other cases, an interest rate does not appear on the face of the note. As we will see, however, there is *implicit* interest, because more is to be repaid at maturity than is owed at the time the note is signed. Notes in which an interest rate is explicitly stated are called **interest-bearing notes.** Notes in which interest is implicit in the agreement are called **non-interest-bearing notes.** We now look at the accounting for each of these types of notes.

INTEREST-BEARING NOTES

Assume that on December 13, 2001, HighTec sells a computer to Baker Corp. at an invoice price of $15,000. Because Baker is short of cash, it gives HighTec a 90-day, 12%

LO 5 Understand how to account for interest-bearing notes receivable.

promissory note. The total amount of interest due on the maturity date is determined as follows:

$$\$15{,}000 \times .12 \times 90/360 = \underline{\$450}$$

The effect of the receipt of the note is as follows:

BALANCE SHEET					INCOME STATEMENT
ASSETS	=	LIABILITIES	+	OWNERS' EQUITY	+ REVENUES – EXPENSES
Notes Receivable 15,000					Sales Revenue 15,000

If we assume that December 31 is the end of HighTec's accounting year, an adjustment is needed to recognize interest earned but not yet received. It is required when a company uses the accrual basis of accounting. The question is: how many days of interest have been earned during December? *It is normal practice to count the day a note matures, but not the day it is signed, in computing interest.* Thus, in our example, interest would be earned for 18 days (December 14 to December 31) during 2001 and for 72 days in 2002:

Month	Number of Days Outstanding
December 2001	18 days
January 2002	31 days
February 2002	28 days
March 2002	13 days (matures on March 13, 2002)
Total days	90 days

Thus, the amount of interest earned during 2001 is $15,000 × .12 × 18/360 or $90. An adjustment is made on December 31 to record interest earned during 2001:

BALANCE SHEET					INCOME STATEMENT
ASSETS	=	LIABILITIES	+	OWNERS' EQUITY	+ REVENUES – EXPENSES
Interest Receivable 90					Interest Revenue 90

On March 13, 2002, HighTec collects the principal amount of the note and interest from Baker:

BALANCE SHEET					INCOME STATEMENT
ASSETS	=	LIABILITIES	+	OWNERS' EQUITY	+ REVENUES – EXPENSES
Cash 15,450					Interest Revenue 360
Notes Receivable (15,000)					
Interest Receivable (90)					

This adjustment accomplishes a number of purposes. First, it removes the amount of $15,000 originally recorded in the Notes Receivable account. Second, it recognizes interest earned during the 72 days in 2002 that the note is outstanding. The calculation of interest earned during 2002 is as follows:

$$\$15{,}000 \times .12 \times 72/360 = \underline{\$360}$$

Third, Interest Receivable for $90 is removed from the records now that the note has been collected. Finally, cash of $15,450 is collected, which represents the principal amount of the note, $15,000, plus interest of $450 for 90 days.

NON-INTEREST-BEARING NOTES

Assume that you walk in to an automobile dealership on November 1, 2001, and find the car of your dreams. After extensive negotiation, the dealer agrees to sell you the car outright for $10,000. Because you are short of cash, you give the dealer $1,000 as a down payment and sign a promissory note to pay $9,900 in six months. Even though interest is never mentioned, it is *implicitly* built into the transaction. You owe the car dealer $10,000 – $1,000, or $9,000, today, and you have agreed to pay $9,900 in six months. The $900 excess of the amount to be paid in six months over the amount owed today is *interest*. The note is called a non-interest-bearing note because no interest is *explicitly* stated. Anytime it is necessary to pay more in the future than is owed today, interest is involved. The *effective interest rate* can be found as follows:

LO 6 Understand how to account for non-interest-bearing notes receivable.

1. The amount of interest implicit in the note: $9,900 – $9,000, or $900
2. The length of the note: 6 months
3. The number of 6-month periods in a year: 12/6 = 2
4. The amount of interest that would apply to a full year: $900 × 2, or $1,800
5. The effective annual interest rate: $1,800/$9,000, or 20%

In essence, the car dealer had you sign a promissory note in the amount of $9,900 but gave you credit equivalent to only $9,000 in cash—that is, the difference between the value of the car today, $10,000, and the amount of your down payment, $1,000. The dealer deducted interest of $900 in advance and gave you the equivalent of a $9,000 loan. Another name for this non-interest-bearing note is a **discounted note.** On the date the note is signed, the car dealer makes an adjustment as follows:

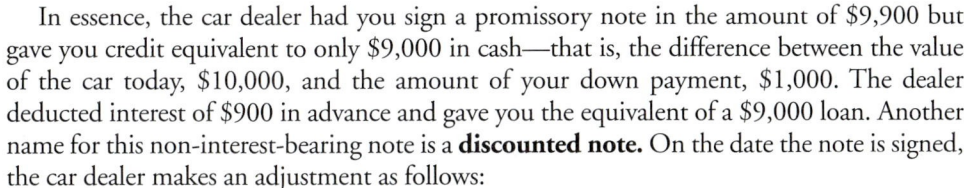

	BALANCE SHEET				INCOME STATEMENT	
ASSETS	=	LIABILITIES	+	OWNERS' EQUITY	+	REVENUES – EXPENSES
Cash	1,000				Sales Revenue	10,000
Notes Receivable	9,900					
Discount on Notes Receivable	(900)					

The cash received represents the down payment. The increase in Notes Receivable of $9,900 is the maturity amount of the promissory note. Sales Revenue represents the amount the car could be sold for today. Discount on Notes Receivable is a contra account to the Notes Receivable account and represents the interest that the dealer will earn over the next six months. As interest is earned, this account will be reduced and Interest Revenue will be increased. For example, at the end of the year, the dealer will make an adjustment to recognize that two months' interest of the total of six months' interest has been earned:

	BALANCE SHEET				INCOME STATEMENT	
ASSETS	=	LIABILITIES	+	OWNERS' EQUITY	+	REVENUES – EXPENSES
Discount on Notes Receivable	300				Interest Revenue	300

The current assets section of the dealer's balance sheet at December 31, 2001, includes the following:

Notes receivable	$9,900	
Less: Discount on notes receivable	600	$9,300

On April 30, the dealer records the collection of the maturity amount of the note and the remaining interest earned:

Notes Receivable | 321

| BALANCE SHEET | | | | | INCOME STATEMENT | |
ASSETS	=	LIABILITIES	+	OWNERS' EQUITY	+	REVENUES – EXPENSES
Cash 9,900					Interest Revenue	600
Notes Receivable (9,900)						
Discount on Notes Receivable 600						

(handwritten note: → why not monthly? 150 at end of each month)

ACCELERATING THE INFLOW OF CASH FROM SALES

LO 7 Explain various techniques that companies use to accelerate the inflow of cash from sales.

Earlier in the chapter, we pointed out why cash sales are preferable to credit sales: credit sales slow down the inflow of cash to the company and create the potential for bad debts. To remain competitive, most businesses find it necessary to grant credit to customers. That is, if one company won't grant credit to a customer, the customer may find another company willing to do so. Companies have found it possible, however, to circumvent the problems inherent in credit sales. In Chapter 5, we discussed the use of sales discounts to motivate timely repayment of accounts receivable. We now consider other approaches that companies use to speed up the flow of cash from sales.

CREDIT CARD SALES

Most retail establishments, as well as many service businesses, accept one or more major credit cards. Among the most common cards are MasterCard, VISA, American Express, Carte Blanche, Discover Card, and Diners Club. Most merchants believe that they must honor at least one or more of these credit cards to remain competitive. In return for a fee, the merchant passes the responsibility for collection on to the credit card company. Thus, the credit card issuer assumes the risk of nonpayment. The basic relationships among the three parties—the customer, the merchant, and the credit card company—are illustrated in Exhibit 7-7. Assume that Joe Smith entertains clients at Club Cafe and charges $100 in meals to his Diners Club credit card. When Joe is presented with his bill at the end of the evening, he is asked to sign a multiple-copy **credit card draft** or invoice. Joe keeps one copy of the draft and leaves the other two copies at Club Cafe. The restaurant keeps one copy as the basis for recording its sales for the day and sends the other copy to Diners Club for payment. Diners Club uses the copy of the draft it gets for two purposes: to reimburse Club Cafe $95 (keeping $5 or 5% of the original sale as a collection fee) and to include Joe Smith's $100 purchase on the monthly bill it mails him.

Assume that total credit card sales on June 5 amount to $800. The effect on the accounting equation is as follows:

If credit card sales accelerate the inflow of cash from sales, then credit card scanners such as this one speed up the process even more.

| BALANCE SHEET | | | | | INCOME STATEMENT | |
ASSETS	=	LIABILITIES	+	OWNERS' EQUITY	+	REVENUES – EXPENSES
Accounts Receivable— Diners Club 800					Sales Revenue	800

Assume that Club Cafe remits the credit card drafts to Diners Club once a week and that the total sales for the week ending June 11 amount to $5,000. Further assume that on June 13, Diners Club pays the amount due to Club Cafe, after deducting a 5% collection fee. The adjustment is as follows:

| BALANCE SHEET | | | | | INCOME STATEMENT | |
ASSETS	=	LIABILITIES	+	OWNERS' EQUITY	+	REVENUES – EXPENSES
Cash 4,750					Collection Fee Expense	(250)
Accounts Receivable— Diners Club (5,000)						

EXHIBIT 7-7   Basic Relationships among Parties with Credit Card Sales

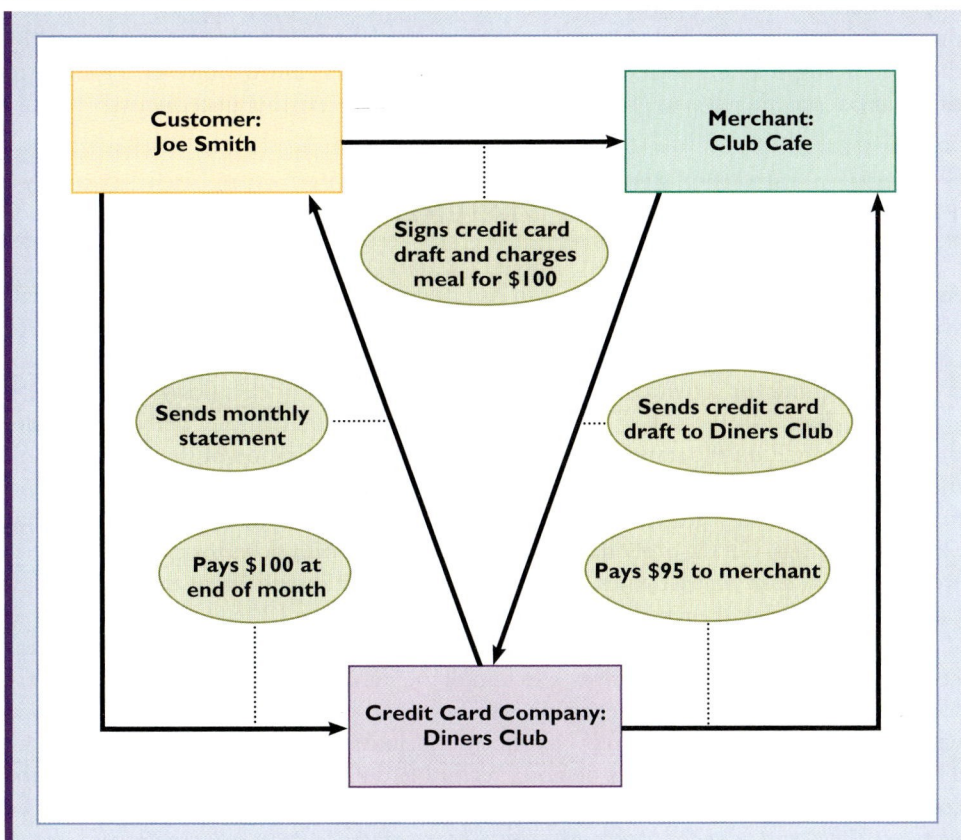

Some credit cards, such as MasterCard and VISA, allow a merchant to present a credit card draft directly for deposit in a bank account, in much the same way the merchant deposits checks, coins, and currency. Obviously, this type of arrangement is even more advantageous for the merchant because the funds are available as soon as the drafts are credited to the bank account. Assume that on July 9, Club Cafe presents VISA credit card drafts to its bank for payment in the amount of $2,000 and that the collection charge is 4%. The effect of the collection is as follows:

		BALANCE SHEET				INCOME STATEMENT	
ASSETS	**=**	**LIABILITIES**	**+**	**OWNERS' EQUITY**	**+**	**REVENUES – EXPENSES**	
Cash	1,920					Collection Fee Expense	(80)
						Sales Revenue	2,000

DISCOUNTING NOTES RECEIVABLE

Promissory notes are negotiable, which means that they can be endorsed and given to someone else for collection. In other words, a company can sign the back of a note, just as it would a check, sell it to a bank, and receive cash before the note's maturity date. This process is called **discounting** and is another way for companies to speed the collection of cash from receivables. A note can be sold immediately to a bank on the date it is issued, or it can be sold after it has been outstanding but before the due date.

When a note is discounted at a bank, it is normally done *with recourse*. This means that if the original customer fails to pay the bank the total amount due on the maturity date of the note, the company that transferred the note to the bank is liable for the full amount. Because there is *uncertainty* as to whether the company will have to make good on any particular note that it discounts at the bank, a *contingent liability* exists from the time the note is discounted until its maturity date. The accounting profession has adopted guidelines to decide whether a particular uncertainty requires that the company record a contingent liability on its balance sheet. Under these guidelines, the contingency created by the discounting of a note with recourse is not recorded as a liability. However, a *footnote* to the financial statements is used to inform the reader of the existing uncertainty.

HOW LIQUID ASSETS AFFECT THE CASH FLOWS STATEMENT

LO 8 Explain the effects of transactions involving liquid assets on the statement of cash flows.

As we discussed earlier in the chapter, cash equivalents are combined with cash on the balance sheet. These items are very near maturity and do not present any significant risk of collectibility. Because of this, any purchases or redemptions of cash equivalents are not considered significant activities to be reported on a statement of cash flows.

The purchase and the sale of investments are considered significant activities and are therefore reported on the statement of cash flows. The classification of these activities on the statement depends on the type of investment. Cash flows from purchases, sales, and maturities of held-to-maturity securities and available-for-sale securities are classified as *investing* activities. On the other hand, these same types of cash flows for trading securities are classified as *operating* activities. We present a complete discussion of the statement of cash flows, including the reporting of investments, in Chapter 12.

The collection of either accounts receivable or notes receivable generates cash for a business and affects the Operating Activities section of the statement of cash flows. Most companies use the indirect method of reporting cash flows and begin the statement of cash flows with the net income of the period. Net income includes the sales revenue of the period. Therefore, a decrease in accounts or notes receivable during the period indicates that the company collected more cash than it recorded in sales revenue. Thus, *a decrease in accounts or notes receivable must be added back to net income because more cash was collected than is reflected in the sales revenue number.* Alternatively, an increase in accounts or notes receivable indicates that the company recorded more sales revenue than cash collected during the period. Therefore, *an increase in accounts or notes receivable requires a deduction from the net income of the period to arrive at cash flow from operating activities.* These adjustments, as well as the cash flows from buying and selling investments, are summarized in Exhibit 7-8. Note that any investments are assumed to be in either held-to-maturity or available-for-sale securities.

EXHIBIT 7-8 How Investments and Receivables Affect the Statement of Cash Flows

Refer back to PepsiCo's statement of cash flows in Exhibit 7-1. Note in the Operating Activities section of the statement that accounts and notes receivable are combined. Does the combined change of $149 million in these two accounts during 1999 indicate an increase or a decrease in the receivables for the year? Because the amount is deducted in the Operating Activities section of the statement, we know that the receivables *increased* during 1999. An increase in receivables means that PepsiCo sold more products on open account and on notes than it actually collected in cash from customers. Thus, the increase is deducted from net income to arrive at the actual cash flow from operating activities.

www.pepsico.com

WARMUP EXERCISES

LO 1   Warmup Exercise 7-1   Composition of Cash

For the following items, indicate whether each should be included (I) or excluded (E) from the line item titled Cash and Cash Equivalents on the balance sheet.

_____ 1. Certificate of deposit maturing in 60 days

_____ 2. Checking account

_____ 3. Certificate of deposit maturing in six months

_____ 4. Savings account

_____ 5. Shares of GM stock

_____ 6. Petty cash

_____ 7. Corporate bonds maturing in 30 days

_____ 8. Certified check

Key to the Solution

Recall the key to classification as part of cash: the amount must be readily available to pay debts and cash equivalents must have an original maturity to the investor of three months or less.

LO 3   Warmup Exercise 7-2   Investments

Indicate whether each of the following events will result in an increase (I), decrease (D), or no effect (NE) on net income for the period.

_____ 1. Trading securities are sold for more than their carrying value.

_____ 2. An interest check is received for held-to-maturity securities.

_____ 3. Available-for-sale securities increase in value during the period.

_____ 4. Available-for-sale securities are sold for less than their carrying value.

_____ 5. Trading securities decrease in value during the period.

_____ 6. Held-to-maturity securities are redeemed on their maturity date at face value.

Key to the Solution

Recall from earlier in the chapter the differences in accounting for the various types of investments.

LO 4   Warmup Exercise 7-3   Accounting for Bad Debts

Brown Corp. ended the year with balances in Accounts Receivable of $60,000 and in Allowance for Doubtful Accounts of $800 (before adjustment). Net sales for the year amounted to $200,000. Determine the effect on the accounting equation, assuming the following:

1. Estimated percentage of net sales uncollectible is 1%.

2. Estimated percentage of year-end accounts receivable uncollectible is 4%.

Key to the Solution

Recall that the percentage of net sales approach does not take into account any existing balance in the allowance account but the percentage of receivables approach does.

Warmup Exercise 7-1

1. I 2. I 3. E 4. I 5. E 6. I 7. E 8. I

Warmup Exercise 7-2

1. I 2. I 3. NE 4. D 5. D 6. NE

Warmup Exercise 7-3

		BALANCE SHEET				INCOME STATEMENT	
ASSETS	=	LIABILITIES	+	OWNERS' EQUITY	+	REVENUES – EXPENSES	
1. Allowance for						Bad Debts Expense	(2,000)
Doubtful Accounts (2,000)							
2. Allowance for						Bad Debts Expense	(1,600)
Doubtful Accounts (1,600)							

REVIEW PROBLEM

The following items pertain to the Current Assets section of the balance sheet for Jackson Corp. at the end of its accounting year, December 31, 2001. Each item must be considered, and any necessary adjustment recognized. Additionally, the accountant for Jackson wants to develop the Current Assets section of the balance sheet as of the end of 2001.

a. Cash in a savings account at the Second State Bank amounts to $13,200.

b. Cash in a checking account at the Second State Bank is $5,775.

c. Cash on hand in the petty cash fund amounts to $400.

d. A 9%, 120-day certificate of deposit was purchased on December 1, 2001, for $10,000.

e. Gross accounts receivable at December 31, 2001, amount to $44,000. Before adjustment, the balance in the Allowance for Doubtful Accounts account is $340. Based on past experience, the accountant estimates that 3% of the gross accounts receivable outstanding at December 31, 2001, will prove to be uncollectible.

f. A customer's 12%, 90-day promissory note in the amount of $6,000 is held at the end of the year. The note has been held for 45 days during 2001.

Required

1. Determine the effect on the accounting equation from the adjustments required in parts **d, e,** and **f.**

2. Prepare the Current Assets section of Jackson's balance sheet as of December 31, 2001. In addition to items **a–f,** the balances in Inventory and Prepaid Insurance on this date are $65,000 and $4,800, respectively.

SOLUTION TO REVIEW PROBLEM

1. The effect on the accounting equation from each item is as follows:

d. Jackson needs an adjustment to record interest earned on the certificate of deposit at the Second State Bank. The CD has been outstanding for 30 days during 2001, and therefore the amount of interest earned is calculated as follows:

$$\$10,000 \times .09 \times 30/360 = \underline{\$75}$$

The effect of the adjustment is as follows:

BALANCE SHEET				INCOME STATEMENT	
ASSETS	=	**LIABILITIES**	+ **OWNERS' EQUITY**	+ **REVENUES – EXPENSES**	
Interest Receivable	75			Interest Revenue	75

e. Based on gross accounts receivable of $44,000 at year-end and an estimate that 3% of this amount will be uncollectible, the balance in the Allowance for Doubtful Accounts should be $1,320 ($44,000 × 3%). Given a current balance of $340, an adjustment for $980 ($1,320 − $340) is needed to bring the balance to the desired amount of $1,320:

BALANCE SHEET				INCOME STATEMENT	
ASSETS	=	**LIABILITIES**	+ **OWNERS' EQUITY**	+ **REVENUES – EXPENSES**	
Allowance for Doubtful Accounts	(980)			Bad Debts Expense	(980)

f. An adjustment is needed to accrue interest on the promissory note ($6,000 × .12 × 45/360 = $90):

BALANCE SHEET				INCOME STATEMENT	
ASSETS	=	**LIABILITIES**	+ **OWNERS' EQUITY**	+ **REVENUES – EXPENSES**	
Interest Receivable	90			Interest Revenue	90

2. The Current Assets section of Jackson's balance sheet appears as follows:

JACKSON CORP.
PARTIAL BALANCE SHEET
DECEMBER 31, 2001

Current Assets

Cash		$ 19,375*
Certificate of deposit		10,000
Accounts receivable	$44,000	
Less: Allowance for doubtful accounts	1,320	42,680
Notes receivable		6,000
Interest receivable		165§
Inventory		65,000
Prepaid insurance		4,800
Total current assets		$148,020

*Savings account	$13,200
Checking account	5,775
Petty cash fund	400
Total	$19,375

§§75 from CD and $90 from promissory note

CHAPTER HIGHLIGHTS

1. **LO 1** The amount of cash reported on the balance sheet includes all items that are readily available to satisfy obligations. Items normally included in cash are coin and currency, petty cash funds, customers' undeposited checks, cashier's checks, certified checks, savings accounts, and checking accounts.

2. **LO 1** Cash equivalents include such items as commercial paper, money market funds, certificates of deposit, and Treasury bills. They are included with cash on the balance sheet and are limited to those investments that are readily convertible to known amounts of cash and have original maturities of three months or less.

3. **LO 2** A bank reconciliation is normally prepared monthly for all checking accounts to reconcile the amount of cash recorded on the books with the amount reported on the bank statement. One popular form for the reconciliation, and the one illustrated in the chapter, reconciles the balance on the bank statement and the balance on the books to the correct balance. Adjustments must be made for all items in the balance per books section of the reconciliation.

4. **LO 2** Many companies use a petty cash fund to disburse small amounts of cash that would otherwise require the use of a check and a more lengthy approval process. The fund is established by writing and cashing a check and placing the coin and currency in a secure place controlled by a custodian. At this point, an adjustment is made to record the establishment of the fund. On presentation of a supporting receipt to the custodian, employees receive disbursements from the fund. The fund is replenished periodically, and an adjustment is made to record the replenishment and to recognize the various expenses incurred.

5. **LO 3** At times, companies invest idle cash in highly liquid financial instruments, such as certificates of deposit. They also invest in the debt and equity securities of other companies. Some investments are made without the intention of influencing or controlling the other company. Accountants classify these investments as held-to-maturity securities, trading securities, or available-for-sale securities. Other investments are made to exert significant influence over the policies of the other companies. The equity method is used in these instances. Finally, companies may buy enough of the common stock of another company to control it. This situation normally results in the presentation of consolidated financial statements.

6. **LO 3** Held-to-maturity securities are bonds that are purchased with the intention of holding them until they mature. The cost method results in the recognition of periodic interest income and the recognition of a gain or loss if the securities are sold prior to when they mature.

7. **LO 3** Trading securities are stocks and bonds held for the short term with the intention of profiting from appreciation in their trading price. Interest or dividends are recognized as income. Trading securities are adjusted to their fair value at the end of each period, and any increase or decrease in value is reported on the income statement.

8. **LO 3** Available-for-sale securities are investments that are not classified as either held-to-maturity or trading securities. The accounting and reporting requirements for this category are similar to the rules for trading securities. The primary difference is that unrealized gains and losses from holding available-for-sale securities (changes in fair value from one period to the next) are not recognized on the income statement. Instead, these amounts are reported as a separate component of stockholders' equity.

9. **LO 4** The allowance method of accounting for bad debts matches the cost associated with uncollectible accounts to the revenue of the period in which the sale took place. One of two variations is used to estimate bad debts under the allowance method. Some companies base bad debts on a percentage of net credit sales. Others use an aging schedule as a basis for relating the amount of bad debts to the balance in Accounts Receivable at the end of the period.

10. **LO 5** A promissory note is a written promise to repay a definite sum of money on demand or at a fixed or determinable date in the future. Situations in which a promissory note is used include the purchase of consumer durables, the lending of money to another party, and the replacement of an existing account receivable. Interest earned but not yet collected should be accrued at the end of an accounting period.

11. **LO 6** The interest on certain promissory notes is implicitly included in the agreement instead of stated explicitly as a percentage of the principal amount of the note. Any difference between the cash purchase price of an item or, in the case of a loan, the amount borrowed and the amount to be repaid at maturity is interest. As is the case for interest-bearing notes, any interest earned but not yet collected is recognized as income at the end of an accounting period.

12. **LO 7** Many businesses accept credit cards in lieu of cash. In return for a fee, the credit card company assumes responsibility for collecting the customer charges. A credit card draft or invoice is the basis for recording a credit card sale and an account receivable. When the drafts are presented to the credit card company for payment, the excess of accounts receivable for these sales over the amount of cash received represents the expense associated with accepting credit cards. In some instances, companies do not have to wait to collect from the credit card company but can instead present the drafts for deposit to their bank account.

13. **LO 7** Because a promissory note is negotiable, it can be sold to another party, such as a bank. The sale of a note is called *discounting* and is a way for a company to accelerate the inflow of cash. If the note is sold or discounted with recourse, the company selling it is contingently liable until the maturity date of the loan. A footnote is used to report this contingency to financial statement readers.

14. **LO 8** Cash equivalents are included with cash on the balance sheet, and therefore changes in them do not appear as significant activities on a statement of cash flows. Purchases and sales of investments do appear in the statement of cash flows. Under the indirect method of preparing the Operating Activities category of the statement of cash flows, increases in accounts and notes receivable are deducted from net income; decreases are added back to net income.

KEY TERMS QUIZ

Because of the large number of terms introduced in this chapter, it has two key terms quizzes. Read each definition below and then write the number of the definition in the blank beside the appropriate term it defines. The solution appears at the end of the chapter.

Quiz 1: Cash and Investments

____ Cash equivalent
____ Bank statement
____ Outstanding check
____ Deposit in transit
____ Bank reconciliation
____ Credit memoranda
____ Debit memoranda

____ Petty cash fund
____ Equity securities
____ Debt securities
____ Held-to-maturity securities
____ Trading securities
____ Available-for-sale securities

1. Additions on a bank statement for such items as interest paid on the account and notes collected by the bank for the customer.

2. An investment that is readily convertible to a known amount of cash and has an original maturity to the investor of three months or less.

3. Deductions on a bank statement for such items as NSF checks and various service charges.

4. A deposit recorded on the books but not yet reflected on the bank statement.

5. Securities issued by corporations as a form of ownership in the business.

6. A check written by a company but not yet presented to the bank for payment.

7. Bonds issued by corporations and governmental bodies as a form of borrowing.

8. A detailed list, provided by the bank, of all the activity for a particular account during the month.

9. A form used by the accountant to reconcile the balance shown on the bank statement for a particular account with the balance shown in the accounting records.

10. Money kept on hand for making minor disbursements in coin and currency rather than by writing checks.

11. Stocks and bonds of other companies bought and held for the purpose of selling them in the near term to generate profits on appreciation in their price.

12. Stocks and bonds that are not classified as either held-to-maturity or trading securities.

13. Investments in bonds of other companies in which the investor has the positive intent and the ability to hold the securities to maturity.

Quiz 2: Receivables

____ Subsidiary ledger
____ Control account
____ Direct write-off method
____ Allowance method
____ Aging schedule
____ Promissory note
____ Maker
____ Payee
____ Note receivable
____ Note payable

____ Principal
____ Maturity date
____ Term
____ Maturity value
____ Interest
____ Interest-bearing note
____ Non-interest-bearing note
____ Discounted note
____ Credit card draft
____ Discounting

1. A method of estimating bad debts on the basis of either the net credit sales of the period or the amount of accounts receivable at the end of the period.

2. The party that will receive the money from a promissory note at some future date.

3. A written promise to repay a definite sum of money on demand or at a fixed or determinable date in the future.

4. A liability resulting from the signing of a promissory note.

5. A multiple-copy document used by a company that accepts a credit card for a sale.

6. An asset resulting from the acceptance of a promissory note from another company.

7. The process of selling a promissory note.

8. The party that agrees to repay the money for a promissory note at some future date.

9. A promissory note in which the interest rate is explicitly stated.

10. A form used to categorize the various individual accounts receivable according to the length of time each has been outstanding.

11. An alternative name for a non-interest-bearing promissory note.

12. The detail for a number of individual items that collectively make up a single general ledger account.

13. A promissory note in which interest is not explicitly stated but is implicit in the agreement.

14. The recognition of bad debts expense at the point an account is written off as uncollectible.

15. The general ledger account that is supported by a subsidiary ledger.

16. The amount of cash received, or the fair value of the products or services received, by the maker when a promissory note is issued.

17. The date that the promissory note is due.

18. The length of time a note is outstanding; that is, the period of time between the date it is issued and the date it matures.

19. The amount of cash the maker is to pay the payee on the maturity date of the note.

20. The difference between the principal amount of the note and its maturity value.

ALTERNATE TERMS

Allowance for doubtful accounts   Allowance for uncollectible accounts

Credit card draft   Invoice

Debt securities   Bonds

Equity securities   Stocks

Net realizable value   Net recoverable amount

Non-interest-bearing note   Discounted note

Short-term investments   Marketable securities

QUESTIONS

1. What is a cash equivalent? Why is it included with cash on the balance sheet?

2. Why does the purchase of an item classified as a cash equivalent *not* appear on the statement of cash flows as an investing activity?

3. A friend says to you: "I understand why it is important to deposit all receipts intact and not keep coin and currency sitting around the business. Beyond this control feature, however, I believe that a company should strive to keep the maximum amount possible in checking accounts to always be able to pay bills on time." How would you evaluate your friend's statement?

4. A friends says to you: "I'm confused. I have a memo included with my bank statement indicating a $20 service charge for printing new checks. If the bank is deducting this amount from my account, why do they call it a 'debit memorandum'? How can you explain this?

5. Different formats for bank reconciliations are possible. What is the format for a bank reconciliation in which a service charge for a lockbox is *added* to the balance per the bank statement? Explain your answer.

6. Stanzel Corp. purchased 1,000 shares of IBM common stock. What will determine whether the shares are classified as trading securities or available-for-sale securities?

7. On December 31, Stockton Inc. invests idle cash in two different certificates of deposit. The first is an 8%, 90-day CD, and the second has an interest rate of 9% and matures in 120 days. How is each of these CDs classified on the December 31 balance sheet?

8. What is the primary difference in the accounting requirements for trading securities and those for available-for-sale securities? How is the primary difference justified?

9. Why are changes in the fair value of trading securities reported in the account *Unrealized* Gains/Losses—Trading Securities even though the gains and losses are reported on the income statement?

10. What is the theoretical justification for the allowance method of accounting for bad debts?

11. In estimating bad debts, why is the balance in Allowance for Doubtful Accounts considered when the percentage of accounts receivable approach is used but not when the percentage of net credit sales approach is used?

12. When estimating bad debts on the basis of a percentage of accounts receivable, what is the advantage to using an aging schedule?

13. What is the distinction between an account receivable and a note receivable?

14. How would you evaluate the following statement? "Given the choice, it would always be better to require an interest-bearing note from a customer as opposed to a non-interest-bearing note. This is because interest on a note receivable is a form of revenue and it is only in the case of an interest-bearing note that interest will be earned."

15. Why does the discounting of a note receivable with recourse result in a contingent liability? Should the liability be reported on the balance sheet?

EXERCISES

LO 2   **Exercise 7-1**   Items on a Bank Reconciliation
Assume that a company is preparing a bank reconciliation for the month of June. It reconciles the bank balance and the book balance to the correct balance. For each of the following items, indicate whether the item is an addition to the bank balance (A-Bank), an addition to the book balance (A-Book), a deduction from the bank balance (D-Bank), a deduction from the book balance (D-Book), or would not appear on the June reconciliation (NA).

_____   **1.**   Check written in June but not yet returned to the bank for payment

_____   **2.**   Customer's NSF check

_____ **3.** Customer's check written in the amount of $54 but recorded on the books in the amount of $45*

_____ **4.** Service charge for new checks

_____ **5.** Principal and interest on a customer's note collected for the company by the bank

_____ **6.** Customer's check deposited on June 30 but not reflected on the bank statement

_____ **7.** Check written on the company's account, paid by the bank, and returned with the bank statement

_____ **8.** Check written on the company's account for $123 but recorded on the books as $132*

_____ **9.** Interest on the checking account for the month of June

*Answer in terms of the adjustment needed to correct for the error.

LO 3 **Exercise 7-2** Certificate of Deposit

On May 31, 2001, Elmer Corp. purchased a 120-day, 9% certificate of deposit for $50,000. The CD was redeemed on September 28, 2001. Determine the effect on the accounting equation of

a. The purchase of the CD.

b. The accrual of interest adjustment for interest earned through June 30, the end of the company's fiscal year.

c. The redemption of the CD.

Assume 360 days in a year.

LO 3 **Exercise 7-3** Classification of Investments

Red Oak makes the following investments in the stock of other companies during 2001. For each investment, indicate how it would be accounted for and reported on; use the following designations: trading security (T), available-for-sale security (AS), equity investee (E), or a subsidiary included in consolidated statements (S).

_____ **1.** 500 shares of ABC common stock to be held for short-term share appreciation

_____ **2.** 20,000 shares of the 50,000 shares of Ace common stock to be held for the long term

_____ **3.** 100 shares of Creston preferred stock to be held for an indefinite period of time

_____ **4.** 80,000 of the 100,000 shares of Orient common stock

_____ **5.** 10,000 of the 40,000 shares of Omaha preferred stock to be held for the long term

LO 3 **Exercise 7-4** Classification of Investments

Fill in the blanks to indicate whether each of the following investments should be classified as a held-to-maturity security (HM), a trading security (T), or an available-for-sale security (AS):

_____ **1.** Shares of IBM stock to be held indefinitely.

_____ **2.** GM bonds due in 10 years. The intent is to hold them until they mature.

_____ **3.** Shares of Motorola stock. Plans are to hold the stock until the price goes up by 10% and then sell it.

_____ **4.** Ford Motor Company bonds due in 15 years. The bonds are part of a portfolio that turns over on the average of every 60 days.

_____ **5.** Chrysler bonds due in 10 years. Plans are to hold them indefinitely.

LO 3 **Exercise 7-5** Purchase and Sale of Bonds

Starship Enterprises enters into the following transactions during 2001 and 2002:

2001
Jan. 1   Purchased $100,000 face value of Northern Lights Inc. bonds at face value. The newly issued bonds have an interest rate of 8% paid semiannually on June 30 and December 31. The bonds mature in five years.
June 30   Received interest on the Northern Lights bonds.
Dec. 31   Received interest on the Northern Lights bonds.

2002
Jan. 1   Sold the Northern Lights Inc. bonds for $102,000.

Assume Starship classifies all bonds as held to maturity.

Required

1. Determine the effect on Starship's accounting equation on each of the preceding dates.
2. Why was Starship able to sell its Northern Lights bonds for $102,000?

LO 3   Exercise 7-6   Investment in Stock

On December 1, 2001, Chicago Corp. purchases 1,000 shares of the preferred stock of Denver Corp. for $40 per share. Chicago expects the price of the stock to increase over the next few months and plans to sell it for a profit. On December 20, 2001, Denver declares a dividend of $1 per share to be paid on January 15, 2002. On December 31, 2001, Chicago's accounting year-end, the Denver stock is trading on the market at $42 per share. Chicago sells the stock on February 12, 2002, at a price of $45 per share.

Required

1. Should Chicago classify its investments as held-to-maturity, trading, or available-for-sale securities? Explain your answer.
2. Determine the effects on the accounting equation of Chicago's purchase of the preferred stock on December 1, 2001, the dividend declared on December 20, 2001, the change in market value at December 31, 2001, and the sale on February 12, 2002.
3. In what category of the balance sheet should Chicago classify its investment on its December 31, 2001, balance sheet?

LO 3   Exercise 7-7   Investment in Stock

On August 15, 2001, Cubs Corp. purchases 5,000 shares of common stock in Sox Inc. at a market price of $15 per share. In addition, Cubs pays brokerage fees of $1,000. Cubs plans to hold the stock indefinitely rather than as a part of its active trading portfolio. The market value of the stock is $13 per share on December 31, 2001, the end of Cubs' accounting year. On July 8, 2002, Cubs sells the Sox stock for $10 per share.

Required

1. Should Cubs classify its investment as held-to-maturity, trading, or available-for-sale securities? Explain your answer.
2. Determine the effects on the accounting equation of Cubs' purchase of the common stock on August 15, 2001, the change in market value at December 31, 2001, and the sale on July 8, 2002.
3. In what category of the balance sheet should Cubs classify its investment on its December 31, 2001, balance sheet?

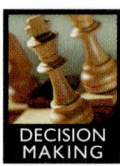

LO 4   Exercise 7-8   Comparison of the Direct Write-Off and Allowance Methods of Accounting for Bad Debts

In its first year of business, Rideaway Bikes has net income of $145,000, exclusive of any adjustment for bad debt expense. The president of the company has asked you to calculate net income under each of two alternatives of accounting for bad debts: the direct write-off method and the allowance method. The president would like to use the method that will result in the higher net income. So far, no adjustments have been made to write off uncollectible accounts or to estimate bad debts. The relevant data are as follows:

Write-offs of uncollectible accounts during the year	$ 10,500
Net credit sales	$650,000
Estimated percentage of net credit sales that will be uncollectible	2%

Required

Compute net income under each of the two alternatives. Does Rideaway have a choice as to which method to use? Should it base its choice on which method will result in the higher net income? (Ignore income taxes.)

LO 4   Exercise 7-9   Allowance Method of Accounting for Bad Debts—Comparison of the Two Approaches

Kandel Company had the following data available for 2001 (before making any adjustments):

Accounts receivable, 12/31/01	$320,100
Allowance for doubtful accounts	2,600
Net credit sales, 2001	834,000

Required

Determine the effect on the accounting equation of the adjustment to recognize bad debts under the following assumptions: (a) bad debt expense is expected to be 2% of net credit sales for the year and (b) Kandel expects it will not be able to collect 6% of the balance in accounts receivable at year-end.

LO 4   Exercise 7-10   Accounts Receivable Turnover for Quaker Oats

The 1999 annual report of Quaker Oats Company reported the following amounts (in millions of dollars).

Net sales	$4,725.2
Trade accounts receivable—net of allowances, December 31, 1999	254.3
Trade accounts receivable—net of allowances, December 31, 1998	283.4

Required

1. Compute Quaker's accounts receivable turnover ratio for 1999. (Assume that all sales are on credit.)

2. What is the average collection period, in days, for an account receivable? Explain your answer.

3. Give some examples of the types of customers you would expect Quaker Oats to have. Do you think the average collection period for sales to these customers is reasonable? What other information do you need to fully answer this question?

LO 5   Exercise 7-11   Interest-Bearing Notes Receivable

On September 1, 2001, Dougherty Corp. accepted a six-month, 7%, $45,000 interest-bearing note from the Rozelle Company in payment of an accounts receivable. Dougherty's year-end is December 31. Rozelle paid the note and interest on the due date.

Required

1. Who is the maker and who is the payee of the note?

2. What is the maturity date of the note?

3. Determine the effect on Dougherty's accounting equation of
   a. The acceptance of the note.
   b. The accrual of interest earned through December 31, 2001, the end of the company's year.
   c. Receipt of payment of the note and interest.

LO 6   Exercise 7-12   Non-Interest-Bearing Note

On May 1, Radtke's Music Mart sold an electronic keyboard to Mary Reynolds. Reynolds made a $300 down payment and signed a 10-month note for $1,625. The normal selling price of the keyboard is $1,800 in cash. Radtke's fiscal year ends December 31. Reynolds paid Radtke in full on the maturity date.

Required

1. How much total interest did Radtke receive on this note?

2. Determine the effect on Radtke's accounting equation on May 1, December 31, and the maturity date.

3. What is the effective interest rate on the note?

LO 7   Exercise 7-13   Credit Card Sales

Darlene's Diner accepts American Express from its customers. Darlene's is closed on Sundays and on that day records the weekly sales and remits the credit card drafts to American Express. For the week ending on Sunday, June 12, cash sales totaled $2,430, and credit card sales amounted to $3,500. On June 15, Darlene's received $3,360 from American Express as payment for the credit card drafts. For the transactions of June 12 and June 15, determine the effect on the accounting equation. As a percentage, what collection fee is American Express charging Darlene?

LO 8   Exercise 7-14   Impact of Transactions Involving Receivables on Statement of Cash Flows

From the following list, identify whether the change in the account balance during the year would be added to or deducted from net income when the indirect method is used to determine cash flows from operating activities.

_____ Increase in accounts receivable

_____ Decrease in accounts receivable

_____ Increase in notes receivable

_____ Decrease in notes receivable

LO 8   Exercise 7-15   Cash Collections—Direct Method

Emily Enterprises' comparative balance sheets included accounts receivable of $224,600 at December 31, 2000, and $205,700 at December 31, 2001. Sales reported on Emily's 2001 income statement amounted to $2,250,000. What is the amount of cash collections that Emily will report in the Operating Activities category of its 2001 statement of cash flows assuming that the direct method is used?

Multi-Concept Exercises

LO 1, 2, 3   Exercise 7-16   Composition of Cash

Using a Y for yes or an N for no, indicate whether each of the following items should be included in cash and cash equivalents on the balance sheet. If an item should not be included in cash and cash equivalents, indicate where it should appear on the balance sheet.

_____ **1.** Checking account at Third County Bank

_____ **2.** Petty cash fund

_____ **3.** Coin and currency

_____ **4.** Postage stamps

_____ **5.** An IOU from an employee

_____ **6.** Savings account at the Ft. Worth Savings & Loan

_____ **7.** A six-month CD

_____ **8.** Undeposited customer checks

_____ **9.** A customer's check returned by the bank and marked NSF

_____ **10.** Sixty-day U.S. Treasury bills

_____ **11.** A cashier's check

LO 1, 3   Exercise 7-17   Classification of Cash Equivalents and Investments on a Balance Sheet

Classify each of the following items as either a cash equivalent (CE), a short-term investment (STI), or a long-term investment (LTI).

_____ **1.** A 120-day certificate of deposit.

_____ **2.** Three hundred shares of GM common stock. The company plans on selling the stock in six months.

_____ **3.** A six-month U.S. Treasury bill.

_____ **4.** A 60-day certificate of deposit.

_____ **5.** Ford Motor Co. bonds maturing in 15 years. The company intends to hold the bonds until maturity.

_____ **6.** Commercial paper issued by ABC Corp., maturing in four months.

_____ **7.** Five hundred shares of Chrysler common stock. The company plans to sell the stock in 60 days to help pay for a note due at that time at the bank.

_____ **8.** Two hundred shares of GE preferred stock. The company intends to hold the stock for 10 years and at that point sell it to help finance construction of a new factory.

_____ **9.** Ten-year U.S. Treasury bonds. The company plans to sell the bonds on the open market in six months.

_____ **10.** A 90-day U.S. Treasury bill.

LO 1, 3, 8 **Exercise 7-18** Cash Equivalents

Systematic Enterprises invested its excess cash in the following instruments during December 2001:

Certificate of deposit, due January 31, 2004	$ 75,000
Certificate of deposit, due March 30, 2002	150,000
Commercial paper, original maturity date February 28, 2002	125,000
Deposit into a money market fund	25,000
Investment in stock	65,000
90-day Treasury bills	100,000
Treasury note, due December 1, 2031	500,000

Required

Determine the amount of cash equivalents that should be combined with cash on the company's balance sheet at December 31, 2001, and for purposes of preparing a statement of cash flows for the year ended December 31, 2001.

LO 1, 8 **Exercise 7-19** Impact of Transactions Involving Cash and Receivables on Statement of Cash Flows

From the following list, identify each item as operating (O), investing (I), financing (F), or not separately reported on the statement of cash flows (N). Assume that the indirect method is used to determine the cash flows from operating activities.

_____ Purchase of cash equivalents

_____ Redemption of cash equivalents

_____ Purchase of available-for-sale securities

_____ Sale of available-for-sale securities

_____ Replenishment of the petty cash fund

_____ Write-off of customer account (under the allowance method)

PROBLEMS

LO 2 **Problem 7-1** Bank Reconciliation

The following information is available to assist you in preparing a bank reconciliation for Calico Corners on May 31, 2001:

a. The balance on the May 31, 2001, bank statement is $8,432.11.

b. Not included on the bank statement is a $1,250.00 deposit made by Calico Corners late on May 31.

c. A comparison between the canceled checks returned with the bank statement and the company records indicated that the following checks are outstanding at May 31:

No. 123	$ 23.40
No. 127	145.00
No. 128	210.80
No. 130	67.32

d. The Cash account on the company's books shows a balance of $9,965.34.

e. The bank acts as a collection agency for interest earned on some municipal bonds held by Calico Corners. The May bank statement indicates interest of $465.00 earned during the month.

f. Interest earned on the checking account and added to Calico Corners' account during May was $54.60. Miscellaneous bank service charges amounted to $50.00.

g. A customer's NSF check in the amount of $166.00 was returned with the May bank statement.

h. A comparison between the deposits listed on the bank statement and the company's books revealed that a customer's check in the amount of $123.45 was recorded on the books during May but was never added to the company's account. The bank erroneously added the check to the account of Calico Closet, which has an account at the same bank.

i. The comparison of deposits per the bank statement with those per the books revealed that another customer's check in the amount of $101.10 was correctly added to the company's account. In recording the check on the company's books, however, the accountant erroneously increased the Cash account $1,011.00.

Required

1. Prepare a bank reconciliation in good form.

2. A friend says to you: "I don't know why companies bother to prepare bank reconciliations—it seems a waste of time. Why don't they just do like I do and adjust the cash account for any difference between what the bank shows as a balance and what shows up in the books?" Explain to your friend *why* a bank reconciliation should be prepared as soon as a bank statement is received.

LO 3 Problem 7-2 Investments in Bonds and Stock

Swartz Inc. enters into the following transactions during 2001:

July 1   Paid $10,000 to acquire on the open market $10,000 face value of Gallatin bonds. The bonds have a stated annual interest rate of 6% with interest paid semiannually on June 30 and December 31. The bonds mature in 5½ years.

Oct. 23   Purchased 600 shares of Eagle Rock common stock at $20 per share.

Nov. 21   Purchased 200 shares of Montana preferred stock at $30 per share.

Dec. 10   Received dividends of $1.50 per share on the Eagle Rock stock and $2.00 per share on the Montana stock.

Dec. 28   Sold 400 shares of Eagle Rock common stock at $25 per share.

Dec. 31   Received interest from the Gallatin bonds.

Dec. 31   Noted market price of $29 per share for the Eagle Rock stock and $26 per share for the Montana stock.

Required

1. Determine the effect on Swartz's accounting equation of each of the preceding transactions. Swartz classifies the bonds as held-to-maturity securities and all stock investments as trading securities.

2. Prepare a partial balance sheet as of December 31, 2001, to indicate the proper presentation of the investments.

3. Indicate the items, and the amount of each, that will appear on the 2001 income statement relative to the investments.

LO 3 Problem 7-3 Investments in Stock

Atlas Superstores occasionally finds itself with excess cash to invest and consequently entered into the following transactions during 2001:

Jan. 15   Purchased 200 shares of Sears common stock at $50 per share, plus $500 in commissions.

May 23   Received dividends of $2 per share on the Sears stock.

June 1   Purchased 100 shares of Ford Motor Co. stock at $74 per share, plus $300 in commissions.

Oct. 20   Sold all the Sears stock at $42 per share, less commissions of $400.

Dec. 15   Received notification from Ford Motor Co. that a $1.50 per share dividend had been declared. The checks will be mailed to stockholders on January 10, 2002.

Dec. 31   Noted that the Ford Motor Co. stock was quoted on the stock exchange at $85 per share.

Required

1. Determine the effect on Atlas's accounting equation of each of the preceding transactions. Assume that Atlas categorizes all investments as available-for-sale securities.

2. What is the total amount that Atlas should report on its income statement from its investments during 2001?

3. Assume all the same facts except that Atlas categorizes all investments as trading securities. How would your answer to part **2** change? Explain why your answer would change.

LO 4 Problem 7-4 Allowance Method for Accounting for Bad Debts

At the beginning of 2001, EZ Tech Company's Accounts Receivable balance was $140,000, and the balance in the Allowance for Doubtful Accounts was $2,350. EZ Tech's sales in 2001 were

$1,050,000, 80% of which were on credit. Collections on account during the year were $670,000. The company wrote off $4,000 of uncollectible accounts during the year.

Required

1. Determine the effect on EZ's accounting equation relative to the sales, collections, and write-offs of accounts receivable during 2001.

2. Determine the effect on EZ's accounting equation of the estimate of bad debts assuming (a) bad debt expense is 3% of credit sales and (b) amounts expected to be uncollectible are 6% of the year-end accounts receivable.

3. What is the net realizable value of accounts receivable on December 31, 2001, under each assumption (**a** and **b**) in part **2**?

4. What effect does the recognition of bad debt expense have on the net realizable value? What effect does the write-off of accounts have on the net realizable value?

LO 4 Problem 7-5 Aging Schedule to Account for Bad Debts

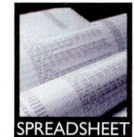
SPREADSHEET

Sparkle Jewels distributes fine stones. It sells on credit to retail jewelry stores and extends terms of 2/10, net 60. For accounts that are not overdue, Sparkle has found that there is a 95% probability of collection. For accounts up to one month past due, the likelihood of collection decreases to 80%. If accounts are between one and two months past due, the probability of collection is 60%, and if an account is more than two months past due, Sparkle Jewels estimates that there is only a 40% chance of collecting the receivable.

On December 31, 2001, the balance in Allowance for Doubtful Accounts is $12,300. The amounts of gross receivables, by age, on this date are as follows:

Category	Amount
Current	$200,000
Past due:	
Less than one month	45,000
One to two months	25,000
More than two months	10,000

Required

1. Prepare a schedule to estimate the amount of uncollectible accounts at December 31, 2001.

2. On the basis of the schedule in part **1,** determine the effect on the accounting equation of the estimate of bad debts at December 31, 2001.

3. Show how accounts receivable would be presented on the December 31, 2001, balance sheet.

LO 4 Problem 7-6 Accounts Receivable Turnover for Compaq Computer and Gateway

The following information was summarized from the 1999 annual report of Compaq Computer   **www.compaq.com**
Corporation:

	(in millions)
Accounts receivable, net, December 31:	
1999	$ 6,685
1998	6,998
Revenue for the year ended December 31:	
1999	38,525
1998	31,169

The following information was summarized from the 1999 annual report of Gateway: **www.gateway.com**

	(in thousands)
Accounts receivable, net:	
December 31, 1999	$ 646,339
December 31, 1998	558,851
Net sales for the year ended:	
December 31, 1999	8,645,561
December 31, 1998	7,467,925

Required

1. Calculate the accounts receivable turnover ratios for Compaq Computer and Gateway for 1999.

2. Calculate the average collection period, in days, for both companies for 1999. Comment on the reasonableness of the collection periods considering the types of companies that you would expect to be customers of Compaq Computer and Gateway.

3. Which company appears to be performing better? What other information should you consider to determine how these companies are performing in this regard?

LO 6 Problem 7-7 Non-Interest-Bearing Note Receivable

Northern Nursery sells a large stock of trees and shrubs to a landscaping business on May 31, 2001. The landscaper makes a down payment of $5,000 and signs a promissory note agreeing to pay $20,000 on August 29, 2001, the end of its busy season. The cash selling price of the nursery stock on May 31 was $24,000.

Required

1. For the transactions on each of the following dates, determine the effect on the accounting equation:
   a. May 31, 2001, to record the receipt of the down payment and the promissory note
   b. June 30, 2001, the end of Northern's fiscal year
   c. August 29, 2001, to record collection of the note

2. Compute the effective rate of interest earned by Northern on the note. Explain your answer.

LO 7 Problem 7-8 Credit Card Sales

Gas stations sometimes sell gasoline at a lower price to customers who pay cash than to customers who use a charge card. A local gas station owner pays 2% of the sales price to the credit card company when customers pay with a credit card. She pays $ .75 per gallon of gasoline and must earn at least $ .25 per gallon of gross margin to stay competitive.

Required

1. Determine the price the owner must charge credit card customers to maintain her gross margin.

2. How much discount could the owner offer to cash customers and still maintain the same gross margin?

LO 8 Problem 7-9 Effects of Changes in Receivable Balances on Statement of Cash Flows

Stegner Inc. reported net income of $130,000 for the year ended December 31, 2001. The following items were included on Stegner's balance sheets at December 31, 2001 and 2000:

	12/31/01	12/31/00
Cash	$105,000	$110,000
Accounts receivable	223,000	83,000
Notes receivable	95,000	100,000

Stegner uses the indirect method to prepare its statement of cash flows. Stegner does not have any other current assets or current liabilities and did not enter into any investing or financing activities during 2001.

Required

1. Prepare Stegner's 2001 statement of cash flows.

2. Draft a brief memo to the owner to explain why cash decreased during a profitable year.

Multi-Concept Problems

LO 1, 3 Problem 7-10 Cash and Liquid Assets on the Balance Sheet

The following accounts are listed in a company's general ledger. The accountant wants to place the items in order of liquidity on the balance sheet.

Accounts receivable

Certificates of deposit (six months)

Trading securities

Prepaid rent

Money market fund

Cash in drawers

Required

Rank the accounts in terms of liquidity. Identify items to be included in the total of cash, and explain why the items not included in cash on the balance sheet are not as liquid as cash. Explain how these items should be classified.

LO 4, 5 Problem 7-11 Accounts and Notes Receivable

Linus Corp. sold merchandise for $5,000 to C. Brown on May 15, 2001, with credit terms of net 30. Subsequent to this, Brown experienced cash flow problems and was unable to pay its debt. On August 10, 2001, Linus stopped trying to collect the outstanding receivable from Brown and wrote the account off as uncollectible. On December 1, 2001, Brown sent Linus a check for $1,000 and offered to sign a two-month, 9%, $4,000 promissory note to satisfy the remaining obligation. Brown paid the entire amount due Linus, with interest, on January 31, 2002. Linus ends its accounting year on December 31 each year, and uses the allowance method to account for bad debts.

Required

1. For each of the transactions during the period from May 15, 2001, to January 31, 2002, determine the effect on Linus's accounting equation.

2. Why would Brown bother to send Linus a check for $1,000 on December 1 and agree to sign a note for the balance, given that such a long period of time had passed since the original purchase?

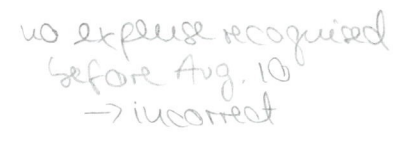

no expense recognized before Aug. 10 → incorrect

Allowance is reinstated

ALTERNATE PROBLEMS

LO 2 Problem 7-1A Bank Reconciliation

The following information is available to assist you in preparing a bank reconciliation for Karen's Catering on March 31, 2001:

a. The balance on the March 31, 2001, bank statement is $6,506.10.

b. Not included on the bank statement is a deposit made by Karen's late on March 31 in the amount of $423.00.

c. A comparison between the canceled checks listed on the bank statement and the company records indicated that the following checks are outstanding at March 31:

No. 112	$ 42.92
No. 117	$307.00
No. 120	$ 10.58
No. 122	$ 75.67

d. The bank acts as a collection agency for checks returned for insufficient funds. The March bank statement indicates that one such check in the amount of $45.00 was collected and deposited and a collection fee of $4.50 was charged.

e. Interest earned on the checking account and credited to Karen's account during March was $4.30. Miscellaneous bank service charges amounted to $22.00.

f. A comparison between the deposits listed on the bank statement and the company's books revealed that a customer's check in the amount of $1,250.00 appears on the bank statement in March but was never credited to the customer's account on the company's books.

g. The comparison of checks cleared per the bank statement with those per the books revealed that the wrong amount was charged to the company's account for a check. The amount of the check was $990.00. The proof machine encoded the check in the amount of $909.00, the amount charged against the company's account.

Required

1. Determine the balance on the books before any adjustments as well as the corrected balance to be reported on the balance sheet.

2. What would you recommend Karen do as a result of the bank error in item **g** above? Why?

LO 3   Problem 7-2A   Investments in Bonds and Stock

Vermont Corp. enters into the following transactions during 2001:

July 1   Paid $10,000 to acquire on the open market $10,000 face value of Maine bonds. The bonds have a stated annual interest rate of 8% with interest paid semiannually on June 30 and December 31. The remaining life of the bonds on the date of purchase is 3½ years.

Oct. 23   Purchased 1,000 shares of Virginia common stock at $15 per share.

Nov. 21   Purchased 600 shares of Carolina preferred stock at $8 per share.

Dec. 10   Received dividends of $.50 per share on the Virginia stock and $1.00 per share on the Carolina stock.

Dec. 28   Sold 700 shares of Virginia common stock at $19 per share.

Dec. 31   Received interest from the Maine bonds.

Dec. 31   The Virginia Stock and the Carolina stock have market prices of $20 per share and $11 per share, respectively.

Required

1. Determine the effect on Vermont's accounting equation of each of the preceding transactions. Vermont classifies the bonds as held-to-maturity securities and all stock investments as trading securities.

2. Prepare a partial balance sheet as of December 31, 2001, to indicate the proper presentation of the investments.

3. Indicate the items, and the amount of each, that will appear on the 2001 income statement relative to the investments.

LO 3   Problem 7-3A   Investments in Stock

Trendy Supercenter occasionally finds itself with excess cash to invest and consequently entered into the following transactions during 2001:

Jan. 15   Purchased 100 shares of IBM common stock at $130 per share, plus $250 in commissions.

May 23   Received dividends of $1 per share on the IBM stock.

June 1   Purchased 200 shares of General Motors stock at $60 per share, plus $300 in commissions.

Oct. 20   Sold all of the IBM stock at $140 per share, less commissions of $400.

Dec. 15   Received notification from General Motors that a $.75 per share dividend had been declared. The checks will be mailed to stockholders on January 10, 2002.

Dec. 31   Noted that the General Motors stock was quoted on the stock exchange at $45 per share.

Required

1. Determine the effect on Trendy's accounting equation of each of the preceding transactions. Assume that Trendy categorizes all investments as available-for-sale securities.

2. What is the total amount of income that Trendy should recognize from its investments during 2001?

3. Assume all of the same facts except that Trendy categorizes all investments as trading securities. How would your answer to part **2** change? Explain why your answer would change.

LO 4   Problem 7-4A   Allowance Method for Accounting for Bad Debts

At the beginning of 2001, Miyazaki Company's Accounts Receivable balance was $105,000 and the balance in the Allowance for Doubtful Accounts was $1,950. Miyazaki's sales in 2001 were $787,500, 80% of which were on credit. Collections on account during the year were $502,500. The company wrote off $3,000 of uncollectible accounts during the year.

Required

1. Determine the effect on Miyazaki's accounting equation related to the sales, collections, and write-offs of accounts receivable during 2001.

2. Determine the effect on Miyazaki's accounting equation of the estimate of bad debts assuming (a) bad debt expense is 3% of credit sales or (b) amounts expected to be uncollectible are 6% of the year-end accounts receivable.

3. What is the net realizable value of accounts receivable on December 31, 2001, under each assumption (**a** and **b**) in part **2?**

4. What effect does the recognition of bad debt expense have on the net realizable value? What effect does the write-off of accounts have on the net realizable value?

LO 4 Problem 7-5A Aging Schedule to Account for Bad Debts

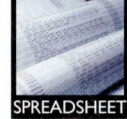

SPREADSHEET

Rough Stuff is a distributor of large rocks. It sells on credit to commercial landscaping companies and extends terms of 2/10, net 60. For accounts that are not overdue, Rough has found that there is a 90% probability of collection. For accounts up to one month past due, the likelihood of collection decreases to 75%. If accounts are between one and two months past due, the probability of collection is 65%, and if an account is more than two months past due, Rough estimates that there is only a 25% chance of collecting the receivable.

On December 31, 2001, the balance in Allowance for Doubtful Accounts is $34,590. The amounts of gross receivables, by age, on this date are as follows:

Category	Amount
Current	$135,000
Past due:	
Less than one month	60,300
One to two months	35,000
More than two months	45,000

Required

1. Prepare a schedule to estimate the amount of uncollectible accounts at December 31, 2001.

2. Rough knows that $40,000 of the $45,000 amount that is more than two months overdue is due from one customer that is in severe financial trouble. It is rumored that the customer will be filing for bankruptcy in the near future. As controller for Rough Stuff, how would you handle this situation?

3. Show how accounts receivable would be presented on the December 31, 2001, balance sheet.

LO 4 Problem 7-6A Accounts Receivable Turnover for Boise Cascade and Georgia-Pacific Corporation

The following information was summarized from the 1999 annual report of Boise Cascade Corporation and Subsidiaries (receivables are net of allowances):

www.boisecascade.com

	(in thousands)
Receivables, December 31:	
1999	$ 663,609
1998	526,359
Sales for the year ended December 31:	
1999	6,952,662
1998	6,162,123

The following information was summarized from the 1999 annual report of Georgia-Pacific Corporation–Georgia Pacific Group (receivables are net of allowances):

www.gp.com

	(in millions)
Receivables:	
January 1, 2000	$ 2,296
December 31, 1998	1,231
Net sales for the year ended:	
January 1, 2000	17,796
December 31, 1998	13,229

Required

1. Calculate the accounts receivable turnover ratios for Boise Cascade and Georgia-Pacific for 1999.

2. Calculate the average collection period, in days, for both companies for 1999. Comment on the reasonableness of the collection periods considering the types of companies that you would expect to be customers of Boise Cascade and Georgia-Pacific.

3. Which company appears to be performing better? What other information should you consider to determine how these companies are performing in this regard?

LO 6 Problem 7-7A Non-Interest-Bearing Note Receivable

Midwest Poultry sells a large stock of birds to a processor on May 31, 2001. The processor makes a $12,000 down payment and signs a $36,900 promissory note agreeing to pay the remainder on August 29, 2001, the end of its busy season. The cash selling price of the birds on May 31 was $48,000.

1. Determine the effect on Midwest's accounting equation on August 29, 2001, to record collection of the note. Midwest's accounting year ends on September 30.

2. Compute the effective rate of interest earned by Midwest on the note. Explain your answer.

LO 7 Problem 7-8A Credit Card Sales

A local fast-food store is considering the use of major credit cards in its outlets. Current annual sales are $800,000 per outlet. The company can purchase the equipment needed to handle credit cards and have an additional phone line installed in each outlet for approximately $800 per outlet. The equipment will be an expense in the year it is installed. The employee training time is minimal. The credit card company will charge a fee equal to 1.5% of sales for the use of credit cards. The company is unable to determine by how much, if any, sales will increase and whether cash customers will use a credit card rather than cash. No other fast-food stores in the local area accept credit cards for sales payment.

Required

1. Assuming only 5% of existing cash customers will use a credit card, what increase in sales is necessary to pay for the credit card equipment in the first year?

2. What other factors might the company consider in addition to an increase in sales dollars?

LO 8 Problem 7-9A Effects of Changes in Receivable Balances on Statement of Cash Flows

St. Charles Antique Market reported a net loss of $6,000 for the year ended December 31, 2001. The following items were included on St. Charles Antique Market's balance sheets at December 31, 2001 and 2000:

	12/31/01	12/31/00
Cash	$ 36,300	$ 3,100
Accounts receivable	79,000	126,000
Notes receivable	112,600	104,800

St. Charles Antique Market uses the indirect method to prepare its statement of cash flows. St. Charles Antique Market does not have any other current assets or current liabilities and did not enter into any investing or financing activities during 2001.

Required

1. Prepare St. Charles Antique Market's 2001 statement of cash flows.

2. Draft a brief memo to the owner to explain why cash increased during such an unprofitable year.

Alternate Multi-Concept Problems

LO 1, 3 Problem 7-10A Cash and Liquid Assets on the Balance Sheet

The following accounts are listed in a company's general ledger:

	December 31, 2001	December 31, 2000
Accounts receivable	$12,300	$10,000
Certificates of deposit (three months)	10,000	10,000
Marketable securities	4,500	4,000
Prepaid rent	1,200	1,500
Money market fund	25,800	28,000
Cash in checking account	6,000	6,000

Required

1. Which items are cash equivalents?

2. Explain where items that are not cash equivalents should be classified on the balance sheet.

3. What are the amount and the direction of change in cash and cash equivalents for 2001? Is the company as liquid at the end of 2001 as it was at the end of 2000? Explain your answer.

LO 4, 5 **Problem 7-11A** Accounts and Notes Receivable

Tweedy Inc. sold merchandise for $6,000 to P.D. Cat on July 31, 2001, with credit terms of net 30. Subsequent to this, Cat experienced cash flow problems and was unable to pay its debt. On December 24, 2001, Tweedy stopped trying to collect the outstanding receivable from Cat and wrote the account off as uncollectible. On January 15, 2002, Cat sent Tweedy a check for $1,500 and offered to sign a two-month, 8%, $4,500 promissory note to satisfy the remaining obligation. Cat paid the entire amount on the note due Tweedy, with interest, on March 15, 2002. Tweedy ends its accounting year on December 31 each year.

Required

1. For each of the transactions during the period from July 31, 2001, to March 15, 2002, determine the effect on Tweedy's accounting equation.

2. Why would Cat bother to send Tweedy a check for $1,500 on January 15 and agree to sign a note for the balance, given that such a long period of time had passed since the original purchase?

CASES

Reading and Interpreting Financial Statements

LO 4 **Case 7-1** Reading and Interpreting Gateway's Financial Statements

Refer to footnote 9 included in Gateway's 1999 annual report.

Required

1. What is the balance in the Allowance for Doubtful Accounts at the end of each of the two years presented? What is the net realizable value at the end of each year?

2. Calculate the ratio of the Allowance for Doubtful Accounts to Gross Accounts Receivable at the end of each of the two years.

3. Why do you think the balance in the Allowance for Doubtful Accounts was increased at the end of 1999? Does this mean that the company expects a higher percentage of bad debts?

LO 3, 8 **Case 7-2** Reading Uno's Statement of Cash Flows

Refer to the financial statements for 1999 included in Uno's annual report.

Required

1. According to the statement of cash flows, what was the increase or decrease in cash during 1999? How does this number relate to any of the numbers on Uno's comparative balance sheets?

2. What was the dollar amount of increase or decrease in accounts receivable for 1999? Why is this number deducted on the statement of cash flows?

Making Financial Decisions

LO 1, 2 Case 7-3 Liquidity

R Montague and J Capulet both distribute films to movie theaters. The following are the current assets for each at the end of the year (all amounts are in millions of dollars):

	R Montague	J Capulet
Cash	$10	$ 5
Six-month certificates of deposit	9	0
Short-term investments in stock	0	6
Accounts receivable	15	23
Allowance for doubtful accounts	(1)	(1)
Total current assets	$33	$33

Required

As a loan officer for the First National Bank of Verona Heights, assume that both companies have come to you asking for a $10 million, six-month loan. If you could lend money to only one of the two, which one would it be? Justify your answer by writing a brief memo to the president of the bank.

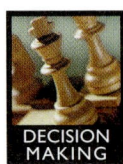

DECISION MAKING

LO 5, 6 Case 7-4 Notes Receivable

Warren Land Development is considering two offers for a lot. Builder A has offered to pay $12,000 down and sign a 10%, $80,000 promissory note, with interest and principal due in one year. Builder B would make a down payment of $20,000 and sign a non-interest-bearing, one-year note for $80,000. The president believes that the deal with Builder A is better because it involves interest and the loan to Builder B does not. The vice president of marketing thinks the offer from Builder B is better because it involves more money "up front." The sales manager is indifferent, reasoning that both builders would eventually pay $100,000 in total and that because the lot was recently appraised at $75,000, both would be paying more than fair market value.

Required

1. Regardless of which offer it accepts, how much revenue should Warren recognize from the sale of the lot? Explain your answer.

2. Which offer do you think Warren should accept? Or is the sales manager correct that it doesn't matter which one is accepted? Explain your answer.

Accounting and Ethics: What Would You Do?

LO 3 Case 7-5 Fair Market Values for Investments

Kennedy Corp. operates a chain of discount stores. The company regularly holds stock of various companies in a trading securities portfolio. One of these investments is 10,000 shares of Clean Air Inc. stock purchased for $100 per share during December 2001.

Clean Air manufactures highly specialized equipment used to test automobile emissions. Unfortunately, the market price of Clean Air's stock dropped during December 2001 and closed the year trading at $75 per share. Kennedy expects the Clean Air stock to experience a turnaround, however, as states pass legislation to require an emissions test on all automobiles.

As controller for Kennedy, you have followed the fortunes of Clean Air with particular interest. You and the company's treasurer are both concerned by the negative impact that a write-down of the stock to fair value would have on Kennedy's earnings for 2001. You have calculated net income for 2001 to be $400,000, exclusive of the recognition of any loss on the stock.

The treasurer comes to you on January 31, 2002, with the following idea:

> Since you haven't closed the books yet for 2001, and we haven't yet released the 2001 financials, let's think carefully about how Clean Air should be classified. I realize that we normally treat these types of investments as trading securities, but if we categorize the Clean Air stock on the balance sheet as available-for-sale rather than a trading security, we won't need to report the adjustment to fair value on the income statement. I don't

see anything wrong with this since we would still report the stock at its fair value on the balance sheet.

DECISION MAKING

Required

1. Compute Kennedy's net income for 2001, under two different assumptions: (a) the stock is classified as a trading security and (b) the stock is classified as an available-for-sale security.

2. Which classification do you believe is appropriate, according to accounting standards? Explain your answer.

3. Would you have any ethical concerns in following the treasurer's advice? Explain your answer.

LO 6 **Case 7-6** Notes Receivable

Patterson Company is a large diversified business with a unit that sells commercial real estate. As a company, Patterson has been profitable in recent years with the exception of the real estate business, where economic conditions have resulted in weak sales. The vice president of the real estate division is aware of the poor performance of his group and needs to find ways to "show a profit."

During the current year the division is successful in selling a 100-acre tract of land for a new shopping center. The original cost of the property to Patterson was $4 million. The buyer has agreed to sign a $10 million note with payments of $2 million due at the end of each of the next five years. The property was appraised late last year at a market value of $7.5 million. The vice president has come to you, the controller, and asked that you record a sale for $10 million with a corresponding increase in Notes Receivable for $10 million.

Required

1. Does the suggestion by the vice president as to how to record the sale violate any accounting principle? If so, explain the principle it violates.

2. What would you do? Write a brief memo to the vice president explaining the proper accounting for the sale.

INTERNET RESEARCH CASE

Case 7-7 PepsiCo

PepsiCo, the number two soft drink maker in the world with major products in snack foods as well, is undergoing changes that it believes will respond to major changes in the grocery business, its biggest customer.

INTERNET

To answer the following questions, examine the chapter-opening text and the financial statements shown in Chapter 7, read the Business Strategxy box that details the changes overtaking PepsiCo in 1998, and access its Web site to focus on both the company and its latest financial information.

www.pepsico.com

1. What are the cash and cash equivalents for PepsiCo for the latest year available?

2. What reason does the company give for the change in cash and equivalents for the most recent year available?

3. What are the short-term investments for the latest year available?

4. What reasons does the company give for the change in short-term investments for the latest year available?

5. What are accounts and notes receivable for the latest year available? Can you tell from the notes how much was for accounts receivable and how much for notes receivable?

6. Comparing the latest annual report with the financial information from 1999 in the textbook, what are three most significant changes to the financial statements? What is the most significant change to PepsiCo as a company?

Quiz 1: Cash and Investments

__2__ Cash equivalent (p. 294)

__8__ Bank statement (p. 297)

__6__ Outstanding check (p. 298)

__4__ Deposit in transit (p. 298)

__9__ Bank reconciliation (p. 298)

__1__ Credit memoranda (p. 298)

__3__ Debit memoranda (p. 299)

__10__ Petty cash fund (p. 301)

__5__ Equity securities (p. 302)

__7__ Debt securities (p. 303)

__13__ Held-to-maturity securities (p. 305)

__11__ Trading securities (p. 305)

__12__ Available-for-sale securities (p. 305)

Quiz 2: Receivables

__12__ Subsidiary ledger (p. 312)

__15__ Control account (p. 312)

__14__ Direct write-off method (p. 313)

__1__ Allowance method (p. 314)

__10__ Aging schedule (p. 317)

__3__ Promissory note (p. 319)

__8__ Maker (p. 319)

__2__ Payee (p. 319)

__6__ Note receivable (p. 319)

__4__ Note payable (p. 319)

__16__ Principal (p. 319)

__17__ Maturity date (p. 319)

__18__ Term (p. 319)

__19__ Maturity value (p. 319)

__20__ Interest (p. 319)

__9__ Interest-bearing note (p. 319)

__13__ Non-interest-bearing note (p. 319)

__11__ Discounted note (p. 321)

__5__ Credit card draft (p. 322)

__7__ Discounting (p. 323)

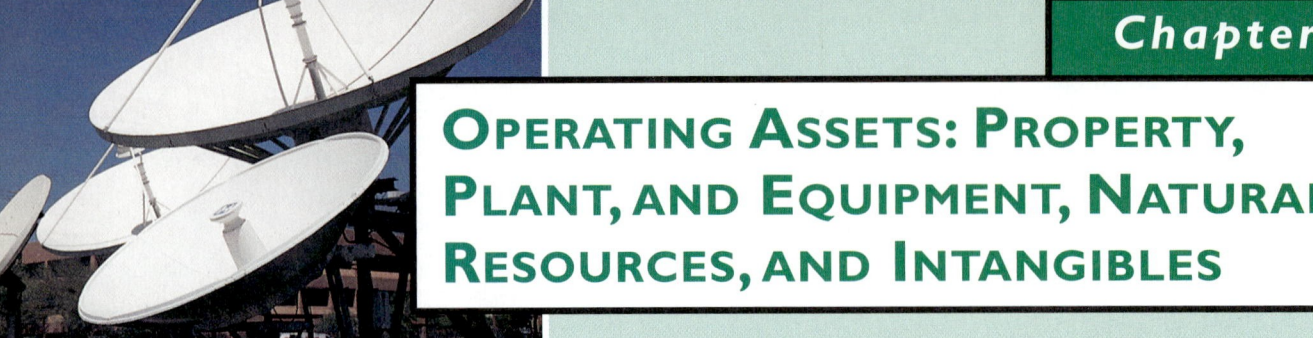

OPERATING ASSETS: PROPERTY, PLANT, AND EQUIPMENT, NATURAL RESOURCES, AND INTANGIBLES

A Look at Previous Chapters

Chapter 2 introduced long-term assets as an important part of a classified balance sheet. The short-term assets of inventory, cash, and receivables were presented in previous chapters.

A Look at This Chapter

This chapter presents long-term operating assets. The first section of the chapter discusses assets that are generally classified as tangible assets or as property, plant, and equipment. We examine asset acquisition issues concerned with use and depreciation, and the sale or disposition of these assets. The second section of the chapter discusses assets generally classified as intangible assets. The accounting issues involved with the acquisition, use, and disposition of intangible assets are examined. The unique features of certain intangible assets are discussed separately.

A Look at Upcoming Chapters

Later chapters discuss the financing of long-term assets. Chapter 10 presents long-term liabilities as a source of financing. Chapter 11 describes the use of stock as a source of funds for financing long-term assets.

FOCUS ON FINANCIAL RESULTS

The media giant Time Warner markets information and entertainment in virtually every medium. The strength of such brands as CNN, TNT, the Cartoon Network, HBO, Time-Life, *People, Time,* and *Sports Illustrated,* of recording artists such as Madonna, Eric Clapton, and Metallica, and of film and TV hits such as The Matrix, Pokémon: The First Movie, The Sopranos, and Sex and the City helped Time Warner's stock price outpace the Standard & Poor's 500 for the third year in a row. That success was capped at the end of 2000 by the FTC's long-awaited approval of the Time Warner-AOL merger, creating the world's biggest media conglomerate.

For sustainable growth, the new firm will leverage its tangible operating assets of plant, property, and equipment and natural resources into new profit opportunities. But intangibles like Time Warner's potent brand names will play as big a part. The company's 1999 annual report acknowledges their power: "The breadth of these brands and their appeal to practically every demographic group ... will give us an unrivaled portfolio."[1]

The merger of AOL and Time Warner will represent the first marriage of a major Internet company and a conventional media firm. Although it took longer than expected for the government to approve the deal, and the business environment the new company faces is continually changing, the result should allow Time Warner to enhance the value of its assets and continue the remarkable appreciation of its stock price in the future.

---

[1]Time Warner's 1999 annual report, p. 4.

TIME WARNER INC.
CONSOLIDATED BALANCE SHEET
December 31,
(millions, except per share amounts)

	1999 Historical[a]
ASSETS	
Current assets	
Cash and equivalents	$ 1,284
Receivables, less allowances of $1.682, $1.513 and $1.007 billion	4,931
Inventories	2,182
Prepaid expenses	1,464
Total current assets	9,861
Noncurrent inventories	4,201
Investments in and amounts due to and from Entertainment Group	—
Other investments	2,096
Property, plant and equipment	8,728
Music catalogues, contracts and copyrights	782
Cable television and sports franchises	8,472
Goodwill	15,458
Other assets	1,641
Total assets	$51,239

(a) The 1999 financial statements reflect the consolidation of the Entertainment Group, which substantially consists of TWE, retroactive to the beginning of 1999. Time Warner's historical financial statements for 1998 have not been changed; however, in order to enhance comparability, pro forma financial statements for 1998 reflecting the consolidation of the Entertainment Group are presented supplementally (Note 1).

Time Warner's 1999 Annual Report

If you were a Time Warner manager, how would you establish the value of intangibles on the balance sheet? How would you determine the life of such assets? How would you evaluate whether the merged company has effectively utilized its intangibles? As you study this chapter, compare the way organizations report tangible and intangible assets on the balance sheet.

After studying this chapter, you should be able to:

LO 1 Understand balance sheet disclosures for operating assets. (p. 350)

LO 2 Determine the acquisition cost of an operating asset. (p. 351)

LO 3 Explain how to calculate the acquisition cost of assets purchased for a lump sum. (p. 352)

LO 4 Describe the impact of capitalizing interest as part of the acquisition cost of an asset. (p. 352)

LO 5 Compare depreciation methods and understand the factors affecting the choice of method. (p. 353)

LO 6 Understand the impact of a change in the estimate of the asset life or residual value. (p. 358)

LO 7 Determine which expenditures should be capitalized as asset costs and which should be treated as expenses. (p. 359)

LO 8 Analyze the effect of the disposal of an asset at a gain or loss. (p. 361)

LO 9 Understand the balance sheet presentation of intangible assets. (p. 365)

LO 10 Describe the proper amortization of intangible assets. (p. 367)

LO 11 Explain the impact that long-term assets have on the statement of cash flows. (p. 370)

OPERATING ASSETS: PROPERTY, PLANT, AND EQUIPMENT

BALANCE SHEET PRESENTATION

LO 1 Understand balance sheet disclosures for operating assets.

Operating assets constitute the major productive assets of many companies. Current assets are important to a company's short-term liquidity; operating assets are absolutely essential to its long-term future. These assets must be used to produce the goods or services the company sells to customers. The dollar amount invested in operating assets may be very large, as is the case with most manufacturing companies. On the other hand, operating assets on the balance sheet may be insignificant to a company's value, as is the case with a computer software firm or many of the so-called Internet firms. Users of financial statements must assess the operating assets to make important decisions. For example, lenders are interested in the value of the operating assets as collateral when making lending decisions. Investors must evaluate whether the operating assets indicate long-term potential and can provide a return to the stockholders.

The terms used to describe the operating assets and the balance sheet presentation of those assets vary somewhat by company. Some firms refer to this category of assets as *fixed* or *plant assets*. Other firms prefer to present operating assets in two categories: *tangible assets* and *intangible assets*. The balance sheet of the toy company Mattel Inc. uses another way to classify operating assets. Mattel presents two classes of operating assets: *property, plant, and equipment* and *other noncurrent assets*. Because the latter term can encompass a variety of items, we will use the more descriptive term *intangible assets* for the second category. We begin by examining the accounting issues concerned with the first category: property, plant, and equipment.

www.mattel.com

The December 31, 1999, balance sheet of Mattel presents property, plant, and equipment as follows (in thousands):

Property, Plant, and Equipment	
Land	$ 35,930
Buildings	276,880
Machinery and equipment	611,948

Capitalized leases		$ 23,271
Leasehold improvements		84,333
		$1,032,362
Less: Accumulated depreciation		474,026
		558,336
Tools, dies, and molds, net		191,158
Property, plant, and equipment, net		$ 749,494

You should note that the acquisition costs of the land, buildings, machinery and equipment, capitalized leases, and leasehold improvements are stated and the amount of accumulated depreciation is deducted to determine the net amount. Tools, dies, and molds are stated at the net amount, meaning that the amount of depreciation has been deducted before the number is presented on the balance sheet. Note that Mattel has assets acquired by capital lease arrangements. (Capital leases are discussed in Chapter 10 and will not be addressed in this chapter.) The account Leasehold Improvements indicates that the company has modified or improved leased assets in a manner that enhances their future service potential. The cost of the improvement is shown separately on the balance sheet.

ACQUISITION OF PROPERTY, PLANT, AND EQUIPMENT

Assets classified as property, plant, and equipment are initially recorded at acquisition cost (also referred to as *historical cost*). As indicated on Mattel's balance sheet, these assets are normally presented on the balance sheet at original acquisition cost minus accumulated depreciation. It is important, however, to define the term *acquisition cost* (also known as original cost) in a more exact manner. What items should be included as part of the original acquisition? **Acquisition cost** should include all the costs that are normal and necessary to acquire the asset and prepare it for its intended use. Items included in acquisition cost would generally include the following:

LO 2 Determine the acquisition cost of an operating asset.

Purchase price

Taxes paid at time of purchase (for example, sales tax)

Transportation charges

Installation costs

An accountant must exercise careful judgment to determine which costs are "normal" and "necessary" and should be included in the calculation of the acquisition cost of operating assets. Acquisition cost should not include expenditures unrelated to the acquisition (for example, repair costs if an asset is damaged during installation) or costs incurred after the asset was installed and use begun.

ACCOUNTING FOR YOUR DECISIONS

You Are an Attorney

You are a newly licensed attorney who just opened a legal firm. As part of your office operations, you have purchased some "slightly used" computers. Should the cost of repairing the computers be considered as part of the acquisition cost?

ANS: If you were aware that the computers needed to be repaired when purchased, the repair costs are part of the cost of acquisition. If the computers were damaged after they were purchased, the costs should be treated as an expense on the income statement.

Group Purchase

Quite often a firm purchases several assets as a group and pays a lump-sum amount. This is most common when a company purchases land and a building situated on it and pays a lump-sum amount for both. It is important to measure separately the acquisition cost of the land and of the building. Land is not a depreciable asset, but the amount allocated to the building is subject to depreciation. In such cases as this, the purchase price should be allocated between land and building on the basis of the proportion of the *fair market value* of each.

For example, assume that on January 1, Payton Company purchased a building and the land that it is situated on for $100,000. The accountant was able to establish that the fair market values of the two assets on January 1 were as follows:

Land	$ 30,000
Building	90,000
Total	$120,000

On the basis of the estimated market values, the purchase price should be allocated as follows:

To land: $100,000 × $30,000/$120,000 = $25,000
To building: $100,000 × $90,000/$120,000 = $75,000

The effect of the purchase on the accounting equation is as follows:

BALANCE SHEET							INCOME STATEMENT
ASSETS		**=**	**LIABILITIES**	**+**	**OWNERS' EQUITY**	**+**	**REVENUES – EXPENSES**
Land	25,000						
Building	75,000						
Cash	(100,000)						

Market value is best established by an independent appraisal of the property. If such appraisal is not possible, the accountant must rely on the market value of other similar assets, on the value of the assets in tax records, or on other available evidence.

These efforts to allocate dollars between land and buildings will permit the appropriate allocation for depreciation. But when an investor or a lender views the balance sheet, he or she is often more interested in the current market value. The best things that can be said about historical cost are that it is a verifiable number and that it is conservative. But it is still up to the lender or the investor to determine the appropriate value for these assets.

Capitalization of Interest

We have seen that acquisition cost may include several items. But should the acquisition cost of an asset include the interest cost necessary to finance the asset? That is, should interest be treated as an asset, or should it be treated as an expense of the period?

Generally, the interest on borrowed money should be treated as an expense of the period. If a company buys an asset and borrows money to finance the purchase, the interest on the borrowed money is not considered part of the asset's cost. Financial statements generally treat investing and financing as separate decisions. Purchase of an asset, an investing activity, is treated as a business decision that is separate from the decision concerning the financing of the asset. Therefore, interest is treated as a period cost and should appear on the income statement as interest expense in the period incurred.

There is one exception to this general guideline, however. If a company *constructs* an asset over a period of time and borrows money to finance the construction, the amount of interest incurred during the construction period is not treated as interest expense. Instead, the interest must be included as part of the acquisition cost of the asset. This is referred to as **capitalization of interest.** The amount of interest that is capitalized (treated as an asset) is based on the *average accumulated expenditures.* The logic of using the average accumulated expenditure is that this number represents an average amount of money tied up in the

project over a year. If it takes $400,000 to construct a building, the interest should not be figured on the full $400,000 because there were times during the year when less than the full amount was being used.

When it costs $400,000 to build an asset and the amount of interest to be capitalized is $10,000, the acquisition cost of the asset is $410,000. The asset should appear on the balance sheet at that amount. Depreciation of the asset should be based on $410,000, less any residual value.

Land Improvements   It is important to distinguish between land and other costs associated with it. The acquisition cost of land should be kept in a separate account because land has an unlimited life and is not subject to depreciation. Other costs associated with land should be recorded in an account such as Land Improvements. For example, the costs of paving a parking lot or landscaping costs are properly treated as **land improvements,** which have a limited life. Therefore, the acquisition costs of land improvements should be depreciated over their useful lives.

Study Tip

Land improvements represent a depreciable asset with a limited life. Land itself is not depreciable.

USE AND DEPRECIATION OF PROPERTY, PLANT, AND EQUIPMENT

All property, plant, and equipment, except land, have a limited life and decline in usefulness over time. The accrual accounting process requires a proper *matching* of expenses and revenue to accurately measure income. Therefore, the accountant must estimate the decline in usefulness of operating assets and allocate the acquisition cost in a manner consistent with the decline in usefulness. This allocation is the process generally referred to as **depreciation.**

Unfortunately, proper matching for operating assets is not easy because of the many factors involved. An asset's decline in usefulness is related to *physical deterioration* factors, such as wear and tear. In some cases, the physical deterioration results from heavy use of the asset in the production process, but it may also result from the passage of time or exposure to the elements.

The decline in an asset's usefulness is also related to *obsolescence* factors. Some operating assets, such as computers, decline in usefulness simply because they have been surpassed by a newer model or newer technology. Finally, the decline in an asset's usefulness is related to a company's *repair and maintenance* policy. A company with an aggressive and extensive repair and maintenance program will not experience a decline in usefulness of operating assets as rapidly as one without such a policy.

Because the decline in an asset's usefulness is related to a variety of factors, several depreciation methods have been developed. In theory, a company should use a depreciation method that allocates the original cost of the asset to the periods benefited and that allows the company to accurately match the expense to the revenue generated by the asset. We will present three methods of depreciation: *straight line, units of production,* and *double declining balance.*

All depreciation methods are based on the asset's original acquisition cost. In addition, all methods require an estimate of two additional factors: the asset's *life* and its *residual value.* The residual value (also referred to as *salvage value*) should represent the amount that could be obtained from selling or disposing of the asset at the end of its useful life. Often this may be a small amount or even zero.

LO 5 Compare depreciation methods and understand the factors affecting the choice of method.

From Concept

TO PRACTICE 8.1

READING UNO'S ANNUAL REPORT
What amount did Uno report as depreciation and amortization in 1999? Where is it disclosed? What depreciation method was used?

Straight-Line Method   The **straight-line method** of depreciation allocates the cost of the asset evenly over time. This method calculates the annual depreciation as follows:

$$\text{Depreciation} = (\text{Acquisition Cost} - \text{Residual Value})/\text{Life}$$

For example, assume that on January 1, 2001, Kemp Company purchased a machine for $20,000. The company estimated that the machine's life would be five years and its residual value at the end of 2005 would be $2,000. The annual depreciation should be calculated as follows:

Property, plant, and equipment (PP&E) constitute operating assets, which show up in the Assets section of the balance sheet. For example, trucks and satellite equipment are essential for installing, maintaining, and operating cable service to customers and should be reported as property, plant, and equipment.

$$\text{Depreciation} = (\text{Acquisition Cost} - \text{Residual Value})/\text{Life}$$
$$\text{Depreciation} = (\$20,000 - \$2,000)/5$$
$$= \$3,600$$

An asset's **book value** is defined as its acquisition cost minus its total amount of accumulated depreciation. Thus, the book value of the machine in this example is $16,400 at the end of 2001:

$$\text{Book Value} = \text{Acquisition Cost} - \text{Accumulated Depreciation}$$
$$\text{Book Value} = \$20,000 - \$3,600$$
$$= \$16,400$$

The book value at the end of 2002 is $12,800:

$$\text{Book Value} = \text{Acquisition Cost} - \text{Accumulated Depreciation}$$
$$\text{Book Value} = \$20,000 - (2 \times \$3,600)$$
$$= \$12,800$$

The most attractive features of the straight-line method are its ease and its simplicity. It is the most popular method for presenting depreciation in the annual report to stockholders.

Units-of-Production Method   In some cases, the decline in an asset's usefulness is directly related to wear and tear as a result of the number of units it produces. In those cases, depreciation should be calculated by the **units-of-production method.** With this method, the asset's life is expressed in terms of the number of units that the asset can produce. The depreciation *per unit* can be calculated as follows:

$$\text{Depreciation per Unit} = (\text{Acquisition Cost} - \text{Residual Value})/$$
$$\text{Total Number of Units in Asset's Life}$$

The annual depreciation for a given year can be calculated based on the number of units produced during that year, as follows:

$$\text{Annual Depreciation} = \text{Depreciation per Unit} \times \text{Units Produced in Current Year}$$

For example, assume that Kemp Company in the previous example wanted to use the units-of-production method for 2001. Also assume that Kemp has been able to estimate that the total number of units that will be produced during the asset's five-year life is 18,000. During 2001, Kemp produced 4,000 units. The depreciation per unit for Kemp's machine can be calculated as follows:

$$\text{Depreciation per Unit} = (\text{Acquisition Cost} - \text{Residual Value})/\text{Life in Units}$$
$$\text{Depreciation per Unit} = (\$20,000 - \$2,000)/18,000$$
$$= \$1 \text{ per Unit}$$

The amount of depreciation that should be recorded as an expense for 2001 is $4,000:

$$\text{Annual Depreciation} = \text{Depreciation per Unit} \times \text{Units Produced in 2001}$$
$$\text{Annual Depreciation} = \$1 \text{ per Unit} \times 4,000 \text{ Units}$$
$$= \$4,000$$

Depreciation will be recorded until the asset produces 18,000 units. The machine cannot be depreciated below its residual value of $2,000.

The units-of-production method is most appropriate when the accountant is able to estimate the total number of units that will be produced over the asset's life. For example, if a factory machine is used to produce a particular item, the life of the asset may be expressed in terms of the number of units produced. Further, the units produced must be related to particular time periods so that depreciation expense can be matched accurately with the related revenue.

Accelerated Depreciation Methods In some cases, more cost should be allocated to the early years of an asset's use and less to the later years. For those assets, an accelerated method of depreciation is appropriate. The term **accelerated depreciation** refers to several depreciation methods by which a higher amount of depreciation is recorded in the early years than in later ones.

One form of accelerated depreciation is the **double declining-balance method.** Under this method, depreciation is calculated at double the straight-line rate but on a declining amount. The first step is to calculate the straight-line rate as a percentage. The straight-line rate for the Kemp asset with a five-year life is

$$100\%/5 \text{ Years} = 20\%.$$

The second step is to double the straight-line rate:

$$2 \times 20\% = 40\%$$

This rate will be applied in all years to the asset's book value at the beginning of each year. As depreciation is recorded, the book value declines. Thus, a constant rate is applied to a declining amount. This constant rate is applied to the full cost or initial book value, not to cost minus residual value, as in the other methods. However, the machine cannot be depreciated below its residual value.

The amount of depreciation for 2001 would be calculated as follows:

$$\text{Depreciation} = \text{Beginning Book Value} \times \text{Rate}$$
$$\text{Depreciation} = \$20,000 \times 40\%$$
$$= \$8,000$$

The amount of depreciation for 2002 would be calculated as follows:

$$\text{Depreciation} = \text{Beginning Book Value} \times \text{Rate}$$
$$\text{Depreciation} = (\$20,000 - \$8,000) \times 40\%$$
$$= \$4,800$$

Study Tip

Residual value is deducted for all depreciation methods except for the double declining-balance method.

The complete depreciation schedule for Kemp Company for all five years of the machine's life would be as follows:

Year	Rate	Book Value At Beginning of Year	Depreciation	Book Value At End of Year
2001	40%	$20,000	$ 8,000	$12,000
2002	40	12,000	4,800	7,200
2003	40	7,200	2,880	4,320
2004	40	4,320	1,728	2,592
2005	40	2,592	592	2,000
Total			$18,000	

In the Kemp Company example, the depreciation for 2005 cannot be calculated as $2,592 × 40% because this would result in an accumulated depreciation amount of more than $18,000. The total amount of depreciation recorded in Years 1 through 4 is $17,408. The accountant should record only $592 depreciation ($18,000 − $17,408) in 2005 so that the remaining value of the machine is $2,000 at the end of 2005.

The double declining-balance method of depreciation results in an accelerated depreciation pattern. This method is most appropriate for assets subject to a rapid decline in usefulness as a result of technical or obsolescence factors. Double declining-balance depreciation is not widely used for financial statement purposes but may be appropriate for certain assets. As discussed earlier, most companies use straight-line depreciation for financial statement purposes because it generally produces the highest net income, especially in growing companies that have a stable or expanding base of assets.

EXHIBIT 8-1　Comparison of Depreciation and Book Values of Straight-Line and Double Declining-Balance Methods

Year	Straight Line		Double Declining Balance	
	Depreciation	Book Value	Depreciation	Book Value
2001	$ 3,600	$16,400	$ 8,000	$12,000
2002	3,600	12,800	4,800	7,200
2003	3,600	9,200	2,880	4,320
2004	3,600	5,600	1,728	2,592
2005	3,600	2,000	592	2,000
Totals	$18,000		$18,000	

Comparison of Depreciation Methods　In this section, you have learned about several methods of depreciating operating assets. Exhibit 8-1 presents a comparison of the depreciation and book values of the Kemp Company asset for 2001–2005 using the straight-line and double declining-balance methods (we have excluded the units-of-production method). Note that both methods result in a depreciation total of $18,000 over the five-year time period. The amount of depreciation per year depends, however, on the method of depreciation chosen.

Nonaccountants often misunderstand the accountant's concept of depreciation. Accountants do not consider depreciation to be a process of *valuing* the asset. That is, depreciation does not describe the increase or decrease in the market value of the asset. Accountants consider depreciation to be a process of *cost allocation.* The purpose is to allocate the original acquisition cost to the periods benefited by the asset. The depreciation method chosen should be based on the decline in the asset's usefulness. A company can choose a different depreciation method for each individual fixed asset or for each class or category of fixed assets.

The choice of depreciation method can have a significant impact on the bottom line. If two companies are essentially identical in every other respect, a different depreciation method for fixed assets can make one company look more profitable than another. Or a company that uses accelerated depreciation for one year can find that its otherwise declining earnings are no longer declining if it switches to straight-line depreciation. Investors should pay some attention to depreciation methods when comparing companies. Statement users must be aware of the different depreciation methods to understand the calculation of income and to compare companies that may not use the same methods.

Some investors ignore depreciation altogether when evaluating a company, not because they do not know that assets depreciate but because they want to focus on cash flow instead of earnings. Depreciation is a "noncash" charge that reduces net income.

Depreciation and Income Taxes　Financial accounting involves the presentation of financial statements to external users of accounting information, users such as investors and creditors. When depreciating an asset for financial accounting purposes, the accountant should choose a depreciation method that is consistent with the asset's decline in usefulness and that properly allocates its cost to the periods that benefit from its use.

Depreciation is also deducted for income tax purposes. Sometimes depreciation is referred to as a *tax shield* because it reduces (as do other expenses) the amount of income tax that would otherwise have to be paid. When depreciating an asset for tax purposes, a company should generally choose a depreciation method that reduces the present value of its tax burden to the lowest possible amount over the life of the asset. Normally, this is best accomplished with an accelerated depreciation method, which allows a company to save more income tax in the early years of the asset. This happens because the higher depreciation charges reduce taxable income more than the straight-line method does. The method allowed for tax purposes is referred to as MACRS, which stands for Modified Accelerated Cost Recovery System. As a form of accelerated depreciation, it results in a larger amount of depreciation in the early years of asset life and a smaller amount in later years.

EXHIBIT 8-2 Management's Choice of Depreciation Method

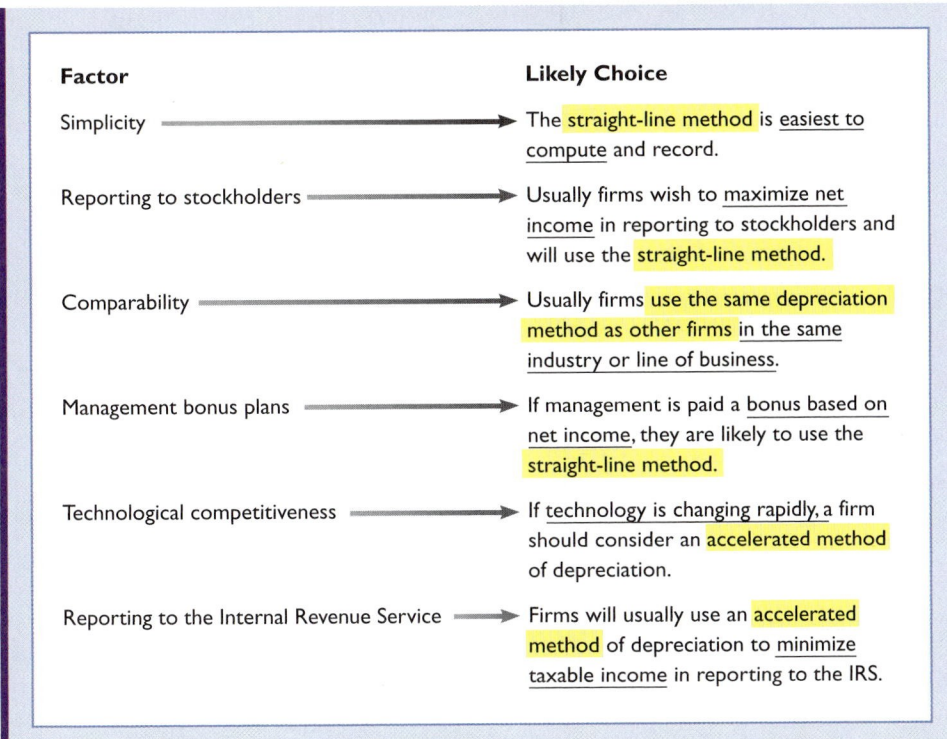

Factor	Likely Choice
Simplicity	The straight-line method is easiest to compute and record.
Reporting to stockholders	Usually firms wish to maximize net income in reporting to stockholders and will use the straight-line method.
Comparability	Usually firms use the same depreciation method as other firms in the same industry or line of business.
Management bonus plans	If management is paid a bonus based on net income, they are likely to use the straight-line method.
Technological competitiveness	If technology is changing rapidly, a firm should consider an accelerated method of depreciation.
Reporting to the Internal Revenue Service	Firms will usually use an accelerated method of depreciation to minimize taxable income in reporting to the IRS.

Choice of Depreciation Method   As we have stated, in theory a company should choose the depreciation method that best allocates the original cost of the asset to the periods benefited by the use of the asset. Theory aside, it is important to examine the other factors that affect a company's decision in choosing a depreciation method or methods. Exhibit 8–2 presents the factors that affect this decision and the likely choice that arises from each factor. Usually, the factors that are the most important are whether depreciation is calculated for presentation on the financial statements to stockholders or is calculated for income tax purposes.

When depreciation is calculated for financial statement purposes, a company generally wants to present the most favorable impression (the highest income) possible. Therefore, most companies choose the straight-line method of depreciation. Exhibit 8–3 indicates the results of a survey in which 600 companies were asked the depreciation method or methods used for their 1998 financial statements. The vast majority (577) used the straight-line method. Twenty-five used the declining-balance method, 9 used the sum-of-the-years'-digits method, 43 used accelerated depreciation but did not specify which form of accelerated depreciation, 36 used the units-of-production method, and 9 used other methods of depreciation. The number of companies does not total to 600 because many companies use different methods for different assets.

If the objective of the company's management is to minimize its income tax liability, then the company will generally not choose the straight-line method for tax purposes. As discussed in the preceding section, accelerated depreciation allows the company to save more on income taxes because depreciation is a tax shield. If we could construct an exhibit, similar to Exhibit 8–3, that indicated the methods of depreciation used for tax purposes, it would indicate that the vast majority of companies do, in fact, use accelerated depreciation for tax purposes.

Therefore, it is not unusual for a company to use *two* depreciation methods for the same asset, one for financial reporting purposes and another for tax purposes. This may seem somewhat confusing, but it is the direct result of the differing goals of financial and tax accounting. See Chapter 10 for more about this issue.

EXHIBIT 8-3   Depreciation Methods Used for Financial Reporting Purposes

Method	Number of Companies	
Straight line		577
Declining balance		25
Sum-of-the-years' digits		9
Other accelerated depreciation methods		43
Units of production		36
Other		9

www.aicpa.org

SOURCE: *Accounting Trends & Techniques*, 53rd ed. (New York: American Institute of Certified Public Accountants, 1999).

LO 6 Understand the impact of a change in the estimate of the asset life or residual value.

Change in Depreciation Estimate   An asset's acquisition cost is known at the time it is purchased, but its life and its residual value must be estimated. These estimates are then used as the basis for depreciating the asset. Occasionally, an estimate of the asset's life or residual value must be altered after the depreciation process has begun. This is an example of an accounting change that is referred to as a **change in estimate.**

Assume the same facts as in the Kemp Company example. The company purchased a machine on January 1, 2001, for $20,000. Kemp estimated that the machine's life would be five years and its residual value at the end of five years would be $2,000. Assume that Kemp has depreciated the machine using the straight-line method for two years. At the beginning of 2003, Kemp believes that the total machine life will be seven years, or another five years beyond the two years the machine has been used. Thus, depreciation must be adjusted to reflect the new estimate of the asset's life.

A change in estimate should be recorded *prospectively,* meaning that the depreciation recorded in prior years is not corrected or restated. Instead, the new estimate should affect the current year and future years. Kemp Company should depreciate the remaining depreciable amount during 2003 through 2007. The amount to be depreciated over that time period should be calculated as follows:

ACCOUNTING FOR YOUR DECISIONS

You Are the Sole Owner

Your accountant has presented you with three sets of financial statements—each with a different depreciation method—and asks you which depreciation method you prefer. You answer that other than for tax purposes, you don't really care. Should you?

ANS: For tax purposes, you would prefer to use the accelerated depreciation method, which minimizes your net income so that you can pay the minimum allowable taxes. For financial statement purposes, you may use a different method. As a sole owner, you may believe that the depreciation method chosen does not matter because you are more concerned with the cash flow of the firm and depreciation is a noncash item. However, the depreciation method is important if you are going to show your statements to external parties—for example, if you must present your statements to a banker in order to get a loan.

Acquisition Cost, Jan. 1, 2001	$20,000
Less: Accumulated Depreciation	
(2 years at $3,600 per year)	7,200
Book Value, Jan. 1, 2003	$12,800
Less: Residual Value	2,000
Remaining Depreciable Amount	$10,800

The remaining depreciable amount should be recorded as depreciation over the remaining life of the machine. In the Kemp Company case, the depreciation amount for 2003 and the following four years would be $2,160:

$$\text{Depreciation} = \text{Remaining Depreciable Amount/Remaining Life}$$

$$\text{Depreciation} = \$10,800/5 \text{ Years}$$

$$= \$2,160$$

If the change in estimate is a material amount, the company should disclose in the footnotes to the 2003 financial statements that depreciation has changed as a result of a change in estimate. The company's auditors have to be very careful that management's decision to change its estimate of the depreciable life of the asset is not simply an attempt to manipulate earnings. Particularly in capital-intensive manufacturing concerns, lengthening the useful life of equipment can have a material impact on earnings.

A change in estimate of an asset's residual value is treated in a manner similar to a change in an asset's life. There should be no attempt to correct or restate the income statements of past periods that were based on the original estimate. Instead, the accountant should use the new estimate of residual value to calculate depreciation for the current and future years.

A change in estimate is not treated the same way as a *change in principle*. If a company changes its *method* of depreciation—for example, from accelerated depreciation to the straight-line method—this constitutes a change in accounting principle and must be disclosed separately on the income statement.

Two-Minute Review

1. *What items should be included when calculating the acquisition cost of an asset?*

2. *Which will be higher in the early years of an asset's life—straight-line depreciation or accelerated depreciation? Which will be higher in the later years? Which will be higher in total over the entire life of the asset?*

Answers:

1. *The general rule for calculating the acquisition cost of an asset is to include all the costs that were necessary to acquire the asset and prepare it for use. Normally, that would include the purchase price but would also include such costs as freight costs, taxes, and installation costs if they were necessary to prepare the asset for use.*

2. *Accelerated depreciation will be higher in the early years of the asset, and straight-line will be higher in the later years. Over the life of the asset, the total amount of depreciation will be the same under all the methods, assuming that the same amount of salvage value is estimated for each of the methods.*

CAPITAL VERSUS REVENUE EXPENDITURES

Accountants must often decide whether certain expenditures related to operating assets should be treated as an addition to the cost of the asset or as an expense. One of the most common examples involving this decision concerns repairs to an asset. Should the repairs constitute capital expenditures or revenue expenditures? A **capital expenditure** is a cost that is added to the acquisition cost of the asset. A **revenue expenditure** is not treated as part of the cost of the asset but as an expense on the income statement. Thus, the company

LO 7 Determine which expenditures should be capitalized as asset costs and which should be treated as expenses.

must decide whether to treat an item as an asset (balance sheet) and depreciate its cost over its life or to treat it as an expense (income statement) of a single period.

The distinction between capital and revenue expenditures is a matter of judgment. Generally, the guideline that should be followed is that if an expenditure increases the life of the asset or its productivity, it should be treated as a capital expenditure and added to the asset account. If an expenditure simply maintains an asset in its normal operating condition, however, it should be treated as an expense. The *materiality* of the expenditure must also be considered. Most companies establish a policy of treating an expenditure smaller than a specified amount as a revenue expenditure (an expense on the income statement).

It is very important that a company not improperly capitalize a material expenditure that should have been written off right away. The capitalization policies of companies are closely watched by Wall Street analysts who try to assess the value of these companies. When a company is capitalizing rather than expensing certain items to artificially boost earnings, that revelation can be very damaging to the stock price.

Expenditures related to operating assets may be classified in several categories. For each type of expenditure, its treatment as capital or revenue should be as follows:

Category	Example	Asset or Expense
Normal maintenance	Repainting	Expense
Minor repair	Replace spark plugs	Expense
Major repair	Replace a vehicle's engine	Asset, if life or productivity is enhanced
Addition	Add a wing to a building	Asset

ACCOUNTING FOR YOUR DECISIONS

You Are the Owner

You are a realtor whose business car has just had its transmission rebuilt for $400. Would you classify this "repair" as a capital expenditure or a revenue expenditure? Why is it important to properly classify the $400?

ANS: If the business car's life is not extended, then the repair should be treated as a revenue expenditure, in which the cost is expensed on the income statement. It is important to properly classify capital and revenue expenditures because capitalizing rather than expensing costs can artificially boost earnings. The opposite effect would occur if costs are expensed and not capitalized.

An item treated as a capital expenditure affects the amount of depreciation that should be recorded over the asset's remaining life. We return to the Kemp Company example to illustrate. Assume again that Kemp purchased a machine on January 1, 2001, for $20,000. Kemp estimated that its residual value at the end of five years would be $2,000 and has depreciated the machine using the straight-line method for 2001 and 2002. At the beginning of 2003, Kemp made a $3,000 overhaul to the machine, extending its life by three years. Because the expenditure qualifies as a capital expenditure, the cost of overhauling the machine should be added to the asset account. The effect on the accounting equation is as follows:

		BALANCE SHEET					INCOME STATEMENT	
ASSETS	=	LIABILITIES	+	OWNERS' EQUITY	+	REVENUES – EXPENSES
Machine	3,000						
Cash	(3,000)						

For the years 2001 and 2002, Kemp recorded depreciation of $3,600 per year:

$$\text{Depreciation} = (\text{Acquisition Cost} - \text{Residual Value})/\text{Life}$$

$$\text{Depreciation} = (\$20,000 - \$2,000)/5$$

$$= \$3,600$$

Beginning in 2003, Kemp should record depreciation of $2,300 per year, computed as follows:

Original Cost, Jan. 1, 2001	$20,000
Less: Accumulated Depreciation (2 years × $3,600)	7,200
Book Value, Jan. 1, 2003	$12,800
Plus: Major Overhaul	3,000
Less: Residual Value	(2,000)
Remaining Depreciable Amount	$13,800

$$\text{Depreciation} = \text{Remaining Depreciable Amount}/\text{Remaining Life}$$

$$\text{Depreciation per year} = \$13,800/6 \text{ Years}$$

$$= \$2,300$$

ENVIRONMENTAL ASPECTS OF OPERATING ASSETS

As the number of the government's environmental regulations has increased, businesses have been required to expend more money complying with them. A common example involves costs to comply with federal requirements to clean up contaminated soil surrounding plant facilities. In some cases, the costs are very large and may exceed the value of the property. Should such costs be considered an expense and recorded entirely in one accounting period, or should they be treated as a capital expenditure and added to the cost of the asset? At the present time, there is little accounting guidance on such issues, and management must exercise careful judgment on a case-by-case basis. It is important, however, for companies at least to conduct a thorough investigation to determine the potential environmental considerations that may affect the value of operating assets and to ponder carefully the accounting implications of new environmental regulations.

Should the costs of cleaning up a contaminated factory be considered an expense of one period or a capital expenditure added to the cost of the plant asset? To make the best decision, management should gather all the facts about the extent of the proposed cleanup and its environmental impact.

DISPOSAL OF PROPERTY, PLANT, AND EQUIPMENT

LO 8 Analyze the effect of the disposal of an asset at a gain or loss.

An asset may be disposed of in any of several ways. One common method is to sell the asset for cash. Sale of an asset involves two important considerations. First, depreciation must be recorded up to the date of sale. If the sale does not occur at the fiscal year-end, usually December 31, depreciation must be recorded for a partial period from the beginning of the year to the date of sale. Second, the company selling the asset must calculate and record the gain or loss on its sale.

Refer again to the Kemp Company example. Assume that Kemp purchased a machine on January 1, 2001, for $20,000, estimating its life to be five years and the residual value to be $2,000. Kemp used the straight-line method of depreciation. Assume that Kemp sold the machine on July 1, 2003, for $12,400. Depreciation for the six-month period from January 1 to July 1, 2003, is $1,800 ($3,600 per year × 1/2 year = $1,800). As of July 1, the balance of the Accumulated Depreciation—Machine account is $9,000, which reflects depreciation for the 2½ years from the date of purchase to the date of sale. The effect on the accounting equation of the sale of the machine is as follows:

BALANCE SHEET						INCOME STATEMENT	
ASSETS	**=**	**LIABILITIES**	**+**	**OWNERS' EQUITY**	**+**	**REVENUES – EXPENSES**	
Accumulated						Gain on Sale	
Depreciation 9,000						of Asset	1,400
Cash 12,400							
Machine (20,000)							

When an asset is sold, all accounts related to it must be removed. In the preceding entry, the Machine account is reduced to eliminate the account, and the Accumulated Depreciation—Machine account is reduced to eliminate it. The **Gain on Sale of Asset** indicates the amount by which the sale price of the machine *exceeds* the book value. Thus, the gain can be calculated as follows:

Asset cost	$20,000
Less: Accumulated depreciation	9,000
Book value	$11,000
Sale price	12,400
Gain on Sale of Asset	$ 1,400

The account Gain on Sale of Asset is an income statement account and should appear in the Other Income/Expense category of the statement. The Gain on Sale of Asset account is not treated as revenue because it does not constitute the company's ongoing or central activity. Instead, it appears as income but in a separate category to denote its incidental nature.

The calculation of a loss on the sale of an asset is similar to that of a gain. Assume in the preceding example that Kemp had sold the machine on July 1, 2003, for $10,000 cash. As in the previous example, depreciation must be recorded to the date of sale, July 1. The effect on the accounting equation of the sale is as follows:

	BALANCE SHEET			INCOME STATEMENT	
ASSETS	**= LIABILITIES**	**+**	**OWNERS' EQUITY**	**+ REVENUES – EXPENSES**	
Accumulated				Loss on Sale	
Depreciation 9,000				of Asset	(1,000)
Cash 10,000					
Machine (20,000)					

The **Loss on Sale of Asset** indicates the amount by which the asset's sales price *is less than* its book value. Thus, the loss could be calculated as follows:

Asset cost	$20,000
Less: Accumulated depreciation	9,000
Book value	$11,000
Sale price	10,000
Loss on Sale of Asset	$ 1,000

The Loss on Sale of Asset account is an income statement account and should appear in the Other Income/Expense category of the income statement.

OPERATING ASSETS: NATURAL RESOURCES

BALANCE SHEET PRESENTATION

Important operating assets for some companies consist of **natural resources,** such as coalfields, oil wells, other mineral deposits, and timberlands. Natural resources share one characteristic: the resource is consumed as it is used. For example, the coal a utility company uses to make electricity is consumed in the process. Most natural resources cannot be replenished in the foreseeable future. Coal and oil, for example, can be replenished only by nature over millions of years. Timberlands may be replenished in a shorter period, but even trees must grow for many years to be usable for lumber.

Natural resources should be carried in the Property, Plant, and Equipment category of the balance sheet as an operating asset. Like other assets in the category, natural resources should initially be recorded at *acquisition cost*. Acquisition cost should include the cost of acquiring the natural resource and the costs necessary to prepare the asset for use. The

	December 31	
	1999	**1998**
	(expressed in thousands)	
Property		
Property and equipment		
Land and land improvements...	70,441	63,307
Buildings and improvements..	613,729	575,509
Machinery and equipment	4,300,250	4,082,724
	4,984,420	4,721,540
Accumulated depreciation...	(2,427,415)	(2,150,385)
	2,557,005	2,571,155
Timber, timberlands, and timber deposits..	294,663	270,570
	2,851,668	2,841,725

Cost of company timber harvested and amortization of logging roads are determined on the basis of the annual amount of timber cut in relation to the total amount of recoverable timber. Timber and timberlands are stated at cost, less the accumulated cost of timber previously harvested.

preparation costs for natural resources may often be very large; for example, a utility may spend large sums to remove layers of dirt before the coal can be mined. These preparation costs should be added to the cost of the asset.

DEPLETION OF NATURAL RESOURCES

When a natural resource is used or consumed, it should be treated as an expense. The process of recording the expense is similar to the depreciation or amortization process, but is usually referred to as *depletion.* The amount of depletion expense each period should reflect the portion of the natural resource that was used during the current year.

Assume, for example, that Local Coal Company purchased a coalfield on January 1, 2001, for $1 million. The company employed a team of engineering experts who estimated the total coal in the field to be 200,000 tons and who determined that the field's residual value after removal of the coal would be zero. Local Coal should calculate the depletion per ton as follows:

$$\text{Depletion per Ton} = (\text{Acquisition Cost} - \text{Residual Value})/\text{Total Number of Tons in Asset's Life}$$

$$= (\$1,000,000 - 0)/200,000 \text{ tons}$$

$$= \$5 \text{ per ton}$$

Depletion expense for each year should be calculated as follows:

$$\text{Depletion Expense} = \text{Depletion per Ton} \times \text{Tons Mined during Year}$$

Assume that Local Coal Company mined 10,000 tons of coal during 2001. The depletion expense for 2001 for Local Coal follows:

$$\$5 \times 10,000 \text{ tons} = \$50,000$$

Local Coal should record the depletion in an Accumulated Depletion—Coalfield account, which would appear as a contra-asset on the balance sheet. Rather than using an accumulated depletion account, some companies may decrease the asset account directly.

There is an interesting parallel between depletion of natural resources and depreciation of plant and equipment. That is, depletion is very similar to depreciation using the units-of-production method. Both require an estimate of the useful life of the asset in terms of the total amount that can be produced (for units-of-production method) or consumed (for depletion) over the asset's life.

www.boisecascade.com

Natural resources may be important assets for some companies. For example, Exhibit 8-4 highlights the asset portion of the 1999 balance sheet and the accompanying footnote of Boise Cascade Corporation. Boise Cascade had timber and timberlands, net of depletion, of $294,663,000 as of December 31, 1999. The footnote indicates that the company records the cost of timber harvested on the basis of annual amount of timber cut in relation to the total amount of recoverable timber.

OPERATING ASSETS: INTANGIBLE ASSETS

Intangible assets are long-term assets with no physical properties. Because one cannot see or touch most intangible assets, it is easy to overlook their importance. Intangibles are recorded as assets, however, because they provide future economic benefits to the company. In fact, an intangible asset may be the most important asset a company owns or controls. For example, a pharmaceutical company may own some property, plant, and equipment, but its most important asset may be its patent for a particular drug or process.

BUSINESS STRATEGY

In the furor surrounding the music industry's lawsuit against Napster, the Internet service that provided a way for computer users to trade music files instead of buying them, media firms (and the public) are becoming much more aware of the value of intangible assets. Determined to head off the possibility of a Napster-like firm in the home video industry, Sony Corp. is preparing the technology and the business partnerships it will need to ensure it can prevent unauthorized parties from delivering movies to consumers electronically.

Sony Corp. is among the leading motion picture production and distribution companies in the United States and worldwide and also leads in music, television production, computer entertainment operations, and online businesses. The company announced early in 2001 that it was preparing to launch its Internet video-on-demand movie service and expected to have several major studios, such as Warner Bros. (a division of Time Warner), MGM, Universal, and Paramount, on board as partners in the new venture.

Other movie companies like Fox and Disney are believed to be investigating similar arrangements, and any deals that are made are likely to be complex. Many regulatory, technical, and copyright issues will have to be resolved in order to deliver movies via the Internet, but at least for now, Sony anticipates that it will rely on the same service model used for pay-per-view, releasing films to its Internet distributors 30 to 60 days after the home video release and months before the films reach premium cable TV channels like HBO and Showtime.

Sony's new service is built on the fact that film companies like Warner Bros. expect future income from intangible assets like the copyrights on their movies. How do you think they can best protect those assets, and how does free distribution on the Internet affect their value? Why would media companies want to make a partnership with Sony's new video-on-demand service a part of their business strategy?

SOURCES: "Net Pix in Sony Sights," Reuters Limited, Jan. 9, 2001, accessed at http://dailynews.yahoo.com/htx/nm/20010109/en/industry-sony_1.html; Christopher Stern, "Satellite, Cable Firms Escalate Competition," *Washington Post*, Aug. 13, 2000, p. E1; Spencer E. Ante, "The Broadband Edge," ABC News.com, Jan. 11, 2000.

EXHIBIT 8-5   Most Common Intangible Assets

Intangible Asset	Description
Patent	Right to use, manufacture, or sell a product; granted by the U.S. Patent Office. Patents have a legal life of 20 years.
Copyright	Right to reproduce or sell a published work. Copyrights are granted for 50 years plus the life of the creator.
Trademark	A symbol or name that allows a product or service to be identified; provides legal protection for 20 years plus an indefinite number of renewal periods.
Goodwill	The excess of the purchase price to acquire a business over the value of the individual net assets acquired.

Likewise, the company that publishes this textbook may consider the copyrights to textbooks to be among its most important revenue-producing assets.

The balance sheet includes the intangible assets that meet the accounting definition of assets. Patents, copyrights, and brand names are included because they are owned by the company and will produce a future benefit that can be identified and measured. The balance sheet, however, would indicate only the acquisition cost of those assets, not the value of the assets to the company or the sales value of the assets.

Of course, the balance sheet does not include all the items that may produce future benefit to the company. A company's employees, its management team, its location, or the intellectual capital of a few key researchers may well provide important future benefits and value. They are not recorded on the balance sheet, however, because they do not meet the accountant's definition of *assets* and cannot be easily identified or measured.

BALANCE SHEET PRESENTATION

Intangible assets are long-term assets and should be shown separately from property, plant, and equipment. Exhibit 8-5 contains a list of the most common intangible assets. Some companies develop a separate category, Intangible Assets, for the various types of intangibles. For example, Exhibit 8-6 presents the Assets section and the accompanying footnote of the 1999 balance sheet of Quaker Oats Company. Note that intangibles account for nearly one-tenth of Quaker's total assets. Quaker presents only one line for intangible assets, but the footnote indicates that intangibles consist primarily of goodwill (see below), which is amortized on a straight-line basis. The presentation of intangible assets varies widely, however.

Exhibit 8-7 presents the Assets section and the accompanying footnote of the 1999 balance sheet of Alberto-Culver Company. Alberto-Culver presents the intangible assets of goodwill and trade names immediately after the Property, Plant, and Equipment category. Both accounts are presented net of the accumulated amortization. The footnote indicates that amortization was computed on the straight-line basis.

The nature of many intangibles is fairly evident, but goodwill is not so easily understood. **Goodwill** represents the amount of the purchase price paid in excess of the market value of the individual net assets when a business is purchased. Goodwill is recorded only when a business is purchased. It is not recorded when a company engages in activities that do not involve the purchase of another business entity. For example, customer loyalty or a good management team may represent "goodwill," but neither meets the accountants' criteria to be recorded as an asset on a firm's financial statements.

Some investors believe that goodwill is not an asset because it is difficult to determine the factors that caused this asset. They prefer to focus their attention on a company's tangible assets. These investors simply reduce the amount shown on the balance sheet by the amount of goodwill, deducting it from total assets and reducing stockholders' equity by the same amount. That is similar to the goodwill accounting that occurs in many foreign countries. International accounting standards allow firms *either* to present goodwill separately as an

From **Concept**

TO PRACTICE 8.2

READING TIME WARNER'S BALANCE SHEET   Which items on Time Warner's 1999 balance sheet should be considered intangible assets?

LO 9 Understand the balance sheet presentation of intangible assets.

www.quakeroats.com

www.alberto-culver.com

**Consolidated
Balance Sheets**

December 31	1999	1998
Assets		
Current Assets		
Cash and cash equivalents	$ 282.9	$ 326.6
Marketable securities	0.3	27.5
Trade accounts receivable – net of allowances	254.3	283.4
Inventories		
Finished goods	186.6	189.1
Grains and raw materials	50.0	48.4
Packaging materials and supplies	29.6	23.9
Total inventories	266.2	261.4
Other current assets	193.0	216.1
Total Current Assets	996.7	1,115.0
Property, Plant and Equipment		
Land	28.2	24.1
Buildings and improvements	407.6	390.2
Machinery and equipment	1,416.1	1,404.5
Property, plant and equipment	1,851.9	1,818.8
Less: Accumulated depreciation	745.2	748.6
Property – Net	1,106.7	1,070.2
Intangible Assets – Net of Amortization	236.9	245.7
Other Assets	55.9	79.4
Total Assets	$ 2,396.2	$ 2,510.3

See accompanying notes to the consolidated financial statements.

Intangibles—Intangible assets consist principally of excess purchase price over net tangible assets of businesses acquired (goodwill) and trademarks. Intangible assets are amortized on a straight-line basis over periods ranging from two to 40 years.

asset *or* to deduct it from stockholders' equity at the time of purchase. The result is that the presentation of goodwill on the financial statements of non-U.S. companies can look much different from that for U.S. companies.

ACQUISITION COST OF INTANGIBLE ASSETS

As was the case with property, plant, and equipment, the acquisition cost of an intangible asset includes all the costs to acquire the asset and prepare it for its intended use. This should include all necessary costs, such as legal costs incurred at the time of acquisition. Acquisition cost also should include those costs that are incurred after acquisition and that are necessary to the existence of the asset. For example, if a firm must pay legal fees to protect a patent from infringement, the costs should be considered part of the acquisition cost and should be included in the patent account.

You should also be aware of one item that is similar to intangible assets but is *not* on the balance sheet. **Research and development costs** are expenditures incurred in the discovery of new knowledge and the translation of research into a design or plan for a new product or service or in a significant improvement to an existing product or service. Firms that engage in research and development do so because they believe such activities provide future benefit to the company. In fact, many firms have become leaders in an industry by engaging in research and development and the discovery of new products or technology. It is often very difficult, however, to identify the amount of future benefits of research and development and to associate those benefits with specific time periods. Because of the difficulty in predicting future benefits, the FASB has ruled that firms are not allowed to treat research and

Consolidated Balance Sheets

Alberto-Culver Company and Subsidiaries

	September 30,	
(In thousands, except share data)	1999	1998
Assets		
Current assets:		
Cash and cash equivalents	$ 55,931	72,395
Short-term investments	1,885	910
Receivables, less allowance for doubtful accounts of		
$8,441 in 1999 and $10,868 in 1998	144,075	129,063
Inventories:		
Raw materials	43,399	37,316
Work-in-process	4,582	6,119
Finished goods	373,907	325,769
Total inventories	421,888	369,204
Prepaid expenses	21,775	19,993
Total current assets	645,554	591,565
Property, plant and equipment:		
Land	13,412	11,328
Buildings and leasehold improvements	142,042	139,622
Machinery and equipment	274,107	257,458
Total property, plant and equipment	429,561	408,408
Accumulated depreciation	190,808	184,932
Property, plant and equipment, net	238,753	223,476
Goodwill, net	172,109	137,599
Trade names, net	72,975	67,158
Other assets	55,143	48,386
	$1,184,534	1,068,184

> **Goodwill and Trade Names** The cost of goodwill and trade names is amortized on a straight-line basis over periods ranging from ten to forty years.

development costs as assets; all such expenditures must be treated as expenses in the period incurred. Many firms, especially high-technology ones, argue that this accounting rule results in seriously understated balance sheets. In their view, an important "asset" is not portrayed on their balance sheet. They also argue that they are at a competitive disadvantage when compared with foreign companies that are allowed to treat at least a portion of research and development as an asset. Users of financial statements somehow need to be aware of those "hidden assets" when analyzing the balance sheets of companies that must expense research and development costs.

It is important to distinguish between patent costs and research and development costs. Patent costs include legal and filing fees necessary to acquire a patent. Such costs are capitalized as an intangible asset, Patent. However, the Patent account should not include the costs of research and development of a new product. Those costs are not capitalized but are treated as an expense, Research and Development.

AMORTIZATION OF INTANGIBLES

Intangibles should be reported on the balance sheet at acquisition cost less accumulated amortization. *Amortization* is very similar to depreciation of property, plant, and equipment. Amortization involves allocating the acquisition cost of the intangible asset to the

LO 10 Describe the proper amortization of intangible assets.

periods benefited by the use of the asset; accounting standards state that the period may generally not exceed 20 years. In most cases, companies use the straight-line method of amortization. You may see instances of an accelerated form of amortization, however, if the decline in usefulness of the intangible asset does not occur evenly over time.

Assume that ML Company developed a patent for a new product on January 1, 2001. The costs involved with patent approval were $10,000, and the company wants to record amortization on the straight-line basis over a five-year life with no residual value. The effect on the accounting equation of the amortization is as follows:

BALANCE SHEET						INCOME STATEMENT	
ASSETS	=	LIABILITIES	+	OWNERS' EQUITY	+	REVENUES – EXPENSES	
Accumulated Amortization (2,000)						Patent Expense	(2,000)

Rather than use an accumulated amortization account, some companies decrease the intangible asset account directly. The asset should be reported on the balance sheet at acquisition cost ($10,000) less accumulated amortization ($2,000), or $8,000, as of December 31, 2001.

Some questions exist about the time period over which to amortize intangible assets. The guideline is that an intangible should be amortized *over its legal life or useful life, whichever is shorter.* For example, a patent has a legal life of 20 years, but many are not useful for that long because new products and technology may surpass them.[2] The patent should be amortized over the number of years in which the firm receives benefits, which may be a period shorter than its legal life.

Certain intangibles have no legal life, and their useful life is very difficult to determine. Goodwill is the primary example. Some accountants argue that goodwill has an unlimited life and should not be amortized. Others argue that the benefits of goodwill are too difficult to determine and this intangible asset should be written off as an expense in its entirety in the year of acquisition. The current accounting guideline takes a compromise approach. Goodwill must be amortized over a period that cannot exceed 20 years. Thus, goodwill must be amortized in a manner similar to the amortization of other intangible assets: over its estimated useful life. But if it is not possible to determine the useful life, the maximum amortization period is 20 years.[3]

---

[2]Patents run for a term of 20 years from the filing date or 17 years from the date they are granted. This textbook will use 20 years as the time period for amortization.

[3]The accounting rules stated in this section are from the FASB Exposure Draft, "Business Combinations and Intangible Assets," September 7, 1999. There is one exception to the 20-year rule. If an intangible asset has identifiable cash flows that will extend beyond 20 years and meets certain other criteria, then the intangible may be amortized over a longer period or in some cases may not be amortized at all.

Finally, it is important to monitor the usefulness of intangible assets as time passes. An intangible asset that will not produce future benefit should be written off as an expense. Assume in the ML example that ML learns on January 1, 2002, when accumulated amortization is $2,000 (or the book value of the patent is $8,000), that a competing company has developed a new product that renders ML's patent worthless. ML has a loss of $8,000, which is the book value of the patent at the time it is deemed to be worthless. The effect on the accounting equation of the patent write-off is as follows:

BALANCE SHEET						INCOME STATEMENT	
ASSETS	=	LIABILITIES	+	OWNERS' EQUITY	+	REVENUES – EXPENSES	
Accumulated						Loss on Patent	(8,000)
Amortization	2,000						
Patent	(10,000)						

The treatment of intangibles with diminished value is consistent with the treatment of all assets. Assets existing on the balance sheet date represent future benefits or revenue. If an item does not have future usefulness, it must be removed from the balance sheet and treated as a loss or expense.

Two-Minute Review

1. What are some examples of intangible assets?

2. Over what time period should intangibles be amortized? What method is generally used?

Answers:

1. Intangibles are assets that have no physical properties. Examples are copyrights, trademarks, patents, franchises, and goodwill.

2. Intangibles should be amortized over the legal life of the asset or the useful life, whichever is shorter. The maximum time period for intangibles is generally twenty years, but in some cases a company may be able to justify a longer time period. Most companies use the straight-line method of amortization. Accelerated methods of amortization are allowed but are not often used.

ANALYZING LONG-TERM ASSETS FOR AVERAGE LIFE AND ASSET TURNOVER

Because long-term assets constitute the major productive assets of most companies, it is important to analyze the age and composition of these assets. We will analyze the assets of Uno in the following section. Analysis of the age of the assets can be accomplished fairly easily for those companies that use the straight-line method of depreciation. A rough measure of the *average life* of the assets can be calculated as follows:

Average Life = Property, Plant, and Equipment/Depreciation Expense

The *average age* of the assets can be calculated as follows:

Average Age = Accumulated Depreciation/Depreciation Expense

At the end of 1999, Uno had property, plant, and equipment of $128,746,000 and accumulated depreciation of $80,149,000. A careful reading of the annual report also indicates depreciation expense of $12,702,000 for 1999. Therefore, the average life of Uno's assets is calculated as follows:

www.pizzeriauno.com

Average Life = Property, Plant, and Equipment/Depreciation Expense

Average Life = $128,746,000/$12,702,000

= 10.14 years

This is a rough estimate because it assumes that the company has purchased assets fairly evenly over time. Because it is an average, it indicates that some assets have a life longer than 10.14 years and others have shorter lives.

The average age of Uno's assets is calculated as follows:

$$\text{Average Age} = \text{Accumulated Depreciation}/\text{Depreciation Expense}$$

$$\text{Average Age} = \$80,149,000/\$12,702,000$$

$$= 6.3 \text{ years}$$

This indicates that Uno's assets are, on average, fairly new and should be productive for several more years.

The asset category of the balance sheet is also important in analyzing the company's *profitability.* The asset turnover ratio is a measure of the productivity of the assets and is measured as follows:

$$\text{Asset Turnover} = \text{Net Sales}/\text{Average Total Assets}$$

This ratio is a measure of how many dollars of assets are necessary for every dollar of sales. If a company is using its assets efficiently, each dollar of assets will create a high amount of sales. Technically, the ratio is based on average *total assets,* but long-term assets often constitute the largest portion of a company's total assets.

HOW LONG-TERM ASSETS AFFECT THE STATEMENT OF CASH FLOWS

LO 11 Explain the impact that long-term assets have on the statement of cash flows.

Determining the impact that acquisition, depreciation, and sale of long-term assets have on the statement of cash flows is important. Each of these business activities influences the statement of cash flows. Exhibit 8-8 illustrates the items discussed in this chapter and their effect on the statement of cash flows.

The acquisition of a long-term asset is an investing activity and should be reflected in the Investing Activities category of the statement of cash flows. The acquisition should appear as a deduction or negative item in that section because it requires the use of cash to purchase the asset. This applies whether the long-term asset is property, plant, and equipment or an intangible asset.

The depreciation or amortization of a long-term asset is *not* a cash item. It was referred to earlier as a noncash charge to earnings. Nevertheless, it must be presented on the state-

EXHIBIT 8-8   Long-Term Assets and the Statement of Cash Flows

Item	Cash Flow Statement	
	Operating Activities	
	Net income	xxx
Depreciation and Amortization		+
Gain on sale of asset		−
Loss on sale of asset		+
	Investing Activities	
Purchase of asset		−
Sale of asset		+
	Financing Activities	

EXHIBIT 8-9 Time Warner Partial Consolidated Statement of Cash Flows

Years Ended December 31, (millions)	1999
	Historical
OPERATIONS	
Net income	$ 1,948
Adjustments for noncash and nonoperating items:	
Extraordinary loss on retirement of debt	12
Depreciation and amortization	2,529
Amortization of film costs	2,294
Noncash interest expense	4
Gain on sale or exchange of cable systems and investments	(2,247)
Excess (deficiency) of distributions over equity in pretax income	
of Entertainment Group	—
Equity in losses of other investee companies after distributions	344
Changes in operating assets and liabilities:	
Receivables	(349)
Inventories	(2,321)
Accounts payable and other liabilities	1,690
Other balance sheet changes	49
Cash provided by operations	3,953
INVESTING ACTIVITIES	
Consolidation of the Entertainment Group's cash and equivalents	87
Investments and acquisitions	(870)
Capital expenditures	(2,231)
Investment proceeds	1,084
Proceeds received from distribution of TWE Senior Capital	—
Cash provided (used) by investing activities	(1,930)

ment of cash flows (if the indirect method is used for the statement) because it was deducted from earnings in calculating the net income figure. Therefore, it must be eliminated or "added back" if the net income amount is used to indicate the amount of cash generated from operations. Thus, depreciation and amortization should be presented in the Operating Activities category of the statement of cash flows as an addition to net income.

The sale or disposition of long-term assets is an investing activity. When an asset is sold, the amount of cash received should be reflected as an addition or a plus amount in the Investing Activities category of the statement of cash flows. If the asset was sold at a gain or loss, however, one additional aspect should be reflected. Because the gain or loss was reflected on the income statement, it should be eliminated from the net income amount presented in the Operating Activities category (if the indirect method is used). A sale of an asset is not an activity related to normal, ongoing operations, and all amounts involved with the sale should be removed from the Operating Activities category. Exhibit 8-9 indicates the Operating and Investing categories of the 1999 statement of cash flows of Time Warner. The company had a net income during 1999; that income, of $1,948 million, is the first line of the Operations category of the cash flow statement. Time Warner's performance is an excellent example of the difference between the net income on the income statement and actual cash flow. Note that the company generated a positive cash flow from operations of $3,953 million. One of the primary reasons was that depreciation and amortization of $2,529 million affected the income statement but do not involve a cash outflow and are therefore added on the cash flow statement. Also note that the Investing Activities category indicates major outlays of cash for new assets: $2,231 million for capital expenditures, which constitute additions to property, plant, and equipment.

www.timewarner.com

From *Concept*

TO PRACTICE 8.3

REFER TO GATEWAY'S CASH FLOW STATEMENT What amount did the company spend on capital expenditures during 1999?

FOCUS ON USERS

This Analyst Often Focuses on Intangible Assets

Aishetu Kolo is a financial analyst working in institutional equity sales trading in Chicago. It is her job to sell blocks of stock to institutional clients. As she forms opinions about the variety of stocks she works with every day, the longevity of the companies behind the stocks is a key factor, which Aishetu often gauges by looking at asset holdings.

Operating assets, for instance, can help her predict the long-term viability of a company because they show the sheer strength of its resources. It is possible for traders like Aishetu to make certain assumptions about a company's longevity if it has a solid operating asset base. This is not to say that companies without huge asset holdings do not have the same potential for long-term health. "When it comes to young companies," Aishetu says, "I often focus on *intangible* assets, such as key personnel, patents on technology, and market share."

It is important to be aware that intangible assets are not the same as other types of assets, however, and should be viewed accordingly. As Aishetu explains, "They can grossly over- or underestimate the true value of the financial position of a company. The exact value of a patent, for instance, can never be fully determined unless you try to buy or sell shares in the company," thereby assigning a price to the asset. This said, intangible assets can have the same value potential as other types of assets. As Aishetu puts it, "Imagine Microsoft without the vision of Bill Gates!"

> "When it comes to young companies, I often focus on *intangible* assets such as key personnel, patents on technology, and market share."
> —Aishetu Kolo

WARMUP EXERCISES

LO 5   Warmup Exercise 8-1   Depreciation Methods
Assume that a company purchases a depreciable asset on January 1 for $10,000. The asset has a four-year life and will have zero residual value at the end of the fourth year.

Required

Calculate depreciation expense for each of the four years using the straight-line method and the double declining-balance method.

LO 5   Warmup Exercise 8-2   Depreciation and Cash Flow
Use the information from Exercise 8-1. Assume that the double declining-balance method will be used for tax purposes and the straight-line method will be used for the financial statement to be given to the stockholders. Also assume that the tax rate is 40%.

Required

How much will the tax savings be in the first year as a result of using the accelerated method of depreciation?

Solutions to Warmup Exercises
Warmup Exercise 8-1

	Straight Line	Double Declining Balance	
Year 1	$2,500*	$10,000 × .50** =	$5,000
2	2,500	($10,000 − $5,000) × .50 =	2,500
3	2,500	($10,000 − $7,500) × .50 =	1,250
4	2,500	($10,000 − $8,750) × .50 =	625

*$10,000/4 years
**Straight-line rate as a percentage is 1 year/4 years or 25%. Double the rate is 25% × 2, or 50%.

Warmup Exercise 8-2

The tax savings is equal to the difference in depreciation between the two methods times the tax rate. Therefore, the tax savings is ($5,000 − $2,500) × .40 = $1,000.

REVIEW PROBLEM

The accountant for Becker Company wants to develop a balance sheet as of December 31, 2001. A review of the asset records has revealed the following information:

a. Asset A was purchased on July 1, 1999, for $40,000 and has been depreciated on the straight-line basis using an estimated life of six years and a residual value of $4,000.

b. Asset B was purchased on January 1, 2000, for $66,000. The straight-line method has been used for depreciation purposes. Originally, the estimated life of the asset was projected to be six years with a residual value of $6,000; however, at the beginning of 2001, the accountant learned that the remaining life of the asset was only three years, with a residual value of $2,000.

c. Asset C was purchased on January 1, 2000, for $50,000. The double declining-balance method has been used for depreciation purposes, with a four-year life and a residual value estimate of $5,000.

Required

1. Assume that these assets represent pieces of equipment. Calculate the acquisition cost, accumulated depreciation, and book value of each asset as of December 31, 2001.

2. How would the assets appear on the balance sheet on December 31, 2001?

3. Assume that Becker Company sold Asset B on January 2, 2002, for $25,000. Calculate the amount of the resulting gain or loss and determine the effect on the accounting equation of the sale. Where would the gain or loss appear on the income statement?

Solution to Review Problem

1.

Asset A

1999	Depreciation	($40,000 − $4,000)/6 × 1/2 Year	=	$ 3,000
2000		($40,000 − $4,000)/6	=	6,000
2001		($40,000 − $4,000)/6	=	6,000
	Accumulated Depreciation			$15,000

Asset B

2000	Depreciation	($66,000 − $6,000)/6	=	$10,000
2001		($66,000 − $10,000 − $2,000)/3	=	18,000
	Accumulated Depreciation			$28,000

Note the impact of the change in estimate on 2001 depreciation.

Asset C

2000	Depreciation	$50,000 × (25% × 2)	=	$25,000
2001		($50,000 − $25,000) × (25% × 2)	=	12,500
	Accumulated Depreciation			$37,500

BECKER COMPANY
SUMMARY OF ASSET COST AND ACCUMULATED DEPRECIATION
AS OF DECEMBER 31, 2001

Asset	Acquisition Cost	Accumulated Depreciation	Book Value
A	$ 40,000	$15,000	$25,000
B	66,000	28,000	38,000
C	50,000	37,500	12,500
Totals	$156,000	$80,500	$75,500

2. The assets would appear in the Long-Term Assets category of the balance sheet as follows:

Equipment	$156,000	
Less: Accumulated depreciation	80,500	
Equipment (net)		$75,500

3.

Asset B Book Value	$38,000
Selling Price	25,000
Loss on Sale of Asset	$13,000

	BALANCE SHEET					INCOME STATEMENT
ASSETS	**=**	**LIABILITIES**	**+**	**OWNERS' EQUITY**	**+**	**REVENUES – EXPENSES**
Cash 25,000						Loss on Sale of Asset (13,000)
Asset B (66,000)						
Accumulated Depreciation 28,000						

The Loss on Sale of Asset account should appear in the Other Income/Other Expense category of the income statement. It is similar to an expense but is not the company's major activity.

CHAPTER HIGHLIGHTS

1. **LO 1** Operating assets are normally presented on the balance sheet in one category for property, plant, and equipment and a second category for intangibles.

2. **LO 1** Operating assets should be presented at original acquisition cost less accumulated depreciation or amortization.

3. **LO 2** Acquisition cost should include all costs necessary to acquire the asset and prepare it for its intended use.

4. **LO 3** When assets are purchased for a lump sum, acquisition cost should be determined as the proportion of the market values of the assets purchased.

5. **LO 4** Interest on assets constructed over time should be capitalized. The amount of interest capitalized should be the average accumulated expenditures times an interest rate.

6. **LO 5** Several depreciation methods are available to describe the decline in usefulness of operating assets. The straight-line method is the most commonly used and assigns the same amount of depreciation to each time period over the asset's life.

7. **LO 5** Accelerated depreciation allocates a greater expense to the earlier years of an asset's life and less to later years. The double declining-balance method is one form of accelerated depreciation.

8. **LO 6** Depreciation is based on an estimate of the life of the asset and the residual value. When it is necessary to change the

estimate, the amount of depreciation expense is adjusted for the current year and future years. Past depreciation amounts are not restated.

9. **LO 7** Capital expenditures are costs that increase an asset's life or its productivity. Capital expenditures should be added to the cost of the asset. Revenue expenditures should be treated as an expense in the period in which they are incurred because they benefit only the current period.

10. **LO 8** The gain or loss on the disposal of an asset is the difference between the asset's book value and its selling price.

11. **LO 9** Intangible assets should be presented on the balance sheet at acquisition cost less accumulated amortization. Acquisition cost should include all costs necessary to acquire the asset.

12. **LO 10** Research and development costs are not treated as an intangible asset. Instead, they are treated as an expense in the year they are incurred.

13. **LO 10** Intangibles should be amortized over the shorter of their legal or useful life. All intangibles, including goodwill, should be amortized over a period not exceeding 20 years.

14. **LO 11** The acquisition of long-term assets should be reflected in the Investing Activities category of the statement of cash flows.

KEY TERMS QUIZ

Read each definition and then write the number of the definition in the blank beside the appropriate term it defines. The solution appears at the end of the chapter.

___ **Acquisition cost**   ___ **Land improvements**

___ **Capitalization of interest**   ___ **Depreciation**

___ Straight-line method
___ Book value
___ Units-of-production method
___ Accelerated depreciation
___ Double declining-balance method
___ Change in estimate
___ Capital expenditure

___ Revenue expenditure
___ Gain on Sale of Asset
___ Loss on Sale of Asset
___ Natural resources
___ Intangible assets
___ Goodwill
___ Research and development costs

1. This amount includes all the costs normally necessary to acquire an asset and prepare it for its intended use.

2. Additions made to a piece of property, such as paving or landscaping a parking lot. The costs are treated separately from land for purposes of recording depreciation.

3. A method by which the same dollar amount of depreciation is recorded in each year of asset use.

4. A method by which depreciation is determined as a function of the number of units the asset produces.

5. The process of treating the cost of interest on constructed assets as a part of the asset cost rather than as an expense.

6. A change in the life of an asset or in its expected residual value.

7. The allocation of the original acquisition cost of an asset to the periods benefited by its use.

8. A cost that improves an operating asset and is added to the asset account.

9. The original acquisition cost of an asset minus the amount of accumulated depreciation.

10. A cost that keeps an operating asset in its normal operating condition and is treated as an expense of the period.

11. An account whose amount indicates that the selling price received on an asset's disposal exceeds its book value.

12. An account whose amount indicates that the book value of an asset exceeds the selling price received on its disposal.

13. A term that refers to several methods by which a higher amount of depreciation is recorded in the early years of an asset's life and a lower amount is recorded in the later years.

14. Long-term assets that have no physical properties—for example, patents, copyrights, and goodwill.

15. A method by which depreciation is recorded at twice the straight-line rate but the depreciable balance is reduced in each period.

16. The amount indicating that the purchase price of a business exceeded the total fair market value of the identifiable net assets at the time the business was acquired.

17. Expenditures incurred in the discovery of new knowledge and the translation of research into a design or plan for a new product.

18. Assets that are consumed during their use—for example, coal or oil.

ALTERNATE TERMS

Accumulated depreciation Allowance for depreciation

Acquisition cost Historical cost

Capitalize Treat as asset

Construction in progress Construction in process

Goodwill Purchase price in excess of the market value of assets

Hidden assets Unrecorded or off–balance sheet assets

Property, Plant, and Equipment Fixed assets

Prospective Current and future years

Residual value Salvage value

Revenue expenditure An expense of the period

QUESTIONS

1. What are several examples of operating assets? Why are operating assets essential to a company's long-term future?

2. What is the meaning of the term *acquisition cost* of operating assets? Give some examples of costs that should be included in the acquisition cost.

3. When assets are purchased as a group, how should the acquisition cost of the individual assets be determined?

4. Why is it important to account separately for the cost of land and building, even when the two assets are purchased together?

5. Under what circumstances should interest be capitalized as part of the cost of an asset?

6. What factors may contribute to the decline in usefulness of operating assets? Should the choice of depreciation method be related to these factors? Must a company choose just one method of depreciation for all assets?

7. Why do you think that most companies use the straight-line method of depreciation?

8. How should the residual value of an operating asset be treated when using the straight-line method? How should it be treated when using the double declining-balance method?

9. Why do many companies use one method to calculate depreciation for the income statement developed for stockholders and another method for income tax purposes?

10. What should a company do if it finds that the original estimate of the life of an asset or the residual value of the asset must be changed?

11. What are the meanings of the terms *capital expenditures* and *revenue expenditures*? What determines whether an item is a capital or revenue expenditure?

12. How is the gain or loss on the sale of an operating asset calculated? Where would the Gain on Sale of Asset account appear on the financial statements?

13. What are several examples of items that constitute intangible assets? In what category of the balance sheet should intangible assets appear?

14. What is the meaning of the term *goodwill*? Give an example of a transaction that would result in the recording of goodwill on the balance sheet.

15. Do you agree with the FASB's ruling that all research and development costs should be treated as an expense on the income statement? Why or why not?

16. Do you agree with some accountants who argue that intangible assets have an unlimited life and, therefore, should not be subject to amortization?

17. When an intangible asset is amortized, should the asset's amortization occur over its legal life or over its useful life? Give an example in which the legal life exceeds the useful life.

18. Suppose that an intangible asset is being amortized over a 10-year time period but a competitor has just introduced a new product that will have a serious negative impact on the asset's value. Should the company continue to amortize the intangible asset over the 10-year life?

EXERCISES

LO 2 Exercise 8-1 Acquisition Cost

Ruby Company purchased a piece of equipment with a list price of $60,000 on January 1, 2001. The following amounts were related to the equipment purchase:

- Terms of the purchase were 2/10, net 30. Ruby paid for the purchase on January 8.
- Freight costs of $1,000 were incurred.
- A state agency required that a pollution-control device be installed on the equipment at a cost of $2,500.
- During installation, the equipment was damaged and repair costs of $4,000 were incurred.
- Architect's fees of $6,000 were paid to redesign the work space to accommodate the new equipment.
- Ruby purchased liability insurance to cover possible damage to the asset. The three-year policy cost $8,000. → *covers future not current risk*
- Ruby financed the purchase with a bank loan. Interest of $3,000 was paid on the loan during 2001. → *expense (always when buy stu.)*

Required

Determine the acquisition cost of the equipment.

LO 3 Exercise 8-2 Lump-Sum Purchase

To add to his growing chain of grocery stores, on January 1, 2001, Danny Marks bought a grocery store of a small competitor for $520,000. An appraiser, hired to assess the value of the assets acquired, determined that the land had a market value of $200,000, the building a market value of $150,000, and the equipment a market value of $250,000.

Required

1. What is the acquisition cost of each asset?
2. Danny plans to depreciate the operating assets on a straight-line basis for 20 years. Determine the amount of depreciation expense for 2001 on these newly acquired assets.
3. How would the assets appear on the balance sheet as of December 31, 2001?

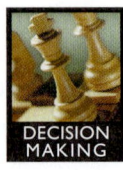

LO 5 Exercise 8-3 Straight-Line and Units-of-Production Methods

Assume that Sample Company purchased factory equipment on January 1, 2001, for $60,000. The equipment has an estimated life of five years and an estimated residual value of $5,000. Sample's accountant is considering whether to use the straight-line or the units-of-production method to depreciate the asset. Because the company is beginning a new production process, the equipment will be used to produce 10,000 units in 2001, but production subsequent to 2001 will increase by 10,000 units each year.

Required

Calculate the depreciation expense, the accumulated depreciation, and the book value of the equipment under both methods for each of the five years of the asset's life. Do you think that the units-of-production method yields reasonable results in this situation?

LO 5 Exercise 8-4 Accelerated Depreciation
Koffman's Warehouse purchased a forklift on January 1, 2001, for $6,000. It is expected to last for five years and have a residual value of $600. Koffman's uses the double declining-balance method for depreciation.

Required

1. Calculate the depreciation expense, the accumulated depreciation, and the book value for each year of the forklift's life.

2. Determine the effect on the accounting equation of the depreciation expense for 2002.

3. Refer to Exhibit 8-2. What factors may have influenced Koffman to use the double declining-balance method?

LO 6 Exercise 8-5 Change in Estimate
Assume that Bloomer Company purchased a new machine on January 1, 2001, for $80,000. The machine has an estimated useful life of nine years and a residual value of $8,000. Bloomer has chosen to use the straight-line method of depreciation. On January 1, 2003, Bloomer discovered that the machine would not be useful beyond December 31, 2006, and estimated its value at that time to be $2,000.

Required

1. Calculate the depreciation expense, the accumulated depreciation, and the book value of the asset for each year, 2001 to 2006.

2. Was the depreciation recorded in 2001 and 2002 wrong? If so, why was it not corrected?

LO 8 Exercise 8-6 Asset Disposal
Assume that Gonzalez Company purchased an asset on January 1, 1999, for $60,000. The asset had an estimated life of six years and an estimated residual value of $6,000. The company used the straight-line method to depreciate the asset. On July 1, 2001, the asset was sold for $40,000 cash.

Required

1. Determine the amount of depreciation for 2001. Also determine the effect on the accounting equation of the sale of the asset.

2. How should the gain or loss on the sale of the asset be presented on the income statement?

LO 8 Exercise 8-7 Asset Disposal
Refer to Exercise 8-6. Assume that Gonzalez Company sold the asset on July 1, 2001, and received $15,000 cash and a note for an additional $15,000.

Required

1. Determine the amount of depreciation for 2001. Also determine the effect on the accounting equation of the sale of the asset.

2. How should the gain or loss on the sale of the asset be presented on the income statement?

LO 10 Exercise 8-8 Amortization of Intangibles
For each of the following intangible assets, indicate the amount of amortization expense that should be recorded for the year 2001 and the amount of accumulated amortization on the balance sheet as of December 31, 2001.

	Goodwill	**Patent**	**Trademark**
Cost	$40,000	$50,000	$80,000
Date of purchase	1/1/94	1/1/96	1/1/99
Useful life	30 yrs.	10 yrs.	20 yrs.
Legal life	undefined	20 yrs.	20 yrs.
Method	SL*	SL	SL

*Represents the straight-line method.

LO 11 Exercise 8-9 Impact of Transactions Involving Operating Assets on Statement of Cash Flows

From the following list, identify each item as operating (O), investing (I), financing (F), or not separately reported on the statement of cash flows (N).

_____ Purchase of land

_____ Proceeds from sale of land

_____ Gain on sale of land

_____ Purchase of equipment

_____ Depreciation expense

_____ Proceeds from sale of equipment

_____ Loss on sale of equipment

LO 11 Exercise 8-10 Impact of Transactions Involving Intangible Assets on Statement of Cash Flows

From the following list, identify each item as operating (O), investing (I), financing (F), or not separately reported on the statement of cash flows (N).

_____ Cost incurred to acquire copyright

_____ Amortization of copyright

_____ Proceeds from sale of patent

_____ Gain on sale of patent

_____ Research and development costs

Multi-Concept Exercises

LO 1, 7 Exercise 8-11 Capital versus Revenue Expenditures

On January 1, 1999, Jose Company purchased a building for $200,000 and a delivery truck for $20,000. The following expenditures have been incurred during 2001, related to the building and the truck:

- The building was painted at a cost of $5,000.
- To prevent leaking, new windows were installed in the building at a cost of $10,000.
- To allow an improved flow of production, a new conveyor system was installed at a cost of $40,000.
- The delivery truck was repainted with a new company logo at a cost of $1,000.
- To allow better handling of large loads, a hydraulic lift system was installed on the truck at a cost of $5,000.
- The truck's engine was overhauled at a cost of $4,000.

Required

1. Determine which of these costs should be capitalized. Also determine the effect on the accounting equation of the capitalized costs. Assume that all costs were incurred on January 1, 2001.

2. Determine the amount of depreciation for the year 2001. The company uses the straight-line method and depreciates the building over 25 years and the truck over 6 years. Assume zero residual value for all assets.

3. How would the assets appear on the balance sheet of December 31, 2001?

LO 4, 5 Exercise 8-12 Capitalization of Interest and Depreciation

During 2001, Mercator Company borrowed $80,000 from a local bank and, in addition, used $120,000 of cash to construct a new corporate office building. Based on average accumulated expenditures, the amount of interest capitalized during 2001 was $8,000. Construction was completed and the building was occupied on January 1, 2002.

Required

1. Determine the acquisition cost of the new building.

2. The building has an estimated useful life of 20 years and a $5,000 salvage value. Assuming that Mercator uses the straight-line basis to depreciate its operating assets, determine the amount of depreciation expense for 2001 and 2002.

LO 9, 10 Exercise 8-13   Research and Development and Patents
Erin Company incurred the following costs during 2001.

a. Research and development costs of $20,000 were incurred. The research was conducted to discover a new product to sell to customers in future years. A product was successfully developed and a patent for the new product was granted during 2001. Erin is unsure of the period benefited by the research but believes the product will result in increased sales over the next five years.

b. Legal costs and application fees of $10,000 for the patent were incurred on January 1, 2001. The patent was granted for a life of 20 years.

c. A patent infringement suit was successfully defended at a cost of $8,000. Assume that all costs were incurred on January 1, 2002.

Required

Determine how the costs in parts **a** and **b** should be presented on Erin's financial statements as of December 31, 2001. Also determine the amount of amortization of intangible assets that Erin should record in 2001 and 2002.

PROBLEMS

LO 1 Problem 8-1   Balance Sheet and Footnote Disclosures for Delta Airlines
The June 30, 1999, balance sheet of Delta Airlines Inc. revealed the following information in the property and equipment category (in millions):

www.deltaairlines.com

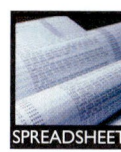
SPREADSHEET

	1999	1998
Flight equipment	$13,389	$11,180
Less: Accumulated depreciation	4,405	3,895
	$ 8,984	$ 7,285
Flight equipment under capital leases	$ 515	$ 515
Less: Accumulated amortization	264	216
	$ 251	$ 299
Ground property and equipment	$ 3,862	$ 3,285
Less: Accumulated depreciation	2,123	1,854
	$ 1,739	$ 1,431

The footnotes that accompany the financial statements revealed the following:

Depreciation and Amortization—Owned flight equipment is depreciated on a straight-line basis over the estimated service lives, which range from 15 to 25 years, to a residual value ranging from 5% to 10% of costs. . . . Ground property and equipment is depreciated on a straight-line basis over the estimated service lives, which range from 3 to 30 years.

Required

1. Assume that Delta Airlines did not dispose of any ground property and equipment during the fiscal year 1999. Calculate the amount of depreciation expense for the year.

2. What was the average life of the ground property and equipment as of 1999?

3. What was the average age of the ground property and equipment as of 1999?

LO 3 Problem 8-2   Lump-Sum Purchase of Assets and Subsequent Events
Carter Development Company purchased, for cash, a large tract of land that was immediately platted and deeded into smaller sections:

Section 1, retail development with highway frontage

Section 2, multifamily apartment development

Section 3, single-family homes in the largest section

DECISION MAKING

Based on recent sales of similar property, the fair market values of the three sections are as follows:

Section 1, $630,000

Section 2, $378,000

Section 3, $252,000

Required

1. What value is assigned to each section of land if the tract was purchased for (a) $1,260,000, (b) $1,560,000, or (c) $1,000,000?

2. How does the purchase of the tract affect the balance sheet?

3. Why would Carter be concerned with the value assigned to each section? Would Carter be more concerned with the values assigned if instead of purchasing three sections of land, it purchased land with buildings? Why or why not?

LO 5 Problem 8-3 Depreciation as a Tax Shield

The term *tax shield* refers to the amount of income tax saved by deducting depreciation for income tax purposes. Assume that Supreme Company is considering the purchase of an asset as of January 1, 2001. The cost of an asset with a five-year life and zero residual value is $100,000. The company will use the straight-line method of depreciation.

Supreme's income for tax purposes before recording depreciation on the asset will be $50,000 per year for the next five years. The corporation is currently in the 35% tax bracket.

Required

Calculate the amount of income tax that Supreme must pay each year if the asset is not purchased. Calculate the amount of income tax that Supreme must pay each year if the asset is purchased. What is the amount of the depreciation tax shield?

LO 5 Problem 8-4 Book versus Tax Depreciation

Griffith Delivery Service purchased a delivery truck for $33,600. The truck has an estimated useful life of six years and no salvage value. For the purposes of preparing financial statements, Griffith is planning to use straight-line depreciation. For tax purposes, Griffith follows MACRS. Depreciation expense using MACRS is $6,720 in Year 1; $10,750 in Year 2; $6,450 in Year 3; $3,870 in each of Years 4 and 5; and $1,940 in Year 6.

Required

1. What is the difference between straight-line and MACRS depreciation expense for each of the six years?

2. Griffith's president has asked why you have used one method for the books and another for calculating taxes. "Can you do this? Is it legal? Don't we take the same total depreciation either way?" he asked. Write a brief memo answering his questions and explaining the benefits of using two methods for depreciation.

LO 5 Problem 8-5 Depreciation and Cash Flow

Ohare Company's only asset as of January 1, 2001, was a limousine. During 2001, only three transactions occurred:

Provided services of $100,000 on account.

Collected all accounts receivable.

Depreciation on the limousine was $15,000.

Required

1. Develop an income statement for Ohare for 2001.

2. Determine the amount of the net cash inflow for Ohare for 2001.

3. Explain in one or more sentences why the amount of the net income on Ohare's income statement does not equal the amount of the net cash inflow.

4. If Ohare developed a cash flow statement for 2001 using the indirect method, what amount would appear in the category titled Cash Flow from Operating Activities?

LO 11 Problem 8-6 Reconstruct Net Book Values Using Statement of Cash Flows

Centralia Stores Inc. had property, plant, and equipment, net of accumulated depreciation of $4,459,000; and intangible assets, net of accumulated amortization, of $673,000 at December 31,

2001. The company's 2001 statement of cash flows, prepared using the indirect method, included the following items.

The Cash Flows from Operating Activities section included three additions to net income: (1) depreciation expense in the amount of $672,000, (2) amortization expense in the amount of $33,000, and (3) the loss on the sale of equipment in the amount of $35,000. The Cash Flows from Operating Activities section also included a subtraction from net income for the gain on the sale of a copyright of $55,000. The Cash Flows from Investing Activities section included outflows for the purchase of a building in the amount of $292,000 and $15,000 for the payment of legal fees to protect a patent from infringement. The Cash Flows from Investing Activities section also included inflows from the sale of equipment in the amount of $315,000 and the sale of a copyright in the amount of $75,000.

Required

1. Determine the book values of the assets that were sold during 2001.

2. Reconstruct the amount of property, plant, and equipment, net of accumulated depreciation, that was reported on the company's balance sheet at December 31, 2000.

3. Reconstruct the amount of intangibles, net of accumulated amortization, that was reported on the company's balance sheet at December 31, 2000.

Multi-Concept Problems

LO 1, 3, 5, 7, 8 **Problem 8-7** Cost of Assets, Subsequent Book Values, and Balance Sheet Presentation

The following events took place at Pete's Painting Company during 2001:

a. On January 1, Pete bought a used truck for $14,000. He added a tool chest and side racks for ladders for $4,800. The truck is expected to last four years and then be sold for $800. Pete uses straight-line depreciation.

b. On January 1, he purchased several items at an auction for $2,400. These items had fair market values as follows:

10 cases of paint trays and roller covers	$ 200
Storage cabinets	600
Ladders & scaffolding	2,400

Pete will use all the paint trays and roller covers this year. The storage cabinets are expected to last nine years, and the ladders and scaffolding for four years.

c. On February 1, Pete paid the city $1,500 for a three-year license to operate the business.

d. On September 1, Pete sold an old truck for $4,800. The truck had cost $12,000 when it was purchased on September 1, 1996. It had been expected to last eight years and have a salvage value of $800.

Required

1. For each situation, explain the value assigned to the asset when it is purchased (or for part **d**, the book value when sold).

2. Determine the amount of depreciation or other expense to be recorded for each asset for 2001.

3. How would these assets appear on the balance sheet as of December 31, 2001?

LO 2, 5 **Problem 8-8** Cost of Assets and the Effect on Depreciation

Early in its first year of business, Toner Company, a fitness and training center, purchased new workout equipment. The acquisition included the following costs:

Purchase price	$150,000
Tax	15,000
Transportation	4,000
Setup*	25,000
Painting*	3,000

*The equipment was adjusted to Toner's specific needs and painted to match the other equipment in the gym.

The bookkeeper recorded an asset, Equipment, $165,000 (purchase price and tax). The remaining costs were expensed for the year. Toner used straight-line depreciation. The equipment was expected to last 10 years with zero salvage value.

Required

1. How much depreciation did Toner report on its income statement related to this equipment in Year 1? What do you believe is the correct amount of depreciation to report in Year 1 related to this equipment?

2. Income is $100,000, before costs related to the equipment are reported. How much income will Toner report in Year 1? What amount of income should it report? You may ignore income tax.

3. Using the equipment as an example, explain the difference between a cost and an expense.

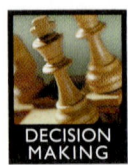

LO 5, 7, 8 Problem 8-9 Capital Expenditures, Depreciation, and Disposal

Merton Company purchased an office building at a cost of $364,000 on January 1, 2000. Merton estimated that the building's life would be 25 years and the residual value at the end of 25 years would be $14,000.

On January 1, 2001, the company made several expenditures related to the building. The entire building was painted and floors were refinished at a cost of $21,000. A federal agency required Merton to install additional pollution-control devices in the building, at a cost of $42,000. With the new devices, Merton believed it was possible to extend the life of the building by an additional six years.

In 2002, Merton altered its corporate strategy dramatically. The company sold the factory building on April 1, 2002, for $392,000 in cash and relocated all operations in another state.

Required

1. Determine the amount of depreciation that should be reflected on the income statement for 2000 and 2001.

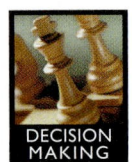

2. Explain why the cost of the pollution-control equipment was not expensed in 2001. What conditions would have allowed Merton to expense the equipment? If Merton has a choice, would it prefer to expense or capitalize the equipment?

3. What amount of gain or loss did Merton record when it sold the building? What amount of gain or loss would have been reported if the pollution-control equipment had been expensed in 2001?

LO 6, 10 Problem 8-10 Amortization of Intangible, Revision of Rate

During 1996, Reynosa Inc.'s R&D department developed a new manufacturing process. R&D costs were $85,000. The process was patented on October 1, 1996. Legal costs to acquire the patent were $11,900. Reynosa decided to expense the patent over the maximum period of time allowed for a patent. Reynosa's fiscal year ends on September 30.

On October 1, 2001, Reynosa's competition announced that it had obtained a patent on a new process that would make Reynosa's patent obsolete in two years.

Required

1. How should Reynosa record the $85,000 and $11,900 costs?

2. How much amortization expense should Reynosa report in each year through the year ended September 30, 2001?

3. How much amortization expense should Reynosa report in the year ended September 30, 2002?

LO 8, 11 Problem 8-11 Purchase and Disposal of Operating Asset and Effects on Statement of Cash Flows

On January 1, 2001, Castlewood Company purchased some machinery for its production line for $104,000. Using an estimated useful life of eight years and a residual value of $8,000, the annual straight-line depreciation of the machinery was calculated to be $12,000. Castlewood used the machinery during 2001 and 2002, but then decided to automate its production process. On December 31, 2002, Castlewood sold the machinery at a loss of $5,000 and purchased new, fully automated machinery for $205,000.

Required

1. How would the preceding transactions be presented on Castlewood's statements of cash flows for the years ended December 31, 2001 and 2002?

2. Why would Castlewood sell at a loss machinery that had a remaining useful life of six years and purchase new machinery with a cost almost twice that of the old?

LO 9, 10, 11 Problem 8-12 Amortization of Intangibles and Effects on Statement of Cash Flows

Tableleaf Inc. purchased a patent a number of years ago. The patent is being amortized on a straight-line basis over its estimated useful life. The company's comparative balance sheets as of December 31, 2001 and 2000, included the following line item:

	12/31/01	12/31/00
Patent, less accumulated amortization of $119,000 (2001) and $102,000 (2000)	$170,000	$187,000

Required

1. How much amortization expense was recorded during 2001?

2. What was the patent's acquisition cost? When was it acquired? What is its estimated useful life? How was the acquisition of the patent reported on that year's statement of cash flows?

3. Assume that Tableleaf uses the indirect method to prepare its statement of cash flows. How is the amortization of the patent reported annually on the statement of cash flows?

4. How would the sale of the patent on January 1, 2002, for $200,000 be reported on the 2002 statement of cash flows?

ALTERNATE PROBLEMS

LO 1 Problem 8-1A Disclosures of Operating Assets

The footnotes to the December 31, 1999, financial statements of TBW included the following disclosures for the Property, Plant, and Equipment account:

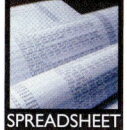
SPREADSHEET

Property, Plant, and Equipment (in millions):	1999	1998
Land and Buildings	$ 963	$ 962
Cable Television Equipment	1,035	941
Furniture, Fixtures, and other Equipment	1,400	1,337
	$3,398	$3,240
Less Accumulated Depreciation	(1,407)	(1,151)
Total	$1,991	$2,089

Required

Assume that TBW disposed of Property, Plant, and Equipment during 1999 with accumulated depreciation of $600 million.

1. Based on the footnote disclosures, what was the amount of depreciation expense for fiscal year 1999 for Property, Plant, and Equipment?

2. What was the average life of the assets in the Property, Plant, and Equipment categories?

3. What was the average age of the assets in the Property, Plant, and Equipment categories?

LO 3 Problem 8-2A Lump-Sum Purchase of Assets and Subsequent Events

Dixon Manufacturing purchased, for cash, three large pieces of equipment. Based on recent sales of similar equipment, the fair market values are as follows:

Piece 1	$200,000
Piece 2	$200,000
Piece 3	$440,000

Required

1. What value is assigned to each piece of equipment if the equipment was purchased for (a) $960,000, (b) $680,000, or (c) $800,000?

2. How does the purchase of the equipment affect total assets?

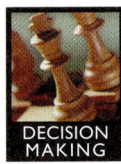

DECISION MAKING

LO 5 **Problem 8-3A** Depreciation as a Tax Shield

The term *tax shield* refers to the amount of income tax saved by deducting depreciation for income tax purposes. Assume that Rummy Company is considering the purchase of an asset as of January 1, 2001. The cost of the asset with a five-year life and zero residual value is $60,000. The company will use the double declining-balance method of depreciation.

Rummy's income for tax purposes before recording depreciation on the asset will be $62,000 per year for the next five years. The corporation is currently in the 30% tax bracket.

Required

Calculate the amount of income tax that Rummy must pay each year if the asset is not purchased and then the amount of income tax that Rummy must pay each year if the asset is purchased. What is the amount of tax shield over the life of the asset? What is the amount of tax shield for Rummy if it uses the straight-line method over the life of the asset? Why would Rummy choose to use the accelerated method?

LO 5 **Problem 8-4A** Book versus Tax Depreciation

Payton Delivery Service purchased a delivery truck for $28,200. The truck will have a useful life of six years and zero salvage value. For the purposes of preparing financial statements, Payton is planning to use straight-line depreciation. For tax purposes, Payton follows MACRS. Depreciation expense using MACRS is $5,650 in Year 1; $9,025 in Year 2; $5,400 in Year 3; $3,250 in each of Years 4 and 5; and $1,625 in Year 6.

Required

1. What would be the difference between straight-line and MACRS depreciation expense for each of the six years?

2. Payton's president has asked why you have used one method for the books and another for calculating taxes. "Can you do this? Is it legal? Don't we take the same total depreciation either way?" she asked. Write a brief memo answering her questions and explaining the benefits of using two methods for depreciation.

LO 10 **Problem 8-5A** Amortization and Cash Flow

Book Company's only asset as of January 1, 2001, was a copyright. During 2001, only three transactions occurred:

Royalties earned from copyright use, $500,000 in cash

Cash paid for advertising and clerical services, $62,500

Amortization of copyright, $50,000

Required

1. What amount of income will Book report in 2001?

2. What is the amount of cash on hand at December 31, 2001?

3. Explain how the cash balance increased from zero at the beginning of the year to its end-of-year balance. Why does the increase in cash not equal the income?

LO 11 **Problem 8-6A** Reconstruct Net Book Values Using Statement of Cash Flows

E-Gen Enterprises Inc. had property, plant, and equipment, net of accumulated depreciation, of $1,555,000; and intangible assets, net of accumulated amortization, of $34,000 at December 31, 2001. The company's 2001 statement of cash flows, prepared using the indirect method, included the following items.

The Cash Flows from Operating Activities section included three additions to net income: (1) depreciation expense in the amount of $205,000, (2) amortization expense in the amount of $3,000, and (3) the loss on the sale of land in the amount of $17,000. The Cash Flows from Operating Activities section also included a subtraction from net income for the gain on the sale of a trademark of $7,000. The Cash Flows from Investing Activities section included outflows for the purchase of equipment in the amount of $277,000 and $6,000 for the payment of legal fees to protect a copyright from infringement. The Cash Flows from Investing Activities section also included inflows from the sale of land in the amount of $187,000 and the sale of a trademark in the amount of $121,000.

Required

1. Determine the book values of the assets that were sold during 2001.

2. Reconstruct the amount of property, plant, and equipment, net of accumulated depreciation, that was reported on the company's balance sheet at December 31, 2000.

3. Reconstruct the amount of intangibles, net of accumulated amortization, that was reported on the company's balance sheet at December 31, 2000.

Alternate Multi-Concept Problems

LO 1, 5, 8, 9, 10   Problem 8-7A   Cost of Assets, Subsequent Book Values, and Balance Sheet Presentation

The following events took place at Tasty-Toppins Inc., a pizza shop that specializes in home delivery, during 2001:

a. January 1, purchased a truck for $16,000 and added a cab and oven at a cost of $10,900. The truck is expected to last five years and be sold for $300 at the end of that time. The company uses straight-line depreciation for its trucks.

b. January 1, purchased equipment for $2,700 from a competitor who was retiring. The equipment is expected to last three years with zero salvage value. The company uses the double declining-balance method to depreciate its equipment.

c. April 1, sold a truck for $1,500. The truck had been purchased for $8,000 exactly five years earlier, had an expected salvage value of $1,000, and was depreciated over an eight-year life using the straight-line method.

d. July 1, purchased a $14,000 patent for a unique baking process to produce a new product. The patent is valid for 15 more years; however, the company expects to produce and market the product for only four years. The patent's value at the end of the four years is indeterminable.

Required

For each situation, explain the amount of depreciation or amortization recorded for each asset in the current year and the book value of each asset at the end of the year. For part **c,** indicate the accumulated depreciation and book value at the time of sale.

LO 2, 5   Problem 8-8A   Cost of Assets and the Effect on Depreciation

Early in its first year of business, Key Inc., a locksmith and security consultant, purchased new equipment. The acquisition included the following costs:

Purchase price	$168,000
Tax	16,500
Transportation	4,400
Setup*	1,100
Operating Cost for First Year	26,400

*The equipment was adjusted to Key's specific needs.

The bookkeeper recorded the asset, Equipment, at $216,400. Key used straight-line depreciation. The equipment was expected to last 10 years with zero residual value.

Required

1. Was $216,400 the proper amount to record for the acquisition cost? If not, explain how each expenditure should be recorded.

2. How much depreciation did Key report on its income statement related to this equipment in Year 1? How much should have been reported?

3. If Key's income before the costs associated with the equipment is $55,000, what amount of income did Key report? What amount should it have reported? You may ignore income tax.

4. Explain how Key should determine the amount to capitalize when recording an asset. What is the effect on the income statement and balance sheet of Key's error?

LO 7, 8   Problem 8-9A   Capital Expenditures, Depreciation, and Disposal

Wagner Company purchased a retail shopping center at a cost of $612,000 on January 1, 2000. Wagner estimated that the life of the building would be 25 years and the residual value at the end of 25 years would be $12,000.

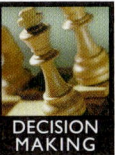

DECISION MAKING

On January 1, 2001, the company made several expenditures related to the building. The entire building was painted and floors were refinished at a cost of $115,200. A local zoning agency required Wagner to install additional fire-protection equipment, including sprinklers and built-in alarms, at a cost of $87,600. With the new protection, Wagner believed it was possible to increase the residual value of the building to $30,000.

In 2002, Wagner altered its corporate strategy dramatically. The company sold the retail shopping center on January 1, 2002, for $360,000 cash.

Required

1. Determine the amount of depreciation that should be reflected on the income statement for 2000 and 2001.

2. Explain why the cost of the fire-protection equipment was not expensed in 2001. What conditions would have allowed Wagner to expense it? If Wagner has a choice, would it prefer to expense or capitalize the improvement?

3. What amount of gain or loss did Wagner record when it sold the building? What amount of gain or loss would have been reported if the fire-protection equipment had been expensed in 2001?

LO 6, 10   Problem 8-10A   Amortization of Intangible, Revision of Rate

Dak Inc. purchased Under Company on January 1, 2001, for $500,000. To determine the value of the assets and liabilities purchased, Dak requested an appraisal of Under's assets and liabilities. The appraiser determined that the fair market values of the items purchased as of January 1, 2001, were as follows:

Assets	Fair Market Value
Cash	$ 75,000
Receivables	125,000
Building	287,500

Liabilities	
Accounts payable	$125,000

Dak decided to amortize any goodwill in the transaction on a straight-line basis over the maximum possible time period.

On January 1, 2002, Dak's accountants determined that the goodwill should be amortized over a shorter period of time. Accordingly, Dak Inc. agreed to amortize all remaining goodwill for a period of 10 more years.

Required

1. Determine the amount of goodwill that resulted from the January 1, 2001, purchase of Under Company and the amount to be amortized in 2001.

2. Determine the amount of goodwill that should be amortized in 2002.

LO 8, 11   Problem 8-11A   Purchase and Disposal of Operating Asset and Effects on Statement of Cash Flows

On January 1, 2001, Mansfield Inc. purchased a medium-size delivery truck for $45,000. Using an estimated useful life of five years and a residual value of $5,000, the annual straight-line depreciation of the truck was calculated to be $8,000. Mansfield used the truck during 2001 and 2002, but then decided to purchase a much larger delivery truck. On December 31, 2002, Mansfield sold the delivery truck at a loss of $12,000 and purchased a new, larger delivery truck for $80,000.

Required

1. How would the preceding transactions be presented on Mansfield's statements of cash flows for the years ended December 31, 2001 and 2002?

2. Why would Mansfield sell a truck that had a remaining useful life of three years at a loss and purchase a new truck with a cost almost twice that of the old?

LO 9, 10, 11 Problem 8-12A Amortization of Intangibles and Effects on Statement of Cash Flows

Quickster Inc. acquired a single trademark a number of years ago. The trademark is being amortized on a straight-line basis over its estimated useful life. The company's comparative balance sheets as of December 31, 2001 and 2000, included the following line item:

	12/31/01	12/31/00
Trademark, less accumulated amortization of $1,661,000 (2001) and $1,510,000 (2000)	$1,357,000	$1,508,000

Required

1. How much amortization expense was recorded during 2001?
2. What was the trademark's acquisition cost? When was it acquired? What is its estimated useful life? How was the acquisition of the trademark reported on that year's statement of cash flows?
3. Assume that Quickster uses the indirect method to prepare its statement of cash flows. How is the amortization of the trademark reported annually on the statement of cash flows?
4. How would the sale of the trademark on January 1, 2002, for $1,700,000 be reported on the 2002 statement of cash flows?

CASES

Reading and Interpreting Financial Statements

LO 1, 9 Case 8-1 Uno Restaurant

Refer to the financial statements and footnotes included in the 1999 annual report of Uno Restaurant.   www.pizzeriauno.com

Required

1. What items does Uno list in the Property, Plant, and Equipment category?
2. What method is used to depreciate the operating assets?
3. What is the estimated useful life of the operating assets?
4. What are the accumulated depreciation and book values of property, plant, and equipment for the most recent fiscal year?
5. Were any assets purchased or sold during the most recent fiscal year?
6. In what category of the balance sheet are intangible assets included?

LO 1, 9 Case 8-2 Gateway

Refer to the financial statements and footnotes included in the 1999 annual report of Gateway.   www.gateway.com

Required

1. What items does Gateway list in the Property, Plant, and Equipment category?
2. What method is used to depreciate the assets?
3. What is the estimated life of the assets?
4. What are the accumulated depreciation and book values of property, plant, and equipment for the most recent fiscal year?
5. What is the amount of intangible assets for the most recent year?

LO 11 Case 8-3 Uno Restaurant's Statement of Cash Flows

Refer to the statement of cash flows in Uno Restaurant's 1999 annual report and answer the following questions: www.pizzeriauno.com

1. What amount of cash was used to purchase property, plant, and equipment during 1999?
2. Did Uno sell any property, plant, and equipment during 1999?
3. What amount was reported for depreciation and amortization during 1999? Does the fact that depreciation and amortization are listed in the Cash Flow from Operating Activities section mean that Uno created cash by reporting depreciation and amortization?

www.gateway.com   Refer to the statement of cash flows in Gateway's 1999 annual report and answer the following questions.

1. What amount of cash was used for capital expenditures during 1999?

2. Did Gateway sell any property, plant, and equipment during 1999?

3. What amount was reported for depreciation and amortization during 1999? Does the fact that depreciation and amortization are listed in the Cash Flow from Operating Activities section mean that Gateway created cash by reporting depreciation and amortization?

Making Financial Decisions

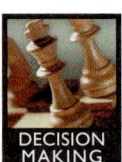

LO 1, 5   **Case 8-5**   Comparing Companies

Assume that you are a financial analyst attempting to compare the financial results of two companies. The 2001 income statement of Straight Company is as follows:

Sales		$720,000
Cost of goods sold		360,000
Gross profit		360,000
Administrative costs	$ 96,000	
Depreciation expense	120,000	216,000
Income before tax		144,000
Tax expense (40%)		57,600
Net income		$ 86,400

Straight Company depreciates all operating assets using the straight-line method for tax purposes and for the annual report provided to stockholders. All operating assets were purchased on the same date, and all assets had an estimated life of five years when purchased. Straight Company's balance sheet reveals that on December 31, 2001, the balance of the Accumulated Depreciation account was $240,000.

You want to compare the annual report of Straight Company to that of Accelerated Company. Both companies are in the same industry, and both have exactly the same assets, sales, and expenses except that Accelerated uses the double declining-balance method for depreciation for income tax purposes and for the annual report provided to stockholders.

Required

Develop Accelerated Company's 2001 income statement. As a financial analyst interested in investing in one of the companies, do you find Straight or Accelerated more attractive? Because depreciation is a noncash expense, should you be indifferent between the two companies? Explain your answer.

LO 5   **Case 8-6**   Depreciation Alternatives

Medsupply Inc. produces supplies used in hospitals and nursing homes. Its sales, production, and costs to produce are expected to remain constant over the next five years. The corporate income tax rate is expected to increase over the next three years. The current rate, 15%, is expected to increase to 20% next year and then to 25% and continue at that rate indefinitely.

Medsupply is considering the purchase of new equipment that is expected to last for five years and to cost $150,000 with zero salvage value. As the controller, you are aware that the company can use one method of depreciation for accounting purposes and another method for tax purposes. You are trying to decide between the straight-line and the double declining-balance methods.

Required

Recommend which method to use for accounting purposes and which to use for tax purposes. Be able to justify your answer on both a numerical and a theoretical basis. How does a noncash adjustment to income, such as depreciation, affect cash flow?

Accounting and Ethics: What Would You Do?

LO 3   **Case 8-7**   Valuing Assets

Denver Company recently hired Terry Davis as an accountant. He was given responsibility for all accounting functions related to fixed asset accounting. Tammy Sharp, Terry's boss, asked him to review all transactions involving the current year's acquisition of fixed assets and to take necessary action to ensure that acquired assets were recorded at proper values. Terry is satisfied that all transactions are proper except for an April 15 purchase of an office building and the land on which it is situated. The purchase price of the acquisition was $200,000. Denver Company has not separately reported the land and building, however.

Terry hired an appraiser to determine the market values of the land and the building. The appraiser reported that his best estimates of the values were $150,000 for the building and $70,000 for the land. When Terry proposed that these values be used to determine the acquisition cost of the assets, Ms. Sharp disagreed. She told Terry to request another appraisal of the property and asked him to stress to the appraiser that the land component of the acquisition could not be depreciated for tax purposes. The second appraiser estimated that the values were $180,000 for the building and $40,000 for the land. Terry and Ms. Sharp agreed that the second appraisal should be used to determine the acquisition cost of the assets.

Required

Did Terry and Ms. Sharp act ethically in this situation? Explain your answer.

LO 5 Case 8-8 Depreciation Estimates

Langsom's Mfg. is planning for a new project. Usually, Langsom's depreciates long-term equipment for 10 years. The equipment for this project is specialized and will have no further use at the end of the project in three years. The manager of the project wants to depreciate the equipment over the usual 10 years and plans on writing off the remaining book value at the end of Year 3 as a loss. You believe that the equipment should be depreciated over the three-year life.

Required

Which method do you think is conceptually better? What should you do if the manager insists on depreciating the equipment over 10 years?

INTERNET RESEARCH CASE

Case 8-9 Time Warner (AOL Time Warner)

Time Warner announced a merger with America Online (AOL), and that merger became final in 2000. AOL, founded in 1985, is the world's largest online service provider, among other attributes. Theirs is a union driven by Time Warner's huge assets in content and media brands, along with its cable systems, and by the potential audience represented by AOL's over 25 million online members. The resulting company, as the Time Warner 1999 annual report states, will have "multiple revenue streams from branded subscriptions, advertising and commerce, and content." You can explore what effect this merger of titans is having on each company's presence on the Web—including the investor's page(s) of the combined AOL Time Warner.

www.aoltimewarner.com

First visit the web site to explore the research opportunities within AOL Time Warner. Explore the site and find out more about the combined company's core businesses. Then answer the following questions.

1. Of Time Warner's intangible assets, which do you think were the most desirable to AOL? Of its tangible assets, which do you think were the most valuable?

2. Explain briefly how management saw Time Warner's and AOL's assets as complementary. In what ways do you think this can make for a stronger company?

3. What is the amount of intangible assets for the combined company? What is the amount of amortization of the intangibles during the current year?

4. What earnings number does the company's management focus on to minimize the effect of amortization (depreciation) of intangible assets?

1	Acquisition cost (p. 351)	**6**	Change in estimate (p. 358)
5	Capitalization of interest (p. 352)	**8**	Capital expenditure (p. 359)
2	Land improvements (p. 353)	**10**	Revenue expenditure (p. 359)
7	Depreciation (p. 353)	**11**	Gain on Sale of Asset (p. 362)
3	Straight-line method (p. 353)	**12**	Loss on Sale of Asset (p. 362)
9	Book value (p. 354)	**18**	Natural resources (p. 362)
4	Units-of-production method (p. 354)	**14**	Intangible assets (p. 364)
13	Accelerated depreciation (p. 355)	**16**	Goodwill (p. 365)
15	Double declining-balance method (p. 355)	**17**	Research and development costs (p. 366)

Part II

INTEGRATIVE PROBLEM

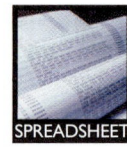
SPREADSHEET

Correct an income statement and statement of cash flows and assess the impact of a change in inventory method; compute the effect of a bad-debt recognition.

The following income statement, statement of cash flows, and additional information are available for PEK Company:

PEK COMPANY
INCOME STATEMENT
FOR THE YEAR ENDED DECEMBER 31, 2001

Sales revenue		$1,250,000
Cost of goods sold		636,500
Gross profit		$ 613,500
Depreciation on plant equipment	$58,400	
Depreciation on buildings	12,000	
Interest expense	33,800	
Other expenses	83,800	188,000
Income before taxes		$ 425,500
Income tax expense (30% rate)		127,650
Net income		$ 297,850

PEK COMPANY
STATEMENT OF CASH FLOWS
FOR THE YEAR ENDED DECEMBER 31, 2001

Cash flows from operating activities:	
Net income	$297,850
Adjustments to reconcile net income to net cash provided by operating activities (includes depreciation expense)	83,200
Net cash provided by operating activities	$381,050
Cash flows from financing activities:	
Dividends	(35,000)
Net increase in cash	$346,050

Additional information:

a. Beginning inventory and purchases for the one product the company sells are as follows:

	Units	Unit Cost
Beginning inventory	50,000	$2.00
Purchases:		
February 5	25,000	2.10
March 10	30,000	2.20
April 15	40,000	2.50
June 16	75,000	3.00
September 5	60,000	3.10
October 3	40,000	3.25

b. During the year, the company sold 250,000 units at $5 each.

c. PEK uses the periodic FIFO method to value its inventory and the straight-line method to depreciate all its long-term assets.

d. During the year-end audit, it was discovered that a January 3, 2001, transaction for the lump-sum purchase of a mixing machine and a boiler was not recorded. The fair market values of the mixing machine and the boiler were $200,000 and $100,000, respectively. Each asset has an estimated useful life of 10 years with no residual value expected. The purchase of the assets was financed by issuing a $270,000 five-year promissory note directly to the seller. Interest of 8% is paid annually on December 31.

Required

1. Prepare a revised income statement and a revised statement of cash flows to take into account the omission of the entry to record the purchase of the two assets. (*Hint:* You will need to take into account any change in income taxes as a result of changes in any income statement items. Assume that income taxes are paid on December 31 of each year.)

2. Assume the same facts as above, except that the company is considering the use of an accelerated method rather than the straight-line method for the assets purchased on January 3, 2001. All other assets would continue to be depreciated on a straight-line basis. Prepare a revised income statement and a revised statement of cash flows, assuming the company decides to use the accelerated method for these two assets rather than the straight-line method resulting in depreciation of $49,091 for 2001.

Treat the answers in requirements 3 and 4 as independent of the other parts.

3. Assume PEK decides to use the LIFO method rather than the FIFO method to value its inventory and recognize cost of goods sold for 2001. Compute the effect (amount of increase or decrease) this would have on cost of goods sold, income tax expense, and net income.

4. Assume PEK failed to record an estimate of bad debts for 2001 (bad debt expense is normally included in "other expenses"). Before any adjustment, the balance in Allowance for Doubtful Accounts is $8,200. The credit manager estimates that 3% of the $800,000 of sales on account will prove to be uncollectible. Based on this information, compute the effect (amount of increase or decrease) of recognition of the bad debt estimate on other expenses, income tax expense, and net income.

STRIDE RITE

Stride Rite Corporation is the familiar, well-known designer and marketer of the leading brand of children's footwear in the United States. Many children have taken their first steps in Stride Rite shoes, including dress shoes, play shoes, boots, sandals, and sneakers for consumers aged six months to 12 years.

The company, based in Lexington, Massachusetts, also sells athletic and casual footwear for children and adults, as well as marine and outdoor recreational footwear and dress shoes. Its new baby collection, introduced in 2000 and designed to mimic barefoot walking and promote natural development, has stepped out quickly and successfully to take its place among the company's other top brand names like Keds, Sperry Top-Sider, Stride-Rite, Grasshoppers, Munchkins, Street Hot, and Tommy Hilfiger.

Under its new Chairman and CEO, David M. Chamberlain, and President and Chief Operating Officer Diane M. Sullivan, the company looks forward to a revival of growth and value in the new century. However, net sales for the fourth quarter of fiscal 2000 decreased 7 percent, to $95.4 million from $102.3 million in the comparable period of fiscal 1999, which included an extra week due to the way the company's fiscal calendar runs. The company incurred a net loss of $685,000 for the quarter, compared to net income of $399,000 for the fourth quarter of the previous year.

For the 2000 fiscal year, net sales totaled $548.3 million, a 4 percent decline from the level achieved in 1999. Earnings were $.58 per share, a slight improvement from fiscal 1999's earnings of $.57 per share as the company's continuing repurchase program yielded a decline in the number of outstanding shares.

The company is "cautiously optimistic" that sales will grow in fiscal 2001. Expected to help spark that growth are more new products like an update of the Keds classic Champion® oxford style and continued innovation in what the company calls "sneaker basics." CEO Chamberlain expressed some concern, however, about the overall sales trends of the company's key retail partners, the stores that distribute its products.

Chamberlain commented in January 2000 that "while the company's performance fell short of our expectations in fiscal 2000, we made solid progress on several important fronts during the year, especially with respect to our two key brands, Stride Rite and Keds." These included the introduction of the Natural Motion Systems™ baby product line, a new design for Stride Rite retail stores, and preparation of the Munchkin® product line for launch in 2001.

The company also plans to expand its store base with a mix of concept stores and outlets, similar to 2000's addition of 24 new retail outlets, and will continue to close underperforming locations as it did in 2000 as well.

The Internet is a growing part of the company's sales and marketing strategy. Stride Rite maintains an informative site at www.stride-rite.com, which features a store locator, and at its interactive site, www.keds.com, customers can place orders for Keds products. In addition, the company has formed a partnership with www.babycenter.com, a popular site for new parents where Stride Rite offers advice on appropriate footwear selections.

Cost-savings moves initiated in recent years have included the gradual transfer of all manufacturing functions overseas. In 1998 Stride Rite closed its last U.S. factory and now buys all its merchandise from foreign makers, mostly in Asia. A new distribution center in Indiana was recently opened.

Questions

1. Stride Rite has developed alliances with Tommy Hilfiger and the Baby Center Web site. Do you think similar partnerships with other firms could help the company improve its market share or financial position? What firms would you suggest for such partnerships?

2. Stride Rite is mainly a wholesaler and therefore relies heavily on its retail partners for the success of its product lines. What do you think the firm can do to improve retail sales in stores? What factors in the retail market can Stride Rite control? Which factors are beyond its control?

3. What impact would you expect the closing of domestic manufacturing operations to have on the firm's financial statements? Where would it have shown up?

Part III

ACCOUNTING FOR LIABILITIES AND OWNERS' EQUITY

A WORD TO STUDENTS ABOUT PART III

By now it's clear that this book is organized along the lines of a balance sheet. That is, Part II covered assets; Part III will cover liabilities and equity. As we'll see, taking on liabilities to pay for assets is one way to provide financing for the future of the company; the other alternative is to issue stock.

Also, the chapters in Part III continue to discuss how the related transactions affect the statement of cash flows, which is key to understanding how companies' statements—and their activities—are interrelated.

Chapter 9

CURRENT LIABILITIES, CONTINGENT LIABILITIES, AND THE TIME VALUE OF MONEY

Study Links

A Look at Previous Chapters

Chapter 2 introduced classified balance sheets, which emphasize the distinction between current and noncurrent assets and liabilities. Current liabilities generally represent items to be paid within one year.

A Look at This Chapter

The first part of this chapter more closely examines the items that appear in the current liability category of the balance sheet. The second part examines whether contingent liabilities should be presented on the balance sheet, disclosed in the footnotes, or ignored altogether. The third part of the chapter presents the concept of the time value of money.

A Look at Upcoming Chapters

Chapter 10 presents the accounting for long-term liabilities. The time value of money concept developed in Chapter 9 will be applied to several long-term liability issues in Chapter 10.

FOCUS ON FINANCIAL RESULTS

JCPenney wants to be "the customer's first choice for the products and services we offer." Right now, the 98-year-old firm is clinging to the No. 5 spot among U.S. retailers.

Through its 1,100 stores in the 50 states, Puerto Rico, and Mexico, its well-known catalog, and a new Web site, the familiar retailer offers family apparel, jewelry, shoes, accessories, and home furnishings that bear national as well as exclusive and private brand names.

Yet, JCPenney's retail business did not perform as well in 1999 as the company had projected.[1] Improving profitability has consistently been a key goal for the firm in recent years. Allen Questrom, the new CEO, may well continue the short- and long-term strategies put in place by his predecessor. They focus on overhauling the department store merchandising process, simplifying pricing, closing underperforming stores, lowering operating costs, and becoming a major e-commerce retailer.

The first two of these objectives have implications for inventory. During 2000 the company worked on reacting more quickly to fast- and slow-selling items to reduce inventory, hoping to take fewer markdowns and yield more profit. Suppliers became an integral part of inventory management during the year.

Managing inventory well also means managing accounts payable, one of JCPenney's current liabilities. That in turn means having enough current assets on hand to pay current liabilities, such as suppliers' bills, on time. So Penney's realizes that its profitability goals are directly linked to effectively managing inventory and the related current liabilities.

[1] JCPenney's 1999 annual report, p. 1.

J. C. PENNEY COMPANY, INC. AND SUBSIDIARIES

($ in millions)	1999	1998
Assets		
Current assets		
Cash (including short-term investments of $1,233 and $95)	$ 1,233	$ 96
Retained interest in JCP Master Credit Card Trust	—	415
Receivables, net (bad debt reserve of $20 and $149)	1,138	4,268
Merchandise inventory (including LIFO reserves of $270 and $227)	5,947	6,060
Prepaid expenses	154	168
Total current assets	8,472	11,007
Property and equipment		
Land and buildings	3,089	3,109
Furniture and fixtures	3,955	4,045
Leasehold improvements	1,151	1,179
Accumulated depreciation	(2,883)	(2,875)
Property and equipment, net	5,312	5,458
Investments, principally held by Direct Marketing	1,827	1,961
Deferred policy acquisition costs	929	847
Goodwill and other intangible assets, net (accumulated amortization of $340 and $227)	3,056	2,941
Other assets	1,292	1,294
Total Assets	$ 20,888	$ 23,508

Liabilities and Stockholders' Equity	1999	1998
Current liabilities		
Accounts payable and accrued expenses	$ 3,351	$ 3,443
Short-term debt	330	1,924
Current maturities of long-term debt	625	438
Deferred taxes	159	107
Total current liabilities	4,465	5,912
Long-term debt	5,844	7,143
Deferred taxes	1,461	1,512
Insurance policy and claims reserves	1,017	946
Other liabilities	873	893
Total Liabilities	13,660	16,406
Stockholders' Equity		
Preferred stock authorized, 25 million shares; issued and outstanding, 0.7 million and 0.8 million shares Series B ESOP convertible preferred	446	475
Common stock, par value 50 cents: authorized, 1,250 million shares; issued and outstanding 261 million and 250 million shares	3,266	2,850
Reinvested earnings	3,590	3,791
Accumulated other comprehensive income/(loss)	(74)	(14)
Total Stockholders' Equity	7,228	7,102
Total Liabilities and Stockholders' Equity	$ 20,888	$ 23,508

JCPenney's 1999 Annual Report

If you were a bank loan officer looking for information about JCPenney's credit rating, what information would you want about current liabilities? While you study this chapter, consider which accounts on JCPenney's balance sheet are current liabilities and how they might influence its financial position.

www.jcpenney.com

After studying this chapter, you should be able to:

LO 1 Identify the components of the current liability category of the balance sheet. (p. 398)

LO 2 Examine how accruals affect the current liability category. (p. 402)

LO 3 Understand how changes in current liabilities affect the statement of cash flows. (p. 403)

LO 4 Determine when contingent liabilities should be presented on the balance sheet or disclosed in footnotes and how to calculate their amounts. (p. 404)

LO 5 Explain the difference between simple and compound interest. (p. 410)

LO 6 Calculate amounts using the future value and present value concepts. (p. 412)

LO 7 Apply the compound interest concepts to some common accounting situations. (p. 417)

LO 8 Understand the deductions and expenses for payroll accounting (Appendix 9A). (p. 427)

LO 9 Determine when compensated absences must be accrued as a liability (Appendix 9A). (p. 430)

CURRENT LIABILITIES

LO 1 Identify the components of the current liability category of the balance sheet.

www.mcdonalds.com

A classified balance sheet presents financial statement items by category in order to provide more information to financial statement users. The balance sheet generally presents two categories of liabilities, current and long-term.

Current liabilities finance the working capital of the company. At any given time during the year, current liabilities may fluctuate substantially. It is important that the company generates sufficient cash flow to retire these debts as they come due. As long as the company's ratio of current assets to current liabilities stays fairly constant from quarter to quarter or year to year, financial statement users are not going to be too concerned.

The current liability portion of the 1999 balance sheet of McDonald's Corporation is highlighted in Exhibit 9-1. Some companies list the accounts in the Current Liabilities category in the order of payment due date. That is, the account that requires payment first is listed first, the account requiring payment next is listed second, and so forth. This allows users of the statement to assess the cash flow implications of each account. McDonald's uses a different approach and lists Notes Payable as the first account.

Current liabilities were first introduced to you in Chapter 2 of this textbook. In general, a **current liability** is an obligation that will be satisfied within one year. Although current liabilities are not due immediately, they are still recorded at face value; that is, the time until payment is not taken into account. If it were, current liabilities would be recorded at a slight discount to reflect interest that would be earned between now and the due date. The face value amount is generally used for all current liabilities because the time period involved is short enough that it is not necessary to record or calculate an interest factor. In addition, when interest rates are low, one need not worry about the interest that could be earned in this short period of time. In Chapter 10, we will find that many long-term liabilities must be stated at their present value on the balance sheet.

The current liability classification is important because it is closely tied to the concept of *liquidity*. Management of the firm must be prepared to pay current liabilities within a very short time period. Therefore, management must have access to liquid assets, cash, or other assets that can be converted to cash in amounts sufficient to pay the current liabilities. Firms that do not have sufficient resources to pay their current liabilities are often said to have a liquidity problem.

A handy ratio to help creditors or potential creditors determine a company's liquidity is the current ratio. A current ratio of current assets to current liabilities of 2:1 is usually a very comfortable margin. If the firm has a large amount of inventory, it is sometimes useful to exclude inventory when computing the ratio. That provides the "quick" ratio. Usually, one would want a quick ratio of at least 1.5:1 to feel secure that the company could pay its

From *Concept*

TO PRACTICE 9.1

READING JCPENNEY'S BALANCE SHEET Refer to JCPenney's balance sheet for 1999. What accounts are listed as current liabilities? What was the change in Accounts Payable from 1998 to 1999?

EXHIBIT 9-1   McDonald's Corporation 1999 Consolidated Balance Sheet

Consolidated balance sheet

(In millions, except per share data)		December 31,	1999	1998
Assets				
Current assets	Cash and equivalents		$ 419.5	$ 299.2
	Accounts and notes receivable		708.1	609.4
	Inventories, at cost, not in excess of market		82.7	77.3
	Prepaid expenses and other current assets		362.0	323.5
	Total current assets		1,572.3	1,309.4
Other assets	Investments in and advances to affiliates		1,002.2	854.1
	Intangible assets–net		1,261.8	973.1
	Miscellaneous		822.4	606.2
	Total other assets		3,086.4	2,433.4
Property and equipment	Property and equipment, at cost		22,450.8	21,758.0
	Accumulated depreciation and amortization		(6,126.3)	(5,716.4)
	Net property and equipment		16,324.5	16,041.6
Total assets			$20,983.2	$19,784.4
Liabilities and shareholders' equity				
Current liabilities	Notes payable		$ 1,073.1	$ 686.8
	Accounts payable		585.7	621.3
	Income taxes		117.2	94.2
	Other taxes		160.1	143.5
	Accrued interest		131.4	132.3
	Other accrued liabilities		660.0	651.0
	Current maturities of long-term debt		546.8	168.0
	Total current liabilities		3,274.3	2,497.1
Other liabilities	Long-term debt		5,632.4	6,188.6
	Other long-term liabilities and minority interests		538.4	492.6
	Deferred income taxes		1,173.6	1,081.9
	Common equity put options		725.4	59.5
Shareholders' equity	Preferred stock, no par value; authorized–165.0 million shares; issued–none			
	Common stock, $.01 par value; authorized–3.5 billion shares; issued–1,660.6 million		16.6	16.6
	Additional paid-in capital		1,288.3	989.2
	Unearned ESOP compensation		(133.3)	(148.7)
	Retained earnings		15,562.8	13,879.6
	Accumulated other comprehensive income		(886.8)	(522.5)
	Common stock in treasury, at cost; 309.8 and 304.4 million shares		(6,208.5)	(4,749.5)
	Total shareholders' equity		9,639.1	9,464.7
Total liabilities and shareholders' equity			$20,983.2	$19,784.4

Highlighted items will require payments within one year

The accompanying financial comments are an integral part of the consolidated financial statements.

bills on time. Of course, the guidelines given for the current ratio, 2:1, and the quick ratio, 1.5:1, are only rules of thumb. The actual current and quick ratios of companies vary widely and depend on the company, the management policies, and the type of industry. Exhibit 9-2 presents the current and quick ratios for the companies that are used as examples in this chapter. The ratios do vary from company to company, yet all are solid companies without liquidity problems.

EXHIBIT 9-2   Current and Quick Ratios of Selected Companies for 1999

Company	Industry	Current Ratio	Quick Ratio
Newell Rubbermaid	consumer products	1.68	1.05
Uno	food	.27	.18
Georgia-Pacific	building products/lumber	1.19	.66
JCPenney	retailing	1.89	.56
Johnson Controls	auto	.90	.78
McDonald's	fast food	.48	.34

Accounting for current liabilities is an area in which U.S. accounting standards are very similar to those of most other countries. Nearly all countries encourage firms to provide a breakdown of liabilities into current and long-term in order to allow users to evaluate liquidity.

ACCOUNTS PAYABLE

Accounts payable represent amounts owed for the purchase of inventory, goods, or services acquired in the normal course of business. Often, Accounts Payable is the first account listed in the current liability category because it requires the payment of cash before other current liabilities. McDonald's is different from most other companies because it lists Notes Payable before Accounts Payable.

Normally, a firm has an established relationship with several suppliers, and formal contractual arrangements with those suppliers are unnecessary. Accounts payable usually do not require the payment of interest, but terms may be given to encourage early payment. For example, terms may be stated as 2/10, n30, which means that a 2% discount is available if payment occurs within the first 10 days and that if payment is not made within 10 days, the full amount must be paid within 30 days.

Timely payment of accounts payable is an important aspect of the management of cash flow. Generally, it is to the company's benefit to take advantage of discounts when they are available. After all, if your supplier is going to give you a 2% discount for paying on Day 10 instead of Day 30, that means you are earning 2% on your money over 20/360 of a year. If you took the 2% discount throughout the year, you would be getting a 36% annual return on your money, because there are 18 periods of 20 days each in a year. It is essential, therefore, that the accounts payable system be established in a manner that alerts management to take advantage of offered discounts.

NOTES PAYABLE

The first current liability on McDonald's balance sheet is notes payable of $1,073.1 million. How is a note payable different from an account payable? The most important difference is that an account payable is not a formal contractual arrangement, whereas a **note payable** is represented by a formal agreement or note signed by the parties to the transaction. Notes payable may arise from dealing with a supplier or from acquiring a cash loan from a bank or creditor. Those notes that are expected to be paid within one year of the balance sheet date should be classified as current liabilities.

The accounting for notes payable depends on whether the interest is paid on the note's due date or is deducted before the borrower receives the loan proceeds. With the first type of note, the terms stipulate that the borrower receives a short-term loan and agrees to repay the principal and interest at the note's due date. For example, assume that Lamanski Company receives a one-year loan from First National Bank on January 1, 2001. The face amount of the note of $1,000 must be repaid on December 31 along with interest at the rate of 12%. The effect of the loan on the financial statements as of January 1 is as follows:

From *Concept*

TO PRACTICE 9.2

READING UNO'S BALANCE SHEET
Refer to Uno's balance sheet. What items are included in the Current Liability portion of the balance sheet?

BALANCE SHEET						INCOME STATEMENT
ASSETS	=	LIABILITIES	+	OWNERS' EQUITY	+	REVENUES – EXPENSES
Cash 1,000		Notes Payable 1,000				

When the loan is repaid on December 31, Lamanski must pay $1,120 ($1,000 of principal and $120 of interest) and must eliminate the Notes Payable account. The effect of the repayment is as follows:

BALANCE SHEET						INCOME STATEMENT
ASSETS	=	LIABILITIES	+	OWNERS' EQUITY	+	REVENUES – EXPENSES
Cash (1,120)		Notes Payable (1,000)				Interest Expense (120)

Banks also use another form of note, one in which the interest is deducted in advance. Suppose that on January 1, 2001, First National Bank granted to Lamanski a $1,000 loan, due on December 31, 2001, but deducted the interest in advance and gave Lamanski the remaining amount of $880 ($1,000 face amount of the note less interest of $120). This is sometimes referred to as *discounting a note* because a Discount on Notes Payable account is established on January 1. The effect is as follows:

BALANCE SHEET						INCOME STATEMENT
ASSETS	=	LIABILITIES	+	OWNERS' EQUITY	+	REVENUES – EXPENSES
Cash 880		Notes Payable 1,000				
		Discount on Notes Payable (120)				

The **Discount on Notes Payable** account should be treated as a reduction of Notes Payable. If a balance sheet was developed immediately after the January 1 loan, the note would appear in the current liability category as follows:

Notes Payable	$1,000
Less: Discount on Notes Payable	120
Net Liability	$ 880

> **Study Tip**
>
> Discount on Notes Payable is a contra-liability account and will be shown as a reduction of the Notes Payable account.

The original balance in the Discount on Notes Payable account represents interest that must be transferred to Interest Expense over the life of the note. Before Lamanski presents its year-end financial statements, it must make an adjustment to transfer the discount to Interest Expense. The effect of the adjustment on December 31 is as follows:

BALANCE SHEET						INCOME STATEMENT
ASSETS	=	LIABILITIES	+	OWNERS' EQUITY	+	REVENUES – EXPENSES
		Discount on Notes Payable 120				Interest Expense (120)

Thus, the balance of the Discount on Notes Payable account is zero, and $120 has been transferred to Interest Expense. When the note is repaid on December 31, 2001, Lamanski must repay the full amount of the note.

It is important to compare the two types of notes payable. In the previous two examples, the stated interest rate on each note was 12%. The dollar amount of interest incurred in each case was $120. However, the interest *rate* on a discounted note, the second example, is always higher than it appears. Lamanski received the use of only $880, yet it was required to repay $1,000. Therefore, the interest rate incurred on the note was actually 120/880, or approximately 13.6%.

CURRENT MATURITIES OF LONG-TERM DEBT

Another account that appears in the current liability category of McDonald's balance sheet is **Current Maturities of Long-Term Debt.** On other companies' balance sheets, this item may appear as Long-Term Debt, Current Portion. This account should appear when a firm has a liability and must make periodic payments. For example, assume that on January 1, 2001, your firm obtained a $10,000 loan from the bank. The terms of the loan require you to make payments in the amount of $1,000 per year for 10 years, payable each January 1, beginning January 1, 2002.

The December 31, 2001, balance sheet should indicate that the liability for the note payable is classified into two portions: a $1,000 current liability that must be repaid within one year and a $9,000 long-term liability. On January 1, 2002, the company must pay $1,000, and should eliminate the current liability of $1,000.

On December 31, 2002, the company should again record the current portion of the liability. Therefore, the 2002 year-end balance sheet should indicate that the liability is classified into two portions: a $1,000 current liability and an $8,000 long-term liability. The process should be repeated each year until the bank loan has been fully paid. When an investor or creditor reads a balance sheet, he or she wants to distinguish between debt that is long-term and debt that is short-term. Therefore, it is important to segregate that portion of the debt that becomes due within one year.

The balance sheet category labeled Current Maturities of Long-Term Debt should include only the amount of principal to be paid. The amount of interest that has been incurred but is unpaid should be listed separately in an account such as Interest Payable.

TAXES PAYABLE

LO 2 Examine how accruals affect the current liability category.

From *Concept*

TO PRACTICE 9.3

READING GATEWAY'S FOOTNOTES
One of Gateway's Current Liabilities is Accrued Royalties. How do the footnotes explain that account?

Corporations pay a variety of taxes, including federal and state income taxes, property taxes, and other taxes. Usually, the largest dollar amount is incurred for state and federal income taxes. Taxes are an expense of the business and should be accrued in the same manner as any other business expense. A company that ends its accounting year on December 31 is not required to calculate the amount of tax owed to the government until the following March 15 or April 15, depending on the type of business. Therefore, year-end financial statements should reflect the amount of taxes incurred as an expense on the income statement and the amount of taxes that will be paid on March 15 or April 15 as a current liability on the balance sheet.

The calculation of the amount of tax a business owes is very complex. For now, the important point is that taxes are an expense when incurred (not when they are paid) and must be recorded as a liability as incurred.

Some analysts prefer to measure a company's profits before it pays taxes for several reasons. For one thing, tax rates change from year to year. A small change in the tax rate may drastically change a firm's profitability. Also, investors should realize that taxes occur in every year but that tax changes are not a recurring element of a business. Additionally, taxes are somewhat beyond the control of a company's management. For these reasons, it is important to consider a firm's operations *before* taxes to better evaluate management's ability to control operations.

OTHER ACCRUED LIABILITIES

McDonald's 1999 balance sheet listed an amount of $660.0 million as current liability under the category of Other Accrued Liabilities. What items might be included in this category?

In previous chapters, especially Chapter 4, we covered many examples of accrued liabilities. **Accrued liabilities** include any amount that has been incurred due to the passage of time but has not been paid as of the balance sheet date. A common example is salary or wages payable. Suppose that your firm has a payroll of $1,000 per day, Monday through Friday, and that employees are paid at the close of work each Friday. Also suppose that

December 31 is the end of your accounting year and falls on a Tuesday. Your firm should reflect the $2,000 of salary incurred, but unpaid, as an expense on the income statement and as a current liability on the balance sheet as of year-end. The amount of the salary payable would be classified as a current liability and could appear in a category such as Other Accrued Liabilities.

Interest is another item that often must be accrued at year-end. Assume that you received a one-year loan of $10,000 on December 1. The loan carries an interest rate of 12%. The income statement developed for the year ending December 31 should reflect one month's interest ($100) as expense even though it may not actually be due. The interest has been incurred and is therefore an expense. The balance sheet should reflect $100 as interest payable. An Interest Payable account representing one month's interest ($100) should be classified as a current liability, assuming that it is to be paid within one year of the December 31 date.

READING THE STATEMENT OF CASH FLOWS FOR CHANGES IN CURRENT LIABILITIES

It is important to understand the impact that current liabilities have on a company's cash flows. Exhibit 9-3 illustrates the placement of current liabilities on the statement of cash flows (using the indirect method) and their effect. Most current liabilities are directly related to a firm's ongoing operations. Therefore, the change in the balance of each current liability account should be reflected in the Operating Activities category of the statement of cash flows. A decrease in a current liability account indicates that cash has been used to pay the liability and should appear as a deduction on the cash flow statement. An increase in a current liability account indicates a recognized expense that has not yet been paid. Look for it as an increase in the Operating Activities category of the cash flow statement.

The cash flow statement of McDonald's Corporation is presented in Exhibit 9-4. Note that one of the items in the Operating Activities category is listed as Taxes and

LO 3 Understand how changes in current liabilities affect the statement of cash flows.

EXHIBIT 9-3 Current Liabilities on the Statement of Cash Flows

Item	Cash Flow Statement
	Operating Activities
	Net income **xxxx**
Increase in current liability	+
Decrease in current liability	−
	Investing Activities
	Financing Activities
Increase in notes payable	+
Decrease in notes payable	−

Other Liabilities of $270.4 million. This means that the balance of those current liabilities increased by $270.4 million, resulting in an increase of cash.

Almost all current liabilities appear in the Operating Activities category of the statement of cash flows, but there are exceptions. If a current liability is not directly related to operating activities, it should not appear in that category. For example, McDonald's uses some notes payable as a means of financing, distinct from operating activities. Therefore, note borrowings and repayments are reflected in the Financing Activities rather than the Operating Activities category (see Exhibit 9-3).

Two-Minute Review

1. What is the definition of current liabilities? Give some examples of items that are typically in the current liability category.

2. How is the current ratio calculated? What is it intended to measure?

3. In which category of the cash flow statement do most current liability items appear?

Answers:

1. Current liabilities are defined as items that will be paid within one year of the balance sheet date. Examples of current liabilities include accounts payable, notes payable if due within one year, taxes payable, and other accrued liabilities. Also, if a portion of a long-term debt will be paid within one year, that portion should be reported as a current liability.

2. The current ratio is calculated as total current assets divided by total current liabilities. It is a measure of the liquidity of the company, or the ability of the company to pay its short-term obligations.

3. Most current liabilities are reported in the operating category of the cash flow statement. You should note that it is the change in the balance of the current liability that is reported.

CONTINGENT LIABILITIES

LO 4 Determine when contingent liabilities should be presented on the balance sheet or disclosed in footnotes and how to calculate their amounts.

We have seen that accountants must exercise a great deal of expertise and judgment in deciding what to record and in determining the amount to record. This is certainly true regarding contingent liabilities. A **contingent liability** is an obligation that involves an existing condition for which the outcome is not known with certainty and depends on

Consolidated statement of cash flows

(In millions)	Years ended December 31,	1999	1998	1997
Operating activities	Net income	$ 1,947.9	$ 1,550.1	$ 1,642.5
	Adjustments to reconcile to cash provided by operations			
	Depreciation and amortization	956.3	881.1	793.8
	Deferred income taxes	52.9	35.4	(1.1)
	Changes in operating working capital items			
	Accounts receivable	(81.9)	(29.9)	(57.6)
	Inventories, prepaid expenses and other current assets	(47.7)	(18.1)	(34.5)
	Accounts payable	(23.9)	(12.7)	52.8
	Taxes and other liabilities	270.4	337.5	221.9
	Refund of U.S. franchisee security deposits			(109.6)
	Other	(65.1)	22.9	(65.9)
	Cash provided by operations	3,008.9	2,766.3	2,442.3
Investing activities	Property and equipment expenditures	(1,867.8)	(1,879.3)	(2,111.2)
	Purchases of restaurant businesses	(340.7)	(131.0)	(235.9)
	Sales of restaurant businesses	241.5	149.0	149.5
	Property sales	20.9	42.5	26.9
	Other	(315.7)	(129.4)	(46.5)
	Cash used for investing activities	(2,261.8)	(1,948.2)	(2,217.2)
Financing activities	Net short-term borrowings (repayments)	116.7	(604.2)	1,097.4
	Long-term financing issuances	902.5	1,461.5	1,037.9
	Long-term financing repayments	(682.8)	(594.9)	(1,133.8)
	Treasury stock purchases	(891.5)	(1,089.8)	(755.1)
	Common and preferred stock dividends	(264.7)	(240.5)	(247.7)
	Series E preferred stock redemption			(358.0)
	Other	193.0	207.6	145.7
	Cash used for financing activities	(626.8)	(860.3)	(213.6)
	Cash and equivalents increase (decrease)	120.3	(42.2)	11.5
	Cash and equivalents at beginning of year	299.2	341.4	329.9
	Cash and equivalents at end of year	$ 419.5	$ 299.2	$ 341.4
Supplemental cash flow disclosures	Interest paid	$ 411.5	$ 406.5	$ 401.7
	Income taxes paid	642.2	545.9	650.8

The accompanying financial comments are an integral part of the consolidated financial statements.

> Note the impact of current liabilities on cash flow

some event that will occur in the future. The actual amount of the liability must be estimated because we cannot clearly predict the future. The important accounting issues are whether contingent liabilities should be recorded and, if so, in what amounts.

This is a judgment call that is usually resolved through discussions among the company's management and its outside auditors. Management usually would rather not disclose contingent liabilities until they come due. The reason is that investors' and creditors' judgment of management is based on the company's earnings, and the recording of a contingent liability must be accompanied by a charge to (reduction in) earnings. Auditors, on the other hand, want management to disclose as much as possible because the auditors are essentially representing the interests of investors and creditors, who want to have as much information as possible.

CONTINGENT LIABILITIES THAT ARE RECORDED

A contingent liability should be accrued and presented on the balance sheet if it is probable and if the amount can be reasonably estimated. But when is an event *probable,* and what does *reasonably estimated* mean? The terms must be defined based on the facts of each situation. A financial statement user would want the company to err on the side of full disclosure. On the other hand, the company should not be required to disclose every remote possibility.

A common contingent liability that must be presented as a liability by firms involves product warranties or guarantees. Many firms sell products for which they provide the customer a warranty against defects that may develop in the products. If a product

> *Study Tip*
>
> Contingent liabilities are recorded only if they are probable and if the amount can be reasonably estimated.

becomes defective within the warranty period, the selling firm ensures that it will repair or replace the item. This is an example of a contingent liability because the expense of fixing a product depends on some of the products becoming defective—an uncertain, although likely, event.

At the end of each period, the selling firm must estimate how many of the products sold in the current year will become defective in the future and the cost of repair or replacement. This type of contingent liability is often referred to as an **estimated liability** to emphasize that the costs are not known at year-end and must be estimated.

As an example, assume that Quickkey Computer sells a computer product for $5,000. When the customer buys the product, Quickkey provides a one-year warranty in case it must be repaired. Assume that in 2001, Quickkey sold 100 computers for a total sales revenue of $500,000. At the end of 2001, Quickkey must record an estimate of the warranty costs that will occur on 2001 sales. Using an analysis of past warranty records, Quickkey estimates that repairs will average 2% of total sales. The 2001 balance sheet should indicate a liability of $10,000 in the account Estimated Liability for Warranty. This liability is classified as a current liability because Quickkey provides a one-year warranty. Quickkey's income statement should reflect a warranty expense of $10,000 to accrue the estimated amount of expense incurred.

The amount of warranty costs that a company presents as an expense is of interest to investors and potential creditors. If the expense as a percentage of sales begins to rise, one might conclude that the product is becoming less reliable.

Warranties are an excellent example of the matching principle. In our Quickkey example, the warranty costs related to 2001 sales were estimated and recorded in 2001. This was done to match the 2001 sales with the expenses related to those sales. If actual repairs of the computers occurred in 2002, they do not result in an expense. The repair costs incurred in 2002 should be treated as a reduction in the liability that had previously been estimated.

Because such items as warranties involve estimation, you may wonder what happens if the amount estimated is not accurate. The company must analyze past warranty records carefully and incorporate any changes in customer buying habits, usage, technological changes, and other changes. Still, even with careful analysis, the actual amount of the expense is not likely to equal the estimated amount. Generally, firms do not change the amount of the expense recorded in past periods for such differences. They may adjust the amount recorded in future periods, however.

Warranties provide an example of a contingent liability that must be estimated and recorded. Another example is premium or coupon offers that accompany many products. Cereal boxes are an everyday example of premium offers. The boxes often allow customers to purchase a toy or game at a reduced price if the purchase is accompanied by cereal box tops or proof of purchase. The offer given to cereal customers represents a contingent liability. At the end of each year, the cereal company must estimate the number of premium offers that will be redeemed and the cost involved and must report a contingent liability for that amount.

Legal claims that have been filed against a firm are also examples of contingent liabilities. In today's business environment, lawsuits and legal claims are a fact of life. They represent a contingent liability because an event has occurred but the outcome of that event, the resolution of the lawsuit, is not known. The defendant in the lawsuit must make a judgment about the outcome of the lawsuit in order to decide whether the item should be recorded on the balance sheet or should be disclosed in the footnotes. If an unfavorable outcome to the legal claim is deemed to be probable, then an amount should be recorded as a contingent liability on the balance sheet. Exhibit 9-5 provides portions of a footnote disclosure that accompanied the 1999 financial statements of Georgia-Pacific Corporation. The note concerned litigation over environmental damage that is alleged to have occurred as a result of the company's activities. Environmental remediation claims are very common for companies in many industries. In this case, Georgia-Pacific believed that an unfavorable outcome had become *probable* and, as a result, recorded a contingent liability (or reserve) for the amount they estimate will be owed at the eventual outcome of this claim.

Product warranties represent a *contingent liability* that must be presented on the balance sheet. This is because some amount of warranty work is *probable* and can be *estimated*. As the level of warranty expense rises, often so does investors' skepticism toward these retailers.

www.gp.com

Note 18

The Corporation is involved in environmental remediation activities at approximately 173 sites, both owned by the Corporation and owned by others, where it has been notified that it is or may be a potentially responsible party under the Comprehensive Environmental Response, Compensation and Liability Act or similar state "superfund" laws.

The Corporation has established reserves for environmental remediation costs for these sites in amounts that it believes are probable and reasonably estimable. Based on analysis of currently available information and previous experience with respect to the cleanup of hazardous substances, the Corporation believes that it is reasonably possible that costs associated with these sites may exceed current reserves by amounts that may prove insignificant or that could range, in the aggregate, up to approximately $56 million.

As you might imagine, firms are not usually eager to record contingent lawsuits as liabilities because the amount of loss is often difficult to estimate. Also, some may view the accountant's decision as an admission of guilt if a lawsuit is recorded as a liability before the courts have finalized a decision. Accountants must often consult with lawyers or other legal experts to determine the probability of the loss of a lawsuit. In cases involving contingencies, it is especially important that the accountant make an independent judgment based on the facts and not be swayed by the desires of other parties.

CONTINGENT LIABILITIES THAT ARE DISCLOSED

Any contingent liability that both is probable and can be reasonably estimated must be reported as a liability. We now must consider contingent liabilities that do not meet the probable criterion or cannot be reasonably estimated. In either case, a contingent liability must be disclosed in the footnotes but not reported on the balance sheet if the contingent liability is at least reasonably possible.

Although information in the footnotes to the financial statements contains very important data on which investors base decisions, some accountants believe that footnote disclosure does not have the same impact as does recording a contingent liability on the balance sheet. For one thing, footnote disclosure does not affect the important financial ratios that investors use to make decisions.

In the previous section, we presented a legal claim involving Georgia-Pacific as an example of a contingent liability that was probable and, therefore, was recorded on the balance sheet as a liability. Most lawsuits, however, are not recorded as liabilities either because the risk of loss is not considered probable or because the amount of the loss cannot be reasonably estimated. If a company does not record a lawsuit as a liability, it must still consider whether the lawsuit should be disclosed in the footnotes. If the risk of loss is

The Company is involved in several legal proceedings relating to the importation and distribution of vinyl mini-blinds made with plastic containing lead stabilizers. In 1996, the Consumer Product Safety Commission found that such stabilizers deteriorate over time from exposure to sunlight and heat, causing lead dust to form on mini-blind surfaces and presenting a health risk to children under six years of age.

Two lawsuits, which were commenced in California in 1996 against a number of companies, including a subsidiary of the Company, alleging failure to warn consumers adequately about the presence of lead in accordance with California law, were resolved during 1998–99. A national, injunction-only, class action settlement covering the Company's subsidiary and several other mini-blinds distributors and retailers was entered in the Superior Court of Passaic County, New Jersey on October 8, 1999.

An additional related lawsuit filed in Illinois in 1997 against a Company subsidiary and other companies is also being dismissed pursuant to the terms of the national settlement entered in New Jersey. The Company's contribution to the settlement and related amounts was not material to the Company's consolidated financial statements.

In December 1998, 13 companies, including a subsidiary of the Company, were named as defendants in another case involving the importation and distribution of vinyl mini-blinds containing lead. The case, filed as a Massachusetts class action in the Superior Court, alleges misrepresentation, breaches of express and implied warranties, negligence, loss of consortium and violation of Massachusetts consumer protection laws. The plaintiffs seek injunctive relief, unspecified damages, compensatory damages for personal injury and court costs.

at least *reasonably possible,* then the company should provide footnote disclosure. This is the course of action taken for most contingent liabilities involving lawsuits.

www.newellco.com

Exhibit 9-6 contains excerpts from the footnotes of the 1999 financial statements of Newell Rubbermaid, Inc., a large company in the consumer products market. The footnote indicates that the company is a defendant in several lawsuits concerning one of its products. The plaintiffs have alleged that the product represents a health risk and have sued for damages. Product liability lawsuits are very common, and many companies have been sued because of allegations that their product causes injury, damage, or health risk to the public. Often, these lawsuits will extend over many years before they are resolved by the courts.

You should note, however, that the Newell Rubbermaid footnote is an example of a contingent liability that has been disclosed in the footnotes *but has not been recorded as a liability on the balance sheet.* Readers of the financial statements, and analysts, must carefully read the footnotes to determine the impact of such contingent liabilities.

ACCOUNTING FOR YOUR DECISIONS

You Are the CEO

You run a high-technology company that grows fast some quarters and disappoints investors in other quarters. As a result, your company's stock price fluctuates widely, and you have attracted the unwanted attention of a law firm that filed a lawsuit on behalf of disgruntled shareholders. How do you reflect this lawsuit on your financial statements?

ANS: Your legal counsel should be consulted to determine whether the plaintiff's case has merit. If a loss is probable and the amount can be estimated, the lawsuit should be recorded as a liability. Unfortunately, lawsuits have become very common for many companies. In some cases, the lawsuits are totally without merit and are frivolous. If your attorneys agree that this case will not result in a loss, then no disclosure would be required.

The amount and the timing of the cash outlays associated with contingent liabilities are especially difficult to determine. Because lawsuits may extend several years into the future, the dollar amount of possible loss may be subject to great uncertainty.

CONTINGENT LIABILITIES VERSUS CONTINGENT ASSETS

Contingent liabilities that are probable and can be reasonably estimated must be presented on the balance sheet before the outcome of the future events is known. This accounting rule applies only to contingent losses or liabilities. It does not apply to contingencies by which the firm may gain. Generally, contingent gains or **contingent assets** are not reported until the gain actually occurs. That is, contingent liabilities may be accrued, but contingent assets are not accrued. Exhibit 9-7 contains a portion of the footnotes from the 1999 financial statements of Johnson Controls, a large company that is a supplier to the automakers. Like many other companies, Johnson Controls has had to accrue rather large amounts for environmental remediation costs. The footnote indicates that Johnson Controls believes that its insurance policies should cover part of the costs. This is an example of a contingent asset because the company may receive some amounts at a future time. The financial statements reveal that Johnson Controls has recorded liabilities related to the remediation costs but has not recorded any of the potential recoveries from insurance even though it appears quite likely that some amount will be received. This may seem inconsistent—it is. Remember, however, that accounting is a discipline based on a conservative set of principles. It is prudent and conservative to delay the recording of a gain until an asset is actually received but to record contingent liabilities in advance.

www.johnsoncontrols.com

Of course, even though the contingent assets are not reported, the information may still be important to investors. Wall Street analysts make their living trying to place a value on contingent assets that they believe will result in future benefits. By buying stock of a company that has unrecorded assets, or advising their clients to do so, investment analysts hope to make money when those assets become a reality.

EXHIBIT 9-7 Footnote Disclosure for Contingent Asset (Proceeds from Insurance) from Johnson Controls' Financial Statements

> NOTE
>
> **15** Contingencies
>
> The Company is involved in a number of proceedings and potential proceedings relating to environmental matters. At September 30, 1999, the Company had an accrued liability of approximately $46 million relating to environmental matters. The Company's environmental liabilities are undiscounted and do not take into consideration any possible recoveries of future insurance proceeds. Because of the uncertainties associated with environmental assessment and remediation activities, the Company's future expenses to remediate the currently identified sites could be considerably higher than the accrued liability. Although it is difficult to estimate the liability of the Company related to these environmental matters, the Company believes that these matters will not have a materially adverse effect upon its capital expenditures, earnings or competitive position.
>
> Additionally, the Company is involved in a number of product liability and various other suits incident to the operation of its businesses. Insurance coverages are maintained and estimated costs are recorded for claims and suits of this nature. It is management's opinion that none of these will have a materially adverse effect on the Company's financial position, results of operations or cash flows.

TIME VALUE OF MONEY CONCEPTS

In this section, we will study the impact that interest has on decision making because of the time value of money. The **time value of money** concept means that people prefer a payment at the present time rather than in the future because of the interest factor. If an amount is received at the present time, it can be invested, and the resulting accumulation will be larger than if the same amount is received in the future. Thus, there is a *time value* to cash receipts and payments. This time value concept is important to every student for two reasons: it affects your personal financial decisions, and it affects accounting valuation decisions.

Exhibit 9-8 indicates some of the personal and accounting decisions affected by the time value of money concept. In your personal life, you make decisions based on the time value of money concept nearly every day. When you invest money, you are interested in how much will be accumulated, and you must determine the *future value* based on the amount of interest that will be compounded. When you borrow money, you must determine the amount of the payments on the loan. You may not always realize it, but the amount of the loan payment is based on the *present value* of the loan, another time value of money concept.

Time value of money is also important because of its implications for accounting valuations. We will discover in Chapter 10 that the issue price of a bond is based on the present value of the cash flows that the bond will produce. The valuation of the bond and the recording of the bond on the balance sheet are based on this concept. Further, the amount that is considered interest expense on the financial statements is also based on time value of money concepts. The bottom portion of Exhibit 9-8 indicates that the valuations of many other accounts, including Notes Receivable and Leases, are based on compound interest calculations.

The time value of money concept is used in virtually every advanced business course. Investment courses, marketing courses, and many other business courses will use the time value of money concept. *In fact, it is probably the most important decision-making tool to master in preparation for the business world.* This section of the text begins with an explanation of how simple interest and compound interest differ and then proceeds to the concepts of present values and future values.

SIMPLE INTEREST

LO 5 Explain the difference between simple and compound interest.

Simple interest is interest earned on the principal amount. If the amount of principal is unchanged from year to year, the interest per year will remain the same. Interest can be calculated by the following formula:

$$I = P \times R \times T,$$

$$PV = \$2,000 \times (1 + .10)^{-2}$$
$$= \$2,000 \times (.826)$$
$$= \$1,652$$

Example 5: A recent magazine article projects that it will cost $120,000 to attend a four-year college 10 years from now. If that is true, how much money would you have to put into an account today to fund that education, assuming a 5% rate of return?

Study Tip

When interest rates *increase*, present values *decrease*. This is called an *inverse relationship*.

Solution:
$$PV = \$120,000(1 + .05)^{-10}$$
$$= \$12,000(.614)$$
$$= \$73,680$$

Tables have also been developed to determine the present value of $1 at various interest rates and number of periods. Table 9-2 on page 424 presents the present value or discount factors for an amount of $1 to be received at a future time. To use the table for our two-year note example, you must read across the line for two periods and down the 10% column to the discount factor of .826. The present value of $2,000 would be calculated as follows:

$$PV = \$2,000(\text{discount factor})$$
$$= \$2,000(.826)$$
$$= \$1,652$$

Two other points are important. First, the example illustrates that the present value amount is always less than the future payment. This happens because of the discount factor. In other words, if we had a smaller amount at the present (the present value), we could invest it and earn interest that would accumulate to an amount equal to the larger amount (the future payment). Second, study of the present value and future value formulas indicates that each is the reciprocal of the other. When we want to calculate a present value amount, we normally use Table 9-2 and multiply a discount factor times the payment. However, we could also use Table 9-1 and divide by the interest factor. Thus, the present value of the $2,000 to be received in the future could also be calculated as follows:

$$PV = \$2,000/1.210$$
$$= \$1,652$$

FUTURE VALUE OF AN ANNUITY

The present value and future value amounts are useful when a single amount is involved. Many accounting situations involve an annuity, however. **Annuity** means a series of payments of equal amounts. We will now consider the calculation of the future value when a series of payments is involved.

Example 6: Suppose that you are to receive $3,000 per year at the end of each of the next four years. Also, assume that each payment could be invested at an interest rate of 10% compounded annually. How much would be accumulated in principal and interest by the end of the fourth year? This is an example of an annuity of payments of equal amounts. A time diagram would portray the payments as follows:

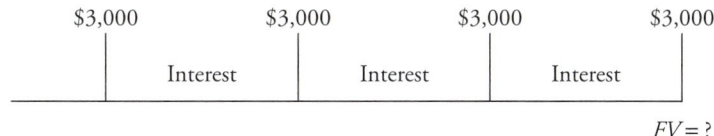

Because we are interested in calculating the future value, we could use the future value of $1 concept and calculate the future value of each $3,000 payment using Table 9-1 as follows:

$$\$3{,}000 \times 1.331 \text{ Interest for 3 Periods} \qquad \$3{,}993$$
$$3{,}000 \times 1.210 \text{ Interest for 2 Periods} \qquad 3{,}630$$
$$3{,}000 \times 1.100 \text{ Interest for 1 Period} \qquad 3{,}300$$
$$3{,}000 \times 1.000 \text{ Interest for 0 Periods} \qquad \underline{3{,}000}$$
$$\text{Total Future Value} \qquad \underline{\underline{\$13{,}923}}$$

It should be noted that four payments would be received but that only three of them would draw interest because the payments are received at the end of each period.

Fortunately, there is an easier method to calculate the **future value of an annuity.** Table 9-3 on page 425 has been constructed to indicate the future value of a series of payments of $1 per period at various interest rates and number of periods. The table can be used for the previous example by reading across the four-period line and down the 10% column to a table factor of 4.641. The future value of an annuity of $3,000 per year can be calculated as follows:

$$FV = \$3{,}000(\text{table factor})$$
$$= \$3{,}000(4.641)$$
$$= \$13{,}923$$

Example 7: You just had a baby girl two weeks ago and are already thinking about college. When she is 15, how much money would be in her college account if you deposit $2,000 into it on each of her 15 birthdays? The interest rate is 10%.

Solution:
$$FV = \$2{,}000(\text{table factor})$$
$$= \$2{,}000(31.772)$$
$$= \$63{,}544$$

When compounding occurs more frequently than annually, adjustments must be made to the interest rate and number of periods, adjustments similar to those discussed previously for single amounts.

Example 8: How would the future value be calculated if the previous example was modified so that we deposited $1,000 semiannually and the interest rate was 10% compounded semiannually (or 5% per period) for 15 years? Table 9-3 could be used by reading across the line for 30 periods and down the column for 5% to obtain a table factor of 66.439. The future value would be calculated as follows:

$$FV = \$1{,}000(\text{table factor})$$
$$= \$1{,}000(66.439)$$
$$= \$66{,}439$$

Comparing the two examples illustrates once again that more frequent compounding results in larger accumulated amounts.

PRESENT VALUE OF AN ANNUITY

Many accounting applications of the time value of money concept concern situations for which we want to know the present value of a series of payments that will occur in the future. This involves calculating the present value of an annuity. An annuity is a series of payments of equal amounts.

Example 9: Suppose that you will receive an annuity of $4,000 per year for four years, with the first received one year from today. The amounts that are received can be invested at a rate of 10% compounded annually. What amount would you need at the present time to have an amount equivalent to the series of payments and interest in the future? To answer this question, you must calculate the **present value of an annuity.** A time diagram of the series of payments would appear as follows:

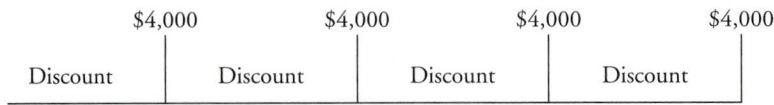

$$PV = ?$$

Because you are interested in calculating the present value, you could refer to the present value of $1 concept and discount each of the $4,000 payments individually using table factors from Table 9-2 as follows:

$4,000 × 0.683 Factor for Four Periods	$ 2,732
4,000 × 0.751 Factor for Three Periods	3,004
4,000 × 0.826 Factor for Two Periods	3,304
4,000 × 0.909 Factor for One Period	3,636
Total Present Value	$12,676

For a problem of any size, it is very cumbersome to calculate the present value of each payment individually. Therefore, tables have been constructed to ease the computational burden. Table 9-4 on page 426 provides table factors to calculate the present value of an annuity of $1 per year at various interest rates and number of periods. The previous example can be solved by reading across the four-year line and down the 10% column to obtain a table factor of 3.170. The present value would then be calculated as follows:

$$PV = \$4,000(\text{table factor})$$
$$= \$4,000(3.170)$$
$$= \$12,680$$

You should note that there is a $4 difference in the present value calculated by the first and second methods. This difference is caused by a small amount of rounding in the table factors that were used.

Example 10: You just won the lottery. You can take your $1 million in a lump sum today, or you can receive $100,000 per year over the next 12 years. Assuming a 5% interest rate, which would you prefer, ignoring tax considerations?

Solution:
$$PV = \$100,000(\text{table factor})$$
$$= \$100,000(8.863)$$
$$= \$886,300$$

Because the present value of the payments over 12 years is less than the $1 million immediate payment, you should prefer the immediate payment.

SOLVING FOR UNKNOWNS

In some cases, the present value or future value amounts will be known but the interest rate or the number of payments must be calculated. The formulas that have been presented thus far can be used for such calculations, but you must be careful to analyze each problem to be sure that you have chosen the correct relationship. We will use two examples to illustrate the power of the time value of money concepts.

LO 7 Apply the compound interest concepts to some common accounting situations.

Assume that you have just purchased a new automobile for $14,420 and must decide how to pay for it. Your local bank has graciously granted you a five-year loan. Because you are a good credit risk, the bank will allow you to make annual payments on the loan at the end of each year. The amount of the loan payments, which include principal and interest, is $4,000 per year. You are concerned that your total payments will be $20,000 ($4,000 per year for five years) and want to calculate the interest rate that is being charged on the loan.

Because the market or present value of the car, as well as the loan, is $14,420, a time diagram of our example would appear as follows:

PV = 14,420

FOCUS ON USERS

Accounts Payables Can Raise Red Flags for This Analyst

Banc One Capital Markets (BOCM) is the investment banking arm of Bank One, which is one of the largest multibank holding companies in the United States. As a BOCM transaction specialist responsible for structuring loans for companies involved in mergers or acquisitions, Philip Yarrow turns to the balance sheet every day to do his job. "I use the balance sheet to evaluate the debt capacity of companies and as a tool to identify potential problems. In the lending business, we consider assets and cash flow to be very important. I use the balance sheet to assess the amount of the assets, focusing on accounts receivable; inventory; and property, plant, and equipment. I also consider the amount of equity a company has, as I decide how much to lend," Phil says.

The balance sheet, and the current liabilities section in particular, can also raise all sorts of red flags to professionals who lend cash to corporations. Phil looks for significant changes in any of the current liabilities accounts—for example, dramatic increases that are not accompanied by similar increases in sales. To him, this kind of imbalance is a sign that the company is struggling to pay its creditors. Phil explains: "If I see accounts receivable going down and accounts payable going up, it could be the early signs of a liquidity crisis. The company may be encouraging customers to pay earlier by offering better terms and holding off longer to pay suppliers because of a lack of cash. This position is unsustainable. Eventually, the suppliers will stop supplying the company with the necessary product it needs to continue business effectively. This will impact the company's cash flow and, therefore, impair the ability of the company to repay its bank loans."

The decision of how to structure a particular financing deal always incorporates analysis of the company's current liabilities position. As Phil says: "By studying the current assets and current liabilities on the company's balance sheets, I can assess the company's need for debt to finance working capital. If the company does have a need for working capital, I would structure a credit arrangement that included a revolving bank loan to allow the company to borrow, repay, and reborrow in a similar manner to a credit card." Liabilities are what enable companies to grow and prosper. However, current liabilities are debts, and they have the potential to impair the solvency of any company. It is Phil's job to figure out whether companies have used debt wisely.

> "If I see accounts receivable going down and accounts payable going up, it could be the early signs of a liquidity crisis."
>
> —Philip Yarrow

The interest rate that we must solve for represents the discount rate that was applied to the $4,000 payments to result in a present value of $14,420. Therefore, the applicable formula is the following:

$$PV = \$4,000(\text{table factor})$$

In this case, PV is known, so the formula can be rearranged as follows:

$$\text{Table Factor} = PV/\$4,000$$
$$= \$14,420/\$4,000$$
$$= 3.605$$

The value of 3.605 represents a table factor in Table 9-4. We must read across the five-year line until we find a table factor of 3.605. In this case, that table factor is found in the 12% column. Therefore, the rate of interest being paid on the auto loan is 12%.

The second example involves solving for the number of interest periods. Assume that you want to accumulate $12,000 as a down payment on a home. You believe that you can save $1,000 per semiannual period, and your bank will pay interest of 8% per year, or 4% per semiannual period. How long will it take you to accumulate the desired amount?

The accumulated amount of $12,000 represents the future value of an annuity of $1,000 per semiannual period. Therefore, we can use the interest factors of Table 9-3 to assist in the solution. The applicable formula in this case is the following:

$$FV = \$1,000(\text{table factor})$$

The future value is known to be $12,000, and we must solve for the interest factor or table factor. Therefore, we can rearrange the formula as follows:

$$\text{Table factor} = FV/\$1,000$$

$$= \$12,000/\$1,000$$

$$= 12.00$$

Using Table 9-3, we must scan down the 4% column until we find a table value that is near 12.00. The closest table value we find is 12.006. That table value corresponds to 10 periods. Therefore, if we deposit $1,000 per semiannual period and invest the money at 4% per semiannual period, it will take 10 semiannual periods (five years) to accumulate $12,000.

WARMUP EXERCISES

LO 1 Warmup Exercise 9-1
A company has the following current assets: Cash, $10,000; Accounts Receivable, $70,000; and Inventory, $20,000. The company also has current liabilities of $40,000. Calculate the company's current ratio and quick ratio.

LO 3 Warmup Exercise 9-2
A company has the following current liabilities at the beginning of the period: Accounts Payable, $30,000; Taxes Payable, $10,000. At the end of the period, the balances of the accounts are as follows: Accounts Payable, $20,000; Taxes Payable, $15,000. What amounts will appear in the cash flow statement, and in what category of the statement will they appear?

LO 6 Warmup Exercise 9-3
A. You invest $1,000 at the beginning of the year. How much will be accumulated in five years if you earn 10% interest compounded annually?

B. You invest $1,000 *per year* at the end of each year for five years. How much will be accumulated in five years if you earn 10% interest compounded annually?

C. You will receive $1,000 in five years. What is the present value of that amount if you can earn 10% interest compounded annually?

D. You will receive $1,000 *per year* at the end of each year for five years. What is the present value of that amount if you can earn 10% interest compounded annually?

SOLUTIONS TO WARMUP EXERCISES

Warmup Exercise 9-1

Current Ratio: Current Assets/Current Liabilities

Cash ($10,000) + Accounts Receivable ($70,000) + Inventory ($20,000) = $100,000

$100,000/$40,000 = 2.5 Current Ratio

Quick Ratio: Quick Assets/Current Liabilities

Cash ($10,000) + Accounts Receivable ($70,000) = $80,000

$80,000/$40,000 = 2.0 Quick Ratio

Warmup Exercise 9-2

The amounts appearing in the cash flow statement should be in the Operating Activities category of the statement. The amounts shown should be the *changes* in the balances of the accounts.

Accounts Payable decreased by $10,000 and should appear as a decrease in the cash flow statement. Taxes Payable increased by $5,000 and should appear as an increase in the cash flow statement.

Warmup Exercise 9-3

A. $FV = \$1{,}000$ (table factor)   using Table 9-1

   $\quad = \$1{,}000 \,(1.611)$ where $i = 10\%$, $n = 5$

   $\quad = \$1{,}611$

B. $FV = \$1{,}000$ (table factor)   using Table 9-3

   $\quad = \$1{,}000 \,(6.105)$ where $i = 10\%$, $n = 5$

   $\quad = \$6{,}105$

C. $PV = \$1{,}000$ (table factor)   using Table 9-2

   $\quad = \$1{,}000 \,(.621)$ where $i = 10\%$, $n = 5$

   $\quad = \$621$

D. $PV = \$1{,}000$ (table factor)   using Table 9-4

   $\quad = \$1{,}000 \,(3.791)$ where $i = 10\%$, $n = 5$

   $\quad = \$3{,}791$

REVIEW PROBLEM

Part A

The accountant for Lunn Express wants to develop a balance sheet as of December 31, 2001. The following items pertain to the liability category and must be considered in order to determine the items that should be reported in the Current Liability section of the balance sheet. You may assume that Lunn began business on January 1, 2001, and, therefore, the beginning balance of all accounts was zero.

a. During 2001, Lunn purchased $100,000 of inventory on account from suppliers. By year-end, $40,000 of the balance has been eliminated as a result of payments. All items were purchased on terms of 2/10, n/30. Lunn uses the gross method of recording payables.

b. On April 1, 2001, Lunn borrowed $10,000 on a one-year note payable from Philips Bank. Terms of the loan indicate that Lunn must repay the principal and 12% interest at the due date of the note.

c. On October 1, 2001, Lunn also borrowed $8,000 from Dove Bank on a one-year note payable. Dove Bank deducted 10% interest in advance and gave to Lunn the net amount. At the due date, Lunn must repay the principal of $8,000.

d. On January 1, 2001, Lunn borrowed $20,000 from Owens Bank by signing a 10-year note payable. Terms of the note indicate that Lunn must make annual payments of principal each January 1 beginning in 2002 and also must pay interest each January 1 in the amount of 8% of the outstanding balance of the loan.

e. The accountant for Lunn has completed an income statement for 2001 that indicates that income before taxes was $10,000. Lunn must pay tax at the rate of 40% and must remit the tax to the Internal Revenue Service by April 15, 2002.

f. As of December 31, 2001, Lunn owes to employees salaries of $3,000 for work performed in 2001. The employees will be paid on the first payday of 2002.

g. During 2001, two lawsuits were filed against Lunn. In the first lawsuit, a customer sued for damages because of an injury that occurred on Lunn's premises. Lunn's legal counsel advised that it is probable that the lawsuit will be settled in 2002 at an amount of $7,000. The second lawsuit involves a patent infringement suit of $14,000 filed against Lunn by a competitor. The legal counsel has advised that there is some possibility that Lunn may be at fault but that a loss does not appear probable at this time.

Part B

a. What amount will be accumulated by January 1, 2005, if $5,000 is invested on January 1, 2001, at 10% interest compounded semiannually?

b. Assume that we are to receive $5,000 on January 1, 2005. What amount at January 1, 2001, is equivalent to the $5,000 that is to be received in 2005? Assume that interest is compounded annually at 10%.

c. What amount will be accumulated by January 1, 2005, if $5,000 is invested each semiannual period for eight periods beginning with June 30, 2001, and ending December 31, 2004? Interest will accumulate at 10% compounded semiannually.

d. Assume that we are to receive $5,000 each semiannual period for eight periods beginning on June 30, 2001. What amount at January 1, 2001, is equivalent to the future series of payments? Assume that interest will accrue at 10% compounded semiannually.

e. Assume that a new bank has begun a promotional campaign to attract savings accounts. The bank advertisement indicates that customers who invest $1,000 will double their money in 10 years. Assuming annual compounding of interest, what rate of interest is the bank offering?

Required

1. Consider all items in part **A.** Develop the Current Liability section of Lunn's balance sheet as of December 31, 2001. To make investment decisions about this company, what additional data would you need? You do not need to consider the footnotes that accompany the balance sheet.

2. Answer the five questions in part **B.**

Solution to Part A

The accountant's decisions for items **a** through **g** of part **A** should be as follows:

a. The balance of the Accounts Payable account should be $60,000. The payables should be reported at the gross amount, and discounts would not be reported until the time of payment.

b. The note payable to Philips Bank of $10,000 should be included as a current liability. Also, interest payable of $900 ($10,000 × 12% × 9/12) should be considered a current liability.

c. The note payable to Dove Bank should be considered a current liability and listed at $8,000 minus the contra account Discount on Note Payable of $600 ($8,000 × 10% × 9/12 remaining).

d. The debt to Owens Bank should be split between current liability and long-term liability with the current portion shown as $2,000. Also, interest payable of $1,600 ($20,000 × 8% × 1 year) should be considered a current liability.

e. Income taxes payable of $4,000 ($10,000 × 40%) are a current liability.

f. Salaries payable of $3,000 represent a current liability.

g. The lawsuit involving the customer must be reported as a current liability of $7,000 because the possibility of loss is probable. The second lawsuit should not be reported but should be disclosed as a footnote to the balance sheet.

LUNN EXPRESS
PARTIAL BALANCE SHEET
AS OF DECEMBER 31, 2001

Current Liabilities

Accounts payable		$60,000
Interest payable ($900 + $1,600)		2,500
Salaries payable		3,000
Taxes payable		4,000
Note payable to Philips Bank		10,000
Note payable to Dove Bank	$8,000	
Less: Discount on note payable	(600)	7,400
Current maturity of long-term debt		2,000
Contingent liability for pending lawsuit		7,000
Total Current Liabilities		$95,900

Other data necessary to make an investment decision might include current assets, total assets, and current liabilities as of December 31, 2000 and 2001. If current assets are significantly larger than current liabilities, you can be comfortable that the company is capable of paying its short-term debt. The dollar amount of current assets and liabilities must be evaluated with regard to the size of the company. The larger the company, the less significant $95,900 in current liabilities would be. Knowing last year's current liabilities would give you an idea about the trend in current liabilities. If they are rising, you would want to know why.

Solution to Part B

a.
$$FV = \$5,000(\text{table factor}) \qquad \text{using Table 9-1}$$
$$= \$5,000(1.477) \qquad \text{where } i = 5\%, n = 8$$
$$= \$7,385$$

b.
$$PV = \$5,000(\text{table factor}) \qquad \text{using Table 9-2}$$
$$= \$5,000(.683) \qquad \text{where } i = 10\%, n = 4$$
$$= \$3,415$$

c.
$$FV \text{ annuity} = \$5,000(\text{table factor}) \qquad \text{using Table 9-3}$$
$$= \$5,000(9.549) \qquad \text{where } i = 5\%, n = 8$$
$$= \$47,745$$

d.
$$PV \text{ annuity} = \$5,000(\text{table factor}) \qquad \text{using Table 9-4}$$
$$= \$5,000(6.463) \qquad \text{where } i = 5\%, n = 8$$
$$= \$32,315$$

e.
$$FV = \$1,000(\text{table factor}) \qquad \text{using Table 9-1}$$

Because the future value is known to be $2,000, the formula can be written as

$$\$2,000 = \$1,000(\text{table factor})$$

and rearranged as

$$\text{Table Factor} = \$2,000/\$1,000 = 2.0.$$

In Table 9-1, the table factor of 2.0 and 10 years correspond with an interest rate of between 7% and 8%.

TABLE 9-1 Future Value of $1

(n) Periods	\multicolumn{12}{c}{Rate of Interest in %}
	2	**3**	**4**	**5**	**6**	**7**	**8**	**9**	**10**	**11**	**12**	**15**
1	1.020	1.030	1.040	1.050	1.060	1.070	1.080	1.090	1.100	1.110	1.120	1.150
2	1.040	1.061	1.082	1.103	1.124	1.145	1.166	1.188	1.210	1.232	1.254	1.323
3	1.061	1.093	1.125	1.158	1.191	1.225	1.260	1.295	1.331	1.368	1.405	1.521
4	1.082	1.126	1.170	1.216	1.262	1.311	1.360	1.412	1.464	1.518	1.574	1.749
5	1.104	1.159	1.217	1.276	1.338	1.403	1.469	1.539	1.611	1.685	1.762	2.011
6	1.126	1.194	1.265	1.340	1.419	1.501	1.587	1.677	1.772	1.870	1.974	2.313
7	1.149	1.230	1.316	1.407	1.504	1.606	1.714	1.828	1.949	2.076	2.211	2.660
8	1.172	1.267	1.369	1.477	1.594	1.718	1.851	1.993	2.144	2.305	2.476	3.059
9	1.195	1.305	1.423	1.551	1.689	1.838	1.999	2.172	2.358	2.558	2.773	3.518
10	1.219	1.344	1.480	1.629	1.791	1.967	2.159	2.367	2.594	2.839	3.106	4.046
11	1.243	1.384	1.539	1.710	1.898	2.105	2.332	2.580	2.853	3.152	3.479	4.652
12	1.268	1.426	1.601	1.796	2.012	2.252	2.518	2.813	3.138	3.498	3.896	5.350
13	1.294	1.469	1.665	1.886	2.133	2.410	2.720	3.066	3.452	3.883	4.363	6.153
14	1.319	1.513	1.732	1.980	2.261	2.579	2.937	3.342	3.797	4.310	4.887	7.076
15	1.346	1.558	1.801	2.079	2.397	2.759	3.172	3.642	4.177	4.785	5.474	8.137
16	1.373	1.605	1.873	2.183	2.540	2.952	3.426	3.970	4.595	5.311	6.130	9.358
17	1.400	1.653	1.948	2.292	2.693	3.159	3.700	4.328	5.054	5.895	6.866	10.761
18	1.428	1.702	2.026	2.407	2.854	3.380	3.996	4.717	5.560	6.544	7.690	12.375
19	1.457	1.754	2.107	2.527	3.026	3.617	4.316	5.142	6.116	7.263	8.613	14.232
20	1.486	1.806	2.191	2.653	3.207	3.870	4.661	5.604	6.727	8.062	9.646	16.367
21	1.516	1.860	2.279	2.786	3.400	4.141	5.034	6.109	7.400	8.949	10.804	18.822
22	1.546	1.916	2.370	2.925	3.604	4.430	5.437	6.659	8.140	9.934	12.100	21.645
23	1.577	1.974	2.465	3.072	3.820	4.741	5.871	7.258	8.954	11.026	13.552	24.891
24	1.608	2.033	2.563	3.225	4.049	5.072	6.341	7.911	9.850	12.239	15.179	28.625
25	1.641	2.094	2.666	3.386	4.292	5.427	6.848	8.623	10.835	13.585	17.000	32.919
26	1.673	2.157	2.772	3.556	4.549	5.807	7.396	9.399	11.918	15.080	19.040	37.857
27	1.707	2.221	2.883	3.733	4.822	6.214	7.988	10.245	13.110	16.739	21.325	43.535
28	1.741	2.288	2.999	3.920	5.112	6.649	8.627	11.167	14.421	18.580	23.884	50.066
29	1.776	2.357	3.119	4.116	5.418	7.114	9.317	12.172	15.863	20.624	26.750	57.575
30	1.811	2.427	3.243	4.322	5.743	7.612	10.063	13.268	17.449	22.892	29.960	66.212

TABLE 9-2 Present Value of $1

(n) Periods	2	3	4	5	6	7	8	9	10	11	12	15
1	0.980	0.971	0.962	0.952	0.943	0.935	0.926	0.917	0.909	0.901	0.893	0.870
2	0.961	0.943	0.925	0.907	0.890	0.873	0.857	0.842	0.826	0.812	0.797	0.756
3	0.942	0.915	0.889	0.864	0.840	0.816	0.794	0.772	0.751	0.731	0.712	0.658
4	0.924	0.888	0.855	0.823	0.792	0.763	0.735	0.708	0.683	0.659	0.636	0.572
5	0.906	0.863	0.822	0.784	0.747	0.713	0.681	0.650	0.621	0.593	0.567	0.497
6	0.888	0.837	0.790	0.746	0.705	0.666	0.630	0.596	0.564	0.535	0.507	0.432
7	0.871	0.813	0.760	0.711	0.665	0.623	0.583	0.547	0.513	0.482	0.452	0.376
8	0.853	0.789	0.731	0.677	0.627	0.582	0.540	0.502	0.467	0.434	0.404	0.327
9	0.837	0.766	0.703	0.645	0.592	0.544	0.500	0.460	0.424	0.391	0.361	0.284
10	0.820	0.744	0.676	0.614	0.558	0.508	0.463	0.422	0.386	0.352	0.322	0.247
11	0.804	0.722	0.650	0.585	0.527	0.475	0.429	0.388	0.350	0.317	0.287	0.215
12	0.788	0.701	0.625	0.557	0.497	0.444	0.397	0.356	0.319	0.286	0.257	0.187
13	0.773	0.681	0.601	0.530	0.469	0.415	0.368	0.326	0.290	0.258	0.229	0.163
14	0.758	0.661	0.577	0.505	0.442	0.388	0.340	0.299	0.263	0.232	0.205	0.141
15	0.743	0.642	0.555	0.481	0.417	0.362	0.315	0.275	0.239	0.209	0.183	0.123
16	0.728	0.623	0.534	0.458	0.394	0.339	0.292	0.252	0.218	0.188	0.163	0.107
17	0.714	0.605	0.513	0.436	0.371	0.317	0.270	0.231	0.198	0.170	0.146	0.093
18	0.700	0.587	0.494	0.416	0.350	0.296	0.250	0.212	0.180	0.153	0.130	0.081
19	0.686	0.570	0.475	0.396	0.331	0.277	0.232	0.194	0.164	0.138	0.116	0.070
20	0.673	0.554	0.456	0.377	0.312	0.258	0.215	0.178	0.149	0.124	0.104	0.061
21	0.660	0.538	0.439	0.359	0.294	0.242	0.199	0.164	0.135	0.112	0.093	0.053
22	0.647	0.522	0.422	0.342	0.278	0.226	0.184	0.150	0.123	0.101	0.083	0.046
23	0.634	0.507	0.406	0.326	0.262	0.211	0.170	0.138	0.112	0.091	0.074	0.040
24	0.622	0.492	0.390	0.310	0.247	0.197	0.158	0.126	0.102	0.082	0.066	0.035
25	0.610	0.478	0.375	0.295	0.233	0.184	0.146	0.116	0.092	0.074	0.059	0.030
26	0.598	0.464	0.361	0.281	0.220	0.172	0.135	0.106	0.084	0.066	0.053	0.026
27	0.586	0.450	0.347	0.268	0.207	0.161	0.125	0.098	0.076	0.060	0.047	0.023
28	0.574	0.437	0.333	0.255	0.196	0.150	0.116	0.090	0.069	0.054	0.042	0.020
29	0.563	0.424	0.321	0.243	0.185	0.141	0.107	0.082	0.063	0.048	0.037	0.017
30	0.552	0.412	0.308	0.231	0.174	0.131	0.099	0.075	0.057	0.044	0.033	0.015

Rate of Interest in %

TABLE 9-3 Future Value of Annuity of $1

(n) Periods	2	3	4	5	6	7	8	9	10	11	12	15
1	1.000	1.000	1.000	1.000	1.000	1.000	1.000	1.000	1.000	1.000	1.000	1.000
2	2.020	2.030	2.040	2.050	2.060	2.070	2.080	2.090	2.100	2.110	2.120	2.150
3	3.060	3.091	3.122	3.153	3.184	3.215	3.246	3.278	3.310	3.342	3.374	3.473
4	4.122	4.184	4.246	4.310	4.375	4.440	4.506	4.573	4.641	4.710	4.779	4.993
5	5.204	5.309	5.416	5.526	5.637	5.751	5.867	5.985	6.105	6.228	6.353	6.742
6	6.308	6.468	6.633	6.802	6.975	7.153	7.336	7.523	7.716	7.913	8.115	8.754
7	7.434	7.662	7.898	8.142	8.394	8.654	8.923	9.200	9.487	9.783	10.089	11.067
8	8.583	8.892	9.214	9.549	9.897	10.260	10.637	11.028	11.436	11.859	12.300	13.727
9	9.755	10.159	10.583	11.027	11.491	11.978	12.488	13.021	13.579	14.164	14.776	16.786
10	10.950	11.464	12.006	12.578	13.181	13.816	14.487	15.193	15.937	16.722	17.549	20.304
11	12.169	12.808	13.486	14.207	14.972	15.784	16.645	17.560	18.531	19.561	20.655	24.349
12	13.412	14.192	15.026	15.917	16.870	17.888	18.977	20.141	21.384	22.713	24.133	29.002
13	14.680	15.618	16.627	17.713	18.882	20.141	21.495	22.953	24.523	26.212	28.029	34.352
14	15.974	17.086	18.292	19.599	21.015	22.550	24.215	26.019	27.975	30.095	32.393	40.505
15	17.293	18.599	20.024	21.579	23.276	25.129	27.152	29.361	31.772	34.405	37.280	47.580
16	18.639	20.157	21.825	23.657	25.673	27.888	30.324	33.003	35.950	39.190	42.753	55.717
17	20.012	21.762	23.698	25.840	28.213	30.840	33.750	36.974	40.545	44.501	48.884	65.075
18	21.412	23.414	25.645	28.132	30.906	33.999	37.450	41.301	45.599	50.396	55.750	75.836
19	22.841	25.117	27.671	30.539	33.760	37.379	41.446	46.018	51.159	56.939	63.440	88.212
20	24.297	26.870	29.778	33.066	36.786	40.995	45.762	51.160	57.275	64.203	72.052	102.444
21	25.783	28.676	31.969	35.719	39.993	44.865	50.423	56.765	64.002	72.265	81.699	118.810
22	27.299	30.537	34.248	38.505	43.392	49.006	55.457	62.873	71.403	81.214	92.503	137.632
23	28.845	32.453	36.618	41.430	46.996	53.436	60.893	69.532	79.543	91.148	104.603	159.276
24	30.422	34.426	39.083	44.502	50.816	58.177	66.765	76.790	88.497	102.174	118.155	184.168
25	32.030	36.459	41.646	47.727	54.865	63.249	73.106	84.701	98.347	114.413	133.334	212.793
26	33.671	38.553	44.312	51.113	59.156	68.676	79.954	93.324	109.182	127.999	150.334	245.712
27	35.344	40.710	47.084	54.669	63.706	74.484	87.351	102.723	121.100	143.079	169.374	283.569
28	37.051	42.931	49.968	58.403	68.528	80.698	95.339	112.968	134.210	159.817	190.699	327.104
29	38.792	45.219	52.966	62.323	73.640	87.347	103.966	124.135	148.631	178.397	214.583	377.170
30	40.568	47.575	56.085	66.439	79.058	94.461	113.283	136.308	164.494	199.021	241.333	434.745

TABLE 9-4 Present Value of Annuity of $1

(n) Periods	\multicolumn{13}{c}{Rate of Interest in %}
	2	**3**	**4**	**5**	**6**	**7**	**8**	**9**	**10**	**11**	**12**	**15**
1	0.980	0.971	0.962	0.952	0.943	0.935	0.926	0.917	0.909	0.901	0.893	0.870
2	1.942	1.913	1.886	1.859	1.833	1.808	1.783	1.759	1.736	1.713	1.690	1.626
3	2.884	2.829	2.775	2.723	2.673	2.624	2.577	2.531	2.487	2.444	2.402	2.283
4	3.808	3.717	3.630	3.546	3.465	3.387	3.312	3.240	3.170	3.102	3.037	2.855
5	4.713	4.580	4.452	4.329	4.212	4.100	3.993	3.890	3.791	3.696	3.605	3.352
6	5.601	5.417	5.242	5.076	4.917	4.767	4.623	4.486	4.355	4.231	4.111	3.784
7	6.472	6.230	6.002	5.786	5.582	5.389	5.206	5.033	4.868	4.712	4.564	4.160
8	7.325	7.020	6.733	6.463	6.210	5.971	5.747	5.535	5.335	5.146	4.968	4.487
9	8.162	7.786	7.435	7.108	6.802	6.515	6.247	5.995	5.759	5.537	5.328	4.772
10	8.983	8.530	8.111	7.722	7.360	7.024	6.710	6.418	6.145	5.889	5.650	5.019
11	9.787	9.253	8.760	8.306	7.887	7.499	7.139	6.805	6.495	6.207	5.938	5.234
12	10.575	9.954	9.385	8.863	8.384	7.943	7.536	7.161	6.814	6.492	6.194	5.421
13	11.348	10.635	9.986	9.394	8.853	8.358	7.904	7.487	7.103	6.750	6.424	5.583
14	12.106	11.296	10.563	9.899	9.295	8.745	8.244	7.786	7.367	6.982	6.628	5.724
15	12.849	11.938	11.118	10.380	9.712	9.108	8.559	8.061	7.606	7.191	6.811	5.847
16	13.578	12.561	11.652	10.838	10.106	9.447	8.851	8.313	7.824	7.379	6.974	5.954
17	14.292	13.166	12.166	11.274	10.477	9.763	9.122	8.544	8.022	7.549	7.120	6.047
18	14.992	13.754	12.659	11.690	10.828	10.059	9.372	8.756	8.201	7.702	7.250	6.128
19	15.678	14.324	13.134	12.085	11.158	10.336	9.604	8.950	8.365	7.839	7.366	6.198
20	16.351	14.877	13.590	12.462	11.470	10.594	9.818	9.129	8.514	7.963	7.469	6.259
21	17.011	15.415	14.029	12.821	11.764	10.836	10.017	9.292	8.649	8.075	7.562	6.312
22	17.658	15.937	14.451	13.163	12.042	11.061	10.201	9.442	8.772	8.176	7.645	6.359
23	18.292	16.444	14.857	13.489	12.303	11.272	10.371	9.580	8.883	8.266	7.718	6.399
24	18.914	16.936	15.247	13.799	12.550	11.469	10.529	9.707	8.985	8.348	7.784	6.434
25	19.523	17.413	15.622	14.094	12.783	11.654	10.675	9.823	9.077	8.422	7.843	6.464
26	20.121	17.877	15.983	14.375	13.003	11.826	10.810	9.929	9.161	8.488	7.896	6.491
27	20.707	18.327	16.330	14.643	13.211	11.987	10.935	10.027	9.237	8.548	7.943	6.514
28	21.281	18.764	16.663	14.898	13.406	12.137	11.051	10.116	9.307	8.602	7.984	6.534
29	21.844	19.188	16.984	15.141	13.591	12.278	11.158	10.198	9.370	8.650	8.022	6.551
30	22.396	19.600	17.292	15.372	13.765	12.409	11.258	10.274	9.427	8.694	8.055	6.566

ACCOUNTING TOOLS: PAYROLL ACCOUNTING

Salaries payable was one of the current liabilities discussed in Chapter 2. At the end of each accounting period, the accountant must accrue salaries that have been earned by the employees but have not yet been paid. To this point, we have not considered the accounting that must be done for payroll deductions and other payroll expenses.

LO 8 Understand the deductions and expenses for payroll accounting.

Payroll deductions and expenses occur not only at year-end but every time, throughout the year, that employees are paid. The amount of cash paid for salaries and wages is the largest cash outflow for many firms. It is imperative that sufficient cash be available not only to meet the weekly or monthly payroll but also to remit the payroll taxes to the appropriate government agencies when required. The purpose of this appendix is to introduce the calculations and the accounting entries that are necessary when payroll is recorded.

The issue of payroll expenses is of great concern to businesses, particularly small entrepreneurial ones. One of the large issues facing companies is how to meet the increasing cost of hiring people. Salary is just one component. How will companies pay salaries plus benefits, such as health insurance, life insurance, disability, unemployment benefits, workers' compensation, and so on? More and more companies are trying to keep their payrolls as small as possible in order to avoid these costs. Unfortunately, this has been a contributing factor in the trends of using more part-time employees and of outsourcing some business functions. Outsourcing, or hiring independent contractors, allows the company to reduce salary expense and the expenses related to fringe benefits. However, it does not necessarily improve the company's profitability. The expenses that are increased as a result of hiring outside contractors must also be considered. A manager must carefully consider all the costs that are affected before deciding whether to hire more employees or go with an independent contractor.

CALCULATION OF GROSS WAGES

We will cover the payroll process by indicating the basic steps that must be performed. The first step is to calculate the **gross wages** of all employees. The gross wage represents the wage amount before deductions. Companies often have two general classes of employees, hourly and salaried. The gross wage of each hourly employee is calculated by multiplying the number of hours worked times his or her hourly wage rate. Salaried employees are not paid on a per-hour basis but at a flat rate per week, month, or year. For both hourly and salaried employees, the payroll accountant must also consider any overtime, bonus, or other salary supplement that may affect gross wages.

CALCULATION OF NET PAY

The second step in the payroll process is to calculate the deductions from each employee's paycheck to determine **net pay.** Deductions from the employees' checks represent a current liability to the employer because the employer must remit the amounts at a future time to the proper agencies or government offices—for example, to the Internal Revenue Service. The deductions that are made depend on the type of company and the employee. The most important deductions are indicated in the following sections.

INCOME TAX

The employer must withhold federal income tax from most employees' paychecks. The amount withheld depends on the employee's earnings and the number of *exemptions* claimed by that employee. An exemption reflects the number of dependents a taxpayer can claim. The more exemptions, the lower is the withholding amount required by the government. Tables are available from the Internal Revenue Service to calculate the proper amount that should be withheld. This amount must be remitted to the Internal Revenue Service periodically; the frequency depends on the company's size and its payroll. Income tax withheld represents a liability to the employer and is normally classified as a current liability.

Many states also have an income tax, and the employer must often withhold additional amounts for the state tax.

FICA—Employees' Share

FICA stands for Federal Insurance Contributions Act; it is commonly called the *social security tax*. The FICA tax is assessed on both the employee and the employer. The employees' portion must be withheld from paychecks at the applicable rate. Currently, the tax is assessed at the rate of 7.65% on the first $72,600 paid to the employee each year. Other rates and special rules apply to certain types of workers and to self-employed individuals. The amounts withheld from the employees' checks must be remitted to the federal government periodically.

FICA taxes withheld from employees' checks represent a liability to the employer until remitted. It is important to remember that the employees' portion of the FICA tax does not represent an expense to the employer.

Voluntary Deductions

If you have ever received a paycheck, you are probably aware that a variety of items was deducted from the amount you earned. Many of these are voluntary deductions chosen by the employee. They may include health insurance, pension or retirement contributions, savings plans, contributions to charities, union dues, and others. Each of these items is deducted from the employees' paychecks, is held by the employer, and is remitted at a future time. Therefore, each represents a current liability to the employer until remitted.

EMPLOYER PAYROLL TAXES

The payroll items discussed thus far do not represent expenses to the employer because they are assessed on the employees and deducted from their paychecks. However, there are taxes that the employer must pay. The two most important are FICA and unemployment taxes.

FICA—Employer's Share

The FICA tax is assessed on both the employee and the employer. The employee amount is withheld from the employees' paychecks and represents a liability but is not an expense to the employer. Normally, an equal amount is assessed on the employer. Therefore, the employer must pay an additional 7.65% of employee wages to the federal government. The employer's portion represents an expense to the employer and should be reflected in a Payroll Tax Expense account or similar type of account. This portion is a liability to the employer until it is remitted.

Unemployment Tax

Most employers must also pay unemployment taxes. The state and federal governments jointly sponsor a program to collect unemployment tax from employers and to pay workers who lose their jobs. The maximum rate of unemployment taxes is 3.4%, of which 2.7% is the state portion and .7% the federal, on an employee's first $7,000 of wages earned each year. The rate is adjusted according to a company's employment history, however. If a company has been fairly stable and few of its employees have filed for unemployment benefits, the rate is adjusted downward.

Unemployment taxes are levied against the employer, not the employee. Therefore, the tax represents an expense to the employer and should be reflected in a Payroll Tax Expense account or similar type of account. The tax also represents a liability to the employer until it is remitted.

AN EXAMPLE

Assume that Kori Company has calculated the gross wages of all employees for the month of July to be $100,000. Also assume that the following amounts have been withheld from the employees' paychecks:

Income tax	$20,000
FICA	7,650
United Way contributions	5,000
Union dues	3,000

In addition, assume that Kori's unemployment tax rate is 3%, that no employees have reached the $7,000 limit, and that Kori's portion of FICA matches the employees' share. We would calculate gross pay and net pay as follows:

Gross pay (or salary expense)		$100,000
Less withholdings:		
Income tax	$20,000	
FICA tax (employees' portion)	7,650	
United Way contributions	5,000	
Union dues	3,000	35,650
Net pay		$ 64,350

In addition, we must consider the employer's payroll taxes:

FICA (employer's share)	$ 7,650
Unemployment taxes	3,000
Total employer's taxes (or payroll tax expense)	$ 10,650

Assume that the amount of the net pay ($64,350) is paid to employees on July 31, but the withholdings and the employer's taxes are not remitted until a later date. We can then consider how Kori's July 31 financial statements would be affected by the July payroll amounts.

Kori's income statement should reflect two expenses for the July payroll:

Salary expense	$100,000
Payroll tax expense	$ 10,650

Kori's balance sheet should reflect the following items in the current liability category until the time that the amounts are remitted:

Income tax payable	$20,000
FICA payable (employees' and employer's share)	15,300
United Way payable	5,000
Union dues payable	3,000
Unemployment taxes payable	3,000

The items listed in the current liability category must be considered of utmost concern to the company. Failure to remit withholdings (for example, income tax withheld from employees' paychecks) on a timely basis can have grave consequences for a firm. The firm must, therefore, take all necessary steps to ensure that adequate cash is available to pay these current liabilities.

COMPENSATED ABSENCES

LO 9 Determine when compensated absences must be accrued as a liability.

Most employers allow employees to accumulate a certain number of sick days and to take a certain number of paid vacation days each year. This causes an accounting question when recording payroll amounts. When should the sick days and vacation days be treated as an expense—in the period they are earned or in the period they are taken by the employee?

The FASB has coined the term **compensated absences.** These are absences from employment, such as vacation, illness, and holidays, for which it is expected that employees will be paid. The FASB has ruled that an expense should be accrued if certain conditions are met: the services have been rendered, the rights (days) accumulate, and payment is probable and can be reasonably estimated. The result of the FASB ruling is that most employers are required to record a liability and an expense for vacation days when earned but sick days are not recorded until employees are actually absent.

Compensated absence is another example of the matching principle at work, and so it is consistent with good accounting theory. Unfortunately, it has also resulted in some complex calculations and additional work for payroll accountants. Part of the complexity is due to unresolved legal issues about compensated absences.

U.S. accounting standards on this issue are much more detailed and extensive than the standards of many foreign countries. As a result, U.S. companies may believe that they are subject to higher record-keeping costs than their foreign competitors.

CHAPTER HIGHLIGHTS

1. **LO 1** Balance sheets generally have two categories of liability: current liabilities and long-term liabilities. Current liabilities are obligations that will be satisfied within one year or within the next operating cycle.

2. **LO 2** Accruals are expenses that have been incurred, but not paid, by the balance sheet date. They increase current liabilities and should be valued at the face amount or the amount necessary to settle the obligation. They are not reported at the present value because of the short time span until payment.

3. **LO 2** Accounts payable represent amounts owed for the purchase of inventory, goods, or services. Accounts payable usually do not require the payment of interest, but a discount may be available to encourage prompt payment.

4. **LO 2** The accounting for notes payable depends on the terms of the note. Some notes payable require the payment of interest at the due date. If so, accounting entries must be made to accrue interest expense to the proper periods. Interest is an expense when incurred, not when paid. Alternatively, the terms of the note may require interest to be deducted in advance. The interest deducted should initially be recorded in a Discount on Notes Payable account and transferred to Interest Expense over the life of the note.

5. **LO 2** Accrued liabilities include any amount that is owed but not actually due as of the balance sheet date. These liabilities may be grouped together in an account, such as Other Accrued Liabilities.

6. **LO 3** The changes in current liabilities affect the cash flow statement and, for most items, are reflected in the Operating Activities category. Decreases in current liabilities indicate a reduction of cash; increases in current liabilities indicate an increase in cash.

7. **LO 4** Contingent liabilities involve an existing condition whose outcome depends on some future event. If a contingent liability is probable and the amount of loss can be reasonably estimated, it should be reported on the balance sheet. If a contingent liability is reasonably possible, it must be disclosed but not reported.

8. **LO 5** Simple interest is interest earned on the principal amount. It is often calculated by the well-known formula of principal times rate times time. Compound interest is calculated on the principal plus previous amounts of interest accumulated.

9. **LO 6** The future value of a single amount represents the amount of interest plus principal that will be accumulated at a future time. The future value of a single amount can be calculated by formula or by the use of Table 9-1.

10. **LO 6** The present value of a single amount represents the amount at a present time that is equivalent to an amount at a future time. The present value of a single amount can be calculated by formula or by the use of Table 9-2.

11. **LO 6** An annuity is a series of payments of equal amount. The future value of an annuity represents the amount that will be accumulated in principal and interest if a series of payments is invested for a specified time and for a specified rate. The future value of an annuity can be calculated by formula or by the use of Table 9-3.

12. **LO 6** The present value of an annuity represents the amount at a present time that is equivalent to a series of payments in the future that will occur for a specified time and at a specified interest or discount rate. The present value of an annuity can be calculated by formula or by the use of Table 9-4.

13. **LO 7** The compound interest concepts are also useful when solving for such unknowns as the number of interest periods or the interest rate on a series of payments using compound interest techniques.

14. **LO 8** There are two types of payroll deductions and expenses. Deductions from the employee's check are made to determine net pay and represent a current liability to the employer. Employer's payroll taxes are also assessed directly on the employer and represent an expense. (Appendix 9A)

15. **LO 9** Compensated absences, such as sick pay and vacation pay, are expenses and must be accrued by the employer if certain conditions are met. (Appendix 9A)

KEY TERMS QUIZ

Read each definition below, and then write the number of the definition in the blank beside the appropriate term it defines. The solution appears at the end of the chapter.

____ Current liability

____ Accounts payable

____ Notes payable

____ Discount on Notes Payable

____ Current Maturities of Long-Term Debt

____ Accrued liability

____ Contingent liability

____ Estimated liability

____ Contingent asset

____ Time value of money

____ Simple interest

____ Compound interest

____ Future value of a single amount

____ Present value of a single amount

____ Annuity

____ Future value of an annuity

____ Present value of an annuity

____ Gross wages (Appendix 9A)

____ Net pay (Appendix 9A)

____ Compensated absences (Appendix 9A)

1. Accounts that will be satisfied within one year or the next operating cycle.

2. The amount needed at the present time to be equivalent to a series of payments and interest in the future.

3. Amounts owed for the purchase of inventory, goods, or services acquired in the normal course of business.

4. A contra-liability account that represents interest deducted from a loan or note in advance.

5. A series of payments of equal amount.

6. The portion of a long-term liability that will be paid within one year of the balance sheet date.

7. A liability that has been incurred but has not been paid as of the balance sheet date.

8. Amounts owed that are represented by a formal contractual agreement. These amounts usually require the payment of interest.

9. A liability that involves an existing condition for which the outcome is not known with certainty and depends on some future event.

10. Interest that is earned or paid on the principal amount only.

11. A contingent liability that is accrued and is reflected on the balance sheet. Common examples are warranties, guarantees, and premium offers.

12. An amount that involves an existing condition dependent on some future event by which the company stands to gain. These amounts are not normally reported.

13. Interest calculated on the principal plus previous amounts of interest accumulated.

14. The concept that indicates that people should prefer to receive an immediate amount at the present time over an equal amount in the future.

15. The amount that will be accumulated in the future when one amount is invested at the present time and accrues interest until the future time.

16. The amount that will be accumulated in the future when a series of payments is invested and accrues interest until the future time.

17. The present amount that is equivalent to an amount at a future time.

18. The amount of an employee's wages before deductions.

19. Employment absences, such as sick days and vacation days, for which it is expected that employees will be paid.

20. The amount of an employee's paycheck after deductions.

ALTERNATE TERMS

Accrued interest   Interest payable

Compensated absences   Accrued vacation or sick pay

Compound interest   Interest on interest

Contingent asset   Contingent gain

Contingent liability   Contingent loss

Current liability   Short-term liability

Current maturities of long-term debt   Long-term debt, current portion

Discounting a note   Interest in advance
FICA   Social security
Future value of an annuity   Amount of an annuity

Gross wages   Gross pay
Income tax liability   Income tax payable
Warranties   Guarantees

1. What is the definition of *current liabilities*? Why is it important to distinguish between current and long-term liabilities?

2. Most firms attempt to pay their accounts payable within the discount period to take advantage of the discount. Why is that normally a sound financial move?

3. Assume that your local bank gives you a $1,000 loan at 10% per year but deducts the interest in advance. Is 10% the "real" rate of interest that you will pay? How could the true interest rate be calculated?

4. Is the account Discount on Notes Payable an income statement or balance sheet account?

5. A firm's year ends on December 31. Its tax is computed and submitted to the IRS on March 15 of the following year. When should the taxes be reported as a liability?

6. What is a contingent liability? Why are contingent liabilities accounted for differently than contingent assets?

7. Many firms believe that it is very difficult to estimate the amount of a possible future contingency. Should a contingent liability be reported even if the dollar amount of the loss is not known? Should it be disclosed in the footnotes?

8. Assume that a lawsuit has been filed against your firm. Your legal counsel has assured you that the likelihood of loss is not probable. How should the lawsuit be disclosed on the financial statements?

9. What is the difference between simple interest and compound interest? Would the amount of interest be higher or lower if the interest is simple rather than compound?

10. What is the effect if interest is compounded quarterly versus annually?

11. Define the terms *present value* and *future value*. How can you determine whether to calculate the present value of an amount versus the future value?

12. What is the meaning of the word *annuity*? Could the present value of an annuity be calculated as a series of single amounts? If so, how?

13. Assume that you know the total dollar amount of a loan and the amount of the monthly payments on the loan. How could you determine the interest rate as a percentage of the loan?

14. The present value and future value concepts are applied to measure the amount of several accounts commonly encountered in accounting. What are some accounts that are valued in this manner?

15. Your employer withholds federal income tax from your paycheck and remits it to the IRS. How is the federal tax treated on the employer's financial statements? (Appendix 9A)

16. Unemployment tax is a tax on the employer rather than on the employee. How should unemployment taxes be treated on the employer's financial statements? (Appendix 9A)

17. What is the meaning of the term *compensated absences*? Give some examples. (Appendix 9A)

18. Do you agree or disagree with the following statement: "Vacation pay should be reported as an expense when the employee takes the vacation"? (Appendix 9A)

EXERCISES

LO 1   Exercise 9-1   Current Liabilities
The items listed below are accounts on Smith's balance sheet of December 31, 2001.

> Taxes Payable
> Accounts Receivable
> Notes Payable, 9%, due in 90 days
> Investment in Bonds
> Capital Stock
> Accounts Payable
> Estimated Warranty Payable in 2002
> Retained Earnings
> Trademark
> Mortgage Payable ($10,000 due every year until 2018)

Required

Identify which of the preceding accounts should be classified as a current liability on Smith's balance sheet. For each item that is not a current liability, indicate the category of the balance sheet in which it would be classified.

LO 1 Exercise 9-2 Current Liabilities

The following items all represent liabilities on a firm's balance sheet.

a. An amount of money owed to a supplier based on the terms 2/20, net 40, for which *no* note was executed

b. An amount of money owed to a creditor on a note due April 30, 2002

c. An amount of money owed to a creditor on a note due August 15, 2003

d. An amount of money owed to employees for work performed during the last week in December

e. An amount of money owed to a bank for the use of borrowed funds due on March 1, 2002

f. An amount of money owed to a creditor as an annual installment payment on a 10-year note

g. An amount of money owed to the federal government, based on the company's annual income

Required

1. For each lettered item, state whether it should be classified as a current liability on the December 31, 2001, balance sheet. Assume that the operating cycle is shorter than one year. If the item should not be classified as a current liability, indicate where on the balance sheet it should be presented.

2. For each item identified as a current liability in part **1,** state the account title that is normally used to report the item on the balance sheet.

3. Why would an investor or creditor be interested in whether an item is a current or a long-term liability?

LO 1 Exercise 9-3 Current Liabilities Section

Jackie Company had the following accounts and balances on December 31, 2001:

Income Taxes Payable	$61,250
Allowance for Doubtful Accounts	17,800
Accounts Payable	24,400
Interest Receivable	5,000
Unearned Revenue	4,320
Wages Payable	6,000
Notes Payable, 10%, due June 2, 2002	1,000
Accounts Receivable	67,500
Discount on Notes Payable	150
Current Maturities of Long-Term Debt	6,900
Interest Payable	3,010

Required

Prepare the Current Liabilities section of Jackie Company's balance sheet as of December 31, 2001.

LO 2 Exercise 9-4 Transaction Analysis

Polly's Cards & Gifts Shop had the following transactions during the year:

a. Polly's purchased inventory on account from a supplier for $8,000. Assume that Polly's uses a periodic inventory system.

b. On May 1, land was purchased for $44,500. A 20% down payment was made, and an 18-month, 8% note was signed for the remainder.

c. Polly's returned $450 worth of inventory purchased in item **a,** which was found broken when the inventory was received.

d. Polly's paid the balance due on the purchase of inventory.

e. On June 1, Polly signed a one-year, $15,000 note to 1st State Bank and received $13,800.

f. Polly's sold 200 gift certificates for $25 each for cash. Sales of gift certificates are recorded as a liability. At year-end, 35% of the gift certificates had been redeemed.

g. Sales for the year were $120,000, of which 90% were for cash. State sales tax of 6% applied to all sales and must be remitted to the state by January 31.

Required

1. Determine the effect on the accounting equation of items **a** through **g**.
2. Assume that Polly's accounting year ends on December 31. Determine the effect of all adjustments necessary to properly reflect the preceding items on the annual financial statements.
3. What is the total of the current liabilities at the end of the year?

LO 2 Exercise 9-5 Current Liabilities and Ratios

Listed here are several accounts that appeared on Kruse's 2001 balance sheet.

Accounts Payable	$ 55,000
Marketable Securities	40,000
Accounts Receivable	180,000
Notes Payable, 12%, due in 60 days	20,000
Capital Stock	1,150,000
Salaries Payable	10,000
Cash	15,000
Equipment	950,000
Taxes Payable	15,000
Retained Earnings	250,000
Inventory	85,000
Allowance for Doubtful Accounts	20,000
Land	600,000

Required

1. Prepare the Current Liabilities section of Kruse's 2001 balance sheet.
2. Compute Kruse's working capital.
3. Compute Kruse's current ratio. What does this ratio indicate about Kruse's condition?

LO 2 Exercise 9-6 Discounts

Each of the following situations involves the use of discounts.

1. How much discount may Seals Inc. take in each of the following transactions? What was the annualized interest rate?

    a. Seals purchases inventory costing $450, 2/10, n/40.

    b. Seals purchases new office furniture costing $1,500, terms 1/10, n/30.

2. Calculate the discount rate Croft Co. received in each of these transactions.

    a. Croft purchased office supplies costing $200 and paid within the discount period with a check for $196.

    b. Croft purchased merchandise for $2,800. It paid within the discount period with a check for $2,674.

LO 2 Exercise 9-7 Notes Payable and Interest

On July 1, 2001, Jo's Flower Shop borrowed $25,000 from the bank. Jo signed a 10-month, 8% promissory note for the entire amount. Jo's uses a calendar year-end.

Required

1. Determine the effect on the accounting equation when the note was issued on July 1.
2. What adjustments would be needed at year end? Determine their effect on the accounting equation.
3. Determine the effect of the May 1 payment of principal and interest.

LO 2 Exercise 9-8 Non-Interest-Bearing Notes Payable

On October 1, 2001, Ratkowski Inc. borrowed $18,000 from 2nd National Bank by issuing a 12-month note. The bank discounted the note at 9%.

Required

1. Determine the effect on the accounting equation of the issuance of the note.
2. What is the effect of the accrual of interest on December 31?
3. Determine the effect of the payment of the note on October 1, 2002.
4. What effective rate of interest did Ratkowski pay?

LO 3 **Exercise 9-9** Impact of Transactions Involving Current Liabilities on Statement of Cash Flows

From the following list, identify whether the change in the account balance during the year would be reported as an operating (O), investing (I), or financing (F) activity, or not separately reported on the statement of cash flows (N). Assume that the indirect method is used to determine the cash flows from operating activities.

_____ Accounts payable

_____ Current maturities of long-term debt

_____ Notes payable

_____ Other accrued liabilities

_____ Salaries and wages payable

_____ Taxes payable

LO 3 **Exercise 9-10** Impact of Transactions Involving Contingent Liabilities on Statement of Cash Flows

From the following list, identify whether the change in the account balance during the year would be reported as an operating (O), investing (I), or financing (F) activity, or not separately reported on the statement of cash flows (N). Assume that the indirect method is used to determine the cash flows from operating activities.

_____ Estimated liability for warranties

_____ Estimated liability for product premiums

_____ Estimated liability for probable loss relating to litigation

LO 3 **Exercise 9-11** Impact of Transactions Involving Payroll Liabilities on Statement of Cash Flows (Appendix 9A)

From the following list, identify whether the change in the account balance during the year would be reported as an operating (O), investing (I), or financing (F) activity, or not separately reported on the statement of cash flows (N). Assume that the indirect method is used to determine the cash flows from operating activities.

_____ Accrued vacation days (compensated absences)

_____ Health insurance premiums payable

_____ FICA payable

_____ Union dues payable

_____ Salary payable

_____ Unemployment taxes payable

LO 4 **Exercise 9-12** Warranties

Clean Corporation manufactures and sells dishwashers. Clean provides all customers with a two-year warranty guaranteeing to repair, free of charge, any defects reported during this time period. During the year, it sold 100,000 dishwashers, for $325 each. Analysis of past warranty records indicates that 12% of all sales will be returned for repair within the warranty period. Clean expects to incur expenditures of $14 to repair each dishwasher. The account Estimated Liability for Warranties had a balance of $120,000 on January 1. Clean incurred $150,000 in actual expenditures during the year.

Required

Determine the effect on the accounting equation of the events related to the warranty transactions during the year. Determine the adjusted ending balance in the Estimated Liability for Warranties account.

LO 5 **Exercise 9-13** Simple versus Compound Interest

Part 1. For each of the following notes, calculate the simple interest due at the end of the term.

Note	Face Value (Principal)	Rate	Term
1	$20,000	4%	6 years
2	20,000	6%	4 years
3	20,000	8%	3 years

Part 2. Now assume that the interest on the notes is compounded annually. Calculate the amount of interest due at the end of the term for each note.

Part 3. Now assume that the interest on the notes is compounded semiannually. Calculate the amount of interest due at the end of the term for each note.

What conclusion can you draw from a comparison of your results in parts **1, 2,** and **3**?

LO 6   Exercise 9-14   Present Value, Future Value

Brian Inc. estimates it will need $150,000 in 10 years to expand its manufacturing facilities. A bank has agreed to pay Brian 5% interest, compounded annually, if the company deposits the entire amount now needed to accumulate $150,000 in 10 years. How much money does Brian need to deposit now?

LO 6   Exercise 9-15   Effect of Compounding Period

Kern Company deposited $1,000 in the bank on January 1, 2001, earning 8% interest. Kern Company withdraws the deposit plus accumulated interest on January 1, 2003. Compute the amount of money Kern withdraws from the bank, assuming that interest is compounded (a) annually, (b) semiannually, and (c) quarterly.

LO 6   Exercise 9-16   Present Value, Future Value

The following situations involve time value of money calculations.

1. A deposit of $7,000 is made on January 1, 2001. The deposit will earn interest at a rate of 8%. How much will be accumulated on January 1, 2006, assuming that interest is compounded (a) annually, (b) semiannually, and (c) quarterly?

2. A deposit is made on January 1, 2001, to earn interest at an annual rate of 8%. The deposit will accumulate to $15,000 by January 1, 2006. How much money was originally deposited, assuming that interest is compounded (a) annually, (b) semiannually, and (c) quarterly?

LO 6   Exercise 9-17   Present Value, Future Value

The following are situations requiring the application of the time value of money.

1. On January 1, 2001, $16,000 is deposited. Assuming an 8% interest rate, calculate the amount accumulated on January 1, 2006, if interest is compounded (a) annually, (b) semiannually, and (c) quarterly.

2. Assume that a deposit made on January 1, 2001, earns 8% interest. The deposit plus interest accumulates to $20,000 on January 1, 2006. How much was invested on January 1, 2001, if interest was compounded (a) annually, (b) semiannually, and (c) quarterly?

LO 7   Exercise 9-18   Annuity

Steve Jones has decided to start saving for his son's college education by depositing $2,000 at the end of every year for 15 years. A bank has agreed to pay interest at the rate of 4% compounded annually. How much will Steve have in the bank immediately after his 15th deposit?

LO 7   Exercise 9-19   Calculation of Years

Kelly Seaver has decided to start saving for her daughter's college education. She wants to accumulate $41,000. The bank will pay interest at the rate of 4% compounded annually. If Kelly plans to make payments of $1,600 at the end of each year, how long will it take her to accumulate $41,000?

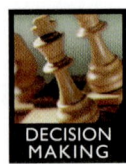

DECISION MAKING

LO 7   Exercise 9-20   Value of Payments

On graduation from college, Susana Lopez signed an agreement to buy a used car. Her annual payments, due at the end of each year for two years, are $1,480. The car dealer used a 12% rate compounded annually to determine the amount of the payments.

Required

1. What should Susana consider the value of the car to be?

2. If she had wanted to make quarterly payments, what would her payments have been, based on the value of the car as determined in part **1**? How much less interest would she have had to pay if she had been making quarterly payments instead of annual payments? What do you think would have happened to the amount of the payment and the interest if she had asked for monthly payments?

LO 8   Exercise 9-21   Payroll Entries (Appendix 9A)

During the month of January, VanderSalm Company's employees earned $385,000. The following rates apply to VanderSalm's gross payroll:

Federal Income Tax Rate	28%	
State Income Tax Rate	5%	
FICA Tax Rate	7.65%	
Federal Unemployment Tax Rate	.8%	
State Unemployment Tax Rate	3.2%	

In addition, employee deductions were $7,000 for health insurance and $980 for union dues.

Required

1. Calculate the withholdings and net pay for wages for the company. Also determine the effect on the accounting equation of the payroll. You may assume that FICA tax applies to all employees.

2. Calculate the employer's portion of payroll taxes for January. Determine the effect on the accounting equation of accruing the employer's portion of the taxes.

3. If the company paid fringe benefits, such as employees' health insurance coverage, how would these contributions affect the payroll entries?

LO 8 Exercise 9-22 Payroll, Employer's Portion (Appendix 9A)
Tasty Bakery Shop has six employees on its payroll. Payroll records include the following information on employee earnings for each employee:

Name	Earnings from 1/1 to 6/30/2001	Earnings for 3rd Quarter, 2001
Dell	$ 23,490	$11,710
Fin	4,240	2,660
Hook	34,100	15,660
Patty	51,000	26,200
Tuss	30,050	19,350
Woo	6,300	3,900
Totals	$149,180	$79,480

FICA taxes are levied at 7.65% on the first $72,600 of each employee's current year's earnings. The unemployment tax rates are .8% for federal and 2.6% for state unemployment. Assume that unemployment taxes are levied on the first $7,000 of each employee's current year's earnings.

Required

1. Calculate the employer's portion of payroll taxes incurred by Tasty Bakery for each employee for the third quarter of 2001. Round your answers to the nearest dollar.

2. Determine the effect on the accounting equation of the employer's portion of payroll taxes.

LO 9 Exercise 9-23 Compensated Absences (Appendix 9A)
Wonder Inc. has a monthly payroll of $72,000 for its 24 employees. In addition to their salary, employees earn one day of vacation and one sick day for each month that they work. There are 20 workdays in a month.

Required

1. Determine the effect on the accounting equation, if any, of recording (a) vacation benefits and (b) sick days.

2. From the owner's perspective, should the company offer the employees vacation and sick pay that accumulates year to year?

Multi-Concept Exercises

LO 6, 7 Exercise 9-24 Compare Alternatives
Jane Bauer has won the lottery and has four options for receiving her winnings:

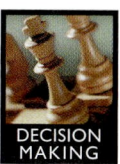

DECISION
MAKING

1. Receive $100,000 at the beginning of the current year
2. Receive $108,000 at the end of the year
3. Receive $20,000 at the end of each year for 8 years
4. Receive $10,000 at the end of each year for 30 years

Jane can invest her winnings at an interest rate of 8% compounded annually at a major bank. Which of the payment options should Jane choose?

LO 6, 7 **Exercise 9-25** Two Situations

The following situations involve the application of the time value of money concepts.

1. Sampson Company just purchased a piece of equipment with a value of $53,300. Sampson financed this purchase with a loan from the bank and must make annual loan payments of $13,000 at the end of each year for the next five years. Interest is compounded annually on the loan. What is the interest rate on the bank loan?

2. Simon Company needs to accumulate $200,000 to repay bonds due in six years. Simon estimates it can save $13,300 at the end of each semiannual period at a local bank offering an annual interest rate of 8% compounded semiannually. Will Simon have enough money saved at the end of six years to repay the bonds?

PROBLEMS

LO 2 **Problem 9-1** Notes and Interest

Glencoe Inc. operates with a June 30 year-end. During 2001, the following transactions occurred:

a. January 1: Signed a one-year, 10% loan for $25,000. Interest and principal are to be paid at maturity.

b. January 10: Signed a line of credit with the Little Local Bank to establish a $400,000 line of credit. Interest of 9% will be charged on all borrowed funds.

c. February 1: Issued a $20,000 non-interest-bearing, six-month note to pay for a new machine. Interest on the note, at 12%, was deducted in advance.

d. March 1: Borrowed $150,000 on the line of credit.

e. June 1: Repaid $100,000 on the line of credit, plus accrued interest.

f. June 30: Made all necessary adjusting entries.

g. August 1: Repaid the non-interest-bearing note.

h. September 1: Borrowed $200,000 on the line of credit.

i. November 1: Issued a three-month, 8%, $12,000 note in payment of an overdue open account.

j. December 31: Repaid the one-year loan (from item **a**) plus accrued interest.

Required

1. Determine the effect on the accounting equation of items **a** through **j**.

2. As of December 31, which notes are outstanding, and how much interest is due on each?

LO 3 **Problem 9-2** Effects of Sara Lee's Current Liabilities on Its Statement of Cash Flows

www.saralee.com   The following items are classified as current liabilities on Sara Lee Corporation's consolidated balance sheet at July 3, 1999, and June 27, 1998 (in millions):

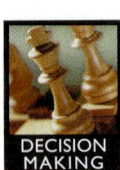

DECISION MAKING

	1999	1998
Notes payable	$1,167	$ 586
Accounts payable	1,782	2,003
Accrued liabilities:		
Payroll and employee benefits	811	684
Advertising and promotions	388	338
Taxes other than payroll and income	91	223
Income taxes	45	159
Other	1,333	1,519
Current maturities of long-term debt	336	221

Required

1. Sara Lee uses the indirect method to prepare its statement of cash flows. Prepare the Operating Activities section of the cash flow statement, which indicates how each item will be reflected as

an adjustment to net income. If you did not include any of the items set forth above, explain why not.

2. How would you decide whether Sara Lee has the ability to pay these liabilities as they become due?

LO 3 Problem 9-3 Effects of Tommy Hilfiger's Changes in Current Assets and Liabilities on Statement of Cash Flows

The following items, listed in alphabetical order, are included in the Current Assets and Current Liabilities categories on the consolidated balance sheet of Tommy Hilfiger Corporation at March 31, 1999 and 1998 (in thousands):

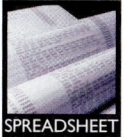

www.tommyhilfiger.com

	1999	1998
Accounts payable	$ 27,310	$ 16,201
Accounts receivable	186,640	104,732
Accrued expenses and other liabilities	188,606	76,197
Short-term borrowings	1,234	–0–
Inventories	222,928	150,947
Other current assets	48,638	25,554

Required

1. Tommy Hilfiger uses the indirect method to prepare its statement of cash flows. Indicate how each item will be reflected as an adjustment to net income in the Operating Activities section of the cash flow statement.

2. If you did not include any of the items set forth above in your answer to part **1,** explain how these items would be reported on the statement of cash flows.

LO 4 Problem 9-4 Warranties

Clearview Company manufactures and sells high-quality television sets. The most popular line sells for $1,000 each and is accompanied by a three-year warranty to repair, free of charge, any defective unit. Average costs to repair each defective unit will be $90 for replacement parts and $60 for labor. Clearview estimates that warranty costs of $12,600 will be incurred during 2001. The company actually sold 600 television sets and incurred replacement part costs of $3,600 and labor costs of $5,400 during the year. The adjusted 2001 ending balance in the Estimated Liability for Warranties account is $10,200.

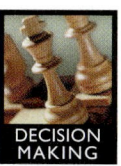

DECISION MAKING

Required

1. How many defective units from this year's sales does Clearview Company estimate will be returned for repair?

2. What percentage of sales does Clearview Company estimate will be returned for repair?

3. What steps should Clearview take if actual warranty costs incurred during 2002 are significantly higher than the estimated liability recorded at the end of 2001?

LO 4 Problem 9-5 Warranties

Bombeck Company sells a product for $1,500. When the customer buys it, Bombeck provides a one-year warranty. Bombeck sold 120 products during 2001. Based on analysis of past warranty records, Bombeck estimates that repairs will average 3% of total sales.

Required

1. Determine the effect on the accounting equation of the estimated liability.

2. Assume that products under warranty must be repaired during 2001 using repair parts from inventory costing $4,950. Determine the effect on the accounting equation for the repair of products.

LO 5 Problem 9-6 Comparison of Simple and Compound Interest

On June 30, 2001, Rolf Inc. borrowed $25,000 from its bank, signing an 8%, two-year note.

Required

1. Assuming that the bank charges simple interest on the note, determine the effect on the accounting equation on each of the following dates:

> December 31, 2001
> December 31, 2002
> June 30, 2003

2. Assume instead that the bank charges 8% on the note, which is compounded semiannually. Determine the effect on the accounting equation on the dates in part **1.**

3. How much additional interest expense will Rolf have in part **2** over part **1**?

LO 6 Problem 9-7 Investment with Varying Interest Rate

Shari Thompson invested $1,000 in a financial institution on January 1, 2001. She leaves her investment in the institution until December 31, 2005. How much money does Shari accumulate if she earned interest, compounded annually, at the following rates?

2001	4%
2002	5%
2003	6%
2004	7%
2005	8%

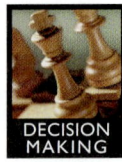

LO 6 Problem 9-8 Comparison of Alternatives

On January 1, 2001, Chen Yu's Office Supply Store plans to remodel the store and install new display cases. Chen has the following options of payment. Chen's interest rate is 8%.

a. Pay $180,000 on January 1, 2001.

b. Pay $196,200 on January 1, 2002.

c. Pay $220,500 on January 1, 2003.

d. Make four annual payments of $55,000 beginning on December 31, 2001.

Required

Which option should he choose? (*Hint:* Calculate the present value of each option as of January 1, 2001.)

LO 8 Problem 9-9 Payroll Amounts (Appendix 9A)

Vivian Company has calculated the gross wages of all employees for the month of August to be $210,000. The following amounts have been withheld from the employees' paychecks:

Income tax	$42,500
FICA	16,000
Heart Fund contributions	5,800
Union dues	3,150

Vivian's unemployment tax rate is 3%, and its portion of FICA matches the employees' share.

Required

1. Determine the effect on the accounting equation of accruing the amount payable to employees.
2. Determine the effect on the accounting equation when the employees are paid.
3. Determine the effect on the accounting equation of recording the employer's payroll costs.
4. Determine the effect on the accounting equation when the withholdings were remitted.

LO 9 Problem 9-10 Compensated Absences (Appendix 9A)

Hetzel Inc. pays its employees every Friday. For every four weeks that employees work, they earn one vacation day. For every six weeks that they work without calling in sick, they earn one sick day. If employees quit or retire, they can receive a lump-sum payment for their unused vacation days and unused sick days.

Required

Write a short memo to the bookkeeper to explain how and when he should report vacation and sick days. Explain how the matching principle applies and why you believe that the timing you recommend is appropriate.

Multi-Concept Problems

LO 2, 5 Problem 9-11 Interest in Advance versus Interest Paid When Loan Is Due

On July 1, 2001, Leach Company needs exactly $103,200 in cash to pay an existing obligation. Leach has decided to borrow from State Bank, which charges 14% interest on loans. The loan will be due in one year. Leach is unsure, however, whether to ask the bank for (a) an interest-bearing loan with interest and principal payable at the end of the year or (b) a loan due in one year but with interest deducted in advance.

Required

1. What will be the face value of the note assuming that
   a. interest is paid when the loan is due?
   b. interest is deducted in advance?

2. Calculate the effective interest rate on the note assuming that
   a. interest is paid when the loan is due.
   b. interest is deducted in advance.

3. Assume that Leach negotiates and signs the one-year note with the bank on July 1, 2001. Also assume that Leach's accounting year ends December 31. Determine the effect on the accounting equation of the issuance of the note and the interest on the note, assuming that
   a. interest is paid when the loan is due.
   b. interest is deducted in advance.

4. Prepare the appropriate balance sheet presentation for July 1, 2001, immediately after the note has been issued, assuming that
   a. interest is paid when the loan is due.
   b. interest is deducted in advance.

LO 1, 4 Problem 9-12 Contingent Liabilities

Listed here are several items for which the outcome of events is unknown at year-end.

a. A company offers a two-year warranty on sales of new computers. It believes that 4% of the computers will require repairs.

b. The company is involved in a trademark infringement suit. The company's legal experts believe an award of $500,000 in the company's favor will be made.

c. A company is involved in an environmental clean-up lawsuit. The company's legal counsel believes it is possible the outcome will be unfavorable but has not been able to estimate the costs of the possible loss.

d. A soap manufacturer has included a coupon offer in the Sunday newspaper supplements. The manufacturer estimates that 25% of the 50-cent coupons will be redeemed.

e. A company has been sued by the federal government for price fixing. The company's legal counsel believes there will be an unfavorable verdict and has made an estimate of the probable loss.

Required

1. Identify which of the items **a** through **e** should be recorded at year-end.

2. Identify which of the items **a** through **e** should not be recorded but should be disclosed in the year-end financial statements.

LO 6, 7 Problem 9-13 Time Value of Money Concepts

The following situations involve the application of the time value of money concept.

1. Janelle Carter deposited $9,750 in the bank on January 1, 1984, at an interest rate of 11% compounded annually. How much has accumulated in the account by January 1, 2001?

2. Mike Smith deposited $21,600 in the bank on January 1, 1991. On January 2, 2001, this deposit has accumulated to $42,487. Interest is compounded annually on the account. What is the rate of interest that Mike earned on the deposit?

3. Lee Spony made a deposit in the bank on January 1, 1994. The bank pays interest at the rate of 8% compounded annually. On January 1, 2001, the deposit has accumulated to $15,000. How much money did Lee originally deposit on January 1, 1994?

4. Nancy Holmes deposited $5,800 in the bank on January 1 a few years ago. The bank pays an interest rate of 10% compounded annually, and the deposit is now worth $15,026. How many years has the deposit been invested?

LO 6, 7 Problem 9-14 Comparison of Alternatives

Brian Imhoff's grandparents want to give him some money when he graduates from high school. They have offered Brian three choices:

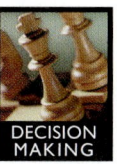
DECISION MAKING

a. Receive $15,000 immediately. Assume that interest is compounded annually.

b. Receive $2,250 at the end of each six months for four years. The first check will be received in six months.

c. Receive $4,350 at the end of each year for four years. Assume interest is compounded annually.

Required

Brian wants to have money for a new car when he graduates from college in four years. Assuming an interest rate of 8%, what option should he choose to have the most money in four years?

ALTERNATE PROBLEMS

LO 2   Problem 9-1A   Notes and Interest
McLaughlin Inc. operates with a June 30 year-end. During 2001, the following transactions occurred:

a. January 1: Signed a one-year, 10% loan for $35,000. Interest and principal are to be paid at maturity.

b. January 10: Signed a line of credit with the Little Local Bank to establish a $560,000 line of credit. Interest of 9% will be charged on all borrowed funds.

c. February 1: Issued a $28,000 non-interest-bearing, six-month note to pay for a new machine. Interest on the note, at 12%, was deducted in advance.

d. March 1: Borrowed $210,000 on the line of credit.

e. June 1: Repaid $140,000 on the line of credit, plus accrued interest.

f. June 30: Made all necessary adjusting entries.

g. August 1: Repaid the non-interest-bearing note.

h. September 1: Borrowed $280,000 on the line of credit.

i. November 1: Issued a three-month, 8%, $16,800 note in payment of an overdue open account.

j. December 31: Repaid the one-year loan (from item **a**) plus accrued interest.

Required

1. Determine the effect on the accounting equation of items **a** through **j**.

2. As of December 31, which notes are outstanding, and how much interest is due on each?

LO 3   Problem 9-2A   Effects of Boeing's Current Liabilities on Its Statement of Cash Flows

The following items are classified as current liabilities on Boeing Company's consolidated statements of financial condition (or balance sheet) at December 31 (in millions):

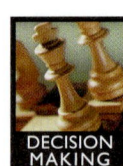

	1999	1998
Accounts payable and other liabilities	$11,269	$11,085
Advances in excess of related costs	1,215	1,251
Income taxes payable	420	569
Short-term debt and current portion of long-term debt	752	869

Required

1. Boeing uses the indirect method to prepare its statement of cash flows. Prepare the Operating Activities section of the cash flow statement, which indicates how each item will be reflected as an adjustment to net income. If you did not include any of the items set forth above, explain why not.

2. How would you decide whether Boeing has the ability to pay these liabilities as they become due?

LO 3   Problem 9-3A   Effects of Nike's Changes in Current Assets and Liabilities on Its Statement of Cash Flows

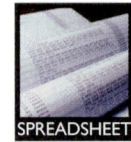

The following items, listed in alphabetical order, are included in the Current Assets and Current Liabilities categories on the consolidated balance sheet of Nike Inc. at May 31, 2000 and 1999 (in millions):

	2000	1999
Accounts payable	$ 543.8	$ 473.6
Accounts receivable	1,567.2	1,540.1
Accrued liabilities	621.9	553.2
Current portion of long-term debt	50.1	1.0
Inventories	1,446.0	1,170.6
Notes payable	924.2	419.1
Prepaid expenses	215.2	219.6

Required

1. Nike uses the indirect method to prepare its statement of cash flows. Indicate how each item will be reflected as an adjustment to net income in the Operating Activities section of the cash flow statement.

2. If you did not include any of the items set forth above in your answer to part **1,** explain how these items would be reported on the statement of cash flows.

LO 4 Problem 9-4A Warranties

Sound Company manufactures and sells high-quality stereo sets. The most popular line sells for $2,000 each and is accompanied by a three-year warranty to repair, free of charge, any defective unit. Average costs to repair each defective unit will be $180 for replacement parts and $120 for labor. Sound estimates that warranty costs of $25,200 will be incurred during 2001. The company actually sold 600 sets and incurred replacement part costs of $7,200 and labor costs of $10,800 during the year. The adjusted 2001 ending balance in the Estimated Liability for Warranties account is $20,400.

Required

1. How many defective units from this year's sales does Sound Company estimate will be returned for repair?

2. What percentage of sales does Sound Company estimate will be returned for repair?

LO 4 Problem 9-5A Warranties

Beck Company sells a product for $3,200. When the customer buys it, Beck provides a one-year warranty. Beck sold 120 products during 2001. Based on analysis of past warranty records, Beck estimates that repairs will average 4% of total sales.

Required

1. Determine the effect on the accounting equation of the estimated liability.

2. Assume that during 2001, products under warranty must be repaired using repair parts from inventory costing $10,200. Determine the effect on the accounting equation for the repair of products.

3. Assume that the balance of the Estimated Liabilities for Warranties account as of the beginning of 2001 was $1,100. Calculate the balance of the account as of the end of 2001.

LO 5 Problem 9-6A Comparison of Simple and Compound Interest

On June 30, 2001, Rolloff Inc. borrowed $25,000 from its bank, signing a 6% note. Principal and interest are due at the end of two years.

Required

1. Assuming that the note earns simple interest for the bank, calculate the amount of interest accrued on each of the following dates:

    December 31, 2001
    December 31, 2002
    June 30, 2003

2. Assume instead that the note earns 6% for the bank but is compounded semiannually. Calculate the amount of interest accrued on the same dates as in part **1.**

3. How much additional interest expense will Rolloff have to pay with semiannual interest?

LO 6 Problem 9-7A Investment with Varying Interest Rate

Trena Thompson invested $2,000 in a financial institution on January 1, 2001. She leaves her investment in the institution until December 31, 2005. How much money will Trena accumulate if she earns interest, compounded annually, at the following rates?

2001	4%
2002	5%
2003	6%
2004	7%
2005	8%

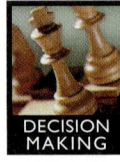

LO 6 Problem 9-8A Comparison of Alternatives

On January 1, 2001, Li Ping's Office Supply Store plans to remodel the store and install new display cases. Li Ping has the following options of payment. Li's interest rate is 8%.

a. Pay $270,000 on January 1, 2001.

b. Pay $294,300 on January 1, 2002.

c. Pay $334,750 on January 1, 2003.

d. Make four annual payments of $82,500 beginning on December 31, 2001.

Required

Which option should Li choose? (*Hint:* Calculate the present value of each option as of January 1, 2001.)

LO 8 Problem 9-9A Payroll Amounts (Appendix 9A)

Calvin Company has calculated the gross wages of all employees for the month of August to be $336,000. The following amounts have been withheld from the employees' paychecks:

Income tax	$68,000
FICA	25,600
Heart Fund contributions	9,280
Union dues	5,040

Calvin's unemployment tax rate is 3%, and its portion of FICA matches the employees' share.

Required

1. Determine the effect on the accounting equation of accruing the amount payable to employees.

2. Determine the effect on the accounting equation when the employees are paid.

3. Determine the effect on the accounting equation of recording the employer's payroll costs.

4. Determine the effect on the accounting equation when the withholdings are remitted.

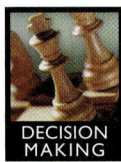

LO 9 Problem 9-10A Compensated Absences (Appendix 9A)

Assume that you are the accountant for a large company with several divisions. The manager of Division B has contacted you with a concern. During 2001, several employees retired from Division B. The company's policy is that employees can be paid for days of sick leave accrued at the time they retire. Payment occurs in the year following retirement. The manager has been told by corporate headquarters that she cannot replace the employees in 2002 because the payment of the accrued sick pay will be deducted from Division B's budget in that year.

Required

In a memo to the manager of Division B, explain the proper accounting for accrued sick pay. Do you think that the policies of corporate headquarters should be revised?

Alternate Multi-Concept Problems

LO 2, 5 Problem 9-11A Interest in Advance versus Interest Paid When Loan Is Due

On July 1, 2001, Moton Company needs exactly $206,400 in cash to pay an existing obligation. Moton has decided to borrow from State Bank, which charges 14% interest on loans. The loan will be due in one year. Moton is unsure, however, whether to ask the bank for (a) an interest-bearing loan with interest and principal payable at the end of the year or (b) a non-interest-bearing loan due in one year but with interest deducted in advance.

Required

1. What will be the face value of the note, assuming that

   a. interest is paid when the loan is due?

   b. interest is deducted in advance?

2. Calculate the effective interest rate on the note, assuming that

   a. interest is paid when the loan is due.

   b. interest is deducted in advance.

3. Assume that Moton negotiates and signs the one-year note with the bank on July 1, 2001. Also assume that Moton's accounting year ends December 31. Determine the effect on the accounting equation of the issuance of the note and the interest on it, assuming that

   a. interest is paid when the loan is due.

   b. interest is deducted in advance.

4. Prepare the appropriate balance sheet presentation for July 1, 2001, immediately after the note has been issued, assuming that

   a. interest is paid when the loan is due.

   b. interest is deducted in advance.

LO 1, 4   Problem 9-12A   Contingent Liabilities

Listed here are several events for which the outcome is unknown at year-end.

a. A company has been sued by the federal government for price fixing. The company's legal counsel believes there will be an unfavorable verdict and has made an estimate of the probable loss.

b. A company is involved in an environmental clean-up lawsuit. The company's legal counsel believes it is possible the outcome will be unfavorable but has not been able to estimate the costs of the possible loss.

c. The company is involved in a trademark infringement suit. The company's legal experts believe an award of $750,000 in the company's favor will be made.

d. A company offers a three-year warranty on sales of new computers. It believes that 6% of the computers will require repairs.

e. A snack food manufacturer has included a coupon offer in the Sunday newspaper supplements. The manufacturer estimates that 30% of the 40-cent coupons will be redeemed.

Required

1. Identify which of the items **a** through **e** should be recorded at year-end.

2. Identify which of the items **a** through **e** should not be recorded but should be disclosed on the year-end financial statements.

LO 6, 7   Problem 9-13A   Time Value of Money Concept

The following situations involve the application of the time value of money concept.

1. Jan Cain deposited $19,500 in the bank on January 1, 1984, at an interest rate of 11% compounded annually. How much has accumulated in the account by January 1, 2001?

2. Mark Schultz deposited $43,200 in the bank on January 1, 1991. On January 2, 2001, this deposit has accumulated to $84,974. Interest is compounded annually on the account. What is the rate of interest that Mark earned on the deposit?

3. Les Hinckle made a deposit in the bank on January 1, 1994. The bank pays interest at the rate of 8% compounded annually. On January 1, 2001, the deposit has accumulated to $30,000. How much money did Les originally deposit on January 1, 1994?

4. Val Hooper deposited $11,600 in the bank on January 1 a few years ago. The bank pays an interest rate of 10% compounded annually, and the deposit is now worth $30,052. For how many years has the deposit been invested?

LO 6, 7   Problem 9-14A   Comparison of Alternatives

Darlene Page's grandparents want to give her some money when she graduates from high school. They have offered Darlene three choices.

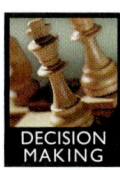

DECISION MAKING

a. Receive $16,000 immediately. Assume that interest is compounded annually.

b. Receive $2,400 at the end of each six months for four years. The first check will be received in six months.

c. Receive $4,640 at the end of each year for four years. Assume interest is compounded annually.

Required

Darlene wants to have money for a new car when she graduates from college in four years. Assuming an interest rate of 8%, what option should she choose to have the most money in four years?

CASES

Reading and Interpreting Financial Statements

LO 1, 2 **Case 9-1** Analysis of Uno Restaurant's Current Liabilities

www.pizzeriauno.com

Refer to Uno's annual report. Using Uno's balance sheet, write a response to the following questions:

1. Uno's total current liabilities increased from $22,280,000 in 1998 to $26,824,000 in 1999. What were the major factors that caused the increase in current liabilities during that time period?

2. Does the increase in Uno's current liabilities indicate that the firm was experiencing liquidity problems? What numbers or ratios could be used to determine its liquidity?

3. The amount listed as Current Portion of Long-Term Debt and Capital Lease Obligations decreased from $4,081,000 in 1998 to $4,075,000 in 1999. What do these amounts represent?

LO 1, 2 **Case 9-2** Analysis of Gateway's Current Liabilities

www.gateway.com

Refer to Gateway's annual report. Using Gateway's balance sheet, write a response to the following questions.

1. Gateway's total current liabilities increased from $1,429,674,000 in 1998 to $1,809,710,000 in 1999. What accounts were the cause of the increase in total current liabilities?

2. Does the increase in Gateway's current liabilities indicate that the firm was experiencing liquidity problems? What numbers or ratios could be used to determine its liquidity?

3. The amount listed as Current Maturities of Long-Term Obligations decreased from $11,415,000 in 1998 to $5,490,000 in 1999. Does the amount of the decrease indicate the amount of the account that was paid during the year?

LO 3 **Case 9-3** Uno Restaurant's Cash Flow Statement

www.pizzeriauno.com

1. Uno's cash flow statement indicates that accounts payable and other liabilities increased by $4,320,000. Where is this amount shown on the statement of cash flows? Does it represent an increase or decrease in cash?

2. In 1999, Uno's repaid $79,490,000 of long-term debt and capital leases. Which category of the statement of cash flows presents those amounts? For the purposes of the statement of cash flows, what category would include short-term borrowings?

3. Uno's October 3, 1999, balance sheet indicated an amount as Deferred Taxes in the Long-Term Assets section. Should it be disclosed in the Operating Activities category of the statement of cash flows?

LO 3 **Case 9-4** Gateway's Cash Flow Statement

www.gateway.com

1. Gateway's Accounts Payable account increased from 1998 to 1999. In which category of the cash flow statement is this reported? Why is it listed as a positive amount?

2. Gateway's net cash provided by operating activities decreased significantly from 1998 to 1999. What were the primary causes for the decrease in cash flow for this time period?

3. What does the account Accrued Royalties mean? Why is it a negative amount in the statement of cash flows for 1999?

LO 3, 4 **Case 9-5** Microsoft Corporation's Contingent Liabilities

www.microsoft.com

Microsoft Corporation has a fiscal year ending on June 30 and uses the indirect method to prepare its statement of cash flows. The notes to its 1999 financial statements include the following:

Contingencies

On May 18, 1998, the Antitrust Division of the U.S. Department of Justice (DOJ) and a group of 20 state Attorneys General filed two antitrust cases against Microsoft in the U.S. District Court for the District of Columbia. The DOJ complaint alleges violations of Sections 1 and 2 of the Sherman Act. The DOJ complaint seeks declaratory relief as to the violations it asserts and preliminary and permanent injunctive relief regarding: the inclusion of Internet browsing software (or other software products) as part of Windows; the terms of agreements regarding non-Microsoft Internet browsing software (or other software products); taking or threatening "action adverse" in consequence of a person's failure to license or distribute Microsoft Internet browsing software (or other software product) or distributing competing products or cooperating with the government; and restrictions on the screens, boot-up sequence, or functions of Microsoft's operating system products. The state Attorneys General allege largely the same claims and various pendent state claims. The states seek declaratory relief and preliminary and permanent injunctive relief similar to that sought by the DOJ, together with statutory penalties under the state law claims. The foregoing description is qualified in its entirety by reference to the full text of the complaints and other papers on file in those actions, case numbers 98-1232 and 98-1233.

On May 22, 1998, Judge Jackson consolidated the two actions. The judge granted Microsoft's motion for summary judgment as to the states' monopoly leverage claim and permitted the remaining claims to proceed to trial. Trial began on October 19, 1998. Microsoft believes the claims are without merit and is defending against them vigorously.

Required

Is disclosure of the complaint in the notes to the financial statements all that is required of Microsoft, or is accrual required? If you decide that accrual is required, what amount should be accrued at June 30, 1999, and how would this contingent liability be reported on Microsoft's balance sheet at June 30, 1999?

Making Financial Decisions

LO 1, 2   Case 9-6   Current Ratio Loan Provision

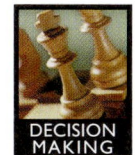

Assume that you are the controller of a small, growing sporting goods company. The prospects for your firm in the future are quite good, but like most other firms, it has been experiencing some cash flow difficulties because all available funds have been used to purchase inventory and finance start-up costs associated with a new business. At the beginning of the current year, your local bank advanced a loan to your company. Included in the loan is the following provision:

The company is obligated to pay interest payments each month for the next five years. Principal is due and must be paid at the end of Year 5. The company is further obligated to maintain a current assets to current liabilities ratio of 2 to 1 as indicated on quarterly statements to be submitted to the bank. If the company fails to meet any loan provisions, all amounts of interest and principal are due immediately upon notification by the bank.

You, as controller, have just gathered the following information as of the end of the first month of the current quarter:

Current Liabilities:	
Accounts payable	$400,000
Taxes payable	100,000
Accrued expenses	50,000
Total Current Liabilities	$550,000

You are concerned about the loan provision that requires a 2:1 ratio of current assets to current liabilities.

Required

1. Indicate what actions could be taken during the next two months to meet the loan provision. Which of the available actions should be recommended?

2. What is the meaning of the term *window-dressing* financial statements? What are the long-run implications of actions taken to window-dress financial statements?

LO 7   Case 9-7   Alternative Payment Options

Kathy Clark owns a small company that makes ice machines for restaurants and food-service facilities. Kathy knows a lot about producing ice machines but is less familiar with the best terms to extend to her customers. One customer is opening a new business and has asked Kathy to consider any of the following options to pay for his new $20,000 ice machine.

a. Term 1: 10% down, the remainder paid at the end of the year plus 8% simple interest.

b. Term 2: 10% down, the remainder paid at the end of the year plus 8% interest, compounded quarterly.

c. Term 3: $0 down, but $21,600 due at the end of the year.

Required

Make a recommendation to Kathy. She believes that 8% is a fair return on her money at this time. Should she accept option **a, b,** or **c,** or take the $20,000 cash at the time of the sale? Justify your recommendation with calculations. What factors, other than the actual amount of cash received from the sale, should be considered?

Accounting and Ethics: What Would You Do?

LO 4 Case 9-8 Warranty Cost Estimate

John Walton is an accountant for ABC Auto Dealers, a large auto dealership in a metropolitan area. ABC sells both new and used cars. New cars are sold with a five-year warranty, the cost of which is carried by the manufacturer. For several years, however, ABC has offered a two-year warranty on used cars. The cost of the warranty is an expense to ABC, and John has been asked by his boss, Mr. Sawyer, to review warranty costs and recommend the amount to accrue on the year-end financial statements.

For the past several years, ABC has recorded as warranty expense 5% of used car sales. John has analyzed past repair records and found that repairs, although fluctuating somewhat from year to year, have averaged near the 5% level. John is convinced, however, that 5% is inadequate for the coming year. He bases his judgment on industry reports of increased repair costs and on the fact that several cars that were recently sold on warranty have experienced very high repair costs. John believes that the current-year repair accrual will be at least 10%. He discussed the higher expense amount with Mr. Sawyer, who is the controller of ABC.

Mr. Sawyer was not happy with John's decision concerning warranty expense. He reminded John of the need to control expenses during the recent sales downturn. He also reminded John that ABC is seeking a large loan from the bank and that the bank loan officers may not be happy with recent operating results, especially if ABC begins to accrue larger amounts for future estimated amounts such as warranties. Finally, Mr. Sawyer reminded John that most of the employees of ABC, including Mr. Sawyer, were members of the company's profit-sharing plan and would not be happy with the reduced share of profits. Mr. Sawyer thanked John for his judgment concerning warranty cost but told him that the accrual for the current year would remain at 5%.

John left the meeting with Mr. Sawyer somewhat frustrated. He was convinced that his judgment concerning the warranty costs was correct. He knew that the owner of ABC would be visiting the office next week and wondered whether he should discuss the matter with him personally at that time. John also had met one of the loan officers from the bank several times and considered calling her to discuss his concern about the warranty expense amount on the year-end statements.

Required

Discuss the courses of action available to John. What should John do concerning his judgment of warranty costs?

LO 4 Case 9-9 Retainer Fees As Sales

Bunch o' Balloons markets balloon arrangements to companies who want to thank clients and employees. Bunch o' Balloons has a unique style that has put it in high demand. Consequently, Bunch o' Balloons has asked clients to establish an account. Clients are asked to pay a retainer fee equal to about three months of client purchases. The fee will be used to cover the cost of arrangements delivered and will be reevaluated at the end of each month. At the end of the current month, Bunch o' Balloons has $43,900 of retainer fees in its possession. The controller is eager to show this amount as sales because "it represents certain sales for the company."

Required

Do you agree with the controller? When should the sales be reported? Why would the controller be eager to report the cash receipts as sales?

Case 9-10   JCPenney

JCPenney hopes a network of retail stores, augmented by catalog sales and a burgeoning e-commerce business, will help the company meet its strategic growth goals and respond to intense competition from other retailers. In recent years, JCPenney has established the company as a family of businesses—department store and catalog, Eckerd drugstores, direct marketing and international operations. Their mission is to change business processes so as to contain expenses, increase revenue and, especially, raise net income.

www.jcpenney.com

INTERNET

JCPenney.com contains a wealth of information about the company. Use this Web site to compare the financial numbers presented in this chapter to the latest numbers available; examine management's plans to improve the company's processes; and find news of interest to investors, analysts, and researchers.

1. Based on the latest information available, determine the total current assets and total current liabilities for JCPenney Company. How do these compare with the amounts of the previous year?

2. Calculate JCPenney's current ratio based on the latest information available.

3. If you were a supplier of merchandise to JCPenney, how might its current ratio effect your willingness to extend credit to the company?

4. What major changes in JCPenney's operations have been implemented in the most current year available? What do you see as the effect, if any, on the financial statements and notes?

SOLUTION TO KEY TERMS QUIZ

1   Current liability (p. 398)

3   Accounts payable (p. 400)

8   Notes payable (p. 400)

4   Discount on Notes Payable (p. 401)

6   Current Maturities of Long-Term Debt (p. 402)

7   Accrued liability (p. 402)

9   Contingent liability (p. 404)

11   Estimated liability (p. 406)

12   Contingent asset (p. 409)

14   Time value of money (p. 410)

10   Simple interest (p. 410)

13   Compound interest (p. 411)

15   Future value of a single amount (p. 412)

17   Present value of a single amount (p. 414)

5   Annuity (p. 415)

16   Future value of an annuity (p. 416)

2   Present value of an annuity (p. 416)

18   Gross wages (p. 427)

20   Net pay (p. 427)

19   Compensated absences (p. 430)

LONG-TERM LIABILITIES

Study Links

A Look at Previous Chapters

The topic of long-term liabilities was introduced in Chapter 2 as an important aspect of a classified balance sheet, which segregates short-term and long-term assets and liabilities. Chapter 9 introduced compound interest and present value calculations as a method used to value long-term liabilities.

A Look at This Chapter

This chapter examines those items that typically appear in the long-term liability category of the balance sheet. The first section of the chapter will cover bonds, an important source of financing for many companies. The second section covers several other important long-term liabilities: leases, pensions, and deferred taxes. Although these liabilities are based on very complex financial arrangements, our primary purpose is to introduce these topics so that you are aware of their existence when reading financial statements.

A Look at Upcoming Chapters

Chapter 11 will examine the presentation of stockholders' equity, the other major category on the right-hand side of the balance sheet.

FOCUS ON FINANCIAL RESULTS

With one of the foremost brands in the world, the Coca-Cola Company reported operating income of nearly $4 billion in 1999. This was a disappointing performance that eventually resulted in the loss of a fifth of the company's workforce worldwide. Despite continued economic turbulence in many of its markets, natural disasters in Turkey and Greece, and a temporary product withdrawal in Belgium and France, the firm pledged to maintain its focus on growth. As its 1999 annual report declares, "We've never lost sight of the fact that first, last and always, we are a consumer growth company."[1]

In 1999 Coca-Cola continued to invest heavily in marketing and infrastructure worldwide. It produced radio spots in 40 different languages, for example, and recorded the accompanying music in 140 different versions adapted to local markets. The company also completed the acquisition of Cadbury Schweppes PLC beverage brands in 155 countries for about $700 million, and it continued to support and strengthen the bottling companies in which it maintains either a controlling or noncontrolling interest.

To expand profitably, Coca-Cola requires more money than it generates in profits. Therefore, it uses a common financing tool: long-term debt. The firm's global presence opens doors to financial markets around the world (the firm deals with approximately 60 different currencies). While most of Coca-Cola's loans in 1999 were in U.S. dollars, management continually adjusts the composition of the debt to accommodate shifting interest rates and currency exchange rates, in order to minimize the overall cost of borrowing.

---

[1]Coca-Cola's 1999 annual report, p. 9.

December 31,	1999	1998
LIABILITIES AND SHARE-OWNERS' EQUITY		
CURRENT		
Accounts payable and accrued expenses	$ 3,714	$ 3,141
Loans and notes payable	5,112	4,459
Current maturities of long-term debt	261	3
Accrued income taxes	769	1,037
TOTAL CURRENT LIABILITIES	9,856	8,640
LONG-TERM DEBT	854	687
OTHER LIABILITIES	902	991
DEFERRED INCOME TAXES	498	424
SHARE-OWNERS' EQUITY		
Common stock, $.25 par value		
Authorized: 5,600,000,000 shares		
Issued: 3,466,371,904 shares in 1999; 3,460,083,686 shares in 1998	867	865
Capital surplus	2,584	2,195
Reinvested earnings	20,773	19,922
Accumulated other comprehensive income and		
unearned compensation on restricted stock	(1,551)	(1,434)
	22,673	21,548
Less treasury stock, at cost (994,796,786 shares in 1999; 994,566,196 shares in 1998)	13,160	13,145
	9,513	8,403
	$ 21,623	$19,145

Coca-Cola's long-term debt

See Notes to Consolidated Financial Statements.

Coca-Cola 1999 annual report

What interest rates does Coca-Cola have to pay on long-term debt? How do accountants record the transactions related to long-term debt? Look for the answers as you study this chapter. Check Coca-Cola's most recent annual report to identify any changes in its long-term liabilities.

www.cocacola.com

BALANCE SHEET PRESENTATION

LO 1 Identify the components of the long-term liability category of the balance sheet.

From **Concept**

TO PRACTICE 10.1

READING COCA-COLA'S BALANCE SHEET Coca-Cola lists three items as long-term liabilities on its 1999 balance sheet. What are those items? Did they increase or decrease?

In general, **long-term liabilities** are obligations that will not be satisfied within one year. Essentially, all liabilities that are not classified as current liabilities are classified as long-term. We will concentrate on the long-term liabilities of bonds or notes, leases, deferred taxes, and pension obligations. On the balance sheet, the items are listed after current liabilities. For example, the Noncurrent Liabilities section of PepsiCo's balance sheet is highlighted in Exhibit 10-1. PepsiCo has acquired financing through a combination of long-term debt, stock issuance, and internal growth or retained earnings. Exhibit 10-1 indicates that long-term debt is one portion of the long-term liability category of the balance sheet. But the balance sheet also reveals two other items that must be considered part of the long-term liability category: deferred income taxes and other liabilities. We begin by looking at a particular type of long-term debt, bonds payable.

BONDS PAYABLE

CHARACTERISTICS OF BONDS

LO 2 Define the important characteristics of bonds payable.

A bond is a security or financial instrument that allows firms to borrow money and repay the loan over a long period of time. The bonds are sold, or *issued,* to investors who have amounts to invest and want a return on their investment. The *borrower* (issuing firm) promises to pay interest on specified dates, usually annually or semiannually. The borrower also promises to repay the principal on a specified date, the *due date* or maturity date.

A bond certificate, illustrated in Exhibit 10-2, is issued at the time of purchase and indicates the *terms* of the bond. Generally, bonds are issued in denominations of $1,000. The denomination of the bond is usually referred to as the **face value** or par value. This is the amount that the firm must pay at the maturity date of the bond.

Firms issue bonds in very large amounts, often in millions in a single issue. After bonds are issued, they may be traded on a bond exchange in the same way that stocks are sold on the stock exchanges. Therefore, bonds are not always held until maturity by the initial investor but may change hands several times before their eventual due date.

EXHIBIT 10-1   PepsiCo Balance Sheet

CONSOLIDATED BALANCE SHEET

(in millions except per share amounts)
PepsiCo, Inc. and Subsidiaries
December 25, 1999 and December 26, 1998

	1999	1998
ASSETS		
Current Assets		
Cash and cash equivalents	$ 964	$ 311
Short-term investments, at cost	92	83
	1,056	394
Accounts and notes receivable, net	1,704	2,453
Inventories	899	1,016
Prepaid expenses and other current assets	514	499
Total Current Assets	4,173	4,362
Property, Plant and Equipment, net	5,266	7,318
Intangible Assets, net	4,735	8,996
Investments in Unconsolidated Affiliates	2,846	1,396
Other Assets	531	588
Total Assets	$ 17,551	$ 22,660
LIABILITIES AND SHAREHOLDERS' EQUITY		
Current Liabilities		
Short-term borrowings	$ 233	$ 3,921
Accounts payable and other current liabilities	3,399	3,870
Income taxes payable	156	123
Total Current Liabilities	3,788	7,914
Long-Term Debt	2,812	4,028
Other Liabilities	2,861	2,314
Deferred Income Taxes	1,209	2,003
Shareholders' Equity		
Capital Stock, par value 1 2/3¢ per share: authorized 3,600 shares, issued 1,726 shares	29	29
Capital in excess of par value	1,081	1,166
Retained earnings	14,066	12,800
Accumulated other comprehensive loss	(989)	(1,059)
	14,187	12,936
Less: repurchased shares, at cost: 271 shares in 1999 and 255 shares in 1998	(7,306)	(6,535)
Total Shareholders' Equity	6,881	6,401
Total Liabilities and Shareholders' Equity	$ 17,551	$ 22,660

PepsiCo's long-term debt

See accompanying Notes to Consolidated Financial Statements.

EXHIBIT 10-2 Bond Certificate

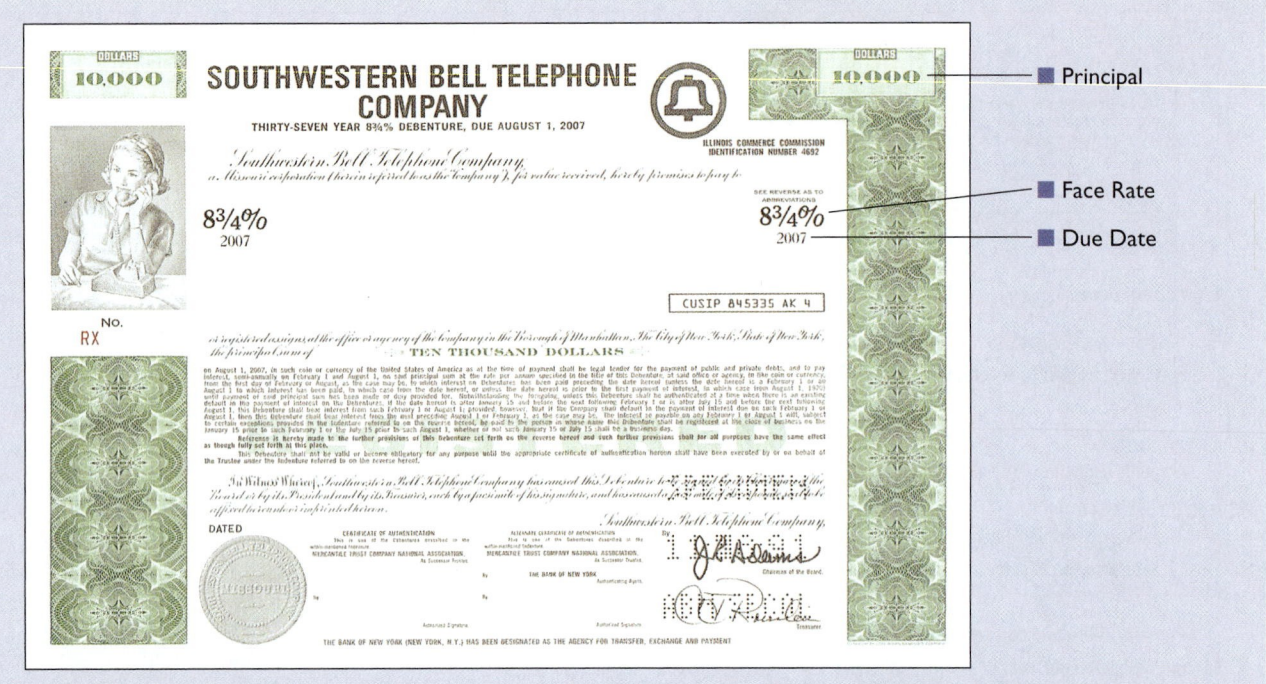

■ Principal

■ Face Rate

■ Due Date

Debenture bonds, like this one from Southwestern Bell Telephone, are backed by the general creditworthiness of the issuing company, not by its assets as collateral. Buyers of such bonds should check the issuer's credit rating, should know how to read the firm's financial statements—and should learn as much as possible about its operations.

Because bond maturities are as long as 30 years, the "secondary" market in bonds—the market for bonds already issued—is a critical factor in a company's ability to raise money. Investors in bonds may want to sell them if interest rates paid by competing investments become more attractive or if the issuer becomes less creditworthy. Buyers of these bonds may be betting that interest rates will reverse course or that the company will get back on its feet. Trading in the secondary market does not affect the financial statements of the issuing company.

We have described the general nature of bonds, but it should not be assumed that all bonds have the same terms and features. Following are some important features that often appear in the bond certificate.

Collateral   The bond certificate should indicate the *collateral* of the loan. Collateral represents the assets that back the bonds in case the issuer cannot make the interest and principal payments and must default on the loan. **Debenture bonds** are not backed by specific collateral of the issuing company. Rather, the investor must examine the general creditworthiness of the issuer. If a bond is a *secured bond*, the certificate indicates specific assets that serve as collateral in case of default.

Due Date   The bond certificate specifies the date that the bond principal must be repaid. Normally, bonds are *term bonds,* meaning that the entire principal amount is due on a single date. Alternatively, bonds may be issued as **serial bonds,** meaning that not all of the principal is due on the same date. For example, a firm may issue serial bonds that have a portion of the principal due each year for the next 10 years. Issuing firms may prefer serial bonds because a firm does not need to accumulate the entire amount for principal repayment at one time.

Other Features   Some bonds are issued as convertible or callable bonds. *Convertible bonds* can be converted into common stock at a future time. This feature allows the investor to buy a security that pays a fixed interest rate but that can be converted at a future date into an equity security (stock) if the issuing firm is growing and profitable. The conversion feature is also advantageous to the issuing firm because convertible bonds normally carry a lower rate of interest.

Callable bonds may be retired before their specified due date. *Callable* generally refers to the issuer's right to retire the bonds. If the buyer or investor has the right to retire the bonds, they are referred to as *redeemable bonds*. Usually, callable bonds stipulate the price to be paid at redemption; this price is referred to as the *redemption price* or the *reacquisition price*. The callable feature is like an insurance policy for the company. Say a bond pays 10%, but interest rates plummet to 6%. Rather than continuing to pay 10%, the company is willing to offer a slight premium over face value for the right to retire those 10% bonds so that it can borrow at 6%. Of course, the investor is invariably disappointed when the company invokes its call privilege.

As you can see, various terms and features are associated with bonds. Each firm seeks to structure the bond agreement in the manner that best meets its financial needs and will attract investors at the most favorable rates.

Bonds are a popular source of financing because of the tax advantages when compared with the issuance of stock. Interest paid on bonds is deductible for tax purposes, but dividends paid on stock are not. This may explain why the amount of debt on many firms' balance sheets has increased in recent years. Debt became popular in the 1980s to finance mergers and again in the early 1990s when interest rates reached 20-year lows. Still, investors and creditors tend to downgrade a company when the amount of debt it has on the balance sheet is deemed to be excessive.

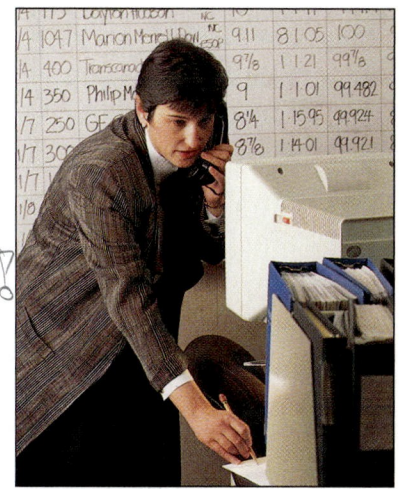

This bond trader assists investors on the secondary market in buying and selling bonds. On the board behind her, she tallies bond availability information, including company name ("Dayton Hudson"), bond rates ("10" for 10%), maturity dates ("1-1-11" for January 1, 2011), and the issue price ("99.479" for 99.479% of face value).

ISSUANCE OF BONDS

When bonds are issued, the issuing firm must recognize the incurrence of a liability in exchange for cash. If bonds are issued at their face amount, the accounting entry is straightforward. For example, assume that on April 1, a firm issues bonds with a face amount of $10,000 and receives $10,000. In this case, the asset Cash and the liability Bonds Payable are both increased by $10,000.

FACTORS AFFECTING BOND PRICE

With bonds payable, two interest rates are always involved. The **face rate of interest** (also called the *stated rate, nominal rate, contract rate,* or *coupon rate*) is the rate specified on the bond certificate. It is the amount of interest that will be paid each interest period. For example, if $10,000 worth of bonds is issued with an 8% annual face rate of interest, then interest of $800 ($10,000 × 8% × 1 year) would be paid at the end of each annual period. Alternatively, bonds often require the payment of interest semiannually. If the bonds in our example required the 8% annual face rate to be paid semiannually (at 4%), then interest of $400 ($10,000 × 8% × ½ year) would be paid each semiannual period.

The second important interest rate is the **market rate of interest** (also called the *effective rate* or *bond yield*). The market rate of interest is the rate that bondholders could obtain by investing in other bonds that are similar to the issuing firm's bonds. The issuing firm does not set the market rate of interest. That rate is determined by the bond market on the basis of many transactions for similar bonds. The market rate incorporates all the "market's" knowledge about economic conditions and all its expectations about future conditions. Normally, issuing firms try to set a face rate that is equal to the market rate. However, because the market rate changes daily, there are almost always small differences between the face rate and the market rate at the time bonds are issued.

In addition to the number of interest payments and the maturity length of the bond, the face rate and the market rate of interest must both be known in order to calculate the issue price of a bond. The **bond issue price** equals the *present value* of the cash flows that the bond will produce. Bonds produce two types of cash flows for the investor, interest receipts and repayment of principal (face value). The interest receipts constitute an annuity of payments each interest period over the life of the bonds. The repayment of principal

LO 3 Determine the issue price of a bond using compound interest techniques.

> *Study Tip*
>
> Calculating the issue price of a bond always involves a calculation of the present value of the cash flows.

(face value) is a one-time receipt that occurs at the end of the term of the bonds. We must calculate the present value of the interest receipts (using Table 9-4) and the present value of the principal amount (using Table 9-2). The total of the two present-value calculations represents the issue price of the bond.

An Example   Suppose that on January 1, 2001, Discount Firm wants to issue bonds with a face value of $10,000. The face or coupon rate of interest has been set at 8%. The bonds will pay interest annually, and the principal amount is due in four years. Also suppose that the market rate of interest for other similar bonds is currently 10%. Because the market rate of interest exceeds the coupon rate, investors will not be willing to pay $10,000 but something less. We want to calculate the amount that will be obtained from the issuance of Discount Firm's bonds.

Discount's bond will produce two sets of cash flows for the investor, an annual interest payment of $800 ($10,000 × 8%) per year for four years and repayment of the principal of $10,000 at the end of the fourth year. To calculate the issue price, we must calculate the present value of the two sets of cash flows. A time diagram portrays the cash flows as follows:

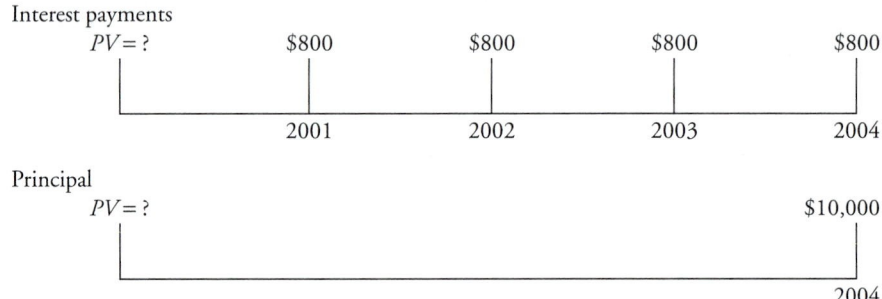

Interest payments

$PV = ?$	$800	$800	$800	$800
	2001	2002	2003	2004

Principal

$PV = ?$ $10,000

2004

We can calculate the issue price by using the compound-interest tables found in Chapter 9, as follows:

$800 × 3.170 (factor from Table 9-4 for 4 periods, 10%)	$2,536
$10,000 × .683 (factor from Table 9-2 for 4 periods, 10%)	6,830
Issue Price	$9,366

The table factors used represent four periods and 10% interest. This is a key point. The issue price of a bond is always calculated using the market rate of interest. The face rate of interest determines the amount of the interest payments, but the market rate determines

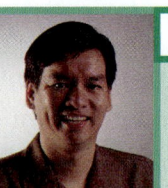

ACCOUNTING FOR YOUR DECISIONS

You Rate the Bonds

One of the factors that determine the rate of interest on a bond is a rating by a rating agency, such as Standard & Poor's or Moody's Investor Service. Bonds with a higher rating are considered less risky and can be issued for a lower rate of interest. You have been given an assignment to rate the bonds issued by PepsiCo. What factors would you consider in your rating?

ANS: There are many factors that affect your evaluation of the riskiness of the company's bonds. One factor would be the amount of debt on PepsiCo's books, which can be found by examining the liability section of the balance sheet. It is important to relate the amount of debt to the total equity of the company; this is often done by computing the debt-to-equity ratio. Another important factor is the company's competitive position within its industry. If PepsiCo can operate profitably, it will generate cash that can be used to pay the interest and principal on the bonds.

Exhibit 10-3 Listing of Bonds on the Bond Market

Bonds	Cur Yld	Vol	Close	Net Chg
IBM 6⅜03	6.5	280	98¾	−¼
IBM 7¼05	7.1	68	101½	+¼

the present value of the payments and the present value of the principal (and, therefore, the issue price).

Our example of Discount Firm reveals that the bonds with a $10,000 face value amount would be issued for $9,366. The bond markets and the financial press often state the issue price as a percentage of the face amount. The percentage for Discount's bonds can be calculated as ($9,366/$10,000) × 100, or 93.66%.

Exhibit 10-3 illustrates how bonds are actually listed in the reporting of the bond markets. The exhibit lists two types of IBM bonds that were traded on a particular day. The portion immediately after the company name—for example, "6⅜03"—indicates that the face rate of interest is 6⅜% and the due date of the bonds is the year 2003. The next column—for example, "6.5"—indicates that the bond investor who purchased the bonds on that day will receive a yield of 6.5%. The column labeled "vol" indicates the number of bonds, in thousands, that were bought and sold during the day. The column labeled "close" indicates the market price of the bonds at the end of the day. For example, the first issue of IBM bonds closed at 98¾, which means that the price was 98¾% of the face value of the bonds. These bonds are trading at a discount because the face rate (6⅜%) is less than the market rate of 6.5%. The bonds in the second issue—"7¼05"—have a face rate of 7¼%, will become due in the year 2005, and closed at 101½, or at a premium. The net change column indicates the change in the bond price that occurred for the day's trading.

www.ibm.com

PREMIUM OR DISCOUNT ON BONDS

Premium or **discount** represents the difference between the face value and the issue price of a bond. We may state the relationship as follows:

LO 4 Understand the effect on the balance sheet of issuance of bonds.

$$\text{Premium} = \text{Issue Price} - \text{Face Value}$$

$$\text{Discount} = \text{Face Value} - \text{Issue Price}$$

In other words, when issue price exceeds face value, the bonds have sold at a premium, and when the face value exceeds the issue price, the bonds have sold at a discount.

We will continue with the Discount Firm example to illustrate the accounting for bonds sold at a discount. Discount Firm's bonds sold at a discount calculated as follows:

$$\text{Discount} = \$10,000 - \$9,366$$

$$\text{Discount} = \$634$$

The effect on Discount Firm's accounting equation as a result of the issuance of the bonds is as follows:

BALANCE SHEET					INCOME STATEMENT
ASSETS	**=**	**LIABILITIES**	**+**	**OWNERS' EQUITY**	**+ REVENUES – EXPENSES**
Cash 9,366		Bonds Payable 10,000			
		Discount on Bonds Payable (634)			

The Discount on Bonds Payable account is shown as a contra liability on the balance sheet in conjunction with the Bonds Payable account and is a deduction from that account. If Discount Firm prepared a balance sheet immediately after the bond issuance, the following would appear in the Long-Term Liabilities category of the balance sheet:

```
Long-Term Liabilities:
  Bonds Payable                              $10,000
  Less: Discount on Bonds Payable                634
                                             $ 9,366
```

The Discount Firm example has illustrated a situation in which the market rate of a bond issue is higher than the face rate. Now, we will examine the opposite situation, when the face rate exceeds the market rate. Again, we are interested in calculating the issue price of the bonds.

Issuing at a Premium   Suppose that on January 1, 2001, Premium Firm wants to issue the same bonds as in the previous example: $10,000 face value bonds, with an 8% face rate of interest and with interest paid annually each year for four years. Assume, however, that the market rate of interest is 6% for similar bonds. The issue price is calculated as the present value of the annuity of interest payments plus the present value of the principal at the market rate of interest. The calculations are as follows:

$800 × 3.465 (factor from Table 9-4 for 4 periods, 6%)	$ 2,772
$10,000 × .792 (factor from Table 9-2 for 4 periods, 6%)	7,920
Issue price	$10,692

We have calculated that the bonds would be issued for $10,692. Because the bonds would be issued at an amount that is higher than the face value amount, they would be issued at a premium. The amount of the premium is calculated as follows:

$$Premium = \$10,692 - \$10,000$$

$$Premium = \$692$$

The effect on the accounting equation of the issuance of the bonds at a premium is as follows:

			BALANCE SHEET					INCOME STATEMENT
	ASSETS	=	LIABILITIES		+	OWNERS' EQUITY	+	REVENUES – EXPENSES
Cash	10,692		Bonds Payable	10,000				
			Premium on Bonds Payable	692				

The account Premium on Bonds Payable is an addition to the Bonds Payable account. If Premium Firm presented a balance sheet immediately after the bond issuance, the Long-Term Liabilities category of the balance sheet would appear as follows:

```
Long-Term Liabilities:
  Bonds Payable                              $10,000
  Plus: Premium on Bonds Payable                 692
                                             $10,692
```

You should learn two important points from the Discount Firm and Premium Firm examples. First, you should be able to determine whether a bond will sell at a premium or discount by the relationship that exists between the face rate and the market rate of interest. *Premium* and *discount* do not mean "good" and "bad." Premium or discount arises solely because of the difference that exists between the face rate and the market rate of interest for a bond issue. The same relationship always exists, so that the following statements hold true:

If Market Rate = Face Rate, THEN bonds are issued at face value amount.

If Market Rate > Face Rate, THEN bonds are issued at a discount.

If Market Rate < Face Rate, THEN bonds are issued at a premium.

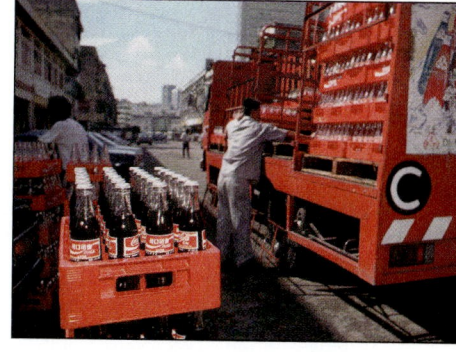

Coke's international sales are a major part of its growth strategy. This Malaysian delivery truck reflects what Coke hopes will be good news in its Middle and Far East Group. In its 1999 annual report, Coke states: "We remain focused on long-term opportunities in these populous markets, and continue to invest in our brands and infrastructure."

The examples also illustrate a second important point. The relationship between interest rates and bond prices is always inverse. To understand the term *inverse relationship*, refer to the Discount Firm and Premium Firm examples. The bonds of the two firms are identical in all respects except for the market rate of interest. When the market rate was 10%, the bond issue price was $9,366 (the Discount Firm example). When the market rate was 6%, the bond issue price increased to $10,692 (the Premium Firm example). The examples illustrate that as interest rates decrease, prices on the bond markets increase and that as interest rates increase, bond prices decrease.

Many investors in the stock market perceive that they are taking a great deal of risk with their capital. In truth, bond investors are taking substantial risk, too. The most obvious risk is that the company will fail and not be able to pay its debts. But another risk is that interest rates on comparable investments will rise. Interest rate risk can have a devastating impact on the current-market value of bonds. One way to minimize interest rate risk is to hold the bond to maturity, at which point the company must pay the face amount.

BOND AMORTIZATION

Purpose of Amortization   The amount of interest expense that should be reflected on a firm's income statement for bonds payable is the true, or effective, interest. The effective interest should reflect the face rate of interest as well as interest that results from issuing the bond at a premium or discount. To reflect that interest component, the amount initially recorded in the Premium on Bonds Payable or the Discount on Bonds Payable account must be amortized or spread over the life of the bond.

Amortization refers to the process of transferring an amount from the discount or premium account to interest expense each time period to adjust interest expense. One commonly used method of amortization is the effective interest method. We will illustrate how to amortize a discount amount and then how to amortize a premium amount.

To illustrate amortization of a discount, we need to return to our Discount Firm example introduced earlier. We have seen that the issue price of the bond could be calculated as $9,366, resulting in a contra-liability balance of $634 in the Discount on Bonds Payable account (see the accounting equation on page 457). But what does the initial balance of the Discount account really represent? The discount should be thought of as additional interest that Discount Firm must pay over and above the 8% face rate. Remember that Discount received only $9,366 but must repay the full principal of $10,000 at the bond due date. For that reason, the $634 of discount is an additional interest cost that must be reflected as interest expense. It is reflected as interest expense by the process of amortization. In other words, interest expense is made up of two components: cash interest and amortization. We will now consider how to amortize premium or discount.

LO 5 Find the amortization of premium or discount using effective interest amortization.

Effective Interest Method: Impact on Expense   The **effective interest method of amortization** amortizes discount or premium in a manner that produces a constant effective interest rate from period to period. The *dollar amount* of interest expense will vary from period to period, but the *rate* of interest will be constant. This interest rate is referred to as the *effective interest rate* and is equal to the market rate of interest at the time the bonds are issued.

To illustrate this point, we introduce two new terms. The **carrying value** of bonds is represented by the following:

Carrying Value = Face Value – Unamortized Discount

For example, the carrying value of the bonds for our Discount Firm example, as of the date of issuance of January 1, 2001, could be calculated as follows:

$$\$10,000 - \$634 = \$9,366$$

In those situations in which there is a premium instead of a discount, carrying value is represented by the following:

Carrying Value = Face Value + Unamortized Premium

For example, the carrying value of the bonds for our Premium Firm example, as of the date of issuance of January 1, 2001, could be calculated as follows:

$$\$10,000 + \$692 = \$10,692$$

The second term has been suggested earlier. The *effective rate of interest* is represented by the following:

Effective Rate = Annual Interest Expense/Carrying Value

Effective Interest Method: An Example   The amortization table in Exhibit 10-4 illustrates effective interest amortization of the bond discount for our Discount Firm example.

As illustrated in Exhibit 10-4, the effective interest method of amortization is based on several important concepts. The relationships can be stated in equation form as follows:

Cash Interest (in Column 1)   = Bond Face Value × Face Rate

Interest Expense (in Column 2)   = Carrying Value × Effective Rate

Discount Amortized (in Column 3) = Interest Expense − Cash Interest

The first column of the exhibit indicates that the cash interest to be paid is $800 ($10,000 × 8%). The second column indicates the annual interest expense at the effective rate of interest (market rate at the time of issuance). This is a constant rate of interest (10% in our example) and is calculated by multiplying the carrying value *as of the beginning of the period* times the market rate of interest. In 2001, the interest expense is $937 ($9,366 × 10%). Note that the amount of interest expense changes each year because the carrying value changes as discount is amortized. The amount of discount amortized each year in Column 3 is the difference between the cash interest in Column 1 and the interest expense in Column 2. Again, note that the amount of discount amortized changes in each of the four years. Finally, the carrying value in Column 4 is the previous year's carrying value plus the discount amortized in

EXHIBIT 10-4   Discount Amortization: Effective Interest Method of Amortization

Date	Column 1 Cash Interest	Column 2 Interest Expense	Column 3 Discount Amortized	Column 4 Carrying Value
	8%	10%	Col. 2 − Col. 1	
1/1/2001	—	—	—	$ 9,366
12/31/2001	$800	$937	$137	9,503
12/31/2002	800	950	150	9,653
12/31/2003	800	965	165	9,818
12/31/2004	800	982	182	10,000

Column 3. When bonds are issued at a discount, the carrying value starts at an amount less than face value and increases each period until it reaches the face value amount.

Exhibit 10-4 is the basis for determining the effect of amortization on the firm's financial statements. The effect of the interest payment and the amortization of discount for 2001 (note the December 31, 2001, line of the table) is as follows:

BALANCE SHEET						INCOME STATEMENT	
ASSETS	**=**	**LIABILITIES**	**+**	**OWNERS' EQUITY**	**+**	**REVENUES – EXPENSES**	
Cash (800)		Discount on Bonds Payable		137		Interest Expense	(937)

contra acc → builds up value of

The balance of the Discount on Bonds Payable account as of December 31, 2001, would be calculated as follows:

Beginning balance, January 1, 2001	$634
Less: Amount amortized	137
Ending balance, December 31, 2001	$497

The December 31, 2001, balance represents the amount *unamortized,* or the amount that will be amortized in future time periods. On the balance sheet presented as of December 31, 2001, the unamortized portion of the discount appears as the balance of the Discount on Bonds Payable account as follows:

Long-term liabilities	
Bonds payable	$10,000
Less: Discount on bonds payable	497
	$ 9,503

The process of amortization would continue for four years, until the balance of the Discount on Bonds Payable account has been reduced to zero. By the end of 2004, all the balance of the Discount on Bonds Payable account will have been transferred to the Interest Expense account and represents an increase in interest expense each period.

The amortization of a premium has an impact opposite that of the amortization of a discount. We will use our Premium Firm example to illustrate. Recall that on January 1, 2001, Premium Firm issued $10,000 face value bonds with a face rate of interest of 8%. At the time the bonds were issued, the market rate was 6%, resulting in an issue price of $10,692 and a balance in the Premium on Bonds Payable account of $692.

The amortization table in Exhibit 10-5 illustrates effective interest amortization of the bond premium for Premium Firm. As the exhibit illustrates, effective interest amortization of a premium is based on the same concepts as amortization of a discount. The following relationships still hold true:

Cash Interest (in Column 1)　　= Bond Face Value × Face Rate

Interest Expense (in Column 2) = Carrying Value　× Effective Rate

The first column of the exhibit indicates that the cash interest to be paid is $800 ($10,000 × 8%). The second column indicates the annual interest expense at the effective rate. In 2001, the interest expense is $642 ($10,692 × 6%). Note, however, two differences between Exhibit 10-4 and Exhibit 10-5. In the amortization of a premium, the cash interest in Column 1 exceeds the interest expense in Column 2. Therefore, the premium amortized is defined as follows:

Premium Amortized (in Column 3) = Cash Interest − Interest Expense

Also note that the carrying value in Column 4 starts at an amount higher than the face value of $10,000 ($10,692) and is amortized downward until it reaches face value. Therefore, the

> **Study Tip**
>
> Amortization of a discount increases interest expense. Amortization of a premium reduces interest expense.

EXHIBIT 10-5 Premium Amortization: Effective Interest Method of Amortization

Date	Column 1 Cash Interest	Column 2 Interest Expense	Column 3 Premium Amortized	Column 4 Carrying Value
	8%	6%	Col. 1 − Col. 2	
1/1/2001	—	—	—	$10,692
12/31/2001	$800	$642	$158	10,534
12/31/2002	800	632	168	10,366
12/31/2003	800	622	178	10,188
12/31/2004	800	612	188	10,000

carrying value at the end of each year is the carrying value at the beginning of the period minus the premium amortized for that year. For example, the carrying value in Exhibit 10-5 at the end of 2001 ($10,534) was calculated by subtracting the premium amortized for 2001 ($158 in Column 3) from the carrying value at the beginning of 2001 ($10,692).

Exhibit 10-5 is the basis for determining the effect of amortization of a premium on the firm's financial statements. The effect of the interest payment and the amortization of premium for 2001 (note the December 31, 2001, line of the table) is as follows:

BALANCE SHEET						INCOME STATEMENT	
ASSETS	**=**	**LIABILITIES**	**+**	**OWNERS' EQUITY**	**+**	**REVENUES − EXPENSES**	
Cash (800)		Premium on Bonds Payable (158)				Interest Expense	(642)

The balance of the Premium on Bonds Payable account as of December 31, 2001, would be calculated as follows:

Beginning balance, January 1, 2001	$692
Less: Amount amortized	158
Ending balance, December 31, 2001	$534

The December 31, 2001, balance represents the amount *unamortized,* or the amount that will be amortized in future time periods. On the balance sheet presented as of December 31, 2001, the unamortized portion of the premium appears as the balance of the Premium on Bonds Payable account as follows:

Long-term liabilities	
Bonds payable	$10,000
Plus: Premium on bonds payable	534
	$10,534

The process of amortization would continue for four years, until the balance of the Premium on Bonds Payable account has been reduced to zero. By the end of 2004, all of the balance of the Premium on Bonds Payable account will have been transferred to the Interest Expense account and represents a reduction of interest expense each period.

Two-Minute Review

1. How do you calculate the issue price of a bond?

2. What effect does amortizing a premium have on the amount of interest expense for the bond? What effect does amortizing a discount have?

NOTE 8 » COMMITMENTS AND CONTINGENCIES

Leases

The Company leases office, warehouse and showroom space, retail stores and office equipment under operating leases, which expire not later than 2023. The Company normalizes fixed escalations in rental expense under its operating leases. Minimum annual rentals under non-cancelable operating leases, excluding operating cost escalations and contingent rental amounts based upon retail sales, are payable as follows: (in thousands)

Fiscal Year Ending March 31,	
2000	$17,038
2001	14,787
2002	13,000
2003	11,166
2004	9,140
Thereafter	38,726

Rent expense was $16,362, $12,551 and $8,911 for the years ended March 31, 1999, 1998 and 1997, respectively.

> Operating leases can be used as an important source of financing.

Operating Leases

You have already accounted for operating leases in previous chapters when recording rent expense and prepaid rent. A rental agreement for a limited time period is also a lease agreement.

Suppose, for example, that Lessee Firm wants to lease a car for a new salesperson. A lease agreement is signed with Lessor Dealer on January 1, 2001, to lease a car for the year for $4,000, payable on December 31, 2001. Typically, a car lease does not transfer title at the end of the term, does not include a bargain-purchase price, and does not last for more than 75% of the car's life. In addition, the present value of the lease payments is not 90% of the car's value. Because the lease does not meet any of the specified criteria, it should be presented as an operating lease. Lessee Firm would simply record lease expense, or rent expense, of $4,000 for the year.

Although operating leases are not recorded on the balance sheet by the lessee, they are mentioned in financial statement footnotes. The FASB requires footnote disclosure of the amount of future lease obligations for leases that are considered operating leases. Exhibit 10-6 provides a portion of the footnote from Tommy Hilfiger Corporation's 1999 annual report. The footnote reveals that Tommy Hilfiger has used operating leases as an important source of financing and has significant off-balance-sheet commitments in future periods as a result. An investor might want to add this off-balance-sheet item to the debt on the balance sheet to get a conservative view of the company's obligations.

www.tommy.com

more advantageous → can be kept off the books

Capital Leases

Capital leases are presented as assets and liabilities by the lessee because they meet one or more of the lease criteria. Suppose that Lessee Firm in the previous example wanted to lease a car for a longer period of time. Assume that on January 1, 2001, Lessee signs a lease agreement with Lessor Dealer to lease a car. The terms of the agreement specify that Lessee will make annual lease payments of $4,000 per year for five years, payable each December 31. Assume also that the lease specifies that at the end of the lease agreement, the title to the car is transferred to Lessee Firm. Lessee must decide how to account for the lease agreement.

The contractual arrangement between Lessee Firm and Lessor Dealer is called a lease agreement, but clearly the agreement is much different from a year-to-year lease arrangement. Essentially, Lessee Firm has acquired the right to use the asset for its entire life and does not need to return it to Lessor Dealer. You may call this agreement a lease, but it actually represents a purchase of the asset by Lessee with payments made over time.

The lease should be treated as a capital lease by Lessee because it meets at least one of the four criteria (it meets the first criterion concerning transfer of title). A capital lease must be recorded at its present value by Lessee as an asset and as an obligation. As of January 1, 2001, we must calculate the present value of the annual payments. If we assume an interest rate of 8%, the present value of the payments is $15,972 ($4,000 × an annuity factor of 3.993 from Table 9-4). The effect on Lessee Firm's accounting equation of treating the lease as a capital lease is as follows:

BALANCE SHEET					INCOME STATEMENT
ASSETS	=	LIABILITIES	+	OWNERS' EQUITY	+	REVENUES – EXPENSES
Leased Asset 15,972		Lease Obligation 15,972			

The Leased Asset account is a long-term asset similar to plant and equipment and represents the fact that Lessee has acquired the right to use and retain the asset. Because the leased asset represents depreciable property, depreciation must be reported for each of the five years of asset use. On December 31, 2001, Lessee presents depreciation of $3,194 ($15,972/5 years), assuming that the straight-line method is adopted. The effect of the depreciation is as follows:

BALANCE SHEET					INCOME STATEMENT
ASSETS	=	LIABILITIES	+	OWNERS' EQUITY	+	REVENUES – EXPENSES
					Depreciation Expense (3,194)
Accumulated Depreciation— Leased Asset (3,194)					

Depreciation of leased assets is referred to as *amortization* by some firms.

On December 31, Lessee Firm also must make a payment of $4,000 to Lessor Dealer. A portion of each payment represents interest on the obligation (loan), and the remainder represents a reduction of the principal amount. Each payment must be separated into its principal and interest components. Generally, the effective interest method is used for that purpose. An effective interest table can be established using the same concepts as were used to amortize a premium or discount on bonds payable.

Exhibit 10-7 illustrates the effective interest method applied to the Lessee Firm example. Note that the table begins with an obligation amount equal to the present value of the payments of $15,972. Each payment is separated into principal and interest amounts so that the amount of the loan obligation at the end of the lease agreement equals zero. The amortization table is the basis for the amounts that are reflected on the financial statement. Exhibit 10-7 indicates that the $4,000 payment in 2001 should be considered as interest of $1,278 (8% of $15,972) and reduction of principal of $2,722. The effect on the accounting equation of the December 31, 2001, payment is as follows:

BALANCE SHEET					INCOME STATEMENT
ASSETS	=	LIABILITIES	+	OWNERS' EQUITY	+	REVENUES – EXPENSES
Cash (4,000)		Lease Obligation (2,722)			Interest Expense (1,278)

Therefore, for a capital lease, Lessee Firm must record both an asset and a liability. The asset is reduced by the process of depreciation. The liability is reduced by reductions of principal using the effective interest method. According to Exhibit 10-7, the total lease obliga-

EXHIBIT 10-7 Lease Amortization: Effective Interest Method of Amortization

Date	Column 1 Lease Payment	Column 2 Interest Expense	Column 3 Reduction of Obligation	Column 4 Lease Obligation
		8%	Col. 1 − Col. 2	
1/1/2001	—	—	—	$15,972
12/31/2001	$4,000	$1,278	$2,722	13,250
12/31/2002	4,000	1,060	2,940	10,310
12/31/2003	4,000	825	3,175	7,135
12/31/2004	4,000	571	3,429	3,706
12/31/2005	4,000	294	3,706	–0–

(handwritten margin notes): just one interest rate for leases · present value of fut. lease payments

tion as of December 31, 2001, is $13,250. This amount must be separated into current and long-term categories. The portion of the liability that will be paid within one year of the balance sheet should be considered a current liability. Reference to Exhibit 10-7 indicates that the liability will be reduced by $2,940 in 2002, and that amount should be considered a current liability. The remaining amount of the liability, $10,310 ($13,250 − $2,940), should be considered long-term. On the balance sheet as of December 31, 2001, Lessee Firm reports the following balances related to the lease obligation:

Assets:		
Leased Assets	$15,972	
Less: Accumulated Depreciation	3,194	
		$12,778
Current Liabilities:		
Lease Obligation		$ 2,940
Long-Term Liabilities:		
Lease Obligation		$10,310

Notice that the depreciated asset does not equal the present value of the lease obligation. That is not unusual. For example, an automobile often may be completely depreciated but still have payments due on it.

The criteria used to determine whether a lease is an operating or a capital lease have provided a standard accounting treatment for all leases. The accounting for leases in foreign countries generally follows guidelines similar to those used in the United States. The criteria used in foreign countries to determine whether a lease is a capital lease are usually less detailed and less specific, however. As a result, capitalization of leases occurs less frequently in foreign countries than in the United States because of the increased use of judgment necessary in applying the accounting rules.

Two-Minute Review

1. When a lease is considered a capital lease to the lessee, what entry is made to initially record the lease agreement?

2. When the lessee makes a lease payment on a capital lease, how is the payment recorded?

(continued)

ANALYZING DEBT TO ASSESS A FIRM'S SOLVENCY

Long-term liabilities are a component of the "capital structure" of the company and are included in the calculation of the debt-to-equity ratio:

$$\text{Debt-to-Equity Ratio} = \frac{\text{Total Liabilities}}{\text{Total Stockholders' Equity}}$$

From *Concept*

TO PRACTICE 10.2

READING UNO RESTAURANT'S BALANCE SHEET Calculate the 1998 and 1999 debt-to-equity ratios for Uno. Did 1999's debt-to-equity ratio go up or down from 1998's?

For example, refer to the Liability category of PepsiCo's balance sheet given in Exhibit 10-1. PepsiCo's total liabilities are $10,670 million (current liabilities of $3,788; long-term debt of $2,812; other liabilities of $2,861; and deferred income taxes of $1,209). Its total stockholders' equity is $6,881 million. Therefore, the debt-to-equity ratio is $10,670/$6,881 or 1.55, which means that PepsiCo has 1.55 times as much debt as equity, a situation that is not uncommon for companies in the beverage industry.

Most investors would prefer to see equity rather than debt on the balance sheet. Debt, and its interest charges, make up a fixed obligation that must be repaid in a finite period of time. In contrast, equity never has to be repaid, and the dividends that are declared on it are optional. Stock investors view debt as a claim against the company that must be satisfied before they get a return on their money.

Other ratios used to measure the degree of debt obligation include the times interest earned ratio and the debt service coverage ratio:

$$\text{Times Interest Earned Ratio} = \frac{\text{Income before Interest and Tax}}{\text{Interest Expense}}$$

$$\text{Debt Service Coverage Ratio} = \frac{\text{Cash Flow from Operations before Interest and Tax}}{\text{Interest and Principal Payments}}$$

Lenders want to be sure that borrowers can pay the interest and repay the principal on a loan. Both of the preceding ratios, which will be explored in more detail in Chapter 13, reflect the degree to which a company can make its debt payments out of current cash flow.

HOW LONG-TERM LIABILITIES AFFECT THE STATEMENT OF CASH FLOWS

LO 8 Explain the effects that transactions involving long-term liabilities have on the statement of cash flows.

www.cocacola.com

Exhibit 10-8 indicates the impact that long-term liabilities have on a company's cash flow and their placement on the cash flow statement.

Most long-term liabilities are related to a firm's financing activities. Therefore, the change in the balance of each long-term liability account should be reflected in the Financing Activities category of the statement of cash flows. The decrease in a long-term liability account indicates that cash has been used to pay the liability. Therefore, in the cash flow statement, a decrease in a long-term liability account should appear as a subtraction or reduction. The increase in a long-term liability account indicates that the firm has obtained additional cash via a long-term obligation. Therefore, an increase in a long-term liability account should appear in the cash flow statement as an addition.

The cash flow statement of Coca-Cola Company is presented in Exhibit 10-9. Note that the Financing Activities category contains two items related to long-term liabilities.

FOCUS ON USERS

Long-Term Liabilities Help Reveal the Company's Future

Philip Yarrow, profiled in the previous chapter, talked about how current liabilities affect lending decisions. Rob Snow, a portfolio manager for FleetBoston Financial, here shares his views on how *long-term liabilities* come into play in his own risk-management and lending decisions. Rob says: "The risk management part of the job relates to performing financial and operational analysis of the companies we do business with, as well as analyzing the performance of the assets in the portfolio. In each of these cases, I am concerned with the long-term viability and success of the companies with whom we do business. The amount and composition of the debt on the company's balance sheet is an excellent predictor of future performance. It is a positive sign when a company is using long-term debt from a stable source to fund assets or activities that support future growth."

So, just as current liabilities reveal a company's near-term viability and its ability to pay back loans, long-term liabilities can help analysts forecast how a company will fare well into the future. In fact, Rob sees long-term liabilities as a company's investment in the future, and he offers an analogy to make the point: "Let's say that you need a car to get to work. You need to work to generate cash. If you can't afford to buy a car today, then you borrow the money to work to generate cash. If you can't afford to buy a car today, then you borrow the money even though the interest you pay on the car loan makes the purchase more expensive. Having the car today will dramatically improve your ability to succeed." Of course, not all debt is beneficial. Rob explains: "The amount of debt and whether it is long-term debt or short-term debt needs to be driven by the company's business model. A company with too much debt may eventually become trapped because it is unable to make interest payments and unable to take on new liabilities as a result of the existing leverage." It is the job of financial analysts like Rob, and Philip Yarrow in Chicago, to make judgments about whether the various liabilities that show up on the balance sheets will translate into a company's future growth.

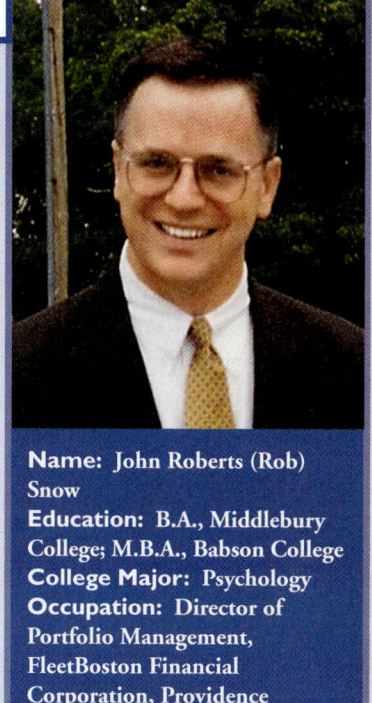

Name: John Roberts (Rob) Snow
Education: B.A., Middlebury College; M.B.A., Babson College
College Major: Psychology
Occupation: Director of Portfolio Management, FleetBoston Financial Corporation, Providence
Age: 32

EXHIBIT 10-8   Long-Term Liabilities on the Statement of Cash Flows

Item	Statement of Cash Flows	
	Operating Activities	
	Net income	xxx
Increase in deferred tax	....	+
Decrease in deferred tax	....	−
	Investing Activities	
	Financing Activities	
Increase in liability	....	+
Decrease in liability	....	−

Consolidated Statements of Cash Flows
The Coca-Cola Company and Subsidiaries

KO_ar 99_p_ 47

Year Ended December 31, (In millions)	1999	1998	1997
OPERATING ACTIVITIES			
Net income	$ 2,431	$ 3,533	$ 4,129
Depreciation and amortization	792	645	626
Deferred income taxes	97	(38)	380
Equity income, net of dividends	292	31	(108)
Foreign currency adjustments	(41)	21	37
Gains on issuances of stock by equity investees	—	(27)	(363)
Gains on sales of assets, including bottling interests	(49)	(306)	(639)
Other operating charges	799	73	60
Other items	119	51	(42)
Net change in operating assets and liabilities	(557)	(550)	(47)
Net cash provided by operating activities	3,883	3,433	4,033
INVESTING ACTIVITIES			
Acquisitions and investments, principally trademarks and bottling companies	(1,876)	(1,428)	(1,100)
Purchases of investments and other assets	(518)	(610)	(459)
Proceeds from disposals of investments and other assets	176	1,036	1,999
Purchases of property, plant and equipment	(1,069)	(863)	(1,093)
Proceeds from disposals of property, plant and equipment	45	54	71
Other investing activities	(179)	(350)	82
Net cash used in investing activities	(3,421)	(2,161)	(500)
FINANCING ACTIVITIES			
Issuances of debt	3,411	1,818	155
Payments of debt	(2,455)	(410)	(751)
Issuances of stock	168	302	150
Purchases of stock for treasury	(15)	(1,563)	(1,262)
Dividends	(1,580)	(1,480)	(1,387)
Net cash used in financing activities	(471)	(1,333)	(3,095)
EFFECT OF EXCHANGE RATE CHANGES ON CASH AND CASH EQUIVALENTS	(28)	(28)	(134)
CASH AND CASH EQUIVALENTS			
Net increase (decrease) during the year	(37)	(89)	304
Balance at beginning of the year	1,648	1,737	1,433
Balance at end of year	$ 1,611	$ 1,648	$ 1,737

> Changes in long-term debt generally affect the financing activities category.

See Notes to Consolidated Financial Statements.

From Concept

TO PRACTICE 10.3

READING GATEWAY'S STATEMENT OF CASH FLOWS   Did Gateway pay off any long-term debt during 1999? Is this a positive or negative amount on the cash flow statement? In which category of the statement do you find the change?

In 1999, long-term debt was issued for $3,411 million and is an addition to cash. This indicates that Coca-Cola increased its cash position by borrowings. Second, the payment of debt is listed as a deduction of $2,455 million. This indicates that Coca-Cola paid long-term liabilities resulting in a reduction of cash.

Although most long-term liabilities are reflected in the Financing Activities category of the statement of cash flows, there are exceptions. The most notable exception involves the Deferred Tax account (discussed in Appendix 10A). The change in this account is reflected in the Operating Activities category of the statement of cash flows. This presentation is necessary because the Deferred Tax account is related to an operating item, income tax expense. For example, in Exhibit 10-9, Coca-Cola listed $97 million in the Operating Activities category of the 1999 statement of cash flows. This indicates that $97 million more was recorded as expense than was paid out in cash. Therefore, the amount is a positive amount in, or an addition to, the Operating Activities category.

WARMUP EXERCISES

Warmup Exercise 10-1

A bond, due in 10 years, with face value of $1,000 and face rate of interest of 8%, is issued when the market rate of interest is 6%.

Required

1. What is the issue price of the bond?
2. What is the amount of premium or discount on the bond at the time of issuance?
3. What amount of interest expense will be shown on the income statement for the first year of the bond?
4. What amount of the premium or discount will be amortized during the first year of the bond?

Warmup Exercise 10-2

You have signed an agreement to lease a car for four years and will make annual payments of $4,000 at the end of each year. (Assume that the lease meets the criteria for a capital lease.)

Required

1. Calculate the present value of the lease payments, assuming an 8% interest rate.
2. Present the effect on the accounting equation of the signing of the lease.
3. When the first lease payment is made, what portion of the payment will be considered interest?

SOLUTION TO WARMUP EXERCISES

Warmup Exercise 10-1

1. The issue price of the bond would be calculated as the present value:

$80 (7.360) = $ 588.80	using Table 9-4 where $i = 6\%$ and $n = 10$
plus $1,000 (.558) = 558.00	using Table 9-2 where $i = 6\%$ and $n = 10$
Issue Price $1,146.80	

2. The amount of the premium is the difference between the issue price and the face value:

$$\text{Premium} = \$1,146.80 - \$1,000$$
$$= \$146.80$$

3. The amount of interest expense can be calculated as follows:

$$\text{Interest Expense} = \$1,146.80 \times .06$$
$$= \$68.81$$

4. The amount that will be amortized can be calculated as follows:

$$\text{Amortized} = \text{Cash Interest} - \text{Interest Expense}$$
$$= (\$1,000 \times .08) - (\$1,146.80 \times .06)$$
$$= \$80.00 - \$68.81$$
$$= \$11.19$$

Warmup Exercise 10-2

1. The present value of the lease payments can be calculated as follows:

$$\text{Present Value} = \$4,000 (3.312) \text{ using Table 9-4 where } i = 8\%, n = 4$$
$$= \$13,248$$

2.

BALANCE SHEET						INCOME STATEMENT
ASSETS	=	LIABILITIES	+	OWNERS' EQUITY	+	REVENUES – EXPENSES
Leased Asset 13,248		Lease Obligation 13,248				

3. The amount of interest can be calculated as follows:

$$\text{Interest} = \$13,248 \times .08$$
$$= \$1,059.84$$

REVIEW PROBLEM

The following items pertain to the liabilities of Brent Foods. You may assume that Brent Foods began business on January 1, 2001, and, therefore, the beginning balance of all accounts was zero.

a. On January 1, 2001, Brent Foods issued bonds with a face value of $50,000. The bonds are due in five years and have a face interest rate of 10%. The market rate on January 1 for similar bonds was 12%. The bonds pay interest annually each December 31. Brent has chosen to use the effective interest method of amortization for any premium or discount on the bonds.

b. On December 31, Brent Foods signed a lease agreement with Cordova Leasing. The agreement requires Brent to make annual lease payments of $3,000 per year for four years, with the first payment due on December 31, 2002. The agreement stipulates that ownership of the property is transferred to Brent at the end of the four-year lease. Assume that an 8% interest rate is used for the leasing transaction.

c. On January 1, 2002, Brent redeems its bonds payable at the specified redemption price of 101. Because this item occurs in 2002, it does not affect the balance sheet prepared for year-end 2001.

Required

1. Determine the effect on the accounting equation of the December 31, 2001 interest adjustment in item **a** and the signing of the lease in item **b**.

2. Develop the Long-Term Liabilities section of Brent Foods's balance sheet as of December 31, 2001, based on items **a** and **b**. You do not need to consider the footnotes that accompany the balance sheet.

3. Would the company prefer to treat the lease in item **b** as an operating lease? Why?

4. Calculate the gain or loss on the bond redemption for item **c** and indicate how it should be reported on the 2002 income statement.

Solution to Review Problem

1. a. The issue price of the bonds on January 1 must be calculated as the present value of the interest payments and the present value of the principal, as follows:

$ 5,000 × 3.605	$18,025
$50,000 × 0.567	28,350
Issue price	$46,375

The amount of the discount is calculated as follows:

$$\$50,000 - \$46,375 = \$3,625$$

The effect of the interest and amortization as of December 31, 2001, is as follows:

BALANCE SHEET					INCOME STATEMENT	
ASSETS	**=**	**LIABILITIES**	**+**	**OWNERS' EQUITY**	**+ REVENUES – EXPENSES**	
Cash (5,000)		Discount on Bonds Payable 565			Interest Expense	(5,565)

The interest expense is calculated using the effective interest method by multiplying the carrying value of the bonds times the market rate of interest ($46,375 × 12%).

Brent must show two accounts in the Long-Term Liabilities section of the balance sheet: Bonds Payable of $50,000 and Discount on Bonds Payable of $3,060 ($3,625 less $565 amortized).

b. The lease meets the criteria to be a capital lease. Brent must report the lease as an asset and report the obligation for lease payments as a liability. The transaction should be reported at the present value of the lease payments, $9,936 (computed by multiplying $3,000 times the annuity factor of 3.312). The effect of treating the lease as a capital lease is as follows:

BALANCE SHEET						INCOME STATEMENT
ASSETS	=	LIABILITIES	+	OWNERS' EQUITY	+	REVENUES − EXPENSES
Leased Asset	9,936	Lease Obligation	9,936			

Because the lease agreement was signed on December 31, 2001, it is not necessary to amortize the Lease Obligation account in 2001. The account should be stated in the Long-Term Liabilities section of Brent's balance sheet at $9,936.

2. The Long-Term Liabilities section of Brent's balance sheet for December 31, 2001, on the basis of items **a** and **b** is as follows:

BRENT FOODS
PARTIAL BALANCE SHEET
AS OF DECEMBER 31, 2001

Long-Term Liabilities:		
Bonds Payable	$50,000	
Less: Unamortized discount on bonds payable	3,060	$46,940
Lease obligation		9,936
Total Long-Term Liabilities		$56,876

3. The company would prefer that the lease be an operating lease because it would not have to report the asset or liability on the balance sheet. This off-balance-sheet financing may give a more favorable impression of the company.

4. Brent must calculate the loss on the bond redemption as the difference between the carrying value of the bonds ($46,940) and the redemption price ($50,000 × 1.01). The amount of the loss is calculated as follows:

$50,500 − $46,940 = $3,560 loss on redemption

The loss should be reported as an extraordinary item on the 2002 income statement.

APPENDIX 10A

ACCOUNTING TOOLS: OTHER LIABILITIES

In this appendix, we will discuss two additional items that are found in the long-term liabilities category of many companies: deferred taxes and pensions. Both items are complex financial arrangements, and our primary purpose is to make you aware of their existence when reading financial statements.

DEFERRED TAX   *equivalent to equity*

The financial statements of most major firms include an item titled Deferred Income Tax or Deferred Tax (see PepsiCo's deferred taxes in Exhibit 10-1 and Coca-Cola's in the chapter opener). In most cases, the account appears in the Long-Term Liabilities section of the balance sheet, and the dollar amount may be large enough to catch the user's attention. For another example, Exhibit 10-10 illustrates the presentation of deferred tax in the 1999 comparative balance sheets of Tribune Company and Subsidiaries. The Deferred Income Taxes account is listed immediately after Long-Term Debt and for Tribune Company should be considered a long-term liability. At the end of 1999, the firm had more than

LO 9 Explain deferred taxes and calculate the deferred tax liability.

www.pepsico.com
www.cocacola.com
www.tribune.com

Liabilities & Shareholders' Equity		Dec. 26, 1999	Dec. 27, 1998
Current Liabilities	Long-term debt due within one year	$ 30,689	$ 29,905
	Accounts payable	176,552	157,708
	Employee compensation and benefits	122,333	114,202
	Contracts payable for broadcast rights	276,307	260,264
	Deferred income	64,419	55,097
	Income taxes	2,226	59,607
	Accrued liabilities	188,070	151,347
	Total current liabilities	860,596	828,130
Long-Term Debt	PHONES debt related to America Online stock	1,328,480	–
	Other long-term debt (less portions due within one year)	1,365,712	1,616,256
Other Non-Current Liabilities	Deferred income taxes	1,251,377	701,778
	Contracts payable for broadcast rights	269,698	268,099
	Compensation and other obligations	251,930	164,690
	Total other non-current liabilities	1,773,005	1,134,567
Commitments and Contingent Liabilities (see Notes 9 and 11)		–	–
Shareholders' Equity	Series B convertible preferred stock (without par value)		
	Authorized: 1,600,000 shares		
	Issued and outstanding: 1,282,665 shares in 1999 and 1,337,926 shares in 1998 (liquidation value $220 per share)	281,093	293,203
	Common stock (without par value) Authorized: 400,000,000 shares; 327,086,632 shares issued	1,018	1,018
	Additional paid-in capital	136,108	209,474
	Retained earnings	4,195,318	2,819,474
	Treasury stock (at cost) 88,071,818 shares in 1999 and 88,255,022 shares in 1998	(1,430,900)	(1,414,661)
	Treasury stock held by Tribune Stock Compensation Fund (at cost) 1,223,384 shares in 1999 and 827,548 shares in 1998	(61,909)	(26,602)
	Unearned compensation related to ESOP	(127,595)	(156,495)
	Accumulated other comprehensive income	476,765	631,206
	Total shareholders' equity	3,469,898	2,356,617
	Total liabilities and shareholders' equity	$8,797,691	$5,935,570

> Deferred tax is a liability for Tribune Company and Subsidiaries

$1,251 million of deferred tax. The size of that account relative to the other liabilities should raise questions concerning its exact meaning. In fact, deferred income taxes represent one of the most misunderstood aspects of financial statements. In this section, we will attempt to address some of the questions concerning deferred taxes.

Deferred tax is an amount that reconciles the differences between the accounting done for purposes of financial reporting to stockholders ("book" purposes) and the accounting done for tax purposes. It may surprise you that U.S. firms are allowed to use accounting methods for financial reporting that differ from those used for tax calculations. The reason is that the Internal Revenue Service defines income and expense differently than does the Financial Accounting Standards Board. As a result, companies tend to use accounting methods that minimize income for tax purposes but maximize income in the annual report to stockholders. This is not true in some foreign countries where financial accounting and

www.irs.gov
www.fasb.org

tax accounting are more closely aligned. Firms in those countries do not report deferred tax because the difference between methods is not significant.

When differences between financial and tax reporting do occur, we can classify them into two types: permanent and temporary. **Permanent differences** occur when an item is included in the tax calculation and is never included for book purposes—or vice versa, when an item is included for book purposes but not for tax purposes.

For example, the tax laws allow taxpayers to exclude interest on certain investments, usually state and municipal bonds, from their income. These are generally called *tax-exempt bonds*. If a corporation buys tax-exempt bonds, it does not have to declare the interest as income for tax purposes. When the corporation develops its income statement for stockholders (book purposes), however, the interest is included and appears in the Interest Income account. Therefore, tax-exempt interest represents a permanent difference between tax and book calculations.

Temporary differences occur when an item affects both the book and the tax calculations but not in the same time period. A difference caused by depreciation methods is the most common type of temporary difference. In previous chapters, you have learned that depreciation may be calculated using a straight-line method or an accelerated method, such as the double declining-balance method. Most firms do not use the same depreciation method for book and tax purposes, however. Generally, straight-line depreciation is used for book purposes and an accelerated method is used for tax purposes because accelerated depreciation lowers taxable income—at least in early years—and, therefore, reduces the tax due. The IRS refers to this accelerated method as the *Modified Accelerated Cost Recovery System (MACRS)*. It is similar to other accelerated depreciation methods in that it allows the firm to take larger depreciation deductions for tax purposes in the early years of the asset and smaller deductions in the later years. Over the life of the depreciable asset, the total depreciation using straight-line is equal to that using MACRS. Therefore, this difference is an example of a temporary difference between book and tax reporting.

The Deferred Tax account is used to reconcile the differences between the accounting for book purposes and for tax purposes. It is important to distinguish between permanent and temporary differences because the FASB has ruled that not all differences should affect the Deferred Tax account. The Deferred Tax account should reflect temporary differences but not items that are permanent differences between book accounting and tax reporting.[4]

Example of Deferred Tax   Assume that Startup Firm begins business on January 1, 2001. During 2001, the firm has sales of $6,000 and has no expenses other than depreciation and income tax at the rate of 40%. Startup has depreciation on only one asset. That asset was purchased on January 1, 2001, for $10,000 and has a four-year life. Startup has decided to use the straight-line depreciation method for financial reporting purposes. Startup's accountants have chosen to use MACRS for tax purposes, however, resulting in $4,000 depreciation in 2001 and a decline of $1,000 per year thereafter.

The depreciation amounts for each of the four years for Startup's asset are as follows:

Year	Tax Depreciation	Book Depreciation	Difference
2001	$ 4,000	$ 2,500	$1,500
2002	3,000	2,500	500
2003	2,000	2,500	(500)
2004	1,000	2,500	(1,500)
Totals	$10,000	$10,000	$–0–

Startup's tax calculation for 2001 is based on the accelerated depreciation of $4,000, as follows:

[4]*Statement of Financial Accounting Standards No. 109*, "Accounting for Income Taxes" (Stamford, Conn.: FASB, 1992).

Sales	$6,000
Depreciation Expense	4,000
Taxable Income	$2,000
× Tax Rate	40%
Tax Payable to IRS	$ 800

For the year 2001, Startup owes $800 of tax to the Internal Revenue Service. This amount is ordinarily recorded as tax payable until the time it is remitted.

Startup wants also to develop an income statement to send to the stockholders. What amount should be shown as tax expense on the income statement? You may guess that the Tax Expense account on the income statement should reflect $800 because that is the amount to be paid to the IRS. That is not true in this case, however. Remember that the tax payable amount was calculated using the depreciation method that Startup chose for tax purposes. The income statement must be calculated using the straight-line method, which Startup uses for book purposes. Therefore, Startup's income statement for 2001 appears as follows:

Sales	$6,000
Depreciation Expense	2,500
Income before Tax	$3,500
Tax Expense (40%)	1,400
Net Income	$2,100

The effect on Startup's financial statements is as follows:

BALANCE SHEET						INCOME STATEMENT	
ASSETS	=	LIABILITIES	+	OWNERS' EQUITY	+	REVENUES – EXPENSES	
		Tax Payable 800				Tax Expense	(1,400)
		Deferred Tax 600					

The Deferred Tax account is a balance sheet account. A balance in it reflects the fact that Startup has received a tax benefit by recording accelerated depreciation, in effect delaying the ultimate obligation to the IRS. To be sure, the amount of deferred tax still represents a liability of Startup. The Deferred Tax account balance of $600 represents the amount of the 2001 temporary difference of $1,500 times the tax rate of 40% ($1,500 × 40% = $600).

What can we learn from the Startup example? First, when you see a firm's income statement, the amount listed as tax expense does not represent the amount of cash paid to the government for taxes. Accrual accounting procedures require that the tax expense amount be calculated using the accounting methods chosen for book purposes.

Second, when you see a firm's balance sheet, the amount in the Deferred Tax account reflects all the temporary differences between the accounting methods chosen for tax and book purposes. The accounting and financial communities are severely divided on whether the Deferred Tax account represents a "true" liability. For one thing, many investment analysts do not view it as a real liability because they have noticed that it continues to grow year after year. Others look at it as a bookkeeping item that is simply there to balance the books. The FASB has taken the stance that deferred tax is an amount that results in a future obligation and meets the definition of a liability. The controversy concerning deferred taxes is likely to continue for many years.

PENSIONS

LO 10 Understand the meaning of a pension obligation and the effect of pensions on the long-term liability category of the balance sheet.

Many large firms establish pension plans to provide income to employees after their retirement. These pension plans often cover a large number of employees and involve millions of dollars. The large amounts in pension funds have become a major force in our economy, representing billions of dollars in stocks and bonds. In fact, pension funds are among the major "institutional investors" that have an enormous economic impact on our stock and bond exchanges.

Pensions are complex financial arrangements that involve difficult estimates and projections developed by specialists and actuaries. Pension plans also involve very difficult accounting issues requiring a wide range of estimates and assumptions about future cash flows.

We will concern ourselves with two accounting questions related to pensions. First, the employer must report the cost of the pension plan as an expense over some time period. How should that expense be reported? Second, the employer's financial statements should reflect a measure of the liability associated with a pension plan. What is the liability for future pension amounts, and how should it be recorded or disclosed? Our discussion will begin with the recording of pension expense.

Pensions on the Income Statement Most pension plans are of the following form:

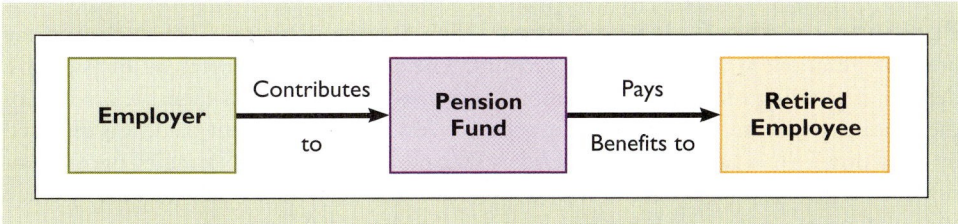

Normally, the employer must make payments to the pension fund at least annually, perhaps more frequently. This is often referred to as *funding the pension* or as the **funding payment.** *Funding* simply means that the employer has contributed cash to the pension fund. The pension fund is usually administered by a trustee, often a bank or other financial institution. The trustee must invest the employer's funds so that they earn interest and dividends sufficient to pay the amounts owed to retired employees.

Our first accounting question concerns the amount that should be shown by the employer as pension expense. This is another example of the difference between cash-basis accounting and accrual accounting. The cash paid as the funding payment is not the same as the expense. When using the accrual basis of accounting, we must consider the amount of pension cost incurred, not the amount paid. Pension expense should be accrued in the period that the employee earns the benefits, regardless of the amount paid to the pension trustee. The amount expensed and the amount paid involve two separate decisions.

The FASB has specified the methods that should be used to calculate the amount of annual pension expense to record on the employer's income statement.[5] The accountant must determine the costs of the separate components of the pension and total them to arrive at the amount of pension expense. The components include the employee's service during the current year, the interest cost, the earnings on pension investments, and other factors. The details of those calculations are beyond our discussion.

To illustrate, suppose that Employer Firm has calculated its annual pension expense to be $80,000 for 2001. Also suppose that Employer has determined that it will make a funding payment of $60,000 to the pension fund. The effect of those decisions on Employer's financial statements is as follows:

BALANCE SHEET						INCOME STATEMENT
ASSETS	=	LIABILITIES	+	OWNERS' EQUITY	+	REVENUES – EXPENSES
Cash (60,000)		Accrued Pension Cost 20,000				Pension Expense (80,000)

↑ debt, liability

The Pension Expense account is an income statement account and is reflected on Employer's 2001 income statement.

[5]*Statement of Financial Accounting Standards No. 87,* "Employers' Accounting for Pension Plans" (Stamford, Conn.: FASB, 1985).

EXHIBIT 10-11   PepsiCo Company's Pension Footnote for 1999

Selected information for plans with accumulated benefit obligation in excess of plan assets:

	Pension	
	1999	1998
Projected benefit obligation	$ (780)	$(1,960)
Accumulated benefit obligation	$ (586)	$(1,661)
Fair value of plan assets	$ 500	$ 1,498

slightly underfunded →

Pensions on the Balance Sheet

The **Accrued Pension Cost** account in the preceding example is a balance sheet account. The account could represent an asset or a liability, depending on whether the amount expensed is more or less than the amount of the funding payment. If the amount expensed is less than the amount paid, it is reported by Employer Firm as an asset and labeled as Prepaid Pension Cost. Normally, the amount expensed is greater than the amount paid, as in the example here. In that case, the Accrued Pension Cost is reported by Employer Firm as a long-term liability.

But what is the meaning of the Accrued Pension Cost account? Is it really a liability? It certainly is not a measure of the amount that is owed to employees at the time of retirement. In fact, the only true meaning that can be given to the account is to say that it is the difference between the amount expensed and the amount funded.[6] In that regard, the Accrued Pension Cost account is inadequate in determining a firm's liability to its employees for future retirement benefits. The FASB requires a great deal of footnote information for pension plans. This footnote section can be used to develop a clearer picture of the status of a firm's pension obligation.

Pension Footnote Information

Readers of financial statements are often interested in the *funding status* of pension plans. This indicates whether sufficient assets are available in the pension fund to cover the amounts to be paid to employees as retirement benefits. We will use the footnote disclosures of an actual firm to illustrate the use of pension information.

Exhibit 10-11 presents portions of the 1999 pension footnote for PepsiCo Company. PepsiCo is a large company with thousands of employees who are covered by the company's pension plans. Analysts who follow the industry must assess whether PepsiCo's pension is adequate for its employees. The amounts on the balance sheet give some indication about the status of the plan, but a more complete picture is provided in the company's footnotes. Fortunately, the footnotes can assist us as we determine whether the pension plans could be considered underfunded. Several items in the footnote must be defined. First, PepsiCo has disclosed the amount of *plan assets* at fair value. This is a measure of the total dollar amount of assets that has been accumulated in the pension fund. The footnote indicates that as of year-end 1999, PepsiCo had assets of $500 million. Second, there are two measures of the amount of pension benefits owed to employees at the time of retirement. One measure is referred to as the **accumulated benefit obligation (ABO).** This is a measure of the amount of pension benefits that would be payable to employees if they were to retire at their existing salary levels. The footnote indicates that as of year-end 1999, PepsiCo had an accumulated benefit obligation of $586 million.

Another measure provides a higher estimate of that obligation. The **projected benefit obligation (PBO)** is a measure of the amount of pension benefits payable to employees if an assumption is made concerning the future salary increases that will be earned by

www.pepsico.com

---

[6]Some pension plans that are underfunded may be required to report an additional amount as a liability. This is referred to as the *minimum liability provision.* Refer to *SFAS No. 87* for more detail.

the employees. This is probably a more realistic view of the amount of the obligation to employees, but it is a less objective number because of the difficulty in estimating future salary increases for employees. The footnote indicates that as of year-end 1999, PepsiCo had a projected benefit obligation of $780 million.

To determine the funding status of the pension plan, we must compare the amount of plan assets with the ABO and PBO. At the end of 1999, PepsiCo had pension plan assets of $500 million, which was less than the PBO. When the amount of assets is less than the amount of the obligation, the plan is referred to as *underfunded*, indicating that at this time, there are not sufficient assets in the pension fund to cover the amount of liability to employees who will retire. Underfunding is also an example of an "off-balance-sheet" liability that investors use to assess the desirability of a company's stock.

PepsiCo's pension plans may be slightly underfunded but overall its pension plans certainly appear to be quite healthy. Not all firms are as fortunate. There have been many press reports of firms whose pension plans are seriously underfunded and for which it is quite questionable whether sufficient assets are available to pay impending retirement benefits. Such underfunded plans must be considered an off-balance-sheet liability by investors or creditors in assessing the company's health.

Users of the financial statements of U.S. firms are somewhat fortunate because the disclosure of pensions on the balance sheet and in the footnotes is quite extensive. The accounting for pensions by firms outside the United States varies considerably. Many countries do not require firms to accrue pension costs, and the expense is reported only when paid to retirees. Furthermore, within the statements and footnotes, there is much less disclosure, making an assessment of the funding status of pensions much more difficult.

POSTRETIREMENT BENEFITS

Pensions represent a benefit paid to employees after their retirement. In addition to pensions, other benefits may be paid to employees after their retirement. For example, many firms promise to pay a portion of retirees' health-care costs. The accounting question is whether postretirement benefits should be considered an expense when paid or during the period that the employee worked for the firm.

A few years ago, most firms treated postretirement benefits as an expense when they were paid to the retiree. It was widely believed that such costs as those for health care after retirement were too uncertain to be accrued as an expense and that such costs did not meet the definition of a liability and, thus, did not merit recording. The result of this expense-as-you-pay accounting was that firms had an obligation that was not recorded as a liability. As health-care costs began to escalate, this unrecorded—and often undisclosed—cost became a concern for many firms as well as for stockholders, analysts, and employees.

The FASB has modified the accounting for other postemployment benefits to be consistent with pension costs. Under the matching principle, postretirement costs must now be accrued as an expense during the period that the employee helps the firm generate revenues and, thus, *earns* the benefits. The accountant must determine the costs of the separate components of postretirement benefits and total them to calculate the amount of the expense. The amount of the expense is reflected on the income statement in the Postretirement Expense account. The balance sheet should normally reflect the Accrued Postretirement Cost account. That account should be classified as a liability in the long-term liability category; it indicates the employer's obligation to present and future retirees.

The dollar amount of the liability represented by postretirement obligations is very large for many companies. For example, in 1999, PepsiCo's obligation to its employees for these retirement costs was $468 million (in addition to its pension plan amounts, disclosed in Exhibit 10-11).

There is still much controversy concerning the accounting for postretirement costs. Many firms object to the accounting requirements because of the uncertainty involved in measuring an obligation that extends far into the future. They also object because the requirements result in reduced profits on the income statement and huge liabilities on the balance sheet. Interestingly, this accounting rule had little impact on the stock market because the investment community already knew the magnitude of the postretirement obligations.

1. **LO 1** Balance sheets generally have two categories of liabilities: current liabilities and long-term liabilities. Long-term liabilities are obligations that will not be satisfied within one year.

2. **LO 2** The terms of a bond payable are given in the bond certificate. The denomination of a bond is its face value. The interest rate stated in the bond certificate is referred to as the *face rate* or *stated rate of interest*. Term bonds all have the same due date. Serial bonds are not all due on the same date. Convertible bonds can be converted into common stock by the bondholders. Callable bonds may be redeemed or retired before their due date.

3. **LO 3** The issue price of a bond is the present value of the cash flows that the bond will provide to the investor. To determine the price, you must calculate the present values of the annuity of interest payments and of the principal amount. The present values must be calculated at the market rate of interest.

4. **LO 4** A bond sells at a discount or premium, depending on the relationship of the face rate to the market rate of interest. If the face rate exceeds the market rate, a bond is issued at a premium. If the face rate is less than the market rate, it will be issued at a discount.

5. **LO 5** Premiums or discounts must be amortized by transferring a portion of the premium or the discount each period to interest expense. The effective interest method of amortization reduces the balance of the premium or discount such that the effective interest rate on the bond is constant over its life.

6. **LO 5** The carrying value of the bond equals the face value plus unamortized premium or minus unamortized discount.

7. **LO 6** When bonds are redeemed before their due date, a gain or loss on redemption results. The gain or loss is the difference between the bond carrying value at the date of redemption and the redemption price. The gain or loss is treated as an extraordinary item on the income statement.

8. **LO 7** A lease, a contractual arrangement between two parties, allows the lessee the right to use property in exchange for making payments to the lessor.

9. **LO 7** There are two major categories of lease agreements: operating and capital. The lessee does not report an operating lease as an asset and does not present the obligation to make payments as a liability. Capital leases are reported as assets and liabilities by the lessee. Leases are reported as capital leases if they meet one or more of four criteria.

10. **LO 7** Capital lease assets must be depreciated by the lessee over the life of the lease agreement. Capital lease payments must be separated into interest expense and reduction of principal using the effective interest method.

11. **LO 8** Long-term liabilities represent methods of financing. Therefore, changes in the balances of long-term liability accounts should be reflected in the Financing Activities category of the statement of cash flows.

12. **LO 9** There are many differences between the accounting for tax purposes and the accounting for financial reporting purposes. Permanent differences occur when an item affects one calculation but never affects the other. Temporary differences affect both book and tax calculations but not in the same time period. (Appendix 10A)

13. **LO 9** The amount of tax payable is calculated using the accounting method chosen for tax purposes. The amount of tax expense is calculated using the accounting method chosen for financial reporting purposes. The Deferred Tax account reconciles the differences between tax expense and tax payable. It reflects all the temporary differences times the tax rate. Deferred taxes is a controversial item on the balance sheet, raising questions as to whether it is a true liability. (Appendix 10A)

14. **LO 10** Pensions represent an obligation to compensate retired employees for service performed while employed. (Appendix 10A)

15. **LO 10** Pension expense is represented on the income statement and is calculated on the basis of several complex components that have been specified by the FASB. (Appendix 10A)

16. **LO 10** Pension expense does not represent the amount of cash paid by the employer to the pension fund. The cash payment is referred to as the *funding payment*. The Accrued Pension account is recorded as the difference between the amount of pension expense and the amount of the funding. (Appendix 10A)

17. **LO 10** The required footnote information on pensions can be used to evaluate the funding status of a firm's pension plan. If the amount of assets in the pension fund exceeds the pension obligation, the fund is considered to be overfunded, generally indicating that it is healthy and well managed. An overfunded plan is an example of an "off-balance-sheet" asset that an investor can count toward the value of the company's stock. (Appendix 10A)

KEY TERMS QUIZ

Read each definition below and then write the number of that definition in the blank beside the appropriate term it defines. The solution appears at the end of the chapter.

_____ **Long-term liability**

_____ **Face value**

_____ **Debenture bonds**

_____ **Serial bonds**

_____ **Callable bonds**

_____ **Face rate of interest**

_____ **Market rate of interest**

_____ **Bond issue price**

_____ **Premium**

_____ **Discount**

_____ **Effective interest method of amortization**

_____ **Carrying value**

___ Gain or loss on redemption
___ Operating lease
___ Capital lease
___ Deferred tax (Appendix 10A)
___ Permanent difference (Appendix 10A)
___ Temporary difference (Appendix 10A)

___ Pension (Appendix 10A)
___ Funding payment (Appendix 10A)
___ Accrued pension cost (Appendix 10A)
___ Accumulated benefit obligation (ABO) (Appendix 10A)
___ Projected benefit obligation (PBO) (Appendix 10A)

1. The principal amount of the bond as stated on the bond certificate.

2. Bonds that do not all have the same due date. A portion of the bonds comes due each time period.

3. The interest rate stated on the bond certificate. It is also called the *nominal* or *coupon rate*.

4. The total of the present value of the cash flows produced by a bond. It is calculated as the present value of the annuity of interest payments plus the present value of the principal.

5. An obligation that will not be satisfied within one year.

6. The excess of the issue price over the face value of bonds. It occurs when the face rate on the bonds exceeds the market rate.

7. Bonds that are backed by the general creditworthiness of the issuer and are not backed by specific collateral.

8. The excess of the face value of bonds over the issue price. It occurs when the market rate on the bonds exceeds the face rate.

9. Bonds that may be redeemed or retired before their specified due date.

10. The process of transferring a portion of premium or discount to interest expense. This method transfers an amount resulting in a constant effective interest rate.

11. The face value of a bond plus the amount of unamortized premium or minus the amount of unamortized discount.

12. The interest rate that bondholders could obtain by investing in other bonds that are similar to the issuing firm's bonds.

13. The difference between the carrying value and the redemption price at the time bonds are redeemed. This amount is presented as an income statement account.

14. A measure of the amount owed to employees for pensions if estimates of future salary increases are incorporated.

15. A lease that does not meet any of four criteria and is not recorded by the lessee.

16. A payment made by the employer to the pension fund or its trustee.

17. A lease that meets one or more of four criteria and is recorded as an asset by the lessee.

18. A difference between the accounting for tax purposes and the accounting for financial reporting purposes. This type of difference affects both book and tax calculations but not in the same time period.

19. The account used to reconcile the difference between the amount recorded as income tax expense and the amount that is payable as income tax.

20. A difference between the accounting for tax purposes and the accounting for financial reporting purposes. This type of difference occurs when an item affects one set of calculations but never affects the other set.

21. An obligation to pay retired employees as compensation for service performed while employed.

22. An account that represents the difference between the amount of pension recorded as an expense and the amount of the funding payment made to the pension fund.

23. A measure of the amount owed to employees for pensions if the employees retire at their existing salary levels.

ALTERNATE TERMS

Accumulated Benefit Obligation   ABO

Bond face value   Bond par value

Bonds payable   Notes payable

Bond retirement   Extinguishment of bonds

Carrying value of bond   Book value of bond

Effective interest amortization   Interest method of amortization

Face rate of interest   Stated rate or nominal rate or coupon rate of interest

Long-term liabilities   Noncurrent liabilities

Market rate of interest   Yield or effective rate of interest

Postretirement costs   Other postemployment benefits

Projected Benefit Obligation   PBO

Redemption price   Reacquisition price

Temporary difference   Timing difference

QUESTIONS

1. Which interest rate, the face rate or the market rate, should be used when calculating the issue price of a bond? Why?

2. What is the tax advantage that companies experience when bonds are issued instead of stock?

3. Does the issuance of bonds at a premium indicate that the face rate is higher or lower than the market rate of interest?

4. How does the effective interest method of amortization result in a constant rate of interest?

5. What is the meaning of the following sentence: "Amortization affects the amount of interest expense"? How does amortization of premium affect the amount of interest expense? How does amortization of discount affect the amount of interest expense?

6. Does amortization of a premium increase or decrease the bond carrying value? Does amortization of a discount increase or decrease the bond carrying value?

7. Is there always a gain or loss when bonds are redeemed? How is the gain or loss calculated?

8. Why is it important to show gains or losses on bond redemption separately on the income statement as an extraordinary item?

9. What are the reasons that not all leases are accounted for in the same manner? Do you think it would be possible to develop a new accounting rule that would treat all leases in the same manner?

10. What is the meaning of the term *off-balance-sheet financing*? Why do some firms want to engage in off-balance-sheet transactions?

11. What are the effects on the financial statements if a lease is considered an operating rather than a capital lease?

12. Should depreciation be reported on leased assets? If so, over what period of time should depreciation occur?

13. Why do firms have a Deferred Tax account? Where should that account be shown on the financial statements? (Appendix 10A)

14. How can you determine whether an item should reflect a permanent or a temporary difference when calculating the deferred tax amount? (Appendix 10A)

15. Does the amount of income tax expense presented on the income statement represent the amount of tax actually paid? Why or why not? (Appendix 10A)

16. When an employer has a pension plan for employees, what information is shown on the financial statements concerning the pension plan? (Appendix 10A)

17. How can you determine whether a pension plan is overfunded or underfunded? (Appendix 10A)

18. What is the difference between the two measures of a pension plan's obligation, the projected benefit obligation and the accumulated benefit obligation? (Appendix 10A)

19. Do you agree with this statement: "All liabilities could be legally enforced in a court of law"? (Appendix 10A)

EXERCISES

LO 2 **Exercise 10-1** Relationships

The following components are computed annually when a bond is issued for other than its face value:

- Cash interest payment
- Interest expense
- Amortization of discount/premium
- Carrying value of bond

Required

State whether each component will increase (I), decrease (D), or remain constant (C) as the bond approaches maturity, given the following situations:

1. Issued at a discount.
2. Issued at a premium.

LO 3 **Exercise 10-2** Issue Price

Youngblood Inc. plans to issue $500,000 face value bonds with a stated interest rate of 8%. They will mature in 10 years. Interest will be paid semiannually. At the date of issuance, assume the market rate is (a) 8%, (b) 6%, and (c) 10%.

Required

For each market interest rate, answer the following questions:

1. What is the amount due at maturity?
2. How much cash interest will be paid every six months?
3. At what price will the bond be issued?

LO 3 **Exercise 10-3** Issue Price

The following terms relate to independent bond issues:

a. 500 bonds; $1,000 face value; 8% stated rate; 5 years; annual interest payments

b. 500 bonds; $1,000 face value; 8% stated rate; 5 years; semiannual interest payments

c. 800 bonds; $1,000 face value; 8% stated rate; 10 years; semiannual interest payments

d. 2,000 bonds; $500 face value; 12% stated rate; 15 years; semiannual interest payments

Required

Assuming the market rate of interest is 10%, calculate the selling price for each bond issue.

LO 4   Exercise 10-4   Impact of Two Bond Alternatives

Yung Chong Company wants to issue 100 bonds, $1,000 face value, in January. The bonds will have a 10-year life and pay interest annually. The market rate of interest on January 1 will be 9%. Yung Chong is considering two alternative bond issues: (a) bonds with a face rate of 8% and (b) bonds with a face rate of 10%.

Required

1. Could the company save money by issuing bonds with an 8% face rate? If it chooses alternative (a), what would be the interest cost as a percentage?

2. Could the company benefit by issuing bonds with a 10% face rate? If it chooses alternative (b), what would be the interest cost as a percentage?

LO 6   Exercise 10-5   Redemption of Bonds

Reynolds Corporation issued $75,000 face value bonds at a discount of $2,500. The bonds contain a call price of 103. Reynolds decides to redeem the bonds early when the unamortized discount is $1,750.

Required

1. Calculate Reynolds Corporation's gain or loss on the early redemption of the bonds.

2. Describe how the gain or loss would be reported on the income statement and in the notes to the financial statements.

LO 6   Exercise 10-6   Redemption of a Bond at Maturity

On March 31, 2001, Sammonds Inc. issued $250,000 face value bonds at a discount of $7,000. The bonds were retired at their maturity date, March 31, 2011.

Required

Assuming the last interest payment and the amortization of discount have already been recorded, calculate the gain or loss on the redemption of the bonds on March 31, 2011. Indicate the effect on the accounting equation of the redemption of the bonds.

LO 7   Exercise 10-7   Leased Asset

Hopper Corporation signed a 10-year capital lease on January 1, 2001. The lease requires annual payments of $8,000 every December 31.

Required

1. Assuming an interest rate of 9%, calculate the present value of the minimum lease payments.

2. Explain why the value of the leased asset and the accompanying lease obligation are not initially reported on the balance sheet at $80,000.

LO 7   Exercise 10-8   Financial Statement Impact of a Lease

Benjamin's Warehouse signed a six-year capital lease on January 1, 2001, with payments due every December 31. Interest is calculated annually at 10%, and the present value of the minimum lease payments is $13,065.

Required

1. Calculate the amount of the annual payment that Benjamin's must make every December 31.

2. Calculate the amount of the lease obligation that would be presented on the December 31, 2002, balance sheet (after two lease payments have been made).

LO 7   Exercise 10-9   Leased Assets

Koffman and Sons signed a four-year lease for a forklift on January 1, 2001. Annual lease payments of $1,510, based on an interest rate of 8%, are to be made every December 31, beginning with December 31, 2001.

Required

1. Assume the lease is treated as an operating lease.
   a. Will the value of the forklift appear on Koffman's balance sheet?
   b. What account will indicate lease payments have been made?
2. Assume the lease is treated as a capital lease.
   a. Indicate the effect on the accounting equation when the lease is signed. Explain why the value of the leased asset is not recorded at $6,040 ($1,510 × 4).
   b. Indicate the effect on the accounting equation of the first lease payment on December 31, 2001.
   c. Calculate the amount of depreciation expense on December 31, 2001.
   d. At what amount would the lease obligation be presented on the balance sheet as of December 31, 2001?

LO 8 Exercise 10-10 Impact of Transactions Involving Bonds on Statement of Cash Flows
From the following list, identify each item as operating (O), investing (I), financing (F), or not separately reported on the statement of cash flows (N).

_____ Proceeds from issuance of bonds payable

_____ Interest expense

_____ Redemption of bonds payable at maturity

LO 8 Exercise 10-11 Impact of Transactions Involving Capital Leases on Statement of Cash Flows
Assume that Garnett Corporation signs a lease agreement with Duncan Company to lease a piece of equipment and determines that the lease should be treated as a capital lease. Garnett records a leased asset in the amount of $53,400 and a lease obligation in the same amount on its balance sheet.

Required

1. Indicate how this transaction would be reported on Garnett's statement of cash flows.
2. From the following list of transactions relating to this lease, identify each item as operating (O), investing (I), financing (F), or not separately reported on the statement of cash flows (N).

   _____ Reduction of lease obligation (principal portion of lease payment)

   _____ Interest expense

   _____ Depreciation expense—leased assets

LO 8 Exercise 10-12 Impact of Transactions Involving Tax Liabilities on Statement of Cash Flows
From the following list, identify each item as operating (O), investing (I), financing (F), or not separately reported on the statement of cash flows (N). For items identified as operating, indicate whether the related amount would be added to or deducted from net income in determining the cash flows from operating activities.

_____ Decrease in taxes payable

_____ Increase in deferred taxes

LO 9 Exercise 10-13 Temporary and Permanent Differences (Appendix 10A)
Madden Corporation wants to determine the amount of deferred tax that should be reported on its 2001 financial statements. It has compiled a list of differences between the accounting conducted for tax purposes and the accounting used for financial reporting (book) purposes.

Required

For each of the following items, indicate whether the difference should be classified as a permanent or a temporary difference.

1. During 2001, Madden received interest on state bonds purchased as an investment. The interest can be treated as tax-exempt interest for tax purposes.
2. During 2001, Madden paid for a life insurance premium on two key executives. Madden's accountant has indicated that the amount of the premium cannot be deducted for income tax purposes.

3. During December 2001, Madden received money for renting a building to a tenant. Madden must report the rent as income on its 2001 tax form. For book purposes, however, the rent will be considered income on the 2002 income statement.

4. Madden owns several pieces of equipment that it depreciates using the straight-line method for book purposes. An accelerated method of depreciation is used for tax purposes, however.

5. Madden offers a warranty on the product it sells. The corporation records the expense of the warranty repair costs in the year the product is sold (the accrual method), for book purposes. For tax purposes, however, Madden is not allowed to deduct the expense until the period when the product is repaired.

6. During 2001, Madden was assessed a large fine by the federal government for polluting the environment. Madden's accountant has indicated that the fine cannot be deducted as an expense for income tax purposes.

LO 9 **Exercise 10-14** Deferred Tax (Appendix 10A)

On January 1, 2001, Kunkel Corporation purchased an asset for $32,000. Assume this is the only asset owned by the corporation. Kunkel has decided to use the straight-line method to depreciate it. For tax purposes, it will be depreciated over three years. It will be depreciated over five years, however, for the financial statements provided to stockholders. Assume that Kunkel Corporation is subject to a 40% tax rate.

Required

Calculate the balance that should be reflected in the Deferred Tax account for Kunkel Corporation for each year 2001 through 2005.

LO 10 **Exercise 10-15** Pension Analysis (Appendix 10A)

The following information was extracted from a footnote found in the 2001 annual report of a company.

Plan Assets	$2.6 billion
Accumulated Benefit Obligation	$1.7 billion
Projected Benefit Obligation	$2.1 billion

Required

1. Determine whether the pension plan is overfunded or underfunded.

2. Explain what your response to part **1** implies about the ability of the plan to provide benefits to future retirees.

Multi-Concept Exercises

LO 4, 5 **Exercise 10-16** Issuance of a Bond at Face Value

On January 1, 2001, Whitefeather Industries issued 300, $1,000 face value bonds. The bonds have a five-year life and pay interest at the rate of 10%. Interest is paid semiannually on July 1 and January 1. The market rate of interest on January 1 was 10%.

Required

1. Calculate the issue price of the bonds and record the issuance of the bonds on January 1, 2001.

2. Explain how the issue price would have been affected if the market rate of interest had been higher than 10%.

3. Determine the effect on the accounting equation of the payment of interest on July 1, 2001.

4. Calculate the amount of interest accrued on December 31, 2001.

LO 4, 5 **Exercise 10-17** Impact of a Discount

Berol Corporation sold 20-year bonds on January 1, 2001. The face value of the bonds was $100,000, and they carry a 9% stated rate of interest, which is paid on December 31 of every year. Berol received $91,526 in return for the issuance of the bonds when the market rate was 10%. Any premium or discount is amortized using the effective interest method.

Required

1. Determine the effect on the accounting equation of the sale of the bonds on January 1, 2001, and the proper balance sheet presentation on this date.

2. Determine the effect on the accounting equation of the payment of interest on December 31, 2001, and the proper balance sheet presentation on this date.

3. Explain why it was necessary for Berol to issue the bonds for only $91,526 rather than $100,000.

LO 4, 5 **Exercise 10-18** Impact of a Premium
Assume the same set of facts for Berol Corporation as in Exercise 10-17 except that it received $109,862 in return for the issuance of the bonds when the market rate was 8%.

Required

1. Determine the effect on the accounting equation of the sale of the bonds on January 1, 2001, and the proper balance sheet presentation on this date.

2. Determine the effect on the accounting equation of the payment of interest on December 31, 2001, and the proper balance sheet presentation on this date.

3. Explain why the company was able to issue the bonds for $109,862 rather than for the face amount.

PROBLEMS

LO 3 **Problem 10-1** Factors That Affect the Bond Issue Price
Becca Company is considering the issue of $100,000 face value, 10-year term bonds. The bonds will pay 6% interest each December 31. The current market rate is 6%; therefore, the bonds will be issued at face value.

Required

1. For each of the following independent situations, indicate whether you believe that the company will receive a premium on the bonds or will issue them at a discount or at face value. Without using numbers, explain your position.

   a. Interest is paid semiannually instead of annually.

   b. Assume instead that the market rate of interest is 7%; the nominal rate is still 6%.

2. For each situation in part **1,** prove your statement by determining the issue price of the bonds given the changes in parts **a** and **b.**

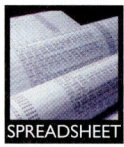

LO 5 **Problem 10-2** Amortization of Discount
Stacy Company issued five-year, 10% bonds with face value of $10,000 on January 1, 2001. Interest is paid annually on December 31. The market rate of interest on this date is 12%, and Stacy Company receives proceeds of $9,275 on the bond issuance.

Required

1. Prepare a five-year table (similar to Exhibit 10-4) to amortize the discount using the effective interest method.

2. What is the total interest expense over the life of the bonds? Cash interest payment? Discount amortization?

3. Determine the effect on the accounting equation of the payment of interest and the amortization of discount on December 31, 2003 (the third year), and determine the balance sheet presentation of the bonds on that date.

LO 5 **Problem 10-3** Amortization of Premium
Assume the same set of facts for Stacy Company as in Problem 10-2 except that the market rate of interest of January 1, 2001, is 8% and the proceeds from the bond issuance equal $10,803.

Required

1. Prepare a five-year table (similar to Exhibit 10-5) to amortize the premium using the effective interest method.

2. What is the total interest expense over the life of the bonds? Cash interest payment? Premium amortization?

3. Determine the effect on the accounting equation of the payment of interest and the amortization of premium on December 31, 2003 (the third year), and determine the balance sheet presentation of the bonds on that date.

LO 6 Problem 10-4 Redemption of Bonds

McGee Company issued $200,000 face value bonds at a premium of $4,500. The bonds contain a call provision of 101. McGee decides to redeem the bonds, due to a significant decline in interest rates. On that date, McGee had amortized only $1,000 of the premium.

Required

1. Calculate the gain or loss on the early redemption of the bonds.

2. Calculate the gain or loss on the redemption, assuming that the call provision is 103 instead of 101.

3. Indicate where the gain or loss should be presented on the financial statements.

4. Why do you suppose the call price is normally higher than 100?

LO 7 Problem 10-5 Financial Statement Impact of a Lease

On January 1, 2001, Muske Trucking Company leased a semitractor and trailer for five years. Annual payments of $28,300 are to be made every December 31, beginning December 31, 2001. Interest expense is based on a rate of 8%. The present value of the minimum lease payments is $113,000 and has been determined to be greater than 90% of the fair market value of the asset on January 1, 2001. Muske uses straight-line depreciation on all assets.

Required

1. Prepare a table similar to Exhibit 10-7 to show the five-year amortization of the lease obligation.

2. Determine the effect on the accounting equation of the lease transaction on January 1, 2001.

3. Determine the effect on the accounting equation of the annual payment, interest expense, and depreciation on December 31, 2002 (the second year of the lease).

4. Prepare the balance sheet presentation as of December 31, 2002, for the leased asset and the lease obligation.

LO 9 Problem 10-6 Deferred Tax (Appendix 10A)

Erinn Corporation has compiled its 2001 financial statements. Included in the Long-Term Liabilities category of the balance sheet are the following amounts:

	2001	2000
Deferred Tax	$180	$100

Included in the income statement are the following amounts related to income taxes:

	2001	2000
Income before Tax	$500	$400
Tax Expense	$200	$160
Net Income	$300	$240

In the footnotes that accompany the 2001 statement are the following amounts:

	2001
Current Provision for Tax	$120
Deferred Portion	80

Required

1. Determine the effect on the accounting equation for income tax expense, deferred tax, and income tax payable.

2. Assume that a stockholder has inquired about the meaning of the numbers recorded and disclosed about deferred tax. Explain why the Deferred Tax liability account exists. Also, what do the terms *current provision* and *deferred portion* mean? Why is the deferred amount in the footnote $80 when the deferred amount on the 2001 balance sheet is $180?

LO 9 Problem 10-7 Deferred Tax Calculations (Appendix 10A)

Wyhowski Inc. reported income from operations, before taxes, for 1999–2001 as follows:

1999	$210,000
2000	240,000
2001	280,000

When calculating income, Wyhowski deducted depreciation on plant equipment. The equipment was purchased January 1, 1999, at a cost of $88,000. The equipment is expected to last three years and have $8,000 salvage value. Wyhowski uses straight-line depreciation for book purposes. For tax purposes, depreciation on the equipment is $50,000 in 1999; $20,000 in 2000; and $10,000 in 2001. Wyhowski's tax rate is 35%.

Required

1. How much did Wyhowski pay in income tax each year?
2. How much income tax expense did Wyhowski record each year?
3. What is the balance in the Deferred Income Tax account at the end of 1999, 2000, and 2001?

LO 10 Problem 10-8 Financial Statement Impact of a Pension (Appendix 10A)

Smith Financial Corporation prepared the following schedule relating to its pension expense and pension-funding payment for the years 1999 through 2001.

Year	Expense	Payment
1999	$100,000	$ 90,000
2000	85,000	105,000
2001	112,000	100,000

At the beginning of 1999, the Prepaid/Accrued Pension Cost account was reported on the balance sheet as an asset with a balance of $4,000.

Required

1. Determine the effect on the accounting equation of Smith Financial Corporation's pension expense for 1999, 2000, and 2001.
2. Calculate the balance in the Prepaid/Accrued Pension Cost account at the end of 2001. Does this represent an asset or a liability?
3. Explain the effects that pension expense, the funding payment, and the balance in the Prepaid/Accrued Pension Cost account have on the 2001 income statement and balance sheet.

Multi-Concept Problems

LO 4, 6 Problem 10-9 Bond Transactions

Brand Company issued $1,000,000 face value, eight-year, 12% bonds on April 1, 2001, when the market rate of interest was 12%. Interest payments are due every October 1 and April 1. Brand uses a calendar year-end.

Required

1. Determine the effect on the accounting equation of the issuance of the bonds on April 1, 2001.
2. Determine the effect on the accounting equation of the interest payment on October 1, 2001.
3. Explain why additional interest must be recorded on December 31, 2001. What impact does this have on the amounts paid on April 1, 2002?
4. Determine the total cash inflows and outflows that occurred on the bonds over the eight-year life.

LO 1, 9, 10 Problem 10-10 Partial Classified Balance Sheet for Tribune Company

www.tribune.com   The following items, listed alphabetically, appear on Tribune Company's consolidated balance sheet at December 26, 1999 (in thousands). The information in parentheses was added to aid in your understanding.

Accounts payable	$ 176,552
Accrued liabilities	188,070
Compensation and other obligations (due after 2000)	251,930
Contracts payable for broadcast rights (the related payments are due during 2000)	276,307
Contracts payable for broadcast rights (the related payments are due after 2000)	269,698
Deferred income (current)	64,419
Deferred income taxes (Long-term)	1,251,377

Employee compensation and benefits (current)	$ 122,333
Income taxes	2,226
Long-term debt due within one year	30,689
Long-term debt (less portions due within one year)	1,365,712
Debt related to America Online stock (long-term)	1,328,480

Required

1. Prepare the Current Liabilities and Long-Term Liabilities sections of Tribune Company's classified balance sheet at December 26, 1999.

2. Tribune Company had total shareholders' equity of $3,469,898 at December 26, 1999. Total stockholders' equity amounted to $2,356,617 and total liabilities $3,578,953 at December 27, 1998. (All amounts are in thousands.) Compute the Tribune Company's debt-to-equity ratio for 1999 and 1998. As an investor, how would you react to the change in this ratio?

3. What other related ratios would the company's lenders use to assess the company? What do these ratios measure?

ALTERNATE PROBLEMS

LO 3   Problem 10-1A   Factors That Affect the Bond Issue Price
Rivera Inc. is considering the issuance of $500,000 face value, 10-year term bonds. The bonds will pay 5% interest each December 31. The current market rate is 5%; therefore, the bonds will be issued at face value.

Required

1. For each of the following independent situations, indicate whether you believe that the company will receive a premium on the bonds or will issue them at a discount or at face value. Without using numbers, explain your position.

   a. Interest is paid semiannually instead of annually.

   b. Assume instead that the market rate of interest is 4%; the nominal rate is still 5%.

2. For each situation in part **1,** prove your statement by determining the issue price of the bonds given the changes in parts **a** and **b.**

LO 5   Problem 10-2A   Amortization of Discount
Ortega Company issued five-year, 5% bonds with face value of $50,000 on January 1, 2001. Interest is paid annually on December 31. The market rate of interest on this date is 8%, and Ortega Company receives proceeds of $44,011 on the bond issuance.

Required

1. Prepare a five-year table (similar to Exhibit 10-4) to amortize the discount using the effective interest method.

2. What is the total interest expense over the life of the bonds? Cash interest payment? Discount amortization?

3. Determine the effect on the accounting equation of the payment of interest on December 31, 2003 (the third year), and the balance sheet presentation of the bonds on that date.

LO 5   Problem 10-3A   Amortization of Premium
Assume the same set of facts for Ortega Company as in Problem 10-2A except that the market rate of interest of January 1, 2001, is 4% and the proceeds from the bond issuance equal $52,230.

Required

1. Prepare a five-year table (similar to Exhibit 10-5) to amortize the premium using the effective interest method.

2. What is the total interest expense over the life of the bonds? Cash interest payment? Premium amortization?

3. Determine the effect on the accounting equation of the payment of interest on December 31, 2003 (the third year), and the balance sheet presentation of the bonds on that date.

LO 6 Problem 10-4A Redemption of Bonds

Elliot Company issued $100,000 face value bonds at a premium of $5,500. The bonds contain a call provision of 101. Elliot decides to redeem the bonds, due to a significant decline in interest rates. On that date, Elliot has amortized only $2,000 of the premium.

Required

1. Calculate the gain or loss on the early redemption of the bonds.

2. Calculate the gain or loss on the redemption, assuming that the call provision is 104 instead of 101.

3. Indicate how the gain or loss would be reported on the income statement and in the notes to the financial statements.

4. Why do you suppose that the call price of the bonds is normally an amount higher than 100?

LO 7 Problem 10-5A Financial Statement Impact of a Lease

On January 1, 2001, Kiger Manufacturing Company leased a factory machine for six years. Annual payments of $21,980 are to be made every December 31, beginning December 31, 2001. Interest expense is based on a rate of 9%. The present value of the minimum lease payments is $98,600 and has been determined to be greater than 90% of the fair market value of the machine on January 1, 2001. Kiger uses straight-line depreciation on all assets.

Required

1. Prepare a table similar to Exhibit 10-7 to show the six-year amortization of the lease obligation.

2. Determine the effect on the accounting equation of the lease transaction on January 1, 2001.

3. Determine the effect on the accounting equation of the annual payment, interest expense, and depreciation on December 31, 2002 (the second year of the lease).

4. Prepare the balance sheet presentation as of December 31, 2002, for the leased asset and the lease obligation.

LO 9 Problem 10-6A Deferred Tax (Appendix 10A)

Thad Corporation has compiled its 2001 financial statements. Included in the Long-Term Liabilities category of the balance sheet are the following amounts:

	2001	2000
Deferred Tax	$180	$200

Included in the income statement are the following amounts related to income taxes:

	2001	2000
Income before Tax	$500	$400
Tax Expense	100	150
Net Income	$400	$250

Required

1. Determine the effect on the accounting equation in 2001 for income tax expense, deferred tax, and income tax payable.

2. Assume that a stockholder has inquired about the meaning of the numbers recorded. Explain why the Deferred Tax liability account exists.

LO 9 Problem 10-7A Deferred Tax Calculations (Appendix 10A)

Clemente Inc. has reported income for book purposes as follows for the past three years:

(in Thousands)	Year 1	Year 2	Year 3
Income before Taxes	$120	$120	$120

Clemente has identified two items that are treated differently in the financial records and in the tax records. The first one is interest income on municipal bonds, which is recognized on the financial reports to the extent of $5,000 each year but does not show up as a revenue item on the company's tax return. The other item is equipment that is depreciated using the straight-line method, at the rate of $20,000 each year, for financial accounting but is depreciated for tax purposes at the rate of $30,000 in Year 1, $20,000 in Year 2, and $10,000 in Year 3.

Required

1. Determine the amount of cash paid for income taxes each year by Clemente. Assume that a 40% tax rate applies to all three years.

2. Calculate the balance in the Deferred Tax account at the end of Years 1, 2, and 3. How does this account appear on the balance sheet?

LO 10 Problem 10-8A Financial Statement Impact of a Pension (Appendix 10A)

Premier Consulting Corporation prepared the following schedule relating to its pension expense and pension-funding payment for the years 1999 through 2001:

Year	Expense	Payment
1999	$100,000	$110,000
2000	85,000	80,000
2001	112,000	100,000

At the beginning of 1999, the Prepaid/Accrued Pension Cost account was reported on the balance sheet as an asset with a balance of $5,000.

Required

1. Determine the effect on the accounting equation of Premier Consulting Corporation's pension expense for 1999, 2000, and 2001.

2. Calculate the balance in the Prepaid/Accrued Pension Cost account at the end of 2001.

3. Explain the effects that pension expense, the funding payment, and the balance in the Prepaid/Accrued Pension Cost account have on the 2001 income statement and balance sheet.

Alternate Multi-Concept Problems

LO 4, 6 Problem 10-9A Financial Statement Impact of a Bond

Worthington Company issued $1,000,000 face value, six-year, 10% bonds on July 1, 2001, when the market rate of interest was 12%. Interest payments are due every July 1 and January 1. Worthington uses a calendar year-end.

Required

1. Determine the effect on the accounting equation of the issuance of the bonds on July 1, 2001.

2. Determine the effect on the accounting equation of the accrual of interest on December 31, 2001.

3. Determine the effect on the accounting equation of the interest payment on January 1, 2002.

4. Calculate the amount of cash that will be paid for the retirement of the bonds on the maturity date.

LO 1, 9, 10 Problem 10-10A Partial Classified Balance Sheet for Boeing

The following items appear on the consolidated balance sheet of Boeing Inc. at December 31, 1999 (in millions). The information in parentheses was added to aid in your understanding.   **www.boeing.com**

Accounts payable and other liabilities	$11,269
Accrued retiree health care	4,877
Advances in excess of related costs	1,215
Deferred income taxes (long-term)	172
Income taxes payable	420
Long-term debt	5,980
Short-term debt and current portion of long-term debt	752

Required

1. Prepare the Current Liabilities and Long-Term Liabilities sections of Boeing's classified balance sheet at December 31, 1999.

2. Boeing had total liabilities of $24,708 and total shareholders' equity of $12,316 at December 31, 1998. Total stockholders' equity amounted to $11,462 at December 31, 1999. (All amounts are in millions.) Compute Boeing's debt-to-equity ratio at December 31, 1999 and 1998. As an investor, how would you react to the change in this ratio?

3. What other related ratios would the company's lenders use to assess the company? What do these ratios measure?

CASES

Reading and Interpreting Financial Statements

LO 1, 7 Case 10-1 Reading and Interpreting Uno's Balance Sheet

www.pizzeriauno.com Refer to the financial statements included in Uno's annual report.

Required

1. What is the total amount of long-term liabilities for Uno's as of October 3, 1999?

2. Uno's has an account titled Long-Term Debt, Net of Current Portion. If that account is a long-term item, why is a portion shown in the current liability category?

3. Footnote 6 indicates that there is a mortgage payable in the long-term debt category. What is the interest rate on the mortgage? What amount of principal payments on debt are due in the next five years?

4. Assume that you are an analyst who must review Uno's financial condition. Assume that Uno's has indicated that it plans to issue debt of nearly $10 million. Your boss is concerned that the amount of long-term debt may be excessive and has asked you to review the financial statements. Prepare a memo to your boss with a response to her concerns. Include in the memo a discussion of the factors that you considered to determine whether the amount of long-term debt is too high.

5. Are any assets pledged as collateral for long-term debt? If so, how much has been pledged?

LO 1, 7 Case 10-2 Reading and Interpreting Gateway's Balance Sheet

www.gateway.com Refer to the financial statements included in Gateway's annual report.

Required

1. What is the total amount of long-term liabilities for Gateway as of December 31, 1999?

2. Gateway has an account for Long-Term Obligations, but a portion of the account is shown in the current liability category. Why?

3. Did the account titled Long-term Obligations, Net of Current Maturities, increase or decrease from 1998 to 1999? What effect would the change have on the cash flows of the company?

4. What factors would you consider to determine if Gateway's long-term debt is too high?

LO 7, 8, 9 Case 10-3 Reading Uno's Statement of Cash Flows

www.pizzeriauno.com Refer to the statement of cash flows in Uno's 1999 annual report.

Required

1. Uno's made repayments of its long-term debt. When payments are made, in which category of the cash flow statement are the payments disclosed?

2. Did the amount of the cash balance increase or decrease in 1999? How much cash was used to repay long-term liabilities?

3. Uno's has a line on the cash flow statement that indicates the proceeds from a revolving line of credit. What is the meaning of that line? How much revolving line of credit exists at year-end?

Making Financial Decisions

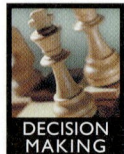
DECISION MAKING

LO 1 Case 10-4 Making a Loan Decision

Assume that you are a loan officer in charge of reviewing loan applications from potential new clients at a major bank. You are considering an application from Molitor Corporation, which is a fairly new company with a limited credit history. It has provided a balance sheet for its most recent fiscal year as follows:

MOLITOR CORPORATION
BALANCE SHEET
DECEMBER 31, 199X

Assets		Liabilities	
Cash	$ 10,000	Accounts payable	$100,000
Receivables	50,000	Notes payable	200,000
Inventory	100,000		
Equipment	500,000		
		Stockholders' Equity	
		Common stock	80,000
		Retained earnings	280,000
Total assets	$660,000	Total liabilities and stockholders' equity	$660,000

Your bank has established certain guidelines that must be met before making a favorable loan recommendation. These include minimum levels for several financial ratios. You are particularly concerned about the bank's policy that loan applicants must have a total-assets-to-debt ratio of at least 2-to-1 to be acceptable. Your initial analysis of Molitor's balance sheet has indicated that the firm has met the minimum total-assets-to-debt ratio requirement. On reading the footnotes that accompany the financial statements, however, you discover the following statement:

> Molitor has engaged in a variety of innovative financial techniques resulting in the acquisition of $200,000 of assets at very favorable rates. The company is obligated to make a series of payments over the next five years to fulfill its commitments in conjunction with these financial instruments. Current generally accepted accounting principles do not require the assets acquired or the related obligations to be reflected on the financial statements.

Required

1. How should this footnote affect your evaluation of Molitor's loan application? Calculate a revised total-assets-to-debt ratio for Molitor.

2. Do you believe that the bank's policy concerning a minimum total-assets-to-debt ratio can be modified to consider financing techniques that are not reflected on the financial statements? Write a statement that expresses your position on this issue.

LO 6 Case 10-5 Bond Redemption Decision

Armstrong Areo Ace, a flight training school, issued $100,000 of 20-year bonds at face value when the market rate was 10%. The bonds have been outstanding for 10 years. The company pays annual interest on January 1. The current rate for similar bonds is 4%. On January 1, the controller would like to purchase the bonds on the open market, retire the bonds, then issue $100,000 of 10-year bonds to pay 4% annual interest.

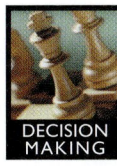

DECISION
MAKING

Required

Draft a memo to the controller advising him to retire the outstanding bonds and issue new debt. Ignore taxes. (*Hint:* Find the selling price of bonds that pay 10% when the market rate is 4%.)

Accounting and Ethics: What Would You Do?

LO 7 Case 10-6 Determination of Asset Life

Jen Latke is an accountant for Hale's Manufacturing Company. Hale's has entered into an agreement to lease a piece of equipment from EZ Leasing. Jen must decide how to report the lease agreement on Hale's financial statements.

Jen has reviewed the lease contract carefully. She has also reviewed the four lease criteria specified in the accounting rules. She has been able to determine that the lease does not meet three of the criteria. However, she is concerned about the criterion that indicates that if the term of the lease is 75% or more of the life of the property, the lease should be classified as a capital lease. Jen is fully aware that Hale's does not want to record the lease agreement as a capital lease but prefers to show it as a type of off-balance-sheet financing.

Jen's reading of the lease contract indicates that the asset has been leased for seven years. She is unsure of the life of such assets, however, and has consulted two sources to determine it. One of them states that equipment similar to that owned by Hale's is depreciated over nine years. The other, a trade publication of the equipment industry, indicates that equipment of this type will usually last for 12 years.

Required

1. How should Jen report the lease agreement in the financial statements?

2. If Jen decides to present the lease as an off-balance-sheet arrangement, has she acted ethically?

LO 10 Case 10-7 Overfunded Pension Plan (Appendix 10A)

Witty Company has sponsored a pension plan for employees for several years. Each year Witty has paid cash to the pension fund, and the pension trustee has used that cash to invest in stocks and bonds. Because the trustee has invested wisely, the amount of the pension assets exceeds the accumulated benefit obligation as of December 31, 2001.

The president of Witty Company wants to pay a dividend to the stockholders at the end of 2001. The president believes that it is important to maintain a stable dividend pattern. Unfortunately, the company, though profitable, does not have enough cash on hand to pay a dividend and must find a way to raise the necessary cash if the dividend is declared. Several executives of the company have recommended that assets be withdrawn from the pension fund. They have pointed out that the fund is currently "overfunded." Further, they have stated that a withdrawal of assets will not have an impact on the financial statements because the overfunding is an "off-balance-sheet item."

Required

Comment on the proposal to withdraw assets from the pension fund to pay a dividend to stockholders. Do you believe it is unethical?

INTERNET RESEARCH CASE

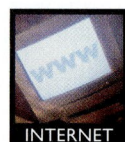

INTERNET

www.cocacola.com

Case 10-8 Coca-Cola

Sold in over 200 countries, Coca-Cola is the most recognized brand name in the world. Sales of Classic Coke, diet Coke, and Sprite provide the company with the cash necessary to pay off debts.

Conduct a search of the World Wide Web, obtain Coca-Cola's most recent annual report, or use library resources to obtain company information to answer the following:

1. Based on the latest information available, what is the amount of Coca-Cola's long-term debt? How does this compare with the long-term debt in the "Focus on Financial Results" in the opening vignette shown at the start of this chapter?

2. What is the face rate on a Coca-Cola bond currently trading on the bond market? How does that rate compare with the current yield for the same bond?

3. During the past three to six months, has the yield for Coca-Cola's bonds increased or decreased?

Optional Research. Obtain information from the company's Web site to determine recent business activities and international expansion that may have affected the amount of long-term debt used by the company.

__5__ Long-term liability (p. 452)

__1__ Face value (p. 452)

__7__ Debenture bonds (p. 454)

__2__ Serial bonds (p. 454)

__9__ Callable bonds (p. 455)

__3__ Face rate of interest (p. 455)

__12__ Market rate of interest (p. 455)

__4__ Bond issue price (p. 455)

__6__ Premium (p. 457)

__8__ Discount (p. 457)

__10__ Effective interest method of amortization (p. 459)

__11__ Carrying value (p. 460)

__13__ Gain or loss on redemption (p. 463)

__15__ Operating lease (p. 466)

__17__ Capital lease (p. 466)

__19__ Deferred tax (p. 476)

__20__ Permanent difference (p. 477)

__18__ Temporary difference (p. 477)

__21__ Pension (p. 479)

__16__ Funding payment (p. 479)

__22__ Accrued pension cost (p. 480)

__23__ Accumulated benefit obligation (ABO) (p. 480)

__14__ Projected benefit obligation (PBO) (p. 480)

STOCKHOLDERS' EQUITY

Study Links

A Look at Previous Chapters
Chapters 9 and 10 covered the current and long-term liability portions of the balance sheet. Liabilities are one source of financing of business activities.

A Look at This Chapter
This chapter examines the other major source of financing available to companies: stock and stock transactions. The discussion centers on the corporate form of organization and the stockholders' equity of corporations. The chapter begins with an overview of the stockholders' equity category of Delta Air Lines and American Airlines (AMR) balance sheets. The impact of stock issuance and repurchase is examined along with the declaration and payment of cash and stock dividends.

A Look at Upcoming Chapters
In Chapter 12 we turn our attention to an expanded discussion of the preparation and use of the statement of cash flows.

FOCUS ON FINANCIAL RESULTS

The airline industry is volatile. Pricing deregulation and the growth of hub-and-spoke routing have squeezed many airlines out of business, and the surviving carriers face conflicts between heightened customer expectations and the need to cut costs. That makes it all the more remarkable that Delta Air Lines could boast, in its fiscal-year 1999 annual report, that diluted earnings per share had grown over 150 percent from 1995 to 1999, the company's 70th year.[1]

Building shareholder value contributes to the stockholders' equity portion of Delta's balance sheet, shown here. For the world's most-flown airline, that goal is paramount and shares attention only with finding capital resources to reinvest in the business. How is stockholders' equity built?

For Delta, building value means adopting innovative technology to speed check-in and boarding; developing a customer-service initiative to ensure reliable and courteous service; continually refurbishing and renovating its fleet of planes and ground facilities; purchasing Atlantic Southeast Airlines to improve its strategic position in the newest air-travel market, regional jet service; and entering business partnerships with Air France, Aeromexico, Korean Air, and Priceline.com.

Since a November 1998 stock split that doubled the number of shares and halved the price of each, Delta's share price has fluctuated within the $40 to $55 range.

---

[1]Delta Air Lines 1999 Annual Report, p. 26.

Delta Air Lines Partial Balance Sheet

	1999	1998
Employee Stock Ownership Plan Preferred Stock:		
Series B ESOP Convertible Preferred Stock, $1.00 par value, $72.00 stated and liquidation value; issued and outstanding 6,547,495 shares at June 30, 1999 and 6,603,429 shares at June 30, 1998	471	475
Unearned compensation under employee stock ownership plan	(276)	(300)
Total Employee Stock Ownership Plan Preferred Stock	195	175
Shareowners' Equity:		
Common stock, $1.50 par value; authorized 450,000,000 shares; issued 179,763,547 shares at June 30, 1999 and 176,566,178 shares at June 30, 1998	270	265
Additional paid-in capital	3,208	3,034
Retained earnings	2,756	1,687
Accumulated other comprehensive income	149	89
Treasury stock at cost, 41,209,828 shares at June 30, 1999 and 26,115,784 shares at June 30, 1998	(1,935)	(1,052)
Total shareowners' equity	4,448	4,023

The accompanying notes are an integral part of these Consolidated Balance Sheets.

Delta Air Lines 1999 annual report

If you were a Delta stockholder, what information about the stock would you want to learn from Delta's balance sheet? What additional information would you want about the company's plans? Use this chapter to help you develop your answers, and look at the financial section of your newspaper or use the Internet to see whether the stock has continued its good performance since the split.

www.deltaairlines.com

After studying this chapter, you should be able to:

LO 1 Identify the components of the Stockholders' Equity category of the balance sheet and the accounts found in each component. (p. 502)

LO 2 Understand the characteristics of common and preferred stock and the differences between the classes of stock. (p. 507)

LO 3 Determine the financial statement impact when stock is issued for cash or for other consideration. (p. 508)

LO 4 Describe the financial statement impact of stock treated as treasury stock. (p. 509)

LO 5 Compute the amount of cash dividends when a firm has issued both preferred and common stock. (p. 512)

LO 6 Understand the difference between cash and stock dividends and the effect of stock dividends. (p. 513)

LO 7 Determine the difference between stock dividends and stock splits. (p. 515)

LO 8 Understand the statement of stockholders' equity and comprehensive income. (p. 517)

LO 9 Understand how investors use ratios to evaluate owners' equity. (p. 519)

LO 10 Explain the effects that transactions involving stockholders' equity have on the statement of cash flows. (p. 522)

AN OVERVIEW OF STOCKHOLDERS' EQUITY

EQUITY AS A SOURCE OF FINANCING

Whenever a company needs to raise money, it must choose from the alternative financing sources that are available. Financing can be divided into two general categories: debt (borrowing from banks or other creditors) and equity (issuing stock). The company's management must consider the advantages and disadvantages of each alternative. Exhibit 11-1 indicates a few of the factors that must be considered.

Issuing stock is a very popular method of financing because of its flexibility. It provides advantages for the issuing company and the investors (stockholders). Investors are primarily concerned with the return on their investment. With stock, the return may be in the form of dividends paid to the investors but may also be the price appreciation of the stock. Stock is popular because it generally provides a higher rate of return (but also a higher

ACCOUNTING FOR YOUR DECISIONS

You Are the Investor

You have the opportunity to buy a company's bonds that pay 8% interest or the same company's stock. The stock has paid an 8% dividend for the last few years. The company is a large, reputable firm and has been profitable during recent times. Should you be indifferent between the two alternatives?

ANS: Interest on bonds is a fixed obligation. Unless the company goes out of business, you can count on receiving the 8% interest if you invest in the bonds. Dividends on stock are not fixed. There is no guarantee that the company will continue to pay 8% as the dividend on your investment. If the company is not profitable, it may decrease the size of the dividend. On the other hand, if the company becomes more profitable, it may pay a larger dividend.

EXHIBIT 11-1 Advantages and Disadvantages of Stock versus Debt Financing

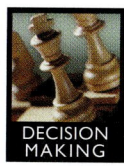
DECISION MAKING

Advantages of Financing with Stock

1. Flexibility → Dividends on stock can be increased in profitable years, reduced when the company is less profitable. Debt interest is fixed. (An advantage for issuing company)

2. Exchanges facilitate trading → Large companies have ready markets for stock through the stock exchanges. (An advantage for issuing company and investors) Sometimes debt is not as widely traded.

3. Return on investment → Stock generally provides a higher return in dividends and in growth than interest on debt. (An advantage for investors)

Disadvantages of Financing with Stock

1. Control → Issuing stock involves giving voting rights to new investors, less control of the company for existing stockholders. (A disadvantage for issuing company)

2. Tax consequences → Interest on debt is tax deductible for the issuing company, dividends on stock are not. (A disadvantage for issuing company)

3. Impact on ratios → Issuing stock decreases several important financial ratios, including earnings per share. (A disadvantage for issuing company)

degree of risk) than can be obtained by creditors who receive interest from lending money. Stock is popular with issuing companies because dividends on stock can be adjusted according to the company's profitability; higher dividends can be paid when the firm is profitable and lower dividends when it is not. Interest on debt financing, on the other hand, is generally fixed and is a legal liability that cannot be adjusted when a company experiences lower profitability.

There are several disadvantages in issuing stock. Stock usually has voting rights, and issuing stock allows new investors to vote. Existing investors may not want to share the control of the company with new stockholders. From the issuing company's viewpoint, there is also a serious tax disadvantage to stock versus debt. As indicated in Chapter 10, interest on debt is tax deductible and results in lower taxes. Dividends on stock, on the other hand, are not tax deductible and do not result in tax savings to the issuing company. Finally, the following sections of this chapter indicate the impact that issuing stock has on the company's financial statements. Issuing stock decreases several important financial ratios, such as earnings per share. Issuing debt does not have a similar effect on the earnings per share ratio.

Management should consider many other factors in deciding between debt and equity financing. The company's goal should be financing the company in a manner that results in the lowest overall cost of capital to the firm. Usually, companies attain that goal by having a reasonable balance of both debt and equity financing.

STOCKHOLDERS' EQUITY ON THE BALANCE SHEET

The basic accounting equation is often stated as follows:

$$\text{Assets} = \text{Liabilities} + \text{Owners' Equity}$$

Owners' equity is viewed as a residual amount. That is, the owners of a corporation have a claim to all assets after the claims represented by liabilities to creditors have been satisfied.

In this chapter, we concentrate on the corporate form of organization and refer to the owners' equity as *stockholders' equity*. Therefore, the basic accounting equation for a corporation can be restated as follows:

$$\text{Assets} = \text{Liabilities} + \text{Stockholders' Equity}$$

The stockholders are the owners of a corporation. They have a residual interest in its assets after the claims of all creditors have been satisfied.

The stockholders' equity category of all corporations has two major components or subcategories:

$$\text{Total Stockholders' Equity} = \text{Contributed Capital}$$
$$+$$
$$\text{Retained Earnings}$$

Contributed capital represents the amount the corporation has received from the sale of stock to stockholders. Retained earnings is the amount of net income that the corporation has earned but not paid as dividends. Instead, the corporation retains and reinvests the income.

Although all corporations maintain the two primary categories of contributed capital and retained earnings, within these categories they use a variety of accounts that have several alternative titles. The next section examines two important items: income and dividends, and their impact on the Retained Earnings account.

From *Concept*

TO PRACTICE 11.1

READING GATEWAY'S ANNUAL REPORT What was the balance of retained earnings for Gateway at the end of 1999? Did the balance increase from the end of 1998?

HOW INCOME AND DIVIDENDS AFFECT RETAINED EARNINGS

The Retained Earnings account plays an important role because it serves as a link between the income statement and the balance sheet. The term *articulated statements* refers to the fact that the information on the income statement is related to the information on the balance sheet. The bridge (or link) between the two statements is the Retained Earnings account. Exhibit 11-2 presents this relationship graphically. As the exhibit indicates, the income statement is used to calculate a company's net income for a given period of time. The amount of the net income is transferred to the statement of retained earnings and is added to the beginning balance of retained earnings (with dividends deducted) to calculate the ending balance of retained earnings. The ending balance of retained earnings is the amount that is portrayed on the balance sheet in the stockholders' equity category. That is why you must always prepare the income statement before you prepare the balance sheet, as you have discovered when developing financial statements in previous chapters of the text.

IDENTIFYING THE COMPONENTS OF THE STOCKHOLDERS' EQUITY SECTION OF THE BALANCE SHEET

LO 1 Identify the components of the Stockholders' Equity category of the balance sheet and the accounts found in each component.

www.amrcorp.com

The liabilities and stockholders' equity portion of the balance sheet of AMR Corporation (American Airlines) is provided in Exhibit 11-3. We will focus on the Stockholders' (Shareholders') Equity category of the balance sheet. All corporations, including AMR, begin the Stockholders' Equity category with a list of the firm's contributed capital. In some cases, there are two categories of stock: common stock and preferred stock (the latter is discussed later in this chapter). Common stock normally carries voting rights, and the common stockholders elect the officers of the corporation and establish its by-laws and governing rules. It is not unusual for corporations to have more than one type of common stock, each with different rights or terms. For example, Continental Airlines, one of AMR's competitors, has two classes of common stock listed on its 1999 balance sheet.

www.continental.com

Number of Shares   It is important to determine the number of shares of stock for each stock account. Corporate balance sheets report the number of shares in three categories: **authorized, issued,** and **outstanding shares.**

To become incorporated, a business must develop articles of incorporation and apply to the proper state authorities for a corporate charter. The corporation must specify the maximum number of shares that it will be allowed to issue. This maximum number of shares is called the *authorized stock.* A corporation applies for authorization to issue many more shares than it will issue immediately, to allow for future growth and other events that may occur over its long life. For example, AMR Corporation indicates that it has 750,000,000 shares of common stock authorized but that only 182,278,766 shares had been issued as of December 31, 1999.

The number of shares *issued* indicates the number of shares that have been sold or transferred to stockholders. The number of shares issued does not necessarily mean, however, that those shares are currently outstanding. The term *outstanding* indicates shares actually in the hands of the stockholders. Shares that have been issued by the corporation and then repurchased are counted as shares issued but not as shares outstanding. Quite often corporations repurchase their own stock as treasury stock (explained in more detail later in this chapter). Treasury stock reduces the number of shares outstanding. The number of AMR's shares of common stock outstanding at December 31, 1999, could be calculated as follows:

Number of shares issued	182,278,766
Less: Treasury stock	34,034,110
Number of shares outstanding	148,244,656

Study Tip

Treasury stock is included in the number of shares issued. It is not part of the number of shares outstanding.

Par Value: The Firm's "Legal Capital"   The Stockholders' Equity category of many balance sheets refers to an amount as the *par value* of the stock. For example,

par value = arbitrary value

EXHIBIT 11-3   AMR Corporation's Partial Balance Sheet

AMR CORPORATION

(in millions, except shares and par value)	December 31, 1999	1998
LIABILITIES AND STOCKHOLDERS' EQUITY		
Current Liabilities		
Accounts payable	$ 1,115	$ 1,047
Accrued salaries and wages	849	917
Accrued liabilities	1,107	973
Air traffic liability	2,255	2,163
Current maturities of long-term debt	302	48
Current obligations under capital leases	236	154
Total current liabilities	5,864	5,302
Long-Term Debt, Less Current Maturities	4,078	2,436
Obligations Under Capital Leases, Less Current Obligations	1,611	1,764
Other Liabilities and Credits		
Deferred income taxes	1,846	1,470
Deferred gains	613	573
Postretirement benefits	1,669	1,598
Other liabilities and deferred credits	1,835	1,614
	5,963	5,255
Commitments and Contingencies		
Stockholders' Equity		
Common stock – $1 par value; shares authorized: 750,000,000;		
Shares issued: 1999 and 1998 – 182,278,766	182	182
Additional paid-in capital	3,061	3,075
Treasury shares at cost: 1999 – 34,034,110; 1998 – 20,927,692	(2,101)	(1,288)
Accumulated other comprehensive income	(2)	(4)
Retained earnings	5,718	4,733
	6,858	6,698
Total Liabilities and Stockholders' Equity	$24,374	$21,455

AMR's contributed capital

AMR's common stock has a par value of $1 per share. **Par value** is an arbitrary amount stated on the face of the stock certificate and represents the legal capital of the corporation. Most corporations set the par value of the stock at very low amounts because there are legal difficulties if stock is sold at less than par. Therefore, par value does not indicate the stock's value or the amount that is obtained when it is sold on the stock exchange; it is simply an arbitrary amount that exists to fulfill legal requirements. A company's legal requirement depends on its state of incorporation. Some states do not require corporations to indicate a par value; others require them to designate the *stated value* of the stock. A stated value is accounted for in the same manner as a par value and appears in the Stockholders' Equity category in the same manner as a par value.

The amount of the par value is the amount that is presented in the stock account. That is, the dollar amount in a firm's stock account can be calculated as its par value per share times number of shares issued. For AMR, the dollar amount appearing in the common stock account can be calculated as follows:

$1 Par Value per Share × 182,278,766 Shares Issued =
$182 million (rounded to millions) Balance in the Common Stock Account

Additional Paid-in Capital   The dollar amounts of the stock accounts in the Stockholders' Equity category do not indicate the amount that was received when the stock was sold to stockholders. The Common Stock and Preferred Stock accounts indicate only the par value of the stock. When stock is issued for an amount higher than the par value, the excess is reported as **additional paid-in capital.** Several alternative titles are used for this account, including Paid-in Capital in Excess of Par, Capital Surplus (an old term that should no longer be used), and Premium on Stock. Regardless of the title, the account represents the amount received in excess of par when stock was issued.

AMR's balance sheet indicates additional paid-in capital of $3,061 million at December 31, 1999. AMR, as well as many other corporations, presents only one amount for additional paid-in capital for all stock transactions. Therefore, we are unable to determine whether the

A prospective stockholder may purchase shares and receive certificates, like this one, either directly from the company or through a stockbroker. Usually, a broker purchases shares in its own name for the investor's account—and the investor never sees a certificate.

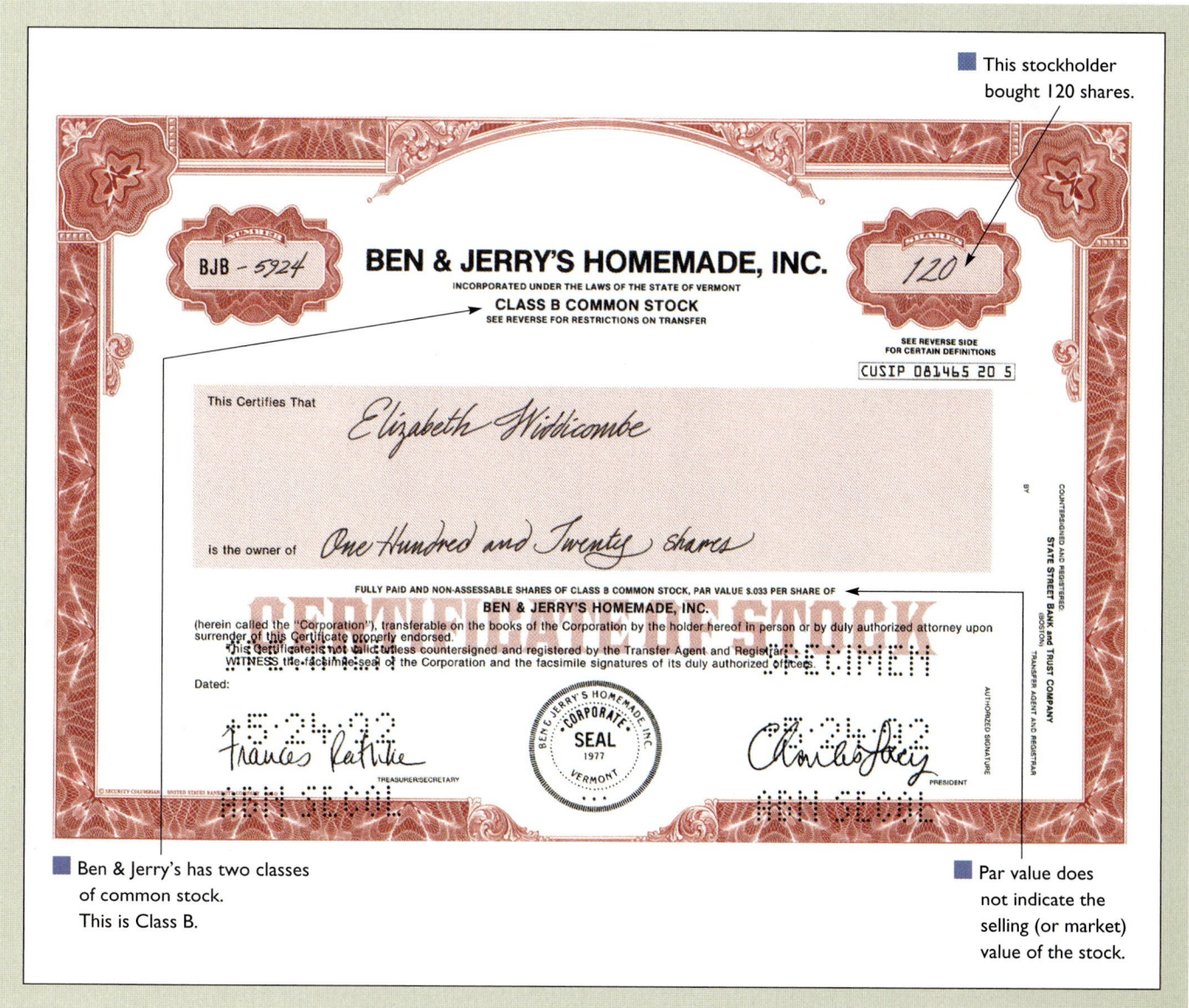

This stockholder bought 120 shares.

Ben & Jerry's has two classes of common stock. This is Class B.

Par value does not indicate the selling (or market) value of the stock.

amount resulted from the issuance of common stock or other stock transactions. As a result, it is often impossible to determine the issue price of each category of stock even with a careful analysis of the balance sheet and the accompanying footnotes.

Retained Earnings: The Amount *Not* Paid as Dividends   **Retained earnings** represents net income that the firm has earned but has *not* paid as dividends. Remember that retained earnings is an amount that is accumulated over the entire life of the corporation and does not represent the income or dividends for a specific year. For example, the balance of the Retained Earnings account on AMR's balance sheet at December 31, 1999, is $5,718 million. That does not mean that AMR had a net income of this amount in 1999; it simply means that over the life of the corporation, AMR has retained $5,718 million more net income than it paid out as dividends to stockholders.

It is also important to remember that the balance of the Retained Earnings account does not mean that liquid assets of that amount are available to the stockholders. Corporations decide to retain income because they have needs other than paying dividends to stockholders. The needs may include the purchase of assets, the retirement of debt, or other financial needs. Money spent for those needs usually benefits the stockholders in the long run, but liquid assets equal to the balance of the Retained Earnings account are not necessarily available to stockholders. In theory, income should be retained whenever the company can reinvest the money and get a better return within the business than the shareholders can get on their own. In summary, retained earnings is a stockholders' equity account. Although the company's assets have increased, retained earnings does not represent a pool of liquid assets.

BUSINESS STRATEGY

The airline industry is in a state of turmoil, with almost as many mergers, acquisitions, expansion plans, and purchase offers flying as planes. American Airlines' parent company, AMR Corp., has offered to purchase TWA, which has filed for bankruptcy. TWA's pilots believe that sale will provide them and other employees with job security and protected benefits. At the same time, Jet Acquisitions Group Inc., a new company made up of aviation experts and investors, has also announced an offer to buy TWA for almost $1 billion, about twice the offer made by AMR Corp.

Meanwhile, United and American, now the world's largest airlines, plan to divide the routes and assets of US Airways between them, giving them control over roughly half the U.S. airline market. Delta is pushing the government to allow other air carriers to close further mergers to balance what it calls "a huge duopoly" and restore the balance of competition. Rival carrier Continental agrees that the deal would create "mega carriers [that] are significantly larger than their next largest competitors."

"These are transactions that clearly threaten competition," said Alfred Kahn, former chairman of the now-defunct Civil Aeronautics Board, speaking before the Senate Judiciary Committee. United and American, however, are insisting that competition will be enhanced and that consumers will reap more choices and greater convenience from the deal. The Justice Department is charged with responsibility for deciding whether the deals can proceed as proposed, be modified, or be challenged in court.

Members of Congress are divided about what course is best for the industry and the nation's air travelers. Unless the companies involved agree to a delay, all parties face a time limit by which the Justice Department must make its decision.

SOURCES: David Leonhardt with Jane L. Levere, "Price of Airline Consolidation," *New York Times*, Jan. 9, 2001, p. C1, C17; David Lawsky, "Delta: Further Mergers May Be Required," Reuters Limited, Feb. 7, 2001, accessed at http://dailynews.yahoo.com/h/nm/20010207/bs/airlines_competition_dc_4.html; "Group of Investors Announces Plans to Offer Almost $1 Billion for TWA," *Wall Street Journal*, Feb. 8, 2001, accessed at http://public.wsj.com/sn/y/SB981601132931107429.html; "TWA Pilots Formally Support Deal," Associated Press, Feb. 16, 2001, accessed at http://www.nytimes.com/aponline/business/AP-WA-Pilots.html.

WHAT IS PREFERRED STOCK?

Many companies have a class of stock called *preferred stock*. One of the advantages of preferred stock is the flexibility it provides because its terms and provisions can be tailored to meet the firm's needs. These terms and provisions are detailed in the stock certificate. Generally, preferred stock offers holders a preference to dividends declared by the corporation. That is, if dividends are declared, the preferred stockholders must receive dividends first, before the holders of common stock.

The dividend rate on preferred stock may be stated in two ways. First, it may be stated as a percentage of the stock's par value. For example, if a stock is presented in the balance sheet as $100 par, 7% preferred stock, its dividend rate is $7 per share ($100 times 7%). Second, the dividend may be stated as a per-share amount. For example, a stock may appear in the balance sheet as $100 par, $7 preferred stock, meaning that the dividend rate is $7 per share. Investors in common stock should note the dividend requirements of the preferred shareholder. The greater the obligation to the preferred shareholder, the less desirable the common stock becomes.

Several important provisions of preferred stock relate to the payment of dividends. Some preferred stock issues have a **cumulative feature,** which means that if a dividend is not declared to the preferred stockholders in one year, dividends are considered to be *in arrears.* Before a dividend can be declared to common stockholders in a subsequent period, the preferred stockholders must be paid all dividends in arrears as well as the current year's dividend. The cumulative feature ensures that the preferred stockholders will receive a dividend before one is paid to common stockholders. It does not guarantee a dividend to preferred stockholders, however. There is no legal requirement mandating that a corporation declare a dividend, and preferred stockholders have a legal right to receive a dividend only when it has been declared.

Some preferred stocks have a **participating feature.** Its purpose is to allow the preferred stockholders to receive a dividend in excess of the regular rate when a firm has been particularly profitable and declares an abnormally large dividend. When the participating feature is present and a firm declares a dividend, the preferred stockholders first have a right to the current year's dividend, and then the common stockholders must receive an equal portion (usually based on the par or stated value of the stocks) of the dividend. The participating feature then applies to any dividend declared in excess of the amounts in the first two steps. The preferred stockholders are allowed to share in the excess, normally on the basis of the total par value of the preferred and common stock. The participating feature is explained in more detail in the section of this chapter concerning dividends.

Preferred stock may also be convertible or callable. The **convertible feature** allows the preferred stockholders to convert their stockholdings to common stock. Convertible preferred stock offers stockholders the advantages of the low risk generally associated with preferred stock and the possibility of the higher return that is associated with common stock. The **callable feature** allows the issuing firm to retire the stock after it has been issued. Normally, the call price is specified as a fixed dollar amount. Firms may exercise the call option to eliminate a certain class of preferred stock so that control of the corporation is maintained in the hands of fewer stockholders. The call option also may be exercised when the dividend rate on the preferred stock is too high and other, more cost-effective financing alternatives are available.

Preferred stock is attractive to many investors because it offers a return in the form of a dividend at a level of risk that is lower than that of most common stocks. Usually, the dividend available on preferred stock is more stable from year to year, and as a result, the market price of the stock is also more stable. In fact, if preferred stock carries certain provisions, the stock is very similar to bonds or notes payable. Management must evaluate whether such securities really represent debt and should be presented in the liability category of the balance sheet or whether they represent equity and should be presented in the equity category. Such a decision involves the concept of *substance over form*. That is, a

LO 2 Understand the characteristics of common and preferred stock and the differences between the classes of stock.

From Concept

TO PRACTICE 11.2

READING DELTA'S ANNUAL REPORT Which financial statements could you look at to identify the different classes of stock issued by Delta? Which classes of stock are issued? How many shares have been issued?

Qwest officials ring the Opening Bell as the first company to be listed on the New York Stock Exchange in the new millennium, on the first day (January 3) of trading in the year 2000.
www.quest.com

company must look not only at the legal form but also at the economic substance of the security to decide whether it is debt or equity.

ISSUANCE OF STOCK

STOCK ISSUED FOR CASH

LO 3 Determine the financial statement impact when stock is issued for cash or for other consideration.

Stock may be issued in several different ways. It may be issued for cash or for noncash assets. When stock is issued for cash, the amount of its par value should be reported in the stock account and the amount in excess of par should be reported in an additional paid-in capital account. For example, assume that on July 1, a firm issued 1,000 shares of $10 par common stock for $15 per share. The effect on the balance sheet is as follows:

BALANCE SHEET						INCOME STATEMENT
ASSETS	=	LIABILITIES	+	OWNERS' EQUITY	+	REVENUES – EXPENSES
Cash	15,000			Common Stock	10,000	
				Additional Paid-in		
				Capital—Common	5,000	

As noted earlier, the Common Stock account and the Additional Paid-in Capital account are both presented in the Stockholders' Equity category of the balance sheet and represent the contributed capital component of the corporation.

If no-par stock is issued, the corporation does not distinguish between common stock and additional paid-in capital. If the firm in the previous example had issued no-par stock on July 1 for $15 per share, the entire amount of $15,000 would be presented in the Common Stock account.

STOCK ISSUED FOR NONCASH CONSIDERATION

Occasionally, stock is issued in return for something other than cash. For example, a corporation may issue stock to obtain land or buildings. When such a transaction occurs, the company faces the difficult task of deciding what value to place on the transaction. This is especially difficult when the market values of the elements of the transaction are not known with complete certainty. According to the general guideline, the transaction should be reported at fair market value. Market value may be indicated by the value of the consideration given (stock) or the value of the consideration received (property), whichever can be most readily determined.

Assume that on July 1, a firm issued 500 shares of $10 par preferred stock to acquire a building. The stock is not widely traded, and the current market value of the stock is not evident. The building has recently been appraised by an independent firm as having a market value of $12,000. In this case, the issuance of the stock affects the balance sheet as follows:

BALANCE SHEET						INCOME STATEMENT
ASSETS	=	LIABILITIES	+	OWNERS' EQUITY	+	REVENUES – EXPENSES
Building	12,000			Preferred Stock	5,000	
				Additional Paid-in		
				Capital—Preferred	7,000	

In other situations, the market value of the stock may be more readily determined and should be used as the best measure of the value of the transaction. Market value may be represented by the current stock-market quotation or by a recent cash sale of the stock. The company should attempt to develop the best estimate of the market value of the non-cash transaction and should neither intentionally overstate nor intentionally understate the assets received by the issuance of stock.

WHAT IS TREASURY STOCK?

The Stockholders' Equity category of AMR's balance sheet in Exhibit 11-3 includes **treasury stock** in the amount of $2,101 million. The Treasury Stock account is created when a corporation buys its own stock sometime after issuing it. For an amount to be treated as treasury stock, (1) it must be the corporation's own stock, (2) it must have been issued to the stockholders at some point, (3) it must have been repurchased from the stockholders, and (4) it must not be retired but must be held for some purpose. Treasury stock is not considered outstanding stock and does not have voting rights.

LO 4 Describe the financial statement impact of stock treated as treasury stock.

A corporation may repurchase stock as treasury stock for several reasons. The most common is to have stock available to distribute to employees for bonuses or as part of an employee-benefit plan. Firms also may buy treasury stock to maintain a favorable market price for the stock or to improve the appearance of the firm's financial ratios. More recently, firms have purchased their stock to maintain control of the ownership and to prevent unwanted takeover or buyout attempts. Of course, the lower the stock price, the more likely a company is to buy back its own stock and wait for the shares to rise in value before reissuing them.

The two methods to account for treasury stock transactions are the cost method and the par value method. We will present the more commonly used cost method. Assume that the Stockholders' Equity section of Rezin Company's balance sheet on December 31, 2000, appears as follows:

Common stock, $10 par value, 1,000 shares issued and outstanding	$10,000
Additional paid-in capital—Common	12,000
Retained earnings	15,000
Total stockholders' equity	$37,000

Assume that on February 1, 2000, Rezin buys 100 of its shares as treasury stock at $25 per share. The effect on Rezin's balance sheet is as follows:

BALANCE SHEET						INCOME STATEMENT	
ASSETS	=	LIABILITIES	+	OWNERS' EQUITY	+	REVENUES – EXPENSES	
Cash (2,500)				Treasury Stock (2,500)			

The purchase of treasury stock does not directly affect the Common Stock account itself. The Treasury Stock account is considered to be a contra account and is subtracted from the total of contributed capital and retained earnings in the Stockholders' Equity section. Treasury Stock is *not* an asset account. When a company buys its own stock, it is contracting its size and reducing the equity of stockholders. Therefore, Treasury Stock is a contra-equity account, not an asset.

The Stockholders' Equity section of Rezin's balance sheet on February 1, 2001, after the purchase of the treasury stock, appears as follows:

Common stock, $10 par value,	$10,000
1,000 shares issued, 900 outstanding	
Additional paid-in capital—Common	12,000
Retained earnings	15,000
Total contributed capital and retained earnings	$37,000
Less: Treasury stock, 100 shares at cost	2,500
Total stockholders' equity	$34,500

Corporations may choose to reissue stock to investors after it has been held as treasury stock. When treasury stock is resold for more than it cost, the difference between the sales price and the cost appears in the Additional Paid-in Capital—Treasury Stock account. For example, if Rezin resold 100 shares of treasury stock on May 1, 2001, for $30 per share, the Treasury Stock account would be reduced by $2,500 (100 shares times $25 per share), and the Additional Paid-in Capital—Treasury Stock account would be increased by $500 (100 shares times the difference between the purchase price of $25 and the reissue price of $30).

When treasury stock is resold for an amount less than its cost, the difference between the sales prices and the cost is deducted from the Additional Paid-in Capital—Treasury Stock account. If that account does not exist, the difference should be deducted from the Retained Earnings account. For example, assume that Rezin Company had resold 100 shares of treasury stock on May 1, 2001, for $20 per share, instead of $30 in the previous example. In this example, Rezin has had no other treasury stock transactions, and, therefore, no balance existed in the Additional Paid-in Capital—Treasury Stock account. Rezin would then reduce the Treasury Stock account by $2,500 (100 shares times $25 per share) and would reduce Retained Earnings by $500 (100 shares times the difference between the purchase price of $25 and the reissue price of $20 per share). Thus, the Additional Paid-in Capital—Treasury Stock account may have a positive balance, but entries that result in a negative balance in the account should not be made.

Note that *income statement accounts are never involved* in treasury stock transactions. Regardless of whether treasury stock is reissued for more or less than its cost, the effect is reflected in the stockholders' equity accounts. It is simply not possible for a firm to engage in transactions involving its own stock and have the result affect the performance of the firm as reflected on the income statement.

Two-Minute Review

1. Where does the Treasury Stock account appear on the balance sheet?
2. What is the effect on stockholders' equity when stock is purchased as treasury stock?
3. How does treasury stock affect the number of shares issued and outstanding?

Answers:

1. Treasury Stock is a contra-equity account, and the balance should appear as a reduction in the Stockholders' Equity category of the balance sheet.

2. When treasury stock is purchased, it reduces total stockholders' equity.

3. Treasury stock is still stock that has been issued and so does not affect the number of shares issued. But it is stock that is held by the company, rather than the stockholders, and the purchase of treasury stock reduces the number of shares of stock outstanding.

RETIREMENT OF STOCK

Retirement of stock occurs when a corporation buys back stock after it has been issued to investors and does not intend to reissue the stock. Retirement often occurs because the corporation wants to eliminate a particular class of stock or a particular group of stockholders. When stock is repurchased and retired, the balances of the stock account and the paid-in capital account that were created when the stock was issued must be eliminated. When the original issue price is higher than the repurchase price of the stock, the difference is reflected in the Paid-in Capital from Stock Retirement account. When the repurchase price of the stock is more than the original issue price, the difference reduces the Retained Earnings account. The general principle for retirement of stock is the same as for treasury stock transactions. No income statement accounts are affected by the retirement. The effect is reflected in the Cash account and the stockholders' equity accounts.

DIVIDENDS: DISTRIBUTION OF INCOME TO SHAREHOLDERS

CASH DIVIDENDS

Corporations may declare and issue several different types of dividends, the most common of which is a cash dividend to stockholders. Cash dividends may be declared quarterly, annually, or at other intervals. Normally, cash dividends are declared on one date, referred to as the *date of declaration,* and are paid out on a later date, referred to as the *payment date.* The dividend is paid to the stockholders that own the stock as of a particular date, the *date of record.*

Generally, two requirements must be met before the board of directors can declare a cash dividend. First, sufficient cash must be available by the payment date to pay to the stockholders. Second, the Retained Earnings account must have a sufficient positive balance. Dividends reduce the balance of the account, and, therefore, Retained Earnings must have a balance before the dividend declaration. Most firms have an established policy concerning the portion of income that will be declared as dividends. The **dividend payout ratio** is calculated as the annual dividend amount divided by the

EXHIBIT 11-4 1999 Dividend Payout Ratios to Common Stockholders in the Retail Industry (all years end in January 2000)

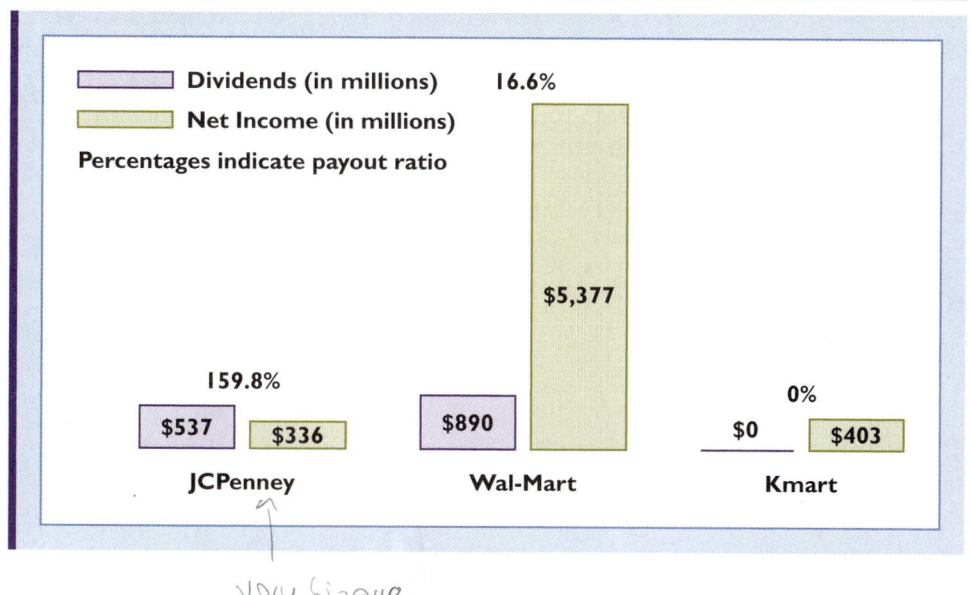

www.jcpenney.com
www.walmart.com
www.bluelight.com

very bizarre

annual net income. The dividend payout ratios of three members of the retail industry are given in Exhibit 11-4. The dividend payout ratio for many firms is 50% or 60% and usually does not exceed 70%. Typically, utilities pay a high proportion of their earnings. In contrast, fast-growing companies in technology often pay nothing to shareholders. Some investors want and need the current income of a high-dividend payout, but others would rather not receive dividend income and prefer to gamble that the stock price will appreciate.

Cash dividends become a liability on the date they are declared. An accounting entry should be recorded on that date to acknowledge the liability and reduce the balance of the Retained Earnings account. For example, assume that on July 1 the board of directors of Grant Company declared a cash dividend of $7,000 to be paid on September 1. Grant reflects the declaration as a reduction of Retained Earnings and an increase in Cash Dividend Payable. The Cash Dividend Payable account is a liability and is normally shown in the Current Liabilities section of the balance sheet. On September 1, when the cash dividend is paid, the Cash Dividend Payable account is eliminated and the Cash account is reduced by $7,000. The important point to remember is that dividends reduce the amount of retained earnings *when declared*. When dividends are paid, the company reduces the liability to stockholders, reflected in the Cash Dividend Payable account.

CASH DIVIDENDS FOR PREFERRED AND COMMON STOCK

LO 5 Compute the amount of cash dividends when a firm has issued both preferred and common stock.

When cash dividends involving more than one class of stock are declared, the corporation must determine the proper amount to allocate to each class of stock. As indicated earlier, the amount of dividends that preferred stockholders have rights to depends on the terms and provisions of the preferred stock. We will illustrate the proper allocation of cash dividends with an example of a firm that has two classes of stock, preferred and common.

Assume that on December 31, 2001, Stricker Company has outstanding 10,000 shares of $10 par, 8% preferred stock and 40,000 shares of $5 par common stock. Stricker was unable to declare a dividend in 1999 or 2000 but wants to declare a $70,000 dividend for 2001. The dividend is to be allocated to preferred and common stockholders in accordance with the terms of the stock agreements.

Noncumulative Preferred Stock   If the terms of the stock agreement indicate that the preferred stock is not cumulative, the preferred stockholders do not have a right to dividends in arrears. The dividends that were not declared in 1999 and 2000 are simply lost and do not affect the distribution of the dividend in 2001. Therefore, the cash dividend declared in 2001 is allocated between preferred and common stockholders as follows:

	To Preferred	To Common
Step 1: Distribute current year dividend to preferred		
(10,000 shares × $10 par × 8% × 1 year)	$8,000	
Step 2: Distribute remaining dividend to common		
($70,000 − $8,000)		$62,000
Total allocated	$8,000	$62,000
Dividend per share		
Preferred: $8,000/10,000 shares	$.80	
Common: $62,000/40,000 shares		$1.55

Cumulative Preferred Stock   If the terms of the stock agreement indicate that the preferred stock is cumulative, the preferred stockholders have a right to dividends in arrears before the current year's dividend is distributed. Therefore, Stricker performs the following steps:

	To Preferred	To Common
Step 1: Distribute dividends in arrears to preferred		
(10,000 shares × $10 par × 8% × 2 years)	$16,000	
Step 2: Distribute current-year dividend to preferred		
(10,000 shares × $10 par × 8% × 1 year)	8,000	
Step 3: Distribute remainder to common		
($70,000 − $24,000)		$46,000
Total allocated	$24,000	$46,000
Dividend per share		
Preferred: $24,000/10,000 shares	$2.40	
Common: $46,000/40,000 shares		$1.15

Cumulative and Participating Preferred Stock If the terms of the stock agreement indicate that the preferred stock is both cumulative and participating, the preferred stockholders have a right to dividends in arrears (the cumulative feature) and to a portion of the current year's dividend that exceeds a specified amount (the participating feature). Assume that Stricker Company preferred stockholders participate in any dividend in excess of 8% of total par value and that the participation is based on the proportion of the total par value of the preferred and common stock. The 2001 dividend is distributed as follows:

	To Preferred	To Common
Step 1: Distribute dividend in arrears to preferred		
(10,000 shares × $10 par × 8% × 2 years)	$16,000	
Step 2: Distribute current-year dividend to preferred		
(10,000 shares × $10 par × 8% × 1 year)	8,000	
Step 3: Distribute equal percentage to common		
(40,000 shares × $5 par × 8%)		$16,000
Step 4: Remainder to preferred and common on basis of total par value		
Preferred:		
($70,000 − $40,000) × $100,000ª/$300,000	10,000	
Common:		
($70,000 − $40,000) × $200,000ᵇ/$300,000		20,000
Total allocated	$34,000	$36,000
Dividend per share		
Preferred: $34,000/10,000 shares	$3.40	
Common: $36,000/40,000 shares		$.90

ª10,000 shares × $10 par
ᵇ40,000 shares × $5 par

The Stricker Company example illustrates the flexibility available with preferred stock. The provisions and terms of the preferred stock can be established to make the stock attractive to investors and to provide an effective form of financing for the corporation. The cumulative and participating features make the preferred stock more attractive. However, these features may make the *common stock* less attractive because more dividends for the preferred stockholders may mean less dividends for the common stockholders.

STOCK DIVIDENDS

Cash dividends are the most popular and widely used form of dividend, but corporations may at times use stock dividends instead of, or in addition to, cash dividends. A **stock dividend** occurs when a corporation declares and issues additional shares of its own stock to its existing stockholders. Firms use stock dividends for several reasons. First, a corporation may simply not have sufficient cash available to declare a cash dividend. Stock dividends

LO 6 Understand the difference between cash and stock dividends and the effect of stock dividends.

do not require the use of the corporation's resources and allow cash to be retained for other purposes. Second, stock dividends result in additional shares of stock outstanding and may decrease the market price per share of stock if the dividend is large (small stock dividends tend to have little effect on market price). The lower price may make the stock more attractive to a wider range of investors and allow enhanced financing opportunities. Finally, stock dividends normally do not represent taxable income to the recipients and may be attractive to some wealthy stockholders.

Similar to cash dividends, stock dividends are normally declared by the board of directors on a specific date, and the stock is distributed to the stockholders at a later date. The corporation recognizes the stock dividend on the date of declaration. Assume that Shah Company's Stockholders' Equity category of the balance sheet appears as follows as of January 1, 2001:

Common stock, $10 par,	
5,000 shares issued and outstanding	$ 50,000
Additional paid-in capital—Common	30,000
Retained earnings	70,000
Total stockholders' equity	$150,000

Assume that on January 2, 2001, Shah declares a 10% stock dividend to common stockholders to be distributed on April 1, 2001. Small stock dividends (usually those of 20 to 25% or less) normally are recorded at the *market value* of the stock as of the date of declaration. Assume that Shah's common stock is selling at $40 per share on that date. Therefore, the total market value of the stock dividend is $20,000 (10% of 5,000 shares outstanding, or 500 shares, times $40 per share). The effect of the stock dividend on January 2, the date of declaration, is as follows:

BALANCE SHEET					INCOME STATEMENT
ASSETS	**=**	**LIABILITIES**	**+**	**OWNERS' EQUITY**	**+** **REVENUES – EXPENSES**
				Retained Earnings (20,000)	
				Common Stock	
				Dividend Distributable 5,000	
				Additional Paid-in	
				Capital—Common 15,000	

The Common Stock Dividend Distributable account represents shares of stock to be issued; it is not a liability account because no cash or assets are to be distributed to the stockholders. Thus, it should be treated as an account in the Stockholders' Equity section of the balance sheet and is a part of the contributed capital component of equity.

Note that the declaration of a stock dividend does not affect the total stockholders' equity of the corporation, although the retained earnings are reduced. That is, the Stockholders' Equity section of Shah's balance sheet on January 2, 2001, is as follows after the declaration of the dividend:

Common stock, $10 par,	
5,000 shares issued and outstanding	$ 50,000
Common stock dividend distributable, 500 shares	5,000
Additional paid-in capital—Common	45,000
Retained earnings	50,000
Total stockholders' equity	$150,000

The account balances are different, but total stockholders' equity is $150,000 both before and after the declaration of the stock dividend. In effect, retained earnings has been capitalized (transferred permanently to the contributed capital accounts). When a corporation actually issues a stock dividend, it is necessary to transfer an amount from the Stock Dividend Distributable account to the appropriate stock account.

Our stock dividend example has illustrated the general rule that stock dividends should be reported at fair market value. That is, in the transaction to reflect the stock dividend, retained earnings is decreased in the amount of the fair market value per share of the stock times the number of shares to be distributed. When a large stock dividend is declared, however, accountants do not follow the general rule we have illustrated. A large stock dividend is a stock dividend of more than 20% to 25% of the number of shares of stock outstanding. In that case, the stock dividend is reported at *par value* rather than at fair market value. That is, Retained Earnings is decreased in the amount of the par value per share times the number of shares to be distributed.

Refer again to the Shah Company example. Assume that instead of a 10% dividend, on January 2, 2001, Shah declares a 100% stock dividend to be distributed on April 1, 2001. The stock dividend results in 5,000 additional shares being issued and certainly meets the definition of a large stock dividend. The effect on the accounting equation on the declaration date is:

BALANCE SHEET					INCOME STATEMENT
ASSETS	=	LIABILITIES	+	OWNERS' EQUITY	+	REVENUES – EXPENSES

Retained Earnings (50,000)
Common Stock
Dividend Distributable 50,000

When the stock is actually distributed, the amount of $50,000 is transferred from the Common Stock Dividend Distributable account to the Common Stock account. The Stockholders' Equity category of Shah's balance sheet as of April 1 after the stock dividend is as follows:

Common stock, $10 par,	
10,000 shares issued and outstanding	$100,000
Additional paid-in capital—Common	30,000
Retained earnings	20,000
Total stockholders' equity	$150,000

Again, you should note that the stock dividend has not affected total stockholders' equity. Shah has $150,000 of stockholders' equity both before and after the stock dividend. The difference between large and small stock dividends is the amount transferred from retained earnings to the contributed capital portion of equity.

STOCK SPLITS

A **stock split** is similar to a stock dividend in that it results in additional shares of stock outstanding and is nontaxable. In fact, firms may use a stock split for nearly the same reasons as a stock dividend: to increase the number of shares, reduce the market price per share, and make the stock more accessible to a wider range of investors. There is an important legal difference, however. Stock dividends do not affect the par value per share of the stock, whereas stock splits reduce the par value per share. There also is an important accounting difference. An accounting transaction is *not recorded* when a corporation declares and executes a stock split. None of the stockholders' equity accounts are affected by the split. Rather, the footnote information accompanying the balance sheet must disclose the additional shares and the reduction of the par value per share.

LO 7 Determine the difference between stock dividends and stock splits.

EXHIBIT 11-5   Gateway's Stockholders' Equity Section

Consolidated Balance Sheets

December 31 (in thousands, except per share amounts)	1998	1999
Stockholders' equity:		
Preferred stock, $.01 par value, 5,000 shares		
authorized, none issued and outstanding	—	—
Class A common stock, nonvoting, $.01 par value,		
1,000 shares authorized; none issued		
and outstanding	—	—
Common stock, $.01 par value, 1,000,000 shares		
authorized; 313,138 shares and 320,016 shares		
issued and outstanding, respectively.	3,131	3,200
Additional paid-in capital	364,421	656,870
Common stock in treasury, at cost, 730 shares in 1999	—	(51,796)
Retained earnings	980,908	1,408,852
Accumulated other comprehensive loss	(4,085)	(8)
Total stockholders' equity	1,344,375	2,017,118
	$2,890,380	$3,954,688

R. STOCK SPLIT. On August 9, 1999, the Company announced that its Board of Directors approved a two-for-one common stock split to be effected in the form of a stock dividend. The shares were distributed on September 7, 1999 to stockholders of record as of August 20, 1999. Share and per share data for all periods presented herein have been restated to reflect the two-for-one common stock split.

Return to the Shah Company example. Assume that on January 2, 2001, Shah issued a 2-for-1 stock split instead of a stock dividend. The split results in an additional 5,000 shares of stock outstanding but should not be recorded in a formal accounting transaction. Therefore, the Stockholders' Equity section of Shah Company immediately after the stock split on January 2, 2001, is as follows:

Common stock, $5 par,	
10,000 shares issued and outstanding	$ 50,000
Additional paid-in capital—Common	30,000
Retained earnings	70,000
Total stockholders' equity	$150,000

You should note that the par value per share has been reduced from $10 to $5 per share of stock as a result of the split. Like a stock dividend, the split does not affect total stockholders' equity because no assets have been transferred. Therefore, the split simply results in more shares of stock with claims to the same net assets of the firm.

www.gateway.com

Exhibit 11-5 presents the stockholders' equity category from Gateway's 1999 balance sheet and the footnote concerning a stock split. The exhibit indicates that Gateway had three classes of stock but had issued only the third class, common stock. As of December 31, 1999, the company had 320,016,000 shares of common stock issued and outstanding. In August 1999, Gateway had declared a 2-for-1 stock split for the common stockholders. This split doubled the number of shares over the number indicated on the 1998 balance sheet. Thus, after the stock split, each stockholder had twice as many shares of stock but still had the same proportional ownership of the company. When a company has a stock split, it restates the number of shares for all previous years also. Although a stock split does

EXHIBIT 11-6   Hewlett-Packard's Statement of Stockholders' Equity, 1999

Consolidated Statement of Shareholders' Equity

| | | Common Stock | | | |
In millions except number of shares in thousands	Number of shares	Par value	Additional Paid-in Capital	Retained earnings	Total
Balance October 31, 1998	1,015,403	10	—	16,909	16,919
1 Shares issued	20,208	—	1,178	—	1,178
2 Shares repurchased	(31,042)	—	(1,178)	(1,465)	(2,643)
3 Dividends	—	—	—	(650)	(650)
4 Net earnings	—	—	—	3,491	3,491
Balance October 31, 1999	**1,004,569**	**$10**	$ —	**$18,285**	**$18,295**

not increase the wealth of the shareholder, it is usually a good sign. Companies with rising stock prices declare a stock split to make the stock more marketable to the small investor, who would be more likely to buy a stock at $50 per share than at $100.

STATEMENT OF STOCKHOLDERS' EQUITY

In addition to a balance sheet, an income statement, and a cash flows statement, many annual reports contain a **statement of stockholders' equity.** The purpose of this statement is to explain all the reasons for the difference between the beginning and the ending balance of each of the accounts in the Stockholders' Equity category of the balance sheet. Of course, if the only changes are the result of income and dividends, a statement of retained earnings is sufficient. When other changes have occurred in stockholders' equity accounts, this more complete statement is necessary.

LO 8 Understand the statement of stockholders' equity and comprehensive income.

The statement of stockholders' equity of Hewlett-Packard Company is presented in Exhibit 11-6 for the year 1999. The statement starts with the beginning balances of each of the accounts as of October 31, 1998. Hewlett-Packard Company stockholders' equity is presented in three categories (the columns on the statement) as of October 31, 1998, as follows (in millions):

www.hp.com

Number of shares	1,015,403
Par value	$10
Retained earnings	$16,909

The statement of stockholders' equity indicates the items or events that affected stockholders' equity during 1999. The items or events were as follows:

Item or Event	Effect on Stockholders' Equity
Shares issued ⟶	Increased additional paid-in capital by $1,178 million
Shares repurchased ⟶	Decreased additional paid-in capital by $1,178 and decreased retained earnings by $1,465 million
Dividends ⟶	Decreased retained earnings by $650 million
Net earnings ⟶	Increased retained earnings by $3,491 million

The last line of the statement of stockholders' equity indicates the ending balances of the stockholders' equity accounts as of the balance sheet date, October 31, 1999. You should note that total stockholders' equity increased during 1999, to $18,295 million at year-end. The statement of stockholders' equity is useful in explaining the reasons for the changes that occurred.

WHAT IS COMPREHENSIVE INCOME?

There has always been some question about which items or transactions should be shown on the income statement and should be included in the calculation of net income. Generally, the accounting rule-making bodies have held that the income statement should reflect an *all-inclusive* approach. That is, all events and transactions that affect income should be shown on the income statement. This approach prevents the manipulation of the income figure by those who would like to show "good news" on the income statement and "bad news" directly on the retained earnings statement or the statement of stockholders' equity. The result of the all-inclusive approach is that the income statement includes items that are not necessarily under management's control, such as losses from natural disasters, and thus the income statement may not be a true reflection of a company's future potential.

The FASB has accepted certain exceptions to the all-inclusive approach and has allowed items to be recorded directly to the stockholders' equity category. This text has discussed one such item: unrealized gains and losses on investment securities. Exhibit 11-7 presents several additional items that are beyond the scope of this text. Such items as these have been excluded from the income statement for various reasons. Quite often, the justification is a concern for the volatility of the net income number. The items we have cited are often large dollar amounts; if included in the income statement, they would cause income to fluctuate widely from period to period. Therefore, the income statement is deemed to be more useful if the items are excluded.

A new term has been coined to incorporate the "income-type" items that escape the income statement. **Comprehensive income** is the net assets increase resulting from all transactions during a time period (except for investments by owners and distributions to owners). Exhibit 11-7 presents the statement of comprehensive income and its relationship

EXHIBIT 11-7 The Relationship of the Income Statement and Statement of Comprehensive Income

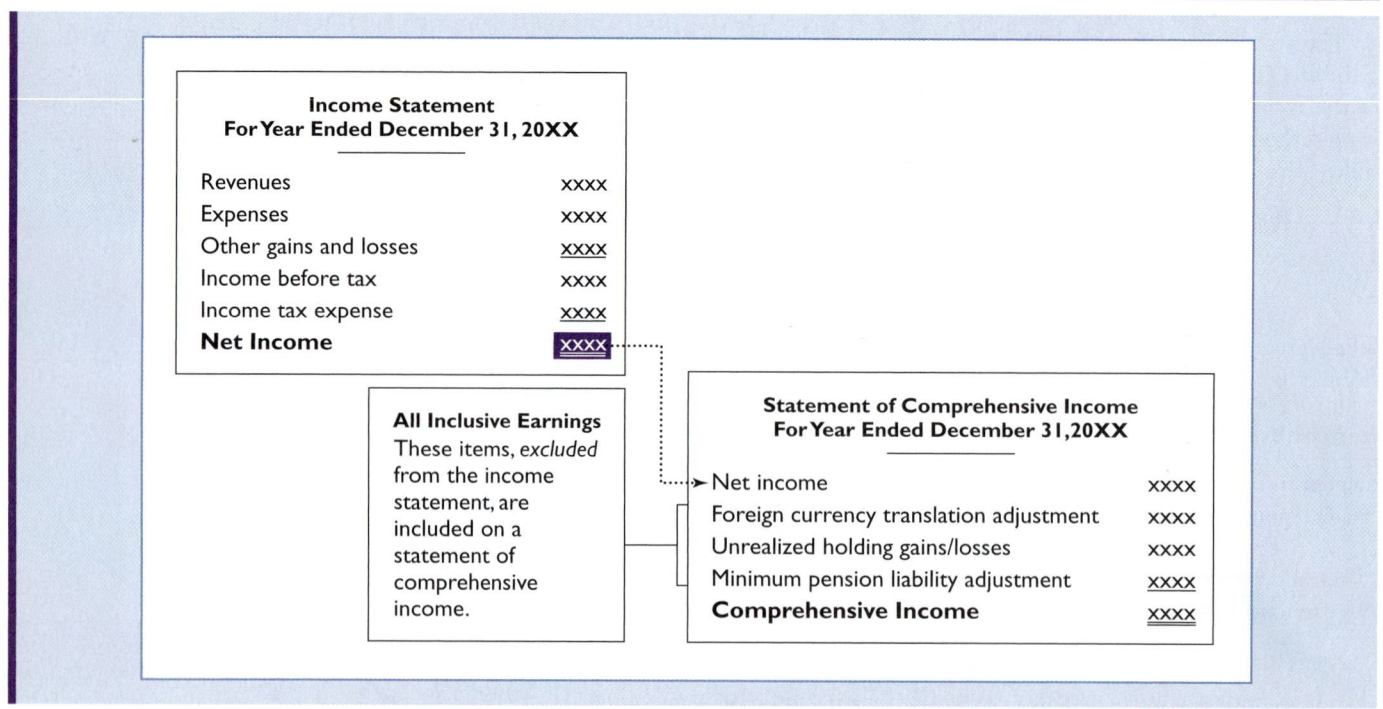

to the traditional income statement. It illustrates that comprehensive income encompasses all the revenues and expenses that are presented on the income statement to calculate net income and also includes items that are not presented on the income statement but affect total stockholders' equity.[2] The comprehensive income measure is truly all-inclusive because it includes such transactions as unrealized gains and prior period adjustments that affect stockholders' equity. Firms are required to disclose comprehensive income because it provides a more complete measure of performance.

WHAT ANALYZING OWNERS' EQUITY REVEALS ABOUT A FIRM'S VALUE

BOOK VALUE PER SHARE

Users of financial statements are often interested in computing the value of a corporation's stock. This is a difficult task because *value* is not a well-defined term and means different things to different users. One measure of value is the book value of the stock. **Book value per share** of common stock represents the rights that each share of common stock has to the net assets of the corporation. The term *net assets* refers to the total assets of the firm minus total liabilities. In other words, net assets equal the total stockholders' equity of the corporation. Therefore, when only common stock is present, book value per share is measured as follows:

LO 9 Understand how investors use ratios to evaluate owners' equity.

$$\text{Book Value per Share} = \frac{\text{Total Stockholders' Equity}}{\text{Number of Shares of Stock Outstanding}}$$

Refer again to the statement of stockholders' equity of Hewlett-Packard that appears in Exhibit 11-6. As of October 31, 1999, the total stockholders' equity is $18,295,000, and the number of outstanding shares of common stock is 1,004,569. Therefore, the book value per share for Hewlett-Packard is $18.21, calculated as follows (shares are in thousands and dollars are in millions):

www.hp.com

$$\$18,295,000/1,004,569 = \$18.21$$

This means that the company's common stockholders have the right to $18.21 per share of net assets in the corporation.

The book value per share indicates the recorded minimum value per share of the stock. In a sense, it indicates the rights of the common stockholders in the event that the company is liquidated. It does not indicate the market value of the common stock. That is, book value per share does not indicate the price that should be paid by those who want to buy or sell the stock on the stock exchange. Book value is also an incomplete measure of value because the corporation's net assets are normally measured on the balance sheet at the original historical cost, not at the current value of the assets. Thus, book value per share does not provide a very accurate measure of the price that a stockholder would be willing to pay for a share of stock. The book value of a stock is often thought to be the "floor" of a stock price. An investor's decision to pay less than book value for a share of stock suggests that he or she thinks that the company is going to continue to lose money, thus shrinking book value.

From Concept

TO PRACTICE 11.3

READING UNO'S ANNUAL REPORT
Refer to Uno's 1999 report. What was the book value per share of the common stock? How did that relate to the market value of the stock?

CALCULATING BOOK VALUE WHEN PREFERRED STOCK IS PRESENT

The focus of the computation of book value per share is always on the value per share of the *common* stock. Therefore, the computation must be adjusted for corporations that have both preferred and common stock. The numerator of the fraction, total stockholders' equity, should be reduced by the rights that preferred stockholders have to the corporation's net assets. Normally, this can be accomplished by deducting the redemption value or liquidation value of the preferred stock along with any dividends in arrears on

---

[2]The format of Exhibit 11-7 is suggested by the FASB. The FASB also allows other possible formats of the statement of comprehensive income.

www.deltaairlines.com

cumulative preferred stock. The denominator should not include the number of shares of preferred stock.

To illustrate the computation of book value per share when both common and preferred stock are present, we will refer to the stockholders' equity category of Delta Air Lines, presented in Exhibit 11-8. When calculating book value per share, we want to consider only the *common* stockholders' equity. Exhibit 11-8 indicates **1** that Delta's total stockholders' equity in 1999 was $4,448 million but also **2** that preferred stockholders had a right to $471 million in the event of liquidation. Therefore, $471 million must be deducted to calculate the rights of the common stockholders:

$$\$4,448 - \$471 = \$3,977 \text{ million common stockholders' equity}$$

The number of shares of common stock *outstanding* can be calculated from Exhibit 11-8 as follows:

$$\begin{array}{rl} 179,763,547 & \text{shares issued} \\ - \ 41,209,828 & \text{treasury shares} \\ \hline 138,553,719 & \text{shares outstanding} \end{array}$$

Therefore, the computation of book value per share is as follows:

$$\$3,977,000,000/138,553,719 = \$28.70 \text{ Book Value per Share}$$

This indicates that if the company were liquidated and the assets sold at their recorded values, the common stockholders would receive $28.70 per share. Of course, if the company went bankrupt and had to liquidate assets at distressed values, stockholders would receive something less than book value.

Two-Minute Review

1. *What effect does a stock dividend have on a firm's stockholders' equity?*
2. *What effect does a stock split have on a firm's stockholders' equity?*
3. *How is book value per share calculated?*

EXHIBIT 11-8 Delta Air Lines Stockholders' Equity Section

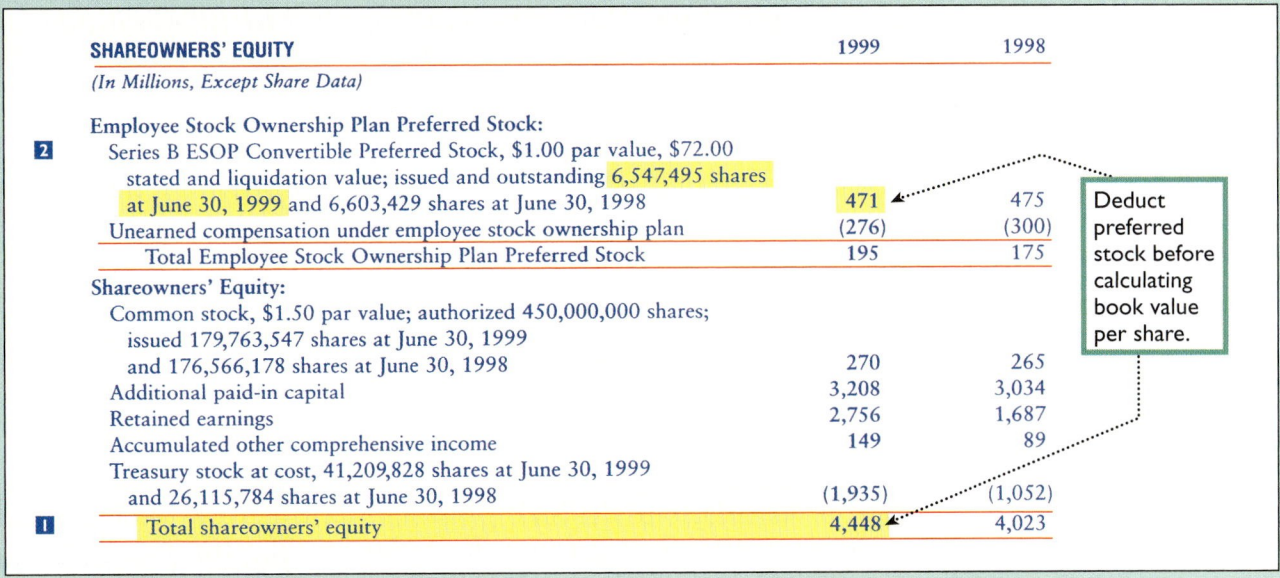

SHAREOWNERS' EQUITY	1999	1998	
(In Millions, Except Share Data)			
Employee Stock Ownership Plan Preferred Stock:			
2 Series B ESOP Convertible Preferred Stock, $1.00 par value, $72.00 stated and liquidation value; issued and outstanding 6,547,495 shares at June 30, 1999 and 6,603,429 shares at June 30, 1998	471	475	Deduct preferred stock before calculating book value per share.
Unearned compensation under employee stock ownership plan	(276)	(300)	
Total Employee Stock Ownership Plan Preferred Stock	195	175	
Shareowners' Equity:			
Common stock, $1.50 par value; authorized 450,000,000 shares; issued 179,763,547 shares at June 30, 1999 and 176,566,178 shares at June 30, 1998	270	265	
Additional paid-in capital	3,208	3,034	
Retained earnings	2,756	1,687	
Accumulated other comprehensive income	149	89	
Treasury stock at cost, 41,209,828 shares at June 30, 1999 and 26,115,784 shares at June 30, 1998	(1,935)	(1,052)	
1 Total shareowners' equity	4,448	4,023	

Answers:

1. *A stock dividend does not change a firm's total stockholders' equity but does affect the balances of accounts within that category of the balance sheet. Generally, a stock dividend will reduce the retained earnings account and will increase the capital stock account.*

2. *A stock split does not affect total stockholders' equity or the accounts within stockholders' equity. No accounting entry is made for a stock split.*

3. *Book value per share is determined by dividing total stockholders' equity (less an amount representing the rights of preferred shareholders) by the number of shares of common stock.*

MARKET VALUE PER SHARE

The market value of the stock is a more meaningful measure of the value of the stock to those financial statement users interested in buying or selling shares of stock. The **market value per share** is the price at which stock is currently selling. When stock is sold on a stock exchange, the price can be determined by its most recent selling price. For example, the listing for General Motors stock on the financial pages of a newspaper may indicate the following:

www.gm.com

52-Week			Daily			
High	**Low**	**Sym**	**High**	**Low**	**Last**	**Change**
59⅜	45¾	GM	57⅞	56½	56½	−⅜

The two left-hand columns indicate the stock price for the last 52-week period. General Motors sold as high as $59⅜ and as low as $45¾ during that time period. The right-hand portion indicates the high and low for the previous day's trading and the closing price. General Motors sold as high as $57⅞ per share and as low as $56½ per share and closed at $56½. For the day, the stock decreased by ⅜ or $0.375 per share.

The market value of the stock depends on many factors. Stockholders must evaluate a corporation's earnings and liquidity as indicated in the financial statements. They must also consider a variety of economic factors and project all the factors into the future to determine the proper market value per share of the stock. Many investors use sophisticated investment techniques, including large databases, to identify factors that affect a company's stock price.

HOW CHANGES IN STOCKHOLDERS' EQUITY AFFECT THE STATEMENT OF CASH FLOWS

LO 10 Explain the effects that transactions involving stockholders' equity have on the statement of cash flows.

It is important to determine the effect that the issuance of stock, the repurchase of stock, and the payment of dividends have on the statement of cash flows. Each of these business activities' impact on cash must be reflected on the statement. Exhibit 11-9 indicates how these stockholders' equity transactions affect cash flow and where the items should be placed on the statement of cash flows.

The issuance of stock is a method to finance business. Therefore, the cash *inflow* from the sale of stock to stockholders should be reflected as an inflow in the Financing Activities section of the statement of cash flows. Generally, companies do not disclose separately the amount received for the par value of the stock and the amount received in excess of par. Rather, one amount is listed to indicate the total inflow of cash.

The repurchase or retirement of stock also represents a financing activity. Therefore, the cash *outflow* should be reflected as a reduction of cash in the Financing Activities section of the statement of cash flows. Again, companies do not distinguish between the amount paid for the par of the stock and the amount paid in excess of par. One amount is generally listed to indicate the total cash outflow to retire stock.

Dividends paid to stockholders represent a cost of financing the business with stock. Therefore, dividends paid should be reflected as a cash *outflow* in the Financing Activities section of the statement of cash flows. It is important to distinguish between the declaration of dividends and the payment of dividends. The cash outflow occurs at the time the dividend is paid and should be reflected on the statement of cash flows in that period.

EXHIBIT 11-9 The Effect of Stockholders' Equity Items on the Statement of Cash Flows

EXHIBIT 11-10   Delta Air Lines 1999 Statement of Cash Flows

CONSOLIDATED STATEMENTS OF CASH FLOWS

FOR THE YEARS ENDED JUNE 30, 1999, 1998 AND 1997

DELTA AIR LINES, INC.

(In Millions)	1999	1998	1997
Cash Flows From Operating Activities:			
Net income	$ 1,101	$ 1,001	$ 854
Adjustments to reconcile net income to cash			
provided by operating activities:			
Restructuring and other non-recurring charges	–	–	52
Depreciation and amortization	961	860	710
Deferred income taxes	418	294	240
Rental expense in excess of (less than) rent payments	10	(17)	(58)
Pension, postretirement and postemployment expense			
in excess of payments	34	179	92
Changes in certain current assets and liabilities:			
Decrease in accounts receivable	339	5	25
(Increase) decrease in prepaid expenses and other			
current assets	(176)	15	(31)
Increase in air traffic liability	152	249	4
Increase in other payables and accrued expenses	12	330	186
Other, net	78	–	(35)
Net cash provided by operating activities	2,929	2,916	2,039
Cash Flows From Investing Activities:			
Property and equipment additions:			
Flight equipment, including advance payments	(2,258)	(1,760)	(1,598)
Ground property and equipment	(561)	(531)	(350)
Decrease (increase) in short-term investments, net	568	(43)	(1)
Proceeds from sale of flight equipment	30	10	8
Acquisition, net of cash acquired	(570)	–	–
Net cash used in investing activities	(2,791)	(2,324)	(1,941)
Cash Flows From Financing Activities:			
Payments on long-term debt and capital			
lease obligations	(154)	(307)	(196)
Payments on notes payable	(277)	–	–
Cash dividends	(43)	(43)	(44)
Issuance of long-term obligations	324	125	–
Issuance of short-term obligations	779	–	–
Issuance of common stock	131	318	38
Income tax benefit from exercise of stock options	34	84	–
Repurchase of common stock	(885)	(354)	(379)
Net cash used in financing activities	(91)	(177)	(581)
Net Increase (Decrease) In Cash and Cash Equivalents	47	415	(483)
Cash and cash equivalents at beginning of year	1,077	662	1,145
Cash and cash equivalents at end of year	$ 1,124	$ 1,077	$ 662

> Changes in stockholders' equity are shown in the Financing Activities category.

The 1999 statement of cash flows for Delta Air Lines is given in Exhibit 11-10. Note in particular three lines in the Financing Activities category of the cash flow statement. First, the cash dividends line indicates cash payments of $43 million for the payment of dividends. Also, a line for the issuance of stock indicates the company had cash inflows during 1999 of $131 million from such transactions. Finally, Delta repurchased stock during the year, and that line indicates that cash payments of $885 million were made to repurchase the stock.

www.deltaairlines.com

Financial Statements Are Interrelated, This Analyst Shows

Chris Morgan is an equity research analyst for Donaldson, Lufkin & Jenrette (DLJ), a full-service investment banking firm with headquarters in New York. As an analyst covering the commercial banking industry, Chris researches and generates financial profiles of banking companies for DLJ's clients, who then use his research to make investment decisions. A company's income statement is paramount to his initial research as he judges a company's earnings potential and its ability to consistently turn a profit. Chris says: "First, I look at the net interest margin, the pretax margin before and after loan loss provisioning, the efficiency ratio (expenses divided by net revenues), the return on assets, and then return on equity."

In addition to looking at earnings, Chris considers the *composition* of earnings to determine the growth potential of a particular company because where earnings *come from* is often as important as their *amount*. Also, the statement of cash flows is an important source of information concerning a company's growth potential. But, the statement often reveals that cash was generated from sources other than earnings and one possible source involves the company's stock. To determine whether stock was involved, Chris might turn from the statement of cash flows to the Stockholder's Equity section of the consolidated balance sheet. He says: "[Looking at] stockholder's equity is useful if a company has engaged in any stock transactions and it is not clear where some of the cash flow is coming from. I also periodically scan the proxy [a statement that is prepared for a company's annual shareholders' meeting] in conjunction with the Shareholders' Equity section to determine the impact of stock options on the share base." Chris's example shows how the financial statements are interrelated and how an analyst moves from statement to statement to develop a precise picture of a company's earnings potential.

> "[Looking at] stockholder's equity is useful if a company has engaged in any stock transactions and it is not clear where some of the cash flow is coming from."
>
> —Chris Morgan

WARMUP EXERCISES

LO 1   Warmup Exercise 11-1

A company has a retained earnings account with a January 1 balance of $500,000. The accountant has reviewed the following information for the current year:

Increase in cash balance	$50,000
Net income	80,000
Dividends declared	30,000
Dividends paid	20,000
Decrease in accounts receivable balance	10,000

Required

Calculate the ending balance of the Retained Earnings account.

Key to the Solution

Cash and accounts receivable do not affect retained earnings. Also, note that dividends are deducted from retained earnings at the time they are declared rather than when they are paid.

LO 2   Warmup Exercise 11-2

A company begins business on January 1 and issues 100,000 shares of common stock. On July 1, the company declares and issues a 2-for-1 stock split. On October 15, the company purchases 20,000 shares of stock as treasury stock and reissues 5,000 shares by the end of the month.

Required

Calculate the number of shares issued and the number of shares outstanding as of the end of the first year of operations.

LO 9 Warmup Exercise 11-3

A. Company A has total stockholders' equity at year-end of $500,000 and has 10,000 shares of stock.

B. Company B has total stockholders' equity at year-end of $500,000 and has 10,000 shares of stock. The company also has 50,000 shares of preferred stock, which has a $1 par value and a liquidation value of $3 per share.

Required

Calculate the book value per share for Company A and Company B.

Key to the Solution

Book value per share is calculated for the common stockholder. If preferred stock is present, an amount must be deducted that represents the amount the preferred stockholder would receive at liquidation.

SOLUTION TO WARMUP EXERCISES

Warmup Exercise 11-1

The ending balance of the Retained Earnings account should be calculated as follows:

Beginning balance	$500,000
Plus: Net income	80,000
Less: Dividends declared	(30,000)
Ending balance	$550,000

Warmup Exercise 11-2

The number of shares of stock issued is 200,000, or 100,000 times 2 because of the stock split. The number of shares outstanding is 185,000, calculated as follows:

Number of shares after split	$100,000 \times 2 = 200,000$
Less purchase of treasury stock	(20,000)
Plus stock reissued	5,000
Total outstanding	185,000 shares

Warmup Exercise 11-3

A. Book value per share is $50, or $500,000/10,000.

B. Book value per share is $35 or ($500,000 − $150,000)/10,000.

REVIEW PROBLEM

Andrew Company was incorporated on January 1, 2001, under a corporate charter that authorized the issuance of 50,000 shares of $5 par common stock and 20,000 shares of $100 par, 8% preferred stock. The following events occurred during 2001. Andrew wants to record the events and develop financial statements on December 31, 2001.

a. Issued for cash 10,000 shares of common stock at $25 per share and 1,000 shares of preferred stock at $110 per share on January 15, 2001.

b. Acquired a patent on April 1 in exchange for 2,000 shares of common stock. At the time of the exchange, the common stock was selling on the local stock exchange for $30 per share.

c. Repurchased 500 shares of common stock on May 1 at $20 per share. The corporation is holding the stock to be used for an employee bonus plan.

d. Declared a cash dividend of $1 per share to common stockholders and an 8% dividend to preferred stockholders on July 1. The preferred stock is noncumulative, nonparticipating. The dividend will be distributed on August 1.

e. Distributed the cash dividend on August 1.

f. Declared and distributed to preferred stockholders a 10% stock dividend on September 1. At the time of the dividend declaration, preferred stock was valued at $130 per share.

g. On December 31, calculated the annual net income for the year to be $200,000.

Required

1. Indicate the effect on the accounting equation of items **a** through **f.**

2. Develop the Stockholders' Equity section of Andrew Company's balance sheet at December 31, 2001. You do not need to consider the footnotes that accompany the balance sheet.

3. Determine the book value per share of the common stock. Assume that the preferred stock can be redeemed at par.

Solution to Review Problem

1. The effects of items **a** through **f** on the accounting equation are as follows:

a.

BALANCE SHEET						INCOME STATEMENT
ASSETS	=	LIABILITIES	+	OWNERS' EQUITY	+	REVENUES – EXPENSES
Cash 360,000				Common Stock 50,000		
				Additional Paid-in		
				Capital—Common 200,000		
				Preferred Stock 100,000		
				Additional Paid-in		
				Capital—Preferred 10,000		

b. The patent received for stock should be recorded at the value of the stock:

BALANCE SHEET						INCOME STATEMENT
ASSETS	=	LIABILITIES	+	OWNERS' EQUITY	+	REVENUES – EXPENSES
Patent 60,000				Common Stock 10,000		
				Additional Paid-in		
				Capital—Common 50,000		

c. Stock reacquired constitutes treasury stock and the effect is as follows:

BALANCE SHEET						INCOME STATEMENT
ASSETS	=	LIABILITIES	+	OWNERS' EQUITY	+	REVENUES – EXPENSES
Cash (10,000)				Treasury Stock (10,000)		

d. A cash dividend should be declared on the number of shares of stock outstanding as of July 1. The effect is as follows:

BALANCE SHEET						INCOME STATEMENT
ASSETS	=	LIABILITIES	+	OWNERS' EQUITY	+	REVENUES – EXPENSES
		Dividends Payable—		Retained Earnings (19,500)		
		Common 11,500				
		Dividends Payable—				
		Preferred 8,000				

The number of common shares outstanding should be calculated as the number of shares issued (12,000) less the number of shares of treasury stock (500). The preferred stock dividend should be calculated as 1,000 shares times $100 par times 8%.

e.

BALANCE SHEET						INCOME STATEMENT
ASSETS	=	LIABILITIES		+	OWNERS' EQUITY	+	REVENUES – EXPENSES

Cash	(19,500)	Dividends Payable—			
		Common	(11,500)		
		Dividends Payable—			
		Preferred	(8,000)		

f. A stock dividend should be based on the number of shares of stock outstanding and should be declared and recorded at the market value of the stock. The impact is as follows:

BALANCE SHEET				INCOME STATEMENT
ASSETS	=	LIABILITIES	+	OWNERS' EQUITY	+	REVENUES – EXPENSES

Retained Earnings	(13,000)	
Preferred Stock	10,000	
Additional Paid-in		
Capital—Preferred	3,000	

The amount of the reduction of retained earnings should be calculated as the number of shares outstanding (1,000) times 10% times $130 per share.

2. The Stockholders' Equity for Andrew Company after completing these transactions appears as follows:

Preferred stock, $100 par, 8%,	
20,000 shares authorized, 1,100 issued	$110,000
Common stock, $5 par,	
50,000 shares authorized, 12,000 issued	60,000
Additional paid-in capital—Preferred	13,000
Additional paid-in capital—Common	250,000
Retained earnings	167,500*
Total contributed capital and retained earnings	$600,500
Less: Treasury stock, 500 shares, common	(10,000)
Total stockholders' equity	$590,500

*$200,000 − $19,500 − $13,000 = $167,500

3. The book value per share of the common stock is calculated as follows:

($590,500 − $110,000)/11,500 shares = $41.78

CHAPTER HIGHLIGHTS

1. LO 1 The Stockholders' Equity category is composed of two parts. Contributed capital is the amount derived from stockholders and other external parties. Retained earnings is the amount of net income not paid as dividends.

2. LO 1 The Stockholders' Equity category reveals the number of shares authorized, issued, and outstanding. Treasury stock is stock that the firm has issued and repurchased but not retired.

3. LO 2 *Preferred stock* refers to a stock that has preference to dividends declared. If a dividend is declared, the preferred stockholders must receive a dividend before the common stockholders.

4. LO 3 When stock is issued for cash, the par value of the stock should be reported in the stock account and the amount in excess of par should be reported in an additional paid-in capital account.

5. LO 3 When stock is issued for a noncash asset, the transaction should reflect the value of the stock given or the value of the property received, whichever is more evident.

6. LO 4 Treasury stock is accounted for as a reduction of stockholders' equity. When treasury stock is reissued and the cost is less than reissue price, the difference is added to additional paid-in capital. When cost exceeds reissue price, additional paid-in capital or retained earnings is reduced for the difference.

7. LO 5 The amount of cash dividends to be paid to common and preferred stockholders depends on the terms of the preferred stock. If the stock is cumulative, preferred stockholders have the right to dividends in arrears before current-year dividends are paid. Participating preferred stock indicates that preferred stockholders can share in the dividend amount that exceeds a specified amount.

8. LO 6 Stock dividends involve the issuance of additional shares of stock. The dividend should normally reflect the fair market value of the additional shares.

9. LO 7 Stock splits are similar to stock dividends except that splits reduce the par value per share of the stock. No accounting transaction is necessary for splits.

10. LO 8 The statement of stockholders' equity reflects the changes in the balances of all stockholder equity accounts.

11. LO 9 Book value per share is calculated as net assets divided by the number of shares of common stock outstanding. It indicates the rights that stockholders have, based on recorded values, to the net assets in the event of liquidation and is therefore not a measure of the market value of the stock.

12. LO 9 When a corporation has both common and preferred stock, the net assets attributed to the rights of the preferred stockholders must be deducted from the amount of net assets to determine the book value per share of the common stock.

13. LO 10 Transactions involving stockholders' equity accounts should be reflected in the Financing Activities category of the statement of cash flows.

KEY TERMS QUIZ

Read each definition below and then write the number of the definition in the blank beside the appropriate term it defines. The solution appears at the end of the chapter.

___ Authorized shares	___ Treasury stock
___ Issued shares	___ Retirement of stock
___ Outstanding shares	___ Dividend payout ratio
___ Par value	___ Stock dividend
___ Additional paid-in capital	___ Stock split
___ Retained earnings	___ Statement of stockholders' equity
___ Cumulative feature	___ Comprehensive income
___ Participating feature	___ Book value per share
___ Convertible feature	___ Market value per share
___ Callable feature	

1. The number of shares sold or distributed to stockholders.

2. An arbitrary amount that is stated on the face of the stock certificate and that represents the legal capital of the firm.

3. Net income that has been made by the corporation but not paid out as dividends.

4. Stock for which holders have a right to dividends in arrears before the current-year dividend is distributed.

5. Allows preferred stock to be returned to the corporation in exchange for common stock.

6. Stock issued by the firm and then repurchased but not retired.

7. The annual dividend amount divided by the annual net income.

8. A statement that reflects the differences between beginning and ending balances for all accounts in the Stockholders' Equity category.

9. Creation of additional shares of stock and reduction of the par value of the stock.

10. Total stockholders' equity divided by the number of shares of common stock outstanding.

11. The amount that reflects the total change in net assets from all sources except investment or withdrawals by the owners of the company.

12. The selling price of the stock as indicated by the most recent stock transactions on, for example, the stock exchange.

13. The maximum number of shares a corporation may issue as indicated in the corporate charter.

14. The number of shares issued less the number of shares held as treasury stock.

15. The amount received for the issuance of stock in excess of the par value of the stock.

16. A provision allowing the preferred stockholders to share, on a percentage basis, in the distribution of an abnormally large dividend.

17. Allows the issuing firm to eliminate a class of stock by paying the stockholders a fixed amount.

18. When the stock of a corporation is repurchased with no intention to reissue at a later date.

19. A corporation's declaration and issuance of additional shares of its own stock to existing stockholders.

Additional paid-in capital Paid-in capital in excess of par value

Additional paid-in capital—treasury stock Paid-in capital from treasury stock transactions

Callable Redeemable

Capital account Owners' equity account

Contributed capital Paid-in capital

Retained earnings Retained income

Small stock dividend Stock dividend less than 20%

Stockholders' equity Owners' equity

QUESTIONS

1. What are the two major components of stockholders' equity? Which accounts generally appear in each component?

2. Corporations disclose the number of shares authorized, issued, and outstanding. What is the meaning of these terms? What causes a difference between the number of shares issued and the number outstanding?

3. Why do firms designate an amount as the par value of stock? Does par value indicate the selling price or market value of the stock?

4. If a firm has a net income for the year, will the balance in the Retained Earnings account equal the net income? What is the meaning of the balance of the account?

5. What is the meaning of the statement that preferred stock has a preference to dividends declared by the corporation? Do preferred stockholders have the right to dividends in arrears on preferred stock?

6. Why might some stockholders be inclined to buy preferred stock rather than common stock? What are the advantages of investing in preferred stock?

7. Why are common shareholders sometimes called *residual owners* when a company has both common and preferred stock outstanding?

8. When stock is issued in exchange for an asset, at what amount should the asset be reported? How could the fair market value be determined?

9. What is treasury stock? Why do firms use it? Where does it appear on a corporation's financial statements?

10. When treasury stock is bought and sold, the transactions do not result in gains or losses reported on the income statement. What account or accounts are used instead? Why are no income statement amounts recorded?

11. Many firms operate at a dividend payout ratio of less than 50%. Why do firms not pay a larger percentage of income as dividends?

12. What is a *stock dividend*? How should it be recorded?

13. Would you rather receive a cash dividend or a stock dividend from a company? Explain.

14. What is the difference between stock dividends and stock splits? How should stock splits be recorded?

15. How is the book value per share calculated? Does the amount calculated as book value per share mean that stockholders will receive a dividend equal to the book value?

16. Can the market value per share of stock be determined by the information on the income statement?

17. What is the difference between a statement of stockholders' equity and a retained earnings statement?

EXERCISES

LO 1 **Exercise 11-1** Stockholders' Equity Accounts

MJ Company has identified the following items. Indicate whether each item is included in an account in the Stockholders' Equity category of the balance sheet. Also indicate whether the item would increase or decrease stockholders' equity.

1. Preferred stock issued by MJ

2. Amount received by MJ in excess of par value when preferred stock was issued

3. Dividends in arrears on MJ preferred stock

4. Cash dividend declared but unpaid on MJ stock

5. Stock dividend declared but unissued by MJ

6. Treasury stock

7. Amount received in excess of cost when treasury stock is reissued by MJ

8. Retained earnings

LO 1 Exercise 11-2 Solve for Unknowns

The Stockholders' Equity category of Zache Company's balance sheet appears below.

Common stock, $10 par, 10,000 shares issued,	
9,200 outstanding	$?
Additional paid-in capital	?
Total contributed capital	$350,000
Retained earnings	100,000
Treasury stock, ? shares at cost	10,000
Total stockholders' equity	?

Required

1. Determine the missing values that are indicated by question marks.

2. What was the cost per share of the treasury stock?

LO 3 Exercise 11-3 Stock Issuance

Horace Company had the following transactions during 2001, its first year of business.

a. Issued 5,000 shares of $5 par common stock for cash at $15 per share.

b. Issued 7,000 shares of common stock on May 1 to acquire a factory building from Barkley Company. Barkley had acquired the building in 1997 at a price of $150,000. Horace estimated that the building was worth $175,000 on May 1, 2001.

c. Issued 2,000 shares of stock on June 1 to acquire a patent. The accountant has been unable to estimate the value of the patent but has determined that Horace's common stock was selling at $25 per share on June 1.

Required

1. Determine each event's impact on the accounting equation.

2. Determine the balance sheet amounts for common stock and additional paid-in capital.

LO 3 Exercise 11-4 Stock Issuances

The following transactions are for Weber Corporation in 2001:

a. On March 1, the corporation was organized and received authorization to issue 5,000 shares of 8%, $100 par value preferred stock and 2,000,000 shares of $10 par value common stock.

b. On March 10, Weber issued 5,000 shares of common stock at $35 per share.

c. On March 18, Weber issued 100 shares of preferred stock at $120 per share.

d. On April 12, Weber issued another 10,000 shares of common stock at $45 per share.

Required

1. Determine the effect on the accounting equation of each of the events.

2. Prepare the Stockholders' Equity section of the balance sheet as of December 31, 2001.

3. Does the balance sheet indicate the market value of the stock at year-end? Explain.

LO 4 Exercise 11-5 Treasury Stock

The Stockholders' Equity category of Bradford Company's balance sheet on January 1, 2001, appeared as follows:

Common stock, $10 par, 10,000 shares issued	
and outstanding	$100,000
Additional paid-in capital	50,000
Retained earnings	80,000
Total stockholders' equity	$230,000

The following transactions occurred during 2001:

a. Reacquired 2,000 shares of common stock at $20 per share on July 1.

b. Reacquired 400 shares of common stock at $18 per share on August 1.

Required

1. Determine the effect on the accounting equation of each event.

2. Assume the company resold the shares of treasury stock at $28 per share on October 1. Did the company benefit from the treasury stock transaction? If so, where is the "gain" presented on the balance sheet?

LO 4 **Exercise 11-6** Treasury Stock Transactions

The stockholders' equity category of Little Joe's balance sheet on January 1, 2001, appeared as follows:

Common stock, $5 par, 40,000 shares issued and outstanding	$200,000
Additional paid-in capital	90,000
Retained earnings	100,000
Total stockholders' equity	$390,000

The following transactions occurred during 2001:

a. Reacquired 5,000 shares of common stock at $20 per share on February 1.

b. Reacquired 1,200 shares of common stock at $13 per share on March 1.

Required

1. Determine each event's impact on the accounting equation.

2. Assume that the treasury stock was reissued on October 1 at $12 per share. Did the company benefit from the treasury stock reissuance? Where is the "gain" or "loss" presented on the financial statements?

3. What effect did the two transactions to purchase treasury stock and the later reissuance of that stock have on the Stockholders' Equity section of the balance sheet?

LO 5 **Exercise 11-7** Cash Dividends

Kerry Company has 1,000 shares of $100 par value, 9% preferred stock and 10,000 shares of $10 par value common stock outstanding. The preferred stock is cumulative and nonparticipating. Dividends were paid in 1997. Since 1997, Kerry has declared and paid dividends as follows:

1998	$ 0
1999	10,000
2000	20,000
2001	25,000

Required

1. Determine the amount of the dividends to be allocated to preferred and common stockholders for each year, 1999 to 2001.

2. If the preferred stock had been noncumulative, how much would have been allocated to the preferred and common stockholders each year?

LO 5 **Exercise 11-8** Cash Dividends

The Stockholders' Equity category of Jackson Company's balance sheet as of January 1, 2001, appeared as follows:

Preferred stock, $100 par, 8%, 2,000 shares issued and outstanding	$200,000
Common stock, $10 par, 5,000 shares issued and outstanding	50,000
Additional paid-in capital	300,000
Total contributed capital	$550,000
Retained earnings	400,000
Total stockholders' equity	$950,000

The footnotes that accompany the financial statements indicate that Jackson has not paid dividends for the two years prior to 2001. On July 1, 2001, Jackson declares a dividend of $100,000 to be paid to preferred and common stockholders on August 1.

Required

1. Determine the amounts of the dividend to be allocated to preferred and common stockholders, assuming that the preferred stock is noncumulative, nonparticipating stock.

2. Determine the effect on the accounting equation of the July 1 and August 1, 2001 events.

3. Determine the amounts of the dividend to be allocated to preferred and common stockholders, assuming instead that the preferred stock is cumulative, nonparticipating stock.

LO 5   Exercise 11-9   Cash Dividends—Participating Feature

Refer to Jackson Company's Stockholders' Equity category in Exercise 11-8. Assume that the footnotes to the financial statements indicate that Jackson has not paid dividends for the two years prior to 2001. On July 1, 2001, Jackson declares a dividend of $100,000 to be paid to preferred and common stockholders on August 1.

Required

1. Determine the amounts of the dividend to be allocated to preferred and common stock, assuming that the preferred stock is cumulative and participates in dividends in proportion to the total par value of preferred and common stock.

2. Determine the effect on the accounting equation of the July 1 and August 1, 2001 events.

LO 6   Exercise 11-10   Stock Dividends

The Stockholders' Equity category of Worthy Company's balance sheet as of January 1, 2001, appeared as follows:

Common stock, $10 par,	
40,000 shares issued and outstanding	$400,000
Additional paid-in capital	100,000
Retained earnings	400,000
Total stockholders' equity	$900,000

The following transactions occurred during 2001:

a. Declared a 10% stock dividend to common stockholders on January 15. At the time of the dividend, the common stock was selling for $30 per share. The stock dividend was to be issued to stockholders on January 30, 2001.

b. Distributed the stock dividend to the stockholders on January 30, 2001.

Required

1. Determine the effect on the accounting equation of the 2001 events.

2. Develop the Stockholders' Equity category of Worthy Company's balance sheet as of January 31, 2001, after the stock dividend was issued. What effect did these transactions have on total stockholders' equity?

LO 7   Exercise 11-11   Stock Dividends versus Stock Splits

Campbell Company wants to increase the number of shares of its common stock outstanding and is considering a stock dividend versus a stock split. The Stockholders' Equity of the firm on its most recent balance sheet appeared as follows:

Common stock, $10 par,	
50,000 shares issued and outstanding	$ 500,000
Additional paid-in capital	750,000
Retained earnings	880,000
Total stockholders' equity	$2,130,000

If a stock dividend is chosen, the firm wants to declare a 100% stock dividend. Because the stock dividend qualifies as a "large stock dividend," it must be recorded at par value. If a stock split is chosen, Campbell will declare a 2-for-1 split.

Required

1. Compare the effects of the stock dividends and stock splits on the accounting equation.
2. Develop the Stockholders' Equity category of Campbell's balance sheet (a) after the stock dividend and (b) after the stock split.

LO 7   Exercise 11-12   Stock Dividends and Stock Splits
Whitacre Company's Stockholders' Equity section of the balance sheet on December 31, 2000, was as follows:

Common stock, $10 par value,	
60,000 shares issued and outstanding	$ 600,000
Additional paid-in capital	480,000
Retained earnings	1,240,000
Total stockholders' equity	$2,320,000

On May 1, 2001, Whitacre declared and issued a 15% stock dividend, when the stock was selling for $20 per share. Then, on November 1, it declared and issued a 2-for-1 stock split.

Required

1. How many shares of stock are outstanding at year-end?
2. What is the par value per share of these shares?
3. Develop the Stockholders' Equity category of Whitacre's balance sheet as of December 31, 2001.

LO 8   Exercise 11-13   Reporting Changes in Stockholders' Equity Items
On May 1, 2000, Ryde Inc. had common stock of $345,000, additional paid-in capital of $1,298,000, and retained earnings of $3,013,000. Ryde did not purchase or sell any common stock during the year. The company reported net income of $556,000 and declared dividends in the amount of $78,000 during the year ended April 30, 2001.

Required

Prepare a financial statement that explains all the reasons for the differences between the beginning and ending balances for the accounts in the Stockholders' Equity category of the balance sheet.

LO 8   Exercise 11-14   Comprehensive Income
Assume that you are the accountant for Ellis Corporation, which has issued its 2001 annual report. You have received an inquiry from a stockholder who has questions about several items in the annual report, including why Ellis has not shown certain transactions on the income statement. In particular, Ellis's 2001 balance sheet revealed two accounts in Stockholders' Equity (Unrealized Gain/Loss— Available-for-Sale Securities and Loss on Foreign Currency Translation Adjustments) for which the dollar amounts involved were not reported on the income statement.

Required

Draft a written response to the stockholder's inquiry that explains the nature of the two accounts and the reason that the amounts involved were not recorded on the 2001 income statement. Do you think the concept of comprehensive income would be useful to explain the impact of all events for Ellis Corporation?

LO 9   Exercise 11-15   Payout Ratio and Book Value per Share
Divac Company has developed a statement of stockholders' equity for the year 2001 as follows:

	Preferred Stock	Paid-in Capital— Preferred	Common Stock	Paid-in Capital— Common	Retained Earnings
Balance Jan. 1	$100,000	$50,000	$400,000	$40,000	$200,000
Stock issued			100,000	10,000	
Net income					80,000
Cash dividend					− 45,000
Stock dividend	10,000	5,000			− 15,000
Balance Dec. 31	$110,000	$55,000	$500,000	$50,000	$220,000

Divac's preferred stock is $100 par, 8% stock. If the stock is liquidated or redeemed, stockholders are entitled to $120 per share. There are no dividends in arrears on the stock. The common stock has a par value of $5 per share.

Required

1. Determine the dividend payout ratio for the common stock.
2. Determine the book value per share of Divac's common stock.

LO 10   Exercise 11-16   Impact of Transactions Involving Issuance of Stock on Statement of Cash Flows

From the following list, identify each item as operating (O), investing (I), financing (F), or not separately reported on the statement of cash flows (N).

_____ Issuance of common stock for cash

_____ Issuance of preferred stock for cash

_____ Issuance of common stock for equipment

_____ Issuance of preferred stock for land and building

_____ Conversion of preferred stock into common stock

LO 10   Exercise 11-17   Impact of Transactions Involving Treasury Stock on Statement of Cash Flows

From the following list, identify each item as operating (O), investing (I), financing (F), or not separately reported on the statement of cash flows (N).

_____ Repurchase common stock as treasury stock

_____ Reissuance of common stock (held as treasury stock)

_____ Retirement of treasury stock

LO 10   Exercise 11-18   Impact of Transactions Involving Dividends on Statement of Cash Flows

From the following list, identify each item as operating (O), investing (I), financing (F), or not separately reported on the statement of cash flows (N).

_____ Payment of cash dividend on common stock

_____ Payment of cash dividend on preferred stock

_____ Distribution of stock dividend

_____ Declaration of stock split

LO 10   Exercise 11-19   Determining Dividends Paid on Statement of Cash Flows

Clifford Company's comparative balance sheet included dividends payable of $80,000 at December 31, 2000, and $100,000 at December 31, 2001. Dividends declared by Clifford during 2001 amounted to $400,000.

Required

1. Calculate the amount of dividends actually paid to stockholders during 2001.
2. How will Clifford report the dividend payments on its 2001 statement of cash flows?

PROBLEMS

LO 1   Problem 11-1   Stockholders' Equity Category

Peeler Company was incorporated as a new business on January 1, 2001. The corporate charter approved on that date authorized the issuance of 1,000 shares of $100 par, 7% cumulative, non-participating preferred stock and 10,000 shares of $5 par common stock. On January 10, Peeler issued for cash 500 shares of preferred stock at $120 per share and 4,000 shares of common at $80 per share. On January 20, it issued 1,000 shares of common stock to acquire a building site, at a time when the stock was selling for $70 per share.

During 2001, Peeler established an employee benefit plan and acquired 500 shares of common stock at $60 per share as treasury stock for that purpose. Later in 2001, it resold 100 shares of the stock at $65 per share.

On December 31, 2001, Peeler determined its net income for the year to be $40,000. The firm declared the annual cash dividend to preferred stockholders and a cash dividend of $5 per share to the common stockholders. The dividends will be paid in 2002.

Required

Develop the Stockholders' Equity category of Peeler's balance sheet as of December 31, 2001. Indicate on the statement the number of shares authorized, issued, and outstanding for both preferred and common stock.

LO 2 Problem 11-2 Evaluating Alternative Investments

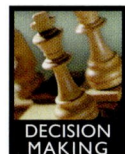

DECISION MAKING

Ellen Hays received a windfall from one of her investments. She would like to invest $100,000 of the money in Linwood Inc., which is offering common stock, preferred stock, and bonds on the open market. The common stock has paid $8 per share in dividends for the past three years and the company expects to be able to perform as well in the current year. The current market price of the common stock is $100 per share. The preferred stock has an 8% dividend rate, cumulative and nonparticipating. The bonds are selling at par with an 8% stated rate.

1. What are the advantages and disadvantages of each type of investment?

2. Recommend one type of investment over the others to Ellen, and justify your reason.

LO 5 Problem 11-3 Dividends for Preferred and Common Stock

The Stockholders' Equity category of Greenbaum Company's balance sheet as of December 31, 2001, appeared as follows:

Preferred stock, $100 par, 8%,	
1,000 shares issued and outstanding	$ 100,000
Common stock, $10 par,	
20,000 shares issued and outstanding	200,000
Additional paid-in capital	250,000
Total contributed capital	$ 550,000
Retained earnings	450,000
Total stockholders' equity	$1,000,000

The footnotes to the financial statements indicate that dividends were not declared or paid for 1999 or 2000. Greenbaum wants to declare a dividend of $59,000 for 2001.

Required

Determine the total and the per-share amounts that should be declared to the preferred and common stockholders under the following assumptions:

1. The preferred stock is noncumulative, nonparticipating.

2. The preferred stock is cumulative, nonparticipating.

3. The preferred stock is cumulative and participating on the basis of the proportion of the total par values of the preferred and common stock.

LO 6 Problem 11-4 Effect of Stock Dividend

Favre Company has a history of paying cash dividends on its common stock. The firm did not have a particularly profitable year, however, in 2001. At the end of the year, Favre found itself without the necessary cash for a dividend and therefore declared a stock dividend to its common stockholders. A 50% stock dividend was declared to stockholders on December 31, 2001. The board of directors is unclear about a stock dividend's effect on Favre's balance sheet and has requested your assistance.

Required

1. Write a statement to indicate the effect that the stock dividend has on the financial statements of Favre Company.

2. A group of common stockholders has contacted the firm to express its concern about the effect of the stock dividend and to question the effect the stock dividend may have on the market price of the stock. Write a statement to address the stockholders' concerns.

Problem 11-5 Dividends and Stock Splits

On January 1, 2001, Frederiksen's Inc.'s Stockholders' Equity category appeared as follows:

Preferred stock, $80 par value, 7%,	
3,000 shares issued and outstanding	$240,000
Common stock, $10 par value,	
15,000 shares issued and outstanding	150,000
Additional paid-in capital—	
Preferred	60,000
Additional paid-in capital—	
Common	225,000
Total contributed capital	$ 675,000
Retained earnings	2,100,000
Total stockholders' equity	$2,775,000

The preferred stock is noncumulative and nonparticipating. During 2001, the following transactions occurred:

a. On March 1, declared a cash dividend of $16,800 on preferred stock. Paid the dividend on April 1.

b. On June 1, declared a 5% stock dividend on common stock. The current market price of the common stock was $18. The stock was issued on July 1.

c. On September 1, declared a cash dividend of $.50 per share on the common stock; paid the dividend on October 1.

d. On December 1, issued a 2-for-1 stock split of common stock, when the stock was selling for $50 per share.

Required

1. Explain each transaction's effect on the stockholders' equity accounts and the total stockholders' equity.

2. Develop the Stockholders' Equity category of the December 31, 2001, balance sheet. Assume the net income for the year was $650,000.

3. Write a paragraph that explains the difference between a stock dividend and a stock split.

LO 8 **Problem 11-6** Statement of Stockholders' Equity

Refer to all the facts in Problem 11-1.

Required

Develop a statement of stockholders' equity for Peeler Company for 2001. The statement should start with the beginning balance of each stockholders' equity account and explain the changes that occurred in each account to arrive at the 2001 ending balances.

LO 8 **Problem 11-7** Wrigley's Comprehensive Income

www.wrigley.com The consolidated statement of common stockholders' equity of Wm. Wrigley Jr. Company for the year ended December 31, 2001, appears at the top of page 537.

Required

1. Which items were included in comprehensive income? If these items had been included on the income statement as part of net income, what would have been the effect?

2. Do you think that the concept of comprehensive income would be useful to explain the impact of all the events that took place during 2001 to the stockholders of Wrigley?

LO 10 **Problem 11-8** Effects of Stockholders' Equity Transactions on Statement of Cash Flows

Refer to all the facts in Problem 11-1.

Required

Indicate how each of the transactions affects the cash flows of Peeler Company, by preparing the Financing Activities section of the 2001 statement of cash flows. Provide an explanation for the exclusion of any of these transactions from the Financing Activities section of the statement.

Wm. Wrigley Jr. Company Consolidated Statement of Stockholders' Equity Including Comprehensive Income

	Common Shares Outstanding	Common Stock	Class B Common Stock	Additional Paid-in Capital	Retained Earnings	Common Stock in Treasury	Other Comprehensive Income	Total Stockholders' Equity
BALANCE DECEMBER 31, 1998	92,896	$12,401	3,095	272	1,184,617	(6,712)	(36,641)	1,157,032
Net earnings					308,183			308,183
Other comprehensive income:								
Currency translation							(38,931)	(38,931)
Unrealized holding gain on marketable equity securities, net of $1,160 tax							2,153	2,153
Total comprehensive income								271,405
Dividends to shareholders					(170,663)			(170,663)
Treasury share purchases	(1,637)					(120,861)		(120,861)
Options exercised and stock awards granted	23			1		1,861		1,862
Conversion from Class B Common to Common	600	80	(80)					
BALANCE DECEMBER 31, 1999	91,882	$12,481	3,015	273	1,322,137	(125,712)	(73,419)	1,138,775

Multi-Concept Problems

LO 1, 4 Problem 11-9 Analysis of Stockholders' Equity

The Stockholders' Equity section of the December 31, 2001, balance sheet of Eldon Company appeared as follows:

Preferred stock, $30 par value,	
5,000 shares authorized, ? shares issued	$120,000
Common stock, ? par,	
10,000 shares authorized, 7,000 shares issued	70,000
Additional paid-in capital—Preferred	6,000
Additional paid-in capital—Common	560,000
Additional paid-in capital—Treasury stock	1,000
Total contributed capital	$757,000
Retained earnings	40,000
Less: Treasury stock, preferred, 100 shares	(3,200)
Total stockholders' equity	?

Required

Determine the following items, based on Eldon's balance sheet:

1. The number of shares of preferred stock issued
2. The number of shares of preferred stock outstanding
3. The average per-share sales price of the preferred stock when issued
4. The par value of the common stock
5. The average per-share sales price of the common stock when issued
6. The cost of the treasury stock per share
7. The total stockholders' equity
8. The per-share book value of the common stock, assuming that there are no dividends in arrears and that the preferred stock can be redeemed at its par value

LO 3, 4, 7 Problem 11-10 Effects of Stockholders' Equity Transactions on the Balance Sheet

The following transactions occurred at Horton Inc. during its first year of operation:

a. Issued 100,000 shares of common stock at $5 each; 1,000,000 shares are authorized at $1 par value.

b. Issued 10,000 shares of common stock for a building and land. The building was appraised for $20,000, but the value of the land is undeterminable. The stock is selling for $10 on the open market.

c. Purchased 1,000 shares of its own common stock on the open market for $16 per share.

d. Declared a dividend of $.10 per share on outstanding common stock. The dividend is to be paid after the end of the first year of operations. Market value of the stock is $26.

e. Declared a 2-for-1 stock split. The market value of the stock was $37 before the stock split.

f. Reported $180,000 of income for the year.

Required

1. Indicate each transaction's effect on the assets, liabilities, and owners' equity of Horton Inc.

2. Prepare the Owners' Equity section of the balance sheet.

3. Write a paragraph that explains the number of shares of stock issued and outstanding at the end of the year.

LO 2, 4 Problem 11-11 Owner's Equity Section of the Balance Sheet

The newly hired accountant at Ives Inc. prepared the following balance sheet:

Assets

Cash	$ 3,500
Accounts receivable	5,000
Treasury stock	500
Plant, property, and equipment	108,000
Retained earnings	1,000
Total assets	$118,000

Liabilities

Accounts payable	$ 5,500
Dividends payable	1,500

Owners' Equity

Common stock, $1 par, 100,000 shares issued	100,000
Additional paid-in capital	11,000
Total liabilities and owners' equity	$118,000

Required

1. Prepare a corrected balance sheet. Write a short explanation for each correction.

2. Why does the Retained Earnings account have a negative balance?

ALTERNATE PROBLEMS

LO 1 Problem 11-1A Stockholders' Equity Category

Kebler Company was incorporated as a new business on January 1, 2001. The corporate charter approved on that date authorized the issuance of 2,000 shares of $100 par 7% cumulative, nonparticipating preferred stock and 20,000 shares of $5 par common stock. On January 10, Kebler issued for cash 1,000 shares of preferred stock at $120 per share and 8,000 shares of common at $80 per share. On January 20, it issued 2,000 shares of common stock to acquire a building site, at a time when the stock was selling for $70 per share.

During 2001, Kebler established an employee benefit plan and acquired 1,000 shares of common stock at $60 per share as treasury stock for that purpose. Later in 2001, it resold 100 shares of the stock at $65 per share.

On December 31, 2001, Kebler determined its net income for the year to be $80,000. The firm declared the annual cash dividend to preferred stockholders and a cash dividend of $5 per share to the common stockholders. The dividend will be paid in 2002.

Required

Develop the Stockholders' Equity category of Kebler's balance sheet as of December 31, 2001. Indicate on the statement the number of shares authorized, issued, and outstanding for both preferred and common stock.

LO 2 Problem 11-2A Evaluating Alternative Investments

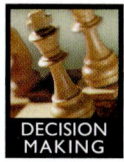

DECISION MAKING

Rob Lowe would like to invest $100,000 in Franklin Inc., which is offering common stock, preferred stock, and bonds on the open market. The common stock has paid $1 per share in dividends for the past three years, and the company expects to be able to double the dividend in the current year. The current market price of the common stock is $10 per share. The preferred stock has an 8% dividend rate. The bonds are selling at par with a 5% stated rate.

Required

1. Explain Franklin's obligation to pay dividends or interest on each instrument.

2. Recommend one type of investment over the others to Rob, and justify your reason.

LO 5 Problem 11-3A Dividends for Preferred and Common Stock

The Stockholders' Equity category of Rausch Company's balance sheet as of December 31, 2001, appeared as follows:

Preferred stock, $100 par, 8%,	
2,000 shares issued and outstanding	$ 200,000
Common stock, $10 par,	
40,000 shares issued and outstanding	400,000
Additional paid-in capital	500,000
Total contributed capital	$1,100,000
Retained earnings	900,000
Total stockholders' equity	$2,000,000

The footnotes to the financial statements indicate that dividends were not declared or paid for 1999 or 2000. Rausch wants to declare a dividend of $118,000 for 2001.

Required

Determine the total and the per-share amounts that should be declared to the preferred and common stockholders under the following assumptions:

1. The preferred stock is noncumulative, nonparticipating.

2. The preferred stock is cumulative, nonparticipating.

3. The preferred stock is cumulative and participating on the basis of the proportion of the total par values of the preferred and common stock.

LO 6 Problem 11-4A Effect of Stock Dividend

Travanti Company has a history of paying cash dividends on its common stock. Although the firm has been profitable this year, the board of directors has been planning construction of a second manufacturing plant. To reduce the amount that they must borrow to finance the expansion, the directors are contemplating replacing their usual cash dividend with a 40% stock dividend. The board is unsure what the effect of a stock dividend will be on the company's balance sheet and has requested your assistance.

Required

1. Write a statement to indicate the effect that the stock dividend has on the financial statements of Travanti Company.

2. A group of common stockholders has contacted the firm to express its concern about the effect of the stock dividend and to question the effect that the stock dividend may have on the market price of the stock. Write a statement to address the stockholders' concerns.

LO 7 Problem 11-5A Dividends and Stock Splits

On January 1, 2001, Svenberg Inc.'s Stockholders' Equity category appeared as follows:

Preferred stock, $80 par value, 8%,	
1,000 shares issued and outstanding	$ 80,000
Common stock, $10 par value,	
10,000 shares issued and outstanding	100,000
Additional paid-in capital—	
Preferred	60,000
Additional paid-in capital—	
Common	225,000
Total contributed capital	465,000
Retained earnings	1,980,000
Total stockholders' equity	$2,445,000

The preferred stock is noncumulative and nonparticipating. During 2001, the following transactions occurred:

a. On March 1, declared a cash dividend of $6,400 on preferred stock. Paid the dividend on April 1.

b. On June 1, declared an 8% stock dividend on common stock. The current market price of the common stock was $26. The stock was issued on July 1.

c. On September 1, declared a cash dividend of $.70 per share on the common stock; paid the dividend on October 1.

d. On December 1, issued a 3-for-1 stock split of common stock, when the stock was selling for $30 per share.

Required

1. Explain each transaction's effect on the stockholders' equity accounts and the total stockholders' equity.

2. Develop the Stockholders' Equity category of the balance sheet. Assume the net income for the year was $720,000.

3. Write a paragraph that explains the difference between a stock dividend and a stock split.

LO 8 Problem 11-6A Statement of Stockholders' Equity

Refer to all the facts in Problem 11-1A.

Required

Develop a statement of stockholders' equity for Kebler Company for 2001. The statement should start with the beginning balance of each stockholders' equity account and explain the changes that occurred in each account to arrive at the 2001 ending balances.

LO 8 Problem 11-7A Intel's Comprehensive Income

www.intel.com The consolidated statement of stockholders' equity of Intel Corporation for the year ended December 26, 1998, appears at the top of page 541.

Required

1. Explain the item that caused Intel's net income to be different from its comprehensive income. What does the term *unrealized gain* mean? What does a positive amount of $545 for unrealized gain mean?

2. Do you think that Intel's stockholders would find the concept of comprehensive income useful to evaluate the performance of the company?

LO 10 Problem 11-8A Effects of Stockholders' Equity Transactions on the Statement of Cash Flows

Refer to all the facts in Problem 11-1A.

Required

Indicate how each of the transactions affects the cash flows of Kebler Company, by preparing the Financing Activities section of the 2001 statement of cash flows. Provide an explanation for the exclusion of any of these transactions from the Financing Activities section of the statement.

Intel Corporation
Consolidated Statements of Stockholders' Equity

(in millions—except per share amounts)	Common Stock and Capital in Excess of Par Value		Retained Earnings	Accumulated Other Com- prehensive Income	Total
	Number of Shares	Amount			
Balance at December 27, 1997	3,256	3,311	15,926	58	19,295
Components of comprehensive income:					
Net income	—	—	6,068	—	6,068
Change in unrealized gain on available-for-sale investments	—	—	—	545	545
Total comprehensive income					6,613
Proceeds from sales of shares through employee stock plans, tax benefit of $415 and other	66	922	—	—	922
Proceeds from exercise of 1998 Step-Up Warrants	155	1,620	—	—	1,620
Proceeds from sales of put warrants	—	40	—	—	40
Reclassification of put warrant obligation, net	—	53	588	—	641
Repurchase and retirement of Common Stock	(162)	(1,124)	(4,462)	—	(5,586)
Cash dividends declared ($.050 per share)	—	—	(168)	—	(168)
Balance at December 26, 1998	3,315	$ 4,822	$17,952	$ 603	$23,377

Alternate Multi-Concept Problems

LO 1, 4 Problem 11-9A Analysis of Stockholders' Equity

The Stockholders' Equity section of the December 31, 2001, balance sheet of Carter Company appeared as follows:

Preferred stock, $50 par value,	
10,000 shares authorized, ? shares issued	$ 400,000
Common stock, ? par value,	
20,000 shares authorized, 14,000 shares issued	280,000
Additional paid-in capital—Preferred	12,000
Additional paid-in capital—Common	980,000
Additional paid-in capital—Treasury stock	2,000
Total contributed capital	$1,674,000
Retained earnings	80,000
Less: Treasury stock, preferred, 200 shares	(12,800)
Total stockholders' equity	$?

Determine the following items, based on Carter's balance sheet.

1. The number of shares of preferred stock issued
2. The number of shares of preferred stock outstanding
3. The average per-share sales price of the preferred stock when issued
4. The par value of the common stock
5. The average per-share sales price of the common stock when issued
6. The cost of the treasury stock per share
7. The total stockholders' equity
8. The per-share book value of the common stock, assuming that there are no dividends in arrears and that the preferred stock can be redeemed at its par value

LO 3, 4, 7 Problem 11-10A Effects of Stockholders' Equity Transactions on the Balance Sheet

The following transactions occurred at Hilton Inc. during its first year of operation:

a. Issued 10,000 shares of common stock at $10 each; 100,000 shares are authorized at $1 par value.

b. Issued 10,000 shares of common stock for a patent, which is expected to be effective for the next 15 years. The value of the patent is undeterminable. The stock is selling for $10 on the open market.

c. Purchased 1,000 shares of its own common stock on the open market for $10 per share.

d. Declared a dividend of $.50 per share of outstanding common stock. The dividend is to be paid after the end of the first year of operations. Market value of the stock is $10.

e. Income for the year is reported as $340,000.

Required

1. Indicate each transaction's effect on the assets, liabilities, and owners' equity of Hilton Inc.

2. Hilton's president has asked you to explain the difference between contributed capital and retained earnings. Discuss these terms as they relate to Hilton.

3. Determine the book value per share of the stock at the end of the year.

LO 2, 4 Problem 11-11A Equity Section of the Balance Sheet

The newly hired accountant at Grainfield Inc. is considering the following list of accounts as he prepares the balance sheet. All the accounts have positive balances. The company is authorized to issue 1,000,000 shares of common stock and 10,000 shares of preferred stock. The treasury stock was purchased at $5 per share.

Treasury stock (common)	$ 15,000
Retained earnings	54,900
Dividends payable	1,500
Common stock, $1 par	100,000
Additional paid-in capital	68,400
Preferred stock, $10 par, 5%	50,000

Required

1. Prepare the Owners' Equity section of the balance sheet for Grainfield.

2. Explain why some of the listed accounts are not shown in the Owners' Equity section.

CASES

Reading and Interpreting Financial Statements

LO 1, 2 Case 11-1 Uno's Stockholders' Equity Category

www.pizzeriauno.com Refer to Uno's 1999 annual report.

Required

1. What are the numbers of shares of preferred stock authorized, issued, and outstanding as of the balance sheet date?

2. What are the number of shares of common stock authorized, issued, and outstanding as of the balance sheet date?

3. Calculate the book value per share of the common stock.

4. The balance of the Retained Earnings account increased during the year. What are the possible factors that affect its balance?

5. The total stockholders' equity as of October 3, 1999, is $80,979,000. Does that mean that stockholders will receive that amount if the company is liquidated?

LO 1, 2 Case 11-2 Gateway's Stockholders' Equity Category

www.gateway.com Refer to Gateway's 1999 annual report.

Required

1. What are the numbers of shares of common stock authorized, issued, and outstanding as of the balance sheet date?

2. Calculate the book value per share of the common stock.

3. The balance of the Retained Earnings account increased during the year. What are the possible factors that affect the balance of this account?

4. The total stockholders' equity as of December 31, 1999, is $2,017,118,000. Does that mean that the stockholders will receive that amount if the company is liquidated?

LO 10 Case 11-3 Reading The Gap's Statement of Cash Flows

A portion of the cash flow statement of The Gap for the year ended January 29, 2000, is as follows (all amounts are in thousands of dollars):

	52 Weeks Ended		
Consolidated Statements of Cash Flows	**Jan. 29, 2000**	**Jan. 30, 1999**	**Jan. 31, 1998**
Cash Flows from Financing Activities			
Net increase in notes payable	84,778	1,357	44,462
Net issuance of long-term debt	311,839	—	495,890
Issuance of common stock	76,211	36,655	23,309
Net purchase of treasury stock	(707,125)	(879,383)	(585,798)
Cash dividends paid	(75,795)	(76,888)	(79,503)
Net cash used for financing activities	(310,092)	(918,259)	(101,640)

Required

1. Explain how each of the items in the Financing Activities category affected the amount of the company's cash. **www.gap.com**

2. The Gap used a large amount of cash to purchase treasury stock during the year. What are possible reasons for buying stock as treasury stock? What will happen to the treasury stock in future time periods?

3. The cash flow statement indicates a use of cash for dividends paid. How do dividends affect the Stockholders' Equity category of the balance sheet?

Making Financial Decisions

LO 1, 2 Case 11-4 Debt versus Preferred Stock

Assume that you are an analyst attempting to compare the financial structures of two companies. In particular, you must analyze the debt and equity categories of the two firms and calculate a debt-to-equity ratio for each firm. The liability and equity categories of First Company at year-end appeared as follows:

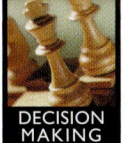

DECISION MAKING

Liabilities	
Accounts payable	$ 500,000
Loan payable	800,000
Stockholders' Equity	
Common stock	300,000
Retained earnings	600,000
Total debt and equity	$2,200,000

First Company's loan payable bears interest at 8%, which is paid annually. The principal is due in five years.

The liability and equity categories of Second Company at year-end appeared as follows:

Liabilities	
Accounts payable	$ 500,000
Stockholders' Equity	
Common stock	300,000
Preferred stock	800,000
Retained earnings	600,000
Total debt and equity	$2,200,000

Second Company's preferred stock is 8%, cumulative stock. A provision of the stock agreement specifies that the stock must be redeemed at face value in five years.

Required

1. It appears that the loan payable of First Company and the preferred stock of Second Company are very similar. What are the differences between the two securities?

2. When calculating the debt-to-equity ratio, do you believe that the Second Company preferred stock should be treated as debt or as stockholders' equity? Write a statement expressing your position on this issue.

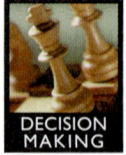

LO 2   Case 11-5   Preferred versus Common Stock

Rohnan Inc. needs to raise $500,000. It is considering two options:

a.   Issue preferred stock, $100 par, 8%, cumulative, nonparticipating, callable at $110. The stock could be issued at par.

b.   Issue common stock, $1 par, market $10. Currently, the company has 400,000 shares outstanding equally in the hands of five owners. The company has never paid a dividend.

Required

Rohnan has asked you to consider both options and make a recommendation. It is equally concerned with cash flow and company control. Write your recommendations.

Accounting and Ethics: What Would You Do?

LO 9   Case 11-6   Inside Information

Jim Brock was an accountant with Hubbard Inc., a large corporation with stock that was publicly traded on the New York Stock Exchange. One of Jim's duties was to manage the corporate reporting department, which was responsible for developing and issuing Hubbard's annual report. At the end of 2001, Hubbard closed its accounting records, and initial calculations indicated a very profitable year. In fact, the net income exceeded the amount that had been projected during the year by the financial analysts who followed Hubbard's stock.

Jim was very pleased with the company's financial performance. In January 2002, he suggested that his father buy Hubbard's stock because he was sure the stock price would increase when the company announced its 2001 results. Jim's father followed the advice and bought a block of stock at $25 per share.

On February 15, 2002, Hubbard announced its 2001 results and issued the annual report. The company received favorable press coverage about its performance, and the stock price on the stock exchange increased to $32 per share.

Required

What was Jim's professional responsibility to Hubbard Inc. concerning the issuance of the 2001 annual report? Did Jim act ethically in this situation?

LO 5   Case 11-7   Dividend Policy

Hancock Inc. is owned by nearly 100 shareholders. Judith Stitch owns 48% of the stock. She needs cash to fulfill her commitment to donate the funds to construct a new art gallery. Some of her friends have agreed to vote for Hancock to pay a larger-than-normal dividend to shareholders. Judith has asked you to vote for the large dividend because she knows that you also support the arts. When informed that the dividend may create a working capital hardship on Hancock, Judith responded: "There is plenty of money in Retained Earnings. The dividend will not affect the cash of the company." Respond to her comment. What ethical questions do you and Judith face? How would you vote?

INTERNET RESEARCH CASE

www.deltaairlines.com

Case 11-8   Delta Air Lines

Delta Air Lines operates in the highly volatile airline industry. It must respond to competition and to innovative technology, and it must do so in ways that continue to build shareholder value.

Conduct a search of the World Wide Web, obtain Delta's most recent annual report, or use library resources to obtain company information to answer the following:

1.   Based on the latest information available, what is Delta's (a) authorized number of common stock shares, (b) issued number of shares, (c) outstanding number of shares, and (d) the average issue price for those shares?

2.   For the most recent year available, what dividend per common share did Delta pay its stockholders?

3. Locate the past 52-week high and low and the most current market price for Delta Air Lines common stock. What financial factors may have affected the company's stock price over the past three to six months? Would you buy Delta stock at this time? Why or why not?

Optional Research. Use an online reservation system to investigate how the prices of Delta Air Lines plane tickets compare with those of the other airlines. Are they higher or lower? Are there some routes where Delta has a competitive advantage?

www.travelocity.com
www.1-800-airfare.com

SOLUTION TO KEY TERMS QUIZ

13 Authorized shares (p. 503)
1 Issued shares (p. 503)
14 Outstanding shares (p. 503)
2 Par value (p. 504)
15 Additional paid-in capital (p. 505)
3 Retained earnings (p. 506)
4 Cumulative feature (p. 507)
16 Participating feature (p. 507)
5 Convertible feature (p. 507)
17 Callable feature (p. 507)

6 Treasury stock (p. 509)
18 Retirement of stock (p. 511)
7 Dividend payout ratio (p. 511)
19 Stock dividend (p. 513)
9 Stock split (p. 515)
8 Statement of stockholders' equity (p. 517)
11 Comprehensive Income (p. 518)
10 Book value per share (p. 519)
12 Market value per share (p. 521)

Part III

INTEGRATIVE PROBLEM

Evaluating financing options for asset acquisition and their impact on financial statements

Following are the financial statements for Griffin Inc. for the year 2001.

GRIFFIN INC.
BALANCE SHEET
AS OF DECEMBER 31, 2001
(IN MILLIONS)

Assets		Liabilities	
Cash	$ 1.6	Current portion of lease	
Other current assets	6.4	obligation	$ 1.0
Leased assets (net of		Other current liabilities	3.0
accumulated depreciation)	7.0	Lease obligation—Long-term	6.0
Other long-term assets	45.0	Other long-term liabilities	6.0
		Total liabilities	$16.0

Preferred stock	$ 1.0
Additional paid-in capital on preferred stock	2.0
Common stock	4.0
Additional paid-in capital on common stock	16.0
Retained earnings	21.0
Total stockholders' equity	$44.0

Total assets	$60.0	Total liabilities and stockholders' equity	$60.0

GRIFFIN INC.
INCOME STATEMENT
FOR THE YEAR ENDED DECEMBER 31, 2001
(IN MILLIONS)

Revenues		$50.0
Expenses:		
Depreciation of leased asset	$ 1.0	
Depreciation—Other assets	3.2	
Interest on leased asset	.5	
Other expenses	27.4	
Income tax (30% rate)	5.4	
Total expenses		(37.5)
Income before extraordinary loss		$12.5
Extraordinary loss (net of $.9 taxes)		(2.1)
Net income		$10.4
EPS before extraordinary loss		$3.10
EPS extraordinary loss		(.53)
EPS—Net income		$2.57

Additional Information:

Griffin Inc. has authorized 500,000 shares of 10%, $10 par value cumulative preferred stock. There were 100,000 shares issued and outstanding at all times during 2001. The firm has also authorized 5 million shares of $1 par common stock, with 4 million shares issued and outstanding.

On January 1, 2001, Griffin Inc. acquired an asset, a piece of specialized heavy equipment, for $8 million with a capital lease. The lease contract indicates that the term of the lease is eight years. Payments of $1.5 million are to be made each December 31. The first lease payment was made December 31, 2001 and consisted of $1 million principal and $.5 million of interest expense. The capital lease is depreciated using the straight-line method over eight years with zero salvage value.

Required

1. Assuming the acquisition of the equipment using a capital lease, indicate the effect on the accounting equation of the acquisition, depreciation, and lease payment.

2. The management of Griffin Inc. is considering the financial statement impact of methods of financing, other than the capital lease, that could have been used to acquire the equipment. For each alternative **a**, **b**, and **c**, indicate the effect on the accounting equation, prepare revised 2001 financial statements and calculate, as revised, the following amounts or ratios:

   Current ratio
   Debt-to-equity ratio
   Net income
   EPS—Net income

Assume that the following alternative actions would have taken place on January 1, 2001.

a. Instead of acquiring the equipment with a capital lease, the company negotiated an operating lease to use the asset. The lease requires annual year-end payments of $1.5 million and results in "off-balance sheet" financing. (*Hint:* The $1.5 million should be treated as rental expense.)

b. Instead of acquiring the equipment with a capital lease, Griffin Inc. issued bonds for $8 million and purchased the equipment with the proceeds of the bond issue. Assume the bond interest of $.5 million was accrued and paid on December 31, 2001. A portion of the principal also is paid each year for eight years. On December 31, 2001, the company paid $1 million of principal and anticipated another $1 million of principal to be paid in 2002. Assume the equipment would have an eight-year life and would be depreciated on a straight-line basis with zero salvage value.

c. Instead of acquiring the equipment with a capital lease, Griffin Inc. issued 200,000 additional shares of 10% preferred stock to raise $8 million and purchased the equipment for $8 million with the proceeds from the stock issue. Dividends on the stock are declared and paid annually. Assume that a dividend payment was made on December 31, 2001. Assume the equipment would have an eight-year life and would be depreciated on a straight-line basis with zero salvage value.

UNO RESTAURANT CORPORATION

Founded in Chicago in 1943, Pizzeria Uno . . . Chicago Bar & Grill, now under the corporate umbrella of **Uno Restaurant Corporation (www.pizzeriauno.com),** has been growing steadily in the competitive $20 billion casual dining industry. With its unique Uno's Original Chicago Deep Dish Pizza and other entrées, appetizers, salads, beverages, and desserts, the retail chain has expanded to include more than 170 restaurants in 29 states, the District of Columbia, Puerto Rico, and Seoul, South Korea. The company's consumer products division supplies Pizzeria Uno–brand food products to theaters, hotels, supermarkets, and American Airlines.

In 1999, the company received two prestigious food industry awards that recognized and highlighted the popularity of the Uno brand: first place winner in the "Choice of Chains" customer survey conducted annually by *Restaurants & Institutions* magazine and the Platinum Award, the survey's highest honor for overall customer satisfaction scores. Also, that year for the first time, Uno's was listed among the nation's top 25 restaurant chains in sales per unit in an annual study conducted by *Nation's Restaurant News.* In fact, 1999 was a record year for revenue, net income, and earnings per share, all of which hit historical highs. Revenues for fiscal year 2000 rose another 8 percent, and the first quarter results for 2001 were up as well. The company invested in refurbishing stores, opening new ones in several locations, and closed a few that were not performing up to expectations.

Aside from attracting widespread industry attention, the company's steady progress toward its operational goals also gratified Uno's managers and shareholders. The firm has improved menus, as well as remodeled some restaurants, and continued its ongoing repositioning strategy, broadening its appeal to the mainstream casual dining market. The company's heightened brand recognition and solid increases in customer satisfaction combined with outstanding financial results to make the company's managers very optimistic about its future. They are targeting ambitious 15 to 20 percent growth rates over the next several years.

Plans for the near term include the continued addition of new restaurants, both company-owned and franchised, for a total of about 20 new stores in 2001. The strong performance of Uno's existing franchise operations, which currently account for about a third of its restaurants, led the company to project that about half the new outlets would be franchised.

In the spring of 2000, the company approved a repurchase of up to 500,000 shares of its common stock, extending a 1.1 million-share stock repurchase program it first announced in 1998 and extended in 1999. As of the publication of its 1999 annual report, the firm had repurchased over 700,000 of its shares. The company carries about $666,000 in capital lease obligations and a $4.6 million mortgage debt. It also relies on a revolving line of credit that it anticipates will help finance the development of additional restaurants as well as provide working capital. Other sources of financing include existing cash balances and cash generated from operations.

Questions

1. Why do you think Uno might be looking to increase the proportion of franchise restaurants it operates? What makes Uno attractive to a franchisee?

2. Current liabilities increased in 1999 as well as revenue. Can you suggest why?

3. What is the purpose of the stock repurchase plan, and why has it been extended?

ADDITIONAL TOPICS IN FINANCIAL REPORTING

A WORD TO STUDENTS ABOUT PART IV

Part IV will be fascinating and even fun—as long as you *keep practicing the concepts and reading the links from chapter to chapter.* **How does the corporation report cash flows?** See Chapter 12 to learn how to evaluate a company based on its cash flows. **Can you find the trends in a company's performance?** Use any set of financial statements you can find to practice the analysis concepts and skills presented in Chapter 13.

e-business

e-business ™

Study Links

A Look at Previous Chapters

In previous chapters, we have seen that assets and liabilities involve important cash flows to a business at one time or another. In Chapter 2, we introduced the statement of cash flows along with the other financial statements.

Chapter 11 completed our examination of the accounting and reporting issues for a company's various assets, liabilities, and equities. Specifically, in that chapter, we considered how companies account for stockholders' equity.

A Look at This Chapter

Now that we have a fuller appreciation of how to account for the various assets and liabilities of a business, we turn our attention in this chapter to an in-depth examination of the statement of cash flows.

A Look at the Upcoming Chapter

Stockholders, creditors, and other groups use financial statements, including the statement of cash flows, to analyze a company. We called attention in earlier chapters to various ratios often used to aid in these analyses. In the final chapter, we discuss the use of ratios and other types of analysis to better understand the financial strength and health of companies.

FOCUS ON FINANCIAL RESULTS

International Business Machines (IBM), the world's top provider of computer hardware, also makes and sells enough software to rank second only to industry powerhouse Microsoft. IBM's service operation is the largest in the world and brings in about 35 percent of the company's sales, a figure that is expected to grow to more than 50 percent within the next five years. IBM also owns Lotus Development, the pioneering maker of Lotus Notes, and Tivoli Systems, whose products help manage corporate computer networks. And, as it expands its international business, IBM bends its focus increasingly to the Internet.

According to CEO Louis Gerstner Jr., IBM plans to capture "a good chunk" of the exploding e-business segment of the information technology marketplace. "The revolution has arrived ... with stunning speed," says the company's 1999 Annual Report. "Any company and every company is a dot-com. *e-business is here.* We're never going back."

If the company successfully rides the ups and downs of the emerging dot-com marketplace, e-business could help replace some of the cash inflow the firm lost in its unsuccessful entry into the retail PC market, from which it withdrew at the end of 1999.

Overall, however, 1999 was another good year for IBM. The firm earned record revenue for the fifth straight year. As you can see from the consolidated statement of cash flows, after using $3.9 billion to buy marketable securities and other investments, and another $5.9 billion for capital expenditures, IBM still had substantial cash available to pay dividends to stockholders, to settle debt, and to invest in its ongoing stock buyback program.

consolidated statement of cash flows

International Business Machines Corporation
and Subsidiary Companies

(Dollars in millions) At December 31:	1999	1998*	1997*
Cash flow from operating activities:			
Net income	**$ 7,712**	$ 6,328	$ 6,093
Adjustments to reconcile net income to cash provided from operating activities:			
Depreciation	**6,159**	4,475	4,018
Amortization of software	**426**	517	983
Deferred income taxes	**(713)**	(606)	358
Gain on disposition of fixed and other assets	**(4,791)**	(261)	(273)
Other changes that (used) provided cash:			
Receivables	**(1,677)**	(2,736)	(3,727)
Inventories	**301**	73	432
Other assets	**(130)**	219	(378)
Accounts payable	**(3)**	362	699
Other liabilities	**2,827**	902	660
Net cash provided from operating activities	**10,111**	9,273	8,865
Cash flow from investing activities:			
Payments for plant, rental machines and other property	**(5,959)**	(6,520)	(6,793)
Proceeds from disposition of plant, rental machines and other property	**1,207**	905	1,130
Investment in software	**(464)**	(250)	(314)
Purchases of marketable securities and other investments	**(3,949)**	(4,211)	(1,617)
Proceeds from marketable securities and other investments	**2,616**	3,945	1,439
Proceeds from sale of the Global Network	**4,880**	—	—
Net cash used in investing activities	**(1,669)**	(6,131)	(6,155)
Cash flow from financing activities:			
Proceeds from new debt	**6,133**	7,567	9,142
Short-term borrowings less than 90 days – net	**276**	499	(668)
Payments to settle debt	**(7,510)**	(5,942)	(4,530)
Preferred stock transactions – net		(5)	(1)
Common stock transactions – net	**(6,645)**	(6,278)	(6,250)
Cash dividends paid	**(879)**	(834)	(783)
Net cash used in financing activities	**(8,625)**	(4,993)	(3,090)
Effect of exchange rate changes on cash and cash equivalents	**(149)**	120	(201)
Net change in cash and cash equivalents	**(332)**	(1,731)	(581)
Cash and cash equivalents at January 1	**5,375**	7,106	7,687
Cash and cash equivalents at December 31	**$ 5,043**	$ 5,375	$ 7,106
Supplemental data:			
Cash paid during the year for:			
Income taxes	**$ 1,904**	$ 1,929	$ 2,472
Interest	**$ 1,574**	$ 1,605	$ 1,475

* Reclassified to conform with 1999 presentation.
The accompanying notes on pages 69 through 93 are an integral part of the financial statements.

IBM's 1999 Annual Report

If you were an IBM stockholder, what evidence from the statement of cash flows would help you determine whether IBM's stock repurchase and its investments in marketable securities will generate long-term benefits? What additional information would you want? Look up IBM's most recent annual report; do you understand how the company has generated and used cash since 1999?

www.ibm.com

After studying this chapter, you should be able to:

LO 1 Explain the purpose of a statement of cash flows. (p. 553)

LO 2 Explain what cash equivalents are and how they are treated on the statement of cash flows. (p. 555)

LO 3 Describe operating, investing, and financing activities, and give examples of each. (p. 556)

LO 4 Describe the difference between the direct and the indirect methods of computing cash flow from operating activities. (p. 560)

LO 5 Prepare a statement of cash flows, using the direct method to determine cash flow from operating activities. (p. 565)

LO 6 Prepare a statement of cash flows, using the indirect method to determine cash flow from operating activities. (p. 576)

LO 7 Use a work sheet to prepare a statement of cash flows, using the indirect method to determine cash flow from operating activities (Appendix 12A). (p. 584)

CASH FLOWS AND ACCRUAL ACCOUNTING

The *bottom line* is a phrase used in many different ways in today's society. "I wish politicians would cut out all the rhetoric and get to the bottom line." "The bottom line is that the manager was fired because the team wasn't winning." "Our company's bottom line is twice what it was last year." This last use of the phrase, in reference to a company's net income, is probably the way in which *bottom line* was first used. In recent years, managers, stockholders, creditors, analysts, and other users of financial statements have become more and more wary of focusing on any one number as an indicator of a company's overall performance. Most experts now agree that there has been a tendency to rely far too heavily on net income and its companion, earnings per share, and, in many cases, to ignore a company's cash flows. As you know by now from your study of accounting, you can't pay bills with net income; you need cash!

www.ibm.com

To understand the difference between a company's bottom line and its cash flow, consider the case of IBM Corporation in 1999. IBM reported net income of over $7.7 billion in 1999. However, as shown in the chapter opener, during this same time period its cash actually decreased by $332 million. How is this possible? First, net income is computed on an accrual basis, not a cash basis. Second, the income statement primarily reflects events related to the operating activities of a business—that is, selling products or providing services.

If you think about it, any one of four combinations is possible. That is, a company's cash position can increase or decrease during a period, and it can report a net profit

EXHIBIT 12-1 Cash Flows and Net Income for Four Technology Companies in 1999 (all amounts in millions of dollars)

Company	Beginning Balance in Cash	Ending Balance in Cash	Increase (Decrease) in Cash	Net Income (Loss)
Intel (fiscal year ended December 25, 1999)	$2,038	$3,695	$1,657	$7,314
IBM	5,375	5,043	(332)	7,712
Lycos (fiscal year ended July 31, 1999)	154	153	(1)	(52)
Amazon.com	26	117	91	(720)

or a net loss. Exhibit 12-1 illustrates this point by showing the performance of four technology-related companies, including IBM, during 1999. Intel is the only one of the four companies that both improved its cash position in 1999 and reported a net profit. As seen in the chapter opener, IBM reported a net profit; nevertheless, it experienced a net decrease in cash during 1999. Lycos reported a net loss in 1999 and also saw its cash decline. Finally, Amazon.com experienced a net loss in 1999, but improved its cash position. To summarize, a company with a profitable year does not necessarily increase its cash position, nor does a company with an unprofitable year always experience a decrease in cash.

PURPOSE OF THE STATEMENT OF CASH FLOWS

The **statement of cash flows** is an important complement to the other major financial statements. It summarizes the operating, investing, and financing activities of a business over a period of time. The balance sheet summarizes the cash on hand and the balances in other assets, liabilities, and owners' equity accounts, providing a snapshot at a specific point in time. The statement of cash flows reports the changes in cash over a period of time and, most important, *explains these changes.*

LO 1 Explain the purpose of a statement of cash flows.

The income statement summarizes performance on an accrual basis. As you have learned in your study of accrual accounting, income on this basis is considered a better indicator of *future* cash inflows and outflows than is a statement limited to current cash flows. The statement of cash flows complements the accrual-based income statement by allowing users to assess a company's performance on a cash basis. As we will see in the following simple example, however, it also goes beyond presenting data related to operating performance and looks at other activities that affect a company's cash position.

AN EXAMPLE

Consider the following discussion between the owner of Fox River Realty and the company accountant. After a successful first year in business in 2000, in which it earned a profit of $100,000, the owner reviews the income statement for the second year, as presented in Exhibit 12-2.

The owner is pleased with the results and asks to see the balance sheet. Comparative balance sheets for the first two years are presented in Exhibit 12-3.

Where Did the Cash Go? At first glance, the owner is surprised to see the significant decline in the Cash account. She immediately presses the accountant for answers. With such a profitable year, where has the cash gone? Specifically, why has cash decreased from $150,000 to $50,000, even though income rose from $100,000 in the first year to $250,000 in the second year?

EXHIBIT 12-2 Income Statement for Fox River Realty

FOX RIVER REALTY	
INCOME STATEMENT	
FOR THE YEAR ENDED DECEMBER 31, 2001	
Revenues	$400,000
Depreciation expense	$ 50,000
All other expenses	100,000
Total expenses	$150,000
Net income	$250,000

EXHIBIT 12-3 Balance Sheets for Fox River Realty

FOX RIVER REALTY
COMPARATIVE BALANCE SHEETS
DECEMBER 31

	December 31	
	2001	**2000**
Cash	$ 50,000	$150,000
Plant and equipment	600,000	350,000
Accumulated depreciation	(150,000)	(100,000)
Total assets	$500,000	$400,000
Notes payable	$100,000	$150,000
Common stock	250,000	200,000
Retained earnings	150,000	50,000
Total equities	$500,000	$400,000

The accountant begins his explanation to the owner by pointing out that income on a cash basis is even *higher* than the reported $250,000. Because depreciation expense is an expense that does not use cash (cash is used when the plant and equipment are purchased, not when they are depreciated), cash provided from operating activities is calculated as follows:

Net income	$250,000
Add back: Depreciation expense	50,000
Cash provided by operating activities	$300,000

Further, the accountant reminds the owner of the additional $50,000 that she invested in the business during the year. Now the owner is even more bewildered: with cash from operations of $300,000 and her own infusion of $50,000, why did cash *decrease* by $100,000? The accountant refreshes the owner's memory on three major outflows of cash during the year. First, even though the business earned $250,000, she withdrew $150,000 in dividends during the year. Second, the comparative balance sheets indicate that notes payable with the bank were reduced from $150,000 to $100,000, requiring the use of $50,000 in cash. Finally, the comparative balance sheets show an increase in plant and equipment for the year from $350,000 to $600,000—a sizable investment of $250,000 in new long-term assets.

Statement of Cash Flows To summarize what happened to the cash, the accountant prepares a statement of cash flows as shown in Exhibit 12-4. Although the owner is not particularly happy with the decrease in cash for the year, she is at least satisfied with the statement as an explanation of where the cash came from and how it was used. The statement summarizes the important cash activities for the year and fills a void created with the presentation of just an income statement and a balance sheet.

REPORTING REQUIREMENTS FOR A STATEMENT OF CASH FLOWS

Accounting standards specify both the basis for preparing the statement of cash flows and the classification of items on the statement.[1] First, the statement must be prepared on a cash basis. Second, the cash flows must be classified into three categories:

---

[1] *Statement of Financial Accounting Standards No. 95,* "Statement of Cash Flows" (Stamford, Conn.: Financial Accounting Standards Board, November 1987).

EXHIBIT 12-4   Statement of Cash Flows for Fox River Realty

FOX RIVER REALTY
STATEMENT OF CASH FLOWS
FOR THE YEAR ENDED DECEMBER 31, 2001

Cash provided (used) by operating activities:	
Net income	$ 250,000
Add back: Depreciation expense	50,000
Net cash provided (used) by operating activities	$ 300,000
Cash provided (used) by investing activities:	
Purchase of new plant and equipment	$(250,000)
Cash provided (used) by financing activities:	
Additional investment by owner	$ 50,000
Cash dividends paid to owner	(150,000)
Repayment of notes payable to bank	(50,000)
Net cash provided (used) by financing activities	$(150,000)
Net increase (decrease) in cash	$(100,000)
Cash balance at beginning of year	150,000
Cash balance at end of year	$ 50,000

- Operating activities
- Investing activities
- Financing activities

We now take a closer look at each of these important requirements in preparing a statement of cash flows.

THE DEFINITION OF CASH: CASH AND CASH EQUIVALENTS

The purpose of the statement of cash flows is to provide information about a company's cash inflows and outflows. Thus, it is essential to have a clear understanding of what the definition of *cash* includes. According to accounting standards, certain items are recognized as being equivalent to cash and are combined with cash on the balance sheet and the statement of cash flows.

Commercial paper (short-term notes issued by corporations), money market funds, and Treasury bills are examples of cash equivalents. To be classified as a **cash equivalent,** an item must be readily convertible to a known amount of cash and have a maturity *to the investor* of three months or less. For example, a three-year Treasury note purchased two months before its maturity is classified as a cash equivalent. The same note purchased two years before maturity is not classified as a cash equivalent but as an investment.

To understand why cash equivalents are combined with cash when preparing a statement of cash flows, assume that a company has a cash balance of $10,000 and no assets that qualify as cash equivalents. Further assume that the $10,000 is used to purchase 90-day Treasury bills. The effect on the accounting equation of the purchase is as follows:

LO 2 Explain what cash equivalents are and how they are treated on the statement of cash flows.

BALANCE SHEET						INCOME STATEMENT	
ASSETS	**=**	**LIABILITIES**	**+**	**OWNERS' EQUITY**	**+**	**REVENUES – EXPENSES**	
Investment in Treasury							
Bills 10,000							
Cash (10,000)							

For record-keeping purposes, it is important to recognize this transaction as a transfer between cash in the bank and an investment in a government security. In the strictest sense, the investment represents an outflow of cash. The purchase of a security with such a short maturity does not, however, involve any significant degree of risk in terms of price changes and thus is not reported on the statement of cash flows as an outflow. Instead, for purposes of classification on the balance sheet and the statement of cash flows, this is merely a transfer *within* the cash and cash equivalents category. The important point is that before the purchase of the Treasury bills, the company had $10,000 in cash and cash equivalents and after the purchase, it still had $10,000 in cash and cash equivalents. *Because nothing changed, the transaction is not reported on the statement of cash flows.*

Now, assume a different transaction in which a company purchases shares of GM common stock for cash. The effect on the accounting equation of this purchase is as follows:

BALANCE SHEET					INCOME STATEMENT
ASSETS	=	LIABILITIES	+	OWNERS' EQUITY	+ REVENUES – EXPENSES
Investment in GM Common Stock 10,000					
Cash (10,000)					

This purchase involves a certain amount of risk for the company making the investment. The GM stock is not convertible to a known amount of cash because its market value is subject to change. Thus, for balance sheet purposes, the investment is not considered a cash equivalent and therefore is not combined with cash but is classified as either a trading security or an available-for-sale security, depending on the company's intent in holding the stock (the distinction between these two types was discussed in Chapter 7). In the preparation of a statement of cash flows, the *investment in stock of another company is considered a significant activity and thus is reported on the statement of cash flows.*

CLASSIFICATION OF CASH FLOWS

LO 3 Describe operating, investing, and financing activities, and give examples of each.

For the statement of cash flows, companies are required to classify activities into three categories: operating, investing, or financing. These categories represent the major functions of an entity, and classifying activities in this way allows users to look at important relationships. For example, one important financing activity for many businesses is borrowing money. Grouping the cash inflows from borrowing money during the period with the cash outflows from repayments of loans during the period makes it easier for analysts and other users of the statements to evaluate the company.

Each of the three types of activities can result both in cash inflows and in cash outflows to the company. Thus, the general format for the statement is as shown in Exhibit 12-5. Note the direct tie between the bottom portion of this statement and the balance sheet. The beginning and ending balances in cash and cash equivalents, shown as the last two lines on the statement of cash flows, are taken directly from the comparative balance sheets. Some companies end their statement of cash flows with the figure for the net increase or decrease in cash and cash equivalents and do not report the beginning and ending balances in cash and cash equivalents directly on the statement of cash flows. Instead, the reader must turn to the balance sheet for these amounts. We now take a closer look at the types of activities that appear in each of the three categories on the statement of cash flows.

Operating Activities   **Operating activities** involve acquiring and selling products and services. The specific activities of a business depend on its type. For example, the purchase of raw materials is an important operating activity for a manufacturer. For a retailer, the purchase of inventory from a distributor constitutes an operating activity. For a realty company, the payment of a commission to a salesperson is an operating activity. All three types of businesses sell either products or services, and their sales are important operating activities.

A statement of cash flows reflects the cash effects, either inflows or outflows, associated with each of these activities. For example, the manufacturer's payment for purchases of raw

EXHIBIT 12-5   Format for the Statement of Cash Flows

THE SMITH CORPORATION
STATEMENT OF CASH FLOWS
FOR THE YEAR ENDED DECEMBER 31, 2001

Cash flows from operating activities:

Inflows	$ xxx	
Outflows	(xxx)	
Net cash provided (used) by operating activities		$xxx

Cash flows from investing activities:

Inflows	xxx	
Outflows	(xxx)	
Net cash provided (used) by investing activities		xxx

Cash flows from financing activities:

Inflows	xxx	
Outflows	(xxx)	
Net cash provided (used) by financing activities		xxx
Net increase (decrease) in cash and cash equivalents		$xxx
Cash and cash equivalents at beginning of year		xxx
Cash and cash equivalents at end of year		$xxx

materials results in a cash outflow. The receipt of cash from collecting an account receivable results in a cash inflow. The income statement reports operating activities on an accrual basis. The statement of cash flows reflects a company's operating activities on a cash basis.

Investing Activities   **Investing activities** involve acquiring and disposing of long-term assets. Replacing worn-out plant and equipment and expanding the existing base of long-term assets are essential to all businesses. In fact, cash paid for these acquisitions, often called *capital expenditures,* is usually the largest single item in the Investing Activities section of the statement. The following excerpt from IBM's 1999 statement of cash flows (also shown in the chapter opener) indicates **1** that the company spent $5,959 million for plant, rental machines, and other property during 1999 (all amounts are in millions of dollars):

Cash flow from investing activities:

1 Payments for plant, rental machines, and other property	(5,959)
2 Proceeds from disposition of plant, rental machines, and other property	1,207
Investment in software	(464)
4 Purchases of marketable securities and other investments	(3,949)
Proceeds from marketable securities and other investments	2,616
3 Proceeds from sale of the Global Network	4,880
Net cash used in investing activities	(1,669)

Sales of long-term assets, such as plant and equipment, are not generally a significant source of cash. These assets are acquired to be used in producing goods and services, or to support this function, rather than to be resold, as is true for inventory. Occasionally, however, plant and equipment may wear out or no longer be needed and are offered for sale. In fact, the excerpt from IBM's report indicates that it generated $1,207 million of cash in 1999 from **2** disposals of plant, rental machines, and other property.

In Chapter 7, we explained why companies sometimes invest in the stocks and bonds of other companies. The classification of these investments on the statement of cash flows depends on the type of investment. The acquisition of one company by another, whether in

the form of a merger or a stock acquisition, is an important *investing* activity to bring to the attention of statement readers. Although IBM did not acquire any other companies during 1999, it did receive $4,880 million from **3** the sale of its Global Network to AT&T. Note that in 1999, IBM spent $3,949 million to buy **4** marketable securities and other investments and generated $2,616 million from selling these investments. According to a footnote to IBM's statements, the company classifies marketable securities as available for sale.

Cash flows from purchases, sales, and maturities of held-to-maturity securities (bonds) and available-for-sale securities (stocks and bonds) are classified as *investing* activities. On the other hand, these same types of cash flows for trading securities are classified as *operating* activities. This apparent inconsistency in the accounting rules is based on the idea that trading securities are held for the express purpose of generating short-term profits and thus are operating in nature.

Financing Activities

All businesses rely on internal financing, external financing, or a combination of the two in meeting their needs for cash. Initially, a new business must have a certain amount of investment by the owners to begin operations. After this, many companies use notes, bonds, and other forms of debt to provide financing.[2] Issuing stock and various forms of debt results in cash inflows that appear as **financing activities** on the statement of cash flows. On the other side, the repurchase of a company's own stock and the repayment of borrowings are important cash outflows to be reported in the Financing Activities section of the statement. Another important activity listed in the Financing Activities section of the statement is the payment of dividends to stockholders. IBM's 1999 statement of cash flows lists most of the common cash inflows and outflows from financing activities (amounts in millions of dollars):

Cash flow from financing activities:	
1 Proceeds from new debt	6,133
Short-term borrowings less than 90 days—net	276
2 Payments to settle debt	(7,510)
Common stock transactions—net	(6,645)
Cash dividends paid	(879)
Net cash used in financing activities	(8,625)

In 1999, IBM **1** received over $6.1 billion from issuing new debt and **2** paid over $7.5 billion to retire old debt. In analyzing IBM, you would probably next read the long-term debt footnote to see whether the company essentially refinanced the old debt with new debt at a lower interest rate and, if it did, what the interest saving is, because this will continue to be a benefit for many years.

Summary of the Three Types of Activities

To summarize the categorization of the activities of a business as operating, investing, and financing, refer to Exhibit 12-6. The exhibit lists examples of each of the three activities along with the related accounts on the balance sheet and the account classifications on the balance sheet.

In the exhibit, operating activities center on the acquisition and sale of products and services and related costs, such as wages and taxes. Two important observations can be made about the cash flow effects from the operating activities of a business. *First, the cash flows from these activities are the cash effects of transactions that enter into the determination of net income.* For example, the sale of a product enters into the calculation of net income. The cash effect of this transaction—that is, the collection of the account receivable—results in a cash inflow from operating activities. *Second, cash flows from operating activities usually relate to an increase or decrease in either a current asset or a current liability.* For example, the payment of taxes to the government results in a decrease in taxes payable, which is a current liability on the balance sheet.

[2]Wm. Wrigley Jr. Company is unusual in this regard in that it relies almost solely on funds generated from stockholders, in the form of common stock, for financing. The company had no short-term notes payable at December 31, 1999, and total long-term liabilities accounted for just slightly over 10% of the total liabilities and stockholders' equity on the balance sheet on that date.

READING GATEWAY'S STATEMENT OF CASH FLOWS According to Gateway's Investing Activities section of its statement of cash flows, what does the company spend a significant amount of cash for every year? What types of expenditures would you expect to find in this category?

Study Tip

Later in the chapter, you will learn a technique to use in preparing the statement of cash flows. Recall the observations made here regarding what types of accounts affect each of the three activities when you get to that section of the chapter.

EXHIBIT 12-6 Classification of Items on the Statement of Cash Flows

Activity	Examples	Effect on Cash	Related Balance Sheet Account	Classification on Balance Sheet
Operating	Collection of customer accounts	Inflow	Accounts receivable	Current asset
	Payment to suppliers for inventory	Outflow	Accounts payable	Current liability
			Inventory	Current asset
	Payment of wages	Outflow	Wages payable	Current liability
	Payment of taxes	Outflow	Taxes payable	Current liability
Investing	Capital expenditures	Outflow	Plant and equipment	Long-term asset
	Purchase of another company	Outflow	Long-term investment	Long-term asset
	Sale of plant and equipment	Inflow	Plant and equipment	Long-term asset
	Sale of another company	Inflow	Long-term investment	Long-term asset
Financing	Issuance of capital stock	Inflow	Capital stock	Stockholders' equity
	Issuance of bonds	Inflow	Bonds payable	Long-term liability
	Issuance of bank note	Inflow	Notes payable	Long-term liability
	Repurchase of stock	Outflow	Treasury stock	Stockholders' equity
	Retirement of bonds	Outflow	Bonds payable	Long-term liability
	Repayment of notes	Outflow	Notes payable	Long-term liability
	Payment of dividends	Outflow	Retained earnings	Stockholders' equity

Note that investing activities normally relate to long-term assets on the balance sheet. For example, the purchase of new plant and equipment increases long-term assets, and the sale of these same assets reduces long-term assets on the balance sheet.

BUSINESS STRATEGY

IBM believes it has seen the future, and the future is now. The company is therefore changing tack. Rather than promoting the continuity the company promised its shareholders in the 1990s, CEO Louis Gerstner Jr. is positioning IBM to take advantage of what he terms "a historic shift" in the way we work, learn, govern, shop, and entertain ourselves.

That shift is powered by the Internet, which Gerstner and many other observers call a new mass medium that will fundamentally change the way we use technology in our lives. IBM sees this change as an opportunity not merely to join the global information network but also to build entirely new ways of doing business. Technology alone is no longer the point—something faster or cheaper is always being invented. But by helping its business customers find new ways to *use* technology, to transform such critical business processes as supply chain management, customer service and support, and product distribution, IBM hopes also reinvent itself as the premier provider of information technology services.

Gerstner sees the long-term future of e-commerce as "a tremendous opportunity for IBM" and has set three goals for the firm: (1) to accelerate its growth in a period of explosive demand for everything IBM produces—hardware, software, services, technology, and expertise; (2) to continue its role as the world's leader in technology innovation and to speed those innovations to market through its own products and those of its business customers; and (3) as more and more IBM products are sold inside other companies' branded products or function behind the scenes in the infrastructure of the Internet, to ensure that the IBM brand remains in the public eye through the quality, reliability, and innovation of its employees.

SOURCES: IBM's 1998 and 1999 annual reports.

One of IBM's many software products is WebSphere, a development platform allowing teams to organize and manage Web development projects. Success of new versions of products like WebSphere will help keep IBM's future bright.
www-4.ibm.com/software/webservers/studio/

Finally, *note that financing activities usually relate to either long-term liabilities or stockholders' equity accounts.* There are exceptions to these observations about the type of balance sheet account involved with each of the three types of activities, but these rules of thumb are useful as we begin to analyze transactions and attempt to determine their classification on the statement of cash flows.

TWO METHODS OF REPORTING CASH FLOW FROM OPERATING ACTIVITIES

LO 4 Describe the difference between the direct and the indirect methods of computing cash flow from operating activities.

Companies use one of two different methods to report the amount of cash flow from operating activities. The first approach, called the **direct method,** involves reporting major classes of gross cash receipts and cash payments. For example, cash collected from customers is reported separately from any interest and dividends received. Each of the major types of cash payments related to the company's operations follows, such as cash paid for inventory, for salaries and wages, for interest, and for taxes. An acceptable alternative to this approach is the **indirect method.** Under the indirect method, net cash flow from operating activities is computed by adjusting net income to remove the effect of all deferrals of past operating cash receipts and payments and all accruals of future operating cash receipts and payments.

Although the direct method is preferred by the Financial Accounting Standards Board, it is used much less frequently than the indirect method in practice. In fact, an annual survey of 600 companies reported that 593 companies used the indirect method and only 7 companies used the direct method.[3]

To compare and contrast the two methods, assume that Boulder Company begins operations as a corporation on January 1, 2001, with the owners' investment of $10,000 in cash. An income statement for 2001 and a balance sheet as of December 31, 2001, are presented in Exhibits 12-7 and 12-8, respectively.

Direct Method   To report cash flow from operating activities under the direct method, we look at each of the items on the income statement and determine how much cash each of these activities either generated or used. For example, revenues for the period were $80,000. Since the balance sheet at the end of the period shows a balance in Accounts Receivable of $13,000, however, Boulder collected only $80,000 − $13,000, or $67,000, from its sales of the period. Thus, the first line on the statement of cash flows in Exhibit 12-9 reports $67,000 in cash collected from customers. Remember that the *net increase* in Accounts Receivable must be deducted from sales to find cash collected. For a new company, this is the same as the ending balance because the company starts the year without a balance in Accounts Receivable.

The same logic can be applied to determine the amount of cash expended for operating purposes. Operating expenses on the income statement are reported at $64,000.

EXHIBIT 12-7   Boulder Company Income Statement

BOULDER COMPANY INCOME STATEMENT FOR THE YEAR ENDED DECEMBER 31, 2001	
Revenues	$80,000
Operating expenses	(64,000)
Income before tax	$16,000
Income tax expense	(4,000)
Net income	$12,000

[3]*Accounting Trends & Techniques,* 53rd ed. (New York: American Institute of Certified Public Accountants, 1999).

EXHIBIT 12-8   Boulder Company Balance Sheet

BOULDER COMPANY
BALANCE SHEET
AS OF DECEMBER 31, 2001

Assets		Liabilities and Stockholders' Equity	
Cash	$15,000	Accounts payable	$ 6,000
Accounts receivable	13,000	Capital stock	10,000
		Retained earnings	12,000
Total	$28,000	Total	$28,000

According to the balance sheet, however, $6,000 of the expense is unpaid at the end of the period as evidenced by the balance in Accounts Payable. Thus, the amount of cash expended for operating purposes as reported on the statement of cash flows in Exhibit 12-9 is $64,000 − $6,000, or $58,000. The other cash payment in the Operating Activities section of the statement is $4,000 for income taxes. Because no liability for income taxes is reported on the balance sheet, we know that $4,000 represents both the income tax expense of the period and the amount paid to the government. The only other item on the statement of cash flows in Exhibit 12-9 is the cash inflow from financing activities for the amount of cash invested by the owner in return for capital stock.

Indirect Method   When the indirect method is used, the first line in the Operating Activities section of the statement of cash flows, as shown in Exhibit 12-10, is the net income of the period. Net income is then *adjusted* to reconcile it to the amount of cash provided by operating activities. As reported on the income statement, this net income figure includes the sales of $80,000 for the period. As we know, however, the amount of cash collected was $13,000 less than this because not all customers paid Boulder the amount due. *The increase in Accounts Receivable for the period is deducted from net income on the statement because the increase indicates that the company sold more during the period than it collected in cash.*

EXHIBIT 12-9   Statement of Cash Flows Using the Direct Method

BOULDER COMPANY
STATEMENT OF CASH FLOWS
FOR THE YEAR ENDED DECEMBER 31, 2001

Cash flows from operating activities

Cash collected from customers	$ 67,000
Cash payments for operating purposes	(58,000)
Cash payments for taxes	(4,000)
Net cash inflow from operating activities	$ 5,000

Cash flows from financing activities

Issuance of capital stock	$ 10,000
Net increase in cash	$ 15,000
Cash balance, beginning of period	–0–
Cash balance, end of period	$ 15,000

EXHIBIT 12-10   Statement of Cash Flows Using the Indirect Method

BOULDER COMPANY
STATEMENT OF CASH FLOWS
FOR THE YEAR ENDED DECEMBER 31, 2001

Cash flows from operating activities	
Net income	$ 12,000
Adjustments to reconcile net income to net cash from operating activities:	
Increase in accounts receivable	(13,000)
Increase in accounts payable	6,000
Net cash inflow from operating activities	$ 5,000
Cash flows from financing activities	
Issuance of capital stock	$ 10,000
Net increase in cash	$ 15,000
Cash balance, beginning of period	–0–
Cash balance, end of period	$ 15,000

From **Concept**

TO PRACTICE 12.2

READING IBM'S STATEMENT OF CASH FLOWS Does IBM use the direct or the indirect method in the Operating Activities section of its statement of cash flows? How can you tell which it is?

The logic for the addition of the increase in Accounts Payable is similar, although the effect is the opposite. The amount of operating expenses deducted on the income statement was $64,000. We know, however, that the amount of cash paid was $6,000 less than this, as the balance in Accounts Payable indicates. *The increase in Accounts Payable for the period is added back to net income on the statement because the increase indicates that the company paid less during the period than it recognized in expense on the income statement.* One observation can be noted about this example. Because this is the first year of operations for Boulder, we wouldn't be too concerned that accounts receivable is increasing faster than accounts payable. If this becomes a trend, however, we would try to improve the accounts receivable collections process.

Two important observations should be made in comparing the two methods illustrated in Exhibits 12-9 and 12-10. First, the amount of cash provided by operating activities is the same under the two methods: $5,000; the two methods are simply different computational approaches to arrive at the cash generated from operations. Second, the remainder of the statement of cash flows is the same, regardless of which method is used. The only difference between the two methods is in the Operating Activities section of the statement.

NONCASH INVESTING AND FINANCING ACTIVITIES

Occasionally, companies engage in important investing and financing activities that do not affect cash. For example, assume that at the end of the year, Wolk Corp. issues capital stock to an inventor in return for the exclusive rights to a patent. Although the patent has no ready market value, the stock could have been sold on the open market for $25,000. The effect on the accounting equation of this transaction is as follows:

BALANCE SHEET						INCOME STATEMENT
ASSETS	=	LIABILITIES	+	OWNERS' EQUITY	+	REVENUES – EXPENSES
Patent 25,000				Capital Stock 25,000		

This transaction does not involve cash and is therefore not reported on the statement of cash flows. However, what if we changed the scenario slightly? Assume that Wolk wants the patent but the inventor is not willing to accept stock in return for it. Instead, Wolk sells

stock on the open market for $25,000 and then pays this amount in cash to the inventor for the rights to the patent.

Consider the effects on the accounting equation of these two transactions. First, the sale of stock increases Cash and Owners' Equity:

BALANCE SHEET						INCOME STATEMENT
ASSETS	=	LIABILITIES	+	OWNERS' EQUITY	+	REVENUES – EXPENSES
Cash 25,000				Capital Stock 25,000		

Next, the acquisition of the patent has the following effect:

BALANCE SHEET						INCOME STATEMENT
ASSETS	=	LIABILITIES	+	OWNERS' EQUITY	+	REVENUES – EXPENSES
Patent 25,000						
Cash (25,000)						

How would each of these two transactions be reported on a statement of cash flows? The first transaction appears as a cash inflow in the Financing Activities section of the statement; the second is reported as a cash outflow in the Investing Activities section. The point is that even though the *form* of this arrangement (with stock sold for cash and then the cash paid to the inventor) differs from the form of the first arrangement (with stock exchanged directly for the patent), the *substance* of the two arrangements is the same. That is, both involve a significant financing activity, the issuance of stock, and an important investing activity, the acquisition of a patent. Because the substance is what matters, accounting standards require that any significant noncash transactions be reported either in a separate schedule or in a footnote to the financial statements. For our transaction in which stock was issued directly to the inventor, presentation in a schedule is as follows:

Supplemental schedule of noncash investing and financing activities

Acquisition of patent in exchange for capital stock $25,000

To this point, we have concentrated on the purpose of a statement of cash flows and the major reporting requirements related to it. We turn our attention next to a methodology to use in actually preparing the statement.

Two-Minute Review

1. *What are cash equivalents, and why are any increases or decreases in them not reported on a statement of cash flows?*

2. *What are the three types of activities reported on a statement of cash flows?*

3. *What are the two methods of reporting cash flow from operating activities, and how do they differ?*

Answers:

1. A cash equivalent is an item readily convertible to a known amount of cash and with an original maturity to the investor of three months or less. Because the maturity date of these items, such as a 60-day certificate of deposit, is so near, they are not considered to carry any significant risks in terms of price changes. Thus, any changes in cash equivalents are not reported on the statement of cash flows.

2. Operating, investing, and financing activities.

3. Direct and indirect methods. The direct method involves reporting major classes of gross cash receipts and cash payments. Under the indirect method, net cash flow from operating activities is computed by adjusting net income to remove the effect of all deferrals of past operating cash receipts and payments and all accruals of future operating cash receipts and payments.

Two interesting observations can be made about the statement of cash flows. First, the "answer" to a statement of cash flows is known before we start to prepare it. That is, the change in cash for the period is known by comparing two successive balance sheets. Thus, it is not the change in cash itself that is emphasized on the statement of cash flows but the *explanations* for the change in cash. That is, each item on a statement of cash flows helps to explain why cash changed by the amount it did during the period. The second important observation about the statement of cash flows relates even more specifically to how we prepare it. Both an income statement and a balance sheet are prepared simply by taking the balances in each of the various accounts in the general ledger and putting them in the right place on the right statement. This is not true for the statement of cash flows, however. Instead, it is necessary to analyze the transactions during the period and attempt to (1) determine which of these affected cash and (2) classify each of the cash effects into one of the three categories.

In the simple examples presented so far in the chapter, we prepared the statement of cash flows without the use of any special tools. In more complex situations, however, some type of methodology is needed. We first will review the basic accounting equation and then illustrate a systematic approach for preparing the statement. Appendix 12A presents a work-sheet approach to the preparation of the statement of cash flows.

THE ACCOUNTING EQUATION AND THE STATEMENT OF CASH FLOWS

The basic accounting equation is as follows:

$$\text{Assets} = \text{Liabilities} + \text{Owners' Equity}$$

Next, consider this refinement of the equation:

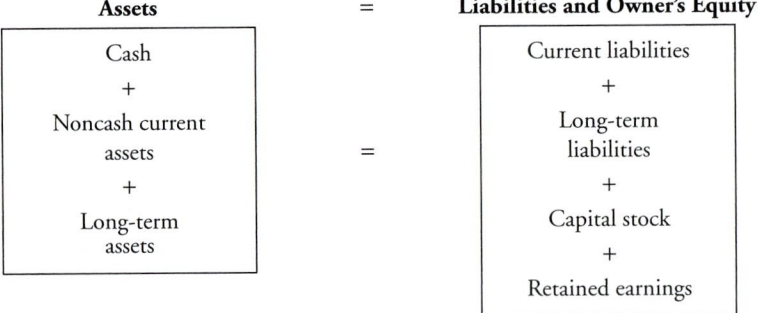

The equation can be rearranged so that only cash is on the left side and all other items are on the right side:

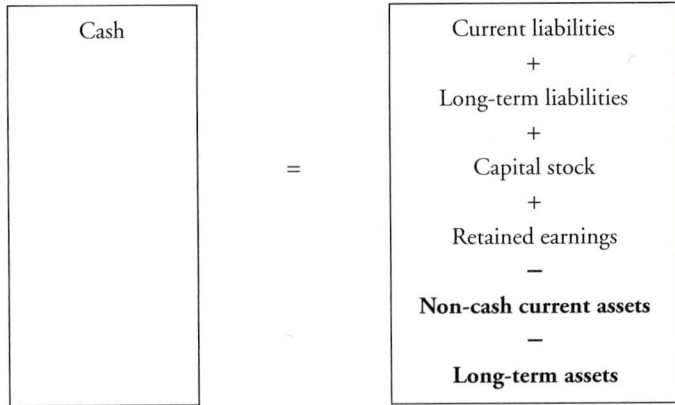

Therefore, any changes in cash must be accompanied by a corresponding change in the right side of the equation. For example, an increase or inflow of cash could result from an *increase* in long-term liabilities in the form of issuing bonds payable, an important financing activity for many companies. Or, an increase in cash could come from a *decrease* in long-term assets in the form of a sale of fixed assets. The various possibilities for inflows (+) and outflows (−) of cash can be summarized by activity as follows:

Activity	Left Side	Right Side	Example
Operating			
	+ Cash	− Noncash current assets	Collect accounts receivable
	− Cash	+ Noncash current assets	Prepay insurance
	+ Cash	+ Current liabilities	Collect customer's deposit
	− Cash	− Current liabilities	Pay suppliers
	+ Cash	+ Retained earnings	Make a cash sale
Investing			
	+ Cash	− Long-term assets	Sell equipment
	− Cash	+ Long-term assets	Buy equipment
Financing			
	+ Cash	+ Long-term liabilities	Issue bonds
	− Cash	− Long-term liabilities	Retire bonds
	+ Cash	+ Capital stock	Issue capital stock
	− Cash	− Capital stock	Buy capital stock
	− Cash	− Retained earnings	Pay dividends

By considering these examples, we see that inflows and outflows of cash relate to increases and decreases in the various balance sheet accounts. We now turn to analyzing these accounts as a way to assemble a statement of cash flows.

PREPARING THE STATEMENT OF CASH FLOWS: DIRECT METHOD

The following steps can be used to prepare a statement of cash flows:

LO 5 Prepare a statement of cash flows, using the direct method to determine cash flow from operating activities.

1. **Set up three schedules with the following headings:**

   a. Cash Flows from Operating Activities

   b. Cash Flows from Investing Activities

   c. Cash Flows from Financing Activities

   As we analyze the transactions that affect each of the noncash balance sheet accounts, any cash effects are entered on the appropriate schedule. When completed, the three schedules contain all the information needed to prepare a statement of cash flows.

2. **Determine the cash flows from operating activities.** Generally, this requires analyzing each item on the *income statement* and the *current asset* and *current liability* accounts. As cash flows are identified in this analysis, they are entered on the schedule of cash flows from operating activities.

3. **Determine the cash flows from investing activities.** Generally, this requires analyzing the *long-term asset* accounts and any additional information provided. As cash flows are indentified in this analysis, they are entered on the schedule of cash flows from investing activities. Any significant noncash activities are entered on a supplemental schedule.

4. **Determine the cash flows from financing activities.** Generally, this requires analyzing the *long-term liability* and *stockholders' equity* accounts and any additional information provided. As cash flows are identified in this analysis, they are entered on the schedule of cash flows from financing activities. Any significant noncash activities are entered on a supplemental schedule.

Remember that these are general rules that the cash effects of changes in current accounts are reported in the operating section, those relating to long-term asset accounts in the investing section, and those relating to long-term liabilities and stockholders' equity in the financing section. The general rules for classification of activities have a few exceptions, but we will not concern ourselves with them.

To illustrate this approach, we will refer to the income statement in Exhibit 12-11 and to the comparative balance sheets and the additional information provided for Julian Corp. in Exhibit 12-12.

Determine the Cash Flows from Operating Activities To do this, we need to consider each of the items on the income statement and any related current assets or liabilities from the balance sheet.

Sales Revenue and Accounts Receivable Sales as reported on the income statement in Exhibit 12-11 amounted to $670,000. Based on the beginning and ending balances in Exhibit 12-12, Accounts Receivable increased during the year by $6,000, from $57,000 to $63,000. *This indicates that Julian had $6,000 more in sales to its customers than it collected in cash from them* (assuming that all sales are on credit). Thus, cash collections must have been $670,000 − $6,000, or $664,000. Another way to look at this is

Beginning accounts receivable	$ 57,000
+ Sales revenue	670,000
− Cash collections	(X)
= Ending accounts receivable	$ 63,000

Solving for X, we can find cash collections:

$$57,000 + 670,000 - X = 63,000$$

$$X = 664,000$$

At this point, note the inflow of cash for $664,000, as shown in the schedule of Cash Flows from Operating Activities, in Exhibit 12-13.

EXHIBIT 12-11 Julian Corp. Income Statement

JULIAN CORP.
INCOME STATEMENT
FOR THE YEAR ENDED DECEMBER 31, 2001

Revenues and gains:		
Sales revenue	$670,000	
Interest revenue	15,000	
Gain on sale of machine	5,000	
Total revenues and gains		$690,000
Expenses and losses:		
Cost of goods sold	$390,000	
Salaries and wages	60,000	
Depreciation	40,000	
Insurance	12,000	
Interest	15,000	
Income taxes	50,000	
Loss on retirement of bonds	3,000	
Total expenses and losses		570,000
Net income		$120,000

EXHIBIT 12-12 Julian Corp. Comparative Balance Sheets

JULIAN CORP.
COMPARATIVE BALANCE SHEETS

	December 31	
	2001	**2000**
Cash	$ 35,000	$ 46,000
Accounts receivable	63,000	57,000
Inventory	84,000	92,000
Prepaid insurance	12,000	18,000
Total current assets	$194,000	$213,000
Long-term investments	$120,000	$ 90,000
Land	150,000	100,000
Property and equipment	320,000	280,000
Accumulated depreciation	(100,000)	(75,000)
Total long-term assets	$490,000	$395,000
Total assets	$684,000	$608,000
Accounts payable	$ 38,000	$ 31,000
Salaries and wages payable	7,000	9,000
Income taxes payable	8,000	5,000
Total current liabilities	$ 53,000	$ 45,000
Notes payable	$ 85,000	$ 35,000
Bonds payable	200,000	260,000
Total long-term liabilities	$285,000	$295,000
Capital stock	$100,000	$ 75,000
Retained earnings	246,000	193,000
Total stockholders' equity	$346,000	$268,000
Total liabilities and stockholders' equity	$684,000	$608,000

Additional Information

1. Long-term investments were purchased for $30,000. The securities are classified as available for sale.
2. Land was purchased by issuing a $50,000 note payable.
3. Equipment was purchased for $75,000.
4. A machine with an original cost of $35,000 and a book value of $20,000 was sold for $25,000.
5. Bonds with a face value of $60,000 were retired by paying $63,000 in cash.
6. Capital stock was issued in exchange for $25,000 in cash.
7. Dividends of $67,000 were paid.

Interest Revenue Julian reported interest revenue on the income statement of $15,000. Did the company actually receive this amount of cash, or was it merely an accrual of revenue earned but not yet received? The answer can be found by examining the current asset section of the balance sheet. *Because there is no Interest Receivable account, the amount of interest earned was the amount of cash received.*

The cash received in interest should be entered in the Schedule of Cash Flows from Operating Activities, as shown in Exhibit 12-13.

Gain on Sale of Machine A gain of $5,000 on the sale of a machine is reported as the next line on the income statement. Any cash received from the sale of a long-term asset is reported in the Investing Activities section of the statement of cash flows.

EXHIBIT 12-13 Schedule of Cash Flows from Operating Activities

CASH FLOWS FROM OPERATING ACTIVITIES

Cash receipts from:	
Sales on account	664,000
Interest	15,000
Cash payments for:	
Inventory purchases	(375,000)
Salaries and wages	(62,000)
Insurance	(6,000)
Interest	(15,000)
Taxes	(47,000)

Thus, we ignore the gain when reporting cash flows from operating activities under the direct method.

Cost of Goods Sold, Inventory, and Accounts Payable Cost of goods sold, as reported on the income statement, amounts to $390,000. Recall that $390,000 is not the amount of cash expended to pay suppliers of inventory. First, cost of goods sold represents the cost of the inventory sold during the period, not the amount purchased. Thus, we must analyze the Inventory account to determine the purchases of the period. Second, the amount of purchases is not the same as the cash paid to suppliers because purchases are normally on account. Thus, we must analyze the Accounts Payable account to determine the cash payments.

Based on the beginning and ending balances from Exhibit 12-12, inventory decreased during the year by $8,000, from $92,000 to $84,000. *This means that the cost of inventory sold was $8,000 more than the purchases of the period.* Thus, purchases must have been $390,000 − $8,000, or $382,000. Another way to look at this is as follows:

Beginning inventory	$ 92,000
+ Purchases	X
− Cost of goods sold	(390,000)
= Ending inventory	$ 84,000

Solving for X, we can find purchases:

$$92,000 + X - 390,000 = 84,000$$

$$X = 382,000$$

Note from Exhibit 12-12 that Accounts Payable increased during the year by $7,000, from $31,000 to $38,000. *This means that Julian's purchases were $7,000 more during the period than its cash payments.* Also, recall that we determined earlier that purchases were $382,000. Thus, cash payments must have been $382,000 − $7,000, or $375,000. Another way to look at this is as follows:

Beginning accounts payable	$ 31,000
+ Purchases	382,000
− Cash payments	(X)
= Ending accounts payable	$ 38,000

Solving for X, we can find cash payments:

$$31,000 + 382,000 - X = 38,000$$

$$X = 375,000$$

At this point, we indicate in the schedule in Exhibit 12-13 that the cash payments for inventory total $375,000.

Salaries and Wages Expense and Salaries and Wages Payable The second expense listed on the income statement in Exhibit 12-11 is salaries and wages of $60,000. However, did Julian *pay* this amount to employees during the year? The answer can be found by examining the Salaries and Wages Payable account in the balance sheet in Exhibit 12-12. From the balance sheet, we note that the liability account decreased by $2,000, from $9,000 to $7,000. *This means that the amount of cash paid to employees was $2,000 more than the amount of expense accrued.* Another way to look at the cash payments of $60,000 + $2,000, or $62,000, is

Beginning salaries and wages payable	$ 9,000
+ Salaries and wages expense	60,000
− Cash payments to employees	(X)
= Ending accounts payable	$ 7,000

Solving for *X,* we can find cash payments:

$$9,000 + 60,000 - X = 7,000$$
$$X = \underline{\underline{62,000}}$$

As you see in Exhibit 12-13, cash paid of $62,000 appears as a cash outflow in the schedule of cash flows from operating activities.

Depreciation Expense The next item on the income statement is depreciation of $40,000. Depreciation of tangible long-term assets, amortization of intangible assets, and depletion of natural resources are different from most other expenses in that they have no effect on cash flow. The only related cash flows are from the purchase and the sale of these long-term assets, and these are reported in the Investing Activities section of the statement of cash flows. Thus, depreciation is not reflected on the schedule of cash flows from operating activities when the direct method is used as in Exhibit 12-13.

ACCOUNTING FOR YOUR DECISIONS

You Are an Entrepreneur

You operate a coffee cart in the lobby of an office building. You started the business this year by investing $5,000 of your own money to buy the coffee cart. Even though you think the cart will last for five years, a friend who has studied accounting has advised you to recognize the entire cost of the cart as an expense the first year. He reasons that "the first year is very crucial to any business and since depreciation is added back in the Operating Activities section of the statement of cash flows, why not add back the maximum amount so that you will maximize the cash flow from operations?" Is your friend's reasoning sound?

ANS: Your friend is correct in stating that depreciation is added back in the Operating Activities section, assuming use of the indirect method. Depreciation is added back, however, only because it was deducted as an expense on the income statement but does not use any cash. Depreciation is not a cash flow, and any manipulation of the amount of depreciation expensed in any one year will not affect the amount of cash generated from operations.

Insurance Expense and Prepaid Insurance According to the income statement in Exhibit 12-11, Julian recorded insurance expense of $12,000 during 2001. This amount is not the cash payments for insurance, however, because Julian has a Prepaid Insurance account on the balance sheet.

Recall from Chapter 4 that as a company buys insurance, it increases its Prepaid Insurance account. As the insurance expires, this account is reduced and an expense is recognized. Note from the balance sheets in Exhibit 12-12 that the Prepaid Insurance account decreased during the year by $6,000, from $18,000 to $12,000. *This means that the amount of cash paid for insurance was $6,000 less than the amount of expense recognized.* Thus, the cash payments must have been $12,000 − $6,000, or $6,000. Another way to look at the cash payments is

Beginning prepaid insurance	$18,000
+ Cash payments for insurance	X
− Insurance expense	(12,000)
= Ending prepaid insurance	$12,000

Solving for X, we can find the amount of cash paid:

$$18,000 + X - 12,000 = 12,000$$
$$X = 6,000$$

Note the cash outflow of $6,000 as entered in Exhibit 12-13 of the schedule of cash flows from operating activities.

Interest Expense The amount of interest expense reported on the income statement is $15,000. Because the balance sheet does not report an accrual of interest owed but not yet paid (an Interest Payable account), we know that $15,000 is also the amount of cash paid. The schedule in Exhibit 12-13 reflects the cash outflow of $15,000 for interest. Whether interest paid is properly classified as an operating activity is subject to considerable debate. The Financial Accounting Standards Board decided in favor of classifying *interest* as an *operating* activity because, unlike dividends, it appears on the income statement. This, it was argued, provides a direct link between the statement of cash flows and the income statement. Many argue, however, that it is inconsistent to classify dividends paid as a financing activity but interest paid as an operating activity. After all, both represent returns paid to providers of capital: interest to creditors and dividends to stockholders.

Income Tax Expense and Income Taxes Payable The income statement in Exhibit 12-11 reports income tax expense of $50,000. We know, however, that this is not necessarily the amount paid to the government during the year. In fact, note the increase in the Income Taxes Payable account on the balance sheets in Exhibit 12-12. The liability increased by $3,000, from $5,000 to $8,000.

This means that the amount of cash paid to the government in taxes was $3,000 less than the amount of expense accrued. Another way to look at the cash payments of $50,000 − $3,000, or $47,000, is

Beginning income taxes payable	$ 5,000
+ Income tax expense	50,000
− Cash payments for taxes	(X)
= Ending income taxes payable	$ 8,000

Solving for X, we can find the amount of cash paid:

$$5,000 + 50,000 - X = 8,000$$
$$X = 47,000$$

As you see by examining Exhibit 12-13, the cash payments for taxes is the last item on the Schedule of Cash Flows from Operating Activities.

Loss on Retirement of Bonds A $3,000 loss on the retirement of bonds is reported as the last item under expenses and losses on the income statement in Exhibit 12-11. Any cash paid to retire a long-term liability is reported in the Financing Activities section of the statement of cash flows. Thus, we ignore the loss when reporting cash flows from operating activities under the direct method.

Compare Net Income with Net Cash Flow from Operating

Activities. At this point, all of the items on the income statement have been analyzed (with the exception of the gain and the loss), as have all the current asset and current liability accounts. All the information needed to prepare the Operating Activities section of the statement of cash flows has been gathered.

To summarize, the preparation of the Operating Activities section of the statement of cash flows requires the conversion of each item on the income statement to a cash basis. The current asset and current liability accounts are analyzed to discover the cash effects of each item on the income statement. Exhibit 12-14 summarizes this conversion process.

EXHIBIT 12-14 Conversion of Income Statement Items to Cash Basis

Income Statement	Amount	Adjustments	Cash Flows
Sales revenue	$670,000		$670,000
		+ Decreases in accounts receivable	–0–
		– Increases in accounts receivable	(6,000)
		Cash collected from customers	$664,000
Interest revenue	15,000		$ 15,000
		+ Decreases in interest receivable	–0–
		– Increases in interest receivable	–0–
		Cash collected in interest	$ 15,000
Gain on sale of machine	5,000	*Not an operating activity*	$ –0–
Cost of goods sold	390,000		$390,000
		+ Increases in inventory	–0–
		– Decreases in inventory	(8,000)
		+ Decreases in accounts payable	–0–
		– Increases in accounts payable	(7,000)
		Cash paid to suppliers	$375,000
Salaries and wages	60,000		$ 60,000
		+ Decreases in salaries/wages payable	2,000
		– Increases in salaries/wages payable	–0–
		Cash paid to employees	$ 62,000
Depreciation	40,000	*No cash flow effect*	$ –0–
Insurance	12,000		$ 12,000
		+ Increases in prepaid insurance	–0–
		– Decreases in prepaid insurance	(6,000)
		Cash paid for insurance	$ 6,000
Interest	15,000		$ 15,000
		+ Decreases in interest payable	–0–
		– Increases in interest payable	–0–
		Cash paid for interest	$ 15,000
Income taxes	50,000		$ 50,000
		+ Decreases in income taxes payable	–0–
		– Increases in income taxes payable	(3,000)
		Cash paid for taxes	$ 47,000
Loss on retirement of bonds	3,000	*Not an operating activity*	$ –0–
Net income	$120,000	Net cash flow from operating activities	$174,000

Note in the exhibit the various adjustments made to put each income statement item on a cash basis. For example, the $6,000 increase in accounts receivable for the period is deducted from sales revenue of $670,000 to arrive at cash collected from customers. Similar adjustments are made to each of the other income statement items with the exception of depreciation, the gain, and the loss. Depreciation is ignored because it does not have an effect on cash flow. The gain relates to the sale of a long-term asset, and any cash effect is reflected in the Investing Activities section of the statement of cash flows. Similarly, the loss resulted from the retirement of bonds, and any cash flow effect is reported in the Financing Activities section. The bottom of the exhibit highlights an important point: Julian reported net income of $120,000 but actually generated $174,000 in cash from operations.

Determine the Cash Flows from Investing Activities   At this point, we turn our attention to the long-term asset accounts and any additional information available about these accounts. Julian has three long-term assets on its balance sheet: Long-Term Investments, Land, and Property and Equipment.

Long-Term Investments   Item 1 in the additional information in Exhibit 12-12 indicates that Julian purchased $30,000 of investments during the year. The $30,000 net increase in the Long-Term Investments account, from $90,000 to $120,000, confirms this (no mention is made of the sale of any investments during 2001). The purchase of investments required the use of $30,000 of cash, as indicated on the Schedule of Cash Flows from Investing Activities in Exhibit 12-15.

Land   Note from the balance sheets in Exhibit 12-12 the $50,000 net increase in land, from $100,000 to $150,000. Item 2 in the additional information indicates that Julian purchased land by issuing a $50,000 note payable. This transaction obviously does not involve cash. It does have both an important financing element and an investing component, however. The issuance of the note is a financing activity, and the acquisition of land is an investing activity. Because no cash was involved, the transaction is reported in a separate schedule instead of directly on the statement of cash flows:

Supplemental schedule of noncash investing and financing activities
Acquisition of land in exchange for note payable $50,000

Property and Equipment   Property and equipment increased by $40,000 during 2001. However, Julian both acquired equipment and sold a machine (items 3 and 4 in the additional information). As we discussed earlier in the chapter, acquisitions of new plant and equipment are important investing activities for most businesses. Thus, the $75,000 expended to acquire new property and equipment appears in the schedule in Exhibit 12-15 as a cash outflow.

As reported in the balance sheets in Exhibit 12-12, the Property and Equipment account increased during the year by only $40,000, from $280,000 to $320,000. Since Julian *added* to this account $75,000, however, we know that it must have *disposed* of some assets as well.

EXHIBIT 12-15   Schedule of Cash Flows from Investing Activities

CASH FLOWS FROM INVESTING ACTIVITIES	
Cash inflows from:	
Sales of machine	25,000
Cash outflows for:	
Purchase of investments	(30,000)
Purchase of plant and equipment	(75,000)

In fact, item 4 in the additional information reports the sale of a machine with an original cost of $35,000. An analysis of the Property and Equipment account at this point confirms this amount:

Beginning property and equipment	$280,000
+ Acquisitions	75,000
− Disposals	(X)
= Ending property and equipment	$320,000

Solving for X, we can find the *cost* of the fixed assets sold during the year:

$$280,000 + 75,000 - X = 320,000$$

$$X = \$35,000$$

The additional information also indicates that the book value of the machine sold was $20,000. This means that if the original cost was $35,000 and the book value was $20,000, the accumulated depreciation on the machine sold must have been $35,000 − $20,000, or $15,000. A similar analysis to the one we just looked at for property and equipment confirms this amount:

Beginning accumulated depreciation	$ 75,000
+ Depreciation expense	40,000
− Accumulated depreciation on assets sold	(X)
= Ending accumulated depreciation	$100,000

Solving for X, we can find the accumulated depreciation on the assets disposed of during the year:

$$75,000 + 40,000 - X = 100,000$$

$$X = \$15,000$$

Finally, we are told in the additional information that the machine was sold for $25,000. *If the selling price was $25,000 and the book value was $20,000, Julian reports a gain on sale of $5,000, an amount that is confirmed on the income statement in Exhibit 12-11.* To summarize, the machine was sold for $25,000, an amount that exceeded its book value of $20,000, thus generating a gain of $5,000. The cash inflow of $25,000 is entered on the Schedule of Cash Flows from Investing Activities in Exhibit 12-15.

Determine the Cash Flows from Financing Activities   These activities generally involve long-term liabilities and stockholders' equity. We first consider Julian's two long-term liabilities, Notes Payable and Bonds Payable, and then the two elements of stockholders' equity, capital stock and retained earnings.

Notes Payable   Recall that item 2 in the additional information reported that Julian purchased land in exchange for a $50,000 note payable. The amount is confirmed on the balance sheets, which show an increase in notes payable of $50,000, from $35,000 to $85,000. In our discussion of investing activities, we already entered this transaction on a supplemental schedule of noncash activities because it was a significant financing activity but did not involve cash.

Bonds Payable   The balance sheets in Exhibit 12-12 report a decrease in bonds payable of $60,000, from $260,000 to $200,000. Item 5 in the additional information in Exhibit 12-12 indicates that bonds with a face value of $60,000 were retired by paying $63,000 in cash. The book value of the bonds retired is the same as the face value of $60,000 because there is no unamortized discount or premium on the records. *When a company has to pay more in cash ($63,000) to settle a debt than the book value of the debt ($60,000), it reports a loss.* In this case, the loss is $3,000, as reported on the income statement in Exhibit 12-11. For purposes of preparing a statement of cash flows with the direct method, however, the important amount is the $63,000 in cash paid to retire the bonds. This amount appears as a cash outflow in the Schedule of Cash Flows from Financing Activities in Exhibit 12-16.

Capital Stock   Exhibit 12-12 indicates an increase in capital stock of $25,000, from $75,000 to $100,000. Julian issued capital stock in exchange for $25,000 in cash, according to item 6 in the additional information in Exhibit 12-12. Some companies issue additional stock after the initial formation of a corporation to raise needed capital. The increase in cash from this issuance is presented as a cash inflow in the Schedule of Cash Flows from Financing Activities, as shown in Exhibit 12-16.

ACCOUNTING FOR YOUR DECISIONS

You Decide for Your Investment Club

You are a member of an investment club and have been given the assignment of analyzing the statements of cash flows for the Norfolk Corp. for the last three years. The company has neither issued nor retired any stock during this time period. You notice that the company's cash balance has increased steadily during this period but that a majority of the increase is due to a large net inflow of cash from financing activities in each of the three years. Should you be concerned?

ANS: The net inflow of cash from financing activities indicates that the company is borrowing more than it is repaying. Certainly borrowing can be an attractive means of financing the purchase of new plant and equipment. At some point, however, the debt, along with interest, will need to be repaid. The company must be able to generate sufficient cash from its operations to make these payments.

Retained Earnings   This account increased during the year by $53,000, from $193,000 to $246,000. Because we know from Exhibit 12-11 that net income was $120,000, however, the company must have declared some dividends. We can determine the amount of cash dividends for 2001 in the following manner:

Beginning retained earnings	$193,000
+ Net income	120,000
− Cash dividends	(X)
= Ending retained earnings	$246,000

Solving for *X*, we can find the amount of cash dividends paid during the year:[4]

$$193,000 + 120,000 - X = 246,000$$

$$X = \$67,000$$

Item 7 in the additional information confirms that this was in fact the amount of dividends paid during the year. The dividends paid appear in the Schedule of Cash Flows from Financing Activities, as presented in Exhibit 12-16.

Using the Three Schedules to Prepare a Statement of Cash Flows

All the information needed to prepare a statement of cash flows is now available in the three schedules, along with the supplemental schedule prepared earlier. From the information gathered in Exhibits 12-13, 12-15, and 12-16, a completed statement of cash flows appears in Exhibit 12-17.

---

[4]Any decrease in Retained Earnings represents the dividends *declared* during the period rather than the amount paid. If there had been a Dividends Payable account, we would analyze it to find the amount of dividends paid. The lack of a balance in such an account at either the beginning or the end of the period tells us that Julian paid the same amount of dividends that it declared during the period.

EXHIBIT 12-16   Schedule of Cash Flows from Financing Activities

CASH FLOWS FROM FINANCING ACTIVITIES	
Cash inflows from:	
Issuance of stock	25,000
Cash outflows for:	
Retirement of bonds	(63,000)
Payment of cash dividends	(67,000)

EXHIBIT 12-17   Completed Statement of Cash Flows for Julian Corp.

JULIAN CORP.
STATEMENT OF CASH FLOWS
FOR THE YEAR ENDED DECEMBER 31, 2001

Cash flows from operating activities

Cash receipts from:	
Sales on account	$ 664,000
Interest	15,000
Total cash receipts	$ 679,000
Cash payments for:	
Inventory purchases	$(375,000)
Salaries and wages	(62,000)
Insurance	(6,000)
Interest	(15,000)
Taxes	(47,000)
Total cash payments	$(505,000)
Net cash provided by operating activities	$ 174,000

Cash flows from investing activities

Purchase of investments	$ (30,000)
Purchase of plant and equipment	(75,000)
Sale of machine	25,000
Net cash used by investing activities	$ (80,000)

Cash flows from financing activities

Retirement of bonds	$ (63,000)
Issuance of stock	25,000
Payment of cash dividends	(67,000)
Net cash used by financing activities	$(105,000)
Net decrease in cash	$ (11,000)
Cash balance, December 31, 2000	$ 46,000
Cash balance, December 31, 2001	$ 35,000

Supplemental schedule of noncash investing and financing activities

Acquisition of land in exchange for note payable	$ 50,000

What does Julian's statement of cash flows tell us? Cash flow from operations totaled $174,000. Cash used to acquire investments and equipment amounted to $80,000, after receiving $25,000 from the sale of a machine. A net amount of $105,000 was used for financing activities. Thus, Julian used more cash than it generated, and that's why the cash balance declined. That's okay for a year or two, but if this continues, the company won't be able to pay its bills.

AN APPROACH TO PREPARING THE STATEMENT OF CASH FLOWS: INDIRECT METHOD

LO 6 Prepare a statement of cash flows, using the indirect method to determine cash flow from operating activities.

The purpose of the Operating Activities section of the statement changes when we use the indirect method. Instead of reporting cash receipts and cash payments, *the objective is to reconcile net income to net cash flow from operating activities.* The other two sections of the completed statement in Exhibit 12-17, the investing and financing sections, are unchanged. The use of the indirect or the direct method for presenting cash flow from operating activities does not affect these two sections.

An approach similar to that used for the direct method can be used to prepare the Operating Activities section of the statement of cash flows under the indirect method.

Net Income Recall that the first line in the Operating Activities section of the statement under the indirect method is net income. That is, we start with the assumptions that all revenues and gains reported on the income statement increase cash flow and that all expenses and losses decrease cash flow. Julian's net income of $120,000, as reported on its income statement in Exhibit 12-11, is reported as the first item in the Operating Activities section of the statement of cash flows as shown in Exhibit 12-18.

From **Concept**

TO **PRACTICE 12.3**

READING UNO'S STATEMENT OF CASH FLOWS Did Accounts Receivable increase or decrease during 1999? Why is the change in this account deducted on the statement of cash flows?

Increase in Accounts Receivable Recall from the balance sheets in Exhibit 12-12 the net increase in Accounts Receivable of $6,000. Because net income includes sales, as opposed to cash collections, the $6,000 *net increase* must be *deducted* to adjust net income to cash from operations, as shown in Exhibit 12-18.

Gain on Sale of Machine The gain itself did not generate any cash, but the *sale* of the machine did. And as we found earlier, the cash generated by selling the machine was reported in the Investing Activities section of the statement. The cash proceeds included the gain. Because the gain is included in the net income figure, it must be *deducted* to determine cash from operations. Also note that the gain is included twice in cash inflows if it is not deducted from the net income figure in the Operating Activities section. Note the deduction of $5,000 in Exhibit 12-18.

Decrease in Inventory As the $8,000 net decrease in the Inventory account indicates, Julian liquidated a portion of its stock of inventory during the year. A net decrease in this account indicates that the company sold more products than it purchased during the year. As shown in Exhibit 12-18, the *net decrease* of $8,000 is *added back* to net income.

Increase in Accounts Payable According to Exhibit 12-12, Julian owed suppliers $31,000 at the start of the year. By the end of the year, the balance had grown to $38,000. Effectively, the company saved cash by delaying the payment of some of its outstanding accounts payable. The *net increase* of $7,000 in this account is *added back* to net income, as shown in Exhibit 12-18.

Decrease in Salaries and Wages Payable Salaries and Wages Payable decreased during the year by $2,000. The rationale for *deducting* the $2,000 *net decrease* in this liability in Exhibit 12-18 follows from what we just said about an increase in Accounts Payable.

JULIAN CORP.
PARTIAL STATEMENT OF CASH FLOWS
FOR THE YEAR ENDED DECEMBER 31, 2001

Net cash flows from operating activities

Net income	$120,000
Adjustments to reconcile net income to net cash provided by operating activities:	
Increase in accounts receivable	(6,000)
Gain on sale of machine	(5,000)
Decrease in inventory	8,000
Increase in accounts payable	7,000
Decrease in salaries and wages payable	(2,000)
Depreciation expense	40,000
Decrease in prepaid insurance	6,000
Increase in income taxes payable	3,000
Loss on retirement of bonds	3,000
Net cash provided by operating activities	$174,000

The payment to employees of $2,000 more than the amount included in expense on the income statement requires an additional deduction under the indirect method.

Depreciation Expense   Depreciation is a noncash expense. Because it was deducted to arrive at net income, we must *add back* $40,000, the amount of depreciation, to find cash from operations. The same holds true for amortization of intangible assets and depletion of natural resources.

Decrease in Prepaid Insurance   This account decreased by $6,000, according to Exhibit 12-12. A decrease in this account indicates that Julian deducted more on the income statement for the insurance expense of the period than it paid in cash for new policies. That is, the cash outlay for insurance protection was not as large as the amount of expense reported on the income statement. Thus, the *net decrease* in the account of $6,000 is *added back* to net income in Exhibit 12-18.

Increase in Income Taxes Payable   Exhibit 12-12 reports a net increase of $3,000 in Income Taxes Payable. The *net increase* of $3,000 in this liability is *added back* to net income in Exhibit 12-18 because the payments to the government were $3,000 less than the amount included on the income statement.

Loss on Retirement of Bonds   The $3,000 loss from retiring bonds was reported on the income statement as a deduction. There are two parts to the explanation for *adding back* the loss to net income to eliminate its effect in the Operating Activities section of the statement. First, any cash outflow from retiring bonds is properly classified as a financing activity, not an operating activity. The entire cash outflow should be reported in one classification rather than being allocated between two classifications. Second, the amount of the cash outflow is $63,000, not $3,000. To summarize, to convert net income to a cash basis, the loss is added back in the Operating Activities section to eliminate its effect. The actual use of cash to retire the bonds is shown in the financing section of the statement.

Summary of Adjustments to Net Income under the Indirect Method

The following is a list of the most common adjustments to net income when the indirect method is used to prepare the Operating Activities section of the statement of cash flows:

Additions to Net Income	Deductions from Net Income
Decrease in accounts receivable	Increase in accounts receivable
Decrease in inventory	Increase in inventory
Decrease in prepayments	Increase in prepayments
Increase in accounts payable	Decrease in accounts payable
Increase in accrued liabilities	Decrease in accrued liabilities
Losses on sales of long-term assets	Gains on sales of long-term assets
Losses on retirements of bonds	Gains on retirements of bonds
Depreciation, amortization, and depletion	

COMPARISON OF THE INDIRECT AND DIRECT METHODS

Earlier in the chapter we pointed out that the amount of cash provided by operating activities is the same under the direct and the indirect methods. The relative merits of the two methods, however, have stirred considerable debate in the accounting profession. The Financial Accounting Standards Board has expressed a strong preference for the direct method but allows companies to use the indirect method.

If a company uses the indirect method, it must separately disclose two important cash payments: income taxes paid and interest paid. Thus, if Julian uses the indirect method, it reports the following either at the bottom of the statement of cash flows or in a footnote:[5]

Income taxes paid	$47,000
Interest paid	$15,000

Advocates of the direct method believe that the information provided with this approach is valuable in evaluating a company's operating efficiency. For example, the use of the direct method allows the analyst to follow any trends in cash receipts from customers and compare them with cash payments to suppliers. The information presented in the Operating Activities section of the statement under the direct method is certainly user-friendly. Someone without a technical background in accounting can easily tell where cash came from and where it went during the period.

Advocates of the indirect method argue two major points. Many companies believe that the use of the direct method reveals too much about their business by telling readers exactly the amount of cash receipts and cash payments from operations. Whether the use of the direct method tells the competition too much about a company is subject to debate. The other argument made for the indirect method is that it focuses attention on the differences between income on an accrual basis and a cash basis. In fact, this reconciliation of net income and cash provided by operating activities is considered to be important enough that *if a company uses the direct method, it must present a separate schedule to reconcile net income to net cash from operating activities.* This schedule, in effect, is the same as the Operating Activities section for the indirect method.

THE USE OF CASH FLOW INFORMATION

The statement of cash flows is a critical disclosure to a company's investors and creditors. Many investors focus on cash flow from operations, rather than net income, as their key statistic. Similarly, many bankers are as concerned with cash flow from operations as they

---

[5]The same *Accounting Trends & Techniques* survey referred to earlier in the chapter (see footnote 3) indicated that of those companies using the indirect method, approximately 55% disclose interest and taxes paid in notes to the financial statements and approximately 45% report these amounts either within or at the bottom of the statement of cash flows.

are with net income because they care about a company's ability to pay its bills. There is the concern that accrual accounting can mask cash flow problems. For example, a company with smooth earnings could be building up accounts receivable and inventory. This may not become evident until the company is in deep trouble.

The statement of cash flows provides investors, analysts, bankers, and other users with a valuable starting point as they attempt to evaluate a company's financial health. From this point, these groups must decide *how* to use the information presented on the statement. They pay particular attention to the *relationships* among various items on the statement, as well as to other financial statement items. In fact, many large banks have their own cash flow models, which typically involve a rearrangement of the items on the statement of cash flows to suit their needs. We now turn our attention to two examples of how various groups use cash flow information.

CREDITORS AND CASH FLOW ADEQUACY

Bankers and other creditors are especially concerned with a company's ability to meet its principal and interest obligations. *Cash flow adequacy* is a measure intended to help in this regard.[6] It gauges the cash available to meet future debt obligations after paying taxes and interest costs and making capital expenditures. Because capital expenditures on new plant and equipment are a necessity for most companies, analysts are concerned with the cash available to repay debt *after* the company has replaced and updated its existing base of long-term assets.

Cash flow adequacy can be computed as follows:

$$\text{Cash Flow Adequacy} = \frac{\text{Cash Flow from Operating Activities} - \text{Capital Expenditures}}{\text{Average Amount of Debt Maturing over Next Five Years}}$$

How could you use the information in an annual report to measure a company's cash flow adequacy? First, whether a company uses the direct or indirect method to report cash flow from operating activities, this number represents cash flow *after* paying interest and taxes. The numerator of the ratio is determined by deducting capital expenditures, as they appear in the Investing Activities section of the statement, from cash flow from operating activities. A disclosure required by the Securities and Exchange Commission provides the information needed to calculate the denominator of the ratio. This regulatory body requires companies to report the annual amount of long-term debt maturing over each of the next five years.

www.sec.gov

IBM's Cash Flow Adequacy As an example of the calculation of this ratio, consider the following amounts from IBM's statement of cash flows for the year ended December 31, 1999 (amounts in millions of dollars):

www.ibm.com

Net cash provided from operating activities	$10,111
Payments for plant, rental machines, and other property	$ 5,959

Note J in IBM's 1999 annual report provides the following information:

Annual maturities in millions of dollars on long-term debt outstanding at December 31, 1999, are as follows: 2000, $5,805; 2001, $2,915; 2002, $2,659; 2003, $1,234; 2004, $489; 2005 and beyond, $6,867.

We can now compute IBM's cash flow adequacy for the year ended December 31, 1999, as follows:

$$\text{Cash Flow Adequacy} = \frac{\$10,111 - \$5,959}{(\$5,805 + \$2,915 + \$2,659 + \$1,234 + \$489)/5} = \frac{\$4,152}{\$2,620.4} = 1.58$$

---

[6]An article appearing in the January 10, 1994, edition of *The Wall Street Journal* reported that Fitch Investors Service Inc. has published a rating system to compare the cash flow adequacy of companies that it rates single-A in its credit ratings. The rating system is intended to help corporate bond investors assess the ability of these companies to meet their maturing debt obligations. Lee Berton, "Investors Have a New Tool for Judging Issuers' Health: 'Cash-Flow Adequacy,'" p. C1.

FOCUS ON USERS

Understanding the Relevance of the Cash Flow Statement to Decision Making

Sara Luedtke is an accountant for The Carlyle Group, a private merchant bank based in Washington, D.C., so she is very familiar with financial statements and the flow of data from one statement to the next. In preparing the statements, accountants like Sara draw relationships among the various line items so that analysts, like the ones discussed in previous chapters, can better evaluate the performance of investments. To illustrate this principle of how the decisions of analysts are affected by the work of accountants, Sara points to the statement of cash flows: "As a private merchant bank, our primary business activity is to invest in ownership of other companies on behalf of investors. Purchases and sales of these companies are called *investing activities,* and our investors review cash flows from these activities to compare how much cash flowed out of the firm into new investments to how much cash flowed into the firm from either sales of, or distributions received from, our investments."

As Sara helps prepare financial statements for the dozens of companies she is responsible for at The Carlyle Group, she is constantly aware that analysts and other external users will interpret her data and base investment decisions on it. Additionally, because The Carlyle Group is itself in the business of buying and selling (i.e., investing in) companies, Sara knows that the financial statements she prepares will be used *internally* for decision making by upper management. If the statements show that investment purchases exceed their sales during the year, for example, The Carlyle Group would need additional cash from investors to fund new investments. Conversely, if The Carlyle Group is selling off more investments than it is buying during a particular period, it would be able to pass some of the excess cash on to investors.

> "[O]ur primary business activity is to invest in ownership of other companies on behalf of investors. Purchases and sales of these companies are called *investing activities, …*"
>
> —Sara Luedtke

Would you feel comfortable lending to IBM if you knew that its ratio of cash flow from operations, after making necessary capital expenditures, to average maturities of debt over the next five years was slightly over 1.5 to 1? Before answering this question, you would want to compare the ratio with the ratios for prior years as well as with the ratio for companies of similar size and in lines of business similar to those of IBM. As a starting point, however, IBM's ratio of 1.58 to 1 indicates that its 1999 cash flow was sufficient to repay its average annual debt over the next five years.

STOCKHOLDERS AND CASH FLOW PER SHARE

As we will see in Chapter 13, one measure of the relative worth of an investment in a company is the ratio of the stock's market price per share to the company's earnings per share (that is, the price/earnings ratio). But many stockholders and Wall Street analysts are even more interested in the price of the stock in relation to the company's cash flow per share. Cash flow for purposes of this ratio is normally limited to cash flow from operating activities. This ratio has been used by these groups to evaluate investments—even though the accounting profession has expressly forbidden the reporting of cash flow per share information in the financial statements. The accounting profession's belief is that this type of information is not an acceptable alternative to earnings per share as an indicator of company performance.

ACCOUNTING FOR YOUR DECISIONS

You Are the Banker

You and your old college roommate are having an argument. You say that cash flow is all that matters when looking at a company's prospects. Your roommate says that the most important number is earnings per share. Who's right?

ANS: You're both wrong. True, bankers are interested in cash flow to make sure that a company can pay back its loans. But earnings per share is important also because it is less easily manipulated. After all, companies can decide when they want to finance expansion, pay down debt, or invest in new businesses. A company with strong earnings can appear weak from a cash flow perspective if it invests too much in new operating assets or other businesses. On the other hand, a company that wants to appear cash-rich can avoid making all the investments that it ought to be making. Although companies can manipulate earnings to some extent, the matching principle ensures that revenues and expenses relating to those revenues take place during the same period.

WARMUP EXERCISES

LO 1   Warmup Exercise 12-1   Purpose of the Statement of Cash Flows

Most companies begin the statement of cash flows by indicating the amount of net income and end it with the beginning and ending cash balances. Why is the statement necessary if net income already appears on the income statement and the cash balances can be found on the balance sheet?

Key to the Solution

Recall the *purpose* of the statement of cash flows as described in the beginning of the chapter.

LO 3   Warmup Exercise 12-2   Classification of Activities

For each of the following activities, indicate whether it should appear on the statement of cash flows as an operating (O), investing (I), or financing (F) activity. Assume the company uses the direct method of reporting in the Operating Activities section.

_____ **1.** New equipment is acquired for cash.

_____ **2.** Thirty-year bonds are issued.

_____ **3.** Cash receipts from the cash register are recorded.

_____ **4.** The biweekly payroll is paid.

_____ **5.** Common stock is issued for cash.

_____ **6.** Land that was being held for future expansion is sold at book value.

Key to the Solution

Recall the general rules for each of the categories: operating activities involve acquiring and selling products and services; investing activities deal with acquiring and disposing of long-term assets; and financing activities are concerned with the raising and repayment of funds in the form of debt and equity.

LO 6   Warmup Exercise 12-3   Adjustments to Net Income with the Indirect Method

Assume that a company uses the indirect method to prepare the Operating Activities section of the statement of cash flows. For each of the following items, indicate whether it would be added to net income (A), deducted from net income (D), or not reported in this section of the statement under the indirect method (NR).

_____ **1.** Decrease in accounts payable

_____ **2.** Increase in accounts receivable

_____ **3.** Decrease in prepaid insurance

_____ 4. Purchase of new factory equipment

_____ 5. Depreciation expense

_____ 6. Gain on retirement of bonds

Key to the Solution

Refer to the summary of adjustments to net income under the indirect method on page 578.

SOLUTIONS TO WARMUP EXERCISES

Warmup Exercise 12-1

The statement of cash flows is a complement to the other statements in that it summarizes the operating, investing, and financing activities over a period of time. Even though the net income and cash balances are available on other statements, the statement of cash flows explains to the reader *why* net income is different than cash flow from operations and *why* cash changed by the amount it did during the period.

Warmup Exercise 12-2

1. I   2. F   3. O   4. O   5. F   6. I

Warmup Exercise 12-3

1. D   2. D   3. A   4. NR   5. A   6. D

REVIEW PROBLEM

An income statement and comparative balance sheets for Dexter Company follow:

DEXTER COMPANY
INCOME STATEMENT
FOR THE YEAR ENDED DECEMBER 31, 2001

Sales revenue	$89,000
Cost of goods sold	57,000
Gross margin	$32,000
Depreciation expense	6,500
Advertising expense	3,200
Salaries expense	12,000
Total operating expenses	$21,700
Operating income	$10,300
Loss on sale of land	2,500
Income before tax	$ 7,800
Income tax expense	2,600
Net income	$ 5,200

DEXTER COMPANY
COMPARATIVE BALANCE SHEETS

	December 31	
	2001	**2000**
Cash	$ 12,000	$ 9,500
Accounts receivable	22,000	18,400
Inventory	25,400	20,500
Prepaid advertising	10,000	8,600
Total current assets	$ 69,400	$ 57,000

	2001	2000
Land	120,000	80,000
Equipment	190,000	130,000
Accumulated depreciation	(70,000)	(63,500)
Total long-term assets	$240,000	$146,500
Total assets	$309,400	$203,500
Accounts payable	$ 15,300	$ 12,100
Salaries payable	14,000	16,400
Income taxes payable	1,200	700
Total current liabilities	$ 30,500	$ 29,200
Capital stock	$200,000	$100,000
Retained earnings	78,900	74,300
Total stockholders' equity	$278,900	$174,300
Total liabilities and stockholders' equity	$309,400	$203,500

Additional Information

1. Land was acquired during the year for $70,000.

2. An unimproved parcel of land was sold during the year for $27,500. Its original cost to Dexter was $30,000.

3. A specialized piece of equipment was acquired in exchange for capital stock in the company. The value of the capital stock was $60,000.

4. In addition to the capital stock issued in item **3,** stock was sold for $40,000.

5. Dividends of $600 were paid.

Required

Prepare a statement of cash flows for 2001 using the direct method in the Operating Activities section of the statement. Include supplemental schedules to report any noncash investing and financing activities and to reconcile net income to net cash provided by operating activities.

Solution to Review Problem

DEXTER COMPANY
STATEMENT OF CASH FLOWS
FOR THE YEAR ENDED DECEMBER 31, 2001

Cash flows from operating activities

Cash collections from customers	$ 85,400
Cash payments:	
To suppliers	$(58,700)
For advertising	(4,600)
To employees	(14,400)
For income taxes	(2,100)
Total cash payments	$(79,800)
Net cash provided by operating activities	$ 5,600

Cash flows from investing activities

Purchase of land	$(70,000)
Sale of land	27,500
Net cash used by investing activities	$(42,500)

Cash flows from financing activities

Issuance of capital stock	$ 40,000
Payment of cash dividends	(600)
Net cash provided by financing activities	$ 39,400
Net increase in cash	$ 2,500
Cash balance, December 31, 2000	9,500
Cash balance, December 31, 2001	$ 12,000

Supplemental schedule of noncash investing and financing activities

Acquisition of specialized equipment in exchange for capital stock	$ 60,000

Reconciliation of net income to net cash provided by operating activities

Net income		$ 5,200
Adjustments to reconcile net income to net cash provided by operating activities:		
Increase in accounts receivable	(3,600)	
Increase in inventory	(4,900)	
Increase in prepaid advertising	(1,400)	
Increase in accounts payable	3,200	
Decrease in salaries payable	(2,400)	
Increase in income taxes payable	500	
Depreciation expense	6,500	
Loss on sale of land	2,500	
Net cash provided by operating activities		$ 5,600

APPENDIX 12A

ACCOUNTING TOOLS: A WORK-SHEET APPROACH TO THE STATEMENT OF CASH FLOWS

LO 7 Use a work sheet to prepare a statement of cash flows, using the indirect method to determine cash flow from operating activities.

In the chapter, we illustrated a systematic approach to aid in the preparation of a statement of cash flows. We now consider the use of a work sheet as an alternative tool to organize the information needed to prepare the statement. We will use the information given in the chapter for Julian Corp. (refer to Exhibits 12-11 and 12-12 for the income statements and comparative balance sheets). Although it is possible to use a work sheet to prepare the statement when the Operating Activities section is prepared under the direct method, we illustrate the use of a work sheet using the more popular *indirect* method.

A work sheet for Julian Corp. is presented in Exhibit 12-19. The following steps were taken in preparing the work sheet:

Step 1: The balances in each account at the end and at the beginning of the period are entered in the first two columns of the work sheet. For Julian, these balances can be found in its comparative balance sheets in Exhibit 12-12. Note that contra assets, liabilities, and owners' equity accounts are bracketed on the work sheet. Because the work sheet lists all balance sheet accounts, the total of the asset balances must equal the total of the liability and owners' equity balances, and, thus, the totals at the bottom for these first two columns equal $0.

Step 2: The additional information listed at the bottom of Exhibit 12-12 is used to record the various investing and financing activities on the work sheet (the following item numbers correspond to the superscript numbers on the work sheet in Exhibit 12-19):

1. Long-term investments were purchased for $30,000. Because this transaction required the use of cash, it is entered as a bracketed amount in the Investing column and as an addition to the Long-term Investments account in the Changes column.

2. Land was acquired by issuing a $50,000 note payable. This transaction is entered on two lines on the work sheet. First, $50,000 is added to the Changes column for Land and as a corresponding deduction in the Noncash column (the last column on the

EXHIBIT 12-19   Julian Corp. Statement of Cash Flows Work Sheet

JULIAN CORP.
STATEMENT OF CASH FLOWS WORK SHEET (INDIRECT METHOD)
(ALL AMOUNTS IN THOUSANDS OF DOLLARS)

| Accounts | Balances | | Changes | Cash Inflows (Outflows) | | | Noncash Activities |
	12/31/01	12/31/00		Operating	Investing	Financing	
Cash	35	46	$(11)^{16}$				
Accounts receivable	63	57	6^{10}	$(6)^{10}$			
Inventory	84	92	$(8)^{11}$	8^{11}			
Prepaid insurance	12	18	$(6)^{12}$	6^{12}			
Long-term investments	120	90	30^{1}		$(30)^{1}$		
Land	150	100	50^{2}				$(50)^{2}$
Property and equipment	320	280	75^{3}		$(75)^{3}$		
			$(35)^{4}$		25^{4}		
Accumulated depreciation	(100)	(75)	15^{4}				
			$(40)^{9}$	40^{9}			
Accounts payable	(38)	(31)	$(7)^{13}$	7^{13}			
Salaries and wages payable	(7)	(9)	2^{14}	$(2)^{14}$			
Income taxes payable	(8)	(5)	$(3)^{15}$	3^{15}			
Notes payable	(85)	(35)	$(50)^{2}$				50^{2}
Bonds payable	(200)	(260)	60^{5}			$(63)^{5}$	
Capital stock	(100)	(75)	$(25)^{6}$			25^{6}	
Retained earnings	(246)	(193)	67^{7}	$(5)^{4}$		$(67)^{7}$	
				3^{5}			
			$(120)^{8}$	120^{8}			
Totals	–0–	–0–	–0–	174	(80)	(105)	–0–
Net decrease in cash				$(11)^{16}$			

SOURCE: The authors are grateful to Jeannie Folk for the development of this work sheet.

work sheet). Likewise, $50,000 is added for Notes Payable to the Changes column and to the Noncash column.

3. Item 3 in the additional information indicates the acquisition of equipment for $75,000. This amount appears on the work sheet as an addition to Property and Equipment in the Changes column and as a deduction (cash outflow) in the Investing column.

4. A machine with an original cost of $35,000 and a book value of $20,000 was sold for $25,000, resulting in four entries on the work sheet. First, the amount of cash received, $25,000, is entered as an addition in the Investing column on the line for property and equipment. On the same line, the cost of the machine, $35,000, is entered as a deduction in the Changes column. The difference between the cost of the machine, $35,000, and its book value, $20,000, is its accumulated depreciation of $15,000. This amount is shown as a deduction from this account in the Changes column. Because the gain

of $5,000 is included in net income, it is deducted in the Operating column (on the Retained Earnings line).

5. Bonds with a face value of $60,000 were retired by paying $63,000 in cash, resulting in the entry of three amounts on the work sheet. The face value of the bonds, $60,000, is entered as a reduction of Bonds Payable in the Changes column. The amount paid to retire the bonds, $63,000, is entered on the same line in the Financing column. The loss of $3,000 is added in the Operating column because it was a deduction to arrive at net income.

6. Capital stock was issued for $25,000. This amount is entered on the Capital Stock line under the Changes column (as an increase in the account) and under the Financing column as an inflow.

7. Dividends of $67,000 were paid. This amount is entered as a reduction in Retained Earnings in the Changes column and as a cash outflow in the Financing Activities column.

Step 3: Because the indirect method is being used, net income of $120,000 for the period is entered as an addition to Retained Earnings in the Operating column of the work sheet (entry 8). The amount is also entered as an increase (bracketed) in the Changes column.

Step 4: Any noncash revenues or expenses are entered on the work sheet on the appropriate lines. For Julian, depreciation expense of $40,000 is added (bracketed) to Accumulated Depreciation in the Changes column and in the Operating column. This entry is identified on the work sheet as entry 9.

Step 5: Each of the changes in the noncash current asset and current liability accounts is entered in the Changes column and in the Operating column. These entries are identified on the work sheet as entries 10 through 15.

Step 6: Totals are determined for the Operating, Investing, and Financing columns and entered at the bottom of the work sheet. The total for the final column, Noncash Activities, of $0, is also entered.

Step 7: The net cash inflow (outflow) for the period is determined by adding the totals of the operating, investing, and financing columns. For Julian, the net cash *outflow* is $11,000, shown as entry 16 at the bottom of the statement. This same amount is then transferred to the line for Cash in the Changes column. Finally, the total of the Changes column at this point should net to $0.

CHAPTER HIGHLIGHTS

1. **LO 1** The purpose of a statement of cash flows is to summarize the cash flows of an entity during a period of time. The cash inflows and outflows are categorized into three activities: operating, investing, and financing.

2. **LO 2** Cash equivalents are convertible to a known amount of cash and are therefore included with cash on the balance sheet. Because such items as commercial paper, money market funds, and Treasury bills do not involve any significant risk, neither their purchase nor their sale is shown as an investing activity on the statement of cash flows.

3. **LO 3** Operating activities are generally the effects of items that enter into the determination of net income, such as the effects of buying and selling products and services. Other operating activities include payments of compensation to employees, taxes to the government, and interest to creditors. Preparation of the Operat-

ing Activities section of the statement of cash flows requires an analysis of the current assets and current liabilities.

4. **LO 3** Investing activities are critical to the success of a business because they involve the replacement of existing productive assets and the addition of new ones. Capital expenditures are normally the single largest cash outflow for most businesses. Occasionally, companies generate cash from the sale of existing plant and equipment. The information needed to prepare the Investing Activities section of the statement of cash flows is found by analyzing the long-term asset accounts.

5. **LO 3** All businesses rely on financing in one form or another. At least initially, all corporations sell stock to raise funds. Many turn to external sources as well, generating cash from the issuance of promissory notes and bonds. The repayment of debt and the reacquisition of capital stock are important uses of cash for some

companies. Given the nature of financing activities, long-term liability and stockholders' equity accounts must be examined in preparing this section of the statement of cash flows.

6. LO 4 Two different methods are acceptable to report cash flow from operating activities. Under the direct method, cash receipts and cash payments related to operations are reported. Under the indirect method, net income is reconciled to net cash flow from operating activities. Regardless of which method is used, the amount of cash generated from operations is the same.

7. LO 5 Preparation of the Operating Activities section under the direct method requires the conversion of income statement items from an accrual basis to a cash basis. Certain items, such as depreciation, do not have a cash effect and are not included on the statement. Gains and losses typically relate to either investing or financing activities and are not included in the Operating Activities section of the statement. When the direct method is used to present cash flow from operating activities, a separate schedule is required to reconcile net income to net cash flow from operating activities. This schedule is the same as the Operating Activities section under the indirect method.

8. LO 6 When the indirect method is used, the reconciliation of net income to net cash flow from operating activities appears on the face of the statement. Adjustments are made for the changes in each of the operating-related current asset and current liability accounts, as well as adjustments for noncash items, such as depreciation. The effects of gains and losses on net income must also be removed to convert to a cash basis. If the indirect method is used, a company must separately disclose the amount of cash paid for taxes and for interest.

9. LO 7 A work sheet is sometimes used in preparing a statement of cash flows. The work sheet acts as a tool to aid in the preparation of the statement. (Appendix 12A)

KEY TERMS QUIZ

Read each definition below and then write the number of that definition in the blank beside the appropriate term it defines. The solution appears at the end of the chapter.

___ Statement of cash flows
___ Cash equivalent
___ Operating activities
___ Investing activities

___ Financing activities
___ Direct method
___ Indirect method

1. Activities concerned with the acquisition and sale of products and services.

2. For preparing the Operating Activities section of the statement of cash flows, the approach in which net income is reconciled to net cash flow from operations.

3. The financial statement that summarizes an entity's cash receipts and cash payments during the period from operating, investing, and financing activities.

4. An item readily convertible to a known amount of cash and with a maturity to the investor of three months or less.

5. Activities concerned with the acquisition and disposal of long-term assets.

6. For preparing the Operating Activities section of the statement of cash flows, the approach in which cash receipts and cash payments are reported.

7. Activities concerned with the raising and repayment of funds in the form of debt and equity.

ALTERNATE TERMS

Bottom line   Net income

Cash flow from operating activities   Cash flow from operations

Statement of cash flows   Cash flows statement

QUESTIONS

1. What is the purpose of the statement of cash flows? As a flows statement, explain how it differs from the income statement.

2. What is a cash equivalent? Why is it included with cash for purposes of preparing a statement of cash flows?

3. Preston Corp. acquires a piece of land by signing a $60,000 promissory note and making a down payment of $20,000. How should this transaction be reported on the statement of cash flows?

4. Hansen Inc. made two purchases during December. One was a $10,000 Treasury bill that matures in 60 days from the date of purchase. The other was a $20,000 investment in Motorola common stock that will be held indefinitely. How should each of these be treated for purposes of preparing a statement of cash flows?

5. Companies are required to classify cash flows as operating, investing, or financing. Which of these three categories do you think will most likely have a net cash *outflow* over a number of years? Explain your answer.

6. A fellow student says to you: "The statement of cash flows is the easiest of the basic financial statements to prepare because you know the answer before you start. You compare the beginning and ending balances in cash on the balance sheet and compute the net inflow or outflow of cash. What could be easier?" Do you agree? Explain your answer.

7. What is your evaluation of the following statement? "Depreciation is responsible for providing some of the highest amounts of cash for capital-intensive businesses. This is obvious by examining the Operating Activities section of the statement of cash flows. Other than the net income of the period, depreciation is often the largest amount reported in this section of the statement."

8. Which method for preparing the Operating Activities section of the statement of cash flows, the direct or the indirect method, do you believe provides more information to users of the statement? Explain your answer.

9. Assume that a company uses the indirect method to prepare the Operating Activities section of the statement of cash flows. Why would a decrease in accounts receivable during the period be added back to net income?

10. Why is it necessary to analyze both inventory and accounts payable in trying to determine cash payments to suppliers when the direct method is used?

11. A company has a very profitable year. What explanations might there be for a decrease in cash?

12. A company reports a net loss for the year. Is it possible that cash could increase during the year? Explain your answer.

13. What effect does a decrease in income taxes payable for the period have on cash generated from operating activities? Does it matter whether the direct or the indirect method is used?

14. Why do accounting standards require a company to separately disclose income taxes paid and interest paid if it uses the indirect method?

15. Is it logical that interest paid is classified as a cash outflow in the *Operating* Activities section of the statement of cash flows but that dividends paid are included in the *Financing* Activities section? Explain your answer.

16. Jackson Company prepays the rent on various office facilities. The beginning balance in Prepaid Rent was $9,600, and the ending balance was $7,300. The income statement reports Rent Expense of $45,900. Under the direct method, what amount would appear for cash paid in rent in the Operating Activities section of the statement of cash flows?

17. Baxter Inc. buys 2,000 shares of its own common stock at $20 per share as treasury stock. How is this transaction reported on the statement of cash flows?

18. Duke Corp. sold a delivery truck for $9,000. Its original cost was $25,000, and the book value at the time of the sale was $11,000. How does the transaction to record the sale appear on a statement of cash flows prepared under the indirect method?

19. Billings Company has a patent on its books with a balance at the beginning of the year of $24,000. The ending balance for the asset was $20,000. The company neither bought nor sold any patents during the year, nor does it use an Accumulated Amortization account. Assuming that the company uses the indirect method in preparing a statement of cash flows, how is the decrease in the Patents account reported on the statement?

20. Ace Inc. declared and distributed a 10% stock dividend during the year. Explain how, if at all, you think this transaction should be reported on a statement of cash flows.

EXERCISES

LO 2 **Exercise 12-1** Cash Equivalents

Metropolis Industries invested its excess cash in the following instruments during December 2001:

Certificate of deposit, due January 31, 2002	$ 35,000
Certificate of deposit, due June 30, 2002	95,000
Investment in City of Elgin bonds, due May 1, 2003	15,000
Investment in Quantum Data stock	66,000
Money Market Fund	105,000
90-day Treasury bills	75,000
Treasury note, due December 1, 2002	200,000

Required

Determine the amount of cash equivalents that should be combined with cash on the company's balance sheet at December 31, 2001, and for purposes of preparing a statement of cash flows for the year ended December 31, 2001.

LO 3 **Exercise 12-2** Classification of Activities

For each of the following transactions reported on a statement of cash flows, fill in the blank to indicate if it would appear in the Operating Activities section (O), in the Investing Activities section (I), or in the Financing Activities section (F). Put an S in the blank if the transaction does not affect cash but is reported in a supplemental schedule of noncash activities. Assume the company uses the direct method in the Operating Activities section.

_____ 1. A company purchases its own common stock in the open market and immediately retires it.

_____ 2. A company issues preferred stock in exchange for land.

_____ 3. A six-month bank loan is obtained.

_____ 4. Twenty-year bonds are issued.

_____ 5. A customer's open account is collected.

_____ 6. Income taxes are paid.

_____ 7. Cash sales for the day are recorded.

_____ 8. Cash dividends are declared and paid.

_____ 9. A creditor is given shares of common stock in the company in return for cancellation of a long-term loan.

_____ 10. A new piece of machinery is acquired for cash.

_____ 11. Stock of another company is acquired as an investment.

_____ 12. Interest is paid on a bank loan.

_____ 13. Factory workers are paid.

LO 3 **Exercise 12-3** Retirement of Bonds Payable on the Statement of Cash Flows—
Indirect Method

Redstone Inc. has the following debt outstanding on December 31, 2001:

10% bonds payable, due 12/31/05	$500,000	
Discount on bonds payable	(40,000)	$460,000

On this date, Redstone retired the entire bond issue by paying cash of $510,000.

Required

1. Determine the effect on the accounting equation of the bond retirement.

2. Describe how the bond retirement would be reported on the statement of cash flows, assuming that Redstone uses the indirect method.

LO 5 **Exercise 12-4** Cash Collections—Direct Method

Stanley Company's comparative balance sheets included accounts receivable of $80,800 at December 31, 2000, and $101,100 at December 31, 2001. Sales reported by Stanley on its 2001 income statement amounted to $1,450,000. What is the amount of cash collections that Stanley will report in the Operating Activities section of its 2001 statement of cash flows assuming that the direct method is used?

LO 5 **Exercise 12-5** Cash Payments—Direct Method

Lester Enterprises' comparative balance sheets included inventory of $90,200 at December 31, 2000, and $70,600 at December 31, 2001. Lester's comparative balance sheets also included accounts payable of $57,700 at December 31, 2000, and $39,200 at December 31, 2001. Lester's accounts payable balances are composed solely of amounts due to suppliers for purchases of inventory on account. Cost of goods sold, as reported by Lester on its 2001 income statement, amounted to $770,900. What is the amount of cash payments for inventory that Lester will report in the Operating Activities section of its 2001 statement of cash flows assuming that the direct method is used?

LO 5 **Exercise 12-6** Operating Activities Section—Direct Method

The following account balances for the noncash current assets and current liabilities of Labrador Company are available:

	December 31	
	2001	**2000**
Accounts receivable	$ 4,000	$ 6,000
Inventory	32,000	25,000
Office supplies	7,000	10,000
Accounts payable	7,500	4,500
Salaries and wages payable	1,500	2,500
Interest payable	500	1,000
Income taxes payable	4,500	3,000

In addition, the income statement for 2001 is as follows:

	2001
Sales revenue	$100,000
Cost of goods sold	75,000
Gross profit	$ 25,000
General and administrative expense	$ 8,000
Depreciation expense	3,000
Total operating expenses	$ 11,000
Income before interest and taxes	$ 14,000
Interest expense	3,000
Income before tax	$ 11,000
Income tax expense	5,000
Net income	$ 6,000

Required

1. Prepare the Operating Activities section of the statement of cash flows using the direct method.

2. What does the use of the direct method reveal about a company that the indirect method does not?

LO 5 **Exercise 12-7** Determination of Missing Amounts—Cash Flow from Operating Activities

The computation of cash provided by operating activities requires analysis of the noncash current asset and current liability accounts. Determine the missing amounts for each of the following independent cases:

Case 1

Accounts receivable, beginning of year	$150,000
Accounts receivable, end of year	100,000
Credit sales for the year	175,000
Cash sales for the year	60,000
Write-offs of uncollectible accounts	35,000
Total cash collections for the year (from cash sales and collections on account)	?

Case 2

Inventory, beginning of year	$ 80,000
Inventory, end of year	55,000
Accounts payable, beginning of year	25,000
Accounts payable, end of year	15,000
Cost of goods sold	175,000
Cash payments for inventory (assume all purchases of inventory are on account)	?

Case 3

Prepaid insurance, beginning of year	$ 17,000
Prepaid insurance, end of year	20,000
Insurance expense	15,000
Cash paid for new insurance policies	?

Case 4

Income taxes payable, beginning of year	$ 95,000
Income taxes payable, end of year	115,000
Income tax expense	300,000
Cash payments for taxes	?

LO 5 **Exercise 12-8** Dividends on the Statement of Cash Flows

The following selected account balances are available from the records of Lewistown Company:

December 31

	2001	2000
Dividends payable	$ 30,000	$ 20,000
Retained earnings	375,000	250,000

Other information available for 2001 follows:

a. Lewistown reported $285,000 net income for the year.

b. It declared and distributed a stock dividend of $50,000 during the year.

c. It declared cash dividends at the end of each quarter and paid them within the next 30 days of the following quarter.

Required

1. Determine the amount of cash dividends *paid* during the year for presentation in the Financing Activities section of the statement of cash flows.

2. Should the stock dividend described in part **b** appear on a statement of cash flows? Explain your answer.

LO 6 **Exercise 12-9** Adjustments to Net Income with the Indirect Method

Assume that a company uses the indirect method to prepare the Operating Activities section of the statement of cash flows. For each of the following items, fill in the blank to indicate whether it would be added to net income (A), deducted from net income (D), or not reported in this section of the statement under the indirect method (NR).

_____ 1. Depreciation expense

_____ 2. Gain on sale of used delivery truck

_____ 3. Bad debts expense

_____ 4. Increase in accounts payable

_____ 5. Purchase of new delivery truck

_____ 6. Loss on retirement of bonds

_____ 7. Increase in prepaid rent

_____ 8. Decrease in inventory

_____ 9. Increase in short-term investments (classified as available-for-sale securities)

_____ 10. Amortization of patents

LO 6 **Exercise 12-10** Operating Activities Section—Indirect Method

The following account balances for the noncash current assets and current liabilities of Suffolk Company are available:

December 31

	2001	2000
Accounts receivable	$43,000	$35,000
Inventory	30,000	40,000
Prepaid rent	17,000	15,000
Totals	$90,000	$90,000
Accounts payable	$26,000	$19,000
Income taxes payable	6,000	10,000
Interest payable	15,000	12,000
Totals	$47,000	$41,000

Net income for 2001 is $40,000. Depreciation expense is $20,000. Assume that all sales and all purchases are on account.

Required

1. Prepare the Operating Activities section of the statement of cash flows using the indirect method.

2. Provide a brief explanation as to why cash flow from operating activities is more or less than the net income of the period.

Multi-Concept Exercises

LO 2, 3 **Exercise 12-11** Classification of Activities

Use the following legend to indicate how each of the following transactions would be reported on the statement of cash flows (assume that the stocks and bonds of other companies are classified as available-for-sale securities):

II = Inflow from investing activities
OI = Outflow from investing activities
IF = Inflow from financing activities
OF = Outflow from financing activities
CE = Classified as a cash equivalent and included with cash for purposes of preparing the statement of cash flows

_____ 1. Purchased a six-month certificate of deposit.

_____ 2. Purchased a 60-day Treasury bill.

_____ 3. Issued 1,000 shares of common stock.

_____ 4. Purchased 1,000 shares of stock in another company.

_____ 5. Purchased 1,000 shares of its own stock to be held in the treasury.

_____ 6. Invested $1,000 in a money market fund.

_____ 7. Sold 500 shares of stock of another company.

_____ 8. Purchased 20-year bonds of another company.

_____ 9. Issued 30-year bonds.

_____ 10. Repaid a six-month bank loan.

LO 3, 5 **Exercise 12-12** Classification of Activities

Use the following legend to indicate how each of the following transactions would be reported on the statement of cash flows (assume that the company uses the direct method in the Operating Activities section):

IO = Inflow from operating activities
OO = Outflow from operating activities
II = Inflow from investing activities
OI = Outflow from investing activities
IF = Inflow from financing activities
OF = Outflow from financing activities
NR = Not reported in the body of the statement of cash flows but included in a supplemental schedule

_____ 1. Collected $10,000 in cash from customers' open accounts for the period.

_____ 2. Paid one of the company's inventory suppliers $500 in settlement of an open account.

_____ 3. Purchased a new copier for $6,000; signed a 90-day note payable.

_____ 4. Issued bonds at face value of $100,000.

_____ 5. Made $23,200 in cash sales for the week.

_____ 6. Purchased an empty lot adjacent to the factory for $50,000. The seller of the land agrees to accept a five-year promissory note as consideration.

_____ 7. Renewed the property insurance policy for another six months. Cash of $1,000 is paid for the renewal.

_____ 8. Purchased a machine for $10,000.

_____ 9. Paid cash dividends of $2,500.

_____ 10. Reclassified as short term a long-term note payable of $5,000 that is due within the next year.

_____ 11. Purchased 500 shares of the company's own stock on the open market for $4,000.

_____ 12. Sold 500 shares of Nike stock for book value of $10,000 (they had been classified as available-for-sale securities).

LO 3, 6 Exercise 12-13 Long-Term Assets on the Statement of Cash Flows—Indirect Method

The following account balances are taken from the records of Martin Corp. for the past two years:

	December 31	
	2001	**2000**
Plant and equipment	$750,000	$500,000
Accumulated depreciation	160,000	200,000
Patents	92,000	80,000
Retained earnings	825,000	675,000

Other information available for 2001 follows:

a. Net income for the year was $200,000.

b. Depreciation expense on plant and equipment was $50,000.

c. Plant and equipment with an original cost of $150,000 were sold for $64,000 (you will need to determine the book value of the assets sold).

d. Amortization expense on patents was $8,000.

e. Both new plant and equipment and patents were purchased for cash during the year.

Required

Indicate, with amounts, how all items related to these long-term assets would be reported in the 2001 statement of cash flows, including any adjustments in the Operating Activities section of the statement. Assume that Martin uses the indirect method.

LO 1, 5 Exercise 12-14 Income Statement, Statement of Cash Flows (Direct Method), and Balance Sheet

The following events occurred at Handsome Hounds Grooming Company during its first year of business:

a. To establish the company, the two owners contributed a total of $50,000 in exchange for common stock.

b. Grooming service revenue for the first year amounted to $150,000, of which $40,000 was on account.

c. Customers owe $10,000 at the end of the year from the services provided on account.

d. At the beginning of the year, a storage building was rented. The company was required to sign a three-year lease for $12,000 per year and make a $2,000 refundable security deposit. The first year's lease payment and the security deposit were paid at the beginning of the year.

e. At the beginning of the year, the company purchased a patent at a cost of $100,000 for a revolutionary system to be used for dog grooming. The patent is expected to be useful for 10 years. The company paid 20% down in cash and signed a four-year note at the bank for the remainder.

f. Operating expenses, including amortization of the patent and rent on the storage building, totaled $80,000 for the first year. No expenses were accrued or unpaid at the end of the year.

g. The company declared and paid a $20,000 cash dividend at the end of the first year.

Required

1. Prepare an income statement for the first year.

2. Prepare a statement of cash flows for the first year, using the direct method in the Operating Activities section.

3. Did the company generate more or less cash flow from operations than it earned in net income? Explain why there is a difference.

4. Prepare a balance sheet as of the end of the first year.

PROBLEMS

LO 6   Problem 12-1   Statement of Cash Flows—Indirect Method
The following balances are available for Chrisman Company:

	December 31	
	2001	**2000**
Cash	$ 8,000	$ 10,000
Accounts receivable	20,000	15,000
Inventory	15,000	25,000
Prepaid rent	9,000	6,000
Land	75,000	75,000
Plant and equipment	400,000	300,000
Accumulated depreciation	(65,000)	(30,000)
Totals	$462,000	$401,000
Accounts payable	$ 12,000	$ 10,000
Income taxes payable	3,000	5,000
Short-term notes payable	35,000	25,000
Bonds payable	75,000	100,000
Common stock	200,000	150,000
Retained earnings	137,000	111,000
Totals	$462,000	$401,000

Bonds were retired during 2001 at face value, plant and equipment were acquired for cash, and common stock was issued for cash. Depreciation expense for the year was $35,000. Net income was reported at $26,000.

Required

1. Prepare a statement of cash flows for 2001, using the indirect method in the Operating Activities section.

2. Did Chrisman generate sufficient cash from operations to pay for its investing activities? How did it generate cash other than from operations? Explain your answers.

LO 7   Problem 12-2   Statement of Cash Flows Using a Work Sheet—Indirect Method (Appendix 12A)
Refer to all the facts in Problem 12-1.

Required

1. Using the format in Appendix 12A, prepare a statement of cash flows work sheet.

2. Prepare a statement of cash flows for 2001, using the indirect method in the Operating Activities section.

3. Did Chrisman generate sufficient cash from operations to pay for its investing activities? How did it generate cash other than from operations? Explain your answers.

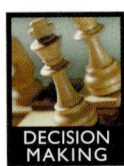
DECISION MAKING

LO 5   Problem 12-3   Statement of Cash Flows—Direct Method
Peoria Corp. has just completed another very successful year, as indicated by the following income statement:

	For the year ended December 31, 2001
Sales revenue	$1,250,000
Cost of goods sold	700,000
Gross profit	$ 550,000
Operating expenses	150,000
Income before interest and taxes	$ 400,000
Interest expense	25,000
Income before taxes	$ 375,000
Income tax expense	150,000
Net income	$ 225,000

Presented below are comparative balance sheets:

	December 31 2001	December 31 2000
Cash	$ 52,000	$ 90,000
Accounts receivable	180,000	130,000
Inventory	230,000	200,000
Prepayments	15,000	25,000
Total current assets	$ 477,000	$ 445,000
Land	$ 750,000	$ 600,000
Plant and equipment	700,000	500,000
Accumulated depreciation	(250,000)	(200,000)
Total long-term assets	$1,200,000	$ 900,000
Total assets	$1,677,000	$1,345,000
Accounts payable	$ 130,000	$ 148,000
Other accrued liabilities	68,000	63,000
Income taxes payable	90,000	110,000
Total current liabilities	$ 288,000	$ 321,000
Long-term bank loan payable	$ 350,000	$ 300,000
Common stock	$ 550,000	$ 400,000
Retained earnings	489,000	324,000
Total stockholders' equity	$1,039,000	$ 724,000
Total liabilities and stockholders' equity	$1,677,000	$1,345,000

Other information follows:

a. Dividends of $60,000 were declared and paid during the year.

b. Operating expenses include $50,000 of depreciation.

c. Land and plant and equipment were acquired for cash, and additional stock was issued for cash. Cash was also received from additional bank loans.

The president has asked you some questions about the year's results. She is very impressed with the profit margin of 18% (net income divided by sales revenue). She is bothered, however, by the decline in the cash balance during the year. One of the conditions of the existing bank loan is that the company maintain a minimum cash balance of $50,000.

Required

1. Prepare a statement of cash flows for 2001, using the direct method in the Operating Activities section.

2. On the basis of your statement in requirement 1, draft a brief memo to the president to explain why cash decreased during such a profitable year. Include in your explanation any recommendations for improving the company's cash flow in future years.

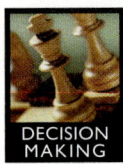

LO 6 Problem 12-4 Statement of Cash Flows—Indirect Method

Refer to all the facts in Problem 12-3.

Required

1. Prepare a statement of cash flows for 2001, using the indirect method in the Operating Activities section.

2. On the basis of your statement in requirement **1,** draft a brief memo to the president to explain why cash decreased during such a profitable year. Include in your explanation any recommendations for improving the company's cash flow in future years.

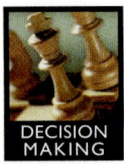

LO 7 Problem 12-5 Statement of Cash Flows Using a Work Sheet—Indirect Method (Appendix 12A)

Refer to all the facts in Problem 12-3.

Required

1. Using the format in Appendix 12A, prepare a statement of cash flows work sheet.

2. Prepare a statement of cash flows for 2001, using the indirect method in the Operating Activities section.

3. On the basis of your statement in requirement **2,** draft a brief memo to the president to explain why cash decreased during such a profitable year. Include in your explanation any recommendations for improving the company's cash flow in future years.

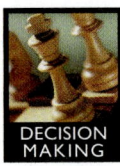

LO 5 Problem 12-6 Statement of Cash Flows—Direct Method

The income statement for Astro Inc. for 2001 follows:

	For the year ended December 31, 2001
Sales revenue	$ 500,000
Cost of goods sold	400,000
Gross profit	$ 100,000
Operating expenses	180,000
Loss before interest and taxes	$ (80,000)
Interest expense	20,000
Net loss	$(100,000)

Presented below are comparative balance sheets:

	December 31	
	2001	**2000**
Cash	$ 95,000	$ 80,000
Accounts receivable	50,000	75,000
Inventory	100,000	150,000
Prepayments	55,000	45,000
Total current assets	$ 300,000	$ 350,000
Land	$ 475,000	$ 400,000
Plant and equipment	870,000	800,000
Accumulated depreciation	(370,000)	(300,000)
Total long-term assets	$ 975,000	$ 900,000
Total assets	$1,275,000	$1,250,000
Accounts payable	$ 125,000	$ 100,000
Other accrued liabilities	35,000	45,000
Interest payable	15,000	10,000
Total current liabilities	$ 175,000	$ 155,000
Long-term bank loan payable	$ 340,000	$ 250,000

Common stock	$ 450,000	$ 400,000
Retained earnings	310,000	445,000
Total stockholders' equity	$ 760,000	$ 845,000
Total liabilities and stockholders' equity	$1,275,000	$1,250,000

Other information follows:

a. Dividends of $35,000 were declared and paid during the year.

b. Operating expenses include $70,000 of depreciation.

c. Land and plant and equipment were acquired for cash, and additional stock was issued for cash. Cash was also received from additional bank loans.

The president has asked you some questions about the year's results. He is disturbed with the $100,000 net loss for the year. He notes, however, that the cash position at the end of the year is improved. He is confused about what appear to be conflicting signals: "How could we have possibly added to our bank accounts during such a terrible year of operations?"

Required

1. Prepare a statement of cash flows for 2001, using the direct method in the Operating Activities section.

2. On the basis of your statement in requirement **1,** draft a brief memo to the president to explain why cash increased during such an unprofitable year. Include in your memo your recommendations for improving the company's bottom line.

LO 6   Problem 12-7   Statement of Cash Flows—Indirect Method
Refer to all the facts in Problem 12-6.

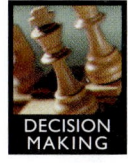

Required

1. Prepare a statement of cash flows for 2001, using the indirect method in the Operating Activities section.

2. On the basis of your statement in requirement **1,** draft a brief memo to the president to explain why cash increased during such an unprofitable year. Include in your memo your recommendations for improving the company's bottom line.

LO 7   Problem 12-8   Statement of Cash Flows Using a Work Sheet—Indirect Method (Appendix 12A)
Refer to all the facts in Problem 12-6.

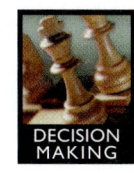

Required

1. Using the format in Appendix 12A, prepare a statement of cash flows work sheet.

2. Prepare a statement of cash flows for 2001, using the indirect method in the Operating Activities section.

3. On the basis of your statement in requirement **2,** draft a brief memo to the president to explain why cash increased during such an unprofitable year. Include in your memo your recommendations for improving the company's bottom line.

LO 6   Problem 12-9   Year-end Balance Sheet and Statement of Cash Flows—Indirect Method
The balance sheet of Terrier Company at the end of 2000 is presented below, along with certain other information for 2001:

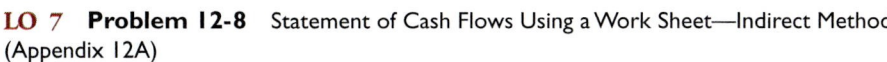

	December 31, 2000
Cash	$ 140,000
Accounts receivable	155,000
Total current assets	$ 295,000
Land	$ 300,000
Plant and equipment	500,000
Accumulated depreciation	(150,000)
Investments	100,000
Total long-term assets	$ 750,000
Total assets	$1,045,000

Current liabilities	$ 205,000
Bonds payable	$ 300,000
Common stock	$ 400,000
Retained earnings	140,000
Total stockholders' equity	$ 540,000
Total liabilities and stockholders' equity	$1,045,000

Other information follows:

a. Net income for 2001 was $70,000.

b. Included in operating expenses was $20,000 in depreciation.

c. Cash dividends of $25,000 were declared and paid.

d. An additional $150,000 of bonds was issued for cash.

e. Common stock of $50,000 was purchased for cash and retired.

f. Cash purchases of plant and equipment during the year were $200,000.

g. An additional $100,000 of bonds was issued in exchange for land.

h. Sales exceeded cash collections on account during the year by $10,000. All sales are on account.

i. The amount of current liabilities remained unchanged during the year.

Required

1. Prepare a statement of cash flows for 2001, using the indirect method in the Operating Activities section. Include a supplemental schedule for noncash activities.

2. Prepare a balance sheet at December 31, 2001.

3. Provide a possible explanation as to why Terrier decided to issue additional bonds for cash during 2001.

LO 7 Problem 12-10 Statement of Cash Flows Using a Work Sheet—Indirect Method (Appendix 12A)
Refer to all the facts in Problem 12-9.

Required

1. Prepare a balance sheet at December 31, 2001.

2. Using the format in Appendix 12A, prepare a statement of cash flows work sheet.

3. Prepare a statement of cash flows for 2001, using the indirect method in the Operating Activities section.

4. Provide a possible explanation as to why Terrier decided to issue additional bonds for cash during 2001.

Multi-Concept Problems

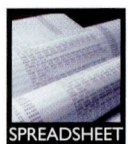
SPREADSHEET

LO 4, 5 Problem 12-11 Statement of Cash Flows—Direct Method
Glendive Corp. is in the process of preparing its statement of cash flows for the year ended June 30, 2001. An income statement for the year and comparative balance sheets follow:

	For the year ended June 30, 2001
Sales revenue	$550,000
Cost of goods sold	350,000
Gross profit	$200,000
General and administrative expenses	$ 55,000
Depreciation expense	75,000
Loss on sale of plant assets	5,000
Total expenses and losses	$135,000
Income before interest and taxes	$ 65,000

	15,000
Interest expense	
Income before taxes	$ 50,000
Income tax expense	17,000
Net income	$ 33,000

	June 30	
	2001	**2000**
Cash	$ 31,000	$ 40,000
Accounts receivable	90,000	75,000
Inventory	80,000	95,000
Prepaid rent	12,000	16,000
Total current assets	$213,000	$226,000
Land	$250,000	$170,000
Plant and equipment	750,000	600,000
Accumulated depreciation	(310,000)	(250,000)
Total long-term assets	$690,000	$520,000
Total assets	$903,000	$746,000
Accounts payable	$155,000	$148,000
Other accrued liabilities	32,000	26,000
Income taxes payable	8,000	10,000
Total current liabilities	$195,000	$184,000
Long-term bank loan payable	$100,000	$130,000
Common stock	$350,000	$200,000
Retained earnings	258,000	232,000
Total stockholders' equity	$608,000	$432,000
Total liabilities and stockholders' equity	$903,000	$746,000

Dividends of $7,000 were declared and paid during the year. New plant assets were purchased for $195,000 in cash during the year. Also, land was purchased for cash. Plant assets were sold during 2001 for $25,000 in cash. The original cost of the assets sold was $45,000, and their book value was $30,000. Additional stock was issued for cash, and a portion of the bank loan was repaid.

Required

1. Prepare a statement of cash flows, using the direct method in the Operating Activities section.

2. Evaluate the following statement: "Whether a company uses the direct or the indirect method to report cash flows from operations is irrelevant because the amount of cash flow from operating activities is the same regardless of which method is used."

LO 4, 6   Problem 12-12   Statement of Cash Flows—Indirect Method
Refer to all the facts in Problem 12-11.

SPREADSHEET

Required

1. Prepare a statement of cash flows for 2001, using the indirect method in the Operating Activities section.

2. Evaluate the following statement: "Whether a company uses the direct or indirect method to report cash flows from operations is irrelevant because the amount of cash flow from operating activities is the same regardless of which method is used."

LO 2, 5   Problem 12-13   Statement of Cash Flows—Direct Method
Lang Company has not yet prepared a formal statement of cash flows for 2001. Comparative balance sheets as of December 31, 2001 and 2000, and a statement of income and retained earnings for the year ended December 31, 2001, follow:

LANG COMPANY
BALANCE SHEET
DECEMBER 31
(THOUSANDS OMITTED)

Assets	2001	2000
Current assets:		
Cash	$ 60	$ 100
U.S. Treasury bills (six-month)	–0–	50
Accounts receivable	610	500
Inventory	720	600
Total current assets	$1,390	$1,250
Long-term assets:		
Land	$ 80	$ 70
Buildings and equipment	710	600
Accumulated depreciation	(180)	(120)
Patents (less amortization)	105	130
Total long-term assets	$ 715	$ 680
Total assets	$2,105	$1,930

Liabilities and Owners' Equity		
Current liabilities:		
Accounts payable	$ 360	$ 300
Taxes payable	25	20
Notes payable	400	400
Total current liabilities	$ 785	$ 720
Term notes payable—due 2005	200	200
Total liabilities	$ 985	$ 920
Owners' equity:		
Common stock outstanding	$ 830	$ 700
Retained earnings	290	310
Total owners' equity	$1,120	$1,010
Total liabilities and owners' equity	$2,105	$1,930

LANG COMPANY
STATEMENT OF INCOME AND RETAINED EARNINGS
FOR THE YEAR ENDED DECEMBER 31, 2001
(THOUSANDS OMITTED)

Sales		$2,408
Less expenses and interest:		
Cost of goods sold	$1,100	
Salaries and benefits	850	
Heat, light, and power	75	
Depreciation	60	
Property taxes	18	
Patent amortization	25	
Miscellaneous expense	10	
Interest	55	2,193
Net income before income taxes		$ 215
Income taxes		105
Net income		$ 110
Retained earnings—January 1, 2001		310
		$ 420
Stock dividend distributed		130
Retained earnings—December 31, 2001		$ 290

Required

1. For purposes of a statement of cash flows, are the U.S. Treasury bills cash equivalents? If not, how should they be classified? Explain your answers.

2. Prepare a statement of cash flows for 2001, using the direct method in the Operating Activities section.

(CMA adapted)

ALTERNATE PROBLEMS

LO 6 Problem 12-1A Statement of Cash Flows—Indirect Method

The following balances are available for Madison Company:

| | December 31 | |
	2001	2000
Cash	$ 12,000	$ 10,000
Accounts receivable	10,000	12,000
Inventory	8,000	7,000
Prepaid rent	1,200	1,000
Land	75,000	75,000
Plant and equipment	200,000	150,000
Accumulated depreciation	(75,000)	(25,000)
Totals	$231,200	$230,000
Accounts payable	$ 15,000	$ 15,000
Income taxes payable	2,500	2,000
Short-term notes payable	20,000	22,500
Bonds payable	75,000	50,000
Common stock	100,000	100,000
Retained earnings	18,700	40,500
Totals	$231,200	$230,000

Bonds were issued during 2001 at face value, and plant and equipment were acquired for cash. Depreciation expense for the year was $50,000. A net loss of $21,800 was reported.

Required

1. Prepare a statement of cash flows for 2001, using the indirect method in the Operating Activities section.

2. Explain briefly how Madison was able to increase its cash balance during a year in which it incurred a net loss.

LO 7 Problem 12-2A Statement of Cash Flows Using a Work Sheet—Indirect Method (Appendix 12A)

Refer to all the facts in Problem 12-1A.

Required

1. Using the format in Appendix 12A, prepare a statement of cash flows work sheet.

2. Prepare a statement of cash flows for 2001, using the indirect method in the Operating Activities section.

3. Explain briefly how Madison was able to increase its cash balance during a year in which it incurred a net loss.

LO 5 Problem 12-3A Statement of Cash Flows—Direct Method

Wabash Corp. has just completed another very successful year, as indicated by the following income statement:

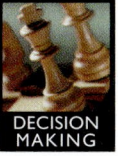

DECISION MAKING

	For the year ended December 31, 2001
Sales revenue	$2,460,000
Cost of goods sold	1,400,000
Gross profit	$1,060,000
Operating expenses	460,000
Income before interest and taxes	$ 600,000
Interest expense	100,000
Income before taxes	$ 500,000
Income tax expense	150,000
Net income	$ 350,000

The following are comparative balance sheets:

	December 31	
	2001	**2000**
Cash	$ 140,000	$ 210,000
Accounts receivable	60,000	145,000
Inventory	200,000	180,000
Prepayments	15,000	25,000
Total current assets	$ 415,000	$ 560,000
Land	$ 600,000	$ 700,000
Plant and equipment	850,000	600,000
Accumulated depreciation	(225,000)	(200,000)
Total long-term assets	$1,225,000	$1,100,000
Total assets	$1,640,000	$1,660,000
Accounts payable	$ 140,000	$ 120,000
Other accrued liabilities	50,000	55,000
Income taxes payable	80,000	115,000
Total current liabilities	$ 270,000	$ 290,000
Long-term bank loan payable	$ 200,000	$ 250,000
Common stock	$ 450,000	$ 400,000
Retained earnings	720,000	720,000
Total stockholders' equity	$1,170,000	$1,120,000
Total liabilities and stockholders' equity	$1,640,000	$1,660,000

Other information follows:

a. Dividends of $350,000 were declared and paid during the year.

b. Operating expenses include $25,000 of depreciation.

c. Land was sold for its book value, and new plant and equipment was acquired for cash.

d. Part of the bank loan was repaid, and additional common stock was issued for cash.

The president has asked you some questions about the year's results. She is very impressed with the profit margin of 14% (net income divided by sales revenue). She is bothered, however, by the decline in the company's cash balance during the year. One of the conditions of the existing bank loan is that the company maintain a minimum cash balance of $100,000.

Required

1. Prepare a statement of cash flows for 2001, using the direct method in the Operating Activities section.

2. On the basis of your statement in requirement **1**, draft a brief memo to the president to explain why cash decreased during such a profitable year. Include in your explanation any recommendations for improving the company's cash flow in future years.

LO 6 Problem 12-4A Statement of Cash Flows—Indirect Method

Refer to all the facts in Problem 12-3A.

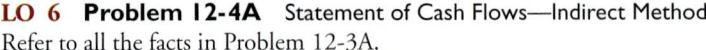

Required

1. Prepare a statement of cash flows for 2001, using the indirect method in the Operating Activities section.

2. On the basis of your statement in requirement **1,** draft a brief memo to the president to explain why cash decreased during such a profitable year. Include in your explanation any recommendations for improving the company's cash flow in future years.

LO 7 **Problem 12-5A** Statement of Cash Flows Using a Work Sheet—Indirect Method (Appendix 12A)
Refer to all the facts in Problem 12-3A.

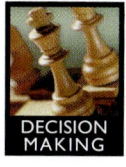
DECISION
MAKING

Required

1. Using the format in Appendix 12A, prepare a statement of cash flows work sheet.

2. Prepare a statement of cash flows for 2001, using the indirect method in the Operating Activities section.

3. On the basis of your statement in requirement **2,** draft a brief memo to the president to explain why cash decreased during such a profitable year. Include in your explanation any recommendations for improving the company's cash flow in future years.

LO 5 **Problem 12-6A** Statement of Cash Flows—Direct Method
The income statement for Pluto Inc. for 2001 follows:

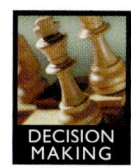
DECISION
MAKING

	For the year ended December 31, 2001
Sales revenue	$350,000
Cost of goods sold	150,000
Gross profit	$200,000
Operating expenses	250,000
Loss before interest and taxes	$ (50,000)
Interest expense	10,000
Net loss	$ (60,000)

Presented below are comparative balance sheets:

	December 31	
	2001	2000
Cash	$ 25,000	$ 10,000
Accounts receivable	30,000	80,000
Inventory	100,000	100,000
Prepayments	36,000	35,000
Total current assets	$191,000	$225,000
Land	$300,000	$200,000
Plant and equipment	500,000	250,000
Accumulated depreciation	(90,000)	(50,000)
Total long-term assets	$710,000	$400,000
Total assets	$901,000	$625,000
Accounts payable	$ 50,000	$ 10,000
Other accrued liabilities	40,000	20,000
Interest payable	22,000	12,000
Total current liabilities	$112,000	$ 42,000
Long-term bank loan payable	$450,000	$100,000
Common stock	$300,000	$300,000
Retained earnings	39,000	183,000
Total stockholders' equity	$339,000	$483,000
Total liabilities and stockholders' equity	$901,000	$625,000

Other information follows:

a. Dividends of $84,000 were declared and paid during the year.

b. Operating expenses include $40,000 of depreciation.

c. Land and plant and equipment were acquired for cash. Cash was received from additional bank loans.

The president has asked you some questions about the year's results. He is disturbed with the net loss of $60,000 for the year. He notes, however, that the cash position at the end of the year is improved. He is confused about what appear to be conflicting signals: "How could we have possibly added to our bank accounts during such a terrible year of operations?"

Required

1. Prepare a statement of cash flows for 2001, using the direct method in the Operating Activities section.

2. On the basis of your statement in requirement **1**, draft a brief memo to the president to explain why cash increased during such an unprofitable year. Include in your memo your recommendations for improving the company's bottom line.

LO 6   Problem 12-7A   Statement of Cash Flows—Indirect Method
Refer to all the facts in Problem 12-6A.

Required

1. Prepare a statement of cash flows for 2001, using the indirect method in the Operating Activities section.

2. On the basis of your statement in requirement **1**, draft a brief memo to the president to explain why cash increased during such an unprofitable year. Include in your memo your recommendations for improving the company's bottom line.

LO 7   Problem 12-8A   Statement of Cash Flows Using a Work Sheet—Indirect Method
(Appendix 12A)
Refer to all the facts in Problem 12-6A.

Required

1. Using the format in Appendix 12A, prepare a statement of cash flows work sheet.

2. Prepare a statement of cash flows for 2001, using the indirect method in the Operating Activities section.

3. On the basis of your statement in requirement **2**, draft a brief memo to the president to explain why cash increased during such an unprofitable year. Include in your memo your recommendations for improving the company's bottom line.

LO 6   Problem 12-9A   Year-end Balance Sheet and Statement of Cash Flows—
Indirect Method
The balance sheet of Poodle Company at the end of 2000 is presented below along with certain other information for 2001:

	December 31, 2000
Cash	$ 155,000
Accounts receivable	140,000
Total current assets	$ 295,000
Land	$ 100,000
Plant and equipment	700,000
Accumulated depreciation	(175,000)
Investments	125,000
Total long-term assets	$ 750,000
Total assets	$1,045,000

Current liabilities	$ 325,000
Bonds payable	$ 100,000
Common stock	$ 500,000
Retained earnings	120,000
Total stockholders' equity	$ 620,000
Total liabilities and stockholders' equity	$1,045,000

Other information follows:

a. Net income for 2001 was $50,000.

b. Included in operating expenses was $25,000 in depreciation.

c. Cash dividends of $40,000 were declared and paid.

d. An additional $50,000 of common stock was issued for cash.

e. Bonds payable of $100,000 were purchased for cash and retired at no gain or loss.

f. Cash purchases of plant and equipment during the year were $60,000.

g. An additional $200,000 of land was acquired in exchange for a long-term note payable.

h. Sales exceeded cash collections on account during the year by $15,000. All sales are on account.

i. The amount of current liabilities decreased by $20,000 during the year.

Required

1. Prepare a statement of cash flows for 2001, using the indirect method in the Operating Activities section. Include a supplemental schedule for noncash activities.

2. Prepare a balance sheet at December 31, 2001.

3. What primary uses did Poodle make of the cash it generated from operating activities?

LO 7   Problem 12-10A   Statement of Cash Flows Using a Work Sheet—Indirect Method (Appendix 12A)
Refer to all the facts in Problem 12-9A.

Required

1. Prepare a balance sheet at December 31, 2001.

2. Using the format in Appendix 12A, prepare a statement of cash flows work sheet.

3. Prepare a statement of cash flows for 2001, using the indirect method in the Operating Activities section.

4. Provide a possible explanation as to why Poodle decided to purchase and retire bonds during 2001.

Alternate Multi-Concept Problems

LO 4, 5   Problem 12-11A   Statement of Cash Flows—Direct Method
Bannack Corp. is in the process of preparing its statement of cash flows for the year ended June 30, 2001. An income statement for the year and comparative balance sheets follow:

	For the year ended June 30, 2001
Sales revenue	$400,000
Cost of goods sold	240,000
Gross profit	$160,000
General and administrative expenses	$ 40,000
Depreciation expense	80,000
Loss on sale of plant assets	10,000
Total expenses and losses	$130,000
Income before interest and taxes	$ 30,000

Interest expense	15,000	
Income before taxes	$ 15,000	
Income tax expense	5,000	
Net income	$ 10,000	

	June 30	
	2001	**2000**
Cash	$ 25,000	$ 40,000
Accounts receivable	80,000	69,000
Inventory	75,000	50,000
Prepaid rent	2,000	18,000
Total current assets	$182,000	$177,000
Land	$ 60,000	$150,000
Plant and equipment	575,000	500,000
Accumulated depreciation	(310,000)	(250,000)
Total long-term assets	$325,000	$400,000
Total assets	$507,000	$577,000
Accounts payable	$145,000	$140,000
Other accrued liabilities	50,000	45,000
Income taxes payable	5,000	15,000
Total current liabilities	$200,000	$200,000
Long-term bank loan payable	$ 75,000	$150,000
Common stock	$100,000	$100,000
Retained earnings	132,000	127,000
Total stockholders' equity	$232,000	$227,000
Total liabilities and stockholders' equity	$507,000	$577,000

Dividends of $5,000 were declared and paid during the year. New plant assets were purchased for $125,000 in cash during the year. Also, land was sold for cash at its book value. Plant assets were sold during 2001 for $20,000 in cash. The original cost of the assets sold was $50,000, and their book value was $30,000. A portion of the bank loan was repaid.

Required

1. Prepare a statement of cash flows for 2001, using the direct method in the Operating Activities section.

2. Evaluate the following statement: "Whether a company uses the direct or the indirect method to report cash flows from operations is irrelevant because the amount of cash flow from operating activities is the same regardless of which method is used."

LO 4, 6 Problem 12-12A Statement of Cash Flows—Indirect Method
Refer to all the facts in Problem 12-11A

Required

1. Prepare a statement of cash flows for 2001, using the indirect method in the Operating Activities section.

2. Evaluate the following statement: "Whether a company uses the direct or the indirect method to report cash flows from operations is irrelevant because the amount of cash flow from operating activities is the same regardless of which method is used."

LO 2, 5 Problem 12-13A Statement of Cash Flows—Direct Method
Shepard Company has not yet prepared a formal statement of cash flows for 2001. Comparative balance sheets as of December 31, 2001 and 2000, and a statement of income and retained earnings for the year ended December 31, 2001, follow:

SHEPARD COMPANY
BALANCE SHEET
DECEMBER 31
(THOUSANDS OMITTED)

Assets	2001	2000
Current assets:		
Cash	$ 50	$ 75
U.S. Treasury bills (six-month)	25	–0–
Accounts receivable	125	200
Inventory	525	500
Total current assets	$ 725	$ 775
Long-term assets:		
Land	$ 100	$ 80
Buildings and equipment	510	450
Accumulated depreciation	(190)	(150)
Patents (less amortization)	90	110
Total long-term assets	$ 510	$ 490
Total assets	$1,235	$1,265

Liabilities and Owners' Equity		
Current liabilities:		
Accounts payable	$ 370	$ 330
Taxes payable	10	20
Notes payable	300	400
Total current liabilities	$ 680	$ 750
Term notes payable—due 2005	200	200
Total liabilities	$ 880	$ 950
Owners' equity:		
Common stock outstanding	$ 220	$ 200
Retained earnings	135	115
Total owners' equity	$ 355	$ 315
Total liabilities and owners' equity	$1,235	$1,265

SHEPARD COMPANY
STATEMENT OF INCOME AND RETAINED EARNINGS
YEAR ENDED DECEMBER 31, 2001
(THOUSANDS OMITTED)

Sales		$1,416
Less expenses and interest:		
Cost of goods sold	$990	
Salaries and benefits	195	
Heat, light, and power	70	
Depreciation	40	
Property taxes	2	
Patent amortization	20	
Miscellaneous expense	2	
Interest	45	1,364
Net income before income taxes		$ 52
Income taxes		12
Net income		$ 40
Retained earnings—January 1, 2001		115
		$ 155
Stock dividend distributed		20
Retained earnings—December 31, 2001		$ 135

Required

1. For purposes of a statement of cash flows, are the U.S. Treasury bills cash equivalents? If not, how should they be classified? Explain your answers.

2. Prepare a statement of cash flows for 2001, using the direct method in the Operating Activities section.

(CMA adapted)

CASES

Reading and Interpreting Financial Statements

LO 2, 3 Case 12-1   Reading and Interpreting Uno's Statement of Cash Flows

www.pizzeriauno.com Refer to Uno's statement of cash flows for 1999 and any other pertinent information in its annual report.

Required

1. As explained in the chapter, cash equivalents are combined with cash on both the balance sheet and the statement of cash flows. Does Uno have any cash equivalents?

2. According to the statement of cash flows, did inventory increase or decrease during the most recent year? Explain your answer.

3. What are the major reasons for the difference between net income and net cash provided by operating activities?

4. Excluding operations, what was Uno's largest source of cash during the most recent year? The largest use of cash?

5. What common type of cash outflow from financing activities is missing from Uno's statement?

LO 2, 3 Case 12-2   Reading and Interpreting Gateway's Statement of Cash Flows

www.gateway.com Refer to Gateway's statement of cash flows for 1999 and any other pertinent information in its annual report.

Required

1. According to a footnote in the annual report, how does the company define cash equivalents?

2. According to the statement of cash flows, did accounts receivable increase or decrease during 1999? Explain your answer.

3. What are the major reasons net cash provided by operating activities is significantly more than net income in 1999?

4. What activity generated $100,000,000 of cash for Gateway in 1999?

5. What common type of cash outflow from financing activities is missing from Gateway's statement?

LO 4 Case 12-3   Reading and Interpreting Sara Lee's Statement of Cash Flows

www.saralee.com Presented below is the Operating Activities section of Sara Lee's 1998 statement of cash flows, along with an excerpt from the Financial Review section of the 1998 annual report (in millions of dollars):

Operating Activities	
Net loss	$ (523)
Adjustments for noncash charges included in net (loss) income:	
Depreciation	427
Amortization of intangibles	191
Restructuring charge	2,040
(Decrease) increase in deferred taxes	(405)
Other noncash credits, net	(5)
Changes in current assets and liabilities, net of businesses acquired and sold	
Decrease in trade accounts receivable	6
(Increase) in inventories	(27)
Decrease in other current assets	34

Increase in accounts payable	20	
Increase in accrued liabilities	177	
Net cash from operating activities	$1,935	

1998 Restructuring In the second quarter of fiscal 1998, the corporation provided for the cost of restructuring its worldwide operations. The planned restructuring activities include the disposition of 116 manufacturing and distribution facilities—86 facilities are owned and 30 are leased. This restructuring provision reduced income before income taxes, net income and basic earnings per share in 1998 by $2,040 million, $1,625 million and $3.46 per share, respectively.

Required

1. Which method, direct or indirect, does Sara Lee use in preparing the Operating Activities section of its statement of cash flows? Explain.

2. Based on your review of this section of Sara Lee's 1998 statement of cash flows, what is the primary reason the company reported a net loss but was able to generate significant cash from operations?

3. Refer to the excerpt from the Financial Review. What was the dollar effect of the 1998 restructuring on income before income taxes? What was the dollar effect of the 1998 restructuring on cash flow during 1998? Relate your answer to the answer you provided in **2.**

Making Financial Decisions

LO 1, 5 Case 12-4 Dividend Decision and the Statement of Cash Flows—Direct Method
Bailey Corp. just completed the most profitable year in its 25-year history. Reported earnings of $1,020,000 on sales of $8,000,000 resulted in a very healthy profit margin of 12.75%. Each year before releasing the financial statements, the board of directors meets to decide on the amount of dividends to declare for the year. For each of the past nine years, the company has declared a dividend of $1 per share of common stock, which has been paid on January 15 of the following year.

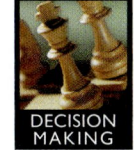
DECISION MAKING

Presented below are the income statement for the year and comparative balance sheets as of the end of the last two years.

	For the year ended December 31, 2001
Sales revenue	$8,000,000
Cost of goods sold	4,500,000
Gross profit	$3,500,000
Operating expenses	1,450,000
Income before interest and taxes	$2,050,000
Interest expense	350,000
Income before taxes	$1,700,000
Income tax expense 40%	680,000
Net income	$1,020,000

	December 31	
	2001	**2000**
Cash	$ 480,000	$ 450,000
Accounts receivable	250,000	200,000
Inventory	750,000	600,000
Prepayments	60,000	75,000
Total current assets	$1,540,000	$1,325,000
Land	$3,255,000	$2,200,000
Plant and equipment	4,200,000	2,500,000
Accumulated depreciation	(1,250,000)	(1,000,000)
Long-term investments	500,000	900,000
Patents	650,000	750,000
Total long-term assets	$7,355,000	$5,350,000
Total assets	$8,895,000	$6,675,000

Accounts payable	$ 350,000	$ 280,000
Other accrued liabilities	285,000	225,000
Income taxes payable	170,000	100,000
Dividends payable	–0–	200,000
Notes payable due within next year	200,000	–0–
Total current liabilities	$1,005,000	$ 805,000
Long-term notes payable	$ 300,000	$ 500,000
Bonds payable	2,200,000	1,500,000
Total long-term liabilities	$2,500,000	$2,000,000
Common stock, $10 par	$2,500,000	$2,000,000
Retained earnings	2,890,000	1,870,000
Total stockholders' equity	$5,390,000	$3,870,000
Total liabilities and stockholders' equity	$8,895,000	$6,675,000

Additional information follows:

a. All sales are on account, as are all purchases.

b. Land was purchased through the issuance of bonds. Additional land (beyond the amount purchased through the issuance of bonds) was purchased for cash.

c. New plant and equipment were acquired during the year for cash. No plant assets were retired during the year. Depreciation expense is included in operating expenses.

d. Long-term investments were sold for cash during the year.

e. No new patents were acquired, and none were disposed of during the year. Amortization expense is included in operating expenses.

f. Notes payable due within next year represents the amount reclassified from long term to short term.

g. Fifty thousand shares of common stock were issued during the year at par value.

As Bailey's controller, you have been asked to recommend to the board whether to declare a dividend this year and, if so, whether the precedent of paying a $1 per share dividend can be maintained. The president is eager to keep the dividend at $1 in view of the successful year just completed. He is also concerned, however, about the effect of a dividend on the company's cash position. He is particularly concerned about the large amount of notes payable that comes due next year. He further notes the aggressive growth pattern in recent years, as evidenced this year by large increases in land and plant and equipment.

Required

1. Using the format in Exhibit 12-14, convert the income statement from an accrual basis to a cash basis.

2. Prepare a statement of cash flows, using the direct method in the Operating Activities section.

3. What do you recommend to the board of directors concerning the declaration of a cash dividend? Should the $1 per share dividend be declared? Should a smaller amount be declared? Should no dividend be declared? Support your answer with any necessary computations. Include in your response your concerns, from a cash flow perspective, about the following year.

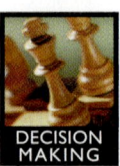

LO 1, 6 Case 12-5 Equipment Replacement Decision and Cash Flows from Operations
Conrad Company has been in operation for four years. The company is pleased with the continued improvement in net income but is concerned about a lack of cash available to replace existing equipment. Land, buildings, and equipment were purchased at the beginning of Year 1. No subsequent fixed asset purchases have been made, but the president believes that equipment will need to be replaced in the near future. The following information is available (all amounts are in millions of dollars):

	Year of Operation			
	Year 1	Year 2	Year 3	Year 4
Net income (loss)	$(10)	$ (2)	$15	$20
Depreciation expense	30	25	15	14
Increase (decrease) in:				
Accounts receivable	32	5	12	20
Inventories	26	8	5	9
Prepayments	0	0	10	5
Accounts payable	15	3	(5)	(4)

Required

1. Compute the cash flow from operations for each of Conrad's first four years of operation.

2. Write a memo to the president explaining why the company is not generating sufficient cash from operations to pay for the replacement of equipment.

Accounting and Ethics: What Would You Do?

LO 1, 6 **Case 12-6** Loan Decision and the Statement of Cash Flows—Indirect Method
Mega Enterprises is in the process of negotiating an extension of its existing loan agreements with a major bank. The bank is particularly concerned with Mega's ability to generate sufficient cash flow from operating activities to meet the periodic principal and interest payments. In conjunction with the negotiations, the controller prepared the following statement of cash flows to present to the bank:

MEGA ENTERPRISES
STATEMENT OF CASH FLOWS
FOR THE YEAR ENDED DECEMBER 31, 2001
(ALL AMOUNTS IN MILLIONS OF DOLLARS)

Cash flows from operating activities

Net income	$ 65
Adjustments to reconcile net income to net	
cash provided by operating activities:	
Depreciation and amortization	56
Increase in accounts receivable	(19)
Decrease in inventory	27
Decrease in accounts payable	(42)
Increase in other accrued liabilities	18
Net cash provided by operating activities	$ 105

Cash flows from investing activities

Acquisitions of other businesses	$(234)
Acquisitions of plant and equipment	(125)
Sale of other businesses	300
Net cash used by investing activities	$ (59)

Cash flows from financing activities

Additional borrowings	$ 150
Repayments of borrowings	(180)
Cash dividends paid	(50)
Net cash used by financing activities	$ (80)
Net decrease in cash	$ (34)
Cash balance, January 1, 2001	42
Cash balance, December 31, 2001	$ 8

During 2001, Mega sold one of its businesses in California. A gain of $150 million was included in 2001 income as the difference between the proceeds from the sale of $450 million and the book value of the business of $300 million. The effect on the accounting equation of the transaction to record the sale is as follows (in millions of dollars):

BALANCE SHEET					INCOME STATEMENT	
ASSETS	**=**	**LIABILITIES**	**+**	**OWNERS' EQUITY**	**+ REVENUES – EXPENSES**	
Cash	450					
California Properties	(300)				Gain on Sale	150

Required

1. Comment on the presentation of the sale of the California business on the statement of cash flows. Does the way in which the sale was reported violate generally accepted accounting principles? Regardless of whether it violates GAAP, does the way in which the transaction was reported on the statement result in a misstatement of the net decrease in cash for the period? Explain your answers.

2. Prepare a revised statement of cash flows for 2001, with the proper presentation of the sale of the California business.

3. Has the controller acted in an unethical manner in the way the sale was reported on the statement of cash flows? Explain your answer.

LO 2, 3 Case 12-7 Cash Equivalents and the Statement of Cash Flows

In December 2001, Rangers Inc. invested $100,000 of idle cash in U.S. Treasury notes. The notes mature on October 1, 2002, at which time Rangers expects to redeem them at face value of $100,000. The treasurer believes that the notes should be classified as cash equivalents because of the plans to hold them to maturity and receive face value. He would also like to avoid presentation of the purchase as an investing activity because the company has made sizable capital expenditures during the year. The treasurer realizes that the decision about classification of the Treasury notes rests with you, as controller.

Required

1. According to generally accepted accounting principles, how should the investment in U.S. Treasury notes be classified for purposes of preparing a statement of cash flows for the year ended December 31, 2001? Explain your answer.

2. As controller for Rangers, what would you do in this situation? What would you tell the treasurer?

INTERNET RESEARCH CASE

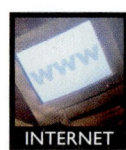

INTERNET

www.ibm.com

Case 12-8 IBM

IBM is firmly in e-business, its annual reports proclaim. Its 1999 annual report, for example, indicates that revenues from e-business services (one of IBM's operations) increased 60 percent to more than $3 billion. While that's still small in comparison to its total revenues of over $87 billion for 1999, the annual report clearly projects e-business affecting many parts of the company, its revenues and expenses, and its operations.

IBM is so large that you can spend hours exploring the Web presence of IBM's various groups in its annual report pages alone. Turn to IBM's Web site to get an overview of the company in the "About IBM" section, review the financial statements and notes for the latest year available, and answer the following questions.

1. What are the groups in which IBM reports its operations on the income statement?

2. Try to determine how pervasive e-business is in the operations and financial contributions IBM touts for each group. (You probably won't find that information directly in the financial statements. For the 1999 annual report, start with the highlights pages, the transformation pages, and the letter to shareholders.)

3. From what you can learn, is IBM truly transforming itself into an e-business powerhouse?

4. Based on the latest financial information, what is the amount of IBM's (a) cash flows from operating activities; (b) cash flows from investing activities; and (c) cash flows from financing

activities? How do these compare to the corresponding numbers from 1999 in the "Focus on Financial Results" vignette at the start of the chapter? What is the trend?

5. What are three major changes in line items you see in the latest year's statement of cash flows? Using information available in the annual report, and in business news services, what changes do they represent within the company?

SOLUTION TO KEY TERMS QUIZ

3 Statement of cash flows (p. 553) **7** Financing activities (p. 558)

4 Cash equivalent (p. 555) **6** Direct method (p. 560)

1 Operating activities (p. 556) **2** Indirect method (p. 560)

5 Investing activities (p. 557)

FINANCIAL STATEMENT ANALYSIS

Study Links

A Look at Previous Chapters

In Chapter 2, we introduced a few key financial ratios and saw the way that investors and creditors use them to better understand a company's financial statements. In many of the subsequent chapters, we introduced ratios relevant to the particular topic being discussed.

A Look at This Chapter

Ratio analysis is one important type of analysis used to interpret financial statements. In this chapter, we expand our discussion of ratio analysis and introduce other valuable techniques used by investors, creditors, and analysts in reaching informed decisions. We will find that ratios and other forms of analyses can provide additional insight beyond that available from merely reading the financial statements.

FOCUS ON FINANCIAL RESULTS

Although its products are variations on the single theme of chewing gum, the 110-year-old Wm. Wrigley Jr. Company has enjoyed a long and highly successful run. In the best year of its first decade, the firm had sales of about $40,000 each month. Now sales reach that number every 10 minutes, with customers in over 150 countries around the world. What accounts for this success?

Basic data for assessing the results of Wrigley's steady investments in marketing and new product innovations appear in the Highlights of Operations section of the company's annual report, pictured here. Net earnings increased from 1998 to 1999 and reached a record level of $308 million. About half those earnings ($154 million) were paid out in dividends to shareholders. However, the company has to make some trade-offs. The more of its earnings it pays in dividends, the less it has available to invest in future growth in such markets as China and Russia, where it has made inroads that it plans to continue broadening, or in new-product development to capture more sales in the U.S. teen market. However, most companies would be envious of the robust return on average equity of over 25 percent in each of the last two years.

	1999	1998
	In thousands of dollars except for per share amounts	
Net Sales	$2,061,602	$2,004,719
Earnings before factory sale	$ 308,183	$ 297,738
—Per Share of Common Stock (basic and diluted)	$ 2.66	$ 2.57
Net Earnings	$ 308,183	$ 304,501
—Per Share of Common Stock (basic and diluted)	$ 2.66	$ 2.63
Dividends Paid	$ 153,812	$ 150,835
—Per Share of Common Stock	$ 1.33	$ 1.30
Additions to Property, Plant and Equipment	$ 127,733	$ 148,027
Stockholders' Equity	$1,138,775	$1,157,032
Return on Average Equity	26.8%	28.4%
Stockholders at Close of Year	38,626	38,052
Average Shares Outstanding (000)	115,861	115,964

About half of earnings paid out as dividends

Wrigley's 1999 Annual Report

If you were considering buying shares of Wrigley stock, you would want to compare Wrigley with alternative investments and assess its ability to generate income and pay dividends. What measures of financial performance would therefore be most important to you? Find the company's most recent annual report and determine whether those measures have improved since 1999.

www.wrigley.com

After studying this chapter, you should be able to:

LO 1 Explain the various limitations and considerations in financial statement analysis. (p. 616)

LO 2 Use comparative financial statements to analyze a company over time (horizontal analysis). (p. 619)

LO 3 Use common-size financial statements to compare various financial statement items (vertical analysis). (p. 622)

LO 4 Compute and use various ratios to assess liquidity. (p. 626)

LO 5 Compute and use various ratios to assess solvency. (p. 631)

LO 6 Compute and use various ratios to assess profitability. (p. 634)

PRECAUTIONS IN STATEMENT ANALYSIS

Various groups have different purposes for analyzing a company's financial statements. For example, a banker is primarily interested in the likelihood that a loan will be repaid. Certain ratios, as we will see, indicate the ability to repay principal and interest. A stockholder, on the other hand, is concerned with a fair return on the amount invested in the company. Again, certain ratios are helpful in assessing the return to the stockholder. The managers of a business are also interested in the tools of financial statement analysis because various outside groups judge managers by using certain key ratios. Fortunately, most financial statements provide information about financial performance. Publicly held corporations are required to include in their annual reports a section that reviews the past year, with management's comments on its performance as measured by selected ratios and other forms of analysis.

Before we turn to various techniques commonly used in the financial analysis of a company, it is important to understand some of the limitations and other considerations in statement analysis.

WATCH FOR ALTERNATIVE ACCOUNTING PRINCIPLES

LO 1 Explain the various limitations and considerations in financial statement analysis.

Every set of financial statements is based on various assumptions. For example, a cost-flow method must be assumed in valuing inventory and recognizing cost of goods sold. The accountant chooses FIFO, LIFO, or one of the other acceptable methods. The analyst or other user finds this type of information in the footnotes to the financial statements. The selection of a particular inventory valuation method has a significant effect on certain key ratios. Recognition of the acceptable alternatives is especially important in comparing two or more companies. *Changes* in accounting methods, such as a change in the depreciation method, also make comparing results for a given company over time more difficult. Again, the reader must turn to the footnotes for information regarding these changes.

TAKE CARE WHEN MAKING COMPARISONS

Users of financial statements often place too much emphasis on summary indicators and key ratios, such as the current ratio and the earnings per share amount. No single ratio is capable of telling the user everything there is to know about a particular company. The calculation of various ratios for a company is only a starting point. One technique we discuss is the comparison of ratios for different periods of time. Has the ratio gone up or down from last year? What is the percentage of increase or decrease in the ratio over the last five years? Recognizing trends in ratios is important in analyzing any company.

The potential investor must also recognize the need to compare one company with others in the same industry. For example, a particular measure of performance may cause an investor to conclude that the company is not operating efficiently. Comparison with an industry standard, however, might indicate that the ratio is normal for companies in that industry. Various organizations publish summaries of selected ratios for a sample of companies in the

United States. The ratios are usually organized by industry. Dun & Bradstreet's *Industry Norms and Key Business Ratios,* for example, is an annual review that organizes companies into five major industries and approximately 800 specific lines of business.

Although industry comparisons are useful, caution is necessary in interpreting the results of such analyses. Few companies in today's economy operate in a single industry. Exceptions exist (Wrigley is almost exclusively in the business of making and selling chewing gum), but most companies cross the boundaries of a single industry. *Conglomerates,* companies operating in more than one industry, present a special challenge to the analyst. Keep in mind also the point made earlier about alternative accounting methods. It is not unusual to find companies in the same industry using different inventory valuation techniques or depreciation methods.

Finally, many corporate income statements contain nonoperating items, such as extraordinary items, cumulative effects from accounting changes, and gains and losses from discontinued operations. When these items exist, the reader must exercise extra caution in making comparisons. To assess the future prospects of a group of companies, you may want to compare income statements *before* taking into account the effects these items have on income.

UNDERSTAND THE POSSIBLE EFFECTS OF INFLATION

Inflation, or an increase in the level of prices, is another important consideration in analyzing financial statements. The statements, to be used by outsiders, are based on historical costs and are not adjusted for the effects of increasing prices. For example, consider the following trend in a company's sales for the past three years:

	2001	2000	1999
Net sales	$121,000	$110,000	$100,000

BUSINESS STRATEGY

Wrigley Co. faces the same difficulties abroad as do many other marketers of consumer products. Currency fluctuations introduce short-term risks, and local economies can become unstable. Retail sales in many regions are generally down, and although international markets are large and therefore attractive to many U.S. firms, success abroad will be hard-won. Yet Wrigley, a traditional family-run firm, perseveres. Sometimes the company selectively raises prices to compensate for currency devaluations, but then it faces declines in sales volume. This might lead the firm to try a new-product introduction or a bigger ad campaign.

In Hong Kong in 1998, Wrigley adopted a three-part strategy to increase volume when retail sales in general were dropping 15 percent due to economic difficulties there. First, Extra for Kids, a new product that had been successful in Europe, was introduced in Hong Kong in June of that year. Next, an aggressive distribution campaign and the use of front-end displays for Wrigley products earned the firm prime display space at all Wellcome stores, the biggest supermarket chain in Hong Kong. Small stores and nontraditional outlets made up an important distribution component for Wrigley, too. Finally, Wrigley turned a poor economic environment into a marketing asset. With advertising spending down in Hong Kong, the company was able to trade additional discounts and bonus TV spots for an increase in its advertising presence in the media, just when it was needed.

The techniques suited this conservative but steadily growing firm. They weren't flashy or innovative, but they were well executed. The strategy of "leave no stone unturned" allowed Wrigley to post a 14 percent gain in volume in an otherwise depressed economy, and the following year, international volume increased again.

SOURCES: "All Around Wrigley: Country Update," accessed at www.wrigley.com/aaw/country1998.htm, December 22, 1999; Wrigley's 1999 Annual Report; William Heuslein, "Wm. Wrigley Jr. Co.: Getting Unstuck," *Forbes,* January 8, 2001, accessed at www.forbes.com.

www.wrigley.com

As measured by the actual dollars of sales, sales have increased by 10% each year. Caution is necessary in concluding that the company is better off in each succeeding year because of the increase in sales *dollars.* Assume, for example, that 1999 sales of $100,000 are the result of selling 100,000 units at $1 each. Are 2000 sales of $110,000 the result of selling 110,000 units at $1 each or of selling 100,000 units at $1.10 each? Although on the surface it may seem unimportant which result accounts for the sales increase, the answer can have significant ramifications. If the company found it necessary to increase selling price to $1.10 in the face of increasing *costs,* it may be no better off than it was in 1999 in terms of gross profit. On the other hand, if the company is able to increase sales revenue by 10% primarily based on growth in unit sales, then its performance would be considered stronger than if the increase is merely due to a price increase. The point to be made is one of caution: published financial statements are stated in historical costs and therefore have not been adjusted for the effects of inflation.

Fortunately, inflation has been relatively subdued in the past several years. During the late 1970s, the FASB actually required a separate footnote in the financial statements to calculate the effects of inflation. The requirement was abandoned in the mid-1980s when inflation had subsided and the profession decided that the cost of providing inflation-adjusted information exceeded the benefits to the users.

EXHIBIT 13-1   Comparative Balance Sheets—Horizontal Analysis

Read from earlier year to later year. Usually, this is from right to left.

HENDERSON COMPANY
COMPARATIVE BALANCE SHEETS
DECEMBER 31, 2001 AND 2000
(ALL AMOUNTS IN THOUSANDS OF DOLLARS)

The base year is normally on the right.

	December 31		Increase (Decrease)	
	2001	**2000**	**Dollars**	**Percent**
Cash	$ 320	$ 1,350	$(1,030) **1**	(76)%
Accounts receivable	5,500	4,500	1,000	22
Inventory	**4,750**	**2,750**	**2,000** **2**	**73**
Prepaid insurance	150	200	(50)	(25)
Total current assets	$10,720	$ 8,800	$ 1,920	22
Land	2,000	2,000	–0–	–0–
Buildings and equipment	6,000	4,500	1,500	33
Accumulated depreciation	(1,850)	(1,500)	(350)	(23)
Total long-term assets	$ 6,150	$ 5,000	$ 1,150	23
Total assets	$16,870	$13,800	$ 3,070	22
Accounts payable	**$ 4,250**	**$ 2,500**	**$ 1,750** **3**	**70**
Taxes payable	2,300	2,100	200	10
Notes payable	600	800	(200)	(25)
Current portion of bonds	100	100	–0–	–0–
Total current liabilities	$ 7,250	$ 5,500	$ 1,750	32
Bonds payable	700	800	(100)	(13)
Total liabilities	$ 7,950	$ 6,300	$ 1,650	26
Preferred stock, $5 par	500	500	–0–	–0–
Common stock, $1 par	1,000	1,000	–0–	–0–
Retained earnings	7,420	6,000	1,420	24
Total stockholders' equity	$ 8,920	$ 7,500	$ 1,420	19
Total liabilities and stockholders' equity	$16,870	$13,800	$ 3,070	22

Dollar change from year to year.

Percentage change from one year to the next year.

In **horizontal analysis,** read right to left to compare one year's results with the next as a dollar amount of change and as a percentage of change from year to year.

NOTE: Referenced amounts boldfaced for convenience.

We are now ready to analyze a set of financial statements. We will begin by looking at the comparative statements of a company for a two-year period. The analysis of the statements over a series of years is often called **horizontal analysis.** We will then see how the statements can be recast in what are referred to as *common-size statements.* The analysis of common-size statements is called **vertical analysis.** Finally, we will consider the use of a variety of ratios to analyze a company.

HORIZONTAL ANALYSIS

Comparative balance sheets for a hypothetical entity, Henderson Company, are presented in Exhibit 13-1. The increase or decrease in each of the major accounts on the balance sheet is shown in both absolute dollars and as a percentage. The base year for computing the percentage increase or decrease in each account is the first year, 2000, and is normally shown on the right side. By reading across from right to left (thus the term *horizontal analysis*), the analyst can quickly spot any unusual changes in accounts from the previous year. Three accounts stand out: **1** Cash decreased by 76%, **2** Inventory increased by 73%, and **3** Accounts Payable increased by 70%. (These lines are also boldfaced for convenience.) Individually, each of these large changes is a red flag. Taken together, these changes send the financial statement user the warning that the business may be deteriorating. Each of these large changes should be investigated further.

Exhibit 13-2 shows comparative statements of income and retained earnings for Henderson for 2001 and 2000. At first glance, **1** the 20% increase in sales to $24 million appears

LO 2 Use comparative financial statements to analyze a company over time (horizontal analysis).

EXHIBIT 13-2 Comparative Statements of Income and Retained Earnings—Horizontal Analysis

HENDERSON COMPANY
COMPARATIVE STATEMENTS OF INCOME AND RETAINED EARNINGS
FOR THE YEARS ENDED DECEMBER 31, 2001 AND 2000
(ALL AMOUNTS IN THOUSANDS OF DOLLARS)

	December 31		Increase (Decrease)		
	2001	2000	Dollars		Percent
Net sales	$24,000	$20,000	$ 4,000	**1**	20%
Cost of goods sold	18,000	14,000	4,000	**2**	29
Gross profit	$ 6,000	$ 6,000	$ –0–		–0–
Selling, general, and administrative					
expense	3,000	2,000	1,000	**3**	50
Operating income	$ 3,000	$ 4,000	$(1,000)	**4**	(25)
Interest expense	140	160	(20)		(13)
Income before tax	$ 2,860	$ 3,840	$ (980)		(26)
Income tax expense	1,140	1,540	(400)		(26)
Net income	$ 1,720	$ 2,300	$ (580)		(25)
Preferred dividends	50	50			
Income available to common	$ 1,670	$ 2,250			
Common dividends	250	250			
To retained earnings	$ 1,420	$ 2,000			
Retained earnings, 1/1	6,000	4,000			
Retained earnings, 12/31	$ 7,420	$ 6,000			

These three increases in revenue and expenses resulted in an operating income *decrease* of 25%.

NOTE: Referenced amounts boldfaced for convenience.

EXHIBIT 13-3   Wrigley Financial Summary

selected financial data

	1999	1998	1997	1996
OPERATING DATA				
Net Sales	$2,061,602	2,004,719	1,937,021	1,835,987
Cost of Sales	854,931	848,363	847,366	814,483
Income Taxes	136,247	136,378	122,614	128,840
Earnings before factory closure and sale in 1998-96, nonrecurring gain on sale of Singapore property in 1994, and cumulative effect of accounting changes in 1992	308,183	297,738	273,771	243,262
—Per Share of Common Stock (basic and diluted)	2.66	2.57	2.36	2.10
Net Earnings	308,183	304,501	271,626	230,272
—Per Share of Common Stock (basic and diluted)	2.66	2.63	2.34	1.99
Dividends Paid	153,812	150,835	135,680	118,308
—Per Share of Common Stock	1.33	1.30	1.17	1.02
—As a Percent of Net Earnings	50%	50%	50%	51%
Dividends Declared				
—Per Share of Common Stock	1.48	1.31	1.19	1.02
Average Shares Outstanding	115,861	115,964	115,964	115,983
OTHER FINANCIAL DATA				
Net Property, Plant and Equipment	$ 559,140	520,090	430,474	388,149
Total Assets	$1,547,745	1,520,855	1,343,126	1,233,543
Working Capital	$ 551,921	624,546	571,857	511,272
Stockholders' Equity	$1,138,775	1,157,032	985,379	897,431
Return on Average Equity	26.8%	28.4%	28.9%	27.2%
Stockholders at Close of Year	38,626	38,052	36,587	34,951
Employees at Close of Year	9,300	9,200	8,200	7,800
Market Price of Stock—High	$ 100.625	104.313	82.063	62.875
—Low	$ 66.500	70.938	54.563	48.375

Net sales has increased every year in the 11-year period.

EXHIBIT 13-3   Wrigley Financial Summary (continued)

1995	1994	1993	1992	1991	1990	1989
					In thousands of dollars and shares except for per share amounts	
1,754,931	1,596,551	1,428,504	1,286,921	1,148,875	1,110,639	992,853
778,019	697,442	617,156	572,468	507,795	508,957	451,773
126,492	122,746	103,944	83,730	79,362	70,897	64,277
223,739	205,767	174,891	148,573	128,652	117,362	106,149
1.93	1.77	1.50	1.27	1.09	1.00	.90
223,739	230,533	174,891	141,295	128,652	117,362	106,149
1.93	1.98	1.50	1.21	1.09	1.00	.90
111,401	104,694	87,344	72,511	64,609	58,060	53,506
.96	.90	.75	.62	.55	.49	.45
50%	45%	50%	51%	50%	49%	50%
.99	.94	.75	.63	.55	.51	.47
116,066	116,358	116,511	117,055	117,517	117,743	118,035
347,491	289,420	239,868	222,137	201,386	188,959	171,951
1,099,219	978,834	815,324	711,372	625,074	563,665	498,624
458,683	413,414	343,132	299,149	276,047	229,735	186,588
796,852	688,470	575,182	498,935	463,399	401,386	342,994
30.1%	36.5%	32.6%	29.4%	29.8%	31.5%	32.6%
28,959	24,078	18,567	14,546	11,086	10,497	10,218
7,300	7,000	6,700	6,400	6,250	5,850	5,750
54.000	53.875	46.125	39.875	27.000	19.750	17.917
42.875	38.125	29.500	22.125	16.375	14.583	11.833

promising, but management was not able to limit the increase in either **2** cost of goods sold or **3** selling, general, and administrative expense to 20%. The analysis indicates that cost of goods sold increased by 29% and selling, general, and administrative expense increased by 50%. The increases in these two expenses more than offset the increase in sales and resulted in **4** a decrease in operating income of 25%.

Companies that experience sales growth often become lax about controlling expenses. Their managements sometimes forget that it is the bottom line that counts, not the top line. Perhaps the salespeople are given incentives to increase sales without considering the costs of the sales. Maybe management is spending too much on overhead, including its own salaries. The owners of the business will have to address these concerns if they want to get a reasonable return on their investment.

Horizontal analysis can be extended to include more than two years of results. At a minimum, publicly held companies are required to include income statements and statements of cash flows for the three most recent years and balance sheets as of the end of the two most recent years. Many annual reports include, as supplementary information, financial summaries of operations for extended periods of time. As illustrated in Exhibit 13-3, for example, Wrigley includes an 11-year summary of selected financial data, such as net sales, dividends paid, return on average equity, and total assets. Note the increase in net sales in every year over the 11-year period. Also note, however, that Wrigley does not include in the summary the gross profit ratio (gross profit divided by net sales). A comparison of the trend in this ratio would help to determine whether the company has effectively controlled the cost to manufacture its products. The summary does show that Wrigley has reported an increase in net earnings before any nonrecurring gains and accounting changes for 10 consecutive years, an enviable record for any company.

Tracking items over a series of years, a practice called *trend analysis,* can be a very powerful tool for the analyst. Advanced statistical techniques are available for analyzing trends in financial data and, most important, for projecting those trends to future periods. Some of the techniques, such as time series analysis, have been used extensively in forecasting sales trends.

Historically, attention has focused on the balance sheet and income statement in analyzing a company's position and results of operation. Only recently have analysts and other users begun to appreciate the value in incorporating the statement of cash flows into their analyses.

Comparative statements of cash flows for Henderson appear in Exhibit 13-4. Henderson's financing activities remained constant over the two-year period, as indicated in that section of the statements. Each year the company paid $200,000 on notes, another $100,000 to retire bonds, and $300,000 to stockholders in dividends. Cash outflow from investing activities slowed down somewhat in 2001, with the purchase of $1,500,000 in new buildings, compared with $2,000,000 the year before.

The most noticeable difference between Henderson's statements of cash flows for the two years is in the Operating Activities section. Operations **1** generated almost $2 million less in cash in 2001 than in 2000 ($1.07 million in 2001 versus $2.95 million in 2000). The decrease in net income **2** was partially responsible for this reduction in cash from operations. However, the increases in **3** accounts receivable and **4** inventories in 2001 had a significant impact on the decrease in cash generated from operating activities.

VERTICAL ANALYSIS

Often, it is easier to examine comparative financial statements if they have been standardized. *Common-size statements* recast all items on the statement as a percentage of a selected item on the statement. This excludes size as a relevant variable in the analysis. One could use this type of analysis to compare Wal-Mart with the smaller Kmart or to compare IBM with the much smaller Apple Computer. It is also a convenient way to compare the same company from year to year.

Vertical analysis involves looking at the relative size and composition of various items on a particular financial statement. Common-size comparative balance sheets for Henderson Company are presented in Exhibit 13-5. Note that all asset accounts are stated as

From Concept

TO PRACTICE 13.1

READING GATEWAY'S ANNUAL REPORT Where does Gateway's annual report provide a financial summary? How many years does it include? In terms of a trend over time, which item on the summary do you think is the most significant?

From Concept

TO PRACTICE 13.2

READING WRIGLEY'S ANNUAL REPORT Refer to Wrigley's financial highlights in Exhibit 13-3. Compute the company's gross profit ratio for each of the 11 years. Is there a noticeable upward or downward trend in the ratio over this time period?

LO 3 Use common-size financial statements to compare various financial statement items (vertical analysis).

EXHIBIT 13-4   Comparative Statements of Cash Flows—Horizontal Analysis

HENDERSON COMPANY
COMPARATIVE STATEMENTS OF CASH FLOWS
FOR THE YEARS ENDED DECEMBER 31, 2001 AND 2000
(ALL AMOUNTS IN THOUSANDS OF DOLLARS)

	2001	2000	Increase (Decrease) Dollars	Increase (Decrease) Percent
Net Cash Flows from Operating Activities				
2 Net income	$1,720	$2,300	$ (580)	(25)%
Adjustments:				
Depreciation expense	350	300		
Changes in:				
3 Accounts receivable	(1,000)	500		
4 Inventory	(2,000)	(300)		
Prepaid insurance	50	50		
Accounts payable	1,750	(200)		
Taxes payable	200	300		
Net cash provided by operating activities **1** Unfavorable	$1,070 ⟵.........	$2,950	$(1,880)	(64)%
Net Cash Flows from Investing Activities				
Purchase of buildings	$(1,500)	$(2,000)	$ (500)	(25)%
Net Cash Flows from Financing Activities				
Repayment of notes	$ (200)	$ (200)	–0–	–0–
Retirement of bonds	(100)	(100)	–0–	–0–
Cash dividends—preferred	(50)	(50)	–0–	–0–
Cash dividends—common	(250)	(250)	–0–	–0–
Net cash used by financing activities	$ (600)	$ (600)	–0–	–0–
Net increase (decrease) in cash	$ (1,030)	$ 350		
Beginning cash balance	1,350	1,000		
Ending cash balance	$ 320	$ 1,350		
Supplemental Information				
Interest paid	$ 140	$ 160		
Income taxes paid	$ 940	$ 1,440		

NOTE: Referenced amounts boldfaced for convenience.

a percentage of total assets. Similarly, all liability and stockholders' equity accounts are stated as a percentage of total liabilities and stockholders' equity. The combination of the comparative balance sheets for the two years and the common-size feature allows the analyst to spot critical changes in the composition of the assets. We noted in Exhibit 13-1 that cash had decreased by 76% over the two years. The decrease of cash from 9.8% of total assets to only 1.9% **1** is highlighted in Exhibit 13-5.

One can also observe in the exhibit that **2** total current assets have continued to represent just under two-thirds (63.5%) of total assets. If cash has decreased significantly in terms of the percentage of total assets, what accounts have increased to maintain current assets at two-thirds of total assets? We can quickly determine from the data in Exhibit 13-5 that **3** although inventory represented 19.9% of total assets at the end of 2000, the percentage is up to 28.1% at the end of 2001. This change in the relative composition of current assets between cash and inventory may have important implications. The change, for instance, may signal that the company is having trouble selling inventory.

EXHIBIT 13-5   Common-Size Comparative Balance Sheets—Vertical Analysis

HENDERSON COMPANY
COMMON-SIZE COMPARATIVE BALANCE SHEETS
DECEMBER 31, 2001 AND 2000
(ALL AMOUNTS IN THOUSANDS OF DOLLARS)

	December 31, 2001		December 31, 2000	
	Dollars	Percent	Dollars	Percent
Cash	$ 320	1.9%	$ 1,350	[1] 9.8%
Accounts receivable	5,500	32.6	4,500	32.6
Inventory	4,750	28.1	2,750	[3] 19.9
Prepaid insurance	150	0.9	200	1.5
Total current assets	$10,720	[2] 63.5%	$ 8,800	63.8%
Land	2,000	11.9	2,000	14.5
Buildings and equipment, net	4,150	24.6	3,000	21.7
Total long-term assets	$ 6,150	36.5	$ 5,000	36.2
Total assets	$ 16,870	100.0%	$13,800	100.0
Accounts payable	$ 4,250	25.2%	$ 2,500	18.1%
Taxes payable	2,300	13.6	2,100	15.2
Notes payable	600	3.6	800	5.8
Current portion of bonds	100	0.6	100	0.7
Total current liabilities	$ 7,250	[4] 43.0%	$ 5,500	39.8%
Bonds payable	700	[5] 4.1	800	5.8
Total liabilities	$ 7,950	47.1%	$ 6,300	45.6%
Preferred stock, $5 par	500	3.0	500	3.6
Common stock, $1 par	1,000	5.9	1,000	7.3
Retained earnings	7,420	44.0	6,000	43.5
Total stockholders' equity	$ 8,920	[6] 52.9%	$ 7,500	54.4%
Total liabilities and stockholders' equity	$ 16,870	100.0%	$13,800	100.0%

Compare percentages across years to spot year-to-year trends.

In **vertical analysis**, compare each line item as a percentage of total (100%) to highlight a company's overall condition.

NOTE: Referenced amounts boldfaced for convenience.

Total current liabilities [4] represent a slightly higher percentage of total liabilities and stockholders' equity at the end of 2001 than at the end of 2000. The increase is balanced by a slight decrease in the relative percentages of [5] long-term debt (the bonds) and of [6] stockholders' equity. We will return later to further analysis of the composition of both the current and the noncurrent accounts.

Common-size comparative income statements for Henderson are presented in Exhibit 13-6. The *base,* or benchmark, to which all other items in the income statement are compared is [1] net sales. Again, observations from the comparative statements alone are further confirmed by examining the common-size statements. Although the **gross profit ratio**—*gross profit as a percentage of net sales*—was 30% in 2000, the same ratio for 2001 is only 25% [2]. Recall the earlier observation that although sales increased by 20% from one year to the next, [3] cost of goods sold increased by 29% and as can be seen in Exhibit 13-6, it now is 75% of net sales, compared to 70% in the prior year.

In addition to the gross profit ratio, an important relationship from Exhibit 13-6 is the *ratio of net income to net sales,* or **profit margin ratio.** The ratio, an overall indicator of management's ability to control expenses, reflects the amount of income for each

HENDERSON COMPANY
COMMON-SIZE COMPARATIVE INCOME STATEMENTS
FOR THE YEARS ENDED DECEMBER 31, 2001 AND 2000
(ALL AMOUNTS IN THOUSANDS OF DOLLARS)

	2001		2000	
	Dollars	**Percent**	**Dollars**	**Percent**
Net sales	$24,000	**1** 100.0%	$20,000	100.0%
Cost of goods sold	**3** 18,000	75.0	14,000	70.0
Gross profit	$ 6,000	**2** 25.0%	$ 6,000	30.0%
Selling, general, and administrative				
expense	3,000	12.5	2,000	10.0
Operating income	$ 3,000	12.5%	$ 4,000	20.0%
Interest expense	140	0.6	160	0.8
Income before tax	$ 2,860	11.9%	$ 3,840	19.2%
Income tax expense	1,140	4.8	1,540	7.7
Net income	$ 1,720	**4** 7.1%	$ 2,300	11.5%

Gross profit as a percentage of sales is the **gross profit ratio.**

The ratio of net income to net sales is the **profit margin ratio.**

NOTE: Referenced amounts boldfaced for convenience.

dollar of sales. Some analysts prefer to look at income before tax, rather than final net income, because taxes are not typically an expense that can be controlled. Further, if the company does not earn a profit before tax, it will incur no tax expense. Note **4** the decrease in Henderson's profit margin: from 11.5% in 2000 to 7.1% in 2001 (or from 19.2% to 11.9% on a before-tax basis).

Two-Minute Review

1. Explain the basic difference between horizontal and vertical analysis.

2. Assume that you are concerned about whether accounts receivable has been increasing over the last few years. Which type of analysis, horizontal or vertical, would you perform to help address your concern?

3. Assume that you are concerned about whether selling and administrative expenses were unreasonable this past year given the level of sales. Which type of analysis, horizontal or vertical, would you perform to help address your concern?

Answers:

1. Horizontal analysis is used to compare a particular financial statement item over a period of time, whereas vertical analysis allows someone to compare various financial statement items within a single period. With vertical analysis, all the items are stated as a percentage of a specific item on that statement, such as sales on the income statement or total assets on the balance sheet.

2. Horizontal analysis could be used to examine the trend in accounts receivable over recent years.

3. Vertical analysis could be used to examine the relationship between selling and administrative expenses and sales. However, you may also want to compare this percentage with the ratio in prior years (thus, you would be performing horizontal analysis as well).

LO 4 Compute and use various ratios to assess liquidity.

Two ratios were discussed in the preceding section: the *gross profit ratio* and the *profit margin ratio*. A ratio is simply the relationship, normally stated as a percentage, between two financial statement amounts. In this section, we consider a wide range of ratios used by management, analysts, and others for a variety of purposes. We classify the ratios in three main categories according to their use in performing (1) liquidity analysis, (2) solvency analysis, and (3) profitability analysis.

Liquidity is a relative measure of the nearness to cash of the assets and liabilities of a company. Nearness to cash deals with the length of time before cash is realized. Various ratios are used to measure liquidity, and they basically concern the company's ability to pay its debts as they come due. Recall the distinction between the current and long-term classifications on the balance sheet. Current assets are assets that will be either converted into cash or consumed within one year or the operating cycle, if the cycle is longer than one year. The operating cycle for a manufacturing company is the length of time between the purchase of raw materials and the eventual collection of any outstanding account receivable from the sale of the product. Current liabilities are a company's obligations that require the use of current assets or the creation of other current liabilities to satisfy them.

The nearness to cash of the current assets is indicated by their placement on the balance sheet. Current assets are listed on the balance sheet in descending order of their nearness to cash. Liquidity is, of course, a matter of degree, with cash being the most liquid of all assets. With few exceptions, such as prepaid insurance, most current assets are convertible into cash. However, accounts receivable is closer to being converted into cash than is inventory. An account receivable need only be collected to be converted to cash. An item of inventory must first be sold, and then, assuming that sales of inventory are on account, the account must be collected before cash is realized.

WORKING CAPITAL

Working capital is the excess of current assets over current liabilities at a point in time:

$$\text{Working Capital} = \text{Current Assets} - \text{Current Liabilities}$$

Reference to Henderson's comparative balance sheets in Exhibit 13-1 indicates the following:

	December 31	
	2001	**2000**
Current assets	$10,720,000	$8,800,000
Current liabilities	7,250,000	5,500,000
Working capital	$ 3,470,000	$3,300,000

The management of working capital is an extremely important task for any business. A comparison of Henderson's working capital at the end of each of the two years indicates a slight increase in the degree of protection for short-term creditors of the company. Management must always strive for the ideal balance of current assets and current liabilities. The amount of working capital is limited in its informational value, however. For example, it tells us nothing about the composition of the current accounts. Also, the dollar amount of working capital may not be useful for comparison with other companies of different sizes in the same industry. Working capital of $3,470,000 may be adequate for Henderson Company, but it might signal impending bankruptcy for a company much larger than Henderson.

CURRENT RATIO

The **current ratio** is one of the most widely used of all financial statement ratios and is calculated as follows:

$$\text{Current Ratio} = \frac{\text{Current Assets}}{\text{Current Liabilities}}$$

For Henderson Company, the ratio at each year-end is as follows:

December 31

2001	2000
$\dfrac{\$10,720,000}{\$7,250,000} = 1.48 \text{ to } 1$	$\dfrac{\$8,800,000}{\$5,500,000} = 1.60 \text{ to } 1$

At the end of 2001, Henderson had $1.48 of current assets for every $1 of current liabilities. Is this current ratio adequate? Or is it a sign of impending financial difficulties? There is no definitive answer to either question. Some analysts use a rule of thumb of 2:1 for the current ratio as a sign of short-term financial health. The answer depends first on the industry. Companies in certain industries have historically operated with current ratios much less than 2:1.

A second concern in interpreting the current ratio involves the composition of the current assets. Cash is usually the only acceptable means of payment for most liabilities. Therefore, it is important to consider the makeup, or *composition,* of the current assets. Refer to Exhibit 13-5 and Henderson's common-size balance sheets. Not only did the current ratio decline during 2001 but also the proportion of the total current assets made up by inventory increased whereas the proportion made up by accounts receivable remained the same. Recall that accounts receivable is only one step removed from cash, whereas inventory requires both sale and collection of the subsequent account.

ACID-TEST RATIO

The **acid-test** or **quick ratio** is a stricter test of a company's ability to pay its current debts as they are due. Specifically, it is intended to deal with the composition problem because it *excludes* inventories and prepaid assets from the numerator of the fraction:

$$\text{Acid-Test or Quick Ratio} = \frac{\text{Quick Assets}}{\text{Current Liabilities}}$$

where

$$\text{Quick Assets} = \text{Cash} + \text{Marketable Securities} + \text{Current Receivables}$$

Henderson's quick assets consist of only cash and accounts receivable, and its quick ratios are as follows:

December 31

2001	2000
$\dfrac{\$320,000 + \$5,500,000}{\$7,250,000} = 0.80 \text{ to } 1$	$\dfrac{\$1,350,000 + \$4,500,000}{\$5,500,000} = 1.06 \text{ to } 1$

Does the quick ratio of less than 1:1 at the end of 2001 mean that Henderson will be unable to pay creditors on time? *For many companies, an acid-test ratio below 1 is not desirable because it may signal the need to liquidate marketable securities to pay bills, regardless of the current trading price of the securities.* Although the quick ratio is a better indication of short-term debt-paying ability than the current ratio, it is still not perfect. For example, we would want to know the normal credit terms that Henderson extends to its customers, as well as the credit terms that the company receives from its suppliers.

Assume that Henderson requires its customers to pay their accounts within 30 days and that the normal credit terms extended by Henderson's suppliers allow payment anytime within 60 days. The relatively longer credit terms extended by Henderson's suppliers give it some cushion in meeting its obligations. The due date of the $2,300,000 in taxes payable could also have a significant effect on the company's ability to remain in business.

CASH FLOW FROM OPERATIONS TO CURRENT LIABILITIES

Two limitations exist with either the current ratio or the quick ratio as a measure of liquidity. First, almost all debts require the payment of cash. Thus, a ratio that focuses on cash is more useful. Second, both ratios focus on liquid assets at a *point in time.* Cash flow from operating activities, as reported on the statement of cash flows, can be used to indicate the flow of cash during the year to cover the debts due.[1] The **cash flow from operations to current liabilities ratio** is computed as follows:

$$\text{Cash Flow from Operations to Current Liabilities Ratio} = \frac{\text{Net Cash Provided by Operating Activities}}{\text{Average Current Liabilities}}$$

Note the use of *average* current liabilities in the denominator. This results in a denominator that is consistent with the numerator, which reports the cash flow over a period of time. Because we need to calculate the *average* current liabilities for both years, it is necessary to add the ending balance sheet for 1999 for use in the analysis. The balance sheet for Henderson on December 31, 1999, is given in Exhibit 13-7. The ratio for Henderson for each year is as follows:

2001	2000
$\dfrac{\$1,070,000}{(\$7,250,000 + \$5,500,000)/2} = 16.8\%$	$\dfrac{\$2,950,000}{(\$5,500,000 + \$5,600,000)/2} = 53.2\%$

Two factors are responsible for the large decrease in this ratio from 2000 to 2001. First, cash generated from operations during 2001 was less than half what it was during 2000 (the numerator). Second, average current liabilities were smaller in 2000 than in 2001 (the denominator). In examining the health of the company in terms of its liquidity, an analyst would concentrate on the reason for these decreases.

ACCOUNTS RECEIVABLE ANALYSIS

The analysis of accounts receivable is an important component in the management of working capital. A company must be willing to extend credit terms that are liberal enough to attract and maintain customers, but at the same time, management must continually monitor the accounts to ensure collection on a timely basis. One measure of the efficiency of the collection process is the **accounts receivable turnover ratio:**

$$\text{Accounts Receivable Turnover Ratio} = \frac{\text{Net Credit Sales}}{\text{Average Accounts Receivable}}$$

Note an important distinction between this ratio and either the current or the quick ratio. Although both of those ratios measure liquidity at a point in time and all numbers come from the balance sheet, a turnover ratio is an *activity* ratio and consists of an activity (sales, in this case) divided by a base to which it is naturally related (accounts receivable). Because an activity such as sales is for a period of time (a year, in this case), the base should be stated as an average for that same period of time.

The accounts receivable turnover ratios for both years can now be calculated (we assume that all sales are on account):

2001	2000
$\dfrac{\$24,000,000}{(\$5,500,000 + \$4,500,000)/2} = 4.8 \text{ times}$	$\dfrac{\$20,000,000}{(\$4,500,000 + \$5,000,000)/2} = 4.2 \text{ times}$

Accounts turned over, on average, 4.2 times in 2000, compared with 4.8 times in 2001. This means that the average number of times accounts were collected during each year was

---

[1]For a detailed discussion on the use of information contained in the statement of cash flows in performing ratio analysis, see Charles A. Carslaw and John R. Mills, "Developing Ratios for Effective Cash Flow Statement Analysis," *Journal of Accountancy* (November 1991), pp. 63–70.

EXHIBIT 13-7 Henderson's Balance Sheet, End of 1999

HENDERSON COMPANY
BALANCE SHEET
DECEMBER 31, 1999
(ALL AMOUNTS IN THOUSANDS OF DOLLARS)

Cash	$ 1,000
Accounts receivable	5,000
Inventory	2,450
Prepaid insurance	250
Total current assets	$ 8,700
Land	2,000
Buildings and equipment, net	1,300
Total long-term assets	$ 3,300
Total assets	$12,000
Accounts payable	$ 2,700
Taxes payable	1,800
Notes payable	1,000
Current portion of bonds	100
Total current liabilities	$ 5,600
Bonds payable	900
Total liabilities	$ 6,500
Preferred stock, $5 par	500
Common stock, $1 par	1,000
Retained earnings	4,000
Total stockholders' equity	$ 5,500
Total liabilities and stockholders' equity	$12,000

between four and five times. What does this mean about the average length of time that an account was outstanding? Another way to measure efficiency in the collection process is to calculate the **number of days' sales in receivables:**

$$\text{Number of Days' Sales in Receivables} = \frac{\text{Number of Days in the Period}}{\text{Accounts Receivable Turnover}}$$

For simplicity, we assume 360 days in a year:

2001	**2000**
$\dfrac{360 \text{ Days}}{4.8 \text{ Times}} = 75 \text{ Days}$	$\dfrac{360 \text{ Days}}{4.2 \text{ Times}} = 86 \text{ Days}$

The average number of days an account is outstanding, or the average collection period, is 75 days in 2001, down from 86 days in 2000. Is this acceptable? The answer depends on the company's credit policy. If Henderson's normal credit terms require payment within 60 days, further investigation is needed, even though the number of days outstanding has decreased from the previous year.

Management needs to be concerned with both the collectibility of an account as it ages and the cost of funds tied up in receivables. For example, a $1 million average receivable balance that requires an additional month to collect suggests that the company is forgoing $10,000 in profits if we assume that the money could be reinvested in the business to earn 1% per month, or 12% per year.

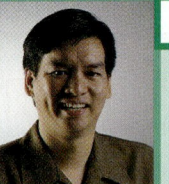

INVENTORY ANALYSIS

A similar set of ratios can be calculated to analyze the efficiency in managing inventory. The **inventory turnover ratio** is as follows:

$$\text{Inventory Turnover Ratio} = \frac{\text{Cost of Goods Sold}}{\text{Average Inventory}}$$

The ratio for each of the two years follows:

2001	2000
$\dfrac{\$18,000,000}{(\$4,750,000 + \$2,750,000)/2} = 4.8$ times	$\dfrac{\$14,000,000}{(\$2,750,000 + \$2,450,000)/2} = 5.4$ times

Henderson was slightly more efficient in 2000 in moving its inventory. The number of "turns" each year varies widely for different industries. For example, a wholesaler of perishable fruits and vegetables may turn over inventory at least 50 times per year. An airplane manufacturer, however, may turn over its inventory once or twice a year. What does the number of turns per year tell us about the average length of time it takes to sell an item of inventory? The **number of days' sales in inventory** is an alternative measure of the company's efficiency in managing inventory. It is the number of days between the date an item of inventory is purchased and the date it is sold:

$$\text{Number of Days' Sales in Inventory} = \frac{\text{Number of Days in the Period}}{\text{Inventory Turnover}}$$

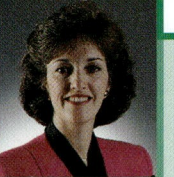

The number of days' sales in inventory for Henderson is as follows:

2001	2000
$\dfrac{360 \text{ Days}}{4.8 \text{ Times}} = 75 \text{ Days}$	$\dfrac{360 \text{ Days}}{5.4 \text{ Times}} = 67 \text{ Days}$

This measure can reveal a great deal about inventory management. For example, an unusually low turnover (and, of course, high number of days in inventory) may signal a large amount of obsolete inventory or problems in the sales department. Or, it may indicate that the company is pricing its products too high and the market is reacting by reducing demand for the company's products.

CASH OPERATING CYCLE

The **cash to cash operating cycle** is the length of time between the purchase of merchandise for sale, assuming a retailer or wholesaler, and the eventual collection of the cash from the sale. One method to approximate the number of days in a company's operating cycle involves combining two measures:

$$\text{Cash to Cash Operating Cycle} = \text{Number of Days' Sales in Inventory}$$
$$+ \text{ Number of Days' Sales in Receivables}$$

Henderson's operating cycles for 2001 and 2000 are as follows:

2001	2000
75 Days + 75 Days = 150 Days	67 Days + 86 Days = 153 Days

The average length of time between the purchase of inventory and the collection of cash from sale of the inventory was 150 days in 2001. Note that although the length of the operating cycle did not change significantly from 2000 to 2001, the composition did change: the increase in the average number of days in inventory was offset by the decrease in the average number of days in receivables.

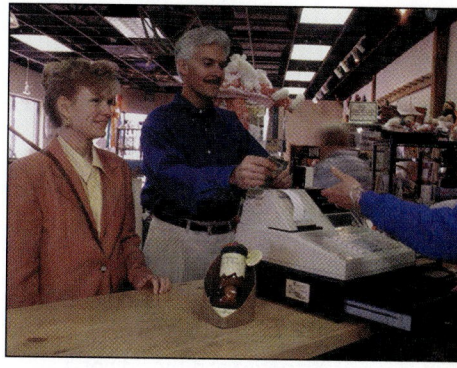

Due to the perishable nature of their products, grocery chains have high inventory turnovers and short cash to cash operating cycles. Firms in other segments have relatively longer cycles.

SOLVENCY ANALYSIS

Solvency refers to a company's ability to remain in business over the long term. It is related to liquidity but differs in time. Although liquidity relates to the firm's ability to pay next year's debts as they come due, solvency concerns the ability of the firm to stay financially healthy over the period of time that existing debt (short and long term) will be outstanding.

LO 5 Compute and use various ratios to assess solvency.

DEBT-TO-EQUITY RATIO

Capital structure is the focal point in solvency analysis. This refers to the composition of the right side of the balance sheet and the mix between debt and stockholders' equity. The composition of debt and equity in the capital structure is an important determinant of the cost of capital to a company. We will have more to say later about the effects that the mix of debt and equity has on profitability. For now, consider the **debt-to-equity ratio:**

$$\text{Debt-to-Equity Ratio} = \frac{\text{Total Liabilities}}{\text{Total Stockholders' Equity}}$$

Henderson's debt-to-equity ratio at each year-end is as follows:

December 31	
2001	**2000**
$\dfrac{\$7,950,000}{\$8,920,000} = 0.89 \text{ to } 1$	$\dfrac{\$6,300,000}{\$7,500,000} = 0.84 \text{ to } 1$

The 2001 ratio indicates that for every $1 of capital that stockholders provided, creditors provided $.89. Variations of the debt-to-equity ratio are sometimes used to assess solvency. For example, an analyst might calculate the ratio of total liabilities to the sum of total liabilities and stockholders' equity. This results in a ratio that differs from the debt-to-equity ratio, but the objective of the measure is the same—to determine the degree to which the company relies on outsiders for funds.

What is an *acceptable* ratio of debt to equity? As with all ratios, the answer depends on the company, the industry, and many other factors. You should not assume that a lower debt-to-equity ratio is better. Certainly taking on additional debt is risky. Many companies are able to benefit from borrowing money, however, by putting the cash raised to good uses in their businesses. Later in the chapter, we discuss the concept of leverage: using borrowed money to benefit the company and its stockholders.

In the 1980s, investors and creditors tolerated a much higher debt-to-equity ratio than is considered prudent today. The savings and loan crisis in the 1980s prompted the federal government to enact regulations requiring financial institutions to have a lower proportion of debt-to-equity. By the mid-1990s, investors and creditors were demanding that all types of companies display lower debt-to-equity ratios.

> ### Study Tip
>
> The elements in many ratios are intuitive and should not require memorization to remember. For example, it is logical that the debt-to-equity ratio is computed by dividing total liabilities by total stockholders' equity.

TIMES INTEREST EARNED

The debt-to-equity ratio is a measure of the company's overall long-term financial health. Management must also be aware of its ability to meet current interest payments to creditors. The **times interest earned ratio** indicates the company's ability to meet current-year interest payments out of current-year earnings:

$$\text{Times Interest Earned Ratio} = \frac{\text{Net Income} + \text{Interest Expense} + \text{Income Tax Expense}}{\text{Interest Expense}}$$

Both interest expense and income tax expense are added back to net income in the numerator because interest is a deduction in arriving at the amount of income subject to tax. Stated slightly differently, if a company had just enough income to cover the payment of interest, tax expense would be zero. The greater the interest coverage is, the better, as far as lenders are concerned. Bankers often place more importance on the times interest earned ratio than even on earnings per share. The ratio for Henderson for each of the two years indicates a great deal of protection in this regard:

2001	2000
$\dfrac{\$1,720,000 + \$140,000 + \$1,140,000}{\$140,000}$	$\dfrac{\$2,300,000 + \$160,000 + \$1,540,000}{\$160,000}$
= 21.4 to 1	= 25 to 1

DEBT SERVICE COVERAGE

Two problems exist with the times interest earned ratio as a measure of the ability to pay creditors. First, the denominator of the fraction considers only *interest*. Management must also be concerned with the *principal* amount of loans maturing in the next year. The second problem deals with the difference between the cash and the accrual bases of accounting. The numerator of the times interest earned ratio is not a measure of the *cash* available to repay loans. Keep in mind the various noncash adjustments, such as depreciation, that enter into the determination of net income. Also, recall that the denominator of the times interest earned ratio is a measure of interest expense, not interest payments. The **debt service coverage ratio** is a measure of the amount of cash that is generated from operating activities during the year and that is available to repay interest due and any maturing principal amounts (that is, the amount available to "service" the debt):

$$\frac{\text{Debt Service}}{\text{Coverage Ratio}} = \frac{\text{Cash Flow from Operations before Interest and Tax Payments}}{\text{Interest and Principal Payments}}$$

Some analysts use an alternative measure in the numerator of this ratio, as well as for other purposes. The alternative is referred to as EBITDA, which stands for earnings before interest, taxes, depreciation, and amortization. Whether EBITDA is a good substitute for cash flow from operations before interest and tax payments depends on whether there were significant changes in current assets and current liabilities during the period. If significant changes in these accounts occurred during the period, cash flow from operations before interest and tax payments is a better measure of a company's ability to cover interest and debt payments.

Cash flow from operations is available on the comparative statement of cash flows in Exhibit 13-4. As was the case with the times interest earned ratio, the net cash provided by operating activities is adjusted to reflect the amount available *before* paying interest and taxes.

Keep in mind that the income statement in Exhibit 13-2 reflects the *expense* for interest and taxes each year. The amounts of interest and taxes *paid* each year are shown as supplemental information at the bottom of the statement of cash flows in Exhibit 13-4 and are relevant in computing the debt service coverage ratio.

We must include any principal payments with interest paid in the denominator of the debt service coverage ratio. According to the Financing Activities section of the statements of cash flows in Exhibit 13-4, Henderson repaid $200,000 each year on the notes payable and $100,000 each year on the bonds. The debt service coverage ratios for the two years are calculated as follows:

2001

$$\frac{\$1,070,000 + \$140,000 + \$940,000}{\$140,000 + \$200,000 + \$100,000} = 4.89 \text{ times}$$

2000

$$\frac{\$2,950,000 + \$160,000 + \$1,440,000}{\$160,000 + \$200,000 + \$100,000} = 9.89 \text{ times}$$

Like Henderson's times interest earned ratio, its debt service coverage ratio decreased during 2001. According to the calculations, however, Henderson still generated almost $5 of cash from operations during 2001 to "cover" every $1 of required interest and principal payments.

CASH FLOW FROM OPERATIONS TO CAPITAL EXPENDITURES RATIO

One final measure is useful in assessing the solvency of a business. The **cash flow from operations to capital expenditures ratio** measures a company's ability to use operations to finance its acquisitions of productive assets. To the extent that a company is able to do this, it should rely less on external financing or additional contributions by the owners to replace and add to the existing capital base. The ratio is computed as follows:

$$\frac{\text{Cash Flow from Operations}}{\text{to Capital Expenditures Ratio}} = \frac{\text{Cash Flow from Operations} - \text{Total Dividends Paid}}{\text{Cash Paid for Acquisitions}}$$

Note that the numerator of the ratio measures the cash flow *after* meeting all dividend payments.[2] The calculation of the ratios for Henderson follows:

2001	2000

$$\frac{\$1,070,000 - \$300,000}{\$1,500,000} = 51.3\% \qquad \frac{\$2,950,000 - \$300,000}{\$2,000,000} = 132.5\%$$

---

[2]Dividends paid are reported on the statement of cash flows in the Financing Activities section. The amount *paid* should be used for this calculation rather than the amount declared, which appears on the statement of retained earnings.

Although the amount of capital expenditures was less in 2001 than in 2000, the company generated considerably less cash from operations in 2001 to cover these acquisitions. In fact, the ratio of less than 100% in 2001 indicates that Henderson was not able to finance all its capital expenditures from operations *and* cover its dividend payments.

Two-Minute Review

1. Explain the difference between liquidity and solvency as it relates to a company's financial position.

2. Assume that you are a supplier and are considering whether to sell to a company on account. Which of the two, liquidity or solvency, are you more concerned with?

Answers:

1. Liquidity is a relative measure of the nearness to cash of the assets and liabilities of a company. Measures of liquidity are intended to determine the company's ability to pay its debts as they come due. Solvency refers to a company's ability to remain in business over the long term. Liquidity and solvency are certainly related, but the latter takes a much more long-term view of the financial health of the company.

2. Because you need to assess the ability of the company to pay its account on a timely basis, you would be more concerned with the liquidity of the company over the short term.

PROFITABILITY ANALYSIS

LO 6 Compute and use various ratios to assess profitability.

Liquidity analysis and solvency analysis deal with management's ability to repay short- and long-term creditors. Creditors are concerned with a company's profitability because a profitable company is more likely to be able to make principal and interest payments. Of course, stockholders care about a company's profitability because it affects the market price of the stock and the ability of the company to pay dividends. Various measures of **profitability** indicate how well management is using the resources at its disposal to earn a return on the funds invested by various groups. Two frequently used profitability measures, the gross profit ratio and the profit margin ratio, were discussed earlier in the chapter. We now turn to other measures of profitability.

RATE OF RETURN ON ASSETS

Before computing the rate of return, we must answer an important question: *Return to whom? Every return ratio is a measure of the relationship between the income earned by the company and the investment made in the company by various groups.* The broadest rate of return ratio is the **return on assets ratio** because it considers the investment made by *all* providers of capital, from short-term creditors to bondholders to stockholders. Therefore, the denominator, or base, for the return on assets ratio is average total liabilities and stockholders' equity—which, of course, is the same as average total assets.

The numerator of a return ratio will be some measure of the company's income for the period. The income selected for the numerator must match the investment or base in the denominator. For example, if average total assets is the base in the denominator, it is necessary to use an income number that is applicable to all providers of capital. Therefore, the income number used in the rate of return on assets is income *after* adding back interest expense. This adjustment considers creditors as one of the groups that have provided funds to the company. In other words, we want the amount of income before either creditors or stockholders have been given any distributions (that is, interest to creditors or dividends to stockholders). Interest expense must be added back on a net-of-tax basis. Because net income is on an after-tax basis, for consistency purposes interest must also be placed on a net, or after-tax, basis.

The return on assets ratio is as follows:

$$\text{Return on Assets Ratio} = \frac{\text{Net Income} + \text{Interest Expense, Net of Tax}}{\text{Average Total Assets}}$$

If we assume a 40% tax rate (which *is* the actual ratio of income tax expense to income before tax for Henderson), its return on assets ratios are as follows:

		2001		2000
Net income		$ 1,720,000		$ 2,300,000
Add back:				
Interest expense	$140,000		$160,000	
× (1 − tax rate)	0.6	84,000	0.6	96,000
Numerator		$ 1,804,000		$ 2,396,000
Assets, beginning of year		$13,800,000		$12,000,000
Assets, end of year		16,870,000		13,800,000
Total		$30,670,000		$25,800,000
Denominator:				
Average total assets				
(total above divided by 2)		$15,335,000		$12,900,000
		$ 1,804,000		$ 2,396,000
		$15,335,000		$12,900,000
Return on assets ratio		= 11.76%		= 18.57%

COMPONENTS OF RETURN ON ASSETS

What caused Henderson's return on assets to decrease so dramatically from the previous year? The answer can be found by considering the two individual components that make up the return on assets ratio. The first of these components is the **return on sales ratio** and is calculated as follows:

$$\text{Return on Sales Ratio} = \frac{\text{Net Income} + \text{Interest Expense, Net of Tax}}{\text{Net Sales}}$$

The return on sales ratios for Henderson for the two years follow:

2001	2000
$\dfrac{\$1,720,000 + \$84,000}{\$24,000,000} = 7.52\%$	$\dfrac{\$2,300,000 + \$96,000}{\$20,000,000} = 11.98\%$

The ratio for 2001 indicates that for every $1 of sales, the company was able to earn a profit, before the payment of interest, of between 7 and 8 cents, as compared with a return of almost 12 cents on the dollar in 2000.

The other component of the rate of return on assets is the **asset turnover ratio.** The ratio is similar to both the inventory turnover and the accounts receivable turnover ratios because it is a measure of the relationship between some activity (net sales, in this case) and some investment base (average total assets):

$$\text{Asset Turnover Ratio} = \frac{\text{Net Sales}}{\text{Average Total Assets}}$$

For Henderson, the ratio for each of the two years follows:

2001	2000
$\dfrac{\$24,000,000}{\$15,335,000} = 1.57 \text{ times}$	$\dfrac{\$20,000,000}{\$12,900,000} = 1.55 \text{ times}$

It now becomes evident that the explanation for the decrease in Henderson's return on assets lies in the drop in the return on sales, since the asset turnover ratio was almost the same. To summarize, note the relationship among the three ratios:

$$\text{Return on Assets} = \text{Return on Sales} \times \text{Asset Turnover}$$

For 2001, Henderson's return on assets consists of the following:

$$\frac{\$1,804,000}{\$24,000,000} \times \frac{\$24,000,000}{\$15,335,000} = 7.52\% \times 1.57 = 11.8\%$$

Finally, notice that net sales cancels out of both ratios, leaving the net income adjusted for interest divided by average assets as the return on assets ratio.

RETURN ON COMMON STOCKHOLDERS' EQUITY

Reasoning similar to that used to calculate return on assets can be used to calculate the return on capital provided by the common stockholder. Because we are interested in the return to the common stockholder, our base is no longer average total assets but average common stockholders' equity. Similarly, the appropriate income figure for the numerator is net income less preferred dividends because we are interested in the return to the common stockholder after all claims have been settled. Income taxes and interest expense have already been deducted in arriving at net income, but preferred dividends have not been deducted, because dividends are a distribution of profits, not an expense.

The **return on common stockholders' equity ratio** is computed as follows:

$$\text{Return on Common Stockholders' Equity Ratio} = \frac{\text{Net Income} - \text{Preferred Dividends}}{\text{Average Common Stockholders' Equity}}$$

The average common stockholders' equity for Henderson is calculated using information from Exhibits 13-1 and 13-7:

| | Account Balances at December 31 | | |
	2001	2000	1999
Common stock, $1 par	$1,000,000	$1,000,000	$1,000,000
Retained earnings	7,420,000	6,000,000	4,000,000
Total common equity	$8,420,000	$7,000,000	$5,000,000

Average common equity:
2000: ($7,000,000 + $5,000,000)/2 = $6,000,000
2001: ($8,420,000 + $7,000,000)/2 = $7,710,000

Net income less preferred dividends—or "income available to common," as it is called—can be found by referring to net income on the income statement and to preferred dividends on the statement of retained earnings. The combined statement of income and retained earnings in Exhibit 13-2 gives the relevant amounts for the numerator. Henderson's return on equity for the two years is as follows:

2001	2000
$\dfrac{\$1,720,000 - \$50,000}{\$7,710,000} = 21.66\%$	$\dfrac{\$2,300,000 - \$50,000}{\$6,000,000} = 37.50\%$

Even though Henderson's return on stockholders' equity ratio decreased significantly from one year to the next, most stockholders would be very happy to achieve these returns on their money. Very few investments offer much more than 10% return unless substantial risk is involved.

RETURN ON ASSETS, RETURN ON EQUITY, AND LEVERAGE

The return on assets for 2001 was 11.8%. But the return to the common stockholders was much higher: 21.7%. How do you explain this phenomenon? Why are the stockholders receiving a higher return on their money than all the providers of money combined are getting? A partial answer to these questions can be found by reviewing the cost to Henderson of the various sources of capital.

Exhibit 13-1 indicates that notes, bonds, and preferred stock are the primary sources of capital other than common stock (accounts payable and taxes payable are *not* included because they represent interest-free loans to the company from suppliers and the government). These sources and the average amount of each outstanding during 2001 follow:

	Account Balances at December 31		
	2001	**2000**	**Average**
Notes payable	$ 600,000	$ 800,000	$ 700,000
Current portion of bonds	100,000	100,000	100,000
Bonds payable—Long-term	700,000	800,000	750,000
Total liabilities	$1,400,000	$1,700,000	$1,550,000
Preferred stock	$ 500,000	$ 500,000	$ 500,000

What was the cost to Henderson of each of these sources? The cost of the money provided by the preferred stockholders is clearly the amount of dividends of $50,000. The cost as a percentage is $50,000/$500,000, or 10%. The average cost of the borrowed money can be approximated by dividing the 2001 interest expense of $140,000 by the average of the notes payable and bonds payable of $1,550,000. The result is an average cost of these two sources of $140,000/$1,550,000, or approximately 9%.

The concept of **leverage** refers to the practice of using borrowed funds and amounts received from preferred stockholders in an attempt to earn an overall return that is higher than the cost of these funds. Recall the rate of return on assets for 2001: 11.8%. Because this return is on an after-tax basis, it is necessary, for comparative purposes, to convert the average cost of borrowed funds to an after-tax basis. Although we computed an average cost for borrowed money of 9%, the actual cost of the borrowed money is 5.4% [9% × (100% − 40%)] after taxes. Because dividends are *not* tax-deductible, the cost of the money provided by preferred stockholders is 10%, as calculated earlier.

Has Henderson successfully employed favorable leverage? That is, has it been able to earn an overall rate of return on assets that is higher than the amounts that it must pay creditors and preferred stockholders? Henderson has been successful in using outside money: neither of the sources must be paid a rate in excess of the 11.8% overall rate on assets used. Also, keep in mind that Henderson has been able to borrow some amounts on an interest-free basis. As mentioned earlier, the accounts payable and taxes payable represent interest-free loans from suppliers and the government, although the loans are typically for a short period of time, such as 30 days.

In summary, the excess of the 21.7% return on equity over the 11.8% return on assets indicates that the Henderson management has been successful in employing leverage; that is, there is favorable leverage. Is it possible to be unsuccessful in this pursuit? That is, can there be unfavorable leverage? If the company must pay more for the amounts provided by creditors and preferred stockholders than it can earn overall, as indicated by the return on assets, there will, in fact, be unfavorable leverage. This may occur when interest requirements are high and net income is low. A company would likely have a high debt-to-equity ratio as well when there is unfavorable leverage.

EARNINGS PER SHARE

Earnings per share is one of the most quoted statistics for publicly traded companies. Stockholders and potential investors want to know what their share of profits is, not just the total dollar amount. Presentation of profits on a per-share basis also allows the stockholder to relate earnings to what he or she paid for a share of stock or to the current trading price of a share of stock.

In simple situations, such as our Henderson Company example, earnings per share (EPS) is calculated as follows:

$$\text{Earnings per Share} = \frac{\text{Net Income} - \text{Preferred Dividends}}{\text{Weighted Average Number of Common Shares Outstanding}}$$

Because Henderson had 1,000,000 shares of common stock outstanding throughout both 2000 and 2001, its EPS for each of the two years is as follows:

2001	2000
$\dfrac{\$1,720,000 - \$50,000}{1,000,000 \text{ shares}} = \$1.67 \text{ per share}$	$\dfrac{\$2,300,000 - \$50,000}{1,000,000 \text{ shares}} = \$2.25 \text{ per share}$

A number of complications can arise in the computation of EPS, and the calculations can become exceedingly complex for a company with many different types of securities in its capital structure. These complications are beyond the scope of this book and are discussed in more advanced accounting courses.

PRICE/EARNINGS RATIO

Earnings per share is an important ratio for an investor because of its relationship to dividends and market price. Stockholders hope to earn a return by receiving periodic dividends or eventually selling the stock for more than they paid for it, or both. Although earnings are related to dividends and market price, the latter two are of primary interest to the stockholder.

We mentioned earlier the desire of investors to relate the earnings of the company to the market price of the stock. Now that we have stated Henderson's earnings on a per-share basis, we can calculate the **price/earnings (P/E) ratio.** What market price is relevant? Should we use the market price that the investor paid for a share of stock, or should we use the current market price? Because earnings are based on the most recent evaluation of the company for accounting purposes, it seems logical to use current market price, which is based on the stock market's current assessment of the company. Therefore, the ratio is computed as follows:

$$\text{Price/Earnings Ratio} = \frac{\text{Current Market Price}}{\text{Earnings per Share}}$$

Assume that the current market price for Henderson's common stock is $15 per share at the end of 2001 and $18 per share at the end of 2000. The price/earnings ratio for each of the two years is as follows:

2001	2000
$\dfrac{\$15 \text{ per Share}}{\$1.67 \text{ per Share}} = 9 \text{ to } 1$	$\dfrac{\$18 \text{ per Share}}{\$2.25 \text{ per Share}} = 8 \text{ to } 1$

What is normal for a P/E ratio? As is the case for all other ratios, it is difficult to generalize as to what is good or bad. The P/E ratio compares the stock market's assessment of a company's performance with its success as reflected on the income statement. A relatively high P/E ratio may indicate that a stock is overpriced by the market; one that is relatively low could indicate that it is underpriced.

The P/E ratio is often thought to indicate the "quality" of a company's earnings. For example, assume that two companies have identical EPS ratios of $2 per share. Why should investors be willing to pay $20 per share (or 10 times earnings) for the stock of one company but only $14 per share (or 7 times earnings) for the stock of the other company? First, we must realize that many factors in addition to the reported earnings of the company affect market prices. General economic conditions, the outlook for the particular

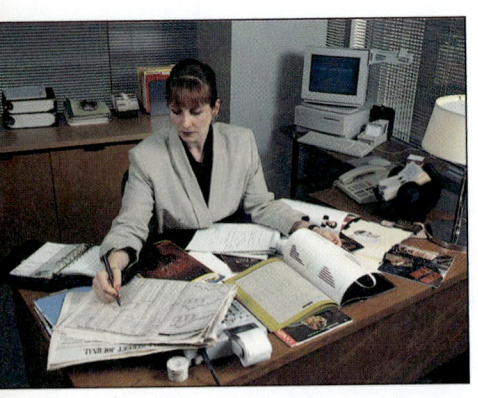

Making financial decisions requires having the right tools at hand, including the annual reports of companies under consideration and recent stock market quotations, printed in most large newspapers.

industry, and pending lawsuits are just three examples of the various factors that can affect the trading price of a company's stock. The difference in P/E ratios for the two companies may reflect the market's assessment of the accounting practices of the companies, however. Assume that the company with a market price of $20 per share uses LIFO in valuing inventory and that the company trading at $14 per share uses FIFO. The difference in prices may indicate that investors believe that even though the companies have the same EPS, the LIFO company is "better off" because it will have a lower amount of taxes to pay. (Recall that in a period of inflation, the use of LIFO results in more cost of goods sold, less income, and therefore less income taxes.) Finally, aside from the way investors view the accounting practices of different companies, they also consider the fact that, to a large extent, earnings reflect the use of historical costs, as opposed to fair market values, in assigning values to assets. Investors must consider the extent to which a company's assets are worth more than what was paid for them.

ACCOUNTING FOR YOUR DECISIONS

You Are the CEO

You have just been promoted to the chief executive officer position at Orange Computer, a company that has recently fallen on hard times. Sales and earnings have been sluggish. Part of the reason that the prior CEO was dismissed by the board was the lagging stock price. Although the typical computer company stock price is roughly 25 times earnings, Orange Computer is languishing at just 8 times earnings. What can you do to restore the company's stock price?

ANS: The best way to boost your company's stock price is to restore earnings to levels comparable to that of other companies in the industry. If investors see that you are cutting costs, boosting sales, and restoring earnings, they may see a future earnings and dividends stream from Orange Computer that matches other competing investments. Consider the case of Lou Gerstner, IBM's CEO. Since Gerstner joined the company, IBM's earnings have experienced a dramatic turnaround, from a loss of $5 billion in 1992, to a profit of $7.7 billion in 1999. By the third quarter of 1999, IBM's common stock was trading at an all-time high.

DIVIDEND RATIOS

Two ratios are used to evaluate a company's dividend policies: the **dividend payout ratio** and the **dividend yield ratio.** The dividend payout ratio is the ratio of the common dividends per share to the earnings per share:

$$\text{Dividend Payout Ratio} = \frac{\text{Common Dividends per Share}}{\text{Earnings per Share}}$$

Exhibit 13-2 indicates that Henderson paid $250,000 in common dividends each year, or with 1 million shares outstanding, $.25 per share. The two payout ratios are as follows:

2001	2000
$\dfrac{\$.25}{\$1.67} = 15.0\%$	$\dfrac{\$.25}{\$2.25} = 11.1\%$

Henderson management was faced with an important financial policy decision in 2001. Should the company maintain the same dividend of $.25 per share, even though EPS dropped significantly? Many companies prefer to maintain a level dividend pattern, hoping that a drop in earnings is only temporary.

From **Concept**

TO PRACTICE 13.3

READING UNO'S ANNUAL REPORT
Refer to Uno's statement of cash flows. Why is it not possible to compute Uno's dividend payout ratio for 1999? Why do you think the company has adopted the policy it has concerning the payment of dividends?

The second dividend ratio of interest to stockholders is the dividend yield ratio:

$$\text{Dividend Yield Ratio} = \frac{\text{Common Dividends per Share}}{\text{Market Price per Share}}$$

The yield to Henderson's stockholders would be calculated as follows:

2001	2000
$\dfrac{\$.25}{\$15} = 1.7\%$	$\dfrac{\$.25}{\$18} = 1.4\%$

As we see, Henderson common stock does not provide a high yield to its investors. The relationship between the dividends and the market price indicates that investors buy the stock for reasons other than the periodic dividend return.

The dividend yield is very important to investors who depend on dividend checks to pay their living expenses. Utility stocks are popular among retirees because these shares have dividend yields as high as 5%. That is considered a good investment with relatively low risk and some opportunity for gains in the stock price. On the other hand, investors who want to put money into growing companies are willing to forgo dividends if it means the potential for greater price appreciation.

Quote		Quotes sponsored by **Salomon Smith Barney**	
WWY Wrigley (Wm Jr) Co			**Last:** 73 $^{15}/_{16}$
News | Charts | Profile | Financials | Analysis | Insiders | SEC			
Last:	73 $^{15}/_{16}$	**Market:**	NYSE
Change:	-$^{15}/_{16}$ (-1.3%)	**Market Capitalization:**	8,559.52 (mil)
Volume:	224,700	**Average Volume:**	270,000
Bid:	N/A	**Dividend/Share:**	0.350
Ask:	N/A	**Yield:**	1.800
Open:	74 $^{5}/_{8}$	**P/E:**	27.000
Previous Close:	74 $^{7}/_{8}$	**Ex-Dividend:**	01/12
Day's Range:	73 $^{3}/_{4}$ - 74 $^{3}/_{4}$	**52 Week Range:**	66 $^{1}/_{2}$ - 100.62

Most major newspapers provide summaries of company stock performance on the leading stock exchanges. Immediate tracking of this information is available online, however, such as this stock quote for Wrigley found at Netscape.com, with data from Salomon Smith Barney. The price/earnings ratio (P/E) and the dividend yield ("yield") are two of the statistics included.

SUMMARY OF SELECTED FINANCIAL RATIOS

We have now completed our review of the various ratios used to assess a company's liquidity, solvency, and profitability. For ease of reference, Exhibit 13-8 summarizes the ratios discussed in this chapter. Keep in mind that this list is not all-inclusive and that certain ratios used by analysts and others may be specific to a particular industry or type of business.

ACCOUNTING FOR YOUR DECISIONS

You Decide on a Stock Purchase

You are starting college and your parents have agreed to help pay your tuition. They will put money into a stock fund for four years and allow you to use the dividends from the fund to pay your quarterly tuition. Should you advise your parents to find a stock with a relatively low dividend yield ratio if it has an above-average return on stockholders' equity?

ANS: Regardless of how attractive a company's return on equity ratio might be, you need cash on a regular basis to pay tuition. You should advise your parents to find a stock with a relatively high dividend yield ratio.

WARMUP EXERCISES

LO 4, 5, 6   Warmup Exercise 13-1   Types of Ratios
Fill in the blanks on the following page to indicate whether each of the following ratios is concerned with a company's liquidity (L), its solvency (S), or its profitability (P).

EXHIBIT 13-8 Summary of Selected Financial Ratios

Liquidity Analysis

Working capital

$$\text{Current Assets} - \text{Current Liabilities}$$

Current ratio

$$\frac{\text{Current Assets}}{\text{Current Liabilities}}$$

Acid-test ratio (quick ratio)

$$\frac{\text{Cash} + \text{Marketable Securities} + \text{Current Receivables}}{\text{Current Liabilities}}$$

Cash flow from operations to current liabilities ratio

$$\frac{\text{Net Cash Provided by Operating Activities}}{\text{Average Current Liabilities}}$$

Accounts receivable turnover ratio

$$\frac{\text{Net Credit Sales}}{\text{Average Accounts Receivable}}$$

Number of days' sales in receivables

$$\frac{\text{Number of Days in the Period}}{\text{Accounts Receivable Turnover}}$$

Inventory turnover ratio

$$\frac{\text{Cost of Goods Sold}}{\text{Average Inventory}}$$

Number of days' sales in inventory

$$\frac{\text{Number of Days in the Period}}{\text{Inventory Turnover}}$$

Cash to cash operating cycle

Number of Days' Sales in Inventory +
Number of Days' Sales in Receivables

Solvency Analysis

Debt-to-equity ratio

$$\frac{\text{Total Liabilities}}{\text{Total Stockholders' Equity}}$$

Times interest earned ratio

$$\frac{\text{Net Income} + \text{Interest Expense} + \text{Income Tax Expense}}{\text{Interest Expense}}$$

Debt service coverage ratio

$$\frac{\text{Cash Flow from Operations before Interest and Tax Payments}}{\text{Interest and Principal Payments}}$$

_____ 1. Return on assets ratio

_____ 2. Current ratio

_____ 3. Debt-to-equity ratio

_____ 4. Earnings per share

_____ 5. Inventory turnover ratio

_____ 6. Gross profit ratio

Key to the Solution

Review the summary of selected ratios in Exhibit 13-8.

LO 4 Warmup Exercise 13-2 Accounts Receivable Turnover

Company A reported sales during the year of $1,000,000. Its average accounts receivable balance during the year was $250,000. Company B reported sales during the same year of $400,000 and had an average accounts receivable balance of $40,000.

Required

1. Compute the accounts receivable turnover for both companies.

2. What is the average length of time each company takes to collect its receivables?

Key to the Solution

Review the summary of selected ratios in Exhibit 13-8.

CHAPTER 13 Financial Statement Analysis

EXHIBIT 13-8   Summary of Selected Financial Ratios (continued)

Cash flow from operations to capital expenditures ratio	$\dfrac{\text{Cash Flow from Operations} - \text{Total Dividends Paid}}{\text{Cash Paid for Acquisitions}}$
Profitability Analysis	
Gross profit ratio	$\dfrac{\text{Gross Profit}}{\text{Net Sales}}$
Profit margin ratio	$\dfrac{\text{Net Income}}{\text{Net Sales}}$
Return on assets ratio	$\dfrac{\text{Net Income} + \text{Interest Expense, Net of Tax}}{\text{Average Total Assets}}$
Return on sales ratio	$\dfrac{\text{Net Income} + \text{Interest Expense, Net of Tax}}{\text{Net Sales}}$
Asset turnover ratio	$\dfrac{\text{Net Sales}}{\text{Average Total Assets}}$
Return on common stockholders' equity ratio	$\dfrac{\text{Net Income} - \text{Preferred Dividends}}{\text{Average Common Stockholders' Equity}}$
Earnings per share	$\dfrac{\text{Net Income} - \text{Preferred Dividends}}{\text{Weighted Average Number of Common Shares Outstanding}}$
Price/earnings ratio	$\dfrac{\text{Current Market Price}}{\text{Earnings per Share}}$
Dividend payout ratio	$\dfrac{\text{Common Dividends per Share}}{\text{Earnings per Share}}$
Dividend yield ratio	$\dfrac{\text{Common Dividends per Share}}{\text{Market Price per Share}}$

LO 6   Warmup Exercise 13-3   Earnings per Share

A company reported net income during the year of $90,000 and paid dividends of $15,000 to its common stockholders and $10,000 to its preferred stockholders. During the year, 20,000 shares of common stock were outstanding and 10,000 shares of preferred stock were outstanding.

Required

Compute earnings per share for the year.

Key to the Solution

Recall that earnings per share only has relevance to the common stockholders, and therefore it is a measure of the earnings per common share outstanding, after taking into account any claims of preferred stockholders.

SOLUTIONS TO WARMUP EXERCISES

Warmup Exercise 13-1

1. P   2. L   3. S   4. P   5. L   6. P

Warmup Exercise 13-2

1. Company A turns over its accounts receivable, on the average, 4 times during the year ($1,000,000/$250,000) and Company B, 10 times during the year ($400,000/$40,000).

2. Assuming 360 days in a year, Company A takes, on the average, 90 days to collect its accounts receivable, and Company B takes, on the average, 36 days.

Warmup Exercise 13-3

Earnings per share: ($90,000 − $10,000)/20,000 shares = $4 per share.

REVIEW PROBLEM

On the following pages are the comparative financial statements for Wm. Wrigley Jr. Company, the chewing gum manufacturer, as shown in its 1999 annual report.

Required

1. Compute the following ratios for the two years 1999 and 1998, either for each year or as of the end of each of the years, as appropriate. Beginning balances for 1998 are not available; that is, you do not have a balance sheet as of the end of 1997. Therefore, to be consistent, use year-end balances for both years where you would normally use average amounts for the year. To compute the return on assets ratio, you will need to find the tax rate. Use the relationship between income taxes and earnings before taxes to find the rate for each year.

   a. Current ratio
   b. Quick ratio
   c. Cash flow from operations to current liabilities ratio
   d. Number of days' sales in receivables
   e. Number of days' sales in inventory
   f. Debt-to-equity ratio
   g. Debt service coverage ratio
   h. Cash flow from operations to capital expenditures ratio
   i. Return on assets ratio
   j. Return on common stockholders' equity ratio

2. Comment on Wrigley's liquidity. Has it improved or declined over the two-year period?

3. Does Wrigley appear to be solvent to you? Does there appear to be anything unusual about its capital structure?

4. Comment on Wrigley's profitability. Would you buy stock in the company?

Solution to Review Problem

1. Ratios:

   a. 1999: $803,746/$251,825 = 3.19
      1998: $843,172/$218,626 = 3.86

   b. 1999: ($288,386 + $18,528 + $181,720)/$251,825 = 1.94
      1998: ($214,572 + $137,112 + $171,537)/$218,626 = 2.39

   c. 1999: $358,036/$251,825 = 1.42
      1998: $323,847/$218,626 = 1.48

   d. 1999: 360 days/[($2,061,602/$181,720)] = 360/11.34 = 32 days
      1998: 360 days/[($2,004,719/$171,537)] = 360/11.69 = 31 days

   e. 1999: 360 days/[($854,931/$257,670)] = 360/3.32 = 108 days
      1998: 360 days/[($848,363/$256,108)] = 360/3.31 = 109 days

   f. 1999: ($251,825 + $44,963 + $112,182)/$1,138,775 = 0.36
      1998: ($218,626 + $40,312 + $104,885)/$1,157,032 = 0.31

   g. 1999: ($358,036 + $130,562 + $709)/$709 = 690
      1998: ($323,847 + $133,530 + $1,164)/$1,164 = 394

consolidated statement of earnings

	1999	1998	1997
	In thousands of dollars except for per share amounts		
EARNINGS			
Revenues:			
Net sales	**$2,061,602**	2,004,719	1,937,021
Investment and other income	**17,636**	18,636	17,153
Total revenues	**2,079,238**	2,023,355	1,954,174
Costs and expenses:			
Cost of sales	**854,931**	848,363	847,366
Costs (Gains) related to factory closure and sale	—	(10,404)	3,300
Selling, distribution and general administrative	**779,168**	743,902	708,310
Interest	**709**	615	958
Total costs and expenses	**1,634,808**	1,582,476	1,559,934
Earnings before income taxes	**444,430**	440,879	394,240
Income taxes	**136,247**	136,378	122,614
Net earnings	**$ 308,183**	304,501	271,626
PER SHARE AMOUNTS			
Net earnings per share of Common Stock (basic and diluted)	**$ 2.66**	2.63	2.34
Dividends paid per share of Common Stock	**$ 1.33**	1.30	1.17

See accompanying accounting policies and notes.

---

h. 1999: ($358,036 − $153,812)/$127,733 = 1.60

1998: ($323,847 − $150,835)/$148,027 = 1.17

i. 1999: $308,183 + [$709(1 − .31*)]/$1,547,745 = 19.9%

1998: $304,501 + [$615(1 − .31*)]/$1,520,855 = 20.0%

j. 1999: $308,183/$1,138,775 = 27.1%

1998: $304,501/$1,157,032† = 26.3%

---

*Tax rate for each of the two years:
1999: $136,247/$444,430 = .31
1998: $136,378/$440,879 = .31

†In addition to its common stock, Wrigley has outstanding Class B common stock. Because this is a second class of stock (similar in many respects to preferred stock), the contributed capital attributable to it should be deducted from total stockholders' equity in the denominator. Similarly, any dividends paid on the Class B common stock should be deducted from net income in the numerator to find the return to the regular common stockholders. We have ignored the difficulties involved in determining these adjustments in our calculations of return on equity.

consolidated statement of cash flows

	1999	1998	1997
			In thousands of dollars
OPERATING ACTIVITIES			
Net earnings	$ 308,183	304,501	271,626
Adjustments to reconcile net earnings to net cash provided by operating activities:			
Depreciation	61,225	55,774	50,439
(Gain) Loss on sales of property, plant and equipment	390	168	(1,141)
Gain related to factory sale	—	(10,404)	—
(Increase) Decrease in:			
Accounts receivable	(21,174)	(12,297)	(19,977)
Inventories	(9,894)	(6,299)	(26,916)
Other current assets	2,807	1,310	(19,053)
Other assets and deferred charges	(22,277)	(17,350)	11,123
Increase (Decrease) in:			
Accounts payable	13,519	4,499	1,549
Accrued expenses	9,734	(3,869)	16,182
Income and other taxes payable	2,649	(4,445)	1,779
Deferred income taxes	2,024	9,826	(2,608)
Other noncurrent liabilities	10,850	2,433	11,475
Net cash provided by operating activities	358,036	323,847	294,478
INVESTING ACTIVITIES			
Additions to property, plant and equipment	(127,733)	(148,027)	(126,509)
Proceeds from property retirements	7,909	10,662	6,888
Purchases of short-term investments	(32,078)	(109,292)	(156,553)
Maturities of short-term investments	150,300	92,676	153,550
Net cash used in investing activities	(1,602)	(153,981)	(122,624)
FINANCING ACTIVITIES			
Dividends paid	(153,812)	(150,835)	(135,680)
Common Stock purchased	(121,268)	(7,679)	(3,676)
Net cash used in financing activities	(275,080)	(158,514)	(139,356)
Effect of exchange rate changes on cash and cash equivalents	(7,540)	(3,407)	(7,104)
Net increase in cash and cash equivalents	73,814	7,945	25,394
Cash and cash equivalents at beginning of year	214,572	206,627	181,233
Cash and cash equivalents at end of year	$ 288,386	214,572	206,627
SUPPLEMENTAL CASH FLOW INFORMATION			
Income taxes paid	$ 130,562	133,530	126,925
Interest paid	$ 709	1,164	900
Interest and dividends received	$ 17,579	19,458	16,598

See accompanying accounting policies and notes.

consolidated balance sheet

	1999	1998
	In thousands of dollars	
ASSETS		
Current assets:		
Cash and cash equivalents	$ 288,386	$ 214,572
Short-term investments, at amortized cost	18,528	137,112
Accounts receivable		
(less allowance for doubtful accounts: **1999— $9,194;** 1998— $7,564)	181,720	171,537
Inventories —		
Finished goods	60,885	64,934
Raw materials and supplies	196,785	191,174
	257,670	256,108
Other current assets	42,301	48,816
Deferred income taxes—current	15,141	15,027
Total current assets	803,746	843,172
Marketable equity securities, at fair value	43,201	39,888
Deferred charges and other assets	114,796	92,183
Deferred income taxes—noncurrent	26,862	25,522
Property, plant and equipment, at cost:		
Land	37,527	36,013
Buildings and building equipment	312,663	310,212
Machinery and equipment	712,585	642,556
	1,062,775	988,781
Less accumulated depreciation	503,635	468,691
Net property, plant and equipment	559,140	520,090
TOTAL ASSETS	$1,547,745	$1,520,855

2. Both the current ratio and the quick ratio declined during 1999. Although the amount of cash flow from operations was up in 1999, the ratio of cash flow from operations to current liabilities declined due to the relatively large increase in current liabilities. Wrigley appears to be quite liquid and should have no problems meeting its short-term obligations.

3. Wrigley is extremely solvent. Its capital structure reveals that it does not rely in any significant way on long-term debt to finance its business. The amount of noncurrent liabilities is only about 10% of total liabilities and stockholders' equity at the end of each year. In fact, a majority of Wrigley's debt is in the form of interest-free current liabilities. Most revealing is the debt service coverage ratio of 690 times in 1999 and 394 times in 1998. The total interest expense each year is insignificant.

	1999	1998
	In thousands of dollars and shares	

LIABILITIES AND STOCKHOLDERS' EQUITY

Current liabilities:

	1999	1998
Accounts payable	$ 86,583	76,691
Accrued expenses	74,816	67,848
Dividends payable	40,073	23,222
Income and other taxes payable	49,654	49,491
Deferred income taxes—current	699	1,374
Total current liabilities	251,825	218,626
Deferred income taxes—noncurrent	44,963	40,312
Other noncurrent liabilities	112,182	104,885

Stockholders' equity:

Preferred Stock—no par value

    Authorized: 20,000 shares
    Issued: None

Common Stock—no par value

	1999	1998
Common Stock Authorized: 400,000 shares Issued: **1999—93,607 shares;** 1998—93,007 shares	12,481	12,401
Class B Common Stock—convertible Authorized: 80,000 shares Issued and outstanding: **1999—22,614 shares;** 1998—23,214 shares	3,015	3,095
Additional paid-in capital	273	272
Retained earnings	1,322,137	1,184,617
Common Stock in treasury, at cost (**1999—1,725 shares;** 1998—111 shares)	(125,712)	(6,712)
Accumulated other comprehensive income—		
Foreign currency translation adjustment	(100,270)	(61,339)
Unrealized holding gains on marketable equity securities	26,851	24,698
	(73,419)	(36,641)
Total stockholders' equity	1,138,775	1,157,032
TOTAL LIABILITIES AND STOCKHOLDERS' EQUITY	$1,547,745	1,520,855

See accompanying accounting policies and notes.

4. The return on assets for 1999 is 19.9%, and the return on common stockholders' equity is 27.1%. These return ratios indicate a very profitable company. It should be noted that the company paid half its 1999 earnings in dividends. Wrigley appears to be a very sound investment, but many other factors, including information on the current market price of the stock, should be considered before making a decision.

CHAPTER HIGHLIGHTS

1. **LO 1** Various parties, including management, creditors, stockholders, and others, perform financial statement analysis. Care must be exercised, however, in all types of financial analysis. For example, the existence of alternative accounting principles can make comparing different companies difficult. Published financial statements are not adjusted for the effects of inflation, and thus comparisons over time must be made with caution.

2. **LO 2** Horizontal analysis uses comparative financial statements to examine the increases and decreases in items from one period to the next. The analysis can look at the change in items over an extended period of time. Many companies present a summary of selected financial items for a 5- or 10-year period.

3. **LO 3** Vertical analysis involves stating all items on a particular financial statement as a percentage of one item on the statement. For example, all expenses on a common-size income statement are stated as a percentage of net sales. This technique, along with horizontal analysis, can be useful in spotting problem areas within a company.

4. **LO 4** Ratios can be categorized according to their primary purpose. Liquidity ratios indicate the company's ability to pay its debts as they are due. The focus of liquidity analysis is on a company's current assets and current liabilities.

5. **LO 5** Solvency ratios deal with a company's long-term financial health—that is, its ability to repay long-term creditors. The right side of the balance sheet is informative in this respect because it reports on the various sources of capital to the business.

6. **LO 6** Profitability ratios measure how well management has used the assets at its disposal to earn a return for the various providers of capital. Return on assets indicates the return to all providers; return on common stockholders' equity measures the return to the residual owners of the business. Certain other ratios are used to relate a company's performance according to the financial statements with its performance in the stock market.

KEY TERMS QUIZ

Because of the number of terms introduced in this chapter, there are two key terms quizzes. For each quiz, read each definition below and then write the number of that definition in the blank beside the appropriate term it defines. The solution appears at the end of the chapter.

Quiz 1:

_____ Horizontal analysis

_____ Vertical analysis

_____ Gross profit ratio

_____ Profit margin ratio

_____ Liquidity

_____ Working capital

_____ Current ratio

_____ Acid-test or quick ratio

_____ Cash flow from operations to current liabilities ratio

_____ Accounts receivable turnover ratio

_____ Number of days' sales in receivables

_____ Inventory turnover ratio

_____ Number of days' sales in inventory

_____ Cash to cash operating cycle

1. A stricter test of liquidity than the current ratio; excludes inventory and prepayments from the numerator.

2. Current assets minus current liabilities.

3. The ratio of current assets to current liabilities.

4. A measure of the average age of accounts receivable.

5. A measure of the ability to pay current debts from operating cash flows.

6. A measure of the number of times accounts receivable are collected in a period.

7. A measure of how long it takes to sell inventory.

8. The length of time from the purchase of inventory to the collection of any receivable from the sale.

9. A measure of the number of times inventory is sold during a period.

10. Gross profit to net sales.

11. A comparison of various financial statement items within a single period with the use of common-size statements.

12. Net income to net sales.

13. The nearness to cash of the assets and liabilities.

14. A comparison of financial statement items over a period of time.

Quiz 2:

_____ Solvency

_____ Debt-to-equity ratio

_____ Times interest earned ratio

_____ Debt service coverage ratio

_____ Cash flow from operations to capital expenditures ratio

_____ Profitability

_____ Return on assets ratio

_____ Return on sales ratio

_____ Asset turnover ratio

_____ Return on common stockholders' equity ratio

_____ Leverage

_____ Earnings per share

_____ Price/earnings (P/E) ratio

_____ Dividend payout ratio

_____ Dividend yield ratio

1. A measure of a company's success in earning a return for the common stockholders.

2. The relationship between a company's performance according to the income statement and its performance in the stock market.

3. The ability of a company to remain in business over the long term.

4. A variation of the profit margin ratio; measures earnings before payments to creditors.

5. A company's bottom line stated on a per-share basis.

6. The percentage of earnings paid out as dividends.

7. The ratio of total liabilities to total stockholders' equity.

8. A measure of the ability of a company to finance long-term asset acquisitions with cash from operations.

9. A measure of a company's success in earning a return for all providers of capital.

10. The relationship between net sales and total assets.

11. The relationship between dividends and the market price of a company's stock.

12. The use of borrowed funds and amounts contributed by preferred stockholders to earn an overall return higher than the cost of these funds.

13. An income statement measure of the ability of a company to meet its interest payments.

14. A statement of cash flows measure of the ability of a company to meet its interest and principal payments.

15. How well management is using company resources to earn a return on the funds invested by various groups.

ALTERNATE TERMS

Acid-test ratio   Quick ratio

Horizontal analysis   Trend analysis

Number of days' sales in receivables   Average collection period

Price/earnings ratio   P/E ratio

QUESTIONS

1. Two companies are in the same industry. Company A uses the LIFO method of inventory valuation, and Company B uses FIFO. What difficulties does this present when comparing the two companies?

2. You are told to compare the company's results for the year, as measured by various ratios, with one of the published surveys that arranges information by industry classification. What are some of the difficulties you may encounter when making comparisons using industry standards?

3. What types of problems does inflation cause in analyzing financial statements?

4. Distinguish between horizontal and vertical analysis. Why is the analysis of common-size statements called *vertical* analysis? Why is horizontal analysis sometimes called *trend* analysis?

5. A company experiences a 15% increase in sales over the previous year. However, gross profit actually decreased by 5% from the previous year. What are some of the possible causes for an increase in sales but a decline in gross profit?

6. A company's total current assets have increased by 5% over the prior year. Management is concerned, however, about the composition of the current assets. Why is the composition of current assets important?

7. Ratios were categorized in the chapter according to their use in performing three different types of analysis. What are the three types of ratios?

8. Describe the operating cycle for a manufacturing company. How would the cycle differ for a retailer?

9. What accounts for the order in which current assets are presented on a balance sheet?

10. A company has a current ratio of 1.25 but an acid-test or quick ratio of only 0.65. How can this difference in the two ratios be explained? What are some concerns that you would have about this company?

11. Explain the basic concept underlying all turnover ratios. Why is it advisable in computing a turnover ratio to use an average in the denominator (for example, average inventory)?

12. Sanders Company's accounts receivable turned over nine times during the year. The credit department extends terms of 2/10, net 30. Does the turnover ratio indicate any problems that management should investigate?

13. The turnover of inventory for Ace Company has slowed from 6.0 times per year to 4.5 times. What are some of the possible explanations for this decrease?

14. How does the operating cycle for a manufacturer differ from the operating cycle for a service company, for example, an airline?

15. What is the difference between liquidity analysis and solvency analysis?

16. Why is the debt service coverage ratio a better measure of solvency than the times interest earned ratio?

17. A friend tells you that the best way to assess solvency is by comparing total debt to total assets. Another friend says that solvency is measured by comparing total debt to total stockholders' equity. Which one is right?

18. A company is in the process of negotiating with a bank for an additional loan. Why will the bank be very interested in the company's debt service coverage ratio?

19. What is the rationale for deducting dividends when computing the ratio of cash flow from operations to capital expenditures?

20. The rate of return on assets ratio is computed by dividing net income and interest expense, net of tax, by average total assets. Why is the numerator net income and interest expense, net of tax, rather than just net income?

21. A company has a return on assets of 14% and a return on common stockholders' equity of 11%. The president of the company has asked you to explain the reason for this difference. What causes the difference? How is the concept of financial leverage involved?

22. What is meant by the "quality" of a company's earnings? Explain why the price/earnings ratio for a company may indicate the quality of earnings.

23. Some ratios are more useful for management, whereas others are better suited to the needs of outsiders, such as stockholders and bankers. What is an example of a ratio that is primarily suited to management use? What is one that is more suited to use by outsiders?

24. The needs of service-oriented companies in analyzing financial statements differ from those of product-oriented companies. Why is this true? Give an example of a ratio that is meaningless to a service business.

EXERCISES

LO 4 Exercise 13-1 Accounts Receivable Analysis

The following account balances are taken from the records of the Faraway Travel Agency:

	December 31		
	2001	**2000**	**1999**
Accounts receivable	$150,000	$100,000	$80,000

	2001	**2000**
Net credit sales	$600,000	$540,000

Faraway extends credit terms requiring full payment in 60 days, with no discount for early payment.

Required

1. Compute Faraway's accounts receivable turnover ratio for 2001 and 2000.
2. Compute the number of days' sales in receivables for 2001 and 2000. Assume 360 days in a year.
3. Comment on the efficiency of Faraway's collection efforts over the two-year period.

LO 4 Exercise 13-2 Inventory Analysis

The following account balances are taken from the records of Lewis Inc., a wholesaler of fresh fruits and vegetables:

	December 31		
	2001	**2000**	**1999**
Merchandise inventory	$ 200,000	$ 150,000	$120,000

	2001	**2000**
Cost of goods sold	$7,100,000	$8,100,000

Required

1. Compute Lewis's inventory turnover ratio for 2001 and 2000.
2. Compute the number of days' sales in inventory for 2001 and 2000. Assume 360 days in a year.
3. Comment on your answers in parts **1** and **2** relative to the company's management of inventory over the two years. What problems do you see in its inventory management?

LO 4 Exercise 13-3 Accounts Receivable and Inventory Analyses for Coca-Cola and Pepsi

The following information was obtained from the 1999 and 1998 financial statements of Coca-Cola Company and Subsidiaries and PepsiCo Inc. and Subsidiaries:

www.cocacola.com
www.pepsico.com

(in millions)		Coca-Cola	PepsiCo
Accounts and notes receivable, net*	12/31/99****	$ 1,798	$ 1,704
	12/31/98	1,666	2,453
Inventories	12/31/99	1,076	899
	12/31/98	890	1,016
Net sales**	1999	19,805	20,367
	1998	18,813	22,348
Cost of goods sold***	1999	6,009	8,198
	1998	5,562	9,330

*Described as "trade accounts receivable" by Coca-Cola.

**Described as "net operating revenues" by Coca-Cola.

***Described as "cost of sales" by PepsiCo.

****PepsiCo's 1999 and 1998 year ends were 12/25/99 and 12/26/98, respectively.

Required

1. Using the information provided above, compute the following for each company for 1999:

   a. Accounts receivable turnover ratio

   b. Number of days' sales in receivables

   c. Inventory turnover ratio

   d. Number of days' sales in inventory

   e. Cash to cash operating cycle

2. Comment briefly on the liquidity of each of these two companies.

LO 4 Exercise 13-4 Liquidity Analyses for Coca-Cola and Pepsi

www.cocacola.com
www.pepsico.com

The following information was summarized from the balance sheets of the Coca-Cola Company and Subsidiaries and PepsiCo Inc. and Subsidiaries at the end of 1999:

(in millions)	Coca-Cola	PepsiCo
Cash and cash equivalents	$1,611	$ 964
Short-term investments/marketable securities	201	92
Accounts, notes, and other receivables, net	1,798	1,704
Inventories	1,076	899
Other current assets	1,794	514
Total current assets	$6,480	$4,173
Current liabilities	$9,856	$3,788
Other liabilities	2,254	6,882
Stockholders' equity	9,513	6,881

Required

1. Using the information provided above, compute the following for each company at the end of 1999:

   a. Current ratio

   b. Quick ratio

2. Comment briefly on the liquidity of each of these two companies. Which appears to be more liquid?

3. What other ratios would help you to more fully assess the liquidity of these companies?

LO 4 Exercise 13-5 Liquidity Analyses for McDonald's and Wendy's

www.mcdonalds.com
www.wendy.com

The following information was summarized from the balance sheets of McDonald's Corporation and Wendy's International Inc. at December 31, 1999 and January 2, 2000, respectively:

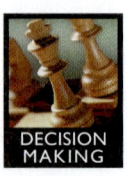

DECISION MAKING

	McDonald's (in millions)	Wendy's (in thousands)
Current Assets:		
Cash and cash equivalents	$ 419.5	$ 210,785
Accounts receivable, net*	708.1	71,763

Notes receivable, net	$ –	$ 7,749
Inventories	82.7	40,271
Other current assets	362.0	19,267
Total current assets	$1,572.3	$ 349,835
Current liabilities	$3,274.3	$ 284,209
Other liabilities	$8,069.8	$ 533,949
Stockholders' equity	$9,639.1	$1,065,439

*McDonald's combines accounts and notes receivable.

Required

1. Using the information provided above, compute the following for each company at year end:
   a. Working capital
   b. Current ratio
   c. Quick ratio

2. Comment briefly on the liquidity of each of these two companies. Which appears to be more liquid?

3. McDonald's reported cash flows from operations of $3,008.9 million during 1999. Wendy's reported cash flows from operations of $291,284 thousand. Current liabilities reported by McDonald's at December 31, 1998, and Wendy's at January 3, 1999, were $2,497.1 million and $249,412 thousand, respectively. Calculate the cash flow from operations to current liabilities ratio for each company. Does the information provided by this ratio change your opinion as to the relative liquidity of each of these two companies?

4. What steps might be taken by McDonald's to cover its short-term cash requirements?

LO 5   Exercise 13-6   Solvency Analyses for Tommy Hilfiger

The following information was obtained from the comparative financial statements included in Tommy Hilfiger Corporation's 2000 annual report (all amounts are in thousands of dollars):   **www.hilfiger.com**

	March 31, 2000	March 31, 1999
Total liabilities	$1,103,807	$1,114,371
Total shareholders' equity	1,277,714	1,092,249

For the Fiscal Years Ended March 31

	2000	1999
Interest expense	$ 41,024	$ 39,525
Provision for income taxes	55,173	72,654
Net income	172,358	173,717
Net cash provided by operating activities	231,209	259,985
Total dividends paid	—	—
Cash used to purchase property and equipment	151,984	79,422
Payments on long-term debt	40,000	10,000

Required

1. Using the information provided above, compute the following for 2000 and 1999:
   a. Debt-to-equity ratio (at each year end)
   b. Times interest earned ratio
   c. Debt service coverage ratio
   d. Cash flow from operations to capital expenditures ratio

2. Comment briefly on the company's solvency.

LO 5   Exercise 13-7   Solvency Analysis

The following information is available from the balance sheets at the ends of the two most recent years and the income statement for the most recent year of Impact Company:

	December 31	
	2001	**2000**
Accounts payable	$ 65,000	$ 50,000
Accrued liabilities	25,000	35,000
Taxes payable	60,000	45,000
Short-term notes payable	–0–	75,000
Bonds payable due within next year	200,000	200,000
Total current liabilities	$ 350,000	$ 405,000
Bonds payable	$ 600,000	$ 800,000
Common stock, $10 par	$1,000,000	$1,000,000
Retained earnings	650,000	500,000
Total stockholders' equity	$1,650,000	$1,500,000
Total liabilities and stockholders' equity	$2,600,000	$2,705,000

	2001
Sales revenue	$1,600,000
Cost of goods sold	950,000
Gross profit	$ 650,000
Selling and administrative expense	300,000
Operating income	$ 350,000
Interest expense	89,000
Income before tax	$ 261,000
Income tax expense	111,000
Net income	$ 150,000

Other Information

a. Short-term notes payable represents a 12-month loan that matured in November 2001. Interest of 12% was paid at maturity.

b. One million dollars of serial bonds had been issued 10 years earlier. The first series of $200,000 matured at the end of 2001, with interest of 8% payable annually.

c. Cash flow from operations was $185,000 in 2001. The amounts of interest and taxes paid during 2001 were $89,000 and $96,000, respectively.

Required

1. Compute the following for Impact Company:
   a. The debt-to-equity ratio at December 31, 2001, and December 31, 2000
   b. The times interest earned ratio for 2001
   c. The debt service coverage ratio for 2001

2. Comment on Impact's solvency at the end of 2001. Do the times interest earned ratio and the debt service coverage ratio differ in terms of their indication of Impact's ability to pay its debts?

LO 6 Exercise 13-8   Return Ratios and Leverage

The following selected data are taken from the financial statements of Evergreen Company:

Sales revenue	$ 650,000
Cost of goods sold	400,000
Gross profit	$ 250,000
Selling and administrative expense	100,000
Operating income	$ 150,000
Interest expense	50,000
Income before tax	$ 100,000
Income tax expense (40%)	40,000
Net income	$ 60,000

Accounts payable	$	45,000
Accrued liabilities		70,000
Income taxes payable		10,000
Interest payable		25,000
Short-term loans payable		150,000
Total current liabilities	$	300,000
Long-term bonds payable	$	500,000
Preferred stock, 10%, $100 par	$	250,000
Common stock, no par		600,000
Retained earnings		350,000
Total stockholders' equity		$1,200,000
Total liabilities and stockholders' equity		$2,000,000

Required

1. Compute the following ratios for Evergreen Company:

   a. Return on sales

   b. Asset turnover (assume that total assets at the beginning of the year were $1,600,000)

   c. Return on assets

   d. Return on common stockholders' equity (assume that the only changes in stockholders' equity during the year were from the net income for the year and dividends on the preferred stock)

2. Comment on Evergreen's use of leverage. Has it successfully employed leverage? Explain your answer.

LO 6 **Exercise 13-9** Relationships among Return on Assets, Return on Sales, and Asset Turnover

A company's return on assets is a function of its ability to turn over its investment (asset turnover) and earn a profit on each dollar of sales (return on sales). For each of the following *independent* cases, determine the missing amounts. (*Note:* Assume in each case that the company has no interest expense; that is, net income is used as the definition of income in all calculations.)

Case 1

Net income	$ 10,000
Net sales	$ 80,000
Average total assets	$ 60,000
Return on assets	?

Case 2

Net income	$ 25,000
Average total assets	$250,000
Return on sales	2%
Net sales	?

Case 3

Average total assets	$ 80,000
Asset turnover	1.5 times
Return on sales	6%
Return on assets	?

Case 4

Return on assets	10%
Net sales	$ 50,000
Asset turnover	1.25 times
Net income	?

Case 5

Return on assets	15%
Net income	$ 20,000
Return on sales	5%
Average total assets	?

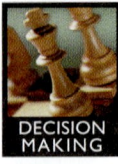

DECISION MAKING

LO 6 Exercise 13-10 EPS, P/E Ratio, and Dividend Ratios

The stockholders' equity section of the balance sheet for Cooperstown Corp. at the end of 2001 appears as follows:

8%, $100 par, cumulative preferred stock, 200,000 shares authorized, 50,000 shares issued and outstanding	$ 5,000,000
Additional paid-in capital on preferred	2,500,000
Common stock, $5 par, 500,000 shares authorized, 400,000 shares issued and outstanding	2,000,000
Additional paid-in capital on common	18,000,000
Retained earnings	37,500,000
Total stockholders' equity	$65,000,000

Net income for the year was $1,300,000. Dividends were declared and paid on the preferred shares during the year, and a quarterly dividend of $.40 per share was declared and paid each quarter on the common shares. The closing market price for the common shares on December 31, 2001, was $24.75 per share.

Required

1. Compute the following ratios for the common stock:
   a. Earnings per share
   b. Price/earnings ratio
   c. Dividend payout ratio
   d. Dividend yield ratio

2. Assume that you are an investment adviser. What other information would you want to have before advising a client regarding the purchase of Cooperstown stock?

LO 6 Exercise 13-11 Earnings per Share and Extraordinary Items

The stockholders' equity section of the balance sheet for Lahey Construction Company at the end of 2001 follows:

9%, $10 par, cumulative preferred stock, 500,000 shares authorized, 200,000 shares issued and outstanding	$ 2,000,000
Additional paid-in capital on preferred	7,500,000
Common stock, $1 par, 2,500,000 shares authorized, 1,500,000 shares issued and outstanding	1,500,000
Additional paid-in capital on common	21,000,000
Retained earnings	25,500,000
Total stockholders' equity	$57,500,000

The lower portion of the 2001 income statement indicates the following:

Net income before tax		$9,750,000
Income tax expense (40%)		(3,900,000)
Income before extraordinary items		$5,850,000
Extraordinary loss from flood	$(6,200,000)	
Less: related tax effect (40%)	2,480,000	(3,720,000)
Net income		$2,130,000

Assume the number of shares outstanding did not change during the year.

Required

1. Compute earnings per share *before* extraordinary items.
2. Compute earnings per share *after* the extraordinary loss.

3. Which of the two EPS ratios is more useful to management? Explain your answer. Would your answer be different if the ratios were to be used by an outsider, for example, by a potential stockholder? Why?

Multi-Concept Exercises

LO 2, 3 **Exercise 13-12** Common-Size Balance Sheets and Horizontal Analysis

Comparative balance sheets for Farinet Company for the past two years are as follows:

	December 31	
	2001	**2000**
Cash	$ 16,000	$ 20,000
Accounts receivable	40,000	30,000
Inventory	30,000	50,000
Prepaid rent	18,000	12,000
Total current assets	$104,000	$112,000
Land	$150,000	$150,000
Plant and equipment	800,000	600,000
Accumulated depreciation	(130,000)	(60,000)
Total long-term assets	$820,000	$690,000
Total assets	$924,000	$802,000
Accounts payable	$ 24,000	$ 20,000
Income taxes payable	6,000	10,000
Short-term notes payable	70,000	50,000
Total current liabilities	$100,000	$ 80,000
Bonds payable	$150,000	$200,000
Common stock	$400,000	$300,000
Retained earnings	274,000	222,000
Total stockholders' equity	$674,000	$522,000
Total liabilities and stockholders' equity	$924,000	$802,000

Required

1. Using the format in Exhibit 13-5, prepare common-size comparative balance sheets for the two years for Farinet Company.

2. What observations can you make about the changes in the relative composition of Farinet's accounts from the common-size balance sheets? List at least five observations.

3. Using the format in Exhibit 13-1, prepare comparative balance sheets for Farinet Company, including columns both for the dollars and for the percentage increase or decrease in each item on the statement.

4. Identify the four items on the balance sheet that experienced the largest change from one year to the next. For each of these, explain where you would look to find additional information about the change.

LO 2, 3 **Exercise 13-13** Common-Size Income Statements and Horizontal Analysis

Income statements for Mariners Corp. for the past two years follow:

	(Amounts in Thousands of Dollars)	
	2001	**2000**
Sales revenue	$60,000	$50,000
Cost of goods sold	42,000	30,000
Gross profit	$18,000	$20,000
Selling and administrative expense	9,000	5,000
Operating income	$ 9,000	$15,000
Interest expense	2,000	2,000
Income before tax	$ 7,000	$13,000
Income tax expense	2,000	4,000
Net income	$ 5,000	$ 9,000

Required

1. Using the format in Exhibit 13-6, prepare common-size comparative income statements for the two years for Mariners Corp.

2. What observations can you make about the common-size statements? List at least four observations.

3. Using the format in Exhibit 13-2, prepare comparative income statements for Mariners Corp., including columns both for the dollars and for the percentage increase or decrease in each item on the statement.

4. Identify the two items on the income statement that experienced the largest change from one year to the next. For each of these, explain where you would look to find additional information about the change.

PROBLEMS

LO 4 Problem 13-1 Effect of Transactions on Working Capital, Current Ratio, and Quick Ratio

(*Note:* Consider completing Problem 13-2 after this problem to ensure that you obtain a clear understanding of the effect of various transactions on these measures of liquidity.)

The following account balances are taken from the records of Liquiform Inc.:

Cash	$ 70,000
Trading securities (short-term)	60,000
Accounts receivable	80,000
Inventory	100,000
Prepaid insurance	10,000
Accounts payable	75,000
Taxes payable	25,000
Salaries and wages payable	40,000
Short-term loans payable	60,000

Required

1. Use the preceding information to compute the amount of working capital and Liquiform's current and quick ratios (round to three decimal points).

2. Determine the effect that each of the following transactions will have on Liquiform's working capital, current ratio, and quick ratio by recalculating each and then indicating whether the measure is increased, decreased, or not affected by the transaction. (For the ratios, round to three decimal points.) Consider each transaction independently; that is, assume that it is the *only* transaction that takes place.

	Effect of Transaction On:		
Transaction	**Working Capital**	**Current Ratio**	**Quick Ratio**
a. Purchased inventory on account for $20,000.			
b. Purchased inventory for cash, $15,000.			
c. Paid suppliers on account, $30,000.			
d. Received cash on account, $40,000.			
e. Paid insurance for next year, $20,000.			
f. Made sales on account, $60,000.			
g. Repaid short-term loans at bank, $25,000.			
h. Borrowed $40,000 at bank for 90 days.			
i. Declared and paid $45,000 cash dividend.			
j. Purchased $20,000 of trading securities (classified as current assets).			
k. Paid $30,000 in salaries.			
l. Accrued additional $15,000 in taxes.			

LO 4 **Problem 13-2** Effect of Transactions on Working Capital, Current Ratio, and Quick Ratio

(*Note:* Consider completing this problem after Problem 13-1 to ensure that you obtain a clear understanding of the effect of various transactions on these measures of liquidity.)

The following account balances are taken from the records of Veriform Inc.:

Cash	$ 70,000
Trading securities (short-term)	60,000
Accounts receivable	80,000
Inventory	100,000
Prepaid insurance	10,000
Accounts payable	75,000
Taxes payable	25,000
Salaries and wages payable	40,000
Short-term loans payable	210,000

Required

1. Use the preceding information to compute the amount of working capital and Veriform's current and quick ratios (round to three decimal points).

2. Determine the effect that each of the following transactions will have on Veriform's working capital, current ratio, and quick ratio by recalculating each and then indicating whether the measure is increased, decreased, or not affected by the transaction. (For the ratios, round to three decimal points.) Consider each transaction independently; that is, assume that it is the *only* transaction that takes place.

	Effect of Transaction On:		
Transaction	Working Capital	Current Ratio	Quick Ratio
a. Purchased inventory on account for $20,000.			
b. Purchased inventory for cash, $15,000.			
c. Paid suppliers on account, $30,000.			
d. Received cash on account, $40,000.			
e. Paid insurance for next year, $20,000.			
f. Made sales on account, $60,000.			
g. Repaid short-term loans at bank, $25,000.			
h. Borrowed $40,000 at bank for 90 days.			
i. Declared and paid $45,000 cash dividend.			
j. Purchased $20,000 of trading securities (classified as current assets).			
k. Paid $30,000 in salaries.			
l. Accrued additional $15,000 in taxes.			

LO 6 **Problem 13-3** Goals for Sales and Return on Assets

DECISION MAKING

The president of Blue Skies Corp. is reviewing with his vice presidents the operating results of the year just completed. Sales increased by 15% from the previous year to $60,000,000. Average total assets for the year were $40,000,000. Net income, after adding back interest expense, net of tax, was $5,000,000.

The president is happy with the performance over the past year but is never satisfied with the status quo. He has set two specific goals for next year: (1) a 20% growth in sales and (2) a return on assets of 15%.

To achieve the second goal, the president has stated his intention to increase the total asset base by 12.5% over the base for the year just completed.

Required

1. For the year just completed, compute the following ratios:

   a. Return on sales

   b. Asset turnover

   c. Return on assets

2. Compute the necessary asset turnover for next year to achieve the president's goal of a 20% increase in sales.

3. Calculate the income needed next year to achieve the goal of a 15% return on total assets. (*Note:* Assume that *income* is defined as net income plus interest, net of tax.)

4. Based on your answers to parts **2** and **3**, comment on the reasonableness of the president's goals. What must the company focus on to attain these goals?

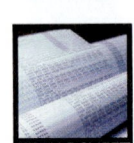

LO 6 Problem 13-4 Goals for Sales and Income Growth

Sunrise Corp. is a major regional retailer. The chief executive officer (CEO) is concerned with the slow growth both of sales and of net income and the subsequent effect on the trading price of the common stock. Selected financial data for the past three years follow.

SUNRISE CORP.
(IN MILLIONS)

	2001	2000	1999
1. Sales	$200.0	$192.5	$187.0
2. Net income	6.0	5.8	5.6
3. Dividends declared and paid	2.5	2.5	2.5
December 31 balances:			
4. Owners' equity	70.0	66.5	63.2
5. Debt	30.0	29.8	30.3
Selected year-end financial ratios			
Net income to sales	3.0%	3.0%	3.0%
Asset turnover	2 times	2 times	2 times
6. Return on owners' equity*	8.6%	8.7%	8.9%
7. Debt to total assets	30.0%	30.9%	32.4%

*Based on year-end balances in owners' equity.

The CEO believes that the price of the stock has been adversely affected by the downward trend of the return on equity, the relatively low dividend payout ratio, and the lack of dividend increases. To improve the price of the stock, she wants to improve the return on equity and dividends. She believes that the company should be able to meet these objectives by (1) increasing sales and net income at an annual rate of 10% a year and (2) establishing a new dividend policy that calls for a dividend payout of 50% of earnings or $3,000,000, whichever is larger.

The 10% annual sales increase will be accomplished through a new promotional program. The president believes that the present net income to sales ratio of 3% will be unchanged by the cost of this new program and any interest paid on new debt. She expects that the company can accomplish this sales and income growth while maintaining the current relationship of total assets to sales. Any capital that is needed to maintain this relationship and that is not generated internally would be acquired through long-term debt financing. The CEO hopes that debt would not exceed 35% of total liabilities and owners' equity.

Required

1. Using the CEO's program, prepare a schedule that shows the appropriate data for the years 2002, 2003, and 2004 for the items numbered 1 through 7 on the preceding schedule.

2. Can the CEO meet all her requirements if a 10% per year growth in income and sales is achieved? Explain your answer.

3. What alternative actions should the CEO consider to improve the return on equity and to support increased dividend payments?

2. Explain the reasons that the CEO might have for wanting to limit debt to 35% of total liabilities and owners' equity.
(CMA adapted)

Multi-Concept Problems

LO 4, 5, 6 Problem 13-5 Basic Financial Ratios

The accounting staff of CCB Enterprises has completed the financial statements for the 2001 calendar year. The statement of income for the current year and the comparative statements of financial position for 2001 and 2000 follow.

CCB ENTERPRISES
STATEMENT OF INCOME
FOR THE YEAR ENDED DECEMBER 31, 2001
(THOUSANDS OMITTED)

Revenue:	
Net sales	$800,000
Other	60,000
Total revenue	$860,000
Expenses:	
Cost of goods sold	$540,000
Research and development	25,000
Selling and administrative	155,000
Interest	20,000
Total expenses	$740,000
Income before income taxes	$120,000
Income taxes	48,000
Net income	$ 72,000

CCB ENTERPRISES
COMPARATIVE STATEMENTS OF FINANCIAL POSITION
DECEMBER 31, 2001 AND 2000
(THOUSANDS OMITTED)

	2001	2000
Assets		
Current assets:		
Cash and short-term investments	$ 26,000	$ 21,000
Receivables, less allowance for doubtful accounts		
($1,100 in 2001 and $1,400 in 2000)	48,000	50,000
Inventories, at lower of FIFO cost or market	65,000	62,000
Prepaid items and other current assets	5,000	3,000
Total current assets	$144,000	$136,000
Other assets:		
Investments, at cost	$106,000	$106,000
Deposits	10,000	8,000
Total other assets	$116,000	$114,000
Property, plant, and equipment:		
Land	$ 12,000	$ 12,000
Buildings and equipment, less		
accumulated depreciation ($126,000 in		
2001 and $122,000 in 2000)	268,000	248,000
Total property, plant, and equipment	$280,000	$260,000
Total assets	$540,000	$510,000
Liabilities and Stockholders' Equity		
Current liabilities:		
Short-term loans	$ 22,000	$ 24,000
Accounts payable	72,000	71,000
Salaries, wages, and other	26,000	27,000
Total current liabilities	$120,000	$122,000
Long-term debt	$160,000	$171,000
Total liabilities	$280,000	$293,000
Stockholders' equity:		
Common stock, at par	$ 44,000	$ 42,000
Paid-in capital in excess of par	64,000	61,000
Total paid-in capital	$108,000	$103,000
Retained earnings	152,000	114,000
Total stockholders' equity	$260,000	$217,000
Total liabilities and stockholders' equity	$540,000	$510,000

Required:

1. Calculate the following financial ratios for 2001 for CCB Enterprises:
    a. Times interest earned
    b. Return on total assets
    c. Return on common stockholders' equity
    d. Debt-equity ratio (at December 31, 2001)
    e. Current ratio (at December 31, 2001)
    f. Quick (acid-test) ratio (at December 31, 2001)
    g. Accounts receivable turnover ratio (assume that all sales are on credit)
    h. Number of days' sales in receivables
    i. Inventory turnover ratio (assume that all purchases are on credit)
    j. Number of days' sales in inventory
    k. Number of days in cash operating cycle

2. Prepare a few brief comments on the overall financial health of CCB Enterprises. For each comment, indicate any information that is not provided in the problem and that you would need to evaluate fully the company's financial health. (CMA adapted)

LO 5, 6   Problem 13-6   Projected Results to Meet Corporate Objectives

Tablon Inc. is a wholly owned subsidiary of Marbel Co. The philosophy of Marbel's management is to allow the subsidiaries to operate as independent units. Corporate control is exercised through the establishment of minimum objectives for each subsidiary, accompanied by substantial rewards for success and penalties for failure. The time period for performance review is long enough for competent managers to display their abilities.

Each quarter the subsidiary is required to submit financial statements. The statements are accompanied by a letter from the subsidiary president explaining the results to date, a forecast for the remainder of the year, and the actions to be taken to achieve the objectives if the forecast indicates that the objectives will not be met.

Marbel management, in conjunction with Tablon management, had set the following objectives for the year ending May 31, 2002. These objectives are similar to those set in previous years.

- Sales growth of 20%
- Return on stockholders' equity of 15%
- A long-term debt-to-equity ratio of not more than 1.0
- Payment of a cash dividend of 50% of net income, with a minimum payment of at least $400,000

Tablon's controller has just completed the financial statements for the six months ended November 30, 2001, and the forecast for the year ending May 31, 2002. The statements are presented below.

After a cursory glance at the financial statements, Tablon's president concluded that not all objectives would be met. At a staff meeting of the Tablon management, the president asked the controller to review the projected results and recommend possible actions that could be taken during the remainder of the year so that Tablon would be more likely to meet the objectives.

TABLON INC.
INCOME STATEMENT
(THOUSANDS OMITTED)

	Year Ended May 31, 2001	Six Months Ended November 30, 2001	Forecast for Year Ending May 31, 2002
Sales	$25,000	$15,000	$30,000
Cost of goods sold	$13,000	$ 8,000	$16,000
Selling expenses	5,000	3,500	7,000
Administrative expenses and interest	4,000	2,500	5,000
Income taxes (40%)	1,200	400	800
Total expenses and taxes	$23,200	$14,400	$28,800
Net income	$ 1,800	$ 600	$ 1,200
Dividends declared and paid	600	0	600
Income retained	$ 1,200	$ 600	$ 600

TABLON INC.
STATEMENT OF FINANCIAL POSITION
(THOUSANDS OMITTED)

	May 31, 2001	November 30, 2001	Forecast for May 31, 2002
Assets			
Cash	$ 400	$ 500	$ 500
Accounts receivable (net)	4,100	6,500	7,100
Inventory	7,000	8,500	8,600
Plant and equipment (net)	6,500	7,000	7,300
Total assets	$18,000	$22,500	$23,500
Liabilities and Equities			
Accounts payable	$ 3,000	$ 4,000	$ 4,000
Accrued taxes	300	200	200
Long-term borrowing	6,000	9,000	10,000
Common stock	5,000	5,000	5,000
Retained earnings	3,700	4,300	4,300
Total liabilities and equities	$18,000	$22,500	$23,500

Required

1. Calculate the projected results for each of the four objectives established for Tablon Inc. State which results will not meet the objectives by year end.

2. From the data presented, identify the factors that seem to contribute to the failure of Tablon Inc. to meet all its objectives.

3. Explain the possible actions that the controller could recommend in response to the president's request.

(CMA adapted)

LO 4, 5, 6 Problem 13-7 Comparison with Industry Averages

Heartland Inc. is a medium-sized company that has been in business for 20 years. The industry has become very competitive in the last few years, and Heartland has decided that it must grow if it is going to survive. It has approached the bank for a sizable five-year loan, and the bank has requested its most recent financial statements as part of the loan package.

The industry in which Heartland operates consists of approximately 20 companies relatively equal in size. The trade association to which all the competitors belong publishes an annual survey of the industry, including industry averages for selected ratios for the competitors. All companies voluntarily submit their statements to the association for this purpose.

Heartland's controller is aware that the bank has access to this survey and is very concerned about how the company fared this past year compared with the rest of the industry. The ratios included in the publication, and the averages for the past year, are as follows:

Ratio	Industry Average
Current ratio	1.23
Acid-test (quick) ratio	0.75
Accounts receivable turnover	33 times
Inventory turnover	29 times
Debt-to-equity ratio	0.53
Times interest earned	8.65 times
Return on sales	6.57%
Asset turnover	1.95 times
Return on assets	12.81%
Return on common stockholders' equity	17.67%

The financial statements to be submitted to the bank in connection with the loan follow:

HEARTLAND INC.
STATEMENT OF INCOME AND RETAINED EARNINGS
FOR THE YEAR ENDED DECEMBER 31, 2001
(THOUSANDS OMITTED)

Sales revenue	$542,750
Cost of goods sold	(435,650)
Gross margin	$107,100
Selling, general, and administrative expenses	(65,780)
Loss on sales of securities	(220)
Income before interest and taxes	$ 41,100
Interest expense	(9,275)
Income before taxes	$ 31,825
Income tax expense	(12,730)
Net income	$ 19,095
Retained earnings, January 1, 2001	58,485
	$ 77,580
Dividends paid on common stock	(12,000)
Retained earnings, December 31, 2001	$ 65,580

HEARTLAND INC.
COMPARATIVE STATEMENTS OF FINANCIAL POSITION
(THOUSANDS OMITTED)

	December 31, 2001	December 31, 2000
Assets		
Current assets:		
Cash	$ 1,135	$ 750
Marketable securities	1,250	2,250
Accounts receivable, net of allowances	15,650	12,380
Inventories	12,680	15,870
Prepaid items	385	420
Total current assets	$ 31,100	$ 31,670
Long-term investments	$ 425	$ 425
Property, plant, and equipment:		
Land	$ 32,000	$ 32,000
Buildings and equipment, net of accumulated depreciation	216,000	206,000
Total property, plant, and equipment	$248,000	$238,000
Total assets	$279,525	$270,095
Liabilities and Stockholders' Equity		
Current liabilities:		
Short-term notes	$ 8,750	$ 12,750
Accounts payable	20,090	14,380
Salaries and wages payable	1,975	2,430
Income taxes payable	3,130	2,050
Total current liabilities	$ 33,945	$ 31,610
Long-term bonds payable	$ 80,000	$ 80,000
Stockholders' equity:		
Common stock, no par	$100,000	$100,000
Retained earnings	65,580	58,485
Total stockholders' equity	$165,580	$158,485
Total liabilities and stockholders' equity	$279,525	$270,095

Required

1. Prepare a columnar report for the controller of Heartland Inc., comparing the industry averages for the ratios published by the trade association with the comparable ratios for Heartland. For Heartland, compute the ratios as of December 31, 2001, or for the year ending December 31, 2001, whichever is appropriate.

2. Briefly evaluate Heartland's ratios relative to the industry averages.

3. Do you think that the bank will approve the loan? Explain your answer.

ALTERNATE PROBLEMS

LO 5   Problem 13-1A   Effect of Transactions on Debt-To-Equity Ratio
(*Note:* Consider completing Problem 13-2A after this problem to ensure that you obtain a clear understanding of the effect of various transactions on this measure of solvency.)

The following account balances are taken from the records of Monet's Garden Inc.:

Current liabilities	$150,000
Long-term liabilities	375,000
Stockholders' equity	400,000

Required

1. Use the information provided above to compute Monet's debt-to-equity ratio (round to three decimal points).

2. Determine the effect that each of the following transactions will have on Monet's debt-to-equity ratio by recalculating the ratio and then indicating whether the ratio is increased, decreased, or not affected by the transaction. (Round to three decimal points.) Consider each transaction independently; that is, assume that it is the *only* transaction that takes place.

Transaction	Effect of Transaction on Debt-To-Equity Ratio
a. Purchased inventory on account for $20,000.	
b. Purchased inventory for cash, $15,000.	
c. Paid suppliers on account, $30,000.	
d. Received cash on account, $40,000.	
e. Paid insurance for next year, $20,000.	
f. Made sales on account, $60,000.	
g. Repaid short-term loans at bank, $25,000.	
h. Borrowed $40,000 at bank for 90 days.	
i. Declared and paid $45,000 cash dividend.	
j. Purchased $20,000 of trading securities (classified as current assets).	
k. Paid $30,000 in salaries.	
l. Accrued additional $15,000 in taxes.	

LO 5   Problem 13-2A   Effect of Transactions on Debt-To-Equity Ratio
(*Note:* Consider completing this problem after Problem 13-1A to ensure that you obtain a clear understanding of the effect of various transactions on this measure of solvency.)

The following account balances are taken from the records of Degas Inc.:

Current liabilities	$ 25,000
Long-term liabilities	125,000
Stockholders' equity	400,000

Required

1. Use the information provided above to compute Degas' debt-to-equity ratio (round to three decimal points).

2. Determine the effect that each of the following transactions will have on Degas's debt-to-equity ratio by recalculating the ratio and then indicating whether the ratio is increased, decreased, or not affected by the transaction. (Round to three decimal points.) Consider each transaction independently; that is, assume that it is the *only* transaction that takes place.

Transaction	Effect of Transaction on Debt-To-Equity Ratio
a. Purchased inventory on account for $20,000.	
b. Purchased inventory for cash, $15,000.	
c. Paid suppliers on account, $30,000.	
d. Received cash on account, $40,000.	
e. Paid insurance for next year, $20,000.	
f. Made sales on account, $60,000.	
g. Repaid short-term loans at bank, $25,000.	
h. Borrowed $40,000 at bank for 90 days.	
i. Declared and paid $45,000 cash dividend.	
j. Purchased $20,000 of trading securities (classified as current assets).	
k. Paid $30,000 in salaries.	
l. Accrued additional $15,000 in taxes.	

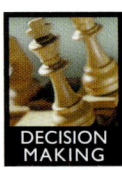

LO 6   Problem 13-3A   Goals for Sales and Return on Assets

The president of Blue Moon Corp. is reviewing with her department managers the operating results of the year just completed. Sales increased by 12% from the previous year to $750,000. Average total assets for the year were $400,000. Net income, after adding back interest expense, net of tax, was $60,000.

The president is happy with the performance over the past year but is never satisfied with the status quo. She has set two specific goals for next year: (1) a 15% growth in sales and (2) a return on assets of 20%.

To achieve the second goal, the president has stated her intention to increase the total asset base by 10% over the base for the year just completed.

Required

1. For the year just completed, compute the following ratios:

    a. Return on sales

    b. Asset turnover

    c. Return on assets

2. Compute the necessary asset turnover for next year to achieve the president's goal of a 15% increase in sales.

3. Calculate the income needed next year to achieve the goal of a 20% return on total assets. (*Note:* Assume that *income* is defined as net income plus interest, net of tax.)

4. Based on your answers to parts 2 and 3, comment on the reasonableness of the president's goals. What must the company focus on to attain these goals?

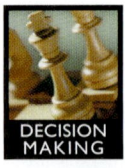

LO 6   Problem 13-4A   Goals for Sales and Income Growth

Sunset Corp. is a major regional retailer. The chief executive officer (CEO) is concerned with the slow growth both of sales and of net income and the subsequent effect on the trading price of the common stock. Selected financial data for the past three years follow.

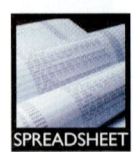

SUNSET CORP.
(IN MILLIONS)

	2001	2000	1999
1. Sales	$100.0	$96.7	$93.3
2. Net income	3.0	2.9	2.8
3. Dividends declared and paid	1.2	1.2	1.2

December 31 balances:

4. Owners' equity	$ 40.0	$38.2	$36.5
5. Debt	10.0	10.2	10.2

Selected year-end financial ratios

Net income to sales	3.0%	3.0%	3.0%
Asset turnover	2 times	2 times	2 times
6. Return on owners' equity*	7.5%	7.6%	7.7%
7. Debt to total assets	20.0%	21.1%	21.8%

*Based on year-end balances in owners' equity.

The CEO believes that the price of the stock has been adversely affected by the downward trend of the return on equity, the relatively low dividend payout ratio, and the lack of dividend increases. To improve the price of the stock, he wants to improve the return on equity and dividends.

He believes that the company should be able to meet these objectives by (1) increasing sales and net income at an annual rate of 10% a year and (2) establishing a new dividend policy that calls for a dividend payout of 60% of earnings or $2,000,000, whichever is larger.

The 10% annual sales increase will be accomplished through a product enhancement program. The president believes that the present net income to sales ratio of 3% will be unchanged by the cost of this new program and any interest paid on new debt. He expects that the company can accomplish this sales and income growth while maintaining the current relationship of total assets to sales. Any capital that is needed to maintain this relationship and that is not generated internally would be acquired through long-term debt financing. The CEO hopes that debt would not exceed 25% of total liabilities and owners' equity.

Required

1. Using the CEO's program, prepare a schedule that shows the appropriate data for the years 2002, 2003, and 2004 for the items numbered 1 through 7 on the preceding schedule.

2. Can the CEO meet all of his requirements if a 10% per-year growth in income and sales is achieved? Explain your answers.

3. What alternative actions should the CEO consider to improve the return on equity and to support increased dividend payments? (CMA adapted)

Alternate Multi-Concept Problems

LO 4, 5, 6 Problem 13-5A Basic Financial Ratios

The accounting staff of SST Enterprises has completed the financial statements for the 2001 calendar year. The statement of income for the current year and the comparative statements of financial position for 2001 and 2000 follow.

SST ENTERPRISES
STATEMENT OF INCOME
YEAR ENDED DECEMBER 31, 2001
(THOUSANDS OMITTED)

Revenue:	
Net sales	$600,000
Other	45,000
Total revenue	$645,000
Expenses:	
Cost of goods sold	$405,000
Research and development	18,000
Selling and administrative	120,000
Interest	15,000
Total expenses	$558,000
Income before income taxes	$ 87,000
Income taxes	27,000
Net income	$ 60,000

SST ENTERPRISES
COMPARATIVE STATEMENTS OF FINANCIAL POSITION
DECEMBER 31, 2001 AND 2000
(THOUSANDS OMITTED)

	2001	2000
Assets		
Current assets:		
Cash and short-term investments	$ 27,000	$ 20,000
Receivables, less allowance for doubtful accounts		
($1,100 in 2001 and $1,400 in 2000)	36,000	37,000
Inventories, at lower of FIFO cost or market	35,000	42,000
Prepaid items and other current assets	2,000	1,000
Total current assets	$100,000	$100,000
Property, plant, and equipment:		
Land	$ 9,000	$ 9,000
Buildings and equipment, less accumulated		
depreciation ($74,000 in 2001 and		
$62,000 in 2000)	191,000	186,000
Total property, plant, and equipment	$200,000	$195,000
Total assets	$300,000	$295,000
Liabilities and Stockholders' Equity		
Current liabilities:		
Short-term loans	$ 20,000	$ 15,000
Accounts payable	80,000	68,000
Salaries, wages, and other	5,000	7,000
Total current liabilities	$105,000	$ 90,000
Long-term debt	15,000	40,000
Total liabilities	$120,000	$130,000
Stockholders' equity:		
Common stock, at par	$ 50,000	$ 50,000
Paid-in capital in excess of par	25,000	25,000
Total paid-in capital	$ 75,000	$ 75,000
Retained earnings	105,000	90,000
Total stockholders' equity	$180,000	$165,000
Total liabilities and stockholders' equity	$300,000	$295,000

Required

1. Calculate the following financial ratios for 2001 for SST Enterprises:

   a. Times interest earned

   b. Return on total assets

   c. Return on common stockholders' equity

   d. Debt-equity ratio (at December 31, 2001)

   e. Current ratio (at December 31, 2001)

   f. Quick (acid-test) ratio (at December 31, 2001)

   g. Accounts receivable turnover ratio (assume that all sales are on credit)

   h. Number of days' sales in receivables

   i. Inventory turnover ratio (assume that all purchases are on credit)

   j. Number of days' sales in inventory

   k. Number of days in cash operating cycle

2. Prepare a few brief comments on the overall financial health of SST Enterprises. For each comment, indicate any information that is not provided in the problem and that you would need to evaluate fully the company's financial health.

(CMA adapted)

Problem 13-6A Projected Results to Meet Corporate Objectives

Grout Inc. is a wholly owned subsidiary of Slait Co. The philosophy of Slait's management is to allow the subsidiaries to operate as independent units. Corporate control is exercised through the establishment of minimum objectives for each subsidiary, accompanied by substantial rewards for success and penalties for failure. The time period for performance review is long enough for competent managers to display their abilities.

Each quarter the subsidiary is required to submit financial statements. The statements are accompanied by a letter from the subsidiary president explaining the results to date, a forecast for the remainder of the year, and the actions to be taken to achieve the objectives if the forecast indicates that the objectives will not be met.

Slait management, in conjunction with Grout management, had set the objectives listed below for the year ending September 30, 2002. These objectives are similar to those set in previous years.

- Sales growth of 10%
- Return on stockholders' equity of 20%
- A long-term debt-to-equity ratio of not more than 1.0
- Payment of a cash dividend of 50% of net income, with a minimum payment of at least $500,000

Grout's controller has just completed preparing the financial statements for the six months ended March 31, 2002, and the forecast for the year ending September 30, 2002. The statements are presented below.

After a cursory glance at the financial statements, Grout's president concluded that not all objectives would be met. At a staff meeting of the Grout management, the president asked the controller to review the projected results and recommend possible actions that could be taken during the remainder of the year so that Grout would be more likely to meet the objectives.

GROUT INC.
INCOME STATEMENT
(THOUSANDS OMITTED)

	Year Ended September 30, 2001	Six Months Ended March 31, 2002	Forecast for Year Ending September 30, 2002
Sales	$10,000	$6,000	$12,000
Cost of goods sold	$ 6,000	$4,000	$ 8,000
Selling expenses	1,500	900	1,800
Administrative expenses and interest	1,000	600	1,200
Income taxes	500	300	600
Total expenses and taxes	$ 9,000	$5,800	$11,600
Net income	$ 1,000	$ 200	$ 400
Dividends declared and paid	500	0	400
Income retained	$ 500	$ 200	$ 0

GROUT INC.
STATEMENT OF FINANCIAL POSITION
(THOUSANDS OMITTED)

	September 30, 2001	March 31, 2002	Forecast for September 30, 2002
Assets			
Cash	$ 400	$ 500	$ 500
Accounts receivable (net)	2,100	3,400	2,600
Inventory	7,000	8,500	8,400
Plant and equipment (net)	2,800	2,500	3,200
Total assets	$12,300	$14,900	$14,700

Liabilities and Equities

Accounts payable	$ 3,000	$ 4,000	$ 4,000
Accrued taxes	300	200	200
Long-term borrowing	4,000	5,500	5,500
Common stock	4,000	4,000	4,000
Retained earnings	1,000	1,200	1,000
Total liabilities and equities	$12,300	$14,900	$14,700

Required

1. Calculate the projected results for each of the four objectives established for Grout Inc. State which results will not meet the objectives by year-end.

2. From the data presented, identify the factors that seem to contribute to the failure of Grout Inc. to meet all of its objectives.

3. Explain the possible actions that the controller could recommend in response to the president's request. (CMA adapted)

LO 4, 5, 6   Problem 13-7A   A Comparison with Industry Averages

Midwest Inc. is a medium-sized company that has been in business for 20 years. The industry has become very competitive in the last few years, and Midwest has decided that it must grow if it is going to survive. It has approached the bank for a sizable five-year loan, and the bank has requested its most recent financial statements as part of the loan package.

The industry in which Midwest operates consists of approximately 20 companies relatively equal in size. The trade association to which all of the competitors belong publishes an annual survey of the industry, including industry averages for selected ratios for the competitors. All companies voluntarily submit their statements to the association for this purpose.

Midwest's controller is aware that the bank has access to this survey and is very concerned about how the company fared this past year compared with the rest of the industry. The ratios included in the publication, and the averages for the past year, are as follows:

Ratio	Industry Average
Current ratio	1.20
Acid-test (quick) ratio	0.50
Inventory turnover	35 times
Debt-to-equity ratio	0.50
Times interest earned	25 times
Return on sales	3%
Asset turnover	3.5 times
Return on common stockholders' equity	20%

The financial statements to be submitted to the bank in connection with the loan follow:

MIDWEST INC.
STATEMENT OF INCOME AND RETAINED EARNINGS
FOR THE YEAR ENDED DECEMBER 31, 2001
(THOUSANDS OMITTED)

Sales revenue	$420,500
Cost of goods sold	(300,000)
Gross margin	$120,500
Selling, general, and administrative expenses	(85,000)
Income before interest and taxes	$ 35,500
Interest expense	(8,600)
Income before taxes	$ 26,900
Income tax expense	(12,000)
Net income	$ 14,900
Retained earnings, January 1, 2001	12,400
	$ 27,300
Dividends paid on common stock	(11,200)
Retained earnings, December 31, 2001	$ 16,100

MIDWEST INC.
COMPARATIVE STATEMENTS OF FINANCIAL POSITION
(THOUSANDS OMITTED)

	December 31, 2001	December 31, 2000
Assets		
Current assets:		
Cash	$ 1,790	$ 2,600
Marketable securities	1,200	1,700
Accounts receivable, net of allowances	400	600
Inventories	8,700	7,400
Prepaid items	350	400
Total current assets	$ 12,440	$ 12,700
Long-term investments	$ 560	$ 400
Property, plant, and equipment:		
Land	$ 12,000	$ 12,000
Buildings and equipment, net of accumulated depreciation	87,000	82,900
Total property, plant, and equipment	$ 99,000	$ 94,900
Total assets	$112,000	$108,000
Liabilities and Stockholders' Equity		
Current liabilities:		
Short-term notes	$ 800	$ 600
Accounts payable	6,040	6,775
Salaries and wages payable	1,500	1,200
Income taxes payable	1,560	1,025
Total current liabilities	$ 9,900	$ 9,600
Long-term bonds payable	$ 36,000	$ 36,000
Stockholders' equity:		
Common stock, no par	$ 50,000	$ 50,000
Retained earnings	16,100	12,400
Total stockholders' equity	$ 66,100	$ 62,400
Total liabilities and stockholders' equity	$112,000	$108,000

Required

1. Prepare a columnar report for the controller of Midwest Inc., comparing the industry averages for the ratios published by the trade association with the comparable ratios for Midwest. For Midwest, compute the ratios as of December 31, 2001, or for the year ending December 31, 2001, whichever is appropriate.

2. Briefly evaluate Midwest's ratios relative to the industry.

3. Do you think that the bank will approve the loan? Explain your answer.

CASES

Reading and Interpreting Financial Statements

LO 2 Case 13-1 Horizontal Analysis for Uno

Refer to Uno's comparative income statements included in its annual report.

Required

1. Prepare a work sheet with the following headings:

	Increase (Decrease) From			
	1998 to 1999		1997 to 1998	
Income Statement Accounts	Dollars	Percent	Dollars	Percent

2. Complete the work sheet using each of the account titles on Uno's income statement. Round dollar amounts to the nearest one-tenth of $1 million and percentages to the nearest one-tenth of a percent.

3. What observations can you make from this horizontal analysis? What is your overall analysis of operations? Have the company's operations improved over the three-year period?

LO 2 **Case 13-2** Horizontal Analysis for Gateway

Refer to Gateway's comparative income statements included in its annual report.

Required

Refer to the requirements in Case 13-1, and respond to each of them for Gateway rather than for Uno.

LO 3 **Case 13-3** Vertical Analysis for Uno

Refer to Uno's financial statements included in its annual report.

Required

1. Using the format in Exhibit 13-6, prepare common-size comparative income statements for 1999 and 1998. Round dollar amounts to the nearest one-tenth of $1 million and percentages to the nearest one-tenth of a percent.

2. What changes do you detect in the income statement relationships from 1998 to 1999?

3. Using the format in Exhibit 13-5, prepare common-size comparative balance sheets at the end of 1999 and 1998. Round dollar amounts to the nearest one-tenth of $1 million and percentages to the nearest one-tenth of a percent.

4. What observations can you make about the relative composition of Uno's assets from the common-size statements? What observations can be made about the changes in the relative composition of liabilities and owners' equity accounts?

LO 3 **Case 13-4** Vertical Analysis for Gateway

Refer to Gateway's financial statements in its annual report.

Required

Refer to the requirements in Case 13-3 and respond to each of them for Gateway rather than for Uno.

LO 4, 5, 6 **Case 13-5** Ratio Analysis for Uno

Refer to Uno's financial statements included in its annual report.

Required

1. Compute the following ratios and other amounts for each of the two years, 1999 and 1998. Because only two years of data are given on the balance sheets, to be consistent you should use year-end balances for each year in lieu of average balances. Assume a 40% tax rate and 360 days to a year. State any other necessary assumptions in making the calculations. Round all ratios to the nearest one-tenth of a percent.

   a. Working capital

   b. Current ratio

   c. Acid-test ratio

   d. Cash flow from operations to current liabilities

   e. Number of days' sales in receivables

   f. Number of days' sales in inventory

   g. Debt-to-equity ratio

   h. Times interest earned

   i. Debt service coverage

j. Cash flow from operations to capital expenditures

k. Asset turnover

l. Return on sales

m. Return on assets

n. Return on common stockholders' equity

2. What is your overall analysis of the financial health of Uno? What do you believe are the company's strengths and weaknesses?

LO 4, 5, 6   Case 13-6   Ratio Analysis for Gateway

Refer to Gateway's financial statements included in its annual report.

Required

Refer to the requirements in Case 13-5, and respond to each of them for Gateway rather than for Uno.

Making Financial Decisions

LO 4, 5, 6   Case 13-7   Acquisition Decision

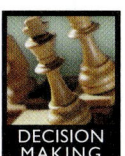

Diversified Industries is a large conglomerate and is continually in the market for new acquisitions. The company has grown rapidly over the last 10 years through buyouts of medium-sized companies. Diversified does not limit itself to companies in any one industry but looks for firms with a sound financial base and the ability to stand on their own financially.

The president of Diversified recently told a meeting of the company's officers: "I want to impress two points on all of you. First, we are not in the business of looking for bargains. Diversified has achieved success in the past by acquiring companies with the ability to be a permanent member of the corporate family. We don't want companies that may appear to be a bargain on paper but can't survive in the long run. Second, a new member of our family must be able to come in and make it on its own—the parent is not organized to be a funding agency for struggling subsidiaries."

Ron Dixon is the vice president of acquisitions for Diversified, a position he has held for five years. He is responsible for making recommendations to the board of directors on potential acquisitions. Because you are one of his assistants, he recently brought you a set of financials for a manufacturer, Heavy Duty Tractors. Dixon believes that Heavy Duty is a "can't-miss" opportunity for Diversified and asks you to confirm his hunch by performing basic financial statement analyses on the company. The most recent income statement and comparative balance sheets for the company follow:

HEAVY DUTY TRACTORS INC.
STATEMENT OF INCOME AND RETAINED EARNINGS
FOR THE YEAR ENDED DECEMBER 31, 2001
(THOUSANDS OMITTED)

Sales revenue	$875,250
Cost of goods sold	542,750
Gross margin	$332,500
Selling, general, and administrative expenses	264,360
Operating income	$ 68,140
Interest expense	45,000
Net income before taxes and extraordinary items	$ 23,140
Income tax expense	9,250
Income before extraordinary items	$ 13,890
Extraordinary gain, less taxes of $6,000	9,000
Net income	$ 22,890
Retained earnings, January 1, 2001	169,820
	$192,710
Dividends paid on common stock	10,000
Retained earnings, December 31, 2001	$182,710

HEAVY DUTY TRACTORS INC.
COMPARATIVE STATEMENTS OF FINANCIAL POSITION
(THOUSANDS OMITTED)

	December 31, 2001	December 31, 2000
Assets		
Current assets:		
Cash	$ 48,500	$ 24,980
Marketable securities	3,750	–0–
Accounts receivable, net of allowances	128,420	84,120
Inventories	135,850	96,780
Prepaid items	7,600	9,300
Total current assets	$324,120	$215,180
Long-term investments	$ 55,890	$ 55,890
Property, plant, and equipment:		
Land	$ 45,000	$ 45,000
Buildings and equipment, less accumulated depreciation of $385,000 in 2001 and $325,000 in 2000	545,000	605,000
Total property, plant, and equipment	$590,000	$650,000
Total assets	$970,010	$921,070
Liabilities and Stockholders' Equity		
Current liabilities:		
Short-term notes	$ 80,000	$ 60,000
Accounts payable	65,350	48,760
Salaries and wages payable	14,360	13,840
Income taxes payable	2,590	3,650
Total current liabilities	$162,300	$126,250
Long-term bonds payable, due 2008	$275,000	$275,000
Stockholders' equity:		
Common stock, no par	$350,000	$350,000
Retained earnings	182,710	169,820
Total stockholders' equity	$532,710	$519,820
Total liabilities and stockholders' equity	$970,010	$921,070

Required

1. How liquid is Heavy Duty Tractors? Support your answer with any ratios that you believe are necessary to justify your conclusion. Also, indicate any other information that you would want to have in making a final determination on its liquidity.

2. In light of the president's comments, should you be concerned about the solvency of Heavy Duty Tractors? Support your answer with the necessary ratios. How does the maturity date of the outstanding debt affect your answer?

3. Has Heavy Duty demonstrated the ability to be a profitable member of the Diversified family? Support your answer with the necessary ratios.

4. What will you tell your boss? Should he recommend to the board of directors that Diversified put in a bid for Heavy Duty Tractors?

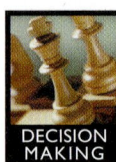

LO 3 Case 13-8 Pricing Decision

BPO's management believes that the company has been successful at increasing sales because it has not increased the selling price of the products, even though its competition has increased prices and costs have increased. Price and cost relationships in Year 1 were established because they represented industry averages. The following income statements are available for BPO's first three years of operation:

	Year 3	Year 2	Year 1
Sales	$125,000	$110,000	$100,000
Cost of goods sold	62,000	49,000	40,000
Gross profit	$ 63,000	$ 61,000	$ 60,000
Operating expenses	53,000	49,000	45,000
Net income	$ 10,000	$ 12,000	$ 15,000

Required

1. Using the format in Exhibit 13-6, prepare common-size comparative income statements for the three years.

2. Explain why net income has decreased while sales have increased.

3. Prepare an income statement for Year 4. Sales volume in units is expected to increase by 10%, and costs are expected to increase by 8%.

4. Do you think BPO should raise its prices or maintain the same selling prices? Explain your answer.

Accounting and Ethics: What Would You Do?

LO 4, 5 Case 13-9 Provisions in a Loan Agreement

As controller of Midwest Construction Company, you are reviewing with your assistant, Dave Jackson, the financial statements for the year just ended. During the review, Jackson reminds you of an existing loan agreement with Southern National Bank. Midwest has agreed to the following conditions:

- The current ratio will be maintained at a minimum level of 1.5 to 1.0 at all times.

- The debt-to-equity ratio will not exceed .5 to 1.0 at any time.

Jackson has drawn up the following preliminary, condensed balance sheet for the year just ended:

MIDWEST CONSTRUCTION COMPANY
BALANCE SHEET
DECEMBER 31
(IN MILLIONS OF DOLLARS)

Current assets	$16	Current liabilities	$10
Long-term assets	64	Long-term debt	15
		Stockholders' equity	55
Total	$80	Total	$80

Jackson wants to discuss two items with you. First, long-term debt currently includes a $5 million note payable, to Eastern State Bank, that is due in six months. The plan is to go to Eastern before the note is due and ask it to extend the maturity date of the note for five years. Jackson doesn't believe that Midwest needs to include the $5 million in current liabilities because the plan is to roll over the note.

Second, in December of this year, Midwest received a $2 million deposit from the state for a major road project. The contract calls for the work to be performed over the next 18 months. Jackson recorded the $2 million as revenue this year because the contract is with the state; there shouldn't be any question about being able to collect.

Required

1. Based on the balance sheet Jackson prepared, is Midwest in compliance with its loan agreement with Southern? Support your answer with any necessary computations.

2. What would you do with the two items in question? Do you see anything wrong with the way Jackson has handled each of them? Explain your answer.

3. Prepare a revised balance sheet based on your answer to part **2.** Also, compute a revised current ratio and debt-to-equity ratio. Based on the revised ratios, is Midwest in compliance with its loan agreement?

LO 4 Case 13-10 Inventory Turnover

Garden Fresh Inc. is a wholesaler of fresh fruits and vegetables. Each year, it submits a set of financial ratios to a trade association. Even though the association doesn't publish the individual ratios for each company, the president of Garden Fresh thinks it is important for public relations that her company look as good as possible. Due to the nature of the fresh fruits and vegetables business, one of the major ratios tracked by the association is inventory turnover. Garden Fresh's inventory stated at FIFO cost was as follows:

	Year Ending December 31	
	2001	**2000**
Fruits	$10,000	$ 9,000
Vegetables	30,000	33,000
Totals	$40,000	$42,000

Sales revenue for the year ending December 31, 2001, is $3,690,000. The company's gross profit ratio is normally 40%.

Based on these data, the president thinks the company should report an inventory turnover ratio of 90 times per year.

Required

1. Explain, using the necessary calculations, how the president came up with an inventory turnover ratio of 90 times.

2. Do you think the company should report a turnover ratio of 90 times? If not, explain why you disagree, and explain, with calculations, what you think the ratio should be.

3. Assume you are the controller for Garden Fresh. What will you tell the president?

INTERNET RESEARCH CASE

www.wrigley.com

Case 13-11   Wrigley

Wrigley is one of the most recognizable chewing gums in the United States and most of its sales are from its international segments. In total, it is the number one maker of chewing gum in the world. After several years of transition, Wrigley believes the new millenium will be an era of growth.

By reading Wrigley's financial statement and notes, and using them to calculate selected financial ratios, as in the review problem, you can develop a current picture of Wrigley's performance that can help you interpret how Wrigley proposes to reach their goal of unparallelled growth.

1. Based on the financial information for the last two years available, compute the ratios required in the review problem on page 644.

2. Comment on Writley's liquidity. Has it improved or declined over the two-year period?

3. Comment on Wrigley's solvency and Wrigley's capital structure.

4. Comment on Wrigley's profitability.

5. By looking at various sources such as the financial news and Wrigley's Financial Data pages, what management plans and initiatives, such as announced increases in building of plants or increases in hiring, are likely to change your analysis of Wrigley's performance the most in future years?

SOLUTIONS TO KEY TERMS QUIZ

Quiz 1:

__14__ Horizontal analysis (p. 619)
__11__ Vertical analysis (p. 619)
__10__ Gross profit ratio (p. 624)
__12__ Profit margin ratio (p. 624)
__13__ Liquidity (p. 626)
__2__ Working capital (p. 626)
__3__ Current ratio (p. 626)
__1__ Acid-test or quick ratio (p. 627)
__5__ Cash flow from operations to current liabilities ratio (p. 628)

__6__ Accounts receivable turnover ratio (p. 628)
__4__ Number of days' sales in receivables (p. 629)
__9__ Inventory turnover ratio (p. 630)
__7__ Number of days' sales in inventory (p. 630)
__8__ Cash to cash operating cycle (p. 631)

Quiz 2:

__3__ Solvency (p. 631)	__10__ Asset turnover ratio (p. 635)
__7__ Debt-to-equity ratio (p. 631)	__1__ Return on common stockholders'
__13__ Times interest earned ratio (p. 632)	equity ratio (p. 636)
__14__ Debt service coverage ratio (p. 632)	__12__ Leverage (p. 637)
__8__ Cash flow from operations to capital	__5__ Earnings per share (p. 637)
expenditures ratio (p. 633)	__2__ Price/earnings (P/E) ratio (p. 638)
__15__ Profitability (p. 634)	__6__ Dividend payout ratio (p. 639)
__9__ Return on assets ratio (p. 634)	__11__ Dividend yield ratio (p. 639)
__4__ Return on sales ratio (p. 635)	

Part IV

INTEGRATIVE PROBLEM

Presented here are comparative balance sheets and a statement of income and retained earnings for Gallagher, Inc., which operates a national chain of sporting goods stores:

GALLAGHER, INC.
COMPARATIVE BALANCE SHEETS
DECEMBER 31, 2001 AND 2000
(ALL AMOUNTS IN THOUSANDS OF DOLLARS)

	December 31	
	2001	2000
Cash	$ 840	$ 2,700
Accounts receivable	12,500	9,000
Inventory	8,000	5,500
Prepaid insurance	100	400
Total current assets	$21,440	$17,600
Land	$ 4,000	$ 4,000
Buildings and equipment	12,000	9,000
Accumulated depreciation	(3,700)	(3,000)
Total long-term assets	$12,300	$10,000
Total assets	$33,740	$27,600
Accounts payable	$ 7,300	$ 5,000
Taxes payable	4,600	4,200
Notes payable	2,400	1,600
Current portion of bonds	200	200
Total current liabilities	$14,500	$11,000
Bonds payable	1,400	1,600
Total liabilities	$15,900	$12,600
Preferred stock, $5 par	$ 1,000	$ 1,000
Common stock, $1 par	2,000	2,000
Retained earnings	14,840	12,000
Total stockholders' equity	$17,840	$15,000
Total liabilities and stockholders' equity	$33,740	$27,600

GALLAGHER, INC.
STATEMENT OF INCOME AND RETAINED EARNINGS
FOR THE YEAR ENDED DECEMBER 31, 2001
(ALL AMOUNTS IN THOUSANDS OF DOLLARS)

Net sales	$48,000
Cost of goods sold	36,000
Gross profit	$12,000
Selling, general and administrative expense	6,000
Operating income	$ 6,000
Interest expense	280
Income before tax	$ 5,720
Income tax expense	2,280
Net income	$ 3,440
Preferred dividends	100
Income available to common	$ 3,340
Common dividends	500
To retained earnings	$ 2,840
Retained earnings, 1/1	12,000
Retained earnings, 12/31	$14,840

Required

1. Prepare a statement of cash flows for Gallagher, Inc. for the year ended December 31, 2001, using the **indirect** method in the Operating Activities section of the statement.

2. Gallagher's management is concerned with both its short-term liquidity and its solvency over the long run. To help it evaluate these, compute the following ratios, rounding all answers to the nearest one-tenth of a percent:

   a. Current ratio

   b. Acid-test ratio

   c. Cash flow from operations to current liabilities ratio

   d. Accounts receivable turnover ratio

   e. Number of days' sales in receivables

   f. Inventory turnover ratio

   g. Number of days' sales in inventory

   h. Debt-to-equity ratio

   i. Debt service coverage ratio

   j. Cash flow from operations to capital expenditures ratio

3. Comment on Gallagher's liquidity and its solvency. What additional information do you need to fully evaluate the company?

VIDEO CASE IV   TERRA LYCOS, INC.

Founded as Lycos in 1995, Terra Lycos (www.terralycos.com) is a rapidly growing Internet service company that in its short history has already reinvented itself more than once. Lycos began as a search engine that guided users to individual Web sites with patented search technology. With the addition of ever-more-powerful navigation technology and tools, the purchase of several other Internet service companies, and, most recently, a merger with Terra Networks S.A. to create Terra Lycos, the firm has long since become a destination in its own right. It also offers an attractive array of free user services such as e-mail, chat rooms, news, shopping, and personal home pages. The youngest company in NASDAQ's history to go public (as Lycos), Terra Lycos now considers its comprehensive network of sites not as a portal but as a "hub," the place at the center of users' experience on the Web.

The Terra Lycos philosophy is that communities are at the core of the hub, personalizing the Web and allowing people with common interests to act as participants rather than observers in a global medium. Its goal? Nothing short of being "the most visited on-line destination in the world."

Users have responded to Terra Lycos's growing network of services with enthusiasm. Visitors to the new hub number over 91 million a month, easily making it one of the most visited sites on the Internet. The Lycos Network includes Tripod, Angelfire, WhoWhere, MailCity, Hotbot, Hot Wired, Wired News, Webmonkey, Quote.com, and others. These top-rated destinations are integrated to allow each user in the Terra Lycos community to locate, retrieve, and manage information tailored to his or her unique interests.

Because Terra Lycos provides its services free to users, it must get most of its revenues from the advertising it carries on its sites and from electronic commerce agreements. Many of Lycos's acquisitions were strategic—the company gained access not only to powerful new technology, highly talented employees, and depth and breadth on the Web, but also to new members. Members join communities, and communities attract advertisers. Tripod and Angelfire in particular have generated significant advertising revenues. Through its addition of the Lycoshop service, Terra Lycos also offers business-to-business e-commerce. The company can build a store for its corporate clients or can link to an existing electronic store front. In addition, the company can add a firm's products to its existing database. All these shopping alternatives draw millions of buyers for its clients every month.

Terra Lycos is growing internationally, with offices in Brazil, Germany, Italy, France, Japan, Korea, Mexico, the United Kingdom, Spain, and the Netherlands and localized services in countries around the world. It has the largest global footprint of any Internet company, operating in 40 countries with 122 sites in 19 different languages.

With its impressive internal growth and savvy acquisitions, Terra Lycos has earned pro forma revenues for 2000, its first year as a combined entity (Terra and Lycos), of $526 million, up 87 percent over the previous year (assuming the companies had been combined for all previous periods). Pro forma losses before interest, taxes, depreciation, amortization, and one-time charges were $348 million for the year. The number of subscribers increased 336 percent to 6.1 million.

Questions

1. What steps has Terra Lycos (or Lycos) taken to reach its operational goals of globalization, convergence, and profitability? What additional strategies do you think it might follow in the future?

2. What do you think are Terra Lycos's financial goals? How can it be sure of meeting them?

3. From watching the video, researching the "About Terra Lycos" page on the company's Web site, and checking the current financial news, determine what you think are some of Terra Lycos's strategic, operational, and competitive goals. How are they related to each other, and to the firm's financial goals?

"From Concept to Practice" assignments, printed in the margins throughout the book, are based on annual reports from Pizzeria Uno, Gateway, and other companies profiled in the opening vignette of each chapter. This Index is a convenient list of these financial statement assignments, which can be used in conjunction with the chapter or as cumulative problems at key points in the course.

CHAPTER 13

13.1 Reading Gateway's Annual Report p. 622
Where does Gateway's annual report provide a financial summary? How many years does it include? In terms of a trend over time, which item on the summary do you think is the most significant?

13.2 Reading Wrigley's Annual Report p. 622
Refer to Wrigley's Financial Highlights in Exhibit 13-3. Compute the company's gross profit ratio for each of the 11 years. Is there a noticeable upward or downward trend in the ratio over this time period?

13.3 Reading Uno's Annual Report p. 639
Refer to Uno's statement of cash flows. Why is it not possible to compute Uno's dividend payout ratio for 1999? Why do you think the company has adopted the policy it has concerning the payment of dividends?

GLOSSARY

Accelerated depreciation   A higher amount of depreciation is recorded in the early years and a lower amount in the later years. (p. 355)

Account   Record used to accumulate amounts for each individual asset, liability, revenue, expense, and component of owners' equity. (p. 101)

Accounting   The process of identifying, measuring, and communicating economic information to various users. (p. 6)

Accounting controls   Procedures concerned with safeguarding the assets or the reliability of the financial statements. (p. 211)

Accounting cycle   A series of steps performed each period and culminating with the preparation of a set of financial statements. (p. 160)

Accounting system   Methods and records used to accurately report an entity's transactions and to maintain accountability for its assets and liabilities. (p. 210)

Accounts payable   Amounts owed for inventory, goods, or services acquired in the normal course of business. (p. 400)

Accounts receivable turnover ratio   A measure of the number of times accounts receivable are collected in a period. (p. 628)

Accrual   Cash has not yet been paid or received, but expense has been incurred or revenue earned. (p. 155)

Accrual basis   A system of accounting in which revenues are recognized when earned and expenses when incurred. (p. 143)

Accrued asset   An asset resulting from the recognition of a revenue before the receipt of cash. (p. 155)

Accrued liability   A liability resulting from the recognition of an expense before the payment of cash. (p. 155, 402)

Accrued pension cost   The difference between the amount of pension recorded as an expense and the amount of the funding payment. (p. 480)

Accumulated benefit obligation (ABO)   A measure of the amount owed to employees for pensions if they retire at their existing salary levels. (p. 480)

Acid-test or quick ratio   A stricter test of liquidity than the current ratio; excludes inventory and prepayments from the numerator. (p. 627)

Acquisition cost   The amount that includes all of the cost normally necessary to acquire an asset and prepare it for its intended use. (p. 351)

Additional paid-in capital   The amount received for the issuance of stock in excess of the par value of the stock. (p. 505)

Adjusting entries   Journal entries made at the end of a period by a company using the accrual basis of accounting. (p. 148)

Administrative controls   Procedures concerned with efficient operation of the business and adherence to managerial policies. (p. 211)

Aging schedule   A form used to categorize the various individual accounts receivable according to the length of time each has been outstanding. (p. 317)

Allowance method   A method of estimating bad debts on the basis of either the net credit sales of the period or the accounts receivable at the end of the period. (p. 314)

American Accounting Association   The professional organization for accounting educators. (p. 20)

American Institute of Certified Public Accountants (AICPA)   The professional organization for certified public accountants. (p. 16)

Annuity   A series of payments of equal amounts. (p. 415)

Asset   A future economic benefit. (p. GS6)

Asset turnover ratio   The relationship between net sales and average total assets. (p. 635)

Audit committee   Board of directors subset that acts as a direct contact between stockholders and the independent accounting firm. (p. 210)

Auditing   The process of examining the financial statements and the underlying records of a company in order to render an opinion as to whether the statements are fairly represented. (p. 18)

Auditors' report   The opinion rendered by a public accounting firm concerning the fairness of the presentation of the financial statements. (p. 18)

Authorized shares   The maximum number of shares a corporation may issue as indicated in the corporate charter. (p. 503)

Available-for-sale securities   Stocks and bonds that are not classified as either held-to-maturity or trading securities. (p. 305)

Balance sheet   The financial statement that summarizes the assets, liabilities, and owners' equity at a specific point in time. (p. 9)

Bank reconciliation   A form used by the accountant to reconcile the balance shown on the bank statement for a particular account with the balance shown in the accounting records. (p. 298)

Bank statement   A detailed list, provided by the bank, of all the activity for a particular account during the month. (p. 297)

Blind receiving report   Form used by the receiving department to account for the quantity and condition of merchandise received from a supplier. (p. 222)

Board of directors   Group composed of key officers of a corporation and outside members responsible for general oversight of the affairs of the entity. (p. 210)

Bond A certificate that represents a corporation's promise to repay a certain amount of money and interest in the future. (p. GS4)

Bond issue price The present value of the annuity of interest payments plus the present value of the principal. (p. 455)

Book value The original cost of an asset minus the amount of accumulated depreciation. (p. 354)

Book value per share Total stockholders equity divided by the number of shares of common stock outstanding. (p. 519)

Business All the activities necessary to provide the members of an economic system with goods and services. (p. GS2)

Business entity Organization operated to earn a profit. (p. GS3)

Callable bonds Bonds that may be redeemed or retired before their specified due date. (p. 455)

Callable feature Allows the firm to eliminate a class of stock by paying the stockholders a specified amount. (p. 507)

Capital expenditure A cost that improves the asset and is added to the asset account. (p. 359)

Capital lease A lease that is recorded as an asset by the lessee. (p. 466)

Capital stock A category on the balance sheet to indicate the owners' contributions to a corporation. (p. GS5)

Capitalization of interest Interest on constructed assets is added to the asset account. (p. 352)

Carrying value The face value of a bond plus the amount of unamortized premium or minus the amount of unamortized discount. (p. 460)

Cash basis A system of accounting in which revenues are recognized when cash is received and expenses when cash is paid. (p. 143)

Cash equivalent An investment that is readily convertible to a known amount of cash and a maturity to the investor of three months or less. (p. 294, 555)

Cash flow from operations to capital expenditures ratio A measure of the ability of a company to finance long-term asset acquisitions with cash from operations. (p. 633)

Cash flow from operations to current liabilities ratio A measure of the ability to pay current debts from operating cash flows. (p. 628)

Cash to cash operating cycle The length of time from the purchase of inventory to the collection of any receivable from the sale. (p. 631)

Change in estimate A change in the life of the asset or in its residual value. (p. 358)

Chart of accounts A numerical list of all the accounts used by a company. (p. 101)

Closing entries Journal entries made at the end of the period to return the balance in all nominal accounts to zero and transfer the net income or loss and the dividends to Retained Earnings. (p. 162)

Comparability For accounting information, the quality that allows a user to analyze two or more companies and look for similarities and differences. (p. 49)

Compensated absences Employee absences for which the employee will be paid. (p. 430)

Compound interest Interest calculated on the principal plus previous amounts of interest. (p. 411)

Comprehensive income The total change in net assets from all sources except investment or withdrawals by the owners. (p. 518)

Conservatism The practice of using the least optimistic estimate when two estimates of amounts are about equally likely. (p. 51)

Consistency For accounting information, the quality that allows a user to compare two or more accounting periods for a single company. (p. 50)

Contingent assets An existing condition for which the outcome is not known but by which the company stands to gain. (p. 409)

Contingent liability An existing condition for which the outcome is not known but depends on some future event. (p. 404)

Contra account An account with a balance that is opposite that of a related account. (p. 150)

Control account The general ledger account that is supported by a subsidiary ledger. (p. 312)

Controller The chief accounting officer for a company. (p. 16)

Convertible feature Allows preferred stock to be exchanged for common stock. (p. 507)

Corporation A form of entity organized under the laws of a particular state; ownership evidenced by shares of stock. (p. GS4)

Cost of goods available for sale Beginning inventory plus cost of goods purchased. (p. 201)

Cost of goods sold Cost of goods available for sale minus ending inventory. (p. 202)

Cost principle Assets recorded at the cost to acquire them. (p. 14)

Credit An entry on the right side of an account. (p. 103)

Credit card draft A multiple-copy document used by a company that accepts a credit card for a sale. (p. 322)

Credit memoranda Additions on a bank statement for such items as interest paid on the account and notes collected by the bank for the customer. (p. 298)

Creditor Someone to whom a company or person has a debt. (p. GS6)

Cumulative feature The right to dividends in arrears before the current-year dividend is distributed. (p. 507)

Current asset An asset that is expected to be realized in cash or sold or consumed during the operating cycle or within one year if the cycle is shorter than one year. (p. 54)

Current liability An obligation that will be satisfied within the next operating cycle or within one year if the cycle is shorter than one year. (p. 57, 398)

Current maturities of long-term debt The portion of a long-term liability that will be paid within one year. (p. 402)

Current ratio Current assets divided by current liabilities. (p. 58, 626)

Current value The amount of cash, or its equivalent, that could be received by selling an asset currently. (p. 141)

Debenture bonds Bonds that are not backed by specific collateral. (p. 454)

Debit An entry on the left side of an account. (p. 103)

Debit memoranda Deductions on a bank statement for such items as NSF checks and various service charges. (p. 299)

Debt securities Bonds issued by corporations and governmental bodies as a form of borrowing. (p. 303)

Debt service coverage ratio A statement of cash flow measure of the ability of a company to meet its interest and principal payments. (p. 632)

Debt-to-equity ratio The ratio of total liabilities to total stockholders' equity. (p. 631)

Deferral Cash has either been paid or received, but expense or revenue has not yet been recognized. (p. 155)

Deferred expense An asset resulting from the payment of cash before the incurrence of expense. (p. 155)

Deferred revenue A liability resulting from the receipt of cash before the recognition of revenue. (p. 155)

Deferred tax The account used to reconcile the difference between the amount recorded as income tax expense and the amount that is payable as income tax. (p. 476)

Deposit in transit A deposit recorded on the books but not yet reflected on the bank statement. (p. 298)

Depreciation The process of allocating the cost of a long-term tangible asset over its useful life. (p. 49, 353)

Direct method For preparing the Operating Activities section of the statement of cash flows, the approach in which cash receipts and cash payments are reported. (p. 560)

Direct write-off method The recognition of bad debts expense at the point an account is written off as uncollectible. (p. 313)

Discount The excess of the face value of bonds over the issue price. (p. 457)

Discount on notes payable A contra liability that represents interest deducted from a loan in advance. (p. 401)

Discounted note An alternative name for a non-interest-bearing promissory note. (p. 321)

Discounting The process of selling a promissory note. (p. 323)

Dividend payout ratio The annual dividend amount divided by the annual net income. (p. 511, 639)

Dividend yield ratio The relationship between dividends and the market price of a company's stock. (p. 639)

Dividends A distribution of the net income of a business to its owners. (p. 11)

Double declining-balance method Depreciation is recorded at twice the straight-line rate, but the balance is reduced each period. (p. 355)

Double-entry system A system of accounting in which every transaction is recorded with equal debits and credits and the accounting equation is kept in balance. (p. 106)

Earnings per share A company's bottom line stated on a per-share basis. (p. 637)

Economic entity concept The assumption that a single, identifiable unit must be accounted for in all situations. (p. GS4)

Effective interest method of amortization The process of transferring a portion of the premium or discount to interest expense; this method results in a constant effective interest rate. (p. 459)

Equity securities Securities issued by corporations as a form of ownership in the business. (p. 302)

Estimated liability A contingent liability that is accrued and reflected on the balance sheet. (p. 406)

Event A happening of consequence to an entity. (p. 94)

Expenses Outflows of assets or incurrences of liabilities resulting from delivering goods, rendering services, or carrying out other activities. (p. GS7, 147)

External event An event involving interaction between an entity and its environment. (p. 94)

Face rate of interest The rate of interest on the bond certificate. (p. 455)

Face value The principal amount of the bond as stated on the bond certificate. (p. 452)

FIFO method An inventory costing method that assigns the most recent costs to ending inventory. (p. 250)

Financial Accounting Standards Board (FASB) The group in the private sector with authority to set accounting standards. (p. 16)

Financial accounting The branch of accounting concerned with the preparation of financial statements for outsider use. (p. 7)

Financing activities Activities concerned with the raising and repayment of funds in the form of debt and equity. (p. 558)

Finished goods A manufacturer's inventory that is complete and ready for sale. (p. 245)

FOB destination point Terms that require the seller to pay for the cost of shipping the merchandise to the buyer. (p. 206)

FOB shipping point Terms that require the buyer to pay for the shipping costs. (p. 206)

Foreign Corrupt Practices Act Legislation intended to increase the accountability of management for accurate records and reliable financial statements. (p. 210)

Funding payment A payment made by the employer to the pension fund or its trustee. (p. 479)

Future value of a single amount Amount accumulated at a future time from a single payment or investment. (p. 412)

Future value of an annuity Amount accumulated in the future when a series of payments is invested and accrues interest. (p. 416)

Gain on sale of asset The excess of the selling price over the asset's book value. (p. 362)

Gain or loss on redemption The difference between the carrying value and the redemption price at the time bonds are redeemed. (p. 463)

General journal The journal used in place of a specialized journal. (p. 109)

General ledger A book, file, hard drive, or other device containing all the accounts. (p. 103)

Generally accepted accounting principles (GAAP) The various methods, rules, practices, and other procedures that have evolved over time in response to the need to regulate the preparation of financial statements. (p. 15)

Going concern The assumption that an entity is not in the process of liquidation and that it will continue indefinitely. (p. 14)

Goodwill The excess of the purchase price of a business over the total market value of identifiable assets. (p. 365)

Gross profit Sales less cost of goods sold. (p. 60)

Gross profit method A technique used to establish an estimate of the cost of inventory stolen, destroyed, or otherwise damaged or of the amount of inventory on hand at an interim date. (p. 263)

Gross profit ratio Gross profit to net sales. (p. 62, 624)

Gross wages The amount of wages before deductions. (p. 427)

Held-to-maturity securities Investments in bonds of other companies in which the investor has the positive intent and the ability to hold the securities to maturity. (p. 365)

Historical cost The amount paid for an asset and used as a basis for recognizing it on the balance sheet and carrying it on later balance sheets. (p. 141)

Horizontal analysis A comparison of financial statement items over a period of time. (p. 619)

Income statement A statement that summarizes revenues and expenses. (p. 9)

Indirect method For preparing the Operating Activities section of the statement of cash flows, the approach in which net income is reconciled to net cash flow from operations. (p. 560)

Intangible assets Assets with no physical properties. (p. 364)

Interest The difference between the principal amount of the note and its maturity value. (p. 319)

Interest-bearing note A promissory note in which the interest rate is explicitly stated. (p. 319)

Interim statements Financial statements prepared monthly, quarterly, or at other intervals less than a year in duration. (p. 163)

Internal audit staff Department responsible for monitoring and evaluating the internal control system. (p. 209)

Internal auditing The department responsible in a company for the review and appraisal of its accounting and administrative controls. (p. 17)

Internal control system Policies and procedures necessary to ensure the safeguarding of an entity's assets, the reliability of its accounting records, and the accomplishment of overall company objectives. (p. 208)

Internal event An event occurring entirely within an entity. (p. 94)

International Accounting Standards Committee (IASC) The organization formed to develop worldwide accounting standards. (p. 16)

Inventory profit The portion of the gross profit that results from holding inventory during a period of rising prices. (p. 255)

Inventory turnover ratio A measure of the number of times inventory is sold during a period. (p. 265, 630)

Investing activities Activities concerned with the acquisition and disposal of long-term assets. (p. 557)

Invoice Form sent by the seller to the buyer as evidence of a sale. (p. 222)

Invoice approval form Form the accounting department uses before making payment to document the accuracy of all the information about a purchase. (p. 222)

Issued shares The number of shares sold or distributed to stockholders. (p. 503)

Journal A chronological record of transactions, also known as the book of original entry. (p. 109)

Journalizing The act of recording journal entries. (p. 109)

Land improvements Costs that are related to land but that have a limited life. (p. 353)

Leverage The use of borrowed funds and amounts contributed by preferred stockholders to earn an overall return higher than the cost of these funds. (p. 637)

Liability An obligation of a business. (p. GS5)

LIFO conformity rule The IRS requirement that if LIFO is used on the tax return, it must also be used in reporting income to stockholders. (p. 254)

LIFO liquidation   The result of selling more units than are purchased during the period, which can have negative tax consequences if a company is using LIFO. (p. 253)

LIFO method   An inventory method that assigns the most recent costs to cost of goods sold. (p. 251)

LIFO reserve   The excess of the value of a company's inventory stated at FIFO over the value stated at LIFO. (p. 254)

Liquidity   The nearness to cash of the assets and liabilities. (p. 58, 626)

Long-term liability   An obligation that will be settled within one year or the current operating cycle. (p. 452)

Loss on sale of asset   The amount by which selling price is less than book value. (p. 362)

Lower-of-cost-or-market (LCM) rule   A conservative inventory valuation approach that is an attempt to anticipate declines in the value of inventory before its actual sale. (p. 260)

Maker   The party that agrees to repay the money for a promissory note at some future date. (p. 319)

Management accounting   The branch of accounting concerned with providing management with information to facilitate planning and control. (p. 6)

Market rate of interest   The rate that investors could obtain by investing in other bonds that are similar to the issuing firm's bonds. (p. 455)

Market value per share   The selling price of the stock as indicated by the most recent transactions. (p. 521)

Matching principle   The association of revenue of a period with all of the costs necessary to generate that revenue. (p. 146)

Materiality   The magnitude of an accounting information omission or misstatement that will affect the judgment of someone relying on the information. (p. 51)

Maturity date   The date that the promissory note is due. (p. 319)

Maturity value   The amount of cash the maker is to pay the payee on the maturity date of the note. (p. 319)

Merchandise inventory   The account wholesalers and retailers use to report inventory held for resale. (p. 244)

Monetary unit   The yardstick used to measure amounts in financial statements; the dollar in the United States. (p. 14)

Moving average   The name given to an average cost method when it is used with a perpetual inventory system. (p. 272)

Multiple-step income statement   An income statement that shows classifications of revenues and expenses as well as important subtotals. (p. 60)

Natural resources   Assets that are consumed during their use. (p. 362)

Net pay   The amount of wages after deductions. (p. 427)

Net sales   Sales revenue less sales returns and allowances and sales discounts. (p. 197)

Nominal accounts   The name given to revenue, expense, and dividend accounts because they are temporary and are closed at the end of the period. (p. 162)

Nonbusiness entity   Organization operated for some purpose other than to earn a profit. (p. GS5)

Non-interest-bearing note   A promissory note in which interest is not explicitly stated but is implicit in the agreement. (p. 319)

Note payable   A liability resulting from the signing of a promissory note. (p. 319, 400)

Note receivable   An asset resulting from the acceptance of a promissory note from another company. (p. 319, 424)

Number of days' sales in inventory   A measure of how long it takes to sell inventory. (p. 265, 630)

Number of days' sales in receivables   A measure of the average age of accounts receivable. (p. 629)

Operating activities   Activities concerned with the acquisition and sale of products and services. (p. 556)

Operating cycle   The period of time between the purchase of inventory and the collection of any receivable from the sale of the inventory. (p. 53)

Operating lease   A lease that does not meet any of the four criteria and is not recorded as an asset by the lessee. (p. 466)

Outstanding check   A check written by a company but not yet presented to the bank for payment. (p. 298)

Outstanding shares   The number of shares issued less the number of shares held as treasury stock. (p. 503)

Owners' equity   The owners' claim on the assets of an entity. (p. 9)

Par value   An arbitrary amount that represents the legal capital of the firm. (p. 504)

Participating feature   Allows preferred stockholders to share on a percentage basis in the distribution of an abnormally large dividend. (p. 507)

Partnership   A business owned by two or more individuals; organization from often used by accounting firms and law firms. (p. GS4)

Payee   The party that will receive the money from a promissory note at some future date. (p. 319)

Pension   An obligation to pay employees for service rendered while employed. (p. 479)

Periodic system   System in which the Inventory account is updated only at the end of the period. (p. 202)

Permanent difference   A difference that affects the tax records but not the accounting records, or vice versa. (p. 477)

Perpetual system   System in which the inventory account is increased at the time of each purchase and decreased at the time of each sale. (p. 202)

Petty cash fund   Money kept on hand for making minor disbursements in coin and currency rather than by writing checks. (p. 301)

Posting   The process of transferring amounts from a journal to the ledger accounts. (p. 109)

Premium   The excess of the issue price over the face value of the bonds. (p. 457)

Present value of a single amount   Amount at a present time that is equivalent to a payment or investment at a future time. (p. 414)

Present value of an annuity   The amount at a present time that is equivalent to a series of payments and interest in the future. (p. 416)

Price/earnings (P/E) ratio   The relationship between a company's performance according to the income statement and its performance in the stock market. (p. 638)

Principal   The amount of cash received, or the fair value of the products or services received, by the maker when a promissory note is issued. (p. 319)

Profit margin   Net income divided by sales. (p. 62)

Profit margin ratio   The amount of income for each dollar of sales. (p. 624)

Profitability   How well management is using company resources to earn a return on the funds invested by various groups. (p. 634)

Projected benefit obligation (PBO)   A measure of the amount owed to employees for pensions if estimates of future salary increases are considered. (p. 480)

Promissory note   A written promise to repay a definite sum of money on demand or at a fixed or determinable date in the future. (p. 319)

Purchase Discounts   Contra-purchases account used to record reductions in purchase price for early payment to a supplier. (p. 206)

Purchase order   Form sent by the purchasing department to the supplier. (p. 219)

Purchase requisition form   Form a department uses to initiate a request to order merchandise. (p. 219)

Purchase Returns and Allowances   Contra-purchases account used in a periodic inventory system when a refund is received from a supplier or a reduction given in the balance owed to a supplier. (p. 205)

Purchases   Account used in a periodic inventory system to record acquisitions of merchandise. (p. 204)

Quantity discount   Reduction in selling price for buying a large number of units of a product. (p. 199)

Raw materials   The inventory of a manufacturer before the addition of any direct labor or manufacturing overhead. (p. 244)

Real accounts   The name given to balance sheet accounts because they are permanent and are not closed at the end of the period. (p. 162)

Recognition   The process of recording an item in the financial statements as an asset, liability, revenue, expense, or the like. (p. 140)

Relevance   The capacity of information to make a difference in a decision. (p. 48)

Reliability   The quality that makes accounting information dependable in representing the events that it purports to represent. (p. 49)

Replacement cost   The current cost of a unit of inventory. (p. 255)

Report of management   Written statement in the annual report indicating the responsibility of management for the financial statements. (p. 209)

Research and development costs   Costs incurred in the discovery of new knowledge. (p. 366)

Retail inventory method   A technique used by retailers to convert the retail value of inventory to a cost basis. (p. 265)

Retained earnings   The part of owners' equity that represents the income earned less dividends paid over the life of an entity. (p. 9, 506)

Retirement of stock   When the stock is repurchased with no intention to reissue at a later date. (p. 511)

Retun on sales ratio   A variation of the profit margin ratio; measures earnings before payments to creditors. (p. 635)

Return on assets ratio   A measure of a company's success in earning a return for all providers of capital. (p. 634)

Return on common stockholders' equity ratio   A measure of a company's success in earning a return for the common stockholders. (p. 636)

Revenue expenditure   A cost that keeps an asset in its normal operating condition and is treated as an expense. (p. 359)

Revenue recognition principle   Revenues are recognized in the income statement when they are realized, or realizable, and earned. (p. 146)

Revenues   Inflows of assets or settlements of liabilities from delivering or producing goods, rendering services, or conducting other activities. (p. GS6, 146)

Sales Discounts   Contra-revenue account used to record discounts given customers for early payment of their accounts. (p. 200)

Sales Returns and Allowances   Contra-revenue account used to record both refunds to customers and reductions of their accounts. (p. 198)

Share of stock   A certificate that acts as ownership in a corporation. (p. GS4)

Securities and Exchange Commission (SEC)   The federal agency with ultimate authority to determine the rules in preparing statements for companies whose stock is sold to the public. (p. 16)

Serial bonds   Bonds that do not all have the same due date; a portion of the bonds comes due each time period. (p. 454)

Simple interest Interest is calculated on the principal amount only. (p. 410)

Single-step income statement An income statement in which all expenses are added together and subtracted from all revenues. (p. 60)

Sole proprietorship Form of organization with a single owner. (p. GS4)

Solvency The ability of a company to remain in business over the long term. (p. 631)

Source document A piece of paper that is used as evidence to record a transaction. (p. 94)

Specific identification method An inventory costing method that relies on matching unit costs with the actual units sold. (p. 249)

Statement of cash flows The financial statement that summarizes an entity's cash receipts and cash payments during the period from operating, investing, and financing activities. (p. 553)

Statement of retained earnings The statement that summarizes the income earned and dividends paid over the life of a business. (p. 11)

Statement of stockholders' equity Reflects the differences between beginning and ending balances for all accounts in the Stockholders' Equity category of the balance sheet. (p. 517)

Stock dividend The issuance of additional shares of stock to existing stockholders. (p. 513)

Stock split The creation of additional shares of stock with a reduction of the par value of the stock. (p. 515)

Stockholder One of the owners of a corporation. (p. GS6)

Stockholders' equity The owners' equity in a corporation. (p. 9)

Straight-line method A method by which the same dollar amount of depreciation is recorded in each year of asset use. (p. 149, 353)

Subsidiary ledger The detail for a number of individual items that collectively make up a single general ledger account. (p. 312)

Temporary difference A difference that affects both book and tax records but not in the same time period. (p. 477)

Term The length of time a note is outstanding; that is, the period of time between the date it is issued and the date it matures. (p. 319)

Time period Artificial segment on the calendar, used as the basis for preparing financial statements. (p. 15)

Time value of money An immediate amount should be preferred over an amount in the future. (p. 410)

Times interest earned ratio An income statement measure of the ability of a company to meet its interest payments. (p. 632)

Trade discount Selling price reduction offered to a special class of customers. (p. 198)

Trading securities Stock and bonds of other companies bought and held for the purpose of selling them in the near term to generate profits on appreciation in their price. (p. 305)

Transaction Any event that is recognized in a set of financial statements. (p. 94)

Transportation-in Adjunct account used to record freight costs paid by the buyer. (p. 204)

Treasurer The officer responsible in an organization for the safeguarding and efficient use of a company's liquid assets. (p. 16)

Treasury stock Stock issued by the firm and then repurchased but not retired. (p. 509)

Trial balance A list of each account and its balance; used to prove equality of debits and credits. (p. 111)

Understandability The quality of accounting information that makes it comprehensible to those willing to spend the necessary time. (p. 48)

Units-of-production method Depreciation is determined as a function of the number of units the asset produces. (p. 354)

Vertical analysis A comparison of various financial statement items within a single period with the use of common-size statements. (p. 619)

Weighted average cost method An inventory costing method that assigns the same unit cost to all units available for sale during the period. (p. 249)

Work in process The cost of unfinished products in a manufacturing company. (p. 245)

Work sheet A device used at the end of the period to gather the information needed to prepare financial statements without actually recording and posting adjusting entries. (p. 161)

Working capital Current assets minus current liabilities. (p. 58, 626)

Chapter 1: page 4, Photo courtesy of Pizzeria Uno; page 16, © Photopia; page 21, Photo courtesy of Lynn Homburg. **Chapter 2:** page 44, Photo courtesy of Gateway Corporation; page 56, © Corel; page 69, Photo courtesy of Matthew Butler. **Chapter 3:** page 92, Reprinted by permission of K2 Corporation; page 95, © PhotoDisc; page 98, © PhotoDisc; page 111, Photo courtesy of Mark Gleason. **Chapter 4:** page 138, © Photopia; page 142, © PhotoDisc; page 162, Photo courtesy of Michael Clarke. **Chapter 5:** page 194, © Photopia; page 199, © PhotoDisc; page 210, © PhotoDisc; page 213, Photo courtesy of Julie Weston. **Chapter 6:** page 242, © Photopia; page 245, © Digital Stock; page 267, Photo courtesy of Kim Anne Starke. **Chapter 7:** page 292, © Don Couch Photography; page 302, Photo courtesy of Barbara Genualdi; page 312, © Don Couch Photography; page 322, © PhotoDisc. **Chapter 8:** page 348, © Don Couch Photography; page 354, © Don Couch Photography; page 361, © Christian Bassu-Picca/Tony Stone Images; page 372, Photo courtesy of Aishetu Kolo. **Chapter 9:** page 396, © Don Couch Photography; page 406, Photo courtesy of Tandy Corporation; page 413, Photo courtesy of Texas Lottery Commission; page 418, Photo courtesy of Philip Yarrow. **Chapter 10:** page 450, © Audrey Gibson/Corbis Images; page 455, © Bill Varie/Image Bank; page 459, © Sergio Dorantes/Corbis Images; page 471, Photo courtesy of John Roberts Snow. **Chapter 11:** page 498, © AP/Wide World Photos; page 507, Photo by Ami Schrager MPG, Inc. provided courtesy of New York Stock Exchange; page 524, Photo courtesy of Christopher Morgan. **Chapter 12:** page 550, Photo courtesy of International Business Machines Corporation. Unauthorized use not permitted; page 559, Logo and photo courtesy of International Business Machines Corporation. Unauthorized use not permitted; page 580, Photo courtesy of Sara Luedtke. **Chapter 13:** page 614, © Photopia; page 631, © PhotoDisc; page 638, © The Stock Yard; page 640, Photo courtesy of Stephen Carmichael.

To the Student: page xxiii, © PhotoDisc. **Getting Started:** page GS2, Photo courtesy of Pizzeria Uno; page GS8, © PhotoDisc

Cover Image Credits: Pizeria Uno, Used by permission of Pizzeria Uno. **Time Warner,** Used by permission of Time Warner. **Walgreen's,** Cover logo used by permission of Walgreen Company. **Circuit City,** © Zaruba Photography for Circuit City. **IBM,** Courtesy of International Business Machines Corporation. Unauthorized use not permitted.

Uno 1999 annual report courtesy of Pizzeria Uno.
Gateway 1999 annual report courtesy of Gateway, Inc.

Video Case I: Tweeter Home Entertainment Group's 1999 Annual Report; "Company Profile," Tweeter Web site, accessed March 7, 2000, www.tweeter.com; "Tweeter Home Entertainment Group Completes Public Offering of 2,550,000 Shares of Common Stock," company press release, February 8, 2000; "Tweeter Home Entertainment Group Reports Record Earnings for Its First Quarter Ending December 31, 1999," company press release, January 20, 2000; Chet Dembeck, "Cyberian Outpost and Tweeter Join Forces: Execs Talk about Venture," E-commerce Times, August 3, 1999, www.ecomercetimes.com. **Video Case II:** "Stride Rite Reports Fourth Quarter Results," company press release, Jan. 9, 2001, accessed at http://biz.yahoo.com/bw/010109/ma_stride_.hrml, Jan. 12, 2001; Stride Rite Annual Report 1999; www.keds.com, accessed Jan. 12, 2001; www.striderite.com, accessed Jan. 12, 2001; www.sperrytopsider.com, accessed Jan. 12, 2001; www.tommy.com, accessed Jan. 12, 2001. **Video Case III:** Uno Restaurant Corporation 1999 Annual Report; Pizzeria Uno . . . Chicago Bar & Grill Web site, www.pizzeriauno.com, accessed April 2000; "Uno's Restaurant Corporation," company capsule accessed March 31, 2000, at www.hoovers.com; and "Uno Increases Stock Repurchase Authorization," PR Newswire, February 28, 2000. **Video Case IV:** The Lycos Network Web site, www.lycos.com, accessed April 2000; Lycos 1998 Annual Report; Lycos, Inc., company capsule, Hoover's Online, March 15, 2000, www.hoovers.com; Katherine Bull, "Ron Sege: Lycos' Executive VP Outlines the Company's New Corporate/Vertical Strategy," Infoworld.com, January 14, 2000.

Cash receipts/disbursements, 217–224
Cash shortages, 303
Cash to cash operating cycle, 631
CD, 295
Certificate of deposit (CD), 295
Change in estimate, 358, 359
Chart of accounts, 101, 102
Check with remittance advice, 224
Clarke, Michael, 162
Classified balance sheet, 53–59
Closing entries, 162
Closing process, 162
Collateral, 454
Common-size statements, 622–625
Common stock, 57, 502, 503
Comparability, 49, 50
Comparative statements, 619–625
Compensated absences, 429
Compound interest, 412
Comprehensive income, 518, 519
Conceptual framework for accounting, 14
Conglomerates, 617
Conservatism, 51, 52
Consistency, 50
Consolidated financial statements, 65, 304
Contingent assets, 409, 410
Contingent liability, 323, 324, **404**–409
Contra account, 150, 198
Contra-revenue account, 198
Contract rate of interest, 455
Contributed capital, 57
Control. *See* Internal control
Control account, 312
Control over cash, 295–301
    bank reconciliation, 298–301
    bank statement, 295–298
    cash management, 295
    petty cash, 301
Controller, 16
Convertible bonds, 454, 455
Convertible feature, 507
Copyright, 365
Corporation, GS4
Cost, 246
Cost of goods available for sale, 201
Cost of goods purchased, 206
Cost of goods sold, 202
Cost principle, 14, 98
Counterbalancing error, 258
Coupon offers, 406
Coupon rate of interest, 455
Credit, 103–105
Credit card draft, 322
Credit card sales, 322, 323
Credit memoranda, 298
Credit terms, 199
Creditor, GS6, 7
Cumulative feature, 507
Current assets, 54–56
Current liabilities, 57, **398**–405
    accounts payable, 400

accrued liabilities, 402, 403
current maturities of long-term debt, 402
notes payable, 400–402
statement of cash flow, and, 403–405
taxes payable, 402
Current maturities of long-term debt, 402
Current ratio, 58, 59, 399, **626,** 627
Current value, 141

D

Date of declaration, 511
Date of record, 511
Debenture bonds, 454
Debit, 103–105
Debit-credit rules, 105
    dividends, 105
    expenses, 104, 105
    revenues, 104
Debit memoranda, 299
Debt securities, 302
Debt service coverage ratio, 470, **632,** 633
Debt-to-equity ratio, 470, **631,** 632
Deferral, 155
Deferred expense, 149, 150, **155,** 156
Deferred revenue, 150–152, **155,** 156
Deferred tax, 475–478
Depletion, 363, 364
Deposit in transit, 298
Depreciation, 49, **353**–359
    accelerated methods, 355
    change in estimate, 358, 359
    choice of method, 357
    double-declining balance method, 355
    income taxes, and, 356
    methods, compared, 356
    straight-line, 353, 354
    units-of-production method, 354
Direct labor, 244
Direct materials, 244, 245
Direct method, 560, 561, 565–576, 578
Direct write-off method, 313
Disclosure, 50, 70
Discount, 457
Discount on notes payable, 401
Discounted note, 321
Discounting, 323
Discounting a note, 401
Dividend payout ratio, 511, 639
Dividend ratios, 639–641
Dividend yield ratio, 639–641
Dividends, 11
    cash, 511–513
    preferred stocks, and, 507
    stock, 513–515
Dividends in arrears, 507
Dollar, 14, 141
Double declining-balance method, 355
Double-entry system, 106
Drexler, Mickey, 200

E

Earned capital, 57
Earnings per share, 637, 638
Economic entity concept, GS4, 14
Economic events, 94
Effective interest method of amortization, 459–462
Effective interest rate, 459
Employer payroll taxes, 428
Employer withholdings, 427, 428
Ending inventory, 201, 204
Environmental regulations, 361
Environmental remediation claims, 406
Equity financing, 500, 501. *See also* Stock
Equity method of accounting, 304
Equity securities, 302
Estimated liability, 406
Ethics
    accountants, 21
    accrual basis of accounting, 159
    management/auditors, 68, 69
Event, 94
Expense, GS7, 148
Expense recognition, 146–148
External event, 94
External users, 6–8

F

Face rate of interest, 455
Face value, 452
Fair value accounting, 310, 311
FASB, 16
FICA tax, 427, 428
FIFO method, 250–252, 271
Financial accounting, 7
Financial Accounting Standards Board (FASB), 16
Financial ratios, 642, 643. *See also* Financial statement analysis
Financial reporting objectives, 46, 47
Financial statement analysis, 614–679
    horizontal analysis, 619–622
    liquidity analysis, 626–631
    precautions, 616–618
    profitability analysis, 634–641
    solvency analysis, 631–634
    trend analysis, 622
    vertical analysis, 622–625
Financial statements
    balance sheet. *See* Balance sheet
    cash flow statement. *See* Statement of cash flows
    income statement. *See* Income statement
    interim, 162, 163
    relationship between, 13
    statement of retained earnings, 11–13
Financing activities, GS5, GS6, **558,** 559
Finished goods, 245
First-in, first-out method (FIFO), 250–252, 271
Fixed assets. *See* Property, plant, and equipment

What's Ahead in 2000?

Uno has never had a "cookie cutter" approach to its business. Our menus change, we offer a variety of specials, and we are always finding new ways to create a positive casual dining experience that keeps guests coming back. We have built a successful organization by ensuring that we have the flexibility to adapt intelligently and quickly to the preferences of our markets. In the coming years we will continue to pursue goal driven strategies that focus on the individual and organizational needs that must be satisfied.

For our guests, we will continue to refine and adapt our restaurants to ensure that there is always something new and different to anticipate with every visit. Great food served in a fun and vibrant atmosphere never goes out of style.

For our employees, we will do everything possible to create a work environment that encourages and recognizes high achievement. By actively working to increase job satisfaction, we build a company based on competence and enthusiasm– ready, willing, and able to take on all challenges.

For our franchise partners, we are committed to helping them succeed in every possible way. As we build the awareness of the Uno brand and all it stands for, we are creating an important asset that enables franchisees to discover new opportunities and to invest with confidence in a proven concept of growing value.

For the customers of our Consumer Products, we will continue to be innovative in creating products that will help them build their business. By backing all our products with the highest standards of quality, we help our customers ensure satisfaction for their customers.

Uno creates value for our shareholders by responding to the needs of our guests, employees, franchisees, and consumer product customers. As we move forward in the 21st century, our goal is to use the lessons of our history wisely in building toward greater successes in the years ahead.

CONSOLIDATED FINANCIAL STATEMENTS

Table of Contents

Pizzeria Uno...Chicago Bar & Grill is famous for it's deep-dish pizza. This signature product, complemented by other entrées, appetizers, salads, beverages and desserts, has created a large and loyal following that has enabled the Company to expand geographically and grow steadily over the years within the casual dining segment of the restaurant industry. At the end of the fiscal year, the Uno Restaurant Corporation system included 98 company-owned and 47 franchised Pizzeria Uno...Chicago Bar & Grill restaurants, 13 franchised Pizzeria Uno Restaurant & Bar and one Mexican restaurant, with locations in 29 states, the District of Columbia, Puerto Rico and Seoul, Korea. The Company also operates a consumer products division which supplies American Airlines, movie theaters, hotel restaurants and supermarkets with Pizzeria Uno brand products.

Financial Highlights	Fiscal Year Ended		
	(Amounts in thousands, except per share data)		
	Oct 3, 1999	Sept. 27, 1998	Sept. 28, 1997
	(53 weeks)		
Revenue	$ 214,233	$ 191,276	$ 178,020
Operating Income	17,987	12,652	6,878
Net Income	9,800	5,387	2,673
Earnings per common share—diluted	$ .84	$ .45	$ .20
Weighted-average shares outstanding– diluted	11,610	12,025	13,209
Shareholders' Equity	$ 80,979	$ 73,669	$ 70,880
System wide restaurant sales			
Company-owned	$ 196,353	$ 174,716	$ 160,045
Franchised	$ 118,443	$ 105,550	$ 102,847

Net Income

Earnings Per Share-Diluted

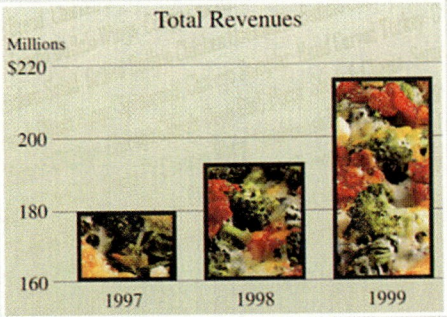

Total Revenues

Uno Award Winners

We would like to honor our 1999 Award Winners for their special contributions during the past year:

Franchise Partner of the Year	Federico Sanchez
General Manager of the Year	Susan Jasie (Company)
	Jeffrey Franklin (Franchise)
Regional Director of the Year	Bruce Knudson
Supplier of the Year	Beatrice Cheese
Founder's Award	Alan Gibson

UNO RESTAURANT CORPORATION
ANNUAL REPORT 1999

1943 1999

Letter to Shareholders

We are pleased to report that 1999 was a record year for your company. Revenue, net income, and earnings per share were the best in Uno's history. Moreover, we had our best year over year increase in comparable store sales since 1994. Sales momentum that began to build in the last half of 1998 accelerated into 1999. The Pizzeria Uno brand is becoming a recognized leader in the casual dining segment of the restaurant industry.

Beyond exceeding our financial goals, excellent progress was made toward our long-term operational goals. We are achieving greater recognition of our Chicago Bar & Grill concept with solid increases in overall guest satisfaction. The combination of financial and operational accomplishments over the past three years has provided Uno with a strong base for continued growth and success in the new millennium.

For the fiscal year ended October 3, 1999, Uno generated net income of $9.8 million, or $.84 per diluted share. That represents a 63% increase over net income of $6.0 million in the prior year, and a 68% increase over diluted per share earnings of $.50 in 1998. Revenues for fiscal year 1999 increased by 12% to $214 million compared to $191 million for fiscal 1998. Fiscal year 1999 reflects 53 weeks of operation compared to 52 weeks in fiscal 1998. (The results for fiscal year 1998 exclude a charge net of taxes of $636,000, or .05 per diluted share, for the cumulative effect of a change in accounting in conjunction with the Company's adoption of SOP 98-5.)

Company-owned comparable store sales improved by 6.1% in 1999, while franchised Pizzeria Uno...Chicago Bar & Grill comparable store sales rose by 5.0%. Average annual unit volume for all full-service Pizzeria Uno...Chicago Bar & Grill units was approximately $2.0 million, a 6.4% increase over 1998. At year-end, Uno had achieved eight consecutive quarters of earnings per share growth of 20% or better, resulting in a compounded earnings per share growth of approximately 39% for the past three years.

During fiscal 1999, the Company opened five full-service restaurants and the franchise system added eight full-service and two quick-service restaurants. We expect to accelerate unit expansion in the year 2000, adding up to 25 new restaurants to the system, 13 to 15 company-owned restaurants and 10 to 12 franchised restaurants.

It is gratifying that the many initiatives launched over the past few years have resulted in our record performance. The repositioning of our concept has been well received by our guests, and it has allowed us to reach a broader portion of the mainstream casual dining market. Now that the repositioning is essentially complete, our focus will be on further improvements in our operations to ensure that every dining experience at a Pizzeria Uno...Chicago Bar & Grill exceeds our guests' expectations.

In 1999, Uno received two prestigious awards that recognize the popularity and power of our brand. In June, Pizzeria Uno...Chicago Bar & Grill was named a first place winner in the "Choice in Chains" customer survey conducted annually by Restaurants & Institutions magazine. Uno received the Platinum Award, the survey's highest honor for top scores in overall customer satisfaction. In July, Uno received further recognition by breaking into the nation's top 100 restaurants list for the first time. Uno was 25th among the top 100 restaurant chains, ranked by sales per unit, in an annual study conducted by Nation's Restaurant News.

Efforts to improve and expand our franchise system continued in 1999. Concept improvements achieved in recent years have enabled us to attract new franchise partners with experience in multi-unit restaurant operations and access to growth capital. We signed three new agreements during the year, which are expected to result in up to 16 new franchise restaurants being opened during the next several years. These agreements and others already in place will provide for expansion, both domestically and abroad. Our goal is to grow our franchised units 20% annually.

Uno's Consumer Products subsidiary, Uno Foods, also established performance milestones this year. Our high quality products are sold in supermarkets, hotels, cinemas, airports, and food courts across the country. We have increased our sales of pizzas to American Airlines

Pizzeria Uno started with the most outrageously delicious deep-dish pizza ever served — and built from there. Today, our full-service restaurants offer a unique casual dining experience that combines a sensational menu, an exciting atmosphere, and tremendous value for our guests. Over the years, we've carefully taken everything that was best about Uno, and made it even better.

PIZZERIA UNO

In 1943, the first Pizzeria Uno opened at the corner of Wabash and Ohio in downtown Chicago. Word began to spread that something new and truly original was happening. If you wanted the world's best deep-dish pizza served in a warm, fun atmosphere, Ike Sewell's upstart restaurant was the only place to go.

PIZZERIA DUE

By 1955, the reputation of Chicago deep-dish pizza had grown to the point where a larger restaurant was needed. opened in a former mansion one block away and was calle Pizzeria Due – but it was still "Number One" in the hearts o its fanatically loyal customers

1943

Ike Sewell

The original Pizzeria Uno on the corner of Wabash and Ohio, Chicago. 1943

1955

Pizzeria Due 1955

In 1963, Uno showed its ability to diversify and satisfy when it opened Su Casa, a new Mexican restaurant next door to Due. Different concept. Different food. Same great response from customers. It was clear that Ike Sewell knew how to run a world-class restaurant.

In 1978, after three years of building trust and friendship, Ike and Aaron shook hands on a deal that would bring the original Chicago deep-dish pizza to the world. Pizzeria Uno was ready for it's national debut.

In 1975, Aaron Spencer discovered the Chicago legend for himself. He tasted the deep-dish pizza and saw the future. Ike Sewell needed some convincing before taking the concept national, but Aaron was equal to the task.

Su Casa 1963

Chicago Deep Dish Pizza

Aaron Spencer and Ike Sewell - 1978

for use aboard domestic and international flights, in both first-class and coach. Late in the year, Uno Foods added new national accounts that are expected to deliver continued growth in fiscal 2000.

In August, the Company appointed three new members to its Board of Directors. They are Tamara P. Davis, Kenneth D. Hill, and James J. Kerasiotes. Ms. Davis is the former President and Chief Executive Officer of UST Leasing Corporation and is a member of several public sector Boards in the field of education. Mr. Hill has more than 40 years of restaurant industry experience and most recently served as Executive Vice President and Chief Operating Officer of Applebee's International, Inc. Mr. Kerasiotes is Chairman and Chief Executive Officer of the Massachusetts Turnpike Authority and has served as Massachusetts' Secretary of Transportation, as well as Chairman of the Massachusetts Bay Transportation Authority. The services of these individuals will be valuable as we continue our efforts to enhance shareholder value.

To support our accelerated expansion strategy, we have added several new executives to the Uno team in 1999. These additional resources bring industry experience, leadership, and add depth to the areas of operations, development, law, human resources and marketing. These individuals will complement our existing well-seasoned management team and play an integral part in the success of our expansion strategy.

In an effort to increase trading volume and to add more liquidity in the Company's stock, as well as to attract broader market coverage, the Company filed a secondary public offering in September. In November, we withdrew the offering due to overall market volatility, weak valuations among the leading public restaurant companies and the price of our stock. We concluded that an offering, although consistent with the aforementioned objectives, was not in the best interest of our shareholders at that time. We continue to monitor market conditions and are prepared to revive our secondary offering when conditions warrant.

Uno's growth is accelerating as we move toward the year 2000. We are a leading company in a growing industry that is gathering momentum. Aging baby boomers are becoming the largest segment of our market and they generate the highest spending per capita on food away from home. Dual income families are projected to increase, and the resulting constraints on time are expected to create more dining out occasions. The economy is healthy and so is Uno. In response to these positive factors, we are targeting 15% to 20% unit growth rates over the next several years.

Uno is well positioned to build upon its leadership in the 21st century. We have the vision, the infrastructure, and the management team to take on the challenges of the years ahead. As we look to the future, we wish to thank the individuals throughout our company who have been responsible for this year's historic performance and achievement. With their continued loyalty and enthusiasm, Uno can move confidently into the new millennium.

Aaron Spencer
Chairman of the Board

Craig S. Miller
President and
Chief Executive Officer

Craig Miller & Aaron Spencer

Building on Success

Many things came together for Uno in 1999. The system-wide changes that we began to put in place five years ago had the desired effects, as our menu and facilities converged upon the goals we set. Our guests noticed the difference and told their friends. In many cases they came back more frequently and brought along friends and family.

With our diverse menu drawing rave reviews from guests, and with people enjoying the authentic Chicago flavor of our repositioned restaurants, performance picked up across the board. The result: a record year in virtually all categories and a strengthened ability to pursue additional opportunities in the years ahead.

For over 20 years, Uno has been a strong competitor in the casual dining industry. The refinements made over the past few years have resulted in a concept with wide appeal in both domestic and international markets. Our performance this year is solid evidence of our ability to execute our strategic plan and gain enthusiastic acceptance in the market place. The demonstrated strength of our concept and strategic plan form the foundation for Uno's continuing growth as we enter the new millennium.

Meeting the Needs and Preferences of Our Guests

Our guests choose Pizzeria Uno...Chicago Bar & Grill for a variety of reasons. It's a great place to come for lunch – whether it's soup and sandwich, a salad, or one of our regular entrees. It's a great place to come for dinner, with appetizers, beverages, charbroiled steaks and hamburgers, grilled chicken dishes, pasta, and fantastic desserts. Our world famous signature dish, the original Chicago deep-dish pizza, or our gourmet thin-crust pizzas are appealing any time of the day.

As we prepared to launch our "Bigger and Better" menu initiative more than a year ago, we faced a difficult question: how do you make superb food even better? We came up with two answers. The first was to examine each recipe and make sure it was not only the very best that could be done, but that it also used only the finest, freshest, and tastiest ingredients. That was a start.

Then we looked at portions, and realized that sometimes "more" really is more. Larger portions translated into better value for our guests. And that was our goal. Give our guests the best we have to offer, and more of it. "Bigger and Better." And it worked.

1979 – 1993

1979

The year was 1979, and Boston met Pizzeria Uno for the first time. It was a bit of a shock. People were used to seeing pizza arrive on a platter the size of a tire. This new kind of pizza came in a dish. It was a meal in itself– a tender crust filled with the finest meats, freshest vegetables, tastiest cheeses, and most flavorful spices. Boston had not experienced anything so satisfying since the Red Sox won the World Series in 1918.

1980

In 1980, the era of franchising began for Uno. The first franchised unit was in Washington D.C., and 20 years later the total number of franchised units had grown to over 60.

1984

In 1984, Craig Miller brought his years of restaurant experience and expertise to Uno, which then consisted of 15 restaurants. He was elected President two years later as company growth began to accelerate and Uno began its move into new geographic markets.

1987

In 1987, on June Uno became a publicly owned comp The successful pu offering provided financial resource fuel new growth a expansion.

1979 Pizzeria Uno opens on Boylston Street in Boston.

1980 The 3rd Company unit opens in Framingham, Mass.

1984

1987 Pizzeria Uno goes

In 1988, Uno opened its 50th restaurant. The location was Nashua, New Hampshire. Word was out: Chicago's favorite pizza traveled well.

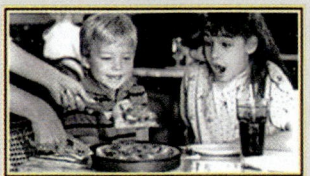

In 1992, Uno opened its 100th restaurant— 100% unit growth in only four years! Uno was making a name for itself as the only full-service casual dining restaurant with a diverse menu and unique "signature" dish that set it apart from the competition.

In 1993, Uno celebrated 50 years of being "Number One" The event was recognized by Chicago Mayor, Richard M. Daley, and the City Council with a city resolution of gratitude and congratulations. There was a black-tie celebration with a main course of — you guessed it – deep-dish pizza. The street in front of the original Pizzeria Uno was honorarily named Ike Sewell Avenue.

100ᵀᴴ Uno Restaurant Opens!

'88   1992   1993

The design and décor of our restaurants is no accident. We experimented with layouts, finishes, and various looks and memorabilia displays. We listened to our guests, refined our approach, and searched for the best and most cost effective ways of achieving our goals. In the end, we chose the current prototype design that lets guests feel and imagine what it was like to be part of old Chicago.

There is simplicity in the design, achieved in part by the use of no nonsense building materials such as exposed brick. There is an openness and honesty to the design, with visible ductwork in the ceiling, advertising signs that hark back to an earlier time, and artful stacks of crates, cartons, and food containers that suggest freshness and abundance.

From the choice of colors, to the use of lighting, to the table service, we create warmth, vitality, and excitement.

We want our guests to feel that they have discovered a bit of America that is authentic and welcoming – where anything and everything on the menu has to be delicious, well prepared, and served with a friendly smile.

With every stroke of artistry that went into the design, we were also monitoring costs. By focusing on simple and easily repeated layouts, along with low maintenance and highly functional materials, we have been able to achieve an improved level of unit economics that makes new construction faster, easier, and less expensive. By enhancing unit economics, Uno is better able to finance expansion, attract qualified franchisers, and build its bottom line.

When we implemented our Bigger and Better menu at Uno restaurants around the country, we began to see increased guest satisfaction. When we started to renovate our existing restaurants to bring them closer to our successful new prototype design, we saw guest satisfaction increase even more.

In June of 1999, Pizzeria Uno...Chicago Bar & Grill was named a first place winner in the prestigious "Choice in Chains" customer survey conducted annually by Restaurants & Institutions magazine. Uno received the Platinum Award, the survey's highest honor, for scoring the highest in overall customer satisfaction in its category. The survey was based on responses from 2,800 consumer households across the country, and Uno's high ranking is a strong indication that our guests view us as a clear leader in casual dining.

Fifty seven years ago, Uno first made a name for itself by bringing together all the right ingredients for a deep-dish pizza with near universal appeal. This year, we once again brought together all the right things to make a great year: Our menu, facility-design, and renovation program are key parts of the story. Our focus on fast, friendly service, and our commitment to find, train, retain, and reward employees is an important piece of the puzzle. Our willingness to listen to our guests and give them everything they want and more than they expect is equally critical. In 1999, all of these things came together allowing Uno to serve up a record year in virtually all categories of performance.

Improved Performance Gives Impetus to Franchising

Uno's franchise partners are located in 29 states across the country, as well as the District of Columbia, Puerto Rico, and Seoul, Korea. The franchise system includes 47 Pizzeria Uno...Chicago Bar & Grill restaurants, and 13 Pizzeria Uno Restaurant & Bar locations. Franchised locations have long been an integral part of Uno's growth strategy and have become an increasing focus of interest over the last two years.

In 1999, Uno signed several new agreements with multi-unit restaurant operators. ADC Development Group, LLC, is scheduled to open three Pizzeria Uno...Chicago Bar & Grill restaurants in Richmond and Charlottesville, Virginia. ADC currently manages six regional Asian restaurants under the name Peking. Another organization, Pizza by Pubs, which currently operates six TGI Friday's restaurants, will open a minimum of three Pizzeria Uno...Chicago Bar & Grill restaurants in eastern Pennsylvania. The Bock Group is an existing Uno franchise partner that has agreed to open another ten locations in suburban Philadelphia and New Jersey.

Success often leads to more success. In the case of franchising, we believe this is especially true. Uno's strong performance over the last two years makes franchising opportunities more attractive than ever before. At the same time, our performance is allowing us to attract individuals and organizations with experience in the casual dining industry and with access to capital, two of the key factors required for franchising success in the casual dining industry.

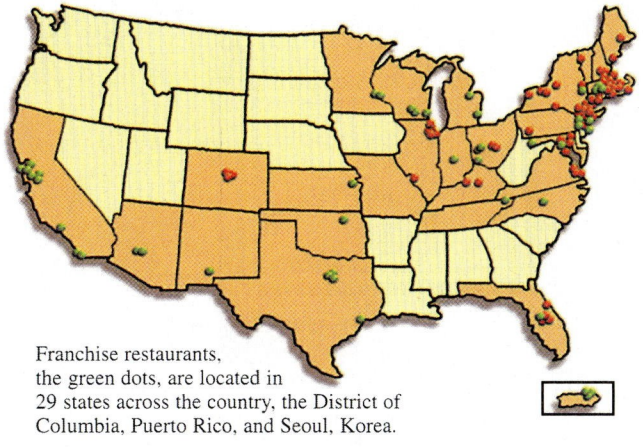

Franchise restaurants, the green dots, are located in 29 states across the country, the District of Columbia, Puerto Rico, and Seoul, Korea.

As competition heated up in the 90's, Uno undertook a far-reaching repositioning program to expand its appeal to customers, franchise operators, and the investment community. Our vision was to reinvent our restaurants, keeping what worked and changing everything else according to our strategic plan. Our goal was to live up to our name: "Uno Is Number One."

1994 - 1999

1994

1994 was the year of the kitchen. Uno added sauté stations, char broilers, grills, and fryers. The result: a new ability to prepare everything with the same high standards as our famous deep-dish pizza.

1995

1995 was the year of the menu. New capabilities in the kitchen meant new offerings to tempt new guests and keep them coming back more often than ever before.

1996

1996 was the year of bricks and mortar. Uno unveiled a new prototype restaurant design to capture the look and feel and honest experience of its Chicago roots.

1997

1997, we emphasized the new
entity of our restaurants with a
light name change – Pizzeria
no...Chicago Bar & Grill.

no was still the place to go for
e world's best tasting pizza, but
ere was so much more. A vari-
y of great foods perfectly pre-
ared. A full selection of bever-
es from the bar. And an atmos-
here that delivered the authentic
arm and excitement of Old
hicago.

no opened its 150th restaurant in
97. Our guests were doing a
rrific job of spreading the word.
y Uno. It's more than you
pect!

1998

1998 arrived and the stage was set for the
strongest performance in Uno history. Nothing
was left to chance as the introduction of the
"Bigger and Better" menu initiative put us over
the top. By consistently delivering a casual dining value that was too good to pass up, we began
to reach new heights of guest satisfaction that set
the stage for continued growth, innovation, and
prosperity in the 21st century.

1999

A Record Year for Uno Foods

In 1999, Uno's Consumer Products subsidiary achieved record revenues, and for the first time in its history revenues exceeded $10 million. In recent years, the division has concentrated on growth in its food service business. Expanding sales to institutional customers including hotels, movie theaters, and airlines accounted for half the division's business, while supermarket sales represented the balance. We expect that institutional sales will grow to approximately sixty percent of total consumer product sales in the coming year.

Uno's deep-dish pizza and thin-crust pizza are available at more than 400 brand name hotels around the country. Approximately 75 cinema complexes including 50 operated by General Cinema offer our products at their concession counters, and we are making inroads with other growing cinema chains. Our business with American Airlines continues to grow, as both deep-dish and thin-crust products have been added to the fare for an increasing number of domestic and international flights.

Uno products today can be found on college campuses, in airports, and in select, upscale food courts. For us, the key to success in these markets is to partner with organizations that value quality. Over the years, we have developed a brand that stands for freshness and excellence, and we build on the strength of that brand name when we work with organizations that meet high standards in the preparation and presentation of our products.

All of our consumer products are handmade at our production facility in Brockton, Massachusetts, where our strict quality control programs ensure that we meet uniformly high standards. Based on this year's accomplishments, we are projecting continued growth in consumer products in the coming year, and our Brockton plant currently has the capacity to handle that growth.

SELECTED FINANCIAL DATA

	Fiscal Year Ended				
	(Amounts in thousands, except per share data)				
	Oct. 3 1999 (53 weeks)	Sept. 27 1998	Sept. 28 1997	Sept. 29 1996	Oct. 1 1995
Income Statement Data:					
REVENUES:					
Restaurant sales	$198,560	$177,343	$164,389	$159,581	$146,100
Consumer product sales	10,568	9,384	9,115	8,351	8,477
Franchise income	5,105	4,549	4,516	4,209	4,129
	214,233	191,276	178,020	172,141	158,706
COSTS AND EXPENSES:					
Cost of food and beverages	54,683	48,567	43,994	44,064	39,420
Labor and benefits	64,700	58,139	54,183	51,868	47,377
Occupancy costs	29,199	27,988	27,045	26,339	22,925
Other operating costs	18,333	18,086	16,067	15,890	13,583
General and administrative	16,629	13,661	13,384	12,155	11,229
Depreciation and amortization	12,702	12,183	12,469	12,964	10,795
Special charges			4,000	3,937	
	196,246	178,624	171,142	167,217	145,329
OPERATING INCOME	17,987	12,652	6,878	4,924	13,377
INTEREST AND OTHER EXPENSE	3,139	3,661	2,827	2,481	1,944
INCOME BEFORE INCOME TAXES	14,848	8,991	4,051	2,443	11,433
Provision for income taxes	5,048	2,968	1,378	757	4,230
INCOME BEFORE CUMULATIVE EFFECT OF CHANGE IN ACCOUNTING PRINCIPLE	9,800	6,023	2,673	1,686	7,203
Cumulative effect of change in accounting principle for pre-opening costs, net of income tax benefit of $313		636			
NET INCOME	$ 9,800	$ 5,387	$ 2,673	$ 1,686	$ 7,203
NET INCOME PER COMMON SHARE:					
Income before cumulative effect of change in accounting principle	$ 0.87	$ 0.50	$ 0.20	$ 0.12	$ 0.54
Cumulative effect of change in accounting principle		(0.05)			
Basic net income per common share....................	$ 0.87	$ 0.45	$ 0.20	$ 0.12	$ 0.54
Diluted net income per common share.................	$ 0.84	$ 0.45	$ 0.20	$ 0.12	$ 0.53
WEIGHTED-AVERAGE SHARES OUTSTANDING					
Basic..	11,313	11,960	13,146	13,963	13,286
Diluted...	11,610	12,025	13,209	14,032	13,600

9

Franchised restaurants which have upgraded and redesigned their restaurants to conform with, or opened as, our Pizzeria Uno...Chicago Bar & Grill concept are included in the table below for all periods presented. Franchised restaurants which have not upgraded and redesigned are included under the caption "Other" for all periods presented. The information under number of restaurants, includes all full-service units, quick-service units, our Su Casa Mexican restaurant and our former Bay Street Grill restaurants. The information under Average Annual Restaurant Sales, under the caption "Other", only includes those franchised restaurants which have not upgraded and redesigned. The table does not include quick-service units, our Su Casa Mexican restaurant in Chicago or our former Bay Street Grill restaurants.

| | Fiscal Year Ended | | | | |
| | (Amounts in thousands, except number of restaurants) | | | | |
	Oct. 3 1999	Sept. 27 1998	Sept. 28 1997	Sept. 29 1996	Oct. 1 1995
Operating Data:	(53 weeks)				
NUMBER OF RESTAURANTS					
Full-Service Pizzeria Uno...Chicago Bar & Grill					
Company-owned	98	94	92	86	79
Franchised	47	42	39	35	33
Other					
Company-owned	1	3	5	6	8
Franchised	18	24	30	32	28
TOTAL AT YEAR END	164	163	166	159	148
SYSTEM WIDE RESTAURANT SALES					
Full-Service Pizzeria Uno...Chicago Bar & Grill					
Company-owned	$196,353	$174,716	$160,045	$151,178	$136,659
Franchised	92,645	75,338	68,861	60,816	55,916
Other					
Company-owned	2,207	2,627	4,344	8,403	9,441
Franchised	25,798	30,212	33,986	35,273	36,529
TOTAL	$317,003	$282,893	$267,236	$255,670	$238,545
AVERAGE ANNUAL RESTAURANT SALES					
Full-Service Pizzeria Uno...Chicago Bar & Grill					
Company-owned	$ 1,972	$ 1,854	$ 1,818	$ 1,846	$ 1,925
Franchised	2,002	1,881	1,858	1,819	1,862
Other					
Franchised	1,132	1,207	1,199	1,223	1,231
Balance Sheet Data:					
Total assets	$149,612	$143,195	$143,732	$135,065	$125,260
Long-term debt, net of current portion	31,612	38,676	42,516	37,085	21,750
Capital lease obligations, net of current portion	489	666	867	1,056	749
Treasury stock	26,826	22,616	19,877	10,653	2,900
Total shareholders' equity	80,979	73,669	70,880	77,136	83,127

MANAGEMENT'S DISCUSSION AND ANALYSIS OF FINANCIAL CONDITION AND RESULTS OF OPERATIONS

Results of Operations

The following table sets forth the percentage relationship to total revenues, unless otherwise indicated, of certain items included in the Company's income statements and operating data for the periods indicated:

	53 Weeks Ended 10/3/99	52 Weeks Ended 9/27/98	52 Weeks Ended 9/28/97
REVENUES:			
Restaurant sales	**92.7%**	92.7%	92.4%
Consumer product sales	**4.9**	4.9	5.1
Franchise income	**2.4**	2.4	2.5
Total	**100.0**	100.0	100.0
COSTS AND EXPENSES:			
Cost of food and beverages (1)	**26.1**	26.0	25.4
Labor and benefits (1)	**30.9**	31.1	31.2
Occupancy costs (1)	**14.0**	15.0	15.6
Other operating costs (1)	**8.8**	9.7	9.3
General and administrative	**7.8**	7.1	7.5
Depreciation and amortization (1)	**6.1**	6.5	7.2
Special charges (1)			2.3
OPERATING INCOME	**8.4**	6.6	3.9
INTEREST AND OTHER EXPENSE	**(1.5)**	(1.9)	(1.6)
INCOME BEFORE INCOME TAXES	**6.9**	4.7	2.3
Provision for income taxes	**2.3**	1.6	.8
INCOME BEFORE CUMULATIVE EFFECT			
OF CHANGE IN ACCOUNTING PRINCIPLE	**4.6**	3.1	1.5
Cumulative effect of change in accounting principle for pre-opening costs, net of income tax benefit		.3	
NET INCOME	**4.6%**	2.8%	1.5%

(1) Percentage of restaurant and consumer product sales

11

Fiscal Year Ended October 3, 1999 (53 weeks)
Compared to Fiscal Year Ended September 27, 1998
(52 weeks)

Total Revenues.
Total revenues increased 12.0% to $214.2 million in
fiscal 1999 from $191.3 million in fiscal 1998.

Restaurant Sales.
Company-owned restaurant sales for the period rose
12.0% to $198.6 million from $177.3 million in fiscal
1998 due primarily to a 6.1% increase in comparable
store sales. Average weekly sales, which includes sales
at comparable stores as well as new restaurants,
increased 6.4% over the prior year, as the latest
variation of our new prototype restaurants (P5)
generated sales volumes approximately 10% higher than
our non-prototype restaurant average. Growth in
operating weeks of full-service Pizzeria Uno...Chicago
Bar & Grill restaurants increased by 5.7% resulting
from the addition of five restaurants during fiscal 1999.

Consumer Product Sales.
Consumer product sales increased 12.6% to $10.6
million in fiscal 1999 from $9.4 million in fiscal 1998.
Sales in the contract food service category grew 38.0%,
primarily as a result of increased shipments to American
Airlines, including initial shipments for new service on
American Airlines international flights, and hotel
accounts. Sales in the supermarket category decreased
18.8% over the same period last year as a 7.5% increase
in Pizzeria Uno branded sales to retail grocers was
offset by the elimination of a large international account
and a reduction in wholesale club store sales.

Franchise Income.
Franchise income, which includes royalty income and
initial franchise fees, increased 12.2% to $5.1 million
from $4.5 million in fiscal 1998. Royalty income
increased 12.0% to $4.9 million in fiscal 1999 from
$4.4 million in fiscal 1998. The increase in royalty
income was primarily due to an 8.1% increase in
average weekly sales for full-service franchised
restaurants. Franchise fees of $160,000 were recorded
for fiscal 1999 compared to $133,000 for fiscal 1998.
Eight full-service franchise restaurants opened and 11
full-service franchise restaurants closed during fiscal
1999, including 10 non-Chicago Bar & Grill restaurants.

Cost of Food and Beverages.
Cost of food and beverage as a percentage of restaurant
and consumer product sales increased to 26.1% for
fiscal 1999 compared to 26.0% for the same period last
year. This increase was due in part to cost increases
associated with the company-wide roll out of the new

menu initiative and slightly higher cheese costs, which
were partially offset by modest menu price increases
during the year. In March 1999 we entered into a fixed
price cheese contract with our cheese supplier for our
mozzarella cheese to help minimize our exposure from
the volatility in the block cheese market which reached
record heights during the summer months.

Labor and Benefits.
Labor costs as a percentage of restaurant and consumer
product sales were down slightly to 30.9% in fiscal
1999 from 31.1% in fiscal 1998 as an increase in the
average wage rate was absorbed by a higher check
average and lower consumer product labor expense.

Occupancy Costs.
Occupancy costs as a percentage of restaurant and
consumer product sales declined to 14.0% in fiscal 1999
from 15.0% in fiscal 1998 due to sales leverage gains.

Other Operating Costs.
Other operating costs as a percentage of restaurant and
consumer product sales declined to 8.8% in fiscal 1999
from 9.7% in fiscal 1998 due to lower advertising and
pre-opening expense.

General and Administrative Expenses.
General and administrative expenses as a percentage of
total revenues increased to 7.8% in fiscal 1999 from
7.1% in fiscal 1998. This increase was primarily due to
higher incentive compensation expense as a result of the
company's strong performance, and increased legal and
professional expense.

Depreciation and Amortization Expense.
Depreciation and amortization expense as a percentage
of restaurant and consumer product sales was down to
6.1% in fiscal 1999 compared to 6.5% in fiscal 1998
due to sales leverage gains.

Operating Income.
Operating income for fiscal 1999 was $18.0 million,
which represents an operating margin of 8.4%.
Operating income for fiscal 1998 was $12.7 million,
which represents an operating margin of 6.6%.

Interest and Other Expense.
Interest and other expense decreased to $3.1 million, or
1.5% of total revenues in fiscal 1999 from $3.7 million,
or 1.9% of total revenues in fiscal 1998. Interest
expense decreased to $3.2 million in fiscal 1999 from
$3.5 million in fiscal 1998 due to a slightly lower
borrowing rate and a lower debt level.

Provision for Income Taxes.

The effective tax rate increased in fiscal 1999 to 34% from 33% in fiscal 1998 due to higher pre-tax profits that shifted us into a higher tax bracket and the diminished impact of tax credits, which remained relatively consistent from fiscal 1998, being applied against a higher pre-tax income amount.

Net Income.

Net income increased to $9.8 million in fiscal 1999 from $5.4 million in fiscal 1998 based on the factors noted above, as 1998 results reflect the adoption of SOP 98-5 "Reporting on the Costs of Start-up Activities" The cumulative effect of this change in accounting principle was $636,000, net of income taxes.

Fiscal Year Ended September 27, 1998 Compared to Fiscal Year Ended September 28, 1997

Total Revenues.

Total revenues increased 7.4% to $191.3 million in fiscal 1998 from $178.0 million in fiscal 1997.

Restaurant Sales.

Company-owned restaurant sales increased 7.9% to $177.3 million from $164.4 million in fiscal 1997, due primarily to a 7.0% increase in operating weeks of full-service Pizzeria Uno...Chicago Bar & Grill restaurants resulting from the addition of four restaurants during the fiscal year. Comparable store sales for the fiscal year ended September 27, 1998 increased by 1.3%, while average weekly sales, which includes sales at comparable stores as well as new restaurants, were 2.0% above the prior year. Sales levels for our latest variations of new prototype restaurants, of which there were seven open during the fiscal year, were 14% above our company-owned restaurant average for the year, partially due to increased sales volumes associated with the honeymoon period following a new restaurant opening.

Consumer Product Sales.

Consumer product sales increased 3.0% to $9.4 million in fiscal 1998 from $9.1 million in fiscal 1997. Sales in the food service category increased significantly as sales to hotel chains increased approximately 117.8% during fiscal 1998. The expansion of movie theater programs and a non-branded program with a national restaurant chain have contributed to our growth in the food service category. Sales volumes decreased in the fresh refrigerated and wholesale club categories as the competition for shelf space has intensified and the presence of fresh prepared food venues has proliferated over the last several years. We continued to test several branded and private label products with various movie theater chains, hotel chains and other food service providers.

Franchise Income.

Franchise income increased 0.7% to $4.5 million in fiscal 1998. Royalty income increased 1.9% in fiscal 1998, as average weekly sales increased by 2.3%. Operating weeks were essentially flat compared to last year, as five new full-service restaurants opened and eight non-Chicago Bar & Grill full-service restaurants closed in fiscal 1998. Initial franchise fees totaled $133,000 for fiscal 1998 compared to $183,000 in fiscal 1997.

Cost of Food and Beverages.

Cost of food and beverages as a percentage of restaurant and consumer product sales increased to 26.0% in fiscal 1998 from 25.4% in fiscal 1997. This increase primarily reflects higher cheese costs and cost increases associated with the system-wide roll out of our new menu initiative.

Labor and Benefits.

Labor and benefits as a percentage of restaurant and consumer product sales decreased slightly to 31.1% in fiscal 1998 from 31.2% in fiscal 1997, as an increase in the average hourly wage rate and increasing salaries for entry level managers were offset by productivity gains in restaurant operations and lower benefits expense.

Occupancy Costs.

Occupancy costs as a percentage of restaurant and consumer product sales decreased to 15.0% in fiscal 1998 from 15.6% in fiscal 1997 due to sales leverage gains and lower security expense.

Other Operating Costs.

Other operating costs as a percentage of restaurant and consumer product sales increased to 9.7% in fiscal 1998 from 9.3% in fiscal 1997, primarily due to $938,000 of pre-opening costs. Previously, in fiscal 1997, these costs were included in the depreciation and amortization category.

General and Administrative Expenses.
General and administrative expenses as a percentage of total revenues decreased to 7.1% in fiscal 1998 from 7.5% in fiscal 1997. This decrease was due to leverage gains associated with higher sales volumes.

Depreciation and Amortization Expense.
Depreciation and amortization expenses as a percentage of restaurant and consumer product sales decreased to 6.5% in fiscal 1998 from 7.2% in fiscal 1997, due to the change in accounting for pre-opening amortization. Excluding this accounting change, depreciation and amortization expense would have been down 0.2% as a percentage of restaurant and consumer product sales due to sales leverage gains.

Special Charges.
In fiscal 1997 we recorded special charges in the amount of $4.0 million, consisting of an asset impairment charge of $3.3 million and restaurant closing costs of $700,000. The $3.3 million asset impairment charge was recorded to reflect a decrease in the carrying value of equipment and improvements at leased properties for two full-service Pizzeria Uno...Chicago Bar & Grill restaurants to their fair market value and resulted from weak operating results and negative cash flow. The restaurant closure costs represent remaining minimum lease payments of one full-service Pizzeria Uno...Chicago Bar & Grill restaurant which was closed during fiscal 1997.

Operating Income.
Operating income was $12.7 million which represents an operating margin of 6.6% for fiscal 1998. For fiscal 1997, operating income was $6.9 million which represents an operating margin of 3.9%. Fiscal 1997 operating income, exclusive of the special charges, was $10.9 million which represents an operating margin of 6.1%. The improvement in operating income and operating margin in fiscal 1998 was primarily due to sales leverage gains in occupancy, depreciation and overhead cost categories.

Interest and Other Expense.
Interest and other expense increased to $3.7 million or 1.9% as a percentage of total revenues in fiscal 1998 from $2.8 million or 1.6% of total revenues in fiscal 1997. This increase was principally due to higher interest expense associated with the increased level of debt due to the repurchase of 1.3 million shares under our "Dutch Auction" tender offer in 1997.

Provision for Income Taxes.
The effective income tax rate decreased to 33.0% for fiscal 1998 from 34% in fiscal 1997, primarily due to the impact of permanent items, which remained consistent in fiscal 1998, being applied against a higher pre-tax income amount.

Cumulative Effect of Change in Accounting Principle.
In fiscal 1998 we elected to adopt the provisions of SOP 98-5 "Reporting the Costs of Start-up Activities," which requires that pre-opening costs be expensed as incurred. In accordance with SOP 98-5, the adoption of this principle is reported as a cumulative effect of a change in accounting and is recognized in the first quarter of fiscal 1998. The cumulative effect of the change in accounting net of applicable taxes was $636,000, or $0.06 per share on a diluted basis.

Liquidity and Sources of Capital
The following table presents a summary of our cash flows for the fifty-three weeks ended October 3, 1999 (in thousands).

Net cash provided by operating activities	$24,764
Net cash used in investing activities	(16,130)
Net cash used in financing activities	(9,912)
Decrease in cash	$(1,278)

Historically, we have leased most of our restaurant locations and pursued a strategy of controlled growth, financing our expansion principally from operating cash flow, public equity offerings, the sale of senior, unsecured notes, and revolving lines of credit. During the fifty-three weeks ended October 3, 1999, our investment in property, equipment and leasehold improvements was $18.9 million.

In fiscal 1999, we opened five restaurants in our existing markets. In fiscal 2000, we currently expect to open approximately 13 to 15 restaurants. We project that the average cash investment required in fiscal 2000 to open a full-service Pizzeria Uno Chicago Bar and Grill restaurant, excluding land and pre-opening costs, will be approximately $1.6 million. The expected capital expenditures for fiscal 2000 are estimated to be approximately $30.0 million of which approximately $22.0 million is expected to be expended for the opening of new restaurants.

As of October 3, 1999, we had outstanding indebtedness of $30.9 million under our $55 million credit facility, $666,000 in capital lease obligations and $4.6 million under our mortgage financing. Advances under the revolving credit facility will accrue interest at the lender's prime rate plus 0-50 basis points, or alternatively, 100-175 basis points above LIBOR, depending upon our level of indebtedness. We anticipate using the revolving credit facility in the future for the development of additional restaurants and for working capital.

In September 1998, our board of directors authorized the repurchase of 1,100,000 shares of our common stock through a "Dutch Auction" tender offer. The terms of the tender offer provided that we would purchase up to 1,100,000 shares (subject to increase under certain circumstances) of our common stock at prices, not in excess of $6.36 nor less than $5.23 per share, specified by tendering stockholders. On October 30, 1998, we completed the repurchase of 302,193 shares at a price of $6.36 per share. The total number of shares purchased represented approximately 3% of the shares outstanding at the time. We used a portion of our $55 million credit facility to purchase the shares tendered.

On April 14, 1999, the board of directors extended the previous 1,100,000 share repurchase program announced on April 22, 1998, for an additional twelve months. To date under this authorization, we have repurchased 704,270 shares, of which 339,185 have been purchased during fiscal 1999.

On September 9, 1999 we filed a registration statement for a proposed public offering of 2,000,000 shares of common stock with the Securities and Exchange Commission. The proposed public offering included 1,000,000 company shares and 1,000,000 shares from an existing shareholder. On November 3, 1999 we withdrew the offering due to overall market volatility and the current share price of our common stock.

We believe that existing cash balances, cash generated from operations and borrowings under our revolving line of credit will be sufficient to fund our capital requirements for the foreseeable future.

We are currently obligated under 98 leases, including 95 leases for Company-owned restaurants, two leases for our executive offices and one lease for a mill shop. We are currently negotiating the renewal of a lease for an office building containing one of our restaurants and continue to pay rent on a tenancy at will basis in the interim.

Year 2000 Compliance

The Year 2000 problem is a result of computer programs being written using two digits rather than four to define the applicable year. Any of our programs that have time sensitive software may recognize the date using "00" as the year 1900 rather than the year 2000, which could result in system failures or miscalculations using existing software. We completed an assessment of our computer systems to identify the systems that could be affected by the "Year 2000" issue and developed and implemented a compliance plan to resolve any issues. We have executed our current plan and believe that we are fully "Year 2000" compliant. However, if unanticipated problems arise from systems or equipment, there could be material adverse effects on the Company's consolidated financial position, results of operations and cash flows.

In addition to the assessment of in-house computer systems, we have assessed the readiness of our vendors, franchise partners and non-information technology equipment for the Year 2000 issue. In terms of our most critical needs, we have received assurances from our major food distributor and our credit card processor that their systems are Year 2000 compliant. We distributed questionnaires to our other business-critical vendors and franchise partners to assess their Year 2000 readiness. We have received assurances from all of our key relationships that they are Year 2000 compliant. We have determined that the most likely worst case scenario would be our inability to acquire food supplies from our food service distributors. We have made arrangements to have adequate inventory on-hand to provide service until an alternative source of supplies becomes available. We believe our operations will not be significantly disrupted if other third parties with whom we have relationships are not Year 2000 compliant. We believe that we will not have any material liability to third parties as a result of any potential noncompliance with Year 2000 issues.

Contingency plans have been developed in the event that there are interruptions critical to our on-going restaurant operations due to the Year 2000 issue. These plans include, but are not limited to, having adequate inventory on-hand to provide service until alternative sources become available, and replacing certain electronic applications with manual processes to provide basic restaurant services. No contingency plans have been developed for the loss of key public services, including gas and electric utilities.

We have expensed all maintenance and modification costs as we incurred them. We have capitalized and depreciated the cost of new software, if material, over its expected useful life. We incurred costs of approximately $150,000 in testing and remediation of all our systems and applications. Approximately $60,000 of the total cost of testing and remediation relates to repair issues and the remainder to replacement of equipment. All costs were budgeted and funded by cash flows from operations. No information technology projects were deferred due to Year 2000 compliance efforts. We did not purse independent verification of our systems because we believe that any effort would be as costly as the remediation effort and was not warranted. The costs related to the Year 2000 compliance project was not material to our financial position or results of operations.

Impact of Inflation

Inflation has not been a major factor in our business for the last several years. We believe we have historically been able to pass on increased costs through menu price increases, but there can be no assurance that we will be able to do so in the future. Future increases in local area construction costs could adversely affect our ability to expand.

Seasonality

Our business is seasonal in nature, with revenues and, to a greater degree, operating income being lower in the first and second fiscal quarters than in other quarters. Our seasonal business pattern is due to our concentration of restaurants in the Northeast, and the resulting lower winter volumes.

Forward-Looking Information

Certain information in this Annual Report on Form 10-K including, but not limited to, statements found in this "Item 7. Management's Discussion and Analysis of Financial Condition and Results of Operations," may be forward-looking statements. Actual results might differ materially from those projected in such forward-looking statements. Among the factors that could cause actual results to differ materially are: the Company's ability to open new restaurants and operate new and existing restaurants profitably, which will depend upon a number of factors including the availability of suitable sites, the negotiation of acceptable lease or purchase terms, the securing of required governmental permits and approvals, the hiring, training and retaining of skilled management, and the availability of adequate financing; changes in local, regional and national economic conditions, especially economic conditions in the areas in which the Company's restaurants are concentrated; increasingly intense competition in the restaurant industry; changes in consumer tastes and eating habits; increases in food, labor, employee benefits and similar costs; and other risks identified from time to time in the Company's periodic reports and the more detailed factors discussed in the Company's Registration Statement on Form S-2 (Reg. No. 333-86765), each as filed with the Securities and Exchange Commission.

Consolidated Balance Sheets

Year ended	October 3 1999	September 27 1998
(Amounts in thousands, except per share data)		
Assets		
Current assets:		
Cash	**$752**	$2,030
Accounts receivable, net	**2,398**	1,784
Inventory	**2,436**	2,296
Prepaid expenses	**1,757**	815
Total current assets	**7,343**	6,925
Property, equipment and leasehold improvements, net	**128,746**	125,323
Deferred income taxes	**10,020**	7,450
Liquor licenses and other assets	**3,503**	3,497
	$149,612	$143,195
Liabilities and shareholders' equity		
Current liabilities:		
Accounts payable	**$ 7,798**	$6,589
Accrued expenses	**8,668**	7,949
Accrued compensation and taxes	**3,369**	2,666
Income taxes payable	**2,914**	995
Current portions of long-term debt and capital lease obligation	**4,075**	4,081
Total current liabilities	**26,824**	22,280
Long-term debt, net of current portion	**31,612**	38,676
Capital lease obligations, net of current portion	**489**	666
Other liabilities	**9,708**	7,904
Commitments and contingencies		
Shareholders' equity:		
Preferred Stock, $1.00 par value; 1,000 shares authorized; no shares issued or outstanding		
Common Stock, $.01 par value, 25,000 shares authorized; 15,375 shares in 1999 and 15,153 shares in 1998 issued	**154**	152
Additional paid-in capital	**55,648**	53,930
Retained earnings	**52,003**	42,203
	107,805	96,285
Treasury Stock (4,100 shares in 1999 and 3,492 shares in 1998) at cost	**(26,826)**	(22,616)
Total shareholders' equity	**80,979**	73,669
	$149,612	$143,195

See accompanying notes.

17

Consolidated Statements of Income

Year ended	October 3 1999	September 27 1998	September 28 1997
(Amounts in thousands, except per share data)	(53 weeks)		
Revenues:			
Restaurant sales	$198,560	$177,343	$164,389
Consumer product sales	10,568	9,384	9,115
Franchise income	5,105	4,549	4,516
	214,233	191,276	178,020
Costs and expenses:			
Cost of food and beverages	54,683	48,567	43,994
Labor and benefits	64,700	58,139	54,183
Occupancy costs	29,199	27,988	27,045
Other operating costs	18,333	18,086	16,067
General and administrative	16,629	13,661	13,384
Depreciation and amortization	12,702	12,183	12,469
Special charges			4,000
	196,246	178,624	171,142
Operating income	17,987	12,652	6,878
Other expense (income):			
Interest expense	3,160	3,527	2,695
Other expense (income)	(21)	134	132
	3,139	3,661	2,827
Income before income taxes	14,848	8,991	4,051
Provision for income taxes	5,048	2,968	1,378
Income before cumulative effect of change in accounting principle	9,800	6,023	2,673
Cumulative effect of change in accounting principle for pre-opening costs, net of income tax benefit of $313		636	
Net income	$9,800	$ 5,387	$2,673
Basic earnings per share:			
Earnings before cumulative effect of change in accounting principle	$ .87	$ .50	$ .20
Cumulative effect of change in accounting principle		(.05)	
	$ .87	$ .45	$ .20
Diluted earnings per share:			
Earnings before cumulative effect of change in accounting principle	$ .84	$ .50	$ .20
Cumulative effect of change in accounting principle		(.05)	
	$ .84	$ .45	$ .20
Basic weighted average shares outstanding	11,313	11,960	13,146
Diluted weighted average shares outstanding	11,610	12,025	13,209

See accompanying notes.

18

Consolidated Statements of Shareholders' Equity

(Amounts in thousands)	Common Stock Shares	Common Stock Amount	Additional Paid-in Capital	Retained Earnings	Treasury Stock	Total
Balance at September 29, 1996	15,068	$151	$53,495	$34,143	$(10,653)	$77,136
Net income				2,673		2,673
Exercise of stock options	62	1	257			258
Purchase of Treasury Stock					(9,224)	(9,224)
Tax benefit from exercise of nonqualified stock options			37			37
Balance at September 28, 1997	15,130	152	53,789	36,816	(19,877)	70,880
Net income				5,387		5,387
Exercise of stock options	23		127			127
Purchase of Treasury Stock					(2,791)	(2,791)
Contribution of Treasury Stock to 401(k) Savings and Employee Stock Ownership Retirement Plan			2		52	54
Tax benefit from exercise of nonqualified stock options			12			12
Balance at September 27, 1998	15,153	152	53,930	42,203	(22,616)	73,669
Net income (53 weeks)				9,800		9,800
Exercise of stock options	222	2	1,515			1,517
Purchase of Treasury Stock					(4,382)	(4,382)
Contribution of Treasury Stock to 401(k) Savings and Employee Stock Ownership Retirement Plan			3		172	175
Tax benefit from exercise of nonqualified stock options			200			200
Balance at October 3, 1999	15,375	$154	$55,648	$52,003	$(26,826)	$80,979

See accompanying notes.

Consolidated Statements of Cash Flows

link between Income Statement & Balance Sheet (handwritten)

Year ended	October 3 1999	September 27 1998	September 28 1997
(Amounts in thousands)			
Operating activities			
Net income	$9,800	$5,387	$ 2,673
Adjustments to reconcile net income to net cash provided by operating activities:			
Cumulative effect of change in accounting principle		636	
Depreciation and amortization	12,823	12,292	12,573
Deferred income taxes	(2,570)	(851)	(2,986)
Contribution of Treasury Stock to 401(k) Savings and Employee Stock Ownership Retirement Plan	175	54	
Provision for deferred rent	184	147	612
Gain on disposal of equipment	(62)	(26)	(15)
Special charges			4,000
Changes in operating assets and liabilities:			
Accounts receivable	(614)	1,039	(367)
Inventory	(140)	30	7
Prepaid expenses	(1,071)	(237)	(1,539)
Accounts payable and other liabilities	4,320	700	4,620
Income taxes payable	1,919	(768)	495
Net cash provided by operating activities	24,764	18,403	20,073
Investing activities			
Additions to property, equipment, and leasehold improvements	(18,860)	(12,141)	(19,982)
Proceeds from sale of fixed assets	2,730	26	300
Net cash used in investing activities	(16,130)	(12,115)	(19,682)
Financing activities			
Proceeds from revolving line of credit	72,243	50,790	71,193
Principal payments on debt and capital lease obligations	(79,490)	(53,882)	(62,997)
Purchase of Treasury Stock	(4,382)	(2,791)	(9,224)
Exercise of stock options	1,717	139	295
Net cash used in financing activities	(9,912)	(5,744)	(733)
Increase (decrease) in cash	(1,278)	544	(342)
Cash at beginning of year	2,030	1,486	1,828
Cash at end of year	$752	$2,030	$1,486

(handwritten: *cash flow from operations*)

(handwritten left margin: *x Big discrepancy good income book for good cash*)

See accompanying notes.

Notes to Consolidated Financial Statements

1. Summary of Significant Accounting Policies

Description of Business

The Company owns and operates 98 Pizzeria Uno...Chicago Bar & Grill casual dining, full-service restaurants primarily from New England to Virginia, as well as Florida, Chicago and Denver, and franchises 60 units in 29 states, the District of Columbia, Puerto Rico and Seoul, Korea. The Company also operates a Mexican restaurant in Chicago and a refrigerated and frozen consumer foods division. The consumer foods business supplies American Airlines, movie theaters, hotel restaurants, supermarkets and wholesale club chains with both frozen and refrigerated Pizzeria Uno brand products, as well as certain private label products.

Basis of Presentation

The consolidated financial statements include the accounts of Uno Restaurant Corporation and its wholly-owned subsidiaries (the Company). All intercompany accounts and transactions have been eliminated in consolidation.

Fiscal Year

The Company's fiscal year ends on the close of business on the Sunday closest to September 30 in each year. The fiscal year ended October 3, 1999 consisted of 53 weeks. Fiscal years 1998 and 1997 consisted of 52 weeks.

Pre-opening Costs

In the third quarter of fiscal 1998, the Company adopted Statement of Position (SOP) 98-5 Reporting the Costs of Start-up Activities which requires that pre-opening costs be expensed as incurred. In accordance with SOP 98-5, the adoption is reported as a cumulative effect of a change in accounting principle and has been recognized retroactively to the first quarter of fiscal 1998. The cumulative effect of the change in accounting principle was $636,000, net of the income tax benefit of $313,000. The impact of adoption on fiscal 1998 results of operations was not material.

Inventory

Inventory, which consists of food, beverages and supplies, is stated at the lower of cost (first-in, first-out method) or market.

Property, Equipment and Leasehold Improvements

Property, equipment and leasehold improvements are recorded at cost. The Company provides for depreciation of buildings and equipment using the straight-line method over 25 and 7 years, respectively. Leasehold improvements are amortized over the shorter of their estimated useful lives or the term of the lease (generally 20 years) using the straight-line method.

Revenue Recognition-Franchise Fees

The Company defers franchise fees until the franchisee opens the restaurant and all services have been substantially performed; at that time, the fee is recorded as income. Royalty income is recorded as earned based on rates provided by the respective franchise agreements. Expenses related to franchise activities amounted to approximately $3,895,000, $3,280,000 and $3,441,000 in fiscal years 1999, 1998 and 1997, respectively.

A summary of full-service franchise unit activity is as follows:

| | Year ended | | |
	October 3 1999	September 27 1998	September 28 1997
Units operating at beginning of year	63	66	63
Units opened	8	5	6
Units closed	(11)	(8)	(3)
Units operating at end of year	60	63	66

Income Taxes

Deferred income taxes are determined utilizing the liability method. Under this method, deferred tax assets and liabilities are determined based on differences between financial reporting and tax basis of assets and liabilities and are measured using the enacted tax rates and laws that will be in effect when the differences are expected to reverse.

Advertising

The Company records advertising expense as incurred. Advertising expense was $5,054,000, $5,257,000 and $4,897,000 for fiscal years 1999, 1998 and 1997, respectively.

Earnings Per Share

Basic earnings per share represents net income divided by the weighted average shares of common stock outstanding during the period. Weighted average shares used in diluted earnings per share include 297,000, 65,000 and 63,000 for fiscal years 1999, 1998 and 1997, respectively, of common stock equivalents arising from stock options using the treasury stock method.

Use of Estimates

The preparation of the consolidated financial statements in conformity with generally accepted accounting principles requires management to make estimates and assumptions that affect the reported amounts of assets and liabilities and the disclosure of contingent assets and liabilities at the date of the consolidated financial statements and the reported amounts of revenues and costs and expenses during the reporting period. Actual results could differ from those estimates.

Stock-Based Compensation

The Company has elected to follow Accounting Principles Board Opinion (APB) No. 25, "Accounting for Stock Issued to Employees" in accounting for its stock-based compensation plans, rather than the alternative fair value accounting method provided for under Statement of Financial Accounting Standard (SFAS) No. 123, "Accounting for Stock-Based Compensation," as this alternative requires the use of option valuation models that were not developed for use in valuing employee stock options. Under APB No. 25, since the exercise price of options granted under these plans equals the market price of the underlying stock on the date of grant, no compensation expense is recognized.

Accounting Pronouncements

In 1999, the Company adopted SFAS No. 130, "Reporting Comprehensive Income" and SFAS No. 131, "Disclosures About Segments of an Enterprise and Related Information," which did not have a material impact on the Company's consolidated financial statements.

In June 1998, the Financial Accounting Standards Board (FASB) issued SFAS No. 133, "Accounting for Derivative Instruments and Hedging Activities,"which is effective for fiscal year 2001. This statement requires all derivatives to be carried on the balance sheet as assets or liabilities at fair value. The accounting for changes in the fair value of the derivatives would depend on the hedging relationship and would be reported in the income statement, or as a component of comprehensive income. The Company believes that the adoption of this new accounting standard will not have a material impact on the Company's consolidated financial statements.

Reclassifications

Certain amounts in the accompanying financial statements have been reclassified to conform with the 1999 presentation.

2. Special Charges

During the third quarter of fiscal 1997, the Company recorded a special charge in the amount of $4.0 million, consisting of an asset impairment charge of $3.3 million and store closing costs of $0.7 million. The $3.3 million asset impairment charge was recorded to reduce the carrying value of equipment and leaseholds at two full-service Uno restaurants to their fair market value and resulted from weak operating results and continuing negative cash flow. The store closure costs represented remaining minimum lease payments of one full-service Uno restaurant which was closed during 1997.

3. Property, Equipment and Leasehold Improvements

Property, equipment and leasehold improvements consist of the following:

	October 3 1999	September 27 1998
	(In thousands)	
Land	**$17,143**	$16,874
Buildings	**28,920**	27,823
Equipment	**58,576**	52,536
Leasehold improvements	**101,326**	93,324
Construction in progress	**2,930**	3,309
	208,895	193,866
Less allowances for depreciation and amortization	**80,149**	68,543
	$128,746	$125,323

4. Related-Party Transactions

The Company leases three buildings from its principal shareholder for a restaurant and corporate office space. Rent expense in the amount of approximately $515,000 was charged to operations in fiscal year 1999 and $505,000 was charged to operations in each of fiscal years 1998 and 1997. The Company believes that the terms of these leases approximate fair rental value.

The Company's Chief Executive Officer and his brother own and operate four franchised restaurants and pay royalties to the Company under standard franchise agreements.

5. Leases

The Company conducts the majority of its operations in leased facilities, which are accounted for as capital or operating leases. The leases typically provide for a base rent plus real estate taxes, insurance and other expenses, plus additional contingent rent based upon revenues of the restaurant. Assets held under capital leases were $2,881,000 at October 3, 1999 and September 27, 1998. Accumulated amortization amounted to $880,000 at October 3, 1999 and $747,000 at September 27, 1998. Capital lease asset amortization is included in depreciation and amortization. At October 3, 1999, the minimum rental commitments under all noncancelable capital and operating leases with initial or remaining terms of more than one year are as follows:

Fiscal Year	Operating Leases	Capital Leases
	(In thousands)	
2000	$9,681	$223
2001	9,802	75
2002	9,861	42
2003	9,515	42
2004	9,392	42
Thereafter	71,026	1,126
	$119,277	1,550
Less amount representing interest		884
Present value of net minimum lease payments		666
Less current portion of obligation under capital leases		177
Long-term obligation under capital leases		$489

Total expenses for all operating leases were as follows:

Fiscal Year	Minimum Lease Rentals	Contingent Rentals	Total
	(In thousands)		
1999	$13,542	$607	$14,149
1998	13,010	689	13,699
1997	12,641	811	13,452

Certain operating lease agreements contain free rent inducements and scheduled rent increases which are being amortized over the terms of the agreements, ranging from 15 to 20 years, using the straight-line method. The deferred rent liability, included in other liabilities, amounted to $4,927,000 at October 3, 1999 and $4,743,000 at September 27, 1998.

6. Financing Arrangements

Long-term debt consists of the following:

	October 3 1999	September 27 1998
	(In thousands)	
Revolving credit and note agreement	$30,915	$37,760
8.75%, 15-year secured mortgage notes payable	4,595	4,796
	35,510	42,556
Less current portion	3,898	3,880
	$31,612	$38,676

In November 1997, the Company amended its credit facility from $50 million to $55 million, which includes a $26.6 million revolver due in October 2002, a $8.4 million term loan due in 20 quarterly installments of $420,000 plus interest commencing on January 31, 1998 and a $20.0 million mortgage facility due in 27 quarterly installments of $500,000 plus interest also commencing on January 31, 1998 with a final payment due in October 2004. The Company is entitled to borrow, at its discretion, amounts which accrue interest at variable rates based on either the LIBOR or prime rate.

Amounts borrowed under the credit facility are secured by certain real properties owned by the Company. At October 3, 1999, interest rates on outstanding borrowings under the revolving line of credit ranged from 6.63% to 8.75%. A commitment fee of approximately 0.38% is accrued on unused borrowings under the new credit agreement. The note agreements contain certain financial and operating covenants, including maintenance of certain levels of net worth and income. At October 3, 1999, the carrying value of the Company's long-term debt approximated fair market value.

Annual principal payments of debt are as follows (in thousands):

Fiscal Year	
2000	$ 3,898
2001	3,918
2002	3,940
2003	13,658
2004	2,309
Thereafter	7,787
	$35,510

The Company has two interest rate swap agreements which convert a portion of its floating rate debt to a fixed-rate basis, thereby reducing the potential impact of interest rate increases on future income. The notional amounts and fair market value under the swap agreements amount to $30 million and $30,000, respectively, at October 3, 1999. The terms range from three to five years with fixed interest rates ranging from

5.80% to 6.04%. The differentials to be paid or received are accrued as interest rates change and are recognized as an adjustment to interest expense related to the debt.

The Company made cash payments of interest of $3,540,000, $3,598,000 and $3,044,000 during fiscal years 1999, 1998 and 1997, respectively. The Company capitalized interest during the construction period of new restaurants which amounted to $157,000 in fiscal year 1999, $127,000 in fiscal year 1998 and $313,000 in fiscal year 1997 and included those amounts in leasehold improvements.

The Company provides certain limited lease financing to qualified franchisees through an agreement with an unaffiliated finance company. The Company's maximum guarantee under the agreement was $714,000 at October 3, 1999. The Company has also guaranteed up to a maximum of $400,000 of future lease payments in the event of default by a specific franchisee.

7. Common Stock Transactions

On September 29, 1998, the Company initiated a Dutch Auction self-tender offer for up to 1,100,000 shares of the Company's common stock and under certain circumstances, reserved the right to purchase in excess of 1,100,000 shares. Under the terms of the offer, the Company invited stockholders to tender their shares at prices ranging from $5.23 to $6.36 per share. On October 30, 1998, the Company completed the tender offer for 302,193 shares of its common stock at $6.36 per share.

8. Prepaid Expenses

Prepaid expenses consist of the following:

	October 3 1999	September 27 1998
	(In thousands)	
Prepaid rent	$1,430	$442
Prepaid operating costs	269	234
Prepaid insurance	58	139
	$1,757	$815

9. Accrued Expenses

Accrued expenses consist of the following:

	October 3 1999	September 27 1998
	(In thousands)	
Accrued store closure	$2,197	$1,826
Accrued rent	1,483	1,372
Accrued insurance	1,627	793
Accrued utilities	653	785
Accrued vacation	737	680
Accrued advertising	482	557
Franchise fee deposits	273	486
Other	1,216	1,450
	$8,668	$7,949

10. Employee Benefit Plans

The Company maintains a 401(k) Savings and Employee Stock Ownership Retirement Plan (the Plan) for all of its eligible employees. The Plan is maintained in accordance with the provisions of Section 401(k) of the Internal Revenue Code and allows all employees with at least one year of service to make annual tax-deferred voluntary contributions up to 15% of their salary. Under the Plan, the Company matches a specified percentage of the employees contributions, subject to certain limitations. Total contributions made to the plan were $225,000, $214,000 and $229,000 in fiscal years 1999, 1998 and 1997, respectively. In 1999 and 1998 respectively, contributions included $175,000 and $54,000 of Uno Restaurant Corporation common stock previously held in Treasury.

The Company sponsors a Deferred Compensation Plan which allows officers to defer up to 20% of their annual compensation. These assets are placed in a rabbi trust and are presented as assets of the Company in the accompanying balance sheet as they are available to the general creditors of the Company in the event of the Company's insolvency. The related liability of $1,308,000 at October 3, 1999 and $880,000 at September 27, 1998 is included in other liabilities in the accompanying balance sheet. Deferred compensation expense in the amounts of $428,000, $153,000 and $161,000 were recorded in fiscal years 1999, 1998 and 1997, respectively.

11. Income Taxes

Deferred taxes are attributable to the following temporary differences:

	October 3 1999	September 27 1998
	(In thousands)	
Deferred tax assets:		
Excess book over tax depreciation	$4,035	$2,327
Deferred rent	1,914	1,937
Accrued expenses	1,910	1,467
Asset impairment charge	1,043	1,211
Franchise fees	900	627
Other	769	376
Total deferred tax assets	10,571	7,945
Deferred tax liabilities:		
Other	551	495
Total deferred tax liabilities	551	495
Net deferred tax assets	$10,020	$7,450

The provision (credit) for income taxes consisted of the following:

	Year ended		
	October 3 1999	September 27 1998	September 28 1997
	(In thousands)		
Current:			
Federal	$6,302	$2,941	$3,448
State	1,316	878	916
	7,618	3,819	4,364
Deferred:			
Federal	(2,069)	(713)	(2,435)
State	(501)	(138)	(551)
	(2,570)	(851)	(2,986)
Income tax expense	$5,048	$2,968	$1,378

A reconciliation of the effective tax rates with the federal statutory rates is as follows:

	Year ended		
	October 3 1999	September 27 1998	September 28 1997
Federal statutory rate	34.3%	34.0%	34.0%
State income taxes, net of federal income tax benefit	4.6	4.6	4.6
Tax credits	(5.1)	(6.5)	(7.1)
Other	.2	.9	2.5
Effective income tax rate	34.0%	33.0%	34.0%

The Company made income tax payments of $5,598,000, $4,545,000 and $3,936,000 during fiscal years 1999, 1998 and 1997, respectively.

12. Stock-Based Compensation

During 1998, the Company's shareholders ratified the 1997 Key Officer Stock Option Plan (the Key Officer Plan) under which options were granted for 1.1 million shares of Common Stock at an exercise price of $6.82 per share, which are fully vested at October 3, 1999. The Key Officer Plan will terminate on August 25, 2007.

During 1998, the Company also established the 1997 Non-Qualified Stock Option Plan for Non-Employee Directors (the 1997 Directors' Plan) which provides for the granting of options to purchase up to 82,500 shares of Common Stock. Options are to be granted at an exercise price equal to the fair market value of the shares of Common Stock at the date of grant and vest one year after date of grant. The 1997 Directors' Plan will terminate on February 26, 2008.

Notes to Consolidated Financial Statements

The Company also has the 1997 Employee Stock Option Plan (the Employee Plan) which provides for the granting of options to purchase up to 1.1 million shares of common stock. Options may be granted at an exercise price not less than fair market value on the date of grant. All options vest at a rate of 20% per year beginning one year after the date of grant. All options terminate ten years after the date of grant.

The Company's 1987 Employee Stock Option Plan which contains similar provisions to the 1997 Plan was terminated during fiscal 1997. The 1.4 million options granted under that plan will continue to vest at a rate of 20% per year beginning one year after the date of grant, with the exception of 103,125 options granted to the President of the Company, which vested immediately at the date of grant. All options terminate ten years after the date of grant, with the exception of the 19,250

options granted to the Chairman, which terminate five years after the date of grant.

The 1989 and 1993 Non-Qualified Stock Option Plans for Non-Employee Directors (the Directors' Plans) provide for up to 111,719 shares of Common Stock issuable upon exercise of options granted under the Directors' Plans. The 1989 and 1993 Directors' Plans terminate on November 10, 1999 and August 17, 2002, but such termination shall not affect the validity of options granted prior to the dates of termination.

Options are granted at an exercise price equal to the fair market value of the shares of Common Stock at the date of grant. Options granted under the Directors' Plans may be exercised commencing one year after the date of grant and ending ten years from the date of grant.

Information regarding the Company's stock option plans is summarized below:

	Year ended					
	October 3 1999		September 27 1998		September 28 1997	
	Options	Weighted-Average Exercise Price	Options	Weighted-Average Exercise Price	Options	Weighted-Average Exercise Price
Outstanding at beginning of period	2,748,410	$6.70	1,361,146	$6.66	1,418,172	$6.62
Granted	281,416	11.09	1,519,908	6.69	232,768	5.99
Exercised	(221,444)	6.85	(20,255)	6.83	(61,233)	4.04
Canceled	(357,751)	6.85	(112,389)	6.21	(228,561)	6.42
Outstanding at end of period	2,450,631	$7.17	2,748,410	$6.70	1,361,146	$6.66
Options exercisable at end of period	1,725,237		1,032,061		760,640	
Options available for grant at end of period	728,309		651,974		939,672	

The weighted-average fair value of options granted during fiscal years 1999, 1998 and 1997, were $4.54, $2.74 and $2.69, respectively. The Company has 3.2 million shares of common stock reserved at October 3, 1999 for the exercise of stock options at October 3, 1999.

The following table presents information about significant option groups outstanding at October 3, 1999:

Exercise Price	Options Outstanding	Weighted-Average Remaining Contractual Life	Options Exercisable	Weighted-Average Exercisable Price
$5.27 - $6.59	902,425	6.9 years	482,286	$5.88
$6.82 - $11.42	1,548,207	7.4 years	1,242,951	$7.13

Notes to Consolidated Financial Statements

Pursuant to the requirements of SFAS No. 123, the following are the pro forma net income and earnings per share for fiscal year 1999, 1998 and 1997 as if the compensation cost for the stock option plans had been determined based on the fair value at the grant date for grants in fiscal year 1999, 1998 and 1997:

	Year ended		
	October 3 1999	September 27 1998	September 28 1997
	(In thousands, except per share information)		
Net income – as reported	**$9,800**	$5,387	$2,673
Basic earnings per share - as reported	**$.87**	$ .45	$ .20
Diluted earnings per share - as reported	**$.84**	$ .45	$ .20
Net income – pro forma	**$9,331**	$4,934	$2,553
Basic earnings per share - pro forma	**$.82**	$.41	$.19
Diluted earnings per share - pro forma	**$.80**	$.41	$.19

The fair value for these options was estimated at the date of grant using the Black-Scholes option pricing model with the following weighted average assumptions for fiscal years 1999, 1998 and 1997, respectively: risk-free interest rates of 6.3%, 5.0% and 6.6%; no dividend yield; the volatility factors of the expected market price of the Company's common stock was 34%, 37% and 40%; and a weighted-average expected life of the options of five years.

The effects on fiscal year 1999, 1998 and 1997 pro forma net income and earnings per share of expensing the fair value of stock options are not necessarily representative of the effects on reported results of operations for future years as the periods presented include only three, two and one years, respectively, of option grants under the Company's plans.

13. Quarterly Financial Data (Unaudited)

	Quarter ended			
	December 27 1998	March 28 1999	June 27 1999	October 3 1999(3)
	(Amounts in thousands, except per share information)			
Revenues	$48,747	$50,251	$53,548	$61,687
Gross profit(1)	9,237	10,037	12,163	15,830
Operating income	3,001	3,082	4,576	7,328
Income before income taxes	2,154	2,229	3,715	6,750
Net income	1,443	1,494	2,488	4,375
Basic earnings per common share	.13	.13	.22	.39
Diluted earnings per common share	.13	.13	.22	.36

	Quarter ended			
	December 28 1997	March 29 1998	June 28 1998	September 27 1998
	(Amounts in thousands, except per share information)			
Revenues	$44,968	$46,682	$48,953	$50,673
Gross profit(1)	8,786	8,939	10,208	11,271
Operating income	2,726	2,286	3,524	4,116
Income before income taxes	1,803	1,351	2,561	3,276
Income before cumulative effect of change in accounting principle	1,208	904	1,717	2,194
Net income(2)	572	904	1,717	2,194
Basic and diluted earnings per common share: Before cumulative effect	.10	.08	.14	.19
Net income	.05	.08	.14	.19

(1) Restaurant and consumer product sales, less cost of food and beverages, labor and benefits, occupancy and other operating expenses, excluding advertising expenses.

(2) The quarter ended December 28, 1997 reflects retroactive application of the cumulative change in accounting principle adopted in the third quarter of fiscal 1998 (see Note 1 – Pre-opening Costs).

(3) The quarter ended October 3, 1999 consisted of 14 weeks compared with 13 weeks for the other quarters presented.

14. Subsequent Event

On November 30, 1999, the Company declared a 10% Common Stock dividend payable on December 23, 1999 to stockholders of record as of December 13, 1999. All share and per share data in the accompanying financial statements have been retroactively adjusted to reflect the stock dividend.

The Board of Directors
Uno Restaurant Corporation

We have audited the accompanying consolidated balance sheets of Uno Restaurant Corporation and subsidiaries (the Company) as of October 3, 1999 and September 27, 1998, and the related consolidated statements of income, shareholders' equity, and cash flows for each of the three years in the period ended October 3, 1999. These financial statements are the responsibility of the Company's management. Our responsibility is to express an opinion on these financial statements based on our audits.

We conducted our audits in accordance with generally accepted auditing standards. Those standards require that we plan and perform the audit to obtain reasonable assurance about whether the financial statements are free of material misstatement. An audit includes examining, on a test basis, evidence supporting the amounts and disclosures in the financial statements. An audit also includes assessing the accounting principles used and significant estimates made by management, as well as evaluating the overall financial statement presentation. We believe that our audits provide a reasonable basis for our opinion.

In our opinion, the financial statements referred to above present fairly, in all material respects, the consolidated financial position of Uno Restaurant Corporation and subsidiaries at October 3, 1999 and September 27, 1998, and the consolidated results of their operations and their cash flows for each of the three years in the period ended October 3, 1999, in conformity with generally accepted accounting principles.

As discussed in Note 1 to the consolidated financial statements, during fiscal year 1998, the Company adopted the provisions of the American Institute of Certified Public Accountants' Statement of Position 98-5, "Reporting the Costs of Start-up Activities."

Ernst + Young LLP

Boston, Massachusetts
October 29, 1999, except for Note 14,
  as to which the date is November 30, 1999

Directors & Officers, Uno Restaurant Corporation

Board of Directors

Aaron D. Spencer
Chairman of the Board

Craig S. Miller
President and Chief Executive Officer

Paul W. MacPhail
*Executive Vice President, Chief
Operating Officer*

James F. Carlin[1][2]
*Former Chairman & Chief
Executive Officer,
Carlin Consolidated, Inc.*

Tamara P. Davis[1][2]
*Former Chief Executive Officer,
UST Leasing Corp.*

John T. Gerlach[1][2][3]
*Director of the Graduate
Business Program,
Sacred Heart University*

Kenneth D. Hill[2]
*Former Chief Operating Officer,
Applebees International Inc.*

James J. Kerasiotes[1]
*Chairman & Chief Executive Officer,
Massachusetts Turnpike Authority*

Stephen J. Sweeney[1][2]
*Former Chairman of the Board,
Boston Edison Company*

[1] Member of the Audit Committee
[2] Member of the Compensation
Committee
[3] Chairman of Executive Committee

Executive Officers

Aaron D. Spencer
Chairman of the Board

Craig S. Miller
President and Chief Executive Officer

Paul W. MacPhail
*Executive Vice President
Chief Operating Officer*

Robert M. Brown
Executive Vice President

Alan M. Fox
*Executive Vice President
President - Uno Foods Inc.*

Robert M. Vincent
*Senior Vice President - Finance
Chief Financial Officer and Treasurer*

Charles A. Jones
Senior Vice President - Development

Larry J. Reeher
Senior Vice President - Human Resources

Holly J. Young
Senior Vice President - Marketing

Staff Officers

Randy M. Clifton
Vice President - Worldwide Franchising

Charles K. Dusenberry II
*Vice President - Construction, Design
and Facilities*

Alan R. Gibson
Vice President - Food and Beverage

George W. Herz II
Vice President - General Counsel

Alan D. LaBatte
Vice President - Information Systems

Subsidiary Officers

Uno Restaurants, Inc.

Kelly C. Baltes
Western Division Vice President

Ralph F. Desiano
New York Division Vice President

William J. Golden
New England Division Vice President

Robert G. Lapointe
Mid-Atlantic Division Vice President

Uno Foods Inc.

Charles J. Kozubal
Senior Vice President

Dieter H. Buehler
Vice President - Plant Operations

Brian J. Whicher
Vice President - Quality Control

Saxet Corporation

Maurice D. Molod
Vice President - Real Estate

Shareholder Information

Form 10-K

The Company's Annual Report on Form 10-K filed with the Securities and Exchange Commission is available without charge upon request and may be obtained by writing to Investor Relations at the Company's Executive Offices.

Common Stock Prices and Dividends

Pursuant to its revolving credit and term loan facility, the Company may not pay cash dividends in excess of 35% of net income for the then most recent four-quarter period. The Company has not paid any cash dividends on its Common Stock and for the foreseeable future intends to continue its policy of retaining earnings to finance the development and growth of the Company. On November 30, 1999 our board of directors declared a 10% stock dividend payable on December 23, 1999 to shareholders of record as of December 13, 1999. The following table, adjusted for the stock split, sets forth the range of high and low sales prices on the New York Stock Exchange (symbol:UNO) for the period from September 29, 1997 to October 3, 1999.

Fiscal Quarter	1998 High	1998 Low
First	6.818	5.682
Second	6.705	5.284
Third	6.989	6.364
Fourth	6.932	5.227

Fiscal Quarter	1999 High	1999 Low
First	6.648	5.284
Second	7.614	6.136
Third	7.955	6.250
Fourth	13.466	8.011

At October 3, 1999 there were approximately 2,200 beneficial owners of the Company's Common Stock.

Executive Offices
Uno Restaurant Corporation
100 Charles Park Road
West Roxbury, MA 02132
617-323-9200
www.pizzeriauno.com

Stock Transfer Agent and Registrar
Chase Mellon Shareholder Services, L.L.C.
East Hartford, CT 06108
860-282-3500

Independent Auditors
Ernst & Young LLP
Boston, MA 02116

Corporate Counsel
Brown, Rudnick, Freed & Gesmer
Boston, MA 02111

Uno Restaurant Corporation

100 Charles Park Road

West Roxbury, MA 02132

www.pizzeriauno.com

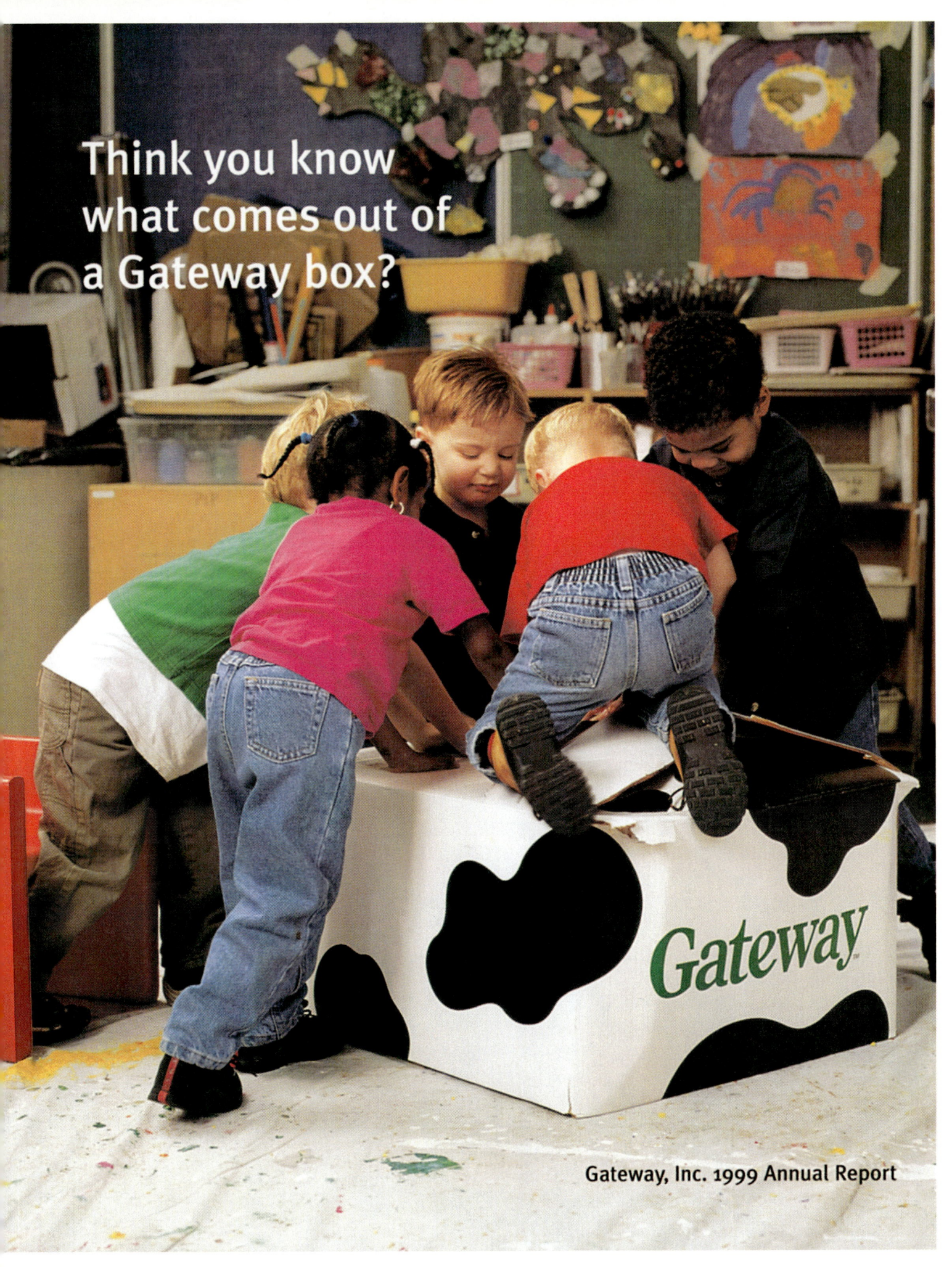

Think you know
what comes out of
a Gateway box?

Gateway, Inc. 1999 Annual Report

Gateway™ is building a global powerhouse to capture the once-in-a-lifetime opportunities of the digital revolution.

The kids at the Kendall Demonstration Elementary School at Gallaudet University were using a Gateway box to build a giraffe.

Pretty much the same process, it turns out.

In January 2000, a representative from Gallaudet University in Washington, D.C., called Gateway to tell us about an interesting Website that features some projects completed by grade school students with the help of their teachers.

This sophisticated Website (www.gallaudet.edu/~pcnmpce/ gatewayboxes/index.html) features the wonderful creations that the deaf students at the University's Kendall Demonstration Elementary School (KDES) made with the boxes in which their Gateway™ computers are shipped.

We took one look at the Website and realized we had found kindred spirits in the kids at KDES. Like them, we look at the Gateway box and see something much bigger…much more exciting and interesting. To us, "the box" is just the door to a world that's filled with opportunities and possibilities. And to us, there was no better way to illustrate Gateway's incredible journey "beyond the box," than through the kids at KDES. We hope you enjoy the trip.

Think again.

A letter to our shareholders from CEO Jeff Weitzen.

I first saw the Gallaudet Website in early January, 2000, and two things immediately struck me.

First, we've got a brand that people just naturally love. And that's not an exaggeration.

Our famous cow-spotted box draws people in and tells them we're approachable, human and connected, so much so that they can have some fun with it... build animals with it... design a Website around it.

That's a rare and invaluable asset in today's world of cold, steely technology brands, particularly as the Internet fans out and becomes simpler and more accessible every day.

It's almost as if the Gateway brand was designed 15 years ago with the coming Internet revolution in mind.

And, of course, I was struck by the obvious metaphor

that serves as the basis of this entire annual report. Like us, these young builders see the box as just the means to an end, a path to a greater destination that's limited only by imagination.

With those two thoughts in my mind, it was hard to look back at 1999 as anything but a great year. It was a year that we took our already strong brand to new heights and laid the foundation for our unique beyond-the-box future.

And along the way, we worked hard to deliver solid financial results. We increased revenues by 16%—about three times the industry growth rate— and grew earnings per share by 25%. We delivered on our promise to diversify our revenue streams beyond the box, exiting 1999 with 20% of our income generated from nonsystem revenues, versus just 3% in the fourth quarter of 1998.

And, in the end, we delivered very healthy returns to our shareholders, as Gateway's stock ended the year 170% higher than it began.

But 2000 is the year that we prove that Gateway looks at the world differently; that we have a unique position in the marketplace; and that, once and for all, we've got the capability to deliver on our vision of the future.

That vision is to Humanize the Digital Revolution, and from a practical standpoint, that means using technology to change the way people live, learn, work and play.

This year, we're going to take our world-class technology and the unparalleled beyond-the-box capabilities we've worked so hard to

build, and bring them to life in new and interesting ways for our clients.

I call it "technology empowerment," using technology to help people and businesses reach higher, do more and go places they've never been.

For example, our innovative Your:)Ware[SM] program will be reborn with fresh bundling offers around solutions like digital photography, on-line financial planning and music downloading, among others.

We'll begin introducing our first wave of Internet appliances to deliver content and applications against very specific needs, all tied together to make the Internet as mobile as today's consumer.

We'll offer our small business clients end-to-end Internet-based solutions

This is the year that we prove that Gateway looks at the world differently; that we have a unique position in the marketplace; and that, once and for all, we've got the capability to deliver on our vision of the future.

that grow with their business through applications like Web hosting, firewall protection and e-mail.

We're also going to take our unique, multichannel distribution model and really beef it up across all channels, extending our brand into literally thousands more points of distribution worldwide.

We'll accomplish all of these tasks both through building our own capabilities and through partnering with best-of-class companies around the world.

To sum it up, 2000 is the year of the "how." This is the year that we take all of our beyond-the-box capabilities and show people how technology can truly change the way they live, learn, work and play.

This is the year we solidify our lifelong relationships with our clients on both the

business and consumer fronts — relationships that will fuel our growth in a way that's far more profitable than anything we've seen before.

And when you think about it, that's the vision that Ted Waitt had when he founded Gateway 15 years ago. Sure, we might have started out as a direct, built-to-order PC maker, but Ted's vision was always much bigger than that. The PC was never the end, it was the means. The PC was always just a tool — our first tool — for showing people a world that's filled with possibilities and opportunities.

On that note, I'll close by thanking Ted, our founder and Chairman, for establishing a brand, a vision and a set of values that have been the cornerstone of the incredible Gateway success story. Equally important, that brand and vision and those values will serve as our compass, pointing us to where we're heading in the future.

And I'm more excited than ever about that future, thanks to the many new tools that our beyond-the-box strategy has yielded. This is the year that we put those tools to work and make 2000 an even better year for our clients, shareholders and employees.

Jeff Weitzen
President and
Chief Executive Officer

How to build a giraffe...or an eagle...or a panda.

They all start out as Gateway boxes, but are quickly transformed into something much more.

The foam braces that cushion the computer during shipment are turned into animal legs. A box is cut at the seam and unfolded lengthwise, then rolled up to make a giraffe's neck.

Soon, wet newspaper drapes a sculpture's skeleton and hardens as papier-mâché. The students decide how to paint their sculpture and then dripping paintbrushes are hard at work, covering every inch of their creation.

Laying the Foundation.

For Gateway, 1999 was the year that we laid the building blocks for an even stronger 2000 and beyond.

It was a year also marked by strong sales, solid financial results and continued strength in our brand. In 1999, Gateway's U.S. consumer business enjoyed 42% unit growth as the company solidified its position as the number-one seller of consumer PCs in the country based on revenue share*. That growth was powered by innovative new products, aggressive Gateway Country® store expansion and a more than 100% increase in sales through Gateway.com over 1998.

We also made great progress in the business-to-business arena, particularly in each of our three core target markets. We grew units 22% in education, 20% in government and 22% in small and medium business.

Overseas, our business in Asia also continued to ramp as we posted unit growth of 65% for the year. The turnaround of our business in Europe remained on track as well, with unit growth of 12% for the year.

But more importantly, 1999 was the year that we described what we wanted to build, then started building it.

In February 1999, we unveiled our beyond-the-box strategy, detailing our move to create multiple, interwoven areas of connection to our clients across our unique, multichannel distribution system. At the time, we said these connections would strengthen our lifelong relationships with clients and also drive a richer, more diverse revenue stream.

Well, a year is an eternity in this industry, and way back in early 1999, no one else was talking about moving beyond the box or the "clicks and mortar" retail approach we pioneered with Gateway Country stores nearly three years ago. A lot of people are talking about all of those things now.

The good news is that we achieved first-mover status in our beyond-the-box strategy. That allowed us to solidify those client relationships early and further establish Gateway as an innovative partner in the new economy. We also learned a lot along the way

*According to GartnerGroup/DataQuest U.S. PC Quarterly Statistics

EXPLOSIVE ISP GROWTH. Gateway achieved fivefold growth in its ISP subscriber base during 1999.

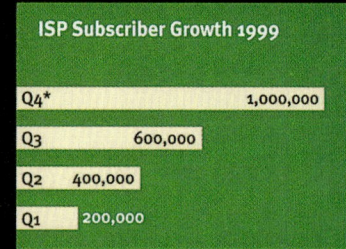

ISP Subscriber Growth 1999

Q4*	1,000,000
Q3	600,000
Q2	400,000
Q1	200,000

*Q4 includes both the Gateway.net® service and AOL users, per the two companies' subscriber-sharing agreement.

chumbo·com

AN INNOVATIVE PARTNER IN THE NEW ECONOMY. Gateway partnered with several best-of-class companies in 1999 to bring new solutions and services to our consumer and business clients.

construction

and created some great new relationships with best-of-breed partners across a number of industry sectors.

Here are some highlights:

Internet Access/Portal. We started the year by becoming the first PC maker to bundle Internet access with the sale of a computer, and our subscriptions to the Gateway.net service took off. By year end, we had a million ISP subscribers, making us the fastest growing fee-based Internet service provider in the United States.

In October, we struck an industry-changing deal with AOL that gave us the infrastructure to handle our explosive ISP growth. The deal also gave us access to AOL's world-class content and portal capabilities. Giving our clients a choice of AOL or the Gateway.net®

service further accelerated our ISP growth, and we exited the year with more than a million joint subscribers as our ISP attach rate rose from 35% to 50% in the fourth quarter.

Peripherals/Software. Also early in the year, we became the first PC maker to launch an online software and peripheral store. We took a minority stake in NECX, an industry-leading e-commerce innovator, and together launched SpotShop.com, offering more than 30,000 software titles and products to our clients.

Training. In 1999, we stepped up our training efforts considerably, launching online training and CD-based training, in addition to our instructor-led training in the more than 400 classrooms we have in

Gateway Country locations throughout the U.S. We refocused those instructor-led courses against the novice user and, by the end of the year, our attach rates for training in Gateway Country locations was over 60%.

Systems. Obviously, our bread and butter has long been the PC, and systems sales still account for the lion's share of our revenue and income stream. On that front, we led the way in 1999 once again with some great product innovations, including our space-saving, all-in-one Gateway Profile™ PC and our new all-in-one Gateway Astro™ PC, whose legacy-free connections make the leap to the Internet a snap. On the portable front, our Solo® 9300 met with rave reviews in both the consumer and business arenas.

DIVERSIFYING THE REVENUE STREAM: Gateway's nonsystem income grew from 3% of total income at the beginning of the year to 20% at the end.

■ System income   □ Nonsystem income

December 31, 1998

December 31, 1999

GATEWAY'S PRODUCT INNOVATIONS. Gateway's great all-in-one PCs, the Gateway Profile and Gateway Astro series, generated a lot of excitement in 1999. Along with the highly powered Solo 9300 laptop, these three innovations captured more than 20 industry accolades in 1999.

Where do the KDES kids get their ideas?

The students are limited only by their own imaginations. Once they come up with something they want to build, they thoroughly research the object by reading about it in books and on-line.

They become immersed in reading and research in a fun way, and they also gain experience in teamwork, cooperation and computer skills.

In many cases, the kids use Gateway computers to search the Internet, communicate with class-mates in other schools and even develop computer-generated models of their final creation.

The Gateway Connection.

The kids at KDES get their vision of what they want to build from the world around them — the books they read, the shows they watch, the things they see on the way to school.

Our own vision to Humanize the Digital Revolution comes from the world around us... through the very real and human connection that Gateway has with our clients, our employees and our communities.

In fact, our vision hasn't changed in the 15 years that have passed since Ted Waitt founded Gateway in an Iowa farmhouse.

We might have started out selling PCs, but our vision never really had anything to do with the technology and the hardware. It was always about people and great client relationships. It was about knowing what real people and real businesses want and need from their technology, and then delivering on those wants and needs. We call those relationships the Gateway Connection.

We stay connected to real people three important ways, and they're all unique to Gateway: our values, our multichannel distribution system and our involvement in local communities. Each of these contributes to our great client relationships and each helps us look at the world and the future very differently from our competitors.

Gateway's Values. Our

values have always been at the heart of our company, long before we ever wrote them down.

In fact, our Vice Chairman, Dave Robino, spoke to our senior management team in 1999 about the importance of Gateway's values and said: "Our goal of great client relationships rests more on our values than it does on products, processes and prices."

How can that be? How can something as "fuzzy" as values play such an important role at a company that competes in a rapidly commoditizing, process-focused, product-centric industry?

Well, one look at our values and it's perfectly clear:

Caring, Respect, Teamwork, Common Sense, Aggressiveness, Honesty, Efficiency and Fun.

It's no coincidence that those eight values, in some

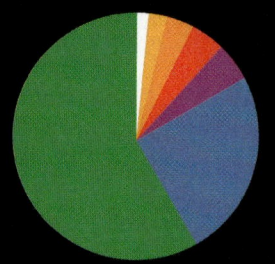

ALMOST A MILLION PEOPLE A DAY VISIT GATEWAY.

- ■ .Net users
- ■ Web visits
- ■ Phone outbound calls
- ■ Tech support calls
- ■ Store traffic
- ■ Phone calls to sales
- ■ Client relations calls

INTERNATIONAL GATEWAY COUNTRY STORE EXPANSION. We added more than 50 Gateway Country stores in Europe and Asia in 1999, including this store in Hong Kong (above).

RAPID U.S. COUNTRY STORE GROWTH. Almost every U.S. resident is within an hour's drive of a Gateway Country store. In 1999, we increased our presence 57% as we expanded to 227 locations, up from 144 the prior year.

GIVING BACK TO OUR COMMUNITIES. Dan Ford is not only a Gateway project manager, but a great example of Gateway values in action as well. He devotes five nights a week to help students with homework at the local community center. He also played a key role in connecting students to computer technology for more effective educational tools.

form or another, are at the heart of any great relationship. And at Gateway, we really do live those values, not just talk about them. As Dave Robino also says: "Our values are the magnetic force that both keeps our best people here and draws new people to us."

That includes both clients and employees, and it's what sets us apart in this wildly competitive industry.

Call, Click or Come In.
Nearly a million people a day connect with Gateway in the U.S. alone, and they connect through the phone, the Web and Gateway Country stores. It's well over a million people worldwide.

And when people connect with us, we're not just taking orders. We're talking. We're asking a lot of questions and we're listening hard to the answers.

This kind of personal relationship with our clients lets us spot opportunities, issues and trends that other technology companies miss. This is especially true in our Gateway Country stores, where our innovative retail atmosphere lets us interact with clients face to face,

around the world. Thanks to Gateway Country stores, we can hear about our clients' needs and concerns directly, while our friendly technicians help them experience our technology solutions firsthand. None of our traditional competitors can make that claim.

Gateway's Community Involvement.
Like a lot of companies, Gateway has a foundation that donates considerable resources to organizations in need. The Gateway Foundation, which is focused on children and education, has provided millions of dollars in funding and technology over the years to schools, youth groups and other charitable outlets around the world.

But Gateway also works hard to foster a sense of true community involvement among its employees worldwide. We have a number of programs, such as Gateway Guardians and Show Your Spots, that encourage employees to donate their time and talents to local organizations, in many cases with paid time off.

Real involvement allows us to give back to the communities where we operate, and it makes great business

sense, too. Because in the end, our vision is to Humanize the Digital Revolution, and if our employees can't connect to their communities in a human way, we'll never be able to achieve that vision.

Just ask Dan Ford, one of our project managers in North Sioux City. Dan runs a volunteer homework tutoring program for underprivileged kids. The program is staffed by local police officers and Gateway employees, and, thanks to a donation by the Gateway Foundation, is powered by Gateway computers.

Dan credits the program's success largely to his hands-on, personal role in setting it up and staying involved in it. In fact, Dan spends about 10 hours a week tutoring kids through the program.

"Working with the kids directly makes me one of them," Dan says. "I'm part of their lives. I open my home and heart to them to really understand what they need, not just what I think they need."

And it started out as just a box.

A friendly giraffe. A personal police car. A school bus. A panda. An eagle.

The kids at KDES looked at a box and saw something more. They opened their minds to a world of possibilities.

You'd never guess their sculptures started out as Gateway boxes (except for the panda, maybe) and that's fine with us.

Because the box itself was never really that important.

What you make with it is.

realization

2000: The Year of the "How."
We've worked hard over the past several years to build a whole new set of capabilities and services to offer our clients.

This is the year that we take those newly found capabilities, bring them all together and apply them to the market in new and innovative ways, showing our consumer and business clients how technology can truly change the way they live, learn, work and play.

Your:)Ware 2.0. Two years ago, Gateway revolutionized the way people purchase technology with the original Your:)Ware program, which bundled technology offerings like hardware, software and Internet access into one easy monthly payment.

Gateway is once again changing the way people think about technology with the launch this year of Your:)Ware 2.0, a new program that delivers solutions-based bundles designed to meet our clients' specific needs.

Gateway Cyber:)Ware, for example, helps people understand how to maximize the Internet through software and an instructor-led course at Gateway Country on surfing the web and using e-mail.

Gateway Money:)Ware helps clients use technology to take control of their financial future. It offers software and on-line tools, plus training that shows clients how technology can help organize home budgets, plan investments and prepare taxes.

Gateway Photo:)Ware includes a digital camera as well as software and in-person training designed to help our clients capture, preserve, organize and share their memories through the PC.

Gateway Music:)Ware helps clients create their own personalized digital music library, with an instructor-led course on downloading music and helpful tools like a CD labeling kit.

All of these solutions are bundled with the PC into one easy monthly payment. And, as new applications arise, Gateway will remain on the cutting edge of bundling those applications into beyond-the-box solutions for consumers.

Web Capabilities Take Businesses to New Heights.
The Internet is a great equalizer, especially for

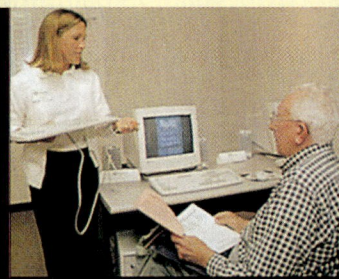

FACE-TO-FACE TRAINING. Gateway Country stores will play a key role in providing training to consumers and business clients this year.

TECHNICAL SOLUTIONS FOR TODAY'S CONSUMERS. With Gateway Photo:)Ware, Gateway clients get everything they need to capture their digital memories forever, and share them with family and friends.

realization

businesses. Through the power and broad reach of the Web, even the smallest businesses can compete with the market leaders.

Just as we plan to take our consumer clients beyond the box with solutions tailored to meet their needs, we'll do the same this year with our business clients, again using the Internet as the centerpiece for many of those solutions.

From training seminars on "How to Build Your Own Web Presence" to providing high-speed, multiuser Internet access and Web development and hosting with best-of-class applications service providers like eSoft, we intend to be the leading provider of end-to-end Internet solutions for small and midsized businesses, and government and educational institutions.

Monthly subscriptions to these services will allow clients to add new capabilities such as network security or hosted applications for human resources management — capabilities that grow with a business's changing needs.

A Brand with Reach. This year, we're going to take the powerful Gateway brand, which already touches more consumers and businesses on a daily basis than any of our competitors, and drive the reach and ubiquity of that brand more aggressively than ever before.

We'll do it through exciting new partnerships like our relationship with OfficeMax, which will create nearly one thousand Gateway stores-within-stores at OfficeMax locations across the U.S.

This innovative hub-and-spoke concept allows us to maintain control of our relationship with the client by creating a no-inventory, direct retail model similar to our Gateway Country store concept, in nearly five times as many outlets.

We'll also expand our brand geographically, with prudent international expansion that takes full advantage of our unique business model.

Beyond the Box. As we look beyond 2000, our move beyond the box won't slow down. We'll always sell PCs, and those PCs will always come in our cow-spotted boxes. But what comes out of those boxes will be so much more.

END-TO-END INTERNET SOLUTIONS FOR BUSINESSES. Gateway helps even the smallest business harness the power of the Internet with applications like Web hosting, firewall protection and e-mail service.

1,000 NEW POINTS OF DISTRIBUTION. Gateway's new store-within-a-store concept at 1,000 OfficeMax locations throughout the U.S. will bring our unique retail atmosphere to more consumers and small businesses than ever before.

OfficeMax

Gallaudet University serves deaf and hard-of-hearing people around the world through a full range of academic, research, and public service programs. Chartered by Congress in 1864, the University has grown steadily in terms of both enrollment and national impact.

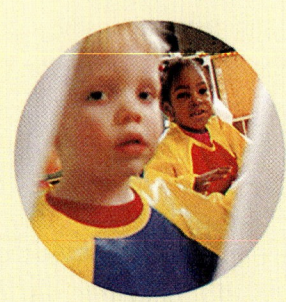

Today approximately 2,000 students, including a limited number of hearing students, are enrolled in undergraduate and graduate degree programs at the University's campus in Washington, D.C. Additional tens of thousands of individuals, including deaf adults and professionals in deafness-related fields, are served nationwide each year through other University programs, including Kendall Demonstration Elementary School (KDES).

Located within the University's campus, KDES serves as a role model in developing and demonstrating cutting-edge educational programs for deaf children. With 135 students enrolled, KDES dedicates itself to a three-fold mission:

Literary skill development, a particular challenge for many children with hearing impairments.

Family education, where parents and siblings can learn skills to build closer and more meaningful relationships with deaf family members.

Student preparation, setting the stage for the successful transition to life in a hearing world.

Gallaudet University is just one example of the thousands of educational clients Gateway supports with products and services suited to best meet students' educational needs. Gateway has sold and delivered hundreds of systems to

Gallaudet over the past five years, and has earned the school's trust with unparalleled service and support.

"We couldn't be happier with the support Gateway has provided to Gallaudet," said Phil Mackall, KDES's director of Information Technology. "Whenever we need a hand, Gateway is there to help."

As a small gesture of appreciation to KDES for the school's amazing degree of generosity and support in producing this annual report, the Gateway Foundation is providing Astro computers for all of the students and faculty members featured in this showcase to use in their classrooms.

Gifts to Gallaudet University and KDES [both 501(c)(3)] can be sent directly to the institution:

Gallaudet University
Corporate/Foundation
    Relations Office
800 Florida Avenue NE
Washington, DC 20002.

Financial Report

Selected Financial Data

(in thousands, except per share amounts)	1995	1996	1997	1998	1999
Operating Results					
Net sales	$ 3,676,328	$ 5,035,228	$ 6,293,680	$ 7,467,925	$ 8,645,561
Gross margin	$ 606,094	$ 936,155	$ 1,076,441	$ 1,546,274	$ 1,899,817
Net income	$ 172,981	$ 250,679	$ 109,797	$ 346,399	$ 427,944
Net income per share:					
Basic	$ 0.60	$ 0.82	$ 0.36	$ 1.11	$ 1.36
Diluted	$ 0.55	$ 0.80	$ 0.35	$ 1.09	$ 1.32
Financial Position					
Total assets	$ 1,124,011	$ 1,673,411	$ 2,039,271	$ 2,890,380	$ 3,954,688
Long-term obligations, net of current maturities	$ 10,805	$ 7,244	$ 7,240	$ 3,360	$ 2,998
Key Ratios					
Days of sales in accounts receivable	29	26	23	22	24
Days inventory on hand	20	17	17	9	9
Days in accounts payable	21	29	27	36	43
Cash conversion cycle	28	14	13	(5)	(10)
Other Data					
Employees (year end, approximate)	9,300	9,700	13,300	19,300	21,000
Weighted average shares outstanding:					
Basic	290,512	305,490	307,680	311,084	313,974
Diluted	315,976	312,474	312,402	317,857	324,421
Closing stock price	$ 6.13	$ 13.39	$ 16.38	$ 25.59	$ 72.06
Market capitalization	$1,828,036	$ 4,111,051	$ 5,049,233	$ 8,013,201	$23,080,353

Management's Discussion and Analysis of Financial Condition and Results of Operations

This Report includes forward-looking statements made based on current management expectations pursuant to the safe harbor provisions of the Private Securities Litigation Reform Act of 1995. These statements are not guarantees of future perform-ance and actual outcomes may differ materially from what is expressed or forecasted. Factors that could cause future results to differ from the Company's expectations include the following: competitive market conditions; infrastructure requirements; availability and cost of suppliers; short product cycles; access to technology; interna-tional operations; credit risk; e-commerce issues; risks of minority investments; risks of acquisition or joint ventures; inventory risks; customer or geo-graphic sales mix; and the Year 2000 transition. For a discussion of these factors, see "Item 1 Business—Factors that May Affect Gateway's Business and Future Results" in the Company's Annual Report on Form 10-K.

Results of Operations

The following table sets forth, for the periods indicated, certain data derived from the Company's consoli-dated income statements:

(dollars in thousands)	1997	Increase (Decrease)	1998	Increase (Decrease)	1999
Net sales	$6,293,680	19%	$7,467,925	16%	$8,645,561
Gross profit	1,076,441	44%	1,546,274	23%	1,899,817
Percentage of net sales	17.1%		20.7%		22.0%
Selling, general and					
administrative expenses	786,168	34%	1,052,047	24%	1,304,147
Percentage of net sales	12.5%		14.1%		15.1%
Nonrecurring expenses	113,842		—		—
Percentage of net sales	1.8%		—		—
Operating income	176,431	180%	494,227	21%	595,670
Percentage of net sales	2.8%		6.6%		6.9%
Net income	109,797	215%	346,399	24%	427,944

SALES. Gateway set new sales records in 1999, shipping more than 4.6 million systems and gener-ating more than $8.6 billion in sales during the year. The Company's 1999 performance eclipsed the prior year's record results, besting 1998 unit shipments and sales by 32% and 16%, respectively, compared to an increase in unit shipments and sales of 37% and 19% in 1998. Domestic and international sales grew 15% and 19%, respectively.

The following table summarizes the Company's net sales for the periods indicated by geographic region:

(dollars in thousands)	1997	Increase (Decrease)	1998	Increase (Decrease)	1999
Net sales					
United States	$5,303,828	21%	$6,412,404	15%	$7,386,537
EMEA	634,616	(10%)	570,191	(5%)	543,182
A-P	355,236	37%	485,330	47%	715,842
Consolidated	$6,293,680	19%	$7,467,925	16%	$8,645,561

In the United States, net sales growth was led by the consumer segment with an increase of 25% in 1999 over 1998 while the business segment grew 5% over the same time period. The consumer and business segments represented 48% and 37%, respectively, of total Company sales in 1999. Consumer growth was driven by the combination of new product introductions, expanding beyond-the-box revenue and continued channel expansion. The Company successfully launched several new PC products in 1999 including the Gateway Profile™, Gateway Profile 2™ and Gateway Astro™ series of all-in-one PC systems. New product introductions provided a unique combination of new form factors and technology with the ability to deliver into targeted price segments such as the sub-$1,000 PC market. In 1999, the Company focused aggressively on diversifying its revenue stream through adding additional, scalable beyond-the-box capabilities by securing a number of strategic alliances. The alliances include a partnership with America Online, Inc. (AOL) to provide Internet access, portal and commerce to Gateway.net and AOL customers. The Company also took an equity stake in NECX Direct LLC (NECX) that leverages NECX's web capabilities and fulfillment engine for sales of software and peripherals. Beyond-the-box revenue including software and peripheral sales, Internet access and portal income, financing, warranty and training revenue accounted for $800M in 1999 sales, up more than 100% versus 1998 and partially mitigating market pricing pressure. The Company also continued to add capability around its three direct channels (phone, stores, web). The Company opened 123 Gateway Country® stores worldwide versus total new store openings of 107 in 1998. At the end of 1999, Gateway had 280 store locations worldwide. In the first year of significant expansion of the store concept internationally, Gateway more than doubled penetration in this channel.

Average unit prices (AUPs) were approximately 13% lower in 1999 compared to a 14% decline in 1998. AUPs continued to decline in 1999 due to a combination of competitive pricing pressure stemming from component cost decreases and significant growth in the sub-$1,000 PC market. The Company expects the industry trend of declining AUPs to continue and intends to mitigate this impact by continuing to diversify its revenue stream as discussed previously.

On the business front, the Company continued to focus on small/medium businesses, government and education. Combined, these three segments grew at 22% in units over the prior year. Gateway also continued to add partners to aggressively pursue the enterprise space. Sales growth in the business segment for the fourth quarter of 1999 was adversely impacted by Year 2000 concerns among large businesses. Management expects that this trend will reverse in 2000 as large businesses and institutions resume normal purchasing patterns.

International continued to execute against Gateway's global strategy. This included aggressive Gateway Country store growth and added beyond the box capabilities. The Asia Pacific region enhanced its unit growth by 65% in 1999 and 63% in 1998. Unit shipments in the European ("EMEA") region increased 12% in 1999, up from a 5% increase in 1998. European volume trends improved significantly during the second half of 1999 as unit shipments increased 24% over the same period of 1998. Unit growth in all regions was offset by the declining AUPs previously discussed.

GROSS PROFIT. Gross profit in 1999 rose to $1.9 billion, an increase of approximately 23% from 1998. As a percentage of sales, gross profit for 1999 increased to 22.0% from 20.7% in 1998 and 17.1% in 1997, improving sequentially every quarter during 1998 and 1999. Improved margins were driven by aggressive supplier management and improved cost structure productivity, effective PC pricing management and the diversified revenue stream from the sale of non-PC services and products discussed above. The increase over 1997 is partially attributable to the adverse effects of excess inventories experienced in the third quarter of 1997.

SELLING, GENERAL AND ADMINISTRATIVE EXPENSES. To support its significant growth, the Company continues to make investments in Gateway Country® stores as discussed above, personnel, systems infrastructure and Internet development, domestically and internationally, resulting in an increase of 24% in selling, general and administrative expenses (SG&A) in 1999 over 1998. SG&A expenses increased 34% in 1998 over 1997. In addition, the Company continues to invest in expanding its presence in the European and Asian markets, building its core systems capability and strengthening its management team. As a percentage of sales, SG&A expenses were 15.1% in 1999, up from 14.1% in 1998 and 12.5% in 1997. The Company expects SG&A expenses to continue to increase in support of its anticipated growth, but at a rate below that of anticipated revenue growth.

OPERATING INCOME. Strong unit growth and gross margin efficiencies contributed to a 21% increase in operating income for 1999. Operating income improved to 6.9% of sales in 1999 from 6.6% in 1998. Operating income in 1999 for the consumer and business segments in the United States was $473.1 million and $474.6 million, respectively, due to increased sales and improved productivity, partially offset by the investment in SG&A. This represents a 60% increase in the consumer segment from 1998 while the business segment declined 15% over 1998 due to the factors discussed above. Non-segment expenses for 1999 totaled $376.3 million, an increase of 5% over 1998. Operating income for the segments includes selling, general and administrative expenses and other overhead charges directly attributable to the segment. Costs excluded from the segments primarily consist of general and administrative expenses that are managed on a corporate-wide basis.

OTHER INCOME, NET. Other income, net includes primarily interest income and expense, gains from the sale of investments, and foreign exchange transaction gains and losses. Other income, net increased to $67.8 million in 1999 from $47.0 million in 1998, due to the additional investment income generated by increases in cash balances and marketable securities.

INCOME TAXES. The Company's annualized effective tax rate decreased to 35.5% for 1999 from the 36.0% recorded in 1998. The effective tax rate for 1999 was favorably impacted by shifts in the geographic distribution of the Company's earnings.

LIQUIDITY AND CAPITAL RESOURCES. The following table presents selected financial statistics and information for the periods indicated:

(dollars in thousands)	1997	1998	1999
Cash and marketable securities	$ 632,249	$ 1,328,467	$ 1,336,371
Days of sales in accounts receivable	23	22	24
Days inventory on hand	17	9	9
Days in accounts payable	27	36	43
Cash conversion cycle	13	(5)	(10)

At December 31, 1999, the Company had cash and cash equivalents of $1.1 billion, marketable securities of $208.7 million and an unsecured committed credit facility with certain banks aggregating $300.0 million, consisting of a revolving line of credit facility and a sub-facility for letters of credit. At December 31, 1999, no amounts were outstanding under the revolving line of credit. Approximately $1.75 million was committed to support outstanding standby letters of credit. Management believes the Company's current sources of working capital, including amounts available under existing credit facilities, will provide adequate flexibility for the Company's financial needs for at least the next 12 months.

The Company generated $731.1 million in cash from operations during 1999, including $589.9 million of net income adjusted for non-cash items. Other significant factors increasing available cash include a decrease in inventory levels of $23.9 million and an increase in accounts payable and other accrued liabilities of $466.1 million, partially offset by an increase in accounts receivable. The Company used approximately $338.2 million for the construction of new facilities, information systems and equipment; $49.6 million to purchase investments in marketable securities, net of proceeds of securities sold; $315.2 million to purchase financing receivables, net of proceeds received for repayment; and $126.9 million to purchase investments in unconsolidated affiliates. As discussed previously, the Company continued to expand the retail Gateway Country stores, bringing the total number of stores worldwide to 280 as of December 31, 1999.

At December 31, 1999, the Company had long-term indebtedness and capital lease obligations of approximately $8.5 million. These obligations relate to the Company's investments in equipment and facilities. The Company anticipates that it will retain all earnings in the foreseeable future for development of its business and will not distribute earnings to its stockholders as dividends.

On April 30, 1999, the Company filed a universal shelf registration statement which contemplates that the Company may from time to time sell up to $1.0 billion of debt or equity securities, which will provide the Company with greater flexibility to respond to acquisition and market opportunities.

In October 1999, the Company entered into a strategic relationship with AOL to combine certain of the companies' sales and distribution channels and capabilities in the development of certain hardware, software and Internet content. As part of the agreement, AOL agreed to invest $800 million in the Company over a three-year period, in a combination of cash and AOL stock. During 1999, AOL purchased 2,725,026 shares of the Company's common stock in exchange for a combination of cash and 1,212,396 shares of AOL common stock.

NEW ACCOUNTING PRONOUNCEMENTS.
In June of 1998, the Financial Accounting Standards Board issued SFAS No. 133, "Accounting for Derivative Instruments and Hedging Activities," which is effective for fiscal years beginning after June 15, 2000. The objective of the statement is to establish accounting and reporting standards for derivative instruments and hedging activities. The Company uses foreign currency forward contracts, a derivative instrument, to hedge foreign currency transactions and anticipated foreign currency transactions. The adoption of this new accounting pronouncement is not expected to be material to the Company's consolidated financial position or results of operations.

In December 1999, the Securities and Exchange Commission issued Staff Accounting Bulletin (SAB) No. 101, "Revenue Recognition in Financial Statements." The objective of this SAB is to provide further guidance on revenue recognition issues in the absence of authoritative literature addressing a specific arrangement or a specific industry. The guidance in the SAB is required to be followed no later than the second fiscal quarter of the fiscal year beginning after December 15, 1999 and is not expected to have a material impact on the Company's financial position or results of operations.

YEAR 2000. The "Year 2000" issue was the result of many existing computer programs and chip-based embedded technology systems using only the last two digits to refer to a year, and therefore, not properly recognizing a year that begins with "20" instead of the familiar "19." If not corrected, many computer applications could fail or create erroneous results.

The Company completed its process toward Year 2000 readiness during 1999 and did not experience an adverse effect on the Company, its business or its financial condition as a result of the date change. During 1999, the Company expensed incremental costs of $13.1 million on Year 2000 remediation efforts and expensed $16.7 million on a life-to-date basis.

QUANTITATIVE AND QUALITATIVE DISCLO-SURES ABOUT MARKET RISK. The results of the Company's foreign operations are affected by changes in exchange rates between certain foreign currencies and the United States dollar. The functional currency for most of the Company's foreign operations is the U.S. dollar. The functional currency for the remaining operations is the local currency in which the subsidiaries operate. Sales made in foreign currencies translate into higher or lower sales in U.S. dollars as the U.S. dollar weakens and strengthens against other currencies. Therefore, changes in exchange rates may negatively affect the Company's consolidated net sales (as expressed in U.S. dollars) and gross margins from foreign operations. The majority of the Company's component purchases are denominated in U.S. dollars.

The Company uses foreign currency forward contracts to hedge foreign currency transactions and probable anticipated foreign currency transactions. These forward contracts are designated as a hedge of international sales by U.S. dollar functional currency entities and intercompany purchases by certain foreign subsidiaries. The principal currencies hedged are the British Pound, Japanese Yen, French Franc, Australian Dollar, Singapore Dollar, and the Deutsche Mark over periods ranging from one to six months. Forward contracts are accounted for on a mark-to-market basis, with realized and unrealized gains or losses recognized currently. Gains or losses arising from forward contracts that are effective as a hedge are included in the basis of the designated transactions. Fluctuations in U.S. dollar currency exchange rates did not have a significant impact on the Company's consolidated financial position, results of operations or cash flows in any given reporting period. Forward contracts designated to hedge foreign currency transaction exposure of $266,471,000 and $303,393,000 were outstanding at December 31, 1998 and 1999, respectively. The estimated fair value of these forward contracts at December 31, 1998 and 1999 was $271,573,000 and $303,917,000, respectively, based on quoted market prices.

Foreign currency exchange contracts are sensitive to changes in foreign currency exchange rates. At December 31, 1999, a hypothetical 10% adverse change in foreign currency exchange rates underlying the Company's open forward contracts would result in an unrealized loss of approximately $32.5 million. Unrealized gains/losses in foreign currency exchange contracts represent the difference between the hypothetical rates and the current market exchange rates. Consistent with the nature of an economic hedge any unrealized gains or losses would be offset by corresponding decreases or increases, respectively, of the underlying transaction being hedged.

The Company is not subject to material market risk with respect to its investment in marketable securities.

To the Stockholders and Board of Directors of
Gateway, Inc.

In our opinion, the accompanying consolidated balance sheets and the related consolidated statements of income, cash flows and changes in stockholders' equity and comprehensive income present fairly, in all material respects, the consolidated financial position of Gateway, Inc. at December 31, 1998 and 1999, and the consolidated results of its operations and its cash flows for each of the three years in the period ended December 31, 1999, in conformity with accounting principles generally accepted in the United States. These financial statements are the responsibility of the Company's management; our responsibility is to express an opinion on these financial statements based on our audits. We conducted our audits of these statements in accordance with auditing standards generally accepted in the United States which require that we plan and perform the audit to obtain reasonable assurance about whether the financial statements are free of material misstatement. An audit includes examining, on a test basis, evidence supporting amounts and disclosures in the financial statements, assessing the accounting principles used and significant estimates made by management, and evaluating the overall financial statement presentation. We believe that our audits provide a reasonable basis for the opinion expressed above.

PricewaterhouseCoopers LLP

PricewaterhouseCoopers LLP
San Diego, California

January 20, 2000

Consolidated Income Statements

For the years ended December 31 (in thousands, except per share amounts)	1997	1998	1999
Net sales	$6,293,680	$7,467,925	$8,645,561
Cost of goods sold	5,217,239	5,921,651	6,745,744
Gross profit	1,076,441	1,546,274	1,899,817
Selling, general and administrative expense	786,168	1,052,047	1,304,147
Nonrecurring expenses	113,842	—	—
Operating income	176,431	494,227	595,670
Other income, net	27,189	47,021	67,809
Income before income taxes	203,620	541,248	663,479
Provision for income taxes	93,823	194,849	235,535
Net income	$ 109,797	$ 346,399	$ 427,944
Net income per share:			
Basic	$ 0.36	$ 1.11	$ 1.36
Diluted	$ 0.35	$ 1.09	$ 1.32
Weighted-average shares outstanding:			
Basic	307,680	311,084	313,974
Diluted	312,402	317,857	324,421

The accompanying notes are an integral part of the consolidated financial statements.

Consolidated Balance Sheets

December 31 (in thousands, except per share amounts)	1998	1999
Assets		
Current assets:		
Cash and cash equivalents	$ 1,169,810	$ 1,127,654
Marketable securities	158,657	208,717
Accounts receivable, net	558,851	646,339
Inventory	167,924	191,870
Other	172,944	522,225
Total current assets	2,228,186	2,696,805
Property, plant and equipment, net	530,988	745,660
Intangibles, net	65,944	52,302
Other assets	65,262	459,921
	$2,890,380	$3,954,688
Liabilities and Stockholders' Equity		
Current liabilities:		
Current maturities of long-term obligations	$ 11,415	$ 5,490
Accounts payable	718,071	898,436
Accrued liabilities	415,265	609,132
Accrued royalties	167,873	153,840
Other current liabilities	117,050	142,812
Total current liabilities	1,429,674	1,809,710
Long-term obligations, net of current maturities	3,360	2,998
Warranty and other liabilities	112,971	124,862
Total liabilities	1,546,005	1,937,570
Commitments and Contingencies (Note 3)		
Stockholders' equity:		
Preferred stock, $.01 par value, 5,000 shares authorized, none issued and outstanding	—	—
Class A common stock, nonvoting, $.01 par value, 1,000 shares authorized; none issued and outstanding	—	—
Common stock, $.01 par value, 1,000,000 shares authorized; 313,138 shares and 320,016 shares issued and outstanding, respectively	3,131	3,200
Additional paid-in capital	364,421	656,870
Common stock in treasury, at cost, 730 shares in 1999	—	(51,796)
Retained earnings	980,908	1,408,852
Accumulated other comprehensive loss	(4,085)	(8)
Total stockholders' equity	1,344,375	2,017,118
	$2,890,380	$3,954,688

The accompanying notes are an integral part of the consolidated financial statements.

Consolidated Statements of Cash Flows

For the years ended December 31 (in thousands)	1997	1998	1999
Cash flows from operating activities:			
Net income	$ 109,797	$ 346,399	$ 427,944
Adjustments to reconcile net income to net cash			
provided by operating activities:			
Depreciation and amortization	86,774	105,524	134,105
Provision for uncollectable accounts receivable	5,688	3,991	28,334
Deferred income taxes	(63,247)	(58,425)	(2,876)
Other, net	42	770	2,381
Nonrecurring expenses	113,842	—	—
Changes in operating assets and liabilities:			
Accounts receivable	(41,950)	(52,164)	(115,822)
Inventory	59,486	81,300	(23,947)
Other assets	(54,513)	451	(185,192)
Accounts payable	66,253	228,921	181,704
Accrued liabilities	48,405	144,899	195,299
Accrued royalties	34,148	8,455	(14,033)
Other current liabilities	35,816	76,278	105,723
Warranty and other liabilities	42,256	21,252	(2,566)
Net cash provided by operating activities	442,797	907,651	731,054
Cash flows from investing activities:			
Capital expenditures	(175,656)	(235,377)	(338,211)
Investment in unconsolidated affiliates	—	—	(126,931)
Purchases of available-for-sale securities	(49,619)	(168,965)	(146,759)
Proceeds from maturities or sales of			
available-for-sale securities	10,985	48,924	97,206
Purchase of financing receivables	—	—	(368,133)
Proceeds from repayment of financing receivables	—	—	52,926
Acquisitions, net of cash acquired	(142,320)	—	—
Other, net	(4,055)	(992)	(1,384)
Net cash (used in) investing activities	(360,665)	(356,410)	(831,286)
Cash flows from financing activities:			
Proceeds from issuances of notes payable	10,000	—	—
Principal payments on long-term obligations			
and notes payable	(15,588)	(13,173)	(6,287)
Purchase of treasury stock	—	—	(122,580)
Proceeds from stock issuance	—	—	100,000
Stock options exercised	5,741	36,159	83,341
Net cash provided by financing activities	153	22,986	54,474
Foreign exchange effect on cash and cash equivalents	(5,044)	1,982	3,602
Net increase (decrease) in cash and cash equivalents	77,241	576,209	(42,156)
Cash and cash equivalents, beginning of year	516,360	593,601	1,169,810
Cash and cash equivalents, end of year	$ 593,601	$1,169,810	$1,127,654

The accompanying notes are an integral part of the consolidated financial statements.

Consolidated Statements of Changes in Stockholders' Equity and Comprehensive Income

For the years ended December 31 (in thousands)	Common Stock Shares	Common Stock Amount	Additional Paid-in Capital	Treasury Stock	Retained Earnings	Accumulated Other Comprehensive Income (Loss)	Total
Balances at December 31, 1996	307,024	$3,070	$ 287,210	$ —	$ 524,712	$ 549	$ 815,541
Comprehensive income:							
Net income	—	—	—	—	109,797	—	109,797
Other comprehensive income:							
Foreign currency translation	—	—	—	—	—	(6,053)	(6,053)
Unrealized gain on available-for-sale securities	—	—	—	—	—	15	15
Comprehensive income							103,759
Stock issuances under employee plans, including tax benefit of $5,003	1,232	10	10,734	—	—	—	10,744
Balances at December 31, 1997	308,256	3,080	297,944	—	634,509	(5,489)	930,044
Comprehensive income:							
Net income	—	—	—	—	346,399	—	346,399
Other comprehensive income:							
Foreign currency translation	—	—	—	—	—	1,549	1,549
Unrealized loss on available-for-sale securities	—	—	—	—	—	(145)	(145)
Comprehensive income							347,803
Stock issuances under employee plans, including tax benefit of $29,769	4,846	49	65,879	—	—	—	65,928
Stock issued to officer	36	2	598	—	—	—	600
Balances at December 31, 1998	313,138	3,131	364,421	—	980,908	(4,085)	1,344,375
Comprehensive income:							
Net income	—	—	—	—	427,944	—	427,944
Other comprehensive income:							
Foreign currency translation	—	—	—	—	—	4,941	4,941
Unrealized loss on available-for-sale securities	—	—	—	—	—	(864)	(864)
Comprehensive income							432,021
Purchase of treasury stock	—	—	—	(122,580)	—	—	(122,580)
Stock issuances under employee plans, including tax benefit of $79,961	4,153	42	92,476	70,784	—	—	163,302
Issuance of common stock	2,725	27	199,973	—	—	—	200,000
Balances at December 31, 1999	320,016	$3,200	$656,870	$ (51,796)	$1,408,852	$ (8)	$ 2,017,118

The accompanying notes are an integral part of the consolidated financial statements.

① Summary of Significant Accounting Policies

Gateway, Inc. (the "Company") is a direct marketer of personal computers ("PCs") and PC-related products and services. The Company develops, manufactures, markets and supports a broad line of desktop and portable PCs, servers, workstations and PC-related products used by individuals, families, businesses, government agencies and educational institutions. The Company also offers and supports PC-related services including training, financing and Internet service.

The significant accounting policies used in the preparation of the consolidated financial statements of the Company are as follows:

A. BASIS OF PRESENTATION. The consolidated financial statements include the accounts of the Company and its wholly-owned subsidiaries. All significant intercompany accounts and transactions have been eliminated.

The Company holds a less than 20% interest in certain unconsolidated affiliates and does not exercise significant influence with respect to such companies. These investments are accounted for using the cost method.

B. USE OF ESTIMATES AND CERTAIN CONCENTRATIONS. The preparation of financial statements in conformity with generally accepted accounting principles requires management to make estimates and assumptions that affect the reported amounts of assets and liabilities and disclosure of contingent assets and liabilities at the date of the financial statements and the reported amounts of revenues and expenses during the reporting period. Actual results could differ from those estimates.

Certain components used by the Company in manufacturing of PC systems are purchased from a limited number of suppliers. An industry shortage or other constraints of any key component could result in delayed shipments and a possible loss of sales, which could affect operating results adversely.

Included in other assets and other current assets are customer financing receivables totaling approximately $300 million. The Company records a reserve for uncollectible accounts based on historical collection experience.

C. CASH AND CASH EQUIVALENTS. The Company considers all highly liquid debt instruments and money market funds with an original maturity of three months or less to be cash equivalents. The carrying amount approximates fair value because of the short maturities of these instruments.

D. MARKETABLE SECURITIES. The carrying amounts of marketable securities used in computing unrealized and realized gains and losses are determined by specific identification. Fair values are determined using quoted market prices. For available-for-sale securities, which are carried at fair value at the balance sheet dates, net unrealized holding gains and losses are reported in accumulated other comprehensive income (loss). Held-to-maturity securities are recorded at amortized cost. Amortization of related discounts or premiums is included in the determination of net income.

Marketable securities at December 31, 1999 and 1998 consisted of available-for-sale mutual funds, commercial paper and debt securities, with market values that approximate their amortized cost. Realized and unrealized gains and losses are not material for any of the periods presented.

E. INVENTORY. Inventory, which is comprised of component parts, subassemblies and finished goods, is valued at the lower of first-in, first-out (FIFO) cost or market. On a quarterly basis, the Company compares on a part by part basis, the amount of the inventory on hand and under commitment with its latest forecasted requirements to determine whether write-downs for excess or obsolete inventory are required.

F. PROPERTY, PLANT AND EQUIPMENT.

Property, plant and equipment are stated at cost. Depreciation is provided using straight-line methods over the assets' estimated useful lives, ranging from four to forty years. Amortization of leasehold improvements is computed using the shorter of the lease term or the estimated useful life of the underlying asset. Upon sale or retirement of property, plant and equipment, the related costs and accumulated depreciation or amortization are removed from the accounts and any gain or loss is included in the determination of net income.

The Company capitalizes costs of purchased software and costs incurred to develop internal use software. Amortization of software costs begins when the software is placed in service and is computed on a straight-line basis over the estimated useful life of the software, ranging from three to five years.

G. INTANGIBLE ASSETS.

Intangible assets principally consist of technology, a customer base and distribution network, an assembled work force and trade name obtained through acquisition. The cost of intangible assets is amortized on a straight-line basis over the estimated periods benefited, ranging from three to ten years.

H. LONG-LIVED ASSETS.

The Company reviews for the impairment of long-lived assets whenever events or changes in circumstances indicate that the carrying amount of an asset may not be recoverable. An impairment loss would be recognized when the sum of the expected undiscounted future net cash flows expected to result from the use of the asset and its eventual disposition is less than its carrying amount.

I. ROYALTIES.

The Company has royalty-bearing license agreements that allow the Company to sell certain hardware and software which is protected by patent, copyright or license. Royalty costs are accrued and included in cost of goods sold when products are shipped or amortized over the period of benefit when the license terms are not specifically related to the units shipped.

J. WARRANTY AND OTHER POST-SALES SUPPORT PROGRAMS.

The Company provides currently for the estimated costs that may be incurred under its warranty and other post-sales support programs.

K. REVENUE RECOGNITION.

The Company generally recognizes revenue from product sales at the time of shipment provided that no significant obligation remains. The Company recognizes revenue from services, such as training and Internet service, upon delivery of the service. For sales involving multiple elements, revenue is allocated to each element based on the relative fair value using vendor specific objective evidence.

Revenue from the sale of extended service plans is deferred and recognized over the extended service period on a straight-line basis. During 1999, the Company also began selling service plans provided by an unrelated third party. These service plans are administered through a third party with all performance obligations and risk of loss transferred to the third party upon sale. Revenue and cost associated with these contracts is recognized at the time of sale.

L. ADVERTISING COSTS:

Advertising costs are charged to expense as incurred.

M. INCOME TAXES:

The provision for income taxes is computed using the liability method, under which deferred tax assets and liabilities are recognized for the expected future tax consequences of temporary differences between the financial reporting and tax bases of assets and liabilities. Deferred tax assets are reduced by a valuation allowance when it is more likely than not that some portion or all of the deferred tax assets will not be realized.

N. NET INCOME PER SHARE.

Basic earnings per common share is computed using the weighted-average number of common shares outstanding during the period. Diluted earnings per common share is computed using the combination of dilutive common stock equivalents and the weighted-average number of common shares outstanding during the period.

The following table sets forth a reconciliation of shares used in the computation of basic and diluted earnings per share.

(in thousands)	1997	1998	1999
Net income for basic and diluted earnings per share	$109,797	$346,399	$427,944
Weighted-average shares for basic earnings per share	307,680	311,084	313,974
Dilutive effect of stock options	4,722	6,773	10,447
Weighted-average shares for diluted earnings per share	312,402	317,857	324,421

O. STOCK-BASED COMPENSATION. The Company measures compensation expense for its employee's and non-employee director's stock-based compensation using the intrinsic value method. Compensation charges related to non-employee stock-based compensation are measured using fair value methods.

P. FOREIGN CURRENCY. The Company uses the U.S. dollar as its functional currency for certain of its international operations and the local currency for all other. For subsidiaries where the local currency is the functional currency, the assets and liabilities are translated into U.S. dollars at exchange rates in effect at the balance sheet date. Income and expense items are translated at the average exchange rates prevailing during the period. Gains and losses from translation are included in accumulated other comprehensive income (loss). Gains and losses resulting from remeasuring monetary asset and liability accounts that are denominated in currencies other than a subsidiary's functional currency are included in "Other income, net."

The Company uses foreign currency forward contracts to hedge foreign currency transactions and probable anticipated foreign currency transactions. These forward contracts are designated as a hedge of international sales by U.S. dollar functional currency entities and intercompany purchases by certain foreign subsidiaries. The principal currencies hedged are the British Pound, Japanese Yen, French Franc, Australian Dollar, Singapore Dollar and the Deutsche Mark over periods ranging from one to six months. Forward contracts are accounted for on a mark-to-market basis, with realized and unrealized gains or losses recognized currently. Gains or losses arising from forward contracts which are effective as

a hedge are included in the basis of the designated transactions. The related receivable or liability with counterparties to the forward contracts is recorded in the consolidated balance sheet. Cash flows from settlements of forward contracts are included in operating activities in the consolidated statements of cash flows. Aggregate transaction gains and losses included in the determination of net income are not material for any period presented. Forward contracts designated to hedge foreign currency transaction exposure of $266,471,000 and $303,393,000 were outstanding at December 31, 1998 and 1999, respectively. The estimated fair value of these forward contracts at December 31, 1998 and 1999 was $271,573,000 and $303,917,000, respectively, based on quoted market prices.

The Company continually monitors its positions with, and the credit quality of, the major international financial institutions which are counterparties to its foreign currency forward contracts, and has not experienced nonperformance by any of these counterparties.

Q. NEW ACCOUNTING PRONOUNCEMENTS. In June of 1998, the Financial Accounting Standards Board issued SFAS No. 133, "Accounting for Derivative Instruments and Hedging Activities" which is effective for fiscal years beginning after June 15, 2000. The objective of the statement is to establish accounting and reporting standards for derivative instruments and hedging activities. The Company uses foreign currency forward contracts, a derivative instrument, to hedge foreign currency transactions and anticipated foreign currency transactions. The adoption of this new accounting pronouncement is not expected to be material to the Company's consolidated financial position or results of operations.

In December 1999, the Securities and Exchange Commission issued Staff Accounting Bulletin (SAB) No. 101, "Revenue Recognition in Financial Statements." The objective of this SAB is to provide further guidance on revenue recognition issues in the absence of authoritative literature addressing a specific arrangement or a specific industry. The guidance in the SAB is required to be followed no later than the second fiscal quarter of the fiscal year beginning

2 Financing Arrangements

A. CREDIT AGREEMENT. The Company is party to an unsecured bank credit agreement (the "Agreement"), totaling $300 million. The Agreement consists of (1) a revolving line of credit facility for committed loans and bid loans; and (2) a sub-facility for letters of credit. Borrowings under the agreement bear interest at the banks' base rate or, at the Company's option, borrowing rates based on a fixed spread over the London Interbank Offered Rate (LIBOR). The Agreement requires the Company to maintain a minimum tangible net worth and maximum debt leverage ratio, as well as minimum fixed

after December 15, 1999 and is not expected to have a material impact on the Company's financial position or results of operations.

R. STOCK SPLIT. On August 9, 1999, the Company announced that its Board of Directors approved a two-for-one common stock split to be effected in the form of a stock dividend. The shares were distributed on September 7, 1999 to stockholders of record as of August 20, 1999. Share and per share data for all periods presented herein have been restated to reflect the two-for-one common stock split.

charge coverage. There were no borrowings outstanding at the end of 1998 and 1999.

At December 31, 1998 and 1999, approximately $2,000,000 and $1,750,000, respectively, was committed to support outstanding standby letters of credit.

B. LONG-TERM OBLIGATIONS. The carrying amount of the Company's long-term obligations approximates fair value, which is estimated based on current rates offered to the Company for obligations of the same remaining maturities. Long-term obligations consist of the following:

December 31 (in thousands)	1998	1999
Notes payable through 2002 with interest rates ranging from 3.90% to 5.50%	$14,408	$8,415
Obligations under capital leases, payable in monthly installments at a fixed rate of 6.5% through 2001	367	73
	14,775	8,488
Less current maturities	11,415	5,490
	$ 3,360	$2,998

The long-term obligations, excluding obligations under capital leases, have the following maturities as of December 31, 1999, in thousands:

2000	$5,430
2001	2,773
2002	212
2003	—
2004	—
	$8,415

3 Commitments and Contingencies

The Company leases certain operating facilities and equipment under non-cancelable operating leases expiring at various dates through 2013. Rent expense was approximately $16,105,000, $25,713,000 and $52,936,000 for 1997, 1998 and 1999, respectively.

Future minimum lease payments under terms of these leases as of December 31, 1999 are as follows:

(in thousands)	Capital Leases	Operating Leases
2000	$60	$ 62,380
2001	18	63,441
2002	5	61,102
2003	—	49,272
2004	—	24,679
Thereafter	—	37,796
Total minimum lease payments	$83	$298,670
Less amount representing interest	10	
Present value of net minimum lease payments	$73	

The Company has entered into licensing and royalty agreements that allow it to use certain hardware and software intellectual properties in its products. Minimum royalty payments due under these agreements for the period 2000 through 2003 total approximately $380,000,000. Total royalty expense is expected to be greater than this minimum amount for these periods.

The Company is a party to various lawsuits and administrative proceedings arising in the ordinary course of its business. The Company evaluates such lawsuits and proceedings on a case-by-case basis, and its policy is to vigorously contest any such claims which it believes are without merit. The Company's management believes that the ultimate resolution of such pending matters will not materially adversely affect the Company's business, financial position, results of operations or cash flows.

4 Income Taxes

The components of the provision for income taxes are as follows:

For the year ended December 31 (in thousands)	1997	1998	1999
Current:			
United States	$154,049	$244,076	$238,799
Foreign	3,021	9,198	(388)
Deferred:			
United States	(49,564)	(40,055)	(13,850)
Foreign	(13,683)	(18,370)	10,974
	$ 93,823	$194,849	$235,535

Income (loss) before income taxes included approximately ($24,000,000), ($13,100,000) and $22,500,000 related to foreign operations for the years ended December 31, 1997, 1998 and 1999, respectively.

A reconciliation of the provision for income taxes and the amount computed by applying the federal statutory income tax rate to income before income taxes is as follows:

(in thousands)	1997	1998	1999
Federal income tax at statutory rate	$ 71,267	$189,437	$232,218
Nondeductible purchased research and development costs	20,704	—	—
Other, net	1,852	5,412	3,317
Provision for income taxes	$ 93,823	$194,849	$235,535

Deferred tax assets and deferred tax liabilities result from temporary differences in the following accounts:

December 31 (in thousands)	1998	1999
U.S. deferred tax assets:		
Inventory	$ 17,721	$ 13,245
Accounts receivable	5,206	7,433
Accrued liabilities	52,143	87,710
Other liabilities	60,539	58,816
Other	8,048	11,651
Total U.S.	143,657	178,855
Foreign deferred tax assets:		
Operating loss carryforwards	33,454	17,928
Deferred costs	2.312	6,662
Other	2,895	8,476
Total foreign	38,661	33,066
Total deferred tax assets	182,318	211,921
U.S. deferred tax liabilities:		
Intangible assets	29,440	46,143
Property, plant & equipment	4,104	13,684
Other	6,507	1,571
Total deferred tax liabilities	40,051	61,398
Net deferred tax assets	$142,267	$150,523

The Company has foreign net operating loss carryforwards of $46,400,000. Of this amount, $27,600,000 expires in the year 2002. The remaining $18,800,000 can be carried forward indefinitely. The Company has assessed its forecast of future taxable income and the expiration of carryforwards and has determined that is it more likely than not that the deferred tax asset relating to foreign net operating loss carryforwards will be realized.

⑤ **Stock Option Plans**

The Company maintains various stock option plans for its employees. Employee options are generally granted at the fair market value of the related common stock at the date of grant. These options generally vest over a four-year period from the date of grant or the employee's initial date of employment. In addition, these options expire, if not exercised, ten years from the date of grant. The Company also maintains option plans for non-employee directors. Option grants to non-employee directors generally have an exercise price equal to the fair market value of the related common stock on the date of grant. These options generally vest over one to three-year periods and expire, if not exercised, ten years from the date of grant.

For all of the Company's stock option plans, options for 5,164,000, 5,456,000 and 5,544,000 shares of common stock were exercisable at December 31, 1997, 1998 and 1999 with a weighted-average exercise price of $4.93, $8.71, and $12.67, respectively. In addition, options for 1,112,000, 560,000, and 126,000 shares of Class A common stock were exercisable at December 31, 1997, 1998 and 1999 with a weighted-average exercise price of $1.01, $0.97, and $0.94, respectively. Class A common stock may be converted into an equal number of shares of common stock at any time. There were 16,656,000, 22,530,000, and 4,504,000 shares of common stock available for grant under the plans at December 31, 1997, 1998 and 1999, respectively.

The following table summarizes activity under the stock option plans for 1997, 1998, and 1999 (in thousands, except per share amounts):

	Common Stock	Weighted-Average Price	Class A Common Stock	Weighted-Average Price
Outstanding, December 31, 1996	10,880	$ 6.10	1,426	$1.06
Granted	10,506	18.04	—	—
Exercised	(926)	5.78	(306)	1.25
Forfeited	(1,550)	11.85	—	—
Outstanding, December 31, 1997	18,910	11.49	1,120	1.01
Granted	12,236	22.59	—	—
Exercised	(4,286)	8.30	(560)	1.05
Forfeited	(2,206)	16.38	—	—
Outstanding, December 31, 1998	24,654	17.10	560	.97
Granted	20,850	37.17	—	—
Exercised	(5,884)	14.12	(434)	.97
Forfeited	(2,824)	25.14	—	—
Outstanding, December 31, 1999	36,796	$28.60	126	$ .94

The following table summarizes information about the Company's Common Stock options outstanding at December 31, 1999 (in thousands, except per share amounts):

	Options Outstanding			Options Exercisable	
Range of Exercise Prices	Number Outstanding at 12/31/1999	Weighted-Average Remaining Contractual Life	Weighted-Average Price	Number Exercisable at 12/31/99	Weighted-Average Price
$ .59–16.32	6,992	6.36	$ 10.38	4,009	$ 8.51
16.75–24.72	6,809	8.09	19.23	1,120	19.73
24.78–30.63	7,057	9.03	28.76	281	26.84
30.88–32.88	9,601	9.37	32.50	260	30.88
32.94–82.50	6,463	9.70	50.09	—	—

The weighted-average fair value per share of options granted during 1997, 1998 and 1999 was $10.81, $13.67, and $22.51, respectively. The fair value of these options was estimated on the date of grant using the Black-Scholes option pricing model with the following weighted-average assumptions used for all grants in 1997, 1998 and 1999: dividend yield of zero percent; expected volatility of 60 percent; risk-free interest rates ranging from 4.5 to 6.6 percent; and expected lives of the options of three and one-half years.

Since all stock options have been granted with exercise prices equal to the fair market value of the related common stock at the date of grant, no compensation expense has been recognized under the Company's stock option plans. Had compensation cost under the plans been determined based on the estimated fair value of the stock options granted in 1997, 1998 and 1999, net income and net income per share would have been reduced to the pro forma amounts indicated below:

(in thousands, except per share amounts)	1997	1998	1999
Net income—as reported	$109,797	$346,399	$427,944
Net income—pro forma	$ 85,804	$297,470	$ 319,494
Net income per share—as reported			
Basic	$ .36	$ 1.11	$ 1.36
Diluted	$ .35	$ 1.09	$ 1.32
Net income per share—pro forma			
Basic	$ .28	$ .96	$ 1.02
Diluted	$ .28	$ .94	$ 0.98

The pro forma effect on net income for 1997, 1998 and 1999 is not fully representative of the pro forma effect on net income in future years because it does not take into consideration pro forma compensation expense related to the vesting of grants made prior to 1997.

6 Retirement Savings Plan

The Company has a 401(k) defined contribution plan which covers employees who have attained 18 years of age and have been employed by the Company for at least six months. Participants may contribute up to 20% of their compensation in any plan year and receive a 50% matching employer contribution of up to 6% of their annual eligible compensation. The Company contributed $2,068,000, $4,730,000, and $6,433,000 to the Plan during 1997, 1998 and 1999, respectively.

7 Nonrecurring Expenses

The Company recorded several nonrecurring pretax charges during the third quarter of 1997 totaling approximately $113,800,000. Of the nonrecurring charges, approximately $59,700,000 was for the write-off of in-process research and development acquired in the purchase of Advanced Logic Research, Inc.(ALR) and certain assets of Amiga Technologies. Also included in the nonrecurring charges was a non-cash write-off of approximately $45,200,000 resulting from the abandonment of a capitalized internal use software project and certain computer equipment. In addition, approximately $8,600,000 was recorded for severance of employees and the closing of a foreign office.

8 Strategic Investments and Alliances

During 1999, the Company entered into a strategic relationship with America Online, Inc.(AOL) to combine certain of the companies' sales and distribution channels and capabilities in the development of certain hardware, software and Internet content. As part of the agreement, AOL agreed to invest $800 million in the Company over a three-year period, in a combination of cash and AOL stock. During 1999, AOL purchased 2,725,026 shares of the Company's common stock in exchange for a combination of cash and 1,212,396 shares of AOL common stock.

During 1999, the Company purchased a 19.9% interest in NECX Direct, LLC, an online e-commerce computer peripheral retailer, and subsequently sold half of that interest to a third party. The purchase price of approximately $77.7 million includes a two-year option to acquire the remaining 80.1% interest for additional consideration. The investment is being accounted for using the cost method.

During the third quarter of 1997, the Company acquired substantially all of the outstanding shares of common stock of ALR, a manufacturer of network servers and personal computers, for a cash purchase price of approximately $196,400,000. The operating results of ALR were not material for all periods presented.

9 Selected Balance Sheet Information

December 31 (in thousands)	1998	1999
Accounts receivable, net:		
Accounts receivable	$ 573,799	$ 662,811
Allowance for uncollectible accounts	(14,948)	(16,472)
	$ 558,851	$ 646,339
Inventory:		
Components and subassemblies	$ 155,746	$ 183,321
Finished goods	12,178	8,549
	$ 167,924	$ 191,870
Property, plant and equipment, net:		
Land	$ 21,784	$ 18,758
Leasehold improvements	57,118	107,317
Buildings	186,361	202,102
Construction in progress	74,105	158,305
Internal use software	94,306	172,501
Office and production equipment	249,924	319,585
Furniture and fixtures	66,578	99,959
Vehicles	15,402	13,477
	765,578	1,092,004
Accumulated depreciation and amortization	(234,590)	(346,344)
	$ 530,988	$ 745,660
Intangibles:		
Intangibles	$ 91,220	$ 91,220
Accumulated amortization	(25,276)	(38,918)
	$ 65,944	$ 52,302
Accrued liabilities:		
Warranty	$ 110,139	$ 142,729
Other	305,126	466,403
	$ 415,265	$ 609,132
Other current liabilities:		
Deferred revenue	$ 61,070	$ 108,603
Other	55,980	34,209
	$ 117,050	$ 142,812

10 Supplemental Statements of Cash Flows Information

(in thousands)	1997	1998	1999
Supplemental disclosure of cash flow information:			
Cash paid during the year for interest	$ 716	$ 930	$ 1,533
Cash paid during the year for income taxes	$163,710	$200,839	$218,944
Supplemental schedule of noncash investing and financing activities:			
Capital lease obligations incurred for the purchase of			
new equipment	$ 4,593	$ 6,741	$ 7,403
Common stock issued in exchange for common stock of investee	—	—	100,000
Acquisitions			
Fair value of assets acquired	$271,189		
Less: Liabilities assumed	70,773		
Cash acquired	58,096		
Acquisitions, net of cash acquired	$142,320		

⑪ Segment Data

The Company's segments are based on the geography and, in the United States (U.S.), by customer class. Geographic segments include the U.S., Europe Middle East Africa (EMEA) and Asia Pacific (A-P). Customer class segments in the U.S. are Consumer and Business. The Company evaluates the performance of its Consumer and Business segments based on sales and operating income, and does not include segment assets or other income and expense items for management reporting purposes. Segment operating income includes selling, general and administrative expenses and other overhead charges directly attributable to the segment and excludes certain expenses managed outside the reporting segment. Costs excluded from the segments primarily consist of general and administrative expenses that are managed on a corporate-wide basis. Certain non-segment operating expenses for prior years have been reclassified to segment specific operating expenses to conform with current year presentation. Segment information prior to 1998 has not been restated to reflect the customer class segments in the U.S. as it is impractical to do so.

The following table sets forth summary information by segment:

(in thousands)	1997	1998	1999
United States			
Net sales:			
Consumer		$3,339,712	$ 4,158,379
Business		3,072,692	3,225,008
	$5,303,828	$6,412,404	$7,383,387
Operating income:			
Consumer		$ 296,390	$ 473,124
Business		560,752	474,599
	$ 597,091	$ 857,142	$ 947,723
Other income, net	25,041	43,600	57,189
Income tax expense	104,552	205,129	224,949
Depreciation and amortization	67,787	83,386	116,142
Segment assets	1,701,654	2,473,627	3,449,240
Long-lived assets	380,757	522,972	1,124,467
EMEA			
Net sales	$ 634,616	$ 570,191	$ 543,182
Operating income (loss)	(11,566)	(6,005)	(8,807)
Other income, net	2,946	1,380	3,584
Income tax expense (benefit)	568	(3,048)	(734)
Depreciation and amortization	6,695	9,820	9,235
Segment assets	187,215	209,820	241,489
Long-lived assets	59,261	57,548	61,676
A-P			
Net sales	$ 355,236	$ 485,330	$ 715,842
Operating income (loss)	(9,733)	1,153	33,049
Other income, net	(798)	2,041	7,036
Income tax expense (benefit)	(11,297)	(7,232)	11,320
Depreciation and amortization	12,292	12,318	8,728
Segment assets	150,402	206,933	263,959
Long-lived assets	34,278	30,184	38,739

A reconciliation of the segments net sales and operating income is as follows:

(in thousands)	1997	1998	1999
Net sales:			
Segment sales	$6,293,680	$7,467,925	$8,642,411
Non-segment sales	—	—	3,150
Total sales	$6,293,680	$7,467,925	$8,645,561
Operating income:			
Segment operating income	$ 575,792	$ 852,290	$ 971,965
Non-segment operating expenses	399,361	358,063	376,295
Total operating income	$ 176,431	$ 494,227	$ 595,670

⑫ Selected Quarterly Financial Data (Unaudited)

The following tables contain selected unaudited consolidated quarterly financial data for the Company:

(in thousands, except per share amounts)	1st Quarter	2nd Quarter	3rd Quarter	4th Quarter
1999:				
Net sales	$ 2,103,411	$1,912,109	$2,178,496	$2,451,545
Gross profit	450,504	421,386	480,049	547,878
Operating income	140,807	122,923	158,779	173,161
Net income	99,579	89,225	113,151	125,989
Net income per share:				
Basic	$ .32	$ .28	$ .36	$ .40
Diluted	$ .31	$ .28	$ .35	$ .38
Weighted-average shares outstanding:				
Basic	312,994	312,886	313,719	316,260
Diluted	321,194	320,314	323,912	330,617
Stock sales price per share:				
High	$ 41.25	$ 38.34	$ 53.88	$ 82.50
Low	$ 26.81	$ 28.53	$ 30.03	$ 46.88
1998:				
Net sales	$1,727,927	$1,618,909	$ 1,815,516	$2,305,573
Gross profit	336,494	333,688	377,807	498,285
Operating income	109,201	83,989	113,355	187,682
Net income	75,871	60,740	80,645	129,143
Net income per share:				
Basic	$ .25	$ .19	$ .26	$ .41
Diluted	$ .24	$ .19	$ .25	$ .41
Weighted-average shares outstanding:				
Basic	309,096	310,854	311,698	312,648
Diluted	315,150	317,774	319,036	319,134
Stock sales price per share:				
High	$ 24.13	$ 29.41	$ 33.56	$ 30.81
Low	$ 16.25	$ 21.28	$ 23.22	$ 20.75

Worldwide Headquarters

Gateway, Inc.
4545 Towne Centre Court
San Diego, California 92121
Telephone: 858-799-3401
Fax: 858-799-3459

Company Information

Copies of the Gateway Annual Report and Form 10-K for the fiscal year 1999 are available to shareholders without charge. If you wish to receive these reports or other company information, please contact:

Investor Relations
Gateway, Inc.
610 Gateway Drive
North Sioux City,
South Dakota 57049-2000
Telephone: 800-846-4503
Fax: 605-232-2757

Annual Meeting

The Annual Meeting of Stockholders of Gateway, Inc. will be held at 9:00 a.m. on Thursday, May 18, 2000, at the Sioux City Convention Center, 801 Fourth Street, Sioux City, Iowa 51101.

Transfer Agent

If you have questions about stock certificates, change of address, consolidation of accounts, transfer of ownership or other stock matters, please contact Gateway's transfer agent:

UMB Bank, n.a.
Securities Transfer Division
P.O. Box 410064
Kansas City, Missouri 64141-0064
Telephone: 800-844-4225
Fax: 816-860-3963
E-mail: sec_xfer@umb.com

Independent Accountants

PricewaterhouseCoopers LLP
San Diego, California

Gateway Board of Directors

THEODORE W. WAITT
Chairman of the Board
Gateway

JEFFREY WEITZEN
President and
Chief Executive Officer
Gateway

CHARLES G. CAREY
Chairman of the Board and
Chief Executive Officer
Fox Television Division
Fox, Inc.
New York, New York

GEORGE H. KRAUSS
Of Counsel
Kutak Rock Law Firm
Omaha, Nebraska

JAMES F. MCCANN
President
1-800-FLOWERS.com, Inc.
Westbury, New York

RICHARD D. SNYDER
President
Avalon Investments, Inc.
Ann Arbor, Michigan

DOUGLAS L. LACEY
Partner
Nichols, Rise & Company
Certified Public Accountants
Sioux City, Iowa

Executive Officers

THEODORE W. WAITT
Chairman of the Board

JEFFREY WEITZEN
President and
Chief Executive Officer

DAVID J. ROBINO
Vice Chairman

R. TODD BRADLEY
Executive Vice President,
Global Operations

VAN M. ANDREWS
Senior Vice President,
Gateway Business

PETER B. ASHKIN
Senior Vice President,
Chief Technology Officer

JOSEPH J. BURKE
Senior Vice President,
Global Business Development

WILLIAM M. ELLIOTT
Senior Vice President,
General Counsel and Secretary

MICHAEL D. HAMMOND
Senior Vice President,
Manufacturing

CLIFFORD S. HOLTZ
Senior Vice President,
Gateway Consumer

JAMES T. POLLARD
Senior Vice President,
Chief Information Officer

JOHN M. RENFRO
Senior Vice President,
Human Resources

JOHN J. TODD
Senior Vice President,
Chief Financial Officer

Design by Addison www.addison.com Major photography by David Katzenstein